HM £7

THE 1993
ELIAS
BASEBALL
ANALYST

THE 1993 ELIAS BASEBALL ANALYST

SEYMOUR SIWOFF, STEVE HIRDT,
TOM HIRDT & PETER HIRDT

A FIRESIDE BOOK • **Published by Simon & Schuster**
New York   London   Toronto   Sydney   Tokyo   Singapore

FIRESIDE
Simon & Schuster Building
Rockefeller Center
1230 Avenue of the Americas
New York, New York 10020

Designed by Bonni Leon
Manufactured in the United States of America

10 9 8 7 6 5 4 3 2 1

Library of Congress Cataloging in Publication Data is available

ISBN: 0-671-73327-3

CONTENTS

ACKNOWLEDGMENTS ix

INTRODUCTION xi

TEAM SECTION 1

American League
Baltimore Orioles 3
Boston Red Sox 6
California Angels 9
Chicago White Sox 12
Cleveland Indians 15
Detroit Tigers 18
Kansas City Royals 21
Milwaukee Brewers 24
Minnesota Twins 27
New York Yankees 30
Oakland Athletics 33
Seattle Mariners 36
Texas Rangers 39
Toronto Blue Jays 42

National League
Atlanta Braves 45
Chicago Cubs 48
Cincinnati Reds 51
Colorado Rockies 54
Florida Marlins 56
Houston Astros 58
Los Angeles Dodgers 61
Montreal Expos 64
New York Mets 67
Philadelphia Phillies 70
Pittsburgh Pirates 73
St. Louis Cardinals 76
San Diego Padres 79
San Francisco Giants 82

BATTER SECTION 85
American League Batters 87
National League Batters 159

PITCHER SECTION 219
American League Pitchers 221
National League Pitchers 265

ROOKIES AND PROSPECTS SECTION 307
Batters 309
Pitchers 321

BALLPARKS SECTION 325
American League 326
National League 329
Rankings 331

ACKNOWLEDGMENTS

In recognition of the invaluable assistance provided by so many of our colleagues, the authors would like to thank the following:

The rest of the Elias Sports Bureau staff: Rocky Avakian, John Carson, Jay Chesler, John Chymczuk, Bryan Fodera, Carl Friedberg, Ken Hirdt, Keung Hui, Frank Labombarda, John Labombarda, Santo Labombarda, Christopher Lasch, Bob Rosen, Alex Stern, Christopher Thorn, Gil Traub, Bob Waterman, and Jon Wynne;

Eliot Cohen, former editor of *Major League Monthly* and coauthor of *The 1990 Baseball Annual;*

Our agent, Nat Sobel, and the rest of his staff, particularly Craig Holden;

At AmeriComp, Jim Bristol and Wendy James;

At Simon & Schuster, Emi Battaglia, Sue Fleming, Stuart Gottesman, Bonni Leon, Tim McGuire, Steve "Motown" Messina, Jay Schweitzer, George Turianski, and especially our editor, Jeff Neuman, whose insight and care help to shape this book every bit as much as we ourselves do.

And special thanks to our families and to those of the people listed here who made individual sacrifices as we rode this book hard to the finish line. Without their support, we wouldn't have made it through the stretch.

INTRODUCTION

Back in the spring of 1975, Gary Carter, Dennis Eckersley, Jim Rice, and Fred Lynn were gearing up for their rookie seasons. And the Elias Sports Bureau was about to undertake a new project of its own—the start of the first baseball database ever compiled to analyze play-by-play data. It seemed to us at the time that there might be an interest among baseball executives in statistics that could identify the strengths and weaknesses of their own players and their opponents to a greater and more meaningful degree than the basic traditional figures did. Until the mid-1970s, there simply was no source for the breakdowns that we now see thrown around on every baseball broadcast, and in every newspaper or periodical that covers baseball—who hits best with runners in scoring position, which pitchers are truly tougher on left-handed batters than on right-handers, and so on.

We had no idea 18 years ago that what we envisioned as a special service to subscribers within the baseball industry would be valued as greatly by fans as by managers, and would become an integral part of a successful annual publication, *The Elias Baseball Analyst.*

This is our ninth edition of the *Analyst.* And true to its roots, it remains a valuable source of information for those in the industry. General managers, managers, players, broadcasters, and writers rely on the accuracy of its statistics. As frustrating as it can be to see and hear our work pirated so often without even a hint of attribution, we take great pride in the fact that so many of the statistics and insights cited on the air or written in newspapers and magazines are taken directly from the *Analyst.* This is one case where fans truly have access to the same information the insiders use.

So what's new for '93? Most notably, the inclusion of essays on baseball's two expansion teams, the Colorado Rockies and the Florida Marlins. The new teams afforded us a chance to examine some interesting related issues. (Be honest—in what other book could you find information on the Seattle Pilots, the Utah Jazz, Marv Throneberry, and George Blanda all within a few pages?)

We have also expanded the Rookies and Prospects Section, which debuted last year, to include more of this season's best first- and second-year players. This material proved extremely popular last year; it's invaluable to any baseball fans looking to put some of the game's bright young stars into historical perspective, and indispensable to those looking for an edge in their fantasy-league drafts.

The other features remain unchanged—team essays, statistics on all players, and the expanded player comments that have been so well received. We hope you enjoy our ninth edition, and will take the time to let us know what you'd like to see next year as we complete our first decade and look forward to the second.

THE 1993
ELIAS
BASEBALL
ANALYST

TEAM SECTION

The Team Section consists of comments and statistics for each of last year's twenty-six major league teams, and comments on the two expansion teams.

The first of three tables that follow the essay of each of last year's teams is the Won-Lost Record by Starting Position chart. This chart lists, for each player on a team, the team's won-lost record in games started by that player at each position, and in the leadoff and cleanup spots in the batting order. In addition, the number of games started by each player against left-handed and right-handed pitchers is listed. The players are listed alphabetically.

WON-LOST RECORD BY STARTING POSITION

Baltimore Orioles	C	1B	2B	3B	SS	LF	CF	RF	DH	P	Leadoff	Cleanup	Starts vs. LH	Starts vs. RH	Total Starts
Manny Alexander	-	-	-	-	-	-	-	-	-		-		-	-	-
Brady Anderson	-	-	-	-	-	83-65	3-4	2-1	-	-	88-70	-	44	114	88-70
Pat Clements	-	-	-	-	-	-	-	-	-	-	-		-	-	-
Storm Davis	-	-	-	-	-	-	-	-	-	1-1	-	-	-	2	1-1
Glenn Davis	-	1-1	-	-	-	-	-	-	53-45	-	-	46-38	32	68	54-46
Rick Dempsey	0-1	-	-	-	-	-	-	-	-	-	-	-	1	-	0-1
Mike Devereaux	-	-	-	-	-	-	86-69	-	-	-	0-2	3-2	45	110	86-69
Mike Flanagan	-	-	-	-	-	-	-	-	-	-	-		-	-	-
Todd Frohwirth	-	-	-	-	-	-	-	-	-	-	-		-	-	-
Leo Gomez	-	-	-	78-58	-	-	-	-	-	-	-	-	37	99	78-58
Chris Hoiles	51-42	-	-	-	-	-	-	-	0-1	-	-	0-2	29	65	51-43
Sam Horn	-	-	-	-	-	-	-	-	26-19	-	-	25-15	-	45	26-19
Tim Hulett	-	-	0-1	9-15	-	-	-	-	5-3	-	-	-	16	17	14-19
Craig Lefferts	-	-	-	-	-	-	-	-	-	1-4	-	-	-	5	1-4
Richie Lewis	-	-	-	-	-	-	-	-	-	1-1	-	-	1	1	1-1
Chito Martinez	-	-	-	-	-	-	26-21	1-2	-	-	-	7	43	27-23
Ben McDonald	-	-	-	-	-	-	-	-	-	19-16	-	-	9	26	19-16
Mark McLemore	-	-	25-27	-	-	-	-	-	1-0	-	1-0	-	7	46	26-27
Luis Mercedes	-	-	-	-	-	1-0	-	7-4	1-0	-	-	-	12	1	9-4
Jose Mesa	-	-	-	-	-	-	-	-	-	3-9	-	-	3	9	3-9
Bob Milacki	-	-	-	-	-	-	-	-	-	11-9	-	-	8	12	11-9
Randy Milligan	-	75-54	-	-	-	-	-	-	2-3	-	-	11-11	41	93	77-57
Alan Mills	-	-	-	-	-	-	-	-	-	2-1	-	-	1	2	2-1
Mike Mussina	-	-	-	-	-	-	-	-	-	21-11	-	-	10	22	21-11
Gregg Olson	-	-	-	-	-	-	-	-	-	-	-	-	-	-	-
Joe Orsulak	-	-	-	-	-	3-7	-	47-41	-	-	0-1	0-1	14	84	50-48
Mark Parent	7-4	-	-	-	-	-	-	-	-	-	-	-	4	7	7-4
Jim Poole	-	-	-	-	-	-	-	-	-	-	-	-	-	-	-
Arthur Rhodes	-	-	-	-	-	-	-	-	-	10-5	-	-	3	12	10-5
Cal Ripken	-	-	-	-	89-73	-	-	-	-	-	-	4-4	46	116	89-73
Billy Ripken	-	-	64-44	-	-	-	-	-	-	-	-	-	40	68	64-44
Steve Scarsone	-	-	0-1	2-0	-	-	-	-	-	-	-	-	1	2	2-1
David Segui	-	13-18	-	-	-	2-1	-	7-6	-	-	-	-	26	21	22-25
Tommy Shields	-	-	-	-	-	-	-	-	-	-	-	-	-	-	-
Rick Sutcliffe	-	-	-	-	-	-	-	-	-	20-16	-	-	11	25	20-16
Jeff Tackett	31-26	-	-	-	-	-	-	-	-	-	-	-	12	45	31-26
Anthony Telford	-	-	-	-	-	-	-	-	-	-	-	-	-	-	-
Jack Voigt	-	-	-	-	-	-	-	-	-	-	-	-	-	-	-
Mark Williamson	-	-	-	-	-	-	-	-	-	-	-	-	-	-	-

Below this chart are the team's batting and pitching totals in a variety of categories and breakdowns. These breakdowns are explained in the introductory text to the Batter Section (see page 85) and the Pitcher Section (see page 219). To see how each team stacks up against the overall totals for its league, compare its totals to the league stat summaries on the next page.

American League

	AB	H	2B	3B	HR	RBI	BB	SO	BA	SA	OBA
Season	77147	20006	3596	386	1776	9222	7704	12196	.259	.385	.328
vs. Left-Handers	20085	5316	1007	86	496	2576	2202	3241	.265	.397	.339
vs. Right-Handers	57062	14690	2589	300	1280	6646	5502	8955	.257	.381	.325
vs. Ground-Ballers	35941	9432	1629	167	704	4274	3494	5501	.262	.376	.330
vs. Fly-Ballers	41206	10574	1967	219	1072	4948	4210	6695	.257	.393	.327
Home Games	37493	9786	1771	216	878	4641	3980	5822	.261	.390	.334
Road Games	39654	10220	1825	170	898	4581	3724	6374	.258	.380	.323
Grass Fields	55086	14215	2414	248	1319	6555	5636	8701	.258	.383	.328
Artificial Turf	22061	5791	1182	138	457	2667	2068	3495	.262	.391	.328
April	9941	2523	469	41	232	1195	1033	1594	.254	.379	.325
May	12874	3311	631	67	333	1596	1350	2044	.257	.394	.329
June	13138	3458	636	62	336	1616	1300	1967	.263	.398	.331
July	12889	3363	576	76	274	1473	1220	1969	.261	.381	.326
August	13598	3569	605	64	317	1681	1383	2204	.262	.386	.333
Sept./Oct.	14707	3782	679	76	284	1661	1418	2418	.257	.372	.325
Leading Off Inn.	18655	4823	891	100	438	438	1595	2800	.259	.387	.321
Runners On	33656	8933	1569	187	759	8205	3736	5253	.265	.391	.337
Bases Empty	43491	11073	2027	199	1017	1017	3968	6943	.255	.381	.321
Runners/Scor. Pos.	19312	5012	892	117	439	7212	2676	3310	.260	.386	.343
Runners On/2 Out	14133	3412	616	91	310	3142	1742	2353	.241	.364	.329
Scor. Pos./2 Out	9145	2119	387	58	196	2760	1350	1612	.232	.351	.335
Late-Inning Pressure	11631	2872	459	41	243	1229	1202	2097	.247	.356	.320
Leading Off	2965	726	121	12	59	59	256	525	.245	.353	.310
Runners On	4885	1214	192	23	97	1083	622	867	.249	.357	.333
Runners/Scor. Pos.	2744	642	101	14	63	969	468	544	.234	.350	.340

RUNS BATTED IN	From 1B	From 2B	From 3B	Scoring Position
Percentage	4.8%	17.9%	42.0%	26.5%

Miscellaneous statistics: Ground outs-to-air outs ratio: 1.07. Leaders in players comments based on 200 plate appearances. . . . Grounded into 1808 double plays in 16,641 opportunities (one per 9.2). Leaders based on 40 opportunities. . . . Drove in 2540 of 4437 runners from third base with less than two outs (57%). Leaders based on 15 opportunities. . . . Base running: Advanced from first base to third on 1455 of 4103 outfield singles (35%); scored from second on 1638 of 2263 (72%). Leaders based on 10 opportunities. . . . Assists per nine innings: first basemen, 0.73; second basemen, 3.04; shortstops, 3.10; third basemen, 2.04. Putouts per nine innings: left fielders, 2.22; center fielders, 2.84; right fielders, 2.15. Leaders based on 500 innings. . . . Opposing base stealers: 1704-for-2564 (66%). Leaders based on 50 attempts.

National League

	AB	H	2B	3B	HR	RBI	BB	SO	BA	SA	OBA
Season	65748	16538	2967	459	1262	7060	5978	11342	.252	.368	.315
vs. Left-Handers	23729	6226	1144	168	484	2646	2116	3853	.262	.386	.323
vs. Right-Handers	42019	10312	1823	291	778	4414	3862	7489	.245	.358	.311
vs. Ground-Ballers	28349	7246	1241	206	493	2965	2523	4616	.256	.366	.319
vs. Fly-Ballers	37399	9292	1726	253	769	4095	3455	6726	.248	.370	.313
Home Games	32121	8248	1521	240	675	3663	3108	5403	.257	.382	.323
Road Games	33627	8290	1446	219	587	3397	2870	5939	.247	.355	.307
Grass Fields	32802	8239	1388	206	643	3441	2906	5523	.251	.365	.313
Artificial Turf	32946	8299	1579	253	619	3619	3072	5819	.252	.372	.318
April	8763	2133	372	67	156	934	854	1632	.243	.355	.313
May	10691	2697	487	75	218	1232	1032	1931	.252	.373	.319
June	10841	2742	525	80	196	1186	1008	1792	.253	.370	.318
July	10926	2720	462	82	213	1035	949	1848	.249	.365	.310
August	11311	2851	494	65	235	1229	983	1861	.252	.370	.313
Sept./Oct.	13216	3395	627	90	244	1444	1152	2278	.257	.373	.318
Leading Off Inn.	16273	4167	735	110	338	338	1197	2650	.256	.377	.310
Runners On	27734	7061	1268	207	544	6342	3035	4819	.255	.374	.326
Bases Empty	38014	9477	1699	252	718	718	2943	6523	.249	.364	.307
Runners/Scor. Pos.	16303	4015	737	125	289	5492	2318	3095	.246	.360	.335
Runners On/2 Out	11835	2706	516	90	212	2392	1489	2188	.229	.341	.319
Scor. Pos./2 Out	7798	1719	343	57	120	2068	1220	1535	.220	.325	.330
Late-Inning Pressure	10660	2680	438	51	210	1108	1127	2011	.251	.361	.325
Leading Off	2741	712	125	17	51	51	229	489	.260	.374	.320
Runners On	4442	1097	172	16	97	995	613	851	.247	.358	.338
Runners/Scor. Pos.	2634	622	92	14	56	871	488	539	.236	.345	.350

RUNS BATTED IN	From 1B	From 2B	From 3B	Scoring Position
Percentage	5.0%	16.5%	39.1%	24.5%

Miscellaneous statistics: Ground outs-to-air outs ratio: 1.15. Leaders in players comments based on 200 plate appearances. . . . Grounded into 1301 double plays in 13,351 opportunities (one per 10.3). Leaders based on 40 opportunities. . . . Drove in 1988 of 3650 runners from third base with less than two outs (54%). Leaders based on 15 opportunities. . . . Base running: Advanced from first base to third on 1025 of 3117 outfield singles (34%); scored from second on 1233 of 1827 (67%). Leaders based on 10 opportunities. . . . Assists per nine innings: first basemen, 0.76; second basemen, 3.02; shortstops, 2.96; third basemen, 1.97. Putouts per nine innings: left fielders, 2.10; center fielders, 2.74; right fielders, 2.01. Leaders based on 500 innings. . . . Opposing base stealers: 1560-for-2301 (68%). Leaders based on 50 attempts.

American League

	W-L	ERA	AB	H	HR	BB	SO	BA	SA	OBA
Season	1134-1134	3.94	77147	20006	1776	7704	12196	.259	.385	.328
vs. Left-Handers			30189	7860	571	3119	4310	.260	.375	.330
vs. Right-Handers			46958	12146	1205	4585	7886	.259	.392	.328
vs. Ground-Ballers			37840	9860	569	3623	5550	.261	.362	.326
vs. Fly-Ballers			39307	10146	1207	4081	6646	.258	.407	.330
Home Games	621-513	3.79	39654	10220	898	3724	6374	.258	.380	.323
Road Games	513-621	4.10	37493	9786	878	3980	5822	.261	.390	.334
Grass Fields	810-810	3.91	55086	14215	1319	5636	8701	.258	.383	.328
Artificial Turf	324-324	4.01	22061	5791	457	2068	3495	.262	.391	.328
April	147-147	3.93	9941	2523	232	1033	1594	.254	.379	.325
May	191-191	4.13	12874	3311	333	1350	2044	.257	.394	.329
June	193-193	4.04	13138	3458	336	1300	1967	.263	.398	.331
July	188-188	3.82	12889	3363	274	1220	1969	.261	.381	.326
August	201-201	4.04	13598	3569	317	1383	2204	.262	.386	.333
Sept./Oct.	214-214	3.70	14707	3782	284	1418	2418	.257	.372	.325
Leading Off Inn.			18655	4823	438	1595	2800	.259	.387	.321
Bases Empty			43491	11073	1017	3968	6943	.255	.381	.321
Runners On			33656	8933	759	3736	5253	.265	.391	.337
Runners/Scor. Pos.			19312	5012	439	2676	3310	.260	.386	.343
Runners On/2 Out			14133	3412	310	1742	2353	.241	.364	.329
Scor. Pos./2 Out			9145	2119	196	1350	1612	.232	.351	.335
Late-Inning Pressure			11631	2872	243	1202	2097	.247	.356	.320
Leading Off			2965	726	59	256	525	.245	.353	.310
Runners On			4885	1214	97	622	867	.249	.357	.333
Runners/Scor. Pos.			2744	642	63	468	544	.234	.350	.340
First 9 Batters			38845	9763	833	4168	6710	.251	.370	.326
Second 9 Batters			20086	5318	455	1861	2901	.265	.390	.329
All Batters Thereafter			18216	4925	488	1675	2585	.270	.412	.334

Miscellaneous statistics: Ground outs-to-air outs ratio: 1.07. Leaders in players comments based on 400 batters faced. . . . Grounded into 1808 double plays in 16,641 opportunities (one per 9.2). Leaders based on 100 innings pitched. . . . Allowed 1207 first-inning runs in 2268 starts (4.32 ERA). . . . Batting support: 4.32 runs per start. Leaders based on 20 starts. . . . Stranded 2215 inherited runners, allowed 1144 to score (66%). Leaders based on 25 inherited runners. . . . Opposing base stealers: 1704-for-2564 (66%). Leaders based on 10 attempts.

National League

	W-L	ERA	AB	H	HR	BB	SO	BA	SA	OBA
Season	972-972	3.50	65748	16538	1262	5978	11342	.252	.368	.315
vs. Left-Handers			28923	7483	553	3085	4847	.259	.377	.331
vs. Right-Handers			36825	9055	709	2893	6495	.246	.361	.303
vs. Ground-Ballers			29530	7299	373	2453	5224	.247	.339	.306
vs. Fly-Ballers			36218	9239	889	3525	6118	.255	.392	.323
Home Games	541-431	3.23	33627	8290	587	2870	5939	.247	.355	.307
Road Games	431-541	3.79	32121	8248	675	3108	5403	.257	.382	.323
Grass Fields	486-486	3.38	32802	8239	643	2906	5523	.251	.365	.313
Artificial Turf	486-486	3.63	32946	8299	619	3072	5819	.252	.372	.318
April	130-130	3.48	8763	2133	156	854	1632	.243	.355	.313
May	158-158	3.74	10691	2697	218	1032	1931	.252	.373	.319
June	162-162	3.53	10841	2742	196	1008	1792	.253	.370	.318
July	162-162	3.08	10926	2720	213	949	1848	.249	.365	.310
August	167-167	3.55	11311	2851	235	983	1861	.252	.370	.313
Sept./Oct.	193-193	3.62	13216	3395	244	1152	2278	.257	.373	.318
Leading Off Inn.			16273	4167	338	1197	2650	.256	.377	.310
Bases Empty			38014	9477	718	2943	6523	.249	.364	.307
Runners On			27734	7061	544	3035	4819	.255	.374	.326
Runners/Scor. Pos.			16303	4015	289	2318	3095	.246	.360	.335
Runners On/2 Out			11835	2706	212	1489	2188	.229	.341	.319
Scor. Pos./2 Out			7798	1719	120	1220	1535	.220	.325	.330
Late-Inning Pressure			10660	2680	210	1127	2011	.251	.361	.325
Leading Off			2741	712	51	229	489	.260	.374	.320
Runners On			4442	1097	97	613	851	.247	.358	.338
Runners/Scor. Pos.			2634	622	56	488	539	.236	.345	.350
First 9 Batters			34839	8461	620	3422	6683	.243	.352	.312
Second 9 Batters			16360	4211	326	1330	2692	.257	.379	.314
All Batters Thereafter			14549	3866	316	1226	1967	.266	.396	.324

Miscellaneous statistics: Ground outs-to-air outs ratio: 1.15. Leaders in players comments based on 400 batters faced. . . . Grounded into 1301 double plays in 13,351 opportunities (one per 10.3). Leaders based on 100 innings pitched. . . . Allowed 982 first-inning runs in 1944 starts (4.10 ERA). . . . Batting support: 3.88 runs per start. Leaders based on 20 starts. . . . Stranded 1645 inherited runners, allowed 808 to score (67%). Leaders based on 25 inherited runners. . . . Opposing base stealers: 1560-for-2301 (68%). Leaders based on 10 attempts.

BALTIMORE ORIOLES

The question just wouldn't go away. Every talk show on which we appeared in the Baltimore area last spring included some form of the following: "Do you guys have any statistics on new ballparks?" Frankly, after Cal Ripken had trashed our "Take a Rest, Cal" campaign with his 1991 MVP season, we welcomed a few comments on other topics. But to a bunch of New Yorkers, the almost religious fervor with which Oriole Park was discussed by the locals seemed somewhat comical. So we prattled on some (politely, we hope) about how the stadium was supposed to be more conducive to home runs by left-handed hitters than right-handers (or was it the other way around?), and how Toronto sure seemed to be doing well since the Skydome opened, and so on. But mostly, we felt like, what's the big deal?

Then we saw the place, and it *is* beautiful—a wonderful place to watch a ballgame; and, as so many have pointed out, much more a "park" than a "stadium." It may not be Versailles, but Oriole Park at Camden Yards is a place to make you feel like a kid again, imagining Paul Blair (or Jim Busby, or Mike Kreevich, depending on your age) racing across the pasture to grab a would-be triple. And if you were already a kid, it was just the place to make you fall in love with baseball—an antidote to seven-time drug offenders, thousand-dollar baseball cards, and three-and-a-half-hour games.

Anyhow, when we considered the various topics that might be included in this Orioles essay, there seemed little doubt that we had to address the new ballpark. Of course, the problem is that a single season's worth of statistics rarely prove much of anything: The Metrodome was tabbed with its "Homerdome" misnomer after apparently increasing home runs by 15 percent in its first season; in the 10 years since then, it has *reduced* them by 2 percent. But if last season is any indication, the hot topic north of the Beltway in 1993 should continue to be Baltimore's lovely new shrine to baseball—made even better this season by its newly imposed no-smoking rules, and meticulously chronicled in Peter Richmond's upcoming book, *Ballpark*. So we've dug around in our files and found a couple of "new-stadium" topics we think you'll find interesting. With so little data available, they may not provide us with any absolute answers, but perhaps they can raise the discussion to a different level, and fans in Texas and Cleveland can use them to whet their appetites for '94.

When the Orioles closed to within a half-game of Toronto in the first week of September, we wondered how many stadiums had hosted postseason games in their first year of operation. The Skydome was obvious because this had occurred there so recently (1989). But what of the older parks?

It turns out that five current stadiums were used for postseason games in their first seasons: Along with the Skydome, there were Fenway Park (1912), Yankee Stadium (1923), and Riverfront and Three Rivers Stadiums, which opened within three weeks of each other in the summer of 1970, and where that season's National League Championship Series between the Reds and Pirates was contested three months later. Oriole Park lost its chance to join the club when Baltimore faded down the stretch with nine losses in 13 games (September 6–20), which expanded Toronto's lead from a half-game to 5½ games. (Two others, no longer in use, also hosted postseason play in their first year of operation: Forbes Field, which opened in 1909, and Braves Field, which opened in 1915—and was used by the Red Sox as their home field in that year's Series, since its capacity was some 10,000 greater than Fenway's.)

Anyway, five out of 26 rookie stadiums in the playoffs or World Series sounded like a lot; in fact, it's a couple more than pure chance would have produced (3.4—and please don't ask what four-tenths of a stadium is). So is it possible, as some talk-show callers suggested, that a team derives some special benefit from its ballpark's inaugural season—that the team rises to the occasion at its new field, so to speak? That didn't seem to be the case with the Orioles last season; their winning percentage was actually 37 points lower at home (43–38, .531) than on the road (46–35, .568). Then again, the Orioles posted a better mark on the road than at Memorial Stadium in 1991 as well. Maybe they just don't like crabs.

This topic required research on more than a single team over a two-year period. The following table lists all teams that launched new ballparks in the last 30 years, except for those that didn't have histories in their previous stadiums long enough to establish a track record (the Dodgers, the Angels, the Mets, and the Astros). The difference between each team's home and road winning percentages is shown for the last full season in their old parks, and the first three years at the new places. (When teams moved during the season, as happened with the Cardinals, the Pirates, the Reds, and the Jays, only the portion of the season after the move was considered.) The averages don't include the White Sox or Orioles, who haven't completed their move-in periods yet:

Year	Team	Old Park	Year One	Year 2	Year 3
1966	Cardinals	+.038	+.063	−.045	−.037
1970	Pirates	+.074	+.145	+.101	+.018
1970	Reds	+.136	+.167	+.160	−.127
1971	Phillies	+.093	+.012	−.048	+.062
1977	Expos	−.004	+.012	+.086	+.198
1982	Twins	+.053	+.173	+.049	+.160
1989	Blue Jays	+.037	+.014	+.025	+.012
1991	White Sox	+.064	+.062	+.160	——
1992	Orioles	−.012	−.037	——	——
	Averages	+.053	+.085	+.041	+.036

Based on the record of the 1992 Orioles alone, you might have concluded that teams need to learn how to take advantage of a new stadium. But the rest of the table indicates just the opposite—generally speaking, an increase in the year of the move, and a decrease thereafter. This is one of those trends for which enough data doesn't exist to actually prove anything. But if you wanted to create a table that *suggests* that teams peak in their first season in a new ballpark, that's what it would look like. And it appears that even after the inclusion of Chicago and Baltimore in the averages, the trend will survive.

Now, about Oriole Park's supposed friendliness to left-handed hitters: There was a lot of talk about that prior to the 1992 season, so it seemed strange that the Orioles didn't go after any solid left-handed home-run hitters. As it happens, the figures for last season indicated that such a skew did in fact exist. But there simply weren't any quality left-handed power hitters available after the 1991 season; only three left-handers who hit even 10 home runs in 1991 were in new uniforms at the start of 1992—first basemen Wally Joyner and Alvin Davis and outfielder Kirk Gibson. Considering that neither Davis nor Gibson lasted the season in the majors, and that Joyner signed a huge contract to play a position that either Glenn Davis or Randy Milligan could capably handle for the Orioles, it's not surprising in retrospect that Baltimore failed to sign a big-swinging lefty. What was the alternative, hiring a private investigator to locate Ken Phelps? (Not with Sam Horn already on the roster.) And when Harold Baines became available in January 1993, they did in fact make their move.

But Camden Yards performed as advertised, showing a big increase in home-run rate by left-handers and a negligible decrease for right-handers—although the basic figures tended to obscure that result. Left-handed batters averaged one home run for every 42 at-bats at Oriole Park; right-handers hit home runs at a rate 15 percent higher (one every 36 ABs). But that was to be expected; after all, with the exception of Brady Anderson and part-timers Horn and Chito Martinez, all of Baltimore's power swings from the right side: Cal Ripken, Glenn Davis, Mike Devereaux, Chris Hoiles, Leo Gomez, and Milligan.

That's why it takes more than the figures at any given stadium to examine its effect on home runs. Imagine if the Astros added Fred McGriff, Barry Bonds, and David Justice to their roster; based on calculations like the one above, you could "prove" that the Astrodome was a good home-run park for left-handed hitters. To determine the actual effect that a team's home field has, you must compare the results there to those compiled in its road games (which serve as a somewhat neutral point of comparison), as in the following table:

| | Left-Handers | | | Right-Handers | | |
	AB	HR	Pct.	AB	HR	Pct.
Oriole Park	2008	48	2.39	3500	96	2.74
Orioles Road Games	2027	32	1.58	3481	96	2.76

Notice that although right-handed hitters had a higher home-run rate than left-handers at Oriole Park, the gap between the two groups was far greater at other stadiums. Again, those gaps exist because Baltimore's best hitters are mostly right-handers. But right-handed hitters performed no better at Camden Yards than they did elsewhere. (Actually the statistics show a

decrease of a half-percent at Oriole Park.) On the other hand, left-handers showed a dramatic 51 percent home-run increase in Baltimore: from one every 63 at-bats elsewhere to one every 42 ABs aiming for the warehouse.

Because the data represent only a single season, which can be misleading, we balanced the home-run figures so that each player contributed an equal amount to both the home and road profiles. (Trust us, you don't want to know the method; if you're curious, it's analogous to the balancing method described in the second half of the Pirates essay.) The adjusted figures showed a smaller but still significant gap: a 29 percent increase for left-handed hitters, a 4 percent decrease for right-handers.

One change in last season's Orioles team that had little to do with the new ballpark was an increased emphasis on speed. In 1991, Baltimore ranked last in the American League with 50 stolen bases, marking the 10th time in 11 seasons that the Orioles ranked among the league's bottom four teams. They also ranked last in scoring from second base on singles to the outfield (64%, compared to a league rate of 73%), and third-to-last in going from first base to third on outfield singles (33%; the A.L. average: 36%).

Last season, Baltimore took a major step forward in all three of those areas. The Orioles stole 89 bases—nearly an 80 percent increase—to rank 10th in the league. They went from first to third on 37 percent of all outfield singles (the sixth-highest rate in the A.L.; league average: 35 percent), and scored from second on 70 percent (ninth in the league; league average: 72 percent).

(This seems an appropriate time to mention that the Orioles hit 36 triples in 1992, to rank third in the A.L. Both the total and the rank were Baltimore's highest since 1973. Based on the other figures mentioned above, a small part of that may have been due to more aggressive baserunning; most was due to the closing of Memorial Stadium, which suppressed triples by roughly 50 percent.)

Did the improvement in Baltimore's speed figures result from the work of first-year Orioles coach Davey Lopes? More likely, it was part of an organization-wide emphasis embodied in the hiring of Lopes. No other American League team has a full-time coach whose explicit responsibilities (as listed in the league's own publication, the *Red Book*) include baserunning. That seems strange at a time when coaching staffs have been routinely expanded to include outfield instructors, strength and conditioning coaches, team psychologists, and other positions of negligible impact. Based on Baltimore's improved baserunning last season, this is an area that other teams ought to investigate.

WON-LOST RECORD BY STARTING POSITION

Baltimore Orioles	C	1B	2B	3B	SS	LF	CF	RF	DH	P	Leadoff	Cleanup	Starts vs. LH	Starts vs. RH	Total Starts
Manny Alexander	-	-	-	-	-	-	-	-	-	-	-	-	-	-	-
Brady Anderson	-	-	-	-	-	83-65	3-4	2-1	-	-	88-70	-	44	114	88-70
Pat Clements	-	-	-	-	-	-	-	-	-	-	-	-	-	-	-
Storm Davis	-	-	-	-	-	-	-	-	-	1-1	-	-	-	2	1-1
Glenn Davis	-	1-1	-	-	-	-	-	-	53-45	-	-	46-38	32	68	54-46
Rick Dempsey	0-1	-	-	-	-	-	-	-	-	-	-	-	1	-	0-1
Mike Devereaux	-	-	-	-	-	-	86-69	-	-	-	0-2	3-2	45	110	86-69
Mike Flanagan	-	-	-	-	-	-	-	-	-	-	-	-	-	-	-
Todd Frohwirth	-	-	-	-	-	-	-	-	-	-	-	-	-	-	-
Leo Gomez	-	-	-	78-58	-	-	-	-	-	-	-	-	37	99	78-58
Chris Hoiles	51-42	-	-	-	-	-	-	-	0-1	-	-	0-2	29	65	51-43
Sam Horn	-	-	-	-	-	-	-	-	26-19	-	-	25-15	-	45	26-19
Tim Hulett	-	-	0-1	9-15	-	-	-	-	5-3	-	-	-	16	17	14-19
Craig Lefferts	-	-	-	-	-	-	-	-	-	1-4	-	-	-	5	1-4
Richie Lewis	-	-	-	-	-	-	-	-	-	1-1	-	-	1	1	1-1
Chito Martinez	-	-	-	-	-	-	26-21	-	1-2	-	-	-	7	43	27-23
Ben McDonald	-	-	-	-	-	-	-	-	-	19-16	-	-	9	26	19-16
Mark McLemore	-	-	25-27	-	-	-	-	-	1-0	-	1-0	-	7	46	26-27
Luis Mercedes	-	-	-	-	-	1-0	-	7-4	1-0	-	-	-	12	1	9-4
Jose Mesa	-	-	-	-	-	-	-	-	-	3-9	-	-	3	9	3-9
Bob Milacki	-	-	-	-	-	-	-	-	-	11-9	-	-	8	12	11-9
Randy Milligan	-	75-54	-	-	-	-	-	-	2-3	-	-	11-11	41	93	77-57
Alan Mills	-	-	-	-	-	-	-	-	-	2-1	-	-	1	2	2-1
Mike Mussina	-	-	-	-	-	-	-	-	-	21-11	-	-	10	22	21-11
Gregg Olson	-	-	-	-	-	-	-	-	-	-	-	-	-	-	-
Joe Orsulak	-	-	-	-	-	3-7	-	47-41	-	-	0-1	0-1	14	84	50-48
Mark Parent	7-4	-	-	-	-	-	-	-	-	-	-	-	4	7	7-4
Jim Poole	-	-	-	-	-	-	-	-	-	-	-	-	-	-	-
Arthur Rhodes	-	-	-	-	-	-	-	-	-	10-5	-	-	3	12	10-5
Cal Ripken	-	-	-	-	89-73	-	-	-	-	-	-	4-4	46	116	89-73
Billy Ripken	-	-	64-44	-	-	-	-	-	-	-	-	-	40	68	64-44
Steve Scarsone	-	-	0-1	2-0	-	-	-	-	-	-	-	-	1	2	2-1
David Segui	-	13-18	-	-	-	2-1	-	7-6	-	-	-	-	26	21	22-25
Tommy Shields	-	-	-	-	-	-	-	-	-	-	-	-	-	-	-
Rick Sutcliffe	-	-	-	-	-	-	-	-	-	20-16	-	-	11	25	20-16
Jeff Tackett	31-26	-	-	-	-	-	-	-	-	-	-	-	12	45	31-26
Anthony Telford	-	-	-	-	-	-	-	-	-	-	-	-	-	-	-
Jack Voigt	-	-	-	-	-	-	-	-	-	-	-	-	-	-	-
Mark Williamson	-	-	-	-	-	-	-	-	-	-	-	-	-	-	-

TEAM TOTALS: BATTING

	AB	H	2B	3B	HR	RBI	BB	SO	BA	SA	OBA
Season	5485	1423	243	36	148	680	647	827	.259	.398	.340
vs. Left-Handers	1459	377	65	7	40	191	181	215	.258	.395	.345
vs. Right-Handers	4026	1046	178	29	108	489	466	612	.260	.399	.338
vs. Ground-Ballers	2721	718	111	14	65	323	307	395	.264	.387	.342
vs. Fly-Ballers	2764	705	132	22	83	357	340	432	.255	.409	.338
Home Games	2679	681	108	19	75	327	323	392	.254	.393	.337
Road Games	2806	742	135	17	73	353	324	435	.264	.403	.342
Grass Fields	4624	1208	195	29	136	574	538	686	.261	.404	.340
Artificial Turf	861	215	48	7	12	106	109	141	.250	.364	.337
April	686	172	41	7	16	96	88	112	.251	.401	.340
May	911	244	44	6	37	137	127	132	.268	.451	.361
June	945	265	37	6	29	120	99	135	.280	.424	.351
July	940	244	43	8	21	114	119	131	.260	.389	.343
August	910	229	33	5	21	115	127	136	.252	.368	.345
Sept./Oct.	1093	269	45	4	24	98	87	181	.246	.360	.303
Leading Off Inn.	1305	335	53	12	43	43	145	183	.257	.415	.336
Runners On	2458	627	108	13	56	588	296	379	.255	.378	.335
Bases Empty	3027	796	135	23	92	92	351	448	.263	.414	.344
Runners/Scor. Pos.	1375	356	64	9	34	526	207	233	.259	.393	.348
Runners On/2 Out	1059	252	51	8	25	239	130	172	.238	.372	.326
Scor. Pos./2 Out	666	162	33	7	17	213	98	109	.243	.390	.345
Late-Inning Pressure	728	173	31	4	15	67	91	125	.238	.353	.324
Leading Off	186	49	9	2	5	5	22	24	.263	.414	.344
Runners On	306	71	14	1	5	57	43	54	.232	.333	.324
Runners/Scor. Pos.	186	39	6	1	3	51	33	35	.210	.301	.319

RUNS BATTED IN	From 1B	From 2B	From 3B	Scoring Position
Totals	73/1866	189/1069	270/635	459/1704
Percentage	3.9%	17.7%	42.5%	26.9%

TEAM TOTALS: PITCHING

	W-L	ERA	AB	H	HR	BB	SO	BA	SA	OBA
Season	89-73	3.79	5531	1419	124	518	846	.257	.380	.322
vs. Left-Handers			2380	591	44	239	345	.248	.357	.316
vs. Right-Handers			3151	828	80	279	501	.263	.398	.326
vs. Ground-Ballers			2774	731	41	238	425	.264	.368	.321
vs. Fly-Ballers			2757	688	83	280	421	.250	.392	.322
Home Games	43-38	3.76	2829	702	69	255	422	.248	.374	.312
Road Games	46-35	3.82	2702	717	55	263	424	.265	.387	.332
Grass Fields	77-60	3.73	4653	1164	103	448	711	.250	.370	.318
Artificial Turf	12-13	4.12	878	255	21	70	135	.290	.436	.344
April	13-8	3.05	680	158	15	65	110	.232	.353	.301
May	16-11	4.31	912	247	30	84	118	.271	.425	.331
June	15-13	4.15	950	251	22	70	127	.264	.397	.315
July	13-14	3.86	931	235	20	98	148	.252	.373	.327
August	16-12	3.69	981	265	20	97	162	.270	.392	.338
Sept./Oct.	16-15	3.53	1077	263	17	104	181	.244	.340	.314
Leading Off Inn.			1348	354	29	106	199	.263	.389	.322
Bases Empty			3127	802	73	282	465	.256	.384	.322
Runners On			2404	617	51	236	381	.257	.376	.321
Runners/Scor. Pos.			1365	347	30	161	236	.254	.376	.327
Runners On/2 Out			999	223	19	124	175	.223	.331	.311
Scor. Pos./2 Out			655	148	11	90	116	.226	.324	.322
Late-Inning Pressure			842	187	11	88	161	.222	.297	.298
Leading Off			215	45	1	18	38	.209	.260	.280
Runners On			329	71	3	63	176	.216	.286	.305
Runners/Scor. Pos.			171	37	0	32	42	.216	.251	.333
First 9 Batters			2628	644	44	275	450	.245	.339	.318
Second 9 Batters			1533	411	41	140	225	.268	.422	.332
All Batters Thereafter			1370	364	39	103	171	.266	.412	.317

WON-LOST RECORD BY STARTING POSITION

Boston Red Sox	C	1B	2B	3B	SS	LF	CF	RF	DH	P	Leadoff	Cleanup	Starts vs. LH	Starts vs. RH	Total Starts
Tommy Barrett	-	-	0-2	-	-	-	-	-	-	-	-	-	-	2	0-2
Wade Boggs	-	-	-	52-62	-	-	-	-	8-13	-	22-33	-	37	98	60-75
Tom Bolton	-	-	-	-	-	-	-	-	-	0-1	-	-	-	1	0-1
Mike Brumley	-	-	-	-	-	-	-	-	-	-	-	-	-	-	-
Tom Brunansky	-	9-9	-	-	-	-	-	36-53	10-7	-	-	37-57	42	82	55-69
Ellis Burks	-	-	-	-	-	-	32-30	-	0-1	-	13-14	-	18	45	32-31
Jack Clark	-	6-6	-	-	-	-	-	-	29-33	-	-	15-13	33	41	35-39
Roger Clemens	-	-	-	-	-	-	-	-	-	22-11	-	-	12	21	22-11
Scott Cooper	-	20-26	-	17-22	-	-	-	-	1-0	-	-	-	8	78	38-48
Danny Darwin	-	-	-	-	-	-	-	-	-	7-8	-	-	4	11	7-8
John Dopson	-	-	-	-	-	-	-	-	-	8-17	-	-	7	18	8-17
John Flaherty	5-16	-	-	-	-	-	-	-	-	-	-	-	7	14	5-16
Tony Fossas	-	-	-	-	-	-	-	-	-	-	-	-	-	-	-
Mike Gardiner	-	-	-	-	-	-	-	-	-	7-11	-	-	6	12	7-11
Jeff Gray	-	-	-	-	-	-	-	-	-	-	-	-	-	-	-
Mike Greenwell	-	-	-	-	-	20-21	-	-	2-3	-	0-1	2-2	12	34	22-24
Greg A. Harris	-	-	-	-	-	-	-	-	-	-	1-1	-	-	2	1-1
Billy Hatcher	-	-	-	-	-	24-38	6-6	-	-	-	20-26	-	21	53	30-44
Joe Hesketh	-	-	-	-	-	-	-	-	-	9-15	-	-	8	16	9-15
Peter Hoy	-	-	-	-	-	-	-	-	-	-	-	-	-	-	-
Daryl Irvine	-	-	-	-	-	-	-	-	-	-	-	-	-	-	-
Steve Lyons	-	2-2	-	-	-	-	-	1-0	-	-	-	-	-	5	3-2
John Marzano	3-12	-	-	-	-	-	-	-	-	-	-	-	3	12	3-12
Tim Naehring	-	-	10-9	4-5	11-11	-	-	-	0-2	-	2-1	-	19	33	25-27
Tony Pena	63-59	-	-	-	-	-	-	-	-	-	-	-	34	88	63-59
Phil Plantier	-	-	-	-	-	6-5	-	27-33	9-13	-	-	-	17	76	42-51
Paul Quantrill	-	-	-	-	-	-	-	-	-	-	-	-	-	-	-
Carlos Quintana	-	-	-	-	-	-	-	-	-	-	-	-	-	-	-
Jeff Reardon	-	-	-	-	-	-	-	-	-	-	-	-	-	-	-
Jody Reed	-	-	63-78	-	-	-	-	-	-	-	23-24	-	45	96	63-78
Luis Rivera	-	-	-	-	35-50	-	-	-	-	-	-	-	25	60	35-50
Ken Ryan	-	-	-	-	-	-	-	-	-	-	-	-	-	-	-
Scott Taylor	-	-	-	-	-	-	-	-	-	-	0-1	-	-	1	0-1
John Valentin	-	-	-	-	27-28	-	-	-	-	-	-	-	12	43	27-28
Mo Vaughn	-	36-46	-	-	-	-	-	-	10-6	-	-	6-2	19	79	46-52
Frank Viola	-	-	-	-	-	-	-	-	-	17-18	-	-	7	28	17-18
Eric Wedge	2-2	-	-	-	-	-	-	-	4-11	-	-	0-1	11	8	6-13
Herm Winningham	-	-	-	-	-	13-12	10-13	-	-	-	-	6-4	3	45	23-25
Matt Young	-	-	-	-	-	-	-	-	-	2-6	-	-	1	7	2-6
Bob Zupcic	-	-	-	-	-	10-13	25-40	9-3	-	-	-	-	39	61	44-56

TEAM TOTALS: BATTING

	AB	H	2B	3B	HR	RBI	BB	SO	BA	SA	OBA
Season	5461	1343	259	21	84	567	591	865	.246	.347	.321
vs. Left-Handers	1445	344	79	5	27	152	175	220	.238	.356	.322
vs. Right-Handers	4016	999	180	16	57	415	416	645	.249	.344	.320
vs. Ground-Ballers	2592	653	119	9	28	277	282	403	.252	.337	.327
vs. Fly-Ballers	2869	690	140	12	56	290	309	462	.241	.356	.315
Home Games	2684	696	149	11	45	308	309	402	.259	.373	.337
Road Games	2777	647	110	10	39	259	282	463	.233	.322	.305
Grass Fields	4650	1157	222	20	70	489	519	726	.249	.350	.325
Artificial Turf	811	186	37	1	14	78	72	139	.229	.329	.295
April	624	145	27	1	6	55	85	122	.232	.308	.323
May	887	222	50	4	11	93	122	147	.250	.353	.341
June	939	235	47	2	17	100	83	140	.250	.359	.313
July	915	224	38	5	16	100	95	136	.245	.350	.315
August	1013	243	49	4	17	107	109	170	.240	.346	.316
Sept./Oct.	1083	274	48	5	17	112	97	150	.253	.354	.318
Leading Off Inn.	1344	316	54	5	18	18	109	194	.235	.323	.298
Runners On	2354	606	122	8	33	516	299	387	.257	.358	.337
Bases Empty	3107	737	137	13	51	51	292	478	.237	.339	.308
Runners/Scor. Pos.	1329	325	64	3	21	471	217	247	.245	.345	.342
Runners On/2 Out	1019	228	43	7	11	200	140	183	.224	.312	.319
Scor. Pos./2 Out	636	135	31	3	6	182	106	125	.212	.299	.325
Late-Inning Pressure	1006	264	49	3	15	107	97	181	.262	.362	.330
Leading Off	254	57	8	0	4	4	21	49	.224	.303	.289
Runners On	427	120	26	2	6	98	48	76	.281	.393	.352
Runners/Scor. Pos.	211	63	13	2	5	92	40	41	.299	.450	.404

RUNS BATTED IN	From 1B	From 2B	From 3B	Scoring Position
Totals	64/1775	172/1036	247/637	419/1673
Percentage	3.6%	16.6%	38.8%	25.0%

TEAM TOTALS: PITCHING

	W-L	ERA	AB	H	HR	BB	SO	BA	SA	OBA
Season	73-89	3.58	5496	1403	107	535	943	.255	.371	.323
vs. Left-Handers			1916	482	27	179	324	.252	.360	.318
vs. Right-Handers			3580	921	80	356	619	.257	.377	.326
vs. Ground-Ballers			2686	666	24	223	428	.248	.331	.308
vs. Fly-Ballers			2810	737	83	312	515	.262	.409	.338
Home Games	44-37	3.52	2860	761	46	256	487	.266	.373	.328
Road Games	29-52	3.65	2636	642	61	279	456	.244	.369	.319
Grass Fields	64-74	3.50	4731	1209	89	460	826	.256	.368	.323
Artificial Turf	9-15	4.09	765	194	18	75	117	.254	.390	.324
April	9-9	2.61	614	135	4	58	148	.220	.296	.289
May	15-12	3.22	880	213	11	68	146	.242	.333	.299
June	11-17	3.98	946	247	28	100	160	.261	.415	.332
July	13-15	3.65	970	262	20	90	133	.270	.388	.334
August	12-18	3.92	1020	276	25	94	185	.271	.394	.336
Sept./Oct.	13-18	3.74	1066	270	19	125	171	.253	.370	.334
Leading Off Inn.			1333	333	29	113	224	.250	.366	.312
Bases Empty			3076	761	62	263	544	.247	.358	.312
Runners On			2420	642	45	272	399	.265	.388	.337
Runners/Scor. Pos.			1416	358	22	202	258	.253	.365	.341
Runners On/2 Out			1010	251	21	123	167	.249	.389	.335
Scor. Pos./2 Out			675	161	12	102	118	.239	.367	.344
Late-Inning Pressure			850	228	15	82	145	.268	.371	.338
Leading Off			210	50	2	20	36	.238	.314	.313
Runners On			362	109	5	45	56	.301	.401	.380
Runners/Scor. Pos.			204	59	3	34	40	.289	.382	.391
First 9 Batters			2689	664	54	277	502	.247	.365	.319
Second 9 Batters			1469	401	28	121	231	.273	.390	.328
All Batters Thereafter			1338	338	25	137	210	.253	.363	.326

BOSTON RED SOX

For the last half-century, as major league baseball underwent such radical changes as the acceptance of African-American players, the abolition of the reserve clause, the widespread use of artificial turf, and the adoption by the American League of the designated hitter rule, the Boston Red Sox remained one of the game's great constants. For nearly 50 years the Red Sox provided their fans with the same product: an explosive offense built around a lineup of right-handed power hitters to exploit the nearness of the left-field wall at Fenway Park, their home since 1912. Jimmie Foxx, Vern Stephens, Jackie Jensen, Tony Conigliaro, Rico Petrocelli, Carlton Fisk, Jim Rice, Tony Armas, Dwight Evans—they launched a 50-year assault on the Green Monster that left opposing managers reluctant to start even their best left-handers at Fenway. So to provide balance, Boston's right-handed power was superbly complemented by three of the best left-handed hitters in major league history—Williams, Yastrzemski, Boggs—and a formidable supporting cast that included Johnny Pesky, Billy Goodman, Pete Runnels, and Fred Lynn. Pitching, speed, defense? Forget it; finesse was not part of the Red Sox vocabulary.

For the most part, Boston's formula proved successful. The Sox endured a period of decline and mediocrity starting in the early 1950s and culminating in consecutive ninth-place finishes in the mid-1960s. But those years only provided the necessary prelude to the Impossible Dream season of 1967, which kicked off a quarter-century during which Boston posted the third-best record in the majors. The top five teams from 1967 through 1991:

Team	Won	Lost	Pct.	GB
Baltimore Orioles	2163	1806	.545	—
Cincinnati Reds	2158	1826	.542	12½
Boston Red Sox	2153	1829	.541	16½
Los Angeles Dodgers	2148	1839	.539	24
New York Yankees	2119	1859	.533	48½

The following graphs will help to illustrate the consistency of Boston's signature product. The first shows the difference in the team's league rank in offense (runs per game) and in defense (opponents' runs per game). Above-the-line values indicate years in which the offense was better; below-the-line values are years in which the pitching was better. Notice that from 1939 through 1989, the Red Sox ranked higher in pitching than in batting only twice, and just barely (by one position in 1943 and 1953).

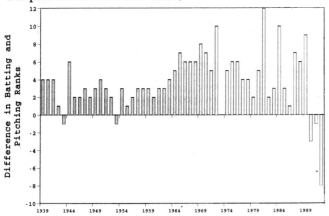

To appreciate how unusual that accomplishment is (and make no mistake—it's an *accomplishment,* not an *achievement,* since it stems in part from a long stretch of sub-par pitching), consider this: Every other non-expansion American League team ranked higher in pitching than in batting at least 16 times during the same 51-year period. The roll call: White Sox, 35; Orioles, 28; Indians, 24; Yankees, 19; Angels (out of 32) and Athletics, 18; Rangers (out of 32) and Tigers, 17; Twins, 16; Royals, 13 (out of 23); Brewers, 8 (out of 23); Mariners, 5 (out of 15); Blue Jays, 5 (out of 15); Red Sox, 2. Of course, Fenway Park itself played a significant role in that trend, but even teams that played in other hitters' parks, like Tiger Stadium, ranked higher in pitching than hitting more often than the Red Sox did.

The next graph contrasts the number of Red Sox home runs hit by right-handed swingers with those of left-handed and switch-hitters. It's standard for a team to get a majority of its home runs from right-handed hitters; for example, 19 of the 26 teams did so last season. (The exceptions were Kansas City in the American League; and Atlanta, Houston, New York, Philadelphia, Pittsburgh, and St. Louis in the National League.) But during the period under consideration, the major league home-run split was just 60–40 in favor of right-handed hitters; Boston's breakdown was more than 2-to-1 in favor of right-handers. That may not seem like a significant variation from the major league average, but over 50 years it represents a margin of nearly 600 more homers for right-handers than a typical team would have produced.

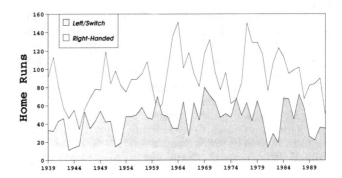

But over the past few seasons, while Boston's image as a right-handed fence-busting force has somehow survived, the Red Sox have become a poor offensive team, with a particular dearth of right-handed power. Even more uncharacteristic, Boston's pitching, led by Roger Clemens, has become nearly the best in the American League. Last season, those two trends almost merged in a conjunction as unlikely as a collision of Neptune and Pluto: As late as August 17, Boston ranked last in home runs but first in ERA (a lead they maintained until September 11). The Red Sox finished the season with a 3.58 ERA to rank a close second to Milwaukee (3.43) in a category in which they haven't led the league since 1914. And only Kansas City and Milwaukee finished the season with fewer homers than the Sox. This may qualify as the greatest sports makeover since surly George Foreman got religion, gained

50 pounds, and became a national folk hero. Boston's rank in runs per game, for and against, along with its home-run totals (overall and by right-handed hitters) for the past 10 years, further emphasizing the suddenness with which the Red Sox have changed their character:

	1983	1984	1985	1986	1987	1988	1989	1990	1991	1992
Hitting	7	2	3	3	4	1	1	7	7	13
Pitching	10	12	6	4	11	7	10	4	6	5
Difference	+3	+10	+3	+1	+7	+6	+9	−3	−1	−8
Total Home Runs	142	181	162	144	174	124	108	106	126	84
Right-Handed HRs	123	113	95	99	102	67	82	84	90	49
RH Percent	87	62	59	69	59	54	76	79	71	58

Perhaps the changes to the character of the Red Sox, and particularly to their offense, were inevitable once the team selected Walt Hriniak as its hitting guru in the late 1970s. In every season from 1969 through 1981, the Red Sox and their opponents hit more home runs at Fenway Park than they hit in Boston's road games. The margin was 26 home runs per season more, suggesting that Fenway caused a 19 percent increase. But as Hriniak became more influential in his role as hitting instructor, the emphasis shifted from blasting home runs over the Green Monster to spanking doubles all around the field. By the mid-1980s, the trend had shifted by 180 degrees: From 1985 through 1987, there were 91 more home runs hit in Red Sox road games than at Fenway Park. But Fenway, it turned out, could be exploited as a hitter's park in other ways. A look at our Ballparks Section indicates that it has the most inflationary effect of any A.L. park on batting average, and the second-highest increase in the majors on doubles and triples.

It has become fashionable in the past few years to attribute the decline of home runs at Fenway to the ring of "600 Club" sky boxes that circle the stadium behind home plate, displacing the old press box to an even higher elevation. The wind patterns, they say, have changed from hitter-friendly to downright inhospitable. Frankly, we haven't trotted our own anemometer and weather vane to Boston, but we can tell you this: The trend toward fewer home runs at Fenway began in the early 1980s, long before the 600 Club was built. Furthermore, the trend has actually ebbed since

the construction of the sky boxes. The following figures contrast the four seasons since the sky boxes were built to the four-year period immediately preceding it:

Years	Fenway Park			Road Games			Fenway Effect
	AB	HR	Rate	AB	HR	Rate	
1985–88	22,287	579	38.5	22,278	655	34.0	−11.6%
1989–92	22,320	463	48.2	21,898	438	50.0	+3.7%

Let's step through those figures. During the four years ending in 1988—Hriniak's last season with the team, when his influence peaked—Boston and its opponents hit one home run every 38 at-bats at Fenway Park, a significantly lower rate than those same teams produced in Boston's road games (one per 34 ABs). As indicated, that margin represents nearly a 12 percent decrease attributable to Fenway. But during the four seasons since then—which is to say, since the construction of the 600 Club—the figures are reversed: Boston and Co. hit home runs at the rate of one per 48 at-bats at Fenway, compared to one per 50 at the opponents' home fields. That may not compare to the effect of Fenway in the 1970s, but it represents a big increase over the Hriniak era.

A final thought: Despite the fact that Fenway Park is no longer an extreme home-run park, and despite the demise of Boston's once powerful right-handed lineup, opposing managers are still reluctant to start left-handed pitchers at Fenway. Notice that the difference between the number of southpaws facing the Red Sox at home and on the road isn't as great as in decades past, but it still exists:

LHP Vs. Boston	1960s	1970s	1980s	1990s
Fenway Park	188	171	214	67
Road Games	229	244	236	75

Over the past 10 years, so much of what typified the Red Sox and their stadium for the previous half-century has been turned on its ear. As popular perception catches up to these very real changes, this vestige should disappear as well, and left-handed pitchers will take their regular turns at Fenway Park.

CALIFORNIA ANGELS

Two years ago, the Detroit Tigers provided a classic example of a high-scoring team with a low batting average: They compensated for the American League's lowest batting average (.247) with major league high totals in home runs (209) and walks (699) to score an average of 5.04 runs per game, the second-highest mark in the league.

The team with the lowest batting average in the A.L. has been the league's lowest-scoring team only half the time recently (in five of the past 10 years, and in 10 of the past 20) and historically (46 times in the league's 92 years of operation). Some readers might have expected that rate to be higher, especially considering how often lazy broadcasters refer to a given team as "the league's best-hitting team"—a frustratingly imprecise term—when what they mean is nothing more than "the team with the highest batting average." So much of a team's offense isn't expressed in its batting average, but it takes a team like the 1991 Tigers to highlight that fact.

Then again, teams like last season's Angels, who finished last in both batting average and scoring average, seemingly underscore the connection between batting average and runs. But the 1992 Angels ranked last in runs per game not just because they batted a league low .243, but for many other reasons as well. The Angels became the 23d team in this century (and only the second in the past 20 years) to score a no-offense hat trick: last in batting average, walks, and extra-base hits.

The Angels who really earned their halos in 1992 were Jim Abbott, Mark Langston, and Julio Valera. To the credit of California's pitching staff, the Angels became only the eighth of those 23 teams to avoid a last-place finish. (Bonus points to any fans who recall that the 1969 Angels actually finished in third place despite a triple-low in offense; no other such team has ever finished in the first division.) Those three Angels starters were all among the six worst-supported pitchers in the American League last season. The following tables show the pitchers who received the most and least batting support in each league last season—that is, the highest and lowest averages of runs scored by their teams in the games they started (minimum: 25 starts). Note the wide gap between Abbott and Kevin Appier, who ranked a distant second among poorly supported A.L. pitchers. As we note in Abbott's individual comments (page 221), his average was the lowest in the American League during the era of the designated hitter:

Highest N.L. Support				Lowest N.L. Support		
Pitcher, Team	W–L	R/G		Pitcher, Team	W–L	R/G
Burkett, S.F.	13–9	4.69		Benes, S.D.	13–14	2.82
Mulholland, Phi.	13–11	4.63		Wilson, S.F.	8–14	3.08
Glavine, Atl.	20–8	4.61		Black, S.F.	10–12	3.11
Harnisch, Hou.	9–10	4.50		Hershiser, L.A.	10–15	3.12
Swindell, Cin.	12–8	4.40		Candiotti, L.A.	11–15	3.13
Fernandez, N.Y.	14–11	4.34		Gooden, N.Y.	10–13	3.26
Hurst, S.D.	14–9	4.34		Henry, Hou.	6–9	3.32
Belcher, Cin.	15–14	4.32		Ke. Gross, L.A.	8–13	3.40
Cone, N.Y.	13–7	4.30		Castillo, Chi.	10–11	3.45
Lefferts, S.D.	13–9	4.30		Schilling, Phi.	14–11	3.46

In the Orioles essay in the 1992 *Analyst,* we noted that poorly supported pitchers who compiled losing records were among those most likely to make a sharp improvement in terms of won-lost record the next season. (If it sounds as if we're about to stray into fantasy-league territory, we are.) We even provided a list of those contenders. The list wasn't foolproof; it included Jeff Ballard, who spent the entire season in the minors, and Allan Anderson and Brian Holman, who were injured for most or all of the year. (We hate when that happens.) But of the other 11 pitchers cited, 10 improved their won-lost records; three did so by at least 10 wins each relative to the .500 mark: Charles Nagy, from 10–15 to 17–10 (from five games below .500 to seven above, or plus-12); Dennis Rasmussen (6–13 to 4–1, plus-10), and Greg Swindell (9–16 to 12–8, plus-11). All things considered, the system performed pretty well in 1992—not surprising in light of its track record, which we documented last year: an average increase of 150 percentage points per pitcher since 1981.

You can easily spot this season's contenders from the tables above—the pitchers with losing records on the low-support lists. And this season, we have a twist that should interest you as well.

In any given season, roughly five pitchers coming off seasons of 25 or more starts will improve their records by 10 or more wins relative to the .500 mark (as Nagy, Rasmussen, and Swindell did last season)—roughly one of every 14 pitchers who meet the starts minimum. Fantasy-league managers could approach draft day with a lot more confidence if they were able to identify the pitchers most likely to do so. Well, there's a simple, commonsense rule for identifying a group of pitchers who historically have had roughly a one-in-three chance of going plus-10 or better in the upcoming season. And, to spare you further suspense, this year's one and only contender is Jim Abbott. (We know you were hoping for someone more obscure; sorry, maybe next year.)

Here's how it works: Pitchers who rank among their league's five worst-supported starters and change teams for the next season are more than four times as likely to go plus-10 or better than the 25-start pitchers. Over the past 30 years, there have been 54 bottom-five pitchers who moved to new teams by the start of the next season; 17 of them improved their records by at least 10 wins, including two of the six greatest increases of the past 15 years (Jerry Koosman and Danny Jackson). The full list:

Highest A.L. Support				Lowest A.L. Support		
Pitcher, Team	W–L	R/G		Pitcher, Team	W–L	R/G
Krueger, Min.	10–6	5.63		Abbott, Cal.	7–15	2.55
Morris, Tor.	21–6	5.44		Appier, K.C.	15–8	3.47
Tapani, Min.	16–11	5.35		Viola, Bos.	13–12	3.49
Stottlemyre, Tor.	12–11	5.30		Langston, Cal.	13–14	3.53
Bosio, Mil.	16–6	5.12		Hanson, Sea.	8–17	3.63
Sanderson, N.Y.	12–11	5.12		Valera, Cal.	8–11	3.68
Gullickson, Det.	14–13	5.06		Hough, Chi.	7–12	3.70
McDonald, Bal.	13–13	5.06		Dopson, Bos.	7–11	3.72
Key, Tor.	13–13	5.00		Ryan, Tex.	5–9	3.81
Moore, Oak.	17–12	4.94		Perez, N.Y.	13–16	3.85

Years	Pitcher	Team	W–L	Supp.	Team	W–L	Supp.	Inc.
1963–64	Roger Craig	NY-N	5–22	2.29	St.L.	7–9	3.47	+15
1964–65	Tracy Stallard	NY-N	10–20	3.29	St.L.	11–8	4.58	+13
1965–66	Al Jackson	NY-N	8–20	2.59	St.L.	13–15	3.00	+10
1966–67	Mike McCormick	Was.	11–14	3.41	S.F.	22–10	4.31	+15
1969–70	Jim McGlothlin	Cal.	8–16	2.86	Cin.	14–10	4.26	+12
1972–73	Carl Morton	Mon.	7–13	2.67	Atl.	15–10	5.27	+11
1972–73	Bill Singer	L.A.	6–16	2.68	Cal.	20–14	4.10	+16
1975–76	Bill Singer	Cal.	7–15	3.48	Tex.	13–10	4.56	+11
1977–78	Vida Blue	Oak.	14–19	3.03	S.F.	18–10	3.91	+13
1977–78	Jon Matlack	NY-N	7–15	3.45	Tex.	15–13	3.06	+10
1978–79	Jerry Koosman	NY-N	3–15	3.28	Min.	20–13	4.51	+19
1979–80	Tom Underwood	Tor.	9–16	3.48	NY-A	13–9	5.64	+11
1980–81	Rick Honeycutt	Sea.	10–17	3.32	Tex.	11–6	4.25	+12
1986–87	Neal Heaton	Min.	7–15	3.66	Mon.	13–10	4.81	+11
1987–88	Danny Jackson	K.C.	9–18	3.35	Cin.	23–8	4.60	+24
1988–89	Mike Moore	Sea.	9–15	3.69	Oak.	19–11	3.97	+14
1991–92	Greg Swindell	Cle.	9–16	3.42	Cin.	12–8	4.40	+11

Although everyone pays it lip service, a pitcher's run support continues to be one of the most underappreciated factors in determining his won-lost record—and one that is obviously out of his control. Over the past 20 years, there have been 23 pitchers whose teams scored an average of fewer than three runs per start (minimum: 25 GS); only two posted winning records—and just barely: Dave Stieb (11–10 with a 3.18 ERA in 1981) and Doug Drabek (14–12 with a 2.80 ERA in 1989). How underappreciated is this factor? In *Baseball America* this winter, Peter Gammons wrote that Jim Abbott would experience a major "comeback" in 1993 because the Yankees would be such an improvement on California's *defense*.

Baseball fans often point to Sandy Koufax's records of 19–5, 26–8, and 27–9 from 1964 through 1966 for notoriously weak-hitting Dodgers teams as examples of successful seasons despite poor support. Well, yes, we'll have to admit that pitchers as good as Koufax can win consistently regardless of the quality of their support. (Of course, there hasn't been a pitcher as good as Koufax since he retired.) But it's worth noting that even Sandy wasn't supported as poorly as you might think. Although the Dodgers ranked eighth in a 10-team league in scoring in each of those seasons, plating an average of 3.75 runs per game during that period, they scored significantly more than that for Koufax: 3.98 runs per game, a mark just barely below the league average for that three-year period (4.05).

All this talk about Los Angeles, the '60s, and scoring reminds us that 1993 is an opportune time to rekindle memories of a small and ultimately insignificant piece of baseball history, but one that has been lamentably forgotten over the past 30 years: Wrigley Field.

If your reaction was "Wrigley Field? *Los Angeles?*" you just proved our point.

The American League expansion of 1961, announced on October 26, 1960, was a hastily arranged move probably designed to get the jump on the National League, which had announced earlier in the month its own expansion plans for 1962. The A.L. plans were approved without ownership for its new team in Los Angeles, and without a stadium in which that team could play. Plans to share the Coliseum were met with a threat of litigation by the Dodgers. It wasn't until after the franchise was awarded on December 6 to a group headed by Gene Autry that a four-year agreement was reached for the new team to rent dates from the Dodgers at their new stadium at Chavez Ravine. But that park was still under construction, and wouldn't be ready for play until 1962. So for one year only, the Angels chose as their home ballpark Wrigley Field, a 35-year-old minor league facility.

Wrigley Field's most notable features were its power alleys, with fences only slightly further from home plate (345 feet) than the distances down the lines (340 feet in left, 338 in right). For just that reason, it was selected as the site for "Home Run Derby," a syndicated television series of the early 1960s still seen occasionally on ESPN. It should have surprised no one that a total of 248 home runs were hit there in 1961 (its only season of major league play), still an all-time major league high. By way of comparison, only 121 home runs were hit in Angels road games in 1961, suggesting that Wrigley Field roughly doubled a player's or a team's home-run output.

Of the nine players with at least 250 at-bats for the Angels in 1961, seven posted the best home-run rates of their careers (that is, fewest at-bats per home run); the names of those players are marked with asterisks in the following table. Seasons of less than 100 ABs weren't considered; but as the table shows, only one of those players had fewer than three other 100-AB seasons:

Player	Years 100+ ABs	1961 Angels AB HR Rate			Highest Other Rate Year Team AB HR Rate				
*Earl Averill	4	323	21	15.4	1959	Cubs	186	10	18.6
*Steve Bilko	6	294	20	14.7	1958	LA-N	188	11	17.1
*Ken Hunt	2	479	25	19.2	1963	Wash.	162	6	27.0
Ted Kluszewski	14	263	15	17.5	1954	Cin.	573	49	11.7
Joe Koppe	6	338	5	67.6	1959	Phil.	422	7	60.3
*Albie Pearson	7	427	7	61.0	1965	Cal.	360	4	90.0
*George Thomas	6	282	13	21.7	1964	Det.	308	12	25.7
*Lee Thomas	8	450	24	18.8	1962	L.A.-A	583	26	22.4
*Leon Wagner	10	453	28	16.2	1962	L.A.-A	612	37	16.5

Baseball trivia to amaze your friends: Zachary Taylor Davis was the architect of both Wrigley Fields, two of the greatest home-run parks in major league history. But lest you think this reflected any preference of his own as to the style of play, he also designed the old Comiskey Park in Chicago, built at the urging of White Sox pitcher Ed Walsh and team owner Charles Comiskey himself to be a home-run hitter's nightmare. (Comiskey said that he wanted a ballpark in which batters had to earn their home runs.)

As discussed in the Rockies essay, the altitude at Mile High Stadium is almost certain to produce a home-run explosion in Denver this season. When the Rockies leave there for Coors Field, their permanent new home starting in 1995, the distances on the fences will change, but the altitude won't—nor will the profusion of home runs it produces, unless the fences are pushed back to Comiskeylike dimensions to compensate. So Wrigley Field in Los Angeles, demolished a quarter-century ago, may eventually lose its place in the record books. But it certainly will never lose its cult status among true baseball fans, or followers of television's cult classics.

WON-LOST RECORD BY STARTING POSITION

California Angels	C	1B	2B	3B	SS	LF	CF	RF	DH	P	Leadoff	Cleanup	Starts vs. LH	Starts vs. RH	Total Starts
Jim Abbott	-	-	-	-	-	-	-	-	-	10-19	-	-	5	24	10-19
Scott Bailes	-	-	-	-	-	-	-	-	-	-	-	-	-	-	-
Bert Blyleven	-	-	-	-	-	-	-	-	-	8-16	-	-	4	20	8-16
Hubie Brooks	-	2-4	-	-	-	-	-	27-41	-	-	-	24-44	19	55	29-45
Mike Butcher	-	-	-	-	-	-	-	-	-	-	-	-	-	-	-
Chuck Crim	-	-	-	-	-	-	-	-	-	-	-	-	-	-	-
Chad Curtis	-	-	-	-	-	20-17	7-25	21-26	-	-	5-4	-	35	81	48-68
Alvin Davis	-	9-11	-	-	-	-	-	-	5-2	-	-	4-4	-	27	14-13
Gary DiSarcina	-	-	-	-	70-85	-	-	-	-	-	-	-	34	121	70-85
Rob Ducey	-	-	-	-	-	8-7	-	0-1	-	-	0-1	-	1	15	8-8
Damion Easley	-	-	-	17-24	1-0	-	-	-	-	-	4-4	-	9	33	18-24
Mark Eichhorn	-	-	-	-	-	-	-	-	-	-	-	-	-	-	-
John Farrell	-	-	-	-	-	-	-	-	-	-	-	-	-	-	-
Junior Felix	-	-	-	-	-	-	62-60	0-1	2-6	-	-	5-3	22	109	64-67
Chuck Finley	-	-	-	-	-	-	-	-	-	16-15	-	-	5	26	16-15
Mike Fitzgerald	25-25	-	-	-	-	3-1	-	3-0	0-1	-	-	-	22	36	31-27
Tim Fortugno	-	-	-	-	-	-	-	-	-	4-1	-	-	1	4	4-1
Steve Frey	-	-	-	-	-	-	-	-	-	-	-	-	-	-	-
Gary Gaetti	-	21-19	-	26-37	-	-	-	-	7-10	-	-	19-20	35	85	54-66
Rene Gonzales	-	0-6	17-19	25-26	0-3	-	-	-	-	-	-	-	22	74	42-54
Jose Gonzalez	-	-	-	-	-	3-5	0-1	0-4	-	-	-	-	12	1	3-10
Joe Grahe	-	-	-	-	-	-	-	-	2-5	-	-	-	2	5	2-5
Bryan Harvey	-	-	-	-	-	-	-	-	-	-	-	-	-	-	-
Hilly Hathaway	-	-	-	-	-	-	-	-	-	-	1-0	-	1	-	1-0
Von Hayes	-	2-1	-	-	-	-	-	37-42	2-2	-	-	14-9	6	80	41-45
Mark Langston	-	-	-	-	-	-	-	-	-	16-16	-	-	7	25	16-16
Scott Lewis	-	-	-	-	-	-	-	-	-	-	1-1	-	-	2	1-1
John Morris	-	-	-	-	-	1-1	-	3-3	2-1	-	-	1-0	1	10	6-5
Greg Myers	1-4	-	-	-	-	-	-	-	-	-	-	-	-	5	1-4
Ken Oberkfell	-	1-0	7-10	-	-	-	-	-	3-1	-	-	1-0	1	21	11-11
John Orton	19-21	-	-	-	-	-	-	-	-	-	-	-	8	32	19-21
Lance Parrish	8-13	-	-	-	-	-	-	0-2	-	-	-	-	4	19	8-15
Luis Polonia	-	-	-	-	-	37-59	-	24-22	-	-	61-81	-	26	116	61-81
Don Robinson	-	-	-	-	-	-	-	-	-	-	3-0	-	1	2	3-0
Bob Rose	-	0-1	11-13	-	-	-	-	-	-	-	-	-	7	18	11-14
Tim Salmon	-	-	-	-	-	-	-	8-13	-	-	-	4-7	4	17	8-13
Dick Schofield	-	-	-	0-1	-	-	-	-	-	-	-	-	-	1	0-1
Luis Sojo	-	-	37-48	4-3	1-1	-	-	-	-	-	-	-	25	69	42-52
Lee Stevens	-	37-48	-	-	-	-	-	0-2	-	-	-	0-3	9	78	37-50
Ron Tingley	19-27	-	-	-	-	-	-	-	-	-	-	-	11	35	19-27
Julio Valera	-	-	-	-	-	-	-	-	-	11-17	-	-	9	19	11-17
Reggie Williams	-	-	-	-	-	3-4	-	-	-	-	-	2-0	2	5	3-4

TEAM TOTALS: BATTING

	AB	H	2B	3B	HR	RBI	BB	SO	BA	SA	OBA
Season	5364	1306	202	20	88	537	416	882	.243	.338	.301
vs. Left-Handers	1250	289	44	2	25	129	112	222	.231	.330	.297
vs. Right-Handers	4114	1017	158	18	63	408	304	660	.247	.340	.302
vs. Ground-Ballers	2552	635	102	6	30	242	196	402	.249	.329	.305
vs. Fly-Ballers	2812	671	100	14	58	295	220	480	.239	.346	.296
Home Games	2637	658	100	10	44	289	204	415	.250	.345	.306
Road Games	2727	648	102	10	44	248	212	467	.238	.331	.296
Grass Fields	4545	1105	165	18	78	454	358	726	.243	.339	.300
Artificial Turf	819	201	37	2	10	83	58	156	.245	.332	.302
April	723	191	36	3	21	101	73	110	.264	.409	.332
May	880	211	30	5	18	78	69	134	.240	.347	.294
June	918	214	35	1	13	86	71	149	.233	.316	.293
July	871	216	33	3	15	96	63	125	.248	.344	.301
August	972	233	34	6	7	85	76	175	.240	.309	.300
Sept./Oct.	1000	241	34	2	14	91	64	189	.241	.321	.291
Leading Off Inn.	1360	332	62	3	19	19	87	221	.244	.336	.294
Runners On	2112	538	69	13	37	486	194	324	.255	.352	.317
Bases Empty	3252	768	133	7	51	51	222	558	.236	.328	.289
Runners/Scor. Pos.	1231	310	41	10	24	438	148	215	.252	.360	.329
Runners On/2 Out	870	190	26	3	13	169	90	146	.218	.300	.295
Scor. Pos./2 Out	565	125	19	3	8	153	71	105	.221	.308	.311
Late-Inning Pressure	875	189	21	2	16	78	73	164	.216	.299	.280
Leading Off	237	50	9	0	3	3	16	53	.211	.287	.264
Runners On	316	71	4	1	9	71	41	54	.225	.329	.318
Runners/Scor. Pos.	179	36	1	1	5	62	34	35	.201	.302	.332

RUNS BATTED IN	From 1B	From 2B	From 3B	Scoring Position
Totals	69/1454	165/954	215/495	380/1449
Percentage	4.7%	17.3%	43.4%	26.2%

TEAM TOTALS: PITCHING

	W-L	ERA	AB	H	HR	BB	SO	BA	SA	OBA
Season	72-90	3.84	5484	1449	130	532	888	.264	.382	.331
vs. Left-Handers			1600	433	27	144	214	.271	.370	.333
vs. Right-Handers			3884	1016	103	388	674	.262	.387	.330
vs. Ground-Ballers			2582	676	36	211	403	.262	.347	.319
vs. Fly-Ballers			2902	773	94	321	485	.266	.413	.341
Home Games	41-40	3.74	2830	753	60	250	447	.266	.371	.326
Road Games	31-50	3.95	2654	696	70	282	441	.262	.393	.335
Grass Fields	63-75	3.75	4693	1237	106	453	756	.264	.375	.330
Artificial Turf	9-15	4.40	791	212	24	79	132	.268	.420	.338
April	11-10	4.19	722	189	17	67	112	.262	.368	.327
May	10-17	3.47	889	219	24	98	159	.246	.369	.321
June	11-17	4.29	940	263	23	85	146	.280	.417	.339
July	14-13	4.10	908	247	27	90	154	.272	.410	.337
August	13-16	3.73	970	249	23	111	146	.257	.371	.336
Sept./Oct.	13-17	3.41	1055	282	16	81	171	.267	.356	.325
Leading Off Inn.			1336	374	38	105	201	.280	.421	.337
Bases Empty			3085	808	81	279	507	.262	.391	.327
Runners On			2399	641	49	253	381	.267	.370	.335
Runners/Scor. Pos.			1369	347	26	190	246	.253	.352	.339
Runners On/2 Out			978	227	20	107	172	.232	.334	.312
Scor. Pos./2 Out			643	141	13	78	118	.219	.322	.308
Late-Inning Pressure			810	209	17	80	136	.258	.357	.325
Leading Off			211	54	6	17	36	.256	.379	.314
Runners On			341	84	6	41	62	.246	.337	.326
Runners/Scor. Pos.			180	36	5	33	43	.200	.311	.321
First 9 Batters			2666	681	69	274	419	.255	.374	.327
Second 9 Batters			1398	364	25	124	237	.260	.361	.321
All Batters Thereafter			1420	404	36	134	232	.285	.418	.348

WON-LOST RECORD BY STARTING POSITION

Chicago White Sox	C	1B	2B	3B	SS	LF	CF	RF	DH	P	Leadoff	Cleanup	Starts vs. LH	Starts vs. RH	Total Starts
Shawn Abner	-	-	-	-	-	5-2	6-5	14-16	-	-	-	-	35	13	25-23
Wilson Alvarez	-	-	-	-	-	-	-	-	-	7-2	-	-	1	8	7-2
George Bell	-	-	-	-	-	8-7	-	76-64	-	-	-	61-46	40	115	84-71
Esteban Beltre	-	-	-	18-14	-	-	-	-	-	-	-	-	16	16	18-14
Joey Cora	-	-	11-10	1-1	0-3	-	-	-	1-0	-	7-5	-	4	23	13-14
Chris Cron	-	0-1	-	-	-	-	-	-	-	-	-	0-1	1	-	0-1
Brian Drahman	-	-	-	-	-	-	-	-	-	-	-	-	-	-	-
Mike Dunne	-	-	-	-	-	-	-	-	-	1-0	-	-	-	1	1-0
Alex Fernandez	-	-	-	-	-	-	-	-	-	13-16	-	-	4	25	13-16
Carlton Fisk	26-25	-	-	-	-	-	-	-	1-0	-	-	1-0	12	40	27-25
Craig Grebeck	-	-	-	2-1	41-41	-	-	-	-	-	-	-	22	63	43-42
Ozzie Guillen	-	-	-	-	7-5	-	-	-	-	-	-	-	5	7	7-5
Scott Hemond	-	-	-	-	-	0-1	-	-	0-1	-	-	-	1	1	0-2
Roberto Hernandez	-	-	-	-	-	-	-	-	-	-	-	-	-	-	-
Greg Hibbard	-	-	-	-	-	-	-	-	-	16-12	-	-	10	18	16-12
Charlie Hough	-	-	-	-	-	-	-	-	-	11-16	-	-	9	18	11-16
Mike Huff	-	-	-	-	-	0-3	-	13-10	-	-	2-0	-	25	1	13-13
Bo Jackson	-	-	-	-	-	-	-	-	-	-	-	-	-	-	-
Shawn Jeter	-	-	-	-	-	-	-	1-3	-	-	1-2	-	-	4	1-3
Lance Johnson	-	-	-	-	-	-	80-71	-	-	-	1-0	-	32	119	80-71
Ron Karkovice	53-45	-	-	-	-	-	-	-	-	-	-	-	31	67	53-45
Terry Leach	-	-	-	-	-	-	-	-	-	-	-	-	-	-	-
Kirk McCaskill	-	-	-	-	-	-	-	-	-	18-16	-	-	8	26	18-16
Jack McDowell	-	-	-	-	-	-	-	-	-	20-14	-	-	10	24	20-14
Matt Merullo	7-5	-	-	-	-	-	-	-	0-1	-	-	0-1	-	13	7-6
Warren Newson	-	-	-	-	-	7-4	-	14-11	1-1	-	2-0	-	-	38	22-16
Donn Pall	-	-	-	-	-	-	-	-	-	-	-	-	-	-	-
Dan Pasqua	-	1-3	-	-	-	-	-	44-36	-	-	-	-	1	83	45-39
Scott Radinsky	-	-	-	-	-	-	-	-	-	-	-	-	-	-	-
Tim Raines	-	-	-	-	-	66-59	-	-	7-7	-	39-48	-	31	108	73-66
Nelson Santovenia	0-1	-	-	-	-	-	-	-	-	-	-	-	-	1	0-1
Steve Sax	-	-	75-66	-	-	-	-	-	-	-	34-21	-	40	101	75-66
Dale Sveum	-	-	-	20-13	-	-	-	-	-	-	-	-	1	32	20-13
Bobby Thigpen	-	-	-	-	-	-	-	-	-	-	-	-	-	-	-
Frank Thomas	-	85-72	-	-	-	-	-	-	0-2	-	-	24-26	42	117	85-74
Robin Ventura	-	-	-	83-74	-	-	-	-	-	-	-	0-2	39	118	83-74

TEAM TOTALS: BATTING

	AB	H	2B	3B	HR	RBI	BB	SO	BA	SA	OBA
Season	5498	1434	269	36	110	686	622	784	.261	.383	.336
vs. Left-Handers	1513	391	82	7	24	168	171	215	.258	.369	.333
vs. Right-Handers	3985	1043	187	29	86	518	451	569	.262	.388	.337
vs. Ground-Ballers	2672	681	125	21	49	317	305	386	.255	.372	.331
vs. Fly-Ballers	2826	753	144	15	61	369	317	398	.266	.393	.339
Home Games	2694	695	129	19	54	341	325	348	.258	.380	.338
Road Games	2804	739	140	17	56	345	297	436	.264	.386	.333
Grass Fields	4578	1210	217	31	97	589	546	635	.264	.389	.342
Artificial Turf	920	224	52	5	13	97	76	149	.243	.353	.301
April	622	166	32	4	10	79	72	82	.267	.379	.344
May	885	205	46	5	13	99	118	146	.232	.339	.320
June	956	252	41	5	19	106	109	138	.264	.377	.338
July	971	263	40	10	17	114	98	118	.271	.385	.340
August	931	252	45	3	26	135	100	115	.271	.409	.339
Sept./Oct.	1133	296	65	9	25	153	125	185	.261	.401	.335
Leading Off Inn.	1327	318	61	10	25	25	118	174	.240	.357	.307
Runners On	2414	679	135	20	45	621	315	353	.281	.410	.359
Bases Empty	3084	755	134	16	65	65	307	431	.245	.362	.316
Runners/Scor. Pos.	1407	382	74	14	26	550	228	229	.271	.399	.361
Runners On/2 Out	1001	246	46	10	21	217	137	157	.246	.375	.339
Scor. Pos./2 Out	648	142	24	5	12	180	105	119	.219	.327	.332
Late-Inning Pressure	780	194	26	4	13	81	89	119	.249	.342	.329
Leading Off	199	50	4	1	5	5	16	25	.251	.357	.317
Runners On	341	86	13	3	1	69	50	61	.252	.317	.348
Runners/Scor. Pos.	188	41	8	1	1	65	38	41	.218	.287	.347

RUNS BATTED IN	From 1B	From 2B	From 3B	Scoring Position
Totals	89/1775	212/1148	275/606	487/1754
Percentage	5.0%	18.5%	45.4%	27.8%

TEAM TOTALS: PITCHING

	W-L	ERA	AB	H	HR	BB	SO	BA	SA	OBA
Season	86-76	3.82	5551	1400	123	550	810	.252	.371	.323
vs. Left-Handers			2151	546	42	220	320	.254	.365	.325
vs. Right-Handers			3400	854	81	330	490	.251	.375	.322
vs. Ground-Ballers			2794	709	48	283	380	.254	.353	.325
vs. Fly-Ballers			2757	691	75	267	430	.251	.390	.321
Home Games	50-32	3.38	2848	691	62	261	432	.243	.347	.309
Road Games	36-44	4.31	2703	709	61	289	378	.262	.397	.339
Grass Fields	78-57	3.81	4656	1166	109	455	689	.250	.367	.320
Artificial Turf	8-19	3.89	895	234	14	95	121	.261	.393	.340
April	11-8	3.74	634	155	17	59	84	.244	.371	.309
May	12-15	3.69	916	223	20	99	142	.243	.365	.322
June	14-14	3.67	957	224	22	96	129	.234	.356	.310
July	13-14	4.24	936	240	21	115	138	.256	.379	.340
August	18-10	3.47	971	252	19	72	142	.260	.360	.317
Sept./Oct.	18-15	4.06	1137	306	24	109	175	.269	.392	.335
Leading Off Inn.			1350	302	25	109	205	.224	.325	.286
Bases Empty			3185	769	71	280	493	.241	.354	.308
Runners On			2366	631	52	270	317	.267	.395	.343
Runners/Scor. Pos.			1318	338	30	187	196	.256	.392	.347
Runners On/2 Out			1035	264	25	125	146	.255	.392	.342
Scor. Pos./2 Out			641	160	18	90	103	.250	.402	.350
Late-Inning Pressure			991	246	23	110	173	.248	.368	.329
Leading Off			250	53	5	24	51	.212	.308	.286
Runners On			425	104	7	55	68	.245	.355	.337
Runners/Scor. Pos.			243	54	5	38	42	.222	.350	.331
First 9 Batters			2622	633	46	290	422	.241	.344	.320
Second 9 Batters			1453	364	38	135	188	.251	.379	.318
All Batters Thereafter			1476	403	39	125	200	.273	.413	.335

CHICAGO WHITE SOX

White Sox outfielders hit only 19 home runs last season. Tim Raines hit 7; Dan Pasqua, 4; George Bell and Lance Johnson, 3 each; and Shawn Abner and Warren Newson, 1 each. (Homers hit while DHing don't count here.) It marked the fourth consecutive season in which Chicago's outfielders produced the fewest home runs in the American League, and the second straight time they trailed the entire majors. No fewer than 13 players hit more home runs during that four-year period than all of Chicago's outfielders combined (100). But last season marked the nadir—at least for now. With the exception of the abbreviated 1981 season, it was the lowest total in the American League since 1949, when White Sox OFs tallied only 19 homers. (Gus Zernial and Catfish Metkovich, 5 each; John Ostrowski and Steve Souchock, 4 each; and Jerry Scala, 1. We know you don't care, but we can't pass up a chance to mention Catfish Metkovich.)

But there's a flip side to this seemingly negative picture. Two White Sox outfielders, Lance Johnson and Tim Raines, were among only 12 in either league to steal at least 40 bases. No other team had more than one OF with 40-plus steals.

Both of those marks are part of a continuing trend in baseball that has seen the profile of a typical starting outfielder swing from power to speed. Last season, outfielders accounted for only 38 percent of all home runs in the majors, the lowest mark in this century. Prior to 1981, that figure had never fallen below 40 percent. The graph below tracks the percentage of home runs and stolen bases that outfielders accounted for. As you can see, these figures were generally similar for the period from 1920 to 1960, but not since 1957 have OFs contributed a larger slice of the overall home-run pie than the steal pie. (Yummy!) And over the past 10 years, the margin between those two figures has ranged from 10 to 17 percent:

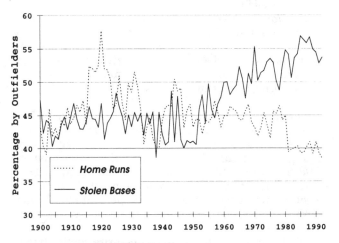

Here's an odd final note: The trend toward more speed and less power among outfielders was rampant in the mid-1980s, primarily on teams that played their home games on artificial turf, perhaps in imitation of the successful Royals and Cardinals teams of the late 1970s and early '80s. From 1983 through 1987, outfielders accounted for 61 percent of all stolen bases on turf teams, but only 37 percent of all home runs. Think of that as plus-24. The gap for teams that played on grass fields was much narrower: 51 percent of steals and 41

percent of homers, or plus-10. But over the past five seasons, the trend has actually swung in the opposite direction, with outfielders on grass-field teams now more speed-dominant than outfielders on teams that play on artificial turf:

	1983	1984	1985	1986	1987	1988	1989	1990	1991	1992
Grass Fields	+ 7	+ 8	+12	+13	+10	+13	+15	+13	+17	+21
Artificial Turf	+24	+23	+26	+23	+23	+20	+17	+14	+ 8	+ 6

Of the 12 outfielders who had at least 30 more stolen bases than home runs last season, only two—Steve Finley and Marquis Grissom—played their home games on a carpet. The other 10 all played on natural grass: Johnson and Raines, Brady Anderson, Brett Butler, Chad Curtis, Darryl Hamilton, Rickey Henderson, Kenny Lofton, Otis Nixon, and Luis Polonia. The mid-'80s movement by turf teams toward speed-dominant outfields made sense, but this latest twist stumps us. It may just serve as a reminder that not every trend has a necessary explanation—or that everything that can be measured should be.

Ask 100 baseball fans how to improve the game and we think a substantial number will suggest that the length of an average game be shortened. Ask 100 White Sox fans how best to shorten the length of a game and a vast majority are sure to suggest that Carlton Fisk be prevented from donning a catcher's mask, shin guards, and chest protector.

Of course, as you all know, this is no joke. Over the past 10 years, the time of an average nine-inning game increased by 15 minutes. And while the *rate* of increase has declined over the past few years, the average has nevertheless risen in every season since 1988, when a sharp one-year decline in scoring momentarily produced shorter games:

1982	1983	1984	1985	1986	1987	1988	1989	1990	1991	1992
2:34	2:36	2:35	2:40	2:44	2:48	2:45	2:46	2:48	2:49.1	2:49.5

Unfortunately the solution to the problem isn't as simple as enforced DHing for Fisk. In an effort to identify the parts of the game most responsible for the additional time, we used a technique called multiple linear regression. Don't panic; it ain't as complex as it sounds. Simply put, we tried to assign a time value to three distinct events that bore a significant relationship to the overall time of a game: (1) batters reaching base; (2) "long plate appearances" (that is, walks and strikeouts); and (3) pitching changes. For the 1992 season, the time of a nine-inning game was approximately equal to: (1.72 times base runners) plus (1.09 times long plate appearances) plus (3.15 times pitching changes) plus an overhead of 97.6 minutes, which includes the time it takes for each team to retire 27 batters, time between innings, time for arguments, and so on. What's interesting is how those values compared to the corresponding regression for 10 years earlier, when nine-inning games were 15 minutes shorter on average:

Year	Overhead	Base Runners	Long PAs	Pitching Changes
1982	98.2	1.38	0.90	3.12
1992	97.6	1.72	1.09	3.15

The most remarkable aspect is that the time required for the overhead—all the regular activities involved in the business of playing a game of baseball—remained for all intents and purposes identical. That means, for instance, that it's wrong to attribute longer games to more commercial time for television, or to the frequency with which batters call for time and step out of the box. So where has the additional time come from? A typical pitching change still adds about as much time to a game now as it did 10 years ago, but the number of pitching changes has risen from 3.15 per game to 4.14, accounting for roughly three minutes per game. The time spent on a walk or strikeout has increased slightly, suggesting that batters may call for time more often on longer plate appearances; the number of walks and strikeouts has increased as well, from 16.2 to 17.4 per game. The net increase of that activity is about four minutes per game.

But by far the most significant increase in the time of a nine-inning baseball game is attributable to the jump from 1.38 to 1.72 minutes for each batter who reaches base. The clear implication is that pitchers are spending more time holding runners close to the bag, whether by throwing to the base, stepping off the rubber, or conferring with their managers and catchers. Even though the number of base runners per game has remained constant (24.2 in both 1982 and 1992), the additional time devoted to each runner has added more than eight minutes to a typical game—roughly half the total increase.

Incidentally, you might be interested to learn that the pattern for games caught by Carlton Fisk is significantly different from that of a typical game. For those who've never fought to stay awake through the late innings of a Fisk-caught marathon, the following table shows what the rest of us already suspected. It shows the length of all nine-inning White Sox games since Fisk signed on, divided into those caught by Fisk and those caught by all others. The games he started behind the plate lasted longer, on average, in each of those 12 seasons:

	1981	1982	1983	1984	1985	1986	1987	1988	1989	1990	1991	1992
Fisk	2:52	2:49	2:49	2:43	2:52	2:54	2:51	2:49	2:56	3:00	3:00	3:01
Others	2:44	2:28	2:38	2:35	2:41	2:43	2:45	2:43	2:51	2:48	2:57	2:49
Diff.	+8	+21	+11	+8	+11	+11	+6	+6	+5	+12	+3	+12

But as you might have suspected, the difference between a Carlton Fisk Special and your run-of-the-mill game lies in the "overhead." Fisk's frequent chats with his pitchers appear to add more than 10 minutes to the game. But note from the figures below that he also seems to lavish attention on relief pitchers; how else do you explain that a typical pitching change is more time consuming with Fisk catching than with other catchers?

Catcher	Overhead	Base Runners	Long PAs	Pitching Changes
Fisk	108.9	1.47	0.94	4.47
Others	98.3	1.48	1.02	3.53

But Fisk is already playing on borrowed time. He caught 54 games last season at age 44; no other player that old has ever caught more than two games in a season. So let's return to the broader problem. What are the possible solutions? Here are a couple:

1. *Place a limit on the number of throws a pitcher can make to each base or the number of times he can step off the rubber for each runner.* If the pitcher reaches his quota without picking the runner off base, the runner is awarded the next base. At first glance, this seems an absurd suggestion, and one not in the spirit of the game. But think about it this way: As the pitcher approaches his limit, the strategic drama builds. If the runner cheats an extra step, does the pitcher use his last throw? It's the kind of subtext that baseball thrives upon, and in its way it's no different from the once-radical notion that foul balls be counted as strikes in an effort to speed up the game nearly a century ago.

2. *Let a batter step out of the box only once per plate appearance.* Anyone remember the classic confrontation between Cliff Johnson of the A's and Ron Davis of the Yankees in Game 1 of the 1981 A.L.C.S.? After striking out three consecutive batters while protecting a 3–1 lead for Tommy John, Davis walked Dwayne Murphy with one out in the eighth, bringing Heathcliff to the plate as the tying run. With a 1–2 count, Johnson went into his own version of Dean Smith's four-corner offense. He started by sauntering to the dugout for a new bat, and six minutes later had drawn a drama-soaked walk that so obviously rattled Davis that Yankees manager Bob Lemon had to remove him from the game. Today, he'd be used to it; a six-minute at-bat would hardly raise an eyebrow anymore. More likely, it would elicit a yawn.

So the batter gets to step out only once. He needs a second time out because something caught in his eye, he needs more pine tar, or he has to call his broker? No problem; it'll just cost him a strike. (Next time he'll think twice before stepping out the first time in order to "get focused.")

3. *Enforce a 20-second rule between throws, even with runners on base.* Make a pitch clock visible from every seat in every ballpark, just as football's play clock and basketball's shot clock are, then watch the fun begin. Encourage fans to count down the final seconds as an opposing pitcher's time expires.

Now please don't cite "the purity of the rules," at least as long as the designated hitter survives. Like it or hate it, the DH rule has set a precedent for making changes to the rules in the interest of a better product. And believe us, the offensive problems faced in 1971 posed a much smaller threat to baseball than the absurd game times do today. The percentage of nine-inning games lasting at least three hours has risen from 13 percent in 1982 to 33 percent last season. We're reminded of a punch line to our favorite comic strip of all time, "Tank McNamara," about football statisticians striking outside a stadium on game day. After warning the fans that they won't even keep track of passes or punts, the stunned fans plead at least for first downs. The statisticians coldly reply, "Desperate times call for desperate measures." Amen.

CLEVELAND INDIANS

Optimism among Cleveland's baseball fans is as rare as snow in the Sahara. It's been 25 years since the Indians finished closer to first place than last, the longest streak in major league history. So for a team that posted its third 100-loss record in seven years in 1991, last season's rebound to fourth place might seem like nothing more than the prelude to another hard fall. But anyone who followed the Indians beyond their slow start last season—and we suspect that eliminates most of you—witnessed what amounted to a nearly unprecedented straight-line rise over the rest of the season, one that caught most baseball fans napping.

Cleveland trailed Toronto by 18½ games on July 11, but nearly kept pace with the new world champions over the second half of the season, posting a 40–34 record after the All-Star break. Nothing illustrates the progress that Cleveland made during the season better than the team's record month by month. The Indians came within one win in September of becoming only the third team in this century to post increasingly better records in every month throughout the season (excluding October):

Year	Team	April	May	June	July	August	Sept.
1973	Boston Red Sox	7–10	13–13	15–12	19–14	18–13	17–11
1984	Kansas City Royals	8–11	12–15	13–14	17–15	17–12	17–11
1992	Cleveland Indians	8–15	11–16	12–15	13–13	16–12	15–12

Now, Boston and Kansas City both had winning records for those seasons as a whole, so this may not necessarily mean anything. But in the next season, the Red Sox held a seven-game lead in August before fading, and the Royals won the 1985 World Series. Regardless, for the first time in years, Indians fans have cause for optimism. Cleveland had the youngest team in the majors in 1992, with an average age of 26 years, 10 months. Over the past 25 years, the youngest team improved its record the next season 18 times. Five of those teams posted 100-point increases, and another—the 1992 Houston Astros—fell one point short of a triple-digit rise. Nearly half of those 25 teams (12 to be exact) won at least a division title within three years; the White Sox or Astros could add to that total this year or next.

Whoa! Indians? Pennant? As Dick Young used to ask, "What's going on here?" Wasn't this supposed to be a civilized discussion among rational men? Well, whenever our imaginations start to run *really* wild like that, we recite this simple mantra: "Super Joe Charboneau."

Charboneau was the middle man in a triumvirate of prodigious Indians rookies, separated by roughly a decade each, who all failed miserably in their attempt to bring respectability to the franchise: Roy Foster in 1970, Charboneau in 1980, and Cory Snyder in 1986. They serve as a collective reminder that no rookie, no matter how promising, comes with a money-back guarantee.

In the 1992 *Analyst,* we introduced a feature that drew more comment from our readers than anything else we published in our first eight editions. "What If?" was a departure from anything we'd done before in that it dealt purely in fantasy, using more than 100 years of

baseball history and the number-crunching power of our computers to evaluate players at various points in their careers and project where they were headed, based on the career tracks of others who had similar statistical profiles. In last year's edition, we used our model to construct imaginary career totals for a number of players whose actual careers were compromised by circumstances beyond their control: What if Joe Jackson hadn't been suspended, and Bo Jackson hadn't been injured? What if the color barrier hadn't delayed the debuts of Jackie Robinson and Luke Easter? What if World War II and the Korean War hadn't taken prime years from Ted Williams, Hank Greenberg, and Joe DiMaggio?

We'll get to some similar scenarios later, but for now we'd like to use that same projection model to demonstrate how unreliable an indicator a promising rookie or sophomore season can be; or, to put it in other terms, how unrealistic our expectations can be for successful first- and second-year players.

Let's first consider Charboneau, who batted .289, hit 23 home runs, and drove in 87 runs as a rookie. You'd think such an auspicious debut season would inevitably lead to bigger and better things. And yet, the list of the five outfielders whose rookie-season statistics most closely matched Charboneau's included no one who played 1000 more games in his major league career, and only one who hit 100 more home runs—and just barely. Note in particular that Roy Foster himself compiled remarkably similar statistics to Charboneau's:

Year	Player	AB	R	H	2B	3B	HR	RBI	BB	SO	BA	Future G	HR
1980	Joe Charboneau	453	76	131	17	2	23	87	49	70	.289	70	6
1964	Sam Bowens	501	58	132	25	2	22	71	42	99	.263	325	22
1970	Roy Foster	477	66	128	26	0	23	60	54	75	.268	198	22
1977	Steve Henderson	350	67	104	16	6	12	65	43	79	.297	986	56
1952	Bob Nieman	478	66	138	22	2	18	74	46	73	.289	970	105
1961	Lee Thomas	452	77	129	11	5	24	70	47	74	.285	895	82

Of course, not all the Charboneau clones proved to be underachievers. Among the players who had Charboneau-like rookie seasons were Frank Howard and Danny Tartabull. But for every Tartabull on the list there was a Floyd Robinson, an Irv Noren, a Jimmie Hall; for every Howard, there was a Willie Smith, a Sam Mele, a Harry Anderson. Hard as it is to imagine, the odds were solidly against Charboneau finishing his career with even 100 home runs. And the same was true, of course, of Foster, whose list of comparable players was naturally quite similar to Charboneau's. Their career tracks demonstrate that a standout rookie season (especially at age 25 or older) is hardly enough to conclude that an All-Star career will follow.

Cory Snyder's failure proves that even a pair of good seasons can be misleading. Snyder batted .272 as a rookie, with 24 home runs in 103 games. Although his batting average dropped to .236 as a sophomore, he hit 33 home runs. Most of the players with the most similar two-year profiles fared a little better than Snyder in the long run. But among the five players with the most similar profiles, only Carlton Fisk reached the 200-HR mark:

| Year | Player | Career Totals After Indicated Year | | | | | | | | | | Career |
		AB	R	H	2B	3B	HR	RBI	BB	SO	BA	HR
1987	Cory Snyder	993	132	249	45	3	57	151	47	289	.251	132+
1970	Nate Colbert	1115	156	279	38	15	62	156	102	300	.250	173
1973	Carlton Fisk	1018	146	274	51	10	50	138	90	194	.269	375+
1970	Bill Melton	1179	146	306	49	3	58	199	122	245	.260	160
1971	Bob Robertson	990	145	265	41	7	56	167	122	241	.268	115
1972	Earl Williams	1081	140	282	42	3	61	179	107	202	.261	138

This seems like a good time to mention that, despite indications to the contrary, fate hasn't always worked against the Indians. For another classic example of players with similar rookie seasons whose careers followed wildly different paths—one that favored the Tribe this time—ask your grandparents if they remember Earl Averill as a rookie center fielder for the Indians in 1929. And if they do, ask them about two other rookies who posted figures uncannily similar to Averill's that season:

Player, Team	G	AB	R	H	2B	3B	HR	RBI	BB	SO	SB	BA
Dale Alexander, Det.	155	626	110	215	43	15	25	137	56	63	5	.343
Earl Averill, Cle.	152	602	110	199	43	13	18	97	64	53	13	.331
Johnny Frederick, Bkn.	148	628	127	206	52	6	24	75	39	34	6	.328

Alexander posted the second-highest batting average ever by an American League rookie. But while undergoing hot-water therapy for a knee sprain in 1933, he suffered leg burns so serious that they eventually ended his career. Frederick set a National League record for doubles by a rookie, but within four years, chronic leg pain limited him to part-time play and pinch-hitting. Only Averill, now enshrined in Cooperstown, was playing in the majors even six years later.

Of course, there are some rookies so spectacular that even a realistic projection model would label them as candidates for the Hall of Fame. That's why the career of Jeff Heath may represent the greatest waste of potential in Indians history. The three most similar rookie seasons were compiled by a pair of Hall of Famers and a nine-time All-Star:

Year	Player	AB	R	H	2B	3B	HR	RBI	BB	SO	BA
1938	Jeff Heath	502	104	172	31	18	21	112	33	55	.343
1975	Fred Lynn	528	103	175	47	7	21	105	62	90	.331
1936	Johnny Mize	414	76	136	30	8	19	93	50	32	.329
1926	Paul Waner	536	101	180	35	22	8	79	66	19	.336

Based on the similarity of Heath's rookie year to those of Lynn, Mize, Waner, Charlie Keller, Bob Meusel, Babe Herman, and Dusty Baker, the computer projections for Heath's career totals are Hall of Fame–caliber: a .313 batting average, with nearly 300 home runs and more than 1200 RBIs. (In fact, Heath had roughly a 20 percent chance to reach the loftier levels of .325, 400 home runs, and 1500 RBIs.)

What a dynamic pair of sluggers Heath and Hal Trosky might have been throughout the 1940s. Trosky completed the 1940 season just before his 28th birthday with career marks of a .314 batting average and more than 500 extra-base hits, including 205 home runs. He drove in 142 runs as a rookie in 1934 and reached the 100-mark in each of the next five seasons as well. The only other players with 100 RBIs in each of their first six seasons were Al Simmons, Joe DiMaggio, and Ted Williams. And the only players with comparable statistical profiles to Trosky's following the 1940 season

are already in the Hall of Fame or are legitimate contenders:

Year	Player	AB	R	H	2B	3B	HR	RBI	BB	SO	BA
1940	Hal Trosky	4055	715	1274	270	53	205	860	405	352	.314
1942	Joe DiMaggio	3978	858	1349	243	82	219	930	404	196	.339
1960	Hank Aaron	4114	714	1309	225	57	219	743	341	378	.318
1964	Orlando Cepeda	4095	646	1266	223	22	222	747	252	616	.309
1980	Jim Rice	3656	596	1124	171	55	196	669	266	687	.307
1983	Eddie Murray	3958	615	1175	208	15	198	697	440	565	.297
1989	Don Mattingly	4022	615	1300	272	15	164	717	314	238	.323

And yet only the most knowledgeable younger fans would know what position Trosky played, in what era he played, or for what team. The explanation: Migraines reduced his effectiveness in 1941 (when a broken finger ended his season in early August) and prompted his retirement after the season. (Trosky made two disappointing comebacks several years later.) What might Trosky have lost? Perhaps a ticket to Cooperstown. Our best-guess figures for the remainder of his career would have given Trosky career totals similar to Billy Williams's Hall of Fame totals:

	G	AB	R	H	2B	3B	HR	RBI	BB	SO	SB	BA
1933–40	1035	4055	715	1274	270	53	205	860	405	352	20	.314
1941–48	1163	4569	710	1347	281	28	180	915	555	411	20	.295
Totals	2198	8624	1425	2621	551	81	385	1775	960	763	40	.304

An earlier generation of Indians fans can only imagine Heath and Trosky tearing up the American League during the 1940s. For the next generation, it's the thought of a late-1960s team led by a pair of pea-throwing left-handers, Herb Score and Sam McDowell, to continue in the tradition of Bob Feller and Bob Lemon. (Score's career ended so prematurely that it's easy to overlook the fact that he was just 32 when Sudden Sam led the league in ERA and strikeouts in 1965.) And if Score had avoided Gil McDougald's line drive and McDowell had avoided the bottle, one or the other would probably have challenged and perhaps broken Walter Johnson's record (at the time) of 3508 career strikeouts. To be sure, both Score and McDowell would have been susceptible to career-threatening arm injuries. For confirmation, look no further than the names on the following lists of comparables. Our best-guess projections are tempered by that possibility, but the optimistic scenario—levels that the pitchers had a 20 percent chance of reaching, and which imply reasonably good health—is spectacular. Score's totals are through the 1956 season, McDowell's after 1970:

Pitcher	W–L	ERA	SO	Pitcher	W–L	ERA	SO
Herb Score	36–19	2.68	508	Sam McDowell	109–92	2.95	1967
Roger Clemens	40–13	3.15	438	Bob Feller	138–72	2.96	1640
Al Downing	26–14	3.18	401	Sandy Koufax	138–78	2.93	2079
Jim Maloney	40–27	3.45	475	Jim Maloney	134–80	3.08	1585
Jim Palmer	39–19	3.07	368	Nolan Ryan	105–98	3.06	1758
Best-Guess	133–112	2.75	2090	Best-Guess	205–164	3.21	3113
Optimistic	232–141	2.49	3558	Optimistic	287–219	3.08	4676

Had enough? Those examples should be enough to make the Carlos Baerga and Charles Nagy Fan Clubs cry uncle. Let's face it—the only thing certain about youth is that you'll outgrow it. And we haven't even discussed Al Rosen. So for even more sobering reminders of how tenuous a commodity potential can be, see the Giants essay for more "What Ifs?"

WON-LOST RECORD BY STARTING POSITION

Cleveland Indians	C	1B	2B	3B	SS	LF	CF	RF	DH	P	Leadoff	Cleanup	Starts vs. LH	Starts vs. RH	Total Starts
Sandy Alomar Jr.	35-49	-	-	-	-	-	-	-	1-0	-	-	-	22	63	36-49
Jack Armstrong	-	-	-	-	-	-	-	-	-	5-18	-	-	6	17	5-18
Brad Arnsberg	-	-	-	-	-	-	-	-	-	-	-	-	-	-	-
Carlos Baerga	-	-	76-84	-	-	-	-	-	0-1	-	-	-	43	118	76-85
Eric Bell	-	-	-	-	-	-	-	-	-	0-1	-	-	-	1	0-1
Albert Belle	-	-	-	-	-	24-28	-	-	48-52	-	-	72-80	41	111	72-80
Denis Boucher	-	-	-	-	-	-	-	-	-	4-3	-	-	4	3	4-3
Mike Christopher	-	-	-	-	-	-	-	-	-	-	-	-	-	-	-
Alex Cole	-	-	-	-	-	5-9	1-2	-	0-3	-	3-5	-	4	16	6-14
Dennis Cook	-	-	-	-	-	-	-	-	-	15-10	-	-	3	22	15-10
Bruce Egloff	-	-	-	-	-	-	-	-	-	-	-	-	-	-	-
Alan Embree	-	-	-	-	-	-	-	-	-	2-2	-	-	1	3	2-2
Felix Fermin	-	-	0-2	2-9	25-22	-	-	-	-	-	-	-	12	48	27-33
Jose Hernandez	-	-	-	-	-	-	-	-	-	-	-	-	-	-	-
Glenallen Hill	-	-	-	-	-	28-22	1-0	4-4	16-16	-	1-0	-	31	60	49-42
Thomas Howard	-	-	-	-	-	19-27	6-12	5-7	1-0	-	7-12	-	25	52	31-46
Brook Jacoby	-	1-4	-	38-39	-	-	-	-	-	-	-	-	32	50	39-43
Reggie Jefferson	-	6-9	-	-	-	-	-	-	4-3	-	-	-	6	16	10-12
Wayne Kirby	-	-	-	-	-	-	-	-	1-0	-	-	-	-	1	1-0
Jesse Levis	4-5	-	-	-	-	-	-	-	-	-	-	-	-	9	4-5
Mark Lewis	-	-	-	0-1	51-62	-	-	-	-	-	-	-	33	81	51-63
Derek Lilliquist	-	-	-	-	-	-	-	-	-	-	-	-	-	-	-
Kenny Lofton	-	-	-	-	-	-	68-72	-	-	-	65-69	-	32	108	68-72
Carlos Martinez	-	15-14	-	13-14	-	-	-	-	2-0	-	-	0-1	30	28	30-28
Jose Mesa	-	-	-	-	-	-	-	-	-	10-5	-	-	4	11	10-5
Dave Mlicki	-	-	-	-	-	-	-	-	-	1-3	-	-	-	4	1-3
Jeff Mutis	-	-	-	-	-	-	-	-	-	0-2	-	-	-	2	0-2
Charles Nagy	-	-	-	-	-	-	-	-	-	19-14	-	-	13	20	19-14
Rod Nichols	-	-	-	-	-	-	-	-	-	7-2	-	-	2	7	7-2
Steve Olin	-	-	-	-	-	-	-	-	-	-	-	-	-	-	-
Junior Ortiz	37-32	-	-	-	-	-	-	-	-	-	-	-	21	48	37-32
Dave Otto	-	-	-	-	-	-	-	-	-	5-11	-	-	6	10	5-11
Tony Perezchica	-	-	-	0-1	0-2	-	-	-	0-1	-	-	-	1	3	0-4
Eric Plunk	-	-	-	-	-	-	-	-	-	-	-	-	-	-	-
Ted Power	-	-	-	-	-	-	-	-	-	-	-	-	-	-	-
David Rohde	-	-	-	0-1	-	-	-	-	-	-	-	-	1	-	0-1
Scott Scudder	-	-	-	-	-	-	-	-	-	8-14	-	-	4	18	8-14
Jeff Shaw	-	-	-	-	-	-	-	-	-	0-1	-	-	-	1	0-1
Joel Skinner	-	-	-	-	-	-	-	-	-	-	-	-	-	-	-
Paul Sorrento	-	54-59	-	-	-	-	-	-	2-9	-	-	3-4	8	116	56-68
Jim Thome	-	-	-	20-17	-	-	-	-	-	-	-	-	3	34	20-17
Mark Whiten	-	-	-	-	-	-	67-75	1-1	-	-	-	1-1	37	107	68-76
Kevin Wickander	-	-	-	-	-	-	-	-	-	-	-	-	-	-	-
Craig Worthington	-	-	-	3-4	-	-	-	-	-	-	-	-	5	2	3-4

TEAM TOTALS: BATTING

	AB	H	2B	3B	HR	RBI	BB	SO	BA	SA	OBA
Season	5620	1495	227	24	127	637	448	885	.266	.383	.323
vs. Left-Handers	1353	386	71	3	30	172	123	220	.285	.409	.347
vs. Right-Handers	4267	1109	156	21	97	465	325	665	.260	.375	.315
vs. Ground-Ballers	2544	672	94	11	50	290	200	384	.264	.369	.321
vs. Fly-Ballers	3076	823	133	13	77	347	248	501	.268	.394	.325
Home Games	2781	786	117	15	62	344	240	429	.283	.402	.341
Road Games	2839	709	110	9	65	293	208	456	.250	.364	.305
Grass Fields	4771	1287	192	22	108	549	390	742	.270	.387	.327
Artificial Turf	849	208	35	2	19	88	58	143	.245	.358	.299
April	795	194	24	1	14	78	60	143	.244	.330	.299
May	917	251	37	4	19	119	81	160	.274	.385	.336
June	909	235	33	4	23	87	59	115	.259	.380	.307
July	898	242	38	4	22	96	61	138	.269	.394	.322
August	973	272	49	6	24	122	84	155	.280	.416	.339
Sept./Oct.	1128	301	46	5	25	135	103	174	.267	.383	.328
Leading Off Inn.	1359	360	50	5	29	29	106	216	.265	.373	.324
Runners On	2393	637	84	12	51	561	208	368	.266	.375	.325
Bases Empty	3227	858	143	12	76	76	240	517	.266	.388	.324
Runners/Scor. Pos.	1354	350	46	7	33	506	153	236	.258	.376	.329
Runners On/2 Out	998	248	31	6	18	203	90	171	.248	.346	.318
Scor. Pos./2 Out	643	148	16	4	13	185	72	123	.230	.328	.314
Late-Inning Pressure	975	241	36	1	21	101	79	182	.247	.351	.308
Leading Off	256	64	11	1	5	5	18	54	.250	.359	.304
Runners On	381	95	14	0	9	89	40	74	.249	.357	.324
Runners/Scor. Pos.	211	52	8	0	7	83	34	42	.246	.384	.348

RUNS BATTED IN	From 1B	From 2B	From 3B	Scoring Position
Totals	66/1720	193/1027	251/599	444/1626
Percentage	3.8%	18.8%	41.9%	27.3%

TEAM TOTALS: PITCHING

	W-L	ERA	AB	H	HR	BB	SO	BA	SA	OBA
Season	76-86	4.11	5615	1507	159	566	890	.268	.407	.336
vs. Left-Handers			2147	585	46	220	307	.272	.392	.341
vs. Right-Handers			3468	922	113	346	583	.266	.416	.333
vs. Ground-Ballers			2791	740	47	265	403	.265	.367	.330
vs. Fly-Ballers			2824	767	112	301	487	.272	.445	.342
Home Games	41-40	4.20	2920	794	94	283	475	.272	.422	.336
Road Games	35-46	4.01	2695	713	65	283	415	.265	.390	.336
Grass Fields	68-69	4.08	4797	1282	141	483	779	.267	.408	.335
Artificial Turf	8-17	4.29	818	225	18	83	111	.275	.401	.341
April	8-15	4.39	799	212	28	82	115	.265	.412	.337
May	11-16	4.12	909	249	21	97	132	.274	.402	.344
June	12-15	4.13	908	248	26	100	160	.273	.411	.345
July	13-13	3.72	921	254	19	70	146	.276	.398	.325
August	16-12	4.23	978	255	27	94	156	.261	.403	.329
Sept./Oct.	16-15	4.08	1100	289	38	123	181	.263	.414	.337
Leading Off Inn.			1348	353	32	120	219	.262	.395	.325
Bases Empty			3131	806	77	307	512	.257	.392	.327
Runners On			2484	701	82	259	378	.282	.425	.346
Runners/Scor. Pos.			1433	384	42	174	233	.268	.400	.338
Runners On/2 Out			1053	288	38	115	170	.274	.433	.349
Scor. Pos./2 Out			688	165	18	84	113	.240	.365	.326
Late-Inning Pressure			926	243	21	93	144	.262	.371	.333
Leading Off			237	63	3	20	35	.266	.346	.328
Runners On			399	94	12	54	65	.236	.368	.327
Runners/Scor. Pos.			218	48	6	38	35	.220	.358	.331
First 9 Batters			2911	732	79	335	534	.251	.383	.330
Second 9 Batters			1460	411	51	134	185	.282	.440	.343
All Batters Thereafter			1244	364	29	97	171	.293	.424	.342

WON-LOST RECORD BY STARTING POSITION

Detroit Tigers	C	1B	2B	3B	SS	LF	CF	RF	DH	P	Leadoff	Cleanup	Starts vs. LH	Starts vs. RH	Total Starts
Scott Aldred	-	-	-	-	-	-	-	-	-	4-9	-	-	4	9	4-9
Skeeter Barnes	-	2-1	-	14-19	-	-	-	-	3-0	-	-	-	35	4	19-20
Dave Bergman	-	16-21	-	-	-	-	-	-	4-5	-	-	-	-	46	20-26
Rico Brogna	-	4-3	-	-	-	-	-	-	2-0	-	-	-	-	9	6-3
Mark Carreon	-	-	-	-	-	31-30	0-1	5-10	7-6	-	-	-	37	53	43-47
Phil Clark	-	-	-	-	-	0-2	-	3-3	3-3	-	-	-	13	1	6-8
Milt Cuyler	-	-	-	-	-	-	37-47	0-1	-	-	1-1	-	24	61	37-48
Rob Deer	-	-	-	-	-	-	-	50-55	1-1	-	-	-	30	77	51-56
John Doherty	-	-	-	-	-	-	-	-	-	6-5	-	-	3	8	6-5
Cecil Fielder	-	52-60	-	-	-	-	-	-	18-25	-	-	70-84	40	115	70-85
Travis Fryman	-	-	-	13-14	62-72	-	-	-	-	-	-	3-2	43	118	75-86
Dan Gakeler	-	-	-	-	-	-	-	-	-	-	-	-	-	-	-
Dan Gladden	-	-	-	-	-	36-49	7-6	-	1-1	-	6-14	-	33	67	44-56
Buddy Groom	-	-	-	-	-	-	-	-	-	1-6	-	-	1	6	1-6
Bill Gullickson	-	-	-	-	-	-	-	-	-	19-15	-	-	10	24	19-15
David Haas	-	-	-	-	-	-	-	-	-	6-5	-	-	3	8	6-5
Shawn Hare	-	1-1	-	-	-	-	-	2-3	-	-	-	-	-	7	3-4
Mike Henneman	-	-	-	-	-	-	-	-	-	-	-	-	-	-	-
John Kiely	-	-	-	-	-	-	-	-	-	-	-	-	-	-	-
Eric King	-	-	-	-	-	-	-	-	-	5-9	-	-	4	10	5-9
Kurt Knudsen	-	-	-	-	-	-	-	-	-	0-1	-	-	-	1	0-1
Chad Kreuter	22-28	-	-	-	-	-	-	-	1-0	-	-	-	21	30	23-28
Les Lancaster	-	-	-	-	-	-	-	-	-	0-1	-	-	-	1	0-1
Mark Leiter	-	-	-	-	-	-	-	-	-	10-4	-	-	5	9	10-4
Scott Livingstone	-	-	-	44-46	-	-	-	-	-	-	-	-	3	87	44-46
Mike Munoz	-	-	-	-	-	-	-	-	-	-	-	-	-	-	-
Gary Pettis	-	-	-	-	-	-	22-23	-	-	-	-	-	11	34	22-23
Tony Phillips	-	-	23-27	4-8	-	8-6	9-10	15-14	14-20	-	68-72	-	43	115	73-85
Kevin Ritz	-	-	-	-	-	-	-	-	-	3-8	-	-	3	8	3-8
Rich Rowland	0-2	0-1	-	-	-	-	-	-	0-2	-	-	-	5	-	0-5
Frank Tanana	-	-	-	-	-	-	-	-	-	16-15	-	-	8	23	16-15
Walt Terrell	-	-	-	-	-	-	-	-	-	5-9	-	-	2	12	5-9
Mickey Tettleton	53-57	-	-	-	-	-	-	0-1	20-20	-	-	2-1	35	116	73-78
Alan Trammell	-	-	-	13-15	-	-	-	-	-	-	-	-	11	17	13-15
Lou Whitaker	-	-	52-60	-	-	-	-	-	1-4	-	-	-	3	114	53-64

TEAM TOTALS: BATTING

	AB	H	2B	3B	HR	RBI	BB	SO	BA	SA	OBA
Season	5515	1411	256	16	182	746	675	1055	.256	.407	.337
vs. Left-Handers	1442	394	72	7	59	228	181	264	.273	.456	.355
vs. Right-Handers	4073	1017	184	9	123	518	494	791	.250	.390	.330
vs. Ground-Ballers	2529	688	131	12	71	370	293	463	.272	.418	.347
vs. Fly-Ballers	2986	723	125	4	111	376	382	592	.242	.398	.328
Home Games	2640	671	126	8	91	366	359	523	.254	.411	.344
Road Games	2875	740	130	8	91	380	316	532	.257	.403	.330
Grass Fields	4673	1191	207	14	164	633	596	886	.255	.410	.339
Artificial Turf	842	220	49	2	18	113	79	169	.261	.388	.325
April	706	161	25	3	31	95	92	128	.228	.404	.318
May	926	233	48	4	35	129	100	184	.252	.425	.326
June	993	281	56	3	34	149	122	196	.283	.448	.363
July	922	225	36	1	22	96	101	176	.244	.357	.318
August	949	242	38	4	32	134	108	185	.255	.405	.328
Sept./Oct.	1019	269	53	1	28	143	152	186	.264	.400	.358
Leading Off Inn.	1299	367	72	5	46	46	143	234	.283	.452	.356
Runners On	2510	657	112	9	83	647	330	457	.262	.413	.343
Bases Empty	3005	754	144	7	99	99	345	598	.251	.402	.331
Runners/Scor. Pos.	1416	382	70	6	50	564	205	275	.270	.434	.352
Runners On/2 Out	1023	245	40	7	36	260	141	200	.239	.398	.333
Scor. Pos./2 Out	657	162	30	5	24	229	97	135	.247	.417	.344
Late-Inning Pressure	764	182	24	1	23	83	86	161	.238	.363	.315
Leading Off	189	40	8	1	3	3	18	45	.212	.312	.287
Runners On	322	79	9	0	12	72	41	61	.245	.385	.324
Runners/Scor. Pos.	171	41	4	0	8	63	27	36	.240	.404	.332

RUNS BATTED IN	From 1B	From 2B	From 3B	Scoring Position
Totals	104/1958	204/1150	256/605	460/1755
Percentage	5.3%	17.7%	42.3%	26.2%

TEAM TOTALS: PITCHING

	W-L	ERA	AB	H	HR	BB	SO	BA	SA	OBA
Season	75-87	4.60	5546	1534	155	564	693	.277	.416	.343
vs. Left-Handers			2137	591	50	220	226	.277	.404	.341
vs. Right-Handers			3409	943	105	344	467	.277	.423	.344
vs. Ground-Ballers			2717	735	54	277	299	.271	.388	.338
vs. Fly-Ballers			2829	799	101	287	394	.282	.443	.348
Home Games	38-42	4.45	2850	792	90	283	363	.278	.426	.343
Road Games	37-45	4.75	2696	742	65	281	330	.275	.405	.343
Grass Fields	63-75	4.59	4753	1314	135	487	595	.276	.416	.343
Artificial Turf	12-12	4.62	793	220	20	77	98	.277	.416	.344
April	7-14	5.72	736	220	24	85	98	.299	.454	.369
May	14-14	4.68	945	263	26	104	121	.278	.419	.351
June	14-14	4.30	968	253	30	104	132	.261	.412	.332
July	13-14	4.17	918	242	20	93	107	.264	.391	.331
August	15-13	4.24	941	266	21	77	108	.283	.403	.337
Sept./Oct.	12-18	4.74	1038	290	34	101	127	.279	.422	.344
Leading Off Inn.			1309	356	39	122	156	.272	.415	.337
Bases Empty			3090	852	92	263	392	.276	.422	.336
Runners On			2456	682	63	301	301	.278	.407	.352
Runners/Scor. Pos.			1391	377	30	229	196	.271	.380	.363
Runners On/2 Out			1021	253	23	140	136	.248	.357	.341
Scor. Pos./2 Out			648	157	12	121	94	.242	.333	.364
Late-Inning Pressure			622	160	21	74	96	.257	.404	.333
Leading Off			160	45	7	17	24	.281	.456	.350
Runners On			265	67	5	37	42	.253	.351	.338
Runners/Scor. Pos.			144	39	2	30	21	.271	.347	.383
First 9 Batters			2938	794	72	326	419	.270	.399	.341
Second 9 Batters			1510	428	36	131	175	.283	.405	.343
All Batters Thereafter			1098	312	47	107	99	.284	.474	.348

DETROIT TIGERS

One of the more remarkable achievements of the 1992 season occurred in relative obscurity on September 27, when Sparky Anderson moved past Hughie Jennings as the all-time winningest manager in Detroit Tigers history. What made that accomplishment truly unique is the fact that Anderson is also the Cincinnati Reds' franchise leader, having passed Bill McKechnie in 1977.

Sparky thus becomes the only manager to top the list of two current franchises, and his feat is far more significant than that of Gil Hodges, the only other manager in the past 70 years to lead two different franchises simultaneously. Hodges sat atop the list of victories for two expansion teams—the Senators/Rangers and the New York Mets—from 1970 until 1987, when Davey Johnson became the Mets' all-time leader in only his fourth season with the team. There had been several similar cases of dual leadership in the early part of the century before teams in the newly formed American League had a chance to establish legitimate records:

• Bill Armour led the Tigers and Indians franchises for one year (1906).
• Clark Griffith led the Senators and the Yankees from 1913 through 1921, when Miller Huggins became the all-time Yankees leader. Griffith was also the White Sox leader in 1904, when he became the Yankees leader. He lost his White Sox lead to Fielder Jones in 1905.
• Miller Huggins became the Yankees leader in 1922, but his total with the Cardinals was surpassed by Branch Rickey a year later.

But the two different franchises Sparky Anderson leads have been in operation throughout the 1900s—a feat unrivaled in major league history. For some perspective, consider this: No player now tops the lists of two current franchises in any of the following categories: games played, runs, hits, extra-base hits, singles, doubles, triples, home runs, RBIs, or walks. No pitcher leads two existing franchises in wins, saves, complete games, or shutouts. The only parallels are those of Rickey Henderson, who leads the Yankees and Athletics in stolen bases; and to a lesser extent Nolan Ryan, who leads a pair of expansion franchises in strikeouts (the Angels and the Astros).

Henderson and Ryan are sure-bet Hall of Famers, likely to be elected in their first seasons of eligibility. And Sparky, too, should earn a bust in the Hall. But unfortunately, it remains to be seen whether that will happen—and as importantly, when—because for some reason, managers aren't elected by the same process as players. Managers are included with executives in a category on which—you guessed it—only the somnolent Veterans Committee votes. And you know what that means: Some of the greatest managers in major league history are still Cooperstown outsiders, most notably Leo Durocher and Earl Weaver. Those managers who do meet the clandestine criteria of the committee's private agenda are often forced to endure a pointless waiting period. And with so many great managers having retired in the past 10 years (like Weaver, Dick Williams, and Whitey Herzog), and a few more nearing the ends of illustrious careers (like

Sparky), the waiting list is sure to grow over the next decade. You see, even if the members of the committee put aside their personal agendas long enough to consider who *really* belongs, the rules permit only one executive or manager to be elected each season.

All sports have informal but nearly unanimous lists of great managers and coaches: George Halas, Bear Bryant, Vince Lombardi, George Allen, Tom Landry, Don Shula, and Bill Walsh in football; Red Auerbach, John Wooden, Adolph Rupp, Bobby Knight, and Pat Riley in basketball; Toe Blake, Al Arbour, and Scotty Bowman in hockey. (A related thought: Why is it that in football, and for some reason only in football, these men are labeled geniuses?) Baseball is no different; any fan could name 10 great managers faster than you could say Tom Trebelhorn, and the lists would be similar: a few relics, like Durocher, Walter Alston, Joe McCarthy, and John McGraw, along with several contemporary managers, like Weaver, Williams, or Billy Martin.

The difference is this: While the football, basketball, and hockey Halls treat their greats with honor, baseball's has adopted a back-of-the-hand attitude that is an affront to the managers themselves, and that betrays a basic ignorance of the crucial role a manager plays. Ask yourself this question: Was there any doubt that Tom Landry would be inducted into the football Hall of Fame in his first year of eligibility? Of course not; the idea is totally ludicrous. And so should be the idea of Earl Weaver not being elected to Cooperstown five years after he retired. The fact that he was not is an embarrassment to the Hall and to the sport itself, yet it's a situation that can be rectified easily and should be addressed immediately.

Here's a suggestion for Ed Stack, the President of the Baseball Hall of Fame: Allow the Baseball Writers Assocation of America to vote for managers by the same rules they use to consider players—that is, managers with 10 years of service become eligible five years after their retirement, or maybe just one year or three years after, considering the advanced ages at which many great managers have stepped down. Walter Alston, for example, retired at 64, was inducted seven years later at 71, and passed away a year later. What took them so long? (Is it possible that a Hall of Fame manager might return to action following induction? Yes, but so what? What would be the harm? Guy Lafleur returned to the NHL with the New York Rangers after being elected to the hockey Hall of Fame, and nothing drastic happened—the Montreal Forum didn't collapse, the Rangers didn't win the Stanley Cup, etc.) And by all means, let's hold a special election as soon as possible to allow the new electorate to play catch-up and correct the years of neglect that occurred under the current set-up. But regardless of the method, the time has come for the Hall of Fame to take the vote on managers away from the Veterans Committee.

Although there's a general consensus on most of the coaches who comprise the elite group in every sport, there's also a universally unresolved issue: Was Lombardi better than Halas? Was Wooden better than Rupp? Was McCarthy better than Durocher? These questions are rarely addressed because there are no widely accepted objective measures for comparing one coach or manager to another. Most fans consider it impossible to isolate a coach's contribution—unlike that of a quarterback, a point guard, or a home-run leader—from the overall success of his team.

But as regular readers of the *Analyst* know, we have developed a system for rating managers based on the premise that, over a period of time, a manager's value is reflected in the difference between the number of games his team wins and the number it was expected to win. It's simply an arithmetic version of the basis on which managers of the year are selected. (Each team's expected-wins total is computed through a complex series of formulas that evaluate its recent past performance and make judgments about the upcoming season.)

According to that method, only five managers in this century added more wins to their teams than Sparky Anderson. The following table lists the all-time top 10 in that category. Four of the seven eligible managers on the list aren't in the Hall of Fame; they are marked with asterisks. Those in the Hall are marked with plus signs:

Manager	Actual Record Won	Lost	Pct.	Expected Record Won	Lost	Pct.	Diff.
+John McGraw	2754	1922	.589	2673	2003	.572	+81
+Joe McCarthy	2126	1335	.614	2062	1399	.596	+64
Billy Martin	1258	1018	.553	1195	1081	.525	+63
+Bill McKechnie	1898	1724	.524	1843	1779	.509	+55
*Dick Williams	1571	1451	.520	1518	1504	.502	+53
Sparky Anderson	1996	1610	.554	1944	1662	.539	+52
*Earl Weaver	1480	1060	.583	1438	1102	.566	+42
Bobby Cox	853	804	.515	812	845	.490	+41
*Billy Southworth	1064	729	.593	1027	766	.573	+37
*Paul Richards	923	901	.506	887	937	.486	+36

As with all traditional baseball statistics, the figures above reflect only regular-season performance. But when his postseason success is included, Sparky leapfrogs over Williams and McKechnie into fourth place. Anderson has a record of 34–21 in postseason play. Only Stengel won more games (37); only McCarthy had a record further above the .500 mark (30–13).

It's too easy to dismiss Sparky Anderson's accomplishments on the basis of the sometimes wacky things he says. But like many managers and coaches, Sparky is a part-time public relations director; as such, you've got to distinguish between what he says and what he truly believes. Did Sparky think Mike Laga was really the best left-handed hitter since Stan Musial? Or that second base prospect Chris Pittaro would force Lou Whitaker to third base? It makes for good copy, but that's about all. When you examine Sparky's record, you can conclude only that he's one of the very best managers in baseball history.

Actually, the thought of Lou Whitaker playing anywhere else is a little difficult to accept—and by "anywhere else" we mean not only other than second base, but also outside Detroit.

So we almost spit our coffee on a Sunday morning late last November when Bill Madden of the New York *Daily News* reported that free agent Whitaker had turned down an offer from the Yankees because "he didn't want to play third base" at this stage of his career. (Whitaker later confirmed the story.) Were they kidding? A 35-year-old career Tigers second baseman being recruited to play in New York at a position he has never played—not even one inning—in his major league career? This was like the Temptations leaving Motown for Windham Hill to sing Broadway show tunes.

Whitaker and Alan Trammell have been as much a Motown institution as Sam and Dave. They broke in together in 1977, and spent 14 seasons as the Tigers' regular second baseman and shortstop, five years longer than any other keystone combo in major league history. Not since 1927, when 40-year-old Ty Cobb signed with the Philadelphia A's after being released by Detroit, has a career Tigers player with as many as 2000 games joined another team. But these things do happen, though a lot less frequently than most might think in the free-agent era. (As we said in the Brewers essay of the 1991 *Analyst*, the freedom to leave also implies the freedom to choose to stay.) The following table lists all the players who played for new teams after spending their entire careers of at least 2000 games with one club. Notice that only two of them played in the free-agent era:

Year	Player	Old Team (Games)	New Team
1926	Max Carey	Pirates (2178)	Dodgers
1927	Ty Cobb	Tigers (2805)	Athletics
1927	Zack Wheat	Dodgers (2322)	Athletics
1933	Joe Judge	Senators (2084)	Dodgers
1934	Sam Rice	Senators (2307)	Indians
1941	Paul Waner	Pirates (2154)	Dodgers
1962	Gil Hodges	Dodgers (2006)	Mets
1965	Yogi Berra	Yankees (2116)	Mets
1967	Eddie Mathews	Braves (2223)	Astros
1972	Willie Mays	Giants (2857)	Mets
1974	Ron Santo	Cubs (2126)	White Sox
1975	Hank Aaron	Braves (3076)	Brewers
1975	Harmon Killebrew	Nats/Twins (2329)	Royals
1975	Billy Williams	Cubs (2213)	Athletics
1979	Pete Rose	Reds (2505)	Phillies
1991	Dwight Evans	Red Sox (2505)	Orioles

So while it may be unusual for a player to join a new team after such a long career, it couldn't be considered rare—at least not as rare as a player making a successful transition to a brand new position at the age of 35. Only five players in major league history accumulated even 100 games at a position at which they had never played before turning 35: three at first base (Dave Philley, Mickey Mantle, and Dwight Evans), one as a catcher (Earle Brucker), and one in the outfield (Bob Thurman). The last two shouldn't count, really, because neither Brucker nor Thurman made his major league debut *at any position* until after he turned 35. As for born-again third basemen, only 27 players made their debuts there at age 35 or older, and none lasted more than 25 games at the position.

Most baseball fans are familiar with the stentorian Yankee Stadium voice that belongs to public address announcer Bob Sheppard. On the list of things you're not likely ever to hear him say: "A-wop bop-a-loo-bop a-lop bam boom" and "Now playing third base (base, base), for the Yankees (Yankees, Yankees), number four (four, four), Lou Whitaker (Whitaker, Whitaker). Number four (four, four)."

KANSAS CITY ROYALS

For many years, the Royals seemed to disprove the widely held assumption that small-market teams can't compete on a level playing field with teams from New York, Los Angeles, Chicago, and so on. Kansas City struck preemptive blows against teams hoping to raid its roster in the early '80s when it signed George Brett, Willie Wilson, and Dan Quisenberry to creative "lifetime" deals. The Royals also established a strong track record of holding on to players who became eligible for free agency, including Larry Gura (1978), Hal McRae (1982 and 1985), Charlie Leibrandt (1987), and Mark Gubicza (1991). And the number of free agents Kansas City signed away from other teams in recent years (Mark Davis, Storm Davis, Kirk Gibson, Mike Boddicker, and David Cone and Greg Gagne last autumn) has more than kept pace with those leaving the Royals (Bill Buckner, Steve Farr, Gerald Perry, and Willie Wilson).

But following the 1991 season, the Royals lost free agent Danny Tartabull to the Yankees and elected not to pursue starting shortstop Kurt Stillwell. Financial considerations were probably a major factor as well when their able-bodied long-standing third baseman Kevin Seitzer was released in late March. It's not our intention here to analyze the ability of a small-market team to compete dollar-for-dollar with baseball's metropolises, but merely to point out the extent to which the free agents Kansas City lost last season contributed to the team's slide to a fifth-place tie with California.

First, some background: The Royals have constructed an unmatched record of consistency. They haven't posted losing marks in consecutive seasons since their first two years of play (1969–70), and they are the only existing major league franchise that has never finished in last place. In fact, just two other teams avoided the cellar in every season from 1969 through 1991, and both of them, Boston and Los Angeles, finished last in 1992. Last season's record of 72–90 was the Royals' worst since 1970.

So what went wrong? Don't blame the pitching. Despite the litany of ex-Royals pitchers now starting elsewhere—Bud Black, David Cone, Danny Jackson, Charlie Leibrandt, Melido Perez, and Bret Saberhagen (not to mention Steve Farr for the bullpen)—Kansas City's staff continued its steady improvement, while an aging lineup continued to decline, as the rankings in the following table show:

Year	Batting Age/Rank	Runs/Rank	Pitching Age/Rank	Runs/Rank
1990	30.2/12th	4.39/6th	27.5/4th	4.40/9th
1991	29.1/8th	4.49/8th	27.8/4th	4.46/7th
1992	29.4/10th	3.77/12th	27.6/2d	4.12/4th

With the responsibility for the team's decline squarely on its offense, it's noteworthy that two specific areas of weakness correspond to the loss of Tartabull and Stillwell: (1) Kansas City ranked last in the American League in home runs; and (2) Royals shortstops batted just .219.

Kansas City hit only 75 home runs, 52 fewer than the league average, and its outfielders hit just 23—half the league average. Tartabull alone hit 25 homers for the Yankees, despite missing 39 games. Remember

how Kevin McReynolds was acquired in the Bret Saberhagen trade to help fill the void left by the loss of Tartabull? While McReynolds accounted for more than half the home runs hit by Royals outfielders last season (13), he also accounted for about half as many as the Royals might have optimistically hoped for. And no outfielder other than Big Mac hit even five homers; the roll call: Brian McRae, 4; Kevin Koslofski, 3; Jim Eisenreich, 2; and Chris Gwynn, 1.

The hole at shortstop opened by Stillwell's departure proved just as difficult to fill as the power vacuum in the outfield. Three different shortstops played at least 50 games, none with any particular distinction: David Howard (74), Curtis Wilkerson (69), and Rico Rossy (51). The .219 batting average compiled by Royals shortstops was 17 points lower than that of any other American League team, and 35 points below the league average. In fact, only two other A.L. teams had lower marks at any position: White Sox right fielders batted .215; Angels catchers hit .216.

Kansas City may ultimately prove to be a litmus test for whether even a financially aggressive team can survive in a small market. Last season's slide was directly traceable to deficiencies created by the organization's inability or unwillingness, at long last, to keep up with the high rollers. If it was the former—that the spirit was willing but the wallet was weak—Kansas City's fifth-place finish just might have been a huge crack in baseball's foundation. But in the wake of the $9 million bonus paid to get David Cone's name on a three-year contract, Kansas City's struggles in '92 look more like a pause than a full stop.

On the heels of Kansas City's disappointing 1992 season, Hal McRae's name is likely to appear near the top of those odious "Managers Most Likely to Lose Their Jobs" lists for 1993. Nevertheless, his long and successful career as a Royals player got us thinking about major leaguers who spent long tenures as both a player and a manager for the same team. McRae himself ranks fourth in Royals history with 1837 games played, behind George Brett (2562), Frank White (2324), and Amos Otis (1891).

So for the sake of argument, let's say McRae presides over a strong rebound this season. He'll still be more than 10 years behind the only two men who played and managed at least 1500 games for the same team: Cap Anson, with the National League's Chicago White Stockings (played 2276 games, managed 2274); and Red Schoendienst, with the Cardinals (played 1795, managed 1999). Schoendienst's mark may be the more impressive, since Anson was usually a player-manager. His total represents 2274 different games, while Schoendienst's total is 3794.

Nine others reached the 1000-game mark in both categories: Lou Boudreau (Indians), Frank Chance (Cubs), Fred Clarke (Pirates), Joe Cronin (Red Sox), Charlie Grimm (Cubs), Bucky Harris (Senators), Mel Ott (Giants), Tris Speaker (Indians), and Bill Terry (Giants).

In one particular area, McRae's team is built in his own image and likeness. McRae ranked among the American League's top three in doubles in five consecutive seasons from 1974 through 1978. He led the league in 1977 and in 1982, and his total of 54 doubles in 1977 was the highest in the majors over the past 40 years. He finished his career with 484 doubles, 449 of them in the American League, and his rate of one every 14.6 at-bats is the sixth highest in A.L. history (minimum: 100 doubles). And what an impressive list that top 10 is—six Hall of Famers, with Boggs a strong candidate. The top 10:

Player	AB	2B	Rate	Player	AB	2B	Rate
Tris Speaker	10208	793	12.9	Hal McRae	6568	449	14.6
Earl Webb	1686	130	13.0	Ted Williams	7706	525	14.7
Hank Greenberg	4791	366	13.1	Nap Lajoie	7501	511	14.7
Bob Fothergill	3265	225	14.5	Harry Heilmann	7297	497	14.7
Joe Cronin	7474	512	14.6	Wade Boggs	6213	422	14.7

Throughout McRae's tenure as a player with the Royals, the team routinely ranked near the top of the league as well. Kansas City ranked second in the A.L. in each of McRae's first three seasons with the team (1973–75), and led the league in each of the next three (1976–78). From 1971 through 1982, the Royals never ranked lower than fourth in the A.L. But their dominance waned in the mid-1980s; in 1987 (when McRae retired after playing 18 games), Kansas City fell to 12th in the league. After rebounding to third place in 1988, they fell back to 10th in 1989.

Over the past three seasons, the last two with McRae back in the dugout, Kansas City has ranked first, third, and first in doubles. So is it the man, or is it Memorex? A glance at the Ballparks Section (p. 325) suggests that it's the down years in the late '80s that are the anomaly. Royals Stadium is the ballpark most likely to turn a single into a double or triple. Take a moment and study that list. We'll wait. . . .

Note in particular that an increase in doubles and triples is one of the *true* universal effects of artificial turf; the 10 fields with synthetic surfaces rank among the top 11 in that category—an extraordinary skew. Although it's been nearly 30 years since the lords of baseball said, "Let there be plastic grass," players, writers, and fans continue to discuss the supposed increase that artificial turf has on batting averages. One of the most common questions asked by hosts and talk-show callers is how many points artificial turf adds to a player's batting average. The answer is: *none*. Some stadiums with synthetic surfaces add points, others subtract points, but it isn't the surface that's responsible, as the following table shows. The major league rank of the 10 carpeted fields in various categories—doubles and triples (individually, and combined as extra-base percentage), two others in which the skew is significant (errors and stolen-base percentage), and two in which it is not (batting average and runs):

Stadium	2B	3B	XB%	E	SB%	BA	Runs
Astrodome	9	6	11	22	1	19	25
Busch Stadium	10	2	7	21	2	16	9
Kingdome	3	9	2	18	9	7	6
Metrodome	2	3	3	23	3	4	4
Olympic Stadium	4	11	5	9	4	13	15
Riverfront Stadium	7	18	9	25	7	6	5
Royals Stadium	5	1	4	6	16	8	16
Skydome	11	5	10	24	6	10	14
Three Rivers Stadium	8	12	8	19	22	20	22
Veterans Stadium	6	8	6	26	8	15	10
Average Rank	6.5	7.5	6.5	19.3	7.8	11.8	12.6

For any category in which the average rank is less than 10, or more than 17, the skew is probably significant. For example, the odds against choosing 10 stadiums at random with an average of 6.5 or less, as with doubles and extra-base hits, are more than 4000-to-1.

For the record, the batting average on artificial turf over the past five years is actually one point lower (.255) than it is on grass (.256). The stolen-base percentage was 50 points higher on turf (.710) than on grass (.660). There was one double or triple for every 17.8 at-bats on turf, one per 20.8 ABs on grass. There were 1.41 errors and 8.29 runs per game on turf, compared to 1.58 and 8.44 on grass.

So the next time someone mentions the effect of artificial turf on batting averages, tell him about Hal McRae, Royals Stadium, doubles and triples, stolen base percentages, and errors. Then kick him in the shin.

Back in 1988, when we first wrote the computer code that has become our projection model for evaluating the future tracks of current players, Gregg Jefferies was one of our favorite test cases. Although he accumulated only 109 at-bats after his late-season call-up, Jefferies's figures were so outstanding that there were few close statistical matches, and the ones that did exist were all spectacular. The most similar season fragments, including the closest of all of them, which has taken place since Jefferies's debut:

Year	Age	Player	AB	R	H	2B	3B	HR	RBI	BB	SO	BA
1988	21	Gregg Jefferies	109	19	35	8	2	6	17	8	10	.321
1990	21	Juan Gonzalez	90	11	26	7	1	4	12	2	18	.289
1915	20	Babe Ruth	92	16	29	10	1	4	21	9	23	.315
1985	21	Jose Canseco	96	16	29	3	0	5	13	4	31	.302
1964	21	Alex Johnson	109	18	33	7	1	4	18	6	26	.303
1932	20	Joe Medwick	106	13	37	12	1	2	12	2	10	.349

Based on those 109 ABs alone, we projected that Jefferies had nearly a 40 percent chance to join the 2500-hit club. But each season since then has reduced the chance that Jefferies would ever hit that high note; he has bounced around within a narrow range from 8 to 12 percent over the past four seasons.

But nothing illustrates the decline in Jefferies's projected hit total better than a list of the players with the closest statistical profiles after each season of his career: 1988—Gonzalez; 1989—Jack Clark; 1990—Carl Yastrzemski; 1991—Carney Lansford; 1992—Jorge Orta.

Of course, as the likelihood of superstardom has declined, so has the chance that Jefferies will prematurely self-destruct; we can now dismiss any players whose careers fizzled or ended before their fourth full season. But as we suggested in the 1992 *Analyst*, Jefferies's upside potential must have been the most compelling factor in the trade of Bret Saberhagen to the Mets. So at this point, it's probably safe to say that the Royals aren't as consoled by the fact that Jefferies has become a reliable regular as they are concerned that they may have acquired nothing more than the next Jorge Orta.

WON-LOST RECORD BY STARTING POSITION

Kansas City Royals	C	1B	2B	3B	SS	LF	CF	RF	DH	P	Leadoff	Cleanup	Starts vs. LH	Starts vs. RH	Total Starts
Kevin Appier	-	-	-	-	-	-	-	-	-	17-13	-	-	8	22	17-13
Luis Aquino	-	-	-	-	-	-	-	-	-	5-8	-	-	6	7	5-8
Juan Berenguer	-	-	-	-	-	-	-	-	-	0-2	-	-	-	2	0-2
Mike Boddicker	-	-	-	-	-	-	-	-	-	2-6	-	-	2	6	2-6
George Brett	-	6-9	-	2-1	-	-	-	-	62-69	-	-	3-3	37	112	70-79
Jeff Conine	-	1-3	-	-	-	10-12	-	-	-	-	-	-	7	19	11-15
Mark Davis	-	-	-	-	-	-	-	-	-	1-5	-	-	2	4	1-5
Jim Eisenreich	-	-	-	-	-	11-10	0-1	26-27	4-4	-	6-5	5-7	6	77	41-42
Tom Gordon	-	-	-	-	-	-	-	-	-	3-8	-	-	3	8	3-8
Mark Gubicza	-	-	-	-	-	-	-	-	-	10-8	-	-	-	18	10-8
Chris Gwynn	-	-	-	-	-	2-2	-	7-7	1-1	-	-	1-1	-	20	10-10
Chris Haney	-	-	-	-	-	-	-	-	-	2-5	-	-	4	3	2-5
Neal Heaton	-	-	-	-	-	-	-	-	-	-	-	-	-	-	-
David Howard	-	-	-	-	27-44	-	-	-	-	-	-	-	21	50	27-44
Gregg Jefferies	-	-	65-81	-	-	-	-	-	-	-	15-20	8-7	39	107	65-81
Joel Johnston	-	-	-	-	-	-	-	-	-	-	-	-	-	-	-
Wally Joyner	-	64-77	-	-	-	-	-	-	0-4	-	-	14-23	38	107	64-81
Kevin Koslofski	-	-	-	-	-	3-4	8-8	8-6	-	-	1-3	-	-	37	19-18
Mike Macfarlane	43-54	-	-	-	-	-	-	-	3-10	-	-	10-16	40	70	46-64
Mike Magnante	-	-	-	-	-	-	-	-	-	3-9	-	-	5	7	3-9
Brent Mayne	26-23	-	-	3-2	-	-	-	-	-	-	-	1-0	-	54	29-25
Brian McRae	-	-	-	-	-	-	64-79	-	-	-	9-16	-	45	98	64-79
Kevin McReynolds	-	-	-	-	-	44-48	-	1-11	1-0	-	-	30-31	32	73	46-59
Rusty Meacham	-	-	-	-	-	-	-	-	-	-	-	-	-	-	-
Bob Melvin	3-13	1-1	-	-	-	-	-	-	-	-	-	0-2	17	1	4-14
Keith Miller	-	-	42-46	-	-	1-13	-	-	1-0	-	34-36	-	30	73	44-59
Dennis Moeller	-	-	-	-	-	-	-	-	-	0-4	-	-	2	2	0-4
Jeff Montgomery	-	-	-	-	-	-	-	-	-	-	-	-	-	-	-
Hipolito Pichardo	-	-	-	-	-	-	-	-	-	14-10	-	-	7	17	14-10
Ed Pierce	-	-	-	-	-	-	-	-	-	1-0	-	-	-	1	1-0
Harvey Pulliam	-	-	-	-	-	-	-	-	0-1	-	-	-	1	-	0-1
Dennis Rasmussen	-	-	-	-	-	-	-	-	-	4-1	-	-	-	5	4-1
Rick Reed	-	-	-	-	-	-	-	-	-	9-9	-	-	4	14	9-9
Rico Rossy	-	-	2-1	1-4	23-22	-	-	-	-	-	-	-	21	32	26-27
Bill Sampen	-	-	-	-	-	-	-	-	-	0-1	-	-	1	-	0-1
Juan Samuel	-	-	5-4	-	-	-	-	5-13	-	-	-	1-2	7	20	10-17
Rich Sauveur	-	-	-	-	-	-	-	-	-	-	-	-	-	-	-
Steve Shifflett	-	-	-	-	-	-	-	-	-	-	-	-	-	-	-
Terry Shumpert	-	-	8-23	-	-	-	-	-	-	-	-	-	10	21	8-23
Gary Thurman	-	-	-	-	-	1-1	0-2	25-26	-	-	-	6-7	39	16	26-29
Curtis Wilkerson	-	-	15-16	1-2	22-24	-	-	-	0-1	-	-	0-1	15	66	38-43
Curt Young	-	-	-	-	-	-	-	-	-	1-1	-	-	1	1	1-1

TEAM TOTALS: BATTING

	AB	H	2B	3B	HR	RBI	BB	SO	BA	SA	OBA
Season	5501	1411	284	42	75	568	439	741	.256	.364	.315
vs. Left-Handers	1655	431	101	13	23	178	135	241	.260	.379	.320
vs. Right-Handers	3846	980	183	29	52	390	304	500	.255	.358	.313
vs. Ground-Ballers	2226	565	109	15	20	227	165	273	.254	.343	.311
vs. Fly-Ballers	3275	846	175	27	55	341	274	468	.258	.379	.318
Home Games	2656	684	134	25	24	288	217	327	.258	.354	.318
Road Games	2845	727	150	17	51	280	222	414	.256	.374	.312
Grass Fields	2214	571	104	12	41	222	165	304	.258	.371	.312
Artificial Turf	3287	840	180	30	34	346	274	437	.256	.360	.317
April	661	137	39	2	10	49	61	99	.207	.318	.281
May	947	249	60	7	17	118	87	124	.263	.395	.327
June	897	242	57	7	9	96	62	114	.270	.379	.319
July	973	259	44	5	12	96	83	124	.266	.359	.326
August	935	261	37	9	16	121	85	128	.279	.389	.343
Sept./Oct.	1088	263	47	12	11	88	61	152	.242	.337	.287
Leading Off Inn.	1356	345	73	13	23	23	90	170	.254	.378	.308
Runners On	2346	604	106	19	31	524	201	315	.257	.358	.317
Bases Empty	3155	807	178	23	44	44	238	426	.256	.369	.314
Runners/Scor. Pos.	1336	328	54	12	17	460	143	197	.246	.342	.318
Runners On/2 Out	1040	267	48	9	17	222	95	134	.257	.369	.325
Scor. Pos./2 Out	676	166	27	6	11	193	76	91	.246	.352	.330
Late-Inning Pressure	891	211	38	6	15	80	92	140	.237	.341	.311
Leading Off	224	53	9	3	5	5	22	33	.237	.371	.316
Runners On	391	83	11	2	6	71	40	64	.212	.297	.286
Runners/Scor. Pos.	213	40	3	1	4	64	25	34	.188	.268	.275

RUNS BATTED IN	From 1B	From 2B	From 3B	Scoring Position
Totals	81/1607	179/1017	233/582	412/1599
Percentage	5.0%	17.6%	40.0%	25.8%

TEAM TOTALS: PITCHING

	W-L	ERA	AB	H	HR	BB	SO	BA	SA	OBA
Season	72-90	3.81	5502	1426	106	512	834	.259	.375	.323
vs. Left-Handers			2206	549	41	206	330	.249	.364	.312
vs. Right-Handers			3296	877	65	306	504	.266	.383	.331
vs. Ground-Ballers			2697	693	35	248	379	.257	.349	.319
vs. Fly-Ballers			2805	733	71	264	455	.261	.400	.327
Home Games	44-37	3.75	2845	738	41	219	416	.259	.367	.314
Road Games	28-53	3.88	2657	688	65	293	418	.259	.385	.333
Grass Fields	22-40	3.94	2062	538	53	224	335	.261	.390	.334
Artificial Turf	50-50	3.73	3440	888	53	288	499	.258	.367	.316
April	3-17	4.16	697	179	14	78	107	.257	.385	.334
May	14-14	4.48	943	250	19	93	161	.265	.385	.329
June	15-12	3.01	905	231	16	62	126	.255	.366	.304
July	13-14	3.08	935	229	14	80	127	.245	.347	.306
August	14-14	4.16	911	231	29	109	150	.254	.398	.335
Sept./Oct.	13-19	4.02	1111	306	14	90	163	.275	.374	.330
Leading Off Inn.			1319	338	21	126	194	.256	.368	.325
Bases Empty			3047	773	58	278	472	.254	.369	.320
Runners On			2455	653	48	234	362	.266	.384	.327
Runners/Scor. Pos.			1383	361	26	168	234	.261	.373	.332
Runners On/2 Out			1020	232	17	115	170	.227	.327	.312
Scor. Pos./2 Out			658	133	8	89	121	.202	.284	.303
Late-Inning Pressure			821	206	17	79	137	.251	.352	.320
Leading Off			211	51	2	15	42	.242	.303	.292
Runners On			343	85	9	39	58	.248	.364	.327
Runners/Scor. Pos.			182	44	5	28	33	.242	.352	.336
First 9 Batters			3079	768	47	309	519	.249	.351	.319
Second 9 Batters			1456	395	25	104	192	.271	.375	.321
All Batters Thereafter			967	263	34	99	123	.272	.454	.341

WON-LOST RECORD BY STARTING POSITION

Milwaukee Brewers	C	1B	2B	3B	SS	LF	CF	RF	DH	P	Leadoff	Cleanup	Starts vs. LH	Starts vs. RH	Total Starts
Andy Allanson	2-6	-	-	-	-	-	-	-	-	-	-	-	4	4	2-6
James Austin	-	-	-	-	-	-	-	-	-	-	-	-	-	-	-
Dante Bichette	-	-	-	-	-	-	-	49-44	0-1	-	-	13-10	36	58	49-45
Ricky Bones	-	-	-	-	-	-	-	-	-	15-13	-	-	6	22	15-13
Chris Bosio	-	-	-	-	-	-	-	-	-	21-12	-	-	7	26	21-12
Alex Diaz	-	-	-	-	-	0-1	0-1	-	-	-	-	-	-	2	0-2
Cal Eldred	-	-	-	-	-	-	-	-	-	12-2	-	-	6	8	12-2
Mike Fetters	-	-	-	-	-	-	-	-	-	-	-	-	-	-	-
Scott Fletcher	-	-	58-41	-	10-6	-	-	-	-	-	2-0	-	35	80	68-47
Jim Gantner	-	-	32-25	5-8	-	-	-	-	-	-	-	-	7	63	37-33
Darryl Hamilton	-	-	-	-	-	12-14	15-8	43-26	-	-	8-9	-	20	98	70-48
Neal Heaton	-	-	-	-	-	-	-	-	-	-	-	-	-	-	-
Doug Henry	-	-	-	-	-	-	-	-	-	-	-	-	-	-	-
Ted Higuera	-	-	-	-	-	-	-	-	-	-	-	-	-	-	-
Darren Holmes	-	-	-	-	-	-	-	-	-	-	-	-	-	-	-
John Jaha	-	18-14	-	-	-	-	-	-	5-2	-	-	2-0	16	23	23-16
Mark Lee	-	-	-	-	-	-	-	-	-	-	-	-	-	-	-
Pat Listach	-	-	-	-	82-63	-	-	-	-	-	66-42	-	39	106	82-63
Tim McIntosh	3-5	3-3	-	-	-	2-1	-	-	1-2	-	-	-	12	8	9-11
Paul Molitor	-	33-15	-	-	-	-	-	57-51	-	-	16-19	-	41	115	90-66
Jaime Navarro	-	-	-	-	-	-	-	-	-	22-12	-	-	13	21	22-12
Dave Nilsson	27-16	-	-	-	-	-	-	-	1-1	-	-	-	5	40	28-17
Edwin Nunez	-	-	-	-	-	-	-	-	-	-	-	-	-	-	-
Jesse Orosco	-	-	-	-	-	-	-	-	-	-	-	-	-	-	-
Dan Plesac	-	-	-	-	-	-	-	-	-	3-1	-	-	2	2	3-1
Ron Robinson	-	-	-	-	-	-	-	-	-	3-5	-	-	1	7	3-5
Bruce Ruffin	-	-	-	-	-	-	-	-	-	1-5	-	-	2	4	1-5
Kevin Seitzer	-	-	1-0	86-60	-	-	-	-	-	-	-	-	41	106	87-60
Bill Spiers	-	-	1-0	-	0-1	-	-	-	-	-	-	-	-	3	2-1
Franklin Stubbs	-	31-28	-	-	-	-	-	-	7-6	-	-	6-9	9	63	38-34
William Suero	-	-	0-3	-	-	-	-	-	0-1	-	-	-	4	-	0-4
B.J. Surhoff	60-43	7-10	-	0-1	-	2-0	-	-	8-1	-	-	8-10	31	101	77-55
Jim Tatum	-	-	-	1-1	-	-	-	-	-	-	-	-	1	1	1-1
Jose Valentin	-	-	0-1	-	-	-	-	-	-	-	-	-	-	1	0-1
Greg Vaughn	-	-	-	-	-	76-54	-	-	3-3	-	-	43-35	37	99	79-57
Bill Wegman	-	-	-	-	-	-	-	-	-	15-20	-	-	5	30	15-20
Robin Yount	-	-	-	-	-	-	77-61	-	9-2	-	20-6	-	40	109	86-63

TEAM TOTALS: BATTING

	AB	H	2B	3B	HR	RBI	BB	SO	BA	SA	OBA
Season	5504	1477	272	35	82	683	511	779	.268	.375	.330
vs. Left-Handers	1283	372	68	13	23	209	134	182	.290	.417	.355
vs. Right-Handers	4221	1105	204	22	59	474	377	597	.262	.362	.322
vs. Ground-Ballers	2535	684	123	14	27	312	226	352	.270	.361	.330
vs. Fly-Ballers	2969	793	149	21	55	371	285	427	.267	.387	.331
Home Games	2580	671	111	17	35	313	271	361	.260	.357	.330
Road Games	2924	806	161	18	47	370	240	418	.276	.391	.330
Grass Fields	4628	1219	212	23	73	549	424	656	.263	.366	.325
Artificial Turf	876	258	60	12	9	134	87	123	.295	.421	.359
April	640	162	22	6	9	82	59	91	.253	.348	.314
May	963	252	50	4	24	112	88	143	.262	.397	.325
June	932	271	50	6	13	129	80	105	.291	.399	.344
July	955	247	48	8	13	103	78	161	.259	.366	.314
August	949	246	47	6	7	121	98	142	.259	.344	.330
Sept./Oct.	1065	299	55	5	16	136	108	137	.281	.387	.347
Leading Off Inn.	1337	357	62	12	19	19	110	184	.267	.374	.325
Runners On	2425	681	124	16	37	638	263	331	.281	.391	.347
Bases Empty	3079	796	148	19	45	45	248	448	.259	.363	.316
Runners/Scor. Pos.	1501	417	77	9	21	578	212	226	.278	.383	.358
Runners On/2 Out	1003	253	44	7	16	242	119	151	.252	.358	.336
Scor. Pos./2 Out	700	169	31	4	9	216	102	114	.241	.336	.343
Late-Inning Pressure	805	215	29	3	13	93	91	109	.267	.359	.340
Leading Off	203	63	5	0	4	4	23	27	.310	.394	.381
Runners On	357	90	12	2	3	83	52	48	.252	.322	.343
Runners/Scor. Pos.	216	52	9	1	3	80	43	30	.241	.333	.357

RUNS BATTED IN	From 1B	From 2B	From 3B	Scoring Position
Totals	74/1632	209/1188	318/678	527/1866
Percentage	4.5%	17.6%	46.9%	28.2%

TEAM TOTALS: PITCHING

	W-L	ERA	AB	H	HR	BB	SO	BA	SA	OBA
Season	92-70	3.43	5468	1344	127	435	793	.246	.371	.305
vs. Left-Handers			2390	581	43	199	259	.243	.351	.301
vs. Right-Handers			3078	763	84	236	534	.248	.386	.308
vs. Ground-Ballers			2575	637	45	212	350	.247	.353	.307
vs. Fly-Ballers			2893	707	82	223	443	.244	.386	.303
Home Games	53-28	2.74	2747	644	51	195	382	.234	.337	.288
Road Games	39-42	4.14	2721	700	76	240	411	.257	.405	.321
Grass Fields	79-59	3.28	4676	1139	98	389	689	.244	.360	.305
Artificial Turf	13-11	4.33	792	205	29	46	104	.259	.434	.304
April	10-9	3.53	633	160	10	59	76	.253	.344	.322
May	13-15	4.40	967	241	31	84	150	.249	.420	.313
June	16-11	3.66	903	223	26	88	117	.247	.383	.315
July	16-12	3.26	968	249	18	63	130	.257	.370	.308
August	15-14	3.20	948	227	23	66	154	.239	.359	.292
Sept./Oct.	22-9	2.71	1049	244	19	75	166	.233	.342	.285
Leading Off Inn.			1354	326	34	97	177	.241	.369	.297
Bases Empty			3256	771	76	239	462	.237	.359	.293
Runners On			2212	573	51	196	331	.259	.388	.321
Runners/Scor. Pos.			1233	306	32	144	198	.248	.384	.324
Runners On/2 Out			914	195	18	89	146	.213	.332	.288
Scor. Pos./2 Out			580	121	14	71	95	.209	.333	.300
Late-Inning Pressure			818	194	10	78	149	.237	.335	.310
Leading Off			220	61	5	15	42	.277	.423	.332
Runners On			327	83	4	43	57	.254	.361	.343
Runners/Scor. Pos.			187	44	3	32	39	.235	.358	.345
First 9 Batters			2607	605	55	253	427	.232	.345	.304
Second 9 Batters			1378	355	35	99	179	.258	.389	.311
All Batters Thereafter			1483	384	37	83	187	.259	.399	.301

MILWAUKEE BREWERS

Seven years ago, in the second edition of the *Analyst*, we wrote about a new basis for platooning, one that we felt could eventually complement traditional lefty-righty maneuvers. Our figures proved that ground-ball hitters enjoyed greater success against fly-ball pitchers than they did against ground-ball pitchers; and fly-ball hitters generally hit better against ground-ballers than they did against fly-ballers. The rule seemed simple to remember in that it mirrored the lefty-righty rules: Matchups of opposites (right-handed batters vs. southpaws, or ground-ball hitters vs. fly-ball pitchers) favor the batter; matchups of like types favor the pitcher.

We demonstrated the trend in various ways in several later editions, and even though the topic became a favorite on talk shows, there seemed little evidence that any managers found our evidence compelling enough to incorporate the principle into their decision-making process. So a few years back, we simply gave up. The only group of men on the entire planet who were in a position to make use of the trend appeared unwilling to blaze the trail.

So we were surprised to learn last August that Brewers manager Phil Garner had decided to use ground-ball tendencies as a basis for late-game substitutions. And we can report that for the season, Brewers relief pitchers had the advantage against 53 percent of the batters they faced. That might not sound like a high rate, but think about it: The issue of changing pitchers probably arises on only, say, 25 percent of all batters faced late in the game. Other factors will often take precedence: a strong lefty-righty skew; the previous history between the players involved; the need for a strikeout or a double-play grounder in a particular situation; and so on. So the potential for making a move based primarily on ground-ball tendencies is probably limited to less than 10 percent of all late-game plate appearances. That's why Garner's 53 percent figure in the table below represents more of a trend than you might think. More significant is the fact that Milwaukee's figure was the highest in the American League last season. And Brewers batters had the advantage on 51.4 percent of all plate appearances from the seventh inning on, the league's second-highest mark. Our only question regarding the following table of those percentages is this: Were Bobby Valentine and Toby Harrah employing the practice in Arlington, too?

appearances last season into one of three categories: (1) ground-ball hitters; (2) neutral hitters; and (3) fly-ball hitters. The classifications are based on their ratios of ground outs to fly outs, with boundaries set to establish groups of similar size; the totals indicate how many members of each group had higher batting averages against each type of pitcher. "GBP" stands for ground-ball pitchers (G/A ratios above the league average), "FBP" for fly-ball pitchers (below the average):

	Better vs. GBP	Better vs. FBP	Pct. Better vs. GBP
Ground-ball hitters	15	19	.441
Neutral hitters	17	18	.486
Fly-ball hitters	23	11	.676

Although the figures do follow the general pattern, the number of players included in a single season isn't large enough to smooth out the edges. But the corresponding table for the 18-year period for which we have ground-ball and fly-ball figures does that very well. The figures include all players with at least 400 plate appearances in a given season in either the American or the National League:

	Better vs. GBP	Better vs. FBP	Pct. Better vs. GBP
Ground-ball hitters	578	474	.549
Neutral hitters	609	451	.575
Fly-ball hitters	674	382	.638

Incidentally, you might be wondering why all three groups, even the ground-ball hitters, have predominantly higher batting averages against ground-ball pitchers than they have vs. fly-ballers. The answer is simple: By the laws of physics, fly-ball pitchers allow more extra-base hits (especially home runs) than worm killers do. Therefore, only fly-ball pitchers who restrict an opponent's on-base potential can be effective enough to pitch in the majors. The bottom line is that even a ground-ball hitter is likely to compile a higher batting average vs. ground-ball pitchers than vs. fly-ball pitchers. It's just that a fly-ball hitter is even more likely to do so.

Recently passed Truth in Statistics legislation obligates us to point out that the skew for handedness is much more pervasive than that for ground- and fly-out tendencies. The table below shows figures for left- and right-handedness that correspond to those shown above:

	Better vs. LHP	Better vs. RHP	Pct. Better vs. LHP
Left-handed hitters	217	756	.223
Right-handed batters	1397	797	.637

But then, we're not arguing that ground-ball tendencies should be the *primary* factor in lineup, pinch-hitting, and pitching change decisions. In fact, since its skews aren't as pronounced as those of lefty-righty platooning, it becomes all the more important that managers be aware of which players follow the general rule and which are the exceptions. (Remember, too,

Relief Pitching				Late-Inning Batting			
Team	BFP	Adv.	Pct.	Team	BFP	Adv.	Pct.
Milwaukee	1605	853	53.1	Texas	2135	1103	51.7
Texas	2003	1058	52.8	Milwaukee	2155	1107	51.4
Chicago	1662	876	52.7	Seattle	2073	1060	51.1
Oakland	2079	1087	52.3	Kansas City	2050	1041	50.8
Seattle	2002	1042	52.0	Oakland	2203	1104	50.1
New York	1775	913	51.4	California	2050	1024	50.0
Detroit	2252	1157	51.4	Minnesota	2103	1048	49.8
Boston	1789	908	50.8	Boston	2210	1095	49.5
California	1790	879	49.1	Detroit	2052	1013	49.4
Kansas City	2328	1140	49.0	Cleveland	2168	1058	48.8
Cleveland	2067	1012	49.0	Toronto	2119	1024	48.3
Toronto	1708	834	48.8	Chicago	2068	982	47.5
Minnesota	1891	898	47.5	New York	2119	1003	47.3
Baltimore	1799	848	47.1	Baltimore	2034	939	46.2
A.L. Totals	26750	13505	50.5	A.L. Totals	29539	14601	49.4

Here's how Milwaukee benefits from the ground-ball platoon practice. The following table classifies all American League batters who made at least 400 plate

that left- and right-handers form a natural black-and-white dichotomy with no overlap. That's not the case with ground- and fly-ball hitters and pitchers, where there's a lot of gray and no absolute distinction.) The lists below show the players with the widest disparities between their career batting averages against ground-ball and fly-ball pitchers (minimum: 100 starts last season):

Better vs. Ground-Ball Pitchers

Player	GBP	FBP	Diff.
Darren Daulton	.261	.205	.056
David Justice	.299	.246	.053
Dave Valle	.256	.208	.048
Junior Felix	.285	.237	.048
Dan Gladden	.293	.248	.045
Dick Schofield	.254	.211	.044
Terry Pendleton	.295	.252	.043
Mark McGwire	.267	.229	.037
Charlie Hayes	.269	.231	.037
Brady Anderson	.256	.223	.033

Better vs. Fly-Ball Pitchers

Player	FBP	GBP	Diff.
Albert Belle	.281	.236	.045
Felix Jose	.306	.264	.042
Tom Pagnozzi	.272	.236	.036
Luis Polonia	.314	.281	.033
Roberto Kelly	.294	.264	.030
Jeff King	.242	.213	.030
Manuel Lee	.267	.239	.028
Delino DeShields	.284	.257	.027
Darryl Hamilton	.304	.279	.025
Jody Reed	.290	.267	.022

Now that Phil Garner has taken the first step, managers who don't make use of ground- and fly-ball data will be at a distinct competitive disadvantage. And frankly, Garner is one manager we're happy to see carrying the banner on this whole ground-ball platooning business. As a rookie last season, Garner led the Brewers to a surprising 92–70 record that left them just four victories behind the world champs-to-be at season's end.

The formulas that we use to determine the number of games a manager and his team are expected to win projected the 1992 Brewers to finish six games below .500, and (after adjusting for extreme variations) attributes seven of the additional wins to Garner. Not all managers who had great first seasons maintained that level of success throughout their careers. (See the table below for examples of those who did not.) But very few recent managers earned figures as high as Garner's in their rookie seasons—only seven others during the expansion era, to be exact. Nevertheless, all three managers with career totals of plus-50 wins or higher since 1961 come from that short list. The highest-rated rookies during the expansion era:

Year	Manager, Team	Expected		Actual		Career Wins
1992	Phil Garner, Mil.	78–84	.484	92–70	.568	+ 7
1986	Hal Lanier, Hou.	80–82	.494	96–66	.593	+ 4
1984	Davey Johnson, Mets	73–89	.451	90–72	.556	+31
1978	George Bamberger, Mil.	71–91	.440	93–69	.574	+10
1970	Sparky Anderson, Cin.	85–77	.527	102–60	.630	+52
1969	Billy Martin, Minn.	82–80	.505	97–65	.599	+63
1967	Dick Williams, Bos.	74–88	.454	92–70	.568	+53
1963	Bob Kennedy, Cubs	68–94	.421	82–80	.506	+ 8
1961	Ralph Houk, Yankees	95–67	.587	109–53	.673	+10

A few observations, then, on Garner's managerial style. In five full seasons under Tom Trebelhorn, the Brewers stole an average of 154 bases a year. Their five-year total of 770 steals was the most of any American League team during that period; only the Athletics came within 100 of Milwaukee's total (718). Yet under Garner, Milwaukee stole 256 bases, nearly 100 more than any other A.L. team, and 80 more than the team record set under Trebelhorn in 1987. It was the highest total by an American League team since 1976, when Oakland stole 341 bases, the highest A.L. total in this century.

Garner also embraced the sacrifice bunt; the Brewers laid down 61 successful sacrifices, to rank second in the league to Oakland (72). Milwaukee's combination of 256 steals and 61 sac bunts undoubtedly help produce the lowest total of double-play ground outs in the A.L. (102)—despite the fact that the Brewers tended slightly more than average toward ground balls and struck out less frequently than any A.L. team except the Royals.

Garner also continued Trebelhorn's tradition of sparse use of pinch hitters. Only 64 Brewers players were announced as pinch hitters last season, the second-lowest total in the league to Toronto (62), and down from 77 under Trebelhorn in 1991.

Who knows whether Garner's aggressive style was responsible for his first-year success, or even whether he will maintain that high standard this season? But it's noteworthy that just one year into his new managerial career, he is already being cited as a role model of sorts by a member of the rookie class of 1993, new Rangers manager Kevin Kennedy. (For more on this, see the Rangers essay.)

MINNESOTA TWINS

Not since the playing days of Harmon Killebrew and Fran Tarkenton has Minneapolis loved an athlete as it does Kirby Puckett. Even before he helped bring two World Series titles to the Twin Cities, Kirby was a local folk hero. So throughout last summer, as word of stalled contract negotiations between Puckett and the Twins spread, his fans adopted the kind of resignation that accompanies news of a dying relative. Only the most optimistic Twins fans harbored much hope that Kirby would return to the team in 1993.

Much of the pessimism was a holdover from the late 1970s, when a promising team was derailed by the free-agent defections of key players still in their primes: Bill Campbell, Lyman Bostock, Tom Burgmeier, Larry Hisle, and Dave Goltz. Additionally, Rod Carew was traded to California to avoid losing him to free agency. Moreover, from 1975 through 1987, only one free agent chose to join the Twins, and only one chose to stay there when given the freedom to leave. In both cases, it was Mike Marshall. To this day, the hurt from those snubs lingers; the Mini-Apple continues to view itself as the small-market town unable to keep its sons from leaving for big-city lights.

There's no question that previous ownership simply refused to play the free-agent market. (It's also important to note that the earlier regime built the foundation for the later championships. As we pointed out in the 1990 *Analyst,* Minnesota's rookie class of 1982 alone—including Tom Brunansky, Gary Gaetti, Kent Hrbek, and Frank Viola—was among the best in baseball history.) But it's time to recognize the fact that since Carl Pohlad purchased the team in 1984, and especially with Andy MacPhail in charge, Minnesota has become competitive in the free-agent market. Although the Twins have continued to lose players since then, most of the losses have been inconsequential, and in some cases actually beneficial.

The following table contrasts the total of free agents that each team has lost with the number of those under the age of 30 who have departed over the past 10 years (labeled "Y&R," for Young and Recent; ages are as of opening day the next season). At least in the case of Minnesota, these categories represent perception and reality. The Twins' reputation as a team damaged by free agency is no longer appropriate:

Team	Tot.	Y&R	Team	Tot.	Y&R
Baltimore	18	1	Atlanta	10	1
Boston	20	0	Chicago	17	2
California	24	1	Cincinnati	17	5
Chicago	18	0	Houston	17	3
Cleveland	14	2	Los Angeles	22	2
Detroit	17	4	Montreal	20	3
Kansas City	14	2	New York	19	2
Milwaukee	16	1	Philadelphia	9	0
Minnesota	27	2	Pittsburgh	26	5
New York	19	0	St. Louis	20	2
Oakland	33	2	San Diego	19	4
Seattle	11	1	San Francisco	18	4
Texas	12	1			
Toronto	14	0			

On a historical basis, only the Oakland A's have lost more free agents than Minnesota. But that applies to today's A's and Twins no more than those bogus football trends that are the mainstay of 1–900 betting services and irresponsible newspapers. (You know, the Bears have won 28 consecutive home games against the spread following defeats of seven points or more—no matter that the streak could date back to Bronco Nagurski and Red Grange for all you know.) Both Oakland and Minnesota have become competitive in the free-agent market since the days of Charles O. Finley and the Griffith family, respectively.

Yes, Minnesota still loses its share of free agents, creating for some the illusion that the Twins can't compete. And the recent losses of John Smiley and Greg Gagne are serious hurdles that jeopardize Minnesota's pennant chances for 1993. But of those who've departed under the current ownership, only Smiley—who, after all, joined the Twins only because he was on the verge of free agency—was under the age of 30, and only 34-year-old Jeff Reardon and 36-year-old Jack Morris (exercising an escape hatch in the free-agent contract that brought him to Minnesota) were coming off seasons in which they ranked among the league's top 10 in a major statistical category. Does anyone in Minneapolis really miss Wally Backman, John Moses, or Terry Leach? Didn't the rapid development of Scott Leius and Pedro Munoz make the departures of Gary Gaetti and Dan Gladden seem downright serendipitous? And considering that Gagne will be a nearly-32-year-old shortstop by the end of the '93 season, maybe this was the right time to say good-bye to him as well.

Puckett's return to Minneapolis was actually typical of the Carl Pohlad/Andy MacPhail regime. Since winning his first title in '87, MacPhail has retained the most valuable members of the team when they became eligible for free agency, including Gaetti in 1987, Randy Bush in 1988, Kent Hrbek in 1989, and Brian Harper in 1991. The only question was money, but there apparently comes a point at which additional dollars that may be available elsewhere are devalued. Why else would Greg Maddux sign with Atlanta and turn down an offer of many millions of dollars more to play for the Yankees? That episode prompted talk in New York of how Gene Michael wasn't as good a salesman as George Steinbrenner, but that misses the real point: It's not the salesman, it's what he's selling—in Steinbrenner's case in the 1970s, more money than anyone else, at a time when relatively few owners were willing to spend. But in today's economic climate, thanks in part to the arbitration procedure, everybody spends big money (or has to). Even before signing their exorbitant new deals, Maddux and Puckett had made millions more in their careers than Steinbrenner paid Reggie to play in New York. So when someone offers a couple million more to a deeper thinker than Barry Bonds, what's the big deal? The hot new commodity for superstar free agents in the 1990s is the security and comfort of playing in a favorable or familiar environment. (Bonds could have gotten some interesting advice about that from his good friend Bobby Bonilla.) And in the end, that's what allows some small-market teams like Minnesota and Kansas City to compete for free agents on equal or better footing than the megalopoli.

While we're on the subject, if it seems to you that over the past few years there have been more superstar free agents than ever before, you're absolutely right.

During the past off-season, seven players became free agents after placing among their league's top three in one of the following categories: runs, hits, home runs, RBIs, batting average, wins, saves, or ERA, or after leading the league in stolen bases. And over the past four years, there were nearly as many free agents available coming off "top-three" seasons (22) as there were over the 13 previous years of free agency (24). The list:

1976: Sal Bando, Bill Campbell, Rollie Fingers, Wayne Garland, Reggie Jackson
1977: Goose Gossage, Larry Hisle, Lyman Bostock
1978: Pete Rose
1979: Don Stanhouse
1980: Ron LeFlore, Don Sutton
1981: None
1982: Hal McRae
1983: Rod Carew
1984: Lee Lacy, Andre Thornton, Bruce Sutter, Rick Sutcliffe
1985: Donnie Moore, Carlton Fisk
1986: Tim Raines, Jack Morris
1987: Paul Molitor, Dave Righetti
1988: None
1989: Rickey Henderson, Nick Esasky, Mark Davis, Storm Davis, Robin Yount
1990: Willie McGee, Brett Butler, Darryl Strawberry, Zane Smith, Danny Darwin, Vince Coleman, Bob Welch
1991: Willie Randolph, Mitch Williams, Tom Candiotti
1992: Greg Maddux, Barry Bonds, Joe Carter, Randy Myers, Paul Molitor, Mark McGwire, Kirby Puckett

This seems an unusual trend, particularly in light of the frequency with which teams now try to lock up their best players with long-term deals, an uncommon practice 10 or 15 years ago. Perhaps players and their agents see "testing the market" as a less drastic step than they did when the process was new. In those first five years, not one of the players above re-signed with his team. Since then, nearly half of them have. Fans should remember this as they watch the gamesmanship that accompanies such season-long negotiations. They ain't gone until they're gone.

Does anyone actually believe in the "sophomore jinx"? We do. Also the "Cy Young Award jinx," the "Most Valuable Player jinx," and the "big free-agent contract jinx."

In fact, we'll go further: Any player having a particularly good year is statistically unlikely to have as good a year the next season. How's that for a jinx?

Webster's defines a *jinx* as something that "brings bad luck" or an "evil spell." Since it's most often applied to second-year players, who presumably offended the gods or something by their precocious starts, let's focus on them. We start with a basic fact: High-profile rookies seldom achieve the same heights as sophomores. Last season, Scott Leius provided a classic example of a second-year decline. His batting average fell by 37 points, from .286 to .249. Other examples? How about Phil Plantier, who fell 85 points short of his rookie-season batting average? Or Leius's teammate Pedro Munoz (down 13 points)? Their performances are typical, but only for rookies *who had high batting averages to begin with*. Of the nine rookies from the class of 1991 who batted at least .250, only two increased their batting averages as sophs last season:

Chuck Knoblauch and Ray Lankford. But among those who batted below .250 in 1991, 9 of 12 posted higher marks in 1992—with no one scrutinizing them for signs of any jinx. The corresponding figures for all rookies over a 50-year period from 1942 through 1991:

Rookie BA		Change in Batting Avg. as a Sophomore		
.250 or Above	228	increases (35%);	429	declines (63%)
Below .250	217	increases (63%);	129	declines (37%)

The flaw lies in thinking there's something special about a *sophomore* jinx. This pattern applies to all players throughout their careers: The higher they bat in season 1, the more difficult it is to match that mark in year 2; the higher in year 2, the tougher in year 3; and so on.

For example, let's look at players in their second and third seasons and see if we can't concoct a "junior jinx." It shouldn't be difficult. The percentage of players who batted higher as juniors than as sophomores is extraordinarily similar to the freshmen/sophomores figures in the table above. Among players who batted .250 or better as sophomores—regardless of what they did as rookies—only 34 percent raised those marks in the following season; but 67 percent of those who batted below .250 as second-year players posted higher marks in their third season. See a trend?

Let's cut through all the bull. The fact is, if you have a good season, it's unlikely you'll do that well next season; have a bad season, you're likely to improve a year later. Any player, any year. Among all players since 1969, only 36 percent improved their batting averages coming off seasons of .250 or better in at least 400 at-bats. The corresponding percentage for those coming off sub-.250 seasons was twice as high: 72 percent. That's not a jinx; it's common sense.

There's a romance about rookies; the best of them hold out the hope of becoming something new and special. They first capture our attention without having shown us a downside or a dark side. Remember Mike Tyson, that sweet-talking 18-year-old knockout machine? Or Monica Seles and Andre Agassi, those polite teenagers destined to erase the bratty image of tennis *wunderkinder*? Hoo boy! A mystique develops around young and talented athletes, and in many cases it's impossible for them to live up to expectations, on and off the field. The sophomore jinx is one of the ways we explain the shortfall without admitting the reality—namely, that these aren't wind-up toys but flesh-and-blood individuals subject to the same pressures and failings as the rest of us.

This may all seem like a lot of numerical and philosophical bluster for a rather minor point and, well, it is. But it strikes us that for all the criticism you hear about "too many statistics" being thrown around—and God only knows that's true—there are also too many *words* tossed about that have no meaning, too—most often by those who damn the numbers. The "sophomore jinx" is one such term; it lets players, writers, and broadcasters say something while saying nothing. If that's all they've got to say, we'd rather they let us watch our baseball in blissful, contemplative silence.

WON-LOST RECORD BY STARTING POSITION

Minnesota Twins	C	1B	2B	3B	SS	LF	CF	RF	DH	P	Leadoff	Cleanup	Starts vs. LH	Starts vs. RH	Total Starts
Paul Abbott	-	-	-	-	-	-	-	-	-	-	-	-	-	-	-
Rick Aguilera	-	-	-	-	-	-	-	-	-	-	-	-	-	-	-
Willie Banks	-	-	-	-	-	-	-	-	-	5-7	-	-	2	10	5-7
Bernardo Brito	-	-	-	-	-	0-1	-	-	1-0	-	-	-	1	1	1-1
Jarvis Brown	-	-	-	-	-	0-1	-	-	-	-	-	-	-	1	0-1
J.T. Bruett	-	-	-	-	-	3-2	6-3	0-1	-	-	5-4	-	-	15	9-6
Randy Bush	-	0-1	-	-	-	2-0	-	6-6	15-8	-	-	-	-	38	23-15
Larry Casian	-	-	-	-	-	-	-	-	-	-	-	-	-	-	-
Chili Davis	-	-	-	-	-	-	-	1-1	62-53	-	-	36-22	28	89	63-54
Tom Edens	-	-	-	-	-	-	-	-	-	-	-	-	-	-	-
Scott Erickson	-	-	-	-	-	-	-	-	-	16-16	-	-	5	27	16-16
Greg Gagne	-	-	-	-	72-59	-	-	-	-	-	-	-	28	103	72-59
Mauro Gozzo	-	-	-	-	-	-	-	-	-	-	-	-	-	-	-
Mark Guthrie	-	-	-	-	-	-	-	-	-	-	-	-	-	-	-
Brian Harper	74-54	-	-	-	-	-	-	-	1-1	-	-	-	31	99	75-55
Donnie Hill	-	-	2-2	0-1	4-3	-	-	-	-	-	-	-	-	12	6-6
Kent Hrbek	-	57-45	-	-	-	-	-	-	3-4	-	-	40-39	16	93	60-49
Terry Jorgensen	-	8-3	-	2-3	-	-	-	-	-	-	-	-	8	8	10-6
Bob Kipper	-	-	-	-	-	-	-	-	-	-	-	-	-	-	-
Chuck Knoblauch	-	-	83-67	-	-	-	-	-	0-1	-	32-33	-	34	117	83-68
Bill Krueger	-	-	-	-	-	-	-	-	-	18-9	-	-	6	21	18-9
Gene Larkin	-	25-23	-	-	-	-	-	19-15	2-2	-	-	-	10	76	46-40
Scott Leius	-	-	-	-	69-48	-	-	-	-	-	-	-	32	85	69-48
Shane Mack	-	-	-	-	-	80-62	4-2	1-1	-	-	-	53-35	32	118	85-65
Pat Mahomes	-	-	-	-	-	-	-	-	-	6-7	-	-	2	11	6-7
Pedro Munoz	-	-	-	-	-	2-3	-	63-47	-	-	-	0-2	34	81	65-50
Mike Pagliarulo	-	-	-	11-15	-	-	-	-	-	-	-	-	-	26	11-15
Derek Parks	1-1	-	-	-	-	-	-	-	-	-	-	-	1	1	1-1
Kirby Puckett	-	-	-	-	-	-	80-67	-	6-3	-	-	14-9	34	122	86-70
Luis Quinones	-	-	-	1-0	-	-	-	-	-	-	-	-	-	1	1-0
Jeff Reboulet	-	-	5-3	7-5	14-10	-	-	-	-	-	-	-	8	36	26-18
Darren Reed	-	-	-	-	-	3-3	-	0-1	-	-	-	-	5	2	3-4
John Smiley	-	-	-	-	-	-	-	-	-	21-13	-	-	7	27	21-13
Kevin Tapani	-	-	-	-	-	-	-	-	-	19-15	-	-	10	24	19-15
Mike Trombley	-	-	-	-	-	-	-	-	-	5-2	-	-	2	5	5-2
Gary Wayne	-	-	-	-	-	-	-	-	-	-	-	-	-	-	-
Lenny Webster	15-17	-	-	-	-	-	-	-	-	-	-	-	4	28	15-17
David West	-	-	-	-	-	-	-	-	-	-	0-3	-	-	3	0-3
Carl Willis	-	-	-	-	-	-	-	-	-	-	-	-	-	-	-

TEAM TOTALS: BATTING

	AB	H	2B	3B	HR	RBI	BB	SO	BA	SA	OBA
Season	5582	1544	275	27	104	701	527	834	.277	.391	.341
vs. Left-Handers	1227	337	68	6	19	158	116	194	.275	.386	.336
vs. Right-Handers	4355	1207	207	21	85	543	411	640	.277	.393	.343
vs. Ground-Ballers	2652	722	117	12	32	306	230	382	.272	.362	.333
vs. Fly-Ballers	2930	822	158	15	72	395	297	452	.281	.418	.349
Home Games	2723	769	132	18	56	352	281	408	.282	.406	.351
Road Games	2859	775	143	9	48	349	246	426	.271	.378	.333
Grass Fields	2166	586	107	4	33	259	183	318	.271	.369	.331
Artificial Turf	3416	958	168	23	71	442	344	516	.280	.405	.348
April	736	200	31	6	15	88	54	86	.272	.391	.323
May	906	277	50	5	21	148	102	123	.306	.442	.377
June	1003	276	56	4	27	144	100	125	.275	.420	.344
July	933	258	42	4	10	103	84	133	.277	.362	.335
August	986	261	49	3	18	99	85	177	.265	.375	.328
Sept./Oct.	1018	272	47	5	13	119	102	190	.267	.361	.339
Leading Off Inn.	1335	385	81	6	36	36	101	207	.288	.439	.346
Runners On	2544	712	127	14	42	639	283	368	.280	.390	.350
Bases Empty	3038	832	148	13	62	62	244	466	.274	.392	.334
Runners/Scor. Pos.	1524	417	76	8	23	573	214	241	.274	.379	.358
Runners On/2 Out	1020	246	45	5	17	223	138	156	.241	.345	.338
Scor. Pos./2 Out	681	156	26	2	9	195	110	107	.229	.313	.344
Late-Inning Pressure	802	211	41	2	5	80	83	146	.263	.338	.335
Leading Off	199	50	10	0	2	2	17	38	.251	.332	.320
Runners On	352	102	22	1	0	75	45	51	.290	.358	.369
Runners/Scor. Pos.	208	56	12	1	0	69	32	34	.269	.337	.364

RUNS BATTED IN	From 1B	From 2B	From 3B	Scoring Position
Totals	78/1812	218/1184	301/683	519/1867
Percentage	4.3%	18.4%	44.1%	27.8%

TEAM TOTALS: PITCHING

	W-L	ERA	AB	H	HR	BB	SO	BA	SA	OBA
Season	90-72	3.70	5472	1391	121	479	923	.254	.382	.316
vs. Left-Handers			2020	526	39	163	332	.260	.384	.316
vs. Right-Handers			3452	865	82	316	591	.251	.382	.316
vs. Ground-Ballers			2625	658	32	253	398	.251	.344	.319
vs. Fly-Ballers			2847	733	89	226	525	.257	.418	.314
Home Games	48-33	3.66	2826	724	56	232	515	.256	.386	.315
Road Games	42-39	3.75	2646	667	65	247	408	.252	.378	.317
Grass Fields	34-28	3.53	2007	490	50	189	315	.244	.369	.310
Artificial Turf	56-44	3.81	3465	901	71	290	608	.260	.390	.319
April	9-12	3.98	689	168	15	74	116	.244	.376	.317
May	18-8	3.78	904	243	24	69	158	.269	.417	.325
June	18-11	3.28	978	254	25	71	154	.260	.393	.309
July	16-11	3.46	921	217	18	88	152	.236	.341	.305
August	12-17	4.27	982	252	25	91	169	.257	.395	.320
Sept./Oct.	17-13	3.54	998	257	14	86	174	.258	.371	.318
Leading Off Inn.			1346	354	29	102	196	.263	.402	.320
Bases Empty			3139	804	72	261	520	.256	.388	.317
Runners On			2333	587	49	218	403	.252	.374	.314
Runners/Scor. Pos.			1389	351	38	148	258	.253	.392	.318
Runners On/2 Out			988	233	22	106	172	.236	.356	.312
Scor. Pos./2 Out			651	149	16	78	116	.229	.346	.313
Late-Inning Pressure			881	215	22	86	167	.244	.367	.314
Leading Off			222	59	7	25	37	.266	.432	.343
Runners On			381	86	8	39	76	.226	.318	.299
Runners/Scor. Pos.			231	49	7	30	51	.212	.320	.302
First 9 Batters			2788	676	65	235	528	.242	.366	.303
Second 9 Batters			1428	369	24	133	220	.258	.373	.320
All Batters Thereafter			1256	346	32	111	175	.275	.430	.335

WON-LOST RECORD BY STARTING POSITION

New York Yankees	C	1B	2B	3B	SS	LF	CF	RF	DH	P	Leadoff	Cleanup	Starts vs. LH	Starts vs. RH	Total Starts
Jesse Barfield	-	-	-	-	-	-	-	15-11	-	-	-	-	12	14	15-11
Tim Burke	-	-	-	-	-	-	-	-	-	-	-	-	-	-	-
Greg Cadaret	-	-	-	-	-	-	-	-	-	4-7	-	-	3	8	4-7
Steve Farr	-	-	-	-	-	-	-	-	-	-	-	-	-	-	-
Mike Gallego	-	-	14-23	-	7-6	-	-	-	-	-	7-5	-	11	39	21-29
Lee Guetterman	-	-	-	-	-	-	-	-	-	-	-	-	-	-	-
John Habyan	-	-	-	-	-	-	-	-	-	-	-	-	-	-	-
Mel Hall	-	-	-	-	-	47-49	-	17-17	3-6	-	-	28-35	31	108	67-72
Charlie Hayes	-	2-1	-	63-74	-	-	-	-	-	-	-	-	48	92	65-75
Shawn Hillegas	-	-	-	-	-	-	-	-	-	2-7	-	-	1	8	2-7
Sterling Hitchcock	-	-	-	-	-	-	-	-	-	1-2	-	-	2	1	1-2
Steve Howe	-	-	-	-	-	-	-	-	-	-	-	-	-	-	-
Mike Humphreys	-	-	-	-	-	1-1	-	-	0-1	-	-	-	3	-	1-2
Dion James	-	-	-	-	-	3-2	5-4	5-13	1-1	-	3-8	-	-	34	14-20
Jeff Johnson	-	-	-	-	-	-	-	-	-	4-4	-	-	2	6	4-4
Scott Kamieniecki	-	-	-	-	-	-	-	-	-	11-17	-	-	10	18	11-17
Pat Kelly	-	-	51-47	-	-	-	-	-	-	-	1-1	-	38	60	51-47
Roberto Kelly	-	-	-	-	-	20-23	44-55	-	-	-	-	-	53	89	64-78
Tim Leary	-	-	-	-	-	-	-	-	-	6-9	-	-	3	12	6-9
Jim Leyritz	3-10	-	-	0-1	-	-	-	2-0	13-13	-	-	-	37	5	18-24
Kevin Maas	-	8-7	-	-	-	-	-	-	25-29	-	-	1-0	1	68	33-36
Don Mattingly	-	63-75	-	-	-	-	-	-	8-7	-	-	12-21	47	106	71-82
Hensley Meulens	-	-	-	1-0	-	-	-	-	-	-	-	-	-	1	1-0
Sam Militello	-	-	-	-	-	-	-	-	-	4-5	-	-	2	7	4-5
Rich Monteleone	-	-	-	-	-	-	-	-	-	-	-	-	-	-	-
Jerry Nielsen	-	-	-	-	-	-	-	-	-	-	-	-	-	-	-
Matt Nokes	49-52	-	-	-	-	-	-	-	-	-	-	1-0	1	100	49-52
Melido Perez	-	-	-	-	-	-	-	-	-	16-17	-	-	16	17	16-17
Scott Sanderson	-	-	-	-	-	-	-	-	-	17-16	-	-	10	23	17-16
Dave Silvestri	-	-	-	-	1-2	-	-	-	-	-	-	-	2	1	1-2
J.T. Snow	-	3-1	-	-	-	-	-	-	-	-	-	-	-	4	3-1
Russ Springer	-	-	-	-	-	-	-	-	-	-	-	-	-	-	-
Andy Stankiewicz	-	-	11-14	-	37-41	-	-	-	-	-	30-33	-	39	64	48-55
Mike Stanley	24-24	0-2	-	-	-	-	-	-	1-3	-	-	0-1	47	7	25-29
Danny Tartabull	-	-	-	-	-	1-0	-	34-33	25-26	-	-	34-29	40	79	60-59
Randy Velarde	-	-	0-2	12-11	31-37	2-9	-	1-4	-	-	6-7	-	40	69	46-63
Bob Wickman	-	-	-	-	-	-	-	-	-	7-1	-	-	2	6	7-1
Bernie Williams	-	-	-	-	-	2-2	27-27	0-3	-	-	29-32	-	22	39	29-32
Gerald Williams	-	-	-	-	-	-	-	2-5	-	-	-	-	5	2	2-5
Mike Witt	-	-	-	-	-	-	-	-	-	-	-	-	-	-	-
Curt Young	-	-	-	-	-	-	-	-	-	4-1	-	-	2	3	4-1

TEAM TOTALS: BATTING

	AB	H	2B	3B	HR	RBI	BB	SO	BA	SA	OBA
Season	5593	1462	281	18	163	703	536	903	.261	.406	.328
vs. Left-Handers	1764	452	85	6	53	242	203	284	.256	.401	.335
vs. Right-Handers	3829	1010	196	12	110	461	333	619	.264	.407	.324
vs. Ground-Ballers	2466	653	113	8	68	309	214	402	.265	.400	.325
vs. Fly-Ballers	3127	809	168	10	95	394	322	501	.259	.410	.330
Home Games	2735	717	135	8	88	373	283	422	.262	.414	.334
Road Games	2858	745	146	10	75	330	253	481	.261	.397	.322
Grass Fields	4700	1221	219	14	145	600	463	757	.260	.405	.328
Artificial Turf	893	241	62	4	18	103	73	146	.270	.409	.323
April	701	183	34	1	19	90	67	116	.261	.394	.329
May	950	250	59	4	33	131	84	161	.263	.438	.325
June	956	226	45	2	29	103	99	171	.236	.379	.309
July	885	221	39	3	27	101	84	147	.250	.392	.317
August	1041	286	44	2	27	132	102	145	.275	.399	.340
Sept./Oct.	1060	296	60	6	28	146	100	163	.279	.426	.343
Leading Off Inn.	1343	338	64	5	38	38	108	207	.252	.392	.311
Runners On	2419	656	132	7	69	609	248	390	.271	.417	.337
Bases Empty	3174	806	149	11	94	94	288	513	.254	.397	.320
Runners/Scor. Pos.	1312	340	66	4	41	519	188	238	.259	.409	.344
Runners On/2 Out	1004	229	41	3	26	226	124	180	.228	.353	.318
Scor. Pos./2 Out	607	132	21	2	17	195	102	110	.217	.343	.335
Late-Inning Pressure	925	230	54	1	27	110	76	167	.249	.397	.309
Leading Off	242	63	15	0	7	7	14	37	.260	.409	.301
Runners On	366	94	23	1	10	93	42	69	.257	.407	.334
Runners/Scor. Pos.	198	53	12	0	7	80	34	44	.268	.434	.367

RUNS BATTED IN	From 1B	From 2B	From 3B	Scoring Position
Totals	103/1820	197/1030	240/581	437/1611
Percentage	5.7%	19.1%	41.3%	27.1%

TEAM TOTALS: PITCHING

	W-L	ERA	AB	H	HR	BB	SO	BA	SA	OBA
Season	76-86	4.21	5517	1453	129	612	851	.263	.394	.338
vs. Left-Handers			2291	626	49	263	317	.273	.399	.348
vs. Right-Handers			3226	827	80	349	534	.256	.392	.331
vs. Ground-Ballers			2777	734	39	280	380	.264	.365	.331
vs. Fly-Ballers			2740	719	90	332	471	.262	.424	.344
Home Games	41-40	4.27	2863	758	70	319	436	.265	.396	.339
Road Games	35-46	4.14	2654	695	59	293	415	.262	.392	.336
Grass Fields	66-71	4.17	4689	1223	115	505	718	.261	.390	.334
Artificial Turf	10-15	4.41	828	230	14	107	133	.278	.419	.359
April	13-8	3.53	679	169	15	86	110	.249	.351	.332
May	13-14	4.19	926	235	22	114	135	.254	.376	.335
June	11-17	4.32	942	253	27	109	145	.269	.427	.350
July	11-15	5.03	909	264	23	93	120	.290	.436	.356
August	13-17	3.75	1001	244	20	113	170	.244	.360	.321
Sept./Oct.	15-15	4.33	1060	288	22	97	171	.272	.408	.334
Leading Off Inn.			1320	361	36	130	178	.273	.412	.342
Bases Empty			3085	813	74	294	483	.264	.392	.331
Runners On			2432	640	55	318	368	.263	.398	.346
Runners/Scor. Pos.			1399	381	34	223	232	.272	.415	.364
Runners On/2 Out			1003	244	19	147	152	.243	.366	.344
Scor. Pos./2 Out			651	158	14	108	105	.243	.376	.353
Late-Inning Pressure			813	205	16	82	136	.252	.360	.322
Leading Off			212	53	5	16	27	.250	.358	.306
Runners On			323	89	6	45	49	.276	.390	.363
Runners/Scor. Pos.			187	45	4	35	26	.241	.369	.352
First 9 Batters			2674	700	56	309	435	.262	.385	.339
Second 9 Batters			1471	377	33	148	211	.256	.383	.325
All Batters Thereafter			1372	376	40	155	205	.274	.424	.348

NEW YORK YANKEES

There was a low-budget movie a few years back—it's become a cult favorite, so maybe you've seen it—called *The Gods Must Be Crazy*, in which a Coke bottle falls from an airplane and lands in an underdeveloped African village. The natives are convinced that the bottle is a gift from the gods, and they adopt it as a religious icon.

For each of the past three seasons, Yankees fans have reacted in a similar fashion to some equally rare apparitions. On a losing team starved for so many years for home-grown talent, the arrival of even semi-promising rookies from within the Yankees system prompted what we referred to in past editions as "rookie hysteria." How else to explain the excitement three years ago over Kevin Maas, Jim Leyritz, and—heaven forbid—Oscar Azocar? Granted, Maas hit his first 15 home runs in just 133 at-bats, an all-time major league record. But the fact that he hit only six more in 121 ABs for the rest of the season, combined with the reality that he didn't make his big-league debut until he was well past his 25th birthday, should have hinted that Maas's fast start was a little fluky. Jim Leyritz? Oscar Azocar? Those were signs of a serious disorder.

The next year it was Wade Taylor, Jeff Johnson, and Scott Kamieniecki that had Yankees fans in a froth. Over their first 25 starts, the three rookie pitchers compiled a 13–9 record with a 3.60 ERA. So what if they went 4–18 with a 7.96 ERA for the rest of the season? These were honest-to-goodness *home-grown* Yankees! Of course, the optimism was again misplaced: Kamieniecki went 6–14 as a sophomore, Johnson was hit hard while getting nearly as many last chances as Steve Howe, and Taylor hasn't been located by Strategic Air Command.

Last season, three more rookie pitchers—Sam Militello, Bob Wickman, and Sterling Hitchcock—arrived amid even greater fanfare. Things nearly got out of hand in August: Militello shut out the Red Sox on one hit over seven innings in his debut, compiled a 3–0 mark with a 2.20 ERA over his first four starts, and it looked like they were going to have to hose down the fans and the media. By this time, Wickman (6–1 despite a 4.11 ERA) and Hitchcock (a strong first outing before being routed in two subsequent starts) came along for the ride on big Sam's coattails.

Why all the excitement over a few good performances by a home-grown pitcher? Remember, this was the same fan base that was outraged when Syd Thrift gave up Al Leiter (!) for Jesse Barfield. While they may not know the details, all Yankees fans understand the following intuitively: Since the debut of Ron Guidry in the mid-1970s, the Yankees have launched the major league career of only one pitcher who won even 30 games for the team: Dave Righetti (74). And since Guidry's retirement after the 1988 season, the Yankees have only 49 wins—an average of 12 per season—from pitchers who made their major league debuts with the team. That's the lowest total in the majors, and roughly one third of the major league average during that time (153):

Toronto	276	Atlanta	227
Milwaukee	231	Cincinnati	184
Chicago	209	Los Angeles	179
Baltimore	206	San Francisco	170
California	198	Montreal	163
Texas	187	Chicago	162
Kansas City	180	St. Louis	145
Detroit	140	San Diego	145
Minnesota	131	New York	133
Boston	127	Pittsburgh	121
Seattle	124	Philadelphia	65
Cleveland	118	Houston	58
Oakland	57		
New York	49		

Oakland's success over the past five years with a staff of imports proves that you don't have to grow your own to compete. But during George Steinbrenner's suspension, the Yankees were reluctant to spend the money it would have taken to land a Mike Moore or a Bob Welch. Melido Perez and Scott Sanderson were inspired acquisitions, but on a completely different level.

But coinciding with Steinbrenner's return, the stakes have just gone up. New York's decision not to resign Sanderson after the 1992 season indicates its confidence that some combination of Militello, Wickman, and Hitchcock can complement Perez and its expensive new acquisitions, Jim Abbott and Jimmy Key. And the money and prospects spent to acquire those two—not to mention Wade Boggs, who'll turn 35 in June—further demonstrates that the Yankees, despite four consecutive losing seasons (their longest streak since 1912–15), are in the race to win it, and soon—perhaps in 1993. With Steinbrenner looking over his shoulder, sophomore manager Buck Showalter may not be as indulgent of any backsliding by Militello, Wickman, or Hitchcock as he and his predecessor, Stump Merrill, were in the past with Taylor, Johnson, and Kamieniecki.

Here's something that may help to explain why the Yankees have chosen to hoard their prospects over the past few seasons. It's been more than 10 years since a Yankees pitcher won at least 15 games while compiling an ERA below 3.00. The last was Rudy May in 1980. But of the 15 pitchers to do so for other teams last season, four are ex-Yankees:

Player	G	GS	CG	W	L	IP	H	HR	BB	SO	ERA
Doug Drabek	34	34	10	15	11	256.2	218	17	54	177	2.77
Mike Morgan	34	34	6	16	8	240.0	203	14	79	123	2.55
Jose Rijo	33	33	2	15	10	211.0	185	15	44	171	2.56
Bob Tewksbury	33	32	5	16	5	233.0	217	15	20	91	2.16

Morgan was traded with Dave Collins to the Blue Jays in 1982 for Dale Murray (who won three games for the Yankees) and Tom Dodd (whose major league career consisted of eight games with the Orioles in 1986). The Yankees threw Fred McGriff and a reported four hundred thousand dollars into the deal—just to even things out. Drabek was traded to the Pirates along with Brian Fisher and Logan Easley following the 1986 season for Rick Rhoden, Cecilio Guante, and Pat Clements, who won a total of 39 games for the Yankees; Drabek has won 92 games for Pittsburgh. Rijo was part of a package that also included Jay Howell and Stan Javier and brought Rickey Henderson to New York in 1985. (No quibble there—Rickey helped keep the Yankees a contender for several years.)

Tewksbury, along with prospects Rich Scheid and Dean Wilkins, was the lure with which the Yankees landed Steve Trout. Trout was an abject failure, winless in 14 appearances (including nine starts) with the Yankees, compiling a 6.60 ERA. Note, though, that the Cubs also gave up on Tewksbury, who has won 38 games since joining the Cardinals.

There are also young hitters whom the Yankees gave away but who are now thriving for other teams: Jay Buhner, traded in 1988 for Ken Phelps; Henderson, sent to Oakland for Eric Plunk, Greg Cadaret, and Luis Polonia; Hal Morris, exiled to Cincinnati (where he came within a hit of a National League batting title) for Tim Leary; Polonia himself, traded to the Angels in 1990 for a washed-up Claudell Washington and a career minor leaguer (who luckily turned into Rich Monteleone, a capable middle-inning reliever); and Deion Sanders, released by the Yankees in 1990. Notice that we haven't even mentioned Dave Winfield, traded for Mike Witt, who apparently ran for Vice President with Ross Perot or something. (See the Winfield comment for more on this.)

Now it's true that almost every team in the majors could compile a list of "the ones that got away." Maybe none would be quite as long as New York's, though wouldn't the Cubs like to have Joe Carter and Rafael Palmeiro back in Chicago? Or how about the Phillies, whose list is short but nevertheless includes Ryne Sandberg, Dave Stewart, Bob Walk, and Charlie Hayes? What makes the Yankees' list different is the number of players involved, the age at which they evicted their now productive alumni, and, as already discussed, how little they got in exchange. There were 11 former Yankees who last season reached at least one of the following threshholds: 25 home runs, 150 hits, 75 runs, 75 RBIs, 25 stolen bases, 10 wins, or 15 saves: Buhner, Henderson, Otis Nixon, Polonia, Sanders, Steve Sax, and Dave Winfield; Drabek, Morgan, Rijo,

and Tewksbury. That's more than double the major league average of five.

But the age at which players like Rijo (19), Morgan (23), Sanders (23), Buhner (24), Drabek (24), Nixon (25), Polonia (25), and Tewksbury (26) were cut loose illustrates the indifference with which the Yankees treated their prospects during the 1980s. That total of eight quality players who were traded, sold, or released before turning 27 is three more than any other team in the majors, and nearly four times the average of the other 25 teams (2.2). And that doesn't even count players like McGriff and Willie McGee, who were traded away long before they had a chance to reach the majors.

If anything, the Yankees have erred in the opposite direction in recent seasons, rejecting numerous offers and watching as the stature of once highly desirable prospects like the Kellys (Roberto and Pat), Hensley Meulens, and Kevin Maas diminished. The organization is now considered one of the best in baseball. But if the price of protecting the Drabeks- and Buhners-to-be is watching some former blue chippers fade, so what? As we pointed out in the 1991 *Analyst*, George Steinbrenner operated much better in the 1970s, filling in the missing pieces of a young foundation built by Gabe Paul, than he did in the 1980s, when an aging infrastructure began to crumble and he tried to buy himself a whole team. That's why New York's commitment to veteran acquisitions this past off-season seemed a bit premature. Given time, Bernie Williams, Gerald Williams, Pat Kelly, or Sam Militello may grow into Mickey Rivers, Willie Randolph, or Ron Guidry, allowing Steinbrenner once again to step to the plate and hit the game-winning home run. But until those prospects develop, all the Yankees may have accomplished is to place additional pressure on them in an environment that's hardly stress-free to begin with. All things considered, it's not that the Yankees are without a plan. It's just that they have one too many.

OAKLAND ATHLETICS

The celebrations after Oakland won last season's A.L. West title were tempered not only by its loss to Toronto in the League Championship Series, but also by two other problems: *(1)* age: the Athletics were the oldest team in baseball in 1992, and by a wide margin; and *(2)* the longest list of looming free agents of any team in either league. The A's, whether by design or plain old common sense, implemented a single strategy to deal with both problems.

First, a look at Oakland's age problem. The following table shows each team's average age—the average of its batters and pitchers. Each player contributes to the pie in proportion to his playing time (plate appearances for batters, innings for pitchers):

	Bat.	Pit.	Avg.		Bat.	Pit.	Avg.
Indians	26.2	27.5	26.8	Astros	26.6	27.3	27.0
Mariners	28.7	27.8	28.3	Phillies	28.1	27.1	27.6
Royals	29.4	27.6	28.5	Expos	27.9	28.6	28.2
Orioles	28.9	28.2	28.5	Braves	29.0	27.6	28.3
Twins	29.2	27.9	28.5	Reds	28.3	28.4	28.4
Angels	28.5	29.3	28.9	Cubs	29.0	27.8	28.4
Rangers	27.7	30.1	28.9	Giants	28.5	28.9	28.7
Brewers	30.4	27.6	29.0	Cardinals	28.9	28.4	28.8
Yankees	28.8	29.5	29.1	Padres	28.8	29.7	29.2
White Sox	29.3	29.6	29.5	Pirates	29.2	29.7	29.5
Blue Jays	29.8	30.3	30.1	Mets	30.6	28.5	29.7
Tigers	30.5	30.5	30.5	Dodgers	28.7	31.4	29.9
Red Sox	29.3	31.7	30.5				
Athletics	30.8	32.5	31.6				

As you can see, the A's not only had the oldest team in the majors last season, but the margin between their average age and that of the Red Sox, the second-oldest team, was 1.1 years. That's a fairly unusual spread; it was only the third time in the past 25 years that a full year or more separated the oldest and second-oldest teams. For the record, the other teams with margins that wide were the 1973 Tigers (still reliving their glory days with Norm Cash, Al Kaline, Jim Northrup, Mickey Lolich, and Woodie Fryman) and the 1979 Yankees (rapidly turning gray with Reggie Jackson, Graig Nettles, Lou Piniella, Catfish Hunter, Tommy John, and Luis Tiant). Like those teams, Oakland had not only the oldest position players in the American League, but the oldest pitchers as well. Unlike those teams, the Athletics were able to recapture past glory with a division title.

It's unusual for a championship team to have to embark on a rebuilding program. Only five other teams won a division or league title with its league's oldest batters and its oldest pitchers. (You want that list, too? All right—the 1910 Cubs, the 1947 Yankees, the 1981 Yankees, the 1982 Angels, and the 1983 Phillies. Now lay off!) But given the age of Oakland's team in 1992, the impending free agency of so many players following the season, and its impressive stockpile of high draft picks made over the past few years, the A's find themselves in a position to do just that. Perhaps "retooling" is a better description; but whatever the label, last season's A.L. West title may have bought the team the year or two of good will it needs to restructure its roster.

Let's look at that list of potential free agents at the conclusion of the 1992 season. They are listed below in order of age, from youngest to oldest, because Oak-

land's solution to both its age and free-agency problems lies therein. Ages are as of opening day 1993:

Age	Player	Age	Player	Age	Player
27	Ruben Sierra	32	Ron Darling	37	Willie Wilson
29	Mark McGwire	33	Randy Ready	38	Jamie Quirk
31	Terry Steinbach	33	Mike Moore	38	Rick Honeycutt
31	Jeff Russell	34	Harold Baines	41	Goose Goosage
32	Kelly Downs	36	Dave Stewart		

As we mentioned earlier, no other team had a list as long as Oakland's. The totals in the following table include only those players designated as free agents immediately following the 1992 season—excluding players like Joe Klink and Jeff Parrett, who were granted free agency when Oakland declined to offer them contracts for 1993:

Athletics	14	Cardinals	10
Blue Jays	12	Dodgers	8
Brewers	9	Mets	7
Tigers	8	Cubs	5
Orioles	6	Reds	5
Twins	6	Phillies	5
Red Sox	5	Giants	5
Angels	5	Braves	4
Rangers	5	Pirates	4
Royals	4	Padres	4
Yankees	4	Expos	3
Mariners	4	Astros	2
Indians	3		
White Sox	2		

Oakland re-signed its three youngest free agents—Sierra, McGwire, and Steinbach—to rich long-term contracts. Two older starters were eligible for free agency: Wilson signed with the Cubs; Baines was offered arbitration, then traded to Baltimore. Of the three pitchers who took regular turns in the rotation throughout the 1992 season, the A's signed only the youngest, Darling; Moore and Stewart signed with the Tigers and Blue Jays, respectively. Honeycutt also accepted a one-year deal, and Gossage signed a minor league contract.

In the end, Oakland fashioned a solution so simple it was downright elegant. The A's retained the services of all of last season's regular starters who were 32 or younger with multiple-year deals. They held onto a few older role players with one-year contracts, and they allowed their oldest free agents to skip town. In so doing, Oakland has already slashed its payroll for the 1993 season by roughly seven million dollars, shaved a year or two from its graying roster, and opened a few positions for those developing prospects should they be ready in '93.

Did the A's have any alternatives? Sure, signing Stewart and Moore was technically an option; but if the millions saved by letting them go helped to corral Sierra, Steinbach, or McGwire, it wasn't really viable. Stewart's contribution was a factor in the team's rebound to another A.L. West title in 1992, but to expect more would be foolhardy. With Eckersley still at the top of his game, Russell was a luxury they couldn't afford. (Remember the signing of Mark Davis by the Royals, whose bullpen already featured Jeff Montgomery and Steve Farr?) Offering Baines arbitration was a low-risk gamble, since Baines was a Type A free agent; if he had declined arbitration and signed elsewhere, Oakland would have received the signing team's first-round draft pick plus another so-called "sandwich" selection between the first and second rounds. Instead, Oakland received two prospects who already have some experience, while continuing to trim the payroll and reduce the team's age.

That's a positive spin on a volatile situation. Although Oakland's common-sense solutions to a challenging off-season must be considered initially successful, it's true nonetheless that for the first time in years the A's approach a new season with several starting positions up for grabs. The losses of Stewart, Moore, Wilson, and Baines reasonable though they were, create voids that must be filled. And to this point, we've mentioned neither the retirement of Carney Lansford nor the trade of Walt Weiss to Florida.

Oakland's third basemen drove in more runs than those of any other American League team last season—97, with Lansford contributing 69 of them. His retirement at the age of 35 is nearly unprecedented. (See his individual player comments on page 120 for more on this.) But for those who subscribe to the theory that there are no great teams without great shortstops—and that, by extension, the A's are losing a vital member of their championship team—the trade of Weiss (for catcher Eric Helfand and pitcher Scott Baker) must have been a shocker.

The fact is, Oakland won without Weiss in 1992. The A's compiled a .594 winning percentage in the 96 games he started (57–39), a .591 mark without him in the lineup (39–27). And they won without Weiss in 1989 as well, when he started only 71 games, missing half the season with a knee injury. That season, the A's had a slightly better mark in the games he missed (56–35, .615) than in the games he started (43–28, .606). Oakland may have trouble defending its title in '93, but it won't be Weiss's departure that prevents a repeat.

But the larger question is this: What's a Weiss worth (as opposed to a *weiss wurst*)? For years, there's been a mystique around shortstops, especially those on winning teams, regardless of their apparent shortcomings. Players at every other position are evaluated almost solely on the basis of their own performance; for some reason, shortstops are often judged more on the basis of their teams' success or failure.

For instance, you've probably heard the old saw that a team can't win a championship with a rookie shortstop. That one was put to rest, or should have been, in 1988, when Weiss and Kevin Elster of the Mets both played regularly as rookies for division winners; another rookie, Jody Reed, shared the position with Spike Owen on the A.L. East champion Red Sox. But such a stupid notion would never have developed in the first place if any of its proponents had cared enough about the facts to simply check them out. Too often, baseball fans (and we use the word *fans* here in the broadest sense to include front-office personnel, managers, players, and the media—the ones usually responsible for such drivel in the first place) would rather sound right than be right. A simple look at the record would have revealed 13 other rookie shortstops whose teams won

at least a division title: Donie Bush (1909 Tigers), Dave Bancroft (1915 Phillies), Swede Risberg (1917 White Sox), Charlie Hollocher (1918 Cubs), Mark Koenig (1926 Yankees), Blondy Ryan (1933 Giants), Phil Rizzuto (1941 Yankees), Alvin Dark (1948 Braves), Tom Tresh (1962 Yankees), Chris Speier (1971 Giants), Frank Taveras (1974 Pirates), Scott Fletcher (1983 White Sox), and Mariano Duncan (1985 Dodgers).

Teams with regular rookie shortstops have played in the postseason nearly as often as teams without them. There have been 139 teams that had rookies play 100 games at shortstop. Fifteen of those teams (11 percent) reached the L.C.S. or World Series. That's only slightly lower than the percentage of teams that reached the postseason without rookie shortstops (211 of 1539 teams, or 14 percent).

The same holds true of the idea that a team can't win a championship without a solid-hitting, good-fielding shortstop. Try telling that to fans of the 1985 Kansas City Royals. They surely haven't forgotten Onix Concepcion and "Late Night" talk-show star Buddy Biancalana. Or, on second thought, maybe they have; that team represented the ultimate in a championship team with little more than a pair of glorified minor league caretakers at shortstop.

What would you think of a shortstop that met *all* of the following criteria: (1) played at least 100 games at shortstop; (2) had a batting average below the league mark excluding pitchers; (3) hit fewer than 10 home runs; (4) drove in fewer than 50 runs; and (5) stole fewer than 10 bases. That ought to cover it: A poor-hitting shortstop with little power, little production, and little speed. You want fielding, too? Okay—let's say he also has to have an error rate worse than the league average. As a reference point, let's mention that last season's only qualifiers were Gary DiSarcina of the Angels, Rafael Belliard of the National League champs and, yes, Walt Weiss, of the A.L. West champs.

Are you getting the idea that teams can do quite well, thank you, without (to be kind) an above-average shortstop? If so, take one giant step—right past the so-called experts who are still scratching their heads over six other teams since 1969 that have won at least a division title with shortstops that met our demanding eligibility requirements: Gene Alley (1971 Pirates), Chris Speier (1971 Giants), Garry Templeton (1984 Padres), Onix Concepcion (1985 Royals), Luis Rivera (1990 Red Sox), and Manuel Lee (1991 Blue Jays). Eight of the 55 teams that had qualifying shortstops have reached the L.C.S. since 1969; that's 15 percent. Of the 553 teams with presumably better shortstops, 88 won their divisions; that's 16 percent.

That's about all we can do—present the facts, which seem to us overwhelmingly in contradiction of the prevailing notion. You've got to take the ball from here and run with it. There's nothing sacrosanct about a shortstop. Teams with good shortstops win a little more often than those with poor ones; but that's not to say that teams with lousy shortstops can't compensate in other areas. They have done so, and will continue to do so. If you still don't agree, please contact the Ray Oyler Fan Club, Detroit, Michigan.

WON-LOST RECORD BY STARTING POSITION

Oakland Athletics	C	1B	2B	3B	SS	LF	CF	RF	DH	P	Leadoff	Cleanup	Starts vs. LH	Starts vs. RH	Total Starts
Harold Baines	-	-	-	-	-	4-2	-	10-3	59-51	-	-	52-38	7	122	73-56
Lance Blankenship	-	3-1	40-29	-	-	9-3	9-2	4-6	-	-	13-7	-	28	78	65-41
Mike Bordick	-	-	49-34	-	39-27	-	-	-	-	-	-	-	36	113	88-61
John Briscoe	-	-	-	-	-	-	-	-	-	0-2	-	-	-	2	0-2
Scott Brosius	-	0-3	-	3-4	-	1-0	-	4-6	-	-	-	-	7	14	8-13
Jerry Browne	-	-	4-3	21-17	-	8-4	12-9	2-2	1-0	-	8-6	-	9	74	48-35
Kevin Campbell	-	-	-	-	-	-	-	-	-	4-1	-	-	-	5	4-1
Jose Canseco	-	-	-	-	-	-	-	46-30	15-5	-	-	-	26	70	61-35
Jim Corsi	-	-	-	-	-	-	-	-	-	-	-	-	-	-	-
Ron Darling	-	-	-	-	-	-	-	-	-	17-16	-	-	4	29	17-16
Kelly Downs	-	-	-	-	-	-	-	-	-	5-8	-	-	4	9	5-8
Kirk Dressendorfer	-	-	-	-	-	-	-	-	-	-	-	-	-	-	-
Dennis Eckersley	-	-	-	-	-	-	-	-	-	-	-	-	-	-	-
Eric Fox	-	-	-	-	-	4-2	9-6	6-4	-	-	9-4	-	5	26	19-12
Goose Gossage	-	-	-	-	-	-	-	-	-	-	-	-	-	-	-
Johnny Guzman	-	-	-	-	-	-	-	-	-	-	-	-	-	-	-
Scott Hemond	3-2	-	-	-	-	0-1	-	1-0	-	-	-	-	5	2	4-3
Dave Henderson	-	-	-	-	-	-	3-5	1-2	2-1	-	-	3-0	5	9	6-8
Rickey Henderson	-	-	-	-	-	62-43	-	3-2	-	-	65-45	-	27	83	65-45
Shawn Hillegas	-	-	-	-	-	-	-	-	-	-	-	-	-	-	-
Rick Honeycutt	-	-	-	-	-	-	-	-	-	-	-	-	-	-	-
Vince Horsman	-	-	-	-	-	-	-	-	-	-	-	-	-	-	-
Dann Howitt	-	-	-	-	-	0-2	2-2	5-2	0-1	-	-	-	-	14	7-7
Mike Kingery	-	-	-	-	-	1-0	2-3	-	-	-	1-0	-	-	6	3-3
Joe Klink	-	-	-	-	-	-	-	-	-	-	-	-	-	-	-
Carney Lansford	-	9-5	-	69-43	-	-	-	-	-	1-0	-	1-0	34	93	79-48
Mark McGwire	-	82-54	-	-	-	-	-	-	-	-	-	39-26	31	105	82-54
Henry Mercedes	-	-	-	-	-	-	-	-	-	-	-	-	-	-	-
Mike Moore	-	-	-	-	-	-	-	-	-	23-13	-	-	5	31	23-13
Troy Neel	-	0-1	-	-	-	0-5	-	6-2	-	-	-	1-0	1	13	6-8
Gene Nelson	-	-	-	-	-	-	-	-	-	-	1-1	-	2	-	1-1
Jeff Parrett	-	-	-	-	-	-	-	-	-	-	-	-	-	-	-
Jamie Quirk	21-20	1-1	-	-	-	-	-	-	-	-	-	-	-	43	22-21
Michael Raczka	-	-	-	-	-	-	-	-	-	-	-	-	-	-	-
Randy Ready	-	1-0	3-0	3-2	-	7-4	-	1-0	6-4	-	-	-	17	14	21-10
Todd Revenig	-	-	-	-	-	-	-	-	-	-	-	-	-	-	-
Jeff Russell	-	-	-	-	-	-	-	-	-	-	-	-	-	-	-
Ruben Sierra	-	-	-	-	-	-	-	15-10	1-0	-	-	-	5	21	16-10
Joe Slusarski	-	-	-	-	-	-	-	-	-	-	9-5	-	3	11	9-5
Terry Steinbach	72-44	0-1	-	-	-	-	-	-	2-0	-	-	0-2	33	86	74-45
Dave Stewart	-	-	-	-	-	-	-	-	-	20-11	-	-	10	21	20-11
Bruce Walton	-	-	-	-	-	-	-	-	-	-	-	-	-	-	-
Walt Weiss	-	-	-	-	57-39	-	-	-	-	-	-	0-1	17	79	57-39
Bob Welch	-	-	-	-	-	-	-	-	-	-	13-7	-	8	12	13-7
Willie Wilson	-	-	-	-	-	59-39	1-1	-	-	-	0-3	-	31	69	60-40
Bobby Witt	-	-	-	-	-	-	-	-	-	4-2	-	-	2	4	4-2

TEAM TOTALS: BATTING

	AB	H	2B	3B	HR	RBI	BB	SO	BA	SA	OBA
Season	5387	1389	219	24	142	693	707	831	.258	.386	.346
vs. Left-Handers	1246	335	55	4	43	175	171	205	.269	.423	.358
vs. Right-Handers	4141	1054	164	20	99	518	536	626	.255	.376	.342
vs. Ground-Ballers	2535	678	100	11	53	327	343	374	.267	.378	.356
vs. Fly-Ballers	2852	711	119	13	89	366	364	457	.249	.394	.337
Home Games	2574	645	97	14	76	334	369	398	.251	.388	.348
Road Games	2813	744	122	10	66	359	338	433	.264	.385	.344
Grass Fields	4493	1137	174	19	116	574	608	691	.253	.378	.344
Artificial Turf	894	252	45	5	26	119	99	140	.282	.431	.356
April	773	211	36	1	23	101	98	129	.273	.411	.354
May	883	223	28	2	20	99	119	139	.253	.357	.339
June	902	228	33	4	29	127	132	128	.253	.395	.351
July	888	243	45	6	21	114	85	135	.274	.409	.341
August	945	242	35	2	28	135	137	160	.256	.386	.356
Sept./Oct.	996	242	42	9	21	117	136	140	.243	.366	.336
Leading Off Inn.	1278	328	51	6	40	40	158	185	.257	.400	.354
Runners On	2434	652	102	12	62	613	338	357	.268	.396	.356
Bases Empty	2953	737	117	12	80	80	369	474	.250	.379	.338
Runners/Scor. Pos.	1407	355	62	6	34	529	233	218	.252	.377	.352
Runners On/2 Out	1039	258	45	4	23	235	166	160	.248	.366	.358
Scor. Pos./2 Out	679	158	30	0	18	213	134	114	.233	.356	.365
Late-Inning Pressure	669	169	16	4	18	96	100	118	.253	.369	.353
Leading Off	171	37	5	2	3	3	22	26	.216	.322	.309
Runners On	273	82	9	2	10	88	55	44	.300	.458	.417
Runners/Scor. Pos.	161	41	6	1	6	77	41	30	.255	.416	.397

RUNS BATTED IN	From 1B	From 2B	From 3B	Scoring Position
Totals	96/1812	185/1112	270/633	455/1745
Percentage	5.3%	16.6%	42.7%	26.1%

TEAM TOTALS: PITCHING

	W-L	ERA	AB	H	HR	BB	SO	BA	SA	OBA
Season	96-66	3.73	5446	1396	129	601	843	.256	.382	.332
vs. Left-Handers			2535	682	48	311	332	.269	.381	.348
vs. Right-Handers			2911	714	81	290	511	.245	.382	.317
vs. Ground-Ballers			2681	710	46	275	389	.265	.378	.334
vs. Fly-Ballers			2765	686	83	326	454	.248	.386	.330
Home Games	51-30	3.49	2764	682	73	289	462	.247	.370	.320
Road Games	45-36	3.98	2682	714	56	312	381	.266	.394	.344
Grass Fields	80-57	3.81	4613	1181	119	522	742	.256	.385	.333
Artificial Turf	16-9	3.28	833	215	10	79	101	.258	.364	.326
April	14-8	3.53	751	190	17	88	116	.253	.386	.333
May	13-14	4.16	882	216	34	98	162	.245	.423	.323
June	18-9	4.45	948	256	25	92	124	.270	.405	.336
July	15-11	3.64	883	240	21	87	133	.272	.398	.341
August	19-10	3.58	969	261	16	117	135	.269	.369	.348
Sept./Oct.	17-14	3.07	1013	233	16	119	173	.230	.320	.312
Leading Off Inn.			1310	347	40	122	198	.265	.413	.335
Bases Empty			3069	787	87	307	463	.256	.396	.330
Runners On			2377	609	42	294	380	.256	.364	.334
Runners/Scor. Pos.			1333	337	26	214	246	.253	.371	.347
Runners On/2 Out			1031	249	18	139	182	.242	.346	.334
Scor. Pos./2 Out			654	149	15	110	125	.228	.356	.341
Late-Inning Pressure			825	174	17	73	187	.211	.310	.278
Leading Off			205	44	7	17	43	.215	.351	.284
Runners On			326	68	3	37	72	.209	.276	.285
Runners/Scor. Pos.			178	33	2	29	48	.185	.253	.292
First 9 Batters			2954	744	62	304	532	.252	.367	.323
Second 9 Batters			1373	361	28	164	170	.263	.382	.343
All Batters Thereafter			1119	291	39	133	141	.260	.421	.340

WON-LOST RECORD BY STARTING POSITION

Seattle Mariners	C	1B	2B	3B	SS	LF	CF	RF	DH	P	Leadoff	Cleanup	Starts vs. LH	Starts vs. RH	Total Starts
Jim Acker	-	-	-	-	-	-	-	-	-	-	-	-	-	-	-
Juan Agosto	-	-	-	-	-	-	-	-	-	1-0	-	-	1	-	1-0
Rich Amaral	-	-	7-5	4-10	0-2	-	-	-	-	-	-	-	9	19	11-17
Shawn Barton	-	-	-	-	-	-	-	-	-	-	-	-	-	-	-
Mike Blowers	-	0-1	-	6-16	-	-	-	-	-	-	-	-	6	17	6-17
Bret Boone	-	-	12-20	-	-	-	-	-	-	-	-	-	11	21	12-20
Scott Bradley	-	-	-	-	-	-	-	-	-	-	-	-	-	-	-
Greg Briley	-	-	3-1	2-2	-	6-9	5-6	1-2	5-5	-	12-9	-	-	47	22-25
Kevin Brown	-	-	-	-	-	-	-	-	-	-	-	-	-	-	-
Jay Buhner	-	-	-	-	-	-	-	60-89	-	-	-	2-0	39	110	60-89
Dave Cochrane	4-3	1-2	-	2-5	-	4-7	-	1-4	0-1	-	-	1-1	14	20	12-22
Henry Cotto	-	-	-	-	-	16-28	5-10	1-3	0-2	-	18-27	-	42	23	22-43
Rich DeLucia	-	-	-	-	-	-	-	-	-	3-8	-	-	4	7	3-8
Brian Fisher	-	-	-	-	-	-	-	-	-	6-8	-	-	5	9	6-8
Dave Fleming	-	-	-	-	-	-	-	-	-	19-14	-	-	8	25	19-14
Mark Grant	-	-	-	-	-	-	-	-	-	3-7	-	-	3	7	3-7
Ken Griffey Jr.	-	-	-	-	-	-	54-82	-	1-2	-	0-1	0-7	37	102	55-84
Eric Gunderson	-	-	-	-	-	-	-	-	-	-	-	-	-	-	-
Erik Hanson	-	-	-	-	-	-	-	-	-	9-21	-	-	9	21	9-21
Gene Harris	-	-	-	-	-	-	-	-	-	-	-	-	-	-	-
Bill Haselman	3-1	-	-	-	-	0-2	-	-	-	-	-	-	2	4	3-3
Bert Heffernan	1-2	-	-	-	-	-	-	-	-	-	-	-	-	3	1-2
Brian Holman	-	-	-	-	-	-	-	-	-	-	-	-	-	-	-
Dann Howitt	-	-	-	-	-	6-4	-	1-0	-	-	-	-	-	11	7-4
Randy Johnson	-	-	-	-	-	-	-	-	-	12-19	-	-	8	23	12-19
Calvin Jones	-	-	-	-	-	-	-	-	-	0-1	-	-	-	1	0-1
Randy Kramer	-	-	-	-	-	-	-	-	-	1-3	-	-	-	4	1-3
Tim Leary	-	-	-	-	-	-	-	-	-	4-4	-	-	1	7	4-4
Pat Lennon	-	-	-	-	-	-	-	-	-	-	-	-	-	-	-
Tino Martinez	-	33-40	-	-	-	-	-	-	14-34	-	-	10-14	16	105	47-74
Edgar Martinez	-	0-2	-	41-61	-	-	-	-	13-15	-	-	4-7	37	95	54-78
Kevin Mitchell	-	-	-	-	-	27-40	-	-	11-15	-	-	38-54	26	67	38-55
John Moses	-	-	-	-	-	3-4	-	-	-	-	-	-	1	6	3-4
Jeff Nelson	-	-	-	-	-	-	-	-	-	-	-	-	-	-	-
Pete O'Brien	-	25-44	-	-	-	-	-	-	14-18	-	-	3-7	6	95	39-62
Clay Parker	-	-	-	-	-	-	-	-	-	3-3	-	-	-	6	3-3
Lance Parrish	11-12	5-9	-	-	-	-	-	6-6	-	-	-	6-8	26	23	22-27
Dennis Powell	-	-	-	-	-	-	-	-	-	-	-	-	-	-	-
Harold Reynolds	-	-	47-76	-	-	-	-	-	-	-	11-23	-	30	93	47-76
Jeff Schaefer	-	-	2-1	-	9-11	-	-	-	-	-	-	-	11	12	11-12
Dave Schmidt	-	-	-	-	-	-	-	-	-	-	-	-	-	-	-
Mike Schooler	-	-	-	-	-	-	-	-	-	-	-	-	-	-	-
Matt Sinatro	4-5	-	-	-	-	-	-	-	-	-	-	-	2	7	4-5
Russ Swan	-	-	-	-	-	-	-	-	-	-	2-7	-	2	7	2-7
Shane Turner	-	-	-	6-9	2-2	-	-	-	-	-	-	-	-	19	8-11
Dave Valle	41-75	-	-	-	-	-	-	-	-	-	-	-	36	80	41-75
Omar Vizquel	-	-	-	-	51-77	-	-	-	-	-	-	23-38	27	101	51-77
Mike Walker	-	-	-	-	-	-	-	-	-	1-2	-	-	1	2	1-2
Kerry Woodson	-	-	-	-	-	-	-	-	-	0-1	-	-	-	1	0-1

TEAM TOTALS: BATTING

	AB	H	2B	3B	HR	RBI	BB	SO	BA	SA	OBA
Season	5564	1466	278	24	149	638	474	841	.263	.402	.323
vs. Left-Handers	1506	420	77	1	49	196	146	220	.279	.429	.344
vs. Right-Handers	4058	1046	201	23	100	442	328	621	.258	.393	.315
vs. Ground-Ballers	2665	709	128	12	63	316	233	401	.266	.394	.327
vs. Fly-Ballers	2899	757	150	12	86	322	241	440	.261	.410	.319
Home Games	2742	736	173	13	78	338	239	417	.268	.426	.329
Road Games	2822	730	105	11	71	300	235	424	.259	.379	.317
Grass Fields	2205	592	85	9	59	260	197	333	.268	.395	.330
Artificial Turf	3359	874	193	15	90	378	277	508	.260	.407	.318
April	703	183	35	2	17	79	57	96	.260	.388	.316
May	926	231	46	6	28	116	79	134	.249	.403	.309
June	941	245	47	3	33	104	75	134	.260	.422	.319
July	996	273	46	5	28	123	88	139	.274	.415	.334
August	970	283	56	3	24	126	103	160	.292	.430	.361
Sept./Oct.	1028	251	48	5	19	90	72	178	.244	.356	.296
Leading Off Inn.	1357	353	71	5	36	36	95	186	.260	.399	.313
Runners On	2397	636	122	10	62	551	223	351	.265	.402	.325
Bases Empty	3167	830	156	14	87	87	251	490	.262	.403	.321
Runners/Scor. Pos.	1354	363	73	8	43	497	158	202	.268	.429	.337
Runners On/2 Out	970	222	50	7	20	193	93	162	.229	.357	.299
Scor. Pos./2 Out	628	139	31	6	15	175	75	101	.221	.361	.306
Late-Inning Pressure	925	244	38	2	20	93	77	176	.264	.374	.321
Leading Off	229	55	11	0	5	5	10	35	.240	.354	.281
Runners On	419	103	14	2	8	81	43	80	.246	.346	.312
Runners/Scor. Pos.	248	58	8	2	6	75	29	52	.234	.355	.307

RUNS BATTED IN	From 1B	From 2B	From 3B	Scoring Position
Totals	76/1730	193/1118	220/535	413/1653
Percentage	4.4%	17.3%	41.1%	25.0%

TEAM TOTALS: PITCHING

	W-L	ERA	AB	H	HR	BB	SO	BA	SA	OBA
Season	64-98	4.55	5519	1467	129	661	894	.266	.400	.348
vs. Left-Handers			1852	507	35	231	250	.274	.395	.353
vs. Right-Handers			3667	960	94	430	644	.262	.402	.345
vs. Ground-Ballers			2649	702	38	327	416	.265	.371	.350
vs. Fly-Ballers			2870	765	91	334	478	.267	.426	.345
Home Games	38-43	4.40	2863	775	63	316	485	.271	.402	.347
Road Games	26-55	4.71	2656	692	66	345	409	.261	.398	.348
Grass Fields	21-41	4.92	2053	538	56	280	320	.262	.406	.353
Artificial Turf	43-57	4.33	3466	929	73	381	574	.268	.396	.344
April	10-11	4.50	704	180	15	77	119	.256	.399	.334
May	11-17	5.56	949	259	28	129	152	.273	.434	.363
June	10-18	4.78	971	282	26	106	123	.290	.422	.364
July	11-17	3.95	959	246	21	102	158	.257	.368	.329
August	13-14	4.37	921	235	23	109	159	.255	.396	.339
Sept./Oct.	9-21	4.19	1015	265	16	138	183	.261	.380	.352
Leading Off Inn.			1313	348	26	121	211	.265	.383	.334
Bases Empty			3001	781	60	326	501	.260	.380	.338
Runners On			2518	686	69	335	393	.272	.423	.358
Runners/Scor. Pos.			1498	400	41	235	247	.267	.419	.363
Runners On/2 Out			1067	276	32	150	184	.259	.421	.355
Scor. Pos./2 Out			701	168	20	122	130	.240	.389	.359
Late-Inning Pressure			732	194	21	114	128	.265	.407	.364
Leading Off			186	47	2	20	29	.253	.339	.332
Runners On			334	94	14	65	54	.281	.479	.391
Runners/Scor. Pos.			195	54	9	48	34	.277	.492	.405
First 9 Batters			2856	743	65	366	482	.260	.393	.347
Second 9 Batters			1383	370	31	151	211	.268	.400	.344
All Batters Thereafter			1280	354	33	144	201	.277	.416	.352

SEATTLE MARINERS

Five years ago, we published our initial research on a topic that had previously been ignored: the tendency of various umpires to favor hitters or pitchers. Each umpire was measured according to the ratio of strike-outs to walks while he worked behind the plate. That's a signature statistic for umpires; although none calls balls and strikes in even 40 games in a season, the strikeout-to-walk ratios of most umps remain fairly constant from one year to the next—much more so than, say, a player's batting average.

The difference between umpires who favor hitters and those who favor pitchers is significant. The table below includes all umpires who worked the plate in at least 10 American League games last season. They are ranked according to their strikeout-to-walk ratios over the past three seasons. Remember, high ratios indicate a "pitcher's umpire" with a wide strike zone resulting in more strikeouts per walk:

Umpire	1992	'90–'92	Umpire	1992	'90–'92
Larry McCoy	1.75	2.04	Mike Reilly	1.84	1.64
Greg Kosc	1.93	2.04	Durwood Merrill	1.71	1.63
Ed Hickox	1.97	1.99	Dale Scott	1.68	1.63
Tim Welke	1.74	1.98	Terry Cooney	1.56	1.60
Ted Hendry	1.98	1.87	Don Denkinger	1.66	1.59
Jim McKean	1.57	1.83	John Shulock	1.47	1.59
Jim Joyce	1.48	1.78	Mark Johnson	1.67	1.57
Drew Coble	1.69	1.77	Rick Reed	1.64	1.57
Al Clark	1.67	1.73	Chuck Meriwether	1.45	1.56
Larry Barnett	1.71	1.72	Dale Ford	1.74	1.55
Vic Voltaggio	1.59	1.70	Terry Craft	1.43	1.54
Larry Young	1.66	1.68	Dave Phillips	1.33	1.49
Gary Cederstrom	1.90	1.67	Tim McClelland	1.51	1.47
Jim Evans	1.65	1.66	Joe Brinkman	1.28	1.46
Rich Garcia	1.55	1.66	Dan Morrison	1.29	1.45
Ken Kaiser	1.80	1.66	Rocky Roe	1.21	1.39
Tim Tschida	1.41	1.65	Derryl Cousins	1.11	1.28

Note the wide disparity between umpires at opposite ends of the continuum: McCoy calls roughly 10 strike-outs for every five walks; Cousins calls only six.

The extremes represented by the Mariners' pitchers, who run the gamut from Dave Fleming (who walked only 2.4 batters per nine innings last season) to Randy Johnson (who averaged more than six walks per nine), provide for some interesting test cases. Seattle's last two managers, Jim Lefebvre and Bill Plummer, may even have tried to keep the wild Johnson off the mound when the two most extreme "hitters' umps" were behind the plate. Although Johnson made 97 starts over the past three seasons, he never took the mound with Cousins calling balls and strikes, and he started only once with Rocky Roe there.

Over the past three seasons, Johnson's record improved markedly and his ERA declined as he encoutered more lenient umpires with larger strike zones. Note also that although the umpires were classified to assign roughly an equal number to each category, Johnson made significantly fewer starts with hitter-favoring umpires. The umpires are designated as favoring hitters or pitchers (or neither) according to their strikeout-to-walk ratios (below 1.55, between 1.55 and 1.72, and above 1.72):

	GS	CG	SHO	W	L	ERA	IP	BB	SO
Hitters' Umpires	24	2	0	6	10	4.45	139.7	99	146
Neutral Umpires	38	5	3	16	13	3.97	253.7	159	264
Pitchers' Umpires	35	6	2	17	12	3.21	238.0	158	253

Dave Fleming is the antithesis of Johnson, and his performance as a starting pitcher over the last two seasons trends accordingly in the opposite direction. His sharp control appears to give him a marked advantage over other pitchers when the home-plate umpire has a small strike zone, and that benefit seems to disappear with more forgiving umpires:

	GS	CG	SHO	W	L	ERA	IP	BB	SO
Hitters' Umpires	11	2	1	7	1	2.53	74.7	20	33
Neutral Umpires	15	5	3	8	5	2.86	104.0	24	50
Pitchers' Umpires	10	0	0	3	4	6.02	61.3	18	39

The records posted by these two suggest that there's an advantage to be gained by gerrymandering your rotation to match control pitchers with hitters' umpires and wild pitchers with wider strike zones. But actually, as we noted when we first did this study in the 1988 *Analyst,* such cases are anomalies; when examined on a league-wide basis, that advantage disappears.

The following table contrasts two groups of pitchers over the past three years—those with the 10 best walk rates in the American League each season, "the Flemings," and those with the 10 worst averages, "the Johnsons" (minimum: 25 starts). Note that for each group of pitchers, only slight differences exist among their won-lost records with each type of umpire. (Winning percentage is the right measure here because it's a pitcher-vs.-pitcher statistic.) The differences are significant only for the Johnsons—the poor-control pitchers—in that the winning percentages trend steadily up in the expected direction. But having stated that, it's important to understand that even for these extreme pitchers, the gain isn't great enough to prompt a manager to twist his rotation around in order to exploit it:

Pitchers	Hitters' Umps		Neutral Umps		Pitchers' Umps	
	W–L	Pct.	W–L	Pct.	W–L	Pct.
The Flemings	131–91	.590	149–86	.634	148–110	.574
The Johnsons	89–98	.476	121–118	.506	128–115	.527

To further support our contention that the differences between umpire groups have only an insignificant effect on a particular pitcher's success or failure, consider the following figures for their National League counterparts over the same three-year period. Again, the group of good control pitchers—the Flemings—consists of the league's top 10 in walks per nine innings each season, and the Johnsons includes the bottom 10. There's no apparent trend:

Pitchers	Hitters' Umps		Neutral Umps		Pitchers' Umps	
	W–L	Pct.	W–L	Pct.	W–L	Pct.
The Flemings	137–92	.598	142–99	.589	129–106	.549
The Johnsons	107–117	.478	92–107	.462	89–99	.473

For the record, here is a listing of the 1992 National League umpires and their strikeout-to-walk ratios for last season and the past three years:

Umpire	1992	'90–'92	Umpire	1992	'90–'92
Ron Barnes	2.43	2.43	Gary Darling	1.53	1.81
Bob Davidson	1.90	2.16	Mike Winters	2.15	1.80
Larry Poncino	2.23	2.16	Brian Gorman	1.88	1.78
Ed Rapuano	2.20	2.07	Jerry Layne	1.91	1.77
Terry Tata	2.21	2.06	Ed Montague	1.81	1.77
Frank Pulli	2.11	2.05	Dana DeMuth	1.78	1.74
Charlie Williams	2.01	2.04	Dutch Rennert	1.70	1.73
Paul Runge	2.07	2.02	Jerry Crawford	1.99	1.72
Greg Bonin	1.93	2.02	Charlie Reliford	2.01	1.69
Doug Harvey	2.05	1.97	Randy Marsh	1.71	1.68
Harry Wendelstedt	1.87	1.92	Phil Cuzzi	1.81	1.67
Gerry Davis	1.73	1.88	Steve Rippley	1.88	1.66
Tom Hallion	2.01	1.87	Joe West	2.02	1.65
Jeff Kellogg	1.86	1.86	Bruce Froemming	1.55	1.59
Jim Quick	1.64	1.83	John McSherry	1.90	1.59
Bill Hohn	1.89	1.81			

We've discussed often the tendency of teams to slide back after several years of steady improvement. So it should have come as no surprise on that basis alone that Seattle, after posting their third consecutive improvement in 1991 (and, in so doing, surpassing the .500 level for the first time), regressed last season. In fact, of 88 teams from 1900 through 1990 that posted steadily better marks for three straight seasons, only one-quarter continued their streaks for a fourth season. But what was unusual about Seattle's retreat was that the Mariners became only the fifth team in this century to wipe out in a single one-year decline the entire gain made over three years of sustained improvement:

Year Team	Year 0	Year 1	Year 2	Year 3	Year 4	Year 5
1926 Pittsburgh Pirates	.552	.565	.588	.621	.549	.610
1964 Kansas City As	.377	.379	.444	.451	.352	.364
1973 Pittsburgh Pirates	.543	.549	.599	.619	.494	.543
1990 Kansas City Royals	.469	.512	.522	.568	.466	.506
1992 Seattle Mariners	.422	.451	.475	.512	.395	—

It would be easy to affix the blame for Seattle's slide to the gamble the team took in trading Bill Swift and two other pitchers to San Francisco for controversial slugger Kevin Mitchell (and pitcher Mike Remlinger)—a trade that failed miserably. Swift made a successful transition from the bullpen to the Giants' starting rotation, and he led the National League with a 2.08 earned run average. Although productive when he played (67 RBIs in 99 games), Mitchell missed nearly half the season with various injuries.

Moreover, the Mitchell trade can be viewed—though unfairly, in our estimation—as a continuation of the philosophy that produced so many dreadful Mariners teams during the 1980s: a craving for a big home-run threat to exploit the hitter-friendly Kingdome that yielded a string of disappointing over-the-hill sluggers, often at the cost of soon-to-be-successful pitchers. The many pitchers traded by Seattle before reaching their prime are enumerated in the Marlins essay (p. 56). Here, we'd like to make the point that regardless of how badly the Mitchell trade failed, it differed from past Mariners deals in a very substantive way: In Mitchell, Seattle acquired a younger player who was much more likely to succeed in Seattle than, for instance, Willie Horton, Richie Zisk, Gorman Thomas, or Steve Balboni.

The other past-prime-time acquisitions seemed rooted in the overly optimistic hope that the Kingdome's looming fences would revitalize some once-booming bats that had gone limp with age. (That rarely happened, and the case of Willie Horton may have provided false hope for years to come.) The following table shows how little those former sluggers had left upon their arrival in Seattle—at least according to our projection model, which forecast their actual performance pretty accurately. (If you're wondering whether such a tool wouldn't provide a nice supplement to a team's own scouting reports, well. . . .) The seasons in the table are each player's first with the Mariners; the ages are as of opening day. Note that Mitchell stands out:

Year	Player	Age	Projected Games	Projected HR	Actual HR
1978	Bob Robertson	31	160	8	8
1979	Willie Horton	36	146	14	37
1981	Jeff Burroughs	30	429	47	10
1981	Richie Zisk	32	598	65	49
1984	Gorman Thomas	33	273	33	43
1987	Gary Matthews	36	111	5	3
1988	Steve Balboni	31	268	29	21
1989	Jeffrey Leonard	33	260	14	34
1990	Pete O'Brien	32	329	27	36+
1992	Kevin Mitchell	30	594	119	9+

Even after his injury-filled 1992 season, the model projects Mitchell to have a good chance to rebound this season and provide the power that Seattle sought two winters ago. Unfortunately for M's fans, if he does, he'll be doing it in a Cincinnati uniform. And the acquisition of Norm Charlton does no more than plug the hole left in the Seattle bullpen by the trade for Mitchell in the first place. The first Mitchell trade was defensible in that he was a recent MVP Award winner available only because of his undesirable excess baggage. The second is understandable, although it smacks of the plug-one-hole-while-creating-another philosophy that besets perennial losers that change their front-office and on-field management as often as the Mariners have. Maybe the best news for M's fans is that general manager Woody Woodward has resisted the temptation that his predecessors could not; after all, he still hasn't brought Matt Nokes, Dan Pasqua, or Franklin Stubbs to Seattle.

TEXAS RANGERS

New Rangers manager Kevin Kennedy at his first press conference: "If I can say anything about my style of managing, it's that I'm very aggressive—I like to make things happen, and I like to run. I plan to bring National League–style baseball to the Rangers, like Phil Garner did last season with the Milwaukee Brewers."

Later that week, Kennedy appeared as a guest on Norm Hitzges's sports talk show on KLIF in Dallas and further explained his philosophy. Kennedy said he would run as often as possible even with a team that had little speed, simply to force the opposing team to defend against all options—an interesting strategy that raises the issue of hidden value in stolen bases.

For many years, there's been an army of supposed baseball "analysts" who have maintained that stolen bases have little or no net effect in constructing runs. The cost of being caught, they claim, so far outweighs the potential advance of a single base that even a high success rate is negated. This has always struck us as a logical conclusion for a mathematician, but certainly not for anyone who spends much time watching baseball. And Kennedy's operating philosophy helps to illustrate why that is so. Baseball is a game of dynamics; each play, each pitch, and each action affects the next, creating new options and eliminating others. How in the world can you isolate any single play—let alone one that is so situation-dependent and starts the carrousel spinning to the extent that a stolen base attempt does—and ascribe an absolute value to it?

Let's look at some figures that help illustrate the cause-and-effect relationship between aggressive base running and the hidden benefits it generates by keeping the opposition back on its heels. Kennedy cited Phil Garner's success as a rookie manager with Milwaukee last season, and the 1992 Brewers provide a classic example of that effect. Notice that along with a huge increase in stolen bases, Brewers opponents committed more errors, more passed balls and wild pitches, and more balks:

		——— Opponents ———		
Year	SB	E	PB/WP	BK
1991	106	115	45	5
1992	256	146	46	8
Diff.	+150	+31	+1	+3

That is a fairly representative trickle-down effect from such a large increase in steals. The following table lists the 1992 Brewers along with nine other recent teams that attempted at least 30 more steals under a new manager than in the previous season. Note the changes in the three categories that reflect defensive adjustments—opponents' errors, passed balls and wild pitches, and balks:

			Increase/Decrease from Previous Year			
Year	Team	New Manager	SBA	E	PB/WP	BK
1984	Cubs	Jim Frey	+ 96	+ 8	+24	+ 3
1985	Expos	Buck Rodgers	+ 77	+11	+ 1	+ 3
1986	Astros	Hal Lanier	+ 86	− 4	+15	+ 1
1986	Braves	Chuck Tanner	+ 45	+ 3	+13	+10
1986	Pirates	Jim Leyland	+ 66	+10	+ 4	+ 1
1986	Padres	Steve Boros	+ 65	+ 8	− 3	+ 3
1987	Padres	Larry Bowa	+125	+12	− 5	+12
1988	Yankees	Martin/Piniella	+ 37	+ 2	+ 5	+55
1990	Indians	John McNamara	+ 34	+34	+ 5	− 3
1990	Reds	Lou Piniella	+ 33	+ 1	− 3	− 1
1992	Brewers	Phil Garner	+197	+31	+ 1	+ 3

Of course, even the mathematicians might have anticipated that passed balls, wild pitches, and balks would increase along with stolen bases: For the 11 teams listed, there were 17 increases in those categories compared to only five declines. And even if the aberrant increase of 55 balks against the Yankees in 1988 is eliminated, the teams gained an average of eight bases from additional wild pitches and balks. That's significant in that it reflects a hidden advantage, but in fact, it's nothing more than window dressing—worth a couple of runs and maybe a victory or two depending on timing.

But the really important increase—and the one that's less obvious in terms of cause and effect—is the average of 11 additional opposition errors, fueled by 10 individual increases and only one decrease. How many runs does 11 errors translate into? The table below suggests an answer to that question. Last season's American League games, classified according to the number of errors each team committed:

Errors	Games	Runs/G	W	L	Pct.
0	1117	3.64	650	467	.582
1	768	4.68	350	418	.456
2	286	5.33	110	176	.385
3	78	6.21	20	58	.256
4	13	6.23	3	10	.231
5	6	8.00	1	5	.167

For the record, an error was worth approximately 0.85 runs in the American League (0.78 runs in the National League), so the addition of 31 opposition errors to Milwaukee's offense last season translated into about 26 runs—or roughly three wins. That may not sound like a lot, but remember that since 1969, 42 divisional races have been decided by three games or less. And contrary to popular belief, in most cases even a great manager is worth only a few wins each season.

So Kevin Kennedy's decision to run as often as possible despite personnel lacking in speed may in fact be a good first step toward adding those couple of wins to Texas's balance sheet. And if Kennedy is right—that even a slow team can benefit from aggressive base running—then, in the event of a tight race, his standard operating procedure just might be a decisive strategy.

We don't know how much Kennedy actually saw of the Rangers last season—not too much probably, considering he had a steady day job. While it's true that Texas ranked only 11th in the American League in stolen bases (81), the Rangers ranked in the middle of the pack in taking an extra base on singles to the outfield:

First Base to Third				Scoring from Second Base			
Team	1Bs	Adv.	Pct.	Team	1Bs	Adv.	Pct.
Cleveland	314	130	.414	Cleveland	148	122	.824
Kansas City	265	104	.392	California	143	117	.818
California	241	93	.386	Kansas City	145	118	.814

Boston	303	116	.383	Chicago	160	130	.813
Minnesota	334	127	.380	Texas	155	114	.735
Baltimore	322	120	.373	Minnesota	200	147	.735
Chicago	298	109	.366	Toronto	176	128	.727
Oakland	313	108	.345	New York	150	107	.713
Texas	270	92	.341	Baltimore	164	114	.695
New York	308	101	.328	Boston	144	96	.667
Milwaukee	282	92	.326	Detroit	166	110	.663
Toronto	271	86	.317	Milwaukee	198	131	.662
Detroit	310	98	.316	Oakland	161	106	.658
Seattle	272	79	.290	Seattle	153	98	.641
A.L. Totals	4103	1455	.355	A.L. Totals	2263	1638	.724

The two players most responsible for Texas's respectable standing on those lists were Jeff Huson and Rafael Palmeiro. Huson ranked third on the Rangers with 38 stolen bases in his first three seasons with the team, so it's no surprise that last season, he exceeded the league average taking extra bases on outfield singles, both going first-to-third (12-for-20) and scoring from second (6-for-7). But Palmeiro stole only 13 bases in his four seasons with the Rangers; his 1992 baserunning figures are more representative of his 12-steal season with the Cubs in 1988: 17-for-39 going from first to third, 13-for-14 scoring from second. So if Kevin Kennedy is going to rev the Rangers' engine as advertised, pencil Huson and Palmeiro in for big increases in steals.

Jeff Heath was a hot-headed outfielder with the Cleveland Indians in the 1930s and 1940s who once fought a teammate who had hit a home run using a bat borrowed from Heath. Heath was highly superstitious and believed that each bat had only a certain number of home runs in it.

We're not buying into Heath's Bat Theory. But at any point in time, each *player* has a certain number of home runs left in him, and our projection model can make an educated guess as to what that total is—how many home runs a given player will hit over the remainder of his career. As of the end of the 1992 season, no player appeared to have more potential home runs in him than Juan Gonzalez.

After two full seasons in the majors, Gonzalez's statistical profile is similar only to those of players who had success as home-run hitters ranging from moderate to extraordinary. The comparisons below—based, of course, on a much broader range of categories than those shown, with heavy weight given to the players' ages—suggest the best- and worst-case scenarios:

Year	Player	Previous Season BA	HR	RBI	Totals to Date BA	HR	RBI	Career HR
1992	Juan Gonzalez	.260	43	109	.259	75	230	75+
1960	Harmon Killebrew	.276	31	80	.250	84	215	573
1965	Willie Stargell	.272	27	107	.266	59	236	475
1987	Jose Canseco	.257	31	113	.253	69	243	235+
1970	Nate Colbert	.259	38	86	.250	62	156	173
1972	Earl Williams	.258	28	87	.261	61	179	138
1980	Bob Horner	.268	35	89	.285	91	250	218

Even the worst-case comparisons we studied (including many not shown above) involve players whose careers continued to flourish for at least a year or two thereafter—with the exception of Dick Kokos, whose promising career was sidetracked by military service in Korea. The implication is unmistakable: Unless his career is compromised by injury or other off-the-field influences, Gonzalez is certain to be a leading home-run hitter for at least the next several years. His upside potential is nearly unlimited. And based on an analysis of the careers of all players with similar statistical profiles to Gonzalez's at about the same age, our best guess is that Gonzalez will hit about 300 more home runs in his career—the highest projected total at this time of any active player. The top 10:

Juan Gonzalez	301	Frank Thomas	221
Ken Griffey	266	Fred McGriff	189
Jose Canseco	244	Gary Sheffield	181
Barry Bonds	239	Albert Belle	149
Mark McGwire	236	Cecil Fielder	148

Gonzalez's total of 301 means that of the players with comparable profiles—weighted for the degree of similarity—half subsequently hit more than 301 home runs, half hit fewer. How accurate can you expect the list to be? We wondered about that ourselves, and ran the corresponding figures as they might have appeared in a hypothetical *1967 Elias Baseball Analyst,* when there was a crop of promising power hitters similar to the current group. Five of the projected top 10 players appear on the actual list of "future home runs" following the 1966 season. We excluded from both lists any members of the rookie class of 1966; Lee May (352) and Reggie Smith (314)—who played a total of 11 games in '66—would have appeared on the "Actual" list:

Projected Leaders		Actual Leaders	
Tony Conigliaro	339	Willie Stargell	383
Dick Allen	288	Tony Perez	363
Frank Robinson	264	Carl Yastrzemski	357
Willie Stargell	242	Willie McCovey	320
Willie McCovey	224	Hank Aaron	313
Willie Horton	212	Willie Horton	267
Boog Powell	205	Dick Allen	262
Willie Mays	186	Billy Williams	256
Tony Oliva	164	Rusty Staub	264
Hank Aaron	152	Joe Morgan	249

We'll close this segment by noting that two players who just missed the current top 10 are of particular interest to Rangers fans: Ruben Sierra (138) and Dean Palmer (135). And with both Gonzalez and Palmer on his side, Jose Canseco may be able to do in Texas what he could not do in Oakland. It's been 20 years since Hank Aaron, Darrell Evans, and Davey Johnson all hit at least 40 home runs for the Braves. Not only are they the only set of three teammates ever to do so, but no *pair* of teammates has done it since then—not even the original Bash Brothers, Canseco and Mark McGwire. Stay tuned.

Texas Rangers	C	1B	2B	3B	SS	LF	CF	RF	DH	P	Leadoff	Cleanup	Starts vs. LH	Starts vs. RH	Total Starts
Gerald Alexander	-	-	-	-	-	-	-	-	-	-	-	-	-	-	-
Floyd Bannister	-	-	-	-	-	-	-	-	-	-	-	-	-	-	-
John Barfield	-	-	-	-	-	-	-	-	-	-	-	-	-	-	-
Brian Bohanon	-	-	-	-	-	-	-	-	-	2-5	-	-	1	6	2-5
Kevin Brown	-	-	-	-	-	-	-	-	-	24-11	-	-	14	21	24-11
Todd Burns	-	-	-	-	-	-	-	-	-	2-8	-	-	6	4	2-8
Mike Campbell	-	-	-	-	-	-	-	-	-	-	-	-	-	-	-
John Cangelosi	-	-	-	-	-	3-2	4-8	2-4	-	-	6-4	-	6	17	9-14
Jose Canseco	-	-	-	-	-	-	-	4-8	5-3	-	-	-	4	16	9-11
Don Carman	-	-	-	-	-	-	-	-	-	-	-	-	-	-	-
Scott Chiamparino	-	-	-	-	-	-	-	-	-	0-4	-	-	1	3	0-4
Cris Colon	-	-	-	-	6-7	-	-	-	-	-	-	-	5	8	6-7
Jack Daugherty	-	2-3	-	-	-	4-3	-	4-1	4-5	-	7-0	-	4	22	14-12
Doug Davis	-	-	-	-	-	-	-	-	-	-	-	-	-	-	-
Mario Diaz	-	-	-	0-1	3-7	-	-	-	-	-	-	-	8	3	3-8
Brian Downing	-	-	1-0	-	-	-	-	-	42-48	-	23-33	2-2	42	49	43-48
Hector Fajardo	-	-	-	-	-	-	-	-	-	-	-	-	-	-	-
Monty Fariss	-	-	3-1	-	-	9-11	1-3	4-7	1-0	-	2-1	-	21	19	18-22
Steve Fireovid	-	-	-	-	-	-	-	-	-	-	-	-	-	-	-
Julio Franco	-	-	3-7	-	-	0-2	-	1-0	7-7	-	8-8	-	11	16	11-16
Jeff Frye	-	-	26-38	-	-	-	-	-	-	-	7-11	-	21	43	26-38
Juan Gonzalez	-	-	-	-	-	10-16	60-57	-	1-3	-	-	22-35	44	103	71-76
Jose Guzman	-	-	-	-	-	-	-	-	-	17-16	-	-	5	28	17-16
Donald Harris	-	-	-	-	-	0-1	3-3	0-1	-	-	-	-	6	2	3-5
Bill Haselman	-	-	-	-	-	-	-	-	-	-	-	-	-	-	-
David Hulse	-	-	-	-	-	-	9-14	1-1	-	-	8-7	-	6	19	10-15
Jeff Huson	-	-	17-15	0-1	28-28	-	-	-	-	-	10-16	-	1	88	45-44
Mike Jeffcoat	-	-	-	-	-	-	-	-	-	1-2	-	-	1	2	1-2
Danilo Leon	-	-	-	-	-	-	-	-	-	-	-	-	-	-	-
Barry Manuel	-	-	-	-	-	-	-	-	-	-	-	-	-	-	-
Terry Mathews	-	-	-	-	-	-	-	-	-	-	-	-	-	-	-
Rob Maurer	-	1-0	-	-	-	-	-	-	-	-	-	-	-	1	1-0
Lance McCullers	-	-	-	-	-	-	-	-	-	-	-	-	-	-	-
Russ McGinnis	3-5	1-1	-	0-1	-	-	-	-	-	-	-	-	9	2	4-7
Al Newman	-	-	27-24	9-7	3-5	-	-	-	-	-	3-2	-	19	56	39-36
Edwin Nunez	-	-	-	-	-	-	-	-	-	-	-	-	-	-	-
Rafael Palmeiro	-	73-81	-	-	-	-	-	-	0-1	-	-	0-1	42	113	73-82
Dean Palmer	-	-	-	68-75	-	-	-	-	-	-	-	-	44	99	68-75
Roger Pavlik	-	-	-	-	-	-	-	-	-	7-5	-	-	3	9	7-5
Dan Peltier	-	-	-	-	-	0-1	-	3-2	-	-	0-1	-	-	6	3-3
Geno Petralli	15-22	-	-	-	-	-	-	-	1-3	-	-	-	1	40	16-25
Kevin Reimer	-	-	-	-	-	51-49	-	-	14-14	-	-	1-3	15	113	65-63
Jeff M. Robinson	-	-	-	-	-	-	-	-	-	3-1	-	-	2	2	3-1
Ivan Rodriguez	57-55	-	-	-	-	-	-	-	-	-	-	-	33	79	57-55
Kenny Rogers	-	-	-	-	-	-	-	-	-	-	-	-	-	-	-
Wayne Rosenthal	-	-	-	-	-	-	-	-	-	-	-	-	-	-	-
Jeff Russell	-	-	-	-	-	-	-	-	-	-	-	-	-	-	-
John Russell	1-1	-	-	-	-	-	-	-	-	-	-	-	2	-	1-1
Nolan Ryan	-	-	-	-	-	-	-	-	-	11-16	-	-	9	18	11-16
Ruben Sierra	-	-	-	-	-	-	-	58-61	2-1	-	-	52-44	36	86	60-62
Dan Smith	-	-	-	-	-	-	-	-	-	0-2	-	-	1	1	0-2
Ray Stephens	1-2	-	-	-	-	-	-	-	-	-	-	-	3	-	1-2
Dickie Thon	-	-	-	-	37-38	-	-	-	-	-	3-2	-	31	44	37-38
Matt Whiteside	-	-	-	-	-	-	-	-	-	-	-	-	-	-	-
Bobby Witt	-	-	-	-	-	-	-	-	-	10-15	-	-	3	22	10-15

TEAM TOTALS: BATTING

	AB	H	2B	3B	HR	RBI	BB	SO	BA	SA	OBA
Season	5537	1387	266	23	159	646	550	1036	.250	.393	.321
vs. Left-Handers	1507	400	71	8	40	185	171	329	.265	.403	.343
vs. Right-Handers	4030	987	195	15	119	461	379	707	.245	.389	.313
vs. Ground-Ballers	2458	621	113	10	72	285	227	424	.253	.395	.319
vs. Fly-Ballers	3079	766	153	13	87	361	323	612	.249	.392	.323
Home Games	2727	689	131	15	71	302	265	541	.253	.390	.322
Road Games	2810	698	135	8	88	344	285	495	.248	.396	.320
Grass Fields	4602	1133	209	19	127	511	445	861	.246	.383	.315
Artificial Turf	935	254	57	4	32	135	105	175	.272	.444	.350
April	802	209	44	3	22	108	89	142	.261	.405	.339
May	978	244	48	5	27	114	88	164	.249	.392	.313
June	921	235	52	4	29	123	113	170	.255	.415	.338
July	873	221	38	9	28	101	79	167	.253	.414	.317
August	989	243	41	2	33	112	91	175	.246	.391	.314
Sept./Oct.	974	235	43	0	20	88	90	218	.241	.347	.310
Leading Off Inn.	1318	334	69	4	32	32	135	221	.253	.385	.328
Runners On	2410	599	115	9	71	558	254	460	.249	.392	.321
Bases Empty	3127	788	151	14	88	88	296	576	.252	.394	.322
Runners/Scor. Pos.	1371	311	56	5	31	450	180	301	.227	.343	.315
Runners On/2 Out	1054	257	55	4	31	241	129	207	.244	.350	.330
Scor. Pos./2 Out	676	149	32	3	16	198	97	146	.220	.348	.323
Late-Inning Pressure	840	184	29	6	25	82	94	188	.219	.357	.301
Leading Off	214	50	8	2	5	5	23	51	.234	.360	.314
Runners On	340	67	8	4	12	69	46	72	.197	.350	.293
Runners/Scor. Pos.	189	31	4	2	4	50	34	50	.164	.270	.289

RUNS BATTED IN	From 1B	From 2B	From 3B	Scoring Position
Totals	100/1744	188/1101	199/550	387/1651
Percentage	5.7%	17.1%	36.2%	23.4%

TEAM TOTALS: PITCHING

	W-L	ERA	AB	H	HR	BB	SO	BA	SA	OBA
Season	77-85	4.09	5568	1471	113	598	1034	.264	.387	.337
vs. Left-Handers			2399	627	42	284	406	.261	.379	.338
vs. Right-Handers			3169	844	71	314	628	.266	.393	.336
vs. Ground-Ballers			2836	771	45	276	494	.272	.385	.337
vs. Fly-Ballers			2732	700	68	322	540	.256	.389	.337
Home Games	36-45	3.89	2844	729	63	297	564	.256	.380	.328
Road Games	41-40	4.29	2724	742	50	301	470	.272	.394	.347
Grass Fields	63-73	3.97	4651	1216	95	514	872	.261	.382	.336
Artificial Turf	14-12	4.72	917	255	18	84	162	.278	.410	.342
April	13-11	4.24	819	225	20	74	136	.275	.414	.333
May	16-12	4.16	965	247	19	113	185	.256	.380	.334
June	14-13	4.47	930	237	21	128	174	.255	.378	.350
July	11-15	3.87	881	229	15	73	164	.260	.375	.318
August	11-18	4.07	996	268	21	124	200	.269	.383	.350
Sept./Oct.	12-16	3.72	977	265	17	86	175	.271	.395	.335
Leading Off Inn.			1339	373	27	116	232	.279	.414	.341
Bases Empty			3043	806	59	304	576	.265	.389	.335
Runners On			2525	665	54	294	458	.263	.384	.339
Runners/Scor. Pos.			1474	378	34	205	285	.256	.387	.341
Runners On/2 Out			1043	248	21	133	199	.238	.352	.331
Scor. Pos./2 Out			675	156	14	101	135	.231	.350	.338
Late-Inning Pressure			920	245	15	93	175	.266	.376	.333
Leading Off			228	62	3	15	47	.272	.390	.322
Runners On			426	113	9	50	77	.265	.369	.337
Runners/Scor. Pos.			252	68	7	40	49	.270	.405	.357
First 9 Batters			2767	730	66	339	517	.264	.403	.346
Second 9 Batters			1365	343	23	136	259	.251	.363	.322
All Batters Thereafter			1436	398	24	123	258	.277	.378	.335

WON-LOST RECORD BY STARTING POSITION

Toronto Blue Jays	C	1B	2B	3B	SS	LF	CF	RF	DH	P	Leadoff	Cleanup	Starts vs. LH	Starts vs. RH	Total Starts
Roberto Alomar	-	-	91-58	-	-	-	-	-	0-1	-	2-1	-	46	104	91-59
Derek Bell	-	-	-	-	-	12-11	5-4	6-1	0-1	-	5-2	-	12	28	23-17
Pat Borders	82-50	-	-	-	-	-	-	-	-	-	-	-	45	87	82-50
Joe Carter	-	2-2	-	-	-	4-2	-	72-51	14-10	-	-	-	48	109	92-65
David Cone	-	-	-	-	-	-	-	-	-	4-3	-	-	1	6	4-3
Ken Dayley	-	-	-	-	-	-	-	-	-	-	-	-	-	-	-
Rob Ducey	-	-	-	-	-	1-1	-	0-1	-	-	-	-	-	3	1-2
Mark Eichhorn	-	-	-	-	-	-	-	-	-	-	-	-	-	-	-
Alfredo Griffin	-	-	1-3	-	22-13	-	-	-	-	-	-	-	8	31	23-16
Kelly Gruber	-	-	-	69-49	-	-	-	-	-	-	-	0-1	34	84	69-49
Juan Guzman	-	-	-	-	-	-	-	-	-	20-8	-	-	8	20	20-8
Tom Henke	-	-	-	-	-	-	-	-	-	-	-	-	-	-	-
Pat Hentgen	-	-	-	-	-	-	-	-	-	1-1	-	-	-	2	1-1
Jeff Kent	-	-	4-5	26-17	-	-	-	-	-	-	-	-	16	36	30-22
Jimmy Key	-	-	-	-	-	-	-	-	-	19-14	-	-	11	22	19-14
Randy Knorr	3-2	-	-	-	-	-	-	-	-	-	-	-	3	2	3-2
Manuel Lee	-	-	-	-	74-52	-	-	-	-	-	-	-	42	84	74-52
Al Leiter	-	-	-	-	-	-	-	-	-	-	-	-	-	-	-
Doug Linton	-	-	-	-	-	-	-	-	-	1-2	-	-	1	2	1-2
Bob MacDonald	-	-	-	-	-	-	-	-	-	-	-	-	-	-	-
Mike Maksudian	-	-	-	-	-	-	-	-	-	-	-	-	-	-	-
Candy Maldonado	-	-	-	-	-	77-51	-	2-0	1-3	-	-	0-1	41	93	80-54
Domingo Martinez	-	1-0	-	-	-	-	-	-	-	-	-	-	1	-	1-0
Jack Morris	-	-	-	-	-	-	-	-	-	25-9	-	-	10	24	25-9
Rance Mulliniks	-	-	-	-	-	-	-	-	-	-	-	-	-	-	-
Greg Myers	7-10	-	-	-	-	-	-	-	-	-	-	-	-	17	7-10
John Olerud	-	79-46	-	-	-	-	-	-	-	-	1-2	-	23	102	79-46
Tom Quinlan	-	-	-	1-0	-	-	-	-	-	-	-	-	1	-	1-0
Ed Sprague	4-4	0-1	-	-	-	-	-	-	1-0	-	-	-	2	8	5-5
Dave Stieb	-	-	-	-	-	-	-	-	-	5-9	-	-	5	9	5-9
Todd Stottlemyre	-	-	-	-	-	-	-	-	-	15-12	-	-	12	15	15-12
Pat Tabler	-	14-17	-	-	-	1-0	-	0-1	-	-	-	1-0	23	10	15-18
Mike Timlin	-	-	-	-	-	-	-	-	-	-	-	-	-	-	-
Rick Trlicek	-	-	-	-	-	-	-	-	-	-	-	-	-	-	-
Duane Ward	-	-	-	-	-	-	-	-	-	-	-	-	-	-	-
Turner Ward	-	-	-	-	-	1-1	2-0	2-0	-	-	-	-	2	4	5-1
Dave Weathers	-	-	-	-	-	-	-	-	-	-	-	-	-	-	-
David Wells	-	-	-	-	-	-	-	-	-	6-8	-	-	1	13	6-8
Devon White	-	-	-	-	-	-	89-62	0-1	-	-	89-63	-	46	106	89-63
Dave Winfield	-	-	-	-	-	-	-	14-12	80-50	-	-	94-62	48	108	94-62
Eddie Zosky	-	-	-	-	0-1	-	-	-	-	-	-	-	-	1	0-1

TEAM TOTALS: BATTING

	AB	H	2B	3B	HR	RBI	BB	SO	BA	SA	OBA
Season	5536	1458	265	40	163	737	561	933	.263	.414	.333
vs. Left-Handers	1435	388	69	4	41	193	183	230	.270	.410	.354
vs. Right-Handers	4101	1070	196	36	122	544	378	703	.261	.416	.326
vs. Ground-Ballers	2794	753	144	12	76	373	273	460	.270	.411	.336
vs. Fly-Ballers	2742	705	121	28	87	364	288	473	.257	.417	.330
Home Games	2641	688	129	24	79	366	295	439	.261	.417	.337
Road Games	2895	770	136	16	84	371	266	494	.266	.411	.330
Grass Fields	2237	598	106	14	72	292	204	380	.267	.424	.330
Artificial Turf	3299	860	159	26	91	445	357	553	.261	.407	.335
April	769	209	43	1	19	94	78	138	.272	.404	.339
May	915	219	35	6	30	103	86	153	.239	.389	.310
June	926	253	47	11	32	142	96	147	.273	.451	.343
July	869	227	46	5	22	116	102	139	.261	.402	.341
August	1035	276	48	9	37	137	78	181	.267	.438	.320
Sept./Oct.	1022	274	46	8	23	145	121	175	.268	.396	.347
Leading Off Inn.	1337	355	68	9	34	34	90	218	.266	.406	.315
Runners On	2440	649	111	25	80	654	284	413	.266	.430	.342
Bases Empty	3096	809	154	15	83	83	277	520	.261	.401	.326
Runners/Scor. Pos.	1395	376	69	16	41	551	190	252	.270	.430	.352
Runners On/2 Out	1033	271	51	11	36	272	150	174	.262	.438	.362
Scor. Pos./2 Out	683	176	36	8	21	233	105	113	.258	.426	.363
Late-Inning Pressure	646	165	27	2	17	78	74	121	.255	.382	.332
Leading Off	162	45	9	0	3	3	14	28	.278	.389	.335
Runners On	294	71	13	2	6	67	36	59	.241	.361	.322
Runners/Scor. Pos.	165	39	7	1	4	58	24	40	.236	.364	.326

RUNS BATTED IN	From 1B	From 2B	From 3B	Scoring Position
Totals	102/1742	218/1091	254/638	472/1729
Percentage	5.9%	20.0%	39.8%	27.3%

TEAM TOTALS: PITCHING

	W-L	ERA	AB	H	HR	BB	SO	BA	SA	OBA
Season	96-66	3.91	5432	1346	124	541	954	.248	.371	.318
vs. Left-Handers			2165	534	38	240	348	.247	.348	.322
vs. Right-Handers			3267	812	86	301	606	.249	.386	.315
vs. Ground-Ballers			2656	698	39	255	406	.263	.364	.329
vs. Fly-Ballers			2776	648	85	286	548	.233	.377	.308
Home Games	53-28	3.74	2765	677	60	269	488	.245	.369	.315
Road Games	43-38	4.09	2667	669	64	272	466	.251	.373	.322
Grass Fields	32-31	4.28	2052	518	50	227	354	.252	.377	.328
Artificial Turf	64-35	3.69	3380	828	74	314	600	.245	.367	.312
April	16-7	3.67	784	183	21	81	147	.233	.371	.308
May	15-12	3.53	887	206	24	100	123	.232	.366	.311
June	14-12	4.03	892	236	19	89	150	.265	.383	.333
July	16-10	3.57	849	209	17	78	159	.246	.366	.311
August	14-16	5.93	1009	288	25	109	168	.285	.424	.357
Sept./Oct.	21-9	2.69	1011	224	18	84	207	.222	.314	.285
Leading Off Inn.			1330	304	33	106	210	.229	.353	.288
Bases Empty			3157	740	75	285	553	.234	.356	.303
Runners On			2275	606	49	256	401	.266	.392	.339
Runners/Scor. Pos.			1311	347	28	196	245	.265	.396	.354
Runners On/2 Out			971	229	17	129	236	.236	.344	.332
Scor. Pos./2 Out			625	153	11	106	123	.245	.362	.360
Late-Inning Pressure			780	166	17	70	163	.213	.319	.279
Leading Off			198	39	4	17	38	.197	.308	.264
Runners On			304	67	7	29	68	.220	.332	.287
Runners/Scor. Pos.			172	32	5	21	41	.186	.308	.272
First 9 Batters			2666	649	53	276	524	.243	.354	.316
Second 9 Batters			1409	369	37	141	218	.262	.400	.330
All Batters Thereafter			1357	328	34	124	212	.242	.372	.310

TORONTO BLUE JAYS

A funny thing happened on the way to Toronto's first world championship. The Jays may be able to look back now and laugh at the collapse of their pitching staff in August, but it was no joke during the first week of September, when Baltimore moved to within a half-game of the Jays and the Brewers came within four-and-a-half. It appeared that Toronto would sink or swim based on whether its starting rotation could rebound, and at the Skydome life preservers were selling like Labatt's.

Before those problems arose, the Blue Jays had opened a comfortable cushion of 4½ games over Baltimore. Despite injuries to Dave Stieb and Juan Guzman, the pitching staff still appeared to be strong, with Jack Morris, Jimmy Key, and Todd Stottlemyre pitching in turn. But starting August 3, the Blue Jays' starters fell to pieces. This was no ordinary slump; it was the pitching collapse of the season, reaching historic proportions for a team with playoff aspirations. Over a 25-game stretch, Toronto starters compiled an ERA of 7.01; 10 failed to complete five innings. In less than four weeks, Toronto's team ERA rose by a half-run per game, from 3.70 to 4.20, and its American League rank plummeted from third to 12th. For the month of August, the Blue Jays compiled a 5.93 ERA and allowed an average of 6.03 runs per game, the highest single-month mark in more than 50 years by a team that reached postseason play. The following table puts those figures in perspective—on the left, the only teams with ERAs above 5.00 in any month last season; on the right, the only teams to reach postseason play after allowing more than six runs per game in any month:

Team	ERA	(Month)	Year	Team	Runs	(Month)
Blue Jays	5.93	(Aug.)	1941	Yankees	6.43	(May)
Tigers	5.72	(Apr.)	1930	Cardinals	6.36	(June)
Mariners	5.56	(May)	1908	Tigers	6.33	(Apr.)
Phillies	5.14	(Apr.)	1930	Athletics	6.20	(May)
Cubs	5.12	(Sept.)	1927	Pirates	6.20	(June)
Yankees	5.03	(July)	1992	Blue Jays	6.03	(Aug.)

Here's an interesting question: Did the collapse of Toronto's starting rotation help or hurt the team's chances of winning its first world championship? We're serious—without the collapse, it's possible there would have been no need to trade for David Cone. And without Cone, well, who knows? On August 27, the Jays traded rookie second baseman Jeff Kent and center-field prospect Ryan Thompson to the Mets for Cone, who, like the Jays' own starters, had struggled throughout August. (He went 0–3 with a 4.15 ERA in his last four starts with the Mets—a slump that was blamed by many on a 166-pitch, complete-game performance in mid-July.)

Cone's problems continued in his first start for Toronto, a highly publicized Saturday afternoon start that had the Skydome rockin'. He allowed a season-high seven runs in 6⅔ innings and took his fourth consecutive loss. And while he won only four of seven starts for Toronto, he was masterful during September; his only losses were by scores of 2–1 (to the Indians) and 1–0 (to the Red Sox). His record of 4–3 for the Jays was far better than it looks; they scored more than three runs only once in his seven starts. Did Cone's presence also contribute to the rebound by the rest of Toronto's

starters? It sounds unlikely to us, even if Jack Morris says it's true. But while we'll never know for certain, it's a fact that the rest of the Jays' rotation bounced back with a 2.98 ERA during September and October, the best in the A.L. during that time.

At first glance, Cone's record in four postseason starts (1–1) was no better than his deceptively mediocre regular-season record for the Jays. But once again, consider the circumstances: His lone postseason victory came in a crucial game—what some would call a "must game"—Game 2 of the A.L.C.S., after Oakland had taken the opener at the Skydome and all Canada seemed ready to concede the series to the A's. Cone also pitched six strong innings in the final game of the World Series before turning a 2–1 lead over to Stottlemyre to start the seventh inning. Years from now, fans might look at nothing more than the statistical record of Cone's two months with Toronto and wonder what all the fuss was about.

Cone was also the latest in a continuing trend toward hired guns brought in to help contending teams win pennants. Think about it—in each of the past seven seasons, the ultimate A.L. East champion made at least one key acquisition during the season: 1986 Red Sox—Dave Henderson, Spike Owen, and Tom Seaver; 1987 Tigers—Bill Madlock (released by the Dodgers) and Doyle Alexander; 1988 Red Sox—Mike Boddicker; 1989 Blue Jays—Mookie Wilson (all right—this one's a stretch, but we really miss Mookie); 1990 Red Sox—Tom Brunansky; 1991 Blue Jays—Tom Candiotti; 1992 Blue Jays—David Cone.

But by no means has this trend been limited to the A.L. East. The Braves acquired closers late in each of the past two seasons: Alejandro Pena in 1991 and Jeff Reardon in 1992. The Pirates picked up Zane Smith for their 1990 pennant drive and Steve Buechele in 1991; last season, they traded Buechele for Danny Jackson in July to stablize their rotation. The A's have spared no expense, acquiring Rickey Henderson and Ken Phelps in 1989 and Harold Baines, Willie McGee, and Willie Randolph in 1990, not to mention last season's block-buster in which they picked up Ruben Sierra, Bobby Witt, and Jeff Russell for Jose Canseco (addition by subtraction, some would say).

Although in general the incidence of players working for more than one team in a season is on the decline, it has increased for division winners. The percentage of multiteam players ranged from 6.4 percent to 8.2 percent over the five years ending in 1990, but fell to 4.5 percent in 1991 and 5.7 percent last season. (Incidentally, look for a sharp increase in 1993; this percentage usually spikes in expansion seasons. The highest rate in the past 40 years was 11.8 percent in 1961; the highest since then was 9.0 percent in 1969; and the highest since *then* was 8.7 percent in 1977.) But the rate for players who finished the season with different teams than the ones they started with was higher on division winners than on other teams 10 times in the past 12 seasons:

	1981	1982	1983	1984	1985	1986	1987	1988	1989	1990	1991	1992
Winners	7.9	8.1	6.1	6.7	6.9	6.3	11.9	4.4	9.4	10.3	7.1	8.0
Others	3.3	5.0	5.3	4.9	5.4	6.7	6.5	6.7	8.0	7.6	4.1	5.3

Evidence of a growing trend: Division winners had a higher pecentage than other teams eight times during the 1980s, five times during the 1970s, four times during the 1960s, and not at all during the 1950s.

Cone was one of the most successful in-season acquisitions ever made, but in our estimation, not the very best. Our nominations for the best ever follow. The criteria we used were: *(1)* the player's performance; *(2)* the team's need; and *(3)* timeliness—that is, how late in the season the player joined his new team. (That last item functioned mostly as a tie-breaker.)

1. The Tigers acquire Doyle Alexander from the Braves for minor league pitcher John Smoltz, Aug. 12, 1987.

Alexander posted a 9–0 record in 11 starts for Detroit. Anything less would have been futile, since the Tigers won the pennant on the final day of the regular season, following the most spectacular final-week comeback in major league history. Detroit trailed Toronto by 3½ games with eight games to play. Alexander defeated the Jays on the final Friday of the season. He pitched a better game versus Toronto the previous Sunday, allowing only two runs (one earned) in 10⅔ innings, but earning no decision in a Tigers victory.

2. The Cubs acquire Rick Sutcliffe from the Indians, with Ron Hassey and George Frazier, for Joe Carter, Mel Hall, Don Schulze, and minor league pitcher Darryl Banks, June 13, 1984.

Sutcliffe won 13 of his first 15 starts after joining the Cubs, as Chicago built its lead over the Mets to 5½ games. He was so dominant that he won the National League Cy Young Award despite making only 20 starts. He won the opening game of the N.L.C.S. over San Diego (and hit a home run in the game), but lost the decisive game.

3. The Cardinals acquire Lou Brock from the Cubs, with Jack Spring and Paul Toth, for Ernie Broglio, Bobby Shantz, and Doug Clemens, June 15, 1964.

Brock, a third-year player for Chicago, was three days shy of his 25th birthday and batting .251 with only two home runs in more than 200 at-bats when St. Louis, seven games out at the time, dipped into its starting rotation to grab him. He wound up second in the N.L. in stolen bases (43) and fifth in batting average (.315), helping the Cards steal the closest three-way race in baseball history. (Give this deal bonus credit as "the gift that keeps on giving.")

4. The Mets acquire Donn Clendenon from the Expos for pitchers Steve Renko, Bill Carden, and Dave Colon and infielder Kevin Collins, June 15, 1969.

This was the Mets' only trade of the 1969 season, and it was a dandy. (For more on the deal, see the Marlins essay.) Clendenon was acquired to platoon at first base with Ed Kranepool, but won an everyday starting job by September. He batted .291 with runners in scoring position after joining the Mets. And he was named the Most Valuable Player in the World Series victory over the Orioles even after not playing in the N.L.C.S. against the Braves, who started three right-handers.

5. The Braves acquire Alejandro Pena from the Mets for Tony Castillo and Joe Roa, Aug. 28, 1991.

Atlanta became desperate for a closer after Juan Berenguer, who led the team in saves (17), was injured in mid-August. Pena was absolutely perfect, converting all 11 save opportunities and earning a pair of wins as well—all of which were needed, since the Braves didn't nail down the division title until the next-to-last day of the season.

Those are the best, but many others deserve a call. Honorable mention goes to:

Orval Overall and Jack Taylor (1906 Cubs): Both went 12–3 for a runaway pennant winner that finished the season 116–36.

Hank Borowy (1945 Cubs): Compiled an 11–2 mark for Chicago after they paid nearly one hundred grand for him in late July.

Al Gionfriddo (1947 Dodgers): He batted only .177 in 37 regular-season games for Brooklyn. But in the World Series, he made perhaps the most famous catch in baseball history, if not for. . . .

Vic Wertz (1954 Indians): Cleveland didn't need his 14 home runs as it cruised to a 111-win, eight-game victory in the A.L. And even his 8-for-16 performance couldn't help the Tribe avoid a four-game sweep by the Giants. But he did get a 450-foot assist on Willie Mays's most famous putout.

Red Schoendienst (1957 Braves): Batted .310 for Milwaukee, who traded its light-hitting second baseman Danny O'Connell for him (along with outfielder Bobby Thomson and pitcher Ray Crone).

Pedro Ramos (1964 Yankees): Unhittable in the role made famous by Luis Arroyo. He allowed only three runs in 21⅔ innings, striking out 21 batters and walking none.

Woodie Fryman (1972 Tigers): Posted a 10–3 record and a 2.05 ERA in 14 starts for a team that won its division on the next-to-last day of the season.

Bill Madlock (1979 Pirates, 1985 Dodgers, and 1987 Tigers): A lifetime achievement award; he batted .328, .360, and .279 after joining champs-to-be, compared to .261, .251, and .180 for the teams he left. Forget Don Baylor—Madlock was the ultimate hired gun.

Don Sutton (1982 Brewers): Won four games down the stretch, including a tie-breaking, final-game victory over Jim Palmer and the Orioles.

Cesar Cedeno (1985 Cardinals): Batted .434 in 28 games after St. Louis lost its only true offensive threat, Jack Clark, with a rib-cage injury. Whitey Herzog said (surprise!), "We would not have won without him."

As a final note, it's worth considering what some teams sacrificed to acquire players whom they hoped would help bring them a title. For example, the first two players on our list, Doyle Alexander and Rick Sutcliffe, both cost their new teams dearly, as did Sutton (Kevin Bass), Smith (Moises Alou), and McGee (Felix Jose). That may eventually prove to be the case with Cone and the Blue Jays as well. Not many second basemen have the potential to hit 20 home runs in a season, as Jeff Kent does. But Pat Gillick has been down this road before; only a year earlier, he traded three promising young players (Glenallen Hill, Mark Whiten, and Denis Boucher) for Tom Candiotti. And as a neutral third-party commentator named Earl Weaver once said of the Cubs losing Joe Carter in the Sutcliffe deal: It doesn't matter; they won the pennant.

ATLANTA BRAVES

As baseball fans, we have a sense that the past two postseasons have had more than their share of drama. As statisticians, we can prove that the degree to which this is true is unprecedented. No team in major league history has played as many postseason games over a two-year period as the Braves did in 1991–92: 27 of a potential 28 games. It will likely take an expansion of the playoffs—and make no mistake, that's coming, whether you like it or not—for a team to top that total. But even if, aided by tier upon tier of made-for-cable playoffs ("Stay tuned as Hefty Bags presents the climactic game of the Ben and Jerry's National League East Division Bracket One Semifinal Series, leading up to the Pepto Bismol Finals!"), some team equals or surpasses the Braves' total statistically, it's going to be tough to top them for drama.

Five of Atlanta's games (19 percent) were decided in extra innings, including four of 13 (31 percent) in the World Series. Since 1903, only 10 percent of all postseason games—and only 9 percent of World Series games—have required overtime. The deciding run scored in the winning team's final at-bat in 11 of the Braves' games (41 percent) and in eight of their World Series games (62 percent). The all-time figures: The deciding run was scored in the winning team's final at-bat in 21 percent of all postseason games, and 19 percent of all World Series games. From Game 2 of the 1991 World Series through Game 3 of the 1992 World Series, seven of the nine World Series games were decided on the winning team's final at-bat. The guys who drove in the winning run were hardly the Magnificent Seven: Scott Leius, Mark Lemke, Jerry Willard, Kirby Puckett, Gene Larkin, Ed Sprague, and Candy Maldonado. More like Kirby and the Six Dwarfs.

The bottom of the ninth inning of Game 7 of the National League Championship Series may have been the best ending to a postseason game in major league history. That's quite a statement, but a comparison to the other great endings of the past will back it up. There have been 141 postseason series since 1903: 89 World Series, 48 League Championship Series, and the four "mini-playoffs" (officially called the Division Series, dormant but not extinct) following the 1981 split season. Atlanta's victory in Game 7 over Pittsburgh marked only the seventh time that a decisive postseason game—*decisive* meaning the series is tied and in its final game) had a sudden-death ending. The others:

- 1912 World Series, Game 8 (there had been one tie game earlier in the Series): The Red Sox trailed the Giants, 2–1, in bottom of 10th. Following New York center fielder Fred Snodgrass's "$30,000 muff" of a fly ball, Tris Speaker's single knocked in the tying run and Larry Gardner's "scoring fly ball" (there was no "sacrifice fly" rule then, so Vin Scully would have fit right in) won it.
- 1924 World Series, Game 7: The Senators and the Giants were tied 3–3 in 12th inning when a grounder hit by Washington's Earl McNeely took a bizarre hop over the head of third baseman Fred Lindstrom to drive in the winning run.
- 1960 World Series, Game 7: The Pirates and the Yankees were tied 9–9 when Bill Mazeroski led

off the bottom of the ninth with a home run off Ralph Terry—still the only home run ever to end a World Series.
- 1972 N.L. Championship Series, Game 5: The Reds trailed the Pirates 3–2 in the bottom of the ninth. Johnny Bench's leadoff homer off Dave Giusti tied the game, and Bob Moose's two-out wild pitch allowed pinch runner George Foster to score the winning run.
- 1976 A.L. Championship Series, Game 5: The Yankees and the Royals were tied 6–6 when Chris Chambliss led off the bottom of the ninth with a homer off Mark Littell.
- 1991 World Series, Game 7: With the Twins and Braves scoreless in 10th inning, Dan Gladden led off with a double, and Gene Larkin delivered the game-winning pinch-hit single with one out.

Each of these games was thrilling in its own right, but Game 7 of the 1992 National League Championship Series had an added dimension: It was the first postseason sudden-death ending in which a team *went from losing to winning* on the game's final pitch. (Bobby Thomson's home run was not in a postseason game.) And so we'd like to honor that inning in a special manner.

For only the second time in *Analyst* history (we also did it for Game 5 of the 1986 American League Championship Series between Boston and California), we'd like to run the final inning of the Pirates-Braves series through our own statistical VCR. Only this time, we'll have the advantage of hitting the PAUSE button whenever the fancy hits us, letting us consider all the elements that made up that uniquely exciting final frame.

A quick reset. For the first time in Championship Series history the same starting pitchers—in this case, John Smoltz and Doug Drabek—hooked up for a third time in one series. (It has happened nine times in World Series play.) While Smoltz had beaten Drabek in Games 1 and 4 of this series, *one starter has never beaten another three times in any postseason series.* The Pirates scored a run in the first on a sacrifice fly by Orlando Merced and one in the sixth on an RBI single by Andy Van Slyke. The Braves' best chance to score—a bases-loaded, none-out situation in the sixth—went unfulfilled when Jeff Blauser lined into a double play and Terry Pendleton lined out. Pittsburgh failed to add to its lead in the seventh, when Steve Avery came out of the bullpen to retire Van Slyke with the bases loaded, and in the eighth, when David Justice threw out Merced trying to score from first on Jeff King's double.

Drabek had pitched a strong eighth inning (two strikeouts and a foul out), and headed into the ninth protecting a 2–0 lead. Despite all of the heroics of the previous year's postseason, in franchise history (including Milwaukee and Boston) *the Braves had never won any of the 22 postseason games in which they trailed going into the ninth inning.* Pendleton led off, bringing to the plate *a .348 career postseason batting average (8-for-23) in Late-Inning Pressure Situations.* But he owns just *a .231 average (9-for-39) vs. Drabek* over six years of regular-season play, and Drabek had *held him hitless in 15 at-bats* in L.C.S. play. Pendleton ripped a deep liner to the right field corner that seemed playable but went uncaught by Cecil Espy (who had just entered the game after pinch-running for the injured Lloyd McClendon in the top of the inning). A double.

Next up, Justice, the tying run. *A fly-ball hitter against a ground-ball pitcher* gives the theoretical advantage to the batter. Right-hander Stan Belinda and left-hander Bob Patterson, *both extreme fly-ball pitchers,* were warming up, but Leyland was committed to Drabek. Justice grounded to second, where Jose Lind tried to backhand the ball, but it deflected off his glove. Lind *made only six errors all season* en route to his first Gold Glove Award (he also had made one in Game 3 of the L.C.S.), but now his name will stand alongside Snodgrass's as having made a pivotal error in the final inning of the climactic game of a postseason series.

First and third, Sid Bream up. Bunt? A successful one would have moved the tying run to second base and would have avoided the chance of a double play. But Bream, who had three sacrifices during the season, is surprisingly not a double-play threat. Due in large part to his propensity for hitting the ball in the air, he *ranked fifth on the National League's toughest-to-double list (three DP grounders in 76 opportunities).* Bream never got the bunt sign and a four-pitch walk followed; only one of the four pitches was close.

After watching his ace throw 129 pitches while working his third game in nine days, Jim Leyland decided to bring in Belinda to face Ron Gant. Unlike Drabek, Belinda gets most of his outs in the air, and induced *only one double-play grounder (back on April 20, no less) in 46 double-play situations* during the season. Even more alarming was his record on inherited runners: *He stranded only 10 while allowing 18 to score.* His "stranded rate" of 36 percent was *the worst among 124 major league relief pitchers* who had inherited at least 20 runners from previous pitchers.

Meanwhile, Bobby Cox elected to leave Bream in the game as the potential winning run. He had three nonpitchers left on the bench (Brian Hunter, who would be his first pinch hitter, and catchers Francisco Cabrera and Javier Lopez); he also had Tom Glavine, who had started Game 6, and who would be the pitcher least likely to see action if Game 7 went to extra innings. Managers are often reluctant to send a pitcher onto the basepaths, but Glavine is a good athlete, a good hitter, and a fine runner who has been *used as a pinch runner* 11 times in his major league career. But Cox was a bit shy of players (Hunter would have played left field with Gant playing in the infield had the game gone to the 10th inning), and had he used Glavine to run for Bream, further extra-inning adjustments would have been necessary (such as having Cabrera play first base). He left Bream running at first base.

Gant's propensity to pull the ball has been documented, and the Pirates defensed him accordingly through the series. (Gant had only nine hits to right field in 1991; he had 25 in 1992.) Barry Bonds had played him virtually in the left field corner throughout the playoffs; but the only putout he recorded on Gant had been a marvelous running catch in left-center in Game 5. (On the other hand, he had an excellent view of Gant's grand-slam homer in Game 2.) This time, his positioning paid off: Gant ripped a half fly/half line drive to the warning track near the corner; the ball was only slightly less toward the corner than Pendleton's double to right field that started the inning. But Bonds was in perfect position to make the catch. A run scored, but potential tying run Justice held at second. It was one of those plays that the crowd cheers because the home team has scored a run, but the result of the play was really nothing but a plus for the Pirates.

That brought up Damon Berryhill, who had only four hits in the seven-game series. If only Greg Olson, the Braves' regular catcher, hadn't broken his leg in September! Olson thrives on these situations: a .247 career hitter who has batted *.275 with runners on base and .304 with runners on base in Late-Inning Pressure Situations.* Berryhill is a .236 career hitter who has hit *only .243 and .245, respectively, in those same runners-on-base categories.* But Berryhill walked on five pitches (two of which seemed close enough to rip), loading the bases.

Some folks have suggested that the change of home-plate umpires from John McSherry to Randy Marsh worked against the Bucs. (Big Mac took ill in the second inning and Marsh took his place.) But McSherry's reputation is that of *a hitter's umpire who doesn't give pitchers the low strike;* those tendencies are supported by the numbers in the umpires' tables listed in the Seattle Mariners essay (page 37). There was actually some concern before the game that he would give Drabek, who pitches low, some trouble.

Rafael Belliard was due next; Cox, with no left-handed hitters available, sent Hunter up as a pinch-hitter. The lack of a lefty doesn't hurt too much against Belinda, *who has been more trouble for lefties (.203) than righties (.225)* during his career. But Hunter is not a good hitter against right-handed pitchers (*.272 career hitter vs. lefties, only .215 vs. righties).* He also has hit *only .189 in 74 Late-Inning Pressure Situation at-bats in two years in Atlanta.* Form held true here: Hunter popped weakly to Lind behind second base.

Bases loaded, two outs, Cabrera batting for Jeff Reardon. He had faced Belinda just once in their respective major league careers; that confrontation, on July 29, 1991, *resulted in a home run.* Cabrera had only 268 at-bats spread over four years in the majors, and just 10 in 1992. But he's a *.329 hitter (25-for-76) with runners in scoring position,* and had already earned a spot in Braves' lore with a ninth-inning, two-out, three-run homer off Rob Dibble to tie an important game in August 1991 that Atlanta went on to win in 13 innings.

Ball one, ball two. A line drive pulled foul. On the 2–1 pitch, Cabrera lined his hit to left. Bream managed to huff and puff his way home from second, LaValliere's desperate lunge with the ball came up inches short, and it was over.

Could the inning have been played differently? Of course, by both managers in many different ways. Someday, computer programs will be written and disk space allocated so that it will be replayed electronically *ad nauseam.* But of all the hundreds of possibilities, we got to see the best.

Before one of the Championship Series games in Atlanta, Francisco Cabrera approached former President Jimmy Carter and asked to pose with him for a photograph. We just wonder which one of them asked for the reprints to send out with his Christmas cards.

WON-LOST RECORD BY STARTING POSITION

Atlanta Braves	C	1B	2B	3B	SS	LF	CF	RF	DH	P	Leadoff	Cleanup	Starts vs. LH	Starts vs. RH	Total Starts
Steve Avery	-	-	-	-	-	-	-	-	-	17-18	-	-	12	23	17-18
Rafael Belliard	-	-	-	-	51-39	-	-	-	-	-	-	-	15	75	51-39
Juan Berenguer	-	-	-	-	-	-	-	-	-	-	-	-	-	-	-
Damon Berryhill	43-32	-	-	-	-	-	-	-	-	-	-	-	13	62	43-32
Mike Bielecki	-	-	-	-	-	-	-	-	-	6-8	-	-	3	11	6-8
Jeff Blauser	-	-	7-11	-	47-25	-	-	-	-	-	-	-	42	48	54-36
Pedro Borbon	-	-	-	-	-	-	-	-	-	-	-	-	-	-	-
Sid Bream	-	63-43	-	-	-	-	-	-	-	-	-	-	-	106	63-43
Francisco Cabrera	-	-	-	-	-	-	-	-	-	-	-	-	-	-	-
Vinny Castilla	-	-	-	2-1	-	-	-	-	-	-	-	-	1	2	2-1
Mark Davis	-	-	-	-	-	-	-	-	-	-	-	-	-	-	-
Nick Esasky	-	-	-	-	-	-	-	-	-	-	-	-	-	-	-
Marvin Freeman	-	-	-	-	-	-	-	-	-	-	-	-	-	-	-
Ron Gant	-	-	-	-	-	72-48	10-7	-	-	-	-	21-17	50	87	82-55
Tom Glavine	-	-	-	-	-	-	-	-	-	22-11	-	-	8	25	22-11
Pat Gomez	-	-	-	-	-	-	-	-	-	-	-	-	-	-	-
Tommy Gregg	-	-	-	-	-	-	0-1	-	-	-	0-1	-	-	1	0-1
Brian Hunter	-	34-21	-	-	-	-	-	1-3	-	-	-	-	51	8	35-24
David Justice	-	-	-	-	-	-	-	82-52	-	-	-	66-44	35	99	82-52
Ryan Klesko	-	1-0	-	-	-	-	-	-	-	-	-	1-0	-	1	1-0
Charlie Leibrandt	-	-	-	-	-	-	-	-	-	22-9	-	-	13	18	22-9
Mark Lemke	-	-	74-40	0-1	-	-	-	-	-	-	-	-	45	70	74-41
Javier Lopez	2-0	-	-	-	-	-	-	-	-	-	-	-	1	1	2-0
Steve Lyons	-	-	-	-	-	-	-	1-1	-	-	-	-	-	2	1-1
Kent Mercker	-	-	-	-	-	-	-	-	-	-	-	-	-	-	-
David Nied	-	-	-	-	-	-	-	-	-	1-1	-	-	-	2	1-1
Melvin Nieves	-	-	-	-	-	0-1	1-0	-	-	-	-	-	-	2	1-1
Otis Nixon	-	-	-	-	-	1-0	56-33	12-3	-	-	69-36	-	47	58	69-36
Greg Olson	53-32	-	-	-	-	-	-	-	-	-	-	-	37	48	53-32
Alejandro Pena	-	-	-	-	-	-	-	-	-	-	-	-	-	-	-
Terry Pendleton	-	-	-	96-62	-	-	-	-	-	-	-	1-0	50	108	96-62
Jeff Reardon	-	-	-	-	-	-	-	-	-	-	-	-	-	-	-
Armando Reynoso	-	-	-	-	-	-	-	-	-	1-0	-	-	1	-	1-0
Ben Rivera	-	-	-	-	-	-	-	-	-	-	-	-	-	-	-
Deion Sanders	-	-	-	-	-	5-4	32-23	1-5	-	-	-	29-27	4	66	38-32
Lonnie Smith	-	-	-	-	-	20-11	-	-	-	-	-	9-3	17	14	20-11
Pete Smith	-	-	-	-	-	-	-	-	-	11-0	-	-	3	8	11-0
John Smoltz	-	-	-	-	-	-	-	-	-	18-17	-	-	11	24	18-17
Mike Stanton	-	-	-	-	-	-	-	-	-	-	-	-	-	-	-
Randy St. Claire	-	-	-	-	-	-	-	-	-	-	-	-	-	-	-
Jeff Treadway	-	-	17-13	-	-	-	-	-	-	-	-	-	-	30	17-13
Jerry Willard	-	-	-	-	-	-	-	-	-	-	-	-	-	-	-
Mark Wohlers	-	-	-	-	-	-	-	-	-	-	-	-	-	-	-

TEAM TOTALS: BATTING

	AB	H	2B	3B	HR	RBI	BB	SO	BA	SA	OBA
Season	5480	1391	223	48	138	641	493	924	.254	.388	.316
vs. Left-Handers	1719	465	76	15	56	234	140	265	.271	.430	.323
vs. Right-Handers	3761	926	147	33	82	407	353	659	.246	.368	.313
vs. Ground-Ballers	2355	626	104	20	55	286	226	395	.266	.397	.331
vs. Fly-Ballers	3125	765	119	28	83	355	267	529	.245	.380	.304
Home Games	2636	681	106	19	72	326	271	434	.258	.395	.328
Road Games	2844	710	117	29	66	315	222	490	.250	.381	.304
Grass Fields	4008	1024	158	32	107	469	379	694	.255	.391	.320
Artificial Turf	1472	367	65	16	31	172	114	230	.249	.378	.303
April	708	167	31	9	17	73	56	144	.236	.377	.293
May	991	263	42	8	24	110	82	152	.265	.397	.322
June	832	222	29	8	23	104	74	133	.267	.404	.327
July	830	189	34	8	16	78	65	135	.228	.346	.285
August	1018	277	46	7	27	138	99	151	.272	.411	.336
Sept./Oct.	1101	273	41	8	31	138	117	209	.248	.384	.321
Leading Off Inn.	1355	358	57	10	35	35	91	221	.264	.399	.312
Runners On	2269	580	101	23	53	556	264	366	.256	.390	.329
Bases Empty	3211	811	122	25	85	85	229	558	.253	.386	.306
Runners/Scor. Pos.	1366	350	60	18	31	489	192	237	.256	.395	.338
Runners On/2 Out	986	221	48	9	21	204	126	163	.224	.355	.314
Scor. Pos./2 Out	653	145	28	7	16	179	95	117	.222	.360	.322
Late-Inning Pressure	692	168	30	6	27	91	86	118	.243	.421	.328
Leading Off	180	49	8	1	8	8	19	27	.272	.461	.342
Runners On	280	67	14	2	11	75	47	42	.239	.421	.344
Runners/Scor. Pos.	177	42	9	2	8	67	35	23	.237	.446	.347

RUNS BATTED IN	From 1B	From 2B	From 3B	Scoring Position
Totals	77/1594	192/1065	234/572	426/1637
Percentage	4.8%	18.0%	40.9%	26.0%

TEAM TOTALS: PITCHING

	W-L	ERA	AB	H	HR	BB	SO	BA	SA	OBA
Season	98-64	3.14	5467	1321	89	489	948	.242	.345	.305
vs. Left-Handers			2023	518	38	225	359	.256	.362	.332
vs. Right-Handers			3444	803	51	264	589	.233	.334	.289
vs. Ground-Ballers			2421	556	28	202	426	.230	.312	.289
vs. Fly-Ballers			3046	765	61	287	522	.251	.370	.317
Home Games	51-30	3.10	2780	684	45	225	470	.246	.344	.303
Road Games	47-34	3.19	2687	637	44	264	478	.237	.346	.307
Grass Fields	76-44	2.95	4071	975	67	353	669	.239	.340	.301
Artificial Turf	22-20	3.70	1396	346	22	136	279	.248	.358	.317
April	11-11	3.03	705	168	13	67	142	.238	.356	.306
May	12-16	4.06	975	260	17	103	171	.267	.387	.339
June	19-6	2.83	817	184	14	67	136	.225	.318	.283
July	16-9	2.52	857	192	14	75	140	.224	.326	.288
August	19-10	3.71	1005	256	18	85	163	.255	.368	.313
Sept./Oct.	21-12	2.67	1108	261	13	92	196	.236	.313	.296
Leading Off Inn.			1358	337	25	100	237	.248	.356	.303
Bases Empty			3199	772	53	243	541	.241	.346	.298
Runners On			2268	549	36	246	407	.242	.343	.315
Runners/Scor. Pos.			1297	298	17	189	260	.230	.316	.324
Runners On/2 Out			984	223	22	124	171	.227	.346	.316
Scor. Pos./2 Out			631	137	10	104	118	.217	.312	.332
Late-Inning Pressure			973	228	17	95	160	.234	.330	.304
Leading Off			241	59	5	23	39	.245	.349	.316
Runners On			401	99	6	52	75	.247	.329	.332
Runners/Scor. Pos.			235	51	1	38	48	.217	.255	.324
First 9 Batters			2735	665	52	266	522	.243	.352	.312
Second 9 Batters			1327	325	17	116	223	.245	.345	.303
All Batters Thereafter			1405	331	20	107	203	.236	.330	.293

WON-LOST RECORD BY STARTING POSITION

Chicago Cubs	C	1B	2B	3B	SS	LF	CF	RF	DH	P	Leadoff	Cleanup	Starts vs. LH	Starts vs. RH	Total Starts
Alex Arias	-	-	-	-	10-18	-	-	-		-	0-2	-	11	17	10-18
Paul Assenmacher	-	-	-	-	-	-	-	-		-	-	-	-	-	-
Shawn Boskie	-	-	-	-	-	-	-	-		6-12	-	-	8	10	6-12
Steve Buechele	-	-	32-29	-	-	-	-	-		-	-	1-0	25	36	32-29
Jim Bullinger	-	-	-	-	-	-	-	-		3-6	-	-	3	6	3-6
Frank Castillo	-	-	-	-	-	-	-	-		14-19	-	-	10	23	14-19
Kal Daniels	-	-	-	-	-	15-9	-	-		-	-	7-3	3	21	15-9
Doug Dascenzo	-	-	-	-	-	4-3	33-35	3-3		-	19-19	-	41	40	40-41
Andre Dawson	-	-	-	-	-	-	-	61-76		-	-	52-60	57	80	61-76
Shawon Dunston	-	-	-	-	4-13	-	-	-		-	4-12	-	6	11	4-13
Joe Girardi	33-37	-	-	-	-	-	-	-		-	-	-	41	29	33-37
Mark Grace	-	74-83	-	-	-	-	-	-		-	-	5-3	58	99	74-83
Mike Harkey	-	-	-	-	-	-	-	-		5-3	-	-	4	4	5-3
Jeff Hartsock	-	-	-	-	-	-	-	-		-	-	-	-	-	-
Jessie Hollins	-	-	-	-	-	-	-	-		-	-	-	-	-	-
Danny Jackson	-	-	-	-	-	-	-	-		6-13	-	-	5	14	6-13
Jeff Kunkel	-	1-0	-	0-1	1-1	-	-	-		-	-	-	4	-	2-2
Greg Maddux	-	-	-	-	-	-	-	-		21-14	-	-	13	22	21-14
Derrick May	-	-	-	-	-	33-39	-	9-4		-	-	1-0	12	73	42-43
Chuck McElroy	-	-	-	-	-	-	-	-		-	-	-	-	-	-
Mike Morgan	-	-	-	-	-	-	-	-		21-13	-	-	15	19	21-13
Ken Patterson	-	-	-	-	-	-	-	-		0-1	-	-	-	1	0-1
Jorge Pedre	-	-	-	-	-	-	-	-		-	-	-	-	-	-
Fernando Ramsey	-	-	-	-	-	-	2-4	-		-	-	-	5	1	2-4
Dennis Rasmussen	-	-	-	-	-	-	-	-		0-1	-	-	1	-	0-1
Jeff D. Robinson	-	-	-	-	-	-	-	-		2-2	-	-	2	2	2-2
Luis Salazar	-	3-0	-	13-17	4-4	11-15	-	-		-	-	-	47	20	31-36
Rey Sanchez	-	-	0-2	-	35-32	-	-	-		-	9-9	-	29	40	35-34
Ryne Sandberg	-	-	77-80	-	-	-	-	-		-	-	12-17	58	99	77-80
Bob Scanlan	-	-	-	-	-	-	-	-		-	-	-	-	-	-
Gary Scott	-	-	-	15-10	-	-	-	-		-	-	-	8	17	15-10
Heathcliff Slocumb	-	-	-	-	-	-	-	-		-	-	-	-	-	-
Dave Smith	-	-	-	-	-	-	-	-		-	-	-	-	-	-
Dwight Smith	-	-	-	-	-	4-9	11-12	5-1		-	5-9	0-1	-	42	20-22
Sammy Sosa	-	-	-	-	-	-	32-33	-		-	16-12	-	21	44	32-33
Doug Strange	-	-	0-2	7-12	-	-	-	-		-	1-0	-	2	19	7-14
Hector Villanueva	13-13	1-1	-	-	-	-	-	-		-	-	-	14	14	14-14
Jose Vizcaino	-	-	-	11-15	25-16	-	-	-		-	20-18	-	21	46	36-31
Chico Walker	-	-	0-1	-	-	2-0	-	-		-	2-0	-	1	2	2-1
Jerome Walton	-	-	-	-	-	8-8	-	-		-	2-3	-	16	-	8-8
Rick Wilkins	32-34	-	-	-	-	-	-	-		-	-	-	8	58	32-34

TEAM TOTALS: BATTING

	AB	H	2B	3B	HR	RBI	BB	SO	BA	SA	OBA
Season	5590	1420	221	41	104	566	417	816	.254	.364	.307
vs. Left-Handers	2008	525	92	17	25	194	132	262	.261	.362	.307
vs. Right-Handers	3582	895	129	24	79	372	285	554	.250	.365	.308
vs. Ground-Ballers	2396	637	95	22	43	262	164	330	.266	.378	.316
vs. Fly-Ballers	3194	783	126	19	61	304	253	486	.245	.354	.301
Home Games	2768	711	120	25	59	297	238	411	.257	.382	.316
Road Games	2822	709	101	16	45	269	179	405	.251	.346	.299
Grass Fields	3907	990	155	32	77	405	305	578	.253	.369	.308
Artificial Turf	1683	430	66	9	27	161	112	238	.255	.354	.305
April	653	139	24	5	10	60	54	106	.213	.311	.274
May	939	222	29	8	16	91	84	151	.236	.335	.299
June	962	257	43	6	17	109	57	129	.267	.377	.309
July	840	206	30	5	21	67	73	121	.245	.368	.308
August	1047	272	42	10	15	97	67	152	.260	.362	.308
Sept./Oct.	1149	324	53	7	25	142	82	157	.282	.406	.331
Leading Off Inn.	1375	328	58	8	24	24	93	201	.239	.345	.290
Runners On	2381	608	97	18	45	507	191	370	.255	.368	.310
Bases Empty	3209	812	124	23	59	59	226	446	.253	.361	.305
Runners/Scor. Pos.	1262	328	52	8	23	431	143	203	.260	.368	.330
Runners On/2 Out	1032	247	38	6	13	197	100	159	.239	.326	.311
Scor. Pos./2 Out	622	146	24	2	8	175	83	106	.235	.318	.329
Late-Inning Pressure	930	239	24	0	20	85	83	140	.257	.347	.322
Leading Off	238	63	13	0	4	4	19	40	.265	.370	.324
Runners On	398	102	7	0	10	75	38	64	.256	.349	.323
Runners/Scor. Pos.	215	53	3	0	6	66	30	35	.247	.344	.336

RUNS BATTED IN	From 1B	From 2B	From 3B	Scoring Position
Totals	85/1759	176/987	201/507	377/1494
Percentage	4.8%	17.8%	39.6%	25.2%

TEAM TOTALS: PITCHING

	W-L	ERA	AB	H	HR	BB	SO	BA	SA	OBA
Season	78-84	3.39	5440	1337	107	575	901	.246	.366	.320
vs. Left-Handers			2727	687	57	327	442	.252	.375	.334
vs. Right-Handers			2713	650	50	248	459	.240	.356	.306
vs. Ground-Ballers			2457	576	28	229	414	.234	.321	.302
vs. Fly-Ballers			2983	761	79	346	487	.255	.402	.335
Home Games	43-38	2.92	2817	669	49	279	479	.237	.349	.307
Road Games	35-46	3.92	2623	668	58	296	422	.255	.384	.334
Grass Fields	58-56	3.07	3854	921	72	379	645	.239	.354	.308
Artificial Turf	20-28	4.21	1586	416	35	196	256	.262	.395	.349
April	7-13	4.04	644	154	12	77	117	.239	.354	.324
May	13-15	3.02	924	223	12	100	168	.241	.345	.316
June	18-10	2.86	925	212	13	95	144	.229	.337	.302
July	11-13	2.43	799	183	16	87	139	.229	.349	.306
August	18-12	2.76	1001	248	21	92	148	.248	.357	.313
Sept./Oct.	11-21	5.12	1147	317	33	124	185	.276	.431	.351
Leading Off Inn.			1344	325	17	114	213	.242	.362	.308
Bases Empty			3172	759	59	266	524	.239	.356	.303
Runners On			2268	578	48	309	377	.255	.380	.343
Runners/Scor. Pos.			1344	318	18	249	249	.237	.340	.350
Runners On/2 Out			967	223	21	165	169	.231	.358	.347
Scor. Pos./2 Out			648	137	6	142	117	.211	.309	.358
Late-Inning Pressure			948	249	13	123	175	.263	.357	.349
Leading Off			242	63	4	23	42	.260	.360	.327
Runners On			411	102	4	75	82	.248	.336	.364
Runners/Scor. Pos.			241	53	1	60	55	.220	.299	.373
First 9 Batters			2857	682	48	333	508	.239	.345	.320
Second 9 Batters			1339	343	35	128	209	.256	.403	.325
All Batters Thereafter			1244	312	24	114	184	.251	.374	.316

CHICAGO CUBS

With due deference to his hometown of Hoboken, New Jersey, and notwithstanding the photographs that adorn Tommy Lasorda's office at Dodger Stadium, Frank Sinatra's favorite city must surely be Chicago. After all, not one but two of his most famous "city songs" have been devoted to it. And while neither of these songs may possess the current allure of "New York, New York" to the karaoke set (never has one tune been mangled so badly by so many), the titles say it all: "Chicago" (that's the song with "On State Street, that great street"), and "My Kind of Town" ("Chicago is"). No less a Chicagoan than Mike Ditka even quoted from "My Way" during his farewell remarks in January.

But there's one Sinatra standard that all too rarely has been applicable to that toddlin' town's favorite baseball team: "Here's to the Winners." The Cubs have produced only two seasons in the last 20 in which they won more games than they lost, although those two suggest yet another title, "All or Nothing at All"—in both 1984 and 1989, the Cubs won a division title.

It's too bad that two of their biggest stars, Andre Dawson and Greg Maddux, were not singing "Our Love Is Here to Stay," as last winter the Cubs lost each to free agency. Maddux had led the team in wins in each of the past five years, and Dawson led the team in RBIs in each of the past three (and in five of the past six). Talk about a "Serenade in Blue": no team had ever had to sustain such a one-two punch before. Surprisingly, few teams have had to cope with *either* kind of loss.

Since the major leagues began compiling RBIs as an official category in 1920, Dawson is only the 20th player to start a season with a new team after having led his previous team in RBIs in each of the previous three (or more) years. Dave Winfield is the only other such player who left his team as a free agent. Think about that: Among all of the big hitters who have changed teams as free agents over the past 17 years, only one had been his team's leading RBI man in each of the three previous seasons. The full list:

Year	Player	Old	New	Years*
1932	Babe Herman	Dodgers	Reds	3
1935	Joe Cronin	Senators	Red Sox	5
1936	Jimmie Foxx	Athletics	Red Sox	4
1938	Zeke Bonura	White Sox	Senators	4
1943	Bob Johnson	Athletics	Senators	7
1948	Dixie Walker	Dodgers	Pirates	3
1957	Del Ennis	Phillies	Cardinals	5
1964	Don Demeter	Phillies	Tigers	3
1964	Norm Siebern	Athletics	Orioles	4
1970	Dick Allen	Phillies	Cardinals	4
1975	Bobby Murcer	Yankees	Giants	4
1976	Rusty Staub	Mets	Tigers	3
1977	Jeff Burroughs	Rangers	Braves	4
1977	George Scott	Brewers	Red Sox	5
1981	Dave Winfield	Padres	Yankees	4
1982	George Foster	Reds	Mets	6
1982	Steve Kemp	Tigers	White Sox	3
1985	George Hendrick	Cardinals	Pirates	5
1990	Joe Carter	Indians	Padres	4
1993	Andre Dawson	Cubs	Red Sox	3

*Previous years leading old team in RBIs.

To find the last pitcher to start a season on a new club after leading his previous team in wins in each of the last three years, you have to go back to 1978, when Vida Blue was traded by Oakland to San Francisco. (The last pitcher to move after at least *five* such seasons in a row—Maddux's total—was Fergie Jenkins, whom the Cubs traded to Texas following the 1973 season; he had led the Cubs in wins in each of the previous seven years.) Over the same since-1920 span as the previous list, Maddux is only the 16th such pitcher to move, and only Catfish Hunter had left his old team as a free agent:

Year	Player	Old	New	Years*
1925	Urban Shocker	Browns	Yankees	5
1926	Jimmy Ring	Phillies	Giants	4
1933	Lefty Stewart	Browns	Senators	3
1933	Earl Whitehill	Tigers	Senators	3
1934	Lefty Grove	Athletics	Red Sox	4
1934	Red Lucas	Reds	Pirates	5
1954	Murry Dickson	Pirates	Phillies	3
1956	Bob Porterfield	Senators	Red Sox	4
1966	Al Jackson	Mets	Cardinals	3
1972	Rick Wise	Phillies	Cardinals	3
1972	Sam McDowell	Indians	Giants	3
1974	Fergie Jenkins	Cubs	Rangers	7
1975	Catfish Hunter	Athletics	Yankees	3
1977	Lynn McGlothen	Cardinals	Giants	3
1978	Vida Blue	Athletics	Giants	3
1993	Greg Maddux	Cubs	Braves	5

*Previous years leading old team in wins.

Only the '92 Cubs show up as the "old" team on both lists. It's enough to make Jim Lefebvre cry, "They Can't Take That Away From Me." But they have, and so the Cubs face a unique set of circumstances as they try to enter 1993 with "High Hopes." They have fortified themselves with some off-season additions of their own: pitchers Jose Guzman, Greg Hibbard, Randy Myers, and Dan Plesac, and outfielders Candy Maldonado and Willie Wilson (yes, old Astroturf Willie romping around on God's green grass in the Friendly Confines). The question is, what kind of team are they joining?

The 1992 Cubs ranked 10th in the National League in runs scored, beating out only the Giants and the Dodgers. Their average of only 3.66 per game was their lowest since 1981 and their lowest in a full season since 1963. And that was *with* Dawson.

Meanwhile, led by Maddux and Mike Morgan, Chicago's pitchers held their opponents to 3.85 runs per game, the sixth-lowest rate in the National League. It marked only the third time since 1980 that the Cubs have not finished among the bottom three teams in the league in that category. In the two other years (1984, eighth; 1989, fifth) they had their division-winning teams; it should be noted that those were also the only two years in the past 25 in which Cubs batters led the league in runs scored.

One reason that the Cubs both scored and yielded fewer runs than they have in the past is that the "Summer Wind" was blowing in (rather than out) at Wrigley Field for so much of 1992. There were 612 runs scored in 81 games there last season; there were 605 runs scored in the Cubs' 81 road games. That's the narrowest difference between the runs scored in those sets of games since 1959, the last year that there were more runs scored in the Cubs' road games than in their home games. (Back then, of course, the stadiums of the other National League teams were considerably more like Wrigley Field than they are today.) Despite last year's totals, Wrigley is still the best hitters' park in baseball taken over the last five years as a whole (see page 331).

All of these numbers taken together paint a picture of a very unCubslike year: one in which they ranked better within the National League in runs allowed than in runs scored. It was only the second time in the 24 years since divisional play that they have done that, the fewest among all 26 major league teams. Curiously, the Cubs' American League counterpart, the Boston Red Sox, also stood better in their league in preventing runs than in scoring them in 1992, only the third time in the past 24 years that they have done so. In the following table, the first number represents the number of times since 1969 that a team ranked higher within its league in runs scored than in runs allowed (each calculated per game); the second represents the number of times the team ranked higher in runs allowed; the third represents the number of times that the rankings were identical:

American League	Bat.	Pit.	Same	National League	Bat.	Pit.	Same
Baltimore	4	15	5	Atlanta	15	5	4
Boston	20	3	1	Chicago	21	2	1
California	6	16	2	Cincinnati	18	4	2
Chicago	12	11	1	Houston	10	12	2
Cleveland	14	9	1	Los Angeles	4	18	2
Detroit	13	7	4	Montreal	6	15	3
Kansas City	6	15	3	New York	7	15	2
Milwaukee	12	9	3	Philadelphia	14	8	2
Minnesota	13	8	3	Pittsburgh	16	8	0
New York	9	12	3	St. Louis	11	11	2
Oakland	10	11	3	San Diego	4	17	3
Seattle	7	7	2	San Francisco	12	9	3
Texas	9	14	1				
Toronto	8	6	2				

It's odd indeed that the Red Sox and the Cubs, teams that have had that separated-at-birth look for so much of their respective histories, had such similar seasons. For years, the words "Cubs" and "runs" had gone together—on both lines of the line score—like "Love and Marriage" (or at least as well as "horse" and "carriage"). The same holds true for the Red Sox. The Cubs had led the National League in runs scored over the previous 10 years, from 1982–91, while the Red Sox had led the American League in runs over the same span.

These two teams each play their home games in old, storied hitters' parks, but the difference between their mashball teams of the past and their milquetoast squads of 1992 was like "Night and Day." And in the

same year as an offensive decline, each team's pitching staff did much better than anyone would have expected. But think about that for a minute: According to some baseball theorists, shouldn't the won-lost records of those teams have been *better* in 1992 because of their improved pitching, whatever their troubles at the plate? After all, we're often reminded, "pitching is 75 percent of the game." Or is it 80 percent? Or 83.4? So we are often told.

It's strange that in a game in which every run that's scored corresponds with one that is allowed, pitching has assumed this bigger-than-life reputation as the far more important element in the offense/defense equation. Granted, an individual pitcher is often many times more important to the outcome of a particular game than a typical position player would be. Still, how could anyone suggest that run prevention is any more or any less important than run scoring? Offense and defense are, of course, equally important.

We looked at every team since 1901 that either scored the most runs in its league or allowed the fewest, and then looked to that year's final standings to see how these teams made out. If baseball were really 75 (or more) percent pitching, we would expect teams that allowed the fewest runs to be far more successful over the course of the years than teams that led in runs scored. The results are summarized here, with the chart indicating the number of teams that finished in first place after leading their league in runs scored or runs allowed:

	A.L.	N.L.	Total
First-place finishes, most runs scored	51	46	97
First-place finishes, fewest runs allowed	47	48	95

For the two leagues combined, 53 percent of the best-hitting teams have finished in first place, compared to 52 percent of the best-pitching teams. With nearly a century's worth of data behind us, teams that led their league in scoring runs have actually won slightly more pennants and division titles than teams that have led their league in run prevention.

The 1992 records of the Cubs (78–84) and the Red Sox (73–89) should serve as a reminder that pitching is not "That Old Black Magic" that through some kind of "Witchcraft" automatically makes champions out of teams regardless of their batting orders. Basing one's baseball beliefs on such a theory would, in the long run, only leave a person "Bewitched, Bothered and Bewildered."

CINCINNATI REDS

Who's got the best starting staff in the N.L. West? The winner by acclamation would certainly be the Braves, and there's no doubt that Atlanta has the youngest and perhaps the most spectacular staff assembled, at least in terms of potential for future accomplishments, since the 1968 Cubs (Ferguson Jenkins, Bill Hands, Ken Holtzman, and Joe Niekro), the 1969 Mets (Tom Seaver, Jerry Koosman, Nolan Ryan, and Tug McGraw), and the 1970 Cardinals (Bob Gibson, Steve Carlton, Mike Torrez, and Jerry Reuss). Tom Glavine and Greg Maddux have won the last two Cy Young Awards, and it wouldn't shock anyone if John Smoltz and Steve Avery won the next two. Glavine, the oldest of the four, will barely be 27 years old on opening day. If another 27-year-old, Pete Smith, returns to his late-1992 form, Atlanta's rotation has no weak link.

But Atlanta isn't the only team in the division with a rotation that's young, deep, or renowned. Despite the loss of free agent Greg Swindell to the division-rival Astros (who are themselves vastly improved, having added not only Swindell but also Doug Drabek), the Reds have a four-deep rotation that may well tempt new manager Tony Perez to re-institute the four-man rotation that Reds pitching coach Jim Kaat used to great advantage in 1984.

Cincinnati's rotation boasts a pair of Reds veterans, Tom Browning and Jose Rijo, and the past two winters' acquisitions, Tim Belcher (from the Dodgers a year ago for Eric Davis) and John Smiley (a free-agent addition this past off-season). They lack the pizzaz of the Braves' pitchers, the lavish contracts of Houston's new top two, and the reputations of the Dodgers' Orel Hershiser and Ramon Martinez, but at their best, Cincinnati's big four could be as good or better than any or all of their division rivals. Each has a career winning percentage of .550 or better, and although they have pitched for winning teams, all have consistently exceeded their teams' percentages. And with the exception of Browning (a question mark coming off a serious knee injury that curtailed his 1992 season in June), all are in their primes. Ages are as of opening day:

Pitcher	Last Season			Career Statistics			
	Age	W–L	ERA	W–L	Pct.	Team	Diff.
Tim Belcher	31	15–14	3.91	65–52	.556	.535	+.021
Tom Browning	32	6–5	5.07	113–80	.585	.506	+.079
Jose Rijo	27	15–10	2.56	83–68	.550	.503	+.047
John Smiley	28	16–9	3.21	76–51	.598	.535	+.063

Previous editions of the *Analyst* have rated pitchers on the difference between their career records and those of a hypothetical "replacement pitcher." The replacement represents a sixth man—a theoretical .400 pitcher—who would have joined the rotation if the pitcher in question weren't available. (The composite winning percentage of all pitchers who made between 5 and 15 starts in any of the last 10 seasons was .400.)

Pitchers with winning percentages at least 100 points better than their imaginary replacements are generally consistent winners, at least if they pitch for competitive clubs. There were 54 such pitchers who started at least 15 games last season, and at least 100 in their careers. As of January 1, four were still hunting for jobs (Bert Blyleven, Kelly Downs, Bill Krueger, and Scott Sanderson). Of the remaining 50, there were far more in the N.L. West (18)—the most pitching-rich division in baseball—than in any of the other divisions. (The A.L. West had 12, the two eastern divisions had 10 each.)

Could it be that the team with the best rotation in the division with the best starters will be Cincinnati? It's a stretch, but at the very least the addition of Smiley this season offsets the loss of Swindell, allowing the Reds to remain competitive with their divisional rivals who have loaded up on pitching. And the ultimate answer to that question may be tied to how Cincinnati decides to deal with the number-five spot in its rotation. The early favorite for the spot is Chris Hammond, a minor league superstar who has compiled only a 14–19 record in several shots at the big time. But if we may make a modest proposal, we would suggest that the best thing the Reds can do with that fifth spot might be to ignore it altogether. Browning, Belcher, and Rijo have all pitched very well in the past with three days between starts. And although the four-man rotation has been out of fashion for quite some time now, this seems a reasonable spot for its return.

Although Browning has made only 12 starts over the past three seasons on three days' rest, he took regular turns with three days between starts in each of his five previous seasons, and his record on so-called "short rest" has been excellent:

Year	3 Days Between Starts						All Other Starts					
	GS	CG	W	L	IP	ERA	GS	CG	W	L	IP	ERA
1984	0	0	0	0	0.0	——	3	0	1	0	23.1	1.54
1985	23	5	15	3	167.0	3.07	15	1	5	6	94.1	4.39
1986	17	3	7	5	105.1	3.84	22	1	7	8	138.0	3.78
1987	6	0	2	4	33.1	5.67	25	2	8	9	147.2	4.94
1988	13	2	7	2	90.1	3.89	23	3	11	3	160.1	3.14
1989	10	3	5	3	72.0	2.88	27	6	10	9	177.2	3.60
1990	7	0	4	2	37.0	5.59	28	2	11	7	190.2	3.45
1991	4	0	1	2	19.1	4.66	32	1	13	12	211.0	4.14
1992	1	0	0	0	5.0	3.60	15	0	6	5	82.0	5.16
Totals	81	13	41	21	529.1	3.74	190	16	72	59	1225.0	3.92

Rijo has a career record of 8–7 with an impressive 1.97 ERA in 17 starts on three days' rest. Belcher's record is even better: 4-1, 1.82 in eight starts. And while Smiley has made only one career start on a three-day rest, all things considered, the factors couldn't be much more weighted in favor of a four-man experiment.

When most fans think of the Reds, they think of hitting, not pitching. Cincinnati has ranked higher in pitching (runs allowed per game) than in batting (runs per game) only three times in the past 21 seasons. But that's basically an illusion, attributable to Riverfront Stadium, one of the best—and certainly the most underrated—hitters' parks in baseball. Based only on road-game statistics, to eliminate the effect of Cincinnati's home field, the Reds have ranked higher in pitching than in hitting 10 times in the last 11 years.

Nevertheless, Cincinnati's long history has featured more accomplished sluggers than hurlers. Only two National League teams—Chicago and Philadelphia, with six each—have had more 200–home-run hitters than the Reds, whose five include Johnny Bench (389), Frank Robinson (324), Tony Perez (287), Ted Kluszewski (251), and George Foster (244). But Cincinnati, along with their partners in pigment, the Red Sox, are the only current pre-expansion franchises for which no pitcher has won 200 games. Roger Clemens, barring injury, will need only three more years to erase Boston's name from that slate, leaving only the Reds with the expansion teams. Tom Browning is a fine pitcher, and has been for some time now. But even so, it will probably surprise you to learn that he needs only four more wins to crack the Reds' all-time top 10 in victories, and only a pair of mediocre seasons to move into the top five:

Pitcher	W	L	Pitcher	W	L
Eppa Rixey	179	148	Frank Dwyer	132	101
Paul Derringer	161	150	Joe Nuxhall	130	109
Bucky Walters	160	107	Pete Donohue	127	110
Dolf Luque	153	152	Noodles Hahn	126	90
Jim Maloney	134	81	Johnny Vander Meer	116	116

What's significant about this rather unimposing list isn't the pitchers who are there, it's the ones that aren't—but who once looked like mortal locks to scale its upper reaches. They form a cautionary tale for those who have already sent their checks for World Series tickets to Fulton County Stadium. As a special treat for those who wrote asking for more "What Ifs," here are a few words on some great Reds pitchers from the not-too-distant past, only one of whom appears on the list above.

Since 1960, only 10 National League pitchers won as many as 60 games before their 25th birthdays. Three of them pitched for the Reds, and all three made their major league debuts between 1960 and 1970: Jim Maloney, Gary Nolan, and Don Gullett. Collectively, those three pitchers won only 137 games after turning 25, or 79 fewer than they won up to that point. The group listed in the table below, is ranked by wins at age 25; the other seven pitchers won an average of 73 games before and 61 after—a margin that will shrink, of course, until years from now (we assume) when Gooden and Maddux retire:

Pitcher	Tot.	Bef.	Aft.	Pitcher	Tot.	Bef.	Aft.
Dwight Gooden	142+	100	42+	Ken Holtzman	174	65	109
Larry Dierker	139	83	56	Ray Sadecki	135	65	70
Don Gullett	109	80	29	Dick Ellsworth	115	62	53
Fernando Valenzuela	141	78	63	Greg Maddux	95+	61	34+
Gary Nolan	110	76	34	Jim Maloney	134	60	74

Cincinnati seems to have been struck by particularly bad luck with the health of its promising young pitchers' arms. Note that Gullett and Nolan had the fewest wins after turning 25 among those 10 pitchers. And keep in mind that the Reds had another outstanding young pitcher in 1970 who failed to make the list above because he blew out his arm even more quickly than Nolan and Gullett: Wayne Simpson, who posted a 14–3 record with a 3.02 ERA as a 21-year-old rookie in 1970. And just to complete a five-man rotation of Reds frustration, let's add Mario Soto, whose promising future evaporated quickly after an outstanding 18–7 season in 1984 at age 28.

The following table suggests what might have been in Cincinnati. Each of the Reds pitchers mentioned above has been paired with a pitcher who had a similar statistical profile before fortune—in one case bad, in the other good—drove his career in the opposite direction. As you study the figures, keep in mind that the oldest of the Reds pitchers—Maloney—was only 37 years old when the youngest—Soto—made his big-league debut in 1977. Ages are as of October 1:

Year	Age	Pitcher	Season W–L	ERA	Career to Date W–L	IP	H	SO	ERA
1969	29	Jim Maloney	12–5	2.77	134–80	1802	1457	1585	3.08
1991	29	Roger Clemens	18–10	2.62	134–61	1784	1500	1665	2.85
1970	22	Gary Nolan	18–7	3.26	49–27	737	626	581	2.92
1973	24	Vida Blue	20–9	3.27	53–28	808	609	629	2.72
1970	21	Wayne Simpson	14–3	3.02	14–3	176	125	119	3.02
1963	22	Al Downing	13–5	2.56	13–6	186	121	184	2.81
1974	23	Don Gullett	17–11	3.04	65–37	902	776	615	3.14
1978	24	Dennis Eckersley	20–8	2.99	60–40	901	774	705	3.16
1984	28	Mario Soto	18–7	3.53	77–58	1250	964	1123	3.22
1968	28	Mickey Lolich	17–9	3.19	83–63	1248	1104	1065	3.53

What if all five of those pitchers had remained healthy? That's probably asking too much. But what if, say, Maloney and Simpson had stayed sound even a few years longer, joining a still-healthy Gullett and Nolan in the rotation for the Big Red Machine of the mid-1970s? There might have been no need for any discussion of which was the greatest team in major league history. Of course, add such a powerful starting staff to those teams and the 1975 World Series might not have lasted six games; Carlton Fisk might never have shown us his command of body English. Sometimes venturing into the "What If" universe leaves the game poorer, not richer. It's a tool that should be used only for good, not evil.

WON-LOST RECORD BY STARTING POSITION

Cincinnati Reds	C	1B	2B	3B	SS	LF	CF	RF	DH	P	Leadoff	Cleanup	Starts vs. LH	Starts vs. RH	Total Starts
Troy Afenir	6-4	-	-	-	-	-	-	-	-	-	-	-	7	3	6-4
Bobby Ayala	-	-	-	-	-	-	-	-	-	4-1	-	-	2	3	4-1
Scott Bankhead	-	-	-	-	-	-	-	-	-	-	-	-	-	-	-
Tim Belcher	-	-	-	-	-	-	-	-	-	19-15	-	-	16	18	19-15
Freddie Benavides	-	-	13-10	-	12-9	-	-	-	-	-	-	-	26	18	25-19
Geronimo Berroa	-	-	-	-	-	1-2	-	-	-	-	-	-	3	-	1-2
Tom Bolton	-	-	-	-	-	-	-	-	-	4-4	-	-	4	4	4-4
Scott Bradley	-	-	-	-	-	-	-	-	-	-	-	-	-	-	-
Glenn Braggs	-	-	-	-	-	22-22	-	10-14	-	-	-	6-10	48	20	32-36
Jeff Branson	-	-	10-7	0-1	-	-	-	-	-	-	-	-	-	18	10-8
Keith Brown	-	-	-	-	-	-	-	-	-	1-1	-	-	1	1	1-1
Tom Browning	-	-	-	-	-	-	-	-	-	8-8	-	-	9	7	8-8
Jacob Brumfield	-	-	-	-	-	-	1-1	0-1	-	-	1-1	-	3	-	1-2
Norm Charlton	-	-	-	-	-	-	-	-	-	-	-	-	-	-	-
Darnell Coles	-	9-8	-	7-7	-	1-1	-	0-1	-	-	-	4-1	27	7	17-17
Tim Costo	-	6-4	-	-	-	-	-	-	-	-	-	1-0	5	5	6-4
Rob Dibble	-	-	-	-	-	-	-	-	-	-	-	-	-	-	-
Bill Doran	-	7-8	52-39	-	-	-	-	-	-	-	-	-	30	76	59-47
Steve Foster	-	-	-	-	-	-	-	-	-	0-1	-	-	-	1	0-1
Gary Green	-	-	-	-	0-1	-	-	-	-	-	-	-	1	-	0-1
Willie Greene	-	-	-	15-9	-	-	-	-	-	-	-	0-1	6	18	15-9
Chris Hammond	-	-	-	-	-	-	-	-	-	16-10	-	-	7	19	16-10
Billy Hatcher	-	-	-	-	-	11-9	-	-	-	-	-	0-1	15	5	11-9
Dwayne Henry	-	-	-	-	-	-	-	-	-	-	-	-	-	-	-
Cesar Hernandez	-	-	-	-	-	1-1	2-1	-	-	-	3-1	-	5	-	3-2
Milt Hill	-	-	-	-	-	-	-	-	-	-	-	-	-	-	-
Barry Larkin	-	-	-	-	78-62	-	-	-	-	-	-	-	57	83	78-62
Dave Martinez	-	8-9	-	-	-	2-1	44-32	1-1	-	-	4-5	-	3	95	55-43
Tony Menendez	-	-	-	-	-	-	-	-	-	-	-	-	-	-	-
Hal Morris	-	60-43	-	-	-	-	-	-	-	-	-	10-9	29	74	60-43
Joe Oliver	78-59	-	-	-	-	-	-	-	-	-	-	-	52	85	78-59
Paul O'Neill	-	-	-	-	-	-	-	79-55	-	-	-	42-27	35	99	79-55
Tim Pugh	-	-	-	-	-	-	-	-	-	4-3	-	-	2	5	4-3
Jeff Reed	2-3	-	-	-	-	-	-	-	-	-	-	-	-	5	2-3
Jose Rijo	-	-	-	-	-	-	-	-	-	18-15	-	-	10	23	18-15
Bip Roberts	-	-	15-16	13-16	-	39-23	8-3	-	-	-	72-57	0-1	42	91	75-58
Scott Ruskin	-	-	-	-	-	-	-	-	-	-	-	-	-	-	-
Chris Sabo	-	-	-	55-39	-	-	-	-	-	-	-	21-21	43	51	55-39
Reggie Sanders	-	-	-	-	-	13-13	35-35	-	-	-	10-7	6-2	49	47	48-48
Greg Swindell	-	-	-	-	-	-	-	-	-	16-14	-	-	10	20	16-14
Dan Wilson	2-3	-	-	-	-	-	-	-	-	-	-	-	1	4	2-3
Rick Wrona	2-3	-	-	-	-	-	-	-	-	-	-	-	1	4	2-3

TEAM TOTALS: BATTING

	AB	H	2B	3B	HR	RBI	BB	SO	BA	SA	OBA
Season	5460	1418	281	44	99	606	563	888	.260	.382	.328
vs. Left-Handers	2074	552	120	14	41	240	212	349	.266	.397	.334
vs. Right-Handers	3386	866	161	30	58	366	351	539	.256	.372	.325
vs. Ground-Ballers	2147	558	107	17	36	231	210	332	.260	.376	.324
vs. Fly-Ballers	3313	860	174	27	63	375	353	556	.260	.385	.332
Home Games	2625	687	146	18	60	327	291	422	.262	.400	.336
Road Games	2835	731	135	26	39	279	272	466	.258	.365	.322
Grass Fields	1675	429	77	16	20	158	139	278	.256	.357	.311
Artificial Turf	3785	989	204	28	79	448	424	610	.261	.393	.336
April	717	179	27	7	10	67	78	109	.250	.349	.324
May	892	231	51	9	13	109	101	155	.259	.380	.336
June	891	236	49	6	21	118	78	150	.265	.404	.322
July	906	238	48	7	16	91	95	138	.263	.384	.331
August	978	245	55	4	23	108	113	158	.251	.385	.327
Sept./Oct.	1076	289	51	11	16	113	98	178	.269	.381	.330
Leading Off Inn.	1322	361	58	13	28	28	118	210	.273	.400	.334
Runners On	2424	611	125	14	39	546	298	383	.252	.363	.330
Bases Empty	3036	807	156	30	60	60	265	505	.266	.396	.327
Runners/Scor. Pos.	1459	350	71	9	22	490	242	255	.240	.346	.341
Runners On/2 Out	994	218	45	7	16	201	132	170	.219	.327	.313
Scor. Pos./2 Out	675	149	29	5	11	179	114	121	.221	.327	.337
Late-Inning Pressure	715	190	40	6	9	89	82	138	.266	.376	.339
Leading Off	175	47	9	3	1	1	24	40	.269	.371	.357
Runners On	326	88	19	2	6	86	46	46	.270	.396	.355
Runners/Scor. Pos.	189	50	9	2	1	72	38	30	.265	.349	.378

RUNS BATTED IN	From 1B	From 2B	From 3B	Scoring Position
Totals	74/1729	173/1123	260/664	433/1787
Percentage	4.3%	15.4%	39.2%	24.2%

TEAM TOTALS: PITCHING

	W-L	ERA	AB	H	HR	BB	SO	BA	SA	OBA
Season	90-72	3.46	5419	1362	109	470	1060	.251	.375	.312
vs. Left-Handers			2156	562	39	238	421	.261	.391	.334
vs. Right-Handers			3263	800	70	232	639	.245	.365	.297
vs. Ground-Ballers			2338	584	34	193	484	.250	.352	.307
vs. Fly-Ballers			3081	778	75	277	576	.253	.393	.316
Home Games	53-28	3.11	2753	666	60	232	565	.242	.368	.302
Road Games	37-44	3.83	2666	696	49	238	495	.261	.383	.322
Grass Fields	22-26	3.76	1591	419	30	145	277	.263	.388	.326
Artificial Turf	68-46	3.34	3828	943	79	325	783	.246	.370	.306
April	11-10	3.95	725	185	13	64	154	.255	.382	.314
May	15-11	3.40	874	213	15	84	167	.244	.348	.311
June	18-9	3.53	894	226	21	70	175	.253	.391	.309
July	15-12	3.07	900	240	19	87	148	.264	.399	.328
August	12-17	4.08	971	249	26	70	209	.256	.398	.308
Sept./Oct.	19-13	2.91	1047	249	15	95	207	.238	.339	.304
Leading Off Inn.			1346	339	38	102	228	.252	.401	.307
Bases Empty			3203	782	62	240	618	.244	.363	.299
Runners On			2216	580	47	230	442	.262	.393	.329
Runners/Scor. Pos.			1274	324	27	170	286	.254	.387	.335
Runners On/2 Out			944	212	16	111	209	.225	.340	.311
Scor. Pos./2 Out			616	132	9	86	151	.214	.325	.314
Late-Inning Pressure			853	203	22	89	230	.238	.366	.312
Leading Off			224	59	8	16	57	.263	.438	.315
Runners On			332	89	9	48	79	.268	.404	.357
Runners/Scor. Pos.			214	51	6	38	59	.238	.379	.346
First 9 Batters			2867	680	51	280	646	.237	.348	.307
Second 9 Batters			1373	364	31	87	244	.265	.396	.310
All Batters Thereafter			1179	318	27	103	170	.270	.417	.326

COLORADO ROCKIES

Baseball fans love to talk about ballparks: Fenway Park's Green Monster, Wrigley's ivy-covered walls, Yankee Stadium's death valley, Mount Rainier rising beyond the center field fence at Seattle's Sicks Stadium. There was a time, it seemed, when each major league ballpark had an idiosyncrasy or two that made it unique and reassuringly familiar. But over the past 20 years, as the familiar nooks and crannies of parks like Forbes Field and Crosley Field have given way to impersonal structural clones like Three Rivers Stadium and Riverfront Stadium, many fans shifted their attention to differences that are statistical instead of physical—measured instead of felt. A new kind of ballpark discussion has sprung up: the effect of a player's home field on his performance.

The proliferation of analytical statistics such as those found in the *Analyst*'s Ballparks Section has fueled the discussion to such a point that no analysis of a trade seems complete without a reference to the benefits or disadvantages of the players' new home stadiums. And why not? After all, some players have taken extreme advantage of their home surroundings. For instance, Wade Boggs has a career batting average more than 60 points higher at Fenway Park (.369) than anywhere else (.307). Mel Ott was a good power hitter on the road, but it was the Polo Grounds, with its right-field seats just 257 feet from home plate, that made him one of the greatest home-run hitters in major league history; Ott's total of 323 home runs at the Polo Grounds is the highest ever by any player at one stadium.

Ever since the Colorado Rockies were awarded a major league franchise, power hitters—seduced by tales of 500-foot home runs by wannabes like Joey Meyer and John Jaha of the Triple-A Denver Zephyrs—have drooled in anticipation of launching moon balls into the light air at Mile High Stadium. Imagine if they also knew that, before he became baseball's most lovable buffoon and light beer spokesman, Marv Throneberry was considered one of the hottest prospects in baseball based on three consecutive seasons as the American Assocation home-run and RBI champion while playing in Denver (1955–57); and that the Denver team has led its league in home runs nine times in the past 20 years, with seven individual home-run leaders during that time (Cliff Johnson, Roger Freed, Frank Ortenzio, Randy Bass, Lloyd McClendon, Brad Komminsk, and Greg Vaughn).

A year from now, we'll be able to check the 1994 Ballparks Section for a clue about how great an effect Denver's altitude has on home runs. But for the time being, and in the absence of comprehensive baseball statistics, it seemed logical to examine some other sports to gauge whether the altitude effect has been exaggerated. Our findings were consistent with the notion that even Roger Maris's record of 61 home runs in a season might not be safe when major league baseball debuts a mile above sea level.

First, a little football history: Prior to 1969, there had been only two field goals in NFL history of 55 yards or longer: one by Bert Rechichar of the Baltimore Colts in 1953, the other—technically not an NFL field goal—by George Blanda of the AFL's Houston Oilers in 1961. (After further review, we'll allow that one.)

But since 1969, longer and more accurate kickers with a totally different style have nailed 33 field goals of at least 55 yards. What's truly remarkable is that eight of them have been kicked at Mile High Stadium. Think about that for a moment: From 1969 through 1992, there were more than 4700 NFL games played outside of Denver, producing only 25 long-distance field goals. During that same period, nearly one-quarter of all 55-yard field goals were kicked in fewer than 200 regular-season games at Mile High Stadium:

Site	Games	FG / Rate
Mile High Stadium	180	8 / One every 23 games
Other Stadiums	4734	25 / One every 189 games

Denver's own kickers had little impact on those figures. The Broncos have had some pretty accurate kickers over the years, including Bobby Howfield, Jim Turner, and Rich Karlis. But the only long-distance threat to wear the Orange and Blue was Fred Steinfort, and he lasted just two seasons with Denver in the early 1980s. No, this trend has little to do with Denver's kickers, and everything to do with its altitude. (Keep that in mind the next time you watch a team run its two-minute drill at Mile High Stadium. Once they move inside their opponents' 40-yard line, they're in field-goal range.)

Denver's punters have benefited greatly, too. The Broncos have had eight punters in their 33-year history who made at least 100 kicks. Every one of them had a higher average in Denver than he had elsewhere, by margins ranging from a little more than two yards per kick by their first punter, George Herring, to more than four yards per punt by Luke Prestridge:

Punter	Home	Road	Diff.
George Herring	40.0	37.9	+2.1
James Fraser	45.2	43.1	+2.1
Bob Scarpitto	45.5	43.2	+2.3
Bill Van Heusen	43.0	40.5	+2.5
Bucky Dilts	39.3	36.2	+3.1
Luke Prestridge	44.1	39.9	+4.2
Chris Norman	42.3	38.2	+4.1
Mike Horan	44.5	40.6	+3.9

And that's not simply a traditional home-field advantage: Over more than 30 years of play, the Broncos' opponents also have a higher average in Denver (43.3) than they have when hosting the Broncos (41.1).

One of the NFL's most durable records is Sammy Baugh's average of 51.4 yards per punt, set more than 50 years ago in 1940. No punter has come within even five yards of that mark since Gary Collins of the Browns did it—and just barely—28 years ago (46.7). Who knows if Slingin' Sammy's record will ever be broken? But if the record does fall, there's a good chance it will be surpassed by a punter for the Denver Broncos. And while it may be some time before the Rockies have a chance to develop some legitimate prospects of their own, the unique conditions in Denver make Coors Field—Colorado's home of the future—the most likely site for the next assault on Maris's sixty-one.

Another noteworthy Broncos trend: They have the greatest home-field advantage in the NFL. Since 1980,

Denver has posted the league's best regular-season record in home games despite a road-game record 10 games below the .500 mark. The difference between Denver's winning percentage at home and on the road is 306 percentage points, the largest in the NFL. The following table shows the five largest home-field advantages since 1980:

Team	Home Games			Road Games			Diff.
	W	L	Pct.	W	L	Pct.	
Denver Broncos	76	25	.752	42	56	.429	+.323
Houston Oilers	60	40	.600	32	68	.320	+.280
Kansas City Chiefs	62	37	.626	35	64	.356	+.270
Pittsburgh Steelers	64	35	.646	40	61	.396	+.250
Buffalo Bills	66	35	.653	40	59	.404	+.249

That might be a coincidence, but the following table strongly suggests that it's not. You see, the same situation exists in the NBA, where the Denver Nuggets, for the 10-year period ending with the 1991–92 season, also had the greatest margin between home and road records. The Broncos were the only NFL team with a margin as great as 300 points; and the Nuggets were the only NBA team with a margin of 400 points:

Team	Home Games			Road Games			Diff.
	W	L	Pct.	W	L	Pct.	
Denver Nuggets	284	126	.693	120	290	.293	+.400
Utah Jazz	312	98	.761	152	258	.371	+.390
Phoenix Suns	295	115	.720	148	262	.361	+.359
Seattle SuperSonics	279	131	.680	132	278	.322	+.358
Portland Trail Blazers	320	90	.780	176	234	.429	+.351

Guess which cities rank 1–2–3 in elevation among NBA locales? Is it coincidental that it's Denver (5280 feet), Salt Lake City (4260), and Phoenix (1090)? Okay, Phoenix may be a stretch, since it's barely in third place in differential and in altitude. (Atlanta is next at 1050.) But the others?

These figures remind us that an acquaintance who lived in Denver for many years once explained that whenever his family took a vacation, they needed a few days to get acclimated to the lower altitude. Which raises the question: Do the huge margins between the home and road winning percentages reflect the inability of opposing teams to play to their potential in Denver? Or is it that the Broncos and Nuggets find it difficult to cope with life at sea level?

There is some evidence that the latter is true—that the statistical home-field advantage may be more accurately described as a large road-field disadvantage. If that were the case—that the Nuggets, for example, had more trouble playing on the road than their opponents had in Denver—their road-game winning percentage would be worst early in a road trip. The reasoning is simple: As the trip progressed, the Nuggets would presumably become more physically acclimated to the thicker air down below. And frankly, we're not sure how to interpret the figures that appear below. The "Early Games" are road games played either one or two days after the teams' last home game; "Later Games" are all other road games. The combined totals for Denver and Utah support the "road-field disadvantage" theory. But if we look only at the Nuggets, the trend disappears; the Jazz alone are responsible for the overall trend:

Team	Early Games		Late Games		Diff.
Denver Nuggets	44–113	.280	75–176	.299	+.019
Utah Jazz	47–100	.320	104–152	.406	+.086
Totals	91–213	.299	179–328	.353	+.054
Other Teams	1128–2276	.331	1990–3621	.355	+.024

If we redefine the categories slightly, so that early games include any games played less than a week since the teams' last home game, a similar but frustratingly paradoxical pattern appears:

Team	Early Games		Late Games		Diff.
Denver Nuggets	93–245	.275	26–44	.371	+.096
Utah Jazz	123–207	.373	28–45	.384	+.011
Totals	216–452	.323	54–89	.378	+.055
Other Teams	2554–4947	.340	564–944	.374	+.034

Once again, the combined totals for Denver and Utah show a much greater early-game disadvantage than those of other teams. But this time, it's the Nuggets who are wholly responsible. Our best guess is this: Close your eyes to the details, and look at the big picture. The Nuggets and Jazz have the widest disparities in the NBA between their home and road performance. But when the two teams are considered together, the difference is significantly greater during the early part of any road trip than it is later in the trip, suggesting that the altitude effect represents more a disadvantage on the road than an advantage at home.

FLORIDA MARLINS

In the rush to judgment following last November's expansion draft, labels were affixed to the Marlins and the Rockies with the speed of a garment-district sweatshop. The draft wasn't a half-hour old before the Marlins were branded "the team of the future," and the Rockies were judged to be putting "the best team possible" on the field in 1993. Remember, this was based on *the first three or four picks for each team*. In the days that followed, the media seemed incapable of choosing between two mutually exclusive scenarios, so they reported both—often in the same report: No one, it seemed, could resist compiling what some went so far as to call "projected starting lineups," based only on draft-day selections; still, most reminded us that the rosters would be significantly different by opening day on account of inevitable trades, additions of free agents, and so on. But fans scanning this season's Rockies and Marlins box scores for clues about their future might do better to stick to tea leaves. Four previous expansions that gave birth to 10 teams have proven that the first-year rosters of new teams provide few clues to their success, either short- or long-term.

That's not to say that none of the players who appeared for past expansion teams in their inaugural seasons achieved success. Actually, you could put together a pretty fair ball club based solely on those first-year rosters:

Starting Pitchers: Dean Chance, Jim Clancy, Joe Niekro, Claude Osteen, and Steve Renko.
Relief Pitchers: Tom Burgmeier, Dave Giusti, Ron Kline, Mike Marshall, and Don McMahon.
Starting Lineup: Nate Colbert (1B), Julio Cruz (2B), Bob Bailey (3B), Jim Fregosi (SS), Lou Piniella (LF), Ruppert Jones (CF), Rusty Staub (RF), Ernie Whitt (C), and Leon Wagner (DH).
Bench: Bob Aspromonte, Ed Brinkman, Rick Cerone, Ed Kranepool, Jerry Morales, and Craig Reynolds.

That's a 25-man roster that could have done some serious damage a few decades ago. But let's be realistic: It represents the best of the talent culled by all the expansion teams in four different seasons. No one team could ever have had the foresight or the luck to grab more than a handful of them. (And four of them weren't expansion-draft picks at all: McMahon, Niekro, and Osteen were acquired in midseason deals; Kranepool was signed by the Mets out of high school during their first season.)

But to return to our original point: The performance of past teams in their infancy provided no indication of their successes or failures down the road. The Mets posted the worst first-year record (40–120), but became the quickest to win a World Series. The Angels had the best inaugural season (70–91) and topped the .500 mark quickest, just a year later with an 86–76 record—a mark they didn't surpass until 16 years later. And before you conclude that there's an inverse relationship—the poorer the first year, the better the prognosis—note that the only other team to play above .400 in its first season, the Kansas City Royals, was enormously successful within 10 years. Here are the 10 expansion teams, ranked by their first-season records,

along with the number of seasons they took to reach .500 and to win their first title, and their average winning percentages for years 6 through 10 and years 11 through 15:

Year	Team	First Season W–L	Pct.	First .500	First Title	Years 6–10	Years 11–15
1961	Los Angeles Angels	70–91	.435	2	19	.475	.462
1969	Kansas City Royals	69–93	.426	3	8	.568	.529
1962	Houston Colt .45s	64–96	.400	8	19	.494	.480
1977	Seattle Mariners	64–98	.395	15	—	.436	.451
1969	Seattle Pilots	64–98	.395	10	13	.481	.528
1961	Washington Senators	61–100	.379	9	—	.447	.437
1977	Toronto Blue Jays	54–107	.335	7	9	.567	.554
1969	San Diego Padres	52–110	.321	10	16	.451	.478
1969	Montreal Expos	52–110	.321	11	13	.466	.527
1962	New York Mets	40–120	.250	8	8	.525	.476

If you see any pattern there, well, we know a fine ophthalmologist who can squeeze you in on Thursday at three. There just isn't any link between how Colorado and Florida will perform this season and what they'll accomplish over the next 5 to 15 years.

It is worth noting, however, that in the long run, the expansion teams with young first-year pitching staffs have outperformed those with older pitchers by a wide margin. The following table ranks the 10 expansion teams from youngest to oldest (with each pitcher contributing to the team average in proportion to the number of innings he pitched). Note that with the exception of the Padres, the general rule prevails: the younger the better. The winning percentages listed below are for years 6 through 15:

Year	Team	Age	Pct.	Year	Team	Age	Pct.
1969	Padres	25.2	.465	1961	Angels	27.8	.468
1969	Royals	25.7	.549	1969	Pilots	28.7	.505
1977	Blue Jays	26.4	.561	1977	Mariners	28.9	.443
1962	Mets	27.1	.500	1962	Colt .45s	29.1	.487
1969	Expos	27.1	.496	1961	Senators	29.7	.442

The difference between the average winning percentage for the five youngest teams (.514) and the five oldest teams (.469) is significant—equivalent to an average of seven wins per team per season. The odd part is that the trend has little or nothing to do with the actual pitchers from each team's first season: Only one pitcher who threw 100 innings for a first-year team did so for that same team more than five years later: Steve Renko for the Expos. In fact, only four others who pitched 100 innings for expansion teams in year 6 pitched for them *at all* in year 1: Dean Chance for the Angels, Dave Giusti for the Colts/Astros, Al Fitzmorris for the Royals, and Jim Clancy for the Blue Jays; they combined for 180 innings in year 1. But the marked difference in success between expansion teams with young staffs and those with older pitchers suggests a difference in philosophy that translates into success or failure over a period of time.

A noteworthy example that we've cited before: During their first seven years of operation, the Mets carefully guarded any pitcher in their system who showed even a glimmer of major league potential. That strategy paid off by the late 1960s, when the Mets flaunted one of the finest young starting rotations in history. But until June 1969, when they dealt the promising minor leaguer Renko (who eventually won 134 games during a 15-year major league career), only one of the 22 pitchers whom New York traded subsequently won even 25 games in his career. And the exception, Bob Miller, was a journeyman reliever who compiled a losing record for other teams after leaving the Mets (57–58).

Just as impressive as the accuracy with which three different Mets general managers identified the 22 discarded pitchers is the loot they were able to extract in return for them. It may have been crystal clear to George Weiss, Bing Devine, and Johnny Murphy that pitchers like Tom Parsons, Dennis Ribant, Jack Fisher, and Billy Wynne had little potential, but that surely wasn't true of their colleagues around the majors. Those pitchers alone brought the Mets Jerry Grote (for Parsons), Don Cardwell (in a 2-for-2 deal for Ribant), and Tommie Agee and Al Weis (for Fisher, Wynne, and Tommy Davis)—all of them key ingredients in their 1969 championship season. The Mets even acquired the manager who led them to their first Series title, Gil Hodges, by surrendering pitcher Bill Denehy to the Washington Senators as part of a settlement; Denehy never won another game in the majors.

The Mets separated the potential haves (like Seaver, Koosman, Gentry, McGraw, McAndrew, and Ryan) from the have-nots with unerring accuracy. And only when the front office saw an opportunity to acquire a player who might help win a pennant did they part with a pitcher of Renko's potential. Of course, they were right even in that judgment: The player they acquired for Renko was World Series MVP Donn Clendenon.

For an example of the opposite approach, look no further than the Seattle Mariners, the most unsuccessful of the 10 expansion teams, with only one winning record in 16 years of play. (It's worth noting here that there was no relationship between the age of a team's position players and its future success or lack thereof.) The 1977 Mariners had five rookie regulars—Ruppert Jones, Craig Reynolds, Jose Baez, Carlos Lopez, and Juan Bernhardt—in a lineup that was the youngest in the American League. On the other hand, their pitching staff, while hardly ancient, had no regular contributor under the age of 25; it was the 11th-oldest staff in a 14-team league. As for a commitment to develop a young pitching staff within the organization, it was nonexistent. At age 39, Diego Segui was their opening-day starter and made 40 appearances despite an 0–7 record. Before the end of 1982, the Mariners had traded Rick Honeycutt, Bud Black, and Shane Rawley, and lost Floyd Bannister to free agency. Meanwhile, seduced by the availability of veteran sluggers on the free-agent market, Seattle signed aging Willie Horton and the ultimately forgettable Bruce Bochte. The Mariners also made a series of trades for declining players with 30–home run pedigrees, forsaking their own younger talent, like Ruppert Jones, in its wake.

By 1979, Seattle's third season of operation, the Mariners had spun around by 180 degrees: The Mariners had a staff of promising young pitchers that would soon be dismantled in an effort to restock their suddenly aging and unproductive lineup. A streak of 14 consecutive seasons without a winning record? There's the recipe in a nutshell.

Only two players on first-year teams led their leagues in major batting or pitching categories: Dick Donovan of the 1961 Washington Senators led the American League in earned run average (2.40), and Tommy Harper of the 1969 Seattle Pilots led the A.L. in stolen bases (73). With those diminished expectations in mind, here are some leaders lists made up only of first-year expansion-team players:

Batting Average: Bob Bailor, Blue Jays, .310; Rusty Staub, Expos, .302; Albie Pearson, Angels, .288; Roman Mejias, Colt .45s, .286; Lee Thomas, Angels, .284.
Home Runs: Frank Thomas, Mets, 34; Rusty Staub, Expos, 29; Leon Wagner, Angels, 28; Leroy Stanton, Mariners, 27; Ken Hunt, Angels, and Don Mincher, Pilots, 25.
Runs Batted In: Frank Thomas, Mets, 94; Dan Meyer, Mariners, and Leroy Stanton, Mariners, 90; Ken Hunt, Angels, 84; Coco Laboy, Expos, 83.
Runs: Albie Pearson, Angels, 92; Rusty Staub, Expos, 89; Wayne Comer, Pilots, 88; Ruppert Jones, Mariners, 85; Roman Mejias, Colt .45s, 82.
Hits: Rusty Staub, Expos, 166; Roman Mejias, Colt .45s, 162; Dan Meyer, Mariners, 159; Ruppert Jones, Mariners, 157; Bob Bailor, Blue Jays, 154.
Doubles: Danny O'Connell, Senators, 30; Tommy Davis, Pilots, Ken Hunt, Angels, and Coco Laboy, Expos, 29; Ruppert Jones, Mariners, Rusty Staub, Expos, Bill Stein, Mariners, and Gary Sutherland, Expos, 26.
Triples: Nate Colbert, Padres, Marty Keough, Senators, Charlie Neal, Mets, and Al Spangler, Colt .45s, 9; Ruppert Jones, Mariners, and Merritt Ranew, Colt .45s, 8.
Bases on Balls: Rusty Staub, Expos, 110; Albie Pearson, Angels, 96; Tommy Harper, Pilots, 95; Mike Fiore, Royals, 84; Wayne Comer, Pilots, 82.
Stolen Bases: Tommy Harper, Pilots, 73; Pat Kelly, Royals, 40; Joe Foy, Royals, 37; Dave Collins, Mariners, 25; Chuck Hinton, Senators, 22.

Wins: Gene Brabender, Pilots, and Dave Lemanczyk, Blue Jays, 13; Diego Segui, Pilots, Wally Bunker, Royals, Bennie Daniels, Senators, Glenn Abbott, Mariners, and Ken McBride, Angels, 12.
Earned Run Average: Dick Donovan, Senators, 2.40; Dick Farrell, Colt .45s, 3.01; Wally Bunker, Royals, 3.23; Roger Nelson, Royals, 3.31; Bennie Daniels, Senators, 3.44.
Complete Games: Roger Craig, Mets, and Jay Hook, Mets, 13; Al Jackson, Mets, Jerry Garvin, Blue Jays, and Bennie Daniels, Senators, 12.
Shutouts: Bill Stoneman, Expos, 5; Al Jackson, Mets, and Bill Butler, Royals, 4; Joe Niekro, Padres, 3; seven pitchers tied with 2.
Saves: Enrique Romo, Mariners, 16; Diego Segui, Pilots, 12; Moe Drabowsky, Royals, Dave Sisler, Senators, and Art Fowler, Angels, 11. (Sisler and Fowler are based on the unofficial, pre-1969 saves figures listed in the *Baseball Encyclopedia*.)
Strikeouts: Dick Farrell, Colt .45s, 203; Bill Stoneman, Expos, 185; Ken McBride, Angels, 180; Ken Johnson, Colt .45s, 178; Bill Butler, Royals, 156.

WON-LOST RECORD BY STARTING POSITION

Houston Astros	C	1B	2B	3B	SS	LF	CF	RF	DH	P	Leadoff	Cleanup	Starts vs. LH	Starts vs. RH	Total Starts
Eric Anthony	-	-	-	-	-	-	-	55-55	-	-	-	19-30	40	70	55-55
Jeff Bagwell	-	77-80	-	-	-	-	-	-	-	-	-	43-30	64	93	77-80
Craig Biggio	-	-	79-78	-	-	-	-	-	-	-	79-77	-	63	94	79-78
Willie Blair	-	-	-	-	-	-	-	-	-	3-5	-	-	2	6	3-5
Joe Boever	-	-	-	-	-	-	-	-	-	-	-	-	-	-	-
Ryan Bowen	-	-	-	-	-	-	-	-	-	2-7	-	-	3	6	2-7
Ken Caminiti	-	-	-	66-62	-	-	-	-	-	-	-	-	54	74	66-62
Casey Candaele	-	-	1-3	10-14	18-23	2-3	-	-	-	-	-	1-1	31	43	31-43
Andujar Cedeno	-	-	-	-	37-32	-	-	-	-	-	-	-	25	44	37-32
Benny Distefano	-	2-0	-	-	-	2-1	0-2	-	-	-	-	-	-	7	4-3
Steve Finley	-	-	-	-	-	-	76-77	-	-	-	1-3	-	56	97	76-77
Luis Gonzalez	-	-	-	-	-	50-46	-	-	-	-	-	12-10	16	80	50-46
Juan Guerrero	-	-	2-4	9-6	0-1	-	-	-	-	-	-	-	8	14	11-11
Pete Harnisch	-	-	-	-	-	-	-	-	-	20-14	-	-	20	14	20-14
Butch Henry	-	-	-	-	-	-	-	-	-	14-14	-	-	9	19	14-14
Xavier Hernandez	-	-	-	-	-	-	-	-	-	-	-	-	-	-	-
Pete Incaviglia	-	-	-	-	-	24-25	-	20-22	-	-	-	7-11	54	37	44-47
Chris Jones	-	-	-	-	-	3-4	0-1	2-0	-	-	-	-	9	1	5-5
Doug Jones	-	-	-	-	-	-	-	-	-	-	-	-	-	-	-
Jimmy Jones	-	-	-	-	-	-	-	-	-	11-12	-	-	10	13	11-12
Darryl Kile	-	-	-	-	-	-	-	-	-	8-14	-	-	8	14	8-14
Rob Mallicoat	-	-	-	-	-	-	-	-	-	-	-	-	-	-	-
Rob Murphy	-	-	-	-	-	-	-	-	-	-	-	-	-	-	-
Al Osuna	-	-	-	-	-	-	-	-	-	-	-	-	-	-	-
Mark Portugal	-	-	-	-	-	-	-	-	-	11-5	-	-	5	11	11-5
Rafael Ramirez	-	-	-	17-20	-	-	-	-	-	-	-	-	17	20	17-20
Shane Reynolds	-	-	-	-	-	-	-	-	-	2-3	-	-	1	4	2-3
Karl Rhodes	-	-	-	-	-	-	-	-	-	-	-	-	-	-	-
Ernest Riles	-	2-1	1-0	3-1	-	-	-	-	-	-	-	-	-	8	6-2
Rich Scheid	-	-	-	-	-	-	-	-	-	0-1	-	-	-	1	0-1
Scott Servais	31-28	-	-	-	-	-	-	-	-	-	-	-	49	10	31-28
Mike Simms	-	-	-	-	-	-	-	4-2	-	-	-	-	4	2	4-2
Eddie Taubensee	42-46	-	-	-	-	-	-	-	-	-	-	-	7	81	42-46
Eddie Tucker	8-7	-	-	-	-	-	-	-	-	-	-	-	8	7	8-7
Denny Walling	-	-	-	-	-	-	-	-	-	-	-	-	-	-	-
Brian Williams	-	-	-	-	-	-	-	-	-	10-6	-	-	6	10	10-6
Eric Yelding	-	-	-	-	-	-	-	-	-	-	-	-	-	-	-
Gerald Young	-	-	-	-	-	0-1	5-3	-	-	-	-	-	7	2	5-4

TEAM TOTALS: BATTING

	AB	H	2B	3B	HR	RBI	BB	SO	BA	SA	OBA
Season	5480	1350	255	38	96	582	506	1025	.246	.359	.313
vs. Left-Handers	2035	522	105	15	39	233	222	368	.257	.380	.331
vs. Right-Handers	3445	828	150	23	57	349	284	657	.240	.347	.303
vs. Ground-Ballers	2379	598	97	20	35	252	216	409	.251	.353	.318
vs. Fly-Ballers	3101	752	158	18	61	330	290	616	.243	.364	.310
Home Games	2733	685	145	22	49	288	275	540	.251	.374	.323
Road Games	2747	665	110	16	47	294	231	485	.242	.345	.304
Grass Fields	1634	402	57	6	26	173	130	279	.246	.336	.305
Artificial Turf	3846	948	198	32	70	409	376	746	.246	.369	.317
April	695	155	30	5	11	55	52	173	.223	.328	.281
May	960	226	52	3	13	95	79	178	.235	.336	.299
June	929	238	45	10	19	120	102	171	.256	.388	.332
July	856	208	34	10	17	80	78	138	.243	.366	.307
August	982	248	42	6	16	116	96	155	.253	.356	.322
Sept./Oct.	1058	275	52	4	20	116	99	210	.260	.373	.327
Leading Off Inn.	1354	342	69	7	23	23	110	244	.253	.365	.313
Runners On	2341	578	107	17	41	527	259	436	.247	.360	.323
Bases Empty	3139	772	148	21	55	55	247	589	.246	.359	.306
Runners/Scor. Pos.	1387	318	52	9	19	442	204	304	.229	.321	.326
Runners On/2 Out	976	213	38	5	17	181	124	203	.218	.320	.315
Scor. Pos./2 Out	649	129	20	4	10	157	108	158	.199	.288	.323
Late-Inning Pressure	942	248	40	4	28	114	113	175	.263	.403	.343
Leading Off	242	65	8	0	7	7	20	43	.269	.388	.327
Runners On	391	108	16	2	14	100	63	77	.276	.435	.374
Runners/Scor. Pos.	238	63	8	2	8	82	57	57	.265	.416	.401

RUNS BATTED IN	From 1B	From 2B	From 3B	Scoring Position
Totals	89/1619	161/1094	236/605	397/1699
Percentage	5.5%	14.7%	39.0%	23.4%

TEAM TOTALS: PITCHING

	W-L	ERA	AB	H	HR	BB	SO	BA	SA	OBA
Season	81-81	3.72	5502	1386	114	539	978	.252	.378	.320
vs. Left-Handers			2699	702	49	314	440	.260	.384	.339
vs. Right-Handers			2803	684	65	225	538	.244	.373	.303
vs. Ground-Ballers			2612	665	33	232	470	.255	.352	.317
vs. Fly-Ballers			2890	721	81	307	508	.249	.402	.323
Home Games	47-34	3.04	2843	673	41	269	539	.237	.331	.306
Road Games	34-47	4.47	2659	713	73	270	439	.268	.428	.336
Grass Fields	20-28	4.36	1572	415	44	165	278	.264	.422	.334
Artificial Turf	61-53	3.47	3930	971	70	374	700	.247	.361	.315
April	10-11	2.78	709	163	10	80	146	.230	.326	.308
May	11-17	4.46	938	235	23	108	156	.251	.391	.330
June	14-14	3.82	934	245	17	96	148	.262	.388	.334
July	11-14	3.17	882	226	15	71	138	.256	.372	.314
August	15-14	3.92	981	253	30	81	181	.258	.410	.315
Sept./Oct.	20-11	3.89	1058	264	19	103	209	.250	.370	.319
Leading Off Inn.			1338	358	27	113	220	.268	.395	.329
Bases Empty			3066	784	63	280	543	.256	.383	.322
Runners On			2436	602	51	259	435	.247	.372	.318
Runners/Scor. Pos.			1431	347	27	202	279	.242	.361	.331
Runners On/2 Out			1003	202	23	123	196	.201	.323	.294
Scor. Pos./2 Out			662	141	15	102	132	.213	.337	.322
Late-Inning Pressure			897	217	16	80	177	.242	.353	.310
Leading Off			229	62	4	21	41	.271	.380	.345
Runners On			390	75	5	38	75	.192	.274	.268
Runners/Scor. Pos.			207	44	1	31	42	.213	.280	.308
First 9 Batters			3139	769	51	335	599	.245	.350	.320
Second 9 Batters			1340	322	35	117	235	.240	.380	.303
All Batters Thereafter			1023	295	28	87	144	.288	.462	.345

HOUSTON ASTROS

The past off-season produced the wildest scramble for high-quality free-agent pitchers since Catfish Hunter presaged the coming of the free-agent era by signing with the Yankees following the 1974 season. By the conclusion of the winter meetings in December, no fewer than nine pitchers who ranked among their league's top 10s in wins or ERA had already changed teams, with two of them joining Houston:

Player, Team	W–L	ERA	New Team	Age
Jim Abbott, Cal.	7–15	2.77	Yankees	25
Chris Bosio, Mil	16–6	3.62	Mariners	30
Doug Drabek, Pit.	15–11	2.77	Astros	30
Jose Guzman, Tex.	16–11	3.66	Cubs	29
Charlie Leibrandt, Atl.	15–7	3.36	Rangers	36
Greg Maddux, Cubs	20–11	2.18	Braves	26
Mike Moore, Oak.	17–12	4.12	Tigers	33
John Smiley, Min.	16–9	3.21	Reds	28
Greg Swindell, Cin.	12–8	2.70	Astros	28

And that chart doesn't even include David Cone, who ranked among the top-10 winners in the majors (17–10, 2.81), but failed to make the list in either league because he split his time between the Mets and Blue Jays. (For the record, Cone will be a 30-year-old member of the Kansas City Royals this season.) Not since the winter after the 1915 season—when the Federal League folded and its refugees scrambled for jobs in the American and National Leagues—have as many leading pitchers changed teams.

Just as unusual as the number of top-shelf pitchers who joined new teams this past winter were the ages at which they became available. Five will still be in their twenties on opening day 1993 (assuming it takes place on schedule), and two others will be 30. Only Moore and Leibrandt can be considered "past peak"—and even that's a difficult argument to make in light of their respective 17- and 15-win seasons in 1992. The following table summarizes the ages of all top-10 pitchers who changed teams during the free-agent era (that is, since 1975) at the time of their first start for their new teams. (The figures do not include the pitchers listed above.) More than two-thirds (32 of 47) were 30 or older. In fact, more than half (29) were older, at the time, than Drabek, one of the older pitchers listed above:

<25	25	26	27	28	29	30	31	32	33	34	35	36	37	38	39	40+
1	1	1	5	3	4	5	5	2	5	5	3	2	1	1	1	2

The age of the pitchers who changed teams this December (all via free agency except for Abbott and Leibrandt) is probably the primary factor in the length of the contracts they received. For the past few years, even the most free-spending teams were reluctant to offer contracts longer than three years to any but the best pitchers. (Roger Clemens and Dwight Gooden are examples of those who rated longer-term deals.) All the free agents listed above received four-year deals, with the exception of Maddux, who got a five-year contract, and Moore, who signed on for only three years. (Cone also signed for only three years, and will have to console himself with his nine-million-dollar up-front payment.) The lengthy commitments and the financial levels lavished on these pitchers—none will receive less than three million dollars per season over the life

of his contract—raises the issue of how long these pitchers can be expected to start regularly for their new employers.

Our projection model provides a clear indication of why teams should be hesitant to make long-term commitments to free-agent pitchers, and calls into question the wisdom of the past off-season's deals. Let's focus first on Drabek, who signed a four-year deal for nearly five million dollars a year. The following table shows the pitchers with the most similar statistical profiles. All were 30 years old at the conclusion of the listed seasons, with the exception of Candelaria, who missed by a month:

Year	Player	GS	W	L	ERA	GS	W	L	IP	H	ERA
1992	Doug Drabek	34	15	11	2.77	217	99	70	1494	1353	3.11
1963	Billy O'Dell	33	14	10	3.16	177	77	76	1420	1322	3.16
1973	Nellie Briles	33	14	13	2.84	192	97	82	1521	1495	3.25
1973	Jerry Koosman	35	14	15	2.84	181	79	68	1331	1168	2.87
1983	John Candelaria	32	15	8	3.23	243	110	69	1614	1502	3.14
1991	Jimmy Key	33	16	12	3.05	217	103	68	1479	1419	3.41

The comparisons are based on a broader spectrum of categories than those shown in the table. And the projections under discussion are based on the future career tracks of many other similar pitchers; the more like Drabek, the more they contribute to the projection. The question is this: How many pitchers with profiles similar to Drabek's made 30 starts three years later? A recent pitcher like Key provides no clue to what lies three years down the road. Briles and Koosman started 31 and 32 games, respectively, three years later. Candelaria spent 13 weeks on the disabled list and made only 16 starts. O'Dell had an effective season for the Braves and Pirates—but as a relief pitcher. Among other pitchers who contributed to the formulation of Drabek's most likely path, some, like Warren Spahn, Gaylord Perry, and Rick Reuschel, pitched effectively into their 40s. But others, like Steve Blass and Orel Hershiser, saw their careers curtailed within three years after the point of comparison.

Those are sobering facts for a team that has spent nearly five million dollars annually for at least four years. All things considered, Drabek appears to have only a 40 percent chance of starting at least 30 games in 1995. And that figure drops to 30 percent in 1996, the final season of his new contract. And the news is no better for most of the other pitchers in new uniforms for '93. Here's how Drabek and the others look with regard to their chances of starting 30 or more games a year over the lives of their new contracts, including Cone (who didn't qualify according to the strict criteria outlined earlier), and excluding Abbott (who has two years remaining on his current deal) and Leibrandt (one year to go):

Pitcher	1993	1994	1995	1996	1997
Chris Bosio	53%	40%	29%	22%	
David Cone	77%	58%	45%		
Doug Drabek	50%	46%	40%	30%	
Jose Guzman	58%	41%	32%	26%	
Greg Maddux	67%	63%	62%	48%	30%
Mike Moore	35%	27%	18%		
John Smiley	62%	47%	38%	35%	
Greg Swindell	69%	47%	38%	34%	

Not one of the eight is likely to make 30 starts in the final season of his new contract. Only Cone is likely to do so in the *next-to-last* year of his new deal. (But, of course, Cone was the only one to sign a three-year deal. It's amazing what you can buy for nine million up-front dollars these days.) These projections may seem unreasonably pessimistic, but even in the case of Maddux, the incumbent Cy Young winner and jewel of the 1993 free-agent crop (among pitchers, that is), there are many individual instances of comparable pitchers who went down with injuries the very next season. Have you forgotten how Bret Saberhagen and Mark Gubicza won a total of just nine games in 36 starts for the Royals in 1989? Guzman and Swindell have both suffered serious injuries to their throwing arms in the past—in Guzman's case, serious enough to keep him off the mound for two full years. It seems almost ludicrous, given the cries about the current state of baseball's finances, that any warnings against such spending should be necessary. But it's almost inevitable that among this past off-season's most expensive free agents, at least a few will be collecting millions of dollars by the mid-1990s and providing their teams with little return on their investments. Forget "Baseball Fever/ Catch It"—the national pastime's slogan ought to be *Caveat emptor.*

Have you ever seen an episode of the old *Twilight Zone* series entitled "Steel"? Lee Marvin plays the title role [sic], an ex-boxer who manages a boxing robot in 1974, six years after boxing has been abolished. (How quaint.) Needing a purse in order to afford the repairs for his aging and now-obsolete "fighter," Marvin dons a hood, mimics a robot, and enters the ring to fight a sleek and highly efficient newer model. (Sort of like a metal Dolph Lundgren, which is redundant.) This true man of false steel gets the tar beat out of him, but earns his purse.

We were reminded of that show and its obvious play on words when it was suggested to us last season that it now seems unrealistic to refer to anyone outside of Camden Yards as an "iron man," a term that had traditionally been used for any player who didn't miss a game for an extended period. Over the past few years, such players have become increasingly rare; except for Cal Ripken, no one has played every game of the past two seasons. In fact, over the past 20 years, the only players to put three iron-man seasons together were Sandy Alomar, Sr. (1970–72), Pete Rose (1974–77 and 1979–82), Steve Garvey (1976–82), Toby Harrah (1980–82), Dale Murphy (1982–85), Joe Carter (1989–91), and Ripken, whose current streak of consecutive games began in May 1982. The trend toward fewer players who dance every dance is obvious in the following graph (from which the 1981 season has been omitted):

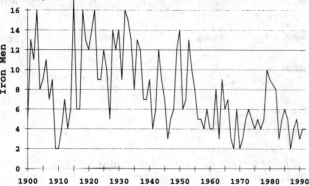

Over the past six years, an average of fewer than four players per year have played every game—or Cal plus 2.7 others, expressed in Ripken notation. Cal can still be called an iron man, but by comparison to players of the past, today's often seem more like tin men, lacking the heart to play every day. Given the overall trend of the above graph, it's possible that there will come a time in the near future when 162-game seasons will be as common as 40-start seasons for pitchers.

So it was somewhat unusual that three Astros players—Jeff Bagwell, Craig Biggio, and Steve Finley—appeared in all 162 Houston games last season. They were the only players other than Ripken to play every game. They were also the 22d set of three teammates to do so in this century, but the first in nearly 20 years. The last five prior to Bagwell, Biggio, and Finley:

Year	Team	Players
1974	Phillies	Larry Bowa, Dave Cash, and Mike Schmidt
1950	Tigers	Johnny Groth, George Kell, and Gerry Priddy
1949	Phillies	Richie Ashburn, Del Ennis, and Granny Hamner
1944	Reds	Eddie Miller, Ray Mueller, and Woody Williams
1934	Tigers	Charlie Gehringer, Marv Owen, and Billy Rogell

No cosmic conclusions here, other than the obvious: that, Ripken and the Astros notwithstanding, there seems little to gain these days by playing every game. There are, of course, factors mitigating against a full dance card. For instance, with the lamentable demise of the doubleheader, 162 games are now being played on an average of 160 dates, leaving few true off-days. Everyone needs a little rest sometimes, and it's become more difficult for modern players to get it without missing a game. Then again, it's not as bad as you might think. Ripken is the extreme example; he's played 1735 games on 1685 dates during the 11-year course of his streak. Even so, he's had 258 in-season days off—roughly one a week. All right, so he often travels on those days; he plays in All-Star games in what we're calling his "spare time," and so on. We're not looking to debate the point, but we think a lot of fans will be surprised that even Ripken had that many days off.

Would it surprise anyone to find that fewer players than ever before take pride in an everyday approach to their craft, or draw satisfaction from it? Or is it that managers more than ever look to rest their starters on occasion, both to get them refreshed and to keep their bench players ready for when they're needed? That's one dispute we'll never be able to answer by the numbers. But at a time when fewer players appear to have the simple ambition to play every day, maybe we should all tip our hats to perhaps the last of a dying breed: on the grand scale of Ripken, and here on the so-far lesser scale of Bagwell, Biggio, and Finley.

LOS ANGELES DODGERS

What was the most unlikely parlay of 1992: *(a)* Perot and Stockdale; *(b)* Clinton and Gore; or *(c)* the Dodgers and Red Sox? If you guessed *(c)*, we think you're right—but, of course, we're not talking about winning their divisions. Last season, Boston and Los Angeles both landed in the cellar, ending the longest streaks of consecutive seasons without a last-place finish in the respective histories of the American and National Leagues. One could easily envision Tommy Lasorda shaking his head and wondering, "Who am I? Why am I here?"

Boston hadn't finished in last place since 1932, a span of 59 consecutive seasons. The Dodgers hadn't landed there in 86 years, since 1905. Only two N.L. teams have had streaks even half as long as Brooklyn-L.A.'s: St. Louis, 71 years (1919–89) and Cincinnati, 44 years (1938–81). The longest streak in NFL history was nowhere near as long: The Chicago Bears went 33 years, from 1936 through 1968, without a last-place finish before posting a 1–13 record in 1969—despite the fact that Gale Sayers led the NFL in rushing. Of course, when the Dodgers began their streak just after the turn of the century, there was no NFL—or for that matter, no NBA. (Of course, basketball itself was about as old as Chelsea Clinton is.) The longest hoop streak was 28 years by the Celtics, extending appropriately from Bob Cousy's first season (1950–51) to John Havlicek's last (1977–78). With the Dodgers' and Red Sox's streaks having ended, the longest current streak in any of the four major team sports is the Montreal Canadiens' all-time NHL span of 52 years. (Hockey historians: Note that Montreal's most recent last-place finish was in 1940, the last time the New York Rangers won the Stanley Cup.) Anyway, the point is that the Dodgers' last-place finish was a historic event, and it deserves a closer look.

You could compose a sizable laundry list of reasons why the Dodgers collapsed last season. We'll absolve Brett Butler and Eric Karros; but nearly every other player contributed in some way. Injuries to Darryl Strawberry and Eric Davis were primary factors. The departure of Tim Belcher and John Wetteland in the Davis trade went uncorrected, and it magnified the importance of disappointing seasons by Ramon Martinez and Roger McDowell. Prospect Jose Offerman was sometimes overmatched at bat and often inept in the field. Mike Scioscia began to look as though he's been on the receiving end of one too many collisions at home plate. Dave Hansen provided no offense; and although they kept their batting averages respectable, Mike Sharperson and Lenny Harris lacked punch. This was a broadly based collapse, best illustrated by the fact that at every position around the diamond, the Dodgers posted a slugging average below the league mark:

Slug. Avg.	C	1B	2B	SS	3B	LF	CF	RF
Dodgers	.310	.402	.340	.333	.317	.327	.382	.358
N.L. Avg.	.357	.422	.361	.340	.397	.400	.398	.399
Margin	−47	−20	−21	−7	−80	−73	−16	−41

that's something they have little control over, and a look at the shortfalls in the table of Dodgers slugging averages indicates that the biggest problems lie in a straight line starting at home plate and running down the left-field line. Los Angeles ranked last in the National League with a .339 slugging average last season, and its .347 mark, with pitchers excluded, was 38 points below the league average; Dodgers catchers, third basemen, and left fielders collectively fell 65 points short of the league marks for those positions.

Let's cut Scioscia some slack. Although he no longer ranks among the best throwing catchers in baseball, his skills behind the plate are still valuable. Dodgers pitchers compiled a far lower ERA with Scioscia catching last season (3.14) than with either of their other catchers, Carlos Hernandez or Mike Piazza (3.81 combined). The Dodgers may not have posted a great record with Scioscia starting (41–58), but they were horrible with the other two in the lineup (22–41).

So if the Dodgers are looking for additional offense— and let's face it, they'd better be—the two spots at which they could get the most bang for their buck would be third base and left field.

But there's another area in which the Dodgers simply must improve if they are to return to contention in the N.L. West. Last season, the Dodgers once again led the majors in errors with 174, the highest total by any team since the 1986 Dodgers committed 181 errors. Los Angeles led the majors for three straight seasons from 1985 through 1987, and they even won a division title in the first of those three seasons—proving that for every rule there is an exception. But the fact is, it's nearly impossible even to contend for a championship with a defense as poor as the Dodgers'.

Consider this: The 1985 Dodgers were one of only three teams in this century to win a title despite leading the majors in errors. The 1965 Minnesota Twins were the only such team to reach the World Series; the 1971 Giants, like the '85 Dodgers, lost in the playoffs. By way of comparison, 33 teams with the *fewest* errors have reached the World Series, the most recent being the 1987 Twins; two others lost in the playoffs.

Although that comparison highlights the extremes, here's a more general trend that may surprise you: Teams that rank last in errors generally compile poorer records than those that rank last in home runs. That may not provide much consolation for the Dodgers, who ranked last in both categories last season. But teams often compensate for a lack of power and still manage to post winning records; seven teams that ranked last in homers did so over the past 20 years, including the Cardinals in 1987, 1989, and 1991. But during that same period, only the 1985 Dodgers won more games than they lost despite a major league high in errors. The following table summarizes the performance of those groups since 1900; the groups have different numbers of teams because of ties for last, in which case we included all the tied teams:

Solutions? A healthy Darryl Strawberry playing right field every day would be the most valuable asset the Dodgers could add to their lineup this season. But

Category	Above .500	.451–.500	.401–.450	.400 & Below	Won–Lost	Pct.
Last in Errors	9	15	29	41	5868–8657	.404
Last in Home Runs	25	22	27	23	6794–8151	.455

Which Dodgers were most responsible for the team's deficient defense? This time, the trend line runs straight up the middle. The team's second basemen and shortstops accounted for 45 more errors than those of the average National League team—that's nearly the entire margin by which the Dodgers exceeded the overall N.L. average (56).

Half of the quartet that committed 32 errors at second base has already been discarded: Juan Samuel was released during the 1992 season, and rookie Eric Young was lost to Colorado in the expansion draft, leaving only regular-starter Lenny Harris and utility-player Mike Sharperson. Clearly, the acquisition of Jody Reed is intended to solve the problem there, and Reed's 14 errors in 142 games last year suggest a distinct improvement. But at shortstop, it was basically a one-man (horror) show: Jose Offerman was responsible for 42 of the team's 52 errors there. And that's hardly good news, since Offerman is regarded as one of the top prospects in the Dodgers organization. Last season, he even displaced Brett Butler—the best leadoff hitter in the league—from the top spot in the Dodgers batting order. Now that's commitment to the future; the question is, what kind of future? (And what kind of commitment?)

Although few teams have been able to win titles while leading the majors in errors, a number have overcome an error-prone shortstop to reach the post-season. In fact, the 1974 Dodgers did so; their shortstop, Bill Russell, committed 39 errors there, a major league high. More recently, the 1982 Braves (Rafael Ramirez) and 1991 Pirates (Jay Bell) won their division with shortstops who led the majors in errors at the position. And during a 15-year period from 1951 through 1965, six such teams reached the Series: the 1951 and 1954 Giants (Alvin Dark), the 1957 and 1958 Braves (Johnny Logan), the 1964 Cardinals (Dick Groat), and the 1965 Twins (MVP Zoilo Versalles).

But does Offerman have the potential to contribute as much at bat as any of those shortstops? Although our projection model finds some remarkable likenesses between Offerman's statistical profile to date and those of several other 23-year-old shortstops who developed into fine offensive players (including Toby Harrah, Roy Smalley, Jr., and Ozzie Smith), the short list of clones also includes Bud Harrelson, Spike Owen, Wayne Tolleson, and—look out below!—Woody Woodward. All things considered, it appears unlikely that Offerman will ever have a 150-hit season. But you be the judge; a comparison of Offerman's statistics last season to those of the pennant-winning shortstops mentioned earlier, all in their primes at the time:

Year	Shortstop	AB	R	H	2B	3B	HR	RBI	BB	SO	SB	BA
1951	Alvin Dark	646	114	196	41	7	14	69	42	39	12	.303
1954	Alvin Dark	644	98	189	26	6	20	70	27	40	5	.293
1957	Johnny Logan	494	59	135	19	7	10	49	31	49	5	.273
1958	Johnny Logan	530	54	120	20	0	11	53	40	57	1	.226
1964	Dick Groat	636	70	186	35	6	1	70	44	42	2	.292
1965	Zoilo Versalles	666	126	182	45	12	19	77	41	122	27	.273
1992	Jose Offerman	534	67	139	20	8	1	30	57	98	23	.260

The bottom line for the Dodgers is this: Last season, they ranked last in the majors in home runs, last in errors, and, although we haven't mentioned this yet, last in runs scored. Not surprisingly, they posted the worst record in baseball (63–99). With so many problems to tend to, you'd think it would be a simple matter to get started on the repairs. But unfortunately, few of the team's many deficiencies overlap. You want to fix the offense? Start with a new third baseman and left fielder. You want to tighten up the defense? Get some help at second base and shortstop. You want to restore some power to the order? Speak to Darryl Strawberry's therapist. Oh, and did we forget to mention that the Dodgers had the oldest pitching staff in the league last season? (Lord, please let Pedro Astacio be the real thing!)

Lacking a single move that addresses several problems at once, it might help to keep this in mind: Some teams overcome a lack of power; a few have even succeeded despite an abundance of errors. But no team since the 1937 Boston Braves has posted even a winning record while scoring the fewest runs in the majors, let alone a record that would place it in pennant contention. An old pitching staff? No need to panic yet—Oakland won pennants in two of the last three years with an even older group. But until the Dodgers get the offense turned around, there's not much point in worrying about pennant winners; respectability will be a stretch.

Now, having said that, we can offer you one of the dead-sure lock bets of 1993: The Dodgers will be included on those lists of the most improved teams at the end of the season. No, we haven't lost our minds; there are two pieces of information to remember: *(1)* The Dodgers had a record of 17–40 in one-run games last year; that's the most one-run losses since 1975, and just two shy of the furthest below .500 in the category in this century. Longtime readers of the *Analyst* know that such a mark is more a measure of bad luck than actual abilities, and is almost certain to even out some the next year. And *(2)* the presence of two expansion teams guarantees extra wins for the 12 older teams, regardless of how they looked last season. So book that bet now, and be careful with your Manager-of-the-Year ballot next October.

WON-LOST RECORD BY STARTING POSITION

Los Angeles Dodgers	C	1B	2B	3B	SS	LF	CF	RF	DH	P	Leadoff	Cleanup	Starts vs. LH	Starts vs. RH	Total Starts
Dave Anderson	-	-	-	5-10	5-1	-	-	-	-	-	-	-	16	5	10-11
Billy Ashley	-	-	-	-	-	0-1	-	7-16	-	-	-	-	9	15	7-17
Pedro Astacio	-	-	-	-	-	-	-	-	-	6-5	-	-	2	9	6-5
Todd Benzinger	-	5-8	-	-	-	9-8	-	13-19	-	-	-	0-2	31	31	27-35
Rafael Bournigal	-	-	-	2-6	-	-	-	-	-	-	-	-	2	6	2-6
Brett Butler	-	-	-	-	-	-	60-92	-	-	-	38-49	-	58	94	60-92
John Candelaria	-	-	-	-	-	-	-	-	-	-	-	-	-	-	-
Tom Candiotti	-	-	-	-	-	-	-	-	-	12-18	-	-	13	17	12-18
Tim Crews	-	-	-	-	-	-	-	-	-	1-1	-	-	-	2	1-1
Kal Daniels	-	3-4	-	-	-	12-9	-	-	-	-	-	-	7	21	15-13
Eric Davis	-	-	-	-	-	25-43	1-1	2-1	-	-	-	15-20	30	43	28-45
Tom Goodwin	-	-	-	-	-	4-9	0-4	-	-	-	-	-	-	17	4-13
Jim Gott	-	-	-	-	-	-	-	-	-	-	-	-	-	-	-
Kevin Gross	-	-	-	-	-	-	-	-	-	10-20	-	-	16	14	10-20
Kip Gross	-	-	-	-	-	-	-	-	-	1-0	-	-	-	1	1-0
Dave Hansen	-	-	-	37-61	-	-	-	-	-	-	-	-	11	87	37-61
Lenny Harris	-	-	23-42	5-5	0-2	1-3	-	4-2	-	-	0-1	-	2	85	33-54
Carlos Hernandez	16-31	-	-	-	-	-	-	-	-	-	-	-	35	12	16-31
Orel Hershiser	-	-	-	-	-	-	-	-	-	13-20	-	-	11	22	13-20
Jay Howell	-	-	-	-	-	-	-	-	-	-	-	-	-	-	-
Stan Javier	-	-	-	-	-	1-4	-	-	-	-	-	-	1	4	1-4
Eric Karros	-	55-87	-	-	-	-	-	-	-	-	-	30-57	59	83	55-87
Pedro Martinez	-	-	-	-	-	-	-	-	-	0-1	-	-	-	1	0-1
Ramon Martinez	-	-	-	-	-	-	-	-	-	10-15	-	-	11	14	10-15
Roger McDowell	-	-	-	-	-	-	-	-	-	-	-	-	-	-	-
Jose Offerman	-	-	-	-	56-90	-	-	-	-	-	23-44	-	58	88	56-90
Bob Ojeda	-	-	-	-	-	-	-	-	-	10-19	-	-	9	20	10-19
Mike Piazza	6-10	-	-	-	-	-	-	-	-	-	-	-	9	7	6-10
Henry Rodriguez	-	-	-	-	-	2-10	-	10-18	-	-	-	-	2	38	12-28
Juan Samuel	-	-	12-17	-	-	-	-	1-0	-	-	-	-	23	7	13-17
Mike Scioscia	41-58	-	-	-	-	-	-	-	-	-	-	-	18	81	41-58
Rudy Seanez	-	-	-	-	-	-	-	-	-	-	-	-	-	-	-
Mike Sharperson	-	-	15-18	16-23	-	-	-	-	-	-	-	-	54	18	31-41
Darryl Strawberry	-	-	-	-	-	1-1	-	16-23	-	-	-	15-18	16	25	17-24
Mitch Webster	-	-	-	-	-	8-11	2-2	10-20	-	-	0-1	3-2	34	19	20-33
Steve Wilson	-	-	-	-	-	-	-	-	-	-	-	-	-	-	-
Eric Young	-	-	13-22	-	-	-	-	-	-	-	2-4	-	21	14	13-22

TEAM TOTALS: BATTING

	AB	H	2B	3B	HR	RBI	BB	SO	BA	SA	OBA
Season	5368	1333	201	34	72	499	503	899	.248	.339	.313
vs. Left-Handers	2007	531	74	9	33	189	197	286	.265	.360	.329
vs. Right-Handers	3361	802	127	25	39	310	306	613	.239	.326	.304
vs. Ground-Ballers	1968	506	79	8	26	173	161	297	.257	.345	.317
vs. Fly-Ballers	3400	827	122	26	46	326	342	602	.243	.335	.312
Home Games	2627	664	96	19	26	247	251	404	.253	.333	.318
Road Games	2741	669	105	15	46	252	252	495	.244	.344	.309
Grass Fields	3965	999	144	25	49	380	380	634	.252	.338	.318
Artificial Turf	1403	334	57	9	23	119	123	265	.238	.341	.301
April	749	190	26	6	13	83	85	137	.254	.356	.330
May	738	178	28	6	16	74	71	137	.241	.360	.309
June	900	222	40	6	8	78	88	148	.247	.331	.314
July	1031	261	34	8	13	98	86	161	.253	.339	.310
August	904	224	33	4	10	78	80	139	.248	.326	.310
Sept./Oct.	1046	258	40	4	12	88	93	177	.247	.327	.310
Leading Off Inn.	1339	336	42	9	13	13	111	198	.251	.325	.310
Runners On	2301	560	92	15	34	461	233	404	.243	.341	.312
Bases Empty	3067	773	109	19	38	38	270	495	.252	.337	.315
Runners/Scor. Pos.	1327	309	56	10	16	408	176	244	.233	.326	.319
Runners On/2 Out	986	220	43	7	14	181	110	191	.223	.324	.306
Scor. Pos./2 Out	648	142	32	5	6	157	92	124	.219	.312	.321
Late-Inning Pressure	972	249	30	4	14	86	94	187	.256	.338	.322
Leading Off	246	67	8	1	1	1	18	37	.272	.325	.325
Runners On	424	90	9	3	8	80	52	92	.212	.304	.297
Runners/Scor. Pos.	239	46	5	3	3	68	42	54	.192	.276	.310

RUNS BATTED IN	From 1B	From 2B	From 3B	Scoring Position
Totals	59/1597	144/1022	224/607	368/1629
Percentage	3.7%	14.1%	36.9%	22.6%

TEAM TOTALS: PITCHING

	W-L	ERA	AB	H	HR	BB	SO	BA	SA	OBA
Season	63-99	3.41	5457	1401	82	553	981	.257	.355	.326
vs. Left-Handers			2638	710	47	343	448	.269	.382	.353
vs. Right-Handers			2819	691	35	210	533	.245	.330	.299
vs. Ground-Ballers			2362	608	24	257	454	.257	.337	.331
vs. Fly-Ballers			3095	793	58	296	527	.256	.369	.322
Home Games	37-44	2.91	2777	702	33	236	508	.253	.337	.312
Road Games	26-55	3.93	2680	699	49	317	473	.261	.374	.340
Grass Fields	51-69	3.25	4075	1039	64	394	711	.255	.350	.322
Artificial Turf	12-30	3.91	1382	362	18	159	270	.262	.371	.338
April	9-13	3.62	749	195	12	77	143	.260	.371	.331
May	13-10	2.83	746	174	7	92	162	.233	.316	.318
June	9-18	3.54	890	223	17	99	157	.251	.367	.324
July	12-19	3.46	1060	281	19	103	194	.265	.366	.331
August	10-18	3.35	932	221	13	91	154	.237	.320	.309
Sept./Oct.	10-21	3.58	1080	307	14	91	171	.284	.381	.339
Leading Off Inn.			1330	351	26	112	246	.264	.382	.322
Bases Empty			3023	779	47	253	549	.258	.359	.318
Runners On			2434	622	35	300	432	.256	.351	.335
Runners/Scor. Pos.			1480	363	20	239	292	.245	.338	.345
Runners On/2 Out			1052	254	21	166	200	.241	.351	.347
Scor. Pos./2 Out			713	166	10	142	143	.233	.325	.362
Late-Inning Pressure			802	226	12	96	143	.282	.365	.359
Leading Off			199	63	4	17	35	.317	.437	.373
Runners On			380	109	5	58	72	.287	.361	.378
Runners/Scor. Pos.			251	70	4	51	46	.279	.355	.394
First 9 Batters			2753	701	37	275	508	.255	.344	.323
Second 9 Batters			1364	345	23	123	249	.253	.363	.317
All Batters Thereafter			1340	355	22	155	224	.265	.372	.341

WON-LOST RECORD BY STARTING POSITION

Montreal Expos	C	1B	2B	3B	SS	LF	CF	RF	DH	P	Leadoff	Cleanup	Starts vs. LH	Starts vs. RH	Total Starts
Moises Alou	-	-	-	-	-	38-24	1-5	5-7	-	-	1-0	2-1	34	46	44-36
Bret Barberie	-	-	10-7	30-27	-	-	-	-	-	-	-	0-2	13	61	40-34
Brian Barnes	-	-	-	-	-	-	-	-	-	8-9	-	-	7	10	8-9
Sean Berry	-	-	-	8-4	-	-	-	-	-	-	-	-	-	12	8-4
Kent Bottenfield	-	-	-	-	-	-	-	-	-	2-2	-	-	-	4	2-2
Eric Bullock	-	-	-	-	-	-	-	-	-	-	-	-	-	-	-
Ivan Calderon	-	-	-	-	-	21-24	-	-	-	-	-	0-1	17	28	21-24
Gary Carter	42-37	2-0	-	-	-	-	-	-	-	-	-	1-0	46	35	44-37
Rick Cerone	9-3	-	-	-	-	-	-	-	-	-	-	-	8	4	9-3
Archi Cianfrocco	-	20-21	-	7-6	-	2-1	-	-	-	-	-	1-0	30	27	29-28
Greg Colbrunn	-	26-18	-	-	-	-	-	-	-	-	-	-	22	22	26-18
Wil Cordero	-	-	6-2	-	13-13	-	-	-	-	-	-	-	11	23	19-15
Delino DeShields	-	-	70-63	-	-	-	-	-	-	-	46-38	-	47	86	70-63
Jeff Fassero	-	-	-	-	-	-	-	-	-	-	-	-	-	-	-
Darrin Fletcher	33-26	-	-	-	-	-	-	-	-	-	-	0-1	-	59	33-26
Tom Foley	-	0-2	1-1	-	14-10	-	-	-	-	-	-	-	3	25	15-13
Mark Gardner	-	-	-	-	-	-	-	-	-	15-15	-	-	12	18	15-15
Jerry Goff	-	-	-	-	-	-	-	-	-	-	-	-	-	-	-
Marquis Grissom	-	-	-	-	-	-	86-70	-	-	-	40-35	-	58	98	86-70
Chris Haney	-	-	-	-	-	-	-	-	-	2-4	-	-	4	2	2-4
Todd Haney	-	-	0-2	-	-	-	-	-	-	-	-	-	2	-	0-2
Gil Heredia	-	-	-	-	-	-	-	-	-	0-1	-	-	-	1	0-1
Ken Hill	-	-	-	-	-	-	-	-	-	21-12	-	-	13	20	21-12
Jonathan Hurst	-	-	-	-	-	-	-	-	-	1-2	-	-	-	3	1-2
Bill Krueger	-	-	-	-	-	-	-	-	-	1-1	-	-	-	2	1-1
Tim Laker	3-8	-	-	-	-	-	-	-	-	-	-	-	5	6	3-8
Bill Landrum	-	-	-	-	-	-	-	-	-	-	-	-	-	-	-
Steve Lyons	-	0-1	-	-	-	-	-	-	-	-	-	-	-	1	0-1
Dennis Martinez	-	-	-	-	-	-	-	-	-	19-13	-	-	13	19	19-13
Matt Maysey	-	-	-	-	-	-	-	-	-	-	-	-	-	-	-
Chris Nabholz	-	-	-	-	-	-	-	-	-	17-15	-	-	10	22	17-15
Bob Natal	0-1	-	-	-	-	-	-	-	-	-	-	-	1	-	0-1
Spike Owen	-	-	-	-	60-52	-	-	-	-	-	-	-	51	61	60-52
Darren Reed	-	-	-	-	-	1-3	-	9-3	-	-	-	-	11	5	10-6
Gilberto Reyes	-	-	-	-	-	-	-	-	-	-	-	-	-	-	-
Bill Risley	-	-	-	-	-	-	-	-	-	1-0	-	-	-	1	1-0
Mel Rojas	-	-	-	-	-	-	-	-	-	-	-	-	-	-	-
Bill Sampen	-	-	-	-	-	-	-	-	-	0-1	-	-	-	1	0-1
Scott Service	-	-	-	-	-	-	-	-	-	-	-	-	-	-	-
Doug Simons	-	-	-	-	-	-	-	-	-	-	-	-	-	-	-
Matt Stairs	-	-	-	-	-	4-4	-	-	-	-	-	-	-	8	4-4
Sergio Valdez	-	-	-	-	-	-	-	-	-	-	-	-	-	-	-
John Vanderwal	-	2-2	-	-	-	21-19	-	1-0	-	-	-	5-3	6	39	24-21
Larry Walker	-	-	-	-	-	-	-	72-65	-	-	-	71-63	49	88	72-65
Tim Wallach	-	36-29	-	42-38	-	-	-	-	-	-	-	7-6	58	87	78-67
John Wetteland	-	-	-	-	-	-	-	-	-	-	-	-	-	-	-
Jerry Willard	-	1-2	-	-	-	-	-	-	-	-	-	-	-	3	1-2
Pete Young	-	-	-	-	-	-	-	-	-	-	-	-	-	-	-

TEAM TOTALS: BATTING

	AB	H	2B	3B	HR	RBI	BB	SO	BA	SA	OBA
Season	5477	1381	263	37	102	601	463	976	.252	.370	.313
vs. Left-Handers	1857	498	95	15	42	223	155	306	.268	.403	.326
vs. Right-Handers	3620	883	168	22	60	378	308	670	.244	.352	.305
vs. Ground-Ballers	2411	607	102	19	35	247	208	374	.252	.353	.314
vs. Fly-Ballers	3066	774	161	18	67	354	255	602	.252	.382	.311
Home Games	2624	673	136	17	50	306	218	438	.256	.378	.316
Road Games	2853	708	127	20	52	295	245	538	.248	.361	.310
Grass Fields	1474	372	63	12	26	156	132	288	.252	.364	.317
Artificial Turf	4003	1009	200	25	76	445	331	688	.252	.371	.311
April	787	188	40	3	16	81	69	147	.239	.358	.303
May	771	196	38	4	24	100	68	156	.254	.407	.318
June	882	227	47	8	12	108	84	143	.257	.370	.321
July	1017	258	36	7	16	98	85	176	.254	.350	.313
August	912	227	41	7	16	98	73	184	.249	.362	.307
Sept./Oct.	1108	285	61	8	18	116	84	170	.257	.375	.313
Leading Off Inn.	1375	370	68	9	33	33	82	205	.269	.404	.314
Runners On	2295	590	112	13	40	539	228	426	.257	.369	.322
Bases Empty	3182	791	151	24	62	62	235	550	.249	.370	.305
Runners/Scor. Pos.	1402	352	70	4	22	464	180	273	.251	.354	.330
Runners On/2 Out	967	221	48	4	12	196	111	194	.229	.324	.314
Scor. Pos./2 Out	653	151	36	2	6	171	95	128	.231	.320	.333
Late-Inning Pressure	819	195	39	4	12	82	76	169	.238	.339	.301
Leading Off	212	55	8	2	4	4	17	41	.259	.373	.314
Runners On	339	79	17	0	5	75	39	67	.233	.327	.306
Runners/Scor. Pos.	206	42	8	0	4	69	32	41	.204	.301	.302

RUNS BATTED IN	From 1B	From 2B	From 3B	Scoring Position
Totals	79/1516	170/1071	250/614	420/1685
Percentage	5.2%	15.9%	40.7%	24.9%

TEAM TOTALS: PITCHING

	W-L	ERA	AB	H	HR	BB	SO	BA	SA	OBA
Season	87-75	3.25	5452	1296	92	525	1014	.238	.343	.309
vs. Left-Handers			2514	609	44	245	482	.242	.348	.313
vs. Right-Handers			2938	687	48	280	532	.234	.339	.305
vs. Ground-Ballers			2423	561	28	200	450	.232	.319	.294
vs. Fly-Ballers			3029	735	64	325	564	.243	.362	.320
Home Games	43-38	3.75	2758	665	48	255	521	.241	.359	.311
Road Games	44-37	2.74	2694	631	44	270	493	.234	.327	.307
Grass Fields	24-18	2.58	1381	328	22	125	233	.238	.328	.304
Artificial Turf	63-57	3.48	4071	968	70	400	781	.238	.348	.310
April	9-14	3.59	783	186	11	86	129	.238	.335	.318
May	12-11	3.82	791	192	17	82	162	.243	.374	.321
June	14-13	3.60	864	203	12	97	159	.235	.346	.316
July	19-11	2.89	1015	255	26	87	187	.251	.376	.314
August	17-10	2.61	901	197	14	82	162	.219	.302	.288
Sept./Oct.	16-16	3.18	1098	263	12	91	215	.240	.328	.298
Leading Off Inn.			1359	343	27	104	243	.252	.375	.310
Bases Empty			3119	747	52	267	568	.239	.347	.305
Runners On			2333	549	40	258	446	.235	.338	.314
Runners/Scor. Pos.			1449	332	25	203	299	.229	.331	.323
Runners On/2 Out			988	205	12	118	194	.207	.285	.298
Scor. Pos./2 Out			683	136	9	98	145	.199	.274	.303
Late-Inning Pressure			855	213	19	93	188	.249	.356	.326
Leading Off			220	69	6	18	41	.314	.486	.366
Runners On			383	77	8	50	88	.201	.282	.300
Runners/Scor. Pos.			230	50	7	42	52	.217	.335	.337
First 9 Batters			2939	693	41	304	628	.236	.334	.312
Second 9 Batters			1389	329	28	110	249	.237	.351	.295
All Batters Thereafter			1124	274	23	111	137	.244	.356	.317

MONTREAL EXPOS

There was near unanimity on last season's top managers. The Baseball Writers Association named Tony LaRussa its American League manager of the year; Jim Leyland won the National League award. The Associated Press, which bestows a single award, named LaRussa its manager of the year; Leyland was the runaway leader among N.L. managers. Both groups placed Phil Garner second and Johnny Oates third among A.L. managers; both had Felipe Alou second and Bobby Cox third in the N.L. (The A.P. had Art Howe tied with Cox.)

But no manager earned as much praise late last season as did Alou, who replaced Tom Runnells as manager of a floundering Expos team on May 21. Montreal had posted a disappointing 17–20 record for Runnells; but for nearly four months after Alou's takeover, the Expos compiled the best mark in the N.L. East, narrowing Pittsburgh's lead from five games to three, before losing 12 of their last 20 games to finish a fading but encouraging second.

The team's turnaround under Alou was not caused by any changes in personnel, as is often the case with midseason managerial changes. The only major changes Alou made were: (1) installing a platoon of Archi Cianfrocco and Greg Colbrunn (who joined the team in early July) at first base, thereby moving Tim Wallach back to third base and demoting disappointing second-year player Bret Barberie to part-time status; (2) replacing Ivan Calderon in left field with Moises Alou; and (3) replacing Chris Haney in the starting rotation with Brian Barnes. The last two weren't even classic "coach's decisions"; they were fueled by injuries (Barnes wasn't available to Runnells, while Calderon was injured in May, and incapacitated shortly after Alou took over). But notice in the following table that the core of the Expos' offense raised its batting average substantially after the change of managers. The table shows individual totals for all starters whose roles remained the same under Alou as under Runnells, and groups the other players together:

Player	Under Runnells				Under Alou				
	G	HR	RBI	BA	G	HR	RBI	BA	Diff.
Gary Carter	23	2	8	.225	72	3	21	.215	−10
Delino DeShields	36	2	13	.270	99	5	43	.301	+31
Darrin Fletcher	16	1	6	.204	67	1	20	.254	+50
Marquis Grissom	37	4	16	.262	122	10	50	.280	+18
Spike Owen	33	3	12	.239	89	4	28	.282	+43
Larry Walker	37	7	25	.287	106	16	68	.306	+19
Tim Wallach	34	1	12	.200	116	8	47	.231	+31
Others	37	7	44	.226	125	28	188	.236	+10

Even though most of the regular Expos starters had higher batting averages under Alou than under Runnells (and all except Carter had higher slugging averages as well), the team's scoring average actually fell from 4.05 runs per game before the change to 3.98 runs thereafter. In fact, Montreal's improvement was attributable to better pitching, and the improvement in its pitching was attributable to its bullpen. Montreal allowed a half-run per game less during Alou's tenure (3.48 per game) than under Runnells's (3.98), despite the fact that its starting pitchers compiled a higher ERA under Alou:

	Under Runnells			Under Alou		
	W–L	Sv	ERA	W–L	Sv	ERA
Starting Pitchers	14–13	—	2.79	51–42	—	3.36
Relief Pitchers	3–7	7	4.91	19–13	42	2.85

Only Chris Nabholz among the starters performed better after Alou replaced Runnells (with before and after ERAs of 3.88 and 3.15, respectively). Ken Hill's ERA rose from 1.79 under Runnells to 2.99 under Alou, Dennis Martinez's mark went from 1.82 to 2.67, and Mark Gardner soared from 2.98 to 4.91. Only the eventual substitution of Brian Barnes (who joined the team in late June) for Chris Haney (who made only one start after the managerial change) kept the rotation's ERA from rising even higher during Alou's tenure.

But the bullpen was a completely different story, and John Wetteland was the key: 0–2 with a 6.48 ERA and six saves in nine opportunities under Runnells; 4–2, 2.03 ERA, 31-for-37 on saves for Alou. Nevertheless, you'd be hard pressed to argue that the new manager handled his closer much differently than did the old one. Neither manager brought Wetteland into a game before the 8th inning all year, but neither pampered him with the Eckersley treatment either. Runnells called for Wetteland in the ninth inning or later in only 8 of his 14 appearances (57%); Alou did so in 31 of 53 (58%). Runnells brought Wetteland in at the start of an inning in 9 of 14 appearances (64%), Alou slightly less often (29 of 53, or 55%). The only difference that can be noted—insignificant as it may be—is this: Runnells never brought Wetteland into a game with the tying or lead run in scoring position. Alou did so six times, and Wetteland thrived in those situations, with a record of 2–0 and three saves in five opportunities, allowing five hits and no earned runs in 8⅔ innings.

But it's foolish to consider Alou's show of confidence in Wetteland as a factor in his closer's form reversal; the latter predated the former, as Wetteland's turnaround began on May 25—his ERA was 6.62 before that, 1.92 thereafter—more than two weeks before Alou first tossed him into one of those pressure cookers. But Wetteland's rebound was exactly the tonic that Montreal needed. The Expos lost four games last season in which they led after seven innings—three in six-plus weeks under Runnells, but only one in four-plus months under Alou.

So, to raise a question that no one really wants to hear at this point (but one that must be asked by anyone with a knowledge of baseball history): As successful as Alou was on a bottom-line basis, was he actively guiding Montreal's mid-1992 turnaround, or was he simply carried along for the ride? The Expos' rebound was impressive, and it clearly coincided with Alou's hiring as manager. But in the absence of any real on-field explanation for the improvement, we're left wondering. And as we'll soon see, the team's before-and-after performance was remarkably similar to that of a pair of recent teams whose managers appeared to sparkle in their first partial seasons, only to be tarnished by declines a year later.

The following table includes a team in each of the two previous seasons that rebounded for new managers as the Expos did for Alou in 1992:

Year	Team	First Manager	W–L	Pct.	Second Manager	W–L	Pct.
1990	Mets	Davey Johnson	20–22	.476	Bud Harrelson	71–49	.592
1991	Royals	John Wathan	16–22	.421	Hal McRae	66–58	.532
1992	Expos	Tom Runnells	17–20	.459	Felipe Alou	70–55	.560

Year	Team	Orig. Manager	W–L	Replacement	W–L
1912	Indians	Harry Davis	54–71	Joe Birmingham	21–7
1940	Cardinals	Ray Blades	14–24	Billy Southworth	69–40
1959	Tigers	Bill Norman	2–15	Jimmy Dykes	74–63
1977	Rangers	Frank Lucchesi	31–31	Billy Hunter	60–33
1988	Padres	Larry Bowa	16–30	Jack McKeon	67–48

We probably don't have to tell you what happened to Harrelson: The Mets collapsed after a strong first half in 1991, and Harrelson came under fire (and spectacularly mishandled the media) and was fired before the end of the season. McRae's second season was only slightly less challenging; a mild second-half rally softened the effect of a disastrous 1–16 start. How much patience will Royals fans, the local media, and, most importantly, team management have this season? We'll tell you in the 1994 *Analyst,* but this much is guaranteed: The good will that McRae earned in 1991 will do him no good in 1993. And if history is any indication, the same rules will apply to Alou this season as well.

What were the most successful in-season managerial changes ever? The simple answer to that is a list of seven replacement managers who took their teams to the League Championship Series or the World Series:

Year	Team	Orig. Manager	W–L	Replacement	W–L
1932	Cubs	Rogers Hornsby	53–44	Charlie Grimm	37–20
1938	Cubs	Charlie Grimm	45–36	Gabby Hartnett	44–27
1978	Yankees	Billy Martin	52–42	Bob Lemon	48–20
1982	Brewers	Buck Rodgers	23–24	Harvey Kuenn	72–43
1983	Phillies	Pat Corrales	43–42	Paul Owens	47–30
1988	Red Sox	John McNamara	43–42	Joe Morgan	46–31
1989	Blue Jays	Jimy Williams	12–24	Cito Gaston	77–49

(An editorial judgment: We omitted from the table the names of Clyde Sukeforth, who managed the Dodgers to victories in the first two games of the 1947 season, and Burt Shotton, who replaced Sukeforth the next day and led the Dodgers to the N.L. title. We also omitted changes made during the divided 1981 season.)

Those changes may represent the ultimate success, but we would add five others that match even the Gaston-for-Williams switch listed above for the magnitude of their turnarounds, but whose teams had fallen too far behind under their original managers to win a title:

If there's a moral here, it's that even the replacements in these two tables—among the most successful in major league history—were subject to a what-have-you-done-lately policy by their bosses that is stunning. Southworth was fortunate; he left the Cardinals before ever posting a subsequent losing record with them. Kuenn was less so; his "voluntary" resignation from the Brewers was prompted by poor health. But Grimm, Lemon, Owens, Morgan, and Hunter were all fired without ever having compiled a losing record; their initial success may have created figurative "no-win" situations.

And here's the ultimate "Win Now" statement: Not one of the replacement managers listed above remained with his team even one full season after his first losing year. Hartnett had another winning year in 1939, but went 75–79 in 1940 and was gone in 1941. Birmingham posted an 86–66 mark in his first full season with the Indians, but fell to 51–102 in 1914 and was dumped after a 12–16 start the next year. Dykes didn't survive even the 1960 season; in fact, he may have suffered the ultimate indignity when he was sent to Cleveland for Joe Gordon in the only swap of managers in major league history. His crime: posting a 44–52 mark for the Tigers a year after leading them to that stunning early-season turnaround. McKeon almost won a division title for San Diego in his second season there, but was banished to the front office the next summer when his Padres fell six games below the .500 mark at midseason, and was fired altogether in September.

Cito Gaston has been fortunate so far. He's kept his job for three seasons since leading the Blue Jays to a stunning come-from-behind A.L. East title as a replacement for Jimy Williams in 1989. Then again, he's put winning numbers on the board in every season since then, and still it was widely believed that anything less than a World Series triumph in 1992 could have cost him his job. Both he and Alou look like they're riding first- or second-line favorites in their races for 1993. But if they fail, don't expect past success to be factored into their job evaluations. Just win, baby? It might be a motto for its originator, Al Davis. But in baseball, it's an order.

NEW YORK METS

During last December's baseball winter meetings, Mets general manager Al Harazin made what at first seemed an odd statement—namely, that he "loved" the trade last August in which the Mets obtained second baseman Jeff Kent and outfielder Ryan Thompson from the Blue Jays for free agent-to-be David Cone. It's hard to imagine a baseball executive falling in love with a trade in which he surrendered his best starting pitcher—under threat of free agency, no less—for a pair of prospects. But aside from the optimism that any GM must feel after acquiring a pair of promising young players, the Cone trade represents a willingness to address the problems of the past two years and start the rebuilding process. Kent and Thompson amount to a bonus for getting started sooner rather than later.

For nearly a decade, the Mets became increasingly reliant on veteran players acquired from other organizations. Of course, that's like saying that Babe Ruth relied on muscle for his home-run stroke. Why not? The Mets enjoyed tremendous success during the second half of the 1980s due in large part to imports like Keith Hernandez, Gary Carter, and Ray Knight. In fact, when New York won 108 games and a World Series in 1986, fewer than half of their plate appearances were by players who made their big-league debuts with the Mets. Note that calculation—the percentage of plate appearances by players who debuted for the team in question. It will be a standard of measure throughout this essay, including in the table below, which shows the percentage of plate appearances by players with their debut teams, for teams that reached postseason play and for all others. Not surprisingly, championship teams had higher percentages than other teams throughout most of this century, but only marginally so during the free-agency era—and not at all in the last three years:

Years	Champs	Others	Years	Champs	Others
1903–09	.372	.397	1950–59	.776	.584
1910–19	.598	.477	1960–69	.689	.551
1920–29	.553	.500	1970–79	.626	.508
1930–39	.684	.572	1980–89	.507	.498
1940–49	.717	.590	1990–92	.482	.491

The effect of free agency is best summarized in these figures: During the 17 seasons since 1976, there has been no significant difference between championship teams (.492) and lesser teams (.494). But during the previous 17 years (that is, from 1959 through 1975), teams that reached postseason play had a far higher rate (.709) than did other teams (.540). Simply put, prior to free agency, it was far more difficult to win a title without a base of talent produced within the organization.

But back to the Mets. As Carter and Hernandez approached retirement, and home-grown players like Lenny Dykstra and Kevin Mitchell were traded away, the Mets were neither inclined to restock their pool from the increasingly expensive free-agent market (at least to the extent necessary to keep their listing ship afloat) nor able to replenish the talent from within their own system.

Last season, the Mets hit bottom in more than one way. Not only was the team's 72–90 record its worst since 1983 (the year before the arrival of Dwight Gooden and Davey Johnson), but only 24 percent of the team's plate appearances came from players who debuted for the Mets. That was the lowest average in the majors last season, and the lowest by any Mets team since—you guessed it—1962, their first year of play. Here's how desperate the situation has become: Last season, only four Mets debutantes started more games for the team than did Ryan Thompson, who joined the team in August. Of those four, one is a pitcher (Gooden); two were cut loose during the off-season (Dave Magadan and Chris Donnels); and the fourth, Todd Hundley, will spend 1993 on probation after batting just .209 in 98 starts last season.

Another symptom: Players who made their first appearance in the majors wearing a Mets uniform produced 543 runs last season (that's a half-run for each run scored or driven in). That total isn't great, though it's hardly damning on its own; seven teams had lower totals, including both National League division winners. New York's problem lies in the fact that the six leading run producers among Mets debutantes played for other teams in 1992: Gregg Jefferies (70½ runs produced), Randy Milligan (62), Kevin Mitchell (57½), Keith Miller (47½), Lenny Dykstra (46), and Mark Carreon (37½). Those who debuted for the Mets *and were still playing for them last season* produced a major league low of 101½ runs. (Those figures do not include runs produced by pitchers.)

Here's an obvious question: Can a team win with so little of its offense home grown? The answer is a qualified yes. Two other teams produced fewer than 200 homemade runs last season: California, which had a record identical to the Mets' (72–90), and San Diego, which posted an 82–80 record. In 1991, the Dodgers went 93–69 despite only 83½ runs produced by players who debuted for them. Then again, look what happened to the Dodgers in 1992. And unfortunately for the Mets and their fans, the Dodgers' fall was symptomatic of a larger pattern: A low total of home-grown runs is not just an indication of current problems, but is also a leading indicator of teams in decline. The table below includes all teams since 1969 that produced fewer than 100 home-grown runs. A few managed a winning record in the year in question, and a few others did so a year later, but most floundered in general over the next few seasons. And, as the group averages indicate, the trend was decidedly downward after the base year:

Year	Team	Runs	Base Year	Base +1	Base +2
1991	Los Angeles Dodgers	83.5	.574	.389	——
1985	Cleveland Indians	78.5	.370	.519	.377
1983	Cleveland Indians	83.5	.432	.463	.370
1983	New York Yankees	88.0	.562	.537	.602
1982	California Angels	31.0	.574	.432	.500
1982	New York Yankees	41.5	.488	.562	.537
1982	Chicago Cubs	71.0	.451	.438	.596
1980	New York Yankees	93.0	.636	.551	.488
1980	Chicago Cubs	61.0	.395	.369	.451
1979	Chicago Cubs	36.5	.494	.395	.369
1978	Chicago Cubs	14.5	.488	.494	.395
1977	Chicago Cubs	43.5	.500	.488	.494
1972	California Angels	54.5	.484	.488	.420
	Averages		.489	.478	.468

That downward trend is what makes Harazin's immediate action so noteworthy. Although it does nothing to revitalize a minor league system that has been conspicuously unproductive in recent seasons, the acquisition of Kent and Thompson is a step toward reversing the trend. And it does so at no expense, if—and here's a big if—you assume that Cone wasn't going to re-sign with the Mets at the end of the 1992 season anyway. One never knows for certain when a player's contract demands are mere brinksmanship on the part of his negotiators. But after going through the arbitration process with Cone in each of the three previous off-seasons and trying to reach multiyear agreements throughout much of that period, you'd think that Harazin had a pretty good take on the situation. Anyway, after losing Darryl Strawberry after the 1990 season, the Mets were roasted for "not getting something for him"; which is to say, for not doing what they did with Cone.

These deals have a way of paying big dividends, even if they're not appreciated by most fans at the time. Four years ago, Seattle nicked the Expos for three valued pitching prospects, including Randy Johnson, for what amounted to a four-month rental of Mark Langston. In 1990, the Expos traded Zane Smith for three minor leaguers, one of whom was Moises Alou; another was Willie Greene. That same season, the Cardinals did with Willie McGee what the Yankees failed to do a year earlier with Rickey Henderson: pried a legitimate young prospect—in this case, Felix Jose—away from the A's. Two years ago, Cleveland rebuilt its outfield with Mark Whiten and Glenallen Hill from Toronto for free agent-to-be Tom Candiotti. And from what we've seen of Jeff Kent, he'll be another name on that list a year or two from now.

Silly as it seems, one of the most popular talk-show questions is why mediocre players make better managers than stars. There's no point in even discussing this without getting at the underlying question: Do they? With Jeff Torborg's playing career as inspiration, we thought it might be worthwhile to document some figures on that question.

Although his playing career had a number of noteworthy exclamation points in the form of the three no-hitters he caught, Torborg nevertheless compiled a .214 batting average during a 10-year career in which he batted 200 times only once (255 ABs in 1973, his final season). Fans often cite his career, and those of some other successful current managers (listed below), as examples of this supposed trend. Their playing statistics, contrasted with their value as a manager (the difference between the number of games they won and the number they were expected to win):

Player	G	AB	R	H	2B	3B	HR	RBI	SB	BA	Wins
Sparky Anderson	152	477	42	104	9	3	0	34	6	.218	+52
Bobby Cox	220	628	50	141	22	2	9	58	3	.225	+41
Tony LaRussa	132	176	15	35	5	2	0	7	0	.199	+35
Tom Kelly	49	127	11	23	5	0	1	11	0	.181	+17

Those examples are appropriately ugly, but you could also construct a table of successful managers who were equally impressive in their playing days. Or have you forgotten about the following:

Player	G	AB	R	H	2B	3B	HR	RBI	SB	BA	Wins
Frank Chance	1286	4295	798	1274	199	80	20	596	405	.297	+20
Joe Cronin	2124	7579	1233	2285	515	118	170	1424	87	.301	+19
Davey Johnson	1435	4797	564	1252	242	18	136	609	33	.261	+31
Al Lopez	1950	5916	613	1547	206	42	52	652	46	.261	+24
John McGraw	1099	3922	1026	1308	127	68	13	462	436	.334	+81

Let's cut to the chase. The following table classifies all managers in this century according to the number of games they played in the majors, a fairly reliable guide to the overall quality of a player. Managers rated as "Plus" are those whose teams won more games than expected according to our projection formula; those rated as "Minus"—well, you get the idea. Successful managers are designated in two subcategories: those who were at least "plus-10" for their careers, and at least "plus-20". There simply aren't any skews worth noting:

Games As Player	Mgrs.	Plus	Minus	+10	+20
0	69	34	35	10	3
1–499	96	36	60	13	7
500–999	71	36	35	10	6
1000–1999	126	49	77	19	9
2000–Up	36	16	20	7	1

Moreover, there are plenty of examples of mediocre players who were unsuccessful as managers. Pat Corrales was a backup catcher for four different teams from 1964 through 1973; he played 63 games as a rookie and never reached that total again. He compiled a record of 571–634 (.474) for the Rangers, Phillies, and Indians, who were expected to win 15 more games than that. Joey Amalfitano (643 games as a player, 66–116 as a manager), Preston Gomez (8, 346–529), Jim Marshall (410, 229–326), and Russ Nixon (906, 231–347) are some other examples of mediocre players who failed as managers. That's the trouble with reasoning based on a handful of examples: It's easy to find the counterexamples that shoot down your premise.

So the next time someone suggests to you that utility infielders, reserve catchers, or career minor leaguers make the best managers, fight back. If he mentions Gene Mauch, tell him about Cronin or Amalfitano. If he mentions Ralph Houk, throw Lopez or Nixon at 'im. He says Earl Weaver, say Davey Johnson or Gomez. And if he's still standing after all that, give up. Some people are like that.

WON-LOST RECORD BY STARTING POSITION

New York Mets	C	1B	2B	3B	SS	LF	CF	RF	DH	P	Leadoff	Cleanup	Starts vs. LH	Starts vs. RH	Total Starts
Kevin Baez	-	-	-	-	2-2	-	-	-	-	-	-	-	2	2	2-2
Kevin Bass	-	-	-	-	-	9-14	-	1-7	-	-	-	1-0	11	20	10-21
Mike Birkbeck	-	-	-	-	-	-	-	-	-	0-1	-	-	-	1	0-1
Bobby Bonilla	-	0-3	-	-	-	-	-	62-59	-	-	-	9-11	45	79	62-62
Daryl Boston	-	-	-	-	-	26-25	6-2	1-5	-	-	10-12	-	6	59	33-32
Tim Burke	-	-	-	-	-	-	-	-	-	-	-	-	-	-	-
Vince Coleman	-	-	-	-	-	15-25	7-13	-	-	-	22-38	-	16	44	22-38
David Cone	-	-	-	-	-	-	-	-	-	17-10	-	-	8	19	17-10
Mark Dewey	-	-	-	-	-	-	-	-	-	-	-	-	-	-	-
Chris Donnels	-	-	3-8	7-14	-	-	-	-	-	-	0-1	-	2	30	10-22
D.J. Dozier	-	-	-	-	-	6-8	-	-	-	-	-	-	10	4	6-8
Kevin Elster	-	-	-	-	2-3	-	-	-	-	-	-	-	2	3	2-3
Sid Fernandez	-	-	-	-	-	-	-	-	-	18-14	-	-	12	20	18-14
Tom Filer	-	-	-	-	-	-	-	-	-	0-1	-	-	-	1	0-1
John Franco	-	-	-	-	-	-	-	-	-	-	-	-	-	-	-
Dave Gallagher	-	-	-	-	-	5-6	4-3	5-11	-	-	-	4-2	24	10	14-20
Paul Gibson	-	-	-	-	-	-	-	-	-	-	1-0	-	-	1	1-0
Dwight Gooden	-	-	-	-	-	-	-	-	-	12-19	-	-	13	18	12-19
Lee Guetterman	-	-	-	-	-	-	-	-	-	-	-	-	-	-	-
Terrel Hansen	-	-	-	-	-	-	-	-	-	-	-	-	-	-	-
Eric Hillman	-	-	-	-	-	-	-	-	-	2-6	-	-	3	5	2-6
Pat Howell	-	-	-	-	-	-	8-13	-	-	-	8-11	-	9	12	8-13
Todd Hundley	46-52	-	-	-	-	-	-	-	-	-	-	-	29	69	46-52
Jeff Innis	-	-	-	-	-	-	-	-	-	-	-	-	-	-	-
Howard Johnson	-	-	-	-	-	8-5	37-45	0-1	-	-	4-3	13-12	34	62	45-51
Barry Jones	-	-	-	-	-	-	-	-	-	-	-	-	-	-	-
Jeff Kent	-	-	13-17	-	0-1	-	-	-	-	-	-	-	14	17	13-18
Dave Magadan	-	1-0	-	41-48	-	-	-	-	-	-	0-1	2-2	29	61	42-48
Rod McCray	-	-	-	-	-	-	-	-	-	-	-	-	-	-	-
Jeff McKnight	-	3-2	2-6	0-1	1-0	-	-	-	-	-	-	0-1	3	12	6-9
Eddie Murray	-	68-84	-	-	-	-	-	-	-	-	-	46-62	51	101	68-84
Junior Noboa	-	-	2-2	-	0-1	-	-	-	-	-	0-3	-	3	2	2-3
Charlie O'Brien	22-29	-	-	-	-	-	-	-	-	-	-	-	27	24	22-29
Bill Pecota	-	-	10-17	10-11	9-11	-	-	-	-	-	-	0-2	26	42	29-39
Willie Randolph	-	-	38-36	-	-	-	-	-	-	-	17-7	-	29	45	38-36
Steve Rosenberg	-	-	-	-	-	-	-	-	-	-	-	-	-	-	-
Bret Saberhagen	-	-	-	-	-	-	-	-	-	8-7	-	-	5	10	8-7
Mackey Sasser	4-9	0-1	-	-	-	3-3	-	1-1	-	-	-	1-1	1	21	8-14
Dick Schofield	-	-	-	-	58-72	-	-	-	-	-	-	-	46	84	58-72
Pete Schourek	-	-	-	-	-	-	-	-	-	8-13	-	-	7	14	8-13
Steve Springer	-	-	1-0	-	-	-	-	-	-	-	-	-	1	-	1-0
Ryan Thompson	-	-	-	-	-	-	9-12	2-4	-	-	7-8	-	10	17	11-16
Joe Vitko	-	-	-	-	-	-	-	-	-	0-1	-	-	1	-	0-1
Chico Walker	-	-	3-4	14-16	-	0-4	1-2	0-2	-	-	0-2	0-1	18	28	18-28
Wally Whitehurst	-	-	-	-	-	-	-	-	-	2-9	-	-	3	8	2-9
Anthony Young	-	-	-	-	-	-	-	-	-	4-9	-	-	4	9	4-9

TEAM TOTALS: BATTING

	AB	H	2B	3B	HR	RBI	BB	SO	BA	SA	OBA
Season	5340	1254	259	17	93	564	572	956	.235	.342	.310
vs. Left-Handers	1916	462	95	8	26	206	191	308	.241	.340	.310
vs. Right-Handers	3424	792	164	9	67	358	381	648	.231	.343	.310
vs. Ground-Ballers	2506	596	121	10	37	246	267	429	.238	.338	.312
vs. Fly-Ballers	2834	658	138	7	56	318	305	527	.232	.345	.308
Home Games	2585	599	123	10	42	270	288	465	.232	.336	.309
Road Games	2755	655	136	7	51	294	284	491	.238	.348	.311
Grass Fields	3707	880	165	14	70	393	388	647	.237	.346	.310
Artificial Turf	1633	374	94	3	23	171	184	309	.229	.333	.309
April	718	171	43	1	10	88	93	129	.238	.343	.330
May	879	199	23	2	16	96	112	151	.226	.312	.314
June	910	212	54	2	19	99	108	159	.233	.359	.317
July	800	196	41	1	11	70	67	137	.245	.340	.303
August	955	224	35	4	22	97	93	159	.235	.349	.304
Sept./Oct.	1078	252	63	7	15	114	99	221	.234	.347	.296
Leading Off Inn.	1345	308	59	3	28	28	110	234	.229	.340	.289
Runners On	2165	538	120	8	40	511	304	363	.248	.367	.339
Bases Empty	3175	716	139	9	53	53	268	593	.226	.325	.288
Runners/Scor. Pos.	1267	283	73	5	27	466	238	239	.223	.353	.341
Runners On/2 Out	915	196	45	3	18	182	140	161	.214	.329	.320
Scor. Pos./2 Out	604	114	31	3	11	162	113	123	.189	.305	.318
Late-Inning Pressure	902	215	46	1	19	102	118	174	.238	.355	.329
Leading Off	233	55	12	1	5	5	18	41	.236	.361	.291
Runners On	363	93	21	0	9	92	68	66	.256	.388	.372
Runners/Scor. Pos.	229	52	14	0	8	87	51	48	.227	.393	.364

RUNS BATTED IN	From 1B	From 2B	From 3B	Scoring Position
Totals	70/1542	165/1016	236/580	401/1596
Percentage	4.5%	16.2%	40.7%	25.1%

TEAM TOTALS: PITCHING

	W-L	ERA	AB	H	HR	BB	SO	BA	SA	OBA
Season	72-90	3.66	5474	1404	98	482	1025	.256	.379	.318
vs. Left-Handers			2369	626	40	256	416	.264	.382	.337
vs. Right-Handers			3105	778	58	226	609	.251	.377	.303
vs. Ground-Ballers			2508	626	22	196	493	.250	.343	.306
vs. Fly-Ballers			2966	778	76	286	532	.262	.411	.328
Home Games	41-40	3.28	2820	707	49	224	528	.251	.370	.308
Road Games	31-50	4.06	2654	697	49	258	497	.263	.390	.328
Grass Fields	57-57	3.36	3887	980	71	320	725	.252	.374	.310
Artificial Turf	15-33	4.40	1587	424	27	162	300	.267	.393	.336
April	13-9	3.81	726	172	9	66	175	.237	.344	.304
May	12-15	3.27	880	221	20	76	198	.251	.373	.310
June	11-17	3.39	968	262	13	86	174	.271	.390	.331
July	13-11	3.01	778	174	12	79	163	.224	.337	.295
August	11-17	3.51	994	255	16	77	146	.257	.382	.313
Sept./Oct.	12-21	4.70	1128	320	28	98	169	.284	.425	.341
Leading Off Inn.			1361	369	29	84	241	.271	.400	.317
Bases Empty			3151	798	59	226	594	.253	.377	.308
Runners On			2323	606	39	256	431	.261	.383	.331
Runners/Scor. Pos.			1367	348	25	194	263	.255	.374	.340
Runners On/2 Out			1010	261	18	133	197	.258	.381	.348
Scor. Pos./2 Out			668	166	13	101	134	.249	.374	.350
Late-Inning Pressure			856	224	18	89	128	.262	.386	.334
Leading Off			224	56	5	16	29	.250	.375	.303
Runners On			335	89	10	54	47	.266	.412	.368
Runners/Scor. Pos.			192	49	7	44	28	.255	.406	.387
First 9 Batters			2761	702	47	253	539	.254	.367	.319
Second 9 Batters			1386	356	15	129	290	.257	.366	.323
All Batters Thereafter			1327	346	36	100	196	.261	.419	.311

WON-LOST RECORD BY STARTING POSITION

Philadelphia Phillies	C	1B	2B	3B	SS	LF	CF	RF	DH	P	Leadoff	Cleanup	Starts vs. LH	Starts vs. RH	Total Starts
Kyle Abbott	-	-	-	-	-	-	-	-	-	3-16	-	-	9	10	3-16
Ruben Amaro Jr.	-	-	-	-	-	10-8	9-14	20-26	-	-	13-19	-	32	55	39-48
Andy Ashby	-	-	-	-	-	-	-	-	-	5-3	-	-	3	5	5-3
Bob Ayrault	-	-	-	-	-	-	-	-	-	-	-	-	-	-	-
Wally Backman	-	-	0-3	-	-	-	-	-	-	-	-	-	-	3	0-3
Jay Baller	-	-	-	-	-	-	-	-	-	-	-	-	-	-	-
Kim Batiste	-	-	-	16-23	-	-	-	-	-	-	-	-	20	19	16-23
Juan Bell	-	-	-	20-25	-	-	-	-	-	-	-	-	22	23	20-25
Cliff Brantley	-	-	-	-	-	-	-	-	-	3-6	-	-	4	5	3-6
Brad Brink	-	-	-	-	-	-	-	-	-	1-6	-	-	7	-	1-6
Braulio Castillo	-	-	-	-	-	-	2-4	6-6	-	-	-	-	8	10	8-10
Wes Chamberlain	-	-	-	-	-	11-14	-	17-28	-	-	-	-	26	44	28-42
Darrin Chapin	-	-	-	-	-	-	-	-	-	-	-	-	-	-	-
Pat Combs	-	-	-	-	-	-	-	-	-	2-2	-	-	2	2	2-2
Danny Cox	-	-	-	-	-	-	-	-	-	3-4	-	-	-	7	3-4
Darren Daulton	61-76	-	-	-	-	-	-	-	-	-	-	17-20	49	88	61-76
Jose DeJesus	-	-	-	-	-	-	-	-	-	-	-	-	-	-	-
Jose DeLeon	-	-	-	-	-	-	-	-	-	1-2	-	-	1	2	1-2
Mariano Duncan	-	-	20-30	1-2	10-16	25-33	-	-	-	-	-	-	61	76	56-81
Len Dykstra	-	-	-	-	-	-	40-45	-	-	-	40-45	-	34	51	40-45
Tommy Greene	-	-	-	-	-	-	-	-	-	7-5	-	-	5	7	7-5
Jeff Grotewold	-	-	-	-	-	0-1	-	-	-	-	-	-	-	1	0-1
Mike Hartley	-	-	-	-	-	-	-	-	-	-	-	-	-	-	-
David Hollins	-	-	-	66-90	-	-	-	-	-	-	-	4-5	65	91	66-90
Ken Howell	-	-	-	-	-	-	-	-	-	-	-	-	-	-	-
Stan Javier	-	-	-	-	-	12-12	19-27	-	-	-	15-25	-	33	37	31-39
Barry Jones	-	-	-	-	-	-	-	-	-	-	-	-	-	-	-
Ricky Jordan	-	25-27	-	-	-	3-6	-	-	-	-	-	6-8	36	25	28-33
John Kruk	-	42-64	-	-	-	2-3	-	12-17	-	-	-	43-59	52	88	56-84
Steve Lake	4-10	-	-	-	-	-	-	-	-	-	-	-	10	4	4-10
Jim Lindeman	-	-	-	-	-	-	1-2	-	-	-	-	-	3	-	1-2
Tony Longmire	-	-	-	-	-	-	-	-	-	-	-	-	-	-	-
Tom Marsh	-	-	-	-	-	7-14	-	8-3	-	-	-	-	20	12	15-17
Greg Mathews	-	-	-	-	-	-	-	-	-	-	1-6	-	1	6	1-6
Joe Millette	-	-	0-1	1-0	12-13	-	-	-	-	-	-	-	9	18	13-14
Mickey Morandini	-	-	48-58	-	-	-	0-1	-	-	-	-	2-2	20	87	48-59
Terry Mulholland	-	-	-	-	-	-	-	-	-	16-16	-	-	12	20	16-16
Dale Murphy	-	-	-	-	-	0-1	-	6-10	-	-	-	0-1	10	7	6-11
Julio Peguero	-	-	-	-	-	-	0-2	-	-	-	-	-	1	1	0-2
Todd Pratt	5-6	-	-	-	-	-	-	-	-	-	-	-	8	3	5-6
Wally Ritchie	-	-	-	-	-	-	-	-	-	-	-	-	-	-	-
Ben Rivera	-	-	-	-	-	-	-	-	-	8-6	-	-	8	6	8-6
Don Robinson	-	-	-	-	-	-	-	-	-	4-4	-	-	4	4	4-4
Steve Scarsone	-	-	2-0	-	-	-	-	-	-	-	-	-	2	-	2-0
Curt Schilling	-	-	-	-	-	-	-	-	-	14-12	-	-	9	17	14-12
Steve Searcy	-	-	-	-	-	-	-	-	-	-	-	-	-	-	-
Keith Shepherd	-	-	-	-	-	-	-	-	-	-	-	-	-	-	-
Dale Sveum	-	3-1	-	2-0	12-14	-	-	-	-	-	-	-	15	17	17-15
Mickey Weston	-	-	-	-	-	-	-	-	-	-	0-1	-	-	1	0-1
Mike Williams	-	-	-	-	-	-	-	-	-	2-3	-	-	2	3	2-3
Mitch Williams	-	-	-	-	-	-	-	-	-	-	-	-	-	-	-

TEAM TOTALS: BATTING

	AB	H	2B	3B	HR	RBI	BB	SO	BA	SA	OBA
Season	5500	1392	255	36	118	638	509	1059	.253	.377	.320
vs. Left-Handers	2286	589	110	12	53	255	189	428	.258	.386	.318
vs. Right-Handers	3214	803	145	24	65	383	320	631	.250	.371	.321
vs. Ground-Ballers	2544	661	116	20	49	284	213	468	.260	.379	.322
vs. Fly-Ballers	2956	731	139	16	69	354	296	591	.247	.375	.318
Home Games	2685	688	133	19	67	342	269	526	.256	.395	.328
Road Games	2815	704	122	17	51	296	240	533	.250	.360	.312
Grass Fields	1463	377	65	7	33	173	118	282	.258	.379	.318
Artificial Turf	4037	1015	190	29	85	465	391	777	.251	.376	.321
April	747	190	30	5	15	102	66	164	.254	.368	.324
May	850	215	46	2	18	105	87	184	.253	.375	.323
June	931	238	52	6	19	96	92	143	.256	.386	.324
July	975	253	37	6	26	119	99	215	.259	.390	.332
August	875	209	37	6	20	95	74	156	.239	.363	.300
Sept./Oct.	1122	287	53	11	20	121	91	197	.256	.376	.316
Leading Off Inn.	1321	337	63	9	23	23	103	243	.255	.369	.316
Runners On	2404	631	114	15	61	581	272	460	.262	.399	.337
Bases Empty	3096	761	141	21	57	57	237	599	.246	.360	.306
Runners/Scor. Pos.	1376	348	59	8	30	487	204	267	.253	.373	.344
Runners On/2 Out	1028	250	46	8	24	126	138	188	.243	.374	.340
Scor. Pos./2 Out	671	153	29	4	11	184	109	122	.228	.332	.341
Late-Inning Pressure	879	230	37	2	15	95	80	193	.262	.359	.330
Leading Off	222	56	11	1	1	1	15	46	.252	.324	.303
Runners On	371	103	16	0	8	88	45	80	.278	.385	.363
Runners/Scor. Pos.	191	51	5	0	6	77	33	41	.267	.387	.378

RUNS BATTED IN	From 1B	From 2B	From 3B	Scoring Position
Totals	99/1766	176/1054	245/610	421/1664
Percentage	5.6%	16.7%	40.2%	25.3%

TEAM TOTALS: PITCHING

	W-L	ERA	AB	H	HR	BB	SO	BA	SA	OBA
Season	70-92	4.11	5401	1387	113	549	851	.257	.384	.326
vs. Left-Handers			2269	603	40	241	311	.266	.381	.336
vs. Right-Handers			3132	784	73	308	540	.250	.386	.318
vs. Ground-Ballers			2306	587	32	210	384	.255	.353	.317
vs. Fly-Ballers			3095	800	81	339	467	.258	.406	.332
Home Games	41-40	3.67	2752	685	49	272	474	.249	.365	.316
Road Games	29-52	4.58	2649	702	64	277	377	.265	.404	.335
Grass Fields	16-26	4.87	1379	371	37	136	212	.269	.413	.333
Artificial Turf	54-66	3.86	4022	1016	76	413	639	.253	.374	.323
April	10-12	5.14	738	195	19	95	131	.264	.404	.349
May	12-13	3.47	860	216	13	95	143	.251	.357	.327
June	12-15	3.78	903	227	16	83	128	.251	.367	.316
July	11-18	4.10	962	254	21	71	146	.264	.398	.314
August	8-18	4.88	874	234	23	100	143	.268	.416	.343
Sept./Oct.	17-16	3.61	1064	261	21	105	160	.245	.367	.312
Leading Off Inn.			1316	354	30	113	191	.269	.405	.329
Bases Empty			3051	779	64	275	457	.255	.379	.319
Runners On			2350	608	49	274	394	.259	.390	.333
Runners/Scor. Pos.			1376	372	26	189	239	.270	.404	.351
Runners On/2 Out			1006	243	14	122	184	.242	.354	.327
Scor. Pos./2 Out			647	163	10	100	120	.252	.371	.357
Late-Inning Pressure			660	177	10	101	112	.268	.394	.365
Leading Off			163	44	3	24	26	.270	.411	.364
Runners On			301	80	7	51	59	.266	.415	.395
Runners/Scor. Pos.			191	57	4	33	37	.298	.466	.395
First 9 Batters			2782	686	63	354	499	.247	.379	.331
Second 9 Batters			1359	355	21	98	200	.261	.366	.312
All Batters Thereafter			1260	346	29	97	152	.275	.415	.326

PHILADELPHIA PHILLIES

Here's a test that will date any baseball fan nearly as well as carbon 14. Answer the following multiple-choice question: Who or what are the Whiz Kids?

(A) A Seattle-based rock band whose members slather their bodies in spreadable processed cheese food;

(B) A not-for-profit organization to aid children with chronic bladder problems; or

(C) The 1950 National League champion Philadelphia Phillies.

If you answered *C,* you're correct; you're also probably at least 40 years old. And if you're past 50, you might even know more than the names of the players on the team.

Back in 1950, the Phillies Whiz Kids were as hot as Hopalong Cassidy, roller derby, and the mambo. But to baseball fans who don't remember eight-team leagues, they are a mystery. Children of the '60s may recall that the name "Whiz Kids" was occasionally invoked by Lindsey Nelson, Red Barber, or other broadcasters of the era, as though it represented something unique and spectacular. But just 10 or 15 years after they burst onto the scene, it seemed that, as with so many fads of the Eisenhower era, every trace of the Whiz Kids had disappeared. Well, not *every* trace—Richie Ashburn was still drawing leadoff walks for the expansion Mets; and Curt Simmons and Robin Roberts were still winning games for a variety of teams. But today, little is remembered about one of the game's special teams, one that shined briefly, but with unusual brilliance, less than a half-century ago. So, as part of our program to expand baseball's historical literacy, we devote this year's Phillies essay to the Whiz Kids.

The 1950 Phillies were coming off a third-place finish that was their best in more than three decades, since they finished second to the 1917 Giants. But more important than that, their roster was loaded with talented "bonus babies" signed during a furious late-1940s spending spree that cost Phillies owner Bob Carpenter an estimated quarter-million dollars for some of the country's best sandlot players. They included Ashburn (who received a $4,500 bonus), Roberts ($25,000), Simmons ($65,000), third baseman Willie Jones ($16,000), and catcher Stan Lopata ($19,000). Although only two key members of the 1950 team were rookies (pitchers Bob Miller and Bubba Church), Philadelphia had the youngest team in the National League.

Despite all its young talent, Philadelphia was selected in a poll of writers to finish fourth in the National League, one position lower than in 1949. But the Whiz Kids—a term coined during training camp by local reporters—led the N.L. throughout much of the spring and most of the summer; by mid-September, the kids were threatening to draw away from the pack completely. Then came a series of blows to the starting rotation: Curt Simmons was lost to military service, Bob Miller (who started the season 8–0) hurt his arm, and Bubba Church was hit below the left eye by a Ted Kluszewski line drive that cost him eight days while he recuperated from plastic surgery. In the end, Philadelphia needed a 10-inning victory over Brooklyn on the final day of the season to avoid a best-of-three tie-breaking playoff with the Dodgers. The Whiz Kids

limped into the World Series and were swept by the Yankees, losing each of the first three games by a single run.

Nevertheless, their heroes were many: Del Ennis led the league with 126 RBIs, and batted .311 with 31 home runs; Ashburn batted .303 and was spectacular in center field; Jones hit 25 home runs, which stands forever as his career high; the veteran catcher Andy Seminick equaled the career highs he'd set a year earlier in home runs (24) and RBIs (68) while raising his batting average by 45 points to .288. And the pitching was sensational, particularly by Roberts (20–11), Simmons (17–8), and Jim Konstanty, who set a major league record with 74 appearances (all in relief) and became the first relief pitcher ever to win a Most Valuable Player award.

Despite its shaky conclusion, the 1950 season should have been a coming-out party for a team so young. Only two other teams in major league history reached the World Series with their league's youngest position players and its youngest pitchers: the 1935 Cubs, who ran second to the Giants in '36 and '37 before returning to the Series in 1938; and the 1943 Cardinals, who lost the Series to the Yankees but returned a year later to beat the Browns, and finished no worse than second for five years thereafter. Since 1950, only two teams with the youngest batters and the youngest pitchers have posted even a winning record; both were preludes to multiple championships: the 1968 Athletics and the 1988 Pirates.

But the Whiz Kids hardly dominated the league throughout the rest of the 1950s. In fact, their September swoon was a harbinger of the trouble ahead; they would never again contend for a league pennant. It wasn't until 1964, when Philadelphia blew a late-September lead and lost the pennant to St. Louis on the final day of the season, that the Phillies would once again finish higher than third place. No team since the Whiz Kids has gone that long after a World Series appearance without as much as a second-place finish. The longest spans in major league history, with the year of the next first- or second-place finish indicated:

Year	Team	Span	Next	Year	Team	Span	Next
1945	Cubs	24	1969	1918	Cubs	11	1929
1918	Red Sox	20	1938	1914	Athletics	11	1925
1944	Browns	16	1960	1960	Pirates	10	1970
1950	Phillies	14	1964	1933	Senators	10	1943
1937	Giants	14	1951	1906	White Sox	10	1916
1973	Mets	11	1984	1982	Brewers	10	1992

Three factors helped prevent the Whiz Kids from becoming perennial contenders: *(1)* an abrupt decline in 1951, attributed by many at the time (including their manager, Eddie Sawyer) to the sins of celebrity and high living in the aftermath of their championship season; *(2)* the evolution of several other powerhouse teams in the National League; and *(3)* the abject failure of the Phillies system to produce any quality players over the next six years.

Although Ashburn and Roberts had great seasons in 1951, most of the other key players from the 1950 team regressed. As the table below indicates, Ashburn was the only regular starter to match his 1950 home-run total in 1951; only he and Jones surpassed their previous season's batting averages. The team fell from fourth in the league with an average of 4.60 runs per game to sixth at 4.21. Goliat's figures do not include five games with the Browns:

	Year	G	AB	R	H	2B	3B	HR	RBI	BB	SB	BA
Ashburn	1950	151	594	84	180	25	14	2	41	63	14	.303
	1951	154	643	92	221	31	5	4	63	50	29	.344
Ennis	1950	153	595	92	185	34	8	31	126	56	2	.311
	1951	144	532	76	142	20	5	15	73	68	4	.267
Goliat	1950	145	483	49	113	13	6	13	64	53	3	.234
	1951	41	138	14	31	2	1	4	15	9	0	.225
Hamner	1950	157	637	78	172	27	5	11	82	39	2	.270
	1951	150	589	61	150	23	7	9	72	29	10	.255
Jones	1950	157	610	100	163	28	6	25	88	61	5	.267
	1951	148	564	79	161	28	5	22	81	60	6	.285
Seminick	1950	130	393	55	113	15	3	24	68	68	0	.288
	1951	101	291	42	66	8	1	11	37	63	1	.227
Sisler	1950	141	523	79	155	29	4	13	83	64	1	.296
	1951	125	428	46	123	20	5	8	52	40	1	.287
Waitkus	1950	154	641	102	182	32	5	2	44	55	3	.284
	1951	145	610	65	157	27	4	1	46	53	0	.257

Although Roberts posted another 20-win season in 1951 (21–15), Simmons was lost to military service for the entire season and Miller pitched only 34 innings as he continued to struggle with arm problems. Konstanty's ERA rose from 2.66 to 4.03 as his record dipped from 16–7 to 4–11, raising the issue of whether he had been overworked in 1950, when he pitched 152 innings in relief during the regular season, then pitched 15 innings more in the World Series, including a start in the opener.

Still, even that broadly based a lapse shouldn't have been cause for alarm; the nucleus of the team was still young, and Simmons was due back in 1952. Of greater concern was the growing strength of the competition. The great rookie class of 1948, of which Ashburn, Roberts, and Simmons were members, had also helped a number of the Phillies' rivals—particularly the Dodgers, who added Duke Snider, Gil Hodges, and Roy Campanella to a lineup that already included Jackie Robinson, the previous year's top rookie. By 1952, tremendous young power hitters were sprouting all over the National League—not only the Dodgers stars mentioned above, but also Eddie Mathews with the Braves and Willie Mays with the Giants. Within two years, Mays would become the dominant player in the league, and Hank Aaron and Joe Adcock would join Mathews on what would be one of the greatest young lineups in major league history.

Unfortunately for the Phillies, their own well ran dry. Have you ever heard of Ted Kazanski? For the seven years starting in 1950, Kazanski, a utility infielder, was the only Phillies rookie who went on to play even 400 games during his entire career (batting .217 in 417 games from 1953 through 1958). The following table lists all Phillies rookies from 1945 through 1960 who played at least 500 games or earned 50 wins—relatively modest totals, wouldn't you say? Note the vacuum from 1950 through 1956:

1946: Del Ennis, Johnny Wyrostek
1948: Richie Ashburn, Robin Roberts, Curt Simmons
1949: Willie Jones, Stan Lopata
1957: Ed Bouchee, Don Cardwell, Turk Farrell, Chico Fernandez, Jack Sanford
1959: Joe Koppe
1960: Ruben Amaro, Clay Dalrymple, Tony Gonzalez

Here's the bottom line: It took the Phillies seven years after losing the 1950 World Series to produce even one rookie who attained career totals of either 500 games or 50 victories. No other Series team ever took more than four years to do so. The only team to reach even four years was the 1957 Yankees, but the abundant talent already on hand allowed the Yankees to extend their dynasty into the mid-1960s.

The 500-game/50-win criterion is purposely lenient. After all, scant qualifiers include Phil Linz, Alvaro Espinoza, Jim Beattie, Charles Hudson, and Atlee Hammaker. Some additional perspective is added by a list of Series teams that failed to produce rookies who reached 1000 games or 100 wins in their first five post-Series seasons: the 1916 Dodgers, the 1939 Reds, and the 1941 Yankees.

Brooklyn went into decline immediately after its appearance in the 1916 World Series; the Dodgers finished in the first division only twice in the next 13 years (an aberrant league title in 1920, and a second-place finish in 1924). Cincinnati's decline was just as marked, only slower to develop: The Reds returned to the Series in 1940, and remained in the first division for another four years thereafter, before enduring a streak of 11 consecutive seasons in the second division. The last of those teams, the 1941 Yankees, may have made the list in part because of servicemen who otherwise would have joined the Yankees during the mid-1940s; we're thinking in particular of Yogi Berra and Vic Raschi. But, like the '57 Yankees, the '41 team was so dominant that an additional influx of rookie talent wasn't necessary. (However, it's worth noting that the period from 1944 through 1948 produced only one A.L. title for the Yankees; it was the only time during a 30-year period starting in 1935 that the Yankees went more than one season without a league championship.)

If there's anything in the story of the Whiz Kids that's applicable to baseball today, it's the realization that few championship teams are powerful enough to remain contenders year after year without an influx of additional talent. Baseball teams don't age in a linear fashion; for example, by 1955 the one-time Whiz Kids had aged to the extent that Philadelphia had the second-oldest lineup in the National League. Teams that appear to stand still are actually shifting into reverse.

Of course, today's teams don't have to rely on their own farm systems to the extent that teams in the 1950s did; the Yankees demonstrated in the first decade of free agency how to stay afloat by throwing money around. This seems particularly topical with regard to the current Atlanta Braves. Most baseball people agree that Atlanta has one of the most talent-laden organizations in baseball. But history proves that this is hardly a case of bringing coals to Newcastle; even winning teams need to fortify their strengths. Those that do not almost inevitably are doomed to a long and humbling decline.

PITTSBURGH PIRATES

For the past few seasons, there were clear and ominous warning signs that the Pittsburgh Pirates would soon cease to exist, at least as we had come to know them through three championship seasons. Arbitration victories two years ago over their two best players made it unlikely that either Barry Bonds or Bobby Bonilla would remain with the team beyond their six-year service periods, so neither departure was at all unexpected. The same could not be said, however, of Pittsburgh's trade last spring of incumbent 20-game-winner John Smiley to the Twins for a pair of prospects. With Doug Drabek also facing free agency after the 1992 season—he eventually left to join the Astros—the implications of the Smiley trade left little to the imagination. The apocalypse was in sight.

But when the Pirates finally came crashing down last winter, it was still shocking to see how little remained of the first National League team in more than a decade to win three consecutive division titles. This was utter devastation—a little bit of Hurricane Andrew in Steel City. Prior to 1991, only six teams in major league history had lost a 100-RBI man from its lineup and a 15-game winner from its rotation during the same off-season. Pittsburgh has done so in each of the past *two* off-seasons:

Year	Team	100+ RBIs	15+ Wins
1901	Phillies	Ed Delahanty	Red Donahue
			Bill Duggleby
			Al Orth
1927	Giants	Rogers Hornsby	Burleigh Grimes
1935	Athletics	Jimmie Foxx	Johnny Marcum
1959	Indians	Rocky Colavito	Cal McLish
1975	Athletics	Reggie Jackson	Ken Holtzman
1991	Pirates	Bobby Bonilla	John Smiley
1992	Pirates	Barry Bonds	Doug Drabek

Not since Charles O. Finley's breakup of the '75 A's had a team lost such big contributors to both its offense and its defense as Pittsburgh suffered prior to the 1992 season. And since it worked so well (don't forget—they still won the division), the Pirates did it again. Then, for good measure, Jose Lind, the trigger man for Pittsburgh's last-inning self-destruction in the 1992 N.L.C.S., and Danny Jackson were handed one-way tickets out of town. And before the winter started, even a cadre of role players including Alex Cole, Cecil Espy, Gary Varsho, and Roger Mason, had found new employers as well. Never before had a team suffered the unredeemed loss of such high-quality players over such a short period of time. And it could be that by the end of the 1993 season, when we can stand back and measure the damage, the dissolution of the 1992 Pirates will be recorded as the most thorough of any defending champion in major league history in terms of quantity as well.

For the record, let's look at the turnover on some of the most turbulent defending champs of the past. First, some background: A typical team changes its makeup from one season to the next by an average of 38 percent. That figure has remained fairly constant throughout this century, with obvious blips on the graph below for the two world wars and the start of the free-agency era. The graph also illustrates a somewhat intuitive fact—namely, that teams that win division or league titles change to a considerably lesser degree than other teams do:

Generally speaking, turnover on the best teams is a bit more than half that on the worst teams. Division and league champions have averaged a 29 percent change, compared to a rate of 52 percent by the more than 200 teams in this century that compiled winning percentages below the .400 mark. And the group of 313 teams that changed its personnel by at least 50 percent includes only two defending champions. In both instances, the vast turnover in personnel was attributable to players who served in the military during World War II: the 1944 Yankees (51.6%) and the 1945 Cardinals (51.7%), who had the highest turnover in this century by a defending champion.

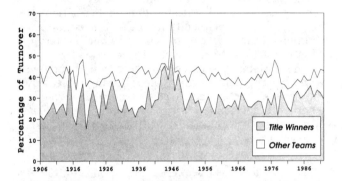

Among championship rosters unaffected by military obligations, none changed more than that of the 1918 Boston Red Sox. Like Pittsburgh's recent makeover, Boston's radical changes were prompted by financial considerations. Red Sox owner Harry Frazee needed to raise cash, so before the start of the 1919 season he began a sell-off of his best players, including pitchers Dutch Leonard and Carl Mays, that would last for years and be a major factor in the start of the Yankees dynasty.

The makeover champ among division winners in the contemporary era was the 1983 Philadelphia Phillies, and the explanation was simple: It was the oldest team in National League history, with two regular starters over the age of 40 by the end of the season (Pete Rose and Joe Morgan), a 41-year-old part-timer (Tony Perez), and three other regulars between the ages of 33 and 35 (Mike Schmidt, Gary Matthews, and Garry Maddox). The pitching staff featured Steve Carlton (38), Tug McGraw (39), and Ron Reed (40); the team leaders in wins (John Denny) and saves (Al Holland) were both past 30.

Philadelphia's reinforcements came in the form of rookie Juan Samuel, Von Hayes (who assumed full-time status in 1984), Glenn Wilson, Sixto Lezcano, Ozzie Virgil, and a variety of role players, including Tim Corcoran, John Wockenfuss, and Len Matuszek. The pitching staff was fortified by the addition of Jerry Koosman and Shane Rawley. If you're looking for a reason for Philadelphia's decline later in the decade, note that only three of those players—Samuel, Virgil, and Matuszek—were developed in the Phillies organization.

That bit of history may spook the Pirates, who sacrificed several outstanding prospects over the past few years to acquire veteran help during pennant races, including Willie Greene and Moises Alou (for

Zane Smith), and dealt a pair of promising pitchers to the Texas Rangers (for Steve Buechele, himself later traded for three months of Danny Jackson). That's hardly a condemnation; three consecutive N.L. East titles is a record that almost any team would trade for, notwithstanding the N.L.C.S. losses. On the other hand, there was the embarrassing administrative blunder that needlessly cost Pittsburgh Wes Chamberlain. Those players would have given the Pirates hope for the future, especially playing alongside the prospects acquired by trading Smiley and Lind, and perhaps shortened the rebuilding process. As it is, Pittsburgh may find itself struggling to keep pace with the expansion teams.

The loss of Barry Bonds alone probably would have been enough to topple Pittsburgh from its position atop the N.L. East. In past editions of the *Analyst,* we have estimated that a typical star player is worth about five wins per season to his team. There is evidence that during Pittsburgh's three-year title run, Bonds was worth roughly double that. The following table shows the Pirates' record over the past seven years divided by whether or not Bonds was in the starting lineup. Focus on the raw won-lost totals; we'll explain the adjusted totals shortly:

Year	Raw Won-Lost Totals				Adjusted Totals	
	With Bonds		Without Bonds		With Bonds	Without
1986	43–65	.398	21–33	.389	21.5–32.5	21–33
1987	60–66	.476	20–16	.556	17.1–18.9	20–16
1988	71–58	.550	14–17	.452	17.1–13.9	14–17
1989	68–77	.469	6–11	.353	8.0–9.0	6–11
1990	85–60	.586	10–7	.588	10.0–7.0	10–7
1991	92–55	.626	6–9	.400	9.4–5.6	6–9
1992	85–53	.616	11–13	.458	14.8–9.2	11–13
Totals	504–434	.537	88–106	.454	97.8–96.2	88–106

The actual totals show that Pittsburgh had a winning percentage 83 points higher when Bonds started than when he sat (the equivalent of 13 wins over a full 162-game schedule). The problem with such a basic calculation is that each season contributes a different proportion of the "With Bonds" totals than it contributes to the "Without Bonds" totals. For example, Bonds started 147 games in 1991, or 16 percent of the totals; in that same season, he accounted for only 8 percent of all games in which he didn't start. That means it's apples and oranges (or, at least, Macintoshes and Rome Beauties).

The adjusted totals proportionately reduce the won-lost figures in games Bonds started so that they represent the same number of games as those he missed in that season. As a result, the adjusted totals are balanced, with each season contributing an equal amount to the "With" and "Without" groups. The difference in the adjusted winning percentages reflects a much more balanced and accurate appraisal of Bonds's value to the Pirates throughout his career: .504 with him, .454

without him—approximately 6.8 wins per season when adjusted for his average of 134 starts per year.

But, of course, Bonds was a far more valuable player over the past three years than he was earlier in his career. The corresponding calculations produce an estimated value of 18 wins per season when restricted to the past three years, but by that point the sample of games is too small to produce a meaningful result. But if we examine the value of all MVPs over a period of time, Bonds's true value over the last three years should become clearer. (Remember that in addition to winning the award in 1990 and 1992, Bonds was runner-up to Terry Pendleton in 1991.)

The following table shows the won-lost totals for the teams of MVPs from 1981 through 1992. When a pitcher won the award, the runner-up has been substituted, and these players are marked with an asterisk:

Year	A.L. MVP	With	W/O	N.L. MVP	With	W/O
1981	*R.Henderson, Oak.	63–44	1–1	Schmidt, Phil.	54–47	5–1
1982	Yount, Mil.	93–60	2–7	Murphy, Atl.	88–73	1–0
1983	C.Ripken, Balt.	98–64	0–0	Murphy, Atl.	85–73	3–1
1984	*Hrbek, Minn.	72–76	9–5	Sandberg, Chi.	95–61	1–4
1985	Mattingly, N.Y.	96–63	1–1	McGee, St.L.	95–51	6–10
1986	*Mattingly, N.Y.	90–72	0–0	*Schmidt, Phil.	82–70	4–5
1987	Bell, Tor.	94–60	2–6	Dawson, Chi.	70–81	6–4
1988	Canseco, Oak.	101–55	3–3	Gibson, L.A.	88–58	6–9
1989	Yount, Mil.	79–81	2–0	Mitchell, S.F.	85–63	7–7
1990	R.Henderson, Oak.	85–47	18–12	Bonds, Pitt.	85–60	10–7
1991	C.Ripken, Balt.	67–95	0–0	Pendleton, Atl.	88–60	6–8
1992	*Puckett, Minn.	86–70	4–2	Bonds, Pitt.	85–53	11–13

The teams of the MVPs listed above compiled a record of 108–106 (.505) when their stars were missing from the starting lineup. With the actual totals adjusted so that each MVP contributed an equal share to the "With" and "Without" totals, the combined winning percentage when they started was .589. The difference between those figures is equivalent to about 12 wins for an MVP who, like Bonds, has started an average of 143 games per season since 1990.

Incidentally, when the same technique was applied to a cross section of star players—specifically, All-Star game starters since 1981—the per-season value was considerably lower: an average of 3.7 wins per season over a full 162 games. (The teams' records were checked not only for the All-Star season but also for the previous year.)

Now let's start adding things up: Minus 10 wins for Bonds, minus another three or four each for Bonilla, Drabek, and Smiley. (Previous editions of the *Analyst* have indicated that starting pitchers and starting position players have roughly equal value.) And Lind may well be worth a win. Not to mention the fact that the estimate of player values assumes that an average backup is available; that may not be the case for Pittsburgh. So it's not too difficult to construct an equation that reduces the Pirates from a 90-win contender to a 70-win also-ran for the upcoming season—a sad ending to a baseball story for the '90s.

WON-LOST RECORD BY STARTING POSITION

Pittsburgh Pirates	C	1B	2B	3B	SS	LF	CF	RF	DH	P	Leadoff	Cleanup	Starts vs. LH	Starts vs. RH	Total Starts
Miguel Batista	-	-	-	-	-	-	-	-	-	-	-	-	-	-	-
Stan Belinda	-	-	-	-	-	-	-	-	-	-	-	-	-	-	-
Jay Bell	-	-	-	-	92-65	-	-	-	-	-	-	-	65	92	92-65
Barry Bonds	-	-	-	-	-	85-53	-	-	-	-	-	63-36	57	81	85-53
Steve Buechele	-	-	-	42-37	-	-	-	-	-	-	-	-	37	42	42-37
Dave Clark	-	-	-	-	-	-	-	1-6	-	-	-	-	-	7	1-6
Alex Cole	-	-	-	-	-	-	0-1	30-15	-	-	30-16	-	2	44	30-16
Victor Cole	-	-	-	-	-	-	-	-	-	1-3	-	-	2	2	1-3
Steve Cooke	-	-	-	-	-	-	-	-	-	-	-	-	-	-	-
Danny Cox	-	-	-	-	-	-	-	-	-	-	-	-	-	-	-
Doug Drabek	-	-	-	-	-	-	-	-	-	20-14	-	-	14	20	20-14
Cecil Espy	-	-	-	-	-	2-5	2-4	7-5	-	-	7-9	0-1	9	16	11-14
Carlos Garcia	-	-	5-2	-	2-0	-	-	-	-	-	-	-	-	9	7-2
Kirk Gibson	-	-	-	-	-	-	-	8-5	-	-	-	8-4	1	12	8-5
Jerry Don Gleaton	-	-	-	-	-	-	-	-	-	-	-	-	-	-	-
Danny Jackson	-	-	-	-	-	-	-	-	-	9-6	-	-	6	9	9-6
Jeff King	-	18-12	10-13	42-22	2-1	-	-	1-0	-	-	11-1	2-4	58	63	73-48
Dennis Lamp	-	-	-	-	-	-	-	-	-	-	-	-	-	-	-
Mike LaValliere	56-31	-	-	-	-	-	-	-	-	-	-	-	-	87	56-31
Jose Lind	-	-	80-51	-	-	-	-	-	-	-	-	-	54	77	80-51
Albert Martin	-	-	-	-	-	1-0	-	-	-	-	-	-	-	1	1-0
Roger Mason	-	-	-	-	-	-	-	-	-	-	-	-	-	-	-
Lloyd McClendon	-	3-2	-	-	-	2-3	-	28-17	-	-	-	23-18	55	-	33-22
Orlando Merced	-	53-34	-	-	-	-	-	4-7	-	-	7-10	7-7	4	94	57-41
Paul Miller	-	-	-	-	-	-	-	-	-	-	-	-	-	-	-
Blas Minor	-	-	-	-	-	-	-	-	-	-	-	-	-	-	-
Denny Neagle	-	-	-	-	-	-	-	-	-	2-4	-	-	4	2	2-4
Vicente Palacios	-	-	-	-	-	-	-	-	-	5-3	-	-	4	4	5-3
Bob Patterson	-	-	-	-	-	-	-	-	-	-	-	-	-	-	-
William Pennyfeather	-	-	-	-	-	-	0-1	-	-	-	-	-	1	-	0-1
Tom Prince	6-4	-	-	-	-	-	-	-	-	-	-	-	7	3	6-4
Gary Redus	-	17-14	-	-	-	1-1	1-0	5-5	-	-	-	23-20	43	1	24-20
Jeff M. Robinson	-	-	-	-	-	-	-	-	-	5-2	-	-	1	6	5-2
Don Slaught	34-31	-	-	-	-	-	-	-	-	-	-	-	58	7	34-31
Zane Smith	-	-	-	-	-	-	-	-	-	14-8	-	-	8	14	14-8
Randy Tomlin	-	-	-	-	-	-	-	-	-	22-11	-	-	11	22	22-11
Andy Van Slyke	-	-	-	-	-	-	93-60	-	-	-	-	-	57	96	93-60
Gary Varsho	-	-	-	-	-	5-4	-	12-6	-	-	8-6	1-0	-	27	17-10
Paul Wagner	-	-	-	-	-	-	-	-	-	1-0	-	-	1	-	1-0
Tim Wakefield	-	-	-	-	-	-	-	-	-	9-4	-	-	5	8	9-4
Bob Walk	-	-	-	-	-	-	-	-	-	8-11	-	-	9	10	8-11
John Wehner	-	5-4	1-0	11-7	-	-	-	-	-	-	-	2-0	12	16	17-11
Kevin Young	-	-	-	1-0	-	-	-	-	-	-	-	-	-	1	1-0

TEAM TOTALS: BATTING

	AB	H	2B	3B	HR	RBI	BB	SO	BA	SA	OBA
Season	5527	1409	272	54	106	656	569	872	.255	.381	.324
vs. Left-Handers	2193	563	121	22	37	250	233	329	.257	.383	.328
vs. Right-Handers	3334	846	151	32	69	406	336	543	.254	.380	.322
vs. Ground-Ballers	2088	510	93	21	27	215	236	336	.244	.348	.323
vs. Fly-Ballers	3439	899	179	33	79	441	333	536	.261	.402	.325
Home Games	2676	707	141	30	51	343	308	413	.264	.396	.339
Road Games	2851	702	131	24	55	313	261	459	.246	.367	.310
Grass Fields	1467	372	76	6	27	154	131	236	.254	.369	.314
Artificial Turf	4060	1037	196	48	79	502	438	636	.255	.386	.328
April	650	155	22	10	13	90	86	98	.238	.363	.329
May	973	260	57	6	17	123	109	161	.267	.391	.342
June	931	225	41	7	16	93	99	146	.242	.352	.313
July	916	216	45	11	18	84	80	147	.236	.368	.295
August	941	250	47	7	15	116	92	152	.266	.378	.330
Sept./Oct.	1116	303	60	13	27	150	103	168	.272	.421	.334
Leading Off Inn.	1362	339	77	12	33	33	103	216	.249	.396	.305
Runners On	2367	631	116	27	46	596	298	363	.267	.397	.345
Bases Empty	3160	778	156	27	60	60	271	509	.246	.370	.308
Runners/Scor. Pos.	1435	384	69	16	26	516	240	268	.268	.392	.355
Runners On/2 Out	994	220	42	9	15	207	153	163	.221	.327	.330
Scor. Pos./2 Out	658	150	30	4	8	181	116	114	.228	.322	.349
Late-Inning Pressure	888	212	36	10	12	96	109	160	.239	.342	.321
Leading Off	231	62	16	3	5	5	25	42	.268	.429	.342
Runners On	362	90	16	4	3	87	58	70	.249	.340	.348
Runners/Scor. Pos.	226	65	10	3	2	83	44	47	.288	.385	.390

RUNS BATTED IN	From 1B	From 2B	From 3B	Scoring Position
Totals	95/1669	212/1108	243/603	455/1711
Percentage	5.7%	19.1%	40.3%	26.6%

TEAM TOTALS: PITCHING

	W-L	ERA	AB	H	HR	BB	SO	BA	SA	OBA
Season	96-66	3.35	5549	1410	101	455	844	.254	.369	.312
vs. Left-Handers			2238	562	40	239	344	.251	.357	.323
vs. Right-Handers			3311	848	61	216	500	.256	.377	.303
vs. Ground-Ballers			2525	639	33	216	395	.253	.345	.314
vs. Fly-Ballers			3024	771	68	239	449	.255	.388	.310
Home Games	53-28	3.04	2834	726	37	231	459	.256	.357	.313
Road Games	43-38	3.68	2715	684	64	224	385	.252	.380	.310
Grass Fields	19-23	3.83	1379	354	35	127	180	.257	.393	.320
Artificial Turf	77-43	3.19	4170	1056	66	328	664	.253	.360	.309
April	15-5	2.49	646	142	10	54	99	.220	.310	.288
May	11-17	4.32	980	272	25	81	142	.278	.421	.332
June	17-11	3.64	958	252	18	70	161	.263	.376	.313
July	12-15	3.33	914	231	16	88	134	.253	.371	.316
August	19-8	3.08	939	238	18	77	142	.253	.356	.312
Sept./Oct.	22-10	3.05	1112	275	14	85	166	.247	.359	.303
Leading Off Inn.			1392	361	18	87	205	.259	.357	.305
Bases Empty			3282	828	51	211	490	.252	.358	.301
Runners On			2267	582	50	244	354	.257	.384	.326
Runners/Scor. Pos.			1333	334	37	195	232	.251	.401	.339
Runners On/2 Out			965	212	10	106	166	.220	.310	.301
Scor. Pos./2 Out			636	129	9	94	120	.203	.310	.309
Late-Inning Pressure			1054	259	26	98	171	.246	.373	.310
Leading Off			268	69	3	20	47	.257	.343	.311
Runners On			432	97	16	53	63	.225	.391	.305
Runners/Scor. Pos.			244	49	14	41	42	.201	.430	.304
First 9 Batters			2906	719	58	260	485	.247	.369	.311
Second 9 Batters			1394	352	18	103	200	.253	.344	.302
All Batters Thereafter			1249	339	25	92	159	.271	.396	.323

WON-LOST RECORD BY STARTING POSITION

St. Louis Cardinals	C	1B	2B	3B	SS	LF	CF	RF	DH	P	Leadoff	Cleanup	Starts vs. LH	Starts vs. RH	Total Starts
Juan Agosto	-	-	-	-	-	-	-	-	-	-	-	-	-	-	-
Luis Alicea	-	-	37-34	-	2-1	-	-	-	-	-	1-1	-	27	47	39-35
Rod Brewer	-	12-10	-	-	-	3-1	-	-	-	-	-	-	3	23	15-11
Ozzie Canseco	-	-	-	-	-	5-2	-	0-1	-	-	-	-	2	6	5-3
Cris Carpenter	-	-	-	-	-	-	-	-	-	-	-	-	-	-	-
Chuck Carr	-	-	-	-	-	2-2	2-3	3-3	-	-	7-8	-	4	11	7-8
Mark Clark	-	-	-	-	-	-	-	-	-	6-14	-	-	11	9	6-14
Rheal Cormier	-	-	-	-	-	-	-	-	-	15-15	-	-	10	20	15-15
Jose DeLeon	-	-	-	-	-	-	-	-	-	7-8	-	-	4	11	7-8
Frank DiPino	-	-	-	-	-	-	-	-	-	-	-	-	-	-	-
Bien Figueroa	-	-	-	1-1	-	-	-	-	-	-	-	-	-	2	1-1
Andres Galarraga	-	39-44	-	-	-	-	-	-	-	-	-	18-14	36	47	39-44
Rich Gedman	13-18	-	-	-	-	-	-	-	-	-	-	-	2	29	13-18
Bernard Gilkey	-	-	-	-	-	41-44	-	0-1	-	-	-	23-22	47	39	41-45
Pedro Guerrero	-	18-10	-	-	-	4-6	-	-	-	-	-	13-9	11	27	22-16
Rex Hudler	-	-	9-3	-	-	-	-	0-2	-	-	1-3	-	9	5	9-5
Tim Jones	-	-	8-5	-	10-15	-	-	-	-	-	-	-	6	32	18-20
Brian Jordan	-	-	-	-	-	14-9	2-4	10-9	-	-	2-3	-	18	30	26-22
Felix Jose	-	-	-	-	-	-	-	63-61	-	-	-	37-39	46	78	63-61
Ray Lankford	-	-	-	-	-	-	79-72	-	-	-	29-28	-	48	103	79-72
Joe Magrane	-	-	-	-	-	-	-	-	-	3-2	-	-	1	4	3-2
Bob McClure	-	-	-	-	-	-	-	-	-	-	-	-	-	-	-
Omar Olivares	-	-	-	-	-	-	-	-	-	15-15	-	-	8	22	15-15
Jose Oquendo	-	-	2-6	2-2	-	-	-	-	-	-	-	-	4	8	4-8
Donovan Osborne	-	-	-	-	-	-	-	-	-	13-16	-	-	10	19	13-16
Tom Pagnozzi	70-61	-	-	-	-	-	-	-	-	-	-	-	54	77	70-61
Geronimo Pena	-	-	24-28	-	-	-	-	-	-	-	-	13-11	17	35	24-28
Mike Perez	-	-	-	-	-	-	-	-	-	-	-	-	-	-	-
Gerald Perry	-	9-13	-	-	-	-	-	-	-	-	-	5-5	3	19	9-13
Stan Royer	-	3-1	-	1-1	-	-	-	-	-	-	-	-	1	5	4-2
Bryn Smith	-	-	-	-	-	-	-	-	-	1-0	-	-	1	-	1-0
Lee Smith	-	-	-	-	-	-	-	-	-	-	-	-	-	-	-
Ozzie Smith	-	-	-	-	68-60	-	-	-	-	-	-	-	47	81	68-60
Scott Terry	-	-	-	-	-	-	-	-	-	-	-	-	-	-	-
Bob Tewksbury	-	-	-	-	-	-	-	-	-	23-9	-	-	11	21	23-9
Milt Thompson	-	-	-	-	-	14-15	-	7-2	-	-	7-3	-	-	38	21-17
Craig Wilson	-	-	3-3	6-8	-	-	-	-	-	-	-	-	9	11	9-11
Tracy Woodson	-	-	2-1	17-9	-	-	-	-	-	-	-	0-1	14	15	19-10
Todd Worrell	-	-	-	-	-	-	-	-	-	-	-	-	-	-	-
Todd Zeile	-	-	-	59-61	-	-	-	-	-	-	-	10-11	40	80	59-61

TEAM TOTALS: BATTING

	AB	H	2B	3B	HR	RBI	BB	SO	BA	SA	OBA
Season	5594	1464	262	44	94	599	495	996	.262	.375	.323
vs. Left-Handers	1903	535	94	13	36	215	171	323	.281	.401	.341
vs. Right-Handers	3691	929	168	31	58	384	324	673	.252	.361	.314
vs. Ground-Ballers	2490	641	106	15	37	238	209	429	.257	.357	.317
vs. Fly-Ballers	3104	823	156	29	57	361	286	567	.265	.389	.328
Home Games	2786	746	119	26	55	312	249	489	.268	.388	.330
Road Games	2808	718	143	18	39	287	246	507	.256	.361	.317
Grass Fields	1473	379	79	9	19	152	129	268	.257	.362	.316
Artificial Turf	4121	1085	183	35	75	447	366	728	.263	.379	.325
April	778	188	34	5	9	63	65	151	.242	.333	.301
May	912	246	37	15	17	117	83	169	.270	.399	.332
June	908	243	51	8	11	91	72	168	.268	.378	.325
July	922	238	37	5	16	70	83	173	.258	.361	.321
August	917	228	45	4	17	102	71	170	.249	.362	.304
Sept./Oct.	1157	321	58	7	24	156	121	165	.277	.402	.345
Leading Off Inn.	1388	370	63	11	26	26	95	217	.267	.384	.316
Runners On	2353	619	103	23	40	545	252	447	.263	.377	.334
Bases Empty	3241	845	159	21	54	54	243	549	.261	.373	.315
Runners/Scor. Pos.	1500	369	69	15	16	471	195	327	.246	.344	.331
Runners On/2 Out	1027	249	45	13	13	234	132	201	.242	.350	.333
Scor. Pos./2 Out	743	174	36	11	5	211	114	154	.234	.332	.342
Late-Inning Pressure	1115	289	41	5	21	103	114	212	.259	.361	.331
Leading Off	293	67	8	2	4	4	21	47	.229	.311	.285
Runners On	440	104	13	1	8	90	62	94	.236	.325	.334
Runners/Scor. Pos.	278	63	10	1	3	79	46	67	.227	.302	.337

RUNS BATTED IN	From 1B	From 2B	From 3B	Scoring Position
Totals	86/1505	204/1162	215/631	419/1793
Percentage	5.7%	17.6%	34.1%	23.4%

TEAM TOTALS: PITCHING

	W-L	ERA	AB	H	HR	BB	SO	BA	SA	OBA
Season	83-79	3.38	5585	1405	118	400	842	.252	.372	.303
vs. Left-Handers			2499	635	55	194	384	.254	.383	.308
vs. Right-Handers			3086	770	63	206	458	.250	.364	.299
vs. Ground-Ballers			2608	642	38	154	407	.246	.339	.290
vs. Fly-Ballers			2977	763	80	246	435	.256	.401	.314
Home Games	45-36	3.21	2877	698	52	203	433	.243	.353	.296
Road Games	38-43	3.56	2708	707	66	197	409	.261	.393	.311
Grass Fields	22-20	3.19	1400	349	34	100	199	.249	.369	.299
Artificial Turf	61-59	3.45	4185	1056	84	300	643	.252	.373	.304
April	11-11	3.12	774	181	12	64	120	.234	.337	.294
May	16-11	3.95	932	235	23	55	146	.252	.385	.296
June	10-16	3.42	888	231	24	68	119	.260	.400	.313
July	11-16	3.16	923	242	21	57	128	.262	.385	.306
August	16-11	3.03	902	211	15	75	148	.234	.341	.291
Sept./Oct.	19-14	3.55	1166	305	23	81	181	.262	.378	.314
Leading Off Inn.			1401	343	29	75	180	.245	.363	.287
Bases Empty			3331	831	69	198	510	.249	.369	.295
Runners On			2254	574	49	202	332	.255	.378	.314
Runners/Scor. Pos.			1342	304	28	142	220	.227	.341	.297
Runners On/2 Out			961	215	19	95	151	.224	.342	.298
Scor. Pos./2 Out			636	131	12	71	110	.206	.311	.290
Late-Inning Pressure			1035	250	25	90	181	.242	.370	.306
Leading Off			283	66	3	13	36	.233	.325	.267
Runners On			388	101	12	45	72	.260	.407	.342
Runners/Scor. Pos.			231	49	7	37	48	.212	.342	.327
First 9 Batters			2999	703	62	243	506	.234	.350	.294
Second 9 Batters			1360	371	32	81	199	.273	.402	.314
All Batters Thereafter			1226	331	24	76	137	.270	.392	.312

ST. LOUIS CARDINALS

It's been three years since Whitey Herzog resigned as manager of the Cardinals. But even under the stewardships of Red Schoendienst (for 24 games after Herzog's resignation) and Joe Torre (since then), the character of the Cardinals has retained Herzog's imprint as though he never left.

Although St. Louis won three National League titles during Whitey's tenure there (more than any other N.L. team during that time), the Cardinals led the league only twice in scoring (runs per game, that is, in 1980 and 1985), and only once in pitching (runs allowed per game, in 1982). But during that same time, even since Herzog's departure, speed and defense have been the team's trademarks. What many don't remember is that before Whitey arrived in St. Louis, the Cardinals hadn't led the league in stolen bases since 1974, and that was hardly a team effort: Lou Brock accounted for 118 of the Cardinals' 172 steals, and Bake McBride for another 30. (Ted Sizemore ranked third on the team with eight.) Since 1980, the year Herzog joined the Cardinals, they've led the N.L. in stolen bases eight times in 13 seasons (including seven straight years from 1982 through 1988, one short of the league record).

Even more impressive has been the team's turnaround on defense. Herzog assumed command of a team that hadn't posted the league's lowest error rate in nearly 30 years—since 1951, when Schoendienst was playing second base. (Herzog himself was a 19-year-old outfielder for the Joplin Miners of the Western Association, and Ozzie Smith was three years from being born.) Since the Herzog era began, St. Louis has led the National League 10 times in 13 years, including a league-record six straight seasons from 1984 through 1989.

(Those who read the Cardinals essay in the 1991 *Analyst* may recall our vow never to use fielding percentage again, but rather its inverse, error rate, which eliminates not only the ambiguity of the term "fielding percentage," but also the imprecise way in which it's expressed. For example, what tells you more: that the Cardinals had a .985 fielding percentage last season, or that they made an average of one error every 67 chances? Do you prefer a statistic in which the range of values in the National League for 1992 was from .972 by the Dodgers to .985 by the Cardinals? Or does it make more baseball sense to say that the Dodgers made one error every 36 chances, and the Cardinals one every 67?)

The following table summarizes a lot of data pertaining to twentieth-century baseball. The first figure in each set of three shows how many times *since 1900* each team led its league in runs per game, opponents' runs per game, stolen bases, and error rates. (We will use these categories to stand for four components of the game: batting, pitching, speed, and defense.) The second figure in each set of three helps put Herzog's effect on the Cardinals in perspective; it shows how many times each team has led the league in that category *since 1980*. The last figure in each set shows *the last time* the team led in that category. Note in particular that no other team has led any category more than five times since 1980 except for St. Louis—which has done it *at least eight times in two different categories*:

	Runs Per Game	Opp. Runs Per Game	Stolen Bases	Error Rate
Orioles	5/0/1971	11/1/1980	4/0/1973	14/5/1991
Red Sox	16/3/1989	9/0/1918	1/0/1935	9/0/1950
Angels	1/0/1979	1/1/1982	1/0/1975	2/1/1985
White Sox	4/1/1983	12/0/1967	29/0/1966	17/0/1962
Indians	7/1/1986	8/0/1956	4/2/1986	10/0/1965
Tigers	18/4/1992	3/1/1984	6/0/1934	10/1/1981
Royals	0/0/—	1/1/1982	4/1/1980	0/0/—
Brewers	2/1/1982	2/2/1992	6/5/1992	1/1/1992
Twins	6/0/1977	5/0/1933	14/0/1948	7/2/1988
Yankees	25/1/1985	26/1/1981	8/1/1985	9/0/1979
Athletics	6/0/1973	10/2/1990	12/3/1991	9/0/1932
Mariners	0/0/—	0/0/—	0/0/—	0/0/—
Rangers	1/1/1991	1/1/1983	2/0/1972	2/1/1983
Blue Jays	1/1/1990	3/3/1991	1/1/1984	2/2/1990

	Runs Per Game	Opp. Runs Per Game	Stolen Bases	Error Rate
Braves	6/2/1983	9/1/1992	1/0/1945	12/0/1969
Cubs	10/2/1989	13/0/1945	4/0/1939	17/1/1983
Reds	9/0/1976	9/1/1990	10/0/1976	17/2/1990
Astros	1/0/1972	4/3/1986	2/0/1979	1/0/1974
Dodgers	12/0/1978	15/3/1991	22/0/1970	8/0/1960
Expos	0/0/—	0/0/—	4/4/1991	0/0/—
Mets	4/4/1990	5/2/1988	0/0/—	0/0/—
Phillies	4/1/1981	4/0/1952	0/0/—	8/0/1979
Pirates	13/2/1992	9/1/1984	15/0/1978	4/0/1920
Cardinals	14/2/1985	9/1/1982	22/8/1992	17/10/1992
Padres	0/0/—	0/0/—	1/1/1980	0/0/—
Giants	20/0/1970	16/1/1987	12/0/1957	9/0/1942

Now, if leading the league in speed or defense were as important as leading the league in batting or pitching, the Cardinals would have won a lot more than three league championships over the past 13 years, and Whitey Herzog would be to managing what Kleenex is to tissues. And although Herzog is widely considered one of the best managers of the contemporary era, it may surprise you to learn how insignificant speed and defense are—at least as compared to scoring runs and preventing your opponent from doing so. Though, when it's phrased that way, it shouldn't surprise you at all. Runs are the forest; speed and defense are the trees—they matter only to the extent that they help a team score runs or prevent them. The following table shows the number of leaders in each category that have reached the World Series (since 1903), and how many have won their divisions (since 1969). It's obvious which categories are more important:

	Runs Per Game	Opp. Runs Per Game	Stolen Bases	Error Rate
Division Winners	27	27	12	14
World Series Teams	81	84	33	48

Apparently, teams leading in batting or pitching are roughly twice as likely to reach the postseason as those that lead in speed or defense. In fact, the difference is greater—much greater; the table above includes a lot of overlapping leaders that skew its results. For example, when the Cardinals went to the 1985 World Series, they led the National League in scoring, steals, and error rate. Would they have won the N.L. title had they not led the league in stolen bases? Possibly. Would they have won the N.L. title had they not led the league in scoring? Not likely. Here's the evidence: 33 of the 178 teams that led their league in stolen bases reached the

World Series (19%). (That includes only the years in which the Series was played: 1903 and 1905 to present.) But if teams that also led the league in pitching are eliminated, the rate drops to 22 of 159 (14%). For teams that led the league in steals but not in scoring, the rate is even lower: 15 of 147 (10%). And if you consider just the stolen-base leaders that topped their leagues in neither batting or pitching, only 8 of 132 reached the Series; that's 6 percent.

A similar degradation occurs for teams that led their league in defense but neither batting nor pitching. The following table gives a clearer indication of how much more important it is to lead the league in batting or pitching than in speed or defense. To net out the leakage from one category to another, it is limited to teams that led the league in only one of the four categories:

	Runs Per Game	Opp. Runs Per Game	Stolen Bases	Error Rate
Division Winners	18	16	3	5
World Series Teams	26	29	3	4

Only three stolen-base leaders have ever appeared in the World Series without also leading the league in runs per game or opponents runs per game: the 1947 Dodgers, the 1967 Cardinals, and the 1980 Royals. The four Series teams that led their league in error rate but nothing else—and, believe us, you're not going to believe number three—were: the 1930 Athletics, the 1956 Dodgers, *the 1961 Yankees,* and the 1987 Twins.

And you know what? Even those figures may overstate the value of leading the league in steals or error rate, and the tip-off to that is the 1961 Yankees. The table below shows the rankings in each of the four categories for the seven Series teams that led only in steals or error rate:

Year	Team	Runs Per Game	Opp. Runs Per Game	Stolen Bases	Error Rate
1930	Phila. Athletics	2	2	7	1
1947	Brooklyn Dodgers	3	3	1	2
1956	Brooklyn Dodgers	2	2	2	1
1961	New York Yankees	2	2	10	1
1967	St.L. Cardinals	2	2	1	7
1980	Kansas City Royals	4	5	1	7
1987	Minnesota Twins	8	9	10	1

Notice that four of the seven teams, while leading the league in neither scoring nor pitching, ranked second in both. Another ranked first in steals, second in fielding, and third in batting and pitching (though in an eight-team league). The only teams that were exceptional in one single area were the two most recent: the '80 Royals (steals) and the '87 Twins (error rate). Think about that: *Only two teams in the entire century* reached the World Series after leading their league in either stolen bases or error rate, but ranking poorly in other areas.

Of course, in Whitey's defense, the Cardinals led the National League not just in steals *or* error rate but in *both* more often than they didn't—seven times in 13 years since 1980, better still in seasons in which

Herzog managed for the entire schedule (six of nine). And five of the 21 teams with that profile have reached the World Series, including St. Louis in 1987 (and 1931). Herzog may have been the first to successfully exploit the fact that base stealers and defensive stars are easier to come by (and work more cheaply) than hitting and pitching stars to build a winning tradition.

All this started us thinking about Dream Teams— no, not Michael, Magic, and Charles, but the players who might make up a Whitey Herzog Dream Team. There won't be any Ruths or Musials on this team— they're too slow and not strong enough defensively. This is a team devoted to the skills that Herzog cultivated in St. Louis, and before that in Kansas City.

Now, the next essay will probably tell you all you want to hear about triple crowns. But before you're worn out on the subject, let's concoct a triple crown around speed and defense; that is, leading the league in stolen bases, error rate, and—for a quick-and-dirty measure of range—assists per game for infielders and catchers, putouts per game for outfielders. Each player was matched only against those who played the same position; outfielders had only to finish among their league's top three in any season. All winners are listed below—multiple winners first, then one-time winners chronologically. The envelope, please:

Catcher: Ray Schalk (1916 and 1922), Billy Sullivan (1906), Bill Killefer (1919).
First Base: Vic Power (1959–60), George Stovall (1909), Joe Judge (1923), Jimmie Foxx (1937), Bill White (1966).
Second Base: Nap Lajoie (1907), Eddie Collins (1910), George Cutshaw (1915), Sparky Adams (1925), Frankie Frisch (1927), Bobby Avila (1953), Horace Clarke (1967).
Third Base: Ossie Bluege (1931), Chris Sabo (1988).
Shortstop: Luis Aparicio (1959–61), Ozzie Smith (1981, 1984, and 1987), Bill Dahlen (1900), Donie Bush (1910), Lou Boudreau (1944), Larry Bowa (1971).
Outfield: Max Carey (1912 and 1917), Terry Moore (1937 and 1940), Jim Landis (1959 and 1962), Harry Bay (1904), Tommy Leach (1907), Tris Speaker (1909), Johnny Mostil (1925), Ethan Allen (1929), Augie Galan (1936), Mike Kreevich (1940), Thurman Tucker (1944), Whitey Lockman (1948), Richie Ashburn (1950), Mickey Mantle (1959), Jose Cardenal (1966), Billy North (1974), Omar Moreno (1981), Brett Butler (1985).

The Dream Team lineup is pretty much filled with multiple winners: Schalk as the catcher; Power at first; Ozzie and Aparicio splitting time at shortstop; and Carey, Moore, and Landis in the pasture. (Let them fight over who plays center.) Second base goes to Frisch because he played for and managed the Redbirds, third base to Bluege on the basis of his first name. That leaves only the pitcher to be determined. In tribute to his seven stolen bases from 1982 to 1985, high in the majors among pitchers during the period of his tenure with the Cardinals, it could only be One Tough Dominican himself—Joaquin Andujar.

SAN DIEGO PADRES

Cable television has spawned an era of media specialization that never ceases to amaze. You want news? Tune in to CNN. You want music? Try MTV or VH-1. Maybe you like classic motion pictures; then AMC is for you. No problem so far, right? But let's say you want the temperature, humidity, and even the comfort index (whatever that is) in any major American city—or *every* major American city? Then turn to The Weather Channel; you might even get some tips on when to plant your turnips or make your foliage drive. If you've got unlimited time and patience, and an insatiable appetite for the mechanics of American government, there's not only C–SPAN, but C–SPAN 2 as well. You like cartoons? Now there's even the Ted Turner–owned Cartoon Channel—24 hours a day, seven days a week, with nothing but Huckleberry Hound, Top Cat, Barney Rubble, and friends.

At its best this narrow focus can be extraordinary. For example, when American troops fought in the Persian Gulf, CNN provided compelling around-the-clock coverage. Sometimes it can be downright silly—or didn't you watch the "planetary premiere" of Madonna's "Erotica" video on MTV?

Of course, if you're a sports freak, there's indispensable ESPN. If it's live and it's important to sports fans, ESPN can take you there. From major news stories like Magic Johnson's first shocking announcement that he was retiring because he had contracted HIV, to cut-ins to no-hitters in progress, to George Brett's 3000th hit live from Anaheim at 12:30 A.M. Eastern time, sports fans can now see more of the stories that are important to them than ever before.

So what's the downside? One is an overemphasis on statistical minutiae and the like. The network too often strains to report unimportant milestones and record "chases" for their own sake, wholly devoid of any baseball context. True baseball stories—its players, events, and issues—give meaning to its statistics, not vice versa. They don't always seem aware of that at ESPN.

For example, last summer ESPN provided breathless nightly updates on Gary Sheffield's pursuit of the National League triple crown—league leaderships in batting average, home runs, and RBIs. We don't have an exact count of how many times ESPN ran a triple-crown update as one of its top stories on the early-evening edition of *SportsCenter,* but it seemed that Sheffield's progress was given as high a priority at ESPN as CNN gave to then-President George Bush's defense of his own crown. Now, we're not saying that a triple crown contender isn't newsworthy. As we'll discuss shortly, they're becoming as rare as two-hour games and two-term commissioners. And Sheffield certainly made an impressive run, albeit one that ultimately fell short. But nearly every night, often among the lead stories? Let's be honest—even in the absence of a close pennant race, Sheffield's flirtation with the triple crown didn't warrant the Persian Gulf treatment. Did such relentless coverage of a tangential semi-event draw viewers to *SportsCenter* or to baseball itself (either at the park or in the comfort of their living room, courtesy of ESPN)? Most fans—excluding fantasy leaguers (which might be as attractive a seating policy as nonalcohol sections)—root for players or teams, not statistics.

*   *   *

The triple-crown watch actually began in early August, when Sheffield passed Andy Van Slyke to move into second place in the National League in batting average (behind John Kruk), while maintaining his 2d-place ranking in both home runs (to Fred McGriff) and RBIs (to Darren Daulton). Four nights later, Sheffield passed Kruk, and less than a week after that he assumed the league lead in RBIs. On August 16, all that separated Sheffield from the lead in the three crown categories was a margin of two home runs; six nights later, he caught McGriff as well.

For the next two weeks, Sheffield played Alydar to Daulton's Affirmed atop the RBI leaders. At the same time, he opened a six-point lead over Van Slyke for the batting lead, but slipped a few home runs behind McGriff. He remained either the leader or runner-up in all three categories as late as September 11; he was among the top three in each through September 25.

But by September 21, Sheffield had fallen nine RBIs behind Daulton, and he was drifting further back in the pack as well, with McGriff, Terry Pendleton, and Barry Bonds all charging. That didn't stop ESPN's game-by-game coverage of Sheffield's progress or reduce its emphasis on his ultimately trivial pursuit. And that could only have been because even a lukewarm challenge to a triple crown has become exceedingly rare.

Sheffield won the league batting title by six points over Van Slyke, and finished third to McGriff and Bonds in homers and a fading fifth in RBIs with nine fewer than the leader, Daulton. It had been seven years since anyone finished as high as fifth in all three crown categories; in 1985 Don Mattingly led the American League in RBIs (145) and ranked third in batting average (.324) and fourth in home runs (35), while Dave Parker led the National League in RBIs (125) and ranked second in homers (34) and fifth in batting average (.312).

One indication that the Triple Crown is growing more difficult is that no one has ranked in his league's top *two* in all three categories since 1967, when Carl Yastrzemski became the last triple-crown winner. That's by far the longest such stretch in triple-crown history (which dates back to 1920, when RBIs became an official statistic). The complete list for the "top-two" crown, with true triple-crown winners marked with an asterisk: George Sisler (1920), Rogers Hornsby (1921, 1922*, and 1925*), Babe Ruth (1923, 1924, 1926, and 1931), Lou Gehrig (1927, 1930, and 1934*), Jimmie Foxx (1932, 1933*, and 1938), Chuck Klein (1933*), Joe Medwick (1937*), Johnny Mize (1940), Ted Williams (1942*, 1946, 1947*, and 1949), Tommy Holmes (1945), Al Rosen (1953), Willie Mays (1955), Mickey Mantle (1956*), Frank Robinson (1966*), and Carl Yastrzemski (1967*).

Here's a question for you: Is a triple crown more likely in baseball or in thoroughbred racing? Since 1919, when Sir Barton became the first mammal to win it in either sport, the score is tied: man 11, equines 11. More important, the frequency in both sports has declined precipitously over the past few decades:

	1919–49	1950–69	1970–92
Man	8	3	0
Horse	8	0	3

Perhaps baseball should adopt the same approach as racing, awarding points in each category to determine a triple-crown "champion." If baseball awarded, say, 10 points to each league's leader in the three crown categories, nine to the runner-up, and so on down to one point for the player who ranks tenth, Sheffield would have earned 24 points last season: 10 for leading the N.L. in batting average; eight for ranking third in home runs; and six for ranking fifth in RBIs. That would have been the highest total in either league; with 20 points, Barry Bonds would have been the runner-up. Leaders in past years would have included Cal Ripken (1991), Ryne Sandberg (1990), Kevin Mitchell (1989), and Jose Canseco (1988).

Better yet, maybe baseball should take a totally different approach to triple crowns, and adopt the cable TV practice of focusing on a smaller universe. How about *team* triple crowns? Last season's five winners would have included Mike Devereaux (.276, 24, 107); Tom Brunansky (.266, 15 HR, 74 RBI—pitiful, ain't it?); Kirby Puckett (.329, 19, 110); Larry Walker (.301, 23, 93); and Terry Pendleton (.311, 21, 105)—but not Sheffield, who finished third in the league in home runs and fifth in RBIs, but only second in each on the Padres behind McGriff. Brunansky but not Sheffield? That'll never do.

If team crowns are irrelevant, then how about *division* triple crowns? After all, the last league crowns occurred just a few years before the start of divisional play. We were surprised to find that only three players have led even their divisions in batting average, home runs, and RBIs in the same season, and none since 1978, when Jim Rice dominated the A.L. East (.315, 46, 139). The others were Billy Williams in 1972 (.333, 37, 122) and George Foster in 1977 (.320, 52, 149).

Rookie triple crowns are pretty interesting, too, not only as an exclamation point for talented current freshmen, but also as a retrospective reminder of those who fizzled. Eric Karros won the National League rookie crown last season, as did Jeff Bagwell in 1991. But no player has won the A.L. rookie triple crown since Reggie Jackson in 1968. The complete list of winners in each league since 1920 follows; in the absence of reliable data on days of service, players are considered rookies only on the basis of previous at-bats:

American League: Bob Meusel, 1920; Alex Metzler, 1927; Dale Alexander, 1929; Bruce Campbell, 1932; Hal Trosky, Sr., 1934; Joe DiMaggio, 1936; Walt Judnich, 1940; Roy Sievers, 1949; Bob Allison, 1959; Tony Oliva, 1964; Willie Horton, 1965; and Reggie Jackson, 1968.

National League: Ray Grimes, 1921; George Grantham, 1923; Del Bissonette, 1928; Joe Medwick, 1933; Frank Robinson, 1956; Orlando Cepeda, 1958; Vada Pinson, 1959; Billy Williams, 1961; Johnny Bench, 1968; Juan Samuel, 1984; Benito Santiago, 1987; Jeff Bagwell, 1991; and Eric Karros, 1992.

But our favorite of all these focused triple crowns is the one suggested by our editor, Jeff Neuman: *position* crowns, which tell us something different, informative, and—get this!—actually worth knowing. Players are considered only at the position at which they played the most games. (Unfortunately, a breakdown of outfield positions into left, center, and right field doesn't exist throughout baseball history, so we've had to include all OFs in a single, highly competitive category.) No player won his position's crown last season. In fact, only Carlos Baerga (second base) and Travis Fryman (shortstop) led in even two categories on a major league level. (Sheffield led third basemen only in home runs; Edgar Martinez and Terry Pendleton led in batting average and RBIs, respectively.)

The last position crown was won by shortstop Cal Ripken in 1991; Ryne Sandberg won at second base in 1990. Over the past 16 years, there have been six crowns, all at either second base or shortstop. The complete list:

First Base: George Sisler, 1920; Lou Gehrig, 1927 and 1934; Jimmie Foxx, 1932–33; Johnny Mize, 1942; Walt Dropo, 1950; Ted Kluszewski, 1954; Willie McCovey, 1968–69.

Second Base: Rogers Hornsby, 1921–22, 1924–25, 1927–29; Charlie Gehringer, 1936; Joe Gordon, 1942; Bobby Doerr, 1944; Jackie Robinson, 1951–52; Joe Morgan, 1976; Ryne Sandberg, 1984 and 1990.

Third Base: Pie Traynor, 1923; Les Bell, 1926; Red Kress, 1931; Don Demeter, 1962; Dick Allen, 1966.

Shortstop: Arky Vaughan, 1935; Vern Stephens, 1945; Ernie Banks, 1958–59; Rico Petrocelli, 1969; Garry Templeton, 1977; Robin Yount, 1982; Alan Trammell, 1987; Cal Ripken, 1991.

Outfield: Ted Williams, 1942; Mickey Mantle, 1956; Billy Williams, 1972.

Catcher: Bob O'Farrell, 1923; Mickey Cochrane, 1927 and 1931; Walker Cooper, 1947; Roy Campanella, 1951 and 1953; Yogi Berra, 1952, 1954, and 1957; Del Crandall, 1960; Joe Torre, 1964–66; Johnny Bench, 1969; Thurman Munson, 1976.

The object of any new statistic should be that it's interesting and informative without being needlessly complex. We think these position crowns are just that. For example, how many of you thought of Jackie Robinson's talents as primarily speed-related? And it sure made us grab our *Baseball Encyclopedia* to take at fresh look at Les Bell.

WON-LOST RECORD BY STARTING POSITION

San Diego Padres	C	1B	2B	3B	SS	LF	CF	RF	DH	P	Leadoff	Cleanup	Starts vs. LH	Starts vs. RH	Total Starts
Larry Andersen	-	-	-	-	-	-	-	-	-	-	-	-	-	-	-
Oscar Azocar	-	-	-	-	-	11-13	-	0-5	-	-	-	-	-	29	11-18
Andy Benes	-	-	-	-	-	-	-	-	-	14-20	-	-	13	21	14-20
Dann Bilardello	6-4	-	-	-	-	-	-	-	-	-	-	-	2	8	6-4
Doug Brocail	-	-	-	-	-	-	-	-	-	1-2	-	-	1	2	1-2
Terry Bross	-	-	-	-	-	-	-	-	-	-	-	-	-	-	-
Jerald Clark	-	3-1	-	-	-	56-51	0-1	7-11	-	-	-	-	48	82	66-64
Pat Clements	-	-	-	-	-	-	-	-	-	-	-	-	-	-	-
Jim Deshaies	-	-	-	-	-	-	-	-	-	7-8	-	-	4	11	7-8
Dave Eiland	-	-	-	-	-	-	-	-	-	3-4	-	-	2	5	3-4
Paul Faries	-	-	0-1	0-1	-	-	-	-	-	-	-	-	1	1	0-2
Tony Fernandez	-	-	-	-	79-76	-	-	-	-	-	79-75	-	54	101	79-76
Jeff Gardner	-	-	0-3	-	-	-	-	-	-	-	-	-	-	3	0-3
Tony Gwynn	-	-	-	-	-	-	-	70-57	-	-	-	-	51	76	70-57
Greg W. Harris	-	-	-	-	-	-	-	-	-	8-12	-	-	7	13	8-12
Gene Harris	-	-	-	-	-	-	-	-	-	1-0	-	-	-	1	1-0
Jeremy Hernandez	-	-	-	-	-	-	-	-	-	-	-	-	-	-	-
Thomas Howard	-	-	-	-	-	-	-	-	-	-	-	-	-	-	-
Bruce Hurst	-	-	-	-	-	-	-	-	-	21-11	-	-	10	22	21-11
Darrin Jackson	-	-	-	-	-	1-0	77-73	-	-	-	1-3	1-2	53	98	78-73
Tom Lampkin	2-3	-	-	-	-	-	-	-	-	-	-	-	-	5	2-3
Craig Lefferts	-	-	-	-	-	-	-	-	-	16-11	-	-	15	12	16-11
Mike Maddux	-	-	-	-	-	-	-	-	-	0-1	-	-	1	-	0-1
Fred McGriff	-	75-76	-	-	-	-	-	-	-	-	-	75-76	54	97	75-76
Jose Melendez	-	-	-	-	-	-	-	-	-	0-3	-	-	-	3	0-3
Randy Myers	-	-	-	-	-	-	-	-	-	-	-	-	-	-	-
Gary Pettis	-	-	-	-	-	-	1-2	0-1	-	-	-	-	-	4	1-3
Rich Rodriguez	-	-	-	-	-	-	-	-	-	0-1	-	-	-	1	0-1
Benito Santiago	52-46	-	-	-	-	-	-	-	-	-	-	-	36	62	52-46
Tim Scott	-	-	-	-	-	-	-	-	-	-	-	-	-	-	-
Frank Seminara	-	-	-	-	-	-	-	-	-	11-7	-	-	6	12	11-7
Gary Sheffield	-	-	-	75-69	-	-	-	-	-	-	-	5-0	54	90	75-69
Craig Shipley	-	-	3-3	2-1	3-4	-	-	-	-	-	0-1	-	6	10	8-8
Phil Stephenson	-	2-0	-	-	3-4	-	-	2-2	-	-	-	-	-	13	7-6
Kurt Stillwell	-	-	55-54	-	-	-	-	-	-	-	2-1	-	37	72	55-54
Tim Teufel	-	2-2	24-19	5-9	-	-	-	-	-	-	-	-	27	34	31-30
Jim Vatcher	-	-	-	-	-	-	0-1	2-2	-	-	-	-	2	3	2-3
Guillermo Velasquez	-	0-1	-	-	-	1-1	-	-	-	-	-	0-1	2	1	1-2
Dan Walters	22-27	-	-	-	-	-	-	-	-	-	-	-	21	28	22-27
Kevin Ward	-	-	-	-	-	10-11	4-3	1-2	-	-	-	1-1	24	7	15-16
Ed Whitson	-	-	-	-	-	-	-	-	-	-	-	-	-	-	-

TEAM TOTALS: BATTING

	AB	H	2B	3B	HR	RBI	BB	SO	BA	SA	OBA
Season	5476	1396	255	30	135	576	453	864	.255	.386	.313
vs. Left-Handers	1812	491	77	14	61	223	145	289	.271	.430	.325
vs. Right-Handers	3664	905	178	16	74	353	308	575	.247	.365	.307
vs. Ground-Ballers	2439	658	116	16	59	259	200	339	.270	.403	.326
vs. Fly-Ballers	3037	738	139	14	76	317	253	525	.243	.373	.302
Home Games	2689	730	126	14	87	320	241	394	.271	.426	.332
Road Games	2787	666	129	16	48	256	212	470	.239	.348	.294
Grass Fields	4047	1041	186	22	113	437	353	605	.257	.398	.317
Artificial Turf	1429	355	69	8	22	139	100	259	.248	.354	.299
April	799	209	34	5	21	85	75	130	.262	.395	.325
May	926	262	49	3	26	120	69	151	.283	.427	.331
June	902	218	39	7	13	89	90	134	.242	.344	.315
July	905	229	44	9	24	91	69	120	.253	.401	.306
August	847	220	36	2	32	97	58	117	.260	.420	.307
Sept./Oct.	1097	258	53	4	19	94	92	212	.235	.343	.296
Leading Off Inn.	1380	382	73	10	34	34	77	203	.277	.418	.317
Runners On	2207	565	89	16	62	503	235	354	.256	.395	.325
Bases Empty	3269	831	166	14	73	73	218	510	.254	.381	.304
Runners/Scor. Pos.	1231	320	55	12	33	426	170	209	.260	.405	.343
Runners On/2 Out	942	214	37	7	26	175	126	187	.227	.364	.320
Scor. Pos./2 Out	585	125	22	4	17	145	100	119	.214	.352	.330
Late-Inning Pressure	839	211	37	4	17	84	79	143	.251	.366	.316
Leading Off	226	63	12	2	6	6	12	39	.279	.429	.315
Runners On	333	86	11	1	7	74	45	58	.258	.360	.344
Runners/Scor. Pos.	197	47	4	0	2	59	33	33	.239	.289	.337

RUNS BATTED IN	From 1B	From 2B	From 3B	Scoring Position
Totals	79/1595	153/980	209/490	362/1470
Percentage	5.0%	15.6%	42.7%	24.6%

TEAM TOTALS: PITCHING

	W-L	ERA	AB	H	HR	BB	SO	BA	SA	OBA
Season	82-80	3.56	5535	1444	111	439	971	.261	.371	.315
vs. Left-Handers			2220	604	54	225	391	.272	.397	.338
vs. Right-Handers			3315	840	57	214	580	.253	.353	.300
vs. Ground-Ballers			2538	665	32	174	429	.262	.342	.310
vs. Fly-Ballers			2997	779	79	265	542	.260	.395	.320
Home Games	45-36	3.61	2833	747	64	225	497	.264	.375	.318
Road Games	37-44	3.50	2702	697	47	214	474	.258	.366	.313
Grass Fields	64-56	3.44	4167	1071	80	331	733	.257	.358	.312
Artificial Turf	18-24	3.94	1368	373	31	108	238	.273	.410	.326
April	12-11	3.62	818	223	20	55	149	.273	.400	.319
May	16-11	4.07	922	238	24	70	164	.258	.384	.310
June	13-14	3.22	931	239	13	81	160	.257	.349	.316
July	15-12	2.84	899	224	13	78	161	.249	.331	.310
August	13-13	4.38	865	243	14	74	128	.281	.388	.335
Sept./Oct.	13-19	3.34	1100	277	24	81	209	.252	.374	.305
Leading Off Inn.			1370	365	35	92	229	.266	.391	.315
Bases Empty			3225	820	64	226	573	.254	.358	.305
Runners On			2310	624	47	213	398	.270	.387	.330
Runners/Scor. Pos.			1327	355	12	161	239	.268	.350	.341
Runners On/2 Out			991	243	20	111	176	.245	.361	.327
Scor. Pos./2 Out			641	156	5	86	115	.243	.323	.338
Late-Inning Pressure			907	244	14	94	162	.269	.353	.337
Leading Off			228	57	4	20	47	.250	.346	.313
Runners On			384	107	0	51	67	.279	.354	.358
Runners/Scor. Pos.			224	64	0	43	36	.286	.308	.388
First 9 Batters			2974	711	45	242	610	.239	.327	.297
Second 9 Batters			1365	377	32	107	218	.276	.403	.327
All Batters Thereafter			1196	356	34	90	143	.298	.441	.346

WON-LOST RECORD BY STARTING POSITION

San Francisco Giants	C	1B	2B	3B	SS	LF	CF	RF	DH	P	Leadoff	Cleanup	Starts vs. LH	Starts vs. RH	Total Starts
Mark Bailey	3-3	-	-	-	-	-	-	-	-	-	-	-	1	5	3-3
Kevin Bass	-	-	-	-	-	20-25	-	8-6	-	-	-	12-12	18	41	28-31
Rod Beck	-	-	-	-	-	-	-	-	-	-	-	-	-	-	-
Mike Benjamin	-	-	-	11-14	-	-	-	-	-	-	-	-	14	11	11-14
Bud Black	-	-	-	-	-	-	-	-	-	11-17	-	-	14	14	11-17
Jeff Brantley	-	-	-	-	-	-	-	-	-	4-0	-	-	4	-	4-0
Dave Burba	-	-	-	-	-	-	-	-	-	3-8	-	-	2	9	3-8
John Burkett	-	-	-	-	-	-	-	-	-	19-13	-	-	15	17	19-13
Larry Carter	-	-	-	-	-	-	-	-	-	1-5	-	-	-	6	1-5
Will Clark	-	61-80	-	-	-	-	-	-	-	-	-	-	50	91	61-80
Royce Clayton	-	-	-	-	40-51	-	-	-	-	-	-	-	29	62	40-51
Craig Colbert	11-11	-	-	4-2	-	-	-	-	-	-	-	-	16	12	15-13
Steve Decker	7-7	-	-	-	-	-	-	-	-	-	-	-	4	10	7-7
Kelly Downs	-	-	-	-	-	-	-	-	-	3-4	-	-	1	6	3-4
Mike Felder	-	-	-	-	-	4-9	18-26	-	-	-	19-31	-	12	45	22-35
Scott Garrelts	-	-	-	-	-	-	-	-	-	-	-	-	-	-	-
Gil Heredia	-	-	-	-	-	-	-	-	-	0-4	-	-	1	3	0-4
Bryan Hickerson	-	-	-	-	-	-	-	-	-	1-0	-	-	1	-	1-0
Steve Hosey	-	-	-	-	-	-	-	7-7	-	-	-	1-1	9	5	7-7
Mike Jackson	-	-	-	-	-	-	-	-	-	-	-	-	-	-	-
Chris James	-	-	-	-	-	27-28	-	1-1	-	-	-	18-15	34	23	28-29
Mark Leonard	-	-	-	-	-	12-18	-	1-1	-	-	-	8-16	3	29	13-19
Darren Lewis	-	-	-	-	-	-	35-42	-	-	-	30-35	-	33	44	35-42
Greg Litton	-	1-2	12-12	0-3	-	-	-	-	-	-	-	-	10	20	13-17
Kirt Manwaring	37-61	-	-	-	-	-	-	-	-	-	-	-	42	56	37-61
Willie McGee	-	-	-	-	-	11-16	36-48	-	-	-	-	13-18	36	75	47-64
Jim McNamara	14-8	-	-	-	-	-	-	-	-	-	-	-	-	22	14-8
Francisco Oliveras	-	-	-	-	-	-	-	-	-	1-6	-	-	3	4	1-6
John Patterson	-	-	7-11	-	-	-	3-2	-	-	-	6-3	-	6	17	10-13
Jim Pena	-	-	-	-	-	-	-	-	-	1-1	-	-	-	2	1-1
Pat Rapp	-	-	-	-	-	-	-	-	-	0-2	-	-	2	-	0-2
Steve Reed	-	-	-	-	-	-	-	-	-	-	-	-	-	-	-
Dave Righetti	-	-	-	-	-	-	-	-	-	0-4	-	-	3	1	0-4
Kevin Rogers	-	-	-	-	-	-	-	-	-	3-3	-	-	-	6	3-3
Andres Santana	-	-	-	-	-	-	-	-	-	-	-	-	-	-	-
Cory Snyder	-	10-8	-	7-6	-	7-8	5-4	13-23	-	-	-	26-31	46	45	42-49
Bill Swift	-	-	-	-	-	-	-	-	-	17-5	-	-	7	15	17-5
Robby Thompson	-	-	53-67	-	-	-	-	-	-	-	-	2-3	48	72	53-67
Jose Uribe	-	-	-	-	21-25	-	-	-	-	-	-	-	17	29	21-25
Matt Williams	-	-	-	61-79	-	-	-	-	-	-	-	7-15	49	91	61-79
Trevor Wilson	-	-	-	-	-	-	-	-	-	8-18	-	-	7	19	8-18
Ted Wood	-	-	-	-	-	2-2	-	6-4	-	-	2-0	-	3	11	8-6

TEAM TOTALS: BATTING

	AB	H	2B	3B	HR	RBI	BB	SO	BA	SA	OBA
Season	5456	1330	220	36	105	532	435	1067	.244	.355	.302
vs. Left-Handers	1919	493	85	14	35	184	129	340	.257	.371	.303
vs. Right-Handers	3537	837	135	22	70	348	306	727	.237	.347	.302
vs. Ground-Ballers	2626	648	105	18	54	272	213	478	.247	.362	.306
vs. Fly-Ballers	2830	682	115	18	51	260	222	589	.241	.348	.299
Home Games	2687	677	130	21	57	285	209	467	.252	.380	.307
Road Games	2769	653	90	15	48	247	226	600	.236	.331	.297
Grass Fields	3982	974	163	25	76	391	322	734	.245	.355	.302
Artificial Turf	1474	356	57	11	29	141	113	333	.242	.354	.302
April	762	202	31	6	11	87	75	144	.265	.365	.330
May	860	199	35	9	18	92	87	186	.231	.356	.305
June	863	204	35	6	18	81	64	168	.236	.353	.291
July	928	228	42	5	19	89	69	187	.246	.363	.301
August	935	227	35	4	22	87	67	168	.243	.359	.298
Sept./Oct.	1108	270	42	6	17	96	73	214	.244	.338	.294
Leading Off Inn.	1357	336	48	9	38	38	104	258	.248	.380	.307
Runners On	2227	550	92	18	43	470	201	447	.247	.362	.309
Bases Empty	3229	780	128	18	62	62	234	620	.242	.350	.297
Runners/Scor. Pos.	1291	304	51	11	24	402	159	297	.235	.348	.315
Runners On/2 Out	988	237	41	12	23	208	97	208	.240	.376	.313
Scor. Pos./2 Out	637	141	26	6	11	167	81	149	.221	.333	.312
Late-Inning Pressure	967	234	38	5	16	81	93	202	.242	.341	.314
Leading Off	243	63	12	1	5	5	21	46	.259	.379	.331
Runners On	415	87	13	1	8	73	50	95	.210	.304	.300
Runners/Scor. Pos.	249	48	7	1	5	62	47	62	.193	.289	.321

RUNS BATTED IN	From 1B	From 2B	From 3B	Scoring Position
Totals	80/1516	169/1028	178/505	347/1533
Percentage	5.3%	16.4%	35.2%	22.6%

TEAM TOTALS: PITCHING

	W-L	ERA	AB	H	HR	BB	SO	BA	SA	OBA
Season	72-90	3.61	5467	1385	128	502	927	.253	.382	.318
vs. Left-Handers			2486	647	49	227	393	.260	.385	.323
vs. Right-Handers			2981	738	79	275	534	.248	.378	.313
vs. Ground-Ballers			2432	590	41	190	418	.243	.350	.300
vs. Fly-Ballers			3035	795	87	312	509	.262	.407	.332
Home Games	42-39	3.15	2783	668	60	219	466	.240	.352	.298
Road Games	30-51	4.10	2684	717	68	283	461	.267	.412	.338
Grass Fields	57-63	3.37	4046	1017	87	331	661	.251	.368	.310
Artificial Turf	15-27	4.29	1421	368	41	171	266	.259	.419	.340
April	12-10	2.61	746	169	15	69	127	.227	.327	.294
May	15-11	4.02	869	218	22	86	152	.251	.377	.318
June	7-19	4.78	869	238	19	96	131	.274	.410	.348
July	16-12	2.77	929	218	11	66	170	.235	.355	.292
August	9-19	3.49	946	246	24	79	137	.260	.394	.318
Sept./Oct.	13-19	3.90	1108	296	27	106	210	.267	.411	.331
Leading Off Inn.			1358	322	27	101	217	.237	.340	.292
Bases Empty			3192	798	75	258	556	.250	.373	.310
Runners On			2275	587	53	244	371	.258	.393	.329
Runners/Scor. Pos.			1283	320	27	185	237	.249	.381	.339
Runners On/2 Out			964	213	16	115	175	.221	.341	.310
Scor. Pos./2 Out			617	125	12	94	130	.203	.332	.315
Late-Inning Pressure			820	190	18	79	184	.232	.340	.301
Leading Off			220	45	2	18	49	.205	.273	.265
Runners On			305	72	9	38	72	.236	.361	.320
Runners/Scor. Pos.			174	35	4	30	46	.201	.305	.312
First 9 Batters			3127	750	65	277	633	.240	.356	.304
Second 9 Batters			1364	372	39	131	176	.273	.430	.337
All Batters Thereafter			976	263	24	94	118	.269	.397	.334

SAN FRANCISCO GIANTS

Every season, for one reason or another, baseball's old guard—writers, broadcasters, former players, and others living in the past—revives its national anthem. Follow the bouncing ball and sing along: "My, how the quality of play has fallen." And this season, its favorite refrain is sure to feature a new verse, blaming expansion for a further dilution of talent and a corresponding decline in the level of play.

One person who should think twice before joining the chorus is the Giants' recently retired general manager, Al Rosen. Rosen's major league career, like the careers of many players of the pre-expansion era, started years later than it should have. His advance as a third baseman in the Indians organization was blocked by perennial All-Star Ken Keltner. So in 1946, when Rosen batted .323 at Pittsfield and led the Canadian-American League in home runs and RBIs, he earned a promotion only to Double-A ball in Oklahoma City. Then after leading the Texas League in batting average, doubles, and RBIs in 1947, he was asked to serve a two-year Triple-A apprenticeship while Keltner played out the string in Cleveland.

Rosen obviously learned his trade well in the bushes: As a 26-year-old rookie in 1950, he led the American League with 37 home runs and compiled a .287 batting average with 116 RBIs. But as with any great season by an older rookie, the lingering question is: Would he have been capable of the same several years earlier? Or put another way, what if Rosen's path to Cleveland hadn't been blocked? By analyzing the careers of players who compiled similar statistics at the same age, our projection model suggests that Rosen was capable of playing in the majors as much as four years before he finally got the call. Of the 25 players with the most comparable statistics at roughly the same age, only three failed to play at least 125 games in the season three years before the point of comparison. Five of them had actually played 750 major league games prior to their Rosen-like seasons:

Year Player	AB	R	H	2B	3B	HR	RBI	BB	SO	BA	Prior Games
1950 Al Rosen	554	100	159	23	4	37	116	100	72	.287	35
1960 Hank Aaron	590	102	172	20	11	40	126	60	63	.292	886
1966 Ron Santo	561	93	175	21	8	30	94	95	78	.312	898
1970 Rusty Staub	569	98	156	23	7	30	94	112	93	.274	991
1974 Johnny Bench	621	108	174	38	2	33	129	80	90	.280	934
1987 Kent Hrbek	477	85	136	20	1	34	90	84	60	.285	761

To say that Rosen wasn't ready to face major league pitching long before 1950 runs counter to overwhelming evidence. Based on a comprehensive survey of Rosen clones, the computer model concluded that Rosen lost more than 400 games and 60 home runs during the time he spent waiting for his chance. Our best guess at filling in those blanks:

Year	G	AB	R	H	2B	3B	HR	RBI	BB	SO	SB	BA
1946	50	183	22	47	9	2	8	31	32	24	2	.257
1947	128	426	60	114	18	3	15	62	55	64	2	.268
1948	143	507	76	141	24	4	21	78	73	70	2	.278
1949	149	541	84	153	26	5	25	89	81	67	3	.282
Totals	470	1657	242	455	77	14	69	260	241	225	9	.275

During his first four seasons with the Indians, Rosen lit up the scoreboard. From 1950 through 1953, he led

the American League in RBIs by a wide margin over runner-up Gus Zernial (468 to 430), and fell one short of Zernial's league-leading total of 133 home runs. (Rosen led the league in home runs in 1950, in RBIs in 1952, and in both in 1953.) But a broken finger suffered during the 1954 season permanently diminished Rosen's effectiveness at the plate, and he retired at age 32 following the 1956 season.

As a result of his late start and premature retirement, Rosen's career totals are modest by comparison to those of many lesser hitters, like Charlie Keller, Wally Post, and Jim Ray Hart. But what if there had been expansion after World War II, creating more jobs for deserving players? What if Rosen had reached the majors in 1946, and then avoided the injury that prematurely ended his career? Our computer projects figures on either side of his four greatest seasons that would have given him career totals similar to those of Gil Hodges, warranting consideration for the Hall of Fame:

Years	G	AB	R	H	2B	3B	HR	RBI	BB	SO	BA
1946–49	470	1657	242	455	77	14	69	260	241	225	.275
1950–53	612	2293	398	683	112	15	132	468	345	245	.298
1954–60	902	3095	461	820	136	13	159	600	443	363	.265
Totals	1984	7045	1101	1958	325	42	360	1328	1029	833	.278

Rosen wasn't the only former star with strong ties to the Bay Area whose big-league career would have started years earlier under other circumstances. Lefty O'Doul was a pitching and hitting star for the San Francisco Seals in the 1920s. He also managed in the Pacific Coast League from 1935 through 1957 (the first 17 years of that period with the Seals) before joining the Giants as a batting instructor.

O'Doul spent the first eight years of his pro career as a pitcher. He achieved his greatest pitching success in 1921, when he posted a 25–9 record for the Seals that earned him a look with the Yankees. But New York barely used him, and soon sent him to the Red Sox, for whom he pitched in 1923. If this were Hollywood, the Sox would have uncovered his latent hitting talent and converted him to a full-time outfielder—retribution for their disastrous sale of Babe Ruth to the Yankees two years earlier. But after one season with Boston in which he posted a 5.43 ERA with 31 walks and only 10 strikeouts—and by the terms of a little-known codicil to the "Curse of the Bambino"—O'Doul was returned to the minors. (Of note: On July 7, he set a major league record that still stands by allowing 13 runs in one inning.)

Actually, it was an arm injury in 1924 that transformed O'Doul into an outfielder. Over the next four seasons, he drove in 566 runs, compiling a .369 batting average. When the Giants brought O'Doul to the majors after he won the Coast League MVP award in 1927, he was already 31 years old. And although he batted .319, even then the Giants didn't realize what they had; Lefty played only 114 games, and after the season he was traded to the Phillies.

The 1929 season hinted at what might have been if the marriage of O'Doul's left-handed swing to the inviting Baker Bowl had taken place 10 years earlier: He led the majors with a .398 batting average, establishing a National League record for hits (254) that has been equaled—by Bill Terry in 1930—but never broken. The list of players with the most comparable seasons at the same age leaves no doubt that O'Doul could have a been superstar throughout the 1920s:

Year	Player	AB	R	H	2B	3B	HR	RBI	BB	SO	BA
1929	Lefty O'Doul	638	152	254	35	6	32	122	76	19	.398
1920	Tris Speaker	552	137	214	50	11	8	107	97	13	.388
1929	Rogers Hornsby	602	156	229	47	8	39	149	87	65	.380
1930	Bill Terry	633	139	254	39	15	23	129	57	33	.401
1936	Earl Averill	614	136	232	39	15	28	126	65	35	.378
1953	Stan Musial	593	127	200	53	9	30	113	105	32	.337

What might O'Doul have accomplished had he played in Philadelphia's Baker Bowl throughout the 1920s? Based on the careers of the players listed above (as well as those of others with similar seasons around age 32—including George Brett, Rod Carew, Tris Speaker, Billy Williams, and Ken Williams), our best guess is that his late start cost Lefty more than 1300 games, 1600 hits, and probably a plaque in upstate New York. Our optimistic scenario (representing figures that O'Doul had about a 20 percent chance of attaining) puts him not only in Cooperstown, but in its high-rent district with the fourth-highest batting average in major league history. The computer model's hypothetical career totals, combining its projections for the years prior to 1929 with O'Doul's actual major league totals thereafter:

	G	AB	R	H	2B	3B	HR	RBI	BB	SO	SB	BA
Actual	970	3264	624	1140	175	41	113	542	333	122	36	.349
Best Guess	2108	7893	1473	2662	475	132	272	1398	727	297	93	.337
Optimistic	2399	8819	1696	3083	543	176	337	1595	866	312	196	.350

To find another deserving player who was ready to start before he got his chance to start, we need look no further than to O'Doul's fellow member of the 254-hit club, Bill Terry. Terry was the last National League player to hit .400. He compiled a career batting average of .341, and was elected to the Hall of Fame in 1954. But Terry was a promising first baseman in the Giants' employ in the early 1920s, when the team put together a string of four consecutive National League titles with George ("Highpockets") Kelly at first base. Kelly himself was only a year older than Terry, but he drove in at least 100 runs in each of those four pennant-winning seasons, including a league-leading total of 136 in 1924.

But manager John McGraw couldn't keep Terry out of the lineup forever, and in 1925, he made a bold move, experimenting with Kelly as a second baseman. Both players topped the .300 mark, but the Giants finished second to Pittsburgh, and the next season Kelly was back at first base and Terry—then 25 years old—was back on the bench. Something had to give, and it did prior to the 1927 season when Kelly was traded to Cincinnati for Edd Roush, culminating an off-season trading flurry that included an exchange of Frankie Frisch for Rogers Hornsby. With Kelly gone, Terry immediately began a streak of both scoring and driving in at least 100 runs in six consecutive seasons, the second longest in National League history. (Only Willie Mays had a longer streak.)

Terry batted .326 with 20 home runs and 121 RBIs in 1927 at age 28. (He posted uncannily similar statistics in 1928.) And history tells us that no one compiles those kinds of numbers at that age unless he was capable of similar play years before. The best example

is Highpockets himself, who posted extraordinarily similar figures as a 28-year-old:

Year	Player	AB	R	H	2B	3B	HR	RBI	BB	SO	BA	Prior Games
1927	Bill Terry	580	101	189	32	13	20	121	46	53	.326	311
1924	George Kelly	571	91	185	37	9	21	136	38	52	.324	717

Terry was lucky only in that the Giants were eventually willing to move Kelly—first to second base, then to Cincinnati—to create a starting position for him. But given an opportunity to play regularly before turning 28, Terry would have posted some impressive totals, especially if his figures approached the high-end projections below, which bear a striking resemblance to those of one of his contemporary Hall of Famers:

	G	AB	R	H	2B	3B	HR	RBI	BB	SO	BA
Best Guess	2035	7846	1333	2610	441	128	191	1282	628	660	.333
Optimistic	2322	8989	1576	3024	538	170	265	1557	797	593	.336
Al Simmons	2215	8761	1507	2927	539	149	307	1827	615	737	.334

Ever heard of Ross Youngs? He's the James A. Garfield of professional baseball—perhaps the least-known player in the Hall of Fame, one who died before he was able to fulfill his potential on the ballfield. Youngs was a teammate of Kelly, Terry, and Frisch, the right fielder on John McGraw's four straight N.L. pennant winners. It was Youngs whom McGraw called "my greatest player." He was stricken with Bright's Disease in 1925, retired in 1926, and passed away in 1927. He was a contemporary of four Hall of Fame outfielders, all of whom compiled similar statistics to his at comparable points in their careers:

		Season Statistics					Career to Date				
Year	Player	AB	H	HR	RBI	BA	AB	H	HR	RBI	BA
1924	Ross Youngs	526	187	10	74	.356	3755	1245	32	496	.332
1927	Goose Goslin	581	194	13	120	.334	3336	1104	73	628	.331
1922	Harry Heilmann	455	162	21	92	.356	3612	1142	71	643	.316
1929	Heinie Manush	574	204	6	81	.355	3310	1119	57	524	.338
1921	Edd Roush	418	147	4	71	.352	3526	1138	25	471	.323

What if Youngs had lived? He would probably have played another six or seven seasons, finished his career with somewhere between 2500 and 3000 hits (his actual total was 1491), and topped the 1000-mark in runs scored (812), RBIs (592), and bases on balls (550). And, in a bizarre twist, Mel Ott probably wouldn't have hit 500 home runs. Not wanting Ott's unique batting style tampered with by a minor league manager, McGraw decided to keep Ott with the Giants after watching him work out in September 1925, despite the fact that Ott was only 16 years old and had never played pro ball. Ott was considered a catcher when he reported to training camp in 1926, but Youngs's illness was probably one of the factors that prompted McGraw to switch Ott to the outfield, and accelerated Ott's rise to stardom by filling the void left by Youngs. (It's said that when McGraw asked Ott if he'd ever played the outfield, the teenager replied, "Yes, but not since I was a kid.") Two years later, Ott was playing regularly at age 19—something O'Doul and Terry must have envied terribly. He hit 511 career home runs, 61 of them before he turned 21 prior to the start of the 1930 season.

That's it for *"What If?" II*. You asked for it, you got it. For those who still haven't had their fill, drop us a line and let us know what direction to take in the 1994 *Analyst*.

BATTER SECTION

The Batter Section is an alphabetical listing of every player who had at least 250 plate appearances last season. Players are listed alphabetically within each league; if he played for both leagues, he is listed in the league where he finished the season.

Column Headings Information

For each player, information is provided in 11 offensive categories.

Sandy Alomar, Jr.

Cleveland Indians	AB	H	2B	3B	HR	RBI	BB	SO	BA	SA	OBA

AB	At-Bats
H	Hits
2B	Doubles
3B	Triples
HR	Home Runs
RBI	Runs Batted In
BB	Bases on Balls
SO	Strikeouts
BA	Batting Average
SA	Slugging Average
OBA	On-Base Average

Season Summary Information

Season	AB	H	2B	3B	HR	RBI	BB	SO	BA	SA	OBA
Season	299	75	16	0	2	26	13	32	.251	.324	.293
vs. Left-Handers	58	11	4	0	0	3	5	6	.190	.259	.277
vs. Right-Handers	241	64	12	0	2	23	8	26	.266	.340	.298
vs. Ground-Ballers	144	44	8	0	1	13	7	11	.306	.382	.342
vs. Fly-Ballers	155	31	8	0	1	13	6	21	.200	.271	.248
Home Games	158	41	7	0	1	15	10	18	.259	.323	.304
Road Games	141	34	9	0	1	11	3	14	.241	.326	.282
Grass Fields	263	67	14	0	2	25	12	29	.255	.331	.297
Artificial Turf	36	8	2	0	0	1	1	3	.222	.278	.263
April	65	14	5	0	1	7	5	8	.215	.338	.271
May	39	8	3	0	0	4	1	6	.205	.282	.262
June	75	18	1	0	1	6	2	8	.240	.293	.269
July	74	24	4	0	0	8	2	4	.324	.378	.351
August	46	11	3	0	0	1	3	6	.239	.304	.300
Sept./Oct.	0	0	0	0	0	0	0	0	—	—	—

Each player's performance for the season is broken down into a variety of special categories. The first line for each player gives his totals for the whole season. This is followed by breakdowns of his performance against left- and right-handed pitchers, against ground-ball and fly-ball pitchers (defined by whether their ground outs-to-air outs ratio is above or below the league average; our research indicates that this is nearly as effective a basis for platooning as "handedness"), in home and road games, on grass fields and artificial turf, and in each month (regular-season October games are grouped with September). For players who played for more than one team, all totals are combined; the "home" totals for Jose Canseco, for example, include games played at Oakland–Alameda County Stadium while with the A's, and at Arlington Stadium while with the Rangers.

Leading Off Inn.	66	21	5	0	0	0	3	8	.318	.394	.357
Runners On	129	24	3	0	2	26	4	13	.186	.256	.228
Bases Empty	170	51	13	0	0	0	9	19	.300	.376	.343
Runners/Scor. Pos.	65	15	2	0	1	24	3	9	.231	.308	.275
Runners On/2 Out	48	11	2	0	0	13	2	5	.229	.271	.275
Scor. Pos./2 Out	26	8	2	0	0	13	2	3	.308	.385	.379

Following these breakdowns, each batter's performance is divided into specific game situations. Totals are given for each batter when he led off an inning, when he batted with bases empty or runners on, with runners in scoring position (on second or third base, or both), with runners on and two out, and with runners in scoring position and two out.

Late-Inning Pressure	60	17	3	0	0	6	2	9	.283	.333	.317
Leading Off	14	5	1	0	0	0	0	1	.357	.429	.357
Runners On	22	5	0	0	0	6	0	4	.227	.227	.261
Runners/Scor. Pos.	14	4	0	0	0	6	0	3	.286	.286	.286

The next group shows the batter's performance in Late-Inning Pressure Situations (LIPS): any plate appearance occurring in the seventh inning or later with the score tied or with the batter's team trailing by one, two, or three runs (or four runs if there are two or more runners on base).

Each player's totals are listed for all late-inning pressure situations, then broken down for his performance leading off the inning, with runners on base, and with runners in scoring position.

RUNS BATTED IN	From 1B	From 2B	From 3B	Scoring Position
Totals	3/99	9/51	12/29	21/80
Percentage	3.0%	17.6%	41.4%	26.3%

The next section, labeled "Runs Batted In," is a measure of the player's ability to drive in runners from each base. For every base, two numbers are listed on the "Totals" line: The first is the number of RBIs credited to the batter for bringing home runners from that base; the second is the total number of opportunities he faced for that situation. Plate appearances that result in a base on balls, hit batsman, sacrifice bunt, or an award of first base for catcher's interference are not treated as "opportunities" if they do not result in a run.

If there is more than one runner on base, there is an "opportunity" to drive in each runner. A single with the bases loaded that scores only the runner from third is an opportunity and an RBI in the "From 3B" line, but an unsuccessful opportunity for both "From 2B" and "From 1B." (The exceptions to this are listed above; a bases-loaded walk is an RBI and opportunity under "From 3B," but goes unrecorded for the other two.)

Also given is the percentage of successful opportunities for each base and a combined total of "From 2B" and "From 3B" to represent runners driven in from scoring position.

The tables are followed by comments for each player. The first of these is a listing of pitchers each batter "loves to face" and "hates to face." The statistics listed for each individual match-up are from all regular-season games since 1975 inclusive. Next are miscellaneous statistics given in text form; these include: the batter's ground outs-to-air outs ratio; his total of double-play ground outs and opportunities (plate appearances with a runner on first and less than two outs); the number and percentage of runners driven in from third base with less than two outs; the direction of balls that reach the outfield, either in the air or on the ground (these may total more than 100 percent because they've been rounded to the nearest whole

percentage); the number and percentage of times he advanced from first to third or scored from second on outfield singles; and fielding statistics (assists per nine innings for infielders, putouts per nine innings for outfielders, and the success rate of opposing base stealers for catchers).

For purposes of comparison, the league totals in all of these categories are listed in the introduction to the Team Section (see page 2).

Roberto Alomar — Bats Left and Right

Toronto Blue Jays	AB	H	2B	3B	HR	RBI	BB	SO	BA	SA	OBA
Season	571	177	27	8	8	76	87	52	.310	.427	.405
vs. Left-Handers	156	48	5	0	5	23	25	17	.308	.436	.414
vs. Right-Handers	415	129	22	8	3	53	62	35	.311	.424	.401
vs. Ground-Ballers	284	90	13	3	2	38	39	24	.317	.405	.402
vs. Fly-Ballers	287	87	14	5	6	38	48	28	.303	.449	.407
Home Games	268	95	14	5	5	49	42	22	.354	.500	.444
Road Games	303	82	13	3	3	27	45	30	.271	.363	.369
Grass Fields	238	64	11	3	2	19	31	24	.269	.366	.353
Artificial Turf	333	113	16	5	6	57	56	28	.339	.471	.439
April	89	34	3	0	3	19	9	9	.382	.517	.439
May	102	32	2	2	2	11	11	8	.314	.431	.391
June	71	22	4	2	1	12	13	5	.310	.465	.424
July	93	24	7	1	0	9	20	11	.258	.355	.395
August	108	35	7	2	1	7	18	9	.324	.454	.421
Sept./Oct.	108	30	4	1	1	18	16	10	.278	.361	.370
Leading Off Inn.	111	39	5	3	2	2	13	6	.351	.505	.419
Runners On	245	83	11	3	6	74	43	19	.339	.482	.438
Bases Empty	326	94	16	5	2	2	44	33	.288	.387	.378
Runners/Scor. Pos.	147	52	8	2	4	68	22	12	.354	.517	.439
Runners On/2 Out	101	33	5	0	3	36	24	4	.327	.465	.460
Scor. Pos./2 Out	78	26	5	0	2	34	14	4	.333	.474	.441
Late-Inning Pressure	61	26	6	0	1	13	11	6	.426	.574	.514
Leading Off	15	6	2	0	1	1	2	1	.400	.733	.471
Runners On	37	17	4	0	0	12	5	3	.459	.568	.524
Runners/Scor. Pos.	23	11	2	0	0	11	3	3	.478	.565	.538

RUNS BATTED IN	From 1B	From 2B	From 3B	Scoring Position
Totals	6/152	32/119	30/61	62/180
Percentage	3.9%	26.9%	49.2%	34.4%

Loves to face: Brian Holman (.500, 9-for-18)
Tim Leary (.469, 15-for-32)
Jack McDowell (.615, 8-for-13, 1 HR)

Hates to face: Roger Clemens (.150, 3-for-20)
Randy Johnson (.167, 3-for-18)
Craig Lefferts (.091, 1-for-11)

Miscellaneous statistics: Ground outs-to-air outs ratio: 1.22 last season, 1.29 for career.... Grounded into 8 double plays in 117 opportunities (one per 15).... Drove in 19 of 22 runners from third base with less than two outs (86%), highest rate in majors.... Direction of balls hit to the outfield: 48% to left field, 27% to center, 24% to right batting left-handed; 39% to left field, 32% to center, 29% to right batting right-handed.... Base running: Advanced from first base to third on 11 of 35 outfield singles (31%); scored from second on 17 of 22 (77%).... Made 2.66 assists per nine innings at second base, lowest rate in A.L.

Comments: Hit safely in all 11 American League Championship Series games in 1991-92, the 4th-longest hitting streak in LCS history. Pete Rose holds the record (15), followed by Greg Luzinski (13) and Don Baylor (12).... Those 11 games were also the first 11 postseason games of his career; he finally was blanked in the World Series opener in Atlanta. Only one player in major league history had a longer streak to start his postseason career (Luzinski's 13-game streak mentioned above).... Became the 2d player in team history to hit over .300 from both sides of the plate in one season; Tony Fernandez did it in 1986. In each of his first four years in the majors, Alomar had hit for a considerably higher average from the left side than from the right; career breakdown: .303 batting left-handed, .264 right-handed.... Ranked 2d in the majors with 62 opposite-field hits; Kirby Puckett led with 64, with three of the top four being switch-hitters (Alomar, Tony Phillips, Tony Fernandez).... Stole third base 12 times in 14 attempts last season; only Marquis Grissom stole third more often (24 times in 26 tries).... Aside from a career-high batting average, he walked 30 more times than his previous career high.... Yearly error totals since 1989: 28, 19, 15, 5.... Batting average of .354 at the SkyDome was the highest by any A.L. player at home. And in Alomar's case, the SkyDome really is home (he lives in the adjacent SkyDome Hotel).

Sandy Alomar Jr. — Bats Right

Cleveland Indians	AB	H	2B	3B	HR	RBI	BB	SO	BA	SA	OBA
Season	299	75	16	0	2	26	13	32	.251	.324	.293
vs. Left-Handers	58	11	4	0	0	3	5	6	.190	.259	.277
vs. Right-Handers	241	64	12	0	2	23	8	26	.266	.340	.298
vs. Ground-Ballers	144	44	8	0	1	13	7	11	.306	.382	.342
vs. Fly-Ballers	155	31	8	0	1	13	6	21	.200	.271	.248
Home Games	158	41	7	0	1	15	10	18	.259	.323	.304
Road Games	141	34	9	0	1	11	3	14	.241	.326	.282
Grass Fields	263	67	14	0	2	25	12	29	.255	.331	.297
Artificial Turf	36	8	2	0	0	1	1	3	.222	.278	.263
April	65	14	5	0	1	7	5	8	.215	.338	.271
May	39	8	3	0	0	4	1	6	.205	.282	.262
June	75	18	1	0	1	6	2	8	.240	.293	.269
July	74	24	4	0	0	8	2	4	.324	.378	.351
August	46	11	3	0	0	1	3	6	.239	.304	.300
Sept./Oct.	0	0	0	0	0	0	0	0	—	—	—
Leading Off Inn.	66	21	5	0	0	0	3	8	.318	.394	.357
Runners On	129	24	3	0	2	26	4	13	.186	.256	.228
Bases Empty	170	51	13	0	0	0	9	19	.300	.376	.343
Runners/Scor. Pos.	65	15	2	0	1	24	3	9	.231	.308	.275
Runners On/2 Out	48	11	2	0	0	13	2	5	.229	.271	.275
Scor. Pos./2 Out	26	8	2	0	0	13	2	3	.308	.385	.379
Late-Inning Pressure	60	17	3	0	0	6	2	9	.283	.333	.317
Leading Off	14	5	1	0	0	0	0	1	.357	.429	.357
Runners On	22	5	0	0	0	6	0	4	.227	.227	.261
Runners/Scor. Pos.	14	4	0	0	0	6	0	3	.286	.286	.286

RUNS BATTED IN	From 1B	From 2B	From 3B	Scoring Position
Totals	3/99	9/51	12/29	21/80
Percentage	3.0%	17.6%	41.4%	26.3%

Loves to face: Greg A. Harris (.400, 4-for-10, 1 HR)
Melido Perez (.455, 5-for-11)
Eric Plunk (2-for-2, 2 BB)

Hates to face: Mark Eichhorn (0-for-8)
Bob Milacki (0-for-13)
Jeff Montgomery (.182, 2-for-11)

Miscellaneous statistics: Ground outs-to-air outs ratio: 0.91 last season, 0.94 for career.... Grounded into 7 double plays in 71 opportunities (one per 10).... Drove in 5 of 14 runners from third base with less than two outs (36%).... Direction of balls hit to the outfield: 47% to left field, 32% to center, 22% to right.... Base running: Advanced from first base to third on 1 of 13 outfield singles (8%), 4th-lowest rate in A.L.; scored from second on 6 of 7 (86%).... Opposing base stealers: 43-for-78 (55%), 3d-lowest rate in A.L.

Comments: Batting average of .286 from the 9th spot in the order tied John Valentin for the highest among major leaguers with at least 100 at-bats in that spot last season. Cleveland had a winning record with Alomar starting in the nine-hole (26-20), and a record of 10-29 when he started in other lineup spots.... Although the Indians' staff posted a 3.81 ERA with Alomar behind the plate, compared to a 4.44 ERA with Junior Ortiz, the club had a losing record with Alomar starting (35-49) and a winning record with Ortiz (37-32).... Opposing base stealers were successful in only four of 12 attempts against the Alomar-Nagy battery.... Indians' catchers combined for only three home runs last season; only the Boston backstops combined for fewer homers (2).... Alomar has hit only two home runs in his last 145 games, compared to 10 homers in 135 major league games prior to that.... Batting average with runners on base was the lowest in the league last season, but his brother excelled in that area (as in most every other area as well), posting the 3d-highest average in the league.... At least Sandy still leads Roberto in All-Star starts, three to two.... Has anyone noticed that players who have changed leagues seem to have an inherent advantage in the All-Star balloting procedure? Who will a casual fan in San Diego (is there any other kind?) vote for among A.L. catchers? Another advantage is having a father and/or brother who is familiar to the voting public. Let's face it, name recognition is the game here. Just ask Roger Clinton.

Brady Anderson   Bats Left

Baltimore Orioles	AB	H	2B	3B	HR	RBI	BB	SO	BA	SA	OBA
Season	623	169	28	10	21	80	98	98	.271	.449	.373
vs. Left-Handers	190	43	8	2	5	26	31	35	.226	.368	.345
vs. Right-Handers	433	126	20	8	16	54	67	63	.291	.485	.386
vs. Ground-Ballers	303	87	15	4	10	44	47	44	.287	.462	.383
vs. Fly-Ballers	320	82	13	6	11	36	51	54	.256	.438	.365
Home Games	313	82	14	2	15	46	48	54	.262	.463	.364
Road Games	310	87	14	8	6	34	50	44	.281	.435	.383
Grass Fields	530	143	22	5	19	65	80	88	.270	.438	.368
Artificial Turf	93	26	6	5	2	15	18	10	.280	.516	.402
April	77	23	6	5	2	18	13	12	.299	.584	.417
May	115	33	8	0	7	19	11	15	.287	.539	.354
June	109	29	4	1	4	11	15	16	.266	.431	.349
July	111	32	3	0	2	13	16	15	.288	.369	.380
August	99	27	2	3	3	11	28	13	.273	.444	.431
Sept./Oct.	112	25	5	1	3	8	15	27	.223	.366	.321
Leading Off Inn.	268	68	12	4	9	9	32	37	.254	.429	.338
Runners On	205	57	9	3	7	66	41	33	.278	.454	.389
Bases Empty	418	112	19	7	14	14	57	65	.268	.447	.365
Runners/Scor. Pos.	134	39	6	3	4	59	32	24	.291	.470	.406
Runners On/2 Out	98	29	6	2	5	36	16	17	.296	.551	.400
Scor. Pos./2 Out	76	23	5	2	3	31	15	13	.303	.539	.418
Late-Inning Pressure	77	22	5	1	1	4	12	14	.286	.416	.385
Leading Off	29	9	2	1	1	1	3	4	.310	.552	.375
Runners On	29	8	2	0	0	3	6	4	.276	.345	.389
Runners/Scor. Pos.	18	4	1	0	0	3	6	4	.222	.278	.400

RUNS BATTED IN	From 1B	From 2B	From 3B	Scoring Position
Totals	8/150	20/111	31/63	51/174
Percentage	5.3%	18.0%	49.2%	29.3%

Loves to face: Mike Boddicker (.400, 8-for-20)
Kevin Tapani (.545, 6-for-11, 1 HR)
Walt Terrell (.563, 9-for-16)

Hates to face: Rod Nichols (0-for-11)
Nolan Ryan (0-for-13)
Dave Stieb (0-for-15)

Miscellaneous statistics: Ground outs-to-air outs ratio: 0.91 last season, 0.92 for career.... Grounded into 2 double plays in 110 opportunities (one per 55), best rate in A.L.... Drove in 19 of 30 runners from third base with less than two outs (63%).... Direction of balls hit to the outfield: 29% to left field, 31% to center, 39% to right.... Base running: Advanced from first base to third on 20 of 35 outfield singles (57%); scored from second on 15 of 19 (79%).... Made 2.43 putouts per nine innings in left field, 2d-highest rate in A.L.

Comments: Led majors in home runs (21), extra-base hits (59), and RBIs (80) from the leadoff spot in the lineup. This on the heels of becoming the first outfielder in major league history to bat .231 or lower in each of his first four seasons in the majors (minimum: 60 games in the outfield each year).... His previous career high in RBIs was 27, a mark he surpassed on May 19 in his 37th game of the season. Before 1992, he had averaged only 36 RBIs for every 162 games played.... Although he eventually shattered career highs in almost every offensive category, his previous history of fine starts had most observers (including us) expecting a sharp decline. He has a career average of .276 in April, but until last season he had hit only .210 from May through October.... With 59 extra-base hits and 53 stolen bases, he joined Marquis Grissom in 1992's 50–50 Club. Only one player in franchise history had done it previously: George Sisler (68 XBH, 51 SB for the 1922 St. Louis Browns).... Ranked third in the league with 10 triples, behind Lance Johnson (12) and teammate Mike Devereaux (11). They became the first pair of Orioles to each reach double figures in that category; the last teammates in franchise history to do it were Bob Dillinger and Whitey Platt on the 1948 Browns.... Led the majors with 749 plate appearances.... Played 158 games last season, including 154 complete games, 2d-highest total in the majors to Travis Fryman's 160. (Ripken went the distance in 153 of his 162 games.)

Carlos Baerga   Bats Left and Right

Cleveland Indians	AB	H	2B	3B	HR	RBI	BB	SO	BA	SA	OBA
Season	657	205	32	1	20	105	35	76	.312	.455	.354
vs. Left-Handers	168	63	9	0	4	35	3	19	.375	.500	.387
vs. Right-Handers	489	142	23	1	16	70	32	57	.290	.440	.343
vs. Ground-Ballers	306	97	15	1	9	51	15	31	.317	.461	.355
vs. Fly-Ballers	351	108	17	0	11	54	20	45	.308	.450	.354
Home Games	329	116	17	0	9	50	18	36	.353	.486	.392
Road Games	328	89	15	1	11	55	17	40	.271	.424	.318
Grass Fields	557	180	25	0	18	89	31	65	.323	.465	.363
Artificial Turf	100	25	7	1	2	16	4	11	.250	.400	.309
April	92	28	3	0	2	10	3	8	.304	.402	.333
May	108	34	3	0	2	18	4	11	.315	.398	.353
June	109	32	7	0	5	16	7	15	.294	.495	.333
July	102	34	5	1	5	19	4	14	.333	.549	.369
August	116	32	7	0	3	21	5	14	.276	.414	.326
Sept./Oct.	130	45	7	0	3	21	12	14	.346	.469	.401
Leading Off Inn.	110	30	6	0	4	4	5	15	.273	.436	.322
Runners On	295	100	11	1	10	95	19	27	.339	.485	.382
Bases Empty	362	105	21	0	10	10	16	49	.290	.431	.331
Runners/Scor. Pos.	182	56	5	0	5	81	17	17	.308	.418	.366
Runners On/2 Out	96	26	4	0	6	28	6	12	.271	.500	.346
Scor. Pos./2 Out	65	17	2	0	4	23	6	9	.262	.477	.360
Late-Inning Pressure	117	37	8	0	2	12	7	12	.316	.436	.367
Leading Off	22	8	2	0	0	0	0	1	.364	.455	.364
Runners On	47	15	3	0	1	11	6	4	.319	.447	.421
Runners/Scor. Pos.	30	9	2	0	1	11	6	3	.300	.467	.436

RUNS BATTED IN	From 1B	From 2B	From 3B	Scoring Position
Totals	10/186	29/125	46/90	75/215
Percentage	5.4%	23.2%	51.1%	34.9%

Loves to face: Jimmy Key (.529, 9-for-17)
Nolan Ryan (.750, 6-for-8, 1 HR)
Bob Welch (.474, 9-for-19, 1 HR)

Hates to face: Scott Erickson (.100, 2-for-20)
Erik Hanson (.133, 2-for-15)
David Wells (.067, 1-for-15, 1 2B)

Miscellaneous statistics: Ground outs-to-air outs ratio: 1.38 last season, 1.49 for career.... Grounded into 15 double plays in 136 opportunities (one per 9.1).... Drove in 40 of 60 runners from third base with less than two outs (67%).... Direction of balls hit to the outfield: 31% to left field, 30% to center, 39% to right batting left-handed; 30% to left field, 39% to center, 31% to right batting right-handed.... Base running: Advanced from first base to third on 10 of 30 outfield singles (33%); scored from second on 17 of 20 (85%).... Made 2.98 assists per nine innings at second base.

Comments: Led the majors with 42 go-ahead RBIs, 17 of which proved to be game-winners, but had built a reputation for clutch run production even before last season. He led rookies with 15 go-ahead RBIs and 10 game-winners in 1990, and led A.L. in percentage of go-ahead RBIs in 1991.... Drove in 105 runs to lead major league second basemen. Of that total, he drove in 40 (of 60) runners from third base with less than two outs; no other player in the majors had as many such opportunities.... Became the first Cleveland player to lead A.L. second basemen in games played since Joe Gordon in 1947.... Became the 5th second baseman to hit 20 home runs and drive in 100 runs in a season in which he batted .300. Those are Triple Crown–type numbers for the position (see the San Diego essay). The others: Rogers Hornsby (five times, all during the 1920s), Charlie Gehringer (1938), Joe Morgan (1976), and Ryne Sandberg (1990).... Took three 0-for-4's in the first three games of the season before getting six hits in a 19-inning game vs. Boston. He had only one more streak all season in which he went hitless in three consecutive games.... Led major league second basemen with 400 putouts, although he ranked next-to-worst among A.L. second basemen (to Steve Sax) in both fielding percentage and errors.... With 1708 plate appearances in three years in the majors, Baerga has walked only 99 times. It is still true that no Caribbean-born player has walked even 90 times in a single major league season.

Harold Baines — Bats Left

Oakland A's	AB	H	2B	3B	HR	RBI	BB	SO	BA	SA	OBA
Season	478	121	18	0	16	76	59	61	.253	.391	.331
vs. Left-Handers	53	13	0	0	1	8	5	16	.245	.302	.310
vs. Right-Handers	425	108	18	0	15	68	54	45	.254	.402	.334
vs. Ground-Ballers	239	63	10	0	7	40	22	20	.264	.393	.321
vs. Fly-Ballers	239	58	8	0	9	36	37	41	.243	.389	.342
Home Games	231	64	8	0	10	46	26	28	.277	.442	.346
Road Games	247	57	10	0	6	30	33	33	.231	.344	.318
Grass Fields	398	103	16	0	15	70	51	48	.259	.412	.339
Artificial Turf	80	18	2	0	1	6	8	13	.225	.287	.292
April	72	14	3	0	1	5	6	15	.194	.278	.256
May	82	20	0	0	1	9	9	8	.244	.280	.309
June	72	19	5	0	5	21	12	7	.264	.542	.365
July	88	29	2	0	1	12	8	13	.330	.386	.385
August	89	21	4	0	4	15	13	12	.236	.416	.333
Sept./Oct.	75	18	4	0	4	14	11	6	.240	.453	.330
Leading Off Inn.	111	27	2	0	2	2	18	14	.243	.315	.349
Runners On	205	63	8	0	12	72	25	22	.307	.522	.373
Bases Empty	273	58	10	0	4	4	34	39	.212	.293	.300
Runners/Scor. Pos.	122	33	3	0	6	57	15	16	.270	.443	.336
Runners On/2 Out	97	26	5	0	7	30	8	12	.268	.536	.324
Scor. Pos./2 Out	55	13	0	0	4	21	7	9	.236	.455	.323
Late-Inning Pressure	59	14	2	0	2	6	6	13	.237	.373	.308
Leading Off	18	2	0	0	0	0	1	4	.111	.111	.158
Runners On	16	7	1	0	1	5	5	3	.438	.688	.571
Runners/Scor. Pos.	10	3	0	0	1	5	3	2	.300	.600	.462

RUNS BATTED IN	From 1B	From 2B	From 3B	Scoring Position
Totals	14/152	18/95	28/55	46/150
Percentage	9.2%	18.9%	50.9%	30.7%

Loves to face: Mike Boddicker (.358, 24-for-67, 4 HR)
Steve Olin (6-for-6, 1 BB)
Nolan Ryan (.368, 7-for-19, 1 2B, 4 HR)

Hates to face: Mark Langston (.139, 5-for-36, 1 HR, 0 BB)
Mark Leiter (.071, 1-for-14)
Melido Perez (.100, 3-for-30, 4 BB)

Miscellaneous statistics: Ground outs-to-air outs ratio: 1.19 last season, 1.30 for career.... Grounded into 11 double plays in 98 opportunities (one per 8.9).... Drove in 21 of 36 runners from third base with less than two outs (58%).... Direction of balls hit to the outfield: 36% to left field, 41% to center, 23% to right.... Base running: Advanced from first base to third on 3 of 23 outfield singles (13%); scored from second on 9 of 12 (75%).... Made 1.71 putouts per nine innings in right field.

Comments: One of only four players to reach double figures in home runs in every season since 1980. The others: Andre Dawson, Eddie Murray, and Lance Parrish. Career total of 241 homers ranks 50th in A.L. history, tied with Jesse Barfield and Cecil Cooper.... Hit eight more homers with men on base than with the bases empty last season, the largest such difference in the majors.... The only player to appear in the postseason under Tony LaRussa for both the White Sox and the Athletics. Five others played during the regular season for LaRussa in both Chicago and Oakland: Tony Bernazard, Dennis Lamp, Vance Law, Gene Nelson, and Jamie Quirk.... Has batted over .300 with runners on base in seven of the last nine seasons.... Ranked 6th in A.L. with five opposite-field home runs last season.... Averaged one strikeout every 8.9 plate appearances last season, establishing a career best for the 2d straight year.... He hasn't had a sacrifice bunt in a regular-season game since 1984, but did lay one down in the 1990 ALCS.... Started 122 of 126 games in which the A's faced right-handed pitchers, but only seven against left-handers. (A's happened to go 7–0 in those games.)... Has batted .364 (12-for-33) in his pinch-hitting appearances over the past three years.... Even though his total of at-bats against left-handed pitchers has decreased in each of the last four seasons, don't think of him as a part-timer yet. Since his debut in 1980, he has qualified for the A.L. batting title in every season except 1990.

George Bell — Bats Right

Chicago White Sox	AB	H	2B	3B	HR	RBI	BB	SO	BA	SA	OBA
Season	627	160	27	0	25	112	31	97	.255	.418	.294
vs. Left-Handers	142	44	8	0	7	28	10	17	.310	.514	.355
vs. Right-Handers	485	116	19	0	18	84	21	80	.239	.390	.276
vs. Ground-Ballers	305	73	10	0	12	53	17	53	.239	.390	.287
vs. Fly-Ballers	322	87	17	0	13	59	14	44	.270	.444	.300
Home Games	326	85	11	0	16	63	14	54	.261	.442	.293
Road Games	301	75	16	0	9	49	17	43	.249	.392	.295
Grass Fields	531	137	19	0	24	103	30	84	.258	.429	.301
Artificial Turf	96	23	8	0	1	9	1	13	.240	.354	.255
April	73	26	2	0	4	13	1	9	.356	.548	.368
May	103	18	4	0	1	14	7	18	.175	.243	.234
June	111	30	6	0	5	22	5	18	.270	.459	.302
July	109	25	5	0	3	20	7	17	.229	.358	.286
August	112	34	5	0	9	25	6	20	.304	.589	.339
Sept./Oct.	119	27	5	0	3	18	5	15	.227	.345	.262
Leading Off Inn.	134	25	6	0	2	2	5	21	.187	.276	.227
Runners On	355	98	17	0	14	101	17	55	.276	.442	.310
Bases Empty	272	62	10	0	11	11	14	42	.228	.386	.273
Runners/Scor. Pos.	212	62	10	0	10	88	16	41	.292	.481	.339
Runners On/2 Out	151	31	5	0	7	38	6	26	.205	.377	.241
Scor. Pos./2 Out	95	19	3	0	4	30	5	21	.200	.358	.248
Late-Inning Pressure	73	19	2	0	2	6	4	14	.260	.370	.299
Leading Off	17	5	1	0	1	1	1	2	.294	.529	.333
Runners On	33	8	0	0	0	4	0	6	.242	.242	.242
Runners/Scor. Pos.	19	4	0	0	0	4	0	5	.211	.211	.211

RUNS BATTED IN	From 1B	From 2B	From 3B	Scoring Position
Totals	16/270	42/180	29/75	71/255
Percentage	5.9%	23.3%	38.7%	27.8%

Loves to face: Scott Bankhead (.448, 13-for-29, 4 2B, 5 HR)
Neal Heaton (.462, 12-for-26, 4 2B, 4 HR, 0 BB)
Kevin Tapani (.500, 9-for-18, 3 2B, 1 HR)

Hates to face: Mike Boddicker (.200, 14-for-70)
Tom Gordon (.091, 2-for-22, 1 HR)
Dave Stewart (.183, 11-for-60, 5 2B, 2 HR)

Miscellaneous statistics: Ground outs-to-air outs ratio: 0.80 last season, 0.75 for career.... Grounded into 29 double plays in 165 opportunities (one per 5.7).... Drove in 22 of 36 runners from third base with less than two outs (61%).... Direction of balls hit to the outfield: 51% to left field, 32% to center, 16% to right.... Base running: Advanced from first base to third on 6 of 27 outfield singles (22%); scored from second on 7 of 10 (70%).... Made 1.96 putouts per nine innings in left field.

Comments: Drove in 57 runs in 50 games (June 22–Aug. 18); no other players had more than 50 RBIs over a 50-game span last season.... Has driven in 909 runs in nine years since becoming a starter in 1984, the most in the majors during that period. The runner-up: Don Mattingly (880). The only active players with at least 900 RBIs over any nine-year period: Eddie Murray (pick just about any nine years of his career, but we like his 931 RBIs from 1977 to 1985) and Dave Winfield (910, 1979–87).... One of only three players with at least 600 plate appearances in each of the last nine seasons. The others: Brett Butler and Cal Ripken.... Became the first player in major league history not to have a triple in three consecutive 500-at-bat seasons.... Career total of 6156 plate appearances is by far the highest among active players without a sacrifice bunt.... Had a career total of just 317 walks at the time of his 250th home run last September. Among the 100 players in major league history who have hit that many homers, only Tony Armas reached the milestone with fewer walks than Bell.... Of the 137 players to play for both the White Sox and Cubs, Bell is the only one to hit 20 home runs for each. (Bell had 20-HR seasons for each; no one else even hit 20 during their *entire tenures* with both the Sox and Cubs.)... Set unwanted career highs last season in strikeouts, strikeout rate, and grounding into double plays (29).... Batted with 255 runners in scoring position last season, the 4th-highest total in the 18 years that we've been keeping track.

Albert Belle — Bats Right

Cleveland Indians

	AB	H	2B	3B	HR	RBI	BB	SO	BA	SA	OBA
Season	585	152	23	1	34	112	52	128	.260	.477	.320
vs. Left-Handers	138	35	10	0	8	27	12	33	.254	.500	.307
vs. Right-Handers	447	117	13	1	26	85	40	95	.262	.470	.325
vs. Ground-Ballers	254	58	8	1	9	43	23	61	.228	.374	.293
vs. Fly-Ballers	331	94	15	0	25	69	29	67	.284	.556	.343
Home Games	285	76	14	1	15	63	28	61	.267	.481	.331
Road Games	300	76	9	0	19	49	24	67	.253	.473	.310
Grass Fields	499	127	21	1	27	93	45	105	.255	.463	.315
Artificial Turf	86	25	2	0	7	19	7	23	.291	.558	.351
April	84	19	5	0	4	13	8	22	.226	.429	.298
May	90	29	3	1	7	21	11	22	.322	.611	.388
June	103	25	2	0	6	14	7	18	.243	.437	.297
July	91	22	3	0	3	16	3	19	.242	.374	.271
August	95	24	4	0	6	19	11	24	.253	.484	.324
Sept./Oct.	122	33	6	0	8	29	12	23	.270	.516	.336
Leading Off Inn.	154	40	4	1	6	6	11	35	.260	.416	.309
Runners On	282	71	12	0	18	96	27	64	.252	.486	.318
Bases Empty	303	81	11	1	16	16	25	64	.267	.469	.323
Runners/Scor. Pos.	155	37	6	0	12	81	19	36	.239	.510	.319
Runners On/2 Out	128	28	3	0	4	23	13	27	.219	.336	.301
Scor. Pos./2 Out	68	12	1	0	3	20	11	16	.176	.324	.300
Late-Inning Pressure	97	24	1	0	4	18	6	23	.247	.381	.287
Leading Off	25	8	0	0	1	1	0	8	.320	.440	.320
Runners On	44	10	1	0	2	16	3	9	.227	.386	.269
Runners/Scor. Pos.	24	4	1	0	1	14	2	4	.167	.333	.226

RUNS BATTED IN	From 1B	From 2B	From 3B	Scoring Position
Totals	18/208	25/107	35/85	60/192
Percentage	8.7%	23.4%	41.2%	31.3%

Loves to face: Chuck Finley (.391, 9-for-23, 3 HR)
Arthur Rhodes (.400, 4-for-10, 2 2B, 2 HR)
Todd Stottlemyre (.429, 6-for-14, 2 HR)

Hates to face: Kevin Appier (.118, 2-for-17, 10 SO)
Roger Clemens (.125, 3-for-24, 12 SO)
Jaime Navarro (0-for-9, 5 SO)

Miscellaneous statistics: Ground outs-to-air outs ratio: 1.01 last season, 1.15 for career.... Grounded into 18 double plays in 132 opportunities (one per 7.3).... Drove in 27 of 49 runners from third base with less than two outs (55%).... Direction of balls hit to the outfield: 41% to left field, 34% to center, 25% to right.... Base running: Advanced from first base to third on 10 of 28 outfield singles (36%); scored from second on 8 of 8 (100%).... Made 2.00 putouts per nine innings in left field.

Comments: Only two players in team history have equaled or surpassed Belle's 1992 totals in homers, RBIs, and runs (81): Hal Trosky (1934 and 1936) and Al Rosen (1950 and 1953).... He hit 28 homers in 1991, followed by 34 last season. Larry Doby is the only player in Indians history to hit at least 28 home runs in three consecutive seasons (1952–54).... Career average of one home run every 18.4 at-bats is 3d-best in Indians history (minimum: 50 HR), behind Rocky Colavito (16.8) and Vic Wertz (17.5).... Snapped a home-run drought of one month (April 23 to May 23) in grand fashion with seven homers over his next 21 at-bats.... Even with the Indians moving in the fences in 1992, he still hit more homers on the road than at home; career totals: 27 at home, 43 on the road.... All of his plate appearances came from the cleanup spot last season.... Batted .326 during his first-inning at-bats, .248 thereafter.... Season total of 124 strikeouts was 8th-highest in team history.... His career rate of runners driven in from scoring position in Late-Inning Pressure Situations (44.2 percent) is the highest of any player since 1975.... Only nine of his 112 RBIs proved to be game-winners; teammate Glenallen Hill drove in only 49 runs, but 10 were game-winners.... On the other hand, Belle drove in more runs in losing causes than any player in the majors: Belle (47), Ken Griffey (46), Darren Daulton (44).

Dante Bichette — Bats Right

Milwaukee Brewers

	AB	H	2B	3B	HR	RBI	BB	SO	BA	SA	OBA
Season	387	111	27	2	5	41	16	74	.287	.406	.318
vs. Left-Handers	119	34	8	2	2	23	9	27	.286	.437	.336
vs. Right-Handers	268	77	19	0	3	18	7	47	.287	.392	.309
vs. Ground-Ballers	190	58	16	2	4	23	10	37	.305	.474	.342
vs. Fly-Ballers	197	53	11	0	1	18	6	37	.269	.340	.295
Home Games	170	41	9	2	3	22	9	33	.241	.371	.280
Road Games	217	70	18	0	2	19	7	41	.323	.433	.348
Grass Fields	327	90	20	2	5	33	14	63	.275	.394	.308
Artificial Turf	60	21	7	0	0	8	2	11	.350	.467	.371
April	37	12	1	0	0	5	1	13	.324	.351	.342
May	91	28	5	0	1	5	6	15	.308	.396	.354
June	77	26	10	2	3	19	3	10	.338	.636	.358
July	48	16	2	0	1	5	0	8	.333	.438	.333
August	74	17	7	0	0	5	4	17	.230	.324	.287
Sept./Oct.	60	12	2	0	0	2	2	11	.200	.233	.222
Leading Off Inn.	94	32	6	1	0	0	3	21	.340	.426	.367
Runners On	176	47	14	1	2	38	8	29	.267	.392	.298
Bases Empty	211	64	13	1	3	3	8	45	.303	.417	.335
Runners/Scor. Pos.	99	23	6	1	1	32	6	20	.232	.343	.269
Runners On/2 Out	76	19	3	1	2	20	4	11	.250	.395	.287
Scor. Pos./2 Out	48	12	1	1	1	17	3	9	.250	.375	.294
Late-Inning Pressure	68	18	1	0	0	3	3	12	.265	.279	.296
Leading Off	24	9	0	0	0	0	1	7	.375	.375	.400
Runners On	24	5	1	0	0	3	1	2	.208	.250	.240
Runners/Scor. Pos.	14	3	1	0	0	3	1	2	.214	.286	.267

RUNS BATTED IN	From 1B	From 2B	From 3B	Scoring Position
Totals	8/123	11/76	17/45	28/121
Percentage	6.5%	14.5%	37.8%	23.1%

Loves to face: Bud Black (.286, 4-for-14, 1 HR)
Tom Candiotti (.308, 4-for-13)

Hates to face: Greg Cadaret (.143, 2-for-14, 7 SO)
Greg Hibbard (.154, 4-for-26)
Greg Swindell (.143, 2-for-14, 8 SO)

Miscellaneous statistics: Ground outs-to-air outs ratio: 1.12 last season, 1.06 for career.... Grounded into 13 double plays in 81 opportunities (one per 6.2).... Drove in 8 of 19 runners from third base with less than two outs (42%).... Direction of balls hit to the outfield: 46% to left field, 26% to center, 28% to right.... Base running: Advanced from first base to third on 5 of 19 outfield singles (26%); scored from second on 4 of 12 (33%), lowest rate in A.L.... Made 1.98 putouts per nine innings in right field, lowest rate in A.L.

Comments: The only player in the majors to bat above .300 in each of the first four months last season.... Increased his batting average by 49 points from 1991 to 1992, but it seems to have cost him some power: His home-run total decreased to five after two consecutive 15-homer seasons. Averaged one homer every 77 at-bats last season, compared to a previous career rate of one every 32 at-bats.... His batting average was a career high, due mostly to his success against right-handed pitchers. He had never batted above .241 vs. right-handers before last season.... Had over 100 plate appearances from each of the fourth, fifth, and sixth spots in the batting order. Among 54 players in the majors with 100 plate appearances from the six-hole, Bichette (.320) was one of six to hit .300 or better from that spot; only Ken Caminiti (.368) and Brian Harper (.336) stood ahead of him.... Career rate of one walk every 24.2 plate appearances is 10th-worst among active players with at least 1000 PAs. Last season's rate of one walk every 25.7 PAs was the worst of his career.... The Brewers were 49–44 with Bichette starting in right field, 43–26 with Darryl Hamilton starting there.... Collected only six outfield assists last season, after a total of 26 over the previous two years.... One of only three men to have played at least 150 games for both the Brewers and the Angels. If you knew that the two others are Joe Lahoud and Ellie Rodriguez, it's time to consider seriously the direction your life has taken.

Lance Blankenship

Bats Right

Oakland A's	AB	H	2B	3B	HR	RBI	BB	SO	BA	SA	OBA
Season	349	84	24	1	3	34	82	57	.241	.341	.393
vs. Left-Handers	89	22	9	0	0	5	30	11	.247	.348	.455
vs. Right-Handers	260	62	15	1	3	29	52	46	.238	.338	.368
vs. Ground-Ballers	158	37	12	1	2	13	45	24	.234	.361	.411
vs. Fly-Ballers	191	47	12	0	1	21	37	33	.246	.325	.377
Home Games	167	43	13	1	1	19	49	24	.257	.365	.439
Road Games	182	41	11	0	2	15	33	33	.225	.319	.346
Grass Fields	307	76	22	1	2	33	77	50	.248	.345	.407
Artificial Turf	42	8	2	0	1	1	5	7	.190	.310	.277
April	72	18	3	0	1	8	11	11	.250	.333	.345
May	72	21	6	0	0	7	19	11	.292	.375	.440
June	84	18	6	1	0	6	22	15	.214	.310	.383
July	12	3	2	0	0	4	2	1	.250	.417	.400
August	51	12	5	0	1	6	9	9	.235	.392	.371
Sept./Oct.	58	12	2	0	1	3	19	10	.207	.293	.418
Leading Off Inn.	82	14	5	0	2	2	20	17	.171	.305	.333
Runners On	158	40	10	1	0	31	36	21	.253	.329	.405
Bases Empty	191	44	14	0	3	3	46	36	.230	.351	.382
Runners/Scor. Pos.	88	17	3	0	0	24	26	13	.193	.227	.390
Runners On/2 Out	64	13	2	1	0	12	15	13	.203	.266	.378
Scor. Pos./2 Out	45	8	1	0	0	10	15	10	.178	.200	.413
Late-Inning Pressure	53	12	1	0	1	3	13	8	.226	.302	.388
Leading Off	13	3	1	0	1	1	2	2	.231	.538	.333
Runners On	22	4	0	0	0	2	9	4	.182	.182	.438
Runners/Scor. Pos.	16	2	0	0	0	2	7	3	.125	.125	.417

RUNS BATTED IN	From 1B	From 2B	From 3B	Scoring Position
Totals	8/117	8/62	15/45	23/107
Percentage	6.8%	12.9%	33.3%	21.5%

Loves to face: Chuck Crim (4-for-4, 1 HR)
Nolan Ryan (.714, 5-for-7)
Frank Viola (.333, 4-for-12, 4 BB)

Hates to face: Roger Clemens (.077, 1-for-13, 2 BB)
Randy Johnson (.067, 1-for-15, 3 BB)
Duane Ward (0-for-6)

Miscellaneous statistics: Ground outs-to-air outs ratio: 0.91 last season, 0.93 for career.... Grounded into 10 double plays in 99 opportunities (one per 10).... Drove in 10 of 21 runners from third base with less than two outs (48%).... Direction of balls hit to the outfield: 55% to left field, 28% to center, 17% to right.... Base running: Advanced from first base to third on 8 of 17 outfield singles (47%); scored from second on 12 of 16 (75%).... Made 3.27 assists per nine innings at second base, 3d-highest rate in A.L.

Comments: He can walk with the best of 'em, even when he's batting ninth in the lineup and no right-thinking pitcher would dare walk him to get to Rickey and Co. at the top of the order. Blankenship walked 43 times while batting ninth last season (he started 68 games there), and his rate of walks from the nine-hole was the highest in the majors among players with at least 20 starts in that spot.... He had drawn only eight walks in 137 total times to the plate in 1989 (one BB every 17.1 PAs), but walked 82 times last year, averaging one every 5.4 plate appearances.... In his career, he has walked in 33 of the 217 innings that he has led off; over the last 18 years, only five players have a higher career rate of walks leading off innings: Jim Wynn, Randy Milligan, Frank Thomas, Gene Tenace, Joe Morgan.... Manny Mota he's not: 2-for-30 lifetime as a pinch hitter (both hits came in 1990); his .067 average is 2d-lowest among active players with at least 25 pinch-hit at-bats.... His .223 average as a second baseman was the lowest among major leaguers with at least 250 plate appearances at that position last season.... Aside from his second base duties, he started four games at first base (while Mark McGwire was disabled) and was one of seven major leaguers to start at least 10 games at each of the outfield positions.... He was the Athletics' 10th-round pick in the 1986 June draft; the only players the A's chose ahead of him who have played in the majors are Scott Hemond (1st round) and Kevin Tapani (2d round).

Wade Boggs

Bats Left

Boston Red Sox	AB	H	2B	3B	HR	RBI	BB	SO	BA	SA	OBA
Season	514	133	22	4	7	50	74	31	.259	.358	.353
vs. Left-Handers	158	43	10	1	1	21	12	13	.272	.367	.326
vs. Right-Handers	356	90	12	3	6	29	62	18	.253	.354	.364
vs. Ground-Ballers	262	66	10	1	2	28	33	11	.252	.355	.337
vs. Fly-Ballers	252	67	12	3	5	22	41	20	.266	.397	.369
Home Games	251	61	13	3	4	26	48	12	.243	.367	.366
Road Games	263	72	9	1	3	24	26	19	.274	.350	.339
Grass Fields	437	111	19	4	6	39	66	27	.254	.357	.353
Artificial Turf	77	22	3	0	1	11	8	4	.286	.364	.353
April	75	19	4	0	0	5	13	6	.253	.307	.360
May	86	25	7	0	3	10	13	3	.291	.477	.380
June	95	23	3	1	3	9	17	4	.242	.389	.363
July	79	24	2	2	0	8	9	3	.304	.380	.371
August	96	19	3	1	1	11	12	4	.198	.281	.286
Sept./Oct.	83	23	3	0	0	7	10	11	.277	.313	.368
Leading Off Inn.	139	35	6	1	1	1	11	6	.252	.331	.311
Runners On	203	58	10	0	2	45	47	17	.286	.365	.412
Bases Empty	311	75	12	4	5	5	27	14	.241	.354	.308
Runners/Scor. Pos.	106	33	6	0	2	44	35	7	.311	.425	.463
Runners On/2 Out	65	16	2	0	1	19	19	6	.246	.323	.417
Scor. Pos./2 Out	40	12	2	0	1	19	16	3	.300	.425	.500
Late-Inning Pressure	93	31	8	0	0	9	11	7	.333	.419	.410
Leading Off	21	7	1	0	0	1	0	2	.333	.381	.364
Runners On	48	17	4	0	0	9	10	3	.354	.438	.475
Runners/Scor. Pos.	19	9	2	0	0	9	9	0	.474	.579	.643

RUNS BATTED IN	From 1B	From 2B	From 3B	Scoring Position
Totals	5/154	18/90	20/46	38/136
Percentage	3.2%	20.0%	43.5%	27.9%

Loves to face: Scott Bankhead (.424, 14-for-33, 0 SO)
Dave Stewart (.371, 23-for-62, 2 HR)
Walt Terrell (.433, 26-for-60, 2 HR)

Hates to face: Randy Johnson (.125, 2-for-16, 8 SO)
Scott Sanderson (.125, 3-for-24)
Bob Welch (.037, 1-for-27, 1 2B, 3 BB)

Miscellaneous statistics: Ground outs-to-air outs ratio: 1.23 last season, 1.35 for career.... Grounded into 10 double plays in 122 opportunities (one per 12).... Drove in 12 of 20 runners from third base with less than two outs (60%).... Direction of balls hit to the outfield: 43% to left field, 36% to center, 21% to right.... Base running: Advanced from first base to third on 10 of 38 outfield singles (26%); scored from second on 6 of 12 (50%).... Made 2.07 assists per nine innings at third base.

Comments: Career batting average fell from .345 to .338 last season, the 3d-largest single-season fall in major league history by a 5000-at-bat veteran. Chuck Klein hit the skids in 1938 (batted .247 and his career average fell from .340 to .333) and a guy named Bill Hallman stumbled in 1901 (batted .185 to go from .283 to .275).... Boggs started 1992 with the 6th-highest career average in history (minimum: 1000 AB), and ended the year 21st, falling behind Willie Keeler, Ted Williams, Tris Speaker, Billy Hamilton, Dan Brouthers, Pete Browning, Dave Orr, Babe Ruth, Harry Heilmann, Bill Terry, Jesse Burkett, George Sisler, Lou Gehrig, Nap Lajoie, and Jake Stenzel. The only other active player in the top 50 is Tony Gwynn (39th at .327).... Prior to 1992, Boggs had hit below .270 in only three of 60 months in the majors (.167 on 3-for-18 in April 1982; .247 in July 1986; .240 in May 1990); he matched that total in the first five months of last season.... His total-base total has dropped in each of the last five seasons.... On July 22, he reached the 6000-at-bat mark with 2046 hits, the most since Ted Williams reached 6000 at-bats with 2088 hits in 1956.... Last season marked the first time since 1980 that Boston didn't have anyone among A.L.'s top ten batters.... Carried a .381 career batting average at Fenway Park into 1992.... Career at Yankee Stadium: .276 with eight extra-base hits in 228 at-bats (.136 on 8-for-59 during the 1990s); he has averaged 26.4 extra-base hits for every 228 at-bats at the Fens.

Pat Borders
Bats Right

Toronto Blue Jays	AB	H	2B	3B	HR	RBI	BB	SO	BA	SA	OBA
Season	480	116	26	2	13	53	33	75	.242	.385	.290
vs. Left-Handers	120	28	8	0	0	9	18	14	.233	.300	.333
vs. Right-Handers	360	88	18	2	13	44	15	61	.244	.414	.274
vs. Ground-Ballers	247	63	18	1	6	33	15	38	.255	.409	.299
vs. Fly-Ballers	233	53	8	1	7	20	18	37	.227	.361	.282
Home Games	231	56	13	1	7	27	16	30	.242	.398	.296
Road Games	249	60	13	1	6	26	17	45	.241	.373	.285
Grass Fields	195	45	9	1	6	22	14	38	.231	.379	.277
Artificial Turf	285	71	17	1	7	31	19	37	.249	.389	.300
April	70	21	5	0	3	8	9	13	.300	.500	.378
May	90	19	2	1	2	4	7	14	.211	.322	.268
June	71	15	3	0	2	8	4	11	.211	.338	.250
July	80	22	6	0	3	15	7	11	.275	.463	.330
August	83	21	5	0	2	7	0	16	.253	.386	.259
Sept./Oct.	86	18	5	1	1	11	6	10	.209	.326	.261
Leading Off Inn.	129	33	6	1	3	3	4	19	.256	.388	.278
Runners On	196	48	11	1	3	43	20	35	.245	.357	.314
Bases Empty	284	68	15	1	10	10	13	40	.239	.405	.273
Runners/Scor. Pos.	106	21	6	1	2	39	17	19	.198	.330	.302
Runners On/2 Out	99	17	4	1	2	19	11	22	.172	.293	.268
Scor. Pos./2 Out	59	11	3	1	2	19	9	14	.186	.373	.304
Late-Inning Pressure	63	12	2	0	1	2	6	10	.190	.270	.261
Leading Off	23	6	0	0	0	0	0	2	.261	.348	.261
Runners On	20	3	0	0	0	1	2	4	.150	.150	.227
Runners/Scor. Pos.	11	1	0	0	0	1	2	2	.091	.091	.231

RUNS BATTED IN	From 1B	From 2B	From 3B	Scoring Position
Totals	6/155	12/86	22/52	34/138
Percentage	3.9%	14.0%	42.3%	24.6%

Loves to face: Todd Burns (.500, 5-for-10, 3 2B)
Charles Nagy (.667, 4-for-6, 3 2B)
Bill Wegman (.455, 5-for-11, 1 HR, 4 SO)

Hates to face: Mike Boddicker (0-for-10)
Kirk McCaskill (.071, 1-for-14, 1 3B)
Frank Viola (.158, 3-for-19)

Miscellaneous statistics: Ground outs-to-air outs ratio: 0.97 last season, 1.12 for career.... Grounded into 11 double plays in 87 opportunities (one per 7.9).... Drove in 14 of 26 runners from third base with less than two outs (54%).... Direction of balls hit to the outfield: 41% to left field, 30% to center, 29% to right.... Base running: Advanced from first base to third on 7 of 25 outfield singles (28%); scored from second on 10 of 15 (67%).... Opposing base stealers: 116-for-167 (69%).

Comments: Although his longest hitting streak during the 1992 regular season was just nine games, he hit safely in all 12 of Toronto's postseason games, becoming the first player in major league history to hit in more than 10 consecutive games in the same postseason. Counting the last two games of the 1991 Championship Series, he has hit safely in 14 consecutive postseason games; the longest postseason hitting streaks of all time: Hank Bauer (17 games), Rickey Henderson (15), Borders (14), Brooks Robinson (14).... His longest streak of consecutive hitless at-bats in the six-game World Series: two.... Led A.L. with 137 games behind the plate.... Became only the 2d A.L. player in the last 14 years to lead major league catchers in assists (88).... He averaged one walk every 15.8 plate appearances last season; although that doesn't put him in a class with Jack Clark or Rickey Henderson, it's quite an improvement for a man who drew only three walks in 160 plate appearances in his rookie season (1988).... Batting average with two outs and runners in scoring position was below .200 for the 4th time in his five-year career.... Hit 10 home runs off left-handers in 1990, but has only one home run in 267 regular-season at-bats against southpaws over the last two seasons. (He also connected off Tom Glavine in Game 4 of the World Series.)... Allowed 31 stolen bases (in 36 attempts) in 12 postseason games last fall, more than double the total vs. any other catcher in any postseason in major league history.

Mike Bordick
Bats Right

Oakland A's	AB	H	2B	3B	HR	RBI	BB	SO	BA	SA	OBA
Season	504	151	19	4	3	48	40	59	.300	.371	.358
vs. Left-Handers	131	44	5	2	1	15	12	12	.336	.427	.393
vs. Right-Handers	373	107	14	2	2	33	28	47	.287	.351	.346
vs. Ground-Ballers	236	73	4	2	2	28	17	27	.309	.369	.364
vs. Fly-Ballers	268	78	15	2	1	20	23	32	.291	.373	.354
Home Games	240	71	7	4	3	25	19	30	.296	.396	.360
Road Games	264	80	12	0	0	23	21	29	.303	.348	.357
Grass Fields	422	119	12	4	3	39	29	53	.282	.351	.335
Artificial Turf	82	32	7	0	0	9	11	6	.390	.476	.474
April	76	27	2	0	0	10	5	9	.355	.382	.390
May	89	31	2	1	1	8	6	8	.348	.427	.385
June	77	18	3	1	1	8	8	12	.234	.338	.314
July	89	26	6	1	0	6	4	12	.292	.382	.337
August	89	24	1	0	0	6	10	8	.270	.281	.358
Sept./Oct.	84	25	5	1	1	10	7	10	.298	.417	.366
Leading Off Inn.	121	42	5	1	2	2	12	8	.347	.455	.410
Runners On	242	73	8	2	1	46	12	33	.302	.364	.341
Bases Empty	262	78	11	2	2	2	28	26	.298	.378	.374
Runners/Scor. Pos.	154	42	7	1	1	45	10	19	.273	.351	.320
Runners On/2 Out	114	34	5	0	1	19	8	14	.298	.368	.360
Scor. Pos./2 Out	77	21	4	0	1	19	6	9	.273	.364	.333
Late-Inning Pressure	55	12	2	1	0	8	3	8	.218	.291	.281
Leading Off	10	3	1	0	0	0	1	0	.300	.600	.417
Runners On	23	4	1	0	0	8	1	4	.174	.217	.214
Runners/Scor. Pos.	17	3	1	0	0	8	1	4	.176	.235	.227

RUNS BATTED IN	From 1B	From 2B	From 3B	Scoring Position
Totals	2/170	17/121	26/65	43/186
Percentage	1.2%	14.0%	40.0%	23.1%

Loves to face: Mark Gubicza (.556, 5-for-9)
Kirk McCaskill (.500, 3-for-6)
Charles Nagy (.538, 7-for-13)

Hates to face: Mark Leiter (0-for-9)
Jaime Navarro (.091, 1-for-11, 1 3B)
Melido Perez (0-for-8)

Miscellaneous statistics: Ground outs-to-air outs ratio: 1.54 last season, 1.61 for career.... Grounded into 10 double plays in 104 opportunities (one per 10).... Drove in 16 of 23 runners from third base with less than two outs (70%).... Direction of balls hit to the outfield: 32% to left field, 32% to center, 35% to right.... Base running: Advanced from first base to third on 9 of 20 outfield singles (45%); scored from second on 14 of 17 (82%).... Made 3.26 assists per nine innings at second base.

Comments: He entered the regular-season finale as a defensive replacement and never came to the plate, presumably to "protect" his .300 batting average. Well, guess what? He was one hit shy of the true .300 mark, ending the season at .2996. "Batting .300" means averaging *at least* 3 hits for every 10 at-bats; rounding a batting average to the next-highest thousandth is an unofficial shorthand for one's actual average. Sorry, Mike, but it seems that someone gets caught on this every other year or so; still, you're in good company: Reggie Jackson's alleged "only .300 season" (in 1980) was similarly spurious.... Other than Carney Lansford, no Athletics infielder has batted .300 or better since both Norm Siebern and Jerry Lumpe did it for Kansas City in 1962.... Bordick finished the regular season with 26 consecutive errorless games at shortstop.... Had only one hit in 19 at-bats in the A.L.C.S.; that ranks among the worst batting performances in L.C.S. history (for a single series; minimum: 15 AB): Gene Alley, 0-for-16 (1972 N.L.C.S.); Aurelio Rodriguez, 0-for-16 (1972 A.L.C.S.); Bordick, .053; Howard Johnson, .056, 1-for-18 (1988 N.L.C.S.)... Career average of .346 on artificial turf, .261 on grass fields.... Led majors with 112 hits from the 8th spot in the lineup. Only Jose Lind (132) and Pat Borders (117) played more games in that spot than Bordick (113).... Batted .283 as a second baseman, but his .323 average at shortstop was the highest of any major leaguer with 200 at-bats from that position.

George Brett
Bats Left

Kansas City Royals	AB	H	2B	3B	HR	RBI	BB	SO	BA	SA	OBA
Season	592	169	35	5	7	61	35	69	.285	.397	.330
vs. Left-Handers	184	51	11	1	0	20	7	24	.277	.348	.320
vs. Right-Handers	408	118	24	4	7	41	28	45	.289	.419	.334
vs. Ground-Ballers	250	67	11	1	1	18	15	36	.268	.332	.313
vs. Fly-Ballers	342	102	24	4	6	43	20	33	.298	.444	.341
Home Games	312	90	19	3	1	35	16	27	.288	.378	.328
Road Games	280	79	16	2	6	26	19	42	.282	.418	.331
Grass Fields	218	61	12	2	5	21	14	33	.280	.422	.328
Artificial Turf	374	108	23	3	2	40	21	36	.289	.382	.331
April	66	13	5	0	2	6	8	7	.197	.364	.303
May	85	26	6	1	0	8	7	12	.306	.400	.366
June	100	26	8	1	1	8	3	6	.260	.390	.288
July	114	34	5	1	1	9	10	18	.298	.386	.360
August	112	34	4	1	2	19	5	11	.304	.411	.328
Sept./Oct.	115	36	7	1	1	11	2	15	.313	.417	.325
Leading Off Inn.	134	36	10	1	3	3	4	15	.269	.425	.295
Runners On	258	80	12	4	2	56	21	30	.310	.411	.361
Bases Empty	334	89	23	1	5	5	14	39	.266	.386	.304
Runners/Scor. Pos.	130	36	5	1	2	50	18	15	.277	.377	.364
Runners On/2 Out	113	36	7	3	1	26	9	12	.319	.460	.369
Scor. Pos./2 Out	62	20	3	1	1	23	8	6	.323	.442	.400
Late-Inning Pressure	90	22	4	0	5	11	8	11	.244	.456	.300
Leading Off	30	8	2	0	2	2	1	3	.267	.533	.290
Runners On	33	6	0	0	2	8	5	4	.182	.364	.275
Runners/Scor. Pos.	17	2	0	0	2	8	4	1	.118	.471	.261

RUNS BATTED IN	From 1B	From 2B	From 3B	Scoring Position
Totals	8/185	24/102	22/48	46/150
Percentage	4.3%	23.5%	45.8%	30.7%

Loves to face: Jim Abbott (.545, 12-for-22, 3 HR)
Gene Nelson (.385, 10-for-26, 5 HR, 0 SO)
Todd Stottlemyre (.571, 12-for-21)

Hates to face: Scott Radinsky (0-for-10)
Rick Sutcliffe (.048, 1-for-21, 3 BB)
Bobby Thigpen (.067, 1-for-15, 2 BB)

Miscellaneous statistics: Ground outs-to-air outs ratio: 1.03 last season, 1.06 for career.... Grounded into 15 double plays in 110 opportunities (one per 7.3).... Drove in 14 of 21 runners from third base with less than two outs (67%).... Direction of balls hit to the outfield: 34% to left field, 39% to center, 27% to right.... Base running: Advanced from first base to third on 8 of 25 outfield singles (32%); scored from second on 8 of 12 (67%).... Made 0.81 assists per nine innings at first base.

Comments: Despite talk of retirement after his 3000th hit, we thought that Brett's return in 1993 was a no-brainer, coming off a 169-hit season. No player in this century retired voluntarily after a season with that many hits. Four were banned in the fall-out over the Black Sox scandal: Happy Felsch, Joe Gedeon, Joe Jackson, and Buck Weaver. Two passed away during the subsequent off-seasons: Chick Stahl and Tony Boeckel.... Career total of 634 doubles ranks 8th, all-time. Within striking distance are the career totals of Carl Yastrzemski (646), Nap Lajoie (648), and Honus Wagner (651).... He is the Royals' all-time leader in singles, doubles, triples, and home runs. Only two other players are franchise leaders in all four of those categories: Stan Musial (St. Louis) and Robin Yount (Milwaukee).... Batted .356 in 90 first-inning at-bats last season, .273 thereafter.... Home-run rate (one every 85 at-bats) was his worst since 1976.... He was hit by as many pitches in 1992 (six) as he was in the previous four years combined.... Brett and Frank White played 1914 games together as teammates, the most in A.L. history, ahead of Dwight Evans and Jim Rice (1845) and Joe Judge and Sam Rice (1780). Does Uncle Ben know about this? The major league record for most games by teammates is 2015 by Ron Santo and Billy Williams.... Highest career batting averages in Late-Inning Pressure Situations in postseason (minimum: 20 AB): Brooks Robinson (.522); Brett (.520); Joe DiMaggio (.455); Pete Rose (.439); Steve Garvey (.438).

Hubie Brooks
Bats Right

California Angels	AB	H	2B	3B	HR	RBI	BB	SO	BA	SA	OBA
Season	306	66	13	0	8	36	12	46	.216	.337	.247
vs. Left-Handers	82	18	2	0	1	8	4	10	.220	.280	.256
vs. Right-Handers	224	48	11	0	7	28	8	36	.214	.357	.244
vs. Ground-Ballers	142	27	6	0	3	13	5	22	.190	.296	.223
vs. Fly-Ballers	164	39	7	0	5	23	7	24	.238	.372	.267
Home Games	150	37	7	0	2	16	7	19	.247	.333	.280
Road Games	156	29	6	0	6	20	5	27	.186	.340	.215
Grass Fields	268	57	11	0	8	33	11	39	.213	.343	.246
Artificial Turf	38	9	2	0	0	3	1	7	.237	.289	.256
April	84	25	5	0	4	19	3	11	.298	.500	.318
May	91	15	2	0	2	7	3	11	.165	.253	.191
June	55	9	3	0	1	4	3	13	.164	.273	.220
July	0	0	0	0	0	0	0	0	.000	.000	.000
August	0	0	0	0	0	0	0	0	—	—	—
Sept./Oct.	76	17	3	0	1	6	3	11	.224	.303	.253
Leading Off Inn.	86	15	4	0	2	2	2	7	.174	.291	.193
Runners On	129	29	6	0	4	32	7	21	.225	.364	.268
Bases Empty	177	37	7	0	4	4	5	25	.209	.316	.231
Runners/Scor. Pos.	78	17	3	0	2	26	6	14	.218	.333	.279
Runners On/2 Out	52	15	2	0	1	12	5	4	.288	.385	.351
Scor. Pos./2 Out	31	10	1	0	1	12	4	2	.323	.452	.400
Late-Inning Pressure	55	12	0	0	2	6	4	8	.218	.327	.283
Leading Off	13	2	0	0	0	0	1	3	.154	.154	.214
Runners On	21	5	0	0	1	5	2	2	.238	.381	.333
Runners/Scor. Pos.	11	2	0	0	1	3	2	1	.182	.182	.357

RUNS BATTED IN	From 1B	From 2B	From 3B	Scoring Position
Totals	5/88	9/54	14/33	23/87
Percentage	5.7%	16.7%	42.4%	26.4%

Loves to face: Tom Glavine (.440, 11-for-25, 1 HR)
Dwight Gooden (.392, 20-for-51, 2 HR)
Rick Honeycutt (.579, 11-for-19)

Hates to face: Joe Magrane (.135, 5-for-37)
Randy Myers (.077, 1-for-13)
Todd Worrell (.095, 2-for-21, 2 BB)

Miscellaneous statistics: Ground outs-to-air outs ratio: 1.16 last season, 1.34 for career.... Grounded into 10 double plays in 58 opportunities (one per 5.8).... Drove in 8 of 21 runners from third base with less than two outs (38%).... Direction of balls hit to the outfield: 33% to left field, 41% to center, 26% to right.... Base running: Advanced from first base to third on 0 of 12 outfield singles (0%), 2d worst in A.L.; scored from second on 8 of 11 (73%).... Made 0.63 assists per nine innings at first base.

Comments: Ernie Banks holds the all-time record for most regular-season games (2528) without ever playing a post-season game, but Brooks leads active players (1536). Others with at least 1400 games: Pete O'Brien (1495), Don Mattingly (1426), and Julio Franco (1402). Brooks played for 2d-place teams in New York (1984) and Los Angeles (1990), but the closest one of his teams ever came to a division title was in 1987, when Montreal finished third, four games behind St. Louis.... Set career-low marks in both hits and batting average for the second straight year. Batting average has decreased in each of the last four years.... You can understand when guys like Mark McGwire and George Bell don't lay down a sacrifice bunt for years at a time, but Hubie Brooks? His last one came in 1983, when Frank Howard managed the Mets. (Guess he didn't dare say no.) ... Streak of three consecutive years with exactly 108 strikeouts was broken in 1991, when he fanned 62 times. But add his 1991 and 1992 strikeout totals together and what do you get?...Averaged one walk every 26.7 trips to the plate last year, the worst rate of his career, after posting the best walk rate of his career in 1991 (one every 9.3 PAs).... Has been an opening-day starter in each of the last 12 years, with a different team in each of the last four.... His 68 starts in the cleanup spot were a team high; the fourth spot in the Angels' lineup produced a .200 batting average last season, the lowest of any lineup slot on any major league club (excluding ninth spot of N.L. clubs).

Jerry Browne　　　　　　　　Bats Left and Right

Oakland A's	AB	H	2B	3B	HR	RBI	BB	SO	BA	SA	OBA
Season	324	93	12	2	3	40	40	40	.287	.364	.366
vs. Left-Handers	49	9	1	0	0	5	3	6	.184	.204	.226
vs. Right-Handers	275	84	11	2	3	35	37	34	.305	.393	.389
vs. Ground-Ballers	138	43	7	0	2	25	22	20	.312	.406	.406
vs. Fly-Ballers	186	50	5	2	1	15	18	20	.269	.333	.335
Home Games	146	41	5	0	1	17	18	20	.281	.336	.369
Road Games	178	52	7	2	2	23	22	20	.292	.388	.364
Grass Fields	277	76	7	2	3	34	37	36	.274	.347	.362
Artificial Turf	47	17	5	0	0	6	3	4	.362	.468	.392
April	9	2	0	0	0	0	1	0	.222	.222	.300
May	61	15	0	0	0	7	5	10	.246	.246	.309
June	73	21	3	0	0	6	9	9	.288	.329	.373
July	54	14	3	1	1	7	9	6	.259	.407	.369
August	78	26	2	0	1	11	10	10	.333	.397	.411
Sept./Oct.	49	15	4	1	1	9	6	5	.306	.490	.362
Leading Off Inn.	77	16	2	0	0	0	8	16	.208	.234	.291
Runners On	140	45	6	1	2	39	18	15	.321	.421	.392
Bases Empty	184	48	6	1	1	1	22	25	.261	.321	.346
Runners/Scor. Pos.	78	25	4	1	2	37	12	7	.321	.474	.392
Runners On/2 Out	61	18	3	0	1	18	12	9	.295	.393	.411
Scor. Pos./2 Out	41	11	2	0	1	17	9	4	.268	.390	.400
Late-Inning Pressure	36	16	2	0	0	6	7	3	.444	.500	.533
Leading Off	9	4	0	0	0	0	2	0	.444	.444	.545
Runners On	12	6	2	0	0	6	2	0	.500	.667	.563
Runners/Scor. Pos.	7	5	2	0	0	6	2	0	.714	1.000	.727

RUNS BATTED IN	From 1B	From 2B	From 3B	Scoring Position
Totals	3/106	13/68	21/38	34/106
Percentage	2.8%	19.1%	55.3%	32.1%

Loves to face: Chuck Crim (.636, 7-for-11, 1 HR)
　　Jimmy Key (.407, 11-for-27, 0 SO)
　　Donn Pall (.625, 5-for-8, 1 HR)
Hates to face: Chuck Finley (.050, 1-for-20, 1 2B)
　　Greg A. Harris (0-for-12)
　　Kirk McCaskill (.083, 2-for-24, 3 BB)

Miscellaneous statistics: Ground outs-to-air outs ratio: 1.24 last season, 1.28 for career.... Grounded into 7 double plays in 80 opportunities (one per 11).... Drove in 14 of 19 runners from third base with less than two outs (74%).... Direction of balls hit to the outfield: 36% to left field, 32% to center, 32% to right batting left-handed; 31% to left field, 46% to center, 23% to right batting right-handed.... Base running: Advanced from first base to third on 5 of 21 outfield singles (24%); scored from second on 1 of 2 (50%).... Made 1.70 assists per nine innings at third base.

Comments: Oakland's leading hitter vs. right-handed pitchers last season. Switch-hitting breakdown was a departure from previous years; he had hit for a higher average from the right side of the plate than he had from the left side in each of his previous six seasons in the majors. Career breakdown: .279 right-handed, .269 left-handed.... Started only nine games against left-handed pitchers last season.... Led A.L. with 16 sacrifice bunts; teammate Mike Bordick was runner-up with 14. Oakland led the league in sacrifice bunts (72) for the first time since 1973.... One of seven former Rangers on the Athletics' postseason roster last season, and that doesn't include Goose Gossage, who was disabled. The others: Harold Baines, Rick Honeycutt, Jeff Russell, Ruben Sierra, Dave Stewart, and Bobby Witt.... Collected four hits in the second postseason start of his career. Six players had four hits in their postseason debut: Frankie Frisch, Monte Irvin, Tommy Leach, Joe Medwick, Mel Ott, and Vic Wertz.... Range is not his strong suit: His career average of 4.4 chances per game at second base is the lowest of any player in A.L. history who played at least 500 games at that position.... Career batting average increases in every month from April through August; April, .199; May, .259; June, .277; July, .294; August, .326.... Need a bases-loaded walk? The Guv'nor's your man: He has drawn 12 walks in 58 career plate appearances with the bases loaded, the highest rate since 1975.

Tom Brunansky　　　　　　　　Bats Right

Boston Red Sox	AB	H	2B	3B	HR	RBI	BB	SO	BA	SA	OBA
Season	458	122	31	3	15	74	66	96	.266	.445	.354
vs. Left-Handers	132	30	10	0	6	20	26	20	.227	.439	.354
vs. Right-Handers	326	92	21	3	9	54	40	76	.282	.448	.354
vs. Ground-Ballers	230	70	20	2	8	47	33	40	.304	.513	.386
vs. Fly-Ballers	228	52	11	1	7	27	33	56	.228	.377	.322
Home Games	217	70	23	1	10	47	32	41	.323	.576	.405
Road Games	241	52	8	2	5	27	34	55	.216	.322	.308
Grass Fields	384	106	28	2	12	61	60	74	.276	.453	.370
Artificial Turf	74	16	3	1	3	13	6	22	.216	.405	.268
April	22	6	0	0	0	1	3	5	.273	.273	.346
May	58	15	7	0	2	11	15	14	.259	.397	.400
June	84	24	12	1	0	6	3	15	.286	.452	.310
July	98	27	6	2	8	32	12	20	.276	.622	.351
August	97	28	5	0	4	13	21	18	.289	.464	.408
Sept./Oct.	99	22	6	0	1	11	12	24	.222	.313	.304
Leading Off Inn.	120	27	2	2	4	4	10	21	.225	.375	.285
Runners On	228	63	18	1	6	65	34	49	.276	.443	.361
Bases Empty	230	59	13	2	9	9	32	47	.257	.448	.347
Runners/Scor. Pos.	115	31	11	1	4	58	20	27	.270	.487	.359
Runners On/2 Out	108	27	6	1	0	20	19	26	.250	.324	.362
Scor. Pos./2 Out	56	14	5	1	0	20	9	14	.250	.375	.354
Late-Inning Pressure	79	21	5	1	4	17	14	20	.266	.506	.376
Leading Off	19	7	0	0	3	3	2	4	.368	.842	.429
Runners On	46	12	4	1	1	14	6	12	.261	.457	.346
Runners/Scor. Pos.	23	8	3	1	0	11	5	6	.348	.565	.464

RUNS BATTED IN	From 1B	From 2B	From 3B	Scoring Position
Totals	13/189	18/85	28/64	46/149
Percentage	6.9%	21.2%	43.8%	30.9%

Loves to face: Jim Abbott (.400, 10-for-25, 5 BB)
　　Mark Eichhorn (.421, 8-for-19, 4 2B, 1 HR)
　　David Wells (.467, 7-for-15, 2 HR)
Hates to face: Rick Aguilera (0-for-10)
　　Randy Johnson (0-for-15, 8 SO)
　　Melido Perez (.105, 2-for-19, 2 2B)

Miscellaneous statistics: Ground outs-to-air outs ratio: 0.87 last season, 0.69 for career.... Grounded into 11 double plays in 120 opportunities (one per 11).... Drove in 18 of 37 runners from third base with less than two outs (49%).... Direction of balls hit to the outfield: 36% to left field, 31% to center, 33% to right.... Base running: Advanced from first base to third on 8 of 29 outfield singles (28%); scored from second on 4 of 10 (40%), 3d-lowest rate in A.L.... Made 2.17 putouts per nine innings in right field.

Comments: Led A.L. in home runs, RBIs, and extra-base hits in July.... His .266 average was the 2d-lowest ever to lead the Red Sox, just slightly higher than Frank Malzone's club-leading .266 mark in 1961. Became the first player to win Boston's triple crown since Jim Rice did it in both 1977 and 1978.... While his season total of 19 go-ahead RBIs did not rank among A.L.'s top 20, his eight go-ahead RBIs from the seventh inning on tied Rickey Henderson for a league high.... Batting average vs. right-handed pitchers was a career high, while his average vs. left-handers was close to a career low. Overall batting average was his best since his .272 as a rookie in 1982.... His longest hitting streak of the year was five games; that matches Chili Davis for the shortest season-high streak among major leaguers who qualified for the batting title.... Yearly home run total has decreased or stayed the same in each of the last five years; he had a career rate of one homer every 21.4 at-bats when he came to Boston, but has averaged one every 30 at-bats with Sox. But don't think that Fenway Park hasn't been good to him; since joining Sox in May 1990, he has a .306 average with 33 homers at home, .202 with 13 dingers on the road.... Has been caught stealing more often than he has stolen successfully in each of the last four seasons, and in seven seasons during his career. Nellie Fox and Dick Schofield, Sr., share the all-time mark of 11 years with a stolen-base percentage below .500.

Jay Buhner
Seattle Mariners — Bats Right

	AB	H	2B	3B	HR	RBI	BB	SO	BA	SA	OBA
Season	543	132	16	3	25	79	71	146	.243	.422	.333
vs. Left-Handers	148	34	4	0	10	25	21	38	.230	.459	.327
vs. Right-Handers	395	98	12	3	15	54	50	108	.248	.408	.335
vs. Ground-Ballers	269	66	5	3	11	45	29	74	.245	.409	.320
vs. Fly-Ballers	274	66	11	0	14	34	42	72	.241	.434	.345
Home Games	263	68	12	3	9	39	38	72	.259	.414	.353
Road Games	280	64	4	0	16	40	33	74	.229	.414	.313
Grass Fields	216	51	1	0	16	39	29	58	.236	.463	.328
Artificial Turf	327	81	15	3	9	40	42	88	.248	.394	.336
April	66	15	2	0	1	5	12	16	.227	.303	.342
May	85	20	0	0	4	17	16	19	.235	.376	.356
June	104	20	2	1	4	12	3	30	.192	.346	.218
July	93	29	2	1	8	19	13	26	.312	.613	.394
August	103	25	4	1	4	15	17	32	.243	.417	.355
Sept./Oct.	92	23	6	0	4	11	10	23	.250	.446	.333
Leading Off Inn.	114	35	5	0	5	5	16	25	.307	.482	.392
Runners On	235	58	7	2	11	65	34	55	.247	.434	.344
Bases Empty	308	74	9	1	14	14	37	91	.240	.412	.324
Runners/Scor. Pos.	135	40	4	2	8	59	28	23	.296	.533	.405
Runners On/2 Out	102	22	1	1	5	27	11	30	.216	.392	.304
Scor. Pos./2 Out	66	18	1	1	5	27	11	13	.273	.545	.385
Late-Inning Pressure	92	22	2	1	5	13	14	25	.239	.446	.340
Leading Off	15	8	1	0	1	1	3	2	.533	.800	.611
Runners On	52	11	1	1	2	10	6	11	.212	.385	.293
Runners/Scor. Pos.	30	8	1	1	1	8	4	4	.267	.467	.353

RUNS BATTED IN	From 1B	From 2B	From 3B	Scoring Position
Totals	9/184	23/115	22/51	45/166
Percentage	4.9%	20.0%	43.1%	27.1%

Loves to face: Mike Boddicker (.500, 6-for-12, 4 2B, 1 HR)
Ben McDonald (.455, 5-for-11, 2 HR)
Dave Stewart (.316, 6-for-19, 1 2B, 3 HR)

Hates to face: Roger Clemens (.067, 1-for-15)
Ted Higuera (0-for-11, 8 SO)
Mark Langston (.100, 2-for-20, 11 SO)

Miscellaneous statistics: Ground outs-to-air outs ratio: 0.74 last season, 0.88 for career.... Grounded into 12 double plays in 131 opportunities (one per 11).... Drove in 14 of 24 runners from third base with less than two outs (58%).... Direction of balls hit to the outfield: 37% to left field, 33% to center, 31% to right.... Base running: Advanced from first base to third on 2 of 30 outfield singles (7%), 3d-lowest rate in A.L.; scored from second on 9 of 15 (60%).... Made 2.13 putouts per nine innings in right field.

Comments: From the Just to Rub It In Department: Buhner hit five home runs against the Yankees last season, the most by any opponent. Remember, the Yankees gave up on Buhner in exchange for Ken Phelps in 1988; since the trade, Buhner has hit 78 home runs for Seattle while no Yankees player has hit more than Don Mattingly's 59.... Career rate of one homer every 19.3 at-bats with Mariners ranks second in franchise history behind Phelps (13.3).... Ranked third in majors with eight opposite-field home runs, behind Danny Tartabull (11) and Fred McGriff (10).... Batted .296 in day games, including an 18-game hitting streak, but only .221 at night. His career figures are almost as lopsided: .285 (one HR every 13.9 AB) in day games; .231 (one HR every 23.3 AB) at night.... Has had five go-ahead RBIs during extra innings over the last two seasons, tying Don Slaught and Rafael Palmeiro for the most in the majors during that time.... Started 149 games in right field, the most in the majors last season. Led A.L. right fielders with 14 assists, four of which started double plays. Also led A.L. in fielding percentage at that position, with only two errors in 329 chances, and ended the season with a streak of 132 consecutive errorless games, the longest by any right fielder in the majors last year.... Came up empty on six stolen-base attempts last season, tying Mickey Tettleton for the biggest oh-fer in the majors. The all-time record: Pete Runnels's legendary 0-for-10 with Washington in 1952.

Ellis Burks
Boston Red Sox — Bats Right

	AB	H	2B	3B	HR	RBI	BB	SO	BA	SA	OBA
Season	235	60	8	3	8	30	25	48	.255	.417	.327
vs. Left-Handers	66	13	2	1	3	8	10	8	.197	.394	.299
vs. Right-Handers	169	47	6	2	5	22	15	40	.278	.426	.339
vs. Ground-Ballers	108	32	6	1	2	13	11	26	.296	.426	.367
vs. Fly-Ballers	127	28	2	2	6	17	14	22	.220	.409	.294
Home Games	108	25	5	2	4	18	12	21	.231	.426	.309
Road Games	127	35	3	1	4	12	13	27	.276	.409	.343
Grass Fields	192	47	5	3	6	24	22	42	.245	.396	.323
Artificial Turf	43	13	3	0	2	6	3	6	.302	.512	.348
April	67	15	3	1	0	5	9	18	.224	.299	.312
May	96	25	4	2	4	17	10	16	.260	.469	.327
June	72	20	1	0	4	8	6	14	.278	.458	.342
July	0	0	0	0	0	0	0	0	.000	.000	.000
August	0	0	0	0	0	0	0	0	—	—	—
Sept./Oct.	0	0	0	0	0	0	0	0	—	—	—
Leading Off Inn.	58	12	0	1	1	1	4	18	.207	.293	.270
Runners On	114	28	8	2	3	25	15	22	.246	.430	.328
Bases Empty	121	32	0	1	5	5	10	26	.264	.405	.326
Runners/Scor. Pos.	65	13	5	0	2	20	11	14	.200	.369	.308
Runners On/2 Out	46	11	3	2	1	11	9	8	.239	.457	.364
Scor. Pos./2 Out	28	6	2	0	1	9	8	5	.214	.393	.389
Late-Inning Pressure	46	11	1	0	2	8	3	13	.239	.391	.280
Leading Off	10	1	0	0	0	0	2	5	.100	.100	.250
Runners On	23	5	1	0	1	7	0	7	.217	.391	.208
Runners/Scor. Pos.	11	2	0	0	1	6	0	4	.182	.455	.167

RUNS BATTED IN	From 1B	From 2B	From 3B	Scoring Position
Totals	6/91	7/51	9/28	16/79
Percentage	6.6%	13.7%	32.1%	20.3%

Loves to face: Erik Hanson (.545, 12-for-22, 2 HR)
Jeff Russell (.450, 9-for-20, 2 HR)
Bill Wegman (.500, 8-for-16, 1 HR)

Hates to face: Jimmy Key (.080, 2-for-25)
Tim Leary (.071, 1-for-14)
Gregg Olson (0-for-10)

Miscellaneous statistics: Ground outs-to-air outs ratio: 0.76 last season, 1.02 for career.... Grounded into 5 double plays in 59 opportunities (one per 12).... Drove in 4 of 13 runners from third base with less than two outs (31%).... Direction of balls hit to the outfield: 51% to left field, 28% to center, 21% to right.... Base running: Advanced from first base to third on 7 of 10 outfield singles (70%), 2d-highest rate in majors; scored from second on 6 of 7 (86%).... Made 2.02 putouts per nine innings in center field, lowest rate in majors.

Comments: Stole 27 bases as a rookie in 1987, but has seen his total decrease on an annual basis: 25, 21, 9, 6, 5. Finished the Red Sox phase of his career with 93 stolen bases; only two Boston players in the last 40 years have accumulated 100 stolen bases: Carl Yastrzemski (168) and Tommy Harper (107).... Only eight Red Sox spent time on the disabled list in 1992, but five of them missed at least 100 days: Burks, Jeff Gray, Mike Greenwell, John Marzano, and Carlos Quintana.... Career breakdown: .296 with 47 home runs at Fenway Park; .267 with 46 homers on the road.... Hit only one home run in 104 at-bats from the cleanup spot. Among major league players with at least 100 at-bats from that spot in the order last season, only Eric Davis had a poorer home run rate.... Most of his clutch-hitting statistics are not good.... His yearly batting averages with runners in scoring position since 1988: .333, .310, .306, .226, .200.... His career rate of runners driven in from third base with less than two outs is only 48.8 percent, after driving in fewer than 40 percent of those runners in each of the last three seasons. Among active players with at least 150 opportunities, only Rob Deer (43.3) and Cory Snyder (45.3) have lower rates.... Although his overall career batting average is still a respectable .281, his career average in Late-Inning Pressure Situations is only .249; his average in LIPS with runners in scoring position is .209 in 110 at-bats; in LIPS with RISP and two outs it's .174 (8-for-46).

Jose Canseco   Bats Right

A's/Rangers	AB	H	2B	3B	HR	RBI	BB	SO	BA	SA	OBA
Season	439	107	15	0	26	87	63	128	.244	.456	.344
vs. Left-Handers	94	24	3	0	7	16	16	33	.255	.511	.372
vs. Right-Handers	345	83	12	0	19	71	47	95	.241	.441	.336
vs. Ground-Ballers	201	47	7	0	11	34	28	60	.234	.433	.333
vs. Fly-Ballers	238	60	8	0	15	53	35	68	.252	.475	.353
Home Games	204	52	4	0	15	39	29	64	.255	.495	.351
Road Games	235	55	11	0	11	48	34	64	.234	.421	.337
Grass Fields	368	94	13	0	23	81	56	106	.255	.478	.358
Artificial Turf	71	13	2	0	3	6	7	22	.183	.338	.266
April	90	22	1	0	6	17	9	24	.244	.456	.310
May	75	16	1	0	4	12	8	17	.213	.387	.286
June	84	25	3	0	8	19	9	21	.298	.619	.368
July	34	6	2	0	1	3	5	7	.176	.324	.300
August	83	21	4	0	3	21	17	35	.253	.410	.382
Sept./Oct.	73	17	4	0	4	15	15	24	.233	.452	.385
Leading Off Inn.	78	23	4	0	7	7	9	18	.295	.615	.368
Runners On	225	57	7	0	11	72	33	57	.253	.431	.353
Bases Empty	214	50	8	0	15	15	30	71	.234	.481	.333
Runners/Scor. Pos.	146	40	3	0	7	63	17	40	.274	.438	.349
Runners On/2 Out	87	20	3	0	3	20	10	23	.230	.368	.316
Scor. Pos./2 Out	65	12	1	0	2	18	8	21	.185	.292	.284
Late Inning Pressure	64	13	2	0	3	10	8	20	.203	.375	.282
Leading Off	17	2	0	0	0	0	1	5	.118	.118	.167
Runners On	30	9	1	0	2	9	4	9	.300	.533	.400
Runners/Scor. Pos.	16	5	0	0	1	7	1	6	.313	.500	.353

RUNS BATTED IN	From 1B	From 2B	From 3B	Scoring Position
Totals	7/145	18/97	36/80	54/177
Percentage	4.8%	18.6%	45.0%	30.5%

Loves to face: Bob Milacki (.357, 5-for-14, 3 HR)
Dave Stieb (.364, 12-for-33, 8 2B, 2 HR)
Todd Stottlemyre (.375, 9-for-24, 7 HR)

Hates to face: Erik Hanson (.053, 1-for-19, 3 BB)
Greg A. Harris (.063, 1-for-16, 10 SO)
Duane Ward (0-for-17, 10 SO)

Miscellaneous statistics: Ground outs-to-air outs ratio: 1.06 last season, 0.84 for career.... Grounded into 16 double plays in 108 opportunities (one per 6.8).... Drove in 30 of 48 runners from third base with less than two outs (63%).... Direction of balls hit to the outfield: 51% to left field, 28% to center, 21% to right.... Base running: Advanced from first base to third on 6 of 20 outfield singles (30%); scored from second on 7 of 10 (70%).... Made 2.29 putouts per nine innings in right field, highest rate in A.L.

Comments: Needs 16 RBIs in his next 28 games to become the first player since Ted Williams to reach the 1000-game mark with as many as 750 RBIs.... Has struck out 998 times in 3655 career at-bats. Only two players in major league history have reached 1000 strikeouts in fewer at-bats: Dave Kingman and Rob Deer.... Became only the fourth player in major league history to be traded during a season in which he had already hit 20 home runs; the others: Dave Kingman (1977), Frank Robinson (1974), and Rico Carty (1978). In the free-agent era, it's easy to imagine a contender trading for such a player. But trading one away?...Batted only .163, averaging one home run every 43 at-bats during the first inning last season. In subsequent innings, he batted .264, and averaged a homer every 14.7 at-bats.... Of his 26 home runs, only one was hit to the opposite field.... His home run rate was his lowest since 1987, his batting average his lowest since 1986.... Over the first four years of his career, he had no home runs in 30 career at-bats with the bases loaded; but after getting his grand-slam swing untracked in the 1988 World Series, he has put together these regular-season numbers with the bags full: .516 (17-for-33), four home runs, two walks.... Caught stealing seven times in 13 attempts last season after being caught just six times in 32 attempts in 1991.... Owns .366 career batting average in Late-Inning Pressure Situations with runners in scoring position, highest among active players (minimum: 25 hits); he stands five points ahead of Don Mattingly and 20 points ahead of Wade Boggs in that category.

Mark Carreon   Bats Right

Detroit Tigers	AB	H	2B	3B	HR	RBI	BB	SO	BA	SA	OBA
Season	336	78	11	1	10	41	22	57	.232	.360	.278
vs. Left-Handers	111	22	1	0	2	8	5	13	.198	.261	.235
vs. Right-Handers	225	56	10	1	8	33	17	44	.249	.409	.299
vs. Ground-Ballers	154	44	7	1	3	21	9	19	.286	.403	.323
vs. Fly-Ballers	182	34	4	0	7	20	13	38	.187	.324	.241
Home Games	151	32	6	1	5	19	14	30	.212	.364	.278
Road Games	185	46	5	0	5	22	8	27	.249	.357	.278
Grass Fields	282	66	10	1	10	35	18	49	.234	.383	.279
Artificial Turf	54	12	1	0	0	6	4	8	.222	.241	.276
April	48	11	1	0	2	7	4	11	.229	.375	.288
May	95	26	4	1	4	16	7	19	.274	.463	.330
June	20	5	0	0	0	0	0	5	.250	.250	.250
July	61	9	2	0	1	3	4	6	.148	.230	.200
August	33	6	1	0	1	3	1	11	.182	.303	.200
Sept./Oct.	79	21	3	0	2	12	6	5	.266	.380	.307
Leading Off Inn.	62	16	2	1	2	2	5	9	.258	.419	.313
Runners On	151	36	5	0	5	36	8	20	.238	.371	.274
Bases Empty	185	42	6	1	5	5	14	37	.227	.351	.281
Runners/Scor. Pos.	89	18	3	0	2	29	7	13	.202	.303	.250
Runners On/2 Out	57	13	1	0	2	10	2	6	.228	.351	.254
Scor. Pos./2 Out	36	6	0	0	1	8	2	4	.167	.250	.211
Late-Inning Pressure	45	9	0	0	0	2	2	4	.200	.200	.234
Leading Off	9	1	0	0	0	0	0	0	.111	.111	.111
Runners On	21	6	0	0	0	2	1	1	.286	.286	.318
Runners/Scor. Pos.	12	2	0	0	0	2	1	1	.167	.167	.231

RUNS BATTED IN	From 1B	From 2B	From 3B	Scoring Position
Totals	6/121	10/77	15/37	25/114
Percentage	5.0%	13.0%	40.5%	21.9%

Loves to face: Steve Avery (.385, 5-for-13, 3 2B)
Rheal Cormier (.417, 5-for-12, 1 HR)
Randy Tomlin (.364, 4-for-11, 1 HR)

Hates to face: Paul Assenmacher (0-for-7, 4 SO)
Tom Glavine (.083, 1-for-12)
Randy Myers (.091, 1-for-11, 4 SO)

Miscellaneous statistics: Ground outs-to-air outs ratio: 0.77 last season, 0.88 for career.... Grounded into 12 double plays in 80 opportunities (one per 6.7).... Drove in 14 of 24 runners from third base with less than two outs (58%).... Direction of balls hit to the outfield: 40% to left field, 33% to center, 27% to right.... Base running: Advanced from first base to third on 6 of 19 outfield singles (32%); scored from second on 7 of 11 (64%).... Made 2.34 putouts per nine innings in left field.

Comments: Rickey Henderson, Brian Hunter, and Carreon were the only nonpitchers in the majors last season who fit the description "bats right, throws left." In major league history, only four such players have had 1000-game careers: Henderson, Hal Chase, Cleon Jones, and 19th-century player Hick Carpenter. Only two others had 500-game careers: Happy Felsch and Carl Warwick.... A footnote goes to Bob Dekas, coordinating producer for CBS baseball and a onetime "bats right, throws left" star at Northwestern. Some friends find it hard to believe that he once shared the Big Ten RBI crown with Dave Winfield (20 each in 1973); we thought it best to record that fact here.... Career total of eight pinch-hit homers is second among active players to Candy Maldonado's nine. Cliff Johnson holds the all-time record with 20 pinch-homers in 273 at-bats, but Carreon's average of one home run every 12.6 pinch-hit at-bats is actually better than Johnson's rate (one every 13.7). Among players with more than five pinch-hit homers, only four have higher rates than Johnson: Jim Ray Hart (one every 11.4 PH-AB), Bob Allison (12.3), Carreon, and Bobby Murcer (13.2).... Has a career average of one home run every 17.6 at-bats during April, but his rate decreases in every month through August: May, 23.0; June, 27.8; July, 31.4; August, 68.5. He starts with a rate similar to Kevin Mitchell's, and ends with a rate like Bill Pecota's.

Joe Carter
Bats Right

Toronto Blue Jays	AB	H	2B	3B	HR	RBI	BB	SO	BA	SA	OBA
Season	622	164	30	7	34	119	36	109	.264	.498	.309
vs. Left-Handers	157	49	14	0	7	20	11	22	.312	.535	.355
vs. Right-Handers	465	115	16	7	27	99	25	87	.247	.486	.294
vs. Ground-Ballers	304	76	14	2	16	55	19	54	.250	.467	.301
vs. Fly-Ballers	318	88	16	5	18	64	17	55	.277	.528	.318
Home Games	301	78	15	3	21	65	17	53	.259	.538	.303
Road Games	321	86	15	4	13	54	19	56	.268	.461	.315
Grass Fields	248	64	14	3	10	43	14	43	.258	.460	.301
Artificial Turf	374	100	16	4	24	76	22	66	.267	.524	.315
April	90	23	6	0	2	11	2	18	.256	.389	.274
May	105	27	4	0	7	19	5	17	.257	.495	.316
June	106	35	4	3	8	23	6	22	.330	.651	.374
July	98	23	5	1	4	15	11	16	.235	.429	.319
August	112	27	8	1	8	26	9	20	.241	.545	.296
Sept./Oct.	111	29	3	2	5	25	3	16	.261	.459	.275
Leading Off Inn.	101	31	7	0	6	6	4	11	.307	.554	.346
Runners On	310	80	7	7	20	105	21	54	.258	.519	.308
Bases Empty	312	84	23	0	14	14	15	55	.269	.478	.311
Runners/Scor. Pos.	179	50	4	6	10	83	17	37	.279	.536	.336
Runners On/2 Out	110	27	3	1	8	38	10	16	.245	.509	.320
Scor. Pos./2 Out	74	20	2	1	6	34	10	11	.270	.568	.372
Late-Inning Pressure	70	14	1	1	3	14	3	12	.200	.371	.227
Leading Off	18	5	0	0	1	1	1	2	.278	.444	.316
Runners On	39	8	1	1	2	13	2	8	.205	.436	.233
Runners/Scor. Pos.	24	4	1	0	1	10	2	6	.167	.333	.214

RUNS BATTED IN	From 1B	From 2B	From 3B	Scoring Position
Totals	22/213	29/140	34/79	63/219
Percentage	10.3%	20.7%	43.0%	28.8%

Loves to face: Tim Leary (.611, 11-for-18, 4 HR)
Jose Mesa (.400, 4-for-10, 2 2B, 2 HR)
Bill Wegman (.415, 17-for-41, 4 2B, 2 3B, 5 HR)
Hates to face: Ron Darling (.105, 2-for-19)
Rich DeLucia (0-for-9, 4 SO)
Jeff Russell (.067, 1-for-15)

Miscellaneous statistics: Ground outs-to-air outs ratio: 0.55 last season (4th-lowest in A.L.), 0.66 for career.... Grounded into 14 double plays in 150 opportunities (one per 11).... Drove in 25 of 49 runners from third base with less than two outs (51%).... Direction of balls hit to the outfield: 48% to left field, 30% to center, 22% to right.... Base running: Advanced from first base to third on 8 of 27 outfield singles (30%); scored from second on 11 of 12 (92%).... Made 2.13 putouts per nine innings in right field.

Comments: Totals over the past seven years: 214 home runs, 772 RBIs, 154 stolen bases. No major league player has ever produced numbers that high in each of those categories over any seven-year span. And only two other players, Willie Mays and Hank Aaron, have ever averaged 30 homers, 100 RBIs, and 20 steals per year over a seven-year period.... Carter leads the majors in RBIs since 1986; that's the highest seven-year total by anyone since Aaron (798) and Frank Robinson (776) from 1961 to 1967. Over the last 40 years, only six players have driven in as many runs over any seven-year span: Aaron, Carter, Robinson, Willie Mays, Ernie Banks, and Jackie Jensen.... Fell two RBIs shy of 100 in 1988, preventing him from becoming the first player since Willie Mays (1959–66) to reach 100 RBIs in seven straight years.... Has missed only nine games over the last five seasons; had a streak of 507 consecutive games snapped in April.... One of 13 players who had 200 or more opportunities to knock in teammates from scoring position last season; he's been over the 200 mark in six of the last seven years.... Led A.L. right fielders with eight errors.... Only one of his 34 regular-season home runs went to the opposite field.... Led A.L. with 13 sacrifice flies.... Became the first player in history to start three consecutive World Series games at different positions in the field; another triumph for the "To DH or not DH" charade under which baseball plays its most important games.

Jack Clark
Bats Right

Boston Red Sox	AB	H	2B	3B	HR	RBI	BB	SO	BA	SA	OBA
Season	257	54	11	0	5	33	56	87	.210	.311	.350
vs. Left-Handers	95	28	6	0	2	14	30	27	.295	.421	.460
vs. Right-Handers	162	26	5	0	3	19	26	60	.160	.247	.278
vs. Ground-Ballers	113	28	5	0	3	20	33	40	.248	.372	.413
vs. Fly-Ballers	144	26	6	0	2	13	23	47	.181	.264	.294
Home Games	116	30	6	0	0	10	27	32	.259	.310	.390
Road Games	141	24	5	0	5	23	29	55	.170	.312	.316
Grass Fields	229	47	11	0	3	24	49	78	.205	.293	.344
Artificial Turf	28	7	0	0	2	9	7	9	.250	.464	.400
April	48	6	1	0	0	1	7	18	.125	.146	.236
May	69	17	2	0	2	18	20	24	.246	.362	.402
June	56	15	4	0	1	5	11	17	.268	.393	.386
July	36	6	1	0	0	2	9	9	.167	.194	.333
August	48	10	3	0	2	7	9	19	.208	.396	.345
Sept./Oct.	0	0	0	0	0	0	0	0	.000	.000	.000
Leading Off Inn.	62	16	0	0	2	2	13	17	.258	.355	.387
Runners On	133	25	6	0	3	31	24	52	.188	.301	.307
Bases Empty	124	29	5	0	2	2	32	35	.234	.323	.395
Runners/Scor. Pos.	73	14	3	0	2	29	16	29	.192	.315	.319
Runners On/2 Out	60	10	3	0	2	10	9	23	.167	.317	.275
Scor. Pos./2 Out	32	4	2	0	1	8	7	14	.125	.281	.282
Late-Inning Pressure	50	12	3	0	0	6	8	13	.240	.300	.350
Leading Off	10	1	0	0	0	0	1	3	.100	.100	.182
Runners On	25	4	2	0	0	6	5	9	.160	.240	.290
Runners/Scor. Pos.	10	1	1	0	0	6	4	4	.100	.200	.333

RUNS BATTED IN	From 1B	From 2B	From 3B	Scoring Position
Totals	4/108	6/49	18/44	24/93
Percentage	3.7%	12.2%	40.9%	25.8%

Loves to face: Rick Honeycutt (.533, 8-for-15, 2 HR, 7 BB)
Craig Lefferts (.455, 5-for-11, 1 2B, 4 HR, 4 BB)
David Wells (.500, 5-for-10, 1 2B, 2 HR)
Hates to face: Mike Boddicker (0-for-16, 7 SO)
Chuck Finley (0-for-11, 6 SO, 5 BB)
Scott Erickson (0-for-10, 3 SO)

Miscellaneous statistics: Ground outs-to-air outs ratio: 1.08 last season, 0.92 for career.... Grounded into 4 double plays in 73 opportunities (one per 18).... Drove in 13 of 24 runners from third base with less than two outs (54%).... Direction of balls hit to the outfield: 49% to left field, 26% to center, 25% to right.... Base running: Advanced from first base to third on 4 of 13 outfield singles (31%); scored from second on 6 of 7 (86%).... Made 0.74 assists per nine innings at first base.

Comments: Started out slowly but tailed off from there: he tied Jesse Barfield for the lowest April batting average in the league. (Things didn't get any better for Barfield.)... Batted a respectable .295 vs. left-handed pitchers, but he had hit .377 and .325 vs. lefties over the two previous seasons.... Played his first major league game in 1975, a year before Robin Yount's big-time debut. Career games played through 1992: Yount 2729, Clark 1994.... Don't leave this page without pondering his home-game batting record. He was the only player in the majors to hit as many as five home runs last season without hitting one at home. Nothing longer than a double in 116 at-bats at Fenway Park; only 10 RBIs in 41 games there. At least he hit for average there (compared to his road-game average, anyway).... Had averaged better than one home run every 20 at-bats for five years in a row from 1987 to 1991 on a tour that took him through Busch Stadium, Yankee Stadium, two years in San Diego's Jack Murphy, and Fenway. But last season? One homer every 51.4 at-bats. No player in major league history had ever fallen from five consecutive 250-at-bat seasons homering better than once every 20 at-bats to a 250-at-bat season with less than one homer every 50 at-bats.... It's a tough year when you've got more cars than extra-base hits.... Welcome to our new game show, "Jack Clark vs. National League Shortstops." In our last show, we saw that Clark was out-hit last year by Rafael Belliard, .211 to .210. But in today's episode, Jack comes back strong, besting Dick Schofield in home runs, five to four.

Scott Cooper

Bats Left

Boston Red Sox	AB	H	2B	3B	HR	RBI	BB	SO	BA	SA	OBA
Season	337	93	21	0	5	33	37	33	.276	.383	.346
vs. Left-Handers	41	11	3	0	1	5	7	6	.268	.415	.375
vs. Right-Handers	296	82	18	0	4	28	30	27	.277	.378	.341
vs. Ground-Ballers	160	45	15	0	0	15	18	18	.281	.375	.352
vs. Fly-Ballers	177	48	6	0	5	18	19	15	.271	.390	.340
Home Games	155	45	6	0	2	10	15	17	.290	.368	.353
Road Games	182	48	15	0	3	23	22	16	.264	.396	.340
Grass Fields	292	81	16	0	5	29	30	28	.277	.384	.343
Artificial Turf	45	12	5	0	0	4	7	5	.267	.378	.365
April	10	1	0	0	0	2	2	2	.100	.100	.231
May	37	9	2	0	0	3	5	1	.243	.297	.333
June	77	21	7	0	0	8	5	7	.273	.364	.313
July	39	10	1	0	0	5	7	9	.256	.282	.370
August	53	15	5	0	0	3	4	7	.283	.377	.333
Sept./Oct.	121	37	6	0	5	12	14	7	.306	.479	.378
Leading Off Inn.	65	20	7	0	1	1	3	4	.308	.462	.338
Runners On	130	35	4	0	0	28	16	16	.269	.300	.345
Bases Empty	207	58	17	0	5	5	21	17	.280	.435	.346
Runners/Scor. Pos.	72	20	2	0	0	28	10	12	.278	.306	.357
Runners On/2 Out	56	11	1	0	0	11	6	10	.196	.214	.274
Scor. Pos./2 Out	36	8	1	0	0	11	3	8	.222	.250	.282
Late-Inning Pressure	72	18	7	0	0	7	5	10	.250	.347	.299
Leading Off	20	4	3	0	0	0	1	2	.200	.350	.238
Runners On	26	8	2	0	0	7	2	4	.308	.385	.357
Runners/Scor. Pos.	12	5	1	0	0	7	1	2	.417	.500	.462

RUNS BATTED IN	From 1B	From 2B	From 3B	Scoring Position
Totals	1/98	9/58	18/35	27/93
Percentage	1.0%	15.5%	51.4%	29.0%

Loves to face: Jim Abbott (3-for-3, 2 2B)
Bill Gullickson (.444, 4-for-9, 1 HR)
Hates to face: Duane Ward (0-for-3, 2 SO)

Miscellaneous statistics: Ground outs-to-air outs ratio: 1.14 last season, 1.08 for career.... Grounded into 5 double plays in 65 opportunities (one per 13).... Drove in 12 of 16 runners from third base with less than two outs (75%).... Direction of balls hit to the outfield: 35% to left field, 30% to center, 35% to right.... Base running: Advanced from first base to third on 8 of 23 outfield singles (35%); scored from second on 5 of 7 (71%).... Made 0.71 assists per nine innings at first base.

Comments: Homerless in 257 career at-bats until September 4, but he smacked five in 116 at-bats from then until the end of the season.... All five of his home runs were solo shots. No A.L. player hit more than five homers last season without hitting at least one with a runner on base.... Owns .326 career batting average at Fenway Park, .260 on the road; but he has hit more doubles in road games than he has at Fenway. That wouldn't be as much of a surprise if this left-handed batter were a pull hitter, but as you can see from the numbers above, he hits his share of balls to the opposite field.... Had five hits in 11 at-bats and drew three walks during extra innings.... Batting average ranked fifth among major league rookies with at least 300 at-bats. Slugging percentage ranked fifth and on-base average ranked fourth among the same group of players.... Cooper, Bob Zupcic, and John Valentin became the third trio of Red Sox rookies in the expansion era to each accumulate at least 200 plate appearances in the same season. The others: Ellis Burks, Mike Greenwell, and Todd Benzinger (1987); Chuck Schilling, Carl Yastrzemski, and Jim Pagliaroni (1961).... Boston's 3d-round selection in the 1986 June draft, and to this day is the only player picked by the Red Sox in that draft who has played in the majors. (Boston's first selection that year actually made the big leagues, but not as a baseball player: Greg McMurtry made it as a wide receiver with the Patriots. If that counts.)

Henry Cotto

Bats Right

Seattle Mariners	AB	H	2B	3B	HR	RBI	BB	SO	BA	SA	OBA
Season	294	76	11	1	5	27	14	49	.259	.354	.294
vs. Left-Handers	168	54	9	0	4	21	14	25	.321	.446	.375
vs. Right-Handers	126	22	2	1	1	6	0	24	.175	.230	.175
vs. Ground-Ballers	113	26	3	0	1	6	4	22	.230	.283	.254
vs. Fly-Ballers	181	50	8	1	4	21	10	27	.276	.398	.318
Home Games	117	29	6	0	2	14	11	18	.248	.350	.315
Road Games	177	47	5	1	3	13	3	31	.266	.356	.278
Grass Fields	140	37	4	1	2	12	3	25	.264	.350	.280
Artificial Turf	154	39	7	0	3	15	11	24	.253	.357	.305
April	26	9	3	0	0	3	2	4	.346	.462	.393
May	37	9	1	0	3	7	3	8	.243	.514	.300
June	46	12	1	0	1	4	3	7	.261	.348	.306
July	55	12	2	0	0	1	1	4	.218	.255	.246
August	55	18	2	0	0	8	4	13	.327	.364	.367
Sept./Oct.	75	16	2	1	1	4	1	13	.213	.307	.224
Leading Off Inn.	96	19	3	0	1	1	1	17	.198	.260	.230
Runners On	114	34	4	1	2	24	8	18	.298	.404	.341
Bases Empty	180	42	7	0	3	3	6	31	.233	.322	.262
Runners/Scor. Pos.	64	19	2	1	1	22	8	10	.297	.406	.370
Runners On/2 Out	52	14	3	1	1	12	2	10	.269	.423	.296
Scor. Pos./2 Out	34	10	2	1	0	10	2	7	.294	.412	.333
Late-Inning Pressure	51	12	1	1	0	4	2	9	.235	.294	.264
Leading Off	8	1	0	0	0	0	0	0	.125	.125	.125
Runners On	27	7	0	1	0	4	2	5	.259	.333	.310
Runners/Scor. Pos.	16	5	0	1	0	4	2	3	.313	.438	.389

RUNS BATTED IN	From 1B	From 2B	From 3B	Scoring Position
Totals	3/86	9/54	10/22	19/76
Percentage	3.5%	16.7%	45.5%	25.0%

Loves to face: John Farrell (.429, 9-for-21, 1 HR)
Jack Morris (.500, 8-for-16, 1 HR)
Curt Young (.391, 9-for-23, 2 HR)
Hates to face: Mark Langston (.152, 5-for-33, 0 BB)
Dave Stewart (.067, 1-for-15)
Frank Viola (.136, 3-for-22)

Miscellaneous statistics: Ground outs-to-air outs ratio: 1.43 last season, 1.35 for career.... Grounded into 2 double plays in 49 opportunities (one per 25).... Drove in 7 of 8 runners from third base with less than two outs (88%).... Direction of balls hit to the outfield: 38% to left field, 36% to center, 26% to right.... Base running: Advanced from first base to third on 8 of 17 outfield singles (47%); scored from second on 9 of 9 (100%).... Made 2.53 putouts per nine innings in left field.

Comments: Stole 23 bases in 25 attempts last season, the best percentage (.920) by any A.L. player. Over the last 50 years, only five A.L. players have had a higher stolen base percentage in a season in which they stole as many bases as Cotto did last year: Amos Otis, 1970 (33-for-35, .943); Jack Perconte, 1985 (31-for-33, .939); Gary Redus, 1988 (26-for-28, .929); Don Baylor, 1972 (24-for-26, .923); Oddibe McDowell, 1987 (24-for-26, .923).... Among active players with at least 100 career stolen bases, only Eric Davis (.875), Tim Raines (.852), and Marquis Grissom (.847) have a higher stolen-base rate than Cotto (.844).... No catcher threw him out attempting to steal second base last season: Pat Borders got him trying to steal third, and Frank Tanana picked him off first on a 1-3-6 caught stealing.... He's a .329 career hitter in April, .253 thereafter; his .237 career mark from September 1 to the end of the season is his lowest in any month.... Has batted .259 in each of the last three even-numbered years. Okay, we promise: no more odd/even-year notes until the Saberhagen comments.... Started all 42 games in which the Mariners faced a southpaw, but only 23 of 120 games against right-handers.... This one may throw you for a loop: his .331 career batting average as a pinch hitter is the highest among active players (minimum: 75 pinch-hit at-bats). He started his career with six hits in his first 45 PH-ABs; since then, he's 33-for-73 (.452), including 19-for-33 (.576) over the last two seasons.

Chad Curtis
Bats Right

California Angels	AB	H	2B	3B	HR	RBI	BB	SO	BA	SA	OBA
Season	441	114	16	2	10	46	51	71	.259	.372	.341
vs. Left-Handers	122	33	6	1	6	22	26	18	.270	.484	.393
vs. Right-Handers	319	81	10	1	4	24	25	53	.254	.329	.318
vs. Ground-Ballers	204	47	6	0	1	11	19	33	.230	.275	.306
vs. Fly-Ballers	237	67	10	2	9	35	32	38	.283	.456	.370
Home Games	201	53	6	1	5	20	24	32	.264	.378	.349
Road Games	240	61	10	1	5	26	27	39	.254	.367	.333
Grass Fields	367	93	13	1	7	31	39	60	.253	.351	.329
Artificial Turf	74	21	3	1	3	15	12	11	.284	.473	.393
April	27	9	2	1	0	4	4	3	.333	.481	.406
May	60	13	2	1	2	3	8	10	.217	.383	.309
June	82	23	2	0	2	14	8	11	.280	.378	.352
July	88	20	4	0	4	9	10	15	.227	.409	.320
August	85	19	2	0	1	7	13	18	.224	.282	.323
Sept./Oct.	99	30	4	0	1	9	8	14	.303	.374	.366
Leading Off Inn.	91	24	2	1	2	2	15	12	.264	.374	.380
Runners On	172	43	7	1	4	40	19	31	.250	.372	.332
Bases Empty	269	71	9	1	6	6	32	40	.264	.372	.347
Runners/Scor. Pos.	106	24	3	1	4	38	10	17	.226	.387	.295
Runners On/2 Out	73	16	2	1	1	13	7	13	.219	.315	.296
Scor. Pos./2 Out	51	10	1	1	1	12	5	8	.196	.314	.268
Late-Inning Pressure	74	18	3	0	2	4	12	16	.243	.365	.356
Leading Off	16	5	1	0	0	0	4	3	.313	.375	.476
Runners On	31	7	1	0	1	3	5	7	.226	.355	.333
Runners/Scor. Pos.	17	2	0	0	1	3	3	3	.118	.294	.250

RUNS BATTED IN	From 1B	From 2B	From 3B	Scoring Position
Totals	4/114	14/81	18/46	32/127
Percentage	3.5%	17.3%	39.1%	25.2%

Loves to face: Derek Lilliquist (2-for-2, 1 HR, 1 BB)
Jack Morris (.600, 3-for-5, 1 2B, 1 HR)
Todd Stottlemyre (.571, 4-for-7, 1 2B, 1 HR)

Hates to face: Chris Bosio (0-for-7)
Juan Guzman (0-for-7, 4 SO)
Kevin Tapani (.111, 1-for-9)

Miscellaneous statistics: Ground outs-to-air outs ratio: 1.39 last season, 1.39 for career.... Grounded into 10 double plays in 86 opportunities (one per 8.6).... Drove in 15 of 23 runners from third base with less than two outs (65%).... Direction of balls hit to the outfield: 32% to left field, 34% to center, 34% to right.... Base running: Advanced from first base to third on 7 of 14 outfield singles (50%); scored from second on 15 of 16 (94%), 2d-highest rate in A.L.... Made 2.03 putouts per nine innings in right field.

Comments: Led A.L. outfielders with 16 assists. In the expansion era, only two rookie outfielders have had more assists: Del Unser (22 in 1968) and Rick Bosetti (17 in 1978).... The only player in the majors last season to appear in at least 35 games in each of the three outfield positions, and the only one to start more than 25 games at all three.... Started all 35 games in which Angels faced a left-handed starter last season; the only other player to do that was Gary Gaetti.... Ranked fifth among major league rookies in games (139), at-bats, runs, hits, and extra-base hits; fourth in RBIs; and third in home runs, stolen bases (43), and walks.... Angels have used a different opening-day starter in right field in each of the last 10 years; from 1983 to 1992: Bobby Clark, Fred Lynn, Reggie Jackson, Ruppert Jones, George Hendrick, Chili Davis, Tony Armas, Claudell Washington, Dave Winfield, Von Hayes. Dan Ford was the last right fielder to start two straight openers for California.... Born on November 6, 1968, one day after we elected Richard Nixon as our president.... Selected by the Angels in the 45th round of the 1989 June draft. (Thank God ESPN doesn't televise *that* baby!) Four of the Angels' first 44 selections from that draft have already made it to the majors: Kyle Abbott (1st round), Joe Grahe (2d round), Tim Salmon (3d round), and Hillary Hathaway (35th round); the latter is related neither to the First Lady nor to Mr. Drysdale's frumpy secretary on "The Beverly Hillbillies."

Milt Cuyler
Bats Left and Right

Detroit Tigers	AB	H	2B	3B	HR	RBI	BB	SO	BA	SA	OBA
Season	291	70	11	1	3	28	10	62	.241	.316	.275
vs. Left-Handers	86	25	2	0	2	8	3	11	.291	.384	.337
vs. Right-Handers	205	45	9	1	1	20	7	51	.220	.288	.249
vs. Ground-Ballers	140	31	8	0	0	11	3	31	.221	.279	.248
vs. Fly-Ballers	151	39	3	1	3	17	7	31	.258	.351	.300
Home Games	148	29	3	0	1	9	7	37	.196	.236	.252
Road Games	143	41	8	1	2	19	3	25	.287	.399	.301
Grass Fields	249	57	9	1	2	21	9	56	.229	.297	.267
Artificial Turf	42	13	2	0	1	7	1	6	.310	.429	.326
April	65	12	3	1	1	7	1	17	.185	.308	.197
May	71	18	1	0	1	8	1	12	.254	.310	.284
June	101	29	7	0	1	11	5	19	.287	.386	.333
July	54	11	0	0	0	2	3	14	.204	.204	.246
August	0	0	0	0	0	0	0	0	.000	.000	.000
Sept./Oct.	0	0	0	0	0	0	0	0	.000	.000	.000
Leading Off Inn.	62	15	3	0	0	0	3	17	.242	.290	.288
Runners On	138	32	5	1	2	27	3	26	.232	.326	.259
Bases Empty	153	38	6	0	1	1	7	36	.248	.307	.290
Runners/Scor. Pos.	74	21	3	1	2	27	2	17	.284	.432	.312
Runners On/2 Out	63	12	0	1	1	14	2	15	.190	.270	.215
Scor. Pos./2 Out	39	10	0	1	1	14	1	11	.256	.385	.275
Late-Inning Pressure	33	6	1	0	0	0	1	7	.182	.212	.250
Leading Off	10	2	1	0	0	0	1	2	.200	.300	.333
Runners On	8	0	0	0	0	0	0	0	.000	.000	.000
Runners/Scor. Pos.	3	0	0	0	0	0	0	1	.000	.000	.000

RUNS BATTED IN	From 1B	From 2B	From 3B	Scoring Position
Totals	2/106	9/58	14/32	23/90
Percentage	1.9%	15.5%	43.8%	25.6%

Loves to face: Dennis Cook (.600, 3-for-5, 1 2B, 1 HR)
Rich DeLucia (.300, 3-for-10, 1 3B, 1 HR)
Jack Morris (.429, 3-for-7, 1 HR, 2 BB)

Hates to face: Chuck Finley (0-for-10)
Erik Hanson (0-for-8)
Tim Leary (0-for-12)

Miscellaneous statistics: Ground outs-to-air outs ratio: 1.48 last season, 1.54 for career.... Grounded into 4 double plays in 64 opportunities (one per 16).... Drove in 8 of 14 runners from third base with less than two outs (57%).... Direction of balls hit to the outfield: 36% to left field, 25% to center, 39% to right batting left-handed; 47% to left field, 27% to center, 27% to right batting right-handed.... Base running: Advanced from first base to third on 4 of 12 outfield singles (33%); scored from second on 11 of 13 (85%).... Made 2.85 putouts per nine innings in center field.

Comments: Became the first player in major league history to steal fewer than 10 bases in his sophomore season after stealing 40 or more bases in his rookie season. Others with large drops: Chris Sabo (46 steals as a rookie, 14 as a sophomore); John Cangelosi, Miguel Dilone, and Larry Lintz all fell from 50 to 21.... A high strikeout rate is an occupational hazard for power hitters, but what about guys like Cuyler? The highest strikeout rates among players with at least 250 at-bats and fewer than five home runs: Alex Cole, one strikeout every 5.0 plate appearances; Cuyler 5.0; Pat Listach, 5.2; Bret Barberie, 5.5; Royce Clayton, 5.6.... Has only two home runs in 388 career at-bats at Tiger Stadium; career breakdown: .224 at home, .275 on the road.... Tigers' center fielders combined for a .225 batting average (lowest in the majors for that position), with four homers and 49 RBIs (fewest in the league). Cuyler started a majority of those games.... One of four Detroit outfielders to spend time on the disabled list last season; he missed the final 71 days of the season.... Owns a career average of .274 with the bases empty, but only .219 with runners on base. Among active players with at least 300 at-bats in each category, only Chris Hoiles (58 points) and Kevin Maas (56 points) have a greater disparity between their career averages in those situations.... Batted .329 in games the Tigers won, .155 in games they lost, the greatest difference among players with 100 at-bats in each category last season.

Chili Davis
Bats Left and Right

Minnesota Twins	AB	H	2B	3B	HR	RBI	BB	SO	BA	SA	OBA
Season	444	128	27	2	12	66	73	76	.288	.439	.386
vs. Left-Handers	121	31	5	0	4	22	13	25	.256	.397	.321
vs. Right-Handers	323	97	22	2	8	44	60	51	.300	.455	.408
vs. Ground-Ballers	224	66	12	1	3	34	36	36	.295	.397	.384
vs. Fly-Ballers	220	62	15	1	9	32	37	40	.282	.482	.387
Home Games	245	67	18	2	6	40	38	42	.273	.437	.364
Road Games	199	61	9	0	6	26	35	34	.307	.442	.412
Grass Fields	146	40	6	0	3	18	26	22	.274	.377	.386
Artificial Turf	298	88	21	2	9	48	47	54	.295	.470	.385
April	65	16	2	1	0	4	12	12	.246	.308	.359
May	69	21	4	1	2	16	14	12	.304	.478	.409
June	82	24	5	0	3	13	13	12	.293	.463	.389
July	89	26	6	0	2	14	10	13	.292	.427	.356
August	89	23	7	0	1	6	13	17	.258	.371	.359
Sept./Oct.	50	18	3	0	4	13	11	10	.360	.660	.469
Leading Off Inn.	105	34	8	2	6	6	10	16	.324	.610	.383
Runners On	210	58	13	0	4	58	47	34	.276	.395	.399
Bases Empty	234	70	14	2	8	8	26	42	.299	.479	.372
Runners/Scor. Pos.	133	35	8	0	1	49	37	27	.263	.346	.409
Runners On/2 Out	89	24	7	0	3	23	25	13	.270	.449	.430
Scor. Pos./2 Out	61	14	5	0	1	18	20	9	.230	.361	.420
Late-Inning Pressure	77	24	4	0	2	14	9	20	.312	.442	.375
Leading Off	13	6	1	0	1	1	2	3	.462	.769	.533
Runners On	35	9	2	0	0	12	6	7	.257	.314	.349
Runners/Scor. Pos.	23	6	1	0	0	11	3	5	.261	.304	.321

RUNS BATTED IN	From 1B	From 2B	From 3B	Scoring Position
Totals	7/150	25/105	22/56	47/161
Percentage	4.7%	23.8%	39.3%	29.2%

Loves to face: David Haas (.667, 4-for-6, 1 HR)
Rick Honeycutt (.393, 11-for-28, 4 HR)
David Wells (.429, 12-for-28, 3 HR)
Hates to face: Ted Higuera (.133, 2-for-15)
Nolan Ryan (.176, 13-for-74, 1 HR)
Frank Viola (.100, 2-for-20, 2 BB)

Miscellaneous statistics: Ground outs-to-air outs ratio: 1.20 last season, 1.21 for career. . . . Grounded into 11 double plays in 108 opportunities (one per 10). . . . Drove in 17 of 27 runners from third base with less than two outs (63%). . . . Direction of balls hit to the outfield: 36% to left field, 32% to center, 33% to right batting left-handed; 38% to left field, 28% to center, 34% to right batting right-handed. . . . Base running: Advanced from first base to third on 17 of 44 outfield singles (39%); scored from second on 8 of 16 (50%). . . . Made 2.40 putouts per nine innings in right field.

Comments: Returns to the Angels, for whom he played 425 games from 1988 to 1990. Believe it or not, that's more games with the Angels than anyone else on the team's current roster. Every other A.L. team ended last season with at least one player with 1000 or more games for the club. . . . Has now played in the American League for five years, after six full seasons in San Francisco. In 874 games with the Giants, Davis had 101 homers and 418 RBIs; although he's played 158 fewer games in the A.L., his A.L. home run and RBI totals (96/400) are comparable to his N.L. totals. . . . For the fifth consecutive season, batted at least 10 points higher from left side than he did from the right. His five-year breakdown: .256 right-handed, .282 left-handed. . . . He's the best against the best: He led all hitters with a .405 batting average against the Blue Jays last season (15-for-37). . . . Ground outs-to-air outs ratio was much higher batting left-handed (1.40) than it was batting right-handed (0.83). . . . On-base percentage has increased in each of the last four seasons, including career-high marks in each of the last two. . . . Ranked fifth on the club in total RBIs, but led the Twins with 11 game-winners. . . . You want consistency? His career batting breakdowns: .270 overall, .271 at home, .269 on the road, .267 in day games, .272 at night, .269 on grass, .271 on artificial turf. He also has batting averages in the .270s in every month except June (.248). Everybody knows that June isn't a chilly month, even in Minnesota.

Glenn Davis
Bats Right

Baltimore Orioles	AB	H	2B	3B	HR	RBI	BB	SO	BA	SA	OBA
Season	398	110	15	2	13	48	37	65	.276	.422	.338
vs. Left-Handers	107	27	3	1	4	18	6	22	.252	.411	.287
vs. Right-Handers	291	83	12	1	9	30	31	43	.285	.426	.356
vs. Ground-Ballers	198	53	6	1	5	21	18	31	.268	.384	.332
vs. Fly-Ballers	200	57	9	1	8	27	19	34	.285	.460	.344
Home Games	200	58	8	1	5	15	12	35	.290	.415	.330
Road Games	198	52	7	1	8	33	25	30	.263	.429	.345
Grass Fields	342	99	14	2	10	40	29	59	.289	.430	.346
Artificial Turf	56	11	1	0	3	8	8	6	.196	.375	.292
April	3	1	0	0	0	0	0	0	.333	.333	.333
May	51	13	1	1	3	9	3	9	.255	.490	.296
June	59	14	1	0	2	5	4	11	.237	.356	.297
July	79	30	3	0	3	14	13	9	.380	.532	.457
August	99	23	6	1	2	8	10	16	.232	.374	.300
Sept./Oct.	107	29	4	0	3	12	7	20	.271	.393	.319
Leading Off Inn.	101	31	4	0	4	4	9	14	.307	.465	.364
Runners On	188	52	6	1	6	41	20	30	.277	.415	.343
Bases Empty	210	58	9	1	7	7	17	35	.276	.429	.333
Runners/Scor. Pos.	99	25	5	1	1	31	10	18	.253	.354	.316
Runners On/2 Out	91	21	3	1	2	15	9	16	.231	.352	.307
Scor. Pos./2 Out	49	10	3	1	1	13	6	10	.204	.367	.304
Late-Inning Pressure	50	12	3	0	2	3	5	9	.240	.420	.309
Leading Off	17	7	2	0	1	1	2	2	.412	.706	.474
Runners On	16	3	0	0	0	1	2	4	.188	.188	.278
Runners/Scor. Pos.	12	1	0	0	0	1	1	3	.083	.083	.154

RUNS BATTED IN	From 1B	From 2B	From 3B	Scoring Position
Totals	6/148	13/75	16/41	29/116
Percentage	4.1%	17.3%	39.0%	25.0%

Loves to face: Neal Heaton (.409, 9-for-22, 4 2B, 2 HR)
Mike Jeffcoat (3-for-3, 2 HR)
Bob Welch (.455, 15-for-33, 2 HR)
Hates to face: Dave Fleming (.091, 1-for-11)
Terry Leach (0-for-10, 3 BB)
Lance McCullers (.050, 1-for-20, 6 SO)

Miscellaneous statistics: Ground outs-to-air outs ratio: 0.90 last season, 0.91 for career. . . . Grounded into 12 double plays in 93 opportunities (one per 7.8). . . . Drove in 10 of 20 runners from third base with less than two outs (50%). . . . Direction of balls hit to the outfield: 44% to left field, 34% to center, 23% to right. . . . Base running: Advanced from first base to third on 8 of 23 outfield singles (35%); scored from second on 3 of 8 (38%). . . . Made 0.50 assists per nine innings at first base.

Comments: Talk about odd combinations: He had a career-high batting average in the same season in which he had a career-low slugging percentage. How odd is that? Only eight other players in major league history have done it, with these parameters: we're considering only seasons of 100 or more games, and a player must have had at least five such seasons (last year was the sixth for Davis). The last player to do it: Gary Ward in 1986. . . . His rate of one home run every 30.6 at-bats was the lowest of his career, and less than half his 1990 rate with Houston (one HR every 14.9 AB). Unfortunately for Davis, his high-average, low-total-bases approach did not result in a lower strikeout rate: one every 6.8 times up last season, compared to one every 6.9 in 1990. . . . Career totals: 80 home runs in home games, 109 on the road. . . . Has received only two intentional passes in 155 A.L. games after getting at least 17 in each of his last three years with Houston. . . . Has missed 238 games over the last three seasons after four consecutive years of 150+ games. . . . Drove in only one of 14 runners from scoring position in Late-Inning Pressure Situations, compared to 27 percent of such runners at other times. . . . In nearly 500 career at-bats, his batting average with runners in scoring position and two outs is .211. . . . Needs 11 homers to reach 200, a level never attained by a major league Davis; but Chili (who needs just three) is odds-on to win the race. Seven Davises have hit 100 home runs, a major league record.

Rob Deer

Bats Right

Detroit Tigers	AB	H	2B	3B	HR	RBI	BB	SO	BA	SA	OBA
Season	393	97	20	1	32	64	51	131	.247	.547	.337
vs. Left-Handers	99	29	3	0	14	21	12	30	.293	.747	.369
vs. Right-Handers	294	68	17	1	18	43	39	101	.231	.480	.326
vs. Ground-Ballers	183	50	9	0	13	31	28	61	.273	.536	.374
vs. Fly-Ballers	210	47	11	1	19	33	23	70	.224	.557	.303
Home Games	173	44	12	0	13	28	24	61	.254	.549	.352
Road Games	220	53	8	1	19	36	27	70	.241	.545	.325
Grass Fields	331	82	16	1	28	57	44	109	.248	.556	.341
Artificial Turf	62	15	4	0	4	7	7	22	.242	.500	.314
April	65	12	3	1	6	12	6	24	.185	.538	.254
May	86	21	4	0	9	14	13	33	.244	.605	.347
June	80	15	2	0	6	12	11	23	.188	.438	.286
July	10	5	0	0	2	2	0	2	.500	1.100	.545
August	40	11	3	0	4	7	1	16	.275	.650	.293
Sept./Oct.	112	33	8	0	5	17	20	33	.295	.500	.406
Leading Off Inn.	90	30	6	0	10	10	10	24	.333	.733	.406
Runners On	179	39	9	0	10	42	27	63	.218	.436	.322
Bases Empty	214	58	11	1	22	22	24	68	.271	.640	.350
Runners/Scor. Pos.	98	21	6	0	5	32	19	41	.214	.429	.339
Runners On/2 Out	72	19	6	0	6	25	14	23	.264	.597	.391
Scor. Pos./2 Out	48	12	5	0	3	19	10	19	.250	.542	.379
Late-Inning Pressure	67	16	4	0	3	6	5	22	.239	.433	.292
Leading Off	11	4	1	0	0	0	1	2	.364	.455	.417
Runners On	27	7	2	0	1	4	3	9	.259	.444	.333
Runners/Scor. Pos.	13	3	0	0	1	4	2	6	.231	.462	.333

RUNS BATTED IN	From 1B	From 2B	From 3B	Scoring Position
Totals	11/150	9/81	12/36	21/117
Percentage	7.3%	11.1%	33.3%	17.9%

Loves to face: Mike Flanagan (.300, 6-for-20, 2 2B, 1 3B, 2 HR)
Greg A. Harris (.235, 4-for-17, 3 HR, 8 BB, 7 SO)
Bob Milacki (.500, 7-for-14, 1 HR)

Hates to face: Erik Hanson (0-for-16, 9 SO)
Nolan Ryan (0-for-14, 10 SO)
Dave Stieb (.043, 1-for-23, 3 BB)

Miscellaneous statistics: Ground outs-to-air outs ratio: 0.50 last season (2d lowest in A.L.), 0.57 for career. . . . Grounded into 8 double plays in 105 opportunities (one per 13). . . . Drove in 6 of 14 runners from third base with less than two outs (43%). . . . Direction of balls hit to the outfield: 61% to left field, 25% to center, 14% to right. . . . Base running: Advanced from first base to third on 7 of 23 outfield singles (30%); scored from second on 4 of 9 (44%). . . . Made 2.24 putouts per nine innings in right field.

Comments: Had 19-day and 26-day stints on the disabled list but still managed to hit 32 home runs in 110 games! Only four other players in major league history reached 30 homers in a season in which they played fewer than 120 games: Mike Schmidt (31 HR in 102 games in strike-shortened 1981), Rudy York (35 HR in 104 games as a rookie in 1937; he didn't become a regular starter until July), Babe Ruth (35 HR in 110 games in 1922; he was suspended until late May), Dick Allen (32 HR in 118 games in 1969; numerous benchings and a suspension marked the tumultuous final season of his first Philadelphia tour). . . . Became the third player with fewer than 70 RBIs in a season of 30+ home runs. The others: Felix Mantilla (30 HR, 64 RBI in 1964) and Brook Jacoby (32 HR, 69 RBI in 1987). . . . Posted career highs in home-run rate and slugging percentage. . . . Reached the 1000-game mark with 1206 strikeouts, the most in major league history. The only other player to whiff 1000 times over his first 1000 games was Dave Kingman (1043); close but no cigar: Bobby Bonds (999), Allen (978), Juan Samuel (977). . . . He's not the man you want at bat with a man on third and less than two outs; he has driven in only 43 percent of runners in such situations, the lowest career rate among active players (minimum: 150 opportunities). . . . If he's ever a midseason threat to Maris's record, remember this: His career home-run rate in April (one HR every 12.1 AB) is his highest in any month, his rate in September (one every 28.0 AB) is his lowest.

Mike Devereaux

Bats Right

Baltimore Orioles	AB	H	2B	3B	HR	RBI	BB	SO	BA	SA	OBA
Season	653	180	29	11	24	107	44	94	.276	.464	.321
vs. Left-Handers	168	59	9	2	9	29	10	24	.351	.589	.383
vs. Right-Handers	485	121	20	9	15	78	34	70	.249	.421	.300
vs. Ground-Ballers	321	86	15	4	9	57	22	45	.268	.424	.314
vs. Fly-Ballers	332	94	14	7	15	50	22	49	.283	.503	.328
Home Games	334	86	12	7	14	54	21	43	.257	.461	.301
Road Games	319	94	17	4	10	53	23	51	.295	.467	.342
Grass Fields	549	148	23	10	22	90	36	82	.270	.468	.314
Artificial Turf	104	32	6	1	2	17	8	12	.308	.442	.360
April	79	22	3	1	4	10	6	14	.278	.494	.329
May	105	23	7	1	4	17	11	12	.219	.419	.294
June	119	41	6	3	4	22	6	13	.345	.546	.373
July	118	29	3	4	3	14	7	21	.246	.415	.287
August	113	33	5	1	6	27	11	12	.292	.513	.352
Sept./Oct.	119	32	5	1	3	17	3	22	.269	.403	.293
Leading Off Inn.	103	27	4	3	5	5	9	13	.262	.505	.321
Runners On	281	74	15	4	9	92	18	39	.263	.441	.305
Bases Empty	372	106	14	7	15	15	26	55	.285	.481	.333
Runners/Scor. Pos.	180	51	12	3	7	86	13	27	.283	.500	.320
Runners On/2 Out	108	26	6	2	5	40	9	11	.241	.472	.299
Scor. Pos./2 Out	83	23	6	2	5	40	9	10	.277	.578	.348
Late-Inning Pressure	86	16	1	1	3	14	5	18	.186	.326	.234
Leading Off	14	0	0	0	0	0	1	3	.000	.000	.067
Runners On	40	12	1	1	3	14	2	5	.300	.600	.333
Runners/Scor. Pos.	30	8	1	1	2	12	2	3	.267	.567	.294

RUNS BATTED IN	From 1B	From 2B	From 3B	Scoring Position
Totals	11/197	33/148	39/78	72/226
Percentage	5.6%	22.3%	50.0%	31.9%

Loves to face: Jim Abbott (.526, 10-for-19, 1 HR)
Jimmy Key (.394, 13-for-33, 2 HR)
Kirk McCaskill (.409, 9-for-22, 2 HR)

Hates to face: Wilson Alvarez (0-for-9)
Kevin Appier (.053, 1-for-19)
Chuck Finley (.129, 4-for-31)

Miscellaneous statistics: Ground outs-to-air outs ratio: 0.79 last season, 0.94 for career. . . . Grounded into 14 double plays in 138 opportunities (one per 10). . . . Drove in 25 of 41 runners from third base with less than two outs (61%). . . . Direction of balls hit to the outfield: 39% to left field, 32% to center, 29% to right. . . . Base running: Advanced from first base to third on 8 of 26 outfield singles (31%); scored from second on 14 of 21 (67%). . . . Made 2.78 putouts per nine innings in center field.

Comments: He technically led major league outfielders with 107 RBIs last season; the top five: Devereaux (107), Juan Gonzalez (105), Kirby Puckett (104), Barry Bonds (103), Joe Carter (103). Hard to believe? We did say *technically*: Gonzalez, Puckett, and Carter all had higher RBI totals than Devereaux for the season, but no one had a higher total as an outfielder. . . . The 2d spot in the Orioles' batting order drove in 110 runs last season, 18 more than the next-highest A.L. team (Detroit). . . . Has hit safely in each of his last 16 games against the Angels, including all 12 games he played against them last season. His career average of .333 against them is his highest against any A.L. club. . . . Batting average vs. left-handed pitchers was a career high, and 4th highest in the league last season. Yearly averages vs. right-handers since 1989: .252, .246, .247, .249. . . . Batted .376 in his first-inning at-bats, .252 thereafter. . . . One of four major leaguers to increase his home-run total in each of the last four seasons. . . . Came to the plate with the bases loaded 29 times last season, collecting 13 hits in 25 at-bats with 38 RBIs; his totals of hits and RBIs were the highest single-season totals by any major league player since we got the bright idea to keep track of bases-loaded situations in 1975 (and Pat Tabler has never even been sent so much as a "thank you"). The old "records" were 11 hits, shared by eight players (including Tabler in 1983), and 34 RBIs by Don Mattingly in his six-grand-slam year of 1987.

Gary DiSarcina
Bats Right

California Angels	AB	H	2B	3B	HR	RBI	BB	SO	BA	SA	OBA
Season	518	128	19	0	3	42	20	50	.247	.301	.283
vs. Left-Handers	114	26	4	0	0	4	5	12	.228	.263	.264
vs. Right-Handers	404	102	15	0	3	38	15	38	.252	.312	.288
vs. Ground-Ballers	248	63	9	0	0	16	10	22	.254	.290	.289
vs. Fly-Ballers	270	65	10	0	3	26	10	28	.241	.311	.277
Home Games	251	59	9	0	2	25	9	21	.235	.295	.269
Road Games	267	69	10	0	1	17	11	29	.258	.307	.296
Grass Fields	435	105	14	0	2	35	18	40	.241	.287	.279
Artificial Turf	83	23	5	0	1	7	2	10	.277	.373	.302
April	62	19	3	0	0	3	6	9	.306	.355	.371
May	80	20	2	0	0	5	5	6	.250	.275	.299
June	85	20	4	0	2	7	2	4	.235	.353	.270
July	84	18	2	0	0	7	4	8	.214	.238	.250
August	103	25	4	0	1	15	1	9	.243	.311	.262
Sept./Oct.	104	26	4	0	0	5	2	14	.250	.288	.271
Leading Off Inn.	122	37	6	0	0	0	4	10	.303	.352	.331
Runners On	209	46	5	0	2	41	9	17	.220	.273	.259
Bases Empty	309	82	14	0	1	1	11	33	.265	.320	.299
Runners/Scor. Pos.	118	27	4	0	0	36	7	14	.229	.263	.282
Runners On/2 Out	88	17	1	0	2	16	6	6	.193	.273	.253
Scor. Pos./2 Out	50	8	0	0	0	11	5	6	.160	.160	.250
Late-Inning Pressure	79	11	1	0	1	7	6	7	.139	.190	.218
Leading Off	22	2	0	0	0	0	0	3	.091	.091	.091
Runners On	31	5	0	0	1	7	6	2	.161	.258	.316
Runners/Scor. Pos.	14	2	0	0	0	5	5	2	.143	.143	.400

RUNS BATTED IN	From 1B	From 2B	From 3B	Scoring Position
Totals	4/141	21/106	14/32	35/138
Percentage	2.8%	19.8%	43.8%	25.4%

Loves to face: Kevin Appier (.500, 5-for-10, 1 HR)
Bob Milacki (.667, 4-for-6, 1 HR)
Melido Perez (.500, 4-for-8)

Hates to face: Kevin Brown (0-for-8)
Dave Stewart (0-for-9)
Kevin Tapani (0-for-9)

Miscellaneous statistics: Ground outs-to-air outs ratio: 1.27 last season, 1.43 for career.... Grounded into 15 double plays in 87 opportunities (one per 5.8).... Drove in 9 of 12 runners from third base with less than two outs (75%).... Direction of balls hit to the outfield: 30% to left field, 36% to center, 34% to right.... Base running: Advanced from first base to third on 12 of 30 outfield singles (40%); scored from second on 12 of 12 (100%), best rate in majors.... Made 3.18 assists per nine innings at shortstop.

Comments: Led major league rookies in games (157) and starts (155). Fell two games shy of the team record for rookies, set by Devon White (159 in 1987). No rookie has played all his team's games since Johnny Ray played 162 for the 1982 Pirates.... Angels led A.L. in games and starts by rookies, as DiSarcina and Chad Curtis became only the third pair of rookies in Angels history to qualify for the batting title in the same season. The others: Jose Cardenal and Paul Schaal (1965); Ken Hunt and Lee Thomas (1961).... Became the fourth rookie in major league history to play as many as 157 games at shortstop. He tied A.L. record, shared by Donie Bush (1907) and Dick Howser (1961), but fell two games shy of Ozzie Smith's major league mark set in 1978. Only one other rookie in Angels history has played as many as 100 games in a season at shortstop: Dick Schofield, 140 games in 1984.... Had been hitless in 13 at-bats in Late-Inning Pressure Situations in parts of 1989, 1990, and 1991 seasons with Angels. Adding those at-bats to the numbers above yields a career average of .120 in LIPS, the lowest among players who have at least 100 LIPS plate appearances since 1975. No other player stands below .150 (Stan Jefferson), and no other active player is below .167 (Junior Felix).... Averaged one walk every 27.7 plate appearances, the lowest rate by any A.L. player last year. The lowest walk rate among rookies this century (minimum: 400 PAs) belongs to Hal Lanier, who walked five times in 401 PAs for the 1964 Giants.

Brian Downing
Bats Right

Texas Rangers	AB	H	2B	3B	HR	RBI	BB	SO	BA	SA	OBA
Season	320	89	18	0	10	39	62	58	.278	.428	.407
vs. Left-Handers	121	34	8	0	3	14	30	30	.281	.421	.429
vs. Right-Handers	199	55	10	0	7	25	32	28	.276	.432	.392
vs. Ground-Ballers	144	35	6	0	6	22	23	26	.243	.410	.363
vs. Fly-Ballers	176	54	12	0	4	17	39	32	.307	.443	.441
Home Games	163	50	12	0	4	16	32	30	.307	.454	.430
Road Games	157	39	6	0	6	23	30	28	.248	.401	.382
Grass Fields	273	80	17	0	9	35	49	48	.293	.454	.412
Artificial Turf	47	9	1	0	1	4	13	10	.191	.277	.377
April	39	10	1	0	2	5	14	6	.256	.436	.482
May	49	14	1	0	2	5	12	5	.286	.429	.435
June	56	13	4	0	1	5	10	12	.232	.357	.358
July	58	16	4	0	3	11	8	14	.276	.500	.373
August	72	23	3	0	2	10	12	11	.319	.444	.424
Sept./Oct.	46	13	5	0	0	3	6	10	.283	.391	.370
Leading Off Inn.	113	34	7	0	4	4	18	13	.301	.469	.402
Runners On	124	32	6	0	4	33	27	29	.258	.403	.404
Bases Empty	196	57	12	0	6	6	35	29	.291	.444	.409
Runners/Scor. Pos.	76	16	3	0	2	28	18	22	.211	.329	.378
Runners On/2 Out	52	13	2	0	0	10	6	13	.250	.288	.350
Scor. Pos./2 Out	41	7	2	0	0	10	4	12	.171	.220	.277
Late-Inning Pressure	47	7	2	0	2	4	6	9	.149	.319	.273
Leading Off	9	3	1	0	1	1	0	1	.333	.778	.333
Runners On	21	1	0	0	1	3	4	5	.048	.190	.231
Runners/Scor. Pos.	14	0	0	0	0	1	3	4	.000	.000	.176

RUNS BATTED IN	From 1B	From 2B	From 3B	Scoring Position
Totals	7/82	12/60	10/32	22/92
Percentage	8.5%	20.0%	31.3%	23.9%

Loves to face: Greg A. Harris (.417, 10-for-24, 2 HR)
Mark Langston (.345, 20-for-58, 4 HR, 14 BB)
Rick Sutcliffe (.385, 5-for-13, 2 2B, 1 HR, 4 BB)

Hates to face: Dennis Eckersley (.163, 8-for-49, 2 HR)
Mike Moore (.125, 6-for-48, 1 HR)
Jaime Navarro (.071, 1-for-14, 1 2B)

Miscellaneous statistics: Ground outs-to-air outs ratio: 0.97 last season, 1.07 for career.... Grounded into 7 double plays in 66 opportunities (one per 9.4).... Drove in 7 of 14 runners from third base with less than two outs (50%).... Direction of balls hit to the outfield: 47% to left field, 29% to center, 24% to right.... Base running: Advanced from first base to third on 5 of 29 outfield singles (17%); scored from second on 8 of 14 (57%).

Comments: Hit at least 10 home runs in each of his last 11 seasons to finish with 275 home runs, the same total as Roger Maris, albeit in 2752 more at-bats.... He hit six homers in his final spring training, tying Dean Palmer and Darren Daulton for the major league lead.... Stands as the Angels' all-time leader in games played (1661), a record that could last into the next century; see the Chili Davis comments.... Career total of 1073 RBIs ranks 53d in A.L. history, but became only the third player in the expansion era to have his season RBI total decline in six straight years. The others: Fred Lynn (1985–90) and Elston Howard (1963–68).... Downing didn't play in the field in the last 603 games of his career; however, in his day, Downing was as close to a mistakeproof outfielder as existed. Among players with at least 500 games in the outfield, Downing's career error rate (one every 220 chances) was the best of all-time; baseball record books, however, generally demand at least 1000 games for qualification in that category.... Ends a 20-year career without ever playing in a World Series, while appearing in just one All-Star Game (1979). But his lone All-Star at-bat (a single off Bruce Sutter) led to a great All-Star moment: He was thrown out trying to score from second on a spectacular throw-catch-and-tag putout executed by Dave Parker and Gary Carter.

Jim Eisenreich — Bats Left
Kansas City Royals

	AB	H	2B	3B	HR	RBI	BB	SO	BA	SA	OBA
Season	353	95	13	3	2	28	24	36	.269	.340	.313
vs. Left-Handers	75	18	4	1	0	7	5	15	.240	.320	.284
vs. Right-Handers	278	77	9	2	2	21	19	21	.277	.345	.321
vs. Ground-Ballers	160	39	8	2	1	15	9	11	.244	.338	.282
vs. Fly-Ballers	193	56	5	1	1	13	15	25	.290	.342	.338
Home Games	160	39	2	3	1	13	14	15	.244	.313	.301
Road Games	193	56	11	0	1	15	10	21	.290	.363	.324
Grass Fields	158	50	10	0	1	14	9	17	.316	.399	.353
Artificial Turf	195	45	3	3	1	14	15	19	.231	.292	.282
April	32	6	0	0	1	3	5	7	.188	.281	.289
May	65	19	5	0	1	9	7	7	.292	.415	.351
June	72	20	4	0	0	4	3	7	.278	.333	.307
July	77	22	2	2	0	7	2	5	.286	.364	.304
August	29	4	0	0	0	2	3	1	.138	.138	.219
Sept./Oct.	78	24	2	1	0	3	4	9	.308	.359	.341
Leading Off Inn.	82	31	5	1	1	1	10	8	.378	.500	.446
Runners On	154	32	5	0	1	27	11	17	.208	.266	.256
Bases Empty	199	63	8	3	1	1	13	19	.317	.402	.358
Runners/Scor. Pos.	97	19	4	0	0	25	9	14	.196	.237	.257
Runners On/2 Out	63	17	4	0	0	13	6	4	.270	.333	.333
Scor. Pos./2 Out	47	11	4	0	0	13	6	3	.234	.319	.321
Late-Inning Pressure	69	18	3	1	1	3	7	12	.261	.377	.325
Leading Off	17	8	0	1	1	1	3	1	.471	.765	.550
Runners On	30	6	1	0	0	2	2	8	.200	.233	.242
Runners/Scor. Pos.	14	0	0	0	0	2	2	6	.000	.000	.118

RUNS BATTED IN	From 1B	From 2B	From 3B	Scoring Position
Totals	2/106	5/71	19/42	24/113
Percentage	1.9%	7.0%	45.2%	21.2%

Loves to face: Lee Guetterman (.545, 6-for-11, 2 2B, 2 BB)
Pete Harnisch (.600, 3-for-5, 1 2B, 1 3B, 2 BB)
Greg Swindell (.462, 6-for-13)

Hates to face: Jim Corsi (0-for-6)
Bill Swift (.211, 4-for-19)

Miscellaneous statistics: Ground outs-to-air outs ratio: 1.06 last season, 1.17 for career.... Grounded into 6 double plays in 77 opportunities (one per 13).... Drove in 12 of 22 runners from third base with less than two outs (55%).... Direction of balls hit to the outfield: 51% to left field, 27% to center, 22% to right.... Base running: Advanced from first base to third on 7 of 20 outfield singles (35%); scored from second on 5 of 6 (83%).... Made 2.25 putouts per nine innings in right field.

Comments: Has hit for a higher average in day games than in night games in each of his last seven seasons in the majors; in each of the last six years, his daytime average has exceeded his nighttime mark by at least 20 points. Career breakdown: .316 under the sun, .261 under the stars. His career average in day games is 10th best among active players (minimum: 500 AB in day games).... Batted .371 (10-for-27) as a pinch hitter last season, lifting his career mark in that role to .301.... Started 77 games against right-handers last season, only six against left-handers, despite a career average that's higher against lefties (.282) than against righties (.276). One of nine active lefty batters for whom that's true (minimum: 1000 plate appearances). Other A.L. players: Ken Griffey (.305, .299); B.J. Surhoff (.273, .266); Jamie Quirk (.278, .237).... Had the best on-base percentage on the team when leading off innings last season. Over the last two years, he has batted .381 in those situations (64-for-168, 14 BB), and has been even better leading off in Late-Inning Pressure Situations: .444 (16-for-35).... Has only two assists in 193 games in the outfield over the past two years.... Royals' right fielders combined for only four home runs last season (two by Eisenreich, one each by McReynolds and Gwynn), the fewest by any team in the majors.... Finished second to Edgar Martinez in A.L. in batting average last season; sorry, that should read "batting average *against Milwaukee*." Edgar hit .394, Eisenreich .391 against the Brew Crew.

Junior Felix — Bats Left and Right
California Angels

	AB	H	2B	3B	HR	RBI	BB	SO	BA	SA	OBA
Season	509	125	22	5	9	72	33	128	.246	.361	.289
vs. Left-Handers	118	32	7	1	3	18	3	30	.271	.424	.285
vs. Right-Handers	391	93	15	4	6	54	30	98	.238	.345	.291
vs. Ground-Ballers	246	63	11	2	3	35	13	57	.256	.354	.289
vs. Fly-Ballers	263	62	11	3	6	37	20	71	.236	.369	.289
Home Games	251	62	8	2	5	32	16	60	.247	.355	.292
Road Games	258	63	14	3	4	40	17	68	.244	.368	.287
Grass Fields	427	104	15	5	9	61	29	110	.244	.365	.290
Artificial Turf	82	21	7	0	0	11	4	18	.256	.341	.287
April	86	25	2	1	3	20	4	19	.291	.442	.319
May	71	20	5	0	2	11	2	17	.282	.437	.293
June	71	17	3	0	0	6	3	15	.239	.282	.263
July	92	18	4	2	1	14	11	19	.196	.315	.286
August	116	29	4	1	2	15	7	32	.250	.353	.290
Sept./Oct.	73	16	4	1	1	6	6	26	.219	.342	.280
Leading Off Inn.	103	23	6	0	3	3	7	30	.223	.369	.273
Runners On	223	68	9	4	2	65	15	45	.305	.408	.339
Bases Empty	286	57	13	1	7	7	18	83	.199	.325	.249
Runners/Scor. Pos.	141	37	2	3	2	59	14	38	.262	.362	.315
Runners On/2 Out	86	24	0	0	1	17	4	15	.279	.314	.319
Scor. Pos./2 Out	59	16	0	0	1	16	3	13	.271	.322	.317
Late-Inning Pressure	74	12	0	0	1	3	4	25	.162	.203	.205
Leading Off	28	5	0	0	1	1	2	9	.179	.286	.233
Runners On	29	6	0	0	0	2	2	8	.207	.207	.258
Runners/Scor. Pos.	18	2	0	0	0	2	2	7	.111	.111	.200

RUNS BATTED IN	From 1B	From 2B	From 3B	Scoring Position
Totals	10/148	19/105	34/63	53/168
Percentage	6.8%	18.1%	54.0%	31.5%

Loves to face: Dennis Lamp (.455, 5-for-11, 1 2B, 1 3B, 1 HR)
Frank Tanana (.400, 6-for-15, 3 2B, 1 HR)

Hates to face: Bill Krueger (0-for-16, 7 SO)
Bret Saberhagen (.083, 1-for-12, 5 SO)

Miscellaneous statistics: Ground outs-to-air outs ratio: 1.54 last season, 1.50 for career.... Grounded into 9 double plays in 102 opportunities (one per 11).... Drove in 27 of 37 runners from third base with less than two outs (73%).... Direction of balls hit to the outfield: 37% to left field, 39% to center, 25% to right batting left-handed; 51% to left field, 29% to center, 20% to right batting right-handed.... Base running: Advanced from first base to third on 6 of 16 outfield singles (38%); scored from second on 15 of 16 (94%), 2d-highest rate in A.L.... Made 2.80 putouts per nine innings in center field.

Comments: Led the Angels with 36 extra-base hits, the lowest total to lead any team since Ron Jackson led the Angels with 29 in 1976. Prior to 1992, the last team without a 40-XBH player was the 1990 Angels, led by Dave Winfield with 39.... Was tied with Cecil Fielder for the A.L. RBI lead at the end of April; his total of 72 RBIs was the lowest to lead any team last season.... Total of 128 strikeouts was sixth highest ever by a player with fewer than 10 home runs. Three of the top six played for the Angels. The top five: Rick Monday, 1968 (143 SO, 8 HR); Ron LeFlore, 1975 (139, 8); Bobby Knoop, 1967 (136, 9); Gary Pettis, 1986 (132, 5);. Ken Hubbs, 1962 (129, 5).... Has improved markedly from the right side of the plate since joining the Angels in 1991; his batting averages: .206 in two seasons with Toronto, .277 with California. Last season was the first in which he batted below .280 from the left side.... Has a career batting average of .167 in Late-Inning Pressure Situations, the lowest in the majors over the last 18 years (minimum: 200 AB). The bottom five: Felix (.167), Kevin Elster (.178), Mike Phillips (.188), Jeff Blauser (.191), and Matt Williams (.191). Felix's batting averages in LIPS since his debut in 1989: .148, .153, .259, .162.... Career rate of one error every 37 chances is ninth worst among active outfielders with at least 400 games. Those with lower averages: Ruben Sierra, Chili Davis, Danny Tartabull, Hubie Brooks, George Bell, Pete Incaviglia, Lonnie Smith, and Glenn Braggs.

Cecil Fielder
Bats Right

Detroit Tigers	AB	H	2B	3B	HR	RBI	BB	SO	BA	SA	OBA
Season	594	145	22	0	35	124	73	151	.244	.458	.325
vs. Left-Handers	134	31	5	0	9	31	24	45	.231	.470	.352
vs. Right-Handers	460	114	17	0	26	93	49	106	.248	.454	.317
vs. Ground-Ballers	275	70	12	0	13	53	26	70	.255	.440	.319
vs. Fly-Ballers	319	75	10	0	22	71	47	81	.235	.473	.331
Home Games	296	76	15	0	18	68	36	66	.257	.490	.339
Road Games	298	69	7	0	17	56	37	85	.232	.426	.312
Grass Fields	513	130	18	0	34	114	64	121	.253	.487	.336
Artificial Turf	81	15	4	0	1	10	9	30	.185	.272	.261
April	78	18	2	0	7	20	7	13	.231	.526	.287
May	75	16	8	0	1	13	9	23	.213	.360	.294
June	113	30	4	0	8	32	16	32	.265	.513	.359
July	107	24	2	0	6	21	12	32	.224	.411	.303
August	104	27	3	0	7	22	11	28	.260	.490	.328
Sept./Oct.	117	30	3	0	6	16	18	23	.256	.436	.356
Leading Off Inn.	162	43	6	0	11	11	19	42	.265	.506	.343
Runners On	295	75	13	0	21	110	43	66	.254	.512	.346
Bases Empty	299	70	9	0	14	14	30	85	.234	.405	.304
Runners/Scor. Pos.	181	48	7	0	10	82	26	41	.265	.470	.346
Runners On/2 Out	131	37	5	0	10	49	17	34	.282	.550	.369
Scor. Pos./2 Out	78	23	2	0	4	34	8	17	.295	.474	.360
Late-Inning Pressure	80	25	1	0	5	19	7	18	.313	.512	.364
Leading Off	20	5	1	0	0	0	0	6	.250	.300	.250
Runners On	39	11	0	0	5	19	4	7	.282	.667	.341
Runners/Scor. Pos.	20	7	0	0	3	15	2	4	.350	.800	.391

RUNS BATTED IN	From 1B	From 2B	From 3B	Scoring Position
Totals	26/217	28/139	35/83	63/222
Percentage	12.0%	20.1%	42.2%	28.4%

Loves to face: Chuck Finley (.304, 7-for-23, 3 HR, 7 BB)
Jimmy Key (.357, 10-for-28, 4 HR)
David Wells (.385, 5-for-13, 2 HR, 5 BB)

Hates to face: Roger Clemens (.048, 1-for-21, 2 BB, 11 SO)
Mark Eichhorn (0-for-12)
Gene Nelson (.050, 1-for-20)

Miscellaneous statistics: Ground outs-to-air outs ratio: 0.88 last season, 0.93 for career. . . . Grounded into 14 double plays in 140 opportunities (one per 10). . . . Drove in 23 of 50 runners from third base with less than two outs (46%). . . . Direction of balls hit to the outfield: 47% to left field, 30% to center, 22% to right. . . . Base running: Advanced from first base to third on 5 of 28 outfield singles (18%); scored from second on 6 of 10 (60%). . . . Made 0.87 assists per nine innings at first base.

Comments: Three-year total of 130 home runs is the highest in the majors since Frank Howard hit 136 from 1968 through 1970, and the 2d highest in Tigers history, behind Hank Greenberg's 132 from 1938 to 1940. . . . Has hit 10 more homers at Tiger Stadium (70) than on the road (60) during that time. . . . Last season's total of 124 RBIs was his lowest in three years since returning to the States. Only 10 other players drove in that many runs in three consecutive seasons; Fielder is the first since Duke Snider (1953–55). Lou Gehrig's eight-year streak was the longest ever (1927–34). . . . Only two other players in this century batted below .250 and drove in at least 120 runs: Harmon Killebrew in 1962 (.243, 126 RBIs) and Gorman Thomas in 1979 (.244, 123). . . . Became the fourth player in major league history to strike out more than 150 times in three consecutive seasons. Others: Rob Deer (4 years, 1986–89); Andres Galarraga (1988–90); Pete Incaviglia (1986–88). . . . Has played in 696 games and never stolen a base. Only two nonpitchers in this century have had careers of at least 700 games without a steal: Russ Nixon (906 games) and Jose Morales (733). . . . Career slugging percentage vs. left-handed pitchers (.582) is 3d highest among active players, behind Frank Thomas (.654) and Dave Hollins (.604). . . . Slugging percentage has dropped at least 50 points in each of the last two seasons (from .592 to .513 to .458). Only one player in major league history has done that three consecutive qualifying seasons: Al Simmons (1931–33).

Scott Fletcher
Bats Right

Milwaukee Brewers	AB	H	2B	3B	HR	RBI	BB	SO	BA	SA	OBA
Season	386	106	18	3	3	51	30	33	.275	.360	.335
vs. Left-Handers	104	32	5	1	0	13	7	10	.308	.375	.360
vs. Right-Handers	282	74	13	2	3	38	23	23	.262	.355	.326
vs. Ground-Ballers	169	46	6	1	1	21	17	17	.272	.337	.349
vs. Fly-Ballers	217	60	12	2	2	30	13	16	.276	.378	.323
Home Games	175	55	11	1	2	26	16	15	.314	.423	.379
Road Games	211	51	7	2	1	25	14	18	.242	.308	.297
Grass Fields	332	92	16	3	3	42	25	30	.277	.370	.332
Artificial Turf	54	14	2	0	0	9	5	3	.259	.296	.349
April	32	11	1	1	0	3	3	3	.344	.438	.400
May	47	14	1	1	1	7	3	3	.298	.426	.333
June	75	23	4	0	1	9	9	6	.307	.360	.388
July	71	15	5	1	1	9	5	6	.211	.352	.263
August	85	26	5	0	0	14	7	6	.306	.365	.368
Sept./Oct.	76	17	2	0	1	9	3	9	.224	.289	.282
Leading Off Inn.	91	23	6	0	1	1	6	8	.253	.352	.299
Runners On	168	53	7	2	2	50	15	11	.315	.417	.380
Bases Empty	218	53	11	1	1	1	15	22	.243	.317	.298
Runners/Scor. Pos.	107	36	5	0	2	47	12	10	.336	.439	.409
Runners On/2 Out	86	30	3	0	2	27	7	6	.349	.453	.404
Scor. Pos./2 Out	61	21	3	0	2	27	6	6	.344	.492	.412
Late-Inning Pressure	56	15	3	0	1	13	4	3	.268	.375	.323
Leading Off	11	3	0	0	0	0	0	0	.273	.273	.273
Runners On	26	9	3	0	1	13	3	1	.346	.577	.419
Runners/Scor. Pos.	17	8	2	0	1	12	2	1	.471	.765	.524

RUNS BATTED IN	From 1B	From 2B	From 3B	Scoring Position
Totals	6/120	17/87	25/51	42/138
Percentage	5.0%	19.5%	49.0%	30.4%

Loves to face: Tim Leary (.476, 10-for-21)
Scott Sanderson (.550, 11-for-20, 2 HR)
David Wells (.417, 5-for-12)

Hates to face: Jim Abbott (.045, 1-for-22)
Kirk McCaskill (.152, 5-for-33)
Todd Stottlemyre (.056, 1-for-18, 2 BB)

Miscellaneous statistics: Ground outs-to-air outs ratio: 1.10 last season, 1.36 for career. . . . Grounded into 4 double plays in 67 opportunities (one per 17). . . . Drove in 16 of 26 runners from third base with less than two outs (62%). . . . Direction of balls hit to the outfield: 41% to left field, 32% to center, 27% to right. . . . Base running: Advanced from first base to third on 9 of 25 outfield singles (36%); scored from second on 13 of 19 (68%). . . . Made 3.36 assists per nine innings at second base, 2d-highest rate in A.L.

Comments: At the age of 34, he stole 17 bases last season—not only a career high, but more than he stole over the previous four years combined. . . . Was 0-for-2 on stolen-base attempts in 1991, but it's not like he barely played; he had 277 at-bats in 90 games. No player in this century came off a no-steal season of 90 games or 250 ABs to swipe as many as Fletcher did in 1992. . . . Incidentally, Fletcher now joins a team on which no player stole even half as many bases as he did in 1992; Boston's leader was Jody Reed with 7. . . . No Red Sox player with 400 ABs had a batting average as high as Fletcher's either; the leader: Tom Brunansky at .266. . . . The only older players to appear in at least 100 games at second base last season were Lou Whitaker and Bill Doran. . . . Led the majors with 45 RBIs from the ninth spot in the batting order last season. . . . Batted over .300 with runners in scoring position four times over a five-year span from 1984 to 1988. Last season's .336 mark was the highest on the Brewers, and it raised his career average to .296. . . . Career breakdown: .294 with runners on base, .241 with the bases empty. . . . Has a career average of .335 vs. the Yankees, .255 against all other teams combined. . . . Has committed only 21 errors in 2196 chances at second base in his American League career (one per 105 chances). He has played 484 A.L. games at second base; no A.L. second baseman with 500 games has an error rate nearly as good. Rich Dauer leads the 500-gamers with an average of one per 79.

Travis Fryman
Bats Right

Detroit Tigers	AB	H	2B	3B	HR	RBI	BB	SO	BA	SA	OBA
Season	659	175	31	4	20	96	45	144	.266	.416	.316
vs. Left-Handers	158	45	7	1	7	31	12	30	.285	.475	.337
vs. Right-Handers	501	130	24	3	13	65	33	114	.259	.397	.309
vs. Ground-Ballers	297	82	16	3	7	40	20	59	.276	.421	.324
vs. Fly-Ballers	362	93	15	1	13	56	25	85	.257	.412	.309
Home Games	319	74	9	2	9	40	22	70	.232	.357	.289
Road Games	340	101	22	2	11	56	23	74	.297	.471	.341
Grass Fields	558	151	22	3	19	78	39	115	.271	.423	.322
Artificial Turf	101	24	9	1	1	18	6	29	.238	.376	.282
April	78	24	1	0	3	7	5	11	.308	.436	.357
May	112	29	5	0	5	18	9	30	.259	.438	.311
June	123	38	10	2	4	25	3	23	.309	.520	.331
July	111	29	7	0	3	16	7	27	.261	.405	.308
August	117	31	4	1	3	14	8	23	.265	.393	.312
Sept./Oct.	118	24	4	1	2	16	13	30	.203	.305	.289
Leading Off Inn.	101	29	6	1	4	4	4	17	.287	.485	.314
Runners On	332	92	17	3	7	83	26	72	.277	.410	.330
Bases Empty	327	83	14	1	13	13	19	72	.254	.422	.301
Runners/Scor. Pos.	194	52	11	2	3	72	13	54	.268	.392	.312
Runners On/2 Out	127	39	5	3	3	38	9	28	.307	.465	.353
Scor. Pos./2 Out	89	27	5	2	2	35	5	25	.303	.472	.340
Late-Inning Pressure	85	16	1	0	5	10	7	25	.188	.376	.245
Leading Off	18	2	0	0	1	1	1	5	.111	.278	.158
Runners On	40	6	1	0	1	6	3	10	.150	.250	.200
Runners/Scor. Pos.	24	3	1	0	1	6	1	8	.125	.292	.148

RUNS BATTED IN	From 1B	From 2B	From 3B	Scoring Position
Totals	11/250	28/151	37/90	65/241
Percentage	4.4%	18.5%	41.1%	27.0%

Loves to face: Kevin Brown (.429, 6-for-14, 1 HR)
Chuck Finley (.409, 9-for-22, 1 HR)
Randy Johnson (.455, 5-for-11, 2 HR, 4 SO)
Hates to face: Chris Bosio (.071, 1-for-14, 7 SO)
Erik Hanson (.063, 1-for-16)
Melido Perez (0-for-16)

Miscellaneous statistics: Ground outs-to-air outs ratio: 0.82 last season, 0.84 for career.... Grounded into 13 double plays in 175 opportunities (one per 13).... Drove in 27 of 52 runners from third base with less than two outs (52%).... Direction of balls hit to the outfield: 42% to left field, 31% to center, 27% to right.... Base running: Advanced from first base to third on 8 of 24 outfield singles (33%); scored from second on 13 of 17 (76%).... Made 3.32 assists per nine innings at shortstop.

Comments: Injuries to Alan Trammell have forced Fryman to split his time between third base and shortstop in three seasons with Detroit—an unusual demand to be made on a player as young as Fryman, who turns 24 in April. The last player to accumulate at least 150 games at two different infield positions prior to his 24th birthday: Cass Michaels (1943–49). The only others to do so: Bruno Betzel, Bill Dahlen, Rogers Hornsby, John Knight, Sibby Sisti, Harry Steinfeldt, and Cecil Travis.... Played 161 games last season; only two players younger than he played as many as 125 games: Juan Gonzalez and Ken Griffey.... Drove in 80 runs as a shortstop, leading the majors in that category. His 14 homers from that position tied Cal Ripken for the major league lead; only one other A.L. shortstop hit more than five (Greg Gagne, 7).... Of his 20 home runs, none were hit to the opposite field, and only one was hit to center.... Led the major leagues in at-bats last season.... Has batted at least 25 points higher against left-handers than he has against right-handers in each of his three seasons in the majors. Career breakdown: .296 vs. LHP, .257 vs. RHP.... Has hit for a higher average on the road than he has at Tiger Stadium in each of his three seasons. Career breakdown: .243, 22 HR at home; .291, 28 HR on the road.... Led the league with a .472 average against the Rangers last season (25-for-53). He also led the league with 16 RBIs against the Blue Jays.

Gary Gaetti
Bats Right

California Angels	AB	H	2B	3B	HR	RBI	BB	SO	BA	SA	OBA
Season	456	103	13	2	12	48	21	79	.226	.342	.267
vs. Left-Handers	124	31	6	0	5	15	8	13	.250	.419	.299
vs. Right-Handers	332	72	7	2	7	33	13	66	.217	.313	.256
vs. Ground-Ballers	212	54	9	1	4	26	8	35	.255	.363	.296
vs. Fly-Ballers	244	49	4	1	8	22	13	44	.201	.324	.242
Home Games	231	60	7	1	8	30	7	40	.260	.403	.289
Road Games	225	43	6	1	4	18	14	39	.191	.280	.246
Grass Fields	378	89	12	1	10	41	17	66	.235	.352	.272
Artificial Turf	78	14	1	1	2	7	4	13	.179	.295	.244
April	66	14	2	1	2	5	4	15	.212	.364	.264
May	92	23	5	0	1	6	5	12	.250	.337	.289
June	82	18	0	0	2	8	4	15	.220	.293	.273
July	73	20	3	0	2	15	3	11	.274	.397	.295
August	66	9	1	1	1	3	4	15	.136	.227	.208
Sept./Oct.	77	19	2	0	4	11	1	11	.247	.429	.266
Leading Off Inn.	107	21	4	0	2	2	1	14	.196	.290	.225
Runners On	195	49	4	2	5	41	14	37	.251	.369	.304
Bases Empty	261	54	9	0	7	7	7	42	.207	.322	.239
Runners/Scor. Pos.	112	28	3	1	3	35	10	24	.250	.375	.315
Runners On/2 Out	89	17	3	0	3	15	5	23	.191	.326	.234
Scor. Pos./2 Out	57	11	3	0	2	13	5	16	.193	.351	.258
Late-Inning Pressure	83	17	3	1	2	9	3	10	.205	.337	.230
Leading Off	30	7	3	0	1	1	1	2	.233	.433	.258
Runners On	23	4	0	1	1	8	1	4	.174	.391	.200
Runners/Scor. Pos.	15	4	0	1	1	8	1	3	.267	.600	.294

RUNS BATTED IN	From 1B	From 2B	From 3B	Scoring Position
Totals	7/136	15/83	14/44	29/127
Percentage	5.1%	18.1%	31.8%	22.8%

Loves to face: Brian Holman (.429, 6-for-14, 2 HR)
Gene Nelson (.452, 14-for-31, 2 HR)
David Wells (.267, 4-for-15, 4 HR)
Hates to face: Kevin Brown (.130, 3-for-23)
Tim Leary (.056, 1-for-18)
Charlie Leibrandt (.103, 4-for-39, 1 HR, 0 BB)

Miscellaneous statistics: Ground outs-to-air outs ratio: 0.81 last season, 0.97 for career.... Grounded into 9 double plays in 84 opportunities (one per 9.3).... Drove in 11 of 21 runners from third base with less than two outs (52%).... Direction of balls hit to the outfield: 41% to left field, 32% to center, 27% to right.... Base running: Advanced from first base to third on 6 of 14 outfield singles (43%); scored from second on 7 of 10 (70%).... Made 2.60 assists per nine innings at third base, highest rate in majors.

Comments: Became the eighth different player in the last eight years to lead the Angels in home runs. His total of 12 home runs was the lowest of any team leader in the majors last season. Except for 1981, the last team whose home-run leader had fewer than 12 was the 1979 Houston Astros; Jose Cruz led them with 9 HRs.... Batted .185 in 151 at-bats from the cleanup spot. The only other major leaguer below the .200 mark with at least 100 ABs from the fourth slot was Eric Davis (.198).... Of note: Gaetti's .300 mark when batting seventh was the highest in the A.L. (minimum: 100 AB).... Was 1-for-28 against the Red Sox last season, 4-for-43 against the White Sox, and 1-for-21 against the Brewers.... On-base percentage leading off innings was the lowest in the A.L. (minimum: 100 PA).... Average of one walk every 23.1 plate appearances last season was the worst of his career.... Has averaged one walk every 20.7 plate appearances since joining the Angels, the 2d-lowest rate in franchise history, behind Willie Smith, whose walk rate was much more generous as a pitcher (3.48 per nine innings) than as a free-swinging outfielder (one per 20.9 PAs).... Career total of 343 double plays as a third baseman ranks seventh in A.L. history, two behind Sal Bando and Eddie Yost, who are tied for fifth. Dare we say it? No one will ever catch Brooks Robinson, whose total of 618 is 200 more than his closest rival, Graig Nettles.... Committed 17 errors in only 67 games at third base last season, and was moved to first base after the All-Star break.

Greg Gagne   Bats Right

Minnesota Twins	AB	H	2B	3B	HR	RBI	BB	SO	BA	SA	OBA
Season	439	108	23	0	7	39	19	83	.246	.346	.280
vs. Left-Handers	105	19	4	0	1	6	6	20	.181	.248	.225
vs. Right-Handers	334	89	19	0	6	33	13	63	.266	.377	.297
vs. Ground-Ballers	217	54	8	0	0	12	13	31	.249	.286	.291
vs. Fly-Ballers	222	54	15	0	7	27	6	52	.243	.405	.268
Home Games	219	50	12	0	1	18	10	48	.228	.297	.265
Road Games	220	58	11	0	6	21	9	35	.264	.395	.294
Grass Fields	164	45	7	0	4	16	7	30	.274	.390	.306
Artificial Turf	275	63	16	0	3	23	12	53	.229	.320	.264
April	62	17	2	0	1	4	3	6	.274	.355	.318
May	83	26	5	0	1	10	6	10	.313	.410	.360
June	79	15	4	0	3	10	3	13	.190	.354	.220
July	75	17	2	0	0	4	2	22	.227	.253	.244
August	81	21	8	0	2	10	4	15	.259	.432	.302
Sept./Oct.	59	12	2	0	0	1	1	17	.203	.237	.217
Leading Off Inn.	102	23	6	0	1	1	4	24	.225	.314	.255
Runners On	180	47	8	0	5	37	8	34	.261	.389	.298
Bases Empty	259	61	15	0	2	2	11	49	.236	.317	.267
Runners/Scor. Pos.	99	28	6	0	2	31	6	18	.283	.404	.327
Runners On/2 Out	76	16	2	0	1	9	3	14	.211	.276	.259
Scor. Pos./2 Out	41	10	1	0	0	7	3	7	.244	.268	.311
Late-Inning Pressure	57	13	1	0	0	2	1	13	.228	.246	.241
Leading Off	15	2	0	0	0	0	1	3	.133	.133	.188
Runners On	26	6	0	0	0	2	0	4	.231	.231	.231
Runners/Scor. Pos.	14	2	0	0	0	2	0	2	.143	.143	.143

RUNS BATTED IN	From 1B	From 2B	From 3B	Scoring Position
Totals	5/128	6/69	21/52	27/121
Percentage	3.9%	8.7%	40.4%	22.3%

Loves to face: Storm Davis (.462, 12-for-26, 2 HR)
Charles Nagy (.529, 9-for-17)
Mike Schooler (3-for-3, 2 2B)
Hates to face: Juan Guzman (0-for-5, 4 SO)
Walt Terrell (.143, 6-for-42)
Bob Welch (.063, 1-for-16, 2 BB)

Miscellaneous statistics: Ground outs-to-air outs ratio: 1.16 last season, 0.98 for career.... Grounded into 11 double plays in 86 opportunities (one per 7.8).... Drove in 16 of 33 runners from third base with less than two outs (48%).... Direction of balls hit to the outfield: 40% to left field, 26% to center, 35% to right.... Base running: Advanced from first base to third on 12 of 21 outfield singles (57%); scored from second on 13 of 14 (93%), 5th-highest rate in A.L.... Made 3.44 assists per nine innings at shortstop, 2d-highest rate in majors.

Comments: Gagne was Minnesota's opening-day starter at shortstop in each of the last seven seasons. He leaves Minneapolis having played 1112 games at shortstop for the Twins, the second highest total in the history of the Washington/Minnesota franchise; Gagne passed Zoilo Versalles last September. George McBride's total of 1444 games at shortstop for the original Washington Senators is suddenly safe—for the time being.... Has hit between 7 and 14 home runs in each of the last seven seasons. No Royals shortstop has ever hit more than 10 homers in a season. U.L. Washington hit 10 in 1982; Kurt Stillwell hit 10 in 1988.... Gagne has hit four postseason home runs, the most ever by a shortstop. Jay Bell, Bert Campaneris, and Alan Trammell each have three.... Last season's batting average vs. left-handers was a career low; his mark vs. right-handers a career high. He had batted at least .280 against left-handed pitchers in each of the previous four seasons. Career breakdown: .261 vs. LHP, .244 vs. RHP.... Slugging percentage was his lowest since his rookie year (1985).... Career average of 48.8 percent driving in runners from third base with less than two outs.... Has batted above .300 in May, and below .200 in June in each of the last two seasons.... Has never walked more than 30 times in a season. The only active player with more games than Gagne who's never topped the 30-walk mark: Luis Salazar.... Committed 18 errors last season, compared to nine in 1991.

Jim Gantner   Bats Left

Milwaukee Brewers	AB	H	2B	3B	HR	RBI	BB	SO	BA	SA	OBA
Season	256	63	12	1	1	18	12	17	.246	.313	.278
vs. Left-Handers	34	7	1	0	0	5	5	0	.206	.235	.300
vs. Right-Handers	222	56	11	1	1	13	7	17	.252	.324	.274
vs. Ground-Ballers	135	37	7	1	0	11	5	10	.274	.341	.296
vs. Fly-Ballers	121	26	5	0	1	7	7	7	.215	.281	.258
Home Games	136	33	6	0	1	10	7	8	.243	.309	.278
Road Games	120	30	6	1	0	8	5	9	.250	.317	.278
Grass Fields	209	47	9	0	1	13	11	15	.225	.282	.262
Artificial Turf	47	16	3	1	0	5	1	2	.340	.447	.347
April	52	15	1	1	0	4	8	4	.288	.346	.383
May	67	13	5	0	0	3	1	6	.194	.269	.203
June	34	7	1	0	0	2	0	2	.206	.235	.200
July	45	13	2	0	0	4	2	3	.289	.333	.319
August	39	10	2	0	1	4	1	1	.256	.385	.275
Sept./Oct.	19	5	1	0	0	1	0	1	.263	.316	.263
Leading Off Inn.	56	14	2	0	1	1	3	4	.250	.339	.288
Runners On	119	32	7	1	0	17	5	6	.269	.345	.294
Bases Empty	137	31	5	0	1	1	7	11	.226	.285	.264
Runners/Scor. Pos.	62	15	4	1	0	15	4	4	.242	.339	.279
Runners On/2 Out	44	11	5	0	0	5	4	4	.250	.364	.313
Scor. Pos./2 Out	27	5	3	0	0	4	3	3	.185	.296	.267
Late-Inning Pressure	45	11	2	0	1	1	5	3	.244	.356	.320
Leading Off	13	4	0	0	1	1	3	0	.308	.538	.438
Runners On	18	3	0	0	0	1	2	2	.167	.167	.250
Runners/Scor. Pos.	10	1	0	0	0	0	2	1	.100	.100	.250

RUNS BATTED IN	From 1B	From 2B	From 3B	Scoring Position
Totals	2/85	6/47	9/26	15/73
Percentage	2.4%	12.8%	34.6%	20.5%

Loves to face: Tom Gordon (.423, 11-for-26)
Joe Grahe (.500, 4-for-8, 1 2B, 1 HR)
Frank Viola (.375, 15-for-40, 1 HR, 0 BB, 0 SO)
Hates to face: Mark Gubicza (.163, 7-for-43, 0 BB)
Bobby Thigpen (0-for-11)
Bobby Witt (.156, 7-for-45)

Miscellaneous statistics: Ground outs-to-air outs ratio: 1.16 last season, 1.38 for career.... Grounded into 9 double plays in 64 opportunities (one per 7.1).... Drove in 7 of 13 runners from third base with less than two outs (54%).... Direction of balls hit to the outfield: 45% to left field, 31% to center, 24% to right.... Base running: Advanced from first base to third on 3 of 11 outfield singles (27%); scored from second on 4 of 8 (50%).... Made 3.17 assists per nine innings at second base.

Comments: Gantner, Robin Yount, and Paul Molitor are the fourth trio of teammates in major league history to each reach the 1800-game mark without playing for another team. Others to do so: Carl Furillo, Gil Hodges, Pee Wee Reese, and Duke Snider with the Dodgers (wow—four of them!); Ernie Banks, Billy Williams, and Ron Santo with the Cubs; George Brett, Frank White, and Willie Wilson with the Royals. Note that none of the groups finished their careers together with their original clubs. Nor will the Brewers' trio, with Molitor having gone north of the border.... Gantner's career totals trail those of both Yount and Molitor in almost every offensive category. An exception: Gantner has been hit by 52 pitches, the most in franchise history. Yount ranks second (43), Molitor third (34).... Has hit for a higher average against ground-ball pitchers than he has against fly-ballers in each of the last seven seasons.... Has hit only three home runs over the last five seasons, all solo shots vs. right-handed pitchers. Of his 47 career homers, only two have been hit against southpaws (both in 1983).... Total of 34 at-bats vs. left-handers without a strikeout wasn't even close to the _Player Analysis_ record held by Marty Barrett, who had 104 at-bats vs. lefties without a strikeout in 1989. (But it was Gantner's lowest AB total vs. LHP since 1979.)... Career total of 1801 games is the most of any active player who has never appeared in an All-Star game. Only two others have as many as 1500 games: Ken Oberkfell (1602) and Rafael Ramirez (1539).

Dan Gladden
Bats Right

Detroit Tigers	AB	H	2B	3B	HR	RBI	BB	SO	BA	SA	OBA
Season	417	106	20	1	7	42	30	64	.254	.357	.304
vs. Left-Handers	124	35	8	1	4	18	12	17	.282	.460	.341
vs. Right-Handers	293	71	12	0	3	24	18	47	.242	.314	.288
vs. Ground-Ballers	199	59	9	1	5	28	14	30	.296	.427	.341
vs. Fly-Ballers	218	47	11	0	2	14	16	34	.216	.294	.270
Home Games	177	40	9	1	3	18	17	26	.226	.339	.291
Road Games	240	66	11	0	4	24	13	38	.275	.371	.314
Grass Fields	354	83	17	1	4	27	27	53	.234	.322	.286
Artificial Turf	63	23	3	0	3	15	3	11	.365	.556	.400
April	85	16	1	1	2	9	6	8	.188	.294	.242
May	25	12	4	0	1	5	0	2	.480	.760	.500
June	60	21	4	0	0	3	6	7	.350	.417	.412
July	75	16	4	0	0	6	6	14	.213	.267	.268
August	93	26	3	0	4	15	7	17	.280	.441	.324
Sept./Oct.	79	15	4	0	0	4	5	16	.190	.241	.235
Leading Off Inn.	102	25	8	0	1	1	10	13	.245	.353	.319
Runners On	190	53	7	1	5	40	13	24	.279	.405	.317
Bases Empty	227	53	13	0	2	2	17	40	.233	.317	.293
Runners/Scor. Pos.	114	30	4	1	4	38	6	14	.263	.421	.288
Runners On/2 Out	81	16	3	1	3	20	6	12	.198	.370	.253
Scor. Pos./2 Out	58	11	2	1	3	20	4	8	.190	.414	.242
Late-Inning Pressure	64	19	4	0	1	7	6	8	.297	.406	.352
Leading Off	20	4	1	0	0	0	1	5	.200	.250	.238
Runners On	26	8	2	0	1	7	3	2	.308	.500	.367
Runners/Scor. Pos.	15	3	1	0	0	5	2	1	.200	.267	.278

RUNS BATTED IN	From 1B	From 2B	From 3B	Scoring Position
Totals	5/149	16/95	14/49	30/144
Percentage	3.4%	16.8%	28.6%	20.8%

Loves to face: Mike Flanagan (.435, 10-for-23, 1 HR)
Jaime Navarro (.533, 8-for-15)
Curt Young (.348, 8-for-23, 2 HR)

Hates to face: Melido Perez (.152, 5-for-33)
Jeff Russell (.125, 4-for-32, 0 BB)
Bobby Witt (.147, 5-for-34)

Miscellaneous statistics: Ground outs-to-air outs ratio: 0.66 last season, 0.94 for career.... Grounded into 10 double plays in 99 opportunities (one per 10).... Drove in 8 of 20 runners from third base with less than two outs (40%).... Direction of balls hit to the outfield: 36% to left field, 38% to center, 27% to right.... Base running: Advanced from first base to third on 8 of 25 outfield singles (32%); scored from second on 7 of 11 (64%).... Made 2.42 putouts per nine innings in left field, 3d-highest rate in A.L.

Comments: Averaged more than 25 stolen bases over the previous eight seasons for the Giants and Twins, but stole only four bases for the Tigers in 1992. His career-low on-base percentage didn't help.... Went from the Metrodome (the extra-base-hit capital of North America) to Tiger Stadium (the hardest place to hit a triple, now that Memorial Stadium is history). He fell from nine triples in 1991 to only one last season.... Batting average against ground-ball pitchers has been at least 50 points higher than his mark vs. fly-ballers in each of his last four seasons. His breakdown since 1989: .304 vs. groundballers, .237 vs. fly-ballers. Over the same period of time the difference in his average against left- and right-handed pitchers is only 15 points (.279 and .264, respectively).... Batted under .200 in both April and September in each of the last two years, while posting a .285 average from May through August for that period.... Batting average in the ultimate clutch category—two outs and runners in scoring position in Late-Inning Pressure Situations—has been below .160 nine times in 10 seasons in the majors. Career average of .128 is 5th lowest since 1975 (minimum: 50 AB), behind Wayne Gross (.107), Tony Bernazard (.113), Barry Bonds (.118), and Jose Lind (.120).... Became the sixth different opening-day starter in the last six years for the Tigers in left field. His predecessors: Larry Herndon, Pat Sheridan, Fred Lynn, Gary Ward, Lloyd Moseby.

Leo Gomez
Bats Right

Baltimore Orioles	AB	H	2B	3B	HR	RBI	BB	SO	BA	SA	OBA
Season	468	124	24	0	17	64	63	78	.265	.425	.356
vs. Left-Handers	104	26	7	0	4	17	23	17	.250	.433	.391
vs. Right-Handers	364	98	17	0	13	47	40	61	.269	.423	.345
vs. Ground-Ballers	256	79	13	0	11	36	27	39	.309	.488	.381
vs. Fly-Ballers	212	45	11	0	6	28	36	39	.212	.349	.328
Home Games	226	59	10	0	6	25	32	34	.261	.385	.358
Road Games	242	65	14	0	11	39	31	44	.269	.463	.355
Grass Fields	381	101	18	0	15	55	48	58	.265	.430	.352
Artificial Turf	87	23	6	0	2	9	15	20	.264	.402	.375
April	66	17	5	0	0	7	10	6	.258	.333	.351
May	76	26	5	0	4	12	8	19	.342	.566	.398
June	79	22	3	0	1	8	14	9	.278	.354	.394
July	92	22	5	0	5	18	11	21	.239	.457	.333
August	84	20	3	0	6	12	15	17	.238	.488	.373
Sept./Oct.	71	17	3	0	1	7	5	6	.239	.324	.282
Leading Off Inn.	92	25	3	0	2	2	10	16	.272	.370	.356
Runners On	231	55	10	0	8	55	28	38	.238	.385	.326
Bases Empty	237	69	14	0	9	9	35	40	.291	.464	.387
Runners/Scor. Pos.	119	27	5	0	5	47	18	21	.227	.395	.320
Runners On/2 Out	96	26	6	0	5	26	8	11	.271	.490	.327
Scor. Pos./2 Out	52	14	3	0	2	19	5	7	.269	.442	.333
Late-Inning Pressure	61	13	3	0	4	10	5	11	.213	.459	.269
Leading Off	17	4	1	0	1	1	2	3	.235	.471	.316
Runners On	26	3	1	0	1	7	1	5	.115	.269	.143
Runners/Scor. Pos.	16	2	1	0	0	5	1	5	.125	.188	.167

RUNS BATTED IN	From 1B	From 2B	From 3B	Scoring Position
Totals	12/192	13/93	22/54	35/147
Percentage	6.3%	14.0%	40.7%	23.8%

Loves to face: Kevin Appier (.500, 7-for-14, 1 HR)
Chuck Finley (.750, 6-for-8, 1 HR)
Donn Pall (.800, 4-for-5, 1 2B, 2 HR, 1 SO)

Hates to face: Mark Leiter (.100, 1-for-10, 5 SO)
Nolan Ryan (0-for-9, 5 SO)
Julio Valera (0-for-7)

Miscellaneous statistics: Ground outs-to-air outs ratio: 0.58 last season (5th lowest in A.L.), 0.62 for career.... Grounded into 14 double plays in 143 opportunities (one per 10).... Drove in 15 of 32 runners from third base with less than two outs (47%).... Direction of balls hit to the outfield: 41% to left field, 34% to center, 25% to right.... Base running: Advanced from first base to third on 11 of 34 outfield singles (32%); scored from second on 8 of 14 (57%).... Made 1.81 assists per nine innings at third base, 3d-lowest rate in A.L.

Comments: Raised his batting average and his walk and home-run totals last season while cutting down on his strikeouts (.233, 16 HR, 40 BB, 82 SO in 1991). Only five other A.L. players did so, including two of his Orioles teammates: Chris Hoiles and Billy Ripken. (In case you were wondering: Baltimore's hitting instructor is Greg Biagini, who managed three seasons at Rochester before joining the O's last season, his first in the majors.)... Led the majors with 10 home runs and 44 RBIs from the seventh spot in the batting order.... Orioles third basemen combined for 19 home runs last season, 3d most in the league, behind Texas (25) and New York (22).... The only infield unit in the league to start at least half of its team's games last season was Gomez, the Ripkens, and Randy Milligan, who started 81 games together.... The Orioles posted a 78–58 record with Gomez starting at third base, but were only 9–15 with Tim Hulett there.... Career batting average of .197 in Late-Inning Pressure Situations, even worse with runners in scoring position (.129), worse still with two outs (.067).... Hasn't hit a home run in 102 career at-bats in April. His rate is one every 24 ABs after that.... Error rate at third base increased from one every 36 chances in 1991 to one every 21 chances last season.... The most pronounced fly-ball hitter on the Orioles last season, with a ratio of 0.58 ground outs-to-air outs. Career batting averages reflect it: .271 vs. ground-ball pitchers, .228 vs. fly-ballers.

Rene Gonzales   Bats Right

California Angels	AB	H	2B	3B	HR	RBI	BB	SO	BA	SA	OBA
Season	329	91	17	1	7	38	41	46	.277	.398	.363
vs. Left-Handers	71	19	3	0	3	11	10	11	.268	.437	.369
vs. Right-Handers	258	72	14	1	4	27	31	35	.279	.388	.361
vs. Ground-Ballers	162	44	9	0	3	14	18	25	.272	.383	.348
vs. Fly-Ballers	167	47	8	1	4	24	23	21	.281	.413	.376
Home Games	168	50	12	0	6	24	22	22	.298	.476	.380
Road Games	161	41	5	1	1	14	19	24	.255	.317	.344
Grass Fields	272	81	15	1	7	35	36	36	.298	.438	.383
Artificial Turf	57	10	2	0	0	3	5	10	.175	.211	.266
April	23	7	2	0	3	6	8	3	.304	.783	.484
May	85	23	2	1	3	13	8	14	.271	.424	.333
June	94	23	8	0	1	10	9	11	.245	.362	.324
July	89	24	3	0	0	6	13	12	.270	.303	.359
August	38	14	2	0	0	3	3	6	.368	.421	.442
Sept./Oct.	0	0	0	0	0	0	0	0	.000	.000	.000
Leading Off Inn.	76	24	5	0	1	1	7	13	.316	.421	.388
Runners On	122	31	3	1	4	35	21	17	.254	.393	.366
Bases Empty	207	60	14	0	3	3	20	29	.290	.401	.361
Runners/Scor. Pos.	65	21	2	1	3	33	15	9	.323	.523	.444
Runners On/2 Out	47	14	2	1	1	16	12	6	.298	.447	.441
Scor. Pos./2 Out	32	11	2	1	1	16	9	5	.344	.563	.488
Late-Inning Pressure	53	8	1	0	1	6	9	9	.151	.226	.274
Leading Off	14	1	0	0	0	0	0	3	.071	.071	.071
Runners On	17	4	0	0	1	6	7	3	.235	.412	.458
Runners/Scor. Pos.	10	3	0	0	0	4	4	2	.300	.300	.500

RUNS BATTED IN	From 1B	From 2B	From 3B	Scoring Position
Totals	4/92	12/46	15/28	27/74
Percentage	4.3%	26.1%	53.6%	36.5%

Loves to face: Alex Fernandez (.800, 4-for-5)
Randy Johnson (.500, 5-for-10, 1 HR)
Dave Stieb (.400, 4-for-10, 1 HR)

Hates to face: Roger Clemens (.125, 2-for-16)
Terry Leach (0-for-10)
Bob Welch (0-for-11)

Miscellaneous statistics: Ground outs-to-air outs ratio: 1.42 last season, 1.54 for career.... Grounded into 17 double plays in 72 opportunities (one per 4.2), worst rate in majors.... Drove in 9 of 14 runners from third base with less than two outs (64%).... Direction of balls hit to the outfield: 37% to left field, 29% to center, 34% to right.... Base running: Advanced from first base to third on 11 of 23 outfield singles (48%); scored from second on 10 of 13 (77%).... Made 2.31 assists per nine innings at third base.

Comments: Although he played in parts of seven seasons from 1984 to 1991, he had never before accumulated as many as 250 at-bats in a season. He hadn't hit higher than .217 since 1987. The only other player since 1980 with four consecutive sub-.220 seasons (minimum: 100 AB) was Gorman Thomas (1983–86). Only three players have had longer streaks during the expansion era: Mike Ryan (8 years, 1965–72), Elrod Hendricks (5, 1972–76); and Ray Oyler (5, 1965–69).... Things looked bleak, but with a change of scenery last season, he posted career highs in home-run and walk rates, as well as batting, slugging, and on-base averages.... Played mostly third base last season, after playing the majority of his games at shortstop in 1991 (for the Blue Jays) and at second base in 1990 (for the Orioles).... Percentage of runners driven in from scoring position was the highest of any A.L. player with at least 50 opportunities last season.... Had played every inning of 42 consecutive games from June 26 through August 10, when a broken left forearm ended his season.... Hit three homers in 71 at-bats against left-handers, after having only one homer against them in 252 previous career at-bats.... Batted .097 with runners in scoring position in 1991 (3-for-31).... Career average is one walk every 9.3 plate appearances, but he has no walks in 36 career PAs leading off innings in Late-Inning Pressure Situations.... One of 21 men to play for both the Expos and the Blue Jays; of them, only Ron Fairly played at least 100 games for both Canadian clubs.

Juan Gonzalez   Bats Right

Texas Rangers	AB	H	2B	3B	HR	RBI	BB	SO	BA	SA	OBA
Season	584	152	24	2	43	109	35	143	.260	.529	.304
vs. Left-Handers	158	40	6	0	8	28	12	43	.253	.443	.302
vs. Right-Handers	426	112	18	2	35	81	23	100	.263	.561	.304
vs. Ground-Ballers	253	69	11	1	19	38	15	62	.273	.549	.316
vs. Fly-Ballers	331	83	13	1	24	71	20	81	.251	.514	.294
Home Games	294	78	18	2	19	50	15	83	.265	.534	.305
Road Games	290	74	6	0	24	59	20	60	.255	.524	.303
Grass Fields	493	126	21	2	36	87	29	125	.256	.525	.298
Artificial Turf	91	26	3	0	7	22	6	18	.286	.549	.337
April	90	24	3	0	4	15	5	17	.267	.433	.299
May	103	26	5	1	3	10	5	21	.252	.408	.284
June	96	28	2	1	11	24	10	31	.292	.677	.352
July	95	22	3	0	8	21	1	24	.232	.516	.248
August	104	27	6	0	12	25	11	28	.260	.663	.330
Sept./Oct.	96	25	5	0	5	14	3	22	.260	.469	.304
Leading Off Inn.	116	26	5	0	7	7	4	30	.224	.448	.268
Runners On	283	70	10	0	16	82	17	73	.247	.452	.285
Bases Empty	301	82	14	2	27	27	18	70	.272	.601	.322
Runners/Scor. Pos.	178	45	7	0	10	69	10	47	.253	.461	.281
Runners On/2 Out	140	35	5	0	8	37	9	36	.250	.457	.300
Scor. Pos./2 Out	89	23	4	0	7	34	5	23	.258	.539	.298
Late-Inning Pressure	85	26	4	0	9	14	7	24	.306	.671	.366
Leading Off	23	8	1	0	2	2	0	5	.348	.652	.375
Runners On	28	7	1	0	3	8	4	5	.250	.607	.344
Runners/Scor. Pos.	13	2	0	0	1	4	4	2	.154	.385	.353

RUNS BATTED IN	From 1B	From 2B	From 3B	Scoring Position
Totals	14/204	28/137	24/74	52/211
Percentage	6.9%	20.4%	32.4%	24.6%

Loves to face: Jim Abbott (.588, 10-for-17, 1 HR)
Tom Gordon (.438, 7-for-16, 2 2B, 2 3B, 1 HR)
Steve Olin (.600, 6-for-10, 2 2B, 2 HR)

Hates to face: Chris Bosio (.067, 1-for-15)
Jimmy Key (.125, 2-for-16)
Mike Moore (.050, 1-for-20, 1 2B)

Miscellaneous statistics: Ground outs-to-air outs ratio: 0.85 last season, 0.83 for career.... Grounded into 16 double plays in 112 opportunities (one per 7.0).... Drove in 18 of 38 runners from third base with less than two outs (47%).... Direction of balls hit to the outfield: 48% to left field, 32% to center, 20% to right.... Base running: Advanced from first base to third on 10 of 32 outfield singles (31%); scored from second on 6 of 9 (67%).... Made 2.72 putouts per nine innings in center field, 3d-lowest rate in A.L.

Comments: Became the 5th-youngest player to hit 40 home runs in a season. Those ahead of him are all Hall of Famers: Mel Ott, Eddie Mathews, Johnny Bench, and Joe DiMaggio; so are the next five behind him: Mathews again, Killebrew, Reggie, Mays, and Aaron.... Gonzalez and Ken Griffey, Jr., both drove in 100 runs in a season twice before their 23d birthdays. Only eight other players in major league history have done that, and all but one of them are in the Hall: Ty Cobb, Joe DiMaggio, Jimmie Foxx, Al Kaline, Eddie Mathews, Mel Ott, Hal Trosky, and Ted Williams.... Gonzalez has 147 extra-base hits in 346 career games, the 30th-highest rate in major league history. Just above him, Barry Bonds and Jose Canseco; just below, Ralph Kiner and Frank Robinson.... Scored only 77 runs last season despite hitting 43 homers. The only other player to hit 40-plus HRs and score fewer than 80 runs: Frank Howard (44 and 79 in 1968).... His total of nine LIPS homers last season was three shy of the record (since 1975) held by George Foster (12 in 1978). Others with 10 in a season: Tony Armas (1982) and Willie Stargell (1979).... Career average of one home run every 12.2 at-bats in Late-Inning Pressure Situations (15 HR in 183 LIPS AB) is the highest in the 18 years we've kept track (minimum: 10 HR).... Has a career average of one home run every 14.5 at-bats from April through August, but only one every 32.0 at-bats in September and October, with a career batting average of .219 in those months.

Craig Grebeck — Bats Right

Chicago White Sox	AB	H	2B	3B	HR	RBI	BB	SO	BA	SA	OBA
Season	287	77	21	2	3	35	30	34	.268	.387	.341
vs. Left-Handers	86	25	8	0	0	9	6	8	.291	.384	.344
vs. Right-Handers	201	52	13	2	3	26	24	26	.259	.388	.339
vs. Ground-Ballers	146	39	11	2	0	13	13	19	.267	.370	.327
vs. Fly-Ballers	141	38	10	0	3	22	17	15	.270	.404	.354
Home Games	134	36	11	1	2	23	18	13	.269	.410	.357
Road Games	153	41	10	1	1	12	12	21	.268	.366	.325
Grass Fields	246	71	18	2	3	32	26	29	.289	.415	.360
Artificial Turf	41	6	3	0	0	3	4	5	.146	.220	.222
April	23	5	2	0	1	6	2	2	.217	.435	.280
May	74	19	6	0	0	8	11	7	.257	.338	.356
June	94	25	7	1	1	7	8	12	.266	.394	.320
July	91	28	6	1	1	14	8	12	.308	.429	.373
August	5	0	0	0	0	0	1	1	.000	.000	.167
Sept./Oct.	0	0	0	0	0	0	0	0	.000	.000	.000
Leading Off Inn.	75	20	4	0	1	1	6	7	.267	.360	.321
Runners On	128	38	13	1	2	34	9	18	.297	.461	.345
Bases Empty	159	39	8	1	1	1	21	16	.245	.327	.337
Runners/Scor. Pos.	68	18	7	0	0	27	7	13	.265	.368	.338
Runners On/2 Out	58	17	6	1	2	17	5	8	.293	.534	.349
Scor. Pos./2 Out	33	7	3	0	0	10	4	7	.212	.303	.297
Late-Inning Pressure	49	10	2	0	1	4	5	8	.204	.306	.278
Leading Off	11	1	0	0	1	1	0	2	.091	.364	.091
Runners On	24	5	1	0	0	3	3	5	.208	.250	.296
Runners/Scor. Pos.	15	2	1	0	0	3	2	5	.133	.200	.235

RUNS BATTED IN	From 1B	From 2B	From 3B	Scoring Position
Totals	7/90	11/59	14/27	25/86
Percentage	7.8%	18.6%	51.9%	29.1%

Loves to face: Mike Magnante (.429, 3-for-7, 3 2B, 1 BB)
Kenny Rogers (.750, 3-for-4, 1 2B, 2 HR)
Matt Young (.571, 8-for-14, 4 SO)

Hates to face: Erik Hanson (.091, 1-for-11)
Randy Johnson (0-for-13)
Mark Langston (0-for-9)

Miscellaneous statistics: Ground outs-to-air outs ratio: 0.72 last season, 0.66 for career.... Grounded into 5 double plays in 62 opportunities (one per 12).... Drove in 9 of 14 runners from third base with less than two outs (64%).... Direction of balls hit to the outfield: 46% to left field, 26% to center, 28% to right.... Base running: Advanced from first base to third on 9 of 17 outfield singles (53%); scored from second on 4 of 7 (57%).... Made 3.42 assists per nine innings at shortstop, 3d-highest rate in majors.

Comments: The Chisox infield unit of Robin Ventura, Grebeck, Sax, and Frank Thomas started 72 games together last season, 2d most of any A.L. combination. (See the Leo Gomez comments for the top unit.)... Acquisition of Steve Sax appeared to leave Grebeck as the White Sox's odd man out. But he got his chance in late April, when Ozzie Guillen, who had started 1042 of 1146 games since joining the White Sox in 1985, tore ligaments in his right knee. The only other shortstops who started as many as 1000 games during that same period: Cal Ripken (1144), Tony Fernandez (1074), and Ozzie Smith (1050). Guillen had never missed more than six starts in a row; in 1991, he missed consecutive starts only once (a 4-game stretch in September). Only as a rookie did Guillen miss as many as 20 starts in one season.... Although he played 19 fewer games last season than he did in 1991, Grebeck came to the plate 65 more times in 1992. In 1991, he started only 62 games, but entered 17 games as a defensive replacement, and nine as a pinch-runner. Last season, he made 85 starts, while appearing only twice as a defensive replacement, and once as a pinch-runner.... Played 85 games at shortstop, driving in 35 runs. White Sox shortstops had 64 RBIs, 4th most in the majors behind Detroit (91), Cincinnati (81), and Baltimore (72).... There were 14 active major leaguers listed at 5'8" or shorter in their club's media guide last season. Of those 14, five played in Chicago: Grebeck, Warren Newson, Joey Cora, Doug Dascenzo, and Tim Raines.

Ken Griffey Jr. — Bats Left

Seattle Mariners	AB	H	2B	3B	HR	RBI	BB	SO	BA	SA	OBA
Season	565	174	39	4	27	103	44	67	.308	.535	.361
vs. Left-Handers	173	62	10	0	12	35	11	23	.358	.624	.413
vs. Right-Handers	392	112	29	4	15	68	33	44	.286	.495	.339
vs. Ground-Ballers	281	90	23	4	11	51	21	25	.320	.548	.371
vs. Fly-Ballers	284	84	16	0	16	52	23	42	.296	.521	.352
Home Games	277	87	22	2	16	51	24	25	.314	.581	.369
Road Games	288	87	17	2	11	52	22	42	.302	.490	.354
Grass Fields	226	70	14	2	9	43	20	31	.310	.509	.368
Artificial Turf	339	104	25	2	18	60	24	36	.307	.552	.357
April	78	20	4	0	2	12	8	7	.256	.385	.322
May	100	34	9	0	7	19	4	14	.340	.640	.368
June	48	12	3	0	5	13	6	8	.250	.625	.345
July	117	38	9	1	4	17	6	15	.325	.521	.360
August	108	35	8	1	6	21	13	11	.324	.583	.402
Sept./Oct.	114	35	6	2	3	21	7	12	.307	.474	.352
Leading Off Inn.	111	31	6	1	5	5	9	10	.279	.486	.333
Runners On	278	97	23	1	17	93	27	30	.349	.622	.406
Bases Empty	287	77	16	3	10	10	17	37	.268	.449	.316
Runners/Scor. Pos.	150	50	11	1	10	76	25	16	.333	.620	.428
Runners On/2 Out	75	26	8	1	4	27	12	6	.347	.640	.437
Scor. Pos./2 Out	48	14	5	1	3	24	11	2	.292	.625	.424
Late-Inning Pressure	84	30	7	0	3	10	12	14	.357	.548	.443
Leading Off	24	7	2	0	1	1	2	4	.292	.500	.346
Runners On	36	11	4	0	1	8	8	4	.306	.500	.432
Runners/Scor. Pos.	18	5	2	0	1	7	7	2	.278	.556	.480

RUNS BATTED IN	From 1B	From 2B	From 3B	Scoring Position
Totals	18/194	32/129	26/46	58/175
Percentage	9.3%	24.8%	56.5%	33.1%

Loves to face: Scott Erickson (.526, 10-for-19)
Tom Gordon (.400, 8-for-20, 3 HR)
Charles Nagy (.412, 7-for-17, 2 2B, 1 3B, 2 HR)

Hates to face: Mike Boddicker (.154, 4-for-26)
Scott Radinsky (0-for-9, 5 SO)
Bob Welch (.154, 4-for-26)

Miscellaneous statistics: Ground outs-to-air outs ratio: 1.07 last season, 1.04 for career.... Grounded into 15 double plays in 155 opportunities (one per 10).... Drove in 19 of 30 runners from third base with less than two outs (63%).... Direction of balls hit to the outfield: 34% to left, 30% to center, 36% to right.... Base running: Advanced from first base to third on 14 of 23 outfield singles (61%); scored from second on 9 of 13 (69%).... Made 2.72 putouts per nine innings in center field.

Comments: Hit the 75th home run of his career on July 9, becoming the 4th-youngest player to reach that milestone. The youngest: Mel Ott, Tony Conigliaro, and Eddie Mathews. Griffey was one day younger than Johnny Bench at the time of his 75th homer.... With 578 major league games already under his belt, Griffey is nevertheless younger than 266 of the 291 rookies who played in the majors last season. He's more than two years younger than either of last season's Rookies of the Year, and he would have been the youngest player to appear for eight different teams last season. Only four players had played more games by their 23d birthdays: Robin Yount (683), Mel Ott (677), Ed Kranepool (648), and Freddie Lindstrom (587).... Over the last 18 years, only two left-handed batters have posted higher career marks against left-handed pitchers: Tony Gwynn (.311) and Rod Carew (.310).... Career batting average is slightly higher against left-handers than against right-handers (.305–.299), but slugging percentage is higher vs. right-handers (.500–.480).... Career average of .311 with one home run every 21.6 at-bats at the Kingdome, compared to .292, one HR per 29.3 at-bats on the road.... Ken's dad was one of many Yankees to have played with Lou Piniella as a teammate and for him as a manager.... Senior played the first six years of his career under Sparky Anderson, but Junior will be playing under his third different manager in as many years.... Posted both the lowest strikeout and walk rates of his career last season.

Kelly Gruber   Bats Right

Toronto Blue Jays	AB	H	2B	3B	HR	RBI	BB	SO	BA	SA	OBA
Season	446	102	16	3	11	43	26	72	.229	.352	.275
vs. Left-Handers	107	26	5	1	3	10	7	20	.243	.393	.291
vs. Right-Handers	339	76	11	2	8	33	19	52	.224	.339	.270
vs. Ground-Ballers	229	60	10	1	7	27	12	34	.262	.406	.298
vs. Fly-Ballers	217	42	6	2	4	16	14	38	.194	.295	.251
Home Games	211	51	8	3	7	28	11	39	.242	.408	.284
Road Games	235	51	8	0	4	15	15	33	.217	.302	.267
Grass Fields	188	44	7	0	4	15	13	23	.234	.335	.286
Artificial Turf	258	58	9	3	7	28	13	49	.225	.364	.266
April	69	17	6	1	3	10	4	10	.246	.493	.284
May	96	24	4	1	5	13	6	16	.250	.469	.298
June	73	14	1	0	0	4	2	9	.192	.205	.213
July	24	6	0	0	1	3	2	5	.250	.375	.321
August	77	15	1	1	0	1	5	14	.195	.234	.262
Sept./Oct.	107	26	4	0	2	12	7	18	.243	.336	.287
Leading Off Inn.	96	21	4	1	0	0	2	15	.219	.281	.242
Runners On	201	49	8	2	6	38	12	35	.244	.393	.284
Bases Empty	245	53	8	1	5	5	14	37	.216	.318	.267
Runners/Scor. Pos.	113	27	5	0	3	30	6	22	.239	.363	.274
Runners On/2 Out	78	19	5	1	1	9	7	15	.244	.372	.314
Scor. Pos./2 Out	46	8	4	0	0	6	4	9	.174	.261	.255
Late-Inning Pressure	56	9	4	0	0	2	3	14	.161	.232	.203
Leading Off	11	2	1	0	0	0	1	4	.182	.273	.250
Runners On	29	3	2	0	0	2	0	7	.103	.172	.103
Runners/Scor. Pos.	14	2	2	0	0	2	0	5	.143	.286	.143

RUNS BATTED IN	From 1B	From 2B	From 3B	Scoring Position
Totals	7/147	11/91	14/44	25/135
Percentage	4.8%	12.1%	31.8%	18.5%

Loves to face: Scott Bankhead (.421, 8-for-19, 1 HR)
Charles Nagy (.400, 8-for-20, 3 2B, 2 HR)
Bob Welch (.412, 7-for-17, 1 HR)

Hates to face: Greg A. Harris (.125, 3-for-24)
Jaime Navarro (.100, 2-for-20)
Nolan Ryan (.091, 2-for-22)

Miscellaneous statistics: Ground outs-to-air outs ratio: 0.83 last season, 1.01 for career. . . . Grounded into 14 double plays in 97 opportunities (one per 6.9). . . . Drove in 12 of 25 runners from third base with less than two outs (48%). . . . Direction of balls hit to the outfield: 34% to left field, 35% to center, 32% to right. . . . Base running: Advanced from first base to third on 8 of 15 outfield singles (53%); scored from second on 11 of 12 (92%). . . . Made 1.89 assists per nine innings at third base.

Comments: His totals have declined in each of the last two seasons in all of the following categories: runs (92, 58, 42); doubles (36, 18, 16); home runs (31, 20, 11); RBIs (118, 65, 43); walks (48, 31, 26); stolen bases (14, 12, 7); batting average (.274, .252, .229); slugging average (.512, .443, .352); and on-base percentage (.330, .308, .275). . . . Good news: Of the 81 other players with similar two-year streaks, only Barry Bonnell added a third year. . . . Blue Jays third basemen combined for a .230 batting average, the lowest of any team in the American League. The Cubs were the only N.L. team with a lower average from that position (.219). . . . He was the only Toronto player to play every inning of the Jays' 22 postseason games in 1989, 1991, and 1992. . . . Had only one hit in 19 at-bats against the Angels last season. He has only two home runs and 17 RBIs in 211 career at-bats against them, his lowest run production totals against any club. If you can't beat 'em, join 'em. . . . Hit a game-tying home run in the eighth inning of the third game of the World Series on the at-bat after he had broken the record for most consecutive hitless at-bats in a single postseason. The old record (22 AB) was shared by Dal Maxvill (1968) and Dave Winfield (1981). . . . Gruber also hit a decisive home run in the second game of the A.L.C.S., with the Jays already down a game to Oakland. The agate for his 1992 postseason says .098 (4-for-41), but he sure made the most of it.

Mel Hall   Bats Left

New York Yankees	AB	H	2B	3B	HR	RBI	BB	SO	BA	SA	OBA
Season	583	163	36	3	15	81	29	53	.280	.429	.310
vs. Left-Handers	179	46	8	1	2	18	8	23	.257	.346	.284
vs. Right-Handers	404	117	28	2	13	63	21	30	.290	.465	.322
vs. Ground-Ballers	259	76	13	2	6	37	8	27	.293	.429	.309
vs. Fly-Ballers	324	87	23	1	9	44	21	26	.269	.429	.311
Home Games	285	70	12	0	7	35	19	19	.246	.361	.292
Road Games	298	93	24	3	8	46	10	34	.312	.493	.328
Grass Fields	495	135	29	0	13	68	27	41	.273	.410	.308
Artificial Turf	88	28	7	3	2	13	2	12	.318	.534	.326
April	80	22	6	0	5	18	2	6	.275	.538	.286
May	112	27	10	1	1	14	4	14	.241	.375	.269
June	108	29	9	0	5	13	4	10	.269	.491	.287
July	88	29	4	0	2	12	9	5	.330	.443	.388
August	105	31	2	1	1	11	5	8	.295	.362	.327
Sept./Oct.	90	25	5	1	1	13	5	10	.278	.389	.313
Leading Off Inn.	120	31	10	0	7	7	4	11	.258	.517	.282
Runners On	292	97	16	2	4	70	13	23	.332	.442	.352
Bases Empty	291	66	20	1	11	11	16	30	.227	.416	.267
Runners/Scor. Pos.	148	46	6	2	2	62	11	19	.311	.419	.343
Runners On/2 Out	115	35	6	0	2	22	7	12	.304	.409	.344
Scor. Pos./2 Out	57	15	2	0	1	18	6	10	.263	.351	.333
Late-Inning Pressure	103	28	9	0	0	8	4	9	.272	.359	.296
Leading Off	27	9	5	0	0	0	1	1	.333	.519	.357
Runners On	46	14	2	0	0	8	2	5	.304	.348	.327
Runners/Scor. Pos.	17	5	0	0	0	7	2	4	.294	.294	.350

RUNS BATTED IN	From 1B	From 2B	From 3B	Scoring Position
Totals	6/231	23/116	37/64	60/180
Percentage	2.6%	19.8%	57.8%	33.3%

Loves to face: Mark Gubicza (.434, 23-for-53, 2 HR)
Todd Stottlemyre (.500, 21-for-42, 1 HR)
Rick Sutcliffe (.667, 6-for-9, 1 HR)

Hates to face: Tom Gordon (.071, 1-for-14)
Tom Henke (0-for-14)
Mark Langston (0-for-11)

Miscellaneous statistics: Ground outs-to-air outs ratio: 0.98 last season, 0.92 for career. . . . Grounded into 13 double plays in 150 opportunities (one per 12). . . . Drove in 31 of 44 runners from third base with less than two outs (70%). . . . Direction of balls hit to the outfield: 26% to left field, 30% to center, 44% to right. . . . Base running: Advanced from first base to third on 7 of 23 outfield singles (30%); scored from second on 12 of 15 (80%). . . . Made 2.29 putouts per nine innings in left field.

Comments: The "Mel Hall of Fame" (most games played by Mels): Ott, 2732; Hall, 1251; Almada, 646; Harder, 584; Stottlemyre, 363; Parnell, 293. . . . Led the American League in doubles as late as July 23, but hit only three in his next 41 games. Only two Yankees have ever led the league in doubles: Lou Gehrig (1927) and Don Mattingly (1984–86). . . . His 103 at-bats in Late-Inning Pressure Situations were the most of any major leaguer without a home run in those situations last season. Four others had at least 100 at-bats without a home run in LIPS: Ozzie Smith (102), Jose Offerman (101), Gregg Jefferies (100), Jody Reed (100). Hall's previous career average was one home run every 20 ABs in LIPS, nearly double his rate at other times (one per 36 AB). . . . Has driven in more than half of the runners from third base with less than two outs in each of his 12 major league seasons. Career rate is 66.9 percent, 5th highest among active players (minimum: 250 opportunities), behind Tony Gwynn (70.4%), Wade Boggs (69.6%), George Brett (69.0%), and Don Mattingly (67.4%). . . . Led the Yankees with 63 home runs over the last four seasons. Of those 63, 41 were hit during the first halves of the season. . . . Hall and Jesse Barfield join a long line of former Yankees who played in Japan, including Roy White, Bill Gullickson, Joe Pepitone, Mike Kekich, Clete Boyer, Ron Davis, Goose Gossage, and, of course, Thad Tillotson.

Darryl Hamilton — Bats Left

Milwaukee Brewers	AB	H	2B	3B	HR	RBI	BB	SO	BA	SA	OBA
Season	470	140	19	7	5	62	45	42	.298	.400	.356
vs. Left-Handers	89	22	3	1	0	13	10	9	.247	.303	.323
vs. Right-Handers	381	118	16	6	5	49	35	33	.310	.423	.363
vs. Ground-Ballers	216	56	7	3	1	34	13	20	.259	.333	.296
vs. Fly-Ballers	254	84	12	4	4	28	32	22	.331	.457	.403
Home Games	233	67	11	4	1	30	26	19	.288	.382	.356
Road Games	237	73	8	3	4	32	19	23	.308	.418	.355
Grass Fields	387	111	18	4	3	48	36	35	.287	.377	.344
Artificial Turf	83	29	1	3	2	14	9	7	.349	.506	.409
April	66	15	1	1	1	11	7	8	.227	.318	.297
May	34	8	2	0	1	3	2	5	.235	.382	.278
June	86	32	3	2	0	11	10	5	.372	.453	.433
July	94	28	8	1	1	9	7	13	.298	.436	.337
August	75	20	5	1	0	16	9	2	.267	.360	.337
Sept./Oct.	115	37	0	2	2	12	10	9	.322	.409	.381
Leading Off Inn.	92	26	7	2	0	0	3	10	.283	.402	.305
Runners On	207	63	5	2	2	59	24	14	.304	.377	.368
Bases Empty	263	77	14	5	3	3	21	28	.293	.418	.345
Runners/Scor. Pos.	136	40	3	1	1	56	19	11	.294	.353	.368
Runners On/2 Out	78	21	1	1	1	24	14	6	.269	.346	.380
Scor. Pos./2 Out	61	17	1	0	1	23	12	6	.279	.344	.397
Late-Inning Pressure	59	20	3	1	1	6	7	4	.339	.475	.409
Leading Off	10	4	2	0	0	0	0	1	.400	.600	.400
Runners On	30	7	0	1	0	5	5	2	.233	.300	.343
Runners/Scor. Pos.	20	3	0	0	0	4	5	2	.150	.150	.320

RUNS BATTED IN	From 1B	From 2B	From 3B	Scoring Position
Totals	3/144	22/108	32/61	54/169
Percentage	2.1%	20.4%	52.5%	32.0%

Loves to face: Kevin Appier (.600, 6-for-10)
Mike Boddicker (.545, 6-for-11)
Bill Gullickson (.400, 4-for-10, 1 HR)

Hates to face: Ron Darling (.125, 2-for-16)
Jimmy Key (.143, 2-for-14)
Jeff Montgomery (0-for-11)

Miscellaneous statistics: Ground outs-to-air outs ratio: 1.73 last season, 1.63 for career.... Grounded into 10 double plays in 109 opportunities (one per 11).... Drove in 24 of 35 runners from third base with less than two outs (69%).... Direction of balls hit to the outfield: 37% to left field, 33% to center, 29% to right.... Base running: Advanced from first base to third on 6 of 20 outfield singles (30%); scored from second on 13 of 18 (72%).... Made 2.27 putouts per nine innings in right field, 2d-highest rate in A.L.

Comments: Certainly one of the 10 most underrated players in the majors. Over the past two years, he has batted .304 and stolen 57 bases. Only one player in either league can match Hamilton's figures in both categories: Bip Roberts.... Led major league outfielders in fielding, handling 289 chances without an error. It was the 10th time in major league history that an outfielder has had that many chances in an errorless season. Others who have done it: Brett Butler, Brian Downing, Curt Flood, Danny Litwhiler, Terry Puhl, Mickey Stanley (twice), Roy White, and Carl Yastrzemski.... The record for consecutive errorless games in the outfield is 266, by Don Demeter (1962–65). Hamilton starts 1993 with an errorless streak of 221 games.... What makes his errorless streak more remarkable is that he's done it from all three outfield positions. Chad Curtis was the only other outfielder to start at least 20 games from each of the three positions last season.... June batting average was the highest in the league.... Career batting average of .344 in Late-Inning Pressure Situations is 3d highest over the 18-year history of *The Player Analysis* (minimum: 50 hits). The top five: Jeff Bagwell (.385), Edgar Martinez (.346), Hamilton (.344), Tony Gwynn (.339), Wade Boggs (.324).... Has batted at least 45 points higher against right-handers than he has against left-handers in each of his four seasons in the majors. Career breakdown: .228 (0 HR) vs. LHP; .307 (8 HR) vs. RHP.

Brian Harper — Bats Right

Minnesota Twins	AB	H	2B	3B	HR	RBI	BB	SO	BA	SA	OBA
Season	502	154	25	0	9	73	26	22	.307	.410	.343
vs. Left-Handers	109	30	6	0	1	13	13	6	.275	.358	.339
vs. Right-Handers	393	124	19	0	8	60	13	16	.316	.425	.344
vs. Ground-Ballers	233	71	11	0	4	36	13	8	.305	.403	.345
vs. Fly-Ballers	269	83	14	0	5	37	13	14	.309	.416	.341
Home Games	241	78	10	0	3	31	15	11	.324	.402	.361
Road Games	261	76	15	0	6	42	11	11	.291	.418	.326
Grass Fields	192	61	11	0	4	36	10	10	.318	.438	.352
Artificial Turf	310	93	14	0	5	37	16	12	.300	.394	.337
April	68	19	2	0	1	7	4	1	.279	.353	.315
May	80	26	7	0	0	17	4	4	.325	.412	.364
June	94	31	5	0	3	13	4	4	.330	.479	.354
July	85	26	6	0	0	10	4	4	.306	.376	.337
August	95	27	2	0	3	14	4	4	.284	.400	.310
Sept./Oct.	80	25	3	0	2	12	6	5	.313	.425	.376
Leading Off Inn.	93	31	5	0	4	4	6	2	.333	.516	.386
Runners On	239	72	11	0	2	66	16	14	.301	.372	.342
Bases Empty	263	82	14	0	7	7	10	8	.312	.445	.344
Runners/Scor. Pos.	147	42	5	0	1	61	13	8	.286	.340	.339
Runners On/2 Out	100	23	3	0	0	20	9	9	.230	.260	.313
Scor. Pos./2 Out	72	16	1	0	0	19	7	6	.222	.236	.317
Late-Inning Pressure	74	21	2	0	1	7	8	3	.284	.351	.365
Leading Off	16	4	0	0	0	0	1	0	.250	.250	.294
Runners On	31	11	2	0	0	6	7	1	.355	.419	.475
Runners/Scor. Pos.	15	5	1	0	0	6	6	0	.333	.400	.522

RUNS BATTED IN	From 1B	From 2B	From 3B	Scoring Position
Totals	6/182	26/119	32/71	58/190
Percentage	3.3%	21.8%	45.1%	30.5%

Loves to face: Chuck Finley (.385, 15-for-39, 1 HR)
Erik Hanson (.583, 7-for-12, 1 HR)
Dave Stewart (.457, 16-for-35)

Hates to face: Mike Magnante (0-for-7)
Melido Perez (.100, 2-for-20, 1 HR)
David Wells (.083, 1-for-12)

Miscellaneous statistics: Ground outs-to-air outs ratio: 0.83 last season, 0.92 for career.... Grounded into 15 double plays in 119 opportunities (one per 7.9).... Drove in 26 of 42 runners from third base with less than two outs (62%).... Direction of balls hit to the outfield: 42% to left field, 31% to center, 26% to right.... Base running: Advanced from first base to third on 7 of 26 outfield singles (27%); scored from second on 10 of 16 (63%).... Opposing base stealers: 118-for-170 (69%).

Comments: Batted over .300 for the third time in the last four years. Over the past 40 years, the only other catchers to compile three .300 seasons: Ted Simmons (7), Thurman Munson (5), Manny Sanguillen (4), Smoky Burgess (4), and Joe Torre (3).... Career batting average of .295 is 3d highest among catchers who played within the last 40 years, behind only Torre (.297) and Sanguillen (.296).... Hitting like that allows the Twins to accept Harper's defensive shortcomings. Last season, he allowed more stolen bases (118) and committed more passed balls (12) than any other catcher in the majors.... Last Twins' catcher to start the All-Star Game: Earl Battey in 1965.... Averaged one strikeout every 24.8 plate appearances last season, the best rate in the league. Over the last 40 years, only four other starting catchers had seasons with lower rates: Burgess, Berra, Mike Scioscia, and Clint Courtney.... Career rate of one walk every 26.7 plate appearances is 4th lowest among active players (minimum: 1000 PA); the bottom three: Ozzie Guillen (one BB every 33.0 PA); Ricky Jordan (28.9); Steve Lake (27.5).... Career rate of one strikeout every 18.1 PAs is 3d lowest among active players, behind Tony Gwynn (one SO every 21.6 PA) and Felix Fermin (18.2).... That adds up to a lot of balls put into play—the highest career percentage, in fact, of any active player (89.4%).... In five seasons with Minnesota, he has a combined average of .304 vs. left-handers, .309 vs. right-handers.

Billy Hatcher   Bats Right

Reds/Red Sox	AB	H	2B	3B	HR	RBI	BB	SO	BA	SA	OBA
Season	409	102	19	2	3	33	22	52	.249	.328	.290
vs. Left-Handers	141	34	6	1	2	7	7	15	.241	.340	.275
vs. Right-Handers	268	68	13	1	1	26	15	37	.254	.321	.298
vs. Ground-Ballers	192	49	8	0	0	19	10	23	.255	.297	.288
vs. Fly-Ballers	217	53	11	2	3	14	12	29	.244	.355	.292
Home Games	191	52	12	0	1	17	14	18	.272	.351	.327
Road Games	218	50	7	2	2	16	8	34	.229	.307	.257
Grass Fields	313	81	15	2	3	30	19	36	.259	.348	.305
Artificial Turf	96	21	4	0	0	3	3	16	.219	.260	.240
April	41	12	1	0	1	4	1	6	.293	.390	.302
May	15	4	0	0	0	1	1	4	.267	.267	.313
June	32	10	2	0	1	4	3	1	.313	.469	.361
July	87	25	7	0	0	6	6	8	.287	.368	.330
August	105	29	5	1	1	12	8	16	.276	.371	.333
Sept./Oct.	129	22	4	1	0	6	3	17	.171	.217	.200
Leading Off Inn.	115	29	4	0	2	2	8	14	.252	.339	.312
Runners On	169	45	8	1	0	30	4	15	.266	.325	.281
Bases Empty	240	57	11	1	3	3	18	37	.237	.329	.296
Runners/Scor. Pos.	103	26	5	0	0	27	4	10	.252	.301	.270
Runners On/2 Out	75	17	3	0	0	12	1	5	.227	.267	.247
Scor. Pos./2 Out	50	8	3	0	0	12	1	5	.160	.220	.176
Late-Inning Pressure	66	23	4	0	1	7	3	9	.348	.455	.377
Leading Off	17	3	0	0	0	0	1	1	.176	.176	.222
Runners On	30	14	2	0	0	6	2	4	.467	.533	.500
Runners/Scor. Pos.	18	9	2	0	0	6	2	1	.500	.611	.550

RUNS BATTED IN	From 1B	From 2B	From 3B	Scoring Position
Totals	4/119	11/85	15/41	26/126
Percentage	3.4%	12.9%	36.6%	20.6%

Loves to face: Dennis Eckersley (.667, 4-for-6, 2 2B)
       Bill Gullickson (.440, 11-for-25, 1 HR, 0 BB)
       Neal Heaton (.444, 8-for-18)

Hates to face: Chris Bosio (0-for-7)
       David Cone (.138, 4-for-29, 1 HR, 6 SO)
       Bob Welch (.100, 2-for-20)

Miscellaneous statistics: Ground outs-to-air outs ratio: 1.34 last season, 1.23 for career. . . . Grounded into 11 double plays in 74 opportunities (one per 6.7). . . . Drove in 9 of 19 runners from third base with less than two outs (47%). . . . Direction of balls hit to the outfield: 25% to left field, 37% to center, 38% to right. . . . Base running: Advanced from first base to third on 10 of 26 outfield singles (38%); scored from second on 8 of 9 (89%). . . . Made 1.86 putouts per nine innings in left field, lowest rate in A.L.

Comments: Came to the Red Sox with a career total of 192 stolen bases. Only two players stole that many bases for the Sox: Harry Hooper (300) and Tris Speaker (266). . . . Has stolen only 15 bases in 32 attempts over the last two seasons (47%), after averaging more than 35 steals per season with a success rate of 77 percent from 1986 through 1990. . . . Started 46 games in the leadoff spot after joining Boston in July. The leadoff spot in the Red Sox's order posted major league lows in batting average (.216), on-base percentage (.282), slugging percentage (.291), runs (78), and stolen bases (8). Wade Boggs (55 starts batting leadoff) and Jody Reed (47) share the blame. . . . Has a career average of .216 as a pinch hitter, with no home runs in 88 at-bats. . . . Career batting average is 35 points higher through June 30 (.282) than it is thereafter (.247). . . . Hasn't homered after August 31 in any of his last four seasons (346 at-bats). . . . Eight straight hits in the 1990 World Series was one indication that he's not bothered by pressure; here's another: His batting average in Late-Inning Pressure Situations has been over .300 in five of his seven full seasons in the majors. Over the last two years, he has 17 hits in 35 at-bats in LIPS with runners in scoring position (.486). . . . Career batting statistics are similar to those of several center fielders of the past who were far superior fielders: Jim Busby, Ken Berry, and Cesar Geronimo.

Charlie Hayes   Bats Right

New York Yankees	AB	H	2B	3B	HR	RBI	BB	SO	BA	SA	OBA
Season	509	131	19	2	18	66	28	100	.257	.409	.297
vs. Left-Handers	150	32	3	0	6	18	9	23	.213	.353	.262
vs. Right-Handers	359	99	16	2	12	48	19	77	.276	.432	.312
vs. Ground-Ballers	232	62	11	2	9	26	11	51	.267	.448	.304
vs. Fly-Ballers	277	69	8	0	9	40	17	49	.249	.375	.291
Home Games	245	54	9	1	7	30	14	44	.220	.351	.267
Road Games	264	77	10	1	11	36	14	56	.292	.462	.325
Grass Fields	422	105	13	2	17	61	23	84	.249	.410	.289
Artificial Turf	87	26	6	0	1	5	5	16	.299	.402	.337
April	77	25	2	0	1	9	0	9	.325	.390	.329
May	97	24	5	0	5	12	5	18	.247	.454	.282
June	90	22	3	1	3	11	9	22	.244	.400	.310
July	84	13	2	0	2	10	2	25	.155	.250	.189
August	106	29	4	1	4	13	9	16	.274	.443	.328
Sept./Oct.	55	18	3	0	3	11	3	10	.327	.545	.362
Leading Off Inn.	135	35	4	2	7	7	7	24	.259	.474	.296
Runners On	213	59	10	0	6	54	15	43	.277	.408	.322
Bases Empty	296	72	9	2	12	12	13	57	.243	.409	.277
Runners/Scor. Pos.	108	28	4	0	2	41	10	22	.259	.352	.317
Runners On/2 Out	108	27	4	0	2	26	9	26	.250	.343	.319
Scor. Pos./2 Out	69	16	1	0	2	23	6	16	.232	.333	.312
Late-Inning Pressure	88	21	4	0	4	7	4	22	.239	.420	.269
Leading Off	32	9	1	0	2	2	2	5	.281	.500	.324
Runners On	36	5	2	0	0	3	1	11	.167	.333	.188
Runners/Scor. Pos.	16	2	0	0	0	2	1	7	.125	.125	.167

RUNS BATTED IN	From 1B	From 2B	From 3B	Scoring Position
Totals	10/164	16/87	22/59	38/146
Percentage	6.1%	18.4%	37.3%	26.0%

Loves to face: Tom Glavine (.381, 8-for-21, 1 HR)
       Les Lancaster (.421, 8-for-19, 1 HR)
       Randy Tomlin (.600, 6-for-10)

Hates to face: Tim Burke (0-for-11)
       Sid Fernandez (.077, 1-for-13, 2 BB, 7 SO)
       Greg Maddux (.087, 2-for-23)

Miscellaneous statistics: Ground outs-to-air outs ratio: 0.86 last season, 0.97 for career. . . . Grounded into 12 double plays in 98 opportunities (one per 8.2). . . . Drove in 13 of 21 runners from third base with less than two outs (62%). . . . Direction of balls hit to the outfield: 29% to left field, 33% to center, 38% to right. . . . Base running: Advanced from first base to third on 5 of 22 outfield singles (23%); scored from second on 6 of 6 (100%). . . . Made 1.85 assists per nine innings at third base.

Comments: Played the same number of games for the Yankees last season as he did for the Phillies in 1991, which makes for an interesting comparison of season totals. Came to the plate 69 more times for New York than he did a year earlier for the Phillies, and set career highs in homers (12 in 1991), RBIs (53), extra-base hits (36), and strikeouts (75). . . . Led A.L. third basemen in fielding as late as July 17 with a rate of one error every 38 chances; finished the season third, behind Kevin Seitzer and Carney Lansford. Neither Graig Nettles nor Clete Boyer ever led the league; the last Yankees third baseman to do so was Red Rolfe in 1936. . . . His home-run total has increased in each season since his debut in 1988 (when he had only 11 ABs): 0, 8, 10, 12, 18. The only other players to raise their totals in every season during that time: Mike Devereaux, Jerald Clark and Edgar Martinez. . . . Drew only 16 walks in 1990, and didn't walk in his first 25 games with New York, but ended the season with a career-high walk rate (one every 19.6 plate appearances). . . . Although he batted 63 points higher against right-handers than he did against lefties last season, his career average is still higher against left-handers (.257) than right-handers (.246). . . . In each of the last two seasons, he has posted his highest monthly batting average during September. . . . Who were the best ever one-season Yankees? How about Bobby Bonds in 1975 (.270, 32 HR, 85 RBI) and Jack Clark in 1988 (.242, 27 HR, 93 RBI)?

Rickey Henderson

Bats Right

Oakland A's	AB	H	2B	3B	HR	RBI	BB	SO	BA	SA	OBA
Season	396	112	18	3	15	46	95	56	.283	.457	.426
vs. Left-Handers	105	28	5	1	5	13	24	17	.267	.476	.403
vs. Right-Handers	291	84	13	2	10	33	71	39	.289	.450	.434
vs. Ground-Ballers	179	51	8	1	3	19	43	23	.285	.391	.427
vs. Fly-Ballers	217	61	10	2	12	27	52	33	.281	.512	.425
Home Games	200	59	8	1	10	27	52	22	.295	.495	.441
Road Games	196	53	10	2	5	19	43	34	.270	.418	.410
Grass Fields	340	103	17	3	14	42	82	41	.303	.494	.440
Artificial Turf	56	9	1	0	1	4	13	15	.161	.232	.342
April	79	18	3	0	3	11	20	21	.228	.380	.384
May	77	26	5	0	3	8	19	8	.338	.519	.474
June	39	10	2	0	1	3	9	4	.256	.385	.396
July	29	8	1	1	1	3	5	1	.276	.483	.382
August	94	29	4	0	4	15	22	11	.309	.479	.451
Sept./Oct.	78	21	3	2	3	6	20	11	.269	.474	.420
Leading Off Inn.	176	54	12	2	8	8	30	25	.307	.534	.411
Runners On	142	41	6	1	4	35	43	21	.289	.430	.455
Bases Empty	254	71	12	2	11	11	52	35	.280	.472	.408
Runners/Scor. Pos.	89	23	2	1	2	28	30	15	.258	.371	.448
Runners On/2 Out	58	17	2	0	0	14	21	8	.293	.328	.488
Scor. Pos./2 Out	45	13	1	0	0	13	16	7	.289	.311	.484
Late-Inning Pressure	46	15	2	1	2	13	15	6	.326	.543	.476
Leading Off	13	3	1	0	0	0	5	2	.231	.308	.444
Runners On	23	9	1	1	1	12	6	3	.391	.652	.484
Runners/Scor. Pos.	16	6	1	1	1	12	4	2	.375	.750	.455

RUNS BATTED IN	From 1B	From 2B	From 3B	Scoring Position
Totals	7/93	15/78	9/30	24/108
Percentage	7.5%	19.2%	30.0%	22.2%

Loves to face: Jimmy Key (.380, 27-for-71, 5 HR)
Ben McDonald (.500, 8-for-16, 2 HR)
Todd Stottlemyre (.364, 4-for-11, 2 HR, 7 BB)

Hates to face: Roger Clemens (.167, 8-for-48, 7 BB)
Scott Kamieniecki (0-for-9, 3 BB)
Nolan Ryan (.118, 2-for-17, 5 BB)

Miscellaneous statistics: Ground outs-to-air outs ratio: 0.71 last season, 1.08 for career.... Grounded into 5 double plays in 75 opportunities (one per 15).... Drove in 5 of 9 runners from third base with less than two outs (56%).... Direction of balls hit to the outfield: 37% to left field, 35% to center, 28% to right.... Base running: Advanced from first base to third on 13 of 23 outfield singles (57%); scored from second on 10 of 16 (63%).... Made 2.35 putouts per nine innings in left field.

Comments: Enters the 1993 season having reached base safely 3336 times. With one season to play before turning 35, Rickey could become only the ninth player to reach 3500 times before his 35th birthday. The others: Hank Aaron, Richie Ashburn, Rogers Hornsby, Eddie Mathews, Stan Musial, Mel Ott, Frank Robinson, and Rusty Staub.... Had reached base safely in 22 consecutive postseason games until David Cone & Co. snapped the streak in the second game of the A.L.C.S. Only two players in history had longer postseason streaks: Boog Powell (25 games) and Lou Gehrig (23).... Five postseason errors (all in A.L.C.S. play) are the most by any outfielder in major league history. Only one other outfielder has committed as many as four: Ross Youngs. (If you've never heard of him, check out page 84 for a quick course in remedial baseball history.) ... Batted .366 leading off the first inning last season, .254 in other at-bats.... Stole 47 bases in 55 attempts on grass fields, but was only 1-for-4 on artificial turf. His stolen-base total has declined in each of the last four seasons (since 1988): 93, 77, 65, 58, 48.... Has drawn at least 80 walks in 11 consecutive seasons, the 3d-longest streak in history, behind Lou Gehrig (13 years) and Eddie Mathews (12).... Career total of 1286 walks leads active players, and it ranks 25th among the all-time leaders. His walk rate last season (one every 5.3 PAs) was the highest of his career.

Glenallen Hill

Bats Right

Cleveland Indians	AB	H	2B	3B	HR	RBI	BB	SO	BA	SA	OBA
Season	369	89	16	1	18	49	20	73	.241	.436	.287
vs. Left-Handers	105	28	7	0	7	18	7	14	.267	.533	.319
vs. Right-Handers	264	61	9	1	11	31	13	59	.231	.398	.274
vs. Ground-Ballers	170	43	7	0	8	24	10	29	.253	.435	.304
vs. Fly-Ballers	199	46	9	1	10	25	10	44	.231	.437	.271
Home Games	179	46	9	0	7	24	12	31	.257	.425	.311
Road Games	190	43	7	1	11	25	8	42	.226	.447	.264
Grass Fields	311	73	12	1	13	39	18	62	.235	.405	.284
Artificial Turf	58	16	4	0	5	10	2	11	.276	.603	.300
April	56	12	2	0	1	4	0	15	.214	.304	.228
May	18	4	2	0	0	1	1	4	.222	.333	.263
June	75	21	3	1	5	12	3	12	.280	.547	.325
July	74	22	4	0	3	7	4	11	.297	.473	.342
August	89	17	4	0	3	13	8	14	.191	.337	.258
Sept./Oct.	57	13	1	0	6	12	4	17	.228	.561	.274
Leading Off Inn.	73	20	2	0	7	7	4	15	.274	.589	.338
Runners On	165	41	9	0	5	36	12	32	.248	.394	.298
Bases Empty	204	48	7	1	13	13	8	41	.235	.471	.278
Runners/Scor. Pos.	87	21	6	0	3	31	7	22	.241	.414	.295
Runners On/2 Out	61	14	2	0	3	13	7	16	.230	.410	.309
Scor. Pos./2 Out	37	7	1	0	2	11	4	10	.189	.378	.268
Late-Inning Pressure	72	14	0	0	6	12	4	25	.194	.444	.256
Leading Off	18	4	0	0	3	3	0	7	.222	.722	.300
Runners On	31	8	0	0	1	7	3	10	.258	.355	.324
Runners/Scor. Pos.	13	4	0	0	0	5	1	4	.308	.308	.357

RUNS BATTED IN	From 1B	From 2B	From 3B	Scoring Position
Totals	5/118	16/74	10/32	26/106
Percentage	4.2%	21.6%	31.3%	24.5%

Loves to face: Scott Erickson (2-for-2, 1 2B, 1 HR, 1 BB)
Mark Guthrie (.583, 7-for-12, 1 HR, 3 SO)
Kirk McCaskill (.500, 4-for-8, 5 BB)

Hates to face: Kenny Rogers (0-for-7, 3 SO)
Kevin Tapani (0-for-9)
Matt Young (.100, 1-for-10)

Miscellaneous statistics: Ground outs-to-air outs ratio: 0.97 last season, 0.92 for career.... Grounded into 11 double plays in 79 opportunities (one per 7.2).... Drove in 9 of 18 runners from third base with less than two outs (50%).... Direction of balls hit to the outfield: 42% to left field, 38% to center, 21% to right.... Base running: Advanced from first base to third on 5 of 22 outfield singles (23%); scored from second on 4 of 4 (100%).... Made 2.11 putouts per nine innings in left field.

Comments: Established a career high in at-bats last season, due to increased playing time against right-handed pitchers. He started 35 of 45 games against right-handers from mid-July to mid-September.... Was the only player to hit two home runs in each of two consecutive games last season. The last player to do so was Barry Larkin (June 27–28, 1991); the last A.L. player: Jose Canseco (1990).... Led A.L. batters with five home runs against the Tigers last season. His four homers at Tiger Stadium tied teammate Carlos Baerga for the most among visiting players.... Scored only 38 runs and drove in 49 despite his 18 home runs. The only other player with that many homers but neither 50 runs nor 50 RBIs last season: Chris Hoiles (20 HR).... Has stolen 23 bases over the past three seasons, but his career statistical profile closely resembles those of many catchers and lumbering one-tool sluggers, like Tom Haller, Johnny Orsino, and Art Shamsky. Most similar active players (offensively speaking): Hoiles, Dante Bichette, and Kevin Maas.... Rate of one strikeout every 5.4 plate appearances last season was the *best* of his career and quite an accomplishment for someone who struck out 211 times in 131 games for Kinston in 1985 (Class A).... Among active players, only Omar Vizquel has more career plate appearances without ever drawing an intentional walk.... Career batting average of .269 vs. ground-ball pitchers, .225 vs. fly-ballers.

Chris Hoiles — Bats Right

Baltimore Orioles	AB	H	2B	3B	HR	RBI	BB	SO	BA	SA	OBA
Season	310	85	10	1	20	40	55	60	.274	.506	.384
vs. Left-Handers	80	23	0	0	4	5	16	7	.287	.438	.406
vs. Right-Handers	230	62	10	1	16	35	39	53	.270	.530	.376
vs. Ground-Ballers	142	44	4	0	12	24	28	30	.310	.592	.428
vs. Fly-Ballers	168	41	6	1	8	16	27	30	.244	.435	.345
Home Games	164	45	6	0	8	20	24	28	.274	.457	.368
Road Games	146	40	4	1	12	20	31	32	.274	.562	.400
Grass Fields	263	75	8	1	19	36	46	50	.285	.540	.392
Artificial Turf	47	10	2	0	1	4	9	10	.213	.319	.339
April	64	21	4	0	5	11	10	12	.328	.625	.413
May	83	22	2	1	5	11	22	13	.265	.494	.419
June	46	11	0	0	4	6	9	10	.239	.500	.368
July	0	0	0	0	0	0	0	0	.000	.000	.000
August	41	10	1	0	1	4	6	7	.244	.341	.340
Sept./Oct.	76	21	3	0	5	8	8	18	.276	.513	.349
Leading Off Inn.	74	23	2	1	8	8	9	12	.311	.689	.386
Runners On	139	29	5	0	3	23	24	32	.209	.309	.323
Bases Empty	171	56	5	1	17	17	31	28	.327	.667	.433
Runners/Scor. Pos.	73	15	3	0	3	23	16	20	.205	.370	.337
Runners On/2 Out	47	9	2	0	2	11	13	13	.191	.362	.377
Scor. Pos./2 Out	30	7	2	0	2	11	10	10	.233	.500	.425
Late-Inning Pressure	40	8	1	0	2	3	2	12	.200	.375	.238
Leading Off	7	2	0	0	1	1	0	2	.286	.714	.286
Runners On	13	1	0	0	0	1	1	4	.077	.077	.143
Runners/Scor. Pos.	8	1	0	0	0	1	0	3	.125	.125	.125

RUNS BATTED IN	From 1B	From 2B	From 3B	Scoring Position
Totals	2/107	7/54	11/31	18/85
Percentage	1.9%	13.0%	35.5%	21.2%

Loves to face: Jim Abbott (.750, 6-for-8)
Jack McDowell (.625, 5-for-8, 1 HR)
Dave Otto (.714, 5-for-7, 2 HR)
Hates to face: Dave Fleming (.111, 1-for-9)
Jack Morris (.091, 1-for-11)
Todd Stottlemyre (0-for-5)

Miscellaneous statistics: Ground outs-to-air outs ratio: 0.72 last season, 0.67 for career.... Grounded into 8 double plays in 82 opportunities (one per 10).... Drove in 7 of 17 runners from third base with less than two outs (41%).... Direction of balls hit to the outfield: 40% to left field, 31% to center, 28% to right.... Base running: Advanced from first base to third on 12 of 28 outfield singles (43%); scored from second on 9 of 11 (82%).... Opposing base stealers: 87-for-109 (80%), highest rate in majors.

Comments: Ranked fifth in the American League in slugging percentage and sixth in on-base average on June 21 when he was hit by a pitch thrown by Tim Leary and suffered a broken wrist.... Jeff Tackett had only 10 major league starts under his belt when Hoiles went down, but started 43 games in Hoiles's absence. Staff ERA was similar with Tackett (3.73) and Hoiles (3.83).... Home-run rate of one every 15.5 at-bats was 4th highest in the league, behind Mark McGwire, Rob Deer, and Juan Gonzalez.... The only A.L. player to increase his home-run rate while decreasing his strikeout rate in each of the last three seasons.... Drove in only 40 runs, the fewest ever by any player in a season with at least 20 home runs.... Of his 32 career home runs, 27 have been solo shots.... Some odd numbers: Hit four more home runs off ground-ball pitchers than he hit vs. fly-ballers. (The only A.L. player with a wider margin in that direction: teammate Leo Gomez—11 vs. GBP, 6 vs. FBP.) And in 1991, Hoiles's gap was even wider—he hit 9 of his 11 HRs vs. ground-ballers.... More funny stuff: Has hit 10 home runs with only 13 RBIs vs. left-handed pitchers. Has only two hits in 45 career at-bats vs. southpaws with runners in scoring position (0-for-17 last season).... Has committed only four errors in his major league career, two on interference, two on stolen-base attempts.... Most games among active nonpitchers who have never stolen a base: Cecil Fielder, 696; Mackey Sasser, 434; Sam Horn, 366; Charlie O'Brien, 339; Greg Myers, 248; Hoiles, 232.

Thomas Howard — Bats Left and Right

Padres/Indians	AB	H	2B	3B	HR	RBI	BB	SO	BA	SA	OBA
Season	361	100	15	2	2	32	17	60	.277	.346	.308
vs. Left-Handers	104	30	3	0	2	11	6	21	.288	.375	.327
vs. Right-Handers	257	70	12	2	0	21	11	39	.272	.335	.300
vs. Ground-Ballers	170	49	5	2	0	17	10	25	.288	.341	.328
vs. Fly-Ballers	191	51	10	0	2	15	7	35	.267	.351	.290
Home Games	181	49	5	2	1	18	9	31	.271	.337	.304
Road Games	180	51	10	0	1	14	8	29	.283	.356	.312
Grass Fields	310	86	13	2	1	28	17	50	.277	.342	.313
Artificial Turf	51	14	2	0	1	4	0	10	.275	.373	.275
April	51	18	2	0	0	2	3	7	.353	.392	.389
May	65	16	2	1	0	4	0	11	.246	.308	.242
June	73	20	4	0	0	7	4	8	.274	.329	.308
July	35	10	0	0	1	5	3	7	.286	.371	.342
August	78	26	4	1	0	9	3	14	.333	.410	.358
Sept./Oct.	59	10	3	0	1	5	4	13	.169	.271	.222
Leading Off Inn.	86	23	4	0	0	5	15	.267	.314	.308	
Runners On	145	46	5	1	1	31	6	24	.317	.386	.340
Bases Empty	216	54	10	1	1	1	11	36	.250	.319	.286
Runners/Scor. Pos.	85	26	2	0	0	27	5	16	.306	.329	.337
Runners On/2 Out	63	20	3	0	0	11	3	9	.317	.365	.348
Scor. Pos./2 Out	43	12	1	0	0	10	3	7	.279	.302	.326
Late-Inning Pressure	70	21	3	0	1	7	3	6	.300	.386	.324
Leading Off	22	7	2	0	0	1	3	.318	.409	.348	
Runners On	26	8	1	0	0	6	2	3	.308	.346	.345
Runners/Scor. Pos.	15	6	0	0	0	5	2	2	.400	.400	.444

RUNS BATTED IN	From 1B	From 2B	From 3B	Scoring Position
Totals	3/95	10/68	17/35	27/103
Percentage	3.2%	14.7%	48.6%	26.2%

Loves to face: Kevin Brown (.571, 4-for-7, 1 2B)
Mike Moore (.571, 4-for-7)
Mike Mussina (2-for-2, 1 BB)
Hates to face: Neal Heaton (.125, 1-for-8, 3 SO)
Scott Kamieniecki (.111, 1-for-9)
Rick Sutcliffe (0-for-6)

Miscellaneous statistics: Ground outs-to-air outs ratio: 1.37 last season, 1.45 for career.... Grounded into 4 double plays in 69 opportunities (one per 17).... Drove in 11 of 16 runners from third base with less than two outs (69%).... Direction of balls hit to the outfield: 39% to left field, 37% to center, 24% to right batting left-handed; 28% to left field, 28% to center, 44% to right batting right-handed.... Base running: Advanced from first base to third on 9 of 20 outfield singles (45%); scored from second on 6 of 6 (100%).... Made 2.28 putouts per nine innings in left field.

Comments: Led the Indians with 53 starts from the 2d spot in the batting order, which produced only 59 RBIs. Considering that Kenny Lofton helped give Cleveland's leadoff spot an above-average on-base percentage and the league's highest stolen-base total, the poor production of their number-two hitters is conspicuous. Others with at least 25 starts batting second for Cleveland: Felix Fermin, Glenallen Hill, and Mark Lewis.... Although Howard batted .296 from the two hole, he drove in only 24 runs (in 64 games), only slightly higher than the average of his mates from that spot. Despite batting behind Lofton for much of the season, Howard didn't drive in a run during the first inning of any game until the final weekend of the season, when he hit a 2-run homer off Baltimore's Craig Lefferts.... Batting average was 5th highest among last season's sophomore class (minimum: 300 AB), behind Bernard Gilkey, .302; Mike Bordick, .300; Chuck Knoblauch, .297; and Ray Lankford, .293.... Hidden value: Howard was one of nine players with more than 10 stolen bases and more than 10 sacrifice bunts last season.... Also had the best GIDP rate on the Indians last season. (See figures above.)... One of seven players to start at least 10 games at each of the three outfield positions last season. He also did that for the Padres in 1991.... Career batting average of .196 (11-for-56) as a pinch hitter.

Kent Hrbek
Bats Left

Minnesota Twins	AB	H	2B	3B	HR	RBI	BB	SO	BA	SA	OBA
Season	394	96	20	0	15	58	71	56	.244	.409	.357
vs. Left-Handers	83	22	5	0	1	9	7	14	.265	.361	.319
vs. Right-Handers	311	74	15	0	14	49	64	42	.238	.421	.366
vs. Ground-Ballers	201	44	8	0	6	28	24	24	.219	.348	.300
vs. Fly-Ballers	193	52	12	0	9	30	47	32	.269	.472	.411
Home Games	193	50	10	0	10	29	31	29	.259	.466	.358
Road Games	201	46	10	0	5	29	40	27	.229	.353	.355
Grass Fields	155	35	8	0	2	21	33	22	.226	.316	.360
Artificial Turf	239	61	12	0	13	37	38	34	.255	.469	.355
April	18	7	3	0	1	4	3	4	.389	.722	.476
May	85	23	6	0	2	11	21	6	.271	.412	.411
June	90	28	5	0	7	20	16	12	.311	.600	.411
July	93	19	4	0	1	11	12	17	.204	.280	.295
August	90	15	1	0	4	11	15	15	.167	.311	.283
Sept./Oct.	18	4	1	0	0	1	4	2	.222	.278	.364
Leading Off Inn.	83	20	5	0	7	7	11	15	.241	.554	.330
Runners On	209	48	10	0	4	47	46	27	.230	.335	.364
Bases Empty	185	48	10	0	11	11	25	29	.259	.492	.348
Runners/Scor. Pos.	124	26	7	0	3	42	35	16	.210	.339	.377
Runners On/2 Out	102	17	2	0	1	14	23	14	.167	.216	.320
Scor. Pos./2 Out	64	10	1	0	1	13	20	7	.156	.219	.357
Late-Inning Pressure	56	14	5	0	0	5	12	8	.250	.339	.382
Leading Off	13	2	1	0	0	0	3	2	.154	.231	.313
Runners On	28	9	3	0	0	5	6	3	.321	.429	.441
Runners/Scor. Pos.	16	5	2	0	0	4	5	3	.313	.438	.476

RUNS BATTED IN	From 1B	From 2B	From 3B	Scoring Position
Totals	7/145	19/95	17/57	36/152
Percentage	4.8%	20.0%	29.8%	23.7%

Loves to face: Dennis Eckersley (.360, 9-for-25, 4 2B, 2 HR, 4 BB)
Bob Milacki (.375, 9-for-24, 3 2B, 3 HR)
Bill Wegman (.400, 14-for-35, 4 HR)

Hates to face: Jimmy Key (.143, 3-for-21)
Charles Nagy (.067, 1-for-15, 2 BB)
Melido Perez (.161, 5-for-31)

Miscellaneous statistics: Ground outs-to-air outs ratio: 1.27 last season, 1.16 for career.... Grounded into 12 double plays in 91 opportunities (one per 7.6).... Drove in 14 of 30 runners from third base with less than two outs (47%).... Direction of balls hit to the outfield: 26% to left field, 37% to center, 37% to right.... Base running: Advanced from first base to third on 7 of 22 outfield singles (32%); scored from second on 9 of 13 (69%).... Made 0.68 assists per nine innings at first base.

Comments: His streak of eight straight seasons with at least 20 home runs was snapped last year, one season shy of Harmon Killebrew's club record.... Last September was his first homerless month since June 1989.... August batting average was the lowest in the American League.... He had batted under .225 in only seven months in his entire career, before doing it in each of the last three months last season.... Average of one walk every 6.6 plate appearances was the highest of his career.... He and Mike Pagliarulo made two trips to the disabled list, but as usual, the Twins were among the healthiest teams in the majors last season. Only two other Twins players visited the D.L. all season: Paul Abbott and Donnie Hill.... In 11 full seasons with the Twins, Hrbek has played 150 or more games in a season only once (158 games in 1985), missing a total of 263 games over those 11 years.... His career-high totals in the following five categories were set in five different seasons: games (158 in 1985), batting average (.312 in 1988), doubles (41 in 1983), home runs (34 in 1987), RBIs (107 in 1984).... Slugging percentage has decreased in each of the last five seasons. (Mike Greenwell is the only other player to do that.) In major league history, no player has done that for more than six straight years. The last of many players with six consecutive declines was Cal Ripken.

Jeff Huson
Bats Left

Texas Rangers	AB	H	2B	3B	HR	RBI	BB	SO	BA	SA	OBA
Season	318	83	14	3	4	24	41	43	.261	.362	.342
vs. Left-Handers	32	9	2	0	1	3	4	10	.281	.438	.361
vs. Right-Handers	286	74	12	3	3	21	37	33	.259	.353	.339
vs. Ground-Ballers	146	37	6	2	1	10	17	16	.253	.342	.329
vs. Fly-Ballers	172	46	8	1	3	14	24	27	.267	.378	.352
Home Games	149	38	6	1	0	12	16	21	.255	.309	.325
Road Games	169	45	8	2	4	12	25	22	.266	.408	.355
Grass Fields	262	73	13	2	3	21	28	35	.279	.378	.345
Artificial Turf	56	10	1	1	1	3	13	8	.179	.286	.329
April	57	16	2	1	0	2	3	9	.281	.351	.317
May	82	18	6	1	1	5	8	9	.220	.354	.297
June	43	14	1	0	0	1	9	6	.326	.349	.434
July	48	15	2	1	2	7	9	8	.313	.521	.407
August	79	18	3	0	1	8	12	11	.228	.304	.323
Sept./Oct.	9	2	0	0	0	1	0	0	.222	.222	.200
Leading Off Inn.	87	23	3	0	1	1	14	12	.264	.333	.366
Runners On	125	28	6	2	1	21	16	22	.224	.328	.304
Bases Empty	193	55	8	1	3	3	25	21	.285	.383	.367
Runners/Scor. Pos.	64	11	5	1	0	18	11	15	.172	.281	.280
Runners On/2 Out	53	11	4	1	1	9	8	10	.208	.377	.323
Scor. Pos./2 Out	38	6	3	1	0	7	6	8	.158	.289	.289
Late-Inning Pressure	48	8	1	1	0	1	6	8	.167	.229	.273
Leading Off	12	2	1	0	0	0	2	2	.167	.250	.286
Runners On	20	3	0	1	0	1	2	4	.150	.250	.261
Runners/Scor. Pos.	11	1	0	1	0	1	2	3	.091	.273	.286

RUNS BATTED IN	From 1B	From 2B	From 3B	Scoring Position
Totals	3/82	8/53	9/27	17/80
Percentage	3.7%	15.1%	33.3%	21.3%

Loves to face: Mark Gubicza (.500, 3-for-6)
Jack McDowell (.381, 8-for-21)
Scott Sanderson (.625, 5-for-8)

Hates to face: Jose Mesa (0-for-9)
Dave Stewart (.091, 1-for-11)
Kevin Tapani (.056, 1-for-18, 1 2B)

Miscellaneous statistics: Ground outs-to-air outs ratio: 1.05 last season, 1.25 for career.... Grounded into 7 double plays in 66 opportunities (one per 9.4).... Drove in 7 of 13 runners from third base with less than two outs (54%).... Direction of balls hit to the outfield: 29% to left field, 28% to center, 42% to right.... Base running: Advanced from first base to third on 12 of 20 outfield singles (60%); scored from second on 6 of 7 (86%).... Made 2.96 assists per nine innings at shortstop.

Comments: This shortstop's most impressive accomplishments have come at second base. Played 47 games there last season, without committing an error; no other A.L. second baseman had a streak that long in 1992.... In his career, he has played 72 games at second base and has yet to commit an error. The major league record for consecutive errorless games at second base is 123 by Ryne Sandberg (1989–1990); the A.L. record is 89, by Jerry Adair (1964–1965). Huson's streak, which extends back to his days with Montreal, is the second longest ever to start a career. (Doug Flynn played his first 77 games at second base without an error.) ... But Huson has played more games at shortstop than anywhere else in each of his five seasons in the majors, and his error rate has improved steadily; chances per error year by year starting in 1989: 8.8, 25.2, 28.2, 31.7.... Started 88 games against right-handed pitchers, but only one against a left-hander last season. Career batting averages are .210 against lefties, .240 against right-handers. Maybe it would be better to platoon on another basis: .215 vs. ground-ballers, .257 vs. fly-ballers.... Has only one hit in his last 28 at-bats as a pinch hitter, dating back to 1990. He has driven in only one run in 48 career at-bats as a pinch hitter.... Career average of .248 on grass fields, .199 on artificial turf.... Has six home runs in his last 472 at-bats since starting his career homerless in 626 at-bats.... The over/under on homers for the remainder of his career: 3.

Brook Jacoby　　　　　　　　　　　Bats Right

Cleveland Indians	AB	H	2B	3B	HR	RBI	BB	SO	BA	SA	OBA
Season	291	76	7	0	4	36	28	54	.261	.326	.324
vs. Left-Handers	97	25	3	0	2	11	8	17	.258	.351	.311
vs. Right-Handers	194	51	4	0	2	25	20	37	.263	.314	.330
vs. Ground-Ballers	132	37	2	0	3	19	11	22	.280	.364	.333
vs. Fly-Ballers	159	39	5	0	1	17	17	32	.245	.296	.317
Home Games	126	39	5	0	3	22	12	22	.310	.421	.362
Road Games	165	37	2	0	1	14	16	32	.224	.255	.295
Grass Fields	241	66	6	0	4	31	23	43	.274	.349	.335
Artificial Turf	50	10	1	0	0	5	5	11	.200	.220	.273
April	49	12	1	0	1	10	2	9	.245	.327	.269
May	71	22	2	0	0	10	9	15	.310	.338	.390
June	56	13	2	0	2	5	7	7	.232	.375	.313
July	32	9	0	0	0	1	1	5	.281	.281	.303
August	57	14	2	0	1	6	5	9	.246	.333	.306
Sept./Oct.	26	6	0	0	0	4	4	9	.231	.231	.323
Leading Off Inn.	59	17	1	0	0	0	4	7	.288	.305	.333
Runners On	134	37	3	0	1	33	17	27	.276	.321	.348
Bases Empty	157	39	4	0	3	3	11	27	.248	.331	.302
Runners/Scor. Pos.	72	22	2	0	1	33	14	18	.306	.375	.400
Runners On/2 Out	63	20	1	0	1	18	8	11	.317	.381	.394
Scor. Pos./2 Out	41	13	0	0	1	18	6	9	.317	.390	.404
Late-Inning Pressure	46	14	1	0	0	6	4	11	.304	.326	.360
Leading Off	10	4	0	0	0	0	1	1	.400	.400	.455
Runners On	19	7	1	0	0	6	3	7	.368	.421	.455
Runners/Scor. Pos.	13	4	1	0	0	6	3	5	.308	.385	.438

RUNS BATTED IN	From 1B	From 2B	From 3B	Scoring Position
Totals	1/100	13/56	18/33	31/89
Percentage	1.0%	23.2%	54.5%	34.8%

Loves to face: Brad Arnsberg (.571, 4-for-7, 2 2B, 2 HR)
Mike Birkbeck (.467, 7-for-15, 1 HR)
Dennis Lamp (.444, 12-for-27, 3 HR, 0 BB)

Hates to face: Roger Clemens (.185, 10-for-54, 1 HR, 24 SO)
Mark Eichhorn (.050, 1-for-20)
David Wells (.053, 1-for-19, 2 BB)

Miscellaneous statistics: Ground outs-to-air outs ratio: 0.89 last season, 1.00 for career.... Grounded into 13 double plays in 67 opportunities (one per 5.2).... Drove in 10 of 15 runners from third base with less than two outs (67%).... Direction of balls hit to the outfield: 33% to left field, 32% to center, 35% to right.... Base running: Advanced from first base to third on 6 of 18 outfield singles (33%); scored from second on 7 of 7 (100%).... Made 2.15 assists per nine innings at third base.

Comments: His 32-home-run season in 1987 remains the best piece of evidence for those espousing that season's lively ball and corked-bat theories. The only other active player to hit 30 home runs in a season without topping the 20 mark at least one other time is Gary Sheffield, who should remedy that shortly. (Davey Johnson, who hit 43 homers in 1973, never hit more than 18 any other time.) ... Played 120 games last season, his lowest total in any full season in the majors. Still, he played over 100 games at third base for the first time since 1989.... He was one of eight different players to start at third base for Cleveland last season, the most of any team in the majors.... After a two-month stint in Oakland to end the 1991 season, Jacoby returned to the Indians last season to post his highest single-season batting average in Cleveland and the lowest road mark of his career. He had hit for a higher average in road games than at Cleveland Stadium in each of his previous eight years with the Tribe.... Fewer than 15 percent of his hits were extra-base hits last season (65 singles, 11 XBH). Prior to 1992, his lowest yearly extra-base hit percentage had been 25 percent (1984).... His rate of grounding into double plays was the worst on the club last season.... Of his 120 career home runs, 80 have been solo shots.... Joins Wade Boggs and Steve Buechele as the only active players with a career stolen base percentage under .400 in at least 25 attempts.

Gregg Jefferies　　　　　　Bats Left and Right

Kansas City Royals	AB	H	2B	3B	HR	RBI	BB	SO	BA	SA	OBA
Season	604	172	36	3	10	75	43	29	.285	.404	.329
vs. Left-Handers	179	46	10	0	3	12	7	11	.257	.363	.282
vs. Right-Handers	425	126	26	3	7	63	36	18	.296	.421	.348
vs. Ground-Ballers	265	68	15	1	4	32	10	13	.257	.366	.280
vs. Fly-Ballers	339	104	21	2	6	43	33	16	.307	.434	.365
Home Games	280	81	15	3	3	37	26	12	.289	.396	.346
Road Games	324	91	21	0	7	38	17	17	.281	.410	.313
Grass Fields	264	72	14	0	6	32	12	10	.273	.394	.301
Artificial Turf	340	100	22	3	4	43	31	19	.294	.412	.349
April	79	16	8	0	0	5	8	5	.203	.304	.270
May	119	34	8	0	1	12	3	6	.286	.378	.303
June	76	25	5	0	3	15	5	2	.329	.513	.361
July	117	39	6	1	3	16	8	8	.333	.479	.370
August	92	30	5	1	1	12	13	2	.326	.435	.411
Sept./Oct.	121	28	4	1	2	15	6	6	.231	.331	.264
Leading Off Inn.	143	44	9	1	3	3	8	6	.308	.448	.349
Runners On	262	71	13	2	3	68	18	10	.271	.370	.308
Bases Empty	342	101	23	1	7	7	25	19	.295	.430	.345
Runners/Scor. Pos.	154	39	1	2	3	61	15	7	.253	.344	.303
Runners On/2 Out	111	32	2	1	3	30	5	5	.288	.405	.363
Scor. Pos./2 Out	87	23	0	1	3	29	11	5	.264	.391	.347
Late-Inning Pressure	100	26	6	0	0	12	10	5	.260	.320	.327
Leading Off	19	5	1	0	0	0	1	2	.263	.316	.300
Runners On	50	12	1	0	0	12	6	1	.240	.260	.321
Runners/Scor. Pos.	34	9	0	0	0	11	4	0	.265	.265	.342

RUNS BATTED IN	From 1B	From 2B	From 3B	Scoring Position
Totals	11/179	23/116	31/64	54/180
Percentage	6.1%	19.8%	48.4%	30.0%

Loves to face: Greg A. Harris (.625, 5-for-8, 1 HR)
Jose Mesa (.615, 8-for-13, 1 HR)
Dave Stewart (.556, 5-for-9, 1 HR)

Hates to face: Rick Honeycutt (0-for-5)
Jack McDowell (.091, 1-for-11)
Bill Wegman (.100, 1-for-10)

Miscellaneous statistics: Ground outs-to-air outs ratio: 1.20 last season, 0.94 for career.... Grounded into 24 double plays in 121 opportunities (one per 5.0), 4th-worst rate in A.L.... Drove in 22 of 28 runners from third base with less than two outs (79%), 2d-highest rate in A.L.... Direction of balls hit to the outfield: 30% to left field, 34% to center, 36% to right batting left-handed; 47% to left field, 31% to center, 22% to right batting right-handed.... Base running: Advanced from first base to third on 12 of 34 outfield singles (35%); scored from second on 16 of 18 (89%).... Made 2.12 assists per nine innings at third base.

Comments: Led American League third basemen with 170 hits last season, 37 more than A.L. batting champ Edgar Martinez.... Jefferies also led all major league third basemen with 19 stolen bases.... Led the Royals in batting vs. right-handed pitchers last season, with his highest average in any full season from the left side of the plate.... Joined Cal Ripken as the only major leaguers with two separate 1992 hitting streaks of at least 15 games.... Now for some bad news: Jefferies also led major league third basemen with 26 errors, and posted the major leagues' highest error rate there (one every 16.4 chances).... Stolen-base percentage (.679) was the lowest of his career. He compiled an 82 percent average in parts of five seasons with the Mets.... Career average of one strikeout every 15.6 plate appearances is 8th best among active players (minimum: 1000 PA).... Career batting average of .208 during April, .287 thereafter.... Had 28 more hits than Mets leader Eddie Murray. Jefferies would have ranked second on the Mets in extra-base hits and RBIs, third in stolen bases.... Will Kansas City's acquisition of Jefferies from the Mets eventually rival their steal of Amos Otis (and pitcher Bob Johnson) for Joe Foy in 1969? Otis accumulated 1993 hits for the Royals, the most by any ex-Mets player after leaving New York. Following Otis on that list: Ken Singleton, 1904; Tim Foli, 1340; Ron Hunt, 955; Hubie Brooks, 906.

Lance Johnson

Bats Left

Chicago White Sox	AB	H	2B	3B	HR	RBI	BB	SO	BA	SA	OBA
Season	567	158	15	12	3	47	34	33	.279	.363	.318
vs. Left-Handers	158	42	3	2	0	14	8	15	.266	.310	.302
vs. Right-Handers	409	116	12	10	3	33	26	18	.284	.384	.324
vs. Ground-Ballers	279	75	7	9	2	28	15	22	.269	.380	.305
vs. Fly-Ballers	288	83	8	3	1	19	19	11	.288	.347	.330
Home Games	274	72	7	4	2	25	20	12	.263	.339	.312
Road Games	293	86	8	8	1	22	14	21	.294	.386	.324
Grass Fields	481	133	8	9	3	36	31	28	.277	.349	.319
Artificial Turf	86	25	7	3	0	11	3	5	.291	.442	.311
April	71	21	1	1	0	4	1	4	.296	.338	.306
May	83	17	1	0	1	4	4	10	.205	.253	.239
June	96	29	5	2	0	7	7	7	.302	.396	.343
July	108	38	0	3	0	11	4	6	.352	.407	.377
August	96	24	1	2	2	9	10	3	.250	.365	.321
Sept./Oct.	113	29	7	4	0	12	8	3	.257	.389	.303
Leading Off Inn.	129	37	0	4	2	2	4	6	.287	.395	.308
Runners On	248	64	8	6	0	44	16	12	.258	.339	.300
Bases Empty	319	94	7	6	3	3	18	21	.295	.382	.332
Runners/Scor. Pos.	142	39	6	5	0	43	14	7	.275	.387	.333
Runners On/2 Out	102	23	1	2	0	14	12	6	.225	.275	.307
Scor. Pos./2 Out	69	13	0	1	0	13	10	6	.188	.217	.291
Late-Inning Pressure	78	18	1	0	0	5	9	9	.231	.244	.311
Leading Off	18	6	0	0	0	0	2	3	.333	.333	.400
Runners On	33	8	0	0	0	5	6	3	.242	.242	.357
Runners/Scor. Pos.	16	4	0	0	0	5	6	2	.250	.250	.440

RUNS BATTED IN	From 1B	From 2B	From 3B	Scoring Position
Totals	4/199	11/115	29/59	40/174
Percentage	2.0%	9.6%	49.2%	23.0%

Loves to face: Luis Aquino (.462, 6-for-13, 2 2B, 2 3B)
Mike Boddicker (.500, 8-for-16)
Joe Grahe (.467, 7-for-15)

Hates to face: Roger Clemens (.147, 5-for-34, 0 BB)
Jaime Navarro (.105, 2-for-19)
Russ Swan (0-for-10)

Miscellaneous statistics: Ground outs-to-air outs ratio: 1.60 last season, 1.85 for career.... Grounded into 20 double plays in 124 opportunities (one per 6.2).... Drove in 22 of 34 runners from third base with less than two outs (65%).... Direction of balls hit to the outfield: 38% to left field, 35% to center, 27% to right.... Base running: Advanced from first base to third on 18 of 27 outfield singles (67%), 4th-highest rate in majors; scored from second on 9 of 9 (100%).... Made 2.86 putouts per nine innings in center field.

Comments: His total of 103 stolen bases over the last three seasons is the highest three-year total by a White Sox player since Rudy Law stole 135 from 1983 to 1985.... Compiled the major leagues' longest hitting streak last season, 25 games—the longest by a White Sox player since Guy Curtright's 26-game streak in 1943. Johnson's was the first 20-game streak by a Chisox player since Ken Berry in 1967.... Has hit safely in each of his last 17 games against the Brewers, including all 12 last season.... Walks exceeded strikeouts for the first time in his career, contributing to his career-high 41 stolen bases. Average of one strikeout every 18.5 plate appearances was the best of his career, by far.... After hitting only two home runs in his first 1900 major league at-bats, he hit two in a span of 23 ABs (August 16–24).... All four of his career home runs have been hit against right-handed pitchers. Has the most career at-bats against left-handed pitchers among active players who are homerless against southpaws. The top three: Johnson (564 AB), Luis Polonia (529), and Rafael Belliard (505).... Has had more than 10 triples but no more than 15 doubles in each of the last two seasons. Since 1900, only five other players have done that in consecutive seasons, the last being Ray Powell (1919–20). Among the other four is Greasy Neale, who had a Hall of Fame career—as coach of the NFL's Philadelphia Eagles.... Lowest career strikeout rates with the bases loaded since 1975: Rico Carty (one every 70 PA); Johnson (59); Jim Spencer (53); Biff Pocoroba (52).

Wally Joyner

Bats Left

Kansas City Royals	AB	H	2B	3B	HR	RBI	BB	SO	BA	SA	OBA
Season	572	154	36	2	9	66	55	50	.269	.386	.336
vs. Left-Handers	192	46	13	0	2	20	15	24	.240	.339	.307
vs. Right-Handers	380	108	23	2	7	46	40	26	.284	.411	.352
vs. Ground-Ballers	238	62	12	0	2	31	19	18	.261	.336	.320
vs. Fly-Ballers	334	92	24	2	7	35	36	32	.275	.422	.348
Home Games	282	75	19	2	1	29	21	21	.266	.358	.324
Road Games	290	79	17	0	8	37	34	29	.272	.414	.349
Grass Fields	223	58	11	0	6	25	25	19	.260	.390	.336
Artificial Turf	349	96	25	2	3	41	30	31	.275	.384	.337
April	81	26	8	0	1	9	7	9	.321	.457	.375
May	67	22	5	0	3	8	2	6	.328	.537	.366
June	105	24	8	0	1	16	7	10	.229	.333	.278
July	110	26	8	0	1	11	12	14	.236	.336	.311
August	107	30	1	1	2	14	12	5	.280	.364	.358
Sept./Oct.	102	26	6	1	1	8	15	6	.255	.363	.350
Leading Off Inn.	125	28	7	1	3	3	7	7	.224	.368	.265
Runners On	261	75	17	1	5	62	27	25	.287	.418	.358
Bases Empty	311	79	19	1	4	4	28	25	.254	.360	.318
Runners/Scor. Pos.	141	40	13	0	3	52	18	11	.284	.440	.372
Runners On/2 Out	112	32	9	1	4	30	15	11	.286	.491	.380
Scor. Pos./2 Out	64	17	7	0	2	22	11	4	.266	.469	.390
Late-Inning Pressure	93	22	4	0	2	11	11	8	.237	.344	.317
Leading Off	21	6	1	0	1	1	2	1	.286	.476	.348
Runners On	46	9	3	0	0	9	5	7	.196	.261	.275
Runners/Scor. Pos.	27	8	3	0	0	9	4	2	.296	.407	.387

RUNS BATTED IN	From 1B	From 2B	From 3B	Scoring Position
Totals	14/179	18/107	25/54	43/161
Percentage	7.8%	16.8%	46.3%	26.7%

Loves to face: Bert Blyleven (.419, 13-for-31, 2 HR)
Jack Morris (.432, 19-for-44, 1 HR)
Dave Stieb (.375, 15-for-40, 4 HR)

Hates to face: Mark Langston (.111, 3-for-27, 1 HR)
Nolan Ryan (.125, 3-for-24, 3 BB)
Kevin Tapani (.150, 3-for-20)

Miscellaneous statistics: Ground outs-to-air outs ratio: 1.06 last season, 0.91 for career.... Grounded into 19 double plays in 107 opportunities (one per 5.6).... Drove in 15 of 23 runners from third base with less than two outs (65%).... Direction of balls hit to the outfield: 32% to left field, 35% to center, 33% to right.... Base running: Advanced from first base to third on 18 of 33 outfield singles (55%); scored from second on 12 of 16 (75%).... Made 0.98 assists per nine innings at first base, 2d-highest rate in majors.

Comments: Slugging percentage was a career low; his on-base and batting averages were both one point above career lows.... Home-run rate (one every 64 at-bats) was less than half his career rate in six years with the Angels (one HR every 28 AB). Joyner matched his career average of eight home runs per season on the road, but added only one at Royals Stadium.... Angels first basemen posted the lowest batting average in the majors at that position last season (.222), but Joyner fans oughtn't gloat—Royals first basemen drove in only four more runs (73) than Angels first basemen (69).... Joyner led A.L. first basemen with 11 stolen bases (a career high).... Started 19 double plays in the field, the most of any major league first baseman.... In the expansion era, only Chris Chambliss, John Mayberry, Jason Thompson, and Cecil Cooper have played 1000 games at first base, but none at any other position. Joyner enters 1993 with 985 games at first base, Will Clark with 995; neither has played a game at any other fielding position.... Career batting- and slugging-average breakdowns: .300, .479 vs. right-handed pitchers; .257, .378 vs. left-handed pitchers.... Fantasy-league alert: Joyner has started quickly but faded in each of the past two seasons, compiling a .338 for April and May, but only a .265 mark from June through October. His highest BA has come in May in each of the past three seasons.

Ron Karkovice
Bats Right

Chicago White Sox	AB	H	2B	3B	HR	RBI	BB	SO	BA	SA	OBA
Season	342	81	12	1	13	50	30	89	.237	.392	.302
vs. Left-Handers	107	24	5	1	4	15	13	30	.224	.402	.314
vs. Right-Handers	235	57	7	0	9	35	17	59	.243	.387	.297
vs. Ground-Ballers	159	35	3	0	6	19	17	36	.220	.352	.307
vs. Fly-Ballers	183	46	9	1	7	31	13	53	.251	.426	.298
Home Games	171	39	6	1	5	18	17	41	.228	.363	.305
Road Games	171	42	6	0	8	32	13	48	.246	.421	.299
Grass Fields	282	66	8	1	9	42	27	72	.234	.365	.306
Artificial Turf	60	15	4	0	4	8	3	17	.250	.517	.286
April	44	11	1	0	1	6	8	9	.250	.341	.370
May	72	12	2	0	1	5	6	25	.167	.236	.231
June	46	11	1	0	3	6	6	15	.239	.457	.340
July	47	9	2	0	1	5	3	5	.191	.298	.250
August	45	10	1	0	1	8	3	9	.222	.311	.271
Sept./Oct.	88	28	5	1	6	20	4	26	.318	.602	.348
Leading Off Inn.	79	20	2	0	4	4	3	19	.253	.430	.280
Runners On	150	37	6	1	6	43	16	43	.247	.420	.327
Bases Empty	192	44	6	0	7	7	14	46	.229	.370	.282
Runners/Scor. Pos.	90	24	3	1	2	34	14	24	.267	.389	.364
Runners On/2 Out	72	18	5	1	2	21	5	18	.250	.431	.299
Scor. Pos./2 Out	47	13	3	1	1	18	4	10	.277	.447	.333
Late-Inning Pressure	43	9	1	0	1	3	4	11	.209	.302	.286
Leading Off	14	5	0	0	0	0	1	0	.357	.357	.400
Runners On	19	2	0	0	0	2	2	7	.105	.105	.217
Runners/Scor. Pos.	13	1	0	0	0	2	1	5	.077	.077	.133

RUNS BATTED IN	From 1B	From 2B	From 3B	Scoring Position
Totals	7/106	14/69	16/43	30/112
Percentage	6.6%	20.3%	37.2%	26.8%

Loves to face: Tim Leary (.625, 5-for-8)
Bobby Witt (.300, 3-for-10, 2 HR)
Curt Young (.556, 5-for-9, 3 SO)

Hates to face: Mark Langston (.111, 2-for-18, 12 SO)
Jaime Navarro (0-for-10)
Matt Young (0-for-10, 6 SO)

Miscellaneous statistics: Ground outs-to-air outs ratio: 0.79 last season, 0.87 for career.... Grounded into 3 double plays in 63 opportunities (one per 21).... Drove in 7 of 21 runners from third base with less than two outs (33%), 3d-lowest rate in majors.... Direction of balls hit to the outfield: 50% to left field, 31% to center, 19% to right.... Base running: Advanced from first base to third on 3 of 18 outfield singles (17%); scored from second on 9 of 10 (90%).... Opposing base stealers: 69-for-102 (68%).

Comments: The White Sox have compiled a better record with Karkovice starting behind the plate than with other starting catchers in each of the past three seasons. Three-year totals: 115–82 (.584) with Karkovice catching, 152–137 (.526) with others.... Had never played more than 75 games in any major league season before last year, when he played 123 games.... Matched his career high for homers in a month in June, and then shattered it in September.... The only player in the majors to increase his extra-base hit total in each of the last five years. No player has done that in six consecutive seasons since Kirk Gibson (1980–85).... Ranked third among major league catchers with 10 stolen bases last season, behind Darren Daulton and B.J. Surhoff (11 each). No other catcher stole more than three bases.... Even though he's batted .246 over his four full seasons with the White Sox, his career average stands at only .226, thanks to two partial seasons (1987–88) in which he went 26-for-200.... Career batting average is .207 in Chicago, .244 elsewhere. Batting average on the road has been higher than at home in six of his seven seasons in the majors.... Of his 36 career home runs, only eight have been hit at Comiskey Park (five new, three old).... Career rate of 42.7 percent of runners driven in from third base with less than two outs is 3d lowest among active players (minimum: 50 opportunities); the only lower rates belong to Dave Valle (42.4) and Bob McIvin (42.5). Karkovice's average has been below 50 percent in five of the last six years.

Pat Kelly
Bats Right

New York Yankees	AB	H	2B	3B	HR	RBI	BB	SO	BA	SA	OBA
Season	318	72	22	2	7	27	25	72	.226	.374	.301
vs. Left-Handers	114	26	5	1	3	7	9	25	.228	.368	.288
vs. Right-Handers	204	46	17	1	4	20	16	47	.225	.377	.307
vs. Ground-Ballers	130	25	6	0	2	10	7	25	.192	.285	.255
vs. Fly-Ballers	188	47	16	2	5	17	18	47	.250	.436	.332
Home Games	176	39	11	2	3	17	16	39	.222	.358	.298
Road Games	142	33	11	0	4	10	9	33	.232	.394	.304
Grass Fields	263	61	17	2	6	23	24	59	.232	.380	.318
Artificial Turf	55	11	5	0	1	4	1	13	.200	.345	.211
April	30	6	2	0	0	0	5	9	.200	.267	.333
May	66	18	6	1	2	8	5	20	.273	.485	.360
June	30	3	0	0	1	1	1	9	.100	.200	.156
July	72	14	3	1	1	5	4	15	.194	.306	.237
August	68	20	5	0	3	11	6	9	.294	.500	.346
Sept./Oct.	52	11	6	0	0	2	4	10	.212	.327	.305
Leading Off Inn.	67	15	3	0	1	1	7	14	.224	.313	.307
Runners On	133	27	9	0	2	22	7	31	.203	.316	.259
Bases Empty	185	45	13	2	5	5	18	41	.243	.416	.330
Runners/Scor. Pos.	62	12	2	0	1	17	5	21	.194	.274	.274
Runners On/2 Out	66	11	4	0	1	11	4	15	.167	.273	.236
Scor. Pos./2 Out	30	4	0	0	1	8	3	10	.133	.233	.257
Late-Inning Pressure	42	10	5	0	0	5	3	10	.238	.357	.306
Leading Off	11	3	2	0	0	0	0	3	.273	.455	.273
Runners On	13	3	2	0	0	5	2	1	.231	.385	.333
Runners/Scor. Pos.	5	1	0	0	0	4	2	1	.200	.200	.400

RUNS BATTED IN	From 1B	From 2B	From 3B	Scoring Position
Totals	5/108	6/53	9/29	15/82
Percentage	4.6%	11.3%	31.0%	18.3%

Loves to face: Goose Gossage (1-for-1, 1 HR, 2 BB)
Kenny Rogers (.750, 3-for-4, 1 2B, 1 HR)
Mark Williamson (.800, 4-for-5, 1 SO)

Hates to face: Kevin Campbell (0-for-8)
Roger Clemens (0-for-9)
Juan Guzman (0-for-4, 4 SO)

Miscellaneous statistics: Ground outs-to-air outs ratio: 0.72 last season, 0.85 for career.... Grounded into 6 double plays in 64 opportunities (one per 11).... Drove in 6 of 15 runners from third base with less than two outs (40%).... Direction of balls hit to the outfield: 44% to left field, 27% to center, 28% to right.... Base running: Advanced from first base to third on 6 of 17 outfield singles (35%); scored from second on 7 of 7 (100%).... Made 3.08 assists per nine innings at second base.

Comments: After playing more at third base than at second base as a rookie in 1991, Kelly stayed in his natural position last year, appearing in 101 games in the field, all at second base.... Yankees second basemen combined for only 42 RBIs, 2d-lowest total in the league last season, ahead of only Rangers second basemen (36).... At 24 years of age, he was the youngest player on the Yankees roster for most of the season; but there are established major league second basemen of All-Star quality even younger: Roberto Alomar, Chuck Knoblauch, Carlos Baerga, and Delino DeShields.... Gave the Yankees some power from the ninth spot. His seven home runs and 31 extra-base hits from the bottom of the order were league highs.... Led the Yankees in bunt singles with eight—twice as many as all his teammates combined.... His three-hit game on September 1 broke a streak of 144 consecutive starts with no more than two hits, dating back to June 26, 1991.... Batting average with runners in scoring position has been below .200 in each of his two major league seasons (career: .190).... Only five players have been hit with as many as 10 pitches over their first 200 games with the Yankees: Don Baylor, 19; Pat Kelly, 15; Joe Sewell, 11; Elliott Maddox, 11; Billy Martin, 10.... If you're a Yankees fan looking for an example of a player whose career started with similar mediocrity but flourished thereafter, check out Frank White in the *Baseball Encyclopedia*. (Then cross your fingers.)

Roberto Kelly
Bats Right

New York Yankees	AB	H	2B	3B	HR	RBI	BB	SO	BA	SA	OBA
Season	580	158	31	2	10	66	41	96	.272	.384	.322
vs. Left-Handers	184	51	9	0	4	21	20	28	.277	.391	.344
vs. Right-Handers	396	107	22	2	6	45	21	68	.270	.381	.310
vs. Ground-Ballers	236	61	15	0	4	29	15	43	.258	.373	.302
vs. Fly-Ballers	344	97	16	2	6	37	26	53	.282	.392	.335
Home Games	296	76	16	1	6	37	21	52	.257	.378	.309
Road Games	284	82	15	1	4	29	20	44	.289	.391	.336
Grass Fields	498	134	27	2	9	56	37	79	.269	.386	.321
Artificial Turf	82	24	4	0	1	10	4	17	.293	.378	.326
April	85	30	6	1	1	14	5	14	.353	.482	.391
May	106	34	5	1	4	16	5	15	.321	.500	.357
June	93	18	5	0	2	10	4	19	.194	.312	.232
July	93	24	4	0	1	8	9	16	.258	.333	.317
August	109	31	7	0	2	9	10	17	.284	.404	.347
Sept./Oct.	94	21	4	0	0	9	8	15	.223	.266	.282
Leading Off Inn.	112	30	8	2	3	3	4	19	.268	.455	.293
Runners On	254	67	15	0	4	60	15	41	.264	.370	.306
Bases Empty	326	91	16	2	6	6	26	55	.279	.396	.334
Runners/Scor. Pos.	145	38	11	0	1	51	13	22	.262	.359	.319
Runners On/2 Out	93	15	3	0	0	15	10	16	.161	.194	.250
Scor. Pos./2 Out	57	11	3	0	0	15	9	8	.193	.246	.303
Late-Inning Pressure	95	22	3	0	2	14	3	17	.232	.326	.260
Leading Off	28	4	0	0	1	1	0	7	.143	.250	.143
Runners On	36	11	3	0	1	13	2	5	.306	.472	.350
Runners/Scor. Pos.	24	7	2	0	0	10	2	3	.292	.375	.333

RUNS BATTED IN	From 1B	From 2B	From 3B	Scoring Position
Totals	9/195	20/105	27/67	47/172
Percentage	4.6%	19.0%	40.3%	27.3%

Loves to face: John Candelaria (.750, 3-for-4, 1 2B, 1 HR, 1 HBP)
Bret Saberhagen (.316, 6-for-19, 2 2B, 1 HR)

Hates to face: Jose Guzman (.167, 4-for-24, 1 HR)
Mike Jackson (0-for-7, 4 SO)
Lee Smith (0-for-4, 2 SO)

Miscellaneous statistics: Ground outs-to-air outs ratio: 1.19 last season, 1.14 for career.... Grounded into 19 double plays in 127 opportunities (one per 6.7).... Drove in 22 of 39 runners from third base with less than two outs (56%).... Direction of balls hit to the outfield: 31% to left field, 35% to center, 34% to right.... Base running: Advanced from first base to third on 10 of 28 outfield singles (36%); scored from second on 11 of 12 (92%).... Made 2.94 putouts per nine innings in center field.

Comments: Should Kelly have the season the Yankees waited five years for, you'll hear stories about how players can't wait to leave New York. Try telling that to Steve Sax. Here are the facts: Over the past 15 years, five batters have had breakthrough seasons immediately following their departure from the Yankees: Oscar Gamble (1977), Toby Harrah (1985), Billy Sample (1986), Ron Kittle (1988), and Don Slaught (1990). Only Gamble's represented a spectacular rise (.297, 31 HR, 83 RBI for the White Sox). Eight had break*downs* after leaving: Sax (1992), Juan Beniquez (1980), Steve Kemp (1985), Butch Wynegar, Dan Pasqua, Jerry Royster, and Mark Salas (all 1988), and Willie Randolph (1989). Much ado about nothing.... Didn't hit a home run in his last 46 games with the Yankees, equaling the longest drought of his career. September was his first homerless month since April 1990.... Hit regularly in three different batting-order positions; the lower he hit, the higher his batting, slugging, and on-base averages rose. Batting 2d (28 games): .236, .274, .308; batting 3d (88 games): .274, .410, .319; batting 5th (31 games): .308, .419, .352.... Batting average with two outs and runners on base was the lowest in the A.L. last season.... Career batting-average breakdown: .302 vs. left-handers, .269 vs. right-handers.... On August 31, Kelly knocked Phil Rizzuto from the Yankees' all-time top 10 in steals. He stole just one base in 28 games thereafter, batting .223 with no homers, and was traded after the season. The "Curse of the Scooter"?

Chuck Knoblauch
Bats Right

Minnesota Twins	AB	H	2B	3B	HR	RBI	BB	SO	BA	SA	OBA
Season	600	178	19	6	2	56	88	60	.297	.358	.384
vs. Left-Handers	124	39	6	2	1	9	17	11	.315	.419	.401
vs. Right-Handers	476	139	13	4	1	47	71	49	.292	.342	.380
vs. Ground-Ballers	285	81	6	5	1	26	38	26	.284	.351	.367
vs. Fly-Ballers	315	97	13	1	1	30	50	34	.308	.365	.400
Home Games	289	83	5	2	0	23	49	23	.287	.318	.388
Road Games	311	95	14	4	2	33	39	37	.305	.395	.381
Grass Fields	242	76	10	2	1	24	23	24	.314	.384	.371
Artificial Turf	358	102	9	4	1	32	65	36	.285	.341	.393
April	80	23	0	0	1	8	8	8	.287	.325	.344
May	99	36	8	1	0	12	16	8	.364	.465	.449
June	95	24	3	1	0	11	22	7	.253	.305	.393
July	103	32	4	2	0	10	10	7	.311	.388	.362
August	115	35	3	1	0	4	8	18	.304	.348	.347
Sept./Oct.	108	28	1	1	1	11	24	12	.259	.315	.400
Leading Off Inn.	166	53	7	1	2	2	20	13	.319	.410	.402
Runners On	241	71	7	4	0	54	35	31	.295	.357	.370
Bases Empty	359	107	12	2	2	2	53	29	.298	.359	.394
Runners/Scor. Pos.	145	38	2	4	0	52	24	20	.262	.331	.346
Runners On/2 Out	84	17	1	1	0	14	15	10	.202	.238	.330
Scor. Pos./2 Out	62	10	0	1	0	13	11	9	.161	.194	.297
Late-Inning Pressure	84	21	2	2	0	11	10	14	.250	.321	.337
Leading Off	24	5	1	0	0	0	3	3	.208	.250	.345
Runners On	35	10	0	1	0	11	5	8	.286	.343	.357
Runners/Scor. Pos.	22	7	0	1	0	11	4	6	.318	.409	.393

RUNS BATTED IN	From 1B	From 2B	From 3B	Scoring Position
Totals	3/163	20/118	31/72	51/190
Percentage	1.8%	16.9%	43.1%	26.8%

Loves to face: Jim Abbott (.400, 8-for-20, 1 HR)
Mike Mussina (.545, 6-for-11, 1 HR)
Bill Wegman (.462, 6-for-13)

Hates to face: Dennis Eckersley (0-for-8)
Juan Guzman (0-for-13)
Mike Magnante (0-for-8)

Miscellaneous statistics: Ground outs-to-air outs ratio: 1.00 last season, 1.18 for career.... Grounded into 8 double plays in 123 opportunities (one per 15).... Drove in 25 of 40 runners from third base with less than two outs (63%).... Direction of balls hit to the outfield: 25% to left field, 38% to center, 38% to right.... Base running: Advanced from first base to third on 24 of 43 outfield singles (56%); scored from second on 24 of 28 (86%).... Made 2.79 assists per nine innings at second base, 2d-lowest rate in A.L.

Comments: Coming off his award-winning rookie season, Knoblauch raised his totals in games, at-bats, runs, hits, home runs, RBIs, walks, stolen bases, batting average, slugging percentage, and on-base average.... Became the first player to lead his league's rookies in hits one season and lead sophomores the next since Kirby Puckett and Juan Samuel (1984–85). Five of the last eight A.L. players to do that have done so for the Twins (or old Washington Senators). Besides Knoblauch and Puckett, they include Gary Ward (1981–82), Tony Oliva (1964–65), and Bob Allison (1959–60). Over the last 30 years, only one player has led the entire majors in hits among rookies and then among sophomores: Ralph Garr (1971–72). Prior to that, many did it, including five rookies of the '50s: Harvey Kuenn (1953), Frank Robinson (1956), Frank Malzone (1957), Orlando Cepeda (1958), and Vada Pinson (1959).... Raised his batting average vs. right-handers by two points from 1991 to 1992, but his mark vs. left-handers leaped by 58 points.... He also sliced his error total by two thirds, from 18 to 6.... Other Rookies of the Year who improved markedly as sophomores: Cal Ripken (1983), Jose Canseco (1987), Bob Horner (1979).... Although his RBI total ranked seventh on the Twins, the only teammate with more game-winning RBIs than Knoblauch (10) was Chili Davis (11).

Carney Lansford

Bats Right

Oakland A's	AB	H	2B	3B	HR	RBI	BB	SO	BA	SA	OBA
Season	496	130	30	1	7	75	43	39	.262	.369	.325
vs. Left-Handers	132	37	12	0	1	17	11	8	.280	.394	.342
vs. Right-Handers	364	93	18	1	6	58	32	31	.255	.360	.319
vs. Ground-Ballers	232	65	11	1	3	39	21	18	.280	.375	.341
vs. Fly-Ballers	264	65	19	0	4	36	22	21	.246	.364	.311
Home Games	218	51	13	1	4	33	19	22	.234	.358	.301
Road Games	278	79	17	0	3	42	24	17	.284	.378	.344
Grass Fields	410	108	26	1	6	65	37	31	.263	.376	.328
Artificial Turf	86	22	4	0	1	10	6	8	.256	.337	.309
April	77	28	9	0	0	11	9	4	.364	.481	.432
May	92	20	3	0	0	12	5	8	.217	.250	.253
June	88	21	4	1	1	9	6	8	.239	.341	.292
July	84	22	5	0	1	9	6	6	.262	.357	.312
August	74	21	7	0	5	23	7	4	.284	.581	.361
Sept./Oct.	81	18	2	0	0	11	10	9	.222	.247	.316
Leading Off Inn.	88	18	3	0	0	0	4	5	.205	.239	.247
Runners On	228	60	15	1	5	73	28	20	.263	.404	.338
Bases Empty	268	70	15	0	2	2	15	19	.261	.340	.313
Runners/Scor. Pos.	147	39	10	0	4	67	20	13	.265	.415	.337
Runners On/2 Out	96	26	7	1	1	34	12	10	.271	.396	.358
Scor. Pos./2 Out	72	22	6	0	1	32	11	7	.306	.431	.398
Late-Inning Pressure	57	14	1	0	1	12	5	6	.246	.316	.317
Leading Off	13	2	0	0	0	0	0	0	.154	.154	.154
Runners On	29	8	0	0	1	12	5	4	.276	.379	.400
Runners/Scor. Pos.	20	5	0	0	1	11	4	2	.250	.400	.375

RUNS BATTED IN	From 1B	From 2B	From 3B	Scoring Position
Totals	12/149	25/129	31/61	56/190
Percentage	8.1%	19.4%	50.8%	29.5%

Loves to face: Scott Bankhead (.500, 12-for-24, 1 HR)
Mike Boddicker (.423, 22-for-52, 4 HR)
Neal Heaton (.522, 12-for-23, 0 SO)

Hates to face: Mark Gubicza (.182, 6-for-33, 0 BB)
Mike Henneman (0-for-11)
Jeff M. Robinson (.143, 4-for-28, 0 BB)

Miscellaneous statistics: Ground outs-to-air outs ratio: 1.11 last season, 1.05 for career.... Grounded into 14 double plays in 110 opportunities (one per 7.9).... Drove in 21 of 32 runners from third base with less than two outs (66%).... Direction of balls hit to the outfield: 33% to left field, 37% to center, 30% to right.... Base running: Advanced from first base to third on 16 of 36 outfield singles (44%); scored from second on 12 of 20 (60%).... Made 1.51 assists per nine innings at third base, lowest rate in majors.

Comments: After missing virtually all of the 1991 season, he came back to drive in 75 runs, the 4th-highest total of his career, and only five shy of his career high (80 in 1980). Athletics third basemen combined for 97 RBIs last season, the most by any team in the American League.... If the retirement sticks, Lansford will be only the third player in the last 40 years to leave the game coming off a season of 75 or more RBIs. The others: Jeffrey Leonard (1990) and Dave Kingman (1986).... The last player to retire following a season with as many RBIs *and hits* as Lansford: Ed Morgan of the 1934 Red Sox.... Hit only seven home runs in 561 at-bats last season, but five came during a span of only 61 ABs (August 2–28).... One of two players in the 92-year history of the Athletics' franchise to play at least 1000 games at third base. His total of 1096 games there is second to Sal Bando's (1446).... Best career postseason error rates at third base (minimum: 15 games): Lansford (one error in 96 chances); Joe Dugan (one per 69); Graig Nettles (one per 61); Billy Johnson (one per 50); Bando (one per 43).... Lansford's career average of 2.52 fielding chances per game ranks 76th among 79 players with 1000 games at third base. Sure, you can reason that he played during a high-strikeout era. But if you adjust all figures to reflect only balls put into play, he ranks one slot *lower*.

Gene Larkin

Bats Left and Right

Minnesota Twins	AB	H	2B	3B	HR	RBI	BB	SO	BA	SA	OBA
Season	337	83	18	1	6	42	28	43	.246	.359	.308
vs. Left-Handers	55	12	6	0	0	5	6	8	.218	.327	.295
vs. Right-Handers	282	71	12	1	6	37	22	35	.252	.365	.311
vs. Ground-Ballers	155	42	8	1	2	22	13	20	.271	.374	.333
vs. Fly-Ballers	182	41	10	0	4	20	15	23	.225	.346	.287
Home Games	153	40	9	0	5	20	16	18	.261	.418	.326
Road Games	184	43	9	1	1	22	12	25	.234	.310	.294
Grass Fields	135	33	7	1	0	13	9	20	.244	.311	.306
Artificial Turf	202	50	11	0	6	29	19	23	.248	.391	.310
April	68	15	5	0	3	12	5	6	.221	.426	.270
May	37	13	1	0	1	9	7	8	.351	.459	.478
June	60	15	2	0	0	5	4	8	.250	.283	.313
July	47	10	1	0	1	2	5	4	.213	.298	.288
August	51	12	5	1	0	3	6	7	.235	.373	.316
Sept./Oct.	74	18	4	0	1	11	1	10	.243	.338	.247
Leading Off Inn.	78	17	7	0	0	0	3	7	.218	.308	.256
Runners On	163	44	9	1	3	39	15	23	.270	.393	.332
Bases Empty	174	39	9	0	3	3	13	20	.224	.328	.286
Runners/Scor. Pos.	94	27	5	0	1	32	11	15	.287	.372	.360
Runners On/2 Out	52	12	1	0	1	10	7	8	.231	.308	.322
Scor. Pos./2 Out	37	9	0	0	0	8	5	5	.243	.243	.333
Late-Inning Pressure	58	16	6	0	0	7	6	10	.276	.379	.354
Leading Off	15	2	1	0	0	0	0	3	.133	.200	.188
Runners On	26	11	5	0	0	7	3	4	.423	.615	.483
Runners/Scor. Pos.	14	6	2	0	0	6	1	1	.429	.571	.467

RUNS BATTED IN	From 1B	From 2B	From 3B	Scoring Position
Totals	7/127	16/76	13/37	29/113
Percentage	5.5%	21.1%	35.1%	25.7%

Loves to face: Mike Boddicker (.300, 6-for-20, 2 HR)
Tim Leary (.500, 5-for-10, 1 HR)
Melido Perez (.333, 7-for-21, 2 HR)

Hates to face: Greg A. Harris (.077, 1-for-13)
Randy Johnson (.067, 1-for-15, 4 BB)
Jeff Montgomery (0-for-11)

Miscellaneous statistics: Ground outs-to-air outs ratio: 0.71 last season, 0.95 for career.... Grounded into 7 double plays in 93 opportunities (one per 13).... Drove in 11 of 23 runners from third base with less than two outs (48%).... Direction of balls hit to the outfield: 24% to left field, 37% to center, 40% to right batting left-handed; 39% to left field, 17% to center, 43% to right batting right-handed.... Base running: Advanced from first base to third on 4 of 16 outfield singles (25%); scored from second on 4 of 9 (44%).... Made 0.63 assists per nine innings at first base.

Comments: Will always be remembered for his game-winning hit in the 10th inning of World Series Game 7. The odd thing is that it came during a streak of 206 regular-season games without a game-winner that spanned more than two years (Aug. 28, 1990–Aug. 30, 1992).... Nevertheless, his career batting average with runners in scoring position in Late-Inning Pressure Situations is .341 (29-for-85), 4th highest among active players with at least 75 at-bats. The top three: Jose Canseco (.366), Don Mattingly (.361), and Wade Boggs (.346).... With Kent Hrbek sidelined, Larkin was Minnesota's opening-day starter at first base, snapping Hrbek's 10-year streak. Minnesota's opening-day first baseman the year before Hrbek arrived was Mickey Hatcher (1981).... Started the first 18 games last season—the only period since the 1990 All-Star break in which he made more than 10 straight starts.... Hit three home runs in April, equaling the highest one-month output of his career, then hit only three more for the rest of the season.... His at-bat total vs. left-handers declined in each of the last three seasons, to a career low in 1992; since 1989: 156, 121, 88, 55.... Career batting averages: .280 at home, .253 on the road.... Over the last three seasons, he's hit 10 of his 13 homers at the Metrodome.... Career home-run rate is one every 70 at-bats, but he is homerless in 80 at-bats as a pinch hitter.... Went 8-for-24 pinch-hitting last season, raising his career pinch BA only to .238.

Manuel Lee — Bats Left and Right

Toronto Blue Jays	AB	H	2B	3B	HR	RBI	BB	SO	BA	SA	OBA
Season	396	104	10	1	3	39	50	73	.263	.316	.343
vs. Left-Handers	118	25	4	0	0	12	15	17	.212	.246	.299
vs. Right-Handers	278	79	6	1	3	27	35	56	.284	.345	.362
vs. Ground-Ballers	197	50	6	0	2	23	24	40	.254	.315	.332
vs. Fly-Ballers	199	54	4	1	1	16	26	33	.271	.317	.354
Home Games	184	41	4	0	1	18	27	36	.223	.261	.321
Road Games	212	63	6	1	2	21	23	37	.297	.363	.363
Grass Fields	161	51	5	1	1	15	16	27	.317	.379	.374
Artificial Turf	235	53	5	0	2	24	34	46	.226	.272	.322
April	65	16	3	0	0	7	7	15	.246	.292	.315
May	80	20	1	0	3	7	8	15	.250	.375	.318
June	82	21	4	1	0	13	14	13	.256	.329	.365
July	77	18	0	0	0	7	10	10	.234	.234	.318
August	78	23	2	0	0	2	6	17	.295	.321	.341
Sept./Oct.	14	6	0	0	0	3	5	3	.429	.429	.579
Leading Off Inn.	92	24	2	0	0	0	13	16	.261	.283	.352
Runners On	157	43	5	0	1	37	19	28	.274	.325	.346
Bases Empty	239	61	5	1	2	2	31	45	.255	.310	.341
Runners/Scor. Pos.	94	31	4	0	1	37	9	17	.330	.404	.377
Runners On/2 Out	61	22	2	0	1	17	13	11	.361	.443	.473
Scor. Pos./2 Out	44	17	2	0	1	17	6	7	.386	.500	.460
Late-Inning Pressure	50	12	0	0	0	1	8	9	.240	.240	.345
Leading Off	13	4	0	0	0	0	3	3	.308	.308	.438
Runners On	17	3	0	0	0	1	3	3	.176	.176	.300
Runners/Scor. Pos.	5	0	0	0	0	1	1	0	.000	.000	.167

RUNS BATTED IN	From 1B	From 2B	From 3B	Scoring Position
Totals	1/111	16/77	19/45	35/122
Percentage	0.9%	20.8%	42.2%	28.7%

Loves to face: Roger Clemens (.421, 8-for-19)
Chuck Finley (.450, 9-for-20)
David Haas (2-for-2, 3 BB)

Hates to face: Luis Aquino (0-for-14)
Bill Gullickson (0-for-13)
Mark Guthrie (.071, 1-for-14)

Miscellaneous statistics: Ground outs-to-air outs ratio: 1.43 last season, 1.78 for career.... Grounded into 8 double plays in 84 opportunities (one per 11).... Drove in 14 of 25 runners from third base with less than two outs (56%).... Direction of balls hit to the outfield: 43% to left field, 30% to center, 27% to right batting left-handed; 20% to left field, 40% to center, 40% to right batting right-handed.... Base running: Advanced from first base to third on 9 of 23 outfield singles (39%); scored from second on 14 of 16 (88%).... Made 2.76 assists per nine innings at shortstop, lowest rate in A.L.

Comments: After committing 19 errors in 1991, he was charged with only seven errors in 525 chances during the 1992 regular season. His average of one error every 75 chances was 2d best among A.L. shortstops, behind Omar Vizquel (one error every 90 chances).... But Lee committed four errors in 55 chances during the postseason. (Roger Peckinpaugh's eight errors at shortstop in the 1925 World Series is the most by any player at any position, or positions, in any postseason.) Three others had six errors in a postseason, regardless of position: second basemen Davey Lopes (1981) and Joe Sewell (1920), and shortstop Honus Wagner (1903).... Fielding could suffer in Arlington. Lee's career error rate at shortstop is 50 percent higher on grass (one every 20 chances) than on artificial turf (one every 30). Difference isn't nearly as wide at second base.... Drew as many walks last season as he did for the two previous seasons combined. His rate of walks (one every 9.1 plate appearances) and his on-base percentage were both career highs.... Only 14 of his 104 hits went for extra bases, the fewest of any player with at least 100 hits last season. The last player with at least 100 hits but fewer than 14 extra-base hits was Felix Fermin in 1989 (115 hits, 10 XBH).... Played 127 games batting in the ninth slot, the most of any major leaguer last season.... Switch-hitting breakdown for 1992 was a departure from his previous career tendency. Career figures: .244 batting left-handed, .272 batting right-handed.

Scott Leius — Bats Right

Minnesota Twins	AB	H	2B	3B	HR	RBI	BB	SO	BA	SA	OBA
Season	409	102	18	2	2	35	34	61	.249	.318	.309
vs. Left-Handers	118	37	5	0	0	10	11	13	.314	.356	.372
vs. Right-Handers	291	65	13	2	2	25	23	48	.223	.302	.283
vs. Ground-Ballers	188	44	13	0	0	17	9	29	.234	.303	.273
vs. Fly-Ballers	221	58	5	2	2	18	25	32	.262	.330	.337
Home Games	221	57	6	2	2	24	21	31	.258	.330	.325
Road Games	188	45	12	0	0	11	13	30	.239	.303	.309
Grass Fields	141	33	8	0	0	8	9	21	.234	.291	.280
Artificial Turf	268	69	10	2	2	27	25	40	.257	.332	.323
April	61	17	2	1	1	10	3	6	.279	.393	.313
May	66	17	2	1	0	5	4	10	.258	.318	.300
June	102	28	6	0	1	7	5	15	.275	.363	.308
July	69	19	4	0	0	8	6	5	.275	.333	.333
August	35	8	3	0	0	3	9	8	.229	.314	.386
Sept./Oct.	76	13	1	0	0	2	7	17	.171	.184	.250
Leading Off Inn.	103	28	8	1	1	1	5	17	.272	.398	.312
Runners On	183	42	6	1	0	33	17	30	.230	.273	.295
Bases Empty	226	60	12	1	2	2	17	31	.265	.354	.320
Runners/Scor. Pos.	126	30	5	1	0	33	9	22	.238	.294	.289
Runners On/2 Out	84	17	3	0	0	15	9	16	.202	.238	.280
Scor. Pos./2 Out	66	12	2	0	0	15	3	13	.182	.212	.217
Late-Inning Pressure	50	13	3	0	0	6	4	8	.260	.320	.315
Leading Off	9	1	0	0	0	0	0	1	.111	.111	.111
Runners On	24	6	2	0	0	6	2	4	.250	.333	.308
Runners/Scor. Pos.	17	5	2	0	0	6	1	3	.294	.412	.333

RUNS BATTED IN	From 1B	From 2B	From 3B	Scoring Position
Totals	1/112	14/100	18/47	32/147
Percentage	0.9%	14.0%	38.3%	21.8%

Loves to face: Ron Darling (.667, 4-for-6)
Donn Pall (.750, 3-for-4, 2 2B, 1 HR)
Matt Young (3-for-3, 1 HR, 1 BB)

Hates to face: Mark Langston (0-for-10)
Melido Perez (.077, 1-for-13, 1 2B)
Bob Welch (0-for-6)

Miscellaneous statistics: Ground outs-to-air outs ratio: 1.55 last season, 1.53 for career.... Grounded into 10 double plays in 68 opportunities (one per 6.8).... Drove in 12 of 24 runners from third base with less than two outs (50%).... Direction of balls hit to the outfield: 35% to left field, 33% to center, 31% to right.... Base running: Advanced from first base to third on 8 of 19 outfield singles (42%); scored from second on 6 of 8 (75%).... Made 2.26 assists per nine innings at third base, 3d-highest rate in A.L.

Comments: Twins third basemen combined for only two home runs, the fewest of any team in the majors last season, and fewer than Mike Pagliarulo and Leius combined for during the 1991 postseason. Their 43 RBIs were the fewest of any A.L. club.... Pags's 100 days on the disabled list afforded Leius lots of playing time against right-handed pitchers. Still, Leius's career batting average vs. left-handers (.307) is 79 points higher than vs. right-handers (.228).... Started the season with only two errors in his first 32 games, finished it with two in his last 48; in between he went 11-for-45.... Batted 39 points higher in Twins' losses (.273) than he did in their victories (.234). Among players with at least 400 plate appearances last season, only nine other players hit for a higher average in defeat than in victory; none had a gap as large as Leius's.... Career batting average of .464 as a pinch hitter (13-for-28) is 2d highest among active players (minimum: 25 AB).... Has hit for a higher average at the Metrodome than on the road in each of his three seasons in the majors. Career breakdown: .293 at home, .227 on the road.... Seven of his eight career home runs have been hit with the bases empty.... One of seven players on the Twins' roster at the end of last season who had played at least 250 games in the majors and played only for Minnesota. The others: Randy Bush, Greg Gagne (gone to Kansas City), Kent Hrbek, Chuck Knoblauch, Gene Larkin, and Kirby Puckett.

Mark Lewis　　　　　　　　　　　　Bats Right

Cleveland Indians	AB	H	2B	3B	HR	RBI	BB	SO	BA	SA	OBA
Season	413	109	21	0	5	30	25	69	.264	.351	.308
vs. Left-Handers	97	28	10	0	2	10	8	13	.289	.454	.343
vs. Right-Handers	316	81	11	0	3	20	17	56	.256	.320	.297
vs. Ground-Ballers	170	52	11	0	1	15	9	27	.306	.388	.344
vs. Fly-Ballers	243	57	10	0	4	15	16	42	.235	.325	.282
Home Games	195	54	13	0	2	17	13	28	.277	.374	.321
Road Games	218	55	8	0	3	13	12	41	.252	.330	.296
Grass Fields	352	92	18	0	5	26	20	57	.261	.355	.301
Artificial Turf	61	17	3	0	0	4	5	12	.279	.328	.348
April	76	22	3	0	1	4	7	12	.289	.368	.341
May	77	22	5	0	2	13	5	13	.286	.429	.333
June	79	17	3	0	0	4	1	12	.215	.253	.225
July	62	12	2	0	1	2	4	12	.194	.274	.254
August	86	29	7	0	1	5	7	15	.337	.453	.394
Sept./Oct.	33	7	1	0	0	2	1	5	.212	.242	.229
Leading Off Inn.	97	28	6	0	2	2	7	17	.289	.412	.343
Runners On	166	45	8	0	1	26	11	26	.271	.337	.313
Bases Empty	247	64	13	0	4	4	14	43	.259	.360	.304
Runners/Scor. Pos.	83	16	4	0	0	22	9	18	.193	.241	.260
Runners On/2 Out	70	17	4	0	0	12	5	15	.243	.300	.303
Scor. Pos./2 Out	43	9	2	0	0	11	4	10	.209	.256	.277
Late-Inning Pressure	64	14	2	0	0	2	5	18	.219	.250	.286
Leading Off	16	4	2	0	0	0	2	5	.250	.375	.333
Runners On	22	4	0	0	0	2	2	6	.182	.182	.280
Runners/Scor. Pos.	10	1	0	0	0	2	2	4	.100	.100	.250

RUNS BATTED IN	From 1B	From 2B	From 3B	Scoring Position
Totals	4/134	7/62	14/44	21/106
Percentage	3.0%	11.3%	31.8%	19.8%

Loves to face:　Scott Lewis (.500, 5-for-10, 3 2B)
　　　　　　　　Mike Moore (.636, 7-for-11)
　　　　　　　　Arthur Rhodes (.667, 4-for-6, 2 2B, 1 HR)

Hates to face:　Jaime Navarro (.118, 2-for-17)
　　　　　　　　Scott Sanderson (0-for-6, 5 SO)
　　　　　　　　Kevin Tapani (0-for-8)

Miscellaneous statistics: Ground outs-to-air outs ratio: 0.83 last season, 0.89 for career.... Grounded into 12 double plays in 86 opportunities (one per 7.2).... Drove in 9 of 22 runners from third base with less than two outs (41%).... Direction of balls hit to the outfield: 36% to left field, 31% to center, 33% to right.... Base running: Advanced from first base to third on 8 of 25 outfield singles (32%); scored from second on 9 of 11 (82%).... Made 2.95 assists per nine innings at shortstop.

Comments: Played 122 games last season at age 23; only one younger player appeared in more games: Ivan Rodriguez (123). Lewis was the 3d-youngest player on an opening-day roster in 1992, older than only Rodriguez and Royce Clayton.... Several Indians shortstops of the past started regularly at a younger age, including Ray Chapman (1913), Julio Franco (1983), and Jay Bell (1988).... Shared the league lead in errors at shortstop with Gary DiSarcina (25). Lewis's error rate of one every 22 chances was 2d worst among major league shortstops to the error machine himself, Jose Offerman (one per 15).... Committed 16 errors in his first 36 games (including 15 over a 20-game stretch), but only nine more in 77 games thereafter.... Committed errors in seven consecutive games from April 28 through May 5, the longest streak by a shortstop since Mariano Duncan's seven-game streak in 1977.... Had only three go-ahead RBIs, the fewest of any A.L. player with at least 400 at-bats.... Batted .277 at home and .252 on the road in both 1991 and 1992.... Career batting average is .321 in April and May, .177 in June and July, .307 from August 1 until season's end.... Had 38 hits in his first 95 at-bats in the majors, but has batted only .244 since then.... Cleveland batting order on July 9 was the youngest in the majors last season (average age: 24 years, 7 months): Kenny Lofton (25 at the time), Mark Lewis (22), Carlos Baerga (23), Albert Belle (25), Paul Sorrento (26), Reggie Jefferson (23), Mark Whiten (25), Jim Thome (21), Sandy Alomar (26).

Pat Listach　　　　　　　Bats Left and Right

Milwaukee Brewers	AB	H	2B	3B	HR	RBI	BB	SO	BA	SA	OBA
Season	579	168	19	6	1	47	55	124	.290	.349	.352
vs. Left-Handers	148	51	7	3	1	18	8	25	.345	.453	.382
vs. Right-Handers	431	117	12	3	0	29	47	99	.271	.313	.342
vs. Ground-Ballers	266	68	6	1	0	21	22	65	.256	.286	.311
vs. Fly-Ballers	313	100	13	5	1	26	33	59	.319	.403	.385
Home Games	267	67	9	1	0	26	22	53	.251	.292	.308
Road Games	312	101	10	5	1	21	33	71	.324	.397	.388
Grass Fields	483	140	17	2	1	37	41	97	.290	.340	.345
Artificial Turf	96	28	2	4	0	10	14	27	.292	.396	.382
April	28	10	1	1	0	1	3	3	.357	.464	.419
May	105	32	2	1	0	7	11	17	.305	.343	.371
June	100	24	1	1	0	9	5	28	.240	.270	.271
July	106	34	5	3	0	11	17	27	.321	.425	.415
August	116	36	5	0	1	10	6	19	.310	.353	.350
Sept./Oct.	124	32	5	0	1	9	13	30	.258	.323	.328
Leading Off Inn.	195	55	4	3	1	1	23	35	.282	.349	.358
Runners On	226	68	9	3	0	46	20	55	.301	.367	.357
Bases Empty	353	100	10	3	1	1	35	69	.283	.337	.348
Runners/Scor. Pos.	145	38	5	1	0	41	15	38	.262	.310	.331
Runners On/2 Out	91	23	4	1	0	14	6	24	.253	.319	.306
Scor. Pos./2 Out	66	11	2	0	0	11	5	20	.167	.197	.236
Late-Inning Pressure	74	21	1	1	0	9	9	14	.284	.324	.357
Leading Off	15	5	0	0	0	0	2	1	.333	.333	.412
Runners On	36	9	0	1	0	9	4	9	.250	.306	.317
Runners/Scor. Pos.	24	6	0	1	0	9	3	5	.250	.333	.321

RUNS BATTED IN	From 1B	From 2B	From 3B	Scoring Position
Totals	5/143	14/113	27/64	41/177
Percentage	3.5%	12.4%	42.2%	23.2%

Loves to face:　Bill Gullickson (.455, 5-for-11)
　　　　　　　　Randy Johnson (3-for-3, 1 HBP)
　　　　　　　　Ben McDonald (.444, 4-for-9)

Hates to face:　John Doherty (.111, 1-for-9, 2 SO)
　　　　　　　　Scott Scudder (0-for-5, 4 SO)
　　　　　　　　Dave Stieb (0-for-7)

Miscellaneous statistics: Ground outs-to-air outs ratio: 1.53 last season, 1.53 for career.... Grounded into 3 double plays in 106 opportunities (one per 35), 5th-best rate in A.L.... Drove in 20 of 36 runners from third base with less than two outs (56%).... Direction of balls hit to the outfield: 55% to left field, 29% to center, 15% to right batting left-handed; 41% to left field, 36% to center, 23% to right batting right-handed.... Base running: Advanced from first base to third on 11 of 29 outfield singles (38%); scored from second on 21 of 28 (75%).... Made 3.16 assists per nine innings at shortstop.

Comments: Led major league rookies in batting average, at-bats, hits, and strikeouts. His 17-game hitting streak was six longer than any other rookie's last season.... Became the ninth shortstop to win the A.L. Rookie of the Year award. Only pitchers (9) and outfielders (13) have won as many. Of the 47 N.L. players who have won the rookie award, only one was a shortstop: Alvin Dark in 1948.... Listach's 168 hits as a shortstop was the 2d-highest total in the majors, behind Tony Fernandez (171). The 2d-highest total among A.L. shortstops was 160 by Cal Ripken.... The last rookie shortstop with at least 150 hits was Julio Franco (153 in 1983). The last with more hits than Listach: Alfredo Griffin (179 in 1979). Two rookie shortstops topped the 200-hit mark: Johnny Pesky (1942) and Harvey Kuenn (1953).... Only three rookies in franchise history played as many as 140 games: Pedro Garcia (160 in 1973), Listach (149 in 1992), and Wayne Comer (147 for the Seattle Pilots in 1969).... Total of 124 strikeouts is the 2d highest ever by a player with fewer than two home runs. Gary Pettis struck out 125 times with one home run in 1985; two years later, he fanned 124 times, again with a single homer.... Here's a streak that's likely to continue (for one more year at least): The Brewers have used a different opening-day starter at shortstop in each of the last five seasons: Dale Sveum (1988), Gary Sheffield (1989), Edgar Diaz (1990), Billy Spiers (1991), and Scott Fletcher (1992).

Scott Livingstone — Bats Left

Detroit Tigers	AB	H	2B	3B	HR	RBI	BB	SO	BA	SA	OBA
Season	354	100	21	0	4	46	21	36	.282	.376	.319
vs. Left-Handers	45	13	2	0	1	7	4	8	.289	.400	.340
vs. Right-Handers	309	87	19	0	3	39	17	28	.282	.372	.316
vs. Ground-Ballers	164	48	9	0	1	22	5	18	.293	.366	.310
vs. Fly-Ballers	190	52	12	0	3	24	16	18	.274	.384	.327
Home Games	175	40	8	0	2	26	12	23	.229	.309	.274
Road Games	179	60	13	0	2	20	9	13	.335	.441	.365
Grass Fields	298	81	18	0	4	44	19	33	.272	.372	.312
Artificial Turf	56	19	3	0	0	2	2	3	.339	.393	.362
April	14	4	0	0	0	1	1	3	.286	.286	.333
May	35	8	1	0	0	0	0	7	.229	.257	.229
June	65	23	5	0	0	8	9	8	.354	.431	.427
July	63	14	2	0	0	7	2	2	.222	.254	.242
August	101	25	6	0	0	15	3	11	.248	.307	.267
Sept./Oct.	76	26	7	0	4	15	6	5	.342	.592	.386
Leading Off Inn.	89	28	6	0	2	2	4	7	.315	.449	.344
Runners On	157	48	7	0	2	44	10	18	.306	.389	.339
Bases Empty	197	52	14	0	2	2	11	18	.264	.365	.303
Runners/Scor. Pos.	93	25	3	0	2	43	6	13	.269	.366	.301
Runners On/2 Out	63	15	2	0	1	13	7	8	.238	.317	.314
Scor. Pos./2 Out	40	8	1	0	1	12	6	6	.200	.300	.304
Late-Inning Pressure	47	10	3	0	1	4	4	4	.213	.340	.269
Leading Off	12	3	1	0	1	1	0	0	.250	.583	.250
Runners On	14	2	0	0	0	3	3	3	.143	.143	.278
Runners/Scor. Pos.	8	0	0	0	0	3	2	3	.000	.000	.182

RUNS BATTED IN	From 1B	From 2B	From 3B	Scoring Position
Totals	4/123	15/79	23/42	38/121
Percentage	3.3%	19.0%	54.8%	31.4%

Loves to face: Scott Erickson (.571, 4-for-7)
Jose Mesa (.444, 4-for-9)
Jack Morris (.667, 6-for-9)

Hates to face: Ron Darling (0-for-6)
Joe Grahe (0-for-7)
Nolan Ryan (0-for-7)

Miscellaneous statistics: Ground outs-to-air outs ratio: 1.12 last season, 1.13 for career.... Grounded into 8 double plays in 80 opportunities (one per 10).... Drove in 19 of 27 runners from third base with less than two outs (70%).... Direction of balls hit to the outfield: 37% to left field, 34% to center, 28% to right.... Base running: Advanced from first base to third on 5 of 16 outfield singles (31%); scored from second on 9 of 13 (69%).... Made 2.02 assists per nine innings at third base.

Comments: Batting average ranked third among major league rookies, behind those of Pat Listach and Kenny Lofton. No Tigers rookie has batted .300 in 40 years, since Harvey Kuenn batted .308 in 1953.... With Livingstone accounting for three-quarters of the at-bats, Tigers rookies combined for a .281 average last season, the highest team average in the majors. The only other Detroit rookie with as many as 50 ABs was Phil Clark, who chipped in with a .407 batting average. Incidentally, even among rookies with as few as 50 at-bats, only six others ever hit .400, including Shoeless Joe Jackson (1911) and Hurricane Bob Hazle (1957).... Was the only rookie to drive in at least 30 percent of runners from scoring position last season (minimum: 100 opportunities).... Was homerless in his first 305 at-bats of the season before hitting four home runs over 31 at-bats (Sept. 10–25).... Started 87 of 119 games in which the Tigers faced a right-handed starter, but only 3 of 43 games vs. southpaws.... Only two other Tigers rookies have played 100 games at third base: Bob Maier (1945) and Steve Boros (1961). Maier, the Tigers' third baseman between Pinky Higgins and George Kell, played only one season in the majors. His last big league game was in the 1945 World Series.... Which reminds us: You know which player with a one-year major league career played the most games? Livingstone's current manager: George ("Sparky") Anderson, 152 games for the 1959 Phillies.

Kenny Lofton — Bats Left

Cleveland Indians	AB	H	2B	3B	HR	RBI	BB	SO	BA	SA	OBA
Season	576	164	15	8	5	42	68	54	.285	.365	.362
vs. Left-Handers	122	45	6	1	0	12	21	15	.369	.434	.466
vs. Right-Handers	454	119	9	7	5	30	47	39	.262	.346	.331
vs. Ground-Ballers	261	68	6	1	2	17	30	15	.261	.314	.339
vs. Fly-Ballers	315	96	9	7	3	25	38	39	.305	.406	.380
Home Games	277	81	7	4	3	22	36	23	.292	.379	.375
Road Games	299	83	8	4	2	20	32	31	.278	.351	.349
Grass Fields	490	140	13	8	5	40	60	46	.286	.376	.365
Artificial Turf	86	24	2	0	0	2	8	8	.279	.302	.340
April	65	14	1	0	0	3	9	5	.215	.231	.320
May	109	33	1	1	1	11	9	7	.303	.367	.356
June	97	24	2	2	0	4	9	5	.247	.309	.311
July	94	23	3	1	2	6	9	8	.245	.362	.317
August	94	32	4	4	2	10	16	12	.340	.532	.436
Sept./Oct.	117	38	3	0	0	8	16	17	.325	.350	.403
Leading Off Inn.	223	57	5	2	2	2	33	25	.256	.323	.354
Runners On	200	57	4	5	2	39	21	16	.285	.385	.354
Bases Empty	376	107	11	3	3	3	47	38	.285	.354	.366
Runners/Scor. Pos.	114	37	1	3	2	37	10	11	.325	.439	.376
Runners On/2 Out	87	25	1	2	1	23	9	11	.287	.379	.361
Scor. Pos./2 Out	59	21	0	1	1	22	7	9	.356	.441	.424
Late-Inning Pressure	94	23	1	0	1	3	12	7	.245	.287	.330
Leading Off	31	8	0	0	0	0	6	2	.258	.258	.378
Runners On	30	4	1	0	1	3	4	3	.133	.267	.235
Runners/Scor. Pos.	14	2	1	0	1	3	2	1	.143	.429	.250

RUNS BATTED IN	From 1B	From 2B	From 3B	Scoring Position
Totals	4/150	19/90	14/37	33/127
Percentage	2.7%	21.1%	37.8%	26.0%

Loves to face: Chuck Finley (.600, 6-for-10)
Bill Gullickson (.556, 5-for-9)
Scott Kamieniecki (.375, 3-for-8, 1 3B, 1 HR)

Hates to face: Jaime Navarro (0-for-7)
Dave Stewart (0-for-6)
Walt Terrell (0-for-8)

Miscellaneous statistics: Ground outs-to-air outs ratio: 1.87 last season (5th highest in A.L.), 1.83 for career.... Grounded into 7 double plays in 105 opportunities (one per 15).... Drove in 7 of 15 runners from third base with less than two outs (47%).... Direction of balls hit to the outfield: 39% to left field, 33% to center, 27% to right.... Base running: Advanced from first base to third on 19 of 27 outfield singles (70%), highest rate in majors; scored from second on 20 of 22 (91%).... Made 3.01 putouts per nine innings in center field, 3d-highest rate in A.L.

Comments: Led the American League with 66 stolen bases, 12 more than runner-up Pat Listach. Only twice previously in this century had rookies captured their league's top two spots in steals. In both previous instances, the players involved were teammates: Danny Murtaugh (18) and Stan Benjamin (17) of the 1941 Phillies; and Minnie Minoso (31) and Jim Busby (26) of the 1951 White Sox.... Have any two rookies ever had seasons as similar, statistically speaking, as Lofton and Listach—even rookies from different seasons? You bet—try Ron Northey (1942) and Tom Veryzer (1975); or, for the same season, Ed Busch and George Kell (1944).... Led major league rookies in plate appearances (651), triples, runs, and walks.... Led A.L. center fielders with 14 assists last season, and tied Juan Gonzalez for the major league lead in errors at that position (8).... Batting average vs. left-handed pitchers was the highest of any left-handed batter in the majors. Since 1975, only three left-handed batters have posted higher single-season averages against southpaws (minimum: 100 AB): Ken Griffey, Sr. (.393 in 1976); Bill Buckner (.389 in 1978); Rod Carew (.371 in 1977).... It was reported that Lofton set an all-time American League record for rookies on September 7, when he stole his 51st and 52d bases of the season, presumably breaking a record of 50, held by Miguel Dilone (1978) and John Cangelosi (1986). In fact, the previous high by an A.L. rookie was 53, by Donie Bush in 1909. Lofton broke the actual mark nearly a week later, on September 13.

Kevin Maas
Bats Left

New York Yankees	AB	H	2B	3B	HR	RBI	BB	SO	BA	SA	OBA
Season	286	71	12	0	11	35	25	63	.248	.406	.305
vs. Left-Handers	54	10	0	0	1	4	2	19	.185	.241	.214
vs. Right-Handers	232	61	12	0	10	31	23	44	.263	.444	.324
vs. Ground-Ballers	140	43	3	0	6	17	9	29	.307	.457	.347
vs. Fly-Ballers	146	28	9	0	5	18	16	34	.192	.356	.267
Home Games	128	27	4	0	7	15	11	28	.211	.406	.270
Road Games	158	44	8	0	4	20	14	35	.278	.405	.333
Grass Fields	240	57	8	0	9	27	23	53	.237	.383	.300
Artificial Turf	46	14	4	0	2	8	2	10	.304	.522	.333
April	32	11	1	0	2	7	7	5	.344	.563	.462
May	60	16	3	0	4	8	5	11	.267	.517	.323
June	82	19	4	0	4	10	6	20	.232	.427	.281
July	54	9	3	0	1	4	7	14	.167	.278	.262
August	37	10	1	0	0	2	0	8	.270	.297	.256
Sept./Oct.	21	6	0	0	0	4	0	5	.286	.286	.273
Leading Off Inn.	77	16	1	0	2	2	6	16	.208	.299	.265
Runners On	112	27	7	0	3	27	14	24	.241	.384	.315
Bases Empty	174	44	5	0	8	8	11	39	.253	.420	.297
Runners/Scor. Pos.	60	11	1	0	2	22	12	15	.183	.300	.303
Runners On/2 Out	50	11	3	0	1	11	6	12	.220	.340	.304
Scor. Pos./2 Out	28	6	1	0	1	10	5	6	.214	.357	.333
Late-Inning Pressure	63	13	2	0	2	7	5	20	.206	.333	.265
Leading Off	11	2	0	0	0	0	1	4	.182	.182	.250
Runners On	29	7	1	0	1	6	3	8	.241	.379	.313
Runners/Scor. Pos.	17	4	0	0	1	6	3	5	.235	.412	.350

RUNS BATTED IN	From 1B	From 2B	From 3B	Scoring Position
Totals	6/91	4/46	14/28	18/74
Percentage	6.6%	8.7%	50.0%	24.3%

Loves to face: Pat Hentgen (2-for-2, 1 2B, 1 HR, 1 BB)
　　　　　　　Kirk McCaskill (.421, 8-for-19, 1 HR)
　　　　　　　Jose Mesa (.615, 8-for-13, 1 HR)

Hates to face: Roger Clemens (.211, 4-for-19)
　　　　　　　Kevin Tapani (.091, 2-for-22, 1 HR)
　　　　　　　Curt Young (.111, 1-for-9)

Miscellaneous statistics: Ground outs-to-air outs ratio: 0.64 last season, 0.58 for career.... Grounded into 1 double play in 53 opportunities (one per 53), 3d-best rate in A.L.... Drove in 9 of 15 runners from third base with less than two outs (60%).... Direction of balls hit to the outfield: 29% to left field, 28% to center, 43% to right.... Base running: Advanced from first base to third on 5 of 13 outfield singles (38%); scored from second on 5 of 8 (63%).... Made 0.26 assists per nine innings at first base.

Comments: Started only one of the 53 games in which the Yankees faced a left-handed starter last season (vs. David West on August 27), compared to 68 of 109 vs. right-handers.... Comparison of directional hitting for 1991 and 1992 shows some progress in using more of the field. Compare last season's figures (listed above) to those for 1991: 21% to left field, 28% to center, 51% to right.... Home-run rate dropped from one every 12 at-bats as a rookie, to one every 22 AB in 1991, to one every 26 ABs last season.... August was his first homerless month since breaking into the majors in June 1990. September was his second such month.... Career batting average is .214 with 27 homers at Yankee Stadium, .255 with 28 homers on the road.... Of 55 career home runs, 39 have been solo shots. Career batting averages: .259 with bases empty, .203 with runners on base, .188 with runners in scoring position.... Good news, bad news: His strikeout rate has decreased in each season, but so has his walk rate. Despite a 28-point increase in his batting average last season, his on-base percentage declined by the same amount.... In 115 career games at first base, he's been charged with 17 errors. Over the last three years, Don Mattingly has committed 12 errors in 359 games.... Only four players in Yankees history have come to the plate as many as 1000 times without a sacrifice bunt: Reggie Jackson, 2707 (although he at least *tried* to bunt for Billy Martin); Maas, 1207; Matt Nokes, 1187; and Claudell Washington, 1051.

Mike Macfarlane
Bats Right

Kansas City Royals	AB	H	2B	3B	HR	RBI	BB	SO	BA	SA	OBA
Season	402	94	28	3	17	48	30	89	.234	.445	.310
vs. Left-Handers	138	36	10	1	7	18	10	28	.261	.500	.331
vs. Right-Handers	264	58	18	2	10	30	20	61	.220	.417	.298
vs. Ground-Ballers	145	32	8	1	5	15	13	30	.221	.393	.325
vs. Fly-Ballers	257	62	20	2	12	33	17	59	.241	.475	.300
Home Games	184	44	16	1	7	21	13	35	.239	.451	.319
Road Games	218	50	12	2	10	27	17	54	.229	.440	.302
Grass Fields	164	40	8	2	8	25	11	36	.244	.463	.313
Artificial Turf	238	54	20	1	9	23	19	53	.227	.433	.307
April	41	7	3	0	1	4	8	13	.171	.317	.352
May	78	17	6	0	4	12	6	20	.218	.449	.299
June	77	19	6	1	1	4	2	17	.247	.390	.266
July	51	9	3	0	0	4	4	13	.176	.235	.263
August	67	19	4	0	7	11	6	15	.284	.657	.360
Sept./Oct.	88	23	6	2	4	13	4	11	.261	.511	.320
Leading Off Inn.	108	28	10	1	5	5	6	26	.259	.509	.322
Runners On	168	32	9	2	6	37	14	31	.190	.375	.285
Bases Empty	234	62	19	1	11	11	16	58	.265	.496	.328
Runners/Scor. Pos.	95	12	4	1	2	25	10	19	.126	.253	.254
Runners On/2 Out	78	13	3	1	3	13	7	16	.167	.346	.270
Scor. Pos./2 Out	49	5	1	1	1	7	5	9	.102	.224	.241
Late-Inning Pressure	67	15	2	2	3	9	8	13	.224	.448	.325
Leading Off	16	5	1	1	1	1	4	3	.313	.688	.450
Runners On	29	5	1	1	1	7	2	5	.172	.379	.273
Runners/Scor. Pos.	15	2	0	0	1	5	1	3	.133	.333	.278

RUNS BATTED IN	From 1B	From 2B	From 3B	Scoring Position
Totals	10/119	7/70	14/44	21/114
Percentage	8.4%	10.0%	31.8%	18.4%

Loves to face: Jim Abbott (.476, 10-for-21, 1 HR)
　　　　　　　Bobby Thigpen (.500, 4-for-8, 1 2B)
　　　　　　　Mark Williamson (.700, 7-for-10, 1 HR)

Hates to face: Randy Johnson (.056, 1-for-18, 1 2B, 3 BB, 11 SO)
　　　　　　　Jack McDowell (.133, 2-for-15)
　　　　　　　Dave Stewart (0-for-11)

Miscellaneous statistics: Ground outs-to-air outs ratio: 0.93 last season, 0.88 for career.... Grounded into 8 double plays in 75 opportunities (one per 9.4).... Drove in 12 of 22 runners from third base with less than two outs (55%).... Direction of balls hit to the outfield: 54% to left field, 22% to center, 24% to right.... Base running: Advanced from first base to third on 2 of 23 outfield singles (9%); scored from second on 8 of 9 (89%).... Opposing base stealers: 67-for-95 (71%), 4th-highest rate in A.L.

Comments: Home-run totals year by year starting with 1989: 2, 6, 13, 17. Macfarlane has increased his total by at least four homers in three straight seasons; Mike Devereaux has done so in each of the last four years. The all-time longest streak: five years, by Whiz Kid Stan Lopata (1952–56).... Third catcher in Royals history to hit as many as 17 home runs in a season; he joins Darrell Porter (1978 and 1979) and Ed Kirkpatrick (1970). (Kirk Patrick—isn't he one of those "SportsCenter" guys?)... With 420 games behind the plate, ranks third in Royals history, behind John Wathan (572) and Porter (492).... Led the American League with 25 doubles as a catcher.... Was hit by 15 pitches last season, tying Shane Mack for the most in the American League. Only three catchers have been hit more often in any season over the last 70 years: Carlton Fisk (17 in 1985); Bill Freehan (20 in 1967, 24 in 1968); Sherm Lollar (16 in 1956).... Had the fewest infield hits of any player with at least 400 at-bats last season (1).... His batting average with runners in scoring position was the lowest in the league last season.... An opening-day start behind the plate for the Royals in 1993 would make him only the third catcher to start three straight season openers for Kansas City. So far, only Wathan (1981–83) and Fran Healy (1974–76) have done that.... Career offensive statistics are comparable to several respected backstops of an earlier generation: Johnny Roseboro, Sherm Lollar, and Tom Haller.

Shane Mack — Bats Right

Minnesota Twins	AB	H	2B	3B	HR	RBI	BB	SO	BA	SA	OBA
Season	600	189	31	6	16	75	64	106	.315	.467	.394
vs. Left-Handers	128	38	10	3	4	24	11	21	.297	.516	.357
vs. Right-Handers	472	151	21	3	12	51	53	85	.320	.453	.403
vs. Ground-Ballers	285	89	10	2	7	34	27	60	.312	.435	.382
vs. Fly-Ballers	315	100	21	4	9	41	37	46	.317	.495	.403
Home Games	286	87	14	5	10	41	36	53	.304	.493	.390
Road Games	314	102	17	1	6	34	28	53	.325	.443	.397
Grass Fields	237	79	15	0	6	26	22	42	.333	.473	.408
Artificial Turf	363	110	16	6	10	49	42	64	.303	.463	.384
April	78	24	3	2	2	9	5	16	.308	.474	.372
May	106	35	4	0	5	18	11	19	.330	.509	.403
June	115	30	10	1	2	12	11	19	.261	.417	.336
July	94	35	4	2	3	17	15	17	.372	.553	.455
August	106	38	6	0	1	8	10	18	.358	.443	.430
Sept./Oct.	101	27	4	1	3	11	12	17	.267	.416	.368
Leading Off Inn.	189	64	14	1	7	7	19	34	.339	.534	.413
Runners On	237	77	10	4	6	65	27	34	.325	.477	.411
Bases Empty	363	112	21	2	10	10	37	72	.309	.460	.382
Runners/Scor. Pos.	141	42	5	2	3	56	21	21	.298	.426	.402
Runners On/2 Out	88	26	4	2	2	28	13	12	.295	.455	.410
Scor. Pos./2 Out	64	18	1	1	2	26	10	9	.281	.422	.403
Late-Inning Pressure	80	21	4	0	1	7	9	17	.262	.350	.344
Leading Off	18	7	2	0	1	1	3	2	.389	.667	.476
Runners On	36	10	1	0	0	6	3	5	.278	.306	.350
Runners/Scor. Pos.	25	7	1	0	0	6	2	4	.280	.320	.357

RUNS BATTED IN	From 1B	From 2B	From 3B	Scoring Position
Totals	10/161	17/103	32/65	49/168
Percentage	6.2%	16.5%	49.2%	29.2%

Loves to face: Chuck Finley (.464, 13-for-28, 1 HR)
Joe Hesketh (.571, 8-for-14, 2 HR)
Scott Sanderson (.700, 7-for-10, 3 HR)

Hates to face: Jim Abbott (.111, 2-for-18, 3 BB)
Tim Leary (.077, 1-for-13, 3 BB)
Bob Welch (.158, 3-for-19)

Miscellaneous statistics: Ground outs-to-air outs ratio: 1.76 last season, 1.64 for career.... Grounded into 8 double plays in 131 opportunities (one per 16).... Drove in 19 of 35 runners from third base with less than two outs (54%).... Direction of balls hit to the outfield: 30% to left field, 29% to center, 41% to right.... Base running: Advanced from first base to third on 18 of 43 outfield singles (42%); scored from second on 19 of 27 (70%).... Made 2.18 putouts per nine innings in left field.

Comments: Starts the 1993 season with a career batting average above .300 by the narrowest of margins—one hit.... Not bad considering he batted .239 as a rookie for the Padres in 1988 and .244 as a sophomore. Only two career .300 hitters began their careers with sub-.250 marks in their first two seasons: George Harper (.303, after batting .205 as a rookie in 1917 and .242 in 1918) and Ken Williams (.319, after batting .242 in 1915 and .111 in 1916). Others who reached 2000 hits after starting with two sub-.250 years: Rabbit Maranville, Brooks Robinson, Rusty Staub, Graig Nettles, Frank White, and Brian Downing.... Mack and Edgar Martinez are the only A.L. players to bat .300 or better in each of the last three seasons (minimum: 300 AB). Two players did it in the other league: Tony Gwynn (10 straight years) and Barry Larkin (4).... Acquired by the Twins from San Diego in the 1989 major league draft—the same draft in which the Padres lost Dave Hollins to the Phillies. Ouch!...Ranked third in the league with 39 infield hits last season, behind Kenny Lofton (49) and Kirby Puckett (41).... Despite his high ratio of ground outs to air outs, he was among the league's toughest batters to double-up (see above).... Batted .387 in 106 at-bats from the 2d spot in the batting order, highest in the majors (minimum: 100 ABs).... Played 150 games in left field, the most of any player in the majors last season.... Over the last two years, he's batted .243 in Late-Inning Pressure Situations, .323 in other at-bats.

Candy Maldonado — Bats Right

Toronto Blue Jays	AB	H	2B	3B	HR	RBI	BB	SO	BA	SA	OBA
Season	489	133	25	4	20	66	59	112	.272	.462	.357
vs. Left-Handers	117	34	4	1	4	16	22	26	.291	.444	.400
vs. Right-Handers	372	99	21	3	16	50	37	86	.266	.468	.342
vs. Ground-Ballers	249	68	15	2	10	37	29	53	.273	.470	.353
vs. Fly-Ballers	240	65	10	2	10	29	30	59	.271	.454	.360
Home Games	219	55	10	3	8	32	27	50	.251	.434	.343
Road Games	270	78	15	1	12	34	32	62	.289	.485	.368
Grass Fields	212	61	8	1	11	27	27	46	.288	.491	.374
Artificial Turf	277	72	17	3	9	39	32	66	.260	.440	.343
April	78	13	3	0	6	8	15	23	.167	.205	.250
May	44	15	5	0	1	5	6	12	.341	.523	.420
June	80	22	7	1	4	14	5	24	.275	.538	.322
July	88	31	1	1	5	13	13	12	.352	.557	.441
August	105	28	5	1	8	18	9	26	.267	.562	.328
Sept./Oct.	94	24	4	1	2	10	18	23	.255	.383	.391
Leading Off Inn.	128	30	4	0	4	4	5	32	.234	.359	.269
Runners On	232	69	13	4	10	56	37	50	.297	.517	.399
Bases Empty	257	64	12	0	10	10	22	62	.249	.412	.316
Runners/Scor. Pos.	115	29	6	2	2	33	25	30	.252	.391	.386
Runners On/2 Out	99	31	6	3	4	27	17	28	.313	.556	.424
Scor. Pos./2 Out	64	15	3	2	1	18	12	19	.234	.391	.364
Late-Inning Pressure	59	19	1	0	2	8	6	17	.322	.441	.385
Leading Off	18	7	0	0	0	0	0	5	.389	.389	.389
Runners On	24	8	1	0	0	6	5	8	.333	.375	.448
Runners/Scor. Pos.	16	4	0	0	0	5	5	6	.250	.250	.429

RUNS BATTED IN	From 1B	From 2B	From 3B	Scoring Position
Totals	17/183	13/80	16/57	29/137
Percentage	9.3%	16.3%	28.1%	21.2%

Loves to face: Mike Jackson (.455, 5-for-11, 2 HR)
Dennis Martinez (.348, 8-for-23, 3 HR)
Todd Worrell (.444, 4-for-9)

Hates to face: Tim Burke (.077, 1-for-13)
Sid Fernandez (.120, 3-for-25)
John Smoltz (0-for-7, 3 SO)

Miscellaneous statistics: Ground outs-to-air outs ratio: 1.01 last season, 1.01 for career.... Grounded into 13 double plays in 127 opportunities (one per 10).... Drove in 9 of 16 runners from third base with less than two outs (56%).... Direction of balls hit to the outfield: 36% to left field, 28% to center, 35% to right.... Base running: Advanced from first base to third on 7 of 25 outfield singles (28%); scored from second on 12 of 17 (71%).... Made 2.06 putouts per nine innings in left field.

Comments: The odds-on favorite to become the first player to homer against each of the current 28 major league clubs. He is the only player currently employed by an N.L. club who has already homered against the older 26.... Leads active players with nine pinch-hit homers, but he hasn't hit any since 1987. In fact, since leaving the National League in 1990, he has only six at-bats as a pinch hitter. He had at least 30 pinch ABs in four different seasons in the N.L. (1984–1986, 1989).... July batting average last season was his highest in any month since June 1987, when he batted .360.... Tied Tim Raines for the major league lead in assists by left fielders last season (12)—little consolation to him when he almost handed the Braves the sixth game of the World Series.... His career postseason batting average is 2d lowest in major league history (minimum: 100 AB). The bottom five: Gene Tenace (.158), Maldonado (.165), Cesar Geronimo (.167), Frank Crosetti (.174), Joe Morgan (.182).... Batted .335 from the seventh inning on, 3d highest in the majors (minimum: 100 at-bats), behind Roberto Alomar (.368) and Edgar Martinez (.357). Candy's average in Late-Inning Pressure Situations was slightly lower (.322).... He's no Jack Clark, but he now has had 20-HR seasons for three different teams: the Giants (1987), Indians (1990), and Jays (1992). Other active players with three or more: Dave Winfield (4 and counting), George Bell, Joe Carter, and Danny Tartabull (3).

Edgar Martinez — Bats Right

Seattle Mariners	AB	H	2B	3B	HR	RBI	BB	SO	BA	SA	OBA
Season	528	181	46	3	18	73	54	61	.343	.544	.404
vs. Left-Handers	141	53	16	0	4	17	18	14	.376	.574	.444
vs. Right-Handers	387	128	30	3	14	56	36	47	.331	.532	.390
vs. Ground-Ballers	251	83	17	0	9	38	28	28	.331	.506	.396
vs. Fly-Ballers	277	98	29	3	9	35	26	33	.354	.578	.412
Home Games	268	84	27	1	11	39	27	37	.313	.545	.377
Road Games	260	97	19	2	7	34	27	24	.373	.542	.432
Grass Fields	206	83	18	2	4	30	25	18	.403	.568	.466
Artificial Turf	322	98	28	1	14	43	29	43	.304	.528	.363
April	67	15	7	0	1	8	11	8	.224	.373	.342
May	103	35	7	3	5	15	9	15	.340	.612	.395
June	108	38	10	0	6	17	8	14	.352	.611	.402
July	98	38	6	0	3	12	12	11	.388	.541	.455
August	114	45	16	0	3	19	9	10	.395	.614	.433
Sept./Oct.	38	10	0	0	0	2	5	3	.263	.263	.341
Leading Off Inn.	97	40	8	0	4	4	8	8	.412	.619	.462
Runners On	227	68	12	1	9	64	24	25	.300	.480	.364
Bases Empty	301	113	34	2	9	9	30	36	.375	.591	.435
Runners/Scor. Pos.	133	41	10	1	8	62	12	14	.308	.579	.358
Runners On/2 Out	89	16	4	0	3	18	5	11	.180	.326	.223
Scor. Pos./2 Out	65	13	4	0	3	18	3	7	.200	.400	.235
Late-Inning Pressure	83	33	9	0	2	7	7	6	.398	.578	.444
Leading Off	25	9	2	0	1	1	1	0	.360	.560	.385
Runners On	28	12	2	0	1	6	3	1	.429	.607	.484
Runners/Scor. Pos.	15	5	1	0	1	6	1	0	.333	.600	.375

RUNS BATTED IN	From 1B	From 2B	From 3B	Scoring Position
Totals	8/145	21/106	26/56	47/162
Percentage	5.5%	19.8%	46.4%	29.0%

Loves to face: Jimmy Key (.400, 12-for-30, 2 HR)
Charles Nagy (.400, 8-for-20, 2 HR)
Rick Sutcliffe (.538, 7-for-13)
Hates to face: Bill Gullickson (.176, 3-for-17)
Jose Mesa (0-for-10)
Nolan Ryan (.053, 1-for-19, 10 SO)

Miscellaneous statistics: Ground outs-to-air outs ratio: 1.13 last season, 1.03 for career.... Grounded into 15 double plays in 117 opportunities (one per 7.8).... Drove in 17 of 25 runners from third base with less than two outs (68%).... Direction of balls hit to the outfield: 37% to left field, 29% to center, 34% to right.... Base running: Advanced from first base to third on 12 of 36 outfield singles (33%); scored from second on 14 of 21 (67%).... Made 2.16 assists per nine innings at third base.

Comments: Now that a Mariners player has won the American League batting title, there remain only four clubs that have never had a player lead their league: the Blue Jays, Astros, Brewers, and Mets. (Of course, you can soon add the Marlins and Rockies.) ... Yearly batting averages since 1989: .240, .302, .307, .343.... The only player to hit better than .300 with more than 10 home runs in each of the last three seasons—an increasingly rare achievement. Only two active players have ever had longer streaks: Don Mattingly (1984–89) and Andre Dawson (1980–82).... Over the 18 years of *The Player Analysis,* only three players have posted higher single-season batting averages in road games (minimum: 75 hits): George Brett (.388 in 1980), Cecil Cooper (.386 in 1980), and Rod Carew (.374 in 1977).... Batting average on grass fields (.403) was the highest single-season average of any player since we started keeping track (minimum: 60 hits).... Career batting average of .333 vs. left-handed pitchers is 2d highest among active players, behind Kirby Puckett (.340).... Career batting average of only .217 in 327 at-bats with two outs and runners on base.... Turned 30 in January, the same day as David Cone. While he's spent only three full seasons in the majors, Martinez is a month older than Len Dykstra, and a few days younger than Devon White.... His statistical profile closely resembles those of two of the game's greatest late starters: Jackie Robinson (after the 1949 season) and Bill Terry (through 1928).

Tino Martinez — Bats Left

Seattle Mariners	AB	H	2B	3B	HR	RBI	BB	SO	BA	SA	OBA
Season	460	118	19	2	16	66	42	77	.257	.411	.316
vs. Left-Handers	101	23	4	0	3	19	5	23	.228	.356	.261
vs. Right-Handers	359	95	15	2	13	47	37	54	.265	.426	.332
vs. Ground-Ballers	215	51	9	2	4	31	23	40	.237	.353	.311
vs. Fly-Ballers	245	67	10	0	12	35	19	37	.273	.461	.321
Home Games	232	62	12	0	10	40	22	34	.267	.448	.326
Road Games	228	56	7	2	6	26	20	43	.246	.373	.307
Grass Fields	178	49	7	1	6	21	14	33	.275	.427	.328
Artificial Turf	282	69	12	1	10	45	28	44	.245	.401	.309
April	62	18	2	1	3	9	3	9	.290	.500	.323
May	79	22	7	0	1	10	8	12	.278	.405	.344
June	87	21	2	1	3	17	5	10	.241	.391	.280
July	65	10	1	0	1	4	8	14	.154	.215	.243
August	96	27	3	0	4	14	7	18	.281	.438	.324
Sept./Oct.	71	20	4	0	4	12	11	14	.282	.507	.376
Leading Off Inn.	107	29	7	0	4	4	2	18	.271	.449	.291
Runners On	204	51	8	2	3	53	27	31	.250	.353	.329
Bases Empty	256	67	11	0	13	13	15	46	.262	.457	.305
Runners/Scor. Pos.	117	32	6	2	3	52	19	18	.274	.436	.359
Runners On/2 Out	91	22	3	2	1	21	16	14	.242	.352	.361
Scor. Pos./2 Out	60	15	3	2	1	21	14	9	.250	.417	.400
Late-Inning Pressure	86	26	6	0	2	13	7	20	.302	.442	.362
Leading Off	18	6	2	0	0	0	0	5	.333	.444	.368
Runners On	45	14	2	0	1	12	6	12	.311	.422	.392
Runners/Scor. Pos.	29	9	2	0	1	12	5	11	.310	.483	.412

RUNS BATTED IN	From 1B	From 2B	From 3B	Scoring Position
Totals	8/155	12/96	30/60	42/156
Percentage	5.2%	12.5%	50.0%	26.9%

Loves to face: Ben McDonald (.545, 6-for-11, 1 HR, 3 SO)
Rod Nichols (.667, 4-for-6, 2 HR)
Dave Stewart (.429, 3-for-7)
Hates to face: Kevin Appier (0-for-11)
Roger Clemens (.125, 2-for-16)
Nolan Ryan (.100, 1-for-10)

Miscellaneous statistics: Ground outs-to-air outs ratio: 1.24 last season, 1.16 for career.... Grounded into 24 double plays in 106 opportunities (one per 4.4), 2d-worst rate in majors.... Drove in 23 of 38 runners from third base with less than two outs (61%).... Direction of balls hit to the outfield: 29% to left field, 28% to center, 43% to right.... Base running: Advanced from first base to third on 5 of 18 outfield singles (28%); scored from second on 8 of 12 (67%).... Made 0.79 assists per nine innings at first base.

Comments: Started 105 of 120 games in which the Mariners faced right-handed pitchers (88%), but only 16 of 42 vs. left-handers (38%).... July batting average was the lowest in the majors.... Seattle DHs led the league with 64 extra-base hits (42 doubles, no triples, 22 home runs). Tino started more games as their designated hitter than anyone else (48).... Grounded into 24 double plays last season, 3d-highest single-season total in Mariners history, behind Jim Presley (29 in 1985) and Bruce Bochte (27 in 1979).... Of his 20 career home runs, 17 have come with the bases empty.... Batted over .300 in the minor leagues in both 1990 and 1991. In four professional seasons, he has career averages of .299 in the minors, .244 in the majors.... Both Tino and Edgar have batted above .300 in Late-Inning Pressure Situations in each of the last two seasons.... Tino and Edgar are the only Martinezes ever to play for the Mariners, but they have had six Joneses, four Nelsons, and four Browns.... For a second consecutive season, the name "Martinez" appeared more times in major league box scores than any other last season (625 times). Runners up: Smith (461), Clark (437), Davis (436), and Bell (428).... That was part of a Latino sweep. Martinezes also hit more home runs than any other group (48)—except for the Gonzalezes (53). And Jose and Juan Guzman accounted for more victories (32) than any other surname in the majors—more than keeping up with the Joneses, who finished second with 31.

Don Mattingly
New York Yankees — Bats Left

	AB	H	2B	3B	HR	RBI	BB	SO	BA	SA	OBA
Season	640	184	40	0	14	86	39	43	.287	.416	.327
vs. Left-Handers	204	58	17	0	2	32	10	18	.284	.397	.318
vs. Right-Handers	436	126	23	0	12	54	29	25	.289	.424	.330
vs. Ground-Ballers	283	81	17	0	7	43	14	18	.286	.420	.320
vs. Fly-Ballers	357	103	23	0	7	43	25	25	.289	.412	.332
Home Games	303	96	22	0	6	42	27	14	.317	.449	.371
Road Games	337	88	18	0	8	44	12	29	.261	.386	.284
Grass Fields	543	163	35	0	13	73	34	37	.300	.430	.340
Artificial Turf	97	21	5	0	1	13	5	6	.216	.299	.250
April	82	19	4	0	2	9	5	4	.232	.354	.276
May	110	29	11	0	4	17	11	10	.264	.473	.331
June	113	35	7	0	3	15	7	7	.310	.451	.347
July	103	34	5	0	1	12	5	5	.330	.408	.355
August	107	30	7	0	1	13	3	8	.280	.374	.298
Sept./Oct.	125	37	6	0	3	20	8	9	.296	.416	.338
Leading Off Inn.	130	33	8	0	3	3	4	7	.254	.385	.281
Runners On	282	88	21	0	8	80	22	22	.312	.472	.355
Bases Empty	358	96	19	0	6	6	17	21	.268	.372	.303
Runners/Scor. Pos.	160	50	13	0	4	69	16	11	.313	.469	.363
Runners On/2 Out	95	27	4	0	1	22	9	8	.284	.358	.346
Scor. Pos./2 Out	59	18	3	0	0	20	7	6	.305	.356	.379
Late-Inning Pressure	101	28	7	0	4	16	9	8	.277	.465	.336
Leading Off	34	8	3	0	2	2	1	3	.235	.500	.257
Runners On	35	12	3	0	2	14	5	3	.343	.600	.425
Runners/Scor. Pos.	18	9	3	0	2	14	3	2	.500	1.000	.571

RUNS BATTED IN	From 1B	From 2B	From 3B	Scoring Position
Totals	14/197	36/128	22/53	58/181
Percentage	7.1%	28.1%	41.5%	32.0%

Loves to face: Bert Blyleven (.409, 18-for-44, 3 HR)
Mark Gubicza (.418, 28-for-67, 4 HR)
Gene Nelson (.455, 10-for-22, 1 HR)

Hates to face: Rick Aguilera (.067, 1-for-15)
Steve Rosenberg (0-for-11)
Kevin Tapani (.091, 2-for-22)

Miscellaneous statistics: Ground outs-to-air outs ratio: 0.76 last season, 0.87 for career.... Grounded into 11 double plays in 138 opportunities (one per 13).... Drove in 17 of 30 runners from third base with less than two outs (57%).... Direction of balls hit to the outfield: 27% to left field, 27% to center, 46% to right.... Base running: Advanced from first base to third on 14 of 40 outfield singles (35%); scored from second on 12 of 22 (55%).... Made 0.85 assists per nine innings at first base.

Comments: His total of 1752 hits since his rookie season of 1983 is the highest 10-year mark by any Yankees player since Lou Gehrig had 2022 hits from 1927 to 1936. Other Yankees with higher 10-year totals: Babe Ruth, 1771 (1923–32); and Earle Combs, 1768 (1925–34).... Led A.L. first basemen in fielding percentage for the fifth time in his career, one shy of the league record of six, held by Stuffy McInnis.... His career error rate at first base (one every 229 chances) is the best in A.L. history, and trails only Steve Garvey (246) and Wes Parker (231) on the all-time list.... Since 1975, only three players have driven in at least 35 percent of runners from scoring position: Thurman Munson (35.2%), Dane Iorg (35.2%), Mattingly (35.1%).... Batted .319 in 135 at-bats from the cleanup position last season. Only one A.L. player had a higher mark batting cleanup (minimum: 100 AB): Robin Yount (.324).... Was retired 245 times on balls hit in the air, the most of any player in the majors.... Struck out more often than he walked for the first time since his rookie season (1983).... Hit more home runs on the road than at Yankee Stadium for the first time since 1983. Career totals: 115 homers at home (one every 24 at-bats); 77 on the road (one every 38 AB).... Has never stolen more than three bases in a season, but he's 10-for-10 over the last five years.... Has hit for a higher average with runners on base than with the bases empty in each of the last six years.... Career batting average is above .300 in every month except April (.272)

Mark McGwire
Oakland A's — Bats Right

	AB	H	2B	3B	HR	RBI	BB	SO	BA	SA	OBA
Season	467	125	22	0	42	104	90	105	.268	.585	.385
vs. Left-Handers	97	32	4	0	14	27	22	14	.330	.804	.447
vs. Right-Handers	370	93	18	0	28	77	68	91	.251	.527	.368
vs. Ground-Ballers	232	61	10	0	15	46	44	50	.263	.500	.378
vs. Fly-Ballers	235	64	12	0	27	58	46	55	.272	.668	.392
Home Games	218	55	8	0	24	52	52	51	.252	.619	.398
Road Games	249	70	14	0	18	52	38	54	.281	.554	.373
Grass Fields	377	96	15	0	34	85	76	96	.255	.565	.379
Artificial Turf	90	29	7	0	8	19	14	9	.322	.667	.411
April	75	25	5	0	10	17	20	12	.333	.800	.480
May	93	22	6	0	8	23	19	27	.237	.559	.360
June	94	26	0	0	8	24	18	25	.277	.532	.389
July	86	22	7	0	6	17	12	18	.256	.547	.359
August	63	16	1	0	6	12	12	15	.254	.556	.364
Sept./Oct.	56	14	3	0	4	11	9	8	.250	.518	.348
Leading Off Inn.	134	42	7	0	16	16	19	22	.313	.724	.399
Runners On	200	51	10	0	15	77	43	43	.255	.530	.378
Bases Empty	267	74	12	0	27	27	47	62	.277	.625	.391
Runners/Scor. Pos.	107	30	9	0	7	61	29	20	.280	.561	.415
Runners On/2 Out	86	25	8	0	5	35	27	19	.291	.558	.460
Scor. Pos./2 Out	52	18	7	0	4	33	17	10	.346	.712	.507
Late-Inning Pressure	61	18	1	0	6	13	12	13	.295	.607	.411
Leading Off	15	5	0	0	2	2	2	5	.333	.733	.412
Runners On	19	6	1	0	2	9	7	1	.316	.684	.500
Runners/Scor. Pos.	10	2	1	0	0	5	5	1	.200	.300	.467

RUNS BATTED IN	From 1B	From 2B	From 3B	Scoring Position
Totals	16/161	17/77	29/53	46/130
Percentage	9.9%	22.1%	54.7%	35.4%

Loves to face: Jim Abbott (.350, 7-for-20, 3 HR)
Mike Boddicker (.269, 7-for-26, 1 2B, 4 HR, 12 BB)
Scott Erickson (.444, 8-for-18, 2 2B, 3 HR)

Hates to face: Roger Clemens (.036, 1-for-28, 1 2B, 3 BB)
Rich DeLucia (.118, 2-for-17)
Nolan Ryan (0-for-9, 6 SO)

Miscellaneous statistics: Ground outs-to-air outs ratio: 0.45 last season (lowest in A.L.), 0.58 for career.... Grounded into 10 double plays in 109 opportunities (one per 11).... Drove in 16 of 28 runners from third base with less than two outs (57%).... Direction of balls hit to the outfield: 50% to left field, 29% to center, 21% to right.... Base running: Advanced from first base to third on 9 of 39 outfield singles (23%); scored from second on 10 of 23 (43%), 5th-lowest rate in A.L.... Made 0.54 assists per nine innings at first base, lowest rate in majors.

Comments: Hit the 200th home run of his career on June 10 in at-bat number 2852. Only four players reached the 200 mark in fewer ABs: Ralph Kiner (2537), Babe Ruth (2580), Harmon Killebrew (2584), and Eddie Mathews (2811).... Over the last two seasons, he has hit 39 home runs at the Oakland Coliseum, 25 elsewhere. But his career home-field deficit remains high at minus 22 (99 at home, 121 on the road).... Career home-run rate in road games is the highest of any active player (one HR every 13.4 AB); career rate at home (one every 15.2 at-bats) ranks third, behind Cecil Fielder and Fred McGriff.... Led A.L. with .585 slugging percentage last season. Over the last 30 years, only Jim Rice (1977–78) has led A.L. in consecutive seasons.... Batting average of .346 with two outs and runners in scoring position was 3d highest in the league, behind Kenny Lofton (.356) and Pedro Munoz (.350).... Career batting average is .281 with runners in scoring position, .236 in other at-bats.... The only player to play every inning of all 32 postseason games for the Athletics since 1988.... Has driven in more than one run in only one of those 32 postseason games; he hit a two-run homer in the first game of the 1992 A.L.C.S.... Batted .209 with no homers during April of 1991. His .333 April batting average last season was the 2d-highest monthly average he ever posted (.351 in September 1987).... Has gone 2264 at-bats since his last triple (June 20, 1988), the longest streak among active players.

Mark McLemore
Bats Left and Right

Baltimore Orioles	AB	H	2B	3B	HR	RBI	BB	SO	BA	SA	OBA
Season	228	56	7	2	0	27	21	26	.246	.294	.308
vs. Left-Handers	58	16	2	0	0	10	5	9	.276	.310	.333
vs. Right-Handers	170	40	5	2	0	17	16	17	.235	.288	.299
vs. Ground-Ballers	129	35	4	2	0	16	13	14	.271	.333	.336
vs. Fly-Ballers	99	21	3	0	0	11	8	12	.212	.242	.271
Home Games	111	22	4	1	0	11	8	12	.198	.252	.250
Road Games	117	34	3	1	0	16	13	14	.291	.333	.362
Grass Fields	192	43	6	2	0	20	15	20	.224	.276	.279
Artificial Turf	36	13	1	0	0	7	6	6	.361	.389	.452
April	33	12	2	0	0	8	4	4	.364	.424	.432
May	53	8	1	0	0	6	9	4	.151	.170	.270
June	40	9	1	0	0	5	3	7	.225	.250	.279
July	40	14	2	2	0	7	4	6	.350	.500	.409
August	15	4	0	0	0	0	0	2	.267	.267	.267
Sept./Oct.	47	9	1	0	0	1	1	3	.191	.213	.208
Leading Off Inn.	35	10	1	0	0	0	6	4	.286	.314	.390
Runners On	120	32	6	1	0	27	11	14	.267	.333	.326
Bases Empty	108	24	1	1	0	0	10	12	.222	.250	.288
Runners/Scor. Pos.	75	23	4	1	0	26	8	8	.307	.387	.369
Runners On/2 Out	56	16	3	1	0	14	5	5	.286	.375	.344
Scor. Pos./2 Out	37	12	2	1	0	13	4	2	.324	.432	.390
Late-Inning Pressure	45	8	1	0	0	3	4	8	.178	.200	.245
Leading Off	6	2	0	0	0	0	2	0	.333	.333	.500
Runners On	22	3	1	0	0	3	1	5	.136	.182	.174
Runners/Scor. Pos.	12	1	0	0	0	2	1	3	.083	.083	.154

RUNS BATTED IN	From 1B	From 2B	From 3B	Scoring Position
Totals	2/82	13/59	12/32	25/91
Percentage	2.4%	22.0%	37.5%	27.5%

Loves to face: John Farrell (.714, 5-for-7)
Mark Langston (.400, 10-for-25, 1 HR)
Bobby Witt (.571, 4-for-7)

Hates to face: Mark Gubicza (.083, 1-for-12)
Eric Plunk (0-for-7, 2 SO)
Bill Wegman (.100, 1-for-10)

Miscellaneous statistics: Ground outs-to-air outs ratio: 1.74 last season, 1.64 for career.... Grounded into 6 double plays in 50 opportunities (one per 8.3).... Drove in 8 of 18 runners from third base with less than two outs (44%).... Direction of balls hit to the outfield: 28% to left field, 39% to center, 32% to right batting left-handed; 29% to left field, 43% to center, 29% to right batting right-handed.... Base running: Advanced from first base to third on 9 of 13 outfield singles (69%), 3d-highest rate in majors; scored from second on 5 of 5 (100%).... Made 3.22 assists per nine innings at second base.

Comments: Started 53 games last season, his highest total since his rookie season of 1987.... Stole 25 bases as a 23-year-old rookie in '87, starting 125 of the first 130 games for California. But he was sent to the minors in late August to make room for veteran Johnny Ray, acquired from the Pirates at the deadline for postseason roster changes. Despite that, he opened the 1988 season as California's regular second baseman, starting 40 of 42 games through May 21, when he injured his elbow. His career never recovered. He returned to active roster in mid-August, but started only 12 games after that.... Started seven consecutive games last September, his longest streak since 1989.... His five career home runs all came in his first 607 major league at-bats. He's 0-for-515 since then.... Orioles second basemen combined for a .236 batting average; among A.L. teams, only the Mariners posted a lower average at that position (.234). O's second sackers also ranked next to last in runs (63), and were tied for last in extra-base hits (24).... Combined with Billy Ripken to give the Orioles 50 consecutive errorless games at second base, the 2d-longest streak by any team last season. The Cubs—or should we say Ryno—had a 60-game streak.... McLemore committed an average of one error every 46 chances.... Batting average with runners in scoring position was a career high.... In 1274 career plate appearances, he's been hit by only one pitch, and has been intentionally walked only once.

Brian McRae
Bats Left and Right

Kansas City Royals	AB	H	2B	3B	HR	RBI	BB	SO	BA	SA	OBA
Season	533	119	23	5	4	52	42	88	.223	.308	.285
vs. Left-Handers	163	38	8	2	3	20	10	27	.233	.362	.282
vs. Right-Handers	370	81	15	3	1	32	32	61	.219	.284	.287
vs. Ground-Ballers	212	50	12	1	1	23	17	38	.236	.316	.299
vs. Fly-Ballers	321	69	11	4	3	29	25	50	.215	.302	.276
Home Games	257	63	12	4	2	34	19	46	.245	.346	.301
Road Games	276	56	11	1	2	18	23	42	.203	.272	.271
Grass Fields	207	41	6	1	0	13	16	32	.198	.237	.258
Artificial Turf	326	78	17	4	4	39	26	56	.239	.353	.303
April	79	14	3	1	1	6	6	9	.177	.278	.235
May	102	21	5	1	0	11	11	20	.206	.275	.281
June	91	25	5	1	0	12	7	14	.275	.385	.323
July	100	23	2	1	0	7	9	11	.230	.270	.313
August	66	14	2	0	1	7	6	12	.212	.288	.274
Sept./Oct.	95	22	6	1	1	9	3	22	.232	.347	.275
Leading Off Inn.	141	32	8	1	0	0	4	17	.227	.298	.264
Runners On	220	53	8	3	3	51	16	44	.241	.345	.290
Bases Empty	313	66	15	2	1	1	26	44	.211	.281	.282
Runners/Scor. Pos.	131	31	2	3	2	44	10	27	.237	.344	.288
Runners On/2 Out	91	21	5	1	1	22	8	15	.231	.341	.293
Scor. Pos./2 Out	63	16	1	1	1	18	7	13	.254	.349	.329
Late-Inning Pressure	85	18	3	1	0	9	10	13	.212	.271	.310
Leading Off	22	2	1	0	0	0	1	2	.091	.136	.231
Runners On	39	11	1	0	0	9	3	7	.282	.359	.318
Runners/Scor. Pos.	21	6	0	1	0	9	2	4	.286	.381	.320

RUNS BATTED IN	From 1B	From 2B	From 3B	Scoring Position
Totals	8/144	18/102	22/57	40/159
Percentage	5.6%	17.6%	38.6%	25.2%

Loves to face: Melido Perez (.600, 6-for-10)
Scott Scudder (.556, 5-for-9)
Kevin Tapani (.563, 9-for-16, 1 HR, 4 SO)

Hates to face: Ron Darling (0-for-12)
Jimmy Key (.071, 1-for-14, 1 3B)
Matt Young (.091, 1-for-11)

Miscellaneous statistics: Ground outs-to-air outs ratio: 1.73 last season, 1.46 for career.... Grounded into 10 double plays in 101 opportunities (one per 10).... Drove in 15 of 25 runners from third base with less than two outs (60%).... Direction of balls hit to the outfield: 38% to left field, 25% to center, 37% to right batting left-handed; 36% to left field, 25% to center, 39% to right batting right-handed.... Base running: Advanced from first base to third on 8 of 19 outfield singles (42%); scored from second on 13 of 15 (87%).... Made 2.94 putouts per nine innings in center field.

Comments: Had the lowest batting average of any major leaguer to qualify for the batting title last season, and the 3d lowest in Royals history, ahead of Fred Patek (.212 in 1972) and Jackie Hernandez (.222 in 1969).... Batting average of .202 from the leadoff slot was 2d lowest in the majors (minimum: 100 AB). Only another second-generation major leaguer, Ruben Amaro, had a lower leadoff BA (.185).... From the 2d spot in the order, McRae had the lowest average in the majors (.175).... Career batting average is .164 during April, .258 thereafter.... Batting, slugging, and on-base averages have dropped in every season since his debut, but his stolen-base percentage is on the rise: 1990—4-for-7 (.571); 1991—20-for-31 (.645); 1992—18-for-23 (.783).... Rate of walks increased from one every 28 plate appearances in 1991 to one every 14 last season. Although his batting average dropped 38 points from 1991 to 1992, his on-base percentage dropped only three points.... His .171 batting average in day games was the 2d lowest in the American League over the past 10 years. Pete Incaviglia batted .161 in 1990—the lowest day-game mark since Paul Blair's memorable .144 in 1975.... This one-time 22-year-old prodigy has become a 25-year-old question mark. At age 25, his father Hal had played in only 87 major league games, compared to 347 for Brian. Of course, Hal had already appeared in a League Championship Series and a World Series with the Reds (1970).

Kevin McReynolds — Bats Right

Kansas City Royals	AB	H	2B	3B	HR	RBI	BB	SO	BA	SA	OBA
Season	373	92	25	0	13	49	67	48	.247	.418	.357
vs. Left-Handers	113	39	11	0	5	22	26	13	.345	.575	.461
vs. Right-Handers	260	53	14	0	8	27	41	35	.204	.350	.309
vs. Ground-Ballers	155	44	10	0	3	16	31	15	.284	.406	.403
vs. Fly-Ballers	218	48	15	0	10	33	36	33	.220	.427	.324
Home Games	186	47	15	0	4	17	34	22	.253	.398	.363
Road Games	187	45	10	0	9	32	33	26	.241	.439	.351
Grass Fields	141	35	5	0	8	24	26	19	.248	.454	.361
Artificial Turf	232	57	20	0	5	25	41	29	.246	.397	.355
April	71	12	1	0	3	5	7	9	.169	.310	.244
May	86	23	8	0	4	14	23	6	.267	.500	.414
June	93	26	7	0	1	13	12	16	.280	.387	.358
July	91	22	6	0	5	15	22	13	.242	.473	.383
August	6	0	0	0	0	0	1	1	.000	.000	.143
Sept./Oct.	26	9	3	0	0	2	2	3	.346	.462	.393
Leading Off Inn.	87	17	7	0	3	3	14	12	.195	.379	.307
Runners On	159	41	8	0	6	42	27	24	.258	.421	.356
Bases Empty	214	51	17	0	7	7	40	24	.238	.416	.358
Runners/Scor. Pos.	85	19	2	0	1	29	21	15	.224	.282	.360
Runners On/2 Out	79	20	4	0	3	19	13	13	.253	.418	.359
Scor. Pos./2 Out	46	10	1	0	1	13	10	9	.217	.304	.357
Late-Inning Pressure	66	13	5	0	2	5	12	11	.197	.364	.321
Leading Off	15	1	0	0	0	0	2	3	.067	.067	.176
Runners On	30	8	2	0	1	4	3	5	.267	.433	.333
Runners/Scor. Pos.	11	2	0	0	0	2	3	2	.182	.182	.357

RUNS BATTED IN	From 1B	From 2B	From 3B	Scoring Position
Totals	10/115	10/58	16/43	26/101
Percentage	8.7%	17.2%	37.2%	25.7%

Loves to face: Ricky Bones (.500, 4-for-8, 2 HR)
Rick Honeycutt (.469, 15-for-32, 1 HR)
Mark Langston (.500, 6-for-12, 1 HR)

Hates to face: Dennis Cook (.071, 1-for-14)
Ron Darling (.120, 3-for-25)
Mike Mussina (0-for-8)

Miscellaneous statistics: Ground outs-to-air outs ratio: 0.54 last season (3d lowest in A.L.), 0.71 for career.... Grounded into 6 double plays in 67 opportunities (one per 11).... Drove in 9 of 19 runners from third base with less than two outs (47%).... Direction of balls hit to the outfield: 36% to left field, 38% to center, 27% to right.... Base running: Advanced from first base to third on 6 of 16 outfield singles (38%); scored from second on 6 of 8 (75%).... Made 2.04 putouts per nine innings in left field, 2d-lowest rate in A.L.

Comments: The only player in the majors whose batting average and RBI totals have decreased in each of the last four years. (He batted .288 with 99 RBIs in 1988.) Only three players in major league history have sustained a similar five-year decline: Johnny Evers (6 years), Eddie Collins and Jake Powell. Both Evers and Collins spent the final years of their streaks as player/coaches. During the 1980s, four years of declining batting averages and RBI totals signaled the end of the line for Jose Cruz, Jody Davis, Fred Lynn, Jason Thompson, and Mike Young. We'll close on a note of optimism for K-Mac: Both Mel Hall and Kevin Seitzer made significant comebacks from four-year slides.... He was the only Royals player to start every game in which the club faced a left-handed starter last season.... Batting average vs. left-handed pitchers was a career high, but his average vs. right-handers was a career low, and the lowest in the American League.... Posted the highest walk rate of his career, averaging one base on balls every 6.6 plate appearances.... Only two other players have appeared in at least 100 games for both the Padres and the Royals: the Kurts—Bevacqua and Stillwell.... Over the last two seasons, he has only two hits in 32 at-bats leading off innings in Late-Inning Pressure Situations. He also reached base twice on walks.... Averaged more than 10 outfield assists per season over the first 10 years of his career, but had only four last season.

Keith Miller — Bats Right

Kansas City Royals	AB	H	2B	3B	HR	RBI	BB	SO	BA	SA	OBA
Season	416	118	24	4	4	38	31	46	.284	.389	.352
vs. Left-Handers	120	32	9	2	0	10	12	15	.267	.375	.333
vs. Right-Handers	296	86	15	2	4	28	19	31	.291	.395	.360
vs. Ground-Ballers	167	55	12	2	2	17	14	14	.329	.461	.401
vs. Fly-Ballers	249	63	12	2	2	21	17	32	.253	.341	.319
Home Games	183	55	8	2	1	17	18	12	.301	.383	.384
Road Games	233	63	16	2	3	21	13	34	.270	.395	.325
Grass Fields	185	48	11	0	2	15	8	26	.259	.351	.305
Artificial Turf	231	70	13	4	2	23	23	20	.303	.420	.387
April	74	22	7	0	1	2	6	11	.297	.432	.366
May	51	16	4	0	1	8	5	5	.314	.451	.386
June	100	27	5	2	1	13	9	14	.270	.390	.357
July	45	17	4	0	0	4	1	4	.378	.467	.404
August	37	7	2	0	1	4	3	3	.189	.324	.302
Sept./Oct.	109	29	2	2	0	7	7	9	.266	.321	.319
Leading Off Inn.	134	31	6	2	1	1	10	10	.231	.328	.299
Runners On	143	41	9	1	1	35	10	16	.287	.385	.358
Bases Empty	273	77	15	3	3	3	21	30	.282	.392	.349
Runners/Scor. Pos.	88	30	6	1	0	32	6	11	.341	.432	.412
Runners On/2 Out	67	20	5	0	0	15	5	8	.299	.373	.373
Scor. Pos./2 Out	44	15	3	0	0	14	3	6	.341	.409	.408
Late-Inning Pressure	64	18	1	0	1	6	5	14	.281	.344	.338
Leading Off	13	2	0	0	0	0	2	1	.154	.154	.267
Runners On	31	10	1	0	1	6	2	6	.323	.452	.371
Runners/Scor. Pos.	20	5	0	0	0	4	0	5	.250	.250	.273

RUNS BATTED IN	From 1B	From 2B	From 3B	Scoring Position
Totals	5/89	17/66	12/33	29/99
Percentage	5.6%	25.8%	36.4%	29.3%

Loves to face: Neal Heaton (.667, 6-for-9)
Jeff Johnson (.571, 4-for-7, 2 2B)
Kevin Tapani (.500, 3-for-6, 1 HR)

Hates to face: Greg A. Harris (0-for-7)
Mark Langston (.063, 1-for-16, 1 2B)
Craig Lefferts (0-for-6)

Miscellaneous statistics: Ground outs-to-air outs ratio: 0.77 last season, 1.01 for career.... Grounded into 1 double play in 54 opportunities (one per 54), 2d-best rate in A.L.... Drove in 8 of 16 runners from third base with less than two outs (50%).... Direction of balls hit to the outfield: 41% to left field, 40% to center, 20% to right.... Base running: Advanced from first base to third on 11 of 20 outfield singles (55%); scored from second on 9 of 13 (69%).... Made 2.86 assists per nine innings at second base.

Comments: His batting average continues to rise. Year by year since 1988: .214, .231, .258, .280, .284. The only other player to raise his batting average in each of those seasons, Bob Melvin, actually has a streak one year longer than Miller's.... His playing time has increased throughout his career as well. Games (and starts) year by year: 1987—25 (13), 1988—40 (13), 1989—57 (32), 1990—88 (53), 1991—98 (62), 1992—106 (103).... Batting average in night games (.327) was roughly double his day-game mark (.164). Career figures: .242 in day games, .285 at night.... Career stolen-base percentage is .889 vs. right-handed pitchers (40-for-45), far better than his .588 mark vs. left-handers (20-for-34).... Career batting average is .251 on grass fields, .296 on artificial turf.... Has a higher career average against right-handed pitchers (.273) than he does against left-handers (.268). Over the last two seasons, the difference is much greater: .299 vs. right-handers, .256 vs. southpaws.... Batted .345 with runners in scoring position in 1991. He and Dwight Smith are the only players to top the .340-mark with RISP in each of the last two years (minimum: 30 AB).... Gregg Jefferies grounded into more than twice as many double plays last season (24) as Miller has in his entire major league career (10).... It was a tough season for Royals second basemen. Miller spent parts of May, June, July, and August on the disabled list (two separate stints), and Terry Shumpert was on the D.L. for 31 days in August and September.

Randy Milligan   Bats Right

Baltimore Orioles	AB	H	2B	3B	HR	RBI	BB	SO	BA	SA	OBA
Season	462	111	21	1	11	53	106	81	.240	.361	.383
vs. Left-Handers	107	30	6	0	3	14	35	22	.280	.421	.462
vs. Right-Handers	355	81	15	1	8	39	71	59	.228	.344	.356
vs. Ground-Ballers	225	48	8	1	2	17	45	38	.213	.284	.347
vs. Fly-Ballers	237	63	13	0	9	36	61	43	.266	.435	.416
Home Games	233	45	5	1	7	26	61	38	.193	.313	.361
Road Games	229	66	16	0	4	27	45	43	.288	.410	.406
Grass Fields	391	89	13	1	11	45	92	64	.228	.350	.377
Artificial Turf	71	22	8	0	0	8	14	17	.310	.423	.416
April	47	10	2	0	2	9	6	10	.213	.383	.315
May	72	22	7	0	1	9	22	9	.306	.444	.474
June	89	22	2	0	4	11	17	14	.247	.404	.374
July	90	20	2	0	1	8	21	17	.222	.278	.363
August	80	23	4	0	2	10	23	12	.287	.412	.443
Sept./Oct.	84	14	4	1	1	6	17	19	.167	.274	.304
Leading Off Inn.	104	23	3	1	4	4	29	18	.221	.385	.396
Runners On	215	53	8	0	5	47	36	34	.247	.353	.355
Bases Empty	247	58	13	1	6	6	70	47	.235	.368	.406
Runners/Scor. Pos.	119	26	5	0	3	42	22	22	.218	.336	.333
Runners On/2 Out	98	22	3	0	1	17	12	12	.224	.286	.315
Scor. Pos./2 Out	58	11	2	0	0	14	8	8	.190	.224	.288
Late-Inning Pressure	63	15	4	0	2	8	12	10	.238	.397	.355
Leading Off	18	4	1	0	1	1	3	3	.222	.444	.333
Runners On	29	7	3	0	1	7	5	4	.241	.448	.343
Runners/Scor. Pos.	21	5	2	0	1	7	3	3	.238	.476	.320

RUNS BATTED IN	From 1B	From 2B	From 3B	Scoring Position
Totals	5/171	15/88	22/55	37/143
Percentage	2.9%	17.0%	40.0%	25.9%

Loves to face: Mark Gubicza (.417, 5-for-12, 1 2B, 1 3B, 2 HR)
Terry Leach (.400, 4-for-10, 1 2B, 2 HR)
Bobby Witt (.400, 8-for-20, 1 HR, 7 BB)
Hates to face: Jack Morris (.053, 1-for-19, 1 2B)
Rod Nichols (.118, 2-for-17)
Nolan Ryan (0-for-13, 8 SO)

Miscellaneous statistics: Ground outs-to-air outs ratio: 1.18 last season, 1.06 for career.... Grounded into 15 double plays in 108 opportunities (one per 7.2).... Drove in 16 of 30 runners from third base with less than two outs (53%).... Direction of balls hit to the outfield: 20% to left field, 36% to center, 44% to right.... Base running: Advanced from first base to third on 13 of 40 outfield singles (33%); scored from second on 6 of 12 (50%).... Made 0.64 assists per nine innings at first base.

Comments: Career rate of one walk every 5.8 plate appearances is 2d highest among active players (minimum: 1000 PA); only Frank Thomas has a higher rate (one BB every 5.4 PA).... Had 329 walks at the time of his 500th game last July. Only two players over the last 40 years have had more walks in their first 500 games: Joe Morgan and Darrell Evans.... Became the first player since 1955, when intentional walks became an official statistic, to draw at least 100 walks in a season without an intentional pass.... Averaged one walk every 4.6 plate appearances leading off innings last season, the 10th-highest rate over the last 18 years, but not the highest of his career: He averaged one walk every 4.4 leadoff PAs in 1990. Those who have had higher single-season rates: John Cangelosi, Jim Wynn, Jack Clark, Dwayne Murphy, Lee Mazzilli, Gary Pettis, and Joe Morgan.... Strikeout rate was the lowest of his career (one every 7.1 PAs).... Orioles first basemen combined for only 63 RBIs, the fewest by any A.L. club last season.... September batting average was his lowest in any month since April 1988 (with Pittsburgh).... His batting average vs. right-handed pitchers was a career low.... One of three active players with at least 2000 plate appearances and no sacrifice bunts. The others: George Bell and Cecil Fielder.... Has been thrown out in his last seven stolen base attempts, dating back to July 1990. The only active player with a longer streak: Jamie Quirk (10). Jay Buhner is also 0-for-his-last-7.

Kevin Mitchell   Bats Right

Seattle Mariners	AB	H	2B	3B	HR	RBI	BB	SO	BA	SA	OBA
Season	360	103	24	0	9	67	35	46	.286	.428	.351
vs. Left-Handers	92	35	5	0	5	27	11	11	.380	.598	.438
vs. Right-Handers	268	68	19	0	4	40	24	35	.254	.369	.320
vs. Ground-Ballers	179	58	14	0	5	38	20	22	.324	.486	.391
vs. Fly-Ballers	181	45	10	0	4	29	15	24	.249	.370	.310
Home Games	207	66	17	0	5	41	17	25	.319	.473	.368
Road Games	153	37	7	0	4	26	18	21	.242	.366	.328
Grass Fields	120	30	5	0	4	25	15	18	.250	.392	.341
Artificial Turf	240	73	19	0	5	42	20	28	.304	.446	.356
April	69	18	4	0	0	8	3	8	.261	.319	.289
May	89	17	3	0	2	11	12	18	.191	.292	.287
June	94	31	9	0	3	12	6	2	.330	.521	.376
July	77	22	7	0	3	24	10	17	.286	.494	.368
August	31	15	1	0	1	11	4	1	.484	.613	.541
Sept./Oct.	0	0	0	0	0	0	0	0	.000	.000	.000
Leading Off Inn.	90	17	5	0	2	2	9	12	.189	.311	.270
Runners On	180	58	16	0	5	63	16	22	.322	.494	.373
Bases Empty	180	45	8	0	4	4	19	24	.250	.361	.328
Runners/Scor. Pos.	113	33	9	0	3	54	12	14	.292	.451	.349
Runners On/2 Out	78	21	7	0	1	20	7	10	.269	.397	.339
Scor. Pos./2 Out	53	11	3	0	0	16	6	6	.208	.264	.288
Late-Inning Pressure	55	15	2	0	0	5	4	8	.273	.309	.322
Leading Off	9	2	0	0	0	0	0	0	.222	.222	.222
Runners On	33	7	1	0	0	5	3	6	.212	.242	.278
Runners/Scor. Pos.	19	2	0	0	0	4	2	4	.105	.105	.190

RUNS BATTED IN	From 1B	From 2B	From 3B	Scoring Position
Totals	11/120	21/81	26/54	47/135
Percentage	9.2%	25.9%	48.1%	34.8%

Loves to face: Steve Avery (4-for-4, 1 HR)
Andy Benes (.350, 7-for-20, 2 2B, 4 HR)
Bruce Hurst (.333, 7-for-21, 1 2B, 5 HR)
Hates to face: Joe Boever (0-for-9)
Jim Gott (0-for-10)
Dave Smith (0-for-9)

Miscellaneous statistics: Ground outs-to-air outs ratio: 0.77 last season, 0.76 for career.... Grounded into 4 double plays in 81 opportunities (one per 20).... Drove in 19 of 28 runners from third base with less than two outs (68%).... Direction of balls hit to the outfield: 38% to left field, 35% to center, 28% to right.... Base running: Advanced from first base to third on 4 of 22 outfield singles (18%); scored from second on 7 of 11 (64%).... Made 2.05 putouts per nine innings in left field, 3d-lowest rate in A.L.

Comments: Was acquired by Seattle to fill the cleanup slot in its batting order. Mitchell's nine homers in 92 games batting cleanup was only slightly better than other Mariners in that spot (7 HR in 84 games). All told, Mariners cleanup hitters combined for only 16 home runs, tying Angels and Royals for the fewest in the league.... Now Mitchell will be asked to fill the same role in Cincinnati, where last season Reds cleanup hitters had only 17 homers, 2d fewest in the National League.... On April 16 last season, Bill Swift (whom Seattle traded to get Mitchell) posted his third win in as many starts and lowered his ERA to 0.70. But to make matters worse, he also raised his batting average to .273—at a time when Mitchell was struggling with a .179 mark. And to add insult, Swift's pair of doubles in that game matched Mitchell's extra-base-hit output for the season as well.... Things got better: Mitchell's batting averages vs. both left-handers and ground-ball pitchers were career highs. He batted .380 against southpaw worm-killers (15-for-39).... Percentage of runners driven in from scoring position was a career high, but drove in only 18.2 percent of those runners in Late-Inning Pressure Situations, compared to 38.1 percent at other times.... Averaged one home run every 40 at-bats last season, the lowest rate of his career.... Averaged one strikeout every 8.7 plate appearances last season, best rate of his career.... Has only one home run in 110 at-bats in Late-Inning Pressure Situations over the last two seasons.

Paul Molitor
Bats Right

Milwaukee Brewers	AB	H	2B	3B	HR	RBI	BB	SO	BA	SA	OBA
Season	609	195	36	7	12	89	73	66	.320	.461	.389
vs. Left-Handers	132	56	11	1	6	32	14	11	.424	.659	.464
vs. Right-Handers	477	139	25	6	6	57	59	55	.291	.407	.369
vs. Ground-Ballers	280	94	16	4	4	41	36	30	.336	.464	.409
vs. Fly-Ballers	329	101	20	3	8	48	37	36	.307	.459	.373
Home Games	286	87	13	4	4	36	43	34	.304	.420	.390
Road Games	323	108	23	3	8	53	30	32	.334	.498	.389
Grass Fields	507	157	27	5	10	68	64	52	.310	.442	.383
Artificial Turf	102	38	9	2	2	21	9	14	.373	.559	.422
April	77	20	3	0	1	12	6	9	.260	.338	.302
May	98	35	6	2	5	13	14	15	.357	.612	.439
June	98	33	7	0	4	15	13	6	.337	.531	.409
July	104	30	3	2	1	15	14	15	.288	.385	.375
August	109	36	5	2	1	21	12	13	.330	.440	.390
Sept./Oct.	123	41	12	1	0	13	14	8	.333	.447	.399
Leading Off Inn.	141	45	12	2	0	0	12	13	.319	.433	.373
Runners On	268	88	14	2	6	83	39	27	.328	.463	.403
Bases Empty	341	107	22	5	6	6	34	39	.314	.460	.378
Runners/Scor. Pos.	164	53	8	2	3	75	32	21	.323	.451	.416
Runners On/2 Out	93	30	3	1	1	24	17	10	.323	.409	.427
Scor. Pos./2 Out	61	17	0	1	1	22	16	7	.279	.361	.429
Late-Inning Pressure	81	26	3	1	1	10	13	13	.321	.420	.417
Leading Off	24	9	1	0	0	0	1	4	.375	.417	.400
Runners On	31	9	1	0	0	9	10	6	.290	.323	.465
Runners/Scor. Pos.	22	7	1	0	0	9	9	4	.318	.364	.515

RUNS BATTED IN	From 1B	From 2B	From 3B	Scoring Position
Totals	10/184	26/125	41/79	67/204
Percentage	5.4%	20.8%	51.9%	32.8%

Loves to face: Rick Aguilera (.556, 5-for-9, 1 HR)
Erik Hanson (.500, 16-for-32, 1 HR)
Neal Heaton (.500, 9-for-18)

Hates to face: Steve Farr (.100, 2-for-20, 2 BB)
Mike Moore (.170, 8-for-47)
Rick Sutcliffe (.111, 3-for-27, 4 BB)

Miscellaneous statistics: Ground outs-to-air outs ratio: 1.02 last season, 1.19 for career.... Grounded into 13 double plays in 135 opportunities (one per 10).... Drove in 34 of 54 runners from third base with less than two outs (63%).... Direction of balls hit to the outfield: 36% to left field, 34% to center, 30% to right.... Base running: Advanced from first base to third on 12 of 35 outfield singles (34%); scored from second on 12 of 18 (67%).... Made 0.55 assists per nine innings at first base.

Comments: Reached the 190-hit mark but fell short of 200 for the third time in the past five years. (He also had a 188-hit season in 1979.) No fewer than 24 other players fell 10 or fewer hits short of the 200 mark three times, including Nellie Fox, a near-miss Hall of Famer, who did so a record five times; and Stan Hack, who had four near misses *and never reached 200.* . . . At the age of 36, he set his career high in RBIs. In the expansion era (since 1961), only seven older players have done that: Alan Ashby, Carlton Fisk, Jose Cruz (*twice*), Lee Lacy, Hal McRae, Cliff Johnson, and Willie Horton.... Batted only five points lower than his 1991 mark. The last A.L. player as old as Molitor with consecutive .320-plus seasons was Ted Williams, who had a five-year streak starting at the age of 36 in 1954. Two N.L. veterans did it in the interim: Stan Musial (1957–58) and Roberto Clemente (1969–71).... Batting average vs. left-handed pitchers was the 2d-highest single-season mark over the 18 years of *The Player Analysis* (minimum: 40 hits vs. LHP). Only Rennie Stennett's .435 average against lefties in 1977 was higher.... Two-year total of 316 games was a career high.... Has only one hit and no RBIs in 17 career at-bats as a pinch hitter.... One of eight players in history to play at least 50 games at each of the infield positions and in the outfield during his career. The others: Bill Almon, Red Kress, Don Money, Joe Quinn, Chico Salmon, Germany Schaefer, Honus Wagner.

Pedro Munoz
Bats Right

Minnesota Twins	AB	H	2B	3B	HR	RBI	BB	SO	BA	SA	OBA
Season	418	113	16	3	12	71	17	90	.270	.409	.298
vs. Left-Handers	122	36	6	1	3	21	6	23	.295	.434	.326
vs. Right-Handers	296	77	10	2	9	50	11	67	.260	.399	.287
vs. Ground-Ballers	187	48	9	1	4	27	8	43	.257	.380	.289
vs. Fly-Ballers	231	65	7	2	8	44	9	47	.281	.433	.306
Home Games	193	53	10	1	8	36	10	39	.275	.461	.314
Road Games	225	60	6	2	4	35	7	51	.267	.364	.285
Grass Fields	179	44	5	1	3	30	6	38	.246	.335	.266
Artificial Turf	239	69	11	2	9	41	11	52	.289	.464	.323
April	69	22	3	0	3	13	3	13	.319	.493	.347
May	70	16	2	0	2	12	3	17	.229	.343	.257
June	63	21	5	0	3	16	3	10	.333	.556	.364
July	69	17	2	0	2	9	2	11	.246	.362	.268
August	54	13	2	1	1	6	1	15	.241	.370	.250
Sept./Oct.	93	24	2	2	1	15	5	24	.258	.355	.300
Leading Off Inn.	102	25	5	0	3	3	5	26	.245	.373	.280
Runners On	193	58	11	1	8	67	9	33	.301	.492	.330
Bases Empty	225	55	5	2	4	4	8	57	.244	.338	.270
Runners/Scor. Pos.	120	38	8	0	6	61	7	21	.317	.533	.351
Runners On/2 Out	93	31	8	1	6	40	4	11	.333	.634	.367
Scor. Pos./2 Out	60	21	6	0	4	34	4	10	.350	.650	.400
Late-Inning Pressure	48	13	2	0	1	5	2	16	.271	.375	.300
Leading Off	17	4	2	0	0	0	1	6	.235	.353	.278
Runners On	14	4	0	0	0	4	1	4	.286	.286	.333
Runners/Scor. Pos.	8	3	0	0	0	4	1	2	.375	.375	.444

RUNS BATTED IN	From 1B	From 2B	From 3B	Scoring Position
Totals	12/147	21/95	26/52	47/147
Percentage	8.2%	22.1%	50.0%	32.0%

Loves to face: Rich DeLucia (.800, 4-for-5, 1 HR)
Jeff Johnson (.400, 4-for-10, 2 HR)
Dave Stewart (.600, 6-for-10, 1 HR)

Hates to face: Jack McDowell (.083, 1-for-12, 2 BB)
Frank Viola (0-for-7)
Bobby Witt (.083, 1-for-12, 7 SO)

Miscellaneous statistics: Ground outs-to-air outs ratio: 1.99 last season (2d highest in A.L.), 1.84 for career.... Grounded into 18 double plays in 80 opportunities (one per 4.4), 3d-worst rate in majors.... Drove in 17 of 31 runners from third base with less than two outs (55%).... Direction of balls hit to the outfield: 23% to left field, 33% to center, 44% to right.... Base running: Advanced from first base to third on 3 of 23 outfield singles (13%); scored from second on 6 of 7 (86%).... Made 2.09 putouts per nine innings in right field.

Comments: Started all 34 games last season in which the Twins faced a left-handed starting pitcher, as did Kirby Puckett and Chuck Knoblauch. Unlike his teammates, Munoz was a part-time starter against right-handers (81 of 128).... Other part-timers against right-handers who started every game vs. southpaws last season: Chad Curtis and Henry Cotto.... Career batting average is 48 points higher vs. left-handers (.307) than vs. right-handers (.259). Home-run rates are nearly identical.... The outfield of Shane Mack, Puckett, and Munoz started 94 games together, the most of any outfield in the majors last season.... Minnesota outfielders led the majors in both batting average (.300) and RBIs (274).... Although he hit eight of his 12 home runs to the opposite field, he had tremendous success when he pulled the ball to the outfield. Of the 39 balls he hit to left field, 33 fell for hits.... Only five other players in the majors hit as many as seven opposite-field homers last season, and all of them had at least 25 total home runs—more than twice Munoz's total.... Walked only 17 times in 439 plate appearances, the 3d-lowest rate among players with at least 400 plate appearances (one BB per 26 PA), behind Mariano Duncan (one per 36) and Gary DiSarcina (one per 28).... Munoz has made 173 career starts, and has never drawn more than one walk in a game....Most comparable statistical profile: Lee May (through 1967).

Al Newman
Bats Left and Right

Texas Rangers	AB	H	2B	3B	HR	RBI	BB	SO	BA	SA	OBA
Season	246	54	5	0	0	12	34	26	.220	.240	.317
vs. Left-Handers	56	15	1	0	0	3	14	9	.268	.286	.423
vs. Right-Handers	190	39	4	0	0	9	20	17	.205	.226	.281
vs. Ground-Ballers	122	28	2	0	0	5	13	11	.230	.246	.304
vs. Fly-Ballers	124	26	3	0	0	7	21	15	.210	.234	.329
Home Games	114	23	3	0	0	3	15	12	.202	.228	.300
Road Games	132	31	2	0	0	9	19	14	.235	.250	.331
Grass Fields	198	43	4	0	0	7	23	23	.217	.237	.302
Artificial Turf	48	11	1	0	0	5	11	3	.229	.250	.373
April	36	8	2	0	0	3	3	4	.222	.278	.282
May	46	10	0	0	0	0	8	5	.217	.217	.333
June	60	14	2	0	0	7	4	4	.233	.267	.292
July	19	3	0	0	0	0	4	2	.158	.158	.304
August	44	12	1	0	0	0	8	6	.273	.295	.385
Sept./Oct.	41	7	0	0	0	2	7	5	.171	.171	.292
Leading Off Inn.	74	19	1	0	0	0	14	10	.257	.270	.375
Runners On	97	24	3	0	0	12	8	5	.247	.278	.305
Bases Empty	149	30	2	0	0	0	26	21	.201	.215	.324
Runners/Scor. Pos.	51	11	2	0	0	12	7	4	.216	.255	.310
Runners On/2 Out	47	8	1	0	0	7	4	2	.170	.191	.235
Scor. Pos./2 Out	27	6	1	0	0	7	4	2	.222	.259	.323
Late-Inning Pressure	25	6	0	0	0	0	5	5	.240	.240	.367
Leading Off	7	2	0	0	0	0	3	1	.286	.286	.500
Runners On	7	2	0	0	0	0	0	1	.286	.286	.286
Runners/Scor. Pos.	2	0	0	0	0	0	0	1	.000	.000	.000

RUNS BATTED IN	From 1B	From 2B	From 3B	Scoring Position
Totals	0/76	4/42	8/19	12/61
Percentage	0.0%	9.5%	42.1%	19.7%

Loves to face: Luis Aquino (.714, 5-for-7)
Erik Hanson (.438, 7-for-16)
Bobby Witt (.375, 9-for-24, 8 BB)
Hates to face: Kevin Appier (0-for-13)
Dennis Eckersley (0-for-10)
Mark Gubicza (.095, 2-for-21)

Miscellaneous statistics: Ground outs-to-air outs ratio: 1.59 last season, 1.68 for career.... Grounded into 5 double plays in 41 opportunities (one per 8.2).... Drove in 3 of 8 runners from third base with less than two outs (38%).... Direction of balls hit to the outfield: 25% to left field, 42% to center, 33% to right batting left-handed; 57% to left field, 29% to center, 14% to right batting right-handed.... Base running: Advanced from first base to third on 5 of 10 outfield singles (50%); scored from second on 4 of 6 (67%).... Made 3.25 assists per nine innings at second base.

Comments: Has only one home run in 2107 career at-bats. Among active players with at least 1000 at-bats, only Newman, Felix Fermin, and Rafael Belliard have fewer than two home runs. (No active player with as many as 1000 at-bats is homerless, though Alex Cole is getting there; he takes an 0-for-916 mark to Mile High Stadium.) ... Has 1971 at-bats since hitting the only home run of his career, off Zane Smith in 1986. Has 1893 at-bats without a home run in the American League.... Could become only the first American League player ever to reach the 2000-AB mark without a homer. Two players went homerless in A.L. careers just short of 2000 ABs: Tom Oliver (1931 ABs from 1930 to 1933) and Irv Hall (1904 ABs, 1943–46).... Hasn't hit anything better than a double in the 1990s. Ron Hunt (in his last three seasons, 1972–1974) is the only other player in major league history to not hit either a triple or a home run in three consecutive seasons of at least 250 plate appearances.... Batted .248 over a two-year period with Minnesota (1989–90); if you subtract those seasons, his career average would stand at .211.... How much did the Rangers miss Julio Franco? Their second basemen combined for only 36 RBIs, the fewest of any team in the majors at that position.... Newman has now played at least 20 games each at second base, third base, and shortstop in six consecutive seasons—twice as long a streak as anyone else's in major league history.

Matt Nokes
Bats Left

New York Yankees	AB	H	2B	3B	HR	RBI	BB	SO	BA	SA	OBA
Season	384	86	9	1	22	59	37	62	.224	.424	.293
vs. Left-Handers	71	14	4	0	5	15	8	18	.197	.465	.275
vs. Right-Handers	313	72	5	1	17	44	29	44	.230	.415	.297
vs. Ground-Ballers	178	43	3	0	12	31	12	32	.242	.461	.294
vs. Fly-Ballers	206	43	6	1	10	28	25	30	.209	.393	.292
Home Games	177	47	4	0	18	41	20	26	.266	.593	.347
Road Games	207	39	5	1	4	18	17	36	.188	.280	.246
Grass Fields	326	72	7	1	21	52	35	55	.221	.442	.299
Artificial Turf	58	14	2	0	1	7	2	7	.241	.328	.258
April	57	13	1	0	3	3	5	9	.228	.404	.290
May	73	17	1	0	4	14	9	11	.233	.411	.310
June	73	12	1	0	2	7	7	15	.164	.260	.244
July	55	12	1	0	4	11	5	9	.218	.455	.286
August	60	13	0	0	6	15	4	9	.217	.517	.262
Sept./Oct.	66	19	5	1	3	9	7	9	.288	.530	.365
Leading Off Inn.	69	17	3	0	2	2	6	8	.246	.377	.316
Runners On	180	40	4	0	12	49	20	34	.222	.444	.295
Bases Empty	204	46	5	1	10	10	17	28	.225	.407	.291
Runners/Scor. Pos.	89	17	2	0	6	37	15	20	.191	.416	.291
Runners On/2 Out	85	17	1	0	7	23	7	19	.200	.459	.261
Scor. Pos./2 Out	51	7	0	0	4	17	7	13	.137	.373	.241
Late-Inning Pressure	65	15	0	0	6	11	9	13	.231	.508	.333
Leading Off	10	4	0	0	0	0	1	0	.400	.400	.455
Runners On	22	5	0	0	3	8	6	6	.227	.636	.452
Runners/Scor. Pos.	11	2	0	0	1	4	7	4	.182	.455	.500

RUNS BATTED IN	From 1B	From 2B	From 3B	Scoring Position
Totals	11/151	11/71	15/41	26/112
Percentage	7.3%	15.5%	36.6%	23.2%

Loves to face: Scott Bankhead (.417, 5-for-12, 2 HR)
Mike Moore (.355, 11-for-31, 3 HR)
Todd Stottlemyre (.340, 16-for-47, 5 HR)
Hates to face: Jose Mesa (0-for-15)
Charles Nagy (.067, 1-for-15, 1 2B)
Nolan Ryan (.105, 2-for-19)

Miscellaneous statistics: Ground outs-to-air outs ratio: 0.72 last season, 0.89 for career.... Grounded into 13 double plays in 91 opportunities (one per 7.0).... Drove in 10 of 19 runners from third base with less than two outs (53%).... Direction of balls hit to the outfield: 16% to left field, 31% to center, 53% to right.... Base running: Advanced from first base to third on 2 of 13 outfield singles (15%); scored from second on 1 of 8 (13%).... Opposing base stealers: 108-for-141 (77%), 2d-highest rate in A.L.

Comments: Yankees catchers combined for 30 home runs last season, tying the Phillies for the most in the majors; Nokes hit 21, Mike Stanley hit 7, and Jim Leyritz hit 2. (Darren Daulton contributed 27 of Philadelphia's total.) It marked the first time that Yankees catchers reached that level since 1963, when Elston Howard hit 28 homers and Yogi Berra hit eight.... According to legend, the '61 team had three catchers who hit 20 home runs each; that's a myth. Although both Yogi and Johnny Blanchard are remembered as catchers, Berra played mostly left field that season, and Blanchard hit four of his homers as a pinch hitter, six others as an outfielder.... Started 100 games against right-handed pitchers last season, but only one against a left-hander.... Disparity between home runs at home and on the road was the greatest in the majors last season. Only two other players were "plus 10" or better at home: Gary Sheffield (23 at home, 10 on the road) and Felix Jose (12 and 2).... Hit six homers in Late-Inning Pressure Situations to tie Mark McGwire and Glenallen Hill for 2d in the league, behind Juan Gonzalez (9).... Hit all 22 home runs to either right or right-center field (none to the opposite field).... Of his 10 opposite-field hits, seven came after the All-Star break, five within an eight-day span in late September.... Yankees team ERA was nearly the same with Nokes catching (4.23) as with Stanley and Leyritz (4.21)—not bad considering that the team indulged its number-one starter, Melido Perez, by allowing him to pitch primarily to Stanley late in the season.

Pete O'Brien
Bats Left

Seattle Mariners	AB	H	2B	3B	HR	RBI	BB	SO	BA	SA	OBA
Season	396	88	15	1	14	52	40	27	.222	.371	.289
vs. Left-Handers	56	12	2	1	1	8	7	6	.214	.339	.288
vs. Right-Handers	340	76	13	0	13	44	33	21	.224	.376	.289
vs. Ground-Ballers	207	39	7	1	5	23	21	19	.188	.304	.261
vs. Fly-Ballers	189	49	8	0	9	29	19	8	.259	.444	.319
Home Games	188	41	9	1	6	27	19	12	.218	.372	.286
Road Games	208	47	6	0	8	25	21	15	.226	.370	.292
Grass Fields	162	34	4	0	6	17	16	11	.210	.346	.276
Artificial Turf	234	54	11	1	8	35	24	16	.231	.389	.298
April	68	16	2	0	6	12	2	4	.235	.529	.254
May	92	18	4	1	5	15	7	7	.196	.424	.250
June	78	19	3	0	1	6	12	5	.244	.321	.344
July	60	11	1	0	2	7	9	6	.183	.300	.286
August	40	6	1	0	0	6	4	4	.150	.175	.217
Sept./Oct.	58	18	4	0	0	6	6	1	.310	.379	.364
Leading Off Inn.	95	21	2	0	6	6	7	3	.221	.432	.275
Runners On	174	45	7	1	5	43	25	15	.259	.397	.340
Bases Empty	222	43	8	0	9	9	15	12	.194	.351	.245
Runners/Scor. Pos.	85	22	5	0	4	39	18	8	.259	.459	.364
Runners On/2 Out	77	18	4	1	2	16	8	6	.234	.390	.306
Scor. Pos./2 Out	43	10	4	0	1	13	6	5	.233	.395	.327
Late-Inning Pressure	70	20	2	0	4	14	9	4	.286	.486	.349
Leading Off	22	5	0	0	1	1	1	0	.227	.364	.261
Runners On	31	9	0	0	3	13	7	4	.290	.581	.381
Runners/Scor. Pos.	17	4	0	0	2	11	4	2	.235	.588	.320

RUNS BATTED IN	From 1B	From 2B	From 3B	Scoring Position
Totals	6/141	15/76	17/36	32/112
Percentage	4.3%	19.7%	47.2%	28.6%

Loves to face: Joe Grahe (.714, 5-for-7)
Pat Mahomes (.600, 3-for-5, 1 HR)
Bobby Witt (.474, 9-for-19, 1 HR)

Hates to face: Gregg Olson (.071, 1-for-14)
Melido Perez (.091, 2-for-22, 2 BB)
Dennis Rasmussen (.118, 2-for-17)

Miscellaneous statistics: Ground outs-to-air outs ratio: 0.72 last season, 0.96 for career.... Grounded into 8 double plays in 93 opportunities (one per 12).... Drove in 12 of 19 runners from third base with less than two outs (63%).... Direction of balls hit to the outfield: 23% to left field, 36% to center, 41% to right.... Base running: Advanced from first base to third on 5 of 17 outfield singles (29%); scored from second on 6 of 9 (67%).... Made 0.78 assists per nine innings at first base.

Comments: Started 95 of 120 games in which the Mariners faced right-handed starting pitchers, but only 6 of 42 against left-handers.... Had accumulated at least 130 at-bats against left-handers in each of his previous nine seasons. Had only five ABs against lefties after August 2.... Average of one strikeout every 16.4 plate appearances last season was the best rate of his career.... Was held homerless in consecutive months for the first time in his career.... Drove in more runs in Mariners' losses (32) than he did in their victories (20). That might not seem unusual, considering that Seattle lost 34 more games than they won. But among A.L. players with at least 25 RBIs last season, only three others drove in a majority in losing causes: Hubie Brooks, Luis Rivera, and Dave Valle.... Had batted under .200 in Late-Inning Pressure Situations in each of his previous three years.... Career average of .135 with two outs and runners in scoring position in Late-Inning Pressure Situations is the lowest over the last 18 years (minimum: 100 AB). Rounding out the bottom five: Hal McRae (.146), Bob Boone (.160), Roy Smalley (.162), and Jeff Burroughs (.168).... Has been an opening-day starter in each of the last 10 seasons (one of 18 major leaguers to do so from 1983 to 1992). Anyone know why?...Sweet Lou will be O'Brien's sixth manager in the last six years, following Bobby Valentine (1988), Doc Edwards and John Hart (1989), Jim Lefebvre (1990–91), and Bill Plummer (1992).

John Olerud
Bats Left

Toronto Blue Jays	AB	H	2B	3B	HR	RBI	BB	SO	BA	SA	OBA
Season	458	130	28	0	16	66	70	61	.284	.450	.375
vs. Left-Handers	97	25	4	0	3	15	22	16	.258	.392	.393
vs. Right-Handers	361	105	24	0	13	51	48	45	.291	.465	.370
vs. Ground-Ballers	246	68	16	0	4	29	35	31	.276	.390	.365
vs. Fly-Ballers	212	62	12	0	12	37	35	30	.292	.519	.386
Home Games	231	61	16	0	4	28	39	30	.264	.385	.368
Road Games	227	69	12	0	12	38	31	31	.304	.515	.383
Grass Fields	164	51	10	0	11	30	28	21	.311	.573	.408
Artificial Turf	294	79	18	0	5	36	42	40	.269	.381	.356
April	67	17	4	0	1	5	17	8	.254	.358	.400
May	68	14	3	0	2	8	8	13	.206	.338	.299
June	88	28	6	0	5	18	10	9	.318	.557	.376
July	74	28	6	0	2	8	10	8	.378	.541	.452
August	66	20	3	0	3	14	11	6	.303	.485	.392
Sept./Oct.	95	23	6	0	3	13	14	17	.242	.400	.336
Leading Off Inn.	85	30	11	0	4	4	10	9	.353	.624	.421
Runners On	218	51	11	0	7	57	31	32	.234	.381	.323
Bases Empty	240	79	17	0	9	9	39	29	.329	.512	.423
Runners/Scor. Pos.	120	26	7	0	3	48	22	19	.217	.350	.327
Runners On/2 Out	90	22	7	0	3	25	19	13	.244	.422	.382
Scor. Pos./2 Out	58	14	5	0	1	20	15	9	.241	.379	.405
Late-Inning Pressure	59	21	4	0	2	9	6	7	.356	.525	.409
Leading Off	13	6	2	0	0	0	0	0	.462	.615	.462
Runners On	27	8	1	0	1	8	5	4	.296	.444	.394
Runners/Scor. Pos.	13	2	0	0	0	5	3	4	.154	.154	.294

RUNS BATTED IN	From 1B	From 2B	From 3B	Scoring Position
Totals	8/168	20/93	22/56	42/149
Percentage	4.8%	21.5%	39.3%	28.2%

Loves to face: Kevin Brown (.478, 11-for-23, 1 HR)
Tim Leary (.385, 5-for-13, 4 2B)
Jaime Navarro (.429, 6-for-14)

Hates to face: Ron Darling (0-for-9)
Tom Gordon (.056, 1-for-18, 1 HR)
Kirk McCaskill (.056, 1-for-18)

Miscellaneous statistics: Ground outs-to-air outs ratio: 1.21 last season, 1.24 for career.... Grounded into 15 double plays in 107 opportunities (one per 7.1).... Drove in 14 of 29 runners from third base with less than two outs (48%).... Direction of balls hit to the outfield: 33% to left field, 33% to center, 34% to right.... Base running: Advanced from first base to third on 6 of 27 outfield singles (22%); scored from second on 4 of 11 (36%), 2d-lowest rate in A.L.... Made 0.66 assists per nine innings at first base.

Comments: Started 102 of 113 games in which Toronto faced right-handed starters, but only 23 of 50 against left-handers.... Led the Blue Jays with five opposite-field home runs in 1991, but didn't hit any to left field last season.... Career average is .353 with runners on base in Late-Inning Pressure Situations, 4th highest over the past 18 years. Above Olerud are his right-handed N.L. clone, Jeff Bagwell (.444), Edgar Martinez (.375), and Mike Ivie (.370).... Career on-base percentage of .403 leading off innings is 3d highest during that same period, behind Frank Thomas (.432) and Wade Boggs (.417).... Career batting average is .323 from June 1 through July 31, but only .240 at other times.... Was pinch-hit for by Ed Sprague during the World Series after being pinch-hit for only three times during the regular season.... Never played a game in the minor leagues; as a result, he is younger than you probably think. He was the youngest in the majors to play at least 50 games at first base last season (born August 5, 1968).... Even with an additional layer of playoff games, Olerud became only the fourth player during the divisional era to start as many as 15 postseason games prior to turning 25. The others: Johnny Bench, Dave Cash, and Willie Randolph. That's parity for you.... Mickey Mantle made 15 postseason starts before turning 22.

Joe Orsulak   Bats Left

Baltimore Orioles	AB	H	2B	3B	HR	RBI	BB	SO	BA	SA	OBA
Season	391	113	18	3	4	39	28	34	.289	.381	.342
vs. Left-Handers	80	20	5	1	0	11	4	10	.250	.338	.307
vs. Right-Handers	311	93	13	2	4	28	24	24	.299	.392	.351
vs. Ground-Ballers	203	51	6	2	0	14	16	17	.251	.300	.312
vs. Fly-Ballers	188	62	12	1	4	25	12	17	.330	.468	.374
Home Games	180	50	5	2	2	18	18	13	.278	.361	.347
Road Games	211	63	13	1	2	21	10	21	.299	.398	.338
Grass Fields	326	96	14	2	4	32	27	25	.294	.387	.355
Artificial Turf	65	17	4	1	0	7	1	9	.262	.354	.273
April	50	11	3	0	0	4	0	9	.220	.280	.220
May	47	10	0	1	0	5	7	5	.213	.255	.333
June	72	26	2	1	1	11	4	10	.361	.458	.395
July	100	37	10	1	1	8	10	4	.370	.520	.427
August	44	12	1	0	0	5	5	2	.273	.295	.360
Sept./Oct.	78	17	2	0	2	6	2	4	.218	.321	.247
Leading Off Inn.	96	22	4	1	1	1	4	5	.229	.323	.267
Runners On	173	52	9	1	2	37	16	21	.301	.399	.368
Bases Empty	218	61	9	2	2	2	12	13	.280	.367	.320
Runners/Scor. Pos.	85	26	5	0	2	36	13	13	.306	.435	.406
Runners On/2 Out	63	16	2	0	1	11	9	11	.254	.333	.365
Scor. Pos./2 Out	34	10	0	0	1	11	7	8	.294	.382	.442
Late-Inning Pressure	57	20	2	1	1	3	5	4	.351	.474	.403
Leading Off	17	5	0	0	0	0	2	2	.294	.294	.368
Runners On	24	8	2	0	0	2	2	2	.333	.417	.385
Runners/Scor. Pos.	10	2	0	0	0	2	2	1	.200	.200	.333

RUNS BATTED IN	From 1B	From 2B	From 3B	Scoring Position
Totals	2/139	16/66	17/32	33/98
Percentage	1.4%	24.2%	53.1%	33.7%

Loves to face: Tom Candiotti (.500, 10-for-20, 3 BB)
Jeff D. Robinson (.400, 4-for-10)
Bryn Smith (.421, 8-for-19)
Hates to face: Lee Guetterman (0-for-7, 2 SO)
Jeff M. Robinson (0-for-12)
Greg Swindell (.091, 1-for-11)

Miscellaneous statistics: Ground outs-to-air outs ratio: 1.19 last season, 1.11 for career.... Grounded into 3 double plays in 98 opportunities (one per 33).... Drove in 12 of 18 runners from third base with less than two outs (67%).... Direction of balls hit to the outfield: 31% to left field, 27% to center, 41% to right.... Base running: Advanced from first base to third on 9 of 20 outfield singles (45%); scored from second on 11 of 16 (69%).... Made 2.25 putouts per nine innings in right field.

Comments: Started 84 of 116 games in which the Orioles faced a right-handed starter, but only 14 of 46 against left-handers.... Career batting average is .239 against left-handers, .286 vs. right-handers. All 37 of his homers have come against right-handers.... Outfield assists dropped from 22 in 132 games in 1991 to only nine in 110 games last season.... Yearly batting averages in home games since 1989: .273, .272, .277, .278. Do you think he noticed the new ballpark in Baltimore? Will he notice he's with a new team in 1993?...Played five consistent seasons in Baltimore, batting within a 20-point range from .269 to .289—the narrowest of any player who batted at least 400 times in each of those seasons. Robby Thompson comes closest (a 23-point range from .241 to .264).... Has hit safely in each of his last 27 games against the White Sox, including all 21 games he played against them over the last two seasons. (Maybe his new manager, Jeff Torborg, based a recommendation on that.)... Which reminds us: Torborg and two of his Mets coaches, Tom McCraw and Mel Stottlemyre, were born within 13 days of one another in November 1941.... Even with the Cashen connection, only four players have appeared in at least 150 games for both the Mets and the Orioles: Tommy Davis, Ray Knight, Eddie Murray, and Ken Singleton.... Could be in for a little culture shock upon his return to the N.L.: The Pirates finished last in the N.L. East in each of the three seasons he spent in Pittsburgh.

Junior Ortiz   Bats Right

Cleveland Indians	AB	H	2B	3B	HR	RBI	BB	SO	BA	SA	OBA
Season	244	61	7	0	0	24	12	23	.250	.279	.296
vs. Left-Handers	65	18	2	0	0	6	6	3	.277	.308	.338
vs. Right-Handers	179	43	5	0	0	18	6	20	.240	.268	.280
vs. Ground-Ballers	110	27	5	0	0	14	5	14	.245	.291	.291
vs. Fly-Ballers	134	34	2	0	0	10	7	9	.254	.269	.301
Home Games	115	34	2	0	0	12	9	12	.296	.313	.362
Road Games	129	27	5	0	0	12	3	11	.209	.248	.233
Grass Fields	199	55	4	0	0	21	12	20	.276	.296	.330
Artificial Turf	45	6	3	0	0	3	0	3	.133	.200	.133
April	21	4	0	0	0	3	4	3	.190	.190	.320
May	53	13	2	0	0	3	2	4	.245	.283	.286
June	19	4	1	0	0	4	1	1	.211	.263	.286
July	21	5	1	0	0	4	0	3	.238	.286	.238
August	41	10	1	0	0	5	1	4	.244	.268	.279
Sept./Oct.	89	25	2	0	0	5	4	8	.281	.303	.319
Leading Off Inn.	58	9	1	0	0	0	2	5	.155	.172	.197
Runners On	110	32	3	0	0	24	7	12	.291	.318	.345
Bases Empty	134	29	4	0	0	0	5	11	.216	.246	.255
Runners/Scor. Pos.	67	20	3	0	0	24	5	8	.299	.343	.347
Runners On/2 Out	57	15	3	0	0	11	4	8	.263	.316	.323
Scor. Pos./2 Out	36	11	3	0	0	11	4	4	.306	.389	.375
Late-Inning Pressure	27	4	0	0	0	1	0	4	.148	.148	.148
Leading Off	9	0	0	0	0	0	0	0	.000	.000	.000
Runners On	6	1	0	0	0	1	0	3	.167	.167	.167
Runners/Scor. Pos.	4	1	0	0	0	1	0	2	.250	.250	.250

RUNS BATTED IN	From 1B	From 2B	From 3B	Scoring Position
Totals	1/80	11/51	12/25	23/76
Percentage	1.3%	21.6%	48.0%	30.3%

Loves to face: Scott Erickson (.429, 3-for-7, 1 2B, 1 HBP)
Joe Grahe (.500, 3-for-6, 2 SO)
Bill Gullickson (.348, 8-for-23)
Hates to face: Cal Eldred (0-for-5, 1 SO)
Chuck Finley (.133, 2-for-15)
Kirk McCaskill (0-for-7)

Miscellaneous statistics: Ground outs-to-air outs ratio: 1.91 last season (4th highest in A.L.), 1.93 for career.... Grounded into 7 double plays in 43 opportunities (one per 6.1).... Drove in 8 of 13 runners from third base with less than two outs (62%).... Direction of balls hit to the outfield: 21% to left field, 40% to center, 40% to right.... Base running: Advanced from first base to third on 4 of 13 outfield singles (31%); scored from second on 4 of 6 (67%).... Opposing base stealers: 59-for-86 (69%).

Comments: Established career highs in games started (69) and games caught (86), topping those he set in 1989 with Pittsburgh (65 and 84, respectively).... Has played 240 games and gone 585 at-bats since his last home run (July 30, 1989, off his current Indians batterymate Dennis Cook). Sounds bad, but it doesn't make the current top 10; 11 active players have longer current homerless streaks.... For the third consecutive season, he was homerless and caught at least 50 games. Since Mike Tresh equaled Bill Bergen's record seven-year streak in 1947, only one other catcher had a streak even three years long: Bob Didier (1969–71).... Indians catchers batted .256 last season, 4th best in the league, behind Minnesota (.298), Oakland (.267), and Baltimore (.259). But Tribe catchers combined for just three homers; only Boston's hit fewer (2).... The league batting average for catchers was .244, the lowest of any position. The top mark belonged to left fielders (.269).... Career total of 579 games behind the plate is 3d highest among active catchers who have never played a game at any other fielding position, behind Mike Scioscia (1395) and Rich Gedman (980).... Each of his last 43 starts came from the ninth spot in the batting order.... Of the three Juniors active in the majors last year, only Felix's first name is actually Junior. The real names of the other two: Adalberto Ortiz, Jr., and Milciades Arturo Noboa, Jr. (Our advice: Stick with Junior; it sounds better than Bert or Millie.)

Rafael Palmeiro

Bats Left

Texas Rangers	AB	H	2B	3B	HR	RBI	BB	SO	BA	SA	OBA
Season	608	163	27	4	22	85	72	83	.268	.434	.352
vs. Left-Handers	178	50	7	3	5	27	20	27	.281	.438	.365
vs. Right-Handers	430	113	20	1	17	58	52	56	.263	.433	.347
vs. Ground-Ballers	275	68	13	1	8	30	30	40	.247	.389	.330
vs. Fly-Ballers	333	95	14	3	14	55	42	43	.285	.471	.370
Home Games	297	78	11	3	8	33	39	38	.263	.401	.354
Road Games	311	85	16	1	14	52	33	45	.273	.466	.350
Grass Fields	510	136	20	4	19	72	59	61	.267	.433	.347
Artificial Turf	98	27	7	0	3	13	13	22	.276	.439	.379
April	85	20	5	1	3	13	9	15	.235	.424	.333
May	105	32	5	1	3	14	17	8	.305	.457	.408
June	101	22	5	0	2	12	12	18	.218	.327	.304
July	109	33	3	2	4	17	6	12	.303	.477	.336
August	113	26	2	0	3	10	13	19	.230	.327	.318
Sept./Oct.	95	30	7	0	7	19	15	11	.316	.611	.411
Leading Off Inn.	114	32	6	1	4	4	10	12	.281	.456	.349
Runners On	259	71	14	2	9	72	39	33	.274	.448	.372
Bases Empty	349	92	13	2	13	13	33	50	.264	.424	.336
Runners/Scor. Pos.	148	40	7	1	4	60	30	21	.270	.412	.390
Runners On/2 Out	94	24	5	1	3	26	26	10	.255	.426	.417
Scor. Pos./2 Out	66	15	3	0	1	21	21	10	.227	.318	.414
Late-Inning Pressure	93	20	1	2	3	11	6	17	.215	.366	.272
Leading Off	27	5	1	1	1	1	1	5	.185	.407	.241
Runners On	34	7	0	1	1	9	4	5	.206	.353	.293
Runners/Scor. Pos.	19	4	0	0	1	8	3	4	.211	.368	.320

RUNS BATTED IN	From 1B	From 2B	From 3B	Scoring Position
Totals	14/193	25/129	24/51	49/180
Percentage	7.3%	19.4%	47.1%	27.2%

Loves to face: Chuck Finley (.476, 10-for-21, 1 HR)
Bill Gullickson (.600, 6-for-10, 2 HR)
Bob Milacki (.571, 8-for-14, 1 HR)
Hates to face: Randy Johnson (.059, 1-for-17)
Jack McDowell (.107, 3-for-28)
Mike Mussina (.071, 1-for-14)

Miscellaneous statistics: Ground outs-to-air outs ratio: 0.90 last season, 0.98 for career.... Grounded into 10 double plays in 145 opportunities (one per 15).... Drove in 20 of 30 runners from third base with less than two outs (67%).... Direction of balls hit to the outfield: 23% to left field, 33% to center, 44% to right.... Base running: Advanced from first base to third on 17 of 39 outfield singles (44%); scored from second on 13 of 14 (93%), 5th-highest rate in A.L.... Made 0.93 assists per nine innings at first base, 3d-highest rate in A.L.

Comments: Power corrupts: His total of 22 opposite-field hits was the lowest in his four seasons with Texas. Two years ago, he had 49 hits to left field—but he hit only 14 home runs that season.... Of his 22 home runs, none were hit to the opposite field, and only one was hit to center.... Batting average was a career low, but his total of walks was a career high. (Both his walk and strikeout rates were career highs.) ... Has driven in five game-winning runs in extra innings over the past two seasons, the most of any player in the majors.... Total of 318 American League games played over the last two seasons trails only Cal Ripken, Joe Carter, and Carlos Baerga.... The only other players with 700-plus plate appearances in each of the last two seasons were fellow A.L.ers Paul Molitor, Ripken, and Frank Thomas.... One of eight players to appear in more than 150 games in each of the last five years. The others: Brett Butler, Joe Carter, Fred McGriff, Eddie Murray, Cal Ripken, Ryne Sandberg, and Ruben Sierra.... Has hit for a higher average against left-handers than against right-handers in three of his five full seasons in the majors. Career breakdown: .289 vs. left-handers, .299 vs. right-handers.... Has stolen only 13 bases in four seasons with Texas, compared to 12 in his final season with the Cubs alone.... Among the 32 players with the most games for the Senators/Rangers, only Toby Harrah and Jim Sundberg finished their careers with the club. Current Rangers Palmeiro and Geno Petralli are on that list.

Dean Palmer

Bats Right

Texas Rangers	AB	H	2B	3B	HR	RBI	BB	SO	BA	SA	OBA
Season	541	124	25	0	26	72	62	154	.229	.420	.311
vs. Left-Handers	143	36	7	0	8	20	18	41	.252	.469	.333
vs. Right-Handers	398	88	18	0	18	52	44	113	.221	.402	.303
vs. Ground-Ballers	241	59	8	0	15	39	33	58	.245	.465	.337
vs. Fly-Ballers	300	65	17	0	11	33	29	96	.217	.383	.289
Home Games	264	64	12	0	11	34	35	76	.242	.413	.337
Road Games	277	60	13	0	15	38	27	78	.217	.426	.286
Grass Fields	447	97	18	0	18	51	53	128	.217	.378	.303
Artificial Turf	94	27	7	0	8	21	9	26	.287	.617	.349
April	76	19	2	0	5	13	14	26	.250	.474	.363
May	101	22	10	0	3	12	3	34	.218	.406	.252
June	94	26	5	0	4	19	14	23	.277	.457	.369
July	90	19	2	0	5	11	16	21	.211	.400	.330
August	78	17	3	0	5	7	5	20	.218	.449	.274
Sept./Oct.	102	21	3	0	4	10	10	30	.206	.353	.277
Leading Off Inn.	112	33	10	0	4	4	16	22	.295	.491	.388
Runners On	232	52	9	0	13	59	23	63	.224	.431	.295
Bases Empty	309	72	16	0	13	13	39	91	.233	.411	.323
Runners/Scor. Pos.	126	23	3	0	3	37	14	37	.183	.278	.262
Runners On/2 Out	91	26	6	0	7	33	11	26	.286	.582	.363
Scor. Pos./2 Out	57	14	2	0	2	21	8	18	.246	.386	.338
Late-Inning Pressure	85	16	3	0	4	9	16	20	.188	.365	.317
Leading Off	21	7	3	0	0	0	5	5	.333	.476	.462
Runners On	32	4	0	0	2	7	6	8	.125	.313	.263
Runners/Scor. Pos.	20	2	0	0	0	3	4	6	.100	.100	.250

RUNS BATTED IN	From 1B	From 2B	From 3B	Scoring Position
Totals	15/171	16/94	15/57	31/151
Percentage	8.8%	17.0%	26.3%	20.5%

Loves to face: Mike Fetters (2-for-2, 2 HR)
Chuck Finley (.400, 4-for-10, 2 2B, 1 HR)
Dave Fleming (.500, 7-for-14, 1 HR)
Hates to face: Mike Mussina (.077, 1-for-13)
Charles Nagy (0-for-8)
Dave Stewart (0-for-12)

Miscellaneous statistics: Ground outs-to-air outs ratio: 0.73 last season, 0.73 for career.... Grounded into 9 double plays in 119 opportunities (one per 13).... Drove in 10 of 30 runners from third base with less than two outs (33%), 3d-lowest rate in majors.... Direction of balls hit to the outfield: 42% to left field, 34% to center, 23% to right.... Base running: Advanced from first base to third on 6 of 22 outfield singles (27%); scored from second on 10 of 16 (63%).... Made 1.80 assists per nine innings at third base, 2d-lowest rate in A.L.

Comments: Batted .227 as a third baseman, the lowest of any A.L. player at that position (minimum: 250 PA), but only slightly lower than Kelly Gruber (.229) and Gary Gaetti (.230).... Led A.L. third basemen with 25 home runs, eight more than runners-up Leo Gomez and Charlie Hayes.... Joins Pete Incaviglia, Jeff Burroughs, and Frank Howard as the only players in franchise history to lead the league in strikeouts.... One of four active players who has a career average of more than one strikeout per game (minimum: 200 games). The others: Rob Deer, Jose Canseco, and Pete Incaviglia.... Spent most of June and July batting 2d, and was the better for it. He hit .270 with only one strikeout every 4.9 plate appearances from that slot, compared to .206 and one SO per 3.6 PAs elsewhere.... Both Palmer and Palmeiro had higher home-run rates from the 2d spot in the order than they had in other at-bats. The pair combined for 19 of the Rangers' 25 homers from the two hole, the most of any club in the majors last season.... Had only one hit in his last 17 at-bats in Late-Inning Pressure Situations.... Career batting average is .247 vs. left-handers, .199 vs. right-handers.... Another interesting career breakdown: .201 on grass fields, .274 on artificial turf.... Similar statistical profiles: Roger Maris (through 1958), John Milner, and Ken ("Hawk") Harrelson. Someone get Palmer to Brooks Brothers—and fast!

Lance Parrish   Bats Right

Angels/Mariners	AB	H	2B	3B	HR	RBI	BB	SO	BA	SA	OBA
Season	275	64	13	1	12	32	24	70	.233	.418	.294
vs. Left-Handers	95	22	7	0	4	10	12	18	.232	.432	.315
vs. Right-Handers	180	42	6	1	8	22	12	52	.233	.411	.282
vs. Ground-Ballers	124	37	5	1	7	15	8	29	.298	.524	.341
vs. Fly-Ballers	151	27	8	0	5	17	16	41	.179	.331	.256
Home Games	135	31	6	0	7	19	10	31	.230	.430	.277
Road Games	140	33	7	1	5	13	14	39	.236	.407	.310
Grass Fields	148	31	4	1	3	16	13	39	.209	.311	.276
Artificial Turf	127	33	9	0	9	16	11	31	.260	.543	.314
April	52	14	1	0	4	10	4	15	.269	.519	.316
May	20	3	1	0	0	1	1	6	.150	.200	.190
June	12	2	0	0	0	0	0	1	.167	.167	.167
July	61	18	2	1	5	13	7	11	.295	.607	.368
August	71	16	4	0	3	5	6	15	.225	.408	.291
Sept./Oct.	59	11	5	0	0	3	6	22	.186	.271	.258
Leading Off Inn.	72	13	2	0	2	2	3	22	.181	.292	.213
Runners On	123	27	6	0	4	24	12	27	.220	.366	.283
Bases Empty	152	37	7	1	8	8	12	43	.243	.461	.303
Runners/Scor. Pos.	72	14	1	0	3	21	9	18	.194	.333	.274
Runners On/2 Out	45	11	1	0	2	10	5	11	.244	.400	.320
Scor. Pos./2 Out	32	8	0	0	2	9	4	8	.250	.438	.333
Late-Inning Pressure	62	8	1	0	1	3	5	23	.129	.194	.191
Leading Off	16	3	0	0	1	1	0	7	.188	.375	.188
Runners On	33	3	1	0	1	2	2	10	.091	.121	.139
Runners/Scor. Pos.	16	1	0	0	0	2	2	7	.063	.063	.158

RUNS BATTED IN	From 1B	From 2B	From 3B	Scoring Position
Totals	5/93	8/58	7/26	15/84
Percentage	5.4%	13.8%	26.9%	17.9%

Loves to face: Rick Aguilera (.385, 5-for-13, 2 2B, 1 HR)
        Jimmy Key (.325, 13-for-40, 4 HR)
        Kirk McCaskill (.400, 6-for-15, 1 2B, 3 HR)

Hates to face: Alex Fernandez (0-for-10)
        Dennis Rasmussen (.087, 2-for-23, 2 BB)
        David Wells (.063, 1-for-16)

Miscellaneous statistics: Ground outs-to-air outs ratio: 0.83 last season, 1.03 for career.... Grounded into 7 double plays in 65 opportunities (one per 9.3).... Drove in 6 of 16 runners from third base with less than two outs (38%).... Direction of balls hit to the outfield: 49% to left field, 23% to center, 28% to right.... Base running: Advanced from first base to third on 0 of 8 outfield singles (0%); scored from second on 3 of 7 (43%).... Opposing base stealers: 59-for-82 (72%), 3d-highest rate in A.L.

Comments: Started last season with the Angels, whose catchers combined for the lowest batting average (.216) and the fewest RBIs (43) of any team in the majors.... Was released by California and signed by Seattle, the only team to use more catchers last season (6) than the Angels (5).... Had two stints on the disabled list by the time he made his Mariners' debut on June 28. Angels catchers spent a total of 171 days on the D.L. last season; John Orton was also disabled twice, and Greg Myers once.... Finished last season with a career total of 1703 games behind the plate, 12th most in major league history. He could pass quite a few guys on that list if he's able to land even a semi-regular catching job this season. Within his reach: Bill Dickey (1712), Ray Schalk (1726), Johnny Bench (1743), Ted Simmons (1772), Gabby Hartnett (1790), and Rick Ferrell (1806).... Has hit at least 10 home runs in each of the last 15 years. Only two players have longer current streaks: Andre Dawson and Eddie Murray (both 16 years).... Didn't waste any last season; his total of 12 home runs was the highest among players who didn't homer in a losing effort.... Hitless in 11 at-bats as a pinch hitter last season, lowering his career average to .196 in that role.... Has batted under .200 in LIPS in four of the last five years.... We think it's a pretty good bet that he'll go down in history as the only man to play for both Ralph Houk and Bill Plummer. The only other active players to have played for Houk: Lou Whitaker, Alan Trammell, and Jack Morris.

Dan Pasqua   Bats Left

Chicago White Sox	AB	H	2B	3B	HR	RBI	BB	SO	BA	SA	OBA
Season	265	56	16	1	6	33	36	57	.211	.347	.305
vs. Left-Handers	18	2	0	0	0	2	2	4	.111	.111	.200
vs. Right-Handers	247	54	16	1	6	31	34	53	.219	.364	.312
vs. Ground-Ballers	130	23	8	0	1	8	15	32	.177	.262	.264
vs. Fly-Ballers	135	33	8	1	5	25	21	25	.244	.430	.344
Home Games	128	24	5	0	2	11	17	27	.188	.273	.284
Road Games	137	32	11	1	4	22	19	30	.234	.416	.325
Grass Fields	225	46	13	1	5	26	34	49	.204	.338	.308
Artificial Turf	40	10	3	0	1	7	2	8	.250	.400	.286
April	45	13	3	1	2	8	5	14	.289	.533	.360
May	56	6	4	0	0	3	9	15	.107	.179	.227
June	14	5	3	0	0	3	1	1	.357	.571	.400
July	26	4	1	0	1	2	6	4	.154	.308	.313
August	62	14	3	0	0	5	6	9	.226	.274	.300
Sept./Oct.	62	14	2	0	3	12	9	14	.226	.403	.319
Leading Off Inn.	58	10	4	0	1	1	7	11	.172	.293	.262
Runners On	117	26	6	1	3	30	16	27	.222	.368	.314
Bases Empty	148	30	10	0	3	3	20	30	.203	.331	.298
Runners/Scor. Pos.	69	14	4	0	2	26	7	17	.203	.348	.266
Runners On/2 Out	51	10	3	0	2	14	8	12	.196	.373	.305
Scor. Pos./2 Out	34	6	2	0	1	11	3	9	.176	.324	.243
Late-Inning Pressure	26	6	1	1	1	3	1	2	.231	.462	.259
Leading Off	7	1	0	0	0	0	1	0	.143	.143	.250
Runners On	12	2	1	1	0	2	0	2	.167	.417	.167
Runners/Scor. Pos.	3	0	0	0	0	0	0	0	.000	.000	.000

RUNS BATTED IN	From 1B	From 2B	From 3B	Scoring Position
Totals	5/94	10/58	12/29	22/87
Percentage	5.3%	17.2%	41.4%	25.3%

Loves to face: Scott Erickson (.400, 6-for-15, 1 2B, 3 HR)
        Mike Moore (.415, 22-for-53, 2 HR)
        Kevin Tapani (.500, 8-for-16, 1 HR)

Hates to face: Roger Clemens (.146, 7-for-48)
        Mike Mussina (0-for-14)
        Nolan Ryan (.120, 3-for-25, 0 BB, 12 SO)

Miscellaneous statistics: Ground outs-to-air outs ratio: 0.76 last season, 0.80 for career.... Grounded into 4 double plays in 65 opportunities (one per 16).... Drove in 8 of 13 runners from third base with less than two outs (62%).... Direction of balls hit to the outfield: 28% to left field, 26% to center, 47% to right.... Base running: Advanced from first base to third on 2 of 7 outfield singles (29%); scored from second on 6 of 6 (100%).... Made 2.21 putouts per nine innings in right field.

Comments: One of three White Sox players to suffer extreme breakdown seasons in 1992. Pasqua's was a 10-to-1 breakdown; that is, there was only one chance in 11 you could have chosen at random a season that bad from his three previous years' worth of at-bats. Carlton Fisk's was slightly less extreme (8-to-1); Steve Sax's was much more so (34-to-1).... Started 83 of 120 games in which the White Sox faced right-handed starters last season, but only 1 of 42 against southpaws.... His 18 at-bats against left-handers were his fewest since his debut season with New York (1985).... Career batting average is .186 with nine home runs against left-handed pitchers, .258 with 101 home runs against right-handers.... Batted .197 as an outfielder, the lowest mark in the majors (minimum: 250 PAs at that position).... Played only right field last season, and committed a career-high six errors.... Career batting average is 61 points higher in day games (.290) than in night games (.229).... Career batting average of .356 against his former team, the Yankees, is the highest among active players against them (minimum: 100 AB). The 2d-highest average vs. New York also belongs to a former Yankee: Luis Polonia (.351).... Comparable offensive players who bounced back from similar off years for at least a few seasons of adequate production: Andy Seminick (1951), Deron Johnson (1968), and Greg Brock (1988). A few who didn't: Jimmie Hall (1969), Mike Epstein (1973), and Willie Aikens (1984).

Tony Pena
Bats Right

Boston Red Sox	AB	H	2B	3B	HR	RBI	BB	SO	BA	SA	OBA
Season	410	99	21	1	1	38	24	61	.241	.305	.284
vs. Left-Handers	111	28	6	0	1	11	2	14	.252	.333	.270
vs. Right-Handers	299	71	15	1	0	27	22	47	.237	.294	.289
vs. Ground-Ballers	193	45	8	1	0	17	11	19	.233	.285	.278
vs. Fly-Ballers	217	54	13	0	1	21	13	42	.249	.323	.289
Home Games	203	56	16	1	1	20	12	30	.276	.379	.316
Road Games	207	43	5	0	0	18	12	31	.208	.232	.252
Grass Fields	349	89	20	1	1	35	20	50	.255	.327	.294
Artificial Turf	61	10	1	0	0	3	4	11	.164	.180	.227
April	55	13	4	0	1	6	2	10	.236	.364	.263
May	77	15	3	0	0	4	4	15	.195	.234	.244
June	71	19	2	0	0	8	4	11	.268	.296	.303
July	66	15	4	0	0	3	6	4	.227	.288	.292
August	68	19	4	0	0	11	4	14	.279	.338	.315
Sept./Oct.	73	18	4	1	0	6	4	7	.247	.329	.286
Leading Off Inn.	98	22	5	0	0	0	4	11	.224	.276	.262
Runners On	190	49	10	0	0	37	8	24	.258	.311	.285
Bases Empty	220	50	11	1	1	1	16	37	.227	.300	.283
Runners/Scor. Pos.	111	27	5	0	0	34	7	17	.243	.288	.283
Runners On/2 Out	91	18	4	0	0	11	5	13	.198	.242	.240
Scor. Pos./2 Out	53	10	2	0	0	10	4	9	.189	.226	.246
Late-Inning Pressure	60	17	4	0	1	2	6	10	.283	.400	.358
Leading Off	19	6	1	0	0	0	1	3	.316	.368	.381
Runners On	20	4	1	0	0	1	1	3	.200	.250	.238
Runners/Scor. Pos.	13	2	1	0	0	1	0	3	.154	.231	.154

RUNS BATTED IN	From 1B	From 2B	From 3B	Scoring Position
Totals	3/129	12/81	22/59	34/140
Percentage	2.3%	14.8%	37.3%	24.3%

Loves to face: Jimmy Key (.476, 10-for-21, 2 HR)
Kenny Rogers (.667, 6-for-9, 2 2B)
Rick Sutcliffe (.370, 20-for-54)

Hates to face: Kirk McCaskill (.053, 1-for-19)
Nolan Ryan (.152, 5-for-33, 0 BB)
Walt Terrell (.097, 3-for-31)

Miscellaneous statistics: Ground outs-to-air outs ratio: 1.97 last season (3d highest in A.L.), 1.64 for career.... Grounded into 11 double plays in 80 opportunities (one per 7.3).... Drove in 15 of 31 runners from third base with less than two outs (48%).... Direction of balls hit to the outfield: 26% to left field, 37% to center, 37% to right.... Base running: Advanced from first base to third on 8 of 21 outfield singles (38%); scored from second on 9 of 14 (64%).... Opposing base stealers: 80-for-119 (67%).

Comments: Red Sox posted a winning record with Pena as the starting catcher (63–59), but played 20 games below .500 with their other catchers starting (John Flaherty, John Marzano, and Eric Wedge: 10–30). No other catcher in either league produced nearly as significant a split. A distant second: The Giants were 14–8 with Jim McNamara catching, compared to 58–82 otherwise.... Boston's staff ERA was 3.49 for Pena, compared to 4.07 for the others.... Pena's throwing has been slightly below the league average during his three seasons with the Sox. Opponents' stolen-base percentage, year by year: .683, .669, .672. The league average during that period: .661.... Thanks to Roger Clemens, Pena led A.L. catchers in putouts for a third consecutive season, the longest streak by an A.L. backstop since Jim Sundberg led for six straight years (1975–80).... Red Sox catchers produced only two home runs last season, the fewest in the majors.... Ranked third in the American League with 13 sac bunts, behind Jerry Browne (16) and Mike Bordick (14). No catcher has ever led the league in that category.... Drove in only one of 17 runners from scoring position in Late-Inning Pressure Situations, compared to a rate of 30 percent at other times.... One of three players to ground into at least 10 double plays in each of the last 11 years. The others: Cal Ripken and Harold Baines.... Turned 35 last June, with a career total of 1498 games caught. Only four catchers caught more games before their 35th birthday: Gary Carter (1779), Johnny Bench (1738), Ted Simmons (1722), and Al Lopez (1570).

Tony Phillips
Bats Left and Right

Detroit Tigers	AB	H	2B	3B	HR	RBI	BB	SO	BA	SA	OBA
Season	606	167	32	3	10	64	114	93	.276	.388	.387
vs. Left-Handers	174	47	9	1	5	23	37	21	.270	.420	.401
vs. Right-Handers	432	120	23	2	5	41	77	72	.278	.375	.382
vs. Ground-Ballers	270	77	15	2	4	36	52	38	.285	.400	.394
vs. Fly-Ballers	336	90	17	1	6	28	62	55	.268	.378	.382
Home Games	289	79	12	1	3	31	64	42	.273	.353	.398
Road Games	317	88	20	2	7	33	50	51	.278	.420	.377
Grass Fields	517	139	25	2	7	45	98	81	.269	.366	.382
Artificial Turf	89	28	7	1	3	19	16	12	.315	.517	.419
April	59	14	1	0	0	3	22	14	.237	.254	.444
May	100	25	5	2	5	23	20	13	.250	.490	.366
June	103	24	6	0	2	10	24	18	.233	.350	.375
July	111	38	6	0	3	9	15	16	.342	.477	.421
August	114	32	7	1	0	10	15	17	.281	.360	.362
Sept./Oct.	119	34	7	0	0	9	18	15	.286	.345	.379
Leading Off Inn.	236	71	12	2	5	5	37	37	.301	.432	.396
Runners On	226	62	14	0	3	57	50	31	.274	.376	.396
Bases Empty	380	105	18	3	7	7	64	62	.276	.395	.382
Runners/Scor. Pos.	124	38	11	0	3	55	28	15	.306	.468	.415
Runners On/2 Out	106	27	9	0	0	23	13	15	.255	.340	.336
Scor. Pos./2 Out	64	17	8	0	0	22	10	9	.266	.391	.365
Late-Inning Pressure	84	20	2	1	2	10	13	20	.238	.357	.340
Leading Off	22	5	1	1	0	0	4	7	.227	.364	.346
Runners On	33	10	1	0	1	9	6	5	.303	.424	.410
Runners/Scor. Pos.	19	7	1	0	1	9	3	1	.368	.579	.455

RUNS BATTED IN	From 1B	From 2B	From 3B	Scoring Position
Totals	9/174	18/88	27/62	45/150
Percentage	5.2%	20.5%	43.5%	30.0%

Loves to face: Todd Burns (.571, 4-for-7, 1 HR)
Dave Stieb (.379, 11-for-29)
Julio Valera (.857, 6-for-7)

Hates to face: Juan Guzman (0-for-12)
Mike Mussina (.067, 1-for-15)
David Wells (.100, 2-for-20)

Miscellaneous statistics: Ground outs-to-air outs ratio: 1.30 last season, 1.17 for career.... Grounded into 13 double plays in 126 opportunities (one per 10).... Drove in 18 of 28 runners from third base with less than two outs (64%).... Direction of balls hit to the outfield: 49% to left field, 28% to center, 22% to right batting left-handed; 34% to left field, 25% to center, 41% to right batting right-handed.... Base running: Advanced from first base to third on 25 of 54 outfield singles (46%); scored from second on 14 of 22 (64%).... Made 3.44 assists per nine innings at second base.

Comments: Tough trivia: Which six players, active in 1992, played under both Tony LaRussa and Sparky Anderson? Answer below.... Started in the leadoff spot in the batting order 140 times last season. Detroit led the major leagues with 119 first-inning runs. (They also allowed the most, 110.) ... Became only the second Tigers player in the last 54 years to lead the major leagues in runs scored. The other was Ron LeFlore in 1978.... Total of 733 plate appearances was 3d highest in Tigers history, behind LeFlore (741) and Rusty Staub (734), both in 1978.... Walked 114 times but finished eight behind team leader Mickey Tettleton. The last A.L. team to have two players with that many walks was the 1949 Philadelphia A's, who had three: Eddie Joost (149), Ferris Fain (136), and Elmer Valo (119).... On-base percentage was a career high.... One of seven players to start at least 10 games at each of the three outfield positions last season.... Batted .313 in his at-bats as an outfielder. Among A.L. players with at least 250 plate appearances at that position, only Kirby Puckett (.331) and Shane Mack (.314) posted higher averages.... Trivia answer: Phillips, Jerry Don Gleaton, Brian Harper, Luis Salazar, Matt Sinatro, and Mickey Tettleton played under both genii.... Older New York baseball fans will regard this as nothing less than heresy, but statistical profile is comparable to those of Big Apple icons Phil Rizzuto (through 1951) and Pee Wee Reese (1950).

Phil Plantier
Bats Left

Boston Red Sox	AB	H	2B	3B	HR	RBI	BB	SO	BA	SA	OBA
Season	349	86	19	0	7	30	44	83	.246	.361	.332
vs. Left-Handers	71	11	1	0	0	1	7	22	.155	.169	.237
vs. Right-Handers	278	75	18	0	7	29	37	61	.270	.410	.356
vs. Ground-Ballers	171	38	6	0	1	12	24	53	.222	.275	.322
vs. Fly-Ballers	178	48	13	0	6	18	20	30	.270	.444	.343
Home Games	201	54	10	0	5	23	22	44	.269	.393	.342
Road Games	148	32	9	0	2	7	22	39	.216	.318	.320
Grass Fields	300	72	14	0	6	27	40	72	.240	.347	.332
Artificial Turf	49	14	5	0	1	3	4	11	.286	.449	.333
April	67	16	5	0	1	9	8	18	.239	.358	.329
May	74	13	7	0	0	2	12	17	.176	.270	.287
June	60	15	2	0	4	12	8	15	.250	.483	.333
July	87	28	3	0	1	5	6	18	.322	.391	.372
August	35	7	0	0	0	0	5	9	.200	.200	.300
Sept./Oct.	26	7	2	0	1	2	5	6	.269	.462	.387
Leading Off Inn.	69	18	5	0	2	2	7	17	.261	.420	.329
Runners On	162	40	10	0	3	26	27	35	.247	.364	.351
Bases Empty	187	46	9	0	4	4	17	48	.246	.358	.316
Runners/Scor. Pos.	90	15	5	0	1	21	23	22	.167	.256	.330
Runners On/2 Out	65	14	0	0	1	10	10	13	.215	.262	.320
Scor. Pos./2 Out	39	6	0	0	0	8	9	8	.154	.154	.313
Late-Inning Pressure	63	17	3	0	1	6	12	12	.270	.365	.395
Leading Off	10	4	0	0	1	1	1	3	.400	.700	.455
Runners On	26	6	3	0	0	5	8	8	.231	.346	.412
Runners/Scor. Pos.	12	2	0	0	0	4	8	4	.167	.167	.500

RUNS BATTED IN	From 1B	From 2B	From 3B	Scoring Position
Totals	4/120	9/78	10/39	19/117
Percentage	3.3%	11.5%	25.6%	16.2%

Loves to face: Jack Armstrong (3-for-3, 1 HR)
  Bill Swift (.750, 3-for-4, 1 2B)

Hates to face: Greg Hibbard (.143, 1-for-7, 2 SO)
  Frank Tanana (0-for-3, 3 SO)

Miscellaneous statistics: Ground outs-to-air outs ratio: 0.84 last season, 0.83 for career.... Grounded into 9 double plays in 81 opportunities (one per 9.0).... Drove in 6 of 20 runners from third base with less than two outs (30%), 2d-lowest rate in majors.... Direction of balls hit to the outfield: 28% to left field, 23% to center, 49% to right.... Base running: Advanced from first base to third on 7 of 22 outfield singles (32%); scored from second on 7 of 10 (70%).... Made 2.21 putouts per nine innings in right field.

Comments: The most disappointing sophomore season of 1992. Plantier hit 11 home runs in just 148 at-bats in 1991, the sixth-highest rate ever by a rookie (minimum: 10 HR), behind Rudy York (35 HR in 375 AB in 1937), Art Shamsky (21-for-234 in 1966), Sam Horn (14-for-158 in 1987), Mark McGwire (49-for-557 in 1987), and Kevin Maas (21-for-254 in 1990).... In 1991, he was 8-for-25 with three home runs and 13 RBIs against left-handed pitchers, but his run production against left-handers last season was among the worst since 1975, when the *Player Analysis* project started. Among players with at least 70 at-bats against lefties, only three others drove in fewer than two runs: Paul Molitor in 1981 (73 AB, no RBIs vs. LHP); Pat Rockett in 1978 (77, 1 RBI); and Chris Speier in 1984 (77 AB, 1 RBI).... Drove in five fewer runs than he did in 1991, despite an increase of more than 200 at-bats—tying the worst such performance since RBIs were officially tabulated starting in 1920. (Frank Bolling in 1957 and Bill Wambsganss in 1924 had similar 5-RBI declines.) Only two other players have had *any* RBI declines in seasons of 200-plus AB increases: Jerry Lumpe (a 2-RBI drop in 1959) and Casey Stengel (4 RBI in 1924).... Has seven homers in 61 career at-bats (one every 8.7) against the Yankees, but only 11 in 451 at-bats against everyone else (one every 41 AB).... Became the fifth different opening-day starter in right field for Boston in the last five years. Since 1988: Mike Greenwell, Dwight Evans, Kevin Romine, Tom Brunansky, Plantier.

Luis Polonia
Bats Left

California Angels	AB	H	2B	3B	HR	RBI	BB	SO	BA	SA	OBA
Season	577	165	17	4	0	35	45	64	.286	.329	.337
vs. Left-Handers	132	30	3	0	0	5	9	25	.227	.250	.280
vs. Right-Handers	445	135	14	4	0	30	36	39	.303	.353	.353
vs. Ground-Ballers	282	81	8	1	0	20	21	23	.287	.323	.334
vs. Fly-Ballers	295	84	9	3	0	15	24	41	.285	.336	.339
Home Games	266	76	11	3	0	19	22	32	.286	.350	.340
Road Games	311	89	6	1	0	16	23	32	.286	.312	.333
Grass Fields	478	136	16	4	0	29	39	49	.285	.335	.337
Artificial Turf	99	29	1	0	0	6	6	15	.293	.303	.333
April	69	19	1	0	0	6	12	1	.275	.290	.378
May	101	29	2	2	0	9	6	11	.287	.347	.324
June	111	34	3	1	0	6	7	16	.306	.351	.345
July	92	34	6	0	0	6	6	11	.370	.435	.408
August	116	29	2	1	0	5	11	10	.250	.284	.318
Sept./Oct.	88	20	3	0	0	3	3	15	.227	.261	.253
Leading Off Inn.	238	64	9	1	0	0	19	33	.269	.315	.323
Runners On	182	55	4	1	0	35	15	17	.302	.335	.351
Bases Empty	395	110	13	3	0	0	30	47	.278	.327	.329
Runners/Scor. Pos.	99	30	4	1	0	35	11	10	.303	.364	.360
Runners On/2 Out	67	21	3	0	0	14	5	8	.313	.358	.361
Scor. Pos./2 Out	46	14	3	0	0	14	5	6	.304	.370	.373
Late-Inning Pressure	80	21	4	0	0	5	5	13	.262	.313	.306
Leading Off	26	7	1	0	0	0	1	7	.269	.308	.296
Runners On	25	7	1	0	0	5	2	2	.280	.320	.357
Runners/Scor. Pos.	16	4	1	0	0	5	2	1	.250	.313	.333

RUNS BATTED IN	From 1B	From 2B	From 3B	Scoring Position
Totals	2/127	13/76	20/43	33/119
Percentage	1.6%	17.1%	46.5%	27.7%

Loves to face: Kevin Appier (.500, 11-for-22)
  Steve Farr (.438, 7-for-16)
  Charles Nagy (.556, 10-for-18)

Hates to face: Mark Gubicza (.222, 10-for-45)
  Kenny Rogers (0-for-14)
  Frank Viola (.083, 1-for-12)

Miscellaneous statistics: Ground outs-to-air outs ratio: 1.72 last season, 1.65 for career.... Grounded into 18 double plays in 97 opportunities (one per 5.4).... Drove in 14 of 23 runners from third base with less than two outs (61%).... Direction of balls hit to the outfield: 43% to left field, 38% to center, 19% to right.... Base running: Advanced from first base to third on 19 of 33 outfield singles (58%); scored from second on 16 of 19 (84%).... Made 2.05 putouts per nine innings in left field.

Comments: Although he has played only 408 games since joining California, Polonia ranks second in games with the Angels among their current players, to Chili Davis, who has rejoined the team (425). Four other A.L. teams lost their only 1000-game veterans during the offseason: Boston (Wade Boggs), Cleveland (Brook Jacoby), Seattle (Harold Reynolds), and Toronto (Rance Mulliniks).... Despite only two and a half years with the Angels, he is about to set the franchise career record for most times caught stealing. Enters the season already having been thrown out 58 times while wearing the halo; that's six fewer than current record holder Rod Carew.... Has something more desirable in common with Carew: They are the only career .300 hitters in Angels history (minimum: 1000 AB).... Career batting average of .331 with two out and runners in scoring position is 2d highest in the 18-year history of *The Player Analysis,* behind Larry Hisle (.332). Rounding out the top five: Thurman Munson (.325), Will Clark (.325), and Wade Boggs (.321).... Has batted .300 or better against right-handed pitchers in five of his six seasons in the majors, but his average against southpaws has decreased in each of the last three years: .310 in 1989, then .294, .238, .227.... Had batted over .300 in Late-Inning Pressure Situations in each of the previous four years.... On April 29, 1990, the Yankees traded Polonia, then 25 years old, to the Angels for 35-year-old Claudell Washington, whose career lasted for only 33 more games after the trade.

Kirby Puckett — Bats Right

Minnesota Twins	AB	H	2B	3B	HR	RBI	BB	SO	BA	SA	OBA
Season	639	210	38	4	19	110	44	97	.329	.490	.374
vs. Left-Handers	125	41	7	0	3	22	12	23	.328	.456	.381
vs. Right-Handers	514	169	31	4	16	88	32	74	.329	.498	.372
vs. Ground-Ballers	297	96	16	2	4	38	23	35	.323	.431	.378
vs. Fly-Ballers	342	114	22	2	15	72	21	62	.333	.541	.371
Home Games	325	113	17	4	9	54	22	53	.348	.508	.392
Road Games	314	97	21	0	10	56	22	44	.309	.471	.356
Grass Fields	238	73	16	0	8	39	15	35	.307	.475	.350
Artificial Turf	401	137	22	4	11	71	29	62	.342	.499	.388
April	88	27	7	2	2	12	3	7	.307	.500	.326
May	107	40	5	1	7	25	3	11	.374	.636	.387
June	119	40	8	1	5	24	7	11	.336	.546	.375
July	103	30	4	0	0	11	8	16	.291	.330	.348
August	111	36	5	0	4	20	9	28	.324	.477	.390
Sept./Oct.	111	37	9	0	1	18	14	24	.333	.441	.405
Leading Off Inn.	120	44	7	0	4	4	5	18	.367	.525	.402
Runners On	327	110	22	2	10	101	32	49	.336	.508	.392
Bases Empty	312	100	16	2	9	9	12	48	.321	.471	.354
Runners/Scor. Pos.	189	65	14	0	6	87	26	35	.344	.513	.417
Runners On/2 Out	104	35	7	1	3	31	15	17	.337	.510	.420
Scor. Pos./2 Out	65	22	5	0	1	25	14	12	.338	.462	.456
Late-Inning Pressure	92	28	6	0	0	8	8	15	.304	.370	.363
Leading Off	23	8	1	0	0	0	1	5	.348	.391	.375
Runners On	39	15	3	0	0	8	5	6	.385	.462	.457
Runners/Scor. Pos.	18	5	0	0	0	5	4	5	.278	.278	.417

RUNS BATTED IN	From 1B	From 2B	From 3B	Scoring Position
Totals	16/228	27/138	48/83	75/221
Percentage	7.0%	19.6%	57.8%	33.9%

Loves to face: Charles Nagy (.556, 10-for-18)
Melido Perez (.488, 20-for-41, 2 HR)
Curt Young (.441, 15-for-34, 2 HR)

Hates to face: Danny Darwin (.143, 4-for-28, 0 BB)
Dennis Eckersley (.063, 1-for-16)
Todd Frohwirth (0-for-13)

Miscellaneous statistics: Ground outs-to-air outs ratio: 1.62 last season, 1.65 for career.... Grounded into 17 double plays in 165 opportunities (one per 10).... Drove in 38 of 51 runners from third base with less than two outs (75%).... Direction of balls hit to the outfield: 28% to left field, 29% to center, 43% to right.... Base running: Advanced from first base to third on 14 of 38 outfield singles (37%); scored from second on 32 of 37 (86%).... Made 2.78 putouts per nine innings in center field.

Comments: Led A.L. in hits for the fourth time in his career, the most of any player since five-time leader Tony Oliva hung 'em up. Other four-time league leaders: Ty Cobb (8 times), Nap Lajoie, Harvey Kuenn, and Nellie Fox (4 each).... Also led the majors in opposite-field hits. The top five: Puckett, 64; Roberto Alomar, 62; Tony Phillips, 61; Tony Fernandez, 60; and John Kruk, 59.... Led the league in total bases for the second time. Don Mattingly is the only other active player to lead the A.L. twice in that category.... Career average of .340 vs. left-handed pitchers is the highest of any player over the last 18 years. His single-season career-*low* mark against southpaws is .299 (1990).... Career batting average is .349 at the Metrodome, .293 on the road.... Has driven in over 30 percent of runners from scoring position in each of his last eight seasons, the second-longest current streak. George Brett has done it in all 18 years that we've tracked that category.... His total of 19 home runs last season was the highest of anyone who didn't hit one in Late-Inning Pressure Situations.... For a few days last June, Puckett led the American League in both singles and extra-base hits—a truly remarkable parlay when you think about it. He finished the season third in singles and only ninth in XBHs, but it's still worth noting that the few players ever to lead their leagues in both categories were all Hall of Famers: Nap Lajoie (1910), Ty Cobb (1911 and 1917), Enos Slaughter (1942), and Stan Musial (1946).

Tim Raines — Bats Left and Right

Chicago White Sox	AB	H	2B	3B	HR	RBI	BB	SO	BA	SA	OBA
Season	551	162	22	9	7	54	81	48	.294	.405	.380
vs. Left-Handers	135	34	3	2	0	11	25	10	.252	.304	.369
vs. Right-Handers	416	128	19	7	7	43	56	38	.308	.438	.383
vs. Ground-Ballers	281	71	11	5	1	20	39	31	.253	.338	.340
vs. Fly-Ballers	270	91	11	4	6	34	42	17	.337	.474	.421
Home Games	263	84	13	4	4	24	41	20	.319	.445	.405
Road Games	288	78	9	5	3	30	40	28	.271	.368	.356
Grass Fields	473	143	21	7	6	44	72	41	.302	.414	.389
Artificial Turf	78	19	1	2	1	10	9	7	.244	.346	.322
April	67	18	3	1	0	6	7	4	.269	.343	.333
May	101	29	7	2	2	7	18	13	.287	.455	.392
June	92	18	2	0	0	7	15	11	.196	.217	.303
July	106	34	4	2	0	12	14	7	.321	.396	.397
August	98	29	4	1	0	7	16	9	.296	.357	.388
Sept./Oct.	87	34	2	3	5	15	11	4	.391	.655	.455
Leading Off Inn.	176	54	8	2	3	3	23	15	.307	.426	.387
Runners On	197	65	9	5	1	48	37	16	.330	.442	.421
Bases Empty	354	97	13	4	6	6	44	32	.274	.384	.354
Runners/Scor. Pos.	108	39	4	4	1	45	29	9	.361	.500	.469
Runners On/2 Out	80	24	3	4	0	20	14	7	.300	.438	.404
Scor. Pos./2 Out	53	16	1	3	0	17	12	5	.302	.434	.431
Late-Inning Pressure	76	25	3	1	2	8	17	6	.329	.474	.452
Leading Off	21	7	0	0	1	1	1	2	.333	.476	.364
Runners On	28	8	1	1	0	6	12	3	.286	.393	.500
Runners/Scor. Pos.	14	3	1	0	0	5	9	2	.214	.286	.522

RUNS BATTED IN	From 1B	From 2B	From 3B	Scoring Position
Totals	5/131	21/97	21/42	42/139
Percentage	3.8%	21.6%	50.0%	30.2%

Loves to face: Bill Gullickson (.394, 13-for-33, 3 HR, 0 SO)
Craig Lefferts (.500, 11-for-22, 1 HR)
Dave Stewart (.500, 11-for-22, 1 HR)

Hates to face: Rick Aguilera (.138, 4-for-29)
David Cone (.148, 4-for-27, 6 SO)
Jaime Navarro (.067, 1-for-15)

Miscellaneous statistics: Ground outs-to-air outs ratio: 1.01 last season, 1.21 for career.... Grounded into 5 double plays in 102 opportunities (one per 20).... Drove in 16 of 23 runners from third base with less than two outs (70%).... Direction of balls hit to the outfield: 32% to left field, 32% to center, 36% to right batting left-handed; 32% to left field, 33% to center, 35% to right batting right-handed.... Base running: Advanced from first base to third on 12 of 35 outfield singles (34%); scored from second on 27 of 34 (79%).... Made 2.50 putouts per nine innings in left field, highest rate in A.L.

Comments: Both Raines and Frank Thomas scored 100-plus runs in each of the last two seasons. No White Sox player had reached the 100 mark for 33 years prior to that, and none had done so in consecutive seasons since Nellie Fox did it for four straight years (1954–57).... After batting in the leadoff spot in each of his first 237 starts with the White Sox, he was dropped to the 2d spot in the batting order over the last two months of the season. He batted .355 from the two slot (100 points higher than he hit batting leadoff), the best such mark in the league (minimum: 200 AB).... Average of one strikeout every 13.4 plate appearances was the best of his career.... Has 13 sacrifice bunts in two seasons with the White Sox; had none in his last four years in Montreal.... Stolen-base percentage (.882) was his best since 1987, the last of four consecutive seasons in which his rate was at least that good.... Was 7-for-7 stealing on artificial turf.... Stole four bases in as many attempts during extra innings last season; the only other players to do that were Luis Polonia and Jose Offerman.... The difference between his career averages from the right and left sides of the plate is only three points (.295 and .298, respectively), but last season was the fifth year in which he batted at least 35 points higher from one side than the other.... Career batting average is .323 in Late-Inning Pressure Situations.

Jody Reed
Boston Red Sox   Bats Right

	AB	H	2B	3B	HR	RBI	BB	SO	BA	SA	OBA
Season	550	136	27	1	3	40	62	44	.247	.316	.321
vs. Left-Handers	154	40	12	1	1	7	21	14	.260	.370	.345
vs. Right-Handers	396	96	15	0	2	33	41	30	.242	.295	.312
vs. Ground-Ballers	247	60	10	1	1	18	30	23	.243	.304	.324
vs. Fly-Ballers	303	76	17	0	2	22	32	21	.251	.327	.320
Home Games	279	77	17	0	2	22	39	21	.276	.358	.364
Road Games	271	59	10	1	1	18	23	23	.218	.273	.276
Grass Fields	479	118	24	1	3	35	53	37	.246	.319	.319
Artificial Turf	71	18	3	0	0	5	9	7	.254	.296	.338
April	75	19	4	0	1	6	12	2	.253	.347	.352
May	114	38	11	1	0	7	11	9	.333	.447	.392
June	106	20	3	0	0	8	8	7	.189	.217	.241
July	83	21	4	0	1	8	11	11	.253	.337	.337
August	103	23	5	0	1	7	13	12	.223	.301	.310
Sept./Oct.	69	15	0	0	0	4	7	3	.217	.217	.289
Leading Off Inn.	156	41	8	0	1	1	15	11	.263	.333	.327
Runners On	204	51	11	0	0	37	36	14	.250	.304	.357
Bases Empty	346	85	16	1	3	3	26	30	.246	.324	.298
Runners/Scor. Pos.	101	24	3	0	0	36	22	9	.238	.267	.362
Runners On/2 Out	80	16	2	0	0	11	16	5	.200	.225	.333
Scor. Pos./2 Out	47	8	1	0	0	11	11	5	.170	.191	.328
Late-Inning Pressure	100	21	4	0	0	7	9	10	.210	.250	.270
Leading Off	20	5	1	0	0	0	6	2	.250	.300	.423
Runners On	44	10	3	0	0	7	3	3	.227	.295	.265
Runners/Scor. Pos.	22	3	0	0	0	7	2	2	.136	.136	.192

RUNS BATTED IN	From 1B	From 2B	From 3B	Scoring Position
Totals	1/162	12/75	24/59	36/134
Percentage	0.6%	16.0%	40.7%	26.9%

Loves to face: Willie Blair (.667, 4-for-6, 1 HR)
Greg Cadaret (.417, 5-for-12)
Pete Harnisch (.400, 4-for-10, 3 BB)

Hates to face: Tom Candiotti (.150, 3-for-20)
Jose Guzman (.143, 2-for-14)
Mike Jackson (.111, 1-for-9)

Miscellaneous statistics: Ground outs-to-air outs ratio: 1.08 last season, 1.00 for career.... Grounded into 17 double plays in 119 opportunities (one per 7.0).... Drove in 19 of 31 runners from third base with less than two outs (61%).... Direction of balls hit to the outfield: 47% to left field, 30% to center, 24% to right.... Base running: Advanced from first base to third on 15 of 30 outfield singles (50%); scored from second on 15 of 20 (75%).... Made 3.38 assists per nine innings at second base, highest rate in A.L.

Comments: Played every inning of every game until mid-June, the longest streak in the majors to start last season.... Was the only Red Sox player to start all 45 games against left-handed pitchers last season. Career batting average is only three points higher against left-handers than vs. right-handers (.282 and .279, respectively).... Has hit only two home runs in 737 career at-bats against southpaws.... Played more games at shortstop than at second base in each of his first three seasons (1987–89), but played only six games at shortstop in 1991 and none last season.... The only player in the majors to collect at least 10 sac bunts in each of the last five seasons. The only other active players with five-year streaks at any time during their careers: his Red Sox replacement, Scott Fletcher, and Ozzie Guillen (6 years each), and new teammate Orel Hershiser.... Career total of 180 doubles in 715 games; among active players, only Don Mattingly had more doubles after that many games.... Career batting average was only 11 points higher at Fenway than elsewhere, but don't expect any more 40-double seasons. (He's had three; only four active players have had more.) Over the last five years, Fenway Park increased doubles by 29 percent, Dodger Stadium decreased them by 19 percent—the highest and lowest figures in the majors. Since Dodger Stadium opened in 1962, only two Dodgers players had 40 doubles in a season: Wes Parker (1970) and Steve Sax (1986); there were nineteen 40-double seasons by the Red Sox during that time.

Kevin Reimer
Texas Rangers   Bats Left

	AB	H	2B	3B	HR	RBI	BB	SO	BA	SA	OBA
Season	494	132	32	2	16	58	42	103	.267	.437	.336
vs. Left-Handers	89	22	4	0	2	8	12	29	.247	.360	.356
vs. Right-Handers	405	110	28	2	14	50	30	74	.272	.454	.332
vs. Ground-Ballers	235	66	16	1	9	32	17	47	.281	.404	.340
vs. Fly-Ballers	259	66	16	1	7	26	25	56	.255	.405	.333
Home Games	239	68	13	2	10	34	20	53	.285	.481	.356
Road Games	255	64	19	0	6	24	22	50	.251	.396	.318
Grass Fields	409	107	23	2	14	48	37	81	.262	.430	.336
Artificial Turf	85	25	9	0	2	10	5	22	.294	.471	.341
April	78	25	9	0	2	12	7	10	.321	.513	.376
May	108	29	7	0	3	12	3	25	.269	.417	.292
June	83	23	4	1	4	16	9	13	.277	.494	.362
July	67	20	6	0	2	3	8	15	.299	.478	.397
August	88	24	4	1	5	13	7	20	.273	.511	.354
Sept./Oct.	70	11	2	0	0	2	8	20	.157	.186	.244
Leading Off Inn.	114	28	7	1	4	4	7	20	.246	.430	.301
Runners On	212	53	9	1	6	48	28	50	.250	.387	.355
Bases Empty	282	79	23	1	10	10	14	53	.280	.475	.321
Runners/Scor. Pos.	123	26	2	1	1	35	17	32	.211	.268	.333
Runners On/2 Out	96	18	3	0	3	21	14	29	.188	.313	.297
Scor. Pos./2 Out	65	10	1	0	1	16	8	20	.154	.215	.257
Late-Inning Pressure	70	19	6	0	3	11	9	22	.271	.486	.350
Leading Off	17	5	0	0	1	1	1	5	.294	.471	.333
Runners On	32	6	3	0	1	9	7	13	.188	.375	.325
Runners/Scor. Pos.	21	3	2	0	0	6	3	9	.143	.238	.240

RUNS BATTED IN	From 1B	From 2B	From 3B	Scoring Position
Totals	10/148	17/100	15/41	32/141
Percentage	6.8%	17.0%	36.6%	22.7%

Loves to face: Kevin Appier (.308, 4-for-13, 2 2B, 2 HR)
Tom Gordon (.444, 4-for-9, 2 2B, 1 HR, 4 SO)
Jose Mesa (.364, 4-for-11, 3 HR)

Hates to face: Chris Bosio (.087, 2-for-23)
Erik Hanson (.091, 1-for-11)
Jack McDowell (.053, 1-for-19, 1 3B)

Miscellaneous statistics: Ground outs-to-air outs ratio: 0.78 last season, 0.89 for career.... Grounded into 10 double plays in 93 opportunities (one per 9.3).... Drove in 9 of 17 runners from third base with less than two outs (53%).... Direction of balls hit to the outfield: 26% to left field, 32% to center, 42% to right.... Base running: Advanced from first base to third on 3 of 19 outfield singles (16%); scored from second on 14 of 17 (82%).... Made 2.12 putouts per nine innings in left field.

Comments: Started 113 games in which the Rangers faced right-handed starters last season, but only 15 of 46 vs. left-handers.... Actually, that's progress; prior to last season, he had started 127 games, but none against a southpaw.... Total of 28 doubles against right-handers was only three short of the major leagues' co-leaders, Kirby Puckett and Frank Thomas.... Led major league outfielders with 11 errors, one more than Juan Gonzalez. They became the first teammates to hold down the top two spots in outfield errors since 1975, when Reggie Jackson and Billy North did it for Oakland.... Career totals: 19 errors in 186 games in the outfield, or one every 9.8 games. The last outfielder with a career rate that high (minimum: 100 games): Sherry Robertson, who retired 40 years ago (20 errors in 163 games from 1940 to 1952).... Career batting average is .305 in Late-Inning Pressure Situations.... No home runs in 69 career at-bats against the Red Sox, the only opposing team against which he hasn't homered.... Has batted in the .260s in each of the last three seasons (.260, .269, .267). No other player has batted within a 10-point range for those three years (minimum: 100 AB in each).... Completed only his second full season in the majors, but shares a birthday with Mark Grace; they'll both turn 29 in July. Reimer, who is five days older than Jose Canseco, played 604 games in parts of six minor league seasons.

Harold Reynolds

Seattle Mariners — Bats Left and Right

Seattle Mariners	AB	H	2B	3B	HR	RBI	BB	SO	BA	SA	OBA
Season	458	113	23	3	3	33	45	41	.247	.330	.316
vs. Left-Handers	116	29	6	0	0	12	17	4	.250	.302	.348
vs. Right-Handers	342	84	17	3	3	21	28	37	.246	.339	.304
vs. Ground-Ballers	222	56	11	1	2	16	22	24	.252	.338	.324
vs. Fly-Ballers	236	57	12	2	1	17	23	17	.242	.322	.308
Home Games	237	62	15	3	2	17	20	20	.262	.376	.326
Road Games	221	51	8	0	1	16	25	21	.231	.281	.305
Grass Fields	183	45	6	0	1	14	22	15	.246	.295	.324
Artificial Turf	275	68	17	3	2	19	23	26	.247	.353	.310
April	78	21	3	1	1	6	7	5	.269	.372	.329
May	94	21	5	1	0	6	13	8	.223	.298	.312
June	98	24	4	1	1	7	8	13	.245	.337	.312
July	89	21	4	0	1	6	7	7	.236	.315	.289
August	57	17	5	0	0	6	8	4	.298	.386	.394
Sept./Oct.	42	9	2	0	0	2	2	4	.214	.262	.256
Leading Off Inn.	133	30	6	2	0	0	11	13	.226	.301	.290
Runners On	184	48	15	0	1	31	17	12	.261	.359	.320
Bases Empty	274	65	8	3	2	2	28	29	.237	.310	.313
Runners/Scor. Pos.	107	30	11	0	1	30	9	8	.280	.411	.325
Runners On/2 Out	76	17	6	0	0	9	10	4	.224	.303	.322
Scor. Pos./2 Out	48	8	3	0	0	8	5	3	.167	.229	.245
Late-Inning Pressure	81	16	0	0	1	6	4	17	.198	.235	.233
Leading Off	27	3	0	0	0	0	1	5	.111	.111	.143
Runners On	27	3	0	0	0	5	1	5	.111	.111	.138
Runners/Scor. Pos.	17	2	0	0	0	5	0	4	.118	.118	.111

RUNS BATTED IN	From 1B	From 2B	From 3B	Scoring Position
Totals	1/129	12/85	17/45	29/130
Percentage	0.8%	14.1%	37.8%	22.3%

Loves to face: Mark Gubicza (.462, 18-for-39)
Mike Henneman (.615, 8-for-13, 1 HR)
Dave Stieb (.469, 15-for-32, 0 BB)

Hates to face: Tom Gordon (.080, 2-for-25, 5 BB)
Dave Stewart (.113, 7-for-62, 7 BB)
Bobby Thigpen (.091, 1-for-11)

Miscellaneous statistics: Ground outs-to-air outs ratio: 1.30 last season, 1.20 for career.... Grounded into 12 double plays in 94 opportunities (one per 7.8).... Drove in 12 of 25 runners from third base with less than two outs (48%).... Direction of balls hit to the outfield: 31% to left field, 24% to center, 46% to right batting left-handed; 26% to left field, 36% to center, 38% to right batting right-handed.... Base running: Advanced from first base to third on 10 of 25 outfield singles (40%); scored from second on 13 of 14 (93%), 5th-highest rate in A.L.... Made 2.94 assists per nine innings at second base.

Comments: Mariners second basemen combined for a .234 batting average, the lowest of any A.L. club last season. The 2d-lowest average in the league at that position belonged to his new team, the Orioles (.236).... Last season's error rate (one every 56.4 chances) was the best of his career, but only slightly better than the major league average for second basemen (one every 56.1 chances).... Played only 140 games last year, after averaging more than 158 games over the previous five years.... Batted .228 in 38 games from the leadoff spot in the batting order, .272 in 63 games from the bottom spot.... Stole only 15 bases after stealing 25 or more in each of the six previous seasons.... Set a career high by grounding into 12 double plays, even though he came to the plate 200 fewer times in 1992 than he did in 1991. The reason: He hit more fly outs than ground outs in '91; last season, he posted his highest ratio of ground outs to fly outs (1.30) since 1987.... Had 11 pinch-hit at-bats last season, more than he had in his entire career through 1992. Career PH figures: .118 (2-for-17).... Has hit for a higher average from the right side of the plate than from the left in each of the last six seasons.... Played two-thirds of an inning in left field on September 11, his only career appearance at any position other than second base.... Leaves the Mariners 11 games short of their all-time record for games played with 1155; Alvin Davis holds the record. The leader among current Mariners players: Dave Valle (711).

Billy Ripken

Baltimore Orioles — Bats Right

Baltimore Orioles	AB	H	2B	3B	HR	RBI	BB	SO	BA	SA	OBA
Season	330	76	15	0	4	36	18	26	.230	.312	.275
vs. Left-Handers	109	25	7	0	0	9	7	5	.229	.294	.280
vs. Right-Handers	221	51	8	0	4	27	11	21	.231	.321	.272
vs. Ground-Ballers	159	33	5	0	2	19	7	15	.208	.277	.249
vs. Fly-Ballers	171	43	10	0	2	17	11	11	.251	.345	.299
Home Games	149	38	5	0	3	22	13	9	.255	.349	.325
Road Games	181	38	10	0	1	14	5	17	.210	.282	.230
Grass Fields	271	59	12	0	4	28	17	19	.218	.306	.270
Artificial Turf	59	17	3	0	0	8	1	7	.288	.339	.300
April	44	8	4	0	0	5	1	7	.182	.273	.200
May	41	10	0	0	1	6	2	2	.244	.317	.311
June	56	11	4	0	1	4	3	3	.196	.321	.246
July	56	16	3	0	2	6	1	3	.286	.446	.298
August	77	18	3	0	0	13	7	9	.234	.273	.294
Sept./Oct.	56	13	1	0	0	2	4	2	.232	.250	.283
Leading Off Inn.	73	13	3	0	0	0	2	8	.178	.219	.200
Runners On	158	43	10	0	1	33	9	11	.272	.354	.320
Bases Empty	172	33	5	0	3	3	9	15	.192	.273	.232
Runners/Scor. Pos.	87	23	3	0	1	30	7	8	.264	.333	.327
Runners On/2 Out	76	23	6	0	0	15	6	8	.303	.382	.361
Scor. Pos./2 Out	47	12	1	0	0	13	5	6	.255	.277	.340
Late-Inning Pressure	17	4	2	0	0	2	1	0	.235	.353	.278
Leading Off	5	1	0	0	0	0	0	0	.200	.200	.200
Runners On	4	1	1	0	0	2	1	0	.250	.500	.400
Runners/Scor. Pos.	1	0	0	0	0	1	1	0	.000	.000	.500

RUNS BATTED IN	From 1B	From 2B	From 3B	Scoring Position
Totals	4/122	11/74	17/42	28/116
Percentage	3.3%	14.9%	40.5%	24.1%

Loves to face: Storm Davis (.462, 6-for-13)
Bill Wegman (.647, 11-for-17, 1 HR)
David Wells (.400, 6-for-15, 1 HR)

Hates to face: Jim Abbott (.091, 1-for-11)
Jack McDowell (.077, 1-for-13)
Dave Stewart (.071, 1-for-14, 1 2B)

Miscellaneous statistics: Ground outs-to-air outs ratio: 1.40 last season, 1.52 for career.... Grounded into 10 double plays in 79 opportunities (one per 7.9).... Drove in 10 of 23 runners from third base with less than two outs (43%).... Direction of balls hit to the outfield: 49% to left field, 27% to center, 24% to right.... Base running: Advanced from first base to third on 4 of 14 outfield singles (29%); scored from second on 5 of 8 (63%).... Made 3.19 assists per nine innings at second base.

Comments: Led major league second basemen in fielding percentage by the narrowest of margins—on two counts: (1) He played only 108 games there, the minimum needed to qualify; and (2) he committed an average of one error every 134.5 chances compared to runner-up Roberto Alomar's rate of one every 134.0. Had Ripken fielded two fewer balls during the season, he and Alomar would have become the first infielders ever to finish in a flat-footed tie for a league lead.... The closest race ever: Frank Duffy edged Fred Stanley for the A.L. shortstop crown in 1976 by a margin equivalent to one error every 116,064 chances.... Based on a 1000-game minimum, Jim Gantner is currently the A.L.'s all-time leader at second base with a rate of one error every 66 chances; but six players with between 500 and 999 games at second have better rates than Gantner. The only one still active is Ripken (one error per 77 chances in 659 games); the others: Rich Dauer, who fell 35 games short (79), Marty Barrett (72), Chuck Schilling (68), Jerry Adair (68), and Cookie Rojas (68).... Pulled 49 percent of the balls he hit to the outfield last season to left field, compared to only 28 percent in 1991.... Batted 7th in his final start of the season, snapping a streak of 149 consecutive starts in which he batted either eighth or ninth.... Total of 57 sacrifice bunts over the past four seasons ranks second in the American League to Felix Fermin (67).... Career batting average is 39 points higher for July through October (.262) than for April through June (.223).

Cal Ripken — Bats Right

Baltimore Orioles

	AB	H	2B	3B	HR	RBI	BB	SO	BA	SA	OBA
Season	637	160	29	1	14	72	64	50	.251	.366	.323
vs. Left-Handers	165	38	6	1	2	13	14	8	.230	.315	.297
vs. Right-Handers	472	122	23	0	12	59	50	42	.258	.383	.332
vs. Ground-Ballers	307	79	13	0	5	29	32	24	.257	.349	.332
vs. Fly-Ballers	330	81	16	1	9	43	32	26	.245	.382	.314
Home Games	312	74	17	1	5	23	31	30	.237	.346	.310
Road Games	325	86	12	0	9	49	33	20	.265	.385	.335
Grass Fields	541	137	24	1	13	59	52	41	.253	.373	.321
Artificial Turf	96	23	5	0	1	13	12	9	.240	.323	.336
April	76	19	6	1	1	11	12	6	.250	.395	.359
May	106	28	4	0	5	11	13	8	.264	.443	.347
June	113	37	4	0	4	16	10	9	.327	.469	.387
July	107	19	4	0	0	10	14	7	.178	.215	.286
August	110	24	4	0	0	11	8	12	.218	.255	.267
Sept./Oct.	125	33	7	0	4	13	7	8	.264	.416	.303
Leading Off Inn.	126	31	5	1	0	0	11	6	.246	.302	.317
Runners On	280	69	9	0	8	66	38	24	.246	.364	.337
Bases Empty	357	91	20	1	6	6	26	26	.255	.367	.311
Runners/Scor. Pos.	145	40	5	0	4	57	30	13	.276	.393	.395
Runners On/2 Out	112	21	4	0	1	18	17	11	.188	.250	.300
Scor. Pos./2 Out	65	17	4	0	1	18	12	4	.262	.369	.385
Late-Inning Pressure	71	19	4	0	0	7	15	3	.268	.324	.398
Leading Off	15	3	1	0	0	0	1	0	.200	.267	.250
Runners On	28	9	1	0	0	7	9	2	.321	.357	.487
Runners/Scor. Pos.	17	5	0	0	0	7	1		.294	.294	.480

RUNS BATTED IN	From 1B	From 2B	From 3B	Scoring Position
Totals	8/204	19/98	31/75	50/173
Percentage	3.9%	19.4%	41.3%	28.9%

Loves to face: Chuck Crim (.529, 9-for-17, 1 HR)
Steve Farr (.348, 8-for-23, 2 2B, 1 HR)
David Wells (.421, 8-for-19, 2 2B, 3 HR)

Hates to face: Juan Guzman (0-for-8)
Tom Henke (.158, 3-for-19)
Eric Plunk (.120, 3-for-25, 1 HR)

Miscellaneous statistics: Ground outs-to-air outs ratio: 0.92 last season, 1.00 for career.... Grounded into 13 double plays in 132 opportunities (one per 10).... Drove in 24 of 45 runners from third base with less than two outs (53%).... Direction of balls hit to the outfield: 42% to left field, 28% to center, 30% to right.... Base running: Advanced from first base to third on 15 of 43 outfield singles (35%); scored from second on 15 of 16 (94%), 2d-highest rate in A.L.... Made 2.78 assists per nine innings at shortstop, 2d-lowest rate in A.L.

Comments: Has played exactly 1800 games, 4th most in franchise history. Needs exactly 162 games—isn't that funny—to tie Mark Belanger for 2d place on that list.... The all-time franchise home-run leader is Eddie Murray with 333, 60 more than Ripken.... Has played at least 160 games in 11 consecutive seasons. Only two other players have had streaks half that long: Billy Williams (8) and Steve Garvey (6).... Has already cracked the American League's all-time top 10 in games at shortstop (1723). This season, he should move past Ed Brinkman (1771), Joe Cronin (1832), and Donie Bush (1867).... Has hit for a higher average in road games than he has in Baltimore in each of the last seven years. Career breakdown: .263 at home, .290 on the road (.304 on artificial turf).... Scored 73 runs and drove in 72; both were career lows.... Failed to hit 20 home runs for the first time in his career.... Has batted under .200 in only four months during his career: August 1981 (.118 in his first month in the majors); April 1982 (.123 in the first month of his first full season); September 1989 (.198); and July 1992 (.178, followed by .218 in August).... Went 73 games without a home run from June 24 through September 13. He had only one previous streak even half that long (40 games in 1989).... Batted .101 (8-for-49) from June 30 through July 23, the lowest 20-game mark of his career. His previous low: .111 (4-for-36) in his first 20 games in the majors.

Luis Rivera — Bats Right

Boston Red Sox

	AB	H	2B	3B	HR	RBI	BB	SO	BA	SA	OBA
Season	288	62	11	1	0	29	26	56	.215	.260	.287
vs. Left-Handers	78	14	3	0	0	7	10	16	.179	.218	.273
vs. Right-Handers	210	48	8	1	0	22	16	40	.229	.276	.293
vs. Ground-Ballers	135	26	5	0	0	11	11	20	.193	.230	.264
vs. Fly-Ballers	153	36	6	1	0	18	15	36	.235	.288	.308
Home Games	127	22	5	0	0	14	9	24	.173	.213	.245
Road Games	161	40	6	1	0	15	17	32	.248	.298	.320
Grass Fields	228	47	7	1	0	23	20	45	.206	.246	.279
Artificial Turf	60	15	4	0	0	6	6	11	.250	.317	.318
April	38	13	2	0	0	2	4	11	.342	.395	.405
May	69	14	1	0	0	8	11	10	.203	.217	.313
June	88	21	6	0	0	11	8	18	.239	.307	.323
July	58	7	1	0	0	3	2	9	.121	.138	.150
August	22	5	1	1	0	5	1	5	.227	.364	.261
Sept./Oct.	13	2	0	0	0	0		3	.154	.154	.154
Leading Off Inn.	70	13	4	0	0	0	8	10	.186	.243	.278
Runners On	132	34	5	1	0	29	11	28	.258	.311	.315
Bases Empty	156	28	6	0	0	0	15	28	.179	.244	.264
Runners/Scor. Pos.	87	23	2	1	0	28	8	20	.264	.310	.326
Runners On/2 Out	71	17	3	1	0	16	6	16	.239	.310	.299
Scor. Pos./2 Out	48	12	1	1	0	15	5	11	.250	.313	.321
Late-Inning Pressure	52	10	3	1	0	3	6	12	.192	.288	.276
Leading Off	16	1	0	0	0	0	2	3	.063	.125	.167
Runners On	16	3	1	1	0	3	3	4	.188	.375	.316
Runners/Scor. Pos.	12	3	1	1	0	3	1	4	.250	.500	.308

RUNS BATTED IN	From 1B	From 2B	From 3B	Scoring Position
Totals	2/86	12/66	15/46	27/112
Percentage	2.3%	18.2%	32.6%	24.1%

Loves to face: Tim Leary (.700, 7-for-10, 1 HR)
Jaime Navarro (.462, 6-for-13, 1 HR)
Kenny Rogers (.500, 6-for-12, 3 2B, 1 3B)

Hates to face: Luis Aquino (.100, 2-for-20)
Nolan Ryan (0-for-10)
Kevin Tapani (0-for-11)

Miscellaneous statistics: Ground outs-to-air outs ratio: 0.91 last season, 0.89 for career.... Grounded into 5 double plays in 45 opportunities (one per 9.0).... Drove in 10 of 22 runners from third base with less than two outs (45%).... Direction of balls hit to the outfield: 38% to left field, 29% to center, 33% to right.... Base running: Advanced from first base to third on 4 of 10 outfield singles (40%); scored from second on 4 of 6 (67%).... Made 3.52 assists per nine innings at shortstop, highest rate in majors.

Comments: Scored only 17 runs in 102 games last season, becoming the first player in Red Sox history to score fewer than 20 runs in a season of at least 100 games. Trivia for Blowhards: Bob Tillman scored 20 runs in 111 games in 1965.... Boston shortstops ranked second in the majors with 120 double plays last season, but most of the credit goes to John Valentin. Rivera turned 56 double plays in 93 games; Valentin turned 45 double plays in only 58 games.... One of three players in the majors with at least 10 go-ahead RBIs, despite having fewer than 30 total RBIs: Rivera (29 RBIs, 10 go-ahead RBIs); Jeff Tackett (24/10); and Von Hayes (29/11).... Has driven in fewer than 50 percent of runners from third base with less than two outs in six of his seven years in the majors (career rate: 48.5%).... Batting average at Fenway Park was the lowest single-season mark by a Red Sox batter in the 18 years of *The Player Analysis* (minimum: 100 AB). Since 1975, only two others failed to reach the .200-mark: Ed Romero (.176 in 1986) and Gary Allenson (.198 in 1979).... Batting average in night games (.191) was 2d lowest in the league, behind teammate Jack Clark (.182).... Doug Griffin, Frank Duffy, Jack Brohamer, Glenn Hoffman, Luis Rivera. Could anyone tells these guys apart from a distance? How did Boston ever miss Woody Woodward and Johnnie LeMaster? (At least there's still time for Walt Weiss.)

Ivan Rodriguez — Bats Right

Texas Rangers	AB	H	2B	3B	HR	RBI	BB	SO	BA	SA	OBA
Season	420	109	16	1	8	37	24	73	.260	.360	.300
vs. Left-Handers	105	29	4	0	2	9	7	14	.276	.371	.319
vs. Right-Handers	315	80	12	1	6	28	17	59	.254	.356	.293
vs. Ground-Ballers	185	45	4	0	4	20	5	28	.243	.330	.266
vs. Fly-Ballers	235	64	12	1	4	17	19	45	.272	.383	.325
Home Games	211	50	5	1	4	19	10	45	.237	.327	.270
Road Games	209	59	11	0	4	18	14	28	.282	.392	.329
Grass Fields	334	82	11	1	6	27	16	61	.246	.338	.279
Artificial Turf	86	27	5	0	2	10	8	12	.314	.442	.375
April	70	22	5	0	1	8	3	9	.314	.429	.347
May	83	21	0	0	4	13	5	19	.253	.398	.292
June	19	5	1	0	2	4	3	3	.263	.632	.364
July	74	18	2	1	1	4	5	15	.243	.338	.291
August	94	24	5	0	0	6	4	13	.255	.309	.286
Sept./Oct.	80	19	3	0	0	2	4	14	.237	.275	.274
Leading Off Inn.	86	26	4	0	2	2	7	10	.302	.419	.362
Runners On	181	43	6	0	4	33	13	35	.238	.337	.286
Bases Empty	239	66	10	1	4	4	11	38	.276	.377	.311
Runners/Scor. Pos.	102	24	2	0	2	28	10	22	.235	.314	.298
Runners On/2 Out	73	17	2	0	1	12	6	17	.233	.301	.291
Scor. Pos./2 Out	46	9	0	0	1	11	5	12	.196	.261	.275
Late-Inning Pressure	70	24	3	0	1	7	7	8	.343	.429	.397
Leading Off	14	6	1	0	0	0	3	0	.429	.500	.529
Runners On	30	7	0	0	1	7	3	4	.233	.333	.294
Runners/Scor. Pos.	17	5	0	0	1	7	3	3	.294	.471	.381

RUNS BATTED IN	From 1B	From 2B	From 3B	Scoring Position
Totals	3/130	10/81	16/39	26/120
Percentage	2.3%	12.3%	41.0%	21.7%

Loves to face: Chris Bosio (.583, 7-for-12)
Dave Fleming (.444, 4-for-9)
Mike Magnante (4-for-4, 1 HR)

Hates to face: Danny Darwin (0-for-6, 3 SO)
Scott Kamieniecki (0-for-6)
Mike Moore (.077, 1-for-13, 1 2B)

Miscellaneous statistics: Ground outs-to-air outs ratio: 1.57 last season, 1.57 for career.... Grounded into 15 double plays in 84 opportunities (one per 5.6).... Drove in 11 of 19 runners from third base with less than two outs (58%).... Direction of balls hit to the outfield: 30% to left field, 30% to center, 39% to right.... Base running: Advanced from first base to third on 7 of 15 outfield singles (47%); scored from second on 5 of 8 (63%).... Opposing base stealers: 53-for-110 (48%), lowest rate in majors.

Comments: Rodriguez is proof positive that the Gold Glove Award for catchers has become little more than a Golden Arm award for the best-throwing catcher. He won the award for 1992 despite leading the majors in errors (15—the most by an A.L. catcher since Andy Allanson was charged with 20 in 1986) and committing 10 passed balls. There have been 70 previous winners of that award; only six led the majors in errors: Earl Battey (1960), Thurman Munson (1974–75), Benito Santiago (1988–89), and Sandy Alomar, Jr. (1990). There seems to be a trend here.... Three of his errors came on catcher's interference, matching Jamie Quirk for the most in the majors. Five came on stolen bases; last season, catchers committed 43 percent of their errors on stolen-base attempts.... Rangers' staff posted a 3.82 ERA with Rodriguez, 4.67 with other catchers.... Had already caught 204 games by the time he turned 21 (last December), the most of any player in major league history. Most games caught prior to adulthood: Rodriguez, 204; Johnny Bench, 180; Del Crandall, 138; Eddie Ainsmith and Butch Wynegar, 137.... No longer the youngest player in the majors. Outfielder Melvin Nieves made his major league debut for the Braves as a pinch hitter on September 1; he won't turn 22 until December 28, 1993—28 days after Rodriguez.... Drew only five walks in 288 plate appearances in 1991 (one every 57.6 PA); that rate increased to one every 18.9 plate appearances last year.... Career rate of one walk every 25.6 plate appearances is about the same as Nolan Ryan's—as a batter (one every 25.2 PA).

Steve Sax — Bats Right

Chicago White Sox	AB	H	2B	3B	HR	RBI	BB	SO	BA	SA	OBA
Season	567	134	26	4	4	47	43	42	.236	.317	.290
vs. Left-Handers	157	36	8	0	1	7	11	7	.229	.299	.278
vs. Right-Handers	410	98	18	4	3	40	32	35	.239	.324	.294
vs. Ground-Ballers	279	63	9	1	1	19	21	23	.226	.276	.284
vs. Fly-Ballers	288	71	17	3	3	28	22	19	.247	.358	.295
Home Games	292	66	14	4	1	21	25	20	.226	.312	.287
Road Games	275	68	12	0	3	26	18	22	.247	.324	.293
Grass Fields	479	113	23	4	2	33	39	35	.236	.313	.293
Artificial Turf	88	21	3	0	2	14	4	7	.239	.341	.272
April	67	18	3	0	0	5	7	5	.269	.313	.338
May	91	19	2	2	0	10	10	6	.209	.275	.282
June	92	19	2	0	1	9	7	5	.207	.261	.263
July	99	25	7	2	1	9	8	8	.253	.394	.312
August	105	23	8	0	1	6	6	12	.219	.324	.259
Sept./Oct.	113	30	4	0	1	8	5	6	.265	.327	.297
Leading Off Inn.	161	32	8	0	1	1	10	13	.199	.267	.246
Runners On	206	49	8	3	2	45	20	14	.238	.335	.303
Bases Empty	361	85	18	1	2	2	23	28	.235	.307	.281
Runners/Scor. Pos.	122	25	3	3	2	44	14	9	.205	.328	.285
Runners On/2 Out	82	16	1	0	0	11	8	3	.195	.207	.283
Scor. Pos./2 Out	53	8	0	0	0	10	5	2	.151	.151	.250
Late-Inning Pressure	77	15	3	1	0	7	6	7	.195	.260	.259
Leading Off	14	4	1	0	0	0	1	0	.286	.357	.333
Runners On	36	6	2	1	0	7	4	3	.167	.278	.262
Runners/Scor. Pos.	23	3	0	1	0	6	3	1	.130	.217	.250

RUNS BATTED IN	From 1B	From 2B	From 3B	Scoring Position
Totals	4/149	15/96	24/62	39/158
Percentage	2.7%	15.6%	38.7%	24.7%

Loves to face: Chuck Crim (.526, 10-for-19)
Neal Heaton (.471, 8-for-17)
Ben McDonald (.545, 6-for-11, 1 HR)

Hates to face: John Dopson (.087, 2-for-23, 3 BB)
Randy Johnson (.038, 1-for-26, 1 2B, 2 BB)
Jack Morris (.100, 2-for-20)

Miscellaneous statistics: Ground outs-to-air outs ratio: 2.18 last season (highest in A.L.), 1.96 for career.... Grounded into 17 double plays in 108 opportunities (one per 6.4).... Drove in 18 of 35 runners from third base with less than two outs (51%).... Direction of balls hit to the outfield: 42% to left field, 22% to center, 36% to right.... Base running: Advanced from first base to third on 11 of 28 outfield singles (39%); scored from second on 13 of 16 (81%).... Made 2.81 assists per nine innings at second base, 3d-lowest rate in A.L.

Comments: The toughest trivia question we've ever asked: Who are the only other players in major league history to play for teams based in New York, Los Angeles, and Chicago, but nowhere else? Answer below.... Charged with 20 errors last year, after committing only 10 in each of his three years with the Yankees.... Became the first player since Tito Fuentes to lead major league second basemen in errors in three different seasons.... Grounded out 275 times last year, the highest total in the majors.... His total of 88 ground outs to the right side made him the major league leader for a third consecutive season.... Batting and on-base averages were career lows.... Has walked more often than he has struck out in each of the last four years.... For the sixth time in his 12-year career, he posted a higher average against right-handers than he did against left-handers. Career batting averages: .292 vs. LHP; .277 vs. RHP.... Batting average in Late-Inning Pressure Situations was the lowest of his career; his career average in LIPS is .301.... Career stolen-base percentage of .714 is awfully low for a perennial 30-base stealer. Over the past 40 years, only one player with at least 400 career steals has a lower success rate than Sax: Brett Butler (.676). Rounding out the bottom of that list: Bobby Bonds (.732), Omar Moreno (.732), Maury Wills (.738), and Lou Brock (.753).... Trivia answer: Carlos May played for the White Sox (1968–76), Yankees (1977–78), and Angels (1978); Billy Wynne played for the Mets (1967), White Sox (1968–70), and Angels (1971).

Kevin Seitzer — Bats Right

Milwaukee Brewers	AB	H	2B	3B	HR	RBI	BB	SO	BA	SA	OBA
Season	540	146	35	1	5	71	57	44	.270	.367	.337
vs. Left-Handers	128	40	10	1	2	17	21	9	.313	.453	.404
vs. Right-Handers	412	106	25	0	3	54	36	35	.257	.340	.315
vs. Ground-Ballers	244	68	12	0	0	21	27	17	.279	.328	.352
vs. Fly-Ballers	296	78	23	1	5	50	30	27	.264	.399	.325
Home Games	259	61	10	1	2	32	30	20	.236	.305	.315
Road Games	281	85	25	0	3	39	27	24	.302	.423	.358
Grass Fields	464	117	26	1	5	55	44	39	.252	.345	.314
Artificial Turf	76	29	9	0	0	16	13	5	.382	.500	.472
April	64	17	4	0	1	9	7	3	.266	.375	.333
May	109	37	11	0	1	12	8	10	.339	.468	.385
June	95	27	4	1	0	13	9	6	.284	.347	.336
July	88	18	4	0	2	14	12	10	.205	.318	.298
August	76	17	5	0	0	8	11	8	.224	.289	.322
Sept./Oct.	108	30	7	0	1	15	10	7	.278	.370	.339
Leading Off Inn.	120	32	4	1	2	2	13	9	.267	.367	.343
Runners On	231	62	18	0	1	67	28	20	.268	.359	.338
Bases Empty	309	84	17	1	4	4	29	24	.272	.372	.336
Runners/Scor. Pos.	150	43	12	0	0	64	24	14	.287	.367	.370
Runners On/2 Out	86	24	8	0	0	24	10	9	.279	.372	.354
Scor. Pos./2 Out	64	20	8	0	0	24	7	6	.313	.438	.380
Late-Inning Pressure	75	24	6	0	1	15	10	6	.320	.440	.386
Leading Off	23	8	0	0	1	1	4	2	.348	.478	.444
Runners On	29	8	2	0	0	14	4	2	.276	.345	.333
Runners/Scor. Pos.	19	5	1	0	0	13	4	2	.263	.316	.346

RUNS BATTED IN	From 1B	From 2B	From 3B	Scoring Position
Totals	6/156	20/116	40/74	60/190
Percentage	3.8%	17.2%	54.1%	31.6%

Loves to face: Eric Bell (.500, 5-for-10, 1 HR)
Alex Fernandez (.750, 3-for-4, 2 HR)
Erik Hanson (.600, 9-for-15)

Hates to face: Scott Bankhead (0-for-11)
Scott Erickson (0-for-12)
Jack McDowell (.045, 1-for-22, 3 BB)

Miscellaneous statistics: Ground outs-to-air outs ratio: 1.26 last season, 1.40 for career.... Grounded into 16 double plays in 113 opportunities (one per 7.1).... Drove in 32 of 48 runners from third base with less than two outs (67%).... Direction of balls hit to the outfield: 28% to left field, 33% to center, 39% to right.... Base running: Advanced from first base to third on 8 of 33 outfield singles (24%); scored from second on 15 of 20 (75%).... Made 1.94 assists per nine innings at third base.

Comments: After leading A.L. third basemen in errors with the Royals in both 1987 and 1988, he became only the second third baseman in Brewers history to lead the league in fielding percentage. The other was Don Money (1973–74).... Some other third basemen who led the league in errors, but later led in fielding percentage: Aurelio Rodriguez, Doug Rader, Ron Santo, and Eddie Yost.... His comeback from four consecutive seasons in which both his batting average and RBI total declined did little to ease the pain of trading Gary Sheffield; Milwaukee third basemen combined for only six home runs, the 2d fewest in the league last season.... Led the majors with 25 doubles in road games.... Career average of .261 on grass fields, .315 on artificial turf.... Led the league with a .444 average against the Mariners last season. Three of the four players to bat .400 or better against Seattle last season were Brewers (Seitzer, Molitor, and Yount).... Career average of .556 (15-for-27) as a pinch hitter. He is the only player in major league history with a pinch average of .500 or better in at least 25 pinch AB, but he's playing for the wrong team. Last season was the ninth straight in which Milwaukee had fewer pinch ABs than any other team in the majors. (Seitzer walked in his only trip as a pinch hitter.)... Career rate of 33.6 percent of runners driven in from scoring position in Late-Inning Pressure Situations is 6th best among active players (minimum: 100 opportunities).

Ruben Sierra — Bats Left and Right

Rangers/A's	AB	H	2B	3B	HR	RBI	BB	SO	BA	SA	OBA
Season	601	167	34	7	17	87	45	68	.278	.443	.323
vs. Left-Handers	171	58	10	3	5	33	14	13	.339	.520	.385
vs. Right-Handers	430	109	24	4	12	54	31	55	.253	.412	.299
vs. Ground-Ballers	284	78	13	2	5	35	11	31	.275	.387	.298
vs. Fly-Ballers	317	89	21	5	12	52	34	37	.281	.492	.345
Home Games	294	71	15	2	10	40	20	37	.241	.408	.285
Road Games	307	96	19	5	7	47	25	31	.313	.476	.359
Grass Fields	506	132	25	3	13	69	34	56	.261	.399	.303
Artificial Turf	95	35	9	4	4	18	11	12	.368	.674	.426
April	88	27	7	1	2	13	7	13	.307	.477	.354
May	117	33	4	1	6	22	6	9	.282	.487	.312
June	91	31	8	2	2	15	5	13	.341	.538	.367
July	104	24	7	1	1	8	7	13	.231	.346	.279
August	100	24	4	1	3	12	6	11	.240	.390	.275
Sept./Oct.	101	28	4	1	3	17	14	9	.277	.426	.359
Leading Off Inn.	137	35	9	2	2	2	8	12	.255	.394	.297
Runners On	293	87	17	1	11	81	30	31	.297	.474	.351
Bases Empty	308	80	17	6	6	6	15	37	.260	.412	.294
Runners/Scor. Pos.	156	44	8	1	5	63	24	18	.282	.442	.358
Runners On/2 Out	124	38	10	1	3	30	16	13	.306	.476	.386
Scor. Pos./2 Out	69	18	5	1	1	22	11	6	.261	.406	.363
Late-Inning Pressure	81	17	2	1	2	13	5	14	.210	.333	.250
Leading Off	23	4	1	1	0	0	1	4	.174	.304	.208
Runners On	34	11	0	0	2	13	3	2	.324	.500	.359
Runners/Scor. Pos.	18	6	0	0	1	11	3	1	.333	.500	.391

RUNS BATTED IN	From 1B	From 2B	From 3B	Scoring Position
Totals	17/226	21/130	32/70	53/200
Percentage	7.5%	16.2%	45.7%	26.5%

Loves to face: Steve Farr (.500, 9-for-18, 1 HR, 6 SO)
Randy Johnson (.441, 15-for-34, 2 HR)
David Wells (.435, 10-for-23, 1 HR)

Hates to face: Todd Frohwirth (0-for-7)
Ted Higuera (.059, 1-for-17)
Gregg Olson (0-for-10, 3 SO)

Miscellaneous statistics: Ground outs-to-air outs ratio: 0.76 last season, 0.89 for career.... Grounded into 11 double plays in 137 opportunities (one per 12).... Drove in 19 of 31 runners from third base with less than two outs (61%).... Direction of balls hit to the outfield: 31% to left field, 29% to center, 40% to right batting left-handed; 47% to left field, 32% to center, 22% to right batting right-handed.... Base running: Advanced from first base to third on 6 of 20 outfield singles (30%); scored from second on 19 of 22 (86%).... Made 2.01 putouts per nine innings in right field, 2d-lowest rate in A.L.

Comments: Made his major league debut on June 1, 1986. Since then, he ranks third in the majors in extra-base hits (430) and fourth in RBIs (673). Joe Carter leads in both categories (with 463 and 743, respectively).... For the fourth straight season, he batted well above .300 from the right side of the plate, but below .300 from the left side; year by year since 1989: .341/.289, .324/.255, .335/.296, .339/.253. Career breakdown: .306 right-handed, .268 left-handed.... While with Texas, he hit 64 home runs on the road, 89 at Arlington Stadium. He'll pay for that in Oakland, which suppresses home runs by 10 percent.... Left Texas as the Rangers' all-time home-run leader (with 153), but failed to dislodge Frank Howard from atop the franchise list (with 246), including 11 years in Washington. No current player poses an immediate threat; the only current Rangers players with more than 50 homers for the team are Juan Gonzalez (75) and Rafael Palmeiro (70).... Has hit 57 sacrifice flies over the past six years, the 2d-highest six-year total in the 40 years that sac flies have been compiled.... Still, his career percentage of driving in runners from third with less than two outs (61%) is barely above the league average (57%).... Has stolen 74 bases in 88 attempts since July 1987 (84%), after starting his career 14-for-33 (42%).... Sierra's power belies the inevitable comparisons to Roberto Clemente, so how about Johnny Callison or Al Kaline? Not as romantic, perhaps, but more accurate.

Luis Sojo
Bats Right

California Angels	AB	H	2B	3B	HR	RBI	BB	SO	BA	SA	OBA
Season	368	100	12	3	7	43	14	24	.272	.378	.299
vs. Left-Handers	95	21	2	0	0	6	5	10	.221	.242	.260
vs. Right-Handers	273	79	10	3	7	37	9	14	.289	.425	.313
vs. Ground-Ballers	172	52	4	0	3	25	6	10	.302	.378	.328
vs. Fly-Ballers	196	48	8	3	4	18	8	14	.245	.378	.275
Home Games	186	50	6	0	2	25	7	8	.269	.333	.294
Road Games	182	50	6	3	5	18	7	16	.275	.423	.305
Grass Fields	304	86	10	3	6	37	12	16	.283	.395	.311
Artificial Turf	64	14	2	0	1	6	2	8	.219	.297	.242
April	0	0	0	0	0	0	0	0	—	—	—
May	6	3	0	0	0	0	0	0	.500	.500	.500
June	52	14	1	0	2	7	1	2	.269	.404	.283
July	108	34	6	0	3	14	0	7	.315	.454	.321
August	107	29	2	3	1	11	4	8	.271	.374	.297
Sept./Oct.	95	20	3	0	1	11	9	7	.211	.274	.276
Leading Off Inn.	67	18	4	0	1	1	3	5	.269	.373	.300
Runners On	154	48	4	2	2	38	5	9	.312	.403	.335
Bases Empty	214	52	8	1	5	5	9	15	.243	.360	.274
Runners/Scor. Pos.	90	32	4	2	2	38	4	6	.356	.511	.385
Runners On/2 Out	51	10	2	0	0	7	3	4	.196	.235	.241
Scor. Pos./2 Out	32	6	2	0	0	7	2	3	.188	.250	.235
Late-Inning Pressure	60	18	1	1	1	6	1	3	.300	.400	.323
Leading Off	12	5	1	0	0	0	0	1	.417	.500	.417
Runners On	23	5	0	0	1	6	1	2	.217	.348	.280
Runners/Scor. Pos.	14	4	0	0	1	6	1	0	.286	.500	.375

RUNS BATTED IN	From 1B	From 2B	From 3B	Scoring Position
Totals	3/97	13/68	20/38	33/106
Percentage	3.1%	19.1%	52.6%	31.1%

Loves to face: Mark Gubicza (.667, 4-for-6, 1 HR)
Charles Nagy (.700, 7-for-10, 1 HR)
Scott Sanderson (.462, 6-for-13)
Hates to face: Greg A. Harris (0-for-9)
Steve Olin (0-for-6)
Kevin Tapani (.143, 2-for-14)

Miscellaneous statistics: Ground outs-to-air outs ratio: 1.09 last season, 1.15 for career.... Grounded into 14 double plays in 72 opportunities (one per 5.1), 5th-worst rate in A.L.... Drove in 18 of 26 runners from third base with less than two outs (69%).... Direction of balls hit to the outfield: 41% to left field, 31% to center, 28% to right.... Base running: Advanced from first base to third on 6 of 16 outfield singles (38%); scored from second on 5 of 6 (83%).... Made 3.16 assists per nine innings at second base.

Comments: One of three players to start at least one game each at second base, third base, and shortstop in each of the last three seasons. The others: Al Newman and Bill Pecota. Normally, that qualifies as trivia, but with Sojo rejoining the Blue Jays this season, he can toss his second baseman's mitt away.... Has made only four starts at shortstop in his three seasons in the bigs, but in 1989 he led all International League shortstops in error rate (one per 23 chances), total chances, and double plays.... His total of seven home runs last season equaled his previous career high at any level of pro ball.... A right-handed batter, he has hit all 11 of his career homers against right-handed pitchers.... There's more: His career average is one strikeout every 17.1 plate appearances against right-handers, one every 13.9 plate appearances vs. left-handers.... Career average of one walk every 26.6 plate appearances is 5th worst among active players (minimum: 750 PA). Who walks less frequently? Ozzie Guillen (33.0), Ricky Jordan (28.9), Steve Lake (27.5), and Brian Harper (26.7).... Stole only seven bases in 18 attempts last season (38.9%), the 3d-lowest rate in club history (minimum: 15 attempts), behind Rick Miller, 1978 (3-for-16, 18.8%) and Rod Carew, 1982 (10-for-27, 37%).... What kind of odds would you have gotten at the beginning of last season that Sojo would hit as many home runs as Hojo?

Paul Sorrento
Bats Left

Cleveland Indians	AB	H	2B	3B	HR	RBI	BB	SO	BA	SA	OBA
Season	458	123	24	1	18	60	51	89	.269	.443	.341
vs. Left-Handers	45	7	1	0	0	4	6	16	.156	.178	.250
vs. Right-Handers	413	116	23	1	18	56	45	73	.281	.472	.351
vs. Ground-Ballers	208	57	11	1	9	29	27	36	.274	.466	.360
vs. Fly-Ballers	250	66	13	0	9	31	24	53	.264	.424	.325
Home Games	226	65	13	1	11	31	27	43	.288	.500	.362
Road Games	232	58	11	0	7	29	24	46	.250	.388	.320
Grass Fields	385	108	21	1	17	53	43	74	.281	.473	.352
Artificial Turf	73	15	3	0	1	7	8	15	.205	.288	.284
April	84	18	1	0	1	7	6	20	.214	.262	.272
May	69	15	1	0	5	15	10	20	.217	.449	.316
June	60	22	3	0	2	6	6	5	.367	.517	.424
July	79	29	7	0	4	9	9	12	.367	.608	.432
August	77	21	5	0	4	12	8	13	.273	.494	.337
Sept./Oct.	89	18	7	1	2	11	12	19	.202	.371	.294
Leading Off Inn.	103	34	6	0	6	6	11	17	.330	.563	.400
Runners On	198	47	10	1	5	47	20	33	.237	.374	.303
Bases Empty	260	76	14	0	13	13	31	56	.292	.496	.370
Runners/Scor. Pos.	115	25	6	1	4	43	14	14	.217	.391	.295
Runners On/2 Out	87	19	5	1	1	18	7	14	.218	.333	.277
Scor. Pos./2 Out	56	10	3	1	1	17	5	7	.179	.321	.246
Late-Inning Pressure	82	18	6	0	2	9	10	21	.220	.366	.304
Leading Off	20	6	3	0	0	0	3	5	.300	.450	.391
Runners On	41	9	2	0	1	8	4	9	.220	.341	.289
Runners/Scor. Pos.	20	5	1	0	1	7	4	4	.250	.450	.375

RUNS BATTED IN	From 1B	From 2B	From 3B	Scoring Position
Totals	8/150	17/86	17/55	34/141
Percentage	5.3%	19.8%	30.9%	24.1%

Loves to face: Dave Stewart (.600, 3-for-5, 2 HR)
Kevin Tapani (.625, 5-for-8, 2 2B, 2 HR, 2 SO)
Bobby Witt (.444, 4-for-9, 1 HR, 3 SO)
Hates to face: Kevin Appier (.182, 2-for-11)
Mike Henneman (0-for-6)
Jack Morris (0-for-15)

Miscellaneous statistics: Ground outs-to-air outs ratio: 1.31 last season, 1.18 for career.... Grounded into 13 double plays in 92 opportunities (one per 7.1).... Drove in 11 of 24 runners from third base with less than two outs (46%).... Direction of balls hit to the outfield: 32% to left field, 35% to center, 32% to right.... Base running: Advanced from first base to third on 14 of 35 outfield singles (40%); scored from second on 8 of 14 (57%).... Made 0.69 assists per nine innings at first base.

Comments: Started 116 of Cleveland's 119 games against right-handed pitchers, but only 8 of 43 against left-handers.... Had only 10 at-bats against left-handers in parts of three seasons with the Twins.... No arguments with how he was used; largest differences between batting averages vs. left- and right-handed pitchers (A.L. qualifying batters): Paul Molitor (133-point difference), Sorrento (125), Kenny Lofton (107), Mike Devereaux (102), Lou Whitaker (89).... Was more an opposite-field hitter for Minnesota; his three-year figures for the Twins: 43% to left field, 35% to center, 22% to right.... Indians first basemen combined for a .276 average (4th highest in the league), but only 70 RBIs (3d fewest).... Became Cleveland's sixth different opening-day starter at first base in the last six seasons, following Pat Tabler, Willie Upshaw, Pete O'Brien, Keith ("Team Leader") Hernandez, and Brook Jacoby.... Will battle Reggie Jefferson and Carlos Martinez for the honor in 1993. Martinez started at first in 24 of 43 games vs. left-handers last season; Jefferson is a switch-hitter who didn't make his season debut until July 4.... Jefferson, incidentally, had 17 hits in a 24-AB span late last season (Sept. 23–28).... Sorrento has a career total of 27 homers in 221 major league games. Potential for a big home-run season is there; he hit 27 in 140 games for Orlando (Triple-A) in 1989.... Has hit four home runs in 35 career at-bats as a pinch hitter. No one else has hit a pinch HR in each of the last three seasons.

Andy Stankiewicz

Bats Right

New York Yankees	AB	H	2B	3B	HR	RBI	BB	SO	BA	SA	OBA
Season	400	107	22	2	2	25	38	42	.268	.348	.338
vs. Left-Handers	136	37	5	1	0	10	10	11	.272	.324	.336
vs. Right-Handers	264	70	17	1	2	15	28	31	.265	.360	.339
vs. Ground-Ballers	179	50	11	1	1	11	15	24	.279	.369	.348
vs. Fly-Ballers	221	57	11	1	1	14	23	18	.258	.330	.337
Home Games	207	61	13	1	2	15	19	18	.295	.396	.354
Road Games	193	46	9	1	0	10	19	24	.238	.295	.321
Grass Fields	350	90	17	2	2	23	33	41	.257	.334	.327
Artificial Turf	50	17	5	0	0	2	5	1	.340	.440	.411
April	39	12	2	0	1	4	8	7	.308	.436	.438
May	34	12	5	0	0	4	1	0	.353	.500	.371
June	105	31	7	1	1	7	12	15	.295	.410	.375
July	101	19	2	0	0	3	7	13	.188	.208	.241
August	62	18	3	0	0	3	3	4	.290	.339	.343
Sept./Oct.	59	15	3	1	0	4	7	3	.254	.339	.333
Leading Off Inn.	137	36	5	0	1	1	15	17	.263	.321	.336
Runners On	136	37	10	1	0	23	10	16	.272	.360	.329
Bases Empty	264	70	12	1	2	2	28	26	.265	.341	.342
Runners/Scor. Pos.	69	21	4	1	0	21	8	11	.304	.391	.372
Runners On/2 Out	54	14	3	1	0	10	3	6	.259	.352	.310
Scor. Pos./2 Out	35	11	3	1	0	10	3	2	.314	.457	.368
Late-Inning Pressure	61	16	5	0	1	6	6	7	.262	.393	.338
Leading Off	12	5	0	0	0	0	1	1	.417	.417	.462
Runners On	25	6	3	0	0	5	2	4	.240	.360	.296
Runners/Scor. Pos.	11	3	1	0	0	4	2	2	.273	.364	.385

RUNS BATTED IN	From 1B	From 2B	From 3B	Scoring Position
Totals	4/107	12/57	7/24	19/81
Percentage	3.7%	21.1%	29.2%	23.5%

Loves to face: Alan Mills (.333, 1-for-3, 1 HR, 3 BB)
                Dave Otto (.429, 3-for-7, 1 2B)
                Kevin Tapani (.500, 3-for-6, 1 BB)

Hates to face: Ricky Bones (0-for-6)
                Dave Fleming (0-for-8)

Miscellaneous statistics: Ground outs-to-air outs ratio: 1.08 last season, 1.08 for career.... Grounded into 13 double plays in 80 opportunities (one per 6.2).... Drove in 5 of 11 runners from third base with less than two outs (45%).... Direction of balls hit to the outfield: 34% to left field, 29% to center, 37% to right.... Base running: Advanced from first base to third on 10 of 26 outfield singles (38%); scored from second on 9 of 14 (64%).... Made 3.32 assists per nine innings at shortstop.

Comments: The last rookie as old as Stankiewicz with as many hits in a season was Ron Washington in 1982 (122). Among other late-blooming rookies who reached triple figures in hits: Coco Laboy (145 hits in 1969) and Ed Charles (154 in 1962).... When he broke camp with the Yankees last spring at 27 years of age, he was the oldest player on any opening-day roster who had never appeared previously in a major league game. As a point of reference, he was born within a couple weeks of Jay Buhner, Ellis Burks, and Barry Bonds.... Over the last 60 years, only two Yankees drove in fewer than 25 runs in a season of at least 400 at-bats: Ruben Amaro (17 RBI in 1967) and Alvaro Espinoza (20 RBI in 1990).... Had the most hits by a Yankees rookie since Willie Randolph had 107 in 1976.... Led the Yankees with 22 infield hits.... The most often used infield combination on the Yankees lineup card started only 32 games together last season: Don Mattingly, Pat Kelly, Stankiewicz, and Charlie Hayes.... Over the past 25 years, only one Yankees shortstop has played in the All-Star Game: Bucky Dent (1980–81).... What's in a name? The most comparable rookie season may have been by an Indians war-time outfielder named Felix *Mackiewicz,* who batted .273 with 2 HR, 37 RBI, 44 BB, and 41 SO in 1945.... The 1992 Long-Name Team: 1B—Galarraga; 2B—Blankenship; 3B—Livingstone; SS—Stankiewicz; LF—McReynolds; CF—Devereaux; RF—Brunansky; C—LaValliere; SP—Kamieniecki.

Terry Steinbach

Bats Right

Oakland A's	AB	H	2B	3B	HR	RBI	BB	SO	BA	SA	OBA
Season	438	122	20	1	12	53	45	58	.279	.411	.345
vs. Left-Handers	110	33	5	0	5	18	11	15	.300	.482	.361
vs. Right-Handers	328	89	15	1	7	35	34	43	.271	.387	.340
vs. Ground-Ballers	193	59	9	1	3	22	23	31	.306	.409	.380
vs. Fly-Ballers	245	63	11	0	9	31	22	27	.257	.412	.317
Home Games	214	49	7	1	3	19	22	26	.229	.313	.301
Road Games	224	73	13	0	9	34	23	32	.326	.504	.386
Grass Fields	367	92	14	1	8	37	40	46	.251	.360	.323
Artificial Turf	71	30	6	0	4	16	5	12	.423	.676	.462
April	24	6	2	0	1	2	4	4	.250	.458	.345
May	79	19	2	0	2	5	7	17	.241	.342	.302
June	80	25	1	1	4	14	10	3	.313	.500	.396
July	85	30	9	0	2	15	6	12	.353	.529	.396
August	94	22	2	0	3	11	10	13	.234	.351	.305
Sept./Oct.	76	20	4	0	0	6	8	9	.263	.316	.329
Leading Off Inn.	87	19	2	0	2	2	8	18	.218	.310	.292
Runners On	209	64	11	1	4	45	22	24	.306	.426	.368
Bases Empty	229	58	9	0	8	8	23	34	.253	.397	.324
Runners/Scor. Pos.	97	33	5	1	3	42	16	11	.340	.505	.422
Runners On/2 Out	80	26	2	0	3	19	14	8	.325	.463	.426
Scor. Pos./2 Out	49	15	1	0	3	18	12	5	.306	.510	.443
Late-Inning Pressure	47	8	0	0	0	4	5	6	.170	.170	.250
Leading Off	10	2	0	0	0	0	3	1	.200	.200	.385
Runners On	22	4	0	0	0	4	2	4	.182	.182	.250
Runners/Scor. Pos.	11	3	0	0	0	4	2	0	.273	.273	.385

RUNS BATTED IN	From 1B	From 2B	From 3B	Scoring Position
Totals	5/177	17/73	19/45	36/118
Percentage	2.8%	23.3%	42.2%	30.5%

Loves to face: Jim Abbott (.476, 10-for-21)
                Danny Darwin (.500, 5-for-10, 3 HR)
                Chuck Finley (.400, 12-for-30, 2 HR)

Hates to face: Kevin Brown (.136, 3-for-22)
                Ben McDonald (.083, 1-for-12)
                Dave Stieb (.063, 1-for-16)

Miscellaneous statistics: Ground outs-to-air outs ratio: 1.05 last season, 1.08 for career.... Grounded into 20 double plays in 121 opportunities (one per 6.1).... Drove in 13 of 21 runners from third base with less than two outs (62%).... Direction of balls hit to the outfield: 29% to left field, 36% to center, 35% to right.... Base running: Advanced from first base to third on 11 of 37 outfield singles (30%); scored from second on 8 of 10 (80%).... Opposing base stealers: 68-for-121 (56%), 4th-lowest rate in A.L.

Comments: Five consecutive opening-day starts is the longest streak by an Athletics catcher since the club settled in Oakland. The franchise record is eight in a row, by Mickey Cochrane (1926–33).... Spent 15 days on the D.L. in April, but established a career-high 124 games behind the plate.... Athletics staff posted an ERA of 3.50 with him behind the plate, 4.24 with other catchers.... Threw out Devon White attempting to steal four times in the A.L.C.S.; White had been caught stealing only four times during the entire regular season.... Committed 10 of Oakland's major league–high 19 errors by backstops.... Career batting average of .262 (one HR every 49 AB) at the Oakland Coliseum, .281 (one HR every 35 AB) on the road.... Batting average of .282 as a catcher was 3d highest in the majors (minimum: 250 PA), behind Don Slaught (.349) and Brian Harper (.308).... More than doubled his total of walks from 1991 to 1992, even though he came to the plate fewer times last season. His average of one walk every 10.8 plate appearances last season was a career best.... Only one hit in 14 at-bats with the bases loaded last season; entered the season with a career mark of .466 (27-for-58) with the bags full.... Batting average with runners in scoring position, year by year since 1987: .250, .256, .264, .297, .285, .340.... Most similar statistical profile: Bob Boone (through 1978).

Lee Stevens   Bats Left

California Angels	AB	H	2B	3B	HR	RBI	BB	SO	BA	SA	OBA
Season	312	69	19	0	7	37	29	64	.221	.349	.288
vs. Left-Handers	44	7	2	0	0	5	4	9	.159	.205	.245
vs. Right-Handers	268	62	17	0	7	32	25	55	.231	.373	.295
vs. Ground-Ballers	146	36	10	0	3	11	13	34	.247	.377	.308
vs. Fly-Ballers	166	33	9	0	4	26	16	30	.199	.325	.270
Home Games	169	31	11	0	2	21	9	40	.183	.284	.223
Road Games	143	38	8	0	5	16	20	24	.266	.427	.358
Grass Fields	275	60	17	0	7	34	25	57	.218	.356	.282
Artificial Turf	37	9	2	0	0	3	4	7	.243	.297	.326
April	46	9	2	0	2	2	5	10	.196	.370	.275
May	53	11	2	0	1	4	5	13	.208	.302	.276
June	71	14	5	0	2	11	5	12	.197	.352	.260
July	37	6	0	0	1	3	2	6	.162	.243	.200
August	42	15	7	0	0	8	5	8	.357	.524	.417
Sept./Oct.	63	14	3	0	1	9	7	15	.222	.317	.300
Leading Off Inn.	80	19	4	0	3	3	6	20	.237	.400	.291
Runners On	118	26	8	0	3	33	16	18	.220	.364	.309
Bases Empty	194	43	11	0	4	4	13	46	.222	.340	.274
Runners/Scor. Pos.	71	18	5	0	2	29	13	13	.254	.408	.360
Runners On/2 Out	57	12	4	0	0	9	10	8	.211	.281	.328
Scor. Pos./2 Out	35	8	2	0	0	8	8	6	.229	.286	.372
Late-Inning Pressure	53	13	4	0	0	3	4	13	.245	.321	.298
Leading Off	13	2	1	0	0	0	2	5	.154	.231	.267
Runners On	16	3	1	0	0	3	2	3	.188	.250	.278
Runners/Scor. Pos.	5	0	0	0	0	3	2	1	.000	.000	.286

RUNS BATTED IN	From 1B	From 2B	From 3B	Scoring Position
Totals	6/79	10/53	14/32	24/85
Percentage	7.6%	18.9%	43.8%	28.2%

Loves to face: Tom Candiotti (.500, 2-for-4, 1 2B)
      Scott Sanderson (.462, 6-for-13, 4 SO)
Hates to face: Greg Hibbard (0-for-11)
      Tim Leary (0-for-5, 5 SO)

Miscellaneous statistics: Ground outs-to-air outs ratio: 1.42 last season, 1.02 for career.... Grounded into 4 double plays in 47 opportunities (one per 12).... Drove in 10 of 16 runners from third base with less than two outs (63%).... Direction of balls hit to the outfield: 41% to left field, 25% to center, 34% to right.... Base running: Advanced from first base to third on 3 of 12 outfield singles (25%); scored from second on 4 of 5 (80%).... Made 0.60 assists per nine innings at first base, 3d-lowest rate in A.L.

Comments: Started 78 games against right-handers last season, but only nine against left-handers.... One of eight different starting first basemen for the Angels last season. Only Oakland and his new team, Montreal, used that many. "Wally World" seems like ages ago.... The Angels had the most unsettled infield in the league last season; their most common infield combination (Stevens, Rene Gonzales, Gary DiSarcina, and Gary Gaetti) started together only 24 times.... Career total of 618 at-bats is the most of any player in the majors in 1992 who has never hit a triple. Next on the list are Bill Gullickson (576) and David Segui (524).... One hit (a home run) in 17 career at-bats with runners in scoring position in Late-Inning Pressure Situations.... One of five selections made by the Angels in the first round of the 1986 June draft. Aside from their own pick, they were awarded four more as compensation for losing Juan Beniquez and Al Holland—both Type A free agents, if you can believe that. Two of those five selections (Daryl Green and Terry Carr) have never played in the majors; three are now playing for other clubs: Stevens (Expos), Roberto Hernandez (White Sox), and Mike Fetters (Brewers). We hate these "Who Was Still Available" lists, but what the hell—California could have chosen Todd Zeile, Bo Jackson, Eric Anthony, Hal Morris, and Kevin Tapani, just to name a few.... Career batting averages: .285 at Triple-A, .225 one level higher.

Franklin Stubbs   Bats Left

Milwaukee Brewers	AB	H	2B	3B	HR	RBI	BB	SO	BA	SA	OBA
Season	288	66	11	1	9	42	27	68	.229	.368	.297
vs. Left-Handers	43	11	1	1	1	10	0	12	.256	.395	.256
vs. Right-Handers	245	55	10	0	8	32	27	56	.224	.363	.303
vs. Ground-Ballers	137	39	8	0	4	21	12	22	.285	.431	.347
vs. Fly-Ballers	151	27	3	1	5	21	15	46	.179	.311	.251
Home Games	101	20	1	0	3	12	9	25	.198	.297	.268
Road Games	187	46	10	1	6	30	18	43	.246	.406	.312
Grass Fields	228	51	6	0	9	33	22	56	.224	.368	.294
Artificial Turf	60	15	5	1	0	9	5	12	.250	.367	.308
April	60	15	3	1	1	10	4	15	.250	.383	.297
May	74	12	2	0	5	12	13	17	.162	.392	.295
June	44	11	2	0	0	6	5	7	.250	.295	.327
July	43	10	1	0	2	6	0	15	.233	.395	.233
August	36	9	3	0	0	6	3	7	.250	.333	.308
Sept./Oct.	31	9	0	0	1	2	2	7	.290	.387	.324
Leading Off Inn.	68	13	1	0	3	3	2	16	.191	.338	.214
Runners On	118	35	7	1	4	37	21	24	.297	.475	.400
Bases Empty	170	31	4	0	5	5	6	44	.182	.294	.215
Runners/Scor. Pos.	77	22	4	1	2	32	16	14	.286	.442	.404
Runners On/2 Out	50	9	1	1	1	11	13	13	.180	.300	.349
Scor. Pos./2 Out	37	6	1	1	0	9	12	9	.162	.243	.367
Late-Inning Pressure	58	14	2	0	3	11	4	10	.241	.431	.290
Leading Off	9	3	0	0	1	1	0	3	.333	.667	.333
Runners On	25	7	2	0	1	9	4	2	.280	.480	.379
Runners/Scor. Pos.	15	5	2	0	1	9	4	2	.333	.667	.474

RUNS BATTED IN	From 1B	From 2B	From 3B	Scoring Position
Totals	6/77	12/62	15/33	27/95
Percentage	7.8%	19.4%	45.5%	28.4%

Loves to face: David Cone (.375, 6-for-16, 3 2B, 1 HR)
      Scott Sanderson (.364, 8-for-22, 2 HR)
      Kevin Tapani (.400, 6-for-15, 3 2B)
Hates to face: Rick Aguilera (.056, 1-for-18)
      Ron Darling (.111, 4-for-36, 1 HR, 6 BB, 19 SO)
      Alex Fernandez (0-for-11, 7 SO)

Miscellaneous statistics: Ground outs-to-air outs ratio: 0.76 last season, 0.71 for career.... Grounded into 2 double plays in 56 opportunities (one per 28).... Drove in 11 of 15 runners from third base with less than two outs (73%).... Direction of balls hit to the outfield: 21% to left field, 23% to center, 56% to right.... Base running: Advanced from first base to third on 7 of 11 outfield singles (64%), 5th-highest rate in majors; scored from second on 3 of 3 (100%).... Made 1.03 assists per nine innings at first base, highest rate in majors.

Comments: Sure has some interesting favorite pitchers, hasn't he?...Batted .219 as a first baseman, the lowest average in the majors last season (minimum: 250 PA).... Started only two double plays in 68 games at first base; the American League average for first basemen is one every 14 games.... Started only four games at first base after August 1.... Started 63 of the 120 games in which the Brewers faced right-handed starters, but only 9 of 42 against left-handers.... Batting average was higher against left-handers than vs. right-handers for the 2d consecutive season. Career figures: .227 vs. LHP, .233 vs. RHP.... Phil Garner, take note: The difference between his career averages against ground-ball pitchers (.276) and fly-ball pitchers (.205) is far greater than vs. left- and right-handers.... The only active player who has hit at least 10 more homers during his career against ground-ball pitchers (56) than he has against fly-ball pitchers (46).... Career batting average is .215 on grass fields, .266 on artificial turf.... Has stolen between 10 and 20 bases in each of the last three years.... Provided a seamless transition from Greg Brock; now turns the reins over to Kevin Reimer. Inspired casting, wouldn't you say?...This concludes our first annual one-page salute to marginal first basemen. Watch for next year's historical retrospective, including Gail Harris/Chuck Harrison and Rocky Nelson/Dick Nen.

B.J. Surhoff
Bats Left

Milwaukee Brewers	AB	H	2B	3B	HR	RBI	BB	SO	BA	SA	OBA
Season	480	121	19	1	4	62	46	41	.252	.321	.314
vs. Left-Handers	126	34	3	1	2	20	11	17	.270	.357	.329
vs. Right-Handers	354	87	16	0	2	42	35	24	.246	.308	.309
vs. Ground-Ballers	221	56	10	0	1	32	15	16	.253	.312	.299
vs. Fly-Ballers	259	65	9	1	3	30	31	25	.251	.328	.327
Home Games	243	68	8	0	3	29	27	20	.280	.350	.349
Road Games	237	53	11	1	1	33	19	21	.224	.291	.278
Grass Fields	403	105	15	1	4	46	40	32	.261	.333	.326
Artificial Turf	77	16	4	0	0	16	6	9	.208	.260	.253
April	66	9	0	0	1	10	4	5	.136	.182	.181
May	65	14	2	0	1	12	2	5	.215	.292	.235
June	95	31	6	0	1	13	7	5	.326	.421	.371
July	86	24	4	0	1	6	9	4	.279	.360	.340
August	78	19	2	0	0	9	12	13	.244	.269	.348
Sept./Oct.	90	24	5	1	0	12	12	9	.267	.344	.346
Leading Off Inn.	113	28	5	0	0	0	11	11	.248	.292	.315
Runners On	218	61	10	1	2	60	24	15	.280	.362	.343
Bases Empty	262	60	9	0	2	2	22	26	.229	.286	.289
Runners/Scor. Pos.	134	40	7	0	2	57	18	7	.299	.396	.366
Runners On/2 Out	94	22	5	1	1	20	13	4	.234	.340	.333
Scor. Pos./2 Out	67	14	3	0	1	17	10	2	.209	.299	.321
Late-Inning Pressure	79	18	2	0	2	12	8	12	.228	.329	.295
Leading Off	16	3	0	0	0	0	1	3	.188	.188	.235
Runners On	41	10	1	0	1	11	5	5	.244	.341	.319
Runners/Scor. Pos.	24	5	1	0	1	11	3	1	.208	.375	.286

RUNS BATTED IN	From 1B	From 2B	From 3B	Scoring Position
Totals	6/137	22/103	30/66	52/169
Percentage	4.4%	21.4%	45.5%	30.8%

Loves to face: Jim Abbott (.583, 7-for-12)
Gary Wayne (.429, 3-for-7, 1 2B, 1 HR, 3 BB)
Bobby Witt (.385, 15-for-39, 2 HR)

Hates to face: Erik Hanson (.147, 5-for-34, 0 BB)
Mike Moore (.121, 4-for-33, 4 BB)
Nolan Ryan (.059, 1-for-17)

Miscellaneous statistics: Ground outs-to-air outs ratio: 1.25 last season, 1.32 for career.... Grounded into 9 double plays in 94 opportunities (one per 10).... Drove in 24 of 34 runners from third base with less than two outs (71%).... Direction of balls hit to the outfield: 35% to left field, 37% to center, 28% to right.... Base running: Advanced from first base to third on 7 of 33 outfield singles (21%); scored from second on 9 of 20 (45%).... Opposing base stealers: 57-for-96 (59%), 5th-lowest rate in A.L.

Comments: Stole 11 bases as a catcher, tying Darren Daulton for the major league lead.... Brewers catchers combined for 15 stolen bases last season, more than one-third of the league total. All other A.L. catchers combined for 28 steals.... Catchers were successful in only 47 percent of their stolen-base attempts, the only position in the league below 50 percent.... The Brewers' three other starting catchers (Andy Allanson, Tim McIntosh, and Dave Nilsson) all spent time on the disabled list last season.... Opponents scored only one run in the 43⅔ innings in which Cal Eldred and Surhoff were battery-mates. Eldred's ERA was 3.02 in 56⅔ innings with other receivers.... Seven of his 17 go-ahead RBIs came after the sixth inning. Only two A.L. players had more go-ahead RBIs from the 7th inning on: Tom Brunansky and Rickey Henderson (8 each).... Career average of .217 with no home runs and only one RBI in 46 at-bats as a pinch hitter.... One of four players active in the majors in 1992 who, at some time in his big league career, has caught and played every infield and outfield position. The others: Steve Lyons, Jose Oquendo, and Bill Pecota (who have all pitched as well; Surhoff hasn't—yet).... Most games played by players known by their initials: U.L. Washington, 907; J.C. Martin, 905; Surhoff, 797; R.J. Reynolds, 786; J.R. Richard, 239. Media survey: Which organization is most likely to report that B.J. "broke the all-time record" when he passes U.L. this summer? (Hint: It will probably conclude, "I did not know that.")

Dale Sveum
Bats Left and Right

Phillies/White Sox	AB	H	2B	3B	HR	RBI	BB	SO	BA	SA	OBA
Season	249	49	13	0	4	28	28	68	.197	.297	.273
vs. Left-Handers	69	14	5	0	0	5	15	24	.203	.275	.345
vs. Right-Handers	180	35	8	0	4	23	13	44	.194	.306	.242
vs. Ground-Ballers	107	21	8	0	1	9	17	25	.196	.299	.299
vs. Fly-Ballers	142	28	5	0	3	19	11	43	.197	.296	.252
Home Games	119	19	5	0	1	13	16	30	.160	.227	.255
Road Games	130	30	8	0	3	15	12	38	.231	.362	.290
Grass Fields	139	36	7	0	4	22	12	30	.259	.396	.310
Artificial Turf	110	13	6	0	0	6	16	38	.118	.173	.228
April	20	4	0	0	0	3	2	5	.200	.200	.261
May	40	6	2	0	0	7	2	15	.150	.200	.186
June	41	5	2	0	0	1	12	12	.122	.171	.321
July	33	9	0	0	2	5	0	7	.273	.455	.273
August	45	10	3	0	1	6	3	10	.222	.356	.265
Sept./Oct.	70	15	6	0	1	6	9	19	.214	.343	.296
Leading Off Inn.	52	11	4	0	1	1	7	11	.212	.346	.305
Runners On	116	27	7	0	2	26	13	30	.233	.345	.299
Bases Empty	133	22	6	0	2	2	15	38	.165	.256	.250
Runners/Scor. Pos.	68	14	5	0	1	24	7	20	.206	.324	.262
Runners On/2 Out	52	14	4	0	1	12	6	11	.269	.404	.345
Scor. Pos./2 Out	35	9	3	0	1	12	4	7	.257	.429	.333
Late-Inning Pressure	51	13	2	0	1	4	7	19	.255	.353	.345
Leading Off	14	3	0	0	0	0	3	5	.214	.214	.353
Runners On	23	7	2	0	0	3	1	7	.304	.391	.333
Runners/Scor. Pos.	13	2	1	0	0	3	1	5	.154	.231	.214

RUNS BATTED IN	From 1B	From 2B	From 3B	Scoring Position
Totals	1/83	9/54	14/33	23/87
Percentage	1.2%	16.7%	42.4%	26.4%

Loves to face: Eric Bell (.429, 3-for-7, 2 HR, 3 BB)
Bill Gullickson (.444, 4-for-9, 2 HR)
Mike Henneman (.556, 5-for-9, 1 HR)

Hates to face: Luis Aquino (0-for-7, 4 SO)
Roger Clemens (.083, 2-for-24, 2 BB, 12 SO)
Jack Morris (.111, 3-for-27, 1 2B, 1 HR)

Miscellaneous statistics: Ground outs-to-air outs ratio: 0.91 last season, 1.00 for career.... Grounded into 6 double plays in 58 opportunities (one per 10).... Drove in 9 of 16 runners from third base with less than two outs (56%).... Direction of balls hit to the outfield: 27% to left field, 39% to center, 35% to right batting left-handed; 43% to left field, 22% to center, 35% to right batting right-handed.... Base running: Advanced from first base to third on 3 of 7 outfield singles (43%); scored from second on 1 of 1 (100%).... Made 3.10 assists per nine innings at shortstop.

Comments: Started 16 games against left-handed pitchers last season: 15 with the Phillies, but only one after joining the White Sox in early August.... Batted under .200 in a season of at least 100 at-bats in both 1990 and 1992. No active player has had three such seasons; the last to do it three times were Steve Jeltz and Rick Dempsey.... His pinch double off Omar Olivares last June snapped a streak of 23 consecutive hitless at-bats as a pinch hitter, dating back to 1987. His career batting average of .059 (2-for-34) as a pinch hitter is the lowest of any active player (minimum: 25 AB).... Was 1-for-19 with 10 strikeouts as a pinch hitter last season.... Career batting average is .248 on grass fields, .186 on artificial turf.... Paul Molitor is the only active player to have played at least 50 games at all four infield positions during his career. With his limited action at first base last season, Sveum became the ninth active player to reach the more modest total of 10 games at each. The list: Molitor, Sveum, Tom Foley, Bill Pecota, Greg Litton, Jose Oquendo, Dave Anderson, Mike Sharperson, and Rene Gonzales.... Hit 25 home runs and drove in 95 runs as a 23-year-old Brewers sophomore in 1987. He has hit 18 home runs since then, and hasn't driven in more than 51 runs in any season since.... Of the 53 players who hit at least 25 home runs in 1987 (an all-time high), fewer than half ever did so again.

Danny Tartabull

Bats Right

New York Yankees	AB	H	2B	3B	HR	RBI	BB	SO	BA	SA	OBA
Season	421	112	19	0	25	85	103	115	.266	.489	.409
vs. Left-Handers	119	34	6	0	11	35	50	29	.286	.613	.494
vs. Right-Handers	302	78	13	0	14	50	53	86	.258	.440	.368
vs. Ground-Ballers	177	46	6	0	8	29	39	50	.260	.429	.390
vs. Fly-Ballers	244	66	13	0	17	56	64	65	.270	.533	.422
Home Games	204	59	10	0	11	48	51	55	.289	.500	.428
Road Games	217	53	9	0	14	37	52	60	.244	.479	.390
Grass Fields	369	103	18	0	22	76	94	103	.279	.507	.424
Artificial Turf	52	9	1	0	3	9	9	12	.173	.365	.295
April	39	12	3	0	1	10	9	14	.308	.462	.438
May	73	19	2	0	3	11	17	23	.260	.411	.396
June	74	16	3	0	2	10	25	22	.216	.338	.414
July	69	15	3	0	8	16	18	20	.217	.609	.375
August	62	18	2	0	5	16	16	15	.290	.565	.436
Sept./Oct.	104	32	6	0	6	22	18	21	.308	.538	.410
Leading Off Inn.	109	23	5	0	3	3	18	32	.211	.339	.323
Runners On	190	56	11	0	15	75	55	48	.295	.589	.449
Bases Empty	231	56	8	0	10	10	48	67	.242	.407	.373
Runners/Scor. Pos.	118	35	7	0	12	67	42	30	.297	.661	.475
Runners On/2 Out	85	22	4	0	6	29	32	22	.259	.518	.462
Scor. Pos./2 Out	52	13	3	0	4	24	24	11	.250	.538	.487
Late-Inning Pressure	72	19	5	0	2	11	13	17	.264	.417	.376
Leading Off	21	5	1	0	0	0	5	7	.238	.286	.385
Runners On	27	7	2	0	2	11	5	4	.259	.556	.375
Runners/Scor. Pos.	19	6	2	0	2	11	4	3	.316	.737	.435

RUNS BATTED IN	From 1B	From 2B	From 3B	Scoring Position
Totals	14/125	23/84	23/52	46/136
Percentage	11.2%	27.4%	44.2%	33.8%

Loves to face: Mark Guthrie (.545, 6-for-11, 2 HR, 6 BB)
Jaime Navarro (.643, 9-for-14, 3 HR, 3 SO)
Dave Stewart (.417, 15-for-36, 5 HR)

Hates to face: Roger Clemens (.167, 6-for-36)
Brian Holman (.160, 4-for-25)
Eric Plunk (.053, 1-for-19, 1 2B, 3 BB)

Miscellaneous statistics: Ground outs-to-air outs ratio: 1.60 last season, 1.13 for career.... Grounded into 7 double plays in 83 opportunities (one per 12).... Drove in 16 of 29 runners from third base with less than two outs (55%).... Direction of balls hit to the outfield: 29% to left field, 32% to center, 39% to right.... Base running: Advanced from first base to third on 8 of 35 outfield singles (23%); scored from second on 12 of 15 (80%).... Made 2.01 putouts per nine innings in right field, 3d-lowest rate in A.L.

Comments: Drove in 47 runs over a 48-game span (June 27–Sept. 12).... Faced left-handed pitchers 56 times with runners in scoring position, drawing 28 walks (half of them intentional). He drove in 31 runs in the remaining 28 at-bats, with 10 hits—*eight of which were home runs*.... Led the majors with 11 opposite-field home runs.... Came within one RBI of leading the Yankees in both homers and RBIs. The last player to lead in both categories in his first season with the Yankees was Babe Ruth (1920).... No one had led the Yankees in homers while playing fewer than 130 games since 1949, when Tommy Henrich hit a team-high 24 home runs in 115 games. (Tartabull played 123 games.) ... The Yankees have had a different home run leader in each of the last six seasons, the team's longest streak since its first eight years in New York (1903–10). Annual club leaders since 1987: Pagliarulo, Clark, Mattingly, Barfield, Nokes, and Tartabull.... Average of one walk every 5.1 plate appearances was the highest rate in A.L. last season.... An exceptional late-season hitter; career RBIs by month: April—71; May—84; June—97; July—103; August—126; September—139. His career batting average through the end of August is .280; from September 1 on, it's .301.... Became only the second player in major league history to have a 25–home-run season for three different clubs before turning 30. The first: Dave Kingman.

Mickey Tettleton

Bats Left and Right

Detroit Tigers	AB	H	2B	3B	HR	RBI	BB	SO	BA	SA	OBA
Season	525	125	25	0	32	83	122	137	.238	.469	.379
vs. Left-Handers	135	37	8	0	8	23	22	28	.274	.511	.373
vs. Right-Handers	390	88	17	0	24	60	100	109	.226	.454	.381
vs. Ground-Ballers	244	57	12	0	15	42	51	60	.234	.467	.362
vs. Fly-Ballers	281	68	13	0	17	41	71	77	.242	.470	.393
Home Games	255	69	16	0	18	41	60	72	.271	.545	.408
Road Games	270	56	9	0	14	42	62	65	.207	.396	.352
Grass Fields	447	108	19	0	29	73	108	125	.242	.479	.386
Artificial Turf	78	17	6	0	3	10	14	12	.218	.410	.337
April	71	19	4	0	7	15	16	17	.268	.620	.402
May	95	19	3	0	3	10	12	19	.200	.326	.287
June	102	29	6	0	8	24	18	33	.284	.578	.392
July	89	22	4	0	4	9	24	26	.247	.427	.400
August	84	15	4	0	4	8	25	17	.179	.369	.364
Sept./Oct.	84	21	4	0	6	17	27	25	.250	.512	.430
Leading Off Inn.	127	35	8	0	9	9	21	29	.276	.551	.383
Runners On	236	53	9	0	13	64	66	65	.225	.428	.386
Bases Empty	289	72	16	0	19	19	56	72	.249	.502	.373
Runners/Scor. Pos.	134	29	7	0	10	58	44	35	.216	.493	.397
Runners On/2 Out	112	19	2	0	5	22	34	33	.170	.321	.363
Scor. Pos./2 Out	71	15	2	0	5	22	23	19	.211	.451	.404
Late-Inning Pressure	71	18	2	0	4	7	14	18	.254	.451	.376
Leading Off	23	5	1	0	1	1	4	7	.217	.391	.333
Runners On	28	8	0	0	2	5	7	7	.286	.500	.429
Runners/Scor. Pos.	10	3	0	0	1	3	6	3	.300	.600	.563

RUNS BATTED IN	From 1B	From 2B	From 3B	Scoring Position
Totals	13/192	19/113	19/55	38/168
Percentage	6.8%	16.8%	34.5%	22.6%

Loves to face: Scott Erickson (.444, 8-for-18)
Joe Hesketh (.462, 6-for-13, 2 2B, 2 HR)
Charles Nagy (.313, 5-for-16, 3 HR)

Hates to face: Bert Blyleven (.048, 1-for-21, 1 3B, 3 BB)
Erik Hanson (0-for-13, 8 SO)
Ron Robinson (0-for-10)

Miscellaneous statistics: Ground outs-to-air outs ratio: 0.58 last season, 1.00 for career.... Grounded into 5 double plays in 121 opportunities (one per 24).... Drove in 16 of 31 runners from third base with less than two outs (52%).... Direction of balls hit to the outfield: 18% to left field, 25% to center, 57% to right batting left-handed; 62% to left field, 23% to center, 15% to right batting right-handed.... Base running: Advanced from first base to third on 6 of 36 outfield singles (17%); scored from second on 7 of 17 (41%), 4th lowest in A.L.... Opposing base stealers: 74-for-113 (65%).

Comments: Technically, he hit only 22 home runs as a catcher; he added nine as a DH and one as on outfielder. But if we call him a catcher (and, after all, he made 110 of his 151 starts at that position), then Tettleton became only the third catcher ever to post consecutive 30-HR seasons. The others: Rudy York (1937–38) and Roy Campanella (1950–51).... Career average of one walk every 6.4 plate appearances is 4th highest among active players (minimum: 1000 PA), behind Frank Thomas (5.4), Randy Milligan (5.8), and Rickey Henderson (6.4).... First Detroit player to lead the league in walks since Eddie Yost in 1960.... Fifth player in major league history with at least 120 walks and 120 strikeouts in the same season; all did it in the past 25 years. The others: Jim Wynn (1969), Frank Howard (1970), Mike Schmidt (1983), and Jack Clark (1987 and 1989).... Became the third Detroit catcher in the last 45 years to lead the league in fielding percentage, joining Bill Freehan and Gus Triandos.... He and Jay Buhner are co-winners of the Pete Runnels Memorial Stop Sign for their 0-for-6 marks on stolen-base attempts last season. (Runnels went 0-for-10 in 1952.) ... Combined with Chad Kreuter to give Detroit the first pair of switch-hitting catchers since Houston paired Mark Bailey with Alan Ashby for four years in the mid-1980s. The last pair before that was Wally Schang and Bubbles Hargrave of the 1926 St. Louis Browns.

Frank Thomas
Bats Right

Chicago White Sox	AB	H	2B	3B	HR	RBI	BB	SO	BA	SA	OBA
Season	573	185	46	2	24	115	122	88	.323	.536	.439
vs. Left-Handers	140	50	15	1	8	26	28	20	.357	.650	.456
vs. Right-Handers	433	135	31	1	16	89	94	68	.312	.499	.433
vs. Ground-Ballers	267	93	22	1	13	62	70	36	.348	.584	.475
vs. Fly-Ballers	306	92	24	1	11	53	52	52	.301	.493	.404
Home Games	292	89	23	2	10	54	64	45	.305	.500	.430
Road Games	281	96	23	0	14	61	58	43	.342	.573	.448
Grass Fields	483	157	37	2	22	101	109	74	.325	.547	.448
Artificial Turf	90	28	9	0	2	14	13	14	.311	.478	.389
April	62	13	4	1	1	7	19	17	.210	.355	.398
May	95	32	7	0	6	22	23	17	.337	.600	.458
June	100	31	6	1	4	21	23	13	.310	.510	.437
July	99	35	7	0	5	18	20	9	.354	.576	.459
August	98	36	5	0	6	22	20	10	.367	.602	.475
Sept./Oct.	119	38	17	0	2	25	17	22	.319	.513	.400
Leading Off Inn.	110	37	10	0	6	6	18	13	.336	.591	.438
Runners On	287	97	25	2	8	99	69	47	.338	.523	.454
Bases Empty	286	88	21	0	16	16	53	41	.308	.549	.423
Runners/Scor. Pos.	174	54	13	0	5	84	45	30	.310	.471	.430
Runners On/2 Out	101	30	6	2	4	30	32	21	.297	.515	.466
Scor. Pos./2 Out	69	19	3	0	4	26	24	15	.275	.493	.462
Late-Inning Pressure	85	23	4	0	3	19	9	12	.271	.424	.344
Leading Off	21	5	0	0	1	1	0	2	.238	.381	.273
Runners On	39	13	3	0	1	17	7	6	.308	.462	.404
Runners/Scor. Pos.	24	9	3	0	1	17	4	3	.375	.625	.448

RUNS BATTED IN	From 1B	From 2B	From 3B	Scoring Position
Totals	18/218	26/132	47/84	73/216
Percentage	8.3%	19.7%	56.0%	33.8%

Loves to face: Joe Hesketh (.833, 5-for-6, 2 2B, 2 HR, 1 SO)
Mark Langston (.444, 8-for-18, 2 HR, 9 BB)
Mike Mussina (.625, 10-for-16, 3 HR)

Hates to face: Greg A. Harris (.077, 1-for-13, 2 BB)
Nolan Ryan (0-for-12, 11 SO)
Frank Viola (.182, 2-for-11)

Miscellaneous statistics: Ground outs-to-air outs ratio: 0.82 last season, 0.92 for career.... Grounded into 19 double plays in 172 opportunities (one per 9.1).... Drove in 37 of 54 runners from third base with less than two outs (69%).... Direction of balls hit to the outfield: 33% to left field, 29% to center, 37% to right.... Base running: Advanced from first base to third on 10 of 43 outfield singles (23%); scored from second on 23 of 26 (88%).... Made 0.59 assists per nine innings at first base, 2d-lowest rate in A.L.

Comments: Career on-base percentage is .447, 3d highest among all players in major league history after their third season, behind only Ted Williams (.474) and Shoeless Joe Jackson (.449).... In three seasons in the majors, he's never gone more than eight consecutive plate appearances without reaching base safely (on a hit, walk, or hit by pitch).... Among active players with at least 1000 at-bats, Thomas has the highest career slugging and on-base averages, by large margins, over Fred McGriff (.542 to .528) and Wade Boggs (.447 to .428), respectively.... The only players in major league history above him in both categories: Lou Gehrig, Babe Ruth, and Ted Williams.... First player since Norm Cash in 1961 (and the eighth in major league history) to reach the 1000-AB mark with at least 50 home runs and a .300 batting average. The others: Chuck Klein, Wally Berger, Bob Johnson, Joe DiMaggio, Rudy York, and Frank Robinson.... Second White Sox player to lead A.L. in extra-base hits since Shoeless Joe did it in 1916. The other: Dick Allen (tied Bobby Murcer in 1972).... Over the last 40 years, only two players have had a higher two-year total of walks than Thomas in 1991 and 1992 (260): Harmon Killebrew (273, 1969–70) and Mickey Mantle (275, 1957–58).... Enters 1993 with 304 walks in 378 games. The most walks after 400 games in the majors: Max Bishop, 327.... His batting average against left-handers has declined in each of the past two seasons—*all the way down to .357*. Year by year: .408, .376, .357.

Dickie Thon
Bats Right

Texas Rangers	AB	H	2B	3B	HR	RBI	BB	SO	BA	SA	OBA
Season	275	68	15	3	4	37	20	40	.247	.367	.293
vs. Left-Handers	99	29	7	2	3	17	11	13	.293	.495	.360
vs. Right-Handers	176	39	8	1	1	20	9	27	.222	.295	.254
vs. Ground-Ballers	124	32	9	2	0	17	10	20	.258	.363	.307
vs. Fly-Ballers	151	36	6	1	4	20	10	20	.238	.371	.282
Home Games	142	37	9	3	2	18	11	24	.261	.408	.306
Road Games	133	31	6	0	2	19	9	16	.233	.323	.280
Grass Fields	234	55	10	3	3	29	17	36	.235	.342	.281
Artificial Turf	41	13	5	0	1	8	3	4	.317	.512	.364
April	66	17	5	0	0	7	7	8	.258	.333	.329
May	72	16	1	1	2	13	3	9	.222	.347	.247
June	75	18	5	0	2	9	8	10	.240	.387	.310
July	52	15	3	2	0	7	1	9	.288	.423	.296
August	7	1	1	0	0	1	1	3	.143	.286	.222
Sept./Oct.	3	1	0	0	0	0	0	1	.333	.333	.333
Leading Off Inn.	65	15	1	0	2	2	4	12	.231	.338	.275
Runners On	121	32	9	2	2	35	11	19	.264	.421	.314
Bases Empty	154	36	6	1	2	2	9	21	.234	.325	.276
Runners/Scor. Pos.	73	21	7	0	0	28	8	15	.288	.384	.337
Runners On/2 Out	52	13	4	0	1	10	7	11	.250	.385	.339
Scor. Pos./2 Out	35	9	3	0	0	8	6	10	.257	.343	.366
Late-Inning Pressure	36	7	1	1	0	3	2	6	.194	.278	.231
Leading Off	12	2	0	0	0	0	0	4	.167	.167	.167
Runners On	15	3	1	1	0	3	2	2	.200	.400	.278
Runners/Scor. Pos.	6	1	1	0	0	2	1	2	.167	.333	.250

RUNS BATTED IN	From 1B	From 2B	From 3B	Scoring Position
Totals	6/90	12/58	15/35	27/93
Percentage	6.7%	20.7%	42.9%	29.0%

Loves to face: Mark Davis (.412, 7-for-17, 2 HR)
Neal Heaton (.389, 7-for-18, 2 HR)
Derek Lilliquist (.833, 5-for-6, 3 2B)

Hates to face: Brian Barnes (.125, 2-for-16)
Mark Langston (.067, 1-for-15, 1 2B)
Scott Scudder (0-for-10)

Miscellaneous statistics: Ground outs-to-air outs ratio: 1.08 last season, 1.11 for career.... Grounded into 2 double plays in 64 opportunities (one per 32).... Drove in 10 of 17 runners from third base with less than two outs (59%).... Direction of balls hit to the outfield: 43% to left field, 31% to center, 27% to right.... Base running: Advanced from first base to third on 1 of 5 outfield singles (20%); scored from second on 11 of 13 (85%).... Made 2.98 assists per nine innings at shortstop.

Comments: Hasn't been hit by a pitch in the last two seasons, and has been hit only four times in 843 games since coming back from that severe beaning by Mike Torrez in 1984. Has been hit a total of nine times in 1302 career games; the only other active players with fewer than 10 HBPs in more than 1300 games: Dave Bergman, Rance Mulliniks, and Pete O'Brien.... The only major leaguer to increase his slugging percentage despite a declining batting average in each of the last two seasons. Only one player in major league history, excluding pitchers, has done that in three straight seasons: Tim McCarver (1964–66).... Committed 15 of the Rangers' 30 errors at shortstop last season. The only A.L. team whose shortstops erred more often: Cleveland (33).... Lack of experience at other positions could hinder his chances of landing a job after being released by the Rangers last fall. Since 1983, Thon has played 953 games at shortstop, two at second base, and one at third base.... He certainly wouldn't turn down a chance to play for Florida or Colorado; four of the five major league teams he has played for are expansion franchises (Angels, Astros, Padres, and Rangers).... Colorado and Florida will be the 11th and 12th expansion teams in modern major league history; the following players have played for five of the previous 10: Floyd Bannister, Juan Beniquez, Thad Bosley, Tommy Davis, Mike Marshall (the pitcher), Bob McClure (who signed a minor league contract with the Marlins over the winter), Willie Montanez, and Leon ("Don't Call Me Bip") Roberts.

Dave Valle

Bats Right

Seattle Mariners	AB	H	2B	3B	HR	RBI	BB	SO	BA	SA	OBA
Season	367	88	16	1	9	30	27	58	.240	.362	.305
vs. Left-Handers	120	34	4	0	4	11	11	16	.283	.417	.348
vs. Right-Handers	247	54	12	1	5	19	16	42	.219	.336	.284
vs. Ground-Ballers	182	53	12	0	4	17	11	25	.291	.423	.340
vs. Fly-Ballers	185	35	4	1	5	13	16	33	.189	.303	.272
Home Games	198	49	14	0	7	19	12	33	.247	.424	.307
Road Games	169	39	2	1	2	11	15	25	.231	.290	.303
Grass Fields	135	28	2	1	1	9	14	24	.207	.259	.289
Artificial Turf	232	60	14	0	8	21	13	34	.259	.422	.315
April	55	15	1	0	1	4	4	16	.273	.345	.328
May	35	10	4	0	1	4	1	4	.286	.486	.324
June	87	21	5	0	4	9	7	11	.241	.437	.313
July	65	11	0	1	1	2	3	9	.169	.246	.206
August	70	21	5	0	1	9	11	12	.300	.414	.402
Sept./Oct.	55	10	1	0	1	2	1	6	.182	.255	.237
Leading Off Inn.	102	23	7	0	3	3	6	10	.225	.382	.295
Runners On	153	32	5	0	1	22	11	26	.209	.261	.269
Bases Empty	214	56	11	1	8	8	16	32	.262	.435	.331
Runners/Scor. Pos.	87	17	5	0	0	20	5	16	.195	.253	.245
Runners On/2 Out	66	12	1	0	0	8	6	10	.182	.197	.250
Scor. Pos./2 Out	39	7	1	0	0	8	4	6	.179	.205	.256
Late-Inning Pressure	44	10	0	0	0	3	3	8	.227	.227	.292
Leading Off	13	0	0	0	0	0	1	2	.000	.000	.133
Runners On	19	6	0	0	0	3	1	2	.316	.316	.350
Runners/Scor. Pos.	11	3	0	0	0	3	0	1	.273	.273	.273

RUNS BATTED IN	From 1B	From 2B	From 3B	Scoring Position
Totals	1/108	11/75	9/30	20/105
Percentage	0.9%	14.7%	30.0%	19.0%

Loves to face: Charlie Leibrandt (.385, 10-for-26)
Charles Nagy (.417, 5-for-12, 1 HR)
Frank Viola (.400, 8-for-20, 1 HR)

Hates to face: Dennis Eckersley (0-for-8)
Tom Gordon (0-for-10, 6 SO)
Ted Higuera (.080, 2-for-25, 3 BB)

Miscellaneous statistics: Ground outs-to-air outs ratio: 1.27 last season, 1.39 for career.... Grounded into 7 double plays in 74 opportunities (one per 11).... Drove in 5 of 10 runners from third base with less than two outs (50%).... Direction of balls hit to the outfield: 34% to left field, 26% to center, 40% to right.... Base running: Advanced from first base to third on 3 of 14 outfield singles (21%); scored from second on 4 of 8 (50%).... Opposing base stealers: 84-for-124 (68%).

Comments: Six consecutive opening-day starts is the longest current streak by any A.L. catcher.... Mariners pitchers compiled a 4.75 ERA for Valle last season, faring much better with Lance Parrish behind the plate (3.50).... Hit the majority of his homers at the Kingdome last season, after hitting only two of 22 there over the previous three years.... Last August was the first month in which he hit .300 or better since May 1989.... One of only three major leaguers to drive in fewer than 20 percent of runners from scoring position in each of the last two seasons (minimum: 75 opportunities each). The others: Rob Deer and Pete Incaviglia.... Has batted .179 with runners in scoring position over the past two years.... One of three players whose RBI total has declined in each of the last five seasons. The others: Brian Downing (6 years), and Pat Tabler (5).... Both he and Jeff Huson have increased their home-run total while their RBI total declined in each of the last two seasons. No player in major league history has done that in three consecutive years.... Has compiled a higher batting average vs. ground-ball pitchers than vs. fly-ballers in each of the past eight seasons. (Has hit below .200 vs. fly-ball pitchers in each of the last three.)... Career batting-average breakdowns: .256 vs. ground-ball pitchers, .208 vs. fly-ball pitchers; .258 vs. left-handers, .214 vs. right-handers.

Greg Vaughn

Bats Right

Milwaukee Brewers	AB	H	2B	3B	HR	RBI	BB	SO	BA	SA	OBA
Season	501	114	18	2	23	78	60	123	.228	.409	.313
vs. Left-Handers	105	26	4	1	6	23	21	19	.248	.476	.370
vs. Right-Handers	396	88	14	1	17	55	39	104	.222	.391	.297
vs. Ground-Ballers	224	51	7	1	6	29	30	53	.228	.348	.319
vs. Fly-Ballers	277	63	11	1	17	49	30	70	.227	.458	.309
Home Games	244	57	8	1	11	42	35	58	.234	.410	.330
Road Games	257	57	10	1	12	36	25	65	.222	.409	.297
Grass Fields	429	99	14	2	20	69	52	108	.231	.413	.315
Artificial Turf	72	15	4	0	3	9	8	15	.208	.389	.305
April	60	16	3	1	4	10	9	13	.267	.550	.357
May	102	16	3	0	5	15	14	26	.157	.333	.259
June	52	8	1	0	1	9	5	12	.154	.231	.237
July	99	25	5	1	3	10	4	29	.253	.414	.288
August	89	19	1	0	4	11	12	22	.213	.360	.308
Sept./Oct.	99	30	5	0	6	23	16	21	.303	.535	.407
Leading Off Inn.	139	33	7	2	7	7	17	25	.237	.468	.321
Runners On	229	53	5	0	12	67	26	63	.231	.410	.317
Bases Empty	272	61	13	2	11	11	34	60	.224	.408	.310
Runners/Scor. Pos.	144	36	2	0	8	58	24	43	.250	.431	.358
Runners On/2 Out	104	24	3	0	5	34	10	32	.231	.404	.316
Scor. Pos./2 Out	74	17	1	0	2	27	9	23	.230	.324	.329
Late-Inning Pressure	77	16	1	0	2	5	12	16	.208	.299	.315
Leading Off	21	5	1	0	1	1	6	2	.238	.429	.407
Runners On	39	9	0	0	0	3	3	9	.231	.231	.286
Runners/Scor. Pos.	20	4	0	0	0	3	3	7	.200	.200	.304

RUNS BATTED IN	From 1B	From 2B	From 3B	Scoring Position
Totals	9/144	26/117	20/62	46/179
Percentage	6.3%	22.2%	32.3%	25.7%

Loves to face: Ron Darling (.375, 6-for-16, 2 HR)
Kirk McCaskill (.471, 8-for-17)
Dave Stewart (.333, 8-for-24, 2 2B, 5 HR, 7 BB)

Hates to face: Roger Clemens (.056, 1-for-18, 10 SO)
Chuck Finley (0-for-14)
Mark Guthrie (0-for-11)

Miscellaneous statistics: Ground outs-to-air outs ratio: 0.63 last season, 0.72 for career.... Grounded into 8 double plays in 100 opportunities (one per 13).... Drove in 11 of 29 runners from third base with less than two outs (38%).... Direction of balls hit to the outfield: 59% to left field, 28% to center, 13% to right.... Base running: Advanced from first base to third on 11 of 26 outfield singles (42%); scored from second on 16 of 20 (80%).... Made 2.26 putouts per nine innings in left field.

Comments: Batting average of .208 from the cleanup spot was the lowest in the majors last season (minimum: 200 AB).... Batted .168 from the 7th inning on, the lowest of any player in the league last season (minimum: 100 AB); among major leaguers, only Dave Martinez had a lower average after the sixth inning (.164).... May batting average was the lowest in A.L. last season.... Hitless in 12 career at-bats as a pinch hitter.... Career batting average is .214 with the bases empty, .259 with runners on base, .281 with runners in scoring position.... Stole 15 bases last season, but was caught stealing just as often. He and Tony Fernandez (20 SB, 20 CS) became the first players to steal as many as 15 bases with a success rate of 50 percent or below since Alfredo Griffin in 1980 (18-for-41).... One of eight players to finish last season on the Brewers roster with at least 250 games in the majors, all with Milwaukee. No other team had as many veterans who spent their entire careers with their original club. (Minnesota was runner-up with 7.) Of those eight players, Paul Molitor has gone to Toronto and Dan Plesac to the Cubs. As of January 31, Jim Gantner was an unsigned free agent.... Career home run rate of one every 21.4 at-bats is 4th highest in Brewers franchise history (minimum: 50 HR), behind Gorman Thomas (17.0), Rob Deer (17.1), and Bill Schroeder (20.9).... His chances of hitting as many as 300 career home runs are 8-to-1; as many as 400, 20-to-1. The over/under: 151.

Mo Vaughn

Bats Left

Boston Red Sox	AB	H	2B	3B	HR	RBI	BB	SO	BA	SA	OBA
Season	355	83	16	2	13	57	47	67	.234	.400	.326
vs. Left-Handers	79	15	3	0	5	14	10	17	.190	.418	.281
vs. Right-Handers	276	68	13	2	8	43	37	50	.246	.395	.339
vs. Ground-Ballers	167	50	7	1	6	29	20	26	.299	.461	.372
vs. Fly-Ballers	188	33	9	1	7	28	27	41	.176	.346	.286
Home Games	202	53	11	2	8	37	24	38	.262	.455	.343
Road Games	153	30	5	0	5	20	23	29	.196	.327	.303
Grass Fields	321	77	15	2	11	51	42	56	.240	.402	.332
Artificial Turf	34	6	1	0	2	6	5	11	.176	.382	.275
April	49	10	1	0	2	7	12	15	.204	.347	.355
May	16	2	0	0	0	4	8	7	.125	.125	.417
June	28	9	2	0	1	3	4	1	.321	.500	.406
July	80	18	3	1	3	13	11	14	.225	.400	.312
August	92	23	3	0	4	14	7	13	.250	.413	.310
Sept./Oct.	90	21	7	1	3	16	5	17	.233	.433	.289
Leading Off Inn.	77	14	5	0	3	3	12	10	.182	.364	.300
Runners On	174	43	10	1	6	50	26	40	.247	.420	.340
Bases Empty	181	40	6	1	7	7	21	27	.221	.381	.312
Runners/Scor. Pos.	100	22	7	0	4	44	19	29	.220	.410	.336
Runners On/2 Out	76	17	6	1	3	24	16	20	.224	.447	.359
Scor. Pos./2 Out	47	11	5	0	1	18	11	14	.234	.404	.379
Late-Inning Pressure	65	18	0	1	1	7	6	12	.277	.354	.347
Leading Off	10	0	0	0	0	0	2	3	.000	.000	.231
Runners On	30	11	0	0	1	7	5	2	.367	.467	.406
Runners/Scor. Pos.	12	5	0	0	1	7	2	1	.417	.667	.500

RUNS BATTED IN	From 1B	From 2B	From 3B	Scoring Position
Totals	11/145	15/75	18/47	33/122
Percentage	7.6%	20.0%	38.3%	27.0%

Loves to face: Mike Boddicker (.750, 3-for-4)
Rich DeLucia (2-for-2, 1 2B, 1 HR, 1 BB)
Kirk McCaskill (.400, 4-for-10, 1 HR)

Hates to face: Kevin Appier (.091, 1-for-11, 5 SO)
Cal Eldred (0-for-6)
Jack Morris (0-for-6)

Miscellaneous statistics: Ground outs-to-air outs ratio: 1.05 last season, 1.04 for career.... Grounded into 9 double plays in 85 opportunities (one per 9.4).... Drove in 14 of 22 runners from third base with less than two outs (64%).... Direction of balls hit to the outfield: 30% to left field, 32% to center, 38% to right.... Base running: Advanced from first base to third on 7 of 18 outfield singles (39%); scored from second on 7 of 14 (50%).... Made 0.71 assists per nine innings at first base.

Comments: Became the fourth Boston player in the last nine years to lead A.L. first basemen in errors, following Bill Buckner (1984), Dwight Evans (1987), and Carlos Quintana (1990). Three other Red Sox first basemen did that earlier in the expansion era: Dick Stuart (twice), Lee Thomas, and George Scott (twice).... Last season was the third in a row in which Boston's regular starter at first base had more errors there (15) than home runs. Vaughn did it in 1991 as well; Quintana did it in 1990.... Boston has used six different opening-day starters at first base in the last six years: Buckner, Evans, Nick Esasky, Billy Jo Robidoux, Quintana, Vaughn.... The infield unit of Vaughn, Jody Reed, Luis Rivera, and Wade Boggs started only 24 games together last season, but it was the most often used combination on the club.... Career batting-average breakdowns: .196 vs. left-handers, .255 vs. right-handers; .295 vs. ground-ball pitchers, .204 vs. fly-ballers; .281 at Fenway Park, .202 on the road; .275 with runners on base, .215 with the bases empty.... His "bats left, throws right" status is a bit more unusual for a first baseman than it is at the other infield positions, but Chris Chambliss, Johnny Mize, Boog Powell, and Kent Hrbek are examples of first basemen who did that.... Last season, there were more than twice as many Seton Hall players in major league baseball (Craig Biggio, Rick Cerone, John Morris, Vaughn, and John Valentin) as in the NBA (Anthony Avent and Mark Bryant).

Randy Velarde

Bats Right

New York Yankees	AB	H	2B	3B	HR	RBI	BB	SO	BA	SA	OBA
Season	412	112	24	1	7	46	38	78	.272	.386	.333
vs. Left-Handers	140	43	10	0	4	22	15	23	.307	.464	.376
vs. Right-Handers	272	69	14	1	3	24	23	55	.254	.346	.310
vs. Ground-Ballers	168	44	7	1	3	17	24	29	.262	.369	.354
vs. Fly-Ballers	244	68	17	0	4	29	14	49	.279	.398	.317
Home Games	198	55	8	0	2	24	20	33	.278	.348	.345
Road Games	214	57	16	1	5	22	18	45	.266	.421	.321
Grass Fields	334	87	12	0	6	36	30	60	.260	.350	.322
Artificial Turf	78	25	12	1	1	10	8	18	.321	.538	.379
April	71	15	4	0	1	6	3	14	.211	.310	.250
May	54	14	3	0	0	3	3	12	.259	.315	.298
June	21	5	0	0	1	4	2	5	.238	.381	.304
July	53	21	8	1	2	6	3	7	.396	.698	.429
August	107	30	3	0	1	13	15	17	.280	.336	.363
Sept./Oct.	106	27	6	0	2	14	12	23	.255	.368	.331
Leading Off Inn.	99	29	6	1	1	1	5	18	.293	.404	.333
Runners On	169	47	9	0	3	42	16	33	.278	.385	.335
Bases Empty	243	65	15	1	4	4	22	45	.267	.387	.331
Runners/Scor. Pos.	92	26	6	0	3	40	13	18	.283	.446	.355
Runners On/2 Out	65	13	1	0	2	15	7	14	.200	.308	.278
Scor. Pos./2 Out	41	10	1	0	2	15	7	8	.244	.415	.354
Late-Inning Pressure	67	18	3	0	2	7	6	12	.269	.403	.329
Leading Off	18	6	2	0	0	0	1	1	.333	.444	.368
Runners On	26	7	0	0	1	6	2	8	.269	.385	.321
Runners/Scor. Pos.	14	5	0	0	1	6	2	2	.357	.571	.438

RUNS BATTED IN	From 1B	From 2B	From 3B	Scoring Position
Totals	5/130	15/69	19/45	34/114
Percentage	3.8%	21.7%	42.2%	29.8%

Loves to face: Bert Blyleven (.600, 6-for-10)
Mike Fetters (.500, 2-for-4, 1 HR)
Joe Hesketh (.500, 5-for-10)

Hates to face: Erik Hanson (.091, 1-for-11)
Jack Morris (.063, 1-for-16, 1 HR)
Bob Welch (0-for-7)

Miscellaneous statistics: Ground outs-to-air outs ratio: 1.44 last season, 1.53 for career.... Grounded into 13 double plays in 96 opportunities (one per 7.4).... Drove in 14 of 24 runners from third base with less than two outs (58%).... Direction of balls hit to the outfield: 30% to left field, 32% to center, 38% to right.... Base running: Advanced from first base to third on 9 of 21 outfield singles (43%); scored from second on 10 of 13 (77%).... Made 3.15 assists per nine innings at shortstop.

Comments: Batting average soared in July when he started driving the ball to left field. As of June 30, he was batting .233; to that point, he had hit only 10 balls to left field on 146 at-bats. From then on, he batted .293, with 34 hits on 45 balls pulled to left field.... Had 10 extra-base hits over a span of 20 at-bats (July 19–26). Prior to that, he'd never had more than six in any single month.... Had never driven in more than eight runs in a month before last August.... Set a career high with 109 starts; his previous high: 65 (1990).... Started 68 games at shortstop, but never had a steady double-play partner. Pat Kelly started at second base in 32 of those games, Andy Stankiewicz in 24, and Mike Gallego in 12.... Career totals of 188 games at third base, 152 at shortstop, 30 at second base, and 30 in the outfield. No other player in Yankees history has ever played as many as 30 games at each of those positions. The last one to play even 10 games at each was Phil Linz.... Career batting average is .280 in day games, .232 at night.... Has driven in only 15 percent of runners from scoring position in Late-Inning Pressure Situations during his career, compared to 25 percent at other times.... Has hit 20 homers in his career, only six at Yankee Stadium. But his batting average is higher in the Bronx (.263) than elsewhere (.239).... Made his major league debut for the Yankees in August 1987. Only three players have appeared in games for the Yankees in each of the last six seasons: Don Mattingly, Velarde, and Roberto Kelly.

Robin Ventura
Bats Left

Chicago White Sox	AB	H	2B	3B	HR	RBI	BB	SO	BA	SA	OBA
Season	592	167	38	1	16	93	93	71	.282	.431	.375
vs. Left-Handers	182	47	12	1	2	28	26	34	.258	.368	.348
vs. Right-Handers	410	120	26	0	14	65	67	37	.293	.459	.387
vs. Ground-Ballers	294	86	18	1	9	46	49	34	.293	.452	.391
vs. Fly-Ballers	298	81	20	0	7	47	44	37	.272	.409	.359
Home Games	285	84	19	1	7	50	49	30	.295	.442	.392
Road Games	307	83	19	0	9	43	44	41	.270	.420	.359
Grass Fields	499	140	32	1	14	84	78	62	.281	.433	.373
Artificial Turf	93	27	6	0	2	9	15	9	.290	.419	.385
April	69	19	6	0	1	11	15	5	.275	.406	.400
May	101	29	7	0	2	15	18	14	.287	.416	.382
June	99	35	6	1	4	14	16	14	.354	.556	.443
July	108	20	3	0	2	8	7	14	.185	.269	.231
August	102	34	8	0	3	23	12	10	.333	.500	.400
Sept./Oct.	113	30	8	0	4	22	25	14	.265	.442	.399
Leading Off Inn.	127	25	6	1	3	3	15	15	.197	.331	.282
Runners On	256	86	21	0	6	83	51	30	.336	.488	.435
Bases Empty	336	81	17	1	10	10	42	41	.241	.387	.325
Runners/Scor. Pos.	149	48	10	0	3	69	38	21	.322	.450	.441
Runners On/2 Out	96	36	10	0	3	30	20	13	.375	.573	.483
Scor. Pos./2 Out	62	20	5	0	1	23	15	12	.323	.452	.455
Late-Inning Pressure	85	22	4	0	2	10	10	12	.259	.376	.333
Leading Off	25	5	1	0	1	1	4	7	.200	.360	.310
Runners On	36	12	3	0	0	8	3	4	.333	.417	.375
Runners/Scor. Pos.	17	7	2	0	0	8	3	2	.412	.529	.476

RUNS BATTED IN	From 1B	From 2B	From 3B	Scoring Position
Totals	17/183	25/115	35/61	60/176
Percentage	9.3%	21.7%	57.4%	34.1%

Loves to face: Kevin Brown (.400, 10-for-25, 1 HR)
Roger Clemens (.379, 11-for-29, 1 HR)
Kevin Tapani (.421, 8-for-19, 2 HR)

Hates to face: Mike Boddicker (.125, 2-for-16)
Tom Gordon (0-for-12)
Jaime Navarro (.100, 2-for-20)

Miscellaneous statistics: Ground outs-to-air outs ratio: 1.01 last season, 1.25 for career.... Grounded into 14 double plays in 140 opportunities (one per 10).... Drove in 28 of 39 runners from third base with less than two outs (72%).... Direction of balls hit to the outfield: 32% to left field, 30% to center, 38% to right.... Base running: Advanced from first base to third on 15 of 42 outfield singles (36%); scored from second on 8 of 11 (73%).... Made 2.40 assists per nine innings at third base, 2d-highest rate in majors.

Comments: Only two rookies during the 1980s batted .300 or better with runners in scoring position in each of their first three seasons in the majors (minimum: 50 AB in each): Tim Raines and Wade Boggs. Ventura and Frank Thomas have both done so in each of their first three years.... Career batting averages: .315 with RISP, .256 in other at-bats.... Drove in seven fewer runs last season than in 1991, but stranded 14 fewer in scoring position. His percentage of driving them in actually rose from 32.3 percent to 34.1.... Led the American League with 93 RBIs and 55 extra-base hits as a third baseman.... Had the most plate appearances (694) of any player who wasn't hit by a pitch last season.... Batted .379 in day games, .248 at night. Previous career average was higher in night games (.267) than day games (.258).... Over the last three years, he's played 147, 151, and a team-record 157 games at third base. Only two other White Sox third basemen have had three seasons, consecutive or otherwise, of even 145 games there: Willie Kamm (6 times in the 1920s) and Bill Melton (1969, 1971, and 1973). Ventura already ranks fifth in franchise history with 471 games at third, behind Kamm (1157), Melton (867), Lee Tannehill (669), and Pete Ward (562).... Most similar offensive profile at same age: Dave Winfield. The only significant differences: stolen bases (advantage Dave) and strikeouts (Ventura).

Omar Vizquel
Bats Left and Right

Seattle Mariners	AB	H	2B	3B	HR	RBI	BB	SO	BA	SA	OBA
Season	483	142	20	4	0	21	32	38	.294	.352	.340
vs. Left-Handers	105	24	4	0	0	5	8	4	.229	.267	.283
vs. Right-Handers	378	118	16	4	0	16	24	34	.312	.376	.356
vs. Ground-Ballers	236	67	7	0	0	10	19	22	.284	.314	.340
vs. Fly-Ballers	247	75	13	4	0	11	13	16	.304	.389	.340
Home Games	241	69	11	3	0	12	17	23	.286	.357	.337
Road Games	242	73	9	1	0	9	15	15	.302	.347	.342
Grass Fields	187	57	7	0	0	9	9	12	.305	.342	.337
Artificial Turf	296	85	13	4	0	12	23	26	.287	.358	.342
April	21	4	0	0	0	1	0	2	.190	.190	.190
May	50	15	1	1	0	3	3	2	.300	.360	.333
June	80	26	6	0	0	1	9	6	.325	.400	.393
July	114	40	8	1	0	8	6	8	.351	.439	.388
August	108	31	1	1	0	4	7	9	.287	.315	.330
Sept./Oct.	110	26	4	1	0	4	7	11	.236	.291	.288
Leading Off Inn.	161	46	6	2	0	0	11	18	.286	.348	.331
Runners On	177	56	9	1	0	21	10	10	.316	.379	.354
Bases Empty	306	86	11	3	0	0	22	28	.281	.337	.331
Runners/Scor. Pos.	101	31	2	1	0	20	5	7	.307	.347	.343
Runners On/2 Out	70	25	1	0	0	12	4	5	.357	.500	.392
Scor. Pos./2 Out	43	13	2	1	0	11	2	5	.302	.395	.333
Late-Inning Pressure	76	19	2	0	0	4	1	9	.250	.276	.260
Leading Off	20	4	1	0	0	0	1	4	.200	.250	.238
Runners On	27	7	1	0	0	4	0	1	.259	.296	.259
Runners/Scor. Pos.	17	6	1	0	0	4	0	0	.353	.412	.353

RUNS BATTED IN	From 1B	From 2B	From 3B	Scoring Position
Totals	3/122	10/88	8/31	18/119
Percentage	2.5%	11.4%	25.8%	15.1%

Loves to face: John Dopson (.556, 5-for-9)
Juan Guzman (.556, 5-for-9)
Jaime Navarro (.400, 10-for-25)

Hates to face: Roger Clemens (.160, 4-for-25, 0 BB)
Kevin Tapani (.160, 4-for-25)
David Wells (0-for-9)

Miscellaneous statistics: Ground outs-to-air outs ratio: 1.21 last season, 1.33 for career.... Grounded into 14 double plays in 87 opportunities (one per 6.2).... Drove in 5 of 15 runners from third base with less than two outs (33%), 3d-lowest rate in majors.... Direction of balls hit to the outfield: 41% to left field, 34% to center, 25% to right batting left-handed; 46% to left field, 26% to center, 28% to right batting right-handed.... Base running: Advanced from first base to third on 8 of 27 outfield singles (30%); scored from second on 4 of 8 (50%).... Made 3.15 assists per nine innings at shortstop.

Comments: Raised his batting average from .230 in 1991, for the greatest breakthrough by a Mariners hitter (rated at 25-to-1) since Bruce Bochte batted .316 with 100 RBIs in 1979.... Breakthrough was attributable entirely to improved hitting from the left side (.230 in 1991); his right-handed batting average actually fell by 1 point.... Led major league shortstops in fielding percentage (one error every 90 chances).... Batted .297 as a shortstop, 2d highest in the majors (minimum: 250 PA), behind Barry Larkin (.304).... Batting average of .323 from the leadoff slot in the order was also highest in the A.L. and 2d in the majors, to Bip Roberts (.325).... Led A.L. in hits during July.... Total of 21 RBIs was the lowest of any player who qualified for the batting title last season.... Drove in only 18 of 119 runners from scoring position (15.1%), the lowest rate by a qualifier since Gary Pettis in 1989 (15-for-101, 14.9%, 18 RBIs)—despite batting above .300 with runners in scoring position (for a second consecutive season, no less).... Most career plate appearances among active players without an intentional walk: Vizquel (1725), Glenallen Hill (975), Nolan Ryan (957), Milt Cuyler (918), Luis Sojo (878).... Hitless in 15 career at-bats as a pinch hitter, the biggest zero of any active player, but not even halfway to the all-time record: Don Kessinger finished his career 0-for-33 as a pinch hitter.

Walt Weiss
Bats Left and Right

Oakland A's	AB	H	2B	3B	HR	RBI	BB	SO	BA	SA	OBA
Season	316	67	5	2	0	21	43	39	.212	.241	.305
vs. Left-Handers	74	10	0	1	0	2	5	3	.135	.162	.190
vs. Right-Handers	242	57	5	1	0	19	38	36	.236	.264	.337
vs. Ground-Ballers	142	27	3	0	0	9	21	19	.190	.211	.289
vs. Fly-Ballers	174	40	2	2	0	12	22	20	.230	.264	.318
Home Games	144	25	3	1	0	8	21	18	.174	.208	.280
Road Games	172	42	2	1	0	13	22	21	.244	.267	.327
Grass Fields	265	56	5	1	0	16	36	33	.211	.238	.306
Artificial Turf	51	11	0	1	0	5	7	6	.216	.255	.300
April	0	0	0	0	0	0	0	0	—	—	—
May	0	0	0	0	0	0	0	0	—	—	—
June	82	19	1	0	0	6	9	6	.232	.244	.304
July	82	20	1	1	0	5	12	11	.244	.280	.330
August	81	18	1	1	0	6	13	12	.222	.259	.330
Sept./Oct.	71	10	2	0	0	4	9	10	.141	.169	.247
Leading Off Inn.	74	17	0	1	0	0	8	7	.230	.257	.305
Runners On	143	31	2	1	0	21	19	16	.217	.245	.301
Bases Empty	173	36	3	1	0	0	24	23	.208	.237	.308
Runners/Scor. Pos.	87	12	2	0	0	20	13	10	.138	.161	.240
Runners On/2 Out	61	13	2	1	0	9	10	5	.213	.279	.324
Scor. Pos./2 Out	45	7	2	0	0	8	8	5	.156	.200	.283
Late-Inning Pressure	34	8	0	0	0	2	11	3	.235	.235	.404
Leading Off	16	2	0	0	0	0	1	1	.125	.125	.176
Runners On	8	5	0	0	0	2	6	0	.625	.625	.688
Runners/Scor. Pos.	1	0	0	0	0	2	4	0	.000	.000	.571

RUNS BATTED IN	From 1B	From 2B	From 3B	Scoring Position
Totals	2/109	6/74	13/35	19/109
Percentage	1.8%	8.1%	37.1%	17.4%

Loves to face: Tom Candiotti (.333, 5-for-15, 3 BB)
Bret Saberhagen (.381, 8-for-21)
Hates to face: Bill Krueger (.091, 1-for-11)
Jeff M. Robinson (.154, 2-for-13)
Greg Swindell (.067, 1-for-15, 1 3B)

Miscellaneous statistics: Ground outs-to-air outs ratio: 1.35 last season, 1.33 for career.... Ground into 10 double plays in 81 opportunities (one per 8.1).... Drove in 9 of 20 runners from third base with less than two outs (45%).... Direction of balls hit to the outfield: 36% to left field, 27% to center, 36% to right batting left-handed; 26% to left field, 33% to center, 41% to right batting right-handed.... Base running: Advanced from first base to third on 8 of 17 outfield singles (47%); scored from second on 3 of 8 (38%).... Made 2.83 assists per nine innings at shortstop, 3d-lowest rate in A.L.

Comments: Batting average from September 1 on was the lowest in A.L.... Batted .213 as a shortstop, the lowest average of any A.L. player at that position (minimum: 250 PA).... Had only three go-ahead RBIs, matching Cleveland's Mark Lewis for the fewest among A.L. players with at least 300 at-bats.... Has hit for a higher average from the left side of the plate than from the right side in each of his six seasons in the majors. Career breakdown: .256 left-handed, .214 right-handed.... All eight of his career homers have been hit from the left side.... Has only three home runs in 1123 at-bats since homering off Scott Bankhead and Tom Niedenfuer in the same game (April 5, 1989).... Has never stolen even 10 bases in a season, but his success rate is close to 80 percent over the last four years (27-for-34, 79%).... Has a career batting average of only .221 at the Oakland Coliseum, compared to a .270 mark on the road.... Hit .333 as a rookie in the 1988 A.L.C.S., but has only five hits in 53 postseason at-bats since then.... Hitless in his last 25 postseason at-bats with runners on base. Only one player in postseason history had a longer streak: Barry Bonds (0-for-28).... Weiss may have a long wait before he has an opportunity to snap that streak.... Has appeared in only 365 of a possible 648 games over the past four seasons.... Most similar statistical profiles, then and now: 1988—Craig Reynolds, Tony Phillips, Ron Gardenhire; 1992—Ruben Amaro, Phil Linz, Wayne Terwilliger.

Lou Whitaker
Bats Left

Detroit Tigers	AB	H	2B	3B	HR	RBI	BB	SO	BA	SA	OBA
Season	453	126	26	0	19	71	81	46	.278	.461	.386
vs. Left-Handers	62	22	6	0	2	15	15	11	.355	.548	.481
vs. Right-Handers	391	104	20	0	17	56	66	35	.266	.448	.370
vs. Ground-Ballers	207	60	13	0	7	34	34	25	.290	.454	.389
vs. Fly-Ballers	246	66	13	0	12	37	47	21	.268	.467	.383
Home Games	228	73	19	0	11	37	50	26	.320	.548	.442
Road Games	225	53	7	0	8	34	31	20	.236	.373	.326
Grass Fields	385	107	23	0	18	61	77	36	.278	.478	.396
Artificial Turf	68	19	3	0	1	10	4	10	.279	.368	.324
April	52	10	1	0	2	3	13	6	.192	.327	.348
May	79	21	6	0	4	11	13	10	.266	.494	.376
June	79	28	8	0	3	11	16	6	.354	.570	.463
July	63	20	4	0	1	9	12	2	.317	.429	.421
August	84	23	1	0	6	21	15	9	.274	.500	.376
Sept./Oct.	96	24	6	0	3	16	12	13	.250	.406	.333
Leading Off Inn.	79	23	6	0	1	1	12	6	.291	.405	.385
Runners On	221	65	10	0	9	61	39	21	.294	.462	.394
Bases Empty	232	61	16	0	10	10	42	25	.263	.461	.378
Runners/Scor. Pos.	111	41	7	0	6	55	20	7	.369	.595	.452
Runners On/2 Out	73	20	2	0	3	21	15	9	.274	.425	.398
Scor. Pos./2 Out	45	15	2	0	3	21	12	3	.333	.578	.474
Late-Inning Pressure	62	15	3	0	1	6	13	12	.242	.339	.373
Leading Off	12	3	1	0	0	0	3	2	.250	.333	.400
Runners On	36	7	0	0	1	6	3	7	.194	.278	.256
Runners/Scor. Pos.	18	4	0	0	1	6	3	3	.222	.389	.333

RUNS BATTED IN	From 1B	From 2B	From 3B	Scoring Position
Totals	6/167	21/91	25/37	46/128
Percentage	3.6%	23.1%	67.6%	35.9%

Loves to face: Bert Blyleven (.385, 25-for-65, 3 HR)
Mike Boddicker (.354, 23-for-65, 4 HR)
Mike Timlin (4-for-4, 2 HR)
Hates to face: Tom Henke (.071, 2-for-28)
Mike Mussina (.056, 1-for-18, 1 2B)
Bill Wegman (.140, 8-for-57, 4 2B, 1 HR)

Miscellaneous statistics: Ground outs-to-air outs ratio: 0.67 last season, 1.04 for career.... Grounded into 9 double plays in 141 opportunities (one per 16).... Drove in 18 of 24 runners from third base with less than two outs (75%).... Direction of balls hit to the outfield: 22% to left field, 35% to center, 43% to right.... Base running: Advanced from first base to third on 8 of 21 outfield singles (38%); scored from second on 14 of 19 (74%).... Made 2.87 assists per nine innings at second base.

Comments: Sparky Anderson has managed the Tigers since June 12, 1979; only Tommy Lasorda has a longer current tenure. Six players spent that entire period with the same team: Whitaker and Alan Trammell, George Brett, Jim Gantner, Paul Molitor, and Robin Yount.... Has played more games for Sparky than any other player (1895), followed by Trammell (1759), Pete Rose (1441), Johnny Bench (1305), and Tom Brookens (1206).... Whitaker and Trammell have played 1741 games together as teammates, 4th most in A.L. history. (See the George Brett comments for the top three.)... Has been an opening-day starter in each of the last 15 years (since 1978), the longest current streak of any A.L. player.... Stands 154 games behind Charlie Gehringer in games played at second base for the Tigers.... Started 114 games against right-handers last season, his highest total in more than 10 years; three starts vs. left-handers was a career low.... Only two other left-handed batters in the A.L. hit above .300 against southpaws (minimum: 50 AB): Kens Lofton and Griffey.... Batting average with runners in scoring position was a career high; percentage of runners driven in from scoring position was highest in A.L. last season.... Has at least one home run in every month since April 1986 (his only HR-less month since April 1983), the longest streak in the league. N.L. players with longer streaks: George Bell, Joe Carter, Andre Dawson, and Ryne Sandberg. (Arbitrary ruling: October homers count for September.)

Devon White
Bats Left and Right

Toronto Blue Jays	AB	H	2B	3B	HR	RBI	BB	SO	BA	SA	OBA
Season	641	159	26	7	17	60	47	133	.248	.390	.303
vs. Left-Handers	179	38	5	0	5	19	13	41	.212	.324	.272
vs. Right-Handers	462	121	21	7	12	41	34	92	.262	.416	.315
vs. Ground-Ballers	331	87	16	2	7	34	25	67	.263	.387	.318
vs. Fly-Ballers	310	72	10	5	10	26	22	66	.232	.394	.288
Home Games	306	81	17	4	7	34	24	64	.265	.415	.321
Road Games	335	78	9	3	10	26	23	69	.233	.367	.286
Grass Fields	255	56	7	3	8	21	17	52	.220	.365	.274
Artificial Turf	386	103	19	4	9	39	30	81	.267	.407	.322
April	93	22	4	0	2	10	6	23	.237	.344	.297
May	112	26	4	1	2	7	11	12	.232	.339	.306
June	107	28	2	3	5	13	8	17	.262	.477	.316
July	107	22	5	1	1	12	7	22	.206	.299	.250
August	103	23	3	1	4	6	2	23	.223	.388	.245
Sept./Oct.	119	38	8	1	3	12	13	26	.319	.479	.386
Leading Off Inn.	233	57	7	2	7	7	14	49	.245	.382	.287
Runners On	241	53	9	3	7	50	22	56	.220	.369	.287
Bases Empty	400	106	17	4	10	10	25	77	.265	.402	.313
Runners/Scor. Pos.	136	31	7	2	2	39	11	31	.228	.353	.285
Runners On/2 Out	108	30	5	2	3	26	14	22	.278	.444	.366
Scor. Pos./2 Out	68	19	4	2	0	20	8	11	.279	.397	.364
Late-Inning Pressure	68	17	2	1	3	9	8	13	.250	.441	.338
Leading Off	8	3	0	0	1	1	2	3	.375	.750	.500
Runners On	37	8	1	1	1	7	3	7	.216	.378	.275
Runners/Scor. Pos.	21	5	0	1	1	7	1	2	.238	.476	.273

RUNS BATTED IN	From 1B	From 2B	From 3B	Scoring Position
Totals	7/170	21/109	15/62	36/171
Percentage	4.1%	19.3%	24.2%	21.1%

Loves to face: Brad Arnsberg (.500, 3-for-6, 2 HR)
Bill Gullickson (.389, 7-for-18, 2 HR)
Brian Holman (.391, 9-for-23)

Hates to face: Kevin Brown (.115, 3-for-26)
Roger Clemens (.125, 7-for-56, 1 HR)
Nolan Ryan (.091, 3-for-33, 3 BB)

Miscellaneous statistics: Ground outs-to-air outs ratio: 1.27 last season, 1.42 for career.... Grounded into 9 double plays in 101 opportunities (one per 11).... Drove in 7 of 28 runners from third base with less than two outs (25%), lowest rate in majors.... Direction of balls hit to the outfield: 34% to left field, 34% to center, 32% to right batting left-handed; 32% to left field, 37% to center, 31% to right batting right-handed.... Base running: Advanced from first base to third on 14 of 27 outfield singles (52%); scored from second on 15 of 19 (79%).... Made 3.05 putouts per nine innings in center field, 2d-highest rate in A.L.

Comments: White and Roberto Alomar batted a combined .388 in the 1992 A.L.C.S., the 4th-highest batting average by a team's one-two hitters in any series in postseason history. The record: .415, by White and Alomar in the 1991 A.L.C.S.... Caught stealing four times in four attempts during the A.L.C.S.... Stole 37 bases in 41 attempts (.902) during the regular season, becoming only the second player in A.L. history with a percentage of .900 or better in a season of at least 35 steals. The other: Willie Wilson in 1984 (47-for-52, .904). It's happened more frequently in the National League: Max Carey (1922), Jimmy Wynn (1965), Bobby Bonds (1969), Davey Lopes (1978–79, 1985), Jerry Mumphrey (1980), Tim Raines (1987), and Eric Davis (1988).... The only A.L. player to homer from both sides of the plate in the same game last season. One was an inside the parker (so give an assist to the official scorer).... The leadoff slot in the Blue Jays batting order had the most strikeouts and the fewest sacrifice bunts (none, matching the Phillies) of any team in the majors.... The outfield of White, Candy Maldonado, and Joe Carter started 93 games together during the regular season, 2d most of any unit in the majors.... Batting average with two outs and runners in scoring position was a career high, after posting marks below .200 in six of his previous seven big league seasons.

Mark Whiten
Bats Left and Right

Cleveland Indians	AB	H	2B	3B	HR	RBI	BB	SO	BA	SA	OBA
Season	508	129	19	4	9	43	72	102	.254	.360	.347
vs. Left-Handers	127	36	7	0	3	8	23	21	.283	.409	.401
vs. Right-Handers	381	93	12	4	6	35	49	81	.244	.344	.328
vs. Ground-Ballers	236	52	5	2	4	13	28	57	.220	.309	.303
vs. Fly-Ballers	272	77	14	2	5	30	44	45	.283	.404	.383
Home Games	260	70	11	3	6	25	32	55	.269	.404	.350
Road Games	248	59	8	1	3	18	40	47	.238	.315	.344
Grass Fields	424	107	17	3	8	37	59	86	.252	.363	.344
Artificial Turf	84	22	2	1	1	6	13	16	.262	.345	.360
April	86	24	0	1	3	12	7	21	.279	.407	.333
May	91	27	7	1	2	8	18	24	.297	.462	.411
June	53	11	2	1	0	2	8	12	.208	.283	.311
July	85	18	5	0	2	9	11	12	.212	.341	.309
August	92	26	4	1	2	8	13	18	.283	.413	.368
Sept./Oct.	101	23	1	0	0	4	15	15	.228	.238	.328
Leading Off Inn.	133	33	5	2	1	1	10	30	.248	.338	.310
Runners On	209	51	6	1	4	38	40	37	.244	.340	.361
Bases Empty	299	78	13	3	5	5	32	65	.261	.375	.336
Runners/Scor. Pos.	113	24	2	0	3	33	30	23	.212	.310	.370
Runners On/2 Out	74	17	1	1	1	8	20	13	.230	.311	.394
Scor. Pos./2 Out	45	4	0	0	0	4	14	12	.089	.089	.305
Late-Inning Pressure	86	21	3	1	3	10	13	20	.244	.407	.343
Leading Off	30	5	1	1	1	1	0	10	.167	.367	.167
Runners On	29	10	1	0	2	9	10	5	.345	.586	.513
Runners/Scor. Pos.	15	4	0	0	2	9	9	3	.267	.667	.542

RUNS BATTED IN	From 1B	From 2B	From 3B	Scoring Position
Totals	5/152	14/93	15/40	29/133
Percentage	3.3%	15.1%	37.5%	21.8%

Loves to face: Kevin Brown (.333, 6-for-18, 2 HR)
Chuck Finley (.500, 8-for-16)
Jack McDowell (.381, 8-for-21)

Hates to face: Alex Fernandez (.100, 1-for-10, 5 SO)
Bill Wegman (0-for-8)
Matt Young (.077, 1-for-13, 1 2B, 2 BB)

Miscellaneous statistics: Ground outs-to-air outs ratio: 1.57 last season, 1.38 for career.... Grounded into 12 double plays in 114 opportunities (one per 10).... Drove in 14 of 22 runners from third base with less than two outs (64%).... Direction of balls hit to the outfield: 32% to left field, 34% to center, 35% to right batting left-handed; 49% to left field, 35% to center, 16% to right batting right-handed.... Base running: Advanced from first base to third on 25 of 40 outfield singles (63%); scored from second on 14 of 17 (82%).... Made 2.26 putouts per nine innings in right field, 3d-highest rate in A.L.

Comments: Has 30 assists in 283 games in the outfield. With Jesse Barfield going to Japan, his average of one assist every 9.4 games is the best among active players (minimum: 250 games in OF).... Whiten threw out 13 runners as a rookie in 1991, 14 last season. The last outfielder with at least 13 assists as both a rookie and sophomore: Carmelo Martinez. The only other active player to have done so: Kirby Puckett.... Word travels fast on these guys. Over the past 15 years, 23 rookie outfielders averaged at least one assist every 10 games. Only four had higher averages as sophomores. (Whiten's increase in assists was attributable to more games played, from 109 to 144; his rate actually decreased.)... Batting average with two outs and runners in scoring position was the lowest in the league last season, and the 7th lowest in the 18 years for which we have the data (minimum: 40 AB). Previous career figures in that category weren't much better (6-for-53).... Joined Brook Jacoby (1988) as the only players in Indians history to reach triple figures in strikeouts but not even double figures in home runs.... Raised his stolen-base total from four in 1991 to 16 last season; Tribe would love to see a rerun of his 49-steal season for Myrtle Beach in 1987.... Stole 119 bases in 569 minor league games.... Also increased his rate of walks, from one every 14.8 plate appearances in 1991 to one every 8.2 PAs last year.

Curtis Wilkerson — Bats Left and Right

Kansas City Royals	AB	H	2B	3B	HR	RBI	BB	SO	BA	SA	OBA
Season	296	74	10	1	2	29	18	47	.250	.311	.292
vs. Left-Handers	68	20	2	0	1	7	6	10	.294	.368	.351
vs. Right-Handers	228	54	8	1	1	22	12	37	.237	.294	.273
vs. Ground-Ballers	129	32	2	0	0	9	7	19	.248	.264	.287
vs. Fly-Ballers	167	42	8	1	2	20	11	28	.251	.347	.295
Home Games	160	43	4	1	2	19	13	20	.269	.344	.326
Road Games	136	31	6	0	0	10	5	27	.228	.272	.250
Grass Fields	110	29	6	0	0	7	4	23	.264	.318	.282
Artificial Turf	186	45	4	1	2	22	14	24	.242	.306	.297
April	22	1	0	0	0	1	0	5	.045	.045	.043
May	51	13	1	1	1	10	4	5	.255	.373	.298
June	47	13	2	0	0	1	4	9	.277	.319	.333
July	65	17	1	0	1	6	3	10	.262	.323	.290
August	53	18	3	0	0	7	4	9	.340	.396	.386
Sept./Oct.	58	12	3	0	0	4	3	9	.207	.259	.258
Leading Off Inn.	78	17	2	0	1	1	2	13	.218	.282	.237
Runners On	112	25	1	1	1	28	10	16	.223	.277	.283
Bases Empty	184	49	9	0	1	1	8	31	.266	.332	.297
Runners/Scor. Pos.	69	17	1	1	1	28	7	12	.246	.333	.309
Runners On/2 Out	49	10	0	1	0	7	4	5	.204	.245	.278
Scor. Pos./2 Out	34	6	0	1	0	7	4	3	.176	.235	.282
Late-Inning Pressure	46	12	2	0	0	4	4	8	.261	.304	.327
Leading Off	15	3	1	0	0	0	1	2	.200	.267	.250
Runners On	11	2	0	0	0	4	1	3	.182	.182	.286
Runners/Scor. Pos.	5	2	0	0	0	4	0	1	.400	.400	.429

RUNS BATTED IN	From 1B	From 2B	From 3B	Scoring Position
Totals	2/76	10/52	15/36	25/88
Percentage	2.6%	19.2%	41.7%	28.4%

Loves to face: Chuck Crim (.667, 4-for-6)
Kirk McCaskill (.391, 9-for-23)
Bob Ojeda (2-for-2, 2 BB)

Hates to face: Bert Blyleven (.125, 4-for-32, 0 BB)
Danny Darwin (0-for-10)
Mike Witt (.136, 3-for-22)

Miscellaneous statistics: Ground outs-to-air outs ratio: 1.35 last season, 1.49 for career.... Grounded into 4 double plays in 55 opportunities (one per 14).... Drove in 14 of 20 runners from third base with less than two outs (70%).... Direction of balls hit to the outfield: 32% to left field, 34% to center, 33% to right batting left-handed; 37% to left field, 30% to center, 33% to right batting right-handed.... Base running: Advanced from first base to third on 4 of 8 outfield singles (50%); scored from second on 8 of 8 (100%).... Made 2.84 assists per nine innings at shortstop.

Comments: How would you like to be a 10-year veteran free agent coming off of a year in which you set a career high in RBIs? Big bucks, right? Well, Wilkerson fits the bill, but that career-high RBI total was only 29. It could be worse: Catcher Matt Sinatro has played parts of 10 major league seasons; his career high in RBIs is *five*. Other active 10-year vets who've never driven in 30 runs in a season: Steve Lake (high of 19) and Otis Nixon (26).... Royals shortstops combined for a .219 batting average, 2d lowest of any team in the majors last year, ahead of only the Mets (.203).... Percentages of runners driven in from scoring position, and from third base with less than two outs, were both career highs.... Batting average from the right side of the plate was also the highest of his career.... Stole 18 bases last season, which topped his total for the previous four years combined.... Has played games at third base, shortstop, and second base in each of the last six seasons, and is one of four active players with career totals of at least 125 games at each. The others: Tony Phillips, Bill Pecota, and Al Newman.... Expansion couldn't have come at a better time. With pinch hitting a more valuable commodity in the senior circuit, you can bet that one line on his free-agent resume shows his .311 batting average as a pinch hitter for the Cubs and Pirates from 1989 through 1991 (23-for-74).... Born on April 26, 1961—the day that Roger Maris hit his first of 61 homers that season, off Detroit's Paul Foytack.

Bernie Williams — Bats Left and Right

New York Yankees	AB	H	2B	3B	HR	RBI	BB	SO	BA	SA	OBA
Season	261	73	14	2	5	26	29	36	.280	.406	.354
vs. Left-Handers	84	25	6	1	1	9	10	11	.298	.429	.379
vs. Right-Handers	177	48	8	1	4	17	19	25	.271	.395	.342
vs. Ground-Ballers	123	31	6	0	2	12	17	21	.252	.350	.348
vs. Fly-Ballers	138	42	8	2	3	14	12	15	.304	.457	.360
Home Games	134	39	8	1	3	13	17	20	.291	.433	.375
Road Games	127	34	6	1	2	13	12	16	.268	.378	.331
Grass Fields	221	60	9	2	5	23	23	30	.271	.398	.343
Artificial Turf	40	13	5	0	0	3	6	6	.325	.450	.413
April	5	1	0	0	0	0	0	2	.200	.200	.200
May	0	0	0	0	0	0	0	0	.000	.000	.000
June	0	0	0	0	0	0	0	0	—	—	—
July	0	0	0	0	0	0	0	0	—	—	—
August	125	31	6	0	4	12	19	16	.248	.392	.352
Sept./Oct.	131	41	8	2	1	14	10	18	.313	.427	.362
Leading Off Inn.	103	27	4	0	1	1	10	17	.262	.330	.327
Runners On	102	28	5	2	2	23	11	12	.275	.422	.345
Bases Empty	159	45	9	0	3	3	18	24	.283	.396	.360
Runners/Scor. Pos.	65	15	2	1	1	20	7	10	.231	.338	.306
Runners On/2 Out	39	7	1	1	1	9	5	4	.179	.333	.273
Scor. Pos./2 Out	30	4	0	1	0	7	3	4	.133	.200	.212
Late-Inning Pressure	42	7	4	0	0	1	4	11	.167	.262	.239
Leading Off	10	2	1	0	0	0	0	2	.200	.300	.200
Runners On	20	2	1	0	0	1	3	5	.100	.150	.217
Runners/Scor. Pos.	15	1	1	0	0	1	2	4	.067	.133	.176

RUNS BATTED IN	From 1B	From 2B	From 3B	Scoring Position
Totals	4/61	6/54	11/28	17/82
Percentage	6.6%	11.1%	39.3%	20.7%

Loves to face: Greg A. Harris (3-for-3)
Eric King (.556, 5-for-9)
Hipolito Pichardo (.600, 3-for-5, 2 2B)

Hates to face: Roger Clemens (.091, 1-for-11, 1 2B)
Bob Milacki (0-for-9)
Dave Stewart (0-for-6)

Miscellaneous statistics: Ground outs-to-air outs ratio: 1.04 last season, 1.23 for career.... Grounded into 5 double plays in 49 opportunities (one per 10).... Drove in 7 of 15 runners from third base with less than two outs (47%).... Direction of balls hit to the outfield: 37% to left field, 25% to center, 38% to right batting left-handed; 48% to left field, 30% to center, 23% to right batting right-handed.... Base running: Advanced from first base to third on 6 of 19 outfield singles (32%); scored from second on 9 of 12 (75%).... Made 3.13 putouts per nine innings in center field.

Comments: Played every inning of his team's 60 games from August 1 until the end of the season. No other player in the majors did so.... In 1991, Williams was the only player not to miss a pitch after the All-Star break.... Reached base safely in each of his last 29 games, and in 48 of his last 49.... Had only three infield singles in 261 at-bats—a surprisingly low total considering his speed, and the fact that he had 177 at-bats from the left side of the plate. Bernie's figures are similar to those of Lance Parrish (3 in 275 AB), Kevin Maas (2-for-286), and Dan Pasqua (2-for-265).... Stole only one base in six attempts against right-handed pitchers, but was 6-for-7 vs. left-handers. League averages: 67 percent vs. RHP, 65 percent vs. LHP.... Drove in only one of 18 runners from scoring position in Late-Inning Pressure Situations.... Career batting average is 90 points higher in day games (.317) than in night games (.227).... Teammate Gerald was the 62d "Williams" to play in the majors. More-common surnames: Smith (122), Johnson (76), Jones (74), Miller (69), Brown (68).... Incidentally, five different Columbus players led the International League in five key offensive categories: BA—J.T. Snow (.313); Hits—Gerald Williams (156); HR—Hensley Meulens (26); XBH—Torey Lovullo (57); SB—Mike Humphreys (37). Meulens also led the league in RBIs (100), with teammates winning the silver and bronze: Lovullo (89), Gerald Williams (86).

Willie Wilson

Bats Left and Right

Oakland A's	AB	H	2B	3B	HR	RBI	BB	SO	BA	SA	OBA
Season	396	107	15	5	0	37	35	65	.270	.333	.329
vs. Left-Handers	121	30	7	0	0	14	13	30	.248	.306	.316
vs. Right-Handers	275	77	8	5	0	23	22	35	.280	.345	.334
vs. Ground-Ballers	188	57	7	2	0	21	13	25	.303	.362	.347
vs. Fly-Ballers	208	50	8	3	0	16	22	40	.240	.308	.313
Home Games	199	54	6	2	0	13	21	33	.271	.322	.339
Road Games	197	53	9	3	0	24	14	32	.269	.345	.318
Grass Fields	313	84	10	3	0	22	27	51	.268	.319	.327
Artificial Turf	83	23	5	2	0	15	8	14	.277	.386	.337
April	73	23	6	1	0	14	5	8	.315	.425	.350
May	74	15	2	1	0	3	11	14	.203	.257	.306
June	61	17	3	0	0	7	11	10	.279	.328	.389
July	81	22	1	1	0	7	4	13	.272	.309	.302
August	38	12	0	1	0	3	1	9	.316	.368	.350
Sept./Oct.	69	18	3	1	0	3	3	11	.261	.333	.292
Leading Off Inn.	77	18	2	1	0	0	8	15	.234	.286	.306
Runners On	197	53	11	1	0	37	17	31	.269	.335	.326
Bases Empty	199	54	4	4	0	0	18	34	.271	.332	.332
Runners/Scor. Pos.	97	23	7	1	0	34	9	17	.237	.330	.300
Runners On/2 Out	94	17	4	0	0	8	6	14	.181	.223	.238
Scor. Pos./2 Out	44	6	4	0	0	8	4	11	.136	.227	.224
Late-Inning Pressure	61	16	1	1	0	4	4	15	.262	.311	.308
Leading Off	18	3	0	1	0	0	1	4	.167	.278	.211
Runners On	27	10	1	0	0	4	2	4	.370	.407	.414
Runners/Scor. Pos.	9	2	0	0	0	3	1	2	.222	.222	.300

RUNS BATTED IN	From 1B	From 2B	From 3B	Scoring Position
Totals	6/163	12/79	19/41	31/120
Percentage	3.7%	15.2%	46.3%	25.8%

Loves to face: Bud Black (.571, 4-for-7)
Doug Drabek (.714, 5-for-7)
Bruce Hurst (.358, 19-for-53)
Hates to face: Dave Righetti (.171, 6-for-35)
Bill Swift (.129, 4-for-31, 4 BB)
Greg Swindell (.158, 3-for-19, 8 SO, 0 BB)

Miscellaneous statistics: Ground outs-to-air outs ratio: 1.73 last season, 1.50 for career.... Grounded into 11 double plays in 94 opportunities (one per 8.5).... Drove in 16 of 21 runners from third base with less than two outs (76%), 5th-highest rate in A.L.... Direction of balls hit to the outfield: 34% to left field, 38% to center, 28% to right batting left-handed; 13% to left field, 42% to center, 45% to right batting right-handed.... Base running: Advanced from first base to third on 7 of 19 outfield singles (37%); scored from second on 12 of 13 (92%).... Made 3.49 putouts per nine innings in center field, highest rate in majors.

Comments: Could return to the leadoff slot in Chicago. For four years from 1981 through 1984, Wilson made 495 starts, all batting leadoff. But over the past three seasons (the last two with Oakland), he started and batted leadoff only 26 times (3 in 1992). Last season, Cubs leadoff hitters posted the lowest N.L. marks in batting average (.248), runs (79), and stolen bases (14). No one player started even 40 games as Chicago's leadoff hitter.... Stole at least 20 bases for the 15th consecutive season. Honus Wagner is the only major leaguer with a longer streak (18 years). Others with 15-year streaks: Lou Brock and Ozzie Smith (whose streak is current, as is Rickey Henderson's 14-year streak).... Moved past Bert Campaneris into fourth place in A.L. history in stolen bases, but he changes leagues 83 behind Eddie Collins for the third spot.... Stole seven bases in the 1992 A.L.C.S., the 2d-highest total ever in a postseason series. Rickey stole eight against the Blue Jays in 1989; others with seven: Ron Gant (1991 N.L.C.S.), Lou Brock (1967 and 1968 World Series).... The feet can still motor, but the arm is gone. He's thrown out only nine runners in 563 games over the past five years; he had 45 assists over his first five seasons.... In two seasons with the Athletics, he hit nothing longer than a double from the right side of the plate. He hit nine triples batting left-handed, no homers from either side. A windy day at Wrigley Field should fix that.

Dave Winfield

Bats Right

Toronto Blue Jays	AB	H	2B	3B	HR	RBI	BB	SO	BA	SA	OBA
Season	583	169	33	3	26	108	82	89	.290	.491	.377
vs. Left-Handers	146	44	7	1	8	28	24	21	.301	.527	.395
vs. Right-Handers	437	125	26	2	18	80	58	68	.286	.478	.370
vs. Ground-Ballers	298	95	13	1	13	54	40	51	.319	.500	.398
vs. Fly-Ballers	285	74	20	2	13	54	42	38	.260	.481	.355
Home Games	268	81	10	2	13	47	47	37	.302	.500	.403
Road Games	315	88	23	1	13	61	35	52	.279	.483	.353
Grass Fields	240	65	17	0	11	46	26	44	.271	.479	.345
Artificial Turf	343	104	16	3	15	62	56	45	.303	.499	.398
April	88	33	3	0	4	12	9	16	.375	.545	.424
May	94	21	5	1	5	15	15	11	.223	.457	.330
June	98	31	9	0	4	17	17	12	.316	.531	.417
July	92	22	7	1	3	11	11	14	.239	.435	.327
August	109	33	6	1	7	32	12	19	.303	.569	.372
Sept./Oct.	102	29	3	0	3	21	18	17	.284	.402	.388
Leading Off Inn.	165	43	9	1	5	5	14	23	.261	.418	.322
Runners On	261	79	16	2	13	95	46	37	.303	.529	.403
Bases Empty	322	90	17	1	13	13	36	52	.280	.460	.354
Runners/Scor. Pos.	165	50	11	1	9	82	35	25	.303	.545	.419
Runners On/2 Out	125	36	7	2	9	44	19	11	.288	.592	.382
Scor. Pos./2 Out	82	21	3	1	7	36	16	7	.256	.573	.378
Late-Inning Pressure	57	13	1	0	3	9	14	12	.228	.404	.380
Leading Off	16	3	0	0	0	0	3	3	.188	.188	.316
Runners On	22	5	0	0	2	7	8	6	.227	.364	.433
Runners/Scor. Pos.	13	4	0	0	1	7	5	5	.308	.538	.500

RUNS BATTED IN	From 1B	From 2B	From 3B	Scoring Position
Totals	16/158	23/117	43/80	66/197
Percentage	10.1%	19.7%	53.8%	33.5%

Loves to face: Kevin Brown (.417, 10-for-24, 4 HR)
Mike Moore (.444, 16-for-36, 2 HR, 13 BB)
Rick Sutcliffe (.400, 14-for-35, 5 HR)
Hates to face: Steve Farr (.143, 3-for-21)
Mike Henneman (.091, 1-for-11)
Jose Mesa (.125, 2-for-16)

Miscellaneous statistics: Ground outs-to-air outs ratio: 1.12 last season, 1.32 for career.... Grounded into 10 double plays in 106 opportunities (one per 11).... Drove in 27 of 43 runners from third base with less than two outs (63%).... Direction of balls hit to the outfield: 41% to left field, 35% to center, 24% to right.... Base running: Advanced from first base to third on 5 of 26 outfield singles (19%); scored from second on 11 of 18 (61%).... Made 2.15 putouts per nine innings in right field.

Comments: Became the oldest player ever to hit a postseason home run; Enos Slaughter is still the oldest to homer in the World Series.... Forget about *how* he played last season; after missing all of 1989 following back surgery, it's amazing that he played *at all* at the age of 40—much less 156 games! Only four players that old played even 140 games in a season: Darrell Evans (1988), Pete Rose (1982 and 1983), Rabbit Maranville (1933), and Honus Wagner (1915).... Missed consecutive games only twice in the last two seasons.... Led the majors with 32 RBIs in August, the highest monthly total of his career.... Became the 13th player to hit 20 home runs in 14 different seasons. Eleven have been elected to the Hall of Fame; the 12th, Mike Schmidt, will join them soon.... Since being traded for Mike Witt on May 11, 1990, he has played more games, hit more homers, driven in more runs, scored more runs, and drawn more walks than any player on the Yankees.... Leads active players in home runs (432), RBIs (1710), and GIDPs (292). The all-time leader in all three categories is Hank Aaron. Home runs and RBIs are out of Winfield's reach, but the GIDP record is not; Big Dave currently ranks sixth, behind Aaron (328), Carl Yastrzemski (323), Jim Rice (315), Brooks Robinson (297), and Rusty Staub (297).... Needs 51 more games in the outfield to match Al Kaline's career total, which ranks sixth all time.... Has hit for a higher average with men on base than he has with the bases empty in eight of his last nine seasons.

Robin Yount
Bats Right

Milwaukee Brewers	AB	H	2B	3B	HR	RBI	BB	SO	BA	SA	OBA
Season	557	147	40	3	8	77	53	81	.264	.390	.325
vs. Left-Handers	125	35	10	1	2	18	16	24	.280	.424	.359
vs. Right-Handers	432	112	30	2	6	59	37	57	.259	.380	.315
vs. Ground-Ballers	255	64	18	0	3	34	24	39	.251	.357	.315
vs. Fly-Ballers	302	83	22	3	5	43	29	42	.275	.417	.333
Home Games	269	72	17	2	3	35	25	35	.268	.379	.327
Road Games	288	75	23	1	5	42	28	46	.260	.399	.323
Grass Fields	465	122	30	2	7	68	42	67	.262	.381	.320
Artificial Turf	92	25	10	1	1	9	11	14	.272	.435	.350
April	64	15	3	0	0	5	6	14	.234	.281	.306
May	103	26	9	0	3	16	10	15	.252	.427	.322
June	90	31	8	0	2	12	11	10	.344	.500	.408
July	99	19	7	0	0	7	5	15	.192	.263	.231
August	87	21	5	2	0	14	10	16	.241	.345	.313
Sept./Oct.	114	35	8	1	3	23	11	11	.307	.474	.359
Leading Off Inn.	121	34	6	0	2	2	10	15	.281	.380	.341
Runners On	265	76	19	3	4	73	30	42	.287	.426	.347
Bases Empty	292	71	21	0	4	4	23	39	.243	.356	.303
Runners/Scor. Pos.	156	45	12	2	1	62	23	25	.288	.410	.359
Runners On/2 Out	118	27	6	1	2	26	11	18	.229	.347	.300
Scor. Pos./2 Out	76	20	6	1	0	22	10	12	.263	.368	.356
Late-Inning Pressure	74	21	4	0	1	8	11	6	.284	.378	.360
Leading Off	17	7	1	0	0	0	4	0	.412	.471	.524
Runners On	34	9	2	0	0	7	7	5	.265	.324	.356
Runners/Scor. Pos.	17	4	1	0	0	7	4	1	.235	.294	.320

RUNS BATTED IN	From 1B	From 2B	From 3B	Scoring Position
Totals	10/181	22/132	37/62	59/194
Percentage	5.5%	16.7%	59.7%	30.4%

Loves to face: Gerald Alexander (.800, 4-for-5, 1 2B, 1 3B)
Mike Flanagan (.443, 35-for-79, 8 2B, 2 3B, 4 HR)
Shawn Hillegas (.429, 6-for-14, 1 2B, 2 HR)

Hates to face: Chuck Finley (.154, 6-for-39)
Mike Mussina (0-for-8)
Bob Welch (.138, 4-for-29)

Miscellaneous statistics: Ground outs-to-air outs ratio: 0.89 last season, 0.96 for career.... Grounded into 9 double plays in 115 opportunities (one per 13).... Drove in 29 of 38 runners from third base with less than two outs (76%), 4th-highest rate in A.L.... Direction of balls hit to the outfield: 31% to left field, 26% to center, 43% to right.... Base running: Advanced from first base to third on 6 of 20 outfield singles (30%); scored from second on 15 of 21 (71%).... Made 2.79 putouts per nine innings in center field.

Comments: Reached the 3000-hit mark on Sept. 9, one week shy of his 37th birthday. Only two players reached that mark at a younger age: Ty Cobb (34) and Hank Aaron (36).... George Brett got his 3000th hit on Sept. 30; he and Yount became the fourth pair to reach 3000 in the same season. The closest were Tris Speaker and Eddie Collins, who did it 16 days apart in 1925.... Needs just 97 games to break into the all-time top 10.... The only player in baseball history to accumulate at least 1000 games at both shortstop (1479) and in the outfield (1007). Only two other players have as many as 400 games at both positions: Harvey Kuenn (748 SS, 826 OF) and Woodie Held (526 SS, 448 OF).... Has driven in 77 runs in each of the last three seasons. (Tom Brunansky had three straight 85s from 1987 through 1989.)... Last season's batting average was his highest since he posted a .318 mark in 1989, the last of his six .300 seasons (including four in a row from '86 through '89).... Has hit 56 home runs over the past four seasons, half of them to right field. The only players with more opposite-field home runs during that time: Fred McGriff (34), Danny Tartabull (32), and Bo Jackson (30).... Last season was his first 40-double season since 1983. The only other players with nine years between 40-double seasons: Bob Johnson (11 years, 1933–44), George Brett (1979–88), Augue Galan (1935–44), and George ("Highpockets") Kelly (1921–29).

Bob Zupcic
Bats Right

Boston Red Sox	AB	H	2B	3B	HR	RBI	BB	SO	BA	SA	OBA
Season	392	108	19	1	3	43	25	60	.276	.352	.322
vs. Left-Handers	133	39	8	1	0	15	13	14	.293	.368	.356
vs. Right-Handers	259	69	11	0	3	28	12	46	.266	.344	.304
vs. Ground-Ballers	197	60	10	1	1	21	11	27	.305	.381	.352
vs. Fly-Ballers	195	48	9	0	2	22	14	33	.246	.323	.292
Home Games	189	50	11	1	3	25	10	32	.265	.381	.310
Road Games	203	58	8	0	0	18	15	28	.286	.325	.333
Grass Fields	332	93	17	1	3	40	22	53	.280	.364	.328
Artificial Turf	60	15	2	0	0	3	3	7	.250	.283	.292
April	5	2	1	0	0	1	0	1	.400	.600	.400
May	46	15	5	0	0	3	4	6	.326	.435	.392
June	50	15	3	0	1	7	1	9	.300	.420	.302
July	80	24	4	0	2	10	7	10	.300	.425	.352
August	109	24	3	0	0	11	7	18	.220	.248	.286
Sept./Oct.	102	28	3	1	0	11	6	16	.275	.324	.312
Leading Off Inn.	76	17	3	0	1	1	5	11	.224	.303	.280
Runners On	155	51	8	1	2	42	7	24	.329	.432	.357
Bases Empty	237	57	11	0	1	1	18	36	.241	.300	.300
Runners/Scor. Pos.	95	28	3	1	2	40	6	18	.295	.411	.324
Runners On/2 Out	68	24	4	1	1	18	3	9	.353	.485	.380
Scor. Pos./2 Out	46	14	2	1	1	17	2	7	.304	.457	.333
Late-Inning Pressure	62	18	4	0	2	15	6	10	.290	.452	.353
Leading Off	15	2	0	0	0	0	2	4	.133	.133	.235
Runners On	30	10	2	0	2	15	2	3	.333	.600	.375
Runners/Scor. Pos.	16	6	1	0	2	14	2	3	.375	.813	.444

RUNS BATTED IN	From 1B	From 2B	From 3B	Scoring Position
Totals	4/108	17/80	19/43	36/123
Percentage	3.7%	21.3%	44.2%	29.3%

Loves to face: Todd Frohwirth (3-for-3)
Mike Henneman (.500, 3-for-6, 1 HR)
Mark Langston (.500, 6-for-12)

Hates to face: Juan Guzman (0-for-5, 4 SO)
Dave Otto (0-for-6)

Miscellaneous statistics: Ground outs-to-air outs ratio: 0.70 last season, 0.71 for career.... Grounded into 6 double plays in 68 opportunities (one per 11).... Drove in 13 of 26 runners from third base with less than two outs (50%).... Direction of balls hit to the outfield: 36% to left field, 39% to center, 25% to right.... Base running: Advanced from first base to third on 10 of 21 outfield singles (48%); scored from second on 13 of 16 (81%).... Made 2.70 putouts per nine innings in center field, 2d-lowest rate in A.L.

Comments: Although the Red Sox lacked a legitimate Rookie-of-the-Year candidate, their rookies combined for more home runs (18) and RBIs (114) than those of any other American League team. The major contributors were Scott Cooper (5 HR, 33 RBI), John Valentin (5 HR, 25 RBI), Eric Wedge (5 HR, 11 RBI), and Zupcic (3 HR, 43 RBI).... Although Tom Brunansky had the highest batting average among the three Red Sox who qualified for the batting title, three of those rookies posted higher averages: Cooper (337 AB), Valentin (185 AB), and Zupcic, all of whom batted .276.... Batting average of .211 from the 3d spot in the batting order was lowest in the majors (minimum: 100 PA).... Seven of his 14 go-ahead RBIs came in the seventh inning or later.... Was hitless in 14 at-bats against the Blue Jays.... He and Dante Bichette were the only major leaguers to bat .300 or better in each of the first four months of the season.... Was one of seven players to start at least 10 games at each of the three outfield positions last season.... Has four career homers, all at Fenway Park.... Has hit two home runs in 11 at-bats with the bases full, two more in 448 ABs with fewer than three runners on base.... The only players listed after Bob Zupcic in *The Baseball Encyclopedia*: Frank Zupo, Paul Zuvella, George Zuverink, and Dutch Zwilling. The Manhattan *White Pages* go all the way up to Archimedes Zzzyandottie. Try and beat that!

Luis Alicea — Bats Left and Right

St. Louis Cardinals	AB	H	2B	3B	HR	RBI	BB	SO	BA	SA	OBA
Season	265	65	9	11	2	32	27	40	.245	.385	.320
vs. Left-Handers	85	25	4	3	0	12	5	10	.294	.412	.340
vs. Right-Handers	180	40	5	8	2	20	22	30	.222	.372	.311
vs. Ground-Ballers	132	28	4	5	0	12	11	18	.212	.318	.269
vs. Fly-Ballers	133	37	5	6	2	20	16	22	.278	.451	.368
Home Games	145	40	6	10	2	18	17	18	.276	.497	.361
Road Games	120	25	3	1	0	14	10	22	.208	.250	.269
Grass Fields	52	7	1	0	0	5	4	12	.135	.154	.193
Artificial Turf	213	58	8	11	2	27	23	28	.272	.441	.350
April	44	5	1	0	0	2	3	9	.114	.136	.163
May	63	22	2	6	1	12	6	5	.349	.619	.425
June	0	0	0	0	0	0	0	0	—	—	—
July	34	10	1	1	0	2	3	6	.294	.382	.351
August	75	16	3	3	0	4	11	12	.213	.333	.322
Sept./Oct.	49	12	2	1	1	12	4	8	.245	.388	.296
Leading Off Inn.	59	12	2	1	0	0	6	8	.203	.271	.299
Runners On	109	28	4	7	0	30	8	16	.257	.422	.309
Bases Empty	156	37	5	4	2	2	19	24	.237	.359	.328
Runners/Scor. Pos.	71	16	3	3	0	25	7	13	.225	.352	.298
Runners On/2 Out	46	8	2	2	0	11	5	5	.174	.304	.283
Scor. Pos./2 Out	39	8	2	2	0	11	4	4	.205	.359	.311
Late-Inning Pressure	55	11	1	1	1	5	7	11	.200	.309	.308
Leading Off	13	3	1	0	0	0	1	2	.231	.308	.375
Runners On	22	3	0	1	0	4	2	5	.136	.227	.200
Runners/Scor. Pos.	16	3	0	1	0	4	1	3	.188	.313	.222

RUNS BATTED IN	From 1B	From 2B	From 3B	Scoring Position
Totals	8/72	11/56	11/31	22/87
Percentage	11.1%	19.6%	35.5%	25.3%

Loves to face: Danny Jackson (.571, 4-for-7, 1 3B)
Darryl Kile (.667, 4-for-6)
Roger McDowell (.500, 3-for-6)
Hates to face: Frank Castillo (0-for-6, 3 SO)
John Smoltz (0-for-7)
Bob Walk (0-for-6)

Miscellaneous statistics: Ground outs-to-air outs ratio: 0.86 last season, 1.00 for career.... Grounded into 5 double plays in 50 opportunities (one per 10).... Drove in 8 of 14 runners from third base with less than two outs (57%).... Direction of balls hit to the outfield: 27% to left field, 31% to center, 42% to right batting left-handed; 28% to left field, 33% to center, 39% to right batting right-handed.... Base running: Advanced from first base to third on 3 of 5 outfield singles (60%); scored from second on 6 of 8 (75%).... Made 3.21 assists per nine innings at second base.

Comments: Tied for 4th in N.L. with 11 triples despite having only 265 at-bats, the lowest total in this century by a player with more than 10 triples. The last player to hit as many triples as Alicea in fewer ABs: Hughie Jennings (12 in 224 AB in 1899).... Only two players in the previous 50 years reached double figures in triples but no doubles: Jorge Orta (1973 White Sox) and Sid Gordon (1943 Giants). Both Alicea and Deion Sanders did that last season.... Posted the highest average from the eighth slot (.310) of any N.L. player (minimum: 100 PA), but hit only .213 when batting elsewhere.... Among active players, only Geronimo Berroa has more career pinch-hit at-bats without ever driving in a run. The top three: Berroa (59), Alicea (50), Jeff Reed (40). Last season, four of his seven appearances as a pinch hitter came with runners in scoring position.... Among N.L. players with at least 50 games at second base last season, only Mark Lemke (0) and Willie Randolph (1) stole fewer bases than Alicea (2).... Cardinals second basemen combined for 10 home runs last season, on the strength of seven by Geronimo Pena. The only other N.L. clubs with double-digit output at that position were the Cubs (26) and Giants (16).... Batted .311 in day games, .220 at night.... Career batting average breakdown: .246 at Busch Stadium, .215 on other artificial turfs, .189 on grass fields. All three of his homers have been hit in St. Louis; all 15 of his triples have been hit on artificial turf.

Moises Alou — Bats Right

Montreal Expos	AB	H	2B	3B	HR	RBI	BB	SO	BA	SA	OBA
Season	341	96	28	2	9	56	25	46	.282	.455	.328
vs. Left-Handers	136	40	11	0	2	14	7	13	.294	.419	.329
vs. Right-Handers	205	56	17	2	7	42	18	33	.273	.478	.327
vs. Ground-Ballers	139	42	12	1	3	27	15	15	.302	.468	.367
vs. Fly-Ballers	202	54	16	1	6	29	10	31	.267	.446	.299
Home Games	143	48	14	2	6	35	11	19	.336	.587	.376
Road Games	198	48	14	0	3	21	14	27	.242	.359	.293
Grass Fields	91	23	9	0	1	10	10	12	.253	.385	.320
Artificial Turf	250	73	19	2	8	46	15	34	.292	.480	.331
April	9	5	2	0	0	1	0	2	.556	.778	.556
May	51	14	4	1	1	4	6	7	.275	.451	.351
June	79	25	6	1	3	22	6	8	.316	.532	.352
July	44	11	5	0	0	5	2	7	.250	.364	.283
August	88	20	6	0	2	8	8	14	.227	.364	.293
Sept./Oct.	70	21	5	0	3	16	3	8	.300	.500	.329
Leading Off Inn.	64	23	8	1	2	2	4	8	.359	.609	.397
Runners On	162	47	13	1	6	53	11	17	.290	.494	.330
Bases Empty	179	49	15	1	3	3	14	29	.274	.419	.326
Runners/Scor. Pos.	113	33	8	1	5	47	11	14	.292	.513	.346
Runners On/2 Out	66	16	3	0	0	13	3	7	.242	.288	.286
Scor. Pos./2 Out	50	13	2	0	0	12	3	6	.260	.300	.315
Late-Inning Pressure	52	15	4	1	3	12	3	7	.288	.577	.321
Leading Off	11	7	3	1	1	1	0	1	.636	1.364	.636
Runners On	27	6	0	0	2	11	0	4	.222	.444	.214
Runners/Scor. Pos.	22	5	0	0	2	11	0	2	.227	.500	.217

RUNS BATTED IN	From 1B	From 2B	From 3B	Scoring Position
Totals	10/100	14/82	23/50	37/132
Percentage	10.0%	17.1%	46.0%	28.0%

Loves to face: Jeff D. Robinson (.500, 2-for-4, 4 BB)
Bob Scanlan (.750, 3-for-4)
Randy Tomlin (.750, 3-for-4, 1 HR)
Hates to face: Kyle Abbott (0-for-7)
Steve Avery (0-for-9)
Ben Rivera (0-for-8, 3 SO)

Miscellaneous statistics: Ground outs-to-air outs ratio: 0.73 last season, 0.78 for career.... Grounded into 5 double plays in 67 opportunities (one per 13).... Drove in 20 of 33 runners from third base with less than two outs (61%).... Direction of balls hit to the outfield: 35% to left field, 28% to center, 37% to right.... Base running: Advanced from first base to third on 5 of 11 outfield singles (45%); scored from second on 10 of 12 (83%).... Made 1.85 putouts per nine innings in left field, 3d-lowest rate in majors.

Comments: His 16 stolen bases tied Reggie Sanders for the N.L. rookie lead.... Stolen base percentage (.889, 16 steals in 18 attempts) was highest of any major league rookie with at least 15 attempts. Since the N.L. started tracking "caught stealing" in 1951, only two other rookies have posted higher stolen-base percentages (minimum: 15 attempts), and both were Expos: Ellis Valentine in 1976 (.933) and Marquis Grissom in 1990 (.917).... Hit the Expos' only grand slam last season, his only hit in eight at-bats with the bases loaded.... Had the highest batting average of any N.L. rookie (minimum: 150 at-bats). Montreal rookies combined for a .256 average, the highest by any N.L. club last season; league batting average for rookies was .229. Expos rookies also led the majors with a combined total of 156 RBIs.... Although he bats from the right side, his walk rate was considerably higher against right-handed pitchers (one every 12.7 PA) than against left-handers (one every 21.1 PA).... Born in Atlanta on July 3, 1966, while his father was playing for the Braves. His dad went 0-for-3 against the Giants and was the only one of the three Alou brothers not to get a hit that day.... Through last season, at least one Alou had played for every N.L. club except the Dodgers, Reds, Phillies, and Cubs.... Robin Yount is the only player still active who had been a major league teammate of Moises's dad, Felipe. You don't remember Felipe with the Brewers? Neither did we: He had just three at-bats for them in 1974.

Ruben Amaro Jr.   Bats Left and Right

Philadelphia Phillies	AB	H	2B	3B	HR	RBI	BB	SO	BA	SA	OBA
Season	374	82	15	6	7	34	37	54	.219	.348	.303
vs. Left-Handers	154	39	8	3	2	17	18	14	.253	.383	.343
vs. Right-Handers	220	43	7	3	5	17	19	40	.195	.323	.275
vs. Ground-Ballers	187	41	11	3	5	17	16	30	.219	.390	.301
vs. Fly-Ballers	187	41	4	3	2	17	21	24	.219	.305	.305
Home Games	169	36	7	4	5	17	15	28	.213	.391	.291
Road Games	205	46	8	2	2	17	22	26	.224	.312	.313
Grass Fields	121	31	5	1	1	10	16	12	.256	.339	.355
Artificial Turf	253	51	10	5	6	24	21	42	.202	.352	.278
April	65	9	3	0	3	7	10	9	.138	.323	.273
May	46	11	2	0	0	5	6	9	.239	.283	.327
June	74	15	3	1	1	7	11	13	.203	.311	.322
July	56	13	0	1	1	3	3	6	.232	.321	.283
August	24	7	0	1	0	0	2	5	.292	.375	.346
Sept./Oct.	109	27	7	3	2	12	5	12	.248	.422	.300
Leading Off Inn.	107	29	6	3	2	2	9	12	.271	.439	.355
Runners On	153	31	6	2	2	29	15	25	.203	.307	.279
Bases Empty	221	51	9	4	5	5	22	29	.231	.376	.320
Runners/Scor. Pos.	84	13	3	2	0	24	12	15	.155	.238	.263
Runners On/2 Out	61	8	2	2	0	10	9	13	.131	.230	.264
Scor. Pos./2 Out	39	6	2	2	0	10	7	8	.154	.308	.298
Late-Inning Pressure	61	12	2	1	1	3	11	13	.197	.311	.329
Leading Off	17	4	1	1	0	0	2	3	.235	.412	.350
Runners On	19	5	0	0	1	3	6	3	.263	.421	.440
Runners/Scor. Pos.	8	1	0	0	0	1	6	1	.125	.125	.500

RUNS BATTED IN	From 1B	From 2B	From 3B	Scoring Position
Totals	6/116	7/70	14/44	21/114
Percentage	5.2%	10.0%	31.8%	18.4%

Loves to face: Mark Clark (.750, 3-for-4, 1 HR, 1 SO)
Sid Fernandez (.400, 4-for-10, 6 fly outs)
Dwight Gooden (.417, 5-for-12)
Hates to face: Doug Drabek (.077, 1-for-13, 1 2B)
Ken Hill (0-for-10)
Jose Rijo (0-for-6)

Miscellaneous statistics: Ground outs-to-air outs ratio: 1.16 last season, 1.20 for career.... Grounded into 11 double plays in 75 opportunities (one per 6.8).... Drove in 9 of 23 runners from third base with less than two outs (39%), 3d-lowest rate in N.L.... Direction of balls hit to the outfield: 33% to left field, 23% to center, 44% to right batting left-handed; 34% to left field, 38% to center, 27% to right batting right-handed.... Base running: Advanced from first base to third on 4 of 21 outfield singles (19%); scored from second on 5 of 7 (71%).... Made 2.11 putouts per nine innings in right field.

Comments: His 28 extra-base hits were more than his father had in any of his 11 years in the majors, and he stands just one home run shy of his dad's career total of eight (in about 1800 fewer at-bats). Junior is a late bloomer who has played only 136 games in the bigs; at the same age, Amaro the elder had already played 459 major league games.... Junior's performance wasn't too good in some categories that weren't recorded back in dad's day: Batting average vs. right-handed pitchers was a major league low; his average with runners on base was 3d lowest in N.L.; and his averages with runners in scoring position or with runners on base and two outs were both 2d lowest in the league.... He batted only .185 when hitting in the first slot, lowest among major league players with at least 100 plate appearances in the leadoff spot.... Had an 0-for-28 streak in April, 2d longest on the team last year to an 0-for-33 by Terry Mulholland.... Amaro and Reggie Sanders shared the distinction of having the most triples among N.L. rookies, and he led all major league rookies in times being hit by a pitch (nine).... The only N.L. player to start at least 10 games in each of the three outfield spots.... Philadelphia outfielders combined to hit just .247 last year, the lowest by any N.L. team. They also combined for the fewest assists (22) by any outfield in either league. Phillies right fielders contributed only four assists to that total, while other teams averaged more than 12 from that spot.

Eric Anthony   Bats Left

Houston Astros	AB	H	2B	3B	HR	RBI	BB	SO	BA	SA	OBA
Season	440	105	15	1	19	80	38	98	.239	.407	.298
vs. Left-Handers	156	33	6	0	5	28	12	44	.212	.346	.269
vs. Right-Handers	284	72	9	1	14	52	26	54	.254	.440	.314
vs. Ground-Ballers	185	46	4	0	8	32	17	32	.249	.400	.314
vs. Fly-Ballers	255	59	11	1	11	48	21	66	.231	.412	.287
Home Games	207	54	8	1	9	36	14	46	.261	.440	.309
Road Games	233	51	7	0	10	44	24	52	.219	.378	.288
Grass Fields	142	31	3	0	8	28	14	30	.218	.408	.285
Artificial Turf	298	74	12	1	11	52	24	68	.248	.406	.305
April	12	2	0	0	0	0	1	3	.167	.167	.231
May	80	21	6	0	2	19	7	14	.262	.412	.318
June	74	20	4	1	3	13	6	19	.270	.473	.325
July	82	20	1	0	7	19	6	16	.244	.512	.292
August	100	19	2	0	3	18	12	24	.190	.300	.277
Sept./Oct.	92	23	2	0	4	11	6	22	.250	.402	.296
Leading Off Inn.	103	19	1	0	2	2	8	24	.184	.252	.243
Runners On	211	59	10	0	11	72	22	43	.280	.483	.342
Bases Empty	229	46	5	1	8	8	16	55	.201	.336	.256
Runners/Scor. Pos.	139	37	7	0	4	56	17	33	.266	.403	.338
Runners On/2 Out	89	22	6	0	2	26	4	24	.247	.382	.280
Scor. Pos./2 Out	70	18	5	0	1	23	3	21	.257	.371	.288
Late-Inning Pressure	79	20	1	0	6	20	6	20	.253	.494	.302
Leading Off	20	5	0	0	1	1	2	5	.250	.400	.318
Runners On	37	13	1	0	4	18	4	10	.351	.703	.405
Runners/Scor. Pos.	26	9	1	0	2	14	4	9	.346	.615	.419

RUNS BATTED IN	From 1B	From 2B	From 3B	Scoring Position
Totals	12/133	22/107	27/59	49/166
Percentage	9.0%	20.6%	45.8%	29.5%

Loves to face: Jose DeLeon (.455, 5-for-11)
Bruce Hurst (.300, 3-for-10, 1 2B, 2 HR, 4 SO)
Les Lancaster (.571, 4-for-7)
Hates to face: Jose DeJesus (0-for-10)
Curt Schilling (0-for-8)
Trevor Wilson (.091, 1-for-11)

Miscellaneous statistics: Ground outs-to-air outs ratio: 1.08 last season, 1.06 for career.... Grounded into 7 double plays in 95 opportunities (one per 14).... Drove in 19 of 27 runners from third base with less than two outs (70%).... Direction of balls hit to the outfield: 27% to left field, 28% to center, 45% to right.... Base running: Advanced from first base to third on 7 of 23 outfield singles (30%); scored from second on 7 of 12 (58%).... Made 1.72 putouts per nine innings in right field, 2d-lowest rate in majors.

Comments: Drove in 80 runs despite his relatively low total of only 105 hits, narrowly missing the N.L. low for hits among 80-RBI men. Bob Bailey had 101 hits and 84 RBIs for Montreal in 1970; the major league low was set by Clyde Vollmer of the Red Sox in 1951 when he had 97 hits and 85 RBIs. In the same vein, Ted Williams had the fewest hits for a 90-RBI man (106 hits, 97 RBIs in 1950), and Rudy York had the fewest hits for a 100-RBI man (115 hits, 103 RBIs in 1937).... Anthony had the only two grand-slam home runs by any Houston player last year.... No doubt about it, he gets his hits at the key times: .178 career average with the bases empty, .250 with runners on base, .319 with runners on base in Late-Inning Pressure Situations.... He was Houston's 34th selection in the 1986 June draft. Among the players selected after him that year, only two have played in the majors: Jesse Levis and Doug Linton.... Career home run rate is better at the Astrodome (one every 24.4 AB) than on the road (one every 25.9 AB).... Led his league in home runs in three consecutive minor league seasons (1987-89).... Rate of walks has decreased in each of his seasons in the majors, to a career low of one every 12.7 plate appearances last year.... His .210 career batting average stands as the 3d-lowest by any nonpitcher in Astros history (minimum: 500 at-bats). Only Luis Pujols (.192) and Hector Torres (.206) stand lower.

Jeff Bagwell
Houston Astros — Bats Right

	AB	H	2B	3B	HR	RBI	BB	SO	BA	SA	OBA
Season	586	160	34	6	18	96	84	97	.273	.444	.368
vs. Left-Handers	210	61	13	3	10	34	38	31	.290	.524	.394
vs. Right-Handers	376	99	21	3	8	62	46	66	.263	.399	.354
vs. Ground-Ballers	259	68	13	4	8	48	35	41	.263	.436	.361
vs. Fly-Ballers	327	92	21	2	10	48	49	56	.281	.450	.374
Home Games	294	76	21	3	8	48	42	50	.259	.432	.355
Road Games	292	84	13	3	10	48	42	47	.288	.455	.382
Grass Fields	172	56	4	1	6	33	24	23	.326	.465	.407
Artificial Turf	414	104	30	5	12	63	60	74	.251	.435	.352
April	78	20	4	1	2	12	13	19	.256	.410	.370
May	105	22	5	0	4	19	11	20	.210	.371	.308
June	97	28	5	0	3	13	17	13	.289	.433	.388
July	88	21	4	3	3	14	12	18	.239	.455	.324
August	105	26	7	2	1	16	16	13	.248	.381	.349
Sept./Oct.	113	43	9	0	5	22	15	14	.381	.593	.459
Leading Off Inn.	135	41	11	1	5	5	20	22	.304	.511	.401
Runners On	268	72	13	2	7	85	48	50	.269	.410	.380
Bases Empty	318	88	21	4	11	11	36	47	.277	.472	.358
Runners/Scor. Pos.	178	47	6	2	5	78	39	35	.264	.404	.385
Runners On/2 Out	100	20	1	1	4	20	25	19	.200	.350	.385
Scor. Pos./2 Out	70	12	0	1	3	18	21	16	.171	.329	.383
Late-Inning Pressure	96	35	5	2	8	25	23	15	.365	.708	.496
Leading Off	25	10	1	0	3	3	5	4	.400	.800	.500
Runners On	41	17	3	1	4	21	15	6	.415	.829	.579
Runners/Scor. Pos.	28	11	1	1	3	17	12	4	.393	.821	.585

RUNS BATTED IN	From 1B	From 2B	From 3B	Scoring Position
Totals	10/173	24/140	44/82	68/222
Percentage	5.8%	17.1%	53.7%	30.6%

Loves to face: Andy Benes (.471, 8-for-17, 1 HR)
Jose DeJesus (.667, 6-for-9, 1 HR)
Randy Myers (.455, 5-for-11, 3 2B, 2 HR)
Hates to face: Tim Belcher (.067, 1-for-15, 1 2B, 3 BB)
Frank Castillo (0-for-13)
Rich Rodriguez (0-for-7, 4 SO)

Miscellaneous statistics: Ground outs-to-air outs ratio: 0.95 last season, 0.94 for career.... Grounded into 17 double plays in 124 opportunities (one per 7.3).... Drove in 39 of 55 runners from third base with less than two outs (71%).... Direction of balls hit to the outfield: 27% to left field, 29% to center, 43% to right.... Base running: Advanced from first base to third on 8 of 31 outfield singles (26%); scored from second on 10 of 17 (59%).... Made 0.85 assists per nine innings at first base.

Comments: Hit for 2d-highest average in N.L. in Late-Inning Pressure Situations last season, giving him a career average of .385 in LIPS, the highest by any player since 1975 (minimum: 50 hits in LIPS). His .444 mark (32-for-72) with runners on base in LIPS is also a major league high since 1975.... Drove in over 30 percent of runners from scoring position in both his rookie and sophomore years. Since 1975, only one N.L. player has driven in at least 30 percent of such runners in each of his first three seasons: Mark Grace (1988–90).... One of only four players in majors to play in all 162 games last season. Besides Cal Ripken, the other three were all Astros: Bagwell, Craig Biggio, and Steve Finley.... Led N.L. with 151 complete games last season.... Tied Joe Carter for most sacrifice flies in the majors (13).... Hit by 12 pitches last season, 2d-highest total in the league.... Had five games with at least four hits, tied for most in the majors with Delino DeShields, George Brett, and Gregg Jefferies.... Started 18 double plays, the most by any N.L. first baseman.... Career batting breakdown: .305 (one HR every 24.5 AB) vs. left-handers, .271 (one HR every 45.3 AB) vs. right-handers.... A .352 career hitter after September 1; maybe he'll get to put that to use in a pennant race this year.

Bret Barberie
Montreal Expos — Bats Left and Right

	AB	H	2B	3B	HR	RBI	BB	SO	BA	SA	OBA
Season	285	66	11	0	1	24	47	62	.232	.281	.354
vs. Left-Handers	67	11	3	0	0	7	9	18	.164	.209	.287
vs. Right-Handers	218	55	8	0	1	17	38	44	.252	.303	.374
vs. Ground-Ballers	134	36	7	0	0	9	26	28	.269	.321	.400
vs. Fly-Ballers	151	30	4	0	1	15	21	34	.199	.245	.311
Home Games	132	38	4	0	0	15	26	23	.288	.318	.414
Road Games	153	28	7	0	1	9	21	39	.183	.248	.300
Grass Fields	93	18	3	0	1	6	10	27	.194	.258	.286
Artificial Turf	192	48	8	0	0	18	37	35	.250	.292	.384
April	70	16	4	0	0	1	14	18	.229	.286	.365
May	30	8	0	0	0	5	6	10	.267	.267	.405
June	19	1	0	0	0	3	4	5	.053	.053	.240
July	51	15	4	0	1	9	9	11	.294	.431	.419
August	51	11	2	0	0	2	2	12	.216	.255	.286
Sept./Oct.	64	15	1	0	0	4	12	6	.234	.250	.351
Leading Off Inn.	77	19	4	0	0	0	3	13	.247	.299	.301
Runners On	107	27	5	0	0	23	20	28	.252	.299	.374
Bases Empty	178	39	6	0	1	1	27	34	.219	.270	.341
Runners/Scor. Pos.	75	17	4	0	0	23	13	18	.227	.280	.348
Runners On/2 Out	42	8	3	0	0	10	7	13	.190	.262	.320
Scor. Pos./2 Out	32	8	3	0	0	10	7	8	.250	.344	.400
Late-Inning Pressure	49	12	3	0	0	7	7	14	.245	.306	.339
Leading Off	14	3	0	0	0	0	0	3	.214	.214	.214
Runners On	22	6	3	0	0	7	3	6	.273	.409	.360
Runners/Scor. Pos.	16	5	3	0	0	7	3	3	.313	.500	.421

RUNS BATTED IN	From 1B	From 2B	From 3B	Scoring Position
Totals	0/64	12/62	11/29	23/91
Percentage	0.0%	19.4%	37.9%	25.3%

Loves to face: Omar Olivares (.385, 5-for-13, 2 BB, 2 HBP)
Bob Walk (.500, 5-for-10)
Anthony Young (4-for-4, 2 BB)
Hates to face: Paul Assenmacher (0-for-5)
Mike Morgan (.100, 1-for-10)
Ben Rivera (0-for-6)

Miscellaneous statistics: Ground outs-to-air outs ratio: 1.25 last season, 1.13 for career.... Grounded into 4 double plays in 52 opportunities (one per 13).... Drove in 8 of 18 runners from third base with less than two outs (44%).... Direction of balls hit to the outfield: 34% to left field, 43% to center, 23% to right batting left-handed; 29% to left field, 33% to center, 38% to right batting right-handed.... Base running: Advanced from first base to third on 7 of 23 outfield singles (30%); scored from second on 5 of 10 (50%), 5th-lowest rate in N.L.... Made 2.25 assists per nine innings at third base, 2d-highest rate in N.L.

Comments: Started nearly 60 percent of games in which Expos faced a right-handed starter (61 of 103), but only 13 of 59 games in which they faced a lefty.... No one expected him to bat .353 again (which he did in 136 at-bats in 1991), but a lot of folks expected more than .232. That kind of a drop-off by a player making the rookie-to-sophomore transition brings back memories of Hurricane Hazle, who batted .403 in 134 at-bats helping the Braves to the 1957 World Championship before falling off to .211 in 114 at-bats the next year. Actually, for a sheer numerical drop, the all-time champ is Royals outfielder Butch Davis, who hit .344 in 122 at-bats in 1983 and .147 in 116 at-bats in 1984.... Batted .183 in road games, 2d worst in the N.L., ahead of only Damon Berryhill (.170).... Career batting breakdown: .317 vs. ground-ball pitchers, .228 vs. fly-ballers.... His walk rate (one every 7.3 plate appearances) was the best among rookies or sophomores with at least 250 trips to the plate last season.... Last year's strikeout rate of one every 5.5 plate appearances was extremely high for a player with only one home run. Since 1969, only two N.L. players have posted higher strikeout rates in seasons of at least 300 plate appearances and fewer than two home runs: Steve Jeltz in 1986 and John Shelby in 1989. It's not quite as uncommon in the American League, where Gary Pettis, Joel Skinner, Manny Lee, and Pat Listach have all done it in recent years.

Kevin Bass — Bats Left and Right

Giants/Mets	AB	H	2B	3B	HR	RBI	BB	SO	BA	SA	OBA
Season	402	108	23	5	9	39	23	70	.269	.418	.308
vs. Left-Handers	144	32	13	1	4	17	3	22	.222	.410	.236
vs. Right-Handers	258	76	10	4	5	22	20	48	.295	.422	.345
vs. Ground-Ballers	187	51	13	2	3	12	12	36	.273	.412	.320
vs. Fly-Ballers	215	57	10	3	6	27	11	34	.265	.423	.297
Home Games	216	63	16	2	7	25	12	41	.292	.481	.329
Road Games	186	45	7	3	2	14	11	29	.242	.344	.283
Grass Fields	298	84	18	2	8	32	16	55	.282	.436	.319
Artificial Turf	104	24	5	3	1	7	7	15	.231	.365	.277
April	38	12	2	1	1	6	4	11	.316	.500	.381
May	72	13	5	2	0	3	2	14	.181	.306	.211
June	63	21	3	0	3	14	4	9	.333	.524	.368
July	69	15	1	0	1	3	6	15	.217	.275	.280
August	86	22	3	0	3	8	4	15	.256	.395	.286
Sept./Oct.	74	25	9	2	1	5	3	6	.338	.554	.364
Leading Off Inn.	106	39	10	3	5	5	1	16	.368	.660	.380
Runners On	182	40	6	0	3	33	17	34	.220	.302	.282
Bases Empty	220	68	17	5	6	6	6	36	.309	.514	.330
Runners/Scor. Pos.	117	24	3	0	1	28	14	21	.205	.256	.284
Runners On/2 Out	82	14	1	0	2	12	8	17	.171	.256	.244
Scor. Pos./2 Out	54	9	0	0	1	10	7	10	.167	.222	.262
Late-Inning Pressure	85	27	5	2	3	9	3	13	.318	.529	.337
Leading Off	25	15	4	2	2	2	0	0	.600	1.160	.600
Runners On	40	9	1	0	1	7	3	8	.225	.325	.273
Runners/Scor. Pos.	26	7	1	0	0	5	3	4	.269	.308	.333

RUNS BATTED IN	From 1B	From 2B	From 3B	Scoring Position
Totals	4/118	13/96	13/43	26/139
Percentage	3.4%	13.5%	30.2%	18.7%

Loves to face: Tim Crews (.667, 6-for-9), Randy Myers (.385, 5-for-13, 2 HR), Armando Reynoso (3-for-3, 1 HR)

Hates to face: Bruce Hurst (.160, 4-for-25, 0 BB), Alejandro Pena (.100, 2-for-20), Todd Worrell (.091, 1-for-11)

Miscellaneous statistics: Ground outs-to-air outs ratio: 1.21 last season, 1.10 for career.... Grounded into 8 double plays in 69 opportunities (one per 8.6).... Drove in 12 of 25 runners from third base with less than two outs (48%).... Direction of balls hit to the outfield: 30% to left field, 40% to center, 30% to right batting left-handed; 37% to left field, 27% to center, 36% to right batting right-handed.... Base running: Advanced from first base to third on 4 of 14 outfield singles (29%); scored from second on 4 of 8 (50%).... Made 2.03 putouts per nine innings in left field.

Comments: Mets' collection of switch-hitters was a big topic of discussion leading into last season, but by the time September rolled around, fans at Shea were watching midseason recruits Kevin Bass and Chico Walker rather than Howard Johnson and Bobby Bonilla. The Mets became the first team in major league history to employ 10 switch-hitting position players during a season (the others: Eddie Murray, Vince Coleman, Todd Hundley, Jeff McKnight, Pat Howell, and Rodney McCray); the 1984 Expos also had 10 switchers, but pitcher Greg Harris was one of them. Note that in the Mets' case, none was a September call-up, either.... Bass batted better than .300 after September 1 for the fifth time in 10 years; three times those September marks have stood above .330.... He and Darren Daulton were the only players to hit four home runs against the Braves last season.... Last season's strikeout rate—one every 6.1 plate appearances—was his worst since 1984, and his rate of runners driven in from scoring position was the lowest of his career.... Over the last 10 years, he's posted a higher average from the left side five times and a higher average from the right side five times. Career breakdown: .273 batting right-handed, .267 batting left-handed.... What does Bass have in common with Hall-of-Famers Warren Spahn and Willie Mays? They all played for the Giants and the Mets in the same season. So did Tommy Herr, Chuck Hiller, Bob Shaw, Mike Phillips, and, yes, Joe Pignatano.

Jay Bell — Bats Right

Pittsburgh Pirates	AB	H	2B	3B	HR	RBI	BB	SO	BA	SA	OBA
Season	632	167	36	6	9	55	55	103	.264	.383	.326
vs. Left-Handers	238	77	19	4	1	20	26	42	.324	.450	.396
vs. Right-Handers	394	90	17	2	8	35	29	61	.228	.343	.282
vs. Ground-Ballers	254	62	12	4	2	16	17	40	.244	.346	.299
vs. Fly-Ballers	378	105	24	2	7	39	38	63	.278	.407	.344
Home Games	302	84	19	3	5	27	33	49	.278	.411	.352
Road Games	330	83	17	3	4	28	22	54	.252	.358	.301
Grass Fields	166	45	11	2	3	18	10	28	.271	.416	.313
Artificial Turf	466	122	25	4	6	37	45	75	.262	.371	.331
April	72	17	2	0	0	5	14	7	.236	.264	.364
May	111	27	7	0	1	10	12	22	.243	.333	.317
June	104	28	6	1	2	10	12	16	.269	.404	.347
July	109	28	8	0	2	4	7	16	.257	.385	.302
August	102	29	7	2	1	13	7	22	.284	.422	.336
Sept./Oct.	134	38	6	3	3	13	3	20	.284	.440	.304
Leading Off Inn.	130	31	6	1	3	3	7	15	.238	.369	.283
Runners On	222	74	17	3	3	49	23	31	.333	.477	.393
Bases Empty	410	93	19	3	6	6	32	72	.227	.332	.289
Runners/Scor. Pos.	120	40	10	1	1	41	13	17	.333	.458	.393
Runners On/2 Out	81	24	9	2	1	23	11	12	.296	.494	.380
Scor. Pos./2 Out	54	16	7	0	1	20	7	7	.296	.481	.377
Late-Inning Pressure	98	29	4	3	2	10	9	12	.296	.459	.355
Leading Off	26	7	1	0	2	2	2	2	.269	.538	.321
Runners On	42	15	3	2	0	8	5	5	.357	.524	.426
Runners/Scor. Pos.	23	9	2	1	0	7	4	3	.391	.565	.481

RUNS BATTED IN	From 1B	From 2B	From 3B	Scoring Position
Totals	10/148	18/85	18/50	36/135
Percentage	6.8%	21.2%	36.0%	26.7%

Loves to face: Paul Assenmacher (.500, 5-for-10, 1 HR), Marvin Freeman (.800, 4-for-5, 1 HR), Danny Jackson (.455, 5-for-11)

Hates to face: Tommy Greene (.053, 1-for-19), Dennis Martinez (.150, 9-for-60), John Smoltz (.077, 2-for-26)

Miscellaneous statistics: Ground outs-to-air outs ratio: 0.90 last season, 1.05 for career.... Grounded into 12 double plays in 121 opportunities (one per 10).... Drove in 11 of 27 runners from third base with less than two outs (41%).... Direction of balls hit to the outfield: 42% to left field, 26% to center, 32% to right.... Base running: Advanced from first base to third on 12 of 31 outfield singles (39%); scored from second on 14 of 19 (74%).... Made 3.35 assists per nine innings at shortstop, highest rate in N.L.

Comments: Career numbers show that he is a much better hitter vs. left-handed pitchers than vs. right-handers, and he is a much better hitter with runners on base than with the bases empty. The breakdowns: .296 vs. lefties, .234 vs. righties; .301 with runners aboard, .227 with the bases empty.... One of eight players who has started 150+ games in each of the past three years.... Led all major league shortstops in assists (526) and chances accepted (794), and led N.L. shortstops in putouts (268) and double plays (94).... Made more outs in the air (208) than any other N.L. player last season.... Hitting streak of 22 games was the longest in the N.L. and the longest by a Pirates player since 1977 when Dave Parker had a pair of 22-game streaks.... Shows symptoms of Sandberg Syndrome: Bell owns .195 career batting average in April, .265 after that.... Batting average with runners on base was 5th best in N.L. as was his mark with runners in scoring position.... On-base percentage leading off innings was 3d worst in league.... Which major league shortstop had the most extra-base hits? Cal Ripken? Barry Larkin? Nope, it was Bell with 51.... Those 51 extra-base hits all came from the second slot in the batting order, which tied Edgar Martinez for the major league high among two-holers. Jay also led N.L. with 87 runs and 55 RBIs from the two hole.... Has 102 career sacrifice bunts; the last nonpitcher to tally 100 sacrifice bunts in fewer plate appearances than Bell was Dick Bartell, who reached that mark in 1932.

Rafael Belliard
Bats Right

Atlanta Braves	AB	H	2B	3B	HR	RBI	BB	SO	BA	SA	OBA
Season	285	60	6	1	0	14	14	43	.211	.239	.255
vs. Left-Handers	61	12	0	0	0	3	1	13	.197	.197	.210
vs. Right-Handers	224	48	6	1	0	11	13	30	.214	.250	.267
vs. Ground-Ballers	128	31	3	0	0	5	8	18	.242	.266	.292
vs. Fly-Ballers	157	29	3	1	0	9	6	25	.185	.217	.224
Home Games	125	25	2	0	0	5	8	12	.200	.216	.259
Road Games	160	35	4	1	0	9	6	31	.219	.256	.251
Grass Fields	206	40	3	0	0	10	11	32	.194	.209	.245
Artificial Turf	79	20	3	1	0	4	3	11	.253	.316	.280
April	55	14	1	0	0	1	4	8	.255	.273	.317
May	71	14	2	0	0	3	2	12	.197	.225	.219
June	46	9	1	0	0	2	3	6	.196	.217	.260
July	50	11	1	0	0	5	3	10	.220	.240	.264
August	38	8	1	1	0	2	1	4	.211	.289	.250
Sept./Oct.	25	4	0	0	0	1	1	3	.160	.160	.192
Leading Off Inn.	62	13	3	1	0	0	4	12	.210	.290	.269
Runners On	120	25	0	0	0	14	7	13	.208	.208	.252
Bases Empty	165	35	6	1	0	0	7	30	.212	.261	.257
Runners/Scor. Pos.	67	12	0	0	0	14	4	8	.179	.179	.225
Runners On/2 Out	57	9	0	0	0	4	7	6	.158	.158	.250
Scor. Pos./2 Out	37	5	0	0	0	4	4	5	.135	.135	.220
Late-Inning Pressure	20	5	0	0	0	2	0	4	.250	.250	.250
Leading Off	5	0	0	0	0	0	0	2	.000	.000	.000
Runners On	8	3	0	0	0	2	0	1	.375	.375	.375
Runners/Scor. Pos.	3	2	0	0	0	2	0	0	.667	.667	.667

RUNS BATTED IN	From 1B	From 2B	From 3B	Scoring Position
Totals	0/84	2/49	12/33	14/82
Percentage	0.0%	4.1%	36.4%	17.1%

Loves to face: Shawn Boskie (.444, 4-for-9)
Terry Mulholland (.417, 5-for-12)
Hates to face: Tim Belcher (.105, 2-for-19)
Kevin Gross (.111, 2-for-18, 2 BB)
Ramon Martinez (.077, 1-for-13)

Miscellaneous statistics: Ground outs-to-air outs ratio: 2.24 last season (2d highest in majors), 1.95 for career.... Grounded into 6 double plays in 58 opportunities (one per 10).... Drove in 9 of 18 runners from third base with less than two outs (50%).... Direction of balls hit to the outfield: 18% to left field, 39% to center, 44% to right.... Base running: Advanced from first base to third on 1 of 12 outfield singles (8%), 3d-lowest rate in N.L.; scored from second on 3 of 4 (75%).... Made 3.02 assists per nine innings at shortstop.

Comments: Braves' 8th-place hitters batted .201 with just 30 RBIs last season, the lowest batting average and RBI total from any lineup spot in the National League (excluding 9th-place hitters). Belliard started 80 games in that spot, the most on the team.... His .223 career batting average ranks 2d lowest among active players (minimum: 1000 at-bats), ahead of only Rob Deer (.222); Deer has outhomered Raffy, 205–1.... Has now gone 1284 at-bats since his home run off Eric Show on May 5, 1987, the 2d-longest current streak among active players.... Only player in the major leagues with at least 50 at-bats but no extra-base hits against left-handers last season; his career totals: 11 extra-base hits in 505 at-bats vs. lefties (seven doubles, four triples). In 1986 he had 122 at-bats vs. lefties with nothing longer than a single, the most by anyone since 1975.... Used 48 times as a defensive replacement, the most such appearances by any N.L. player.... All right, so he can't hit; did you know that he doesn't run, either? He went stealless last season. The last Braves shortstop to play as many games there as Belliard's 139 in a season without a stolen base was Marty Perez in 1972.... Still, he was the last Braves hitter to do something good in 1992: His sacrifice bunt in the 10th inning of World Series Game Six moved potential tying run John Smoltz into scoring position, but Brian Hunter grounded out and Otis Nixon bunted out to end the season.

Todd Benzinger
Bats Left and Right

Los Angeles Dodgers	AB	H	2B	3B	HR	RBI	BB	SO	BA	SA	OBA
Season	293	70	16	2	4	31	15	54	.239	.348	.272
vs. Left-Handers	126	34	5	1	1	16	3	12	.270	.349	.282
vs. Right-Handers	167	36	11	1	3	15	12	42	.216	.347	.264
vs. Ground-Ballers	108	27	8	0	2	11	6	15	.250	.380	.284
vs. Fly-Ballers	185	43	8	2	2	20	9	39	.232	.330	.264
Home Games	143	34	9	1	1	13	8	24	.238	.336	.275
Road Games	150	36	7	1	3	18	7	30	.240	.360	.269
Grass Fields	225	51	12	1	2	17	12	36	.227	.316	.261
Artificial Turf	68	19	4	1	2	14	3	18	.279	.456	.306
April	40	8	4	0	0	2	1	10	.200	.300	.220
May	60	16	3	1	2	14	5	9	.267	.450	.309
June	77	18	5	0	0	4	2	16	.234	.299	.253
July	58	14	3	0	0	4	4	9	.241	.293	.281
August	38	7	1	0	0	2	2	8	.184	.211	.225
Sept./Oct.	20	7	0	1	2	5	1	2	.350	.750	.381
Leading Off Inn.	76	19	5	0	0	0	4	14	.250	.316	.287
Runners On	122	29	6	1	3	30	6	27	.238	.377	.263
Bases Empty	171	41	10	1	1	1	9	27	.240	.327	.278
Runners/Scor. Pos.	69	16	2	1	2	27	4	15	.232	.377	.256
Runners On/2 Out	57	11	1	0	3	14	4	17	.193	.368	.246
Scor. Pos./2 Out	38	8	1	0	2	12	4	10	.211	.395	.286
Late-Inning Pressure	65	17	3	1	1	12	2	15	.262	.385	.275
Leading Off	15	5	1	0	0	0	1	1	.333	.400	.375
Runners On	28	5	1	1	1	12	0	11	.179	.393	.167
Runners/Scor. Pos.	17	4	1	1	1	12	0	5	.235	.588	.211

RUNS BATTED IN	From 1B	From 2B	From 3B	Scoring Position
Totals	5/92	8/55	14/39	22/94
Percentage	5.4%	14.5%	35.9%	23.4%

Loves to face: Steve Avery (.389, 7-for-18)
Tom Glavine (.382, 13-for-34, 2 HR)
Walt Terrell (.353, 6-for-17, 1 2B, 4 HR)
Hates to face: Terry Mulholland (.118, 2-for-17)
Bret Saberhagen (0-for-9, 5 SO)
Bob Tewksbury (0-for-10)

Miscellaneous statistics: Ground outs-to-air outs ratio: 1.09 last season, 1.01 for career.... Grounded into 6 double plays in 54 opportunities (one per 9.0).... Drove in 10 of 18 runners from third base with less than two outs (56%).... Direction of balls hit to the outfield: 31% to left field, 34% to center, 36% to right batting left-handed; 33% to left field, 38% to center, 29% to right batting right-handed.... Base running: Advanced from first base to third on 0 of 8 outfield singles (0%); scored from second on 6 of 9 (67%).... Made 1.64 putouts per nine innings in right field.

Comments: Batting average, on-base percentage, and RBI were all career lows.... Not exactly a Mercedes on the bases; he stole only two bases in six attempts, the fifth straight year that he has been caught stealing more times than he has stolen successfully; the only other current five-year streak in the majors belongs to Mark Lemke. Only nine players in history have had longer streaks, with Nellie Fox holding the record of eight straight seasons (1957–64); the last streak of six years: Tom Veryzer (1975–80). Benzinger's career totals: 19 stolen bases, 28 caught stealings.... An outfield assist in June was his first in 102 games out there, since starting his career in Boston with six assists in his first 43 games in the outfield.... Signed with Giants in mid-January; they would be his fifth major league team, and his fourth since July 1991.... Batted .271 as a pinch hitter last season, quite an improvement over his previous .164 mark in that role.... Hit two pinch-hit homers and two grand-slam homers last season; one of them was the fourth pinch-hit grand-slam for the Dodgers since they went west in 1958.... Now has six home runs in 89 career at-bats with the bases loaded—a rate of one for every 14.8 at-bats; in nonbases-loaded situations, he has averaged one homer for every 51.2 at-bats. No other active player with so pedestrian a home-run rate at other times has such a Ruthian rate when the bags are full (minimum: four grand-slam home runs).

Damon Berryhill
Bats Left and Right

Atlanta Braves	AB	H	2B	3B	HR	RBI	BB	SO	BA	SA	OBA
Season	307	70	16	1	10	43	17	67	.228	.384	.268
vs. Left-Handers	73	17	3	0	1	11	4	10	.233	.315	.269
vs. Right-Handers	234	53	13	1	9	32	13	57	.226	.406	.268
vs. Ground-Ballers	165	41	8	0	6	30	8	34	.248	.406	.284
vs. Fly-Ballers	142	29	8	1	4	13	9	33	.204	.359	.250
Home Games	148	43	9	1	6	24	8	34	.291	.486	.325
Road Games	159	27	7	0	4	19	9	33	.170	.289	.216
Grass Fields	237	58	12	1	7	29	12	52	.245	.392	.283
Artificial Turf	70	12	4	0	3	14	5	15	.171	.357	.221
April	39	11	1	0	3	8	1	4	.282	.538	.300
May	64	11	1	0	3	8	2	17	.172	.328	.197
June	40	12	4	0	0	7	3	11	.300	.400	.349
July	43	6	3	0	0	2	5	12	.140	.209	.240
August	50	12	3	0	3	7	2	8	.240	.480	.264
Sept./Oct.	71	18	4	1	1	11	4	15	.254	.380	.289
Leading Off Inn.	57	16	2	0	2	2	2	9	.281	.421	.305
Runners On	142	32	10	0	4	37	10	35	.225	.380	.271
Bases Empty	165	38	6	1	6	6	7	32	.230	.388	.266
Runners/Scor. Pos.	88	24	8	0	3	35	9	23	.273	.466	.330
Runners On/2 Out	72	14	6	0	1	16	4	21	.194	.319	.237
Scor. Pos./2 Out	49	12	6	0	0	14	4	15	.245	.367	.302
Late-Inning Pressure	52	12	2	1	2	5	3	11	.231	.423	.273
Leading Off	17	5	0	0	1	1	1	3	.294	.471	.333
Runners On	20	4	1	0	0	3	2	4	.200	.250	.273
Runners/Scor. Pos.	14	3	1	0	0	3	2	2	.214	.286	.313

RUNS BATTED IN	From 1B	From 2B	From 3B	Scoring Position
Totals	6/102	17/69	10/37	27/106
Percentage	5.9%	24.6%	27.0%	25.5%

Loves to face: Willie Blair (4-for-4, 2 2B, 1 3B)
Pete Harnisch (.273, 3-for-11, 1 2B, 2 HR, 3 BB)
John Smiley (.667, 4-for-6, 1 HR)

Hates to face: John Franco (0-for-7)
Orel Hershiser (.095, 2-for-21)
Mike Morgan (.100, 1-for-10)

Miscellaneous statistics: Ground outs-to-air outs ratio: 0.80 last season, 1.02 for career.... Grounded into 4 double plays in 50 opportunities (one per 13).... Drove in 8 of 14 runners from third base with less than two outs (57%).... Direction of balls hit to the outfield: 24% to left field, 19% to center, 58% to right batting left-handed; 32% to left field, 32% to center, 36% to right batting right-handed.... Base running: Advanced from first base to third on 4 of 9 outfield singles (44%); scored from second on 1 of 1 (100%).... Opposing base stealers: 71-for-91 (78%), highest rate in N.L.

Comments: We don't know if Damon is a religious sort, but a "thank-you" novena might be in order. He has had the good fortune of playing his home games in two of the majors' best hitters parks in Chicago and Atlanta. That's reflected in his career breakdown of .267 with 17 home runs in home games, .205 with 11 homers in road games.... Last year he hit .170 away from Atlanta, the N.L.'s lowest road batting average.... He has hit 22 of 28 career homers from the left side, but has a higher batting average from the right side (.247) than the left (.232).... Owns the lowest career batting average in Braves' postseason history among players with at least 40 at-bats. At least he's in good company with two other guys under the .200 mark: Berryhill, .130 (6-for-46); Johnny Logan, .154 (8-for-52); Eddie Mathews, .191 (9-for-47).... Had a poor World Series offensively despite his three-run homer off Jack Morris that won Game 1: he went 2-for-22 and fanned 11 times, tying Mathews (1958) and Wayne Garrett (1973) for 2d-most K's in one World Series; Willie Wilson set the record of 12 in 1980.... Think that there were a lot of switch-hitters in the World Series? You're right. Never before had there been seven switchers in the starting lineups (Otis Nixon, Terry Pendleton, Berryhill, Mark Lemke, Devon White, Roberto Alomar, Manuel Lee).... This might surprise you: Atlanta pitchers had a 2.82 ERA in 661⅓ innings with Berryhill catching, 3.47 in 754⅔ innings with Greg Olson back of the plate.

Craig Biggio
Bats Right

Houston Astros	AB	H	2B	3B	HR	RBI	BB	SO	BA	SA	OBA
Season	613	170	32	3	6	39	94	95	.277	.369	.378
vs. Left-Handers	218	60	10	1	3	14	50	22	.275	.372	.410
vs. Right-Handers	395	110	22	2	3	25	44	73	.278	.367	.359
vs. Ground-Ballers	263	77	13	2	2	18	43	45	.293	.380	.397
vs. Fly-Ballers	350	93	19	1	4	21	51	50	.266	.360	.365
Home Games	303	85	19	2	3	17	48	44	.281	.386	.384
Road Games	310	85	13	1	3	22	46	51	.274	.352	.373
Grass Fields	188	48	5	0	1	10	23	25	.255	.298	.343
Artificial Turf	425	122	27	3	5	29	71	70	.287	.400	.394
April	83	26	5	1	1	2	9	13	.313	.434	.380
May	112	32	7	0	3	12	13	25	.286	.429	.357
June	97	25	6	0	1	6	23	14	.258	.351	.402
July	96	24	3	1	0	1	14	12	.250	.302	.357
August	108	35	4	1	1	11	17	8	.324	.407	.430
Sept./Oct.	117	28	7	0	0	7	18	23	.239	.299	.346
Leading Off Inn.	268	76	14	2	4	4	34	42	.284	.396	.370
Runners On	171	46	9	1	1	34	38	31	.269	.351	.404
Bases Empty	442	124	23	2	5	5	56	64	.281	.376	.368
Runners/Scor. Pos.	104	31	6	1	0	32	27	18	.298	.375	.440
Runners On/2 Out	71	19	4	1	1	14	21	13	.268	.394	.447
Scor. Pos./2 Out	45	13	2	1	0	12	16	9	.289	.378	.484
Late-Inning Pressure	97	26	2	0	0	4	20	12	.268	.289	.398
Leading Off	32	11	1	0	0	0	4	4	.344	.375	.417
Runners On	29	7	0	0	0	4	8	6	.241	.241	.421
Runners/Scor. Pos.	17	6	0	0	0	4	8	4	.353	.353	.560

RUNS BATTED IN	From 1B	From 2B	From 3B	Scoring Position
Totals	3/110	15/82	15/44	30/126
Percentage	2.7%	18.3%	34.1%	23.8%

Loves to face: Orel Hershiser (.465, 20-for-43)
Danny Jackson (.667, 6-for-9)
John Wetteland (.556, 5-for-9, 2 HR, 3 SO)

Hates to face: Kevin Gross (.074, 2-for-27, 2 BB)
Ramon Martinez (.087, 2-for-23, 1 HR)
Curt Schilling (0-for-10)

Miscellaneous statistics: Ground outs-to-air outs ratio: 1.11 last season, 1.07 for career.... Grounded into 5 double plays in 80 opportunities (one per 16).... Drove in 11 of 24 runners from third base with less than two outs (46%).... Direction of balls hit to the outfield: 37% to left field, 34% to center, 29% to right.... Base running: Advanced from first base to third on 18 of 55 outfield singles (33%); scored from second on 12 of 18 (67%).... Made 2.64 assists per nine innings at second base, 2d-lowest rate in majors.

Comments: Selected to All-Star squad as an alternate for the second consecutive year; other than pitchers J.R. Richard and Mike Scott, no Houston player has started the All-Star Game since Cesar Cedeno in 1973. That gap of 19 years without a position player starting the All-Star Game is an all-time record; the second-longest streak is 17 years by Indians (1966–82).... Led N.L. with 721 plate appearances.... The second player ever to spend at least one season as a regular starter at both catcher and second base. The other: Tom Daly (1887–1903). The only other active player with even 10 games at both positions: Geno Petralli (535 at C, 13 at 2B).... Played 162 games and stole 38 bases last year in first year as an infielder, after previous single-season highs of 150 games and 25 steals (both in 1990).... Along with a switch of defensive position came a switch in his position in lineup; he took his new leadoff role seriously, walking 94 times after totals of 49, 53, and 53 over the previous three seasons.... Career numbers: .281 vs. righties, .259 vs. lefties.... Has hit for a higher average vs. right-handers than vs. left-handers in each of the last three years; Pat Borders is the only other right-handed batter in majors to have done that (minimum: 100 at-bats vs. both types of pitching each year).... Career breakdown by two-month periods: April–May, .299; June–July, .272; August–October, .256. Last September was his first month with an average below .250 since September of 1989.

Jeff Blauser — Bats Right

Atlanta Braves

	AB	H	2B	3B	HR	RBI	BB	SO	BA	SA	OBA
Season	343	90	19	3	14	46	46	82	.262	.458	.354
vs. Left-Handers	142	43	11	1	9	24	25	30	.303	.585	.402
vs. Right-Handers	201	47	8	2	5	22	21	52	.234	.368	.317
vs. Ground-Ballers	141	35	7	2	4	19	18	39	.248	.411	.345
vs. Fly-Ballers	202	55	12	1	10	27	28	43	.272	.490	.359
Home Games	162	46	9	2	5	19	22	36	.284	.457	.380
Road Games	181	44	10	1	9	27	24	46	.243	.459	.330
Grass Fields	248	69	14	3	11	33	32	57	.278	.492	.367
Artificial Turf	95	21	5	0	3	13	14	25	.221	.368	.318
April	50	9	1	1	1	6	2	16	.180	.300	.212
May	50	15	5	1	0	8	5	13	.300	.440	.368
June	46	7	1	0	2	5	4	13	.152	.304	.231
July	34	7	1	0	4	9	9	11	.206	.588	.372
August	70	23	3	0	3	7	11	10	.329	.500	.415
Sept./Oct.	93	29	8	1	4	11	15	19	.312	.548	.418
Leading Off Inn.	76	24	5	1	4	4	5	17	.316	.566	.358
Runners On	126	34	7	1	6	38	23	36	.270	.484	.387
Bases Empty	217	56	12	2	8	8	23	46	.258	.442	.332
Runners/Scor. Pos.	75	22	5	1	3	31	14	22	.293	.507	.398
Runners On/2 Out	52	11	3	0	3	13	9	15	.212	.442	.328
Scor. Pos./2 Out	38	9	3	0	3	13	7	10	.237	.553	.356
Late-Inning Pressure	53	10	2	0	4	9	8	13	.189	.453	.317
Leading Off	11	2	1	0	1	1	1	3	.182	.545	.250
Runners On	23	5	0	0	2	7	4	5	.217	.478	.357
Runners/Scor. Pos.	15	3	0	0	1	5	1	4	.200	.400	.250

RUNS BATTED IN	From 1B	From 2B	From 3B	Scoring Position
Totals	7/87	12/59	13/34	25/93
Percentage	8.0%	20.3%	38.2%	26.9%

Loves to face: Bud Black (.300, 6-for-20, 2 2B, 1 3B, 1 HR)
Tom Browning (.348, 16-for-46, 1 HR)
Mark Portugal (.462, 6-for-13, 3 HR)
Hates to face: Andy Benes (.136, 3-for-22)
Scott Garrelts (.136, 3-for-22, 1 HR)
Bruce Hurst (.196, 9-for-46, 1 HR)

Miscellaneous statistics: Ground outs-to-air outs ratio: 0.85 last season, 0.91 for career.... Grounded into 2 double plays in 70 opportunities (one per 35).... Drove in 10 of 16 runners from third base with less than two outs (63%).... Direction of balls hit to the outfield: 34% to left field, 26% to center, 40% to right.... Base running: Advanced from first base to third on 3 of 14 outfield singles (21%); scored from second on 9 of 11 (82%).... Made 2.79 assists per nine innings at shortstop.

Comments: During regular season, he started 42 of 51 games in which the Braves faced left-handed starters, but only 48 of 111 vs. right-handers; he then started all 13 postseason games, against any and all handers. Yearly batting averages vs. lefties since 1990: .294, .305, .303.... Slugging percentage vs. lefties ranked 10th in majors last season (minimum: 100 at-bats).... Of his 49 career home runs, 34 have come with the bases empty, and, somewhat surprisingly, 26 have been hit on the road.... Nine of his home runs last season came from the second spot in the lineup; only one other N.L. *team* had more homers from the number-two spot in the lineup (the Cubs had 17). In all, Atlanta's two-hole hitters hit 24 homers, with 14 coming from Terry Pendleton and one from Mark Lemke.... Hit 13 homers in 106 games at shortstop; only Detroit (15) and Baltimore (14) got more home runs from their shortstops than the Braves did (13).... The only Braves shortstop ever to start the All-Star Game was Eddie Miller in 1942—51 years and two cities ago.... Has hit for a higher average in Atlanta than on the road in five of his six seasons in the majors.... Owns .192 career average in Late-Inning Pressure Situations; he has batted below .200 in those situations in each of the last three years. But if he hasn't hit for average in LIPS, he has hit for power: nine LIPS home runs, or one every 19.8 at-bats, over the past three years.... Ended the regular season by batting over .300 in consecutive months for the first time in his career.

Barry Bonds — Bats Left

Pittsburgh Pirates

	AB	H	2B	3B	HR	RBI	BB	SO	BA	SA	OBA
Season	473	147	36	5	34	103	127	69	.311	.624	.456
vs. Left-Handers	222	69	19	3	13	44	55	35	.311	.599	.445
vs. Right-Handers	251	78	17	2	21	59	72	34	.311	.645	.465
vs. Ground-Ballers	163	52	13	1	7	24	49	18	.319	.540	.476
vs. Fly-Ballers	310	95	23	4	27	79	78	51	.306	.668	.445
Home Games	210	71	21	2	15	44	69	35	.338	.671	.498
Road Games	263	76	15	3	19	59	58	34	.289	.586	.418
Grass Fields	147	41	8	1	9	26	28	15	.279	.531	.393
Artificial Turf	326	106	28	4	25	77	99	54	.325	.666	.482
April	63	20	2	0	7	17	11	9	.317	.683	.434
May	101	30	9	0	6	23	20	9	.297	.564	.423
June	41	10	1	1	2	3	16	8	.244	.463	.456
July	83	26	9	3	5	19	19	14	.313	.675	.433
August	83	21	5	0	3	14	28	14	.253	.442	.431
Sept./Oct.	102	40	10	1	11	27	33	15	.392	.833	.537
Leading Off Inn.	125	41	13	1	6	6	25	19	.328	.592	.444
Runners On	222	67	13	3	18	87	77	30	.302	.631	.476
Bases Empty	251	80	23	2	16	16	50	39	.319	.618	.436
Runners/Scor. Pos.	118	37	5	3	13	71	52	16	.314	.737	.508
Runners On/2 Out	95	24	5	3	6	29	42	15	.253	.558	.486
Scor. Pos./2 Out	49	13	2	3	3	22	28	7	.265	.612	.532
Late-Inning Pressure	77	19	5	1	3	10	24	16	.247	.455	.422
Leading Off	15	5	2	0	1	1	4	2	.333	.667	.474
Runners On	29	6	2	0	0	7	15	7	.207	.345	.467
Runners/Scor. Pos.	11	2	0	1	0	6	8	4	.182	.364	.500

RUNS BATTED IN	From 1B	From 2B	From 3B	Scoring Position
Totals	18/161	19/80	32/61	51/141
Percentage	11.2%	23.8%	52.5%	36.2%

Loves to face: Jose DeLeon (.400, 12-for-30, 4 HR)
Tommy Greene (.538, 7-for-13, 3 HR)
Bruce Hurst (.462, 12-for-26, 3 HR)
Hates to face: Paul Assenmacher (.147, 5-for-34, 3 2B, 1 HR)
Cris Carpenter (0-for-8, 3 SO)
Chuck McElroy (.071, 1-for-14, 1 2B)

Miscellaneous statistics: Ground outs-to-air outs ratio: 0.78 last season, 0.83 for career.... Grounded into 9 double plays in 114 opportunities (one per 13).... Drove in 23 of 37 runners from third base with less than two outs (62%).... Direction of balls hit to the outfield: 29% to left field, 25% to center, 46% to right.... Base running: Advanced from first base to third on 12 of 35 outfield singles (34%); scored from second on 19 of 27 (70%).... Made 2.25 putouts per nine innings in left field.

Comments: Ninety-two home runs, 333 RBIs, 134 steals over last three seasons; no player had ever averaged 30 homers, 100 RBIs, and 40 steals over any three-year slice in major league history. Willie Mays (1955–57) and Howard Johnson (1989–91) averaged 30/100/30 over a three-year span.... Only player in majors to drive in more than 35 percent of runners from scoring position in each of last three years.... Career figures: batting .274 and slugging .503 vs. right-handers; .276 and .504 vs. lefties.... Only player in majors to increase his walk rate in each of the last five years.... On-base percentage leading off innings was best in majors.... Started and finished with a flourish: Led N.L. in homers in April, and led the majors in homers from September 1 to the end of the season. Batting average and home runs for Sept./Oct. were the highest in any month of his career.... Had 100 RBIs for a team that finished in first place in each of the last three seasons. The only other N.L. players ever to do that: George Kelly and Irish Meusel of 1922–24 Giants. (Kelly also had 122 RBIs for N.L.-champion 1921 Giants, giving him a four-year streak, the N.L. record.) The last A.L. player with 100 RBIs for three consecutive first-place teams: Roger Maris, 1960–62; Bill Dickey and Joe DiMaggio had four-year streaks, 1936–39.... Bondses hold all-time father/son home run record with 508, of which Bobby hit 186 with Giants; Barry would need 176 with the Giants for the pair to beat the Berras' record of 361 father/son homers with one team (Yankees).

Bobby Bonilla

Bats Left and Right

New York Mets	AB	H	2B	3B	HR	RBI	BB	SO	BA	SA	OBA
Season	438	109	23	0	19	70	66	73	.249	.432	.348
vs. Left-Handers	175	42	7	0	4	21	17	15	.240	.349	.307
vs. Right-Handers	263	67	16	0	15	49	49	58	.255	.487	.373
vs. Ground-Ballers	193	45	12	0	6	27	34	32	.233	.389	.346
vs. Fly-Ballers	245	64	11	0	13	43	32	41	.261	.465	.349
Home Games	196	42	11	0	5	21	31	31	.214	.347	.325
Road Games	242	67	12	0	14	49	35	42	.277	.500	.367
Grass Fields	296	66	13	0	14	44	41	45	.223	.409	.319
Artificial Turf	142	43	10	0	5	26	25	28	.303	.479	.407
April	82	22	3	0	2	14	14	15	.268	.378	.375
May	90	21	3	0	3	15	17	13	.233	.367	.352
June	89	26	11	0	3	14	17	18	.292	.517	.411
July	80	21	4	0	4	11	7	15	.262	.463	.322
August	51	10	1	0	6	14	3	3	.196	.569	.241
Sept./Oct.	46	9	1	0	1	2	8	9	.196	.283	.315
Leading Off Inn.	96	27	5	0	7	7	13	14	.281	.552	.373
Runners On	192	52	11	0	9	60	33	33	.271	.469	.376
Bases Empty	246	57	12	0	10	10	33	40	.232	.402	.325
Runners/Scor. Pos.	117	30	6	0	5	51	23	18	.256	.436	.376
Runners On/2 Out	73	24	6	0	3	23	18	11	.329	.534	.462
Scor. Pos./2 Out	53	15	4	0	1	18	12	9	.283	.415	.415
Late-Inning Pressure	70	20	3	0	5	14	12	12	.286	.543	.390
Leading Off	15	4	0	0	2	2	2	1	.267	.667	.353
Runners On	31	11	2	0	3	12	7	7	.355	.710	.474
Runners/Scor. Pos.	18	5	0	0	2	9	5	5	.278	.611	.435

RUNS BATTED IN	From 1B	From 2B	From 3B	Scoring Position
Totals	10/139	20/87	21/59	41/146
Percentage	7.2%	23.0%	35.6%	28.1%

Loves to face: Tom Browning (.390, 16-for-41, 4 2B, 8 HR)
Frank DiPino (.455, 10-for-22, 1 HR)
Pete Smith (.467, 7-for-15, 3 HR)

Hates to face: Brian Barnes (0-for-8)
Tim Belcher (.162, 6-for-37, 0 BB, 10 SO)
Todd Worrell (.091, 1-for-11, 6 SO)

Miscellaneous statistics: Ground outs-to-air outs ratio: 0.85 last season, 0.90 for career.... Grounded into 11 double plays in 98 opportunities (one per 8.9).... Drove in 14 of 30 runners from third base with less than two outs (47%).... Direction of balls hit to the outfield: 39% to left field, 25% to center, 36% to right batting left-handed; 39% to left field, 36% to center, 26% to right batting right-handed.... Base running: Advanced from first base to third on 4 of 23 outfield singles (17%); scored from second on 10 of 11 (91%), 3d-highest rate in N.L.... Made 2.17 putouts per nine innings in right field, 3d-highest rate in N.L.

Comments: Breakdown of career-low .249 batting average: .277 on the road, but only .214 at Shea, the 7th-lowest home mark in N.L. Four Mets (Bonilla, Howard Johnson, Todd Hundley, and Dick Schofield) finished among the bottom 10 in the league in home batting. Who's to blame (multiple answers permitted)? (a) the players themselves; (b) the fans; (c) the media; (d) official scorer Red Foley; (e) Amy Fisher.... Has hit for a higher average from the left side than the right in each of the last four seasons. His four-year breakdown: .297 left-handed, .254 right-handed.... Had batted under .200 in only one month during his career (July 1989), before doing it in each of the last two months last season.... Two homers on opening day last season gave him a career total of three in season openers. With Gary Carter (6) retired, only three active players have more: Darryl Strawberry, Dave Winfield, and George Brett, each with four.... Had only one sacrifice fly in 1992 after hitting 26 in 1990–91.... Batted .179 with no home runs in 56 first-inning at-bats.... One of five active players with a .300 career average in All-Star Games (minimum: 10 at-bats): Wade Boggs, .368 (7-for-19); Bonilla, .364 (4-for-11); Dave Winfield, .361 (13-for-36); Strawberry, .333 (4-for-12); Tim Raines, .300 (3-for-10). Any of these guys would gladly take an All-Star oh-fer at Oriole Park, just as long as they're there.

Daryl Boston

Bats Left

New York Mets	AB	H	2B	3B	HR	RBI	BB	SO	BA	SA	OBA
Season	289	72	14	2	11	35	38	60	.249	.426	.338
vs. Left-Handers	47	15	3	0	1	4	5	9	.319	.447	.407
vs. Right-Handers	242	57	11	2	10	31	33	51	.236	.421	.325
vs. Ground-Ballers	122	37	6	2	5	19	16	16	.303	.508	.383
vs. Fly-Ballers	167	35	8	0	6	16	22	44	.210	.365	.306
Home Games	140	32	5	1	5	17	16	32	.229	.386	.311
Road Games	149	40	9	1	6	18	22	28	.268	.463	.364
Grass Fields	223	57	7	2	10	29	24	43	.256	.439	.329
Artificial Turf	66	15	7	0	1	6	14	17	.227	.379	.366
April	40	10	1	1	1	4	6	9	.250	.400	.375
May	70	17	2	1	2	10	4	11	.243	.386	.284
June	28	7	2	0	2	3	4	8	.250	.536	.333
July	39	7	4	0	1	4	2	10	.179	.359	.214
August	75	23	2	0	5	8	9	13	.307	.533	.388
Sept./Oct.	37	8	3	0	0	6	13	9	.216	.297	.404
Leading Off Inn.	92	19	3	0	3	3	7	15	.207	.337	.263
Runners On	96	27	4	1	3	27	16	19	.281	.438	.381
Bases Empty	193	45	10	1	8	8	22	41	.233	.420	.315
Runners/Scor. Pos.	54	17	3	1	3	27	13	13	.315	.574	.431
Runners On/2 Out	32	8	2	0	1	5	7	4	.250	.406	.385
Scor. Pos./2 Out	18	4	1	0	1	5	6	3	.222	.444	.417
Late-Inning Pressure	54	12	3	0	3	8	12	16	.222	.444	.382
Leading Off	18	3	1	0	0	0	2	4	.167	.222	.250
Runners On	18	4	2	0	1	6	5	5	.222	.500	.417
Runners/Scor. Pos.	13	4	2	0	1	6	5	4	.308	.692	.526

RUNS BATTED IN	From 1B	From 2B	From 3B	Scoring Position
Totals	2/72	12/48	10/23	22/71
Percentage	2.8%	25.0%	43.5%	31.0%

Loves to face: Pete Smith (.714, 5-for-7, 3 2B)
Bob Tewksbury (.474, 9-for-19)
Bob Walk (.545, 6-for-11, 2 HR)

Hates to face: Andy Benes (.071, 1-for-14, 1 HR)
Rob Dibble (0-for-7, 4 SO)
Greg Maddux (.148, 4-for-27)

Miscellaneous statistics: Ground outs-to-air outs ratio: 0.78 last season, 0.91 for career.... Grounded into 5 double plays in 54 opportunities (one per 11).... Drove in 10 of 19 runners from third base with less than two outs (53%).... Direction of balls hit to the outfield: 26% to left field, 34% to center, 40% to right.... Base running: Advanced from first base to third on 3 of 10 outfield singles (30%); scored from second on 0 of 4 (0%).... Made 1.81 putouts per nine innings in left field.

Comments: Had 334 plate appearances last season, continuing a remarkable streak: In eight straight seasons, this quintessential fourth outfielder has come to the plate at least 200 times but never 400 times. There have been only 10 other players in major league history who have had such streaks of at least eight years: nine catchers (a position that historically has called for shared duty) and a first baseman named Joe Start, who as his name suggests, did it from the start of the National League, from 1876 to 1883 (when team schedules varied from 60 to 84 games). This year, Boston goes for the all-time record of nine straight years, a mark shared by Jose Azcue (1962–70) and Alan Ashby (1978–86); Don Slaught also has a current eight-year streak. But it won't be a piece of cake for Daryl: he signed with the Rockies as a free agent, and he may see more playing time than he has in the past.... Career stolen-base percentage breakdown: .808 (21-for-26) on artificial turf, .667 (76-for-114) on dirt, which is the surface at Mile High Stadium.... Don't be deceived by his high average vs. lefties last season. Career breakdown: .237 with one homer every 111 at-bats vs. left-handers, .252 with one homer every 31 at-bats vs. right-handers.... Has hit .300 or better against ground-ball pitchers in each of the last three years, during which time he compiled a .237 mark against fly-ballers.... Hit three pinch homers last season, but has batted only .203 in that role in his career.

Glenn Braggs
Bats Right

Cincinnati Reds	AB	H	2B	3B	HR	RBI	BB	SO	BA	SA	OBA
Season	266	63	16	3	8	38	36	48	.237	.410	.330
vs. Left-Handers	145	36	7	2	5	24	21	24	.248	.428	.343
vs. Right-Handers	121	27	9	1	3	14	15	24	.223	.388	.314
vs. Ground-Ballers	89	16	4	2	1	10	12	15	.180	.303	.288
vs. Fly-Ballers	177	47	12	1	7	28	24	33	.266	.463	.351
Home Games	117	28	7	2	4	19	19	22	.239	.436	.350
Road Games	149	35	9	1	4	19	17	26	.235	.389	.314
Grass Fields	80	25	7	1	2	12	8	13	.313	.500	.371
Artificial Turf	186	38	9	2	6	26	28	35	.204	.371	.313
April	33	7	1	0	0	3	3	6	.212	.242	.278
May	43	7	1	0	0	4	6	10	.163	.186	.280
June	35	11	4	0	2	9	8	7	.314	.600	.442
July	53	12	3	1	2	6	9	8	.226	.434	.333
August	81	20	6	1	3	12	8	15	.247	.457	.319
Sept./Oct.	21	6	1	1	1	4	2	2	.286	.571	.348
Leading Off Inn.	71	17	3	1	2	2	4	11	.239	.394	.280
Runners On	128	29	9	2	5	35	21	22	.227	.445	.336
Bases Empty	138	34	7	1	3	3	15	26	.246	.377	.325
Runners/Scor. Pos.	77	17	5	1	4	31	15	13	.221	.468	.347
Runners On/2 Out	48	10	1	2	2	10	8	12	.208	.438	.333
Scor. Pos./2 Out	31	7	1	1	2	9	6	2	.226	.516	.368
Late-Inning Pressure	43	17	4	1	1	9	2	7	.395	.605	.426
Leading Off	8	4	2	0	0	0	0	2	.500	.750	.500
Runners On	21	6	2	1	1	9	2	1	.286	.619	.360
Runners/Scor. Pos.	10	3	1	1	0	6	2	0	.300	.600	.429

RUNS BATTED IN	From 1B	From 2B	From 3B	Scoring Position
Totals	6/98	12/66	12/33	24/99
Percentage	6.1%	18.2%	36.4%	24.2%

Loves to face: Steve Avery (.464, 13-for-28, 4 HR)
      Edwin Nunez (.667, 6-for-9, 3 2B, 1 HR)
      Mike Witt (.423, 11-for-26, 3 HR)
Hates to face: Joe Boever (0-for-7)
      Scott Garrelts (.100, 1-for-10)
      Don Robinson (0-for-7)

Miscellaneous statistics: Ground outs-to-air outs ratio: 1.00 last season, 1.24 for career.... Grounded into 10 double plays in 69 opportunities (one per 6.9).... Drove in 10 of 21 runners from third base with less than two outs (48%).... Direction of balls hit to the outfield: 48% to left field, 28% to center, 24% to right.... Base running: Advanced from first base to third on 4 of 14 outfield singles (29%); scored from second on 9 of 15 (60%).... Made 1.46 putouts per nine innings in left field.

Comments: Batted .316 from the seventh inning on, and .395 in Late-Inning Pressure Situations. Among N.L. players with at least 40 at-bats in LIPS, only Brett Butler (.430) and Lenny Dykstra (.420) had higher averages.... Overall batting average was a career low.... Despite last season's figures, he has a higher career average against ground-ball pitchers (.266) than he does against fly-ballers (.251).... Also bucked previous career trend with his grass/artificial breakdown. Career figures: .253 on grass, .266 on artificial turf.... Started 48 of 61 games in which Reds faced a left-handed starting pitcher, but only 20 of 101 in which they went up against a right-hander.... Strikeout rate has improved in each of the last four seasons; only eight other players can make that claim.... Walk rate was also the best of his career.... Homerless streak of 154 at-bats from August 6, 1991, to June 15, 1992, was the longest of his career.... He had 10 assists in his first 57 games in the outfield after joining the Reds in 1990, but only five in 156 games in the outfield after that.... Signed a contract last fall to play in Japan this year; once they get a good look at the body on Braggs, the Japanese may be convinced that they've finally got a weapon that can defeat Godzilla (or at least Charles Barkley). And with so many major leaguers heading to the Far East, how long will it be before we see the first Japanese Baseball Rotisserie League? Maybe if we get them sidetracked with that stuff, we can go back to making the better cars.

Sid Bream
Bats Left

Atlanta Braves	AB	H	2B	3B	HR	RBI	BB	SO	BA	SA	OBA
Season	372	97	25	1	10	61	46	51	.261	.414	.340
vs. Left-Handers	33	8	4	0	1	7	1	5	.242	.455	.265
vs. Right-Handers	339	89	21	1	9	54	45	46	.263	.410	.347
vs. Ground-Ballers	172	53	13	1	5	37	22	23	.308	.483	.383
vs. Fly-Ballers	200	44	12	0	5	24	24	28	.220	.355	.304
Home Games	178	47	11	0	4	32	26	20	.264	.393	.353
Road Games	194	50	14	1	6	29	20	31	.258	.433	.329
Grass Fields	276	70	17	1	7	45	36	39	.254	.399	.337
Artificial Turf	96	27	8	0	3	16	10	12	.281	.458	.352
April	51	9	3	0	0	2	9	9	.176	.235	.300
May	53	16	5	0	2	8	9	3	.302	.509	.413
June	61	15	3	1	0	11	7	11	.246	.328	.319
July	63	18	5	0	2	8	4	7	.286	.460	.324
August	67	20	5	0	4	22	7	5	.299	.552	.355
Sept./Oct.	77	19	4	0	2	10	10	16	.247	.377	.333
Leading Off Inn.	86	19	6	0	4	4	7	11	.221	.430	.280
Runners On	165	50	14	1	3	54	23	20	.303	.455	.383
Bases Empty	207	47	11	0	7	7	23	31	.227	.382	.304
Runners/Scor. Pos.	107	32	10	1	0	45	16	14	.299	.411	.383
Runners On/2 Out	69	23	7	1	0	22	16	9	.333	.464	.465
Scor. Pos./2 Out	49	16	4	1	0	20	11	6	.327	.449	.459
Late-Inning Pressure	40	6	3	0	1	3	4	5	.150	.300	.227
Leading Off	10	2	1	0	0	0	2	2	.200	.300	.333
Runners On	19	3	1	0	1	3	0	0	.158	.368	.158
Runners/Scor. Pos.	12	1	1	0	0	1	0	0	.083	.167	.083

RUNS BATTED IN	From 1B	From 2B	From 3B	Scoring Position
Totals	9/123	21/84	21/45	42/129
Percentage	7.3%	25.0%	46.7%	32.6%

Loves to face: Dwight Gooden (.345, 19-for-55, 3 HR)
      Kevin Gross (.353, 18-for-51, 4 HR)
      Mike Maddux (.529, 9-for-17)
Hates to face: Tim Belcher (.143, 5-for-35, 1 HR)
      Sid Fernandez (.063, 1-for-16)
      Pete Harnisch (.143, 4-for-28)

Miscellaneous statistics: Ground outs-to-air outs ratio: 0.86 last season, 0.98 for career.... Grounded into 3 double plays in 76 opportunities (one per 25).... Drove in 14 of 23 runners from third base with less than two outs (61%).... Direction of balls hit to the outfield: 32% to left field, 34% to center, 34% to right.... Base running: Advanced from first base to third on 6 of 17 outfield singles (35%); scored from second on 2 of 3 (67%).... Made 0.72 assists per nine innings at first base, 3d-lowest rate in N.L.

Comments: From the Anomaly Department: In two seasons with the Braves he has hit twice as many home runs on the road (14) as he has at home.... Has hit a home run in the Championship Series in each of the past three years (one in Atlanta); only three other players have done that: Boog Powell (1969–71), Greg Luzinski (1976–78), and Jay Bell (1990–92).... Has started 12 World Series games and hasn't driven in a run in any of them. The all-time record for World Series starts from the start of a career without an RBI is 13, shared by two Hall of Famers: St. Louis outfielder Chick Hafey (1926–30) and Yankees pitcher Whitey Ford (1950–60).... Bream didn't start a regular-season or postseason game in which a left-hander opposed the Braves in 1992. He was the only player in the majors who started at least 100 games last season, all against one type of pitching.... His current streak: 147 starts since his last start against a lefty: May 27, 1991, vs. Bruce Hurst.... Has driven in career rate of 66.2 percent of runners from third with less than two outs; among active N.L. players only Tony Gwynn (70.4) and Mark Grace (69.8) have higher rates (minimum: 100 chances).... Stole six bases in six attempts during the regular season; only one other N.L. player stole as many bases without being caught (Jacob Brumfield of the Reds). We don't care; we still would have pinch-run Tom Glavine for him in the ninth inning of Game Seven in the N.L.C.S. (But for the sake of one of the all-time video highlights, we're sure glad that Bobby Cox stayed with Sid!)

Steve Buechele

Bats Right

Pirates/Cubs	AB	H	2B	3B	HR	RBI	BB	SO	BA	SA	OBA
Season	524	137	23	4	9	64	52	105	.261	.372	.334
vs. Left-Handers	207	63	17	1	5	26	21	33	.304	.469	.372
vs. Right-Handers	317	74	6	3	4	38	31	72	.233	.309	.310
vs. Ground-Ballers	224	52	6	3	1	22	21	46	.232	.299	.304
vs. Fly-Ballers	300	85	17	1	8	42	31	59	.283	.427	.357
Home Games	276	68	9	3	4	32	27	56	.246	.344	.316
Road Games	248	69	14	1	5	32	25	49	.278	.403	.355
Grass Fields	218	58	14	3	2	27	18	46	.266	.385	.329
Artificial Turf	306	79	9	1	7	37	34	59	.258	.363	.338
April	72	17	4	1	2	15	6	14	.236	.403	.304
May	95	28	6	0	4	15	15	23	.295	.484	.393
June	89	18	3	0	2	10	13	17	.202	.303	.301
July	89	29	3	1	1	7	4	12	.326	.416	.355
August	94	21	4	2	0	11	7	24	.223	.309	.295
Sept./Oct.	85	24	3	0	0	6	7	15	.282	.318	.351
Leading Off Inn.	135	39	12	1	4	4	7	24	.289	.481	.333
Runners On	224	65	8	2	3	58	31	51	.290	.384	.379
Bases Empty	300	72	15	2	6	6	21	54	.240	.363	.298
Runners/Scor. Pos.	146	41	4	2	0	51	26	37	.281	.336	.390
Runners On/2 Out	91	22	1	0	0	21	11	23	.242	.253	.324
Scor. Pos./2 Out	70	18	1	0	0	21	11	20	.257	.271	.358
Late-Inning Pressure	88	18	5	0	0	2	6	22	.205	.261	.271
Leading Off	33	8	4	0	0	0	2	9	.242	.364	.286
Runners On	29	6	1	0	0	2	3	10	.207	.241	.303
Runners/Scor. Pos.	15	4	0	0	0	2	2	8	.267	.267	.389

RUNS BATTED IN	From 1B	From 2B	From 3B	Scoring Position
Totals	6/153	25/113	24/61	49/174
Percentage	3.9%	22.1%	39.3%	28.2%

Loves to face: Bud Black (.343, 12-for-35, 3 HR)
     Pete Harnisch (.375, 3-for-8, 2 HR, 2 BB)
     Bret Saberhagen (.462, 12-for-26, 1 HR, 0 BB)

Hates to face: Tom Candiotti (.192, 5-for-26, 11 SO)
     Mike Jackson (0-for-9)
     Bill Swift (.063, 1-for-16)

Miscellaneous statistics: Ground outs-to-air outs ratio: 0.97 last season, 1.08 for career.... Grounded into 10 double plays in 112 opportunities (one per 11).... Drove in 18 of 34 runners from third base with less than two outs (53%).... Direction of balls hit to the outfield: 32% to left field, 37% to center, 31% to right.... Base running: Advanced from first base to third on 8 of 32 outfield singles (25%); scored from second on 9 of 17 (53%).... Made 2.09 assists per nine innings at third base.

Comments: Stands fifth on the all-time fielding list among third basemen with a career rate of one error every 30.9 chances; the top four: Brooks Robinson (one every 34.8 chances), Ken Reitz (32.9), George Kell (31.9), and Don Money (31.5). But Buechele's rate has increased considerably over the last two seasons, during which he has averaged one error every 23.7 chances; he set a career high with 17 errors in 1992.... Batting average with runners on base was a career high, as was his mark against left-handed pitchers; career breakdown: .277 vs. lefties, .229 vs. righties.... Last year's home run rate, one every 58.2 at-bats, was the lowest of his career.... Had 48 RBIs from the 6th spot in the batting order, the most in the majors.... Cubs third basemen combined for a .219 batting average, the lowest of any team in the majors at that position. That wasn't all Buechele's fault: He batted .274 as a third baseman after he was traded to the Cubs. But the four other players whom the Cubs used at that position batted a pathetic .185, and in 384 at-bats no less: Jose Vizcaino hit .208 in 106 at-bats, Luis Salazar .188 in 112, Doug Strange .169 in 71, and Gary Scott .165 in 91.... Has stolen one base in nine attempts over the last two years; he's 0-for-8 lifetime on artificial turf.... Drove in only two of 17 runners from scoring position in Late-Inning Pressure Situations (11.8%), compared to 30 percent of such runners at other times; if you think that's a bad rate, wait 'til you get a load of Brett Butler's....

Brett Butler

Bats Left

Los Angeles Dodgers	AB	H	2B	3B	HR	RBI	BB	SO	BA	SA	OBA
Season	553	171	14	11	3	39	95	67	.309	.391	.413
vs. Left-Handers	223	66	2	3	1	17	39	31	.296	.345	.402
vs. Right-Handers	330	105	12	8	2	22	56	36	.318	.421	.420
vs. Ground-Ballers	204	53	3	3	1	11	32	25	.260	.319	.364
vs. Fly-Ballers	349	118	11	8	2	28	63	42	.338	.433	.441
Home Games	267	81	4	6	1	19	48	28	.303	.375	.411
Road Games	286	90	10	5	2	20	47	39	.315	.406	.414
Grass Fields	411	131	11	9	3	31	72	45	.319	.411	.421
Artificial Turf	142	40	3	2	0	8	23	22	.282	.331	.389
April	88	26	1	4	1	7	13	12	.295	.432	.386
May	84	20	1	0	0	2	10	17	.238	.250	.330
June	96	26	4	3	0	9	19	11	.271	.375	.391
July	95	42	3	2	1	12	22	9	.442	.547	.547
August	97	29	3	2	1	7	15	11	.299	.402	.398
Sept./Oct.	93	28	2	0	0	2	16	7	.301	.323	.404
Leading Off Inn.	184	53	2	3	2	2	34	24	.288	.364	.405
Runners On	192	59	6	4	1	37	29	26	.307	.396	.396
Bases Empty	361	112	8	7	2	2	66	41	.310	.388	.421
Runners/Scor. Pos.	126	33	5	3	0	34	17	19	.262	.349	.347
Runners On/2 Out	84	27	4	3	1	16	13	14	.321	.476	.412
Scor. Pos./2 Out	63	17	3	2	0	13	8	12	.270	.381	.352
Late-Inning Pressure	93	40	2	0	1	1	19	14	.430	.484	.527
Leading Off	26	12	1	0	1	1	5	3	.462	.615	.548
Runners On	30	7	0	0	0	0	9	8	.233	.233	.410
Runners/Scor. Pos.	18	1	0	0	0	0	8	6	.056	.056	.346

RUNS BATTED IN	From 1B	From 2B	From 3B	Scoring Position
Totals	4/115	13/97	19/59	32/156
Percentage	3.5%	13.4%	32.2%	20.5%

Loves to face: Ryan Bowen (.714, 5-for-7)
     Mike Morgan (.429, 18-for-42, 0 SO)
     John Smoltz (.400, 16-for-40, 13 BB)

Hates to face: John Candelaria (0-for-9)
     Rob Murphy (.083, 1-for-12, 4 SO)
     Al Osuna (0-for-7, 4 BB, 3 SO)

Miscellaneous statistics: Ground outs-to-air outs ratio: 1.94 last season (5th highest in N.L.), 1.35 for career.... Grounded into 4 double plays in 99 opportunities (one per 25).... Drove in 15 of 36 runners from third base with less than two outs (42%).... Direction of balls hit to the outfield: 43% to left field, 35% to center, 22% to right.... Base running: Advanced from first base to third on 19 of 48 outfield singles (40%); scored from second on 10 of 14 (71%).... Made 2.41 putouts per nine innings in center field, 3d-lowest rate in N.L.

Comments: Third player in history to lead N.L. in singles for three years in a row; the others: Ginger Beaumont (1902–04) and Lloyd Waner (1927–29).... Led majors in batting, runs scored, and stolen bases (18) in July; his .442 average was the highest by any major league player in any month in the 1990s.... Hit N.L.-high .362 from second spot in lineup (minimum: 100 PA).... One of four players in major league history to be caught stealing at least 200 times (while that statistic was being recorded); only Lou Brock (307) and Rickey Henderson (240) have been erased more often than Butler (209).... Career stolen-base percentage (.676) is the lowest over the last 40 years among players with at least 400 steals; among players with 300 or more, only Rod Carew had a lower success rate (.654).... Led majors with 24 sacrifice bunts.... Has the top fielding percentage of any outfielder in Dodgers history (one error every 372 chances) with at least 250 games played. He holds the same distinction for the Giants and Indians; among Braves outfielders, he somehow ranks second to Dion James.... Had best average in majors last year in Late-Inning Pressure Situations, and yet he failed to drive in *any* of 21 runners from scoring position in Late-Inning Pressure Situations last season, breaking the mark for LIPS futility set by Ron Kittle in 1984 (0-for-20).... Led the majors in infield hits (70) for the third consecutive season. Rounding out the top five: Kenny Lofton, 49; Craig Biggio, 46; Kirby Puckett, 41; Shane Mack, 39.

Ken Caminiti

Bats Left and Right

Houston Astros	AB	H	2B	3B	HR	RBI	BB	SO	BA	SA	OBA
Season	506	149	31	2	13	62	44	68	.294	.441	.350
vs. Left-Handers	208	63	13	1	7	35	18	29	.303	.476	.357
vs. Right-Handers	298	86	18	1	6	27	26	39	.289	.416	.345
vs. Ground-Ballers	224	65	12	0	4	24	19	21	.290	.397	.348
vs. Fly-Ballers	282	84	19	2	9	38	25	47	.298	.475	.350
Home Games	246	81	18	1	7	34	25	32	.329	.496	.389
Road Games	260	68	13	1	6	28	19	36	.262	.388	.311
Grass Fields	157	47	8	1	3	16	14	19	.299	.420	.355
Artificial Turf	349	102	23	1	10	46	30	49	.292	.450	.347
April	39	12	3	0	2	5	4	6	.308	.538	.372
May	37	9	2	0	0	1	6	5	.243	.297	.349
June	109	38	9	0	3	18	11	13	.349	.514	.402
July	96	30	4	1	2	11	6	7	.313	.438	.352
August	109	30	8	1	3	14	9	17	.275	.450	.331
Sept./Oct.	116	30	5	0	3	13	8	20	.259	.379	.306
Leading Off Inn.	123	42	7	1	3	3	4	12	.341	.488	.362
Runners On	223	62	14	1	6	55	28	27	.278	.430	.353
Bases Empty	283	87	17	1	7	7	16	41	.307	.449	.347
Runners/Scor. Pos.	136	34	8	0	4	45	23	20	.250	.397	.350
Runners On/2 Out	79	17	5	0	1	13	12	10	.215	.316	.319
Scor. Pos./2 Out	52	9	3	0	1	11	11	8	.173	.288	.317
Late-Inning Pressure	88	25	7	0	1	8	15	14	.284	.398	.385
Leading Off	28	9	1	0	0	0	1	3	.321	.357	.345
Runners On	34	8	3	0	1	8	11	5	.235	.412	.413
Runners/Scor. Pos.	19	4	1	0	1	7	10	4	.211	.421	.467

RUNS BATTED IN	From 1B	From 2B	From 3B	Scoring Position
Totals	11/147	14/99	24/66	38/165
Percentage	7.5%	14.1%	36.4%	23.0%

Loves to face: Kevin Gross (.385, 10-for-26, 1 HR)
Chuck McElroy (.750, 6-for-8, 1 HR)
Trevor Wilson (.333, 8-for-24, 2 2B, 3 HR, 0 SO)
Hates to face: Tim Belcher (.154, 6-for-39, 1 HR)
Jay Howell (.125, 2-for-16)
Chris Nabholz (0-for-13)

Miscellaneous statistics: Ground outs-to-air outs ratio: 1.26 last season, 1.05 for career.... Grounded into 14 double plays in 110 opportunities (one per 7.9).... Drove in 20 of 34 runners from third base with less than two outs (59%).... Direction of balls hit to the outfield: 31% to left field, 29% to center, 40% to right batting left-handed; 43% to left field, 35% to center, 22% to right batting right-handed.... Base running: Advanced from first base to third on 12 of 32 outfield singles (38%); scored from second on 13 of 18 (72%).... Made 1.66 assists per nine innings at third base, 2d-lowest rate in N.L.

Comments: The only player in the majors, among qualifiers for the batting title, to increase his batting average by at least 10 points in each of the last two seasons (from .242 to .253 to .294). The last player with a longer streak was Tim Raines, who is the only player in major league history to do that in four consecutive seasons (1983–86).... Led N.L. third basemen in fielding (one error every 29.4 chances), the first Houston third baseman to lead the league since Doug Rader in 1975.... Has been the Astros' opening-day starter at third base each of the last four years; Enos Cabell (1976–80) was the last to start five straight openers at that position for Houston.... Most games at third base by Houston players: Doug Rader, 1116; Bob Aspromonte, 931; Cabell, 744; Caminiti, 679; Phil Garner, 497.... His 679 games at third are the most among active players who have never played at any other position. The all-time record for most games played exclusively at that position is 1672 by Willie Kamm, followed by Frank Baker (1548), Frank Malzone (1370), and Caminiti.... Tied with Mark Grace for most hits in N.L. during month of June last season.... No Houston player has homered at Wrigley Field in eight games since Caminiti did so on July 19, 1991.... Batting average of .289 from left side of the plate was a career high; he had never before hit even .240 from that side. From the right side he has batted over .300 four times. Career averages: .289 batting right-handed, .236 left-handed.

Casey Candaele

Bats Left and Right

Houston Astros	AB	H	2B	3B	HR	RBI	BB	SO	BA	SA	OBA
Season	320	68	12	1	1	18	24	36	.213	.266	.269
vs. Left-Handers	128	34	7	0	1	9	12	11	.266	.344	.331
vs. Right-Handers	192	34	5	1	0	9	12	25	.177	.214	.226
vs. Ground-Ballers	140	26	5	1	1	6	9	11	.186	.257	.232
vs. Fly-Ballers	180	42	7	0	0	12	15	25	.233	.272	.297
Home Games	159	31	6	1	1	9	15	15	.195	.264	.267
Road Games	161	37	6	0	0	9	9	21	.230	.267	.272
Grass Fields	105	24	3	0	0	7	2	15	.229	.257	.245
Artificial Turf	215	44	9	1	1	11	22	21	.205	.270	.280
April	55	11	0	0	1	3	1	8	.200	.255	.211
May	73	13	3	0	0	2	6	8	.178	.219	.241
June	53	12	0	1	0	1	5	8	.226	.264	.305
July	70	13	6	0	0	5	5	3	.186	.271	.241
August	38	11	0	0	0	2	1	5	.289	.289	.300
Sept./Oct.	31	8	3	0	0	5	6	4	.258	.355	.385
Leading Off Inn.	84	19	4	0	1	1	7	6	.226	.310	.301
Runners On	118	23	3	0	0	17	9	16	.195	.220	.246
Bases Empty	202	45	9	1	1	1	15	20	.223	.292	.283
Runners/Scor. Pos.	66	10	2	0	0	17	7	13	.152	.182	.225
Runners On/2 Out	57	12	1	0	0	6	2	9	.211	.228	.250
Scor. Pos./2 Out	36	6	1	0	0	6	2	7	.167	.194	.231
Late-Inning Pressure	73	19	5	0	0	4	9	8	.260	.329	.341
Leading Off	19	4	1	0	0	0	2	1	.211	.263	.318
Runners On	25	6	2	0	0	4	4	6	.240	.320	.323
Runners/Scor. Pos.	13	2	1	0	0	4	4	4	.154	.231	.316

RUNS BATTED IN	From 1B	From 2B	From 3B	Scoring Position
Totals	0/94	6/59	11/30	17/89
Percentage	0.0%	10.2%	36.7%	19.1%

Loves to face: John Burkett (.368, 7-for-19, 1 HR)
Frank Castillo (.667, 6-for-9)
Ramon Martinez (.444, 4-for-9, 2 BB)
Hates to face: Sid Fernandez (.077, 1-for-13)
Dwight Gooden (.148, 4-for-27)
John Smoltz (.056, 1-for-18, 3 BB)

Miscellaneous statistics: Ground outs-to-air outs ratio: 1.07 last season, 1.14 for career.... Grounded into 5 double plays in 60 opportunities (one per 12).... Drove in 10 of 16 runners from third base with less than two outs (63%).... Direction of balls hit to the outfield: 31% to left field, 30% to center, 39% to right batting left-handed; 32% to left field, 26% to center, 42% to right batting right-handed.... Base running: Advanced from first base to third on 2 of 8 outfield singles (25%); scored from second on 2 of 5 (40%).... Made 3.10 assists per nine innings at shortstop.

Comments: Countdown in N.L. rank: Batting average in night games (.206) was 4th lowest in the league; average in home games was 3d lowest; average with runners on base was 2d lowest; average with runners in scoring position was *the* lowest.... Had batted over .300 with runners in scoring position in each of the previous two seasons.... Although his career high for stolen bases in a season is only nine, he has tied an all-time record by improving his stolen base percentage in five consecutive seasons; his yearly percentages since his debut in 1986: .375, .412, .500, .583, .750, .875. Six other players have had five straight years of improvement: Joe DeMaestri, 1954–58; Mike Easler, 1979–83; Dan Gladden, 1984–88; Al Kaline, 1958–62; Billy Sample, 1979–83; and Bill Virdon, 1956–60.... Owns .652 career stolen base percentage (30-for-46) on artificial turf, but only .308 (4-for-13) on dirt infields.... Difference between his career averages from the left and right sides of the plate (.227 left, .289 right) is even greater than Ken Caminiti's.... He has batted .136 (6-for-44) as a pinch hitter over the past two years; in 1990, he went 10-for-30 with three triples in that role.... Has played a plurality of his games at a different position in each of the last three years: in the outfield in 1990, at second base in 1991, at shortstop in 1992; he's the only player in the majors who has done that while playing at least 100 games in each of the last three seasons.

Gary Carter   Bats Right

Montreal Expos	AB	H	2B	3B	HR	RBI	BB	SO	BA	SA	OBA
Season	285	62	18	1	5	29	33	37	.218	.340	.299
vs. Left-Handers	139	32	13	0	2	14	15	15	.230	.367	.301
vs. Right-Handers	146	30	5	1	3	15	18	22	.205	.315	.298
vs. Ground-Ballers	125	32	7	1	3	14	11	12	.256	.400	.314
vs. Fly-Ballers	160	30	11	0	2	15	22	25	.188	.294	.289
Home Games	153	37	9	1	2	15	20	18	.242	.353	.335
Road Games	132	25	9	0	3	14	13	19	.189	.326	.257
Grass Fields	73	13	5	0	1	5	7	10	.178	.288	.250
Artificial Turf	212	49	13	1	4	24	26	27	.231	.358	.316
April	33	9	2	0	0	0	2	3	.273	.333	.314
May	68	17	5	0	3	10	9	13	.250	.456	.338
June	58	12	4	0	0	3	5	8	.207	.276	.288
July	53	8	0	0	0	2	4	3	.151	.151	.207
August	40	7	1	1	2	7	9	4	.175	.400	.314
Sept./Oct.	33	9	6	0	0	7	4	6	.273	.455	.351
Leading Off Inn.	61	10	3	1	1	1	6	11	.164	.295	.239
Runners On	124	30	9	0	3	27	20	16	.242	.387	.347
Bases Empty	161	32	9	1	2	2	13	21	.199	.304	.259
Runners/Scor. Pos.	73	15	6	0	0	19	16	13	.205	.288	.333
Runners On/2 Out	45	7	2	0	1	6	14	5	.156	.267	.367
Scor. Pos./2 Out	31	3	1	0	0	3	10	4	.097	.129	.317
Late-Inning Pressure	49	9	3	0	0	3	4	8	.184	.245	.245
Leading Off	8	0	0	0	0	0	1	3	.000	.000	.111
Runners On	20	4	1	0	0	3	2	2	.200	.250	.273
Runners/Scor. Pos.	14	2	0	0	0	2	2	2	.143	.143	.250

RUNS BATTED IN	From 1B	From 2B	From 3B	Scoring Position
Totals	7/91	8/59	9/24	17/83
Percentage	7.7%	13.6%	37.5%	20.5%

Loved to face: Rheal Cormier (.467, 7-for-15)
Ron Darling (.444, 4-for-9, 2 HR)
Scott Sanderson (.333, 7-for-21, 3 HR)

Hated to face: Steve Avery (.067, 1-for-15)
Dennis Martinez (.071, 2-for-28, 0 BB)
Dave Smith (.059, 1-for-17)

Miscellaneous statistics: Ground outs-to-air outs ratio: 0.55 last season (2d lowest in N.L.), 0.78 for career.... Grounded into 4 double plays in 65 opportunities (one per 16).... Drove in 9 of 13 runners from third base with less than two outs (69%).... Direction of balls hit to the outfield: 41% to left field, 29% to center, 30% to right.... Base running: Advanced from first base to third on 0 of 8 outfield singles (0%); scored from second on 4 of 8 (50%).... Opposing base stealers: 98-for-136 (72%).

Comments: His farewell tour finally came to a close after a four-year run playing Broadway, Ghirardelli Square, Hollywood, and Montreal.... Retired as the all-time major league leader among catchers in putouts (11,785) and total chances (13,109).... Had 247 home runs and 887 RBIs in 10-year peak period from 1977 to 1986; Yogi Berra and Johnny Bench were the only other catchers in history to equal those numbers over a 10-year span.... Five homers last year left him with 324 for his career, of which 298 came as a catcher.... Had more at-bats, extra-base hits, and RBIs last year than in any season since 1988, his last year as an everyday catcher.... Ends his career with a total of six opening-day homers, 5th most in major league history, behind Frank Robinson (8), Babe Ruth, Willie Mays, and Eddie Mathews (7 each).... Opponents stole 98 bases with Carter behind the plate, the most against any N.L. catcher last season.... Had lowest average in N.L. with two outs and runners in scoring position.... One of the greatest performers in All-Star games: nine games behind the plate ranks fourth, behind Berra (14), Bench (11), and Carlton Fisk (10). Only three players hit more All-Star homers than Carter (3): Stan Musial (6), Fred Lynn (4), and Ted Williams (4).... One of six players to play for the Mets, Dodgers, and Giants. One day, when the question is "Who are the two *Hall of Famers* to have played for the Mets, Dodgers, and Giants?", your answer will be "Duke Snider and Gary Carter."

Wes Chamberlain   Bats Right

Philadelphia Phillies	AB	H	2B	3B	HR	RBI	BB	SO	BA	SA	OBA
Season	275	71	18	0	9	41	10	55	.258	.422	.285
vs. Left-Handers	104	27	8	0	3	15	5	15	.260	.423	.291
vs. Right-Handers	171	44	10	0	6	26	5	40	.257	.421	.281
vs. Ground-Ballers	145	39	8	0	3	19	4	27	.269	.386	.293
vs. Fly-Ballers	130	32	10	0	6	22	6	28	.246	.462	.275
Home Games	144	40	10	0	3	19	5	29	.278	.410	.300
Road Games	131	31	8	0	6	22	5	26	.237	.435	.268
Grass Fields	88	23	6	0	4	13	1	17	.261	.466	.275
Artificial Turf	187	48	12	0	5	28	9	38	.257	.401	.289
April	77	16	4	0	3	9	1	21	.208	.377	.228
May	12	2	1	0	0	0	0	5	.167	.250	.167
June	44	15	4	0	2	6	2	2	.341	.568	.362
July	91	25	6	0	2	16	4	18	.275	.407	.302
August	51	13	3	0	2	10	3	9	.255	.431	.296
Sept./Oct.	0	0	0	0	0	0	0	0	.000	.000	.000
Leading Off Inn.	61	17	5	0	3	3	1	14	.279	.508	.290
Runners On	136	34	7	0	3	35	6	25	.250	.368	.283
Bases Empty	139	37	11	0	6	6	4	30	.266	.475	.287
Runners/Scor. Pos.	76	19	3	0	2	31	5	14	.250	.368	.298
Runners On/2 Out	55	14	1	0	3	18	4	9	.255	.436	.305
Scor. Pos./2 Out	35	9	0	0	2	15	4	7	.257	.429	.333
Late-Inning Pressure	45	10	3	0	1	4	1	10	.222	.356	.255
Leading Off	14	1	1	0	0	0	0	2	.071	.143	.071
Runners On	20	4	1	0	0	3	0	6	.200	.250	.238
Runners/Scor. Pos.	3	1	0	0	0	3	0	1	.333	.333	.500

RUNS BATTED IN	From 1B	From 2B	From 3B	Scoring Position
Totals	6/107	12/56	14/38	26/94
Percentage	5.6%	21.4%	36.8%	27.7%

Loves to face: Greg W. Harris (.500, 3-for-6, 2 HR)
Jimmy Jones (3-for-3, 2 2B)
John Smiley (.400, 4-for-10, 2 HR)

Hates to face: Omar Olivares (0-for-9)
Mel Rojas (0-for-8)
Anthony Young (.100, 1-for-10)

Miscellaneous statistics: Ground outs-to-air outs ratio: 0.92 last season, 1.00 for career.... Grounded into 7 double plays in 69 opportunities (one per 10).... Drove in 9 of 20 runners from third base with less than two outs (45%).... Direction of balls hit to the outfield: 38% to left field, 33% to center, 28% to right.... Base running: Advanced from first base to third on 5 of 8 outfield singles (63%); scored from second on 2 of 4 (50%).... Made 1.95 putouts per nine innings in right field.

Comments: Became the Phillies' 10th different opening-day left fielder in the last 10 years. Since 1983, they have used Gary Matthews, Glenn Wilson, Jeff Stone, Gary Redus, Mike Easler, Phil Bradley, Ron Jones, John Kruk, Von Hayes, and Chamberlain. That equals the current high for longest-running opening-day revolving door by one team at one position; the Angels have used 10 different right fielders in their last 10 openers.... Career breakdown: .272 at Veterans Stadium, .224 on the road.... Averaged one walk every 28.9 plate appearances last year, the 5th-lowest rate among major leaguers with at least 250 plate appearances. But two teammates had even lower rates: Ricky Jordan (one BB every 56.8 PA) and Mariano Duncan (one every 35.6). Even with three of the bottom five in that category, would you believe that the Phillies' team rate of walks actually increased from 1991 to 1992?...Of his 24 career home runs, 15 have been hit with runners on base. Consider that last season 57 percent of all major league home runs were solo shots. Only eight other active players have hit at least six more homers with runners on than with the bases empty; among them are teammates Jordan and David Hollins.... Born on April 13, 1966, and his name was immediately in the sports headlines; well, sort of. Lead story in the Philadelphia papers that day: 76ers, led by Chamberlain, had been eliminated from the playoffs by Russell's Celtics the previous day.

Jerald Clark — Bats Right

San Diego Padres	AB	H	2B	3B	HR	RBI	BB	SO	BA	SA	OBA
Season	496	120	22	6	12	58	22	97	.242	.383	.278
vs. Left-Handers	152	42	9	2	6	20	6	26	.276	.480	.306
vs. Right-Handers	344	78	13	4	6	38	16	71	.227	.340	.266
vs. Ground-Ballers	224	61	11	4	4	26	12	37	.272	.411	.311
vs. Fly-Ballers	272	59	11	2	8	32	10	60	.217	.360	.251
Home Games	247	63	9	3	9	34	11	40	.255	.425	.292
Road Games	249	57	13	3	3	24	11	57	.229	.341	.264
Grass Fields	355	95	17	5	12	52	17	61	.268	.445	.302
Artificial Turf	141	25	5	1	0	6	5	36	.177	.227	.216
April	83	15	2	0	4	8	8	19	.181	.349	.261
May	91	17	3	0	0	4	3	18	.187	.220	.211
June	50	11	4	1	0	3	3	8	.220	.340	.273
July	85	32	6	2	3	17	7	14	.376	.600	.424
August	77	21	3	1	2	6	0	10	.273	.416	.291
Sept./Oct.	110	24	4	2	3	20	1	28	.218	.373	.223
Leading Off Inn.	121	33	6	0	2	2	5	22	.273	.372	.302
Runners On	202	51	6	5	7	53	14	40	.252	.436	.303
Bases Empty	294	69	16	1	5	5	8	57	.235	.347	.260
Runners/Scor. Pos.	118	31	2	4	4	45	10	19	.263	.449	.323
Runners On/2 Out	90	20	5	3	4	21	11	25	.222	.478	.307
Scor. Pos./2 Out	54	12	2	2	2	15	9	15	.222	.444	.333
Late-Inning Pressure	84	19	4	0	2	12	3	20	.226	.345	.253
Leading Off	24	4	1	0	0	0	1	5	.167	.208	.200
Runners On	34	11	1	0	2	12	2	8	.324	.529	.361
Runners/Scor. Pos.	20	5	0	0	0	7	1	5	.250	.250	.286

RUNS BATTED IN	From 1B	From 2B	From 3B	Scoring Position
Totals	10/139	17/93	19/44	36/137
Percentage	7.2%	18.3%	43.2%	26.3%

Loves to face: Bud Black (.364, 4-for-11, 2 HR)
Orel Hershiser (.467, 7-for-15)
Mike Morgan (.389, 7-for-18, 1 HR)

Hates to face: Danny Jackson (0-for-13)
Jose Rijo (.053, 1-for-19)
John Smoltz (0-for-11)

Miscellaneous statistics: Ground outs-to-air outs ratio: 0.74 last season, 0.87 for career.... Grounded into 7 double plays in 82 opportunities (one per 12).... Drove in 17 of 26 runners from third base with less than two outs (65%).... Direction of balls hit to the outfield: 38% to left field, 40% to center, 23% to right.... Base running: Advanced from first base to third on 5 of 20 outfield singles (25%); scored from second on 2 of 7 (29%).... Made 2.26 putouts per nine innings in left field, 3d-highest rate in N.L.

Comments: When Clark batted in the sixth spot in San Diego's lineup last season, he hit only .167, the lowest by any N.L. player in that spot (minimum: 100 plate appearances); but from the seventh spot, he produced more extra-base hits (27) than anyone in the majors. Of course, with the Rockies, he may be the cleanup hitter.... Padres left fielders combined to hit .210 last year, the lowest average by any team in the majors at an outfield position. Clark hit .226 in 115 games in left.... Despite last season's breakdown, he still has a higher career mark vs. right-handers (.244) than vs. left-handers (.223).... Has hit for a higher average against ground-ball pitchers than against fly-ballers in each of his five seasons in the majors; career averages: .266 vs. GBP; .210 vs. FBP.... Has driven in 35 of 51 runners from third base with less than two outs, an excellent career rate of 68.6 percent. What makes that unusual is that Clark is a high strikeout hitter (career rate: one every 4.9 plate appearances), exactly the type of guy who is usually less effective in such situations. That 68.6 rate is the best among all active players who average at least five strikeouts for every 100 plate appearances, and it's not close for second.... Had only one triple in 731 career at-bats as of last year's All-Star break, then hit six over the second half of the season.... Has homered against every opposing N.L. club but the Mets (78 career at-bats); he can take aim at them in Rockies' debut on April 5.

Will Clark — Bats Left

San Francisco Giants	AB	H	2B	3B	HR	RBI	BB	SO	BA	SA	OBA
Season	513	154	40	1	16	73	73	82	.300	.476	.384
vs. Left-Handers	205	63	12	0	2	30	21	31	.307	.395	.366
vs. Right-Handers	308	91	28	1	14	43	52	51	.295	.529	.396
vs. Ground-Ballers	229	67	18	1	11	37	44	35	.293	.524	.404
vs. Fly-Ballers	284	87	22	0	5	36	29	47	.306	.437	.367
Home Games	270	91	26	1	11	44	42	39	.337	.563	.422
Road Games	243	63	14	0	5	29	31	43	.259	.379	.342
Grass Fields	379	121	30	1	12	55	61	62	.319	.499	.409
Artificial Turf	134	33	10	0	4	18	12	20	.246	.410	.311
April	81	28	7	1	1	11	16	15	.346	.494	.444
May	94	27	5	0	3	11	16	17	.287	.436	.393
June	71	23	5	0	4	11	10	7	.324	.563	.402
July	92	26	8	0	3	16	8	18	.283	.467	.340
August	96	25	8	0	3	16	14	13	.260	.438	.359
Sept./Oct.	79	25	7	0	2	8	9	12	.316	.481	.374
Leading Off Inn.	84	20	6	1	3	3	7	13	.238	.440	.304
Runners On	210	71	15	0	8	65	44	34	.338	.524	.436
Bases Empty	303	83	25	1	8	8	29	48	.274	.442	.343
Runners/Scor. Pos.	112	37	9	0	5	55	36	27	.330	.545	.459
Runners On/2 Out	74	28	7	0	3	26	22	13	.378	.595	.526
Scor. Pos./2 Out	40	15	5	0	1	20	20	11	.375	.575	.583
Late-Inning Pressure	82	25	7	0	2	12	17	17	.305	.463	.420
Leading Off	22	5	2	0	0	0	1	4	.227	.318	.261
Runners On	32	13	2	0	2	12	15	7	.406	.656	.583
Runners/Scor. Pos.	20	6	2	0	1	10	15	6	.300	.550	.583

RUNS BATTED IN	From 1B	From 2B	From 3B	Scoring Position
Totals	10/148	23/87	24/52	47/139
Percentage	6.8%	26.4%	46.2%	33.8%

Loves to face: Kyle Abbott (.583, 7-for-12)
Ramon Martinez (.368, 14-for-38, 3 2B, 3 HR)
Todd Worrell (.500, 5-for-10, 2 2B, 1 HR)

Hates to face: Mike Harkey (0-for-11)
Randy Myers (.136, 3-for-22, 1 HR, 3 BB, 11 SO)
Chris Nabholz (0-for-12)

Miscellaneous statistics: Ground outs-to-air outs ratio: 0.79 last season, 0.84 for career.... Grounded into 5 double plays in 102 opportunities (one per 20).... Drove in 17 of 33 runners from third base with less than two outs (52%).... Direction of balls hit to the outfield: 38% to left field, 28% to center, 34% to right.... Base running: Advanced from first base to third on 5 of 23 outfield singles (22%); scored from second on 13 of 21 (62%).... Made 0.77 assists per nine innings at first base.

Comments: The only active player (minimum: 1000 games) with a career batting average over .300 and a career slugging percentage over .500. Among the 31 retired players who meet those specs, 26 are in the Hall of Fame; the five who haven't made it to Cooperstown are Wally Berger (.300, .522), Babe Herman (.324, .532), Joe Jackson (.356, .518), Hal Trosky (.302, .522), and Ken Williams (.319, .531).... His .337 average in home games was 4th highest in the league. That makes four different seasons in which he has hit .325 or better at Candlestick, an amazing feat at one of the worst hitters' parks in baseball.... Led N.L. with a .338 mark with runners on base; he has hit for a higher average with runners on base than with the bases empty in each of the last six seasons, by an average difference of 40 points per season.... His .325 career average with two outs and runners in scoring position is 2d best among active players behind Luis Polonia (.331).... Led Giants with 73 RBIs, the fewest by the team leader on any N.L. team last season, and the lowest total to lead San Francisco since 1985 (Jeff Leonard, 62).... One of four players in the expansion era to have hit 25 or more doubles in each of his first seven seasons in the majors. The others: Barry Bonds, Garry Maddox, and Carl Yastrzemski.... Has batted over .300 in each of the last four Aprils and each of the last six Junes, but has a career mark of only .263 in May.... With the bases loaded, Will's evil twin Won't shows up. Career numbers: .208 (15-for-72), one walk, 20 strikeouts.

Royce Clayton   Bats Right

San Francisco Giants	AB	H	2B	3B	HR	RBI	BB	SO	BA	SA	OBA
Season	321	72	7	4	4	24	26	63	.224	.308	.281
vs. Left-Handers	96	24	4	2	0	4	11	21	.250	.333	.327
vs. Right-Handers	225	48	3	2	4	20	15	42	.213	.298	.260
vs. Ground-Ballers	182	34	4	2	2	14	11	34	.187	.264	.232
vs. Fly-Ballers	139	38	3	2	2	10	15	29	.273	.367	.342
Home Games	172	43	3	2	3	15	15	23	.250	.343	.309
Road Games	149	29	4	2	1	9	11	40	.195	.268	.248
Grass Fields	236	56	4	3	3	18	20	39	.237	.318	.296
Artificial Turf	85	16	3	1	1	6	6	24	.188	.282	.239
April	74	16	1	2	0	6	7	15	.216	.284	.280
May	58	12	4	0	2	8	6	12	.207	.379	.277
June	47	9	1	1	1	2	4	9	.191	.319	.255
July	0	0	0	0	0	0	0	0	.000	.000	.000
August	35	11	0	0	0	3	4	3	.314	.314	.385
Sept./Oct.	107	24	1	1	1	5	5	24	.224	.280	.259
Leading Off Inn.	74	22	1	0	2	2	7	14	.297	.392	.358
Runners On	143	32	2	4	1	21	10	25	.224	.315	.271
Bases Empty	178	40	5	0	3	3	16	38	.225	.303	.289
Runners/Scor. Pos.	82	15	1	3	1	20	9	13	.183	.305	.258
Runners On/2 Out	54	14	0	2	0	6	6	8	.259	.333	.333
Scor. Pos./2 Out	32	5	0	1	0	5	5	5	.156	.219	.270
Late-Inning Pressure	58	13	0	0	1	2	9	11	.224	.276	.328
Leading Off	16	8	0	0	1	1	4	2	.500	.688	.600
Runners On	24	4	0	0	0	1	3	2	.167	.167	.259
Runners/Scor. Pos.	12	1	0	0	0	1	3	1	.083	.083	.267

RUNS BATTED IN	From 1B	From 2B	From 3B	Scoring Position
Totals	2/101	8/61	10/33	18/94
Percentage	2.0%	13.1%	30.3%	19.1%

Loves to face: Steve Avery (.600, 3-for-5, 1 2B, 1 3B)
Rheal Cormier (.750, 3-for-4, 1 2B)
Darryl Kile (.429, 3-for-7, 1 HR)
Hates to face: Mark Portugal (0-for-7)
Bob Scanlan (0-for-5)
Frank Seminara (0-for-5)

Miscellaneous statistics: Ground outs-to-air outs ratio: 1.85 last season, 1.72 for career.... Grounded into 11 double plays in 66 opportunities (one per 6.0).... Drove in 9 of 18 runners from third base with less than two outs (50%).... Direction of balls hit to the outfield: 35% to left field, 29% to center, 36% to right.... Base running: Advanced from first base to third on 8 of 13 outfield singles (62%), highest rate in N.L.; scored from second on 1 of 7 (14%).... Made 2.94 assists per nine innings at shortstop.

Comments: Only National League player born in the 1970s to appear in more than 50 games.... Among the youngest players in Giants history to accumulate at least 100 games at shortstop. Three did it at an even younger age: Travis Jackson, Buddy Kerr, and Chris Speier.... Made 91 starts at shortstop last season. N.L. Rookie-of-the-Year Eric Karros was the only N.L. rookie to make 100 starts last season; Todd Hundley (98), Reggie Sanders (96), and Clayton (91) came next.... San Francisco's first-round choice and the 15th player selected in the 1988 June draft; of the first 14 picks, nine have already made their major league debuts. Three shortstops were selected ahead of Clayton: Mark Lewis (2d), Monty Fariss (6th), and Austin Manahan (13th). Manahan is the only one of the three who has not played in the big leagues; he was drafted as a shortstop out of high school, and batted .221 last season as a second baseman for the Carolina Mudcats of the Southern League (AA) in the Pittsburgh system.... Giants shortstops batted .228 last season, but that still beat out those of three N.L. teams: Houston (.227), Philadelphia (.222), and New York (.203).... Clayton had 6th-lowest road average in the league; his average vs. right-handers was 5th lowest.... He struck out 328 times in 381 minor league games from 1989 to 1991.

Alex Cole   Bats Left

Indians/Pirates	AB	H	2B	3B	HR	RBI	BB	SO	BA	SA	OBA
Season	302	77	4	7	0	15	28	67	.255	.315	.318
vs. Left-Handers	49	14	0	2	0	3	6	14	.286	.367	.368
vs. Right-Handers	253	63	4	5	0	12	22	53	.249	.304	.308
vs. Ground-Ballers	137	34	2	4	0	6	12	36	.248	.321	.309
vs. Fly-Ballers	165	43	2	3	0	9	16	31	.261	.309	.326
Home Games	137	41	2	5	0	13	17	30	.299	.387	.378
Road Games	165	36	2	2	0	2	11	37	.218	.255	.266
Grass Fields	128	29	1	0	0	5	14	25	.227	.234	.303
Artificial Turf	174	48	3	7	0	10	14	42	.276	.374	.330
April	32	5	1	0	0	0	3	8	.156	.188	.229
May	47	11	0	0	0	5	5	10	.234	.234	.315
June	17	4	0	0	0	0	2	3	.235	.235	.316
July	68	19	0	4	0	5	7	18	.279	.397	.347
August	59	21	2	1	0	1	5	12	.356	.424	.406
Sept./Oct.	79	17	1	2	0	4	6	16	.215	.278	.267
Leading Off Inn.	114	25	2	1	0	0	12	20	.219	.254	.294
Runners On	91	19	1	3	0	15	10	21	.209	.286	.282
Bases Empty	211	58	3	4	0	0	18	46	.275	.327	.335
Runners/Scor. Pos.	55	12	1	2	0	14	8	15	.218	.309	.308
Runners On/2 Out	42	5	0	0	0	3	3	11	.119	.119	.178
Scor. Pos./2 Out	29	4	0	0	0	3	3	9	.138	.138	.219
Late-Inning Pressure	56	14	1	1	0	5	9	15	.250	.304	.364
Leading Off	20	4	1	0	0	0	4	5	.200	.250	.304
Runners On	18	4	0	1	0	5	4	4	.222	.333	.364
Runners/Scor. Pos.	13	4	0	1	0	5	4	2	.308	.462	.471

RUNS BATTED IN	From 1B	From 2B	From 3B	Scoring Position
Totals	2/58	4/45	9/20	13/65
Percentage	3.4%	8.9%	45.0%	20.0%

Loves to face: Frank Castillo (.400, 4-for-10)
Omar Olivares (.500, 4-for-8)
Jeff D. Robinson (.625, 5-for-8)
Hates to face: Jose Guzman (0-for-8)
Dennis Martinez (.143, 1-for-7, 4 SO)
Mike Morgan (0-for-6)

Miscellaneous statistics: Ground outs-to-air outs ratio: 1.70 last season, 1.49 for career.... Grounded into 4 double plays in 40 opportunities (one per 10).... Drove in 8 of 12 runners from third base with less than two outs (67%).... Direction of balls hit to the outfield: 39% to left field, 40% to center, 21% to right.... Base running: Advanced from first base to third on 7 of 15 outfield singles (47%); scored from second on 8 of 11 (73%).... Made 1.90 putouts per nine innings in right field.

Comments: Homerless in 916 career at-bats in the majors, the highest total of major league at-bats by any active player who hasn't homered. The top five: Cole, Joey Cora (710), Orel Hershiser (555), Bert Blyleven (451), Zane Smith (453). The only other active nonpitcher who is homerless in at least 250 career at-bats is St. Louis's Craig Wilson (313). The all-time mark: 2335 by Bill Holbert, a catcher who played in the '70s and '80s—that's the 1870s and '80s.... The last players to reach the 1000-at-bat mark without a homer: Tom Herr (1982), Mick Kelleher (1981), Luis Gomez (1980), and Don Sutton (1978).... Seven different players started at least 10 games in the leadoff spot for Pittsburgh last season: Cole (46 starts), Gary Redus (43), Orlando Merced (17), Cecil Espy (16), Gary Varsho (14), Jeff King (12), and Kirk Gibson (12).... One of nine left-handed batters active in 1992 with at least 1000 career plate appearances and a higher career average vs. left-handed pitchers (.313) than vs. right-handers (.276).... On-base percentage leading off innings dropped from .433 in 1991; his overall walk rate decreased from one every 7.8 plate appearances in 1991 to one every 11.9 PA in 1992.... Career average with the bases empty (.297) is 44 points higher than with runners on base (.253); among active players with at least 1000 plate appearances, only Kevin Maas (56 points) and Edgar Martinez (48 points) have larger disparities of that type.

Vince Coleman — Bats Left and Right

New York Mets	AB	H	2B	3B	HR	RBI	BB	SO	BA	SA	OBA
Season	229	63	11	1	2	21	27	41	.275	.358	.355
vs. Left-Handers	60	17	4	1	1	9	7	11	.283	.433	.358
vs. Right-Handers	169	46	7	0	1	12	20	30	.272	.331	.354
vs. Ground-Ballers	104	25	4	1	1	10	10	18	.240	.327	.310
vs. Fly-Ballers	125	38	7	0	1	11	17	23	.304	.384	.392
Home Games	119	33	3	0	2	14	17	21	.277	.353	.370
Road Games	110	30	8	1	0	7	10	20	.273	.364	.339
Grass Fields	145	37	3	0	2	14	19	28	.255	.317	.343
Artificial Turf	84	26	8	1	0	7	8	13	.310	.429	.376
April	13	5	2	0	0	2	2	1	.385	.538	.467
May	9	3	0	0	0	1	1	2	.333	.333	.400
June	92	28	4	0	2	10	10	12	.304	.413	.385
July	12	2	1	0	0	0	1	1	.167	.250	.231
August	66	14	2	0	0	5	13	15	.212	.242	.338
Sept./Oct.	37	11	2	1	0	3	0	10	.297	.405	.297
Leading Off Inn.	94	28	6	0	0	0	10	23	.298	.362	.377
Runners On	67	19	4	1	2	21	11	11	.284	.463	.380
Bases Empty	162	44	7	0	0	0	16	30	.272	.315	.344
Runners/Scor. Pos.	45	14	4	1	2	21	9	9	.311	.578	.418
Runners On/2 Out	32	8	1	1	2	11	6	2	.250	.531	.368
Scor. Pos./2 Out	22	6	1	1	2	11	6	2	.273	.682	.429
Late-Inning Pressure	38	9	1	0	1	6	4	7	.237	.342	.310
Leading Off	10	3	0	0	0	0	0	2	.300	.300	.300
Runners On	16	5	1	0	1	6	3	3	.313	.563	.421
Runners/Scor. Pos.	9	3	1	0	1	6	3	2	.333	.778	.500

RUNS BATTED IN	From 1B	From 2B	From 3B	Scoring Position
Totals	0/35	8/39	11/18	19/57
Percentage	0.0%	20.5%	61.1%	33.3%

Loves to face: Tim Belcher (.500, 11-for-22)
Jose Rijo (.417, 5-for-12, 2 3B, 4 SO)
Zane Smith (.429, 24-for-56)
Hates to face: Mike Morgan (.105, 2-for-19)
Pete Smith (.071, 1-for-14, 2 BB)
Randy Tomlin (.050, 1-for-20)

Miscellaneous statistics: Ground outs-to-air outs ratio: 1.63 last season, 1.49 for career.... Grounded into 1 double play in 22 opportunities (one per 22).... Drove in 5 of 7 runners from third base with less than two outs (71%).... Direction of balls hit to the outfield: 44% to left field, 35% to center, 22% to right batting left-handed; 28% to left field, 41% to center, 31% to right batting right-handed.... Base running: Advanced from first base to third on 4 of 8 outfield singles (50%); scored from second on 7 of 9 (78%).... Made 1.54 putouts per nine innings in left field.

Comments: One of five players with declining at-bats totals in each of the last five years; others: Scott Bradley, Eric Davis, Randy Ready, and Pat Tabler. The last guy with a six-year streak was Fred Lynn in the last six years of his career.... One of seven players to make three separate trips to the D.L. last season. The others: Larry Andersen, Ivan Calderon, Lenny Dykstra, Julio Franco, Jose Oquendo, and Bob Welch.... Mets used 12 different starters in the leadoff spot last year, a major league high.... Coleman drove in a career-high 33 percent of runners from scoring position last season. Coming into 1992, his career rate in that category had been the lowest of anyone with as many opportunities as Coleman over the preceding 17 years.... His 1992 ground outs-to-air outs ratio: 1.91 from the left side of the plate, 1.06 from the right side.... On-base percentage has improved in each of the last four years; the problem has been in the "minutes played" column.... Career breakdown shows a late-season breakdown: he has batted .272 from April to August, .229 from September 1 on.... Has already been caught stealing as many times (three) by the Cardinals (in 12 attempts) as he was by the Mets (in 67 attempts).... Career stolen-base analysis: .839 percentage with one steal every 1.5 games on artificial turf; .746 with one every 2.3 games on dirt tracks.... As a team, the Mets ran more and ran better away from Shea last year: 46 steals in 75 tries (.613) at home, 83 in 106 attempts (.783) on the road.

Doug Dascenzo — Bats Left and Right

Chicago Cubs	AB	H	2B	3B	HR	RBI	BB	SO	BA	SA	OBA
Season	376	96	13	4	0	20	27	32	.255	.311	.304
vs. Left-Handers	169	41	7	1	0	10	8	7	.243	.296	.275
vs. Right-Handers	207	55	6	3	0	10	19	25	.266	.324	.326
vs. Ground-Ballers	168	44	6	2	0	6	13	9	.262	.321	.313
vs. Fly-Ballers	208	52	7	2	0	14	14	23	.250	.303	.296
Home Games	202	51	9	4	0	11	14	22	.252	.337	.301
Road Games	174	45	4	0	0	9	13	10	.259	.282	.307
Grass Fields	272	68	10	4	0	12	18	25	.250	.316	.297
Artificial Turf	104	28	3	0	0	8	9	7	.269	.298	.322
April	18	7	0	0	0	1	1	1	.389	.389	.421
May	25	4	0	0	0	1	1	4	.160	.160	.192
June	101	23	3	1	0	6	5	5	.228	.277	.262
July	71	19	3	1	0	3	12	10	.268	.338	.369
August	89	23	5	1	0	5	2	4	.258	.337	.275
Sept./Oct.	72	20	2	1	0	4	6	8	.278	.333	.333
Leading Off Inn.	131	29	6	1	0	0	8	15	.221	.282	.266
Runners On	134	35	1	1	0	20	7	10	.261	.284	.294
Bases Empty	242	61	12	3	0	0	20	22	.252	.326	.309
Runners/Scor. Pos.	78	20	1	0	0	19	5	6	.256	.269	.294
Runners On/2 Out	65	16	0	1	0	13	1	3	.246	.277	.258
Scor. Pos./2 Out	46	13	0	0	0	12	1	3	.283	.283	.298
Late-Inning Pressure	64	12	1	0	0	1	9	6	.188	.203	.288
Leading Off	19	4	1	0	0	0	3	3	.211	.263	.318
Runners On	23	5	0	0	0	1	2	1	.217	.217	.280
Runners/Scor. Pos.	13	3	0	0	0	1	2	1	.231	.231	.333

RUNS BATTED IN	From 1B	From 2B	From 3B	Scoring Position
Totals	1/90	8/69	11/21	19/90
Percentage	1.1%	11.6%	52.4%	21.1%

Loves to face: Dennis Rasmussen (.412, 7-for-17)
Bill Sampen (.667, 4-for-6)
Frank Viola (.571, 8-for-14)
Hates to face: Ron Darling (.100, 1-for-10)
Jim Deshaies (.100, 2-for-20)
John Dopson (0-for-5)

Miscellaneous statistics: Ground outs-to-air outs ratio: 1.42 last season, 1.27 for career.... Grounded into 3 double plays in 59 opportunities (one per 20).... Drove in 6 of 9 runners from third base with less than two outs (67%).... Direction of balls hit to the outfield: 34% to left field, 29% to center, 37% to right batting left-handed; 35% to left field, 36% to center, 29% to right batting right-handed.... Base running: Advanced from first base to third on 6 of 17 outfield singles (35%); scored from second on 10 of 11 (91%), 3d-highest rate in N.L.... Made 2.51 putouts per nine innings in center field.

Comments: Began his career with 242 consecutive errorless games in the outfield, a major league record for the start of a career and a league record for consecutive errorless games at any point in a career. Has committed seven errors in 138 games since his streak was broken.... There's one category in which this little fellow is up there with the big boys: driving in runners from third base with less than two outs. His career rate is 69 percent (35-for-51) to rank tied for 7th (with Jerald Clark) among active players with at least 50 opportunities. The others on the list: David Justice, Delino DeShields, Tony Gwynn, Mark Grace, Wade Boggs, and George Brett.... On the other hand, his on-base percentage leading off innings was the lowest in N.L. last season.... When leading off the *lineup*, he didn't fare much better: he drew only six walks in 187 plate appearances from the top spot, the lowest rate in the league among players up at least 100 times in the leadoff spot; runner-up was teammate Jose Vizcaino (one walk every 29.2 PA).... Batted .429 as a pinch hitter (9-for-21), second in the majors among players with at least 20 pinch-hit at-bats to Willie McGee's .524 (11-for-21).... Became only the fifth Cubs player over the last 30 years to come to the plate at least 400 times in a season without hitting a home run. The others: Don Kessinger (1967, 1973, 1975), Glenn Beckert (1973), Ivan DeJesus (1981), and Larry Bowa (1982, 1984); all of them were middle infielders.

Darren Daulton
Bats Left

Philadelphia Phillies	AB	H	2B	3B	HR	RBI	BB	SO	BA	SA	OBA
Season	485	131	32	5	27	109	88	103	.270	.524	.385
vs. Left-Handers	202	52	16	0	11	40	30	45	.257	.500	.363
vs. Right-Handers	283	79	16	5	16	69	58	58	.279	.541	.399
vs. Ground-Ballers	227	63	14	4	13	52	38	47	.278	.546	.381
vs. Fly-Ballers	258	68	18	1	14	57	50	56	.264	.504	.387
Home Games	229	73	17	4	17	63	46	51	.319	.651	.434
Road Games	256	58	15	1	10	46	42	52	.227	.410	.339
Grass Fields	144	30	8	0	5	26	19	24	.208	.368	.304
Artificial Turf	341	101	24	5	22	83	69	79	.296	.589	.417
April	66	15	4	2	1	16	12	18	.227	.394	.333
May	68	28	9	0	3	16	15	15	.412	.676	.524
June	91	23	4	0	8	23	16	18	.253	.560	.361
July	87	23	3	1	6	21	16	21	.264	.529	.383
August	78	18	4	1	6	15	10	18	.231	.538	.333
Sept./Oct.	95	24	8	1	3	18	19	13	.253	.453	.383
Leading Off Inn.	114	27	7	0	5	5	15	20	.237	.430	.341
Runners On	244	74	17	4	17	99	55	53	.303	.615	.427
Bases Empty	241	57	15	1	10	10	33	50	.237	.432	.338
Runners/Scor. Pos.	134	40	10	1	8	72	35	31	.299	.567	.432
Runners On/2 Out	108	30	7	1	6	30	29	23	.278	.528	.439
Scor. Pos./2 Out	63	16	4	0	3	20	19	16	.254	.460	.434
Late-Inning Pressure	84	17	6	0	2	12	12	23	.202	.345	.316
Leading Off	20	2	1	0	0	0	2	4	.100	.150	.182
Runners On	44	11	5	0	1	11	8	14	.250	.432	.389
Runners/Scor. Pos.	22	5	1	0	1	8	7	7	.227	.409	.433

RUNS BATTED IN	From 1B	From 2B	From 3B	Scoring Position
Totals	26/193	24/105	32/60	56/165
Percentage	13.5%	22.9%	53.3%	33.9%

Loves to face: John Burkett (.571, 8-for-14)
Les Lancaster (.462, 6-for-13)
Bill Swift (.667, 4-for-6, 2 2B, 1 HR)

Hates to face: Sid Fernandez (.100, 2-for-20, 3 BB)
Bill Landrum (0-for-10)
Chris Nabholz (.071, 1-for-14, 4 BB)

Miscellaneous statistics: Ground outs-to-air outs ratio: 0.66 last season, 0.79 for career.... Grounded into 3 double plays in 126 opportunities (one per 42), 5th-best rate in N.L.... Drove in 22 of 30 runners from third base with less than two outs (73%).... Direction of balls hit to the outfield: 19% to left field, 34% to center, 47% to right.... Base running: Advanced from first base to third on 5 of 29 outfield singles (17%); scored from second on 7 of 13 (54%).... Opposing base stealers: 88-for-137 (64%).

Comments: Increased his home-run total from 12 in 1991 to 27 last year, but that wasn't even the greatest increase on his own team; David Hollins went from 6 to 27.... Only six left-handed-hitting catchers have hit at least 25 home runs in a season: Yogi Berra (six times), Bill Dickey (twice), Ed Bailey (1956), Tom Haller (1966), Matt Nokes (1987), and Daulton (1992).... Became only the third catcher with at least 20 homers, 100 RBIs, and 10 stolen bases in one season. The other two: Johnny Bench (1975) and Carlton Fisk (1985).... Hit 16 doubles and 11 home runs vs. left-handed pitchers; among left-handed batters in either league, only Barry Bonds (13), Fred McGriff (13), and Ken Griffey (12) had more home runs; only Bonds (35) and Andy Van Slyke (30) had more extra-base hits.... Those impressive numbers against lefties came with no advance warning: Through 1991, he had a .202 batting average and only four home runs in 322 at-bats vs. lefties.... More runners were caught stealing with Daulton catching (49) than with any other N.L. receiver.... Tied with B.J. Surhoff for the major league lead in stolen bases among catchers last season (11). His career stolen base percentage is .800 (32-for-40); Rickey Henderson, who has a few more attempts, is at .813.... Career average of .261 vs. ground-ball pitchers, .205 vs. fly-ballers. Unusually, he has hit more home runs vs. ground-ballers (40) than vs. fly-ballers (35).... Other great breakthroughs in Phillies history: Tony Taylor, 1970 (.301, 43 points above his prior career mark), and Dolph Camilli, 1936 (.315, 28 HR, 102 RBI).

Eric Davis
Bats Right

Los Angeles Dodgers	AB	H	2B	3B	HR	RBI	BB	SO	BA	SA	OBA
Season	267	61	8	1	5	32	36	71	.228	.322	.325
vs. Left-Handers	89	21	4	0	4	11	23	19	.236	.416	.393
vs. Right-Handers	178	40	4	1	1	21	13	52	.225	.275	.286
vs. Ground-Ballers	100	27	4	0	2	11	9	22	.270	.370	.336
vs. Fly-Ballers	167	34	4	1	3	21	27	49	.204	.293	.318
Home Games	133	31	6	0	1	15	16	30	.233	.301	.316
Road Games	134	30	2	1	4	17	20	41	.224	.343	.333
Grass Fields	194	48	7	1	4	24	26	50	.247	.356	.342
Artificial Turf	73	13	1	0	1	8	10	21	.178	.233	.277
April	71	22	3	0	4	13	10	22	.310	.521	.398
May	42	7	3	0	0	3	6	14	.167	.238	.271
June	43	9	1	0	0	5	4	11	.209	.233	.277
July	83	18	1	1	1	10	12	18	.217	.289	.313
August	18	4	0	0	0	1	2	6	.222	.222	.333
Sept./Oct.	10	1	0	0	0	0	2	0	.100	.100	.308
Leading Off Inn.	56	13	0	0	3	3	4	15	.232	.393	.283
Runners On	133	31	5	1	1	28	23	30	.233	.308	.354
Bases Empty	134	30	3	0	4	4	13	41	.224	.336	.293
Runners/Scor. Pos.	80	22	2	0	1	26	16	16	.275	.338	.406
Runners On/2 Out	61	16	5	0	1	12	13	8	.262	.393	.400
Scor. Pos./2 Out	36	10	2	0	1	11	9	4	.278	.417	.435
Late-Inning Pressure	44	7	1	0	0	6	6	6	.159	.182	.275
Leading Off	11	1	0	0	0	0	1	2	.091	.091	.167
Runners On	20	5	1	0	0	6	4	1	.250	.300	.400
Runners/Scor. Pos.	13	4	1	0	0	6	3	0	.308	.385	.471

RUNS BATTED IN	From 1B	From 2B	From 3B	Scoring Position
Totals	3/91	13/67	11/29	24/96
Percentage	3.3%	19.4%	37.9%	25.0%

Loves to face: Paul Assenmacher (.625, 5-for-8, 2 HR)
Doug Drabek (.333, 9-for-27, 2 2B, 1 3B, 2 HR)
John Smoltz (.556, 10-for-18, 4 HR)

Hates to face: Larry Andersen (.136, 3-for-22)
Cris Carpenter (.091, 1-for-11)
Greg Maddux (.167, 7-for-42)

Miscellaneous statistics: Ground outs-to-air outs ratio: 1.39 last season, 1.08 for career.... Grounded into 9 double plays in 57 opportunities (one per 6.3).... Drove in 8 of 18 runners from third base with less than two outs (44%).... Direction of balls hit to the outfield: 31% to left field, 34% to center, 34% to right.... Base running: Advanced from first base to third on 6 of 14 outfield singles (43%); scored from second on 4 of 4 (100%).... Made 1.70 putouts per nine innings in left field, lowest rate in majors.

Comments: Hit 148 home runs from 1986 to 1990, but has only 16 in two seasons since then. There were 17 players who hit 125 or more homers in that five-year period; only Davis and Jesse Barfield (19) have hit fewer than 20 in the two years since.... Led majors in stolen-base percentage (.950) with 19 steals in 20 tries last season. No catcher threw him out; his only "caught stealing" was a pickoff by Trevor Wilson. He has been at .875 or higher six times in the past seven years; only two other players have had even four such seasons (minimum: 15 attempts) in their entire careers: Tim Raines (5) and Dave Lopes (4).... Needs 34 steals to reach 300 for his career and qualify as the all-time percentage leader. For now, Raines leads at .852 (730 steals, 127 caught); Eric's at .875 (266 steals, 38 caught).... Batted a puny .198 with 13 RBIs in 35 games as a cleanup hitter, the lowest average by any N.L. cleanup hitter (minimum: 100 at-bats). But in 84 at-bats in the 5th spot, he managed a more robust .310 (possibly the first time the word "robust" has been used in connection with Davis).... Eric and Darryl Strawberry started together only 30 times last year, while they combined for 145 days on the disabled list in four trips.... From the *1992 Analyst,* "He will become only the second player in major league history to reach the 200-HR mark without playing more than 135 games in a season. The other: Dave Kingman." One of our more presumptuous moments, don't you think? He's still 18 shy of 200 as we head into '93.

Andre Dawson — Bats Right

Chicago Cubs	AB	H	2B	3B	HR	RBI	BB	SO	BA	SA	OBA
Season	542	150	27	2	22	90	30	70	.277	.456	.316
vs. Left-Handers	195	56	12	1	7	35	10	24	.287	.467	.321
vs. Right-Handers	347	94	15	1	15	55	20	46	.271	.450	.314
vs. Ground-Ballers	230	65	10	1	10	46	13	27	.283	.465	.329
vs. Fly-Ballers	312	85	17	1	12	44	17	43	.272	.449	.306
Home Games	252	77	16	2	13	48	20	34	.306	.540	.357
Road Games	290	73	11	0	9	42	10	36	.252	.383	.279
Grass Fields	365	113	21	2	18	70	26	46	.310	.526	.357
Artificial Turf	177	37	6	0	4	20	4	24	.209	.311	.228
April	59	15	3	0	3	12	1	11	.254	.458	.274
May	104	34	6	0	4	20	4	15	.327	.500	.345
June	81	21	4	0	3	14	5	8	.259	.420	.303
July	92	16	2	0	5	8	7	16	.174	.359	.232
August	95	30	6	1	3	15	11	9	.316	.495	.393
Sept./Oct.	111	34	6	1	4	21	2	11	.306	.486	.322
Leading Off Inn.	124	29	5	1	5	5	8	19	.234	.411	.291
Runners On	282	81	12	1	9	77	16	36	.287	.433	.321
Bases Empty	260	69	15	1	13	13	14	34	.265	.481	.310
Runners/Scor. Pos.	145	41	7	0	2	59	15	22	.283	.372	.341
Runners On/2 Out	139	37	5	1	1	26	9	19	.266	.338	.311
Scor. Pos./2 Out	70	19	4	0	1	24	8	12	.271	.371	.346
Late-Inning Pressure	99	34	4	0	5	13	4	9	.343	.535	.375
Leading Off	27	10	2	0	1	1	1	3	.370	.556	.414
Runners On	47	14	2	0	1	9	2	6	.298	.404	.327
Runners/Scor. Pos.	24	7	2	0	0	7	2	4	.292	.375	.346

RUNS BATTED IN	From 1B	From 2B	From 3B	Scoring Position
Totals	15/210	26/107	27/58	53/165
Percentage	7.1%	24.3%	46.6%	32.1%

Loves to face: Ron Darling (.333, 19-for-57, 4 HR)
Mark Grant (.571, 12-for-21, 3 HR)
Scott Scudder (.750, 3-for-4, 1 2B, 2 HR, 4 BB)
Hates to face: Rich Gossage (.091, 1-for-11)
Bob Kipper (0-for-14)
Bill Sampen (.091, 1-for-11)

Miscellaneous statistics: Ground outs-to-air outs ratio: 1.08 last season, 0.99 for career.... Grounded into 13 double plays in 119 opportunities (one per 9.2).... Drove in 21 of 30 runners from third base with less than two outs (70%).... Direction of balls hit to the outfield: 42% to left field, 33% to center, 25% to right.... Base running: Advanced from first base to third on 8 of 26 outfield singles (31%); scored from second on 7 of 11 (64%).... Made 1.70 putouts per nine innings in right field, lowest rate in majors.

Comments: His next home run will make him the 25th player in major league history to reach the 400 mark for his career (unless Dale Murphy hits two before Dawson gets one). His career average of one walk every 17.5 plate appearances will be the lowest rate among players in the 400-HR Club. The lowest rates to date: Ernie Banks (one walk every 13.6 PA); Dave Kingman (12.2); Billy Williams (10.1). In case you didn't notice, all of them played for the Cubs.... He leaves the National League eight home runs shy of Duke Snider's 10th-place total (407).... Collected more than 50 extra-base hits last season for the 13th time in his career. Only two players in N.L. history have done that more often: Hank Aaron (18) and Stan Musial (16).... Tied with Babe Ruth for 18th place on all-time list of games played in the outfield (2238); Dave Winfield (2437) is the only active player ahead of Dawson.... Had 3d-best average in N.L. in Late-Inning Pressure Situations.... From the Cubs to the Red Sox, a masochist's delight! The only player to appear in at least 200 games for both clubs? Bill Buckner.... Green Monster Alert: All 22 of his home runs last season were hit to left field. But if you think his home run output will increase at Fenway, see page 331 in the Ballparks Section.... Has a career batting average of .304, with one home run every 18.6 at-bats in day games, .264 (one HR every 26.3 AB) at night. He probably can't wait to get a crack at the annual morning game on Patriots Day.

Delino DeShields — Bats Left

Montreal Expos	AB	H	2B	3B	HR	RBI	BB	SO	BA	SA	OBA
Season	530	155	19	8	7	56	54	108	.292	.398	.359
vs. Left-Handers	185	58	6	2	2	21	22	33	.314	.400	.389
vs. Right-Handers	345	97	13	6	5	35	32	75	.281	.397	.343
vs. Ground-Ballers	219	65	3	4	5	24	27	39	.297	.416	.377
vs. Fly-Ballers	311	90	16	4	2	32	27	69	.289	.386	.347
Home Games	271	75	9	4	1	19	23	56	.277	.351	.338
Road Games	259	80	10	4	6	37	31	52	.309	.448	.381
Grass Fields	146	47	8	2	2	24	23	29	.322	.445	.409
Artificial Turf	384	108	11	6	5	32	31	79	.281	.380	.339
April	91	25	2	1	2	6	8	23	.275	.385	.337
May	86	21	4	0	0	7	10	22	.244	.291	.320
June	100	33	4	4	0	9	15	19	.330	.450	.414
July	117	44	5	1	3	13	12	20	.376	.513	.434
August	93	26	3	1	2	20	7	14	.280	.398	.343
Sept./Oct.	43	6	1	1	0	1	2	10	.140	.209	.178
Leading Off Inn.	191	55	2	2	3	3	11	32	.288	.366	.330
Runners On	177	50	6	4	2	51	23	38	.282	.395	.366
Bases Empty	353	105	13	4	5	5	31	70	.297	.399	.356
Runners/Scor. Pos.	115	35	5	1	2	47	19	28	.304	.417	.394
Runners On/2 Out	74	22	2	2	2	24	10	17	.297	.459	.388
Scor. Pos./2 Out	55	18	2	1	2	23	9	11	.327	.509	.422
Late-Inning Pressure	72	22	4	1	1	14	5	17	.306	.431	.342
Leading Off	22	6	0	1	0	0	0	5	.273	.364	.273
Runners On	29	12	2	0	1	14	4	7	.414	.586	.457
Runners/Scor. Pos.	20	8	2	0	1	14	3	4	.400	.650	.440

RUNS BATTED IN	From 1B	From 2B	From 3B	Scoring Position
Totals	6/106	19/92	24/48	43/140
Percentage	5.7%	20.7%	50.0%	30.7%

Loves to face: Rheal Cormier (.500, 5-for-10, 1 HR, 3 SO)
Ramon Martinez (.429, 9-for-21, 1 HR)
Curt Schilling (.400, 6-for-15, 2 HR)
Hates to face: John Franco (0-for-8, 5 SO)
Tom Glavine (.179, 5-for-28)
Trevor Wilson (.067, 1-for-15, 2 BB)

Miscellaneous statistics: Ground outs-to-air outs ratio: 1.58 last season, 1.72 for career.... Grounded into 10 double plays in 82 opportunities (one per 8.2).... Drove in 16 of 23 runners from third base with less than two outs (70%).... Direction of balls hit to the outfield: 34% to left field, 35% to center, 31% to right.... Base running: Advanced from first base to third on 12 of 31 outfield singles (39%); scored from second on 9 of 14 (64%).... Made 2.74 assists per nine innings at second base.

Comments: Already has played more games at second base (410) than any player in Expos history, passing Ron Hunt (388) last year. How big a hole has second base been for Montreal over the years? Until last year, the team record for games by a *pitcher* was higher than Hunt's team record for games by a second baseman. That had been the only case in the N.L. in which the team record for games by a pitcher exceeded the corresponding record for any other position.... Stole 46 bases, second in N.L. behind teammate Marquis Grissom; last pair of teammates to finish one-two in N.L. steals: Omar Moreno and Frank Taveras with 1978 Pirates.... Seven home runs from the leadoff spot in the lineup last season tied him with Deion Sanders for the N.L. high; top spot in the Expos order combined for a league-high 13 homers.... Has driven in 71.1 percent of runners from third base with less than two outs, 2d best among active players, behind David Justice (73.1).... At age 23, he was the youngest N.L. player to appear in more than 125 games last year.... Only four left-handed batters in the league had a higher mark against lefties last season (minimum: 100 AB); DeShields had hit only .217 off southpaws in 1991.... Hit .345 in day games (2d best in N.L.), including the longest day-game situational hitting streak in the league (15 games). Philosophical questions: *(a)* If a tree falls in a forest and no one is around, does it make noise? *(b)* If a player has a hitting streak and doesn't know it (and so faces no daily pressure), should we bother to tell you about it?

Bill Doran
Bats Left and Right

Cincinnati Reds	AB	H	2B	3B	HR	RBI	BB	SO	BA	SA	OBA
Season	387	91	16	2	8	47	64	40	.235	.349	.342
vs. Left-Handers	125	25	5	0	2	11	30	13	.200	.288	.353
vs. Right-Handers	262	66	11	2	6	36	34	27	.252	.378	.337
vs. Ground-Ballers	148	36	5	0	4	14	24	16	.243	.358	.347
vs. Fly-Ballers	239	55	11	2	4	33	40	24	.230	.343	.339
Home Games	197	44	6	0	6	25	34	18	.223	.345	.338
Road Games	190	47	10	2	2	22	30	22	.247	.353	.347
Grass Fields	104	26	5	1	1	9	14	9	.250	.346	.333
Artificial Turf	283	65	11	1	7	38	50	31	.230	.350	.345
April	65	13	2	0	1	10	9	7	.200	.277	.289
May	79	22	6	1	4	13	11	10	.278	.532	.367
June	50	12	2	0	0	4	7	5	.240	.280	.333
July	65	14	4	0	2	7	6	7	.215	.369	.282
August	65	10	0	0	1	8	19	7	.154	.200	.345
Sept./Oct.	63	20	2	1	0	5	12	4	.317	.381	.427
Leading Off Inn.	69	19	1	0	2	2	10	10	.275	.377	.367
Runners On	187	45	9	1	4	43	35	18	.241	.364	.357
Bases Empty	200	46	7	1	4	4	29	22	.230	.335	.328
Runners/Scor. Pos.	105	22	4	0	2	38	31	15	.210	.305	.384
Runners On/2 Out	73	11	1	1	1	12	13	14	.151	.233	.279
Scor. Pos./2 Out	53	7	1	0	1	11	13	12	.132	.208	.303
Late-Inning Pressure	61	15	4	0	2	16	13	10	.246	.410	.373
Leading Off	10	0	0	0	0	0	3	1	.000	.000	.231
Runners On	37	13	4	0	2	16	8	5	.351	.622	.457
Runners/Scor. Pos.	23	9	2	0	1	14	5	5	.391	.609	.483

RUNS BATTED IN	From 1B	From 2B	From 3B	Scoring Position
Totals	4/141	15/86	20/46	35/132
Percentage	2.8%	17.4%	43.5%	26.5%

Loves to face: Chris Haney (.500, 2-for-4, 1 2B, 1 HR)
Joe Hesketh (.364, 8-for-22, 2 HR)
Craig Lefferts (.412, 14-for-34)

Hates to face: David Cone (.156, 5-for-32)
Greg A. Harris (.091, 1-for-11)
Tim Leary (.120, 3-for-25, 3 BB)

Miscellaneous statistics: Ground outs-to-air outs ratio: 0.73 last season, 1.04 for career.... Grounded into 11 double plays in 103 opportunities (one per 9.4).... Drove in 15 of 23 runners from third base with less than two outs (65%).... Direction of balls hit to the outfield: 26% to left field, 30% to center, 44% to right batting left-handed; 40% to left field, 33% to center, 27% to right batting right-handed.... Base running: Advanced from first base to third on 5 of 24 outfield singles (21%); scored from second on 9 of 9 (100%).... Made 2.74 assists per nine innings at second base.

Comments: Of the 59 switch-hitters active in the majors in 1992 with at least 1000 career at-bats, Doran has the smallest disparity in career batting by side of the plate. His career figures: .2669 batting left-handed, .2667 batting right-handed. Over the past three years, however, he has batted .285 from the left side and only .242 from the right, and his .200 mark batting right-handed last season was the 3d lowest by any N.L. player vs. left-handers.... Played 25 games at first base last season, after playing only 30 games at positions other than second base over his previous 10 seasons in majors.... Ranks second all-time among Reds second basemen in career fielding (minimum: 200 games) with one error every 65.4 chances, trailing only Joe Morgan (70.4). Among Houston second basemen, Doran stands third in fielding while Morgan stands seventh.... Strikeout rate (one every 11.4 trips to plate) was the best of his 11-year career.... Had one hit in 14 at-bats as a pinch hitter last season to lower his career mark to .179 (10-for-56, no HR) in that role.... Had lowest batting average in majors in August.... Has hit over .300 from September 1 to the end of the season in each of his three years with Cincinnati; in eight years with Houston, he batted a composite .243 during such periods. Only four other major league players have hit .300 or better in the last month-plus in each of the past three years (minimum: 25 at-bats each year): John Kruk, Eddie Murray, Terry Pendleton, and Ryne Sandberg.

Mariano Duncan
Bats Right

Philadelphia Phillies	AB	H	2B	3B	HR	RBI	BB	SO	BA	SA	OBA
Season	574	153	40	3	8	50	17	108	.267	.389	.292
vs. Left-Handers	231	66	14	1	4	19	6	42	.286	.407	.308
vs. Right-Handers	343	87	26	2	4	31	11	66	.254	.376	.281
vs. Ground-Ballers	270	71	18	2	3	21	9	50	.263	.378	.291
vs. Fly-Ballers	304	82	22	1	5	29	8	58	.270	.398	.292
Home Games	276	67	19	1	3	18	12	56	.243	.351	.277
Road Games	298	86	21	2	5	32	5	52	.289	.423	.305
Grass Fields	158	48	15	1	3	15	2	32	.304	.468	.317
Artificial Turf	416	105	25	2	5	35	15	76	.252	.358	.282
April	90	28	10	0	0	8	1	17	.311	.422	.344
May	110	26	6	1	2	12	1	22	.236	.364	.241
June	114	35	7	1	2	14	4	17	.307	.439	.336
July	105	25	6	0	2	4	6	22	.238	.352	.277
August	84	19	5	1	1	9	4	13	.226	.345	.258
Sept./Oct.	71	20	6	0	1	3	1	17	.282	.408	.292
Leading Off Inn.	111	36	9	2	1	1	3	18	.324	.468	.342
Runners On	235	60	15	1	4	46	7	47	.255	.379	.278
Bases Empty	339	93	25	2	4	4	10	61	.274	.395	.301
Runners/Scor. Pos.	122	30	8	1	4	44	3	27	.246	.426	.262
Runners On/2 Out	82	18	6	1	2	17	4	15	.220	.390	.264
Scor. Pos./2 Out	59	12	4	1	2	17	2	12	.203	.407	.230
Late-Inning Pressure	88	24	3	0	1	7	2	14	.273	.341	.301
Leading Off	24	7	0	0	0	0	0	3	.292	.292	.292
Runners On	34	8	1	0	1	7	2	4	.235	.324	.289
Runners/Scor. Pos.	20	5	0	0	1	7	1	2	.250	.400	.304

RUNS BATTED IN	From 1B	From 2B	From 3B	Scoring Position
Totals	7/178	15/106	20/43	35/149
Percentage	3.9%	14.2%	46.5%	23.5%

Loves to face: Sid Fernandez (.405, 17-for-42)
Bruce Hurst (.400, 14-for-35, 2 HR, 0 BB)
Trevor Wilson (.435, 10-for-23, 1 HR)

Hates to face: Doug Drabek (.179, 5-for-28, 1 HR, 0 BB)
Jim Gott (.077, 1-for-13)
Les Lancaster (0-for-10)

Miscellaneous statistics: Ground outs-to-air outs ratio: 1.41 last season, 1.29 for career.... Grounded into 15 double plays in 129 opportunities (one per 8.6).... Drove in 16 of 25 runners from third base with less than two outs (64%).... Direction of balls hit to the outfield: 29% to left field, 32% to center, 39% to right.... Base running: Advanced from first base to third on 7 of 22 outfield singles (32%); scored from second on 16 of 21 (76%).... Made 2.15 putouts per nine innings in left field.

Comments: Batted over 600 times in his debut season (1985), then played five years without qualifying for the batting title before topping the 600-PA mark again in 1992.... Matched his career high in games (142), and set new highs in hits, doubles, and extra-base hits. His walk rate, however, was the worst of his career (one every 35.6 PA).... Not to say that he ever challenged Chuck Klein's team record of 59 doubles set in 1930, but he joined Pete Rose and Von Hayes as the only Phillies players over the past 50 years to get 40 two-base hits in a season.... Batting average vs. right-handed pitchers was a career high, but his average vs. left-handers slipped from .410 in 1990 to .314 in 1991 to .286 in 1992. Career marks: .305 vs. left-handers, .223 vs. right-handers.... His .324 batting average when leading off an inning contrasts sharply with his .216 career effort in that category over his six previous years in the majors.... Turned in a perfect 15-for-15 performance in stolen base attempts on his home (artificial) turf. His overall percentage of .885 (23-for-26) was 4th-best in team history in the 42 years in which this statistic has been kept officially (minimum: 20 SB). The top marks: Larry Bowa, .914 (32-for-35) in 1977; Bake McBride, .903 (28-for-31) in 1978; Garry Maddox, .889 (24-for-27) in 1975.... Error rate at second base (one every 32.4 chances) was 2d-worst in majors last season (minimum: 50 games); the only guy he beat out was the guy for whom he was traded back in 1989, Lenny Harris.

Len Dykstra
Bats Left

Philadelphia Phillies	AB	H	2B	3B	HR	RBI	BB	SO	BA	SA	OBA
Season	345	104	18	0	6	39	40	32	.301	.406	.375
vs. Left-Handers	146	47	7	0	4	23	16	15	.322	.452	.389
vs. Right-Handers	199	57	11	0	2	16	24	17	.286	.372	.364
vs. Ground-Ballers	158	48	7	0	2	12	12	8	.304	.386	.355
vs. Fly-Ballers	187	56	11	0	4	27	28	24	.299	.422	.391
Home Games	196	60	8	0	5	27	26	18	.306	.423	.385
Road Games	149	44	10	0	1	12	14	14	.295	.383	.361
Grass Fields	55	13	4	0	0	3	4	4	.236	.309	.300
Artificial Turf	290	91	14	0	6	36	36	28	.314	.424	.389
April	29	5	2	0	0	2	3	3	.172	.241	.273
May	101	28	4	0	3	16	13	10	.277	.406	.362
June	102	32	7	0	0	10	10	8	.314	.382	.374
July	58	22	3	0	2	8	9	5	.379	.534	.456
August	55	17	2	0	1	3	5	6	.309	.400	.367
Sept./Oct.	0	0	0	0	0	0	0	0	.000	.000	.000
Leading Off Inn.	150	39	6	0	2	2	16	17	.260	.340	.339
Runners On	101	37	8	0	2	35	15	8	.366	.505	.433
Bases Empty	244	67	10	0	4	4	25	24	.275	.365	.349
Runners/Scor. Pos.	68	25	5	0	1	31	12	6	.368	.485	.440
Runners On/2 Out	50	19	6	0	1	19	10	5	.380	.560	.483
Scor. Pos./2 Out	39	14	4	0	1	17	8	4	.359	.538	.468
Late-Inning Pressure	50	21	3	0	0	10	4	4	.420	.480	.456
Leading Off	10	3	0	0	0	0	0	1	.300	.300	.300
Runners On	20	12	3	0	0	10	4	1	.600	.750	.615
Runners/Scor. Pos.	15	7	2	0	0	9	2	1	.467	.600	.474

RUNS BATTED IN	From 1B	From 2B	From 3B	Scoring Position
Totals	6/67	15/56	12/25	27/81
Percentage	9.0%	26.8%	48.0%	33.3%

Loves to face: Paul Assenmacher (.615, 8-for-13, 1 HR, 3 SO)
Ken Hill (.600, 12-for-20, 1 HR)
Bob Walk (.424, 14-for-33)

Hates to face: Doug Drabek (.167, 8-for-48)
Greg W. Harris (.118, 2-for-17)
Joe Magrane (.087, 2-for-23)

Miscellaneous statistics: Ground outs-to-air outs ratio: 1.10 last season, 1.00 for career.... Grounded into 1 double play in 37 opportunities (one per 37).... Drove in 9 of 13 runners from third base with less than two outs (69%).... Direction of balls hit to the outfield: 25% to left field, 40% to center, 35% to right.... Base running: Advanced from first base to third on 4 of 17 outfield singles (24%); scored from second on 9 of 16 (56%).... Made 3.03 putouts per nine innings in center field, 3d-highest rate in N.L.

Comments: Batting average with runners on base in Late-Inning Pressure Situations was the 2d-highest since 1975 (minimum: 10 hits); Rance Mulliniks hit .684 in 1984.... Batting .374 with runners on base since 1990, best in the majors.... He has batted .290, .309, and .322 against southpaws in the past three years. His composite .305 mark vs. lefties since 1990 is 3d-highest among left-handed batters. Who's ahead of him? Not Boggs, Gwynn, or Mattingly, but Ken Griffey (.325) and David Justice (.306).... Has batted over .300 at Veterans Stadium in each of his three full seasons with the Phillies. Career breakdown: .295 on artificial turf, .274 on grass fields.... Had never been on the disabled list until his automobile accident in May 1991. Since then he has played only 123 games while accumulating 193 days in five separate stints on the DL.... Has not played a game in September since 1990.... Although he's played only 148 games over the last two seasons, he's stolen 54 bases in 63 attempts during that time. He has at least 20 steals and has been successful on at least 85 percent of his attempts in each of the last three seasons. Only two other players have ever had streaks as long: Tim Raines (1983–87) and Eric Davis (1986–88).... One of 51 players to play for both the Mets and Phillies; among them, only Dykstra, Tug McGraw, and Willie Montanez have played at least 250 games for each team.... Watch him for 20 minutes and you could guess that his grandfather played in the NHL.

Mike Felder
Bats Left and Right

San Francisco Giants	AB	H	2B	3B	HR	RBI	BB	SO	BA	SA	OBA
Season	322	92	13	3	4	23	21	29	.286	.382	.330
vs. Left-Handers	88	27	5	0	1	6	5	7	.307	.398	.340
vs. Right-Handers	234	65	8	3	3	17	16	22	.278	.376	.327
vs. Ground-Ballers	160	46	5	2	2	14	9	16	.287	.381	.324
vs. Fly-Ballers	162	46	8	1	2	9	12	13	.284	.383	.337
Home Games	164	43	7	1	1	7	7	16	.262	.335	.299
Road Games	158	49	6	2	3	16	14	13	.310	.430	.362
Grass Fields	239	64	7	2	1	11	14	24	.268	.326	.313
Artificial Turf	83	28	6	1	3	12	7	5	.337	.542	.380
April	36	12	0	0	0	1	1	3	.333	.333	.351
May	51	16	1	3	1	12	4	5	.314	.510	.351
June	54	10	3	0	0	1	5	7	.185	.241	.254
July	52	13	3	0	1	2	3	6	.250	.365	.291
August	63	21	3	0	2	4	3	2	.333	.476	.373
Sept./Oct.	66	20	3	0	0	3	5	6	.303	.348	.356
Leading Off Inn.	116	37	4	0	2	2	8	10	.319	.405	.368
Runners On	94	28	3	2	2	21	7	9	.298	.436	.337
Bases Empty	228	64	10	1	2	2	14	20	.281	.360	.328
Runners/Scor. Pos.	54	14	3	2	1	19	5	6	.259	.444	.306
Runners On/2 Out	40	11	1	2	1	12	4	4	.275	.475	.341
Scor. Pos./2 Out	29	8	1	2	1	12	3	3	.276	.552	.344
Late-Inning Pressure	82	25	3	0	1	6	8	8	.305	.378	.370
Leading Off	22	6	0	0	0	0	2	5	.273	.273	.360
Runners On	34	11	1	0	1	6	3	3	.324	.441	.368
Runners/Scor. Pos.	19	3	1	0	0	4	2	2	.158	.211	.227

RUNS BATTED IN	From 1B	From 2B	From 3B	Scoring Position
Totals	3/64	6/44	10/25	16/69
Percentage	4.7%	13.6%	40.0%	23.2%

Loves to face: John Barfield (.750, 3-for-4, 1 3B)
Bob Milacki (.500, 4-for-8, 2 2B)
Duane Ward (.500, 4-for-8, 1 2B, 1 3B)

Hates to face: Mike Boddicker (.067, 1-for-15)
Roger Clemens (.118, 2-for-17, 2 2B)
Paul Gibson (0-for-14)

Miscellaneous statistics: Ground outs-to-air outs ratio: 1.08 last season, 1.38 for career.... Grounded into 3 double plays in 47 opportunities (one per 16).... Drove in 5 of 13 runners from third base with less than two outs (38%).... Direction of balls hit to the outfield: 27% to left field, 28% to center, 44% to right batting left-handed; 49% to left field, 26% to center, 26% to right batting right-handed.... Base running: Advanced from first base to third on 6 of 12 outfield singles (50%); scored from second on 9 of 10 (90%).... Made 2.53 putouts per nine innings in center field.

Comments: Lou Piniella has got some players with pretty small strike zones up in Seattle: Felder and Greg Briley, standing one atop the other, measure 11 feet, five inches; that's one inch shorter than the walls in left and center field at the Kingdome.... Batted .434 in first inning last season, best in majors among players with 50 first-inning plate appearances.... Seattle's leadoff hitters batted .286 last season, 3d-highest in A.L., but because of a league-low total of only 49 walks, the Mariners stood 10th in the league in the more crucial category for leadoff hitters, on-base percentage (.335). Felder led off 50 games for San Francisco last season; his on-base percentage from that spot was .328.... Rate of walks (one every 16.7 plate appearances) was the 2d-worst of his career; in 1988 with the Brewers, he came to the plate 85 times without drawing a base on balls.... Has hit for a higher average from the right side of the plate than from the left side in six of the last seven seasons. Career breakdown: .279 right-handed, .248 left-handed.... Grounded into three double plays last season after grounding into only one in the previous two years combined.... Baseball belief is that to take advantage of speed, fast runners should hit the ball on the ground; but in 1992, while Felder's ground outs-to-air outs ratio dropped more sharply than George Bush's approval ratings, what do you think happened? He established career highs in both batting average and slugging percentage.

Tony Fernandez

Bats Left and Right

San Diego Padres	AB	H	2B	3B	HR	RBI	BB	SO	BA	SA	OBA
Season	622	171	32	4	4	37	56	62	.275	.359	.337
vs. Left-Handers	207	58	9	0	1	18	22	12	.280	.338	.349
vs. Right-Handers	415	113	23	4	3	19	34	50	.272	.369	.331
vs. Ground-Ballers	288	83	20	3	3	16	23	26	.288	.410	.342
vs. Fly-Ballers	334	88	12	1	1	21	33	36	.263	.314	.333
Home Games	301	85	16	1	3	19	34	35	.282	.372	.355
Road Games	321	86	16	3	1	18	22	27	.268	.346	.320
Grass Fields	461	124	25	4	4	28	48	49	.269	.367	.339
Artificial Turf	161	47	7	0	0	9	8	13	.292	.335	.331
April	86	27	3	0	1	6	5	9	.314	.384	.352
May	107	35	7	1	1	12	8	12	.327	.439	.381
June	101	28	4	2	0	5	15	13	.277	.356	.378
July	104	19	6	0	0	3	7	9	.183	.240	.234
August	93	24	4	1	0	5	10	5	.258	.323	.327
Sept./Oct.	131	38	8	0	2	6	11	14	.290	.397	.345
Leading Off Inn.	276	76	16	4	1	1	19	22	.275	.373	.327
Runners On	172	46	6	0	1	34	18	19	.267	.320	.338
Bases Empty	450	125	26	4	3	3	38	43	.278	.373	.337
Runners/Scor. Pos.	99	27	3	0	1	34	12	11	.273	.333	.353
Runners On/2 Out	78	16	1	0	1	11	9	10	.205	.256	.295
Scor. Pos./2 Out	52	10	0	0	1	11	7	6	.192	.250	.300
Late-Inning Pressure	89	26	4	0	1	6	8	10	.292	.371	.347
Leading Off	28	11	2	0	0	0	2	2	.393	.464	.433
Runners On	33	7	0	0	0	5	3	3	.212	.212	.270
Runners/Scor. Pos.	20	4	0	0	0	5	1	1	.200	.200	.227

RUNS BATTED IN	From 1B	From 2B	From 3B	Scoring Position
Totals	1/110	9/75	23/46	32/121
Percentage	0.9%	12.0%	50.0%	26.4%

Loves to face: Steve Avery (.455, 5-for-11, 4 BB)
Doug Drabek (.412, 7-for-17, 1 3B)
Pete Harnisch (.417, 15-for-36)
Hates to face: Bud Black (.197, 13-for-66)
Chris Nabholz (0-for-12)
Bob Tewksbury (.154, 4-for-26, 0 BB)

Miscellaneous statistics: Ground outs-to-air outs ratio: 0.99 last season, 1.26 for career.... Grounded into 6 double plays in 77 opportunities (one per 13).... Drove in 17 of 25 runners from third base with less than two outs (68%).... Direction of balls hit to the outfield: 38% to left field, 32% to center, 31% to right batting left-handed; 19% to left field, 37% to center, 44% to right batting right-handed.... Base running: Advanced from first base to third on 11 of 32 outfield singles (34%); scored from second on 11 of 17 (65%).... Made 2.70 assists per nine innings at shortstop, lowest rate in majors.

Comments: Season was a mirror image of 1991; compare the figures above to the previous year's: 558 AB, 152 hits, 27 doubles, 5 triples, 4 HR, 38 RBI, 55 BB, 74 SO, .272 BA, .360 SA, .337 OBA.... Still ranks as the top-fielding shortstop in major league history with a career rate of one error every 49.4 chances.... Hasn't made more than one error in a game since August 27, 1988, a span of 630 starts. Only one active shortstop has a streak even half that long: Omar Vizquel (405).... Stole 20 bases in 40 attempts last season for the 2d-worst success rate in major league history among players with at least 20 steals; Jack Fournier of St. Louis went 20-for-42 in 1921. Garry Templeton (28-for-52 in 1977) was the only 20-steal player in the last 50 years to come close to the .500 mark.... Finished 1992 with a 19-game hitting streak, tying Brett Butler for N.L.'s 2d-longest last season.... Had most hits in majors as a shortstop (171) and had the most from the leadoff spot in the lineup (170).... Led N.L. with 60 opposite-field hits last season; he went the other way more often when batting right-handed (44% of his hits went to right field) than when batting left-handed (31% of his hits went to left).... Has hit over .300 when leading off innings in Late-Inning Pressure Situations in each of the last seven years. His career on-base percentage in those situations (.410) is 4th highest in the majors since 1975, behind Wade Boggs (.412), Rickey Henderson (.410), and Mickey Rivers (.410).

Steve Finley

Bats Left

Houston Astros	AB	H	2B	3B	HR	RBI	BB	SO	BA	SA	OBA
Season	607	177	29	13	5	55	58	63	.292	.407	.355
vs. Left-Handers	226	63	8	5	1	19	17	31	.279	.372	.336
vs. Right-Handers	381	114	21	8	4	36	41	32	.299	.428	.366
vs. Ground-Ballers	261	79	11	8	1	26	26	25	.303	.418	.368
vs. Fly-Ballers	346	98	18	5	4	29	32	38	.283	.399	.346
Home Games	294	89	11	7	5	31	35	34	.303	.439	.381
Road Games	313	88	18	6	0	24	23	29	.281	.377	.329
Grass Fields	186	52	12	1	0	11	13	20	.280	.355	.325
Artificial Turf	421	125	17	12	5	44	45	43	.297	.430	.368
April	86	24	4	2	1	7	4	15	.279	.407	.311
May	118	35	8	3	1	7	7	11	.297	.441	.341
June	104	28	5	5	0	10	11	7	.269	.413	.339
July	92	23	1	1	0	4	8	9	.250	.283	.310
August	89	25	6	0	0	13	16	9	.281	.348	.396
Sept./Oct.	118	42	5	2	3	14	12	12	.356	.508	.415
Leading Off Inn.	108	24	4	1	0	0	9	11	.222	.278	.282
Runners On	270	83	11	10	0	50	23	29	.307	.422	.364
Bases Empty	337	94	18	3	5	5	35	34	.279	.395	.349
Runners/Scor. Pos.	142	39	3	5	0	40	18	18	.275	.366	.352
Runners On/2 Out	99	28	2	1	0	13	14	11	.283	.323	.372
Scor. Pos./2 Out	68	17	2	1	0	13	13	8	.250	.309	.370
Late-Inning Pressure	100	31	5	0	2	6	11	9	.310	.420	.375
Leading Off	19	6	1	0	0	0	2	1	.316	.368	.381
Runners On	46	13	1	0	0	4	5	5	.283	.304	.346
Runners/Scor. Pos.	26	6	1	0	0	4	5	4	.231	.269	.344

RUNS BATTED IN	From 1B	From 2B	From 3B	Scoring Position
Totals	12/195	16/118	22/53	38/171
Percentage	6.2%	13.6%	41.5%	22.2%

Loves to face: Orel Hershiser (.450, 9-for-20, 1 HR)
Ramon Martinez (.500, 4-for-8, 2 2B, 1 HR)
Mike Morgan (.346, 9-for-26, 2 HR)
Hates to face: Andy Benes (.125, 3-for-24)
Greg Maddux (.192, 5-for-26, 0 BB)
Bret Saberhagen (.091, 1-for-11)

Miscellaneous statistics: Ground outs-to-air outs ratio: 1.48 last season, 1.45 for career.... Grounded into 10 double plays in 146 opportunities (one per 15).... Drove in 18 of 28 runners from third base with less than two outs (64%).... Direction of balls hit to the outfield: 29% to left field, 38% to center, 32% to right.... Base running: Advanced from first base to third on 9 of 27 outfield singles (33%); scored from second on 16 of 23 (70%).... Made 2.78 putouts per nine innings in center field.

Comments: Hit five home runs, all at the Astrodome, the most by any player last season who did not hit one on the road; in 1991, his first year with the Astros, he hit eight homers, all on the road.... But that slight drop in home runs marked his only decline in any statistical category. In fact, he has improved his batting average, slugging percentage, on-base average, walk rate, and strikeout rate in each of three seasons since his debut with Baltimore in 1989. Also increasing each of those years were his totals in games, plate appearances, at-bats, hits, extra-base hits, doubles, triples, total bases, RBIs, walks, intentional walks, and stolen bases.... Only seven players in major league history have increased both their batting average and their walk rate in four consecutive seasons, most recently Brook Jacoby (1984–87).... One of three players in double-figures in triples in both 1991 and 1992; the others: Mike Devereaux and Lance Johnson. The last player with a longer streak: Juan Samuel (1984–87); the all-time record is 17 straight seasons by Sam Crawford (1900–16).... Drove in 53 runs from the second spot in the lineup; the only N.L. player with more was Jay Bell (55).... Grounded out more often than any other N.L. batter last season (226 times).... Played 158 games in 1991, followed by 162 last season; that's the highest two-year total in Houston's franchise history.... Yearly stolen-base totals since his debut in 1989: 17, 22, 34, 44. Now let's see if he can get into the 50s, the 60s and the 70s in the next three years.

Andres Galarraga — Bats Right

St. Louis Cardinals	AB	H	2B	3B	HR	RBI	BB	SO	BA	SA	OBA
Season	325	79	14	2	10	39	11	69	.243	.391	.282
vs. Left-Handers	125	40	7	1	6	19	5	23	.320	.536	.348
vs. Right-Handers	200	39	7	1	4	20	6	46	.195	.300	.242
vs. Ground-Ballers	148	29	5	1	4	12	5	28	.196	.324	.236
vs. Fly-Ballers	177	50	9	1	6	27	6	41	.282	.446	.321
Home Games	159	42	6	1	4	16	3	36	.264	.390	.298
Road Games	166	37	8	1	6	23	8	33	.223	.392	.268
Grass Fields	77	17	3	1	4	10	3	17	.221	.442	.259
Artificial Turf	248	62	11	1	6	29	8	52	.250	.375	.289
April	6	1	0	0	0	1	0	1	.167	.167	.286
May	34	7	0	0	0	2	1	9	.206	.206	.250
June	79	14	4	1	0	3	1	20	.177	.253	.217
July	90	27	4	1	5	12	4	13	.300	.533	.344
August	98	24	6	0	3	17	3	20	.245	.398	.269
Sept./Oct.	18	6	0	0	2	4	2	6	.333	.667	.381
Leading Off Inn.	79	24	6	1	4	4	1	13	.304	.557	.329
Runners On	144	31	4	1	4	33	8	37	.215	.340	.270
Bases Empty	181	48	10	1	6	6	3	32	.265	.431	.293
Runners/Scor. Pos.	94	18	3	1	1	27	6	26	.191	.277	.269
Runners On/2 Out	63	10	1	0	2	9	5	15	.159	.270	.221
Scor. Pos./2 Out	40	4	0	0	1	7	5	10	.100	.175	.200
Late-Inning Pressure	62	16	2	0	2	9	2	14	.258	.387	.288
Leading Off	15	4	1	0	1	1	0	4	.267	.533	.267
Runners On	25	5	1	0	1	8	0	7	.200	.360	.222
Runners/Scor. Pos.	20	3	1	0	1	8	0	5	.150	.350	.143

RUNS BATTED IN	From 1B	From 2B	From 3B	Scoring Position
Totals	6/90	8/73	15/37	23/110
Percentage	6.7%	11.0%	40.5%	20.9%

Loves to face: Pat Combs (.400, 8-for-20, 7 2B)
Randy Myers (.333, 5-for-15, 2 HR, 4 BB)
Todd Worrell (.421, 8-for-19, 3 2B, 1 3B)
Hates to face: Jose DeLeon (.061, 2-for-33, 1 HR, 3 BB)
Rob Dibble (0-for-8, 8 SO)
Ken Howell (0-for-10, 8 SO)

Miscellaneous statistics: Ground outs-to-air outs ratio: 1.24 last season, 1.45 for career.... Grounded into 8 double plays in 56 opportunities (one per 7.0).... Drove in 12 of 21 runners from third base with less than two outs (57%).... Direction of balls hit to the outfield: 38% to left field, 39% to center, 22% to right.... Base running: Advanced from first base to third on 8 of 18 outfield singles (44%); scored from second on 8 of 11 (73%).... Made 0.74 assists per nine innings at first base.

Comments: Has his piece of basball immortality as the first free agent signed by the Rockies. That could lead to another distinction: He has currently played 942 N.L. regular-season games without ever appearing in a post-season game; only two active National Leaguers have higher totals—Milt Thompson (980) and Tom Foley (952).... Colorado is hoping that his second-half resurgence was no illusion; he batted .296 with a .497 slugging percentage after the All-Star break.... Remember 1987 and 1988? He batted .305 and .302 with 90 or more RBIs each year and a league-leading 184 hits in the latter season. By 1992, respect for him had fallen so low that he was the only N.L. player with at least 10 home runs who was not intentionally walked during the season.... Had 2d-lowest average in N.L with two outs and runners in scoring position last year. He has batted under .200 with runners in scoring position in each of the last two seasons.... Rate of walks last season (one every 31.5 plate appearances) was less than half of his previous career rate (one every 15.0 PA), but his 1992 strikeout rate (one every 5.0 PA) was the best of his career.... Pinch-hitting over the last three seasons: 0-for-15 with eight strikeouts.... His batting averages against left- and right-handed pitchers have been all over the lot. In 1986, he batted .333 vs. left-handers, .234 vs. right-handers; in 1987, .323 and .297; in 1988, .283 and .310; in 1989, .385 and .201. Then the fun really started: in 1990, .226 and .273; in 1991, .180 and .239; last year, .320 and .195.

Ron Gant — Bats Right

Atlanta Braves	AB	H	2B	3B	HR	RBI	BB	SO	BA	SA	OBA
Season	544	141	22	6	17	80	45	101	.259	.415	.321
vs. Left-Handers	177	45	7	3	5	32	17	32	.254	.412	.322
vs. Right-Handers	367	96	15	3	12	48	28	69	.262	.417	.320
vs. Ground-Ballers	248	64	12	3	6	30	19	43	.258	.403	.321
vs. Fly-Ballers	296	77	10	3	11	50	26	58	.260	.426	.320
Home Games	257	71	12	3	10	45	19	44	.276	.463	.336
Road Games	287	70	10	3	7	35	26	57	.244	.373	.307
Grass Fields	398	104	16	3	13	57	30	70	.261	.415	.320
Artificial Turf	146	37	6	3	4	23	15	31	.253	.418	.323
April	77	21	3	0	5	19	10	21	.273	.506	.367
May	110	32	8	2	2	18	13	16	.291	.455	.371
June	93	25	5	1	3	9	5	12	.269	.441	.324
July	95	21	2	1	1	7	1	18	.221	.295	.232
August	69	14	2	1	1	9	11	20	.203	.304	.309
Sept./Oct.	100	28	2	1	5	18	5	14	.280	.470	.311
Leading Off Inn.	120	38	6	0	5	5	3	19	.317	.492	.339
Runners On	246	55	10	4	4	67	26	42	.224	.346	.299
Bases Empty	298	86	12	2	13	13	19	59	.289	.473	.340
Runners/Scor. Pos.	152	39	6	2	3	63	22	24	.257	.382	.343
Runners On/2 Out	96	20	4	1	2	23	13	17	.208	.333	.303
Scor. Pos./2 Out	60	16	3	1	2	23	12	12	.267	.450	.389
Late-Inning Pressure	63	18	3	0	1	5	4	11	.286	.381	.333
Leading Off	23	7	1	0	0	0	0	3	.304	.348	.304
Runners On	24	6	2	0	0	4	3	4	.250	.333	.321
Runners/Scor. Pos.	17	3	1	0	0	4	3	3	.176	.235	.286

RUNS BATTED IN	From 1B	From 2B	From 3B	Scoring Position
Totals	6/170	25/120	32/67	57/187
Percentage	3.5%	20.8%	47.8%	30.5%

Loves to face: Ken Hill (.318, 7-for-22, 3 HR)
Omar Olivares (.600, 6-for-10, 2 2B, 2 HR)
Mark Portugal (.474, 9-for-19, 1 HR)
Hates to face: Sid Fernandez (0-for-10)
Kevin Gross (.148, 4-for-27, 1 HR)
Todd Worrell (0-for-8)

Miscellaneous statistics: Ground outs-to-air outs ratio: 0.84 last season, 0.73 for career.... Grounded into 10 double plays in 118 opportunities (one per 12).... Drove in 23 of 46 runners from third base with less than two outs (50%).... Direction of balls hit to the outfield: 45% to left field, 32% to center, 23% to right.... Base running: Advanced from first base to third on 15 of 27 outfield singles (56%); scored from second on 13 of 16 (81%).... Made 1.94 putouts per nine innings in left field.

Comments: Had 141 hits in both 1991 and 1992; drove in 25 fewer runs last season despite driving in a higher percentage of runners from scoring position than he had the previous year. His extra-base hit total dropped from 70 to 45 (13 fewer doubles, 15 fewer home runs). The Braves looked at all those numbers and gave him a raise of a million dollars.... First Braves player this century to steal at least 30 bases in three consecutive seasons.... Started 50 of the 51 games in which the Braves faced a left-handed starter, 87 of their 111 games against right-handed starters. But he started only one of five vs. right-handers in the World Series when he platooned with Deion Sanders.... Batted .183 (15-for-82) with only one home run in his first-inning at-bats. In subsequent at-bats, he posted a .273 average with one home run every 29 at-bats.... Last year he had by far the most productive April of his career; even with last year factored in, his career batting average in baseball's first month is .191.... His career batting average is .259, but it's only .237 in Late-Inning Pressure Situations. In LIPS with runners on base, it's .195 in 149 at-bats.... Has hit 111 home runs, and has .333 batting average (18-for-54) with the bases loaded, but has never hit a regular-season grand slam. He hit one in Game 2 of last year's Championship Series and just missed another in the ninth inning of Game 7, one that would have turned him into Chris Chambliss, Francisco Cabrera, and Jimmy Carter all rolled into one.

Bernard Gilkey
Bats Right

St. Louis Cardinals	AB	H	2B	3B	HR	RBI	BB	SO	BA	SA	OBA
Season	384	116	19	4	7	43	39	52	.302	.427	.364
vs. Left-Handers	176	62	7	2	2	20	16	18	.352	.449	.402
vs. Right-Handers	208	54	12	2	5	23	23	34	.260	.409	.333
vs. Ground-Ballers	182	55	8	1	2	14	13	22	.302	.390	.348
vs. Fly-Ballers	202	61	11	3	5	29	26	30	.302	.460	.378
Home Games	196	58	11	2	3	20	14	24	.296	.418	.338
Road Games	188	58	8	2	4	23	25	28	.309	.436	.391
Grass Fields	95	28	4	2	1	11	14	17	.295	.411	.391
Artificial Turf	289	88	15	2	6	32	25	35	.304	.433	.355
April	47	14	3	0	0	2	3	9	.298	.362	.340
May	34	10	1	1	0	4	3	5	.294	.382	.351
June	47	18	3	1	0	6	5	9	.383	.489	.434
July	77	20	3	1	1	10	8	12	.260	.364	.326
August	100	23	5	0	3	12	13	13	.230	.370	.319
Sept./Oct.	79	31	4	1	3	9	7	4	.392	.582	.438
Leading Off Inn.	123	34	8	1	2	2	6	17	.276	.407	.310
Runners On	142	48	5	3	5	41	19	15	.338	.521	.406
Bases Empty	242	68	14	1	2	2	20	37	.281	.372	.338
Runners/Scor. Pos.	78	28	3	3	2	35	14	9	.359	.551	.438
Runners On/2 Out	64	19	3	3	0	17	12	4	.297	.438	.408
Scor. Pos./2 Out	45	16	3	3	0	17	11	2	.356	.556	.482
Late-Inning Pressure	88	27	4	0	3	11	7	13	.307	.455	.354
Leading Off	26	7	2	0	1	1	2	4	.269	.462	.321
Runners On	34	8	1	0	2	10	3	6	.235	.441	.289
Runners/Scor. Pos.	14	4	1	0	1	8	1	2	.286	.571	.313

RUNS BATTED IN	From 1B	From 2B	From 3B	Scoring Position
Totals	7/102	15/66	14/29	29/95
Percentage	6.9%	22.7%	48.3%	30.5%

Loves to face: Chris Hammond (.778, 7-for-9)
Danny Jackson (.474, 9-for-19)
Terry Mulholland (.526, 10-for-19)

Hates to face: John Burkett (0-for-8)
Jeff Innis (0-for-7)
Randy Tomlin (.125, 3-for-24)

Miscellaneous statistics: Ground outs-to-air outs ratio: 0.90 last season, 1.03 for career.... Grounded into 5 double plays in 70 opportunities (one per 14).... Drove in 9 of 11 runners from third base with less than two outs (82%).... Direction of balls hit to the outfield: 41% to left field, 25% to center, 34% to right.... Base running: Advanced from first base to third on 8 of 18 outfield singles (44%); scored from second on 13 of 16 (81%).... Made 2.39 putouts per nine innings in left field, 2d-highest rate in N.L.

Comments: Had 3d-highest batting average in N.L. with two outs and runners in scoring position, and had league's 3d-highest average vs. left-handed pitchers. Cardinals were the only N.L. team that had two players bat .350 or higher vs. left-handers (Felix Jose hit .374), and they led N.L. teams with a .281 mark against southpaws.... Started 47 of the 56 games in which Redbirds faced a left-handed starter, but only 39 of 106 games against right-handers.... One of seven Cardinals with at least 10 stolen bases last season; no other N.L. team had more than five.... Walked 39 times in each of the past two seasons, despite coming to the plate 120 more times in 1992.... Grounded into 14 double plays in 1991, one every 4.4 opportunities, which was 4th-worst rate in N.L.; last year he averaged one GIDP every 14 opportunities.... Career breakdown: .251 at Busch Stadium, .291 on other artificial surfaces, .289 on grass fields.... Committed five errors in 231 chances last season (one every 46.2 chances), after making only one in 171 chances in 1991.... Stole 45 or more bases in each of his last three full years in minors (1988–90), but has only 38 steals in 230 games in majors.... With all the talk of the sophomore jinx (and with all of the cable hours available on highlight shows), how come no one has established a Sophomore of the Year Award? Top batting averages by major league sophomores last year (minimum: 300 at-bats): Gilkey, .302; Mike Bordick, .300; Chuck Knoblauch, .297; Ray Lankford, .293.

Joe Girardi
Bats Right

Chicago Cubs	AB	H	2B	3B	HR	RBI	BB	SO	BA	SA	OBA
Season	270	73	3	1	1	12	19	38	.270	.300	.320
vs. Left-Handers	137	41	2	1	0	5	9	16	.299	.328	.342
vs. Right-Handers	133	32	1	0	1	7	10	22	.241	.271	.297
vs. Ground-Ballers	118	27	1	0	1	4	3	18	.229	.263	.254
vs. Fly-Ballers	152	46	2	1	0	8	16	20	.303	.329	.367
Home Games	128	39	1	1	1	7	9	21	.305	.352	.350
Road Games	142	34	2	0	0	5	10	17	.239	.254	.292
Grass Fields	194	51	2	1	1	9	14	31	.263	.299	.313
Artificial Turf	76	22	1	0	0	3	5	7	.289	.303	.337
April	36	10	1	0	0	3	0	5	.278	.306	.270
May	67	20	0	0	1	4	13	11	.299	.343	.412
June	50	14	0	0	0	2	2	9	.280	.280	.321
July	36	10	1	0	0	1	2	2	.278	.306	.316
August	50	11	1	1	0	1	1	6	.220	.280	.235
Sept./Oct.	31	8	0	0	0	1	1	5	.258	.258	.281
Leading Off Inn.	60	17	0	0	0	0	4	9	.283	.283	.328
Runners On	119	31	2	0	0	11	9	15	.261	.277	.310
Bases Empty	151	42	1	1	1	1	10	23	.278	.318	.327
Runners/Scor. Pos.	51	12	2	0	0	11	6	8	.235	.275	.310
Runners On/2 Out	43	11	0	0	0	2	3	7	.256	.256	.304
Scor. Pos./2 Out	20	2	0	0	0	2	3	5	.100	.100	.217
Late-Inning Pressure	47	14	0	0	0	3	3	4	.298	.298	.340
Leading Off	12	4	0	0	0	0	0	0	.333	.333	.333
Runners On	20	6	0	0	0	3	3	2	.300	.300	.391
Runners/Scor. Pos.	9	4	0	0	0	3	2	1	.444	.444	.545

RUNS BATTED IN	From 1B	From 2B	From 3B	Scoring Position
Totals	0/96	5/39	6/21	11/60
Percentage	0.0%	12.8%	28.6%	18.3%

Loves to face: Roger McDowell (.667, 4-for-6)
Mark Portugal (.471, 8-for-17)
Jose Rijo (.455, 5-for-11, 1 HR)

Hates to face: Chris Nabholz (0-for-8)
Alejandro Pena (0-for-8)
Bob Tewksbury (.063, 1-for-16)

Miscellaneous statistics: Ground outs-to-air outs ratio: 1.58 last season, 1.50 for career.... Grounded into 8 double plays in 65 opportunities (one per 8.1).... Drove in 6 of 11 runners from third base with less than two outs (55%).... Direction of balls hit to the outfield: 29% to left field, 35% to center, 37% to right.... Base running: Advanced from first base to third on 2 of 14 outfield singles (14%); scored from second on 3 of 5 (60%).... Opposing base stealers: 46-for-78 (59%), 3d-lowest rate in N.L.

Comments: Equaled the team record for fewest extra-base hits in a season of at least 250 at-bats. Rollie Zeider was the last to do it; that was in 1918, when the last month of the season went unplayed due to the war. The others were Jimmy Slagle (1908) and Germany Schaefer (1902). Over the last 50 years, only two N.L. players have had fewer than five extra-base hits in a season of at least 250 at-bats: Jim Davenport in 1968 and Rafael (didn't he invent this category?) Belliard in 1988.... Season ended with a broken bone in the hand in late September, but he was not placed on the disabled list.... Finished his Cubs career with a total of 299 games behind the plate. Since Randy Hundley, Cubs have had only two catchers last 300 games: Jody Davis (961) and Steve Swisher (361).... Has drawn only one walk for every 18.2 career plate appearances, a rate that is even worse than it looks when you consider that 20 of the 53 walks he has drawn have been intentional.... Career breakdown: .292 vs. left-handers, .242 vs. right-handers, and 6-for-11 as a pinch hitter.... Over four years in the majors, he has had roughly the same number of at-bats in both home and road games; he has driven in almost twice as many runs at Wrigley Field (46) as he has on the road (24).... Owns a mild-mannered .257 career batting average during the first nine innings of games, but goes ballistic in extra innings. His career mark of .423 (11-for-26) in overtime is the highest among all N.L. players over the four years that he's been in the majors (minimum: 25 at-bats).

Luis Gonzalez
Bats Left

Houston Astros	AB	H	2B	3B	HR	RBI	BB	SO	BA	SA	OBA
Season	387	94	19	3	10	55	24	52	.243	.385	.289
vs. Left-Handers	80	28	6	2	1	13	7	11	.350	.512	.404
vs. Right-Handers	307	66	13	1	9	42	17	41	.215	.352	.258
vs. Ground-Ballers	175	34	4	1	4	20	10	20	.194	.297	.238
vs. Fly-Ballers	212	60	15	2	6	35	14	32	.283	.458	.330
Home Games	204	42	10	1	4	25	14	35	.206	.324	.255
Road Games	183	52	9	2	6	30	10	17	.284	.454	.328
Grass Fields	126	35	5	2	3	19	5	14	.278	.421	.316
Artificial Turf	261	59	14	1	7	36	19	38	.226	.368	.277
April	50	6	2	0	1	4	4	11	.120	.220	.196
May	45	9	2	0	0	2	1	7	.200	.244	.217
June	69	22	4	0	5	19	5	7	.319	.594	.365
July	38	9	2	2	0	2	6	7	.237	.395	.341
August	83	28	2	1	2	13	3	6	.337	.458	.360
Sept./Oct.	102	20	7	0	2	15	5	14	.196	.324	.239
Leading Off Inn.	79	23	6	1	4	4	5	12	.291	.544	.333
Runners On	188	47	9	0	4	49	12	23	.250	.362	.296
Bases Empty	199	47	10	3	6	6	12	29	.236	.407	.283
Runners/Scor. Pos.	108	27	4	0	4	45	10	15	.250	.398	.314
Runners On/2 Out	73	16	2	0	3	19	5	12	.219	.370	.278
Scor. Pos./2 Out	48	10	0	0	3	18	5	9	.208	.396	.296
Late-Inning Pressure	65	21	3	0	3	15	5	11	.323	.508	.371
Leading Off	21	7	0	0	1	1	1	4	.333	.476	.364
Runners On	29	13	2	0	2	14	3	4	.448	.724	.500
Runners/Scor. Pos.	17	8	1	0	2	13	3	3	.471	.882	.550

RUNS BATTED IN	From 1B	From 2B	From 3B	Scoring Position
Totals	7/132	17/89	21/42	38/131
Percentage	5.3%	19.1%	50.0%	29.0%

Loves to face: Tim Belcher (.357, 5-for-14, 1 HR)
Greg Maddux (.409, 9-for-22, 3 HR)
Randy Myers (.571, 4-for-7, 2 2B)
Hates to face: Steve Avery (.071, 1-for-14, 1 2B)
Ramon Martinez (0-for-7, 4 SO)
Bret Saberhagen (0-for-7)

Miscellaneous statistics: Ground outs-to-air outs ratio: 0.85 last season, 0.85 for career.... Grounded into 6 double plays in 89 opportunities (one per 15).... Drove in 17 of 22 runners from third base with less than two outs (77%), 2d-highest rate in N.L.... Direction of balls hit to the outfield: 30% to left field, 33% to center, 37% to right.... Base running: Advanced from first base to third on 1 of 9 outfield singles (11%); scored from second on 6 of 10 (60%).... Made 2.73 putouts per nine innings in left field, highest rate in majors.

Comments: Has played the April Fool two years in a row: He had the lowest average in the majors in April 1992 after batting .148 (9-for-61) in April 1991. He and Dan Gladden were the only major leaguers last season who hit below .200 in both April and September (minimum: 50 at-bats in each).... Among left-handed batters with at least 80 at-bats vs. left-handed pitchers last season, only Kenny Lofton (.369) and Ken Griffey (.358) posted higher averages. He batted only .172 in 122 at-bats vs. lefties as a rookie in 1991. He has hit 21 of his 23 career homers off right-handers.... Despite his success against lefties, he started only 16 of the 64 games in which the Astros faced a lefty starter last season; he started 80 of 98 games vs. right-handers.... Drove in nine of 19 runners from scoring position in Late-Inning Pressure Situations (47.4%); his career mark in that category is 40.5% (17-of-42). Among active players with at least 30 opportunities, only Albert Belle has a higher rate (44.2).... Has hit only eight of 23 career home runs at the Astrodome; he hit only .206 there last season, the 4th-lowest home average by any N.L. player.... Hit three home runs in Cincinnati, the most by any visitor. That reminds us of one of our favorite facts from the past: in 1979, a season in which Houston won 89 games and finished 1½ games behind the division-winning Reds, the player who hit the most home runs at the Astrodome was the Reds' George Foster (four); he hit one more than the Astros' leader, Denny Walling.

Mark Grace
Bats Left

Chicago Cubs	AB	H	2B	3B	HR	RBI	BB	SO	BA	SA	OBA
Season	603	185	37	5	9	79	72	36	.307	.430	.380
vs. Left-Handers	225	63	11	1	3	29	17	19	.280	.378	.329
vs. Right-Handers	378	122	26	4	6	50	55	17	.323	.460	.409
vs. Ground-Ballers	250	84	19	2	3	41	28	12	.336	.464	.404
vs. Fly-Ballers	353	101	18	3	6	38	44	24	.286	.405	.363
Home Games	285	80	17	0	5	40	45	18	.281	.393	.373
Road Games	318	105	20	5	4	39	27	18	.330	.462	.387
Grass Fields	418	120	22	3	6	54	56	31	.287	.397	.369
Artificial Turf	185	65	15	2	3	25	16	5	.351	.503	.407
April	67	15	4	1	2	8	15	1	.224	.403	.366
May	105	34	7	3	2	20	18	9	.324	.505	.423
June	94	38	6	0	0	9	9	2	.404	.468	.457
July	94	26	5	1	1	9	13	7	.277	.383	.373
August	121	34	4	0	4	16	9	9	.281	.413	.333
Sept./Oct.	122	38	11	0	0	17	8	8	.311	.402	.341
Leading Off Inn.	108	28	6	1	3	3	16	7	.259	.417	.355
Runners On	265	84	21	2	3	73	31	19	.317	.445	.384
Bases Empty	338	101	16	3	6	6	41	17	.299	.417	.376
Runners/Scor. Pos.	138	45	14	1	1	65	24	13	.326	.464	.413
Runners On/2 Out	85	25	6	1	1	29	15	6	.294	.424	.406
Scor. Pos./2 Out	65	21	6	1	1	29	12	6	.323	.492	.436
Late-Inning Pressure	94	29	1	0	1	14	15	6	.309	.351	.407
Leading Off	17	5	0	0	1	1	2	2	.294	.471	.368
Runners On	44	15	1	0	0	13	9	3	.341	.364	.446
Runners/Scor. Pos.	25	9	1	0	0	13	7	3	.360	.400	.486

RUNS BATTED IN	From 1B	From 2B	From 3B	Scoring Position
Totals	10/189	31/105	29/58	60/163
Percentage	5.3%	29.5%	50.0%	36.8%

Loves to face: Scott Garrelts (.579, 11-for-19, 1 HR)
Mike Maddux (.474, 9-for-19, 1 HR)
Jose Rijo (.455, 15-for-33, 1 HR)
Hates to face: John Franco (.071, 1-for-14, 3 BB)
Mitch Williams (.083, 1-for-12)
Trevor Wilson (.158, 3-for-19)

Miscellaneous statistics: Ground outs-to-air outs ratio: 1.01 last season, 1.19 for career.... Grounded into 14 double plays in 145 opportunities (one per 10).... Drove in 21 of 33 runners from third base with less than two outs (64%).... Direction of balls hit to the outfield: 27% to left field, 35% to center, 38% to right.... Base running: Advanced from first base to third on 15 of 40 outfield singles (38%); scored from second on 11 of 17 (65%).... Made 0.90 assists per nine innings at first base, 3d-highest rate in N.L.

Comments: In each of the last two seasons his total of walks has increased (from 59 to 70 to 72) while his strikeout total has decreased (from 54 to 53 to 36). Only seven players in this century have done that in three consecutive seasons: Muddy Ruel (1923–25), Buddy Lewis (1937–39), Lou Boudreau (1946–48), Jim Northrup (1969–71), Garry Maddox (1973–75), Mike Hargrove (1976–78), and Bob Knepper (1987–89).... N.L.'s 2d-toughest batter to strike out last season, behind Tony Gwynn.... Has walked more than twice as many times as he has struck out against right-handed pitchers in his career (242 walks, 115 strikeouts); the only other active players who have done that (minimum: 500 plate appearances vs. right-handers) are Wade Boggs and Mike Scioscia.... Finished with a .330 road batting average, 2d-best in the league last season; it was his first .300 season away from Wrigley Field.... Batting average on artificial turf was 2d-highest in league and included a 16-game hitting streak on rugs.... Hit safely in 26 consecutive victories by his team, matching Terry Pendleton for N.L.'s longest such streak.... June batting average was highest in the majors, and the highest in any month of his career; his average in April was the 2d lowest of his career.... Led N.L. first basemen in assists for the 3d straight season. The last first baseman to do that was Elbie Fletcher, who had a four-year streak from 1940–43.... Career average stands at .299, three hits shy of the .300 mark.

Marquis Grissom
Bats Right

Montreal Expos	AB	H	2B	3B	HR	RBI	BB	SO	BA	SA	OBA
Season	653	180	39	6	14	66	42	81	.276	.418	.322
vs. Left-Handers	212	57	14	4	6	24	17	26	.269	.458	.325
vs. Right-Handers	441	123	25	2	8	42	25	55	.279	.399	.321
vs. Ground-Ballers	296	79	20	4	3	22	17	26	.267	.392	.312
vs. Fly-Ballers	357	101	19	2	11	44	25	55	.283	.440	.331
Home Games	316	84	24	2	8	31	17	38	.266	.430	.309
Road Games	337	96	15	4	6	35	25	43	.285	.407	.335
Grass Fields	171	48	10	2	1	18	10	27	.281	.380	.324
Artificial Turf	482	132	29	4	13	48	32	54	.274	.432	.322
April	94	26	5	1	3	12	8	8	.277	.447	.333
May	92	24	3	1	2	8	4	19	.261	.380	.299
June	103	32	10	1	0	11	14	11	.311	.427	.395
July	123	31	5	1	2	15	4	16	.252	.358	.277
August	110	29	7	1	4	9	8	16	.264	.455	.311
Sept./Oct.	131	38	9	1	3	11	4	11	.290	.443	.321
Leading Off Inn.	176	54	11	2	5	5	7	25	.307	.477	.337
Runners On	262	72	18	1	4	56	23	34	.275	.397	.333
Bases Empty	391	108	21	5	10	10	19	47	.276	.432	.315
Runners/Scor. Pos.	154	45	12	0	3	50	19	17	.292	.429	.369
Runners On/2 Out	94	27	6	0	3	25	11	12	.287	.447	.362
Scor. Pos./2 Out	68	23	5	0	2	23	9	8	.338	.500	.416
Late-Inning Pressure	86	22	1	1	1	7	7	7	.256	.326	.312
Leading Off	21	7	0	0	0	2	2	3	.333	.333	.391
Runners On	35	8	1	0	0	6	4	0	.229	.257	.308
Runners/Scor. Pos.	24	4	0	0	0	6	3	0	.167	.167	.259

RUNS BATTED IN	From 1B	From 2B	From 3B	Scoring Position
Totals	7/166	20/122	25/57	45/179
Percentage	4.2%	16.4%	43.9%	25.1%

Loves to face: Bruce Hurst (.480, 12-for-25, 1 HR)
Curt Schilling (.688, 11-for-16, 1 HR)
Bob Walk (.421, 8-for-19, 1 HR)

Hates to face: Jim Gott (0-for-7)
Pete Schourek (0-for-9)
Mitch Williams (0-for-11)

Miscellaneous statistics: Ground outs-to-air outs ratio: 1.17 last season, 1.19 for career.... Grounded into 12 double plays in 120 opportunities (one per 10).... Drove in 17 of 32 runners from third base with less than two outs (53%).... Direction of balls hit to the outfield: 31% to left field, 39% to center, 30% to right.... Base running: Advanced from first base to third on 9 of 22 outfield singles (41%); scored from second on 17 of 25 (68%).... Made 2.57 putouts per nine innings in center field.

Comments: Owns higher career stolen base percentage vs. left-handed pitchers (.892, 74-for-83) than vs. right-handers (.817, 103-for-126). That's surprising at first glance since lefties generally hold runners better (1992 major league average: .692 vs. right-handers, .652 vs. left-handers). But Marquis has a penchant for stealing third base, something accomplished more easily against a lefty (1992 figures: .771 stolen-base percentage of third vs. left-handers, .705 vs. right-handers); he stole third 24 times in 26 tries last season, and no other player in the majors swiped third more than 12 times. But hold on: Even more analysis shows that Gris does a better job at stealing *second* vs. lefties (.870, 47-for-54) than vs. right-ies (.804, 82-for-102), and that is a departure from norm (1992 figures for all runners: .629 vs. lefties, .687 vs. righties).... Stole 13 bases vs. St. Louis, the most by any player vs. any opponent in 1992. In his career, he's 19-for-19 against Atlanta.... One of eight players since 1900 with 75 steals in each of two consecutive seasons. Among these eight players, only Vince Coleman (four years) and Tim Raines (three years) extended their streaks farther.... Has batted .344 with two outs and runners in scoring position over the past two seasons, the best average in the majors among the 114 players with at least 100 at-bats in such situations in 1991-92.... Batted sixth in lineup for 13 consecutive games in April; that alone had people looking askance at Tom Runnells.

Tony Gwynn
Bats Left

San Diego Padres	AB	H	2B	3B	HR	RBI	BB	SO	BA	SA	OBA
Season	520	165	27	3	6	41	46	16	.317	.415	.371
vs. Left-Handers	205	67	8	1	3	16	14	5	.327	.420	.368
vs. Right-Handers	315	98	19	2	3	25	32	11	.311	.413	.372
vs. Ground-Ballers	233	80	13	1	3	22	23	6	.343	.446	.401
vs. Fly-Ballers	287	85	14	2	3	19	23	10	.296	.390	.346
Home Games	229	70	8	0	4	15	25	11	.306	.393	.371
Road Games	291	95	19	3	2	26	21	5	.326	.433	.371
Grass Fields	372	108	15	0	5	23	32	15	.290	.371	.344
Artificial Turf	148	57	12	3	1	18	14	1	.385	.527	.438
April	98	34	6	1	0	4	8	4	.347	.429	.393
May	90	35	6	1	4	19	10	0	.389	.611	.446
June	107	27	3	0	2	7	15	3	.252	.336	.341
July	88	23	3	1	0	4	8	4	.261	.318	.323
August	99	33	6	0	0	5	4	3	.333	.394	.359
Sept./Oct.	38	13	3	0	0	2	1	1	.342	.421	.359
Leading Off Inn.	95	34	5	1	0	0	5	1	.358	.432	.390
Runners On	205	66	12	2	4	39	26	9	.322	.459	.393
Bases Empty	315	99	15	1	2	2	20	7	.314	.387	.355
Runners/Scor. Pos.	90	29	9	2	1	32	22	6	.322	.500	.443
Runners On/2 Out	78	27	4	0	2	14	11	4	.346	.474	.427
Scor. Pos./2 Out	39	11	3	0	0	10	10	2	.282	.359	.429
Late-Inning Pressure	66	25	3	0	2	5	10	1	.379	.515	.455
Leading Off	18	7	0	0	0	1	0	.389	.389	.421
Runners On	24	7	1	0	1	4	7	1	.292	.458	.438
Runners/Scor. Pos.	11	3	1	0	0	2	6	1	.273	.364	.500

RUNS BATTED IN	From 1B	From 2B	From 3B	Scoring Position
Totals	7/153	10/75	18/28	28/103
Percentage	4.6%	13.3%	64.3%	27.2%

Loves to face: Jeff Brantley (.647, 11-for-17)
Greg Maddux (.500, 22-for-44, 0 SO)
John Smoltz (.465, 20-for-43, 2 HR)

Hates to face: Frank DiPino (.050, 1-for-20)
Ken Hill (.185, 5-for-27, 0 BB)
Pete Schourek (0-for-10)

Miscellaneous statistics: Ground outs-to-air outs ratio: 1.21 last season, 1.67 for career.... Grounded into 12 double plays in 103 opportunities (one per 8.6).... Drove in 12 of 16 runners from third base with less than two outs (75%), 4th-highest rate in N.L.... Direction of balls hit to the outfield: 38% to left field, 36% to center, 26% to right.... Base running: Advanced from first base to third on 11 of 33 outfield singles (33%); scored from second on 12 of 18 (67%).... Made 2.15 putouts per nine innings in right field.

Comments: Has 10 consecutive years in the .300/300 Club: that's a .300 batting average in a season of at least 300 at-bats. He's halfway to Ty Cobb's record of 20 straight; Honus Wagner and Stan Musial share the N.L. mark with 16 in a row. The only other players active in the postwar era who had streaks of 10 years: Rod Carew, 13 years; Ted Williams, 10 years; Wade Boggs, 10 years. (Ted's streak was ended by the 1952 season, in which he had only 10 at-bats.)... Gwynn trails Boggs, .338 to .327, in career batting average, but there's only a one-point difference in their career marks with runners on base (Boggs .345, Gwynn .344).... Has batted over .300 in seven of his nine Aprils in the majors; he missed by one hit in 1985 (.297) and in 1988 (.299). In all, he has hit .300 or better in 39 of his 61 months in the majors.... Only active player with a career rate of driving in more than 70 percent of runners from third base with less than two outs (minimum: 100 chances).... Toughest batter to strike out in majors last season, with a career-best rate of one whiff every 35.6 times up. He has increased his home-run rate while lowering his strikeout rate in each of the last three seasons. No N.L. player has had a longer streak in this century; Mickey Mantle had a five-year streak, 1952–56.... Led N.L. in batting on plastic turf last year; career breakdown: .333 on turf, .325 on grass.... Makes better in-game adjustments than Jimmy Johnson: He hit only .233 in 120 first-inning at-bats last season, but .343 thereafter.

Dave Hansen
Bats Left

Los Angeles Dodgers	AB	H	2B	3B	HR	RBI	BB	SO	BA	SA	OBA
Season	341	73	11	0	6	22	34	49	.214	.299	.286
vs. Left-Handers	46	9	2	0	0	1	4	8	.196	.239	.255
vs. Right-Handers	295	64	9	0	6	21	30	41	.217	.308	.291
vs. Ground-Ballers	129	27	2	0	2	7	14	15	.209	.271	.287
vs. Fly-Ballers	212	46	9	0	4	15	20	34	.217	.316	.285
Home Games	182	42	4	0	1	10	16	22	.231	.269	.295
Road Games	159	31	7	0	5	12	18	27	.195	.333	.275
Grass Fields	252	55	7	0	3	17	23	33	.218	.282	.284
Artificial Turf	89	18	4	0	3	5	11	16	.202	.348	.290
April	34	5	1	0	1	3	2	4	.147	.265	.194
May	48	12	3	0	2	4	9	4	.250	.438	.368
June	41	7	2	0	1	2	6	6	.171	.293	.277
July	70	19	2	0	1	7	2	10	.271	.343	.288
August	73	14	1	0	0	5	8	10	.192	.205	.277
Sept./Oct.	75	16	2	0	1	1	7	15	.213	.280	.280
Leading Off Inn.	100	24	3	0	3	3	6	11	.240	.360	.283
Runners On	129	22	5	0	1	17	14	22	.171	.233	.248
Bases Empty	212	51	6	0	5	5	20	27	.241	.340	.309
Runners/Scor. Pos.	70	11	2	0	0	13	10	15	.157	.186	.256
Runners On/2 Out	53	9	2	0	1	6	7	11	.170	.264	.267
Scor. Pos./2 Out	35	5	1	0	0	4	6	10	.143	.171	.268
Late-Inning Pressure	64	11	1	0	1	4	6	16	.172	.234	.239
Leading Off	18	2	0	0	0	0	1	5	.111	.111	.158
Runners On	25	2	0	0	0	3	2	9	.080	.080	.143
Runners/Scor. Pos.	13	1	0	0	0	3	1	7	.077	.077	.133

RUNS BATTED IN	From 1B	From 2B	From 3B	Scoring Position
Totals	3/93	5/55	8/29	13/84
Percentage	3.2%	9.1%	27.6%	15.5%

Loves to face: Tim Belcher (.429, 3-for-7)
Shawn Boskie (.750, 3-for-4, 2 2B, 1 HR)
Bill Swift (.385, 5-for-13)

Hates to face: Greg W. Harris (.083, 1-for-12)
Darryl Kile (.091, 1-for-11)
Mike Maddux (0-for-6)

Miscellaneous statistics: Ground outs-to-air outs ratio: 1.30 last season, 1.20 for career.... Grounded into 9 double plays in 64 opportunities (one per 7.1).... Drove in 6 of 14 runners from third base with less than two outs (43%).... Direction of balls hit to the outfield: 38% to left field, 31% to center, 31% to right.... Base running: Advanced from first base to third on 2 of 18 outfield singles (11%); scored from second on 2 of 5 (40%).... Made 1.98 assists per nine innings at third base.

Comments: Major league teams averaged 75 or more RBIs at three positions last season: first base (84.4), right field (76.8), and third base (75.0). Dodgers' puny total of 42 RBIs from their third basemen was the lowest by any major league team at any of these three positions, and their total of 28 extra-base hits from third basemen was lowest in N.L.... Hansen started 98 games at third base: 87 of the 100 games in which the Dodgers faced a right-handed starter, and 11 of 62 against left-handers.... Batting average was the lowest of any sophomore with at least 300 at-bats last season.... He also hit for the lowest average in the majors with runners on base, and had the 3d-lowest mark in the league with runners in scoring position.... Hit a major league low .158 from the 8th slot in the batting order (minimum: 100 PA); strangely, other Dodgers batted .271 from the eight-hole, leaving L.A. with a league-high .248 mark from that spot.... Percentage of runners driven in from scoring position was 4th-lowest in the majors (minimum: 80 opportunities).... Six days younger than Gary Sheffield, he was the youngest N.L. player to appear in at least 100 games at third base last season. In Dodgers' history dating to 1890, only two younger players have had 100-game seasons at third base: Bill Sudakis (1969) and Red Smith (1912 and 1913). No, not the sportswriter.

Lenny Harris
Bats Left

Los Angeles Dodgers	AB	H	2B	3B	HR	RBI	BB	SO	BA	SA	OBA
Season	347	94	11	0	0	30	24	24	.271	.303	.318
vs. Left-Handers	36	5	0	0	0	0	3	6	.139	.139	.205
vs. Right-Handers	311	89	11	0	0	30	21	18	.286	.322	.331
vs. Ground-Ballers	147	46	6	0	0	16	6	9	.313	.354	.340
vs. Fly-Ballers	200	48	5	0	0	14	18	15	.240	.265	.303
Home Games	177	47	5	0	0	15	11	13	.266	.294	.307
Road Games	170	47	6	0	0	15	13	11	.276	.312	.330
Grass Fields	268	75	6	0	0	22	18	18	.280	.302	.323
Artificial Turf	79	19	5	0	0	8	6	6	.241	.304	.302
April	53	18	0	0	0	3	4	2	.340	.340	.386
May	56	13	2	0	0	1	5	7	.232	.268	.295
June	62	19	4	0	0	9	3	5	.306	.371	.338
July	63	15	1	0	0	2	0	3	.238	.254	.238
August	52	14	3	0	0	5	5	3	.269	.327	.345
Sept./Oct.	61	15	1	0	0	10	7	4	.246	.262	.314
Leading Off Inn.	68	15	0	0	0	0	1	4	.221	.221	.232
Runners On	157	47	10	0	0	30	10	10	.299	.363	.341
Bases Empty	190	47	1	0	0	0	14	14	.247	.253	.299
Runners/Scor. Pos.	84	25	10	0	0	30	5	5	.298	.417	.330
Runners On/2 Out	58	20	5	0	0	13	0	6	.345	.431	.356
Scor. Pos./2 Out	36	12	5	0	0	13	0	4	.333	.472	.333
Late-Inning Pressure	61	19	0	0	0	5	5	3	.311	.311	.364
Leading Off	12	4	0	0	0	0	0	0	.333	.333	.333
Runners On	30	10	0	0	0	5	2	1	.333	.333	.375
Runners/Scor. Pos.	16	6	0	0	0	5	2	1	.375	.375	.444

RUNS BATTED IN	From 1B	From 2B	From 3B	Scoring Position
Totals	1/105	13/65	16/33	29/98
Percentage	1.0%	20.0%	48.5%	29.6%

Loves to face: Jose Rijo (.407, 11-for-27)
John Smoltz (.364, 16-for-44)
Bob Tewksbury (.600, 6-for-10)

Hates to face: Jose DeJesus (0-for-11)
Doug Drabek (.048, 1-for-21)
Dwayne Henry (0-for-7)

Miscellaneous statistics: Ground outs-to-air outs ratio: 2.05 last season (3d highest in N.L.), 1.87 for career.... Grounded into 10 double plays in 79 opportunities (one per 7.9).... Drove in 10 of 16 runners from third base with less than two outs (63%).... Direction of balls hit to the outfield: 40% to left field, 36% to center, 24% to right.... Base running: Advanced from first base to third on 6 of 13 outfield singles (46%); scored from second on 5 of 6 (83%).... Made 3.43 assists per nine innings at second base, 2d-highest rate in majors.

Comments: His career fielding numbers demonstrate proof of an easier life through synthetics. At second base, he has committed errors more than three times as frequently on grass fields (one every 27.9 chances) as on artificial turf (one every 89.0 chances). At third base, the difference is nearly as striking: an error every 15.8 chances on grass fields, one every 32.7 chances on artificial turf.... The numbers for 1992 in the majors as a whole show much less of a difference: at second base, one error every 55.2 chances on grass, one every 57.5 chances on artificial turf; at third base, one error every 20.0 chances on grass, one every 20.9 chances on artificial turf.... Fitting in with the program, he made six errors in 27 chances filling in at shortstop last season.... Another in the line of switch-hitters who hit much better one way: .291 career batting average vs. right-handers, .216 vs. left-handers, with only four extra-base hits in 236 career at-bats vs. lefties. Last year 85 of his 87 starts were against right-handers.... Has batted over .300 in Late-Inning Pressure Situations in each of the last two seasons.... Set a club record for most at-bats in a season with neither a triple nor a home run. The old mark was 321 at-bats by Pee Wee Oliver in 1964; Frank Taveras holds the all-time mark, with 562 at-bats for the Mets in 1980....Some numbers just exist, without explanation: Lenny's stolen base percentage is .789 in night games (45-for-57) but only .514 in day games (19-for-37).

David Hollins — Bats Left and Right

Philadelphia Phillies	AB	H	2B	3B	HR	RBI	BB	SO	BA	SA	OBA
Season	586	158	28	4	27	93	76	110	.270	.469	.369
vs. Left-Handers	245	79	16	3	17	45	23	44	.322	.620	.391
vs. Right-Handers	341	79	12	1	10	48	53	66	.232	.361	.355
vs. Ground-Ballers	283	76	11	1	9	45	33	53	.269	.410	.364
vs. Fly-Ballers	303	82	17	3	18	48	43	57	.271	.525	.374
Home Games	291	77	19	2	14	48	46	54	.265	.488	.384
Road Games	295	81	9	2	13	45	30	56	.275	.451	.354
Grass Fields	152	41	5	1	8	27	13	36	.270	.474	.345
Artificial Turf	434	117	23	3	19	66	63	74	.270	.468	.377
April	79	18	2	0	3	16	12	16	.228	.367	.371
May	90	26	7	1	3	11	16	16	.289	.489	.409
June	108	30	3	1	4	11	11	19	.278	.435	.342
July	106	28	6	2	4	19	9	23	.264	.472	.350
August	95	24	4	0	6	14	14	19	.253	.484	.351
Sept./Oct.	108	32	6	0	7	22	14	17	.296	.546	.394
Leading Off Inn.	110	25	6	0	1	1	10	22	.227	.309	.309
Runners On	268	79	11	1	16	82	40	49	.295	.522	.399
Bases Empty	318	79	17	3	11	11	36	61	.248	.425	.343
Runners/Scor. Pos.	164	43	8	0	4	55	33	29	.262	.384	.393
Runners On/2 Out	97	28	3	1	7	36	16	13	.289	.557	.415
Scor. Pos./2 Out	67	14	3	0	1	23	16	7	.209	.299	.376
Late-Inning Pressure	93	25	3	1	4	16	7	20	.269	.452	.352
Leading Off	21	4	0	0	0	0	0	7	.190	.190	.190
Runners On	44	11	2	0	2	14	4	7	.250	.432	.377
Runners/Scor. Pos.	28	8	1	0	2	13	3	4	.286	.536	.412

RUNS BATTED IN	From 1B	From 2B	From 3B	Scoring Position
Totals	18/179	24/132	24/59	48/191
Percentage	10.1%	18.2%	40.7%	25.1%

Loves to face: Butch Henry (.875, 7-for-8, 1 2B, 4 HR, 1 SO)
Bruce Hurst (.500, 7-for-14, 2 HR)
Mike Morgan (.400, 8-for-20, 3 2B, 2 HR)
Hates to face: Paul Assenmacher (.100, 1-for-10)
Greg Maddux (.136, 3-for-22)
Mel Rojas (0-for-7)

Miscellaneous statistics: Ground outs-to-air outs ratio: 0.89 last season, 0.81 for career.... Grounded into 8 double plays in 124 opportunities (one per 16).... Drove in 15 of 30 runners from third base with less than two outs (50%).... Direction of balls hit to the outfield: 33% to left field, 32% to center, 35% to right batting left-handed; 48% to left field, 28% to center, 24% to right batting right-handed.... Base running: Advanced from first base to third on 16 of 27 outfield singles (59%), 4th-highest rate in N.L.; scored from second on 22 of 28 (79%).... Made 1.66 assists per nine innings at third base, 3d-lowest rate in N.L.

Comments: Career breakdown: batting .318 and slugging .604 batting right-handed; .227 and .359 batting left-handed. That .604 slugging percentage vs. lefties ranks second to Frank Thomas (.654) over the past 18 years.... Largest differentials between their batting averages vs. right- and left-handed pitchers among qualifiers for N.L. batting title: Felix Jose (123-point difference), Jay Bell (96), Hollins (90), Barry Larkin (82), Otis Nixon (80). Three of the five are switch-hitters.... Gary Sheffield was the only third baseman in the majors with more home runs last year.... Hollins hit 12 home runs over the last seven weeks of the season; the only major leaguers with more over that span were Barry Bonds (14) and Jose Gonzalez (13).... He is truly the heir to Mike Schmidt: he hit six home runs against the Cubs last season; Schmidt did his greatest damage against the Cubs, hitting 78 in 1004 at-bats.... Hit four opposite-field home runs, tied for 2d most in the league, behind Fred McGriff (10). Others with four: Barry Bonds, David Justice, Larry Walker, and Geronimo Pena; that's right, Geronimo Pena.... Led the majors in being hit by pitches (19), no mean feat since a switch-hitter has a preferable view of every pitch; in fact, that's the highest single-season HBP total by any switcher in major league history. Only two switch-hitters have been hit as many as 50 times in their careers: Pete Rose (107) and Willie Wilson (59).

Todd Hundley — Bats Left and Right

New York Mets	AB	H	2B	3B	HR	RBI	BB	SO	BA	SA	OBA
Season	358	75	17	0	7	32	19	76	.209	.316	.256
vs. Left-Handers	113	20	3	0	4	10	4	32	.177	.310	.217
vs. Right-Handers	245	55	14	0	3	22	15	44	.224	.318	.274
vs. Ground-Ballers	170	38	9	0	1	10	10	40	.224	.294	.272
vs. Fly-Ballers	188	37	8	0	6	22	9	36	.197	.335	.241
Home Games	181	40	8	0	2	16	11	38	.221	.298	.272
Road Games	177	35	9	0	5	16	8	38	.198	.333	.239
Grass Fields	254	56	14	0	3	20	16	53	.220	.311	.274
Artificial Turf	104	19	3	0	4	12	3	23	.183	.327	.211
April	40	6	0	0	2	3		10	.150	.300	.227
May	57	11	2	0	1	5	7	12	.221	.281	.303
June	59	12	5	0	3	13	1	10	.203	.441	.217
July	49	12	3	0	1	2	2	10	.245	.367	.275
August	62	13	4	0	0	1	3	17	.210	.274	.258
Sept./Oct.	91	21	3	0	0	9	3	17	.231	.264	.250
Leading Off Inn.	97	20	5	0	2	3		19	.206	.320	.320
Runners On	139	32	6	0	3	28	14	25	.230	.338	.306
Bases Empty	219	43	11	0	4	4	5	51	.196	.301	.221
Runners/Scor. Pos.	82	13	3	0	2	26	10	19	.159	.268	.260
Runners On/2 Out	55	9	2	0	0	6	6	11	.164	.200	.246
Scor. Pos./2 Out	40	5	2	0	0	6	3	9	.125	.175	.186
Late-Inning Pressure	71	19	6	0	0	3	4	19	.268	.352	.325
Leading Off	22	7	2	0	0	0	0	6	.318	.409	.318
Runners On	23	5	0	0	0	3	4	7	.217	.217	.357
Runners/Scor. Pos.	13	0	0	0	0	3	2	5	.000	.000	.188

RUNS BATTED IN	From 1B	From 2B	From 3B	Scoring Position
Totals	4/106	7/72	14/40	21/112
Percentage	3.8%	9.7%	35.0%	18.8%

Loves to face: Mike Morgan (.364, 4-for-11)
Bob Tewksbury (.429, 3-for-7, 1 HR)
Mitch Williams (.500, 2-for-4, 1 HR)
Hates to face: Cliff Brantley (0-for-8, 3 SO)
Ken Hill (0-for-9)
Danny Jackson (0-for-8)

Miscellaneous statistics: Ground outs-to-air outs ratio: 1.04 last season, 1.04 for career.... Grounded into 8 double plays in 80 opportunities (one per 10).... Drove in 10 of 20 runners from third base with less than two outs (50%).... Direction of balls hit to the outfield: 28% to left field, 29% to center, 42% to right batting left-handed; 42% to left field, 44% to center, 14% to right batting right-handed.... Base running: Advanced from first base to third on 3 of 9 outfield singles (33%); scored from second on 7 of 11 (64%).... Opposing base stealers: 89-for-122 (73%), 5th-highest rate in N.L.

Comments: Turned 23 last May; he was the youngest player to play in at least 100 N.L. games last season.... Made 98 starts, 2d-highest total of any N.L. rookie (Eric Karros had 142).... Caught 121 games, a Mets rookie record; Mike Fitzgerald (107 games in 1983) was the only other Mets rookie to catch over 100 games.... Over the last 60 years, only one man caught at least 100 games in a season for a New York club at a younger age: Thurman Munson in 1970. Old-time New Yorkers to do it: Shanty Hogan with Giants in 1928, Bill Dickey with Yankees in 1929 and 1930, Al Lopez with Dodgers in 1930 and 1931.... Opponents stole 89 bases against Hundley; among all N.L. catchers only Gary Carter (98) yielded more.... Mets pitchers had a 3.33 ERA in 892⅓ innings with Hundley catching, 4.11 in 427⅓ innings with Charlie O'Brien, 4.68 in 127 innings with Mackey Sasser.... Sorry, Todd, Randy, and the whole Hundley family; now it's time to talk about hitting: Batted .221 at Shea, .198 on the road, joining teammate Dick Schofield as the only N.L. players to finish in the bottom 10 in both home and road batting average.... Had the lowest batting average in the league in night games (.200), 6th lowest on artificial turf, 4th lowest with runners in scoring position, and the lowest in the majors vs. left-handers.... Batted .211 as a catcher, lowest among all major league backstops (minimum: 250 PA); Mets catchers combined for 2d-lowest average in majors, ahead of only the Angels (.216).

Brian Hunter
Bats Right

Atlanta Braves	AB	H	2B	3B	HR	RBI	BB	SO	BA	SA	OBA
Season	238	57	13	2	14	41	21	50	.239	.487	.292
vs. Left-Handers	155	42	10	1	12	32	16	23	.271	.581	.326
vs. Right-Handers	83	15	3	1	2	9	5	27	.181	.313	.225
vs. Ground-Ballers	93	22	7	1	4	17	11	17	.237	.462	.308
vs. Fly-Ballers	145	35	6	1	10	24	10	33	.241	.503	.281
Home Games	107	31	5	1	9	23	15	24	.290	.607	.362
Road Games	131	26	8	1	5	18	6	26	.198	.389	.229
Grass Fields	167	40	8	1	11	28	19	35	.240	.497	.306
Artificial Turf	71	17	5	1	3	13	2	15	.239	.465	.257
April	41	3	1	0	2	3	1	13	.073	.244	.093
May	53	18	4	1	2	11	4	9	.340	.566	.367
June	31	9	2	1	3	8	2	4	.290	.710	.314
July	27	3	1	0	1	3	1	4	.111	.259	.138
August	49	14	4	0	3	8	5	11	.286	.551	.352
Sept./Oct.	37	10	1	0	3	8	8	9	.270	.541	.391
Leading Off Inn.	57	10	3	0	3	3	7	15	.175	.386	.266
Runners On	94	21	8	1	4	31	8	19	.223	.457	.264
Bases Empty	144	36	5	1	10	10	13	31	.250	.507	.312
Runners/Scor. Pos.	56	11	5	0	1	23	5	13	.196	.339	.232
Runners On/2 Out	42	7	3	0	0	5	3	10	.167	.238	.222
Scor. Pos./2 Out	32	4	1	0	0	4	2	9	.125	.156	.176
Late-Inning Pressure	33	5	2	0	3	7	6	12	.152	.485	.268
Leading Off	12	1	1	0	0	0	3	3	.083	.167	.267
Runners On	11	2	1	0	1	5	2	6	.182	.545	.267
Runners/Scor. Pos.	7	1	0	0	1	4	2	4	.143	.571	.273

RUNS BATTED IN	From 1B	From 2B	From 3B	Scoring Position
Totals	5/72	6/43	16/33	22/76
Percentage	6.9%	14.0%	48.5%	28.9%

Loves to face: Terry Mulholland (.385, 5-for-13, 1 HR)
Donovan Osborne (.625, 5-for-8, 2 HR)
Pete Schourek (.500, 2-for-4, 2 HR)

Hates to face: Frank Castillo (0-for-6, 3 SO)
Bob Tewksbury (.111, 1-for-9)

Miscellaneous statistics: Ground outs-to-air outs ratio: 0.43 last season (lowest rate in majors), 0.61 for career.... Grounded into 2 double plays in 50 opportunities (one per 25).... Drove in 15 of 19 runners from third base with less than two outs (79%), highest rate in N.L.... Direction of balls hit to the outfield: 57% to left field, 25% to center, 18% to right.... Base running: Advanced from first base to third on 4 of 9 outfield singles (44%); scored from second on 3 of 7 (43%).... Made 0.83 assists per nine innings at first base.

Comments: The only player who started all 51 games in which Braves faced a left-handed starter last season. And for good reason: He has 18 homers in 276 at-bats vs. left-handers over the past two seasons; David Hollins (20 homers in 290 at-bats) is the only N.L. player with a better home-run rate vs. lefties in that time.... Career breakdowns: .272 vs. left-handers, .215 vs. right-handers; .278 at Atlanta, .215 on the road.... Had nine homers from the 6th spot in the lineup, the most by any N.L. player.... Committed as many errors in six games in the outfield as he did in 92 games at first base (two). Teammate Melvin Nieves, the youngest player in the majors last season, did even worse: three errors in six games in the outfield.... Averaged one home run every 17 at-bats, the highest rate among major league sophomores in 1992. Only three players in Braves history have posted higher home-run rates than Hunter in their post-rookie season (minimum: 10 HR): Eddie Mathews in 1953 (one HR every 12.3 AB); Wes Covington in 1957 (15.6); Bob Horner in 1979 (14.8).... Call him "Big Game" Hunter in the N.L.C.S., where he owns a career average of .304 (7-for-23) and hit a key home run in Game 7 in 1991; but the name doesn't apply in the World Series, where he has hit only .192 (5-for-26). Last year, he came up empty as the penultimate hitter in each series; pinch-hitting in key situations, he popped out (pre-Cabrera) vs. Stan Belinda and grounded out (pre–Otis Nixon's bunt) vs. Jimmy Key.

Pete Incaviglia
Bats Right

Houston Astros	AB	H	2B	3B	HR	RBI	BB	SO	BA	SA	OBA
Season	349	93	22	1	11	44	25	99	.266	.430	.319
vs. Left-Handers	170	48	13	1	7	27	16	50	.282	.494	.344
vs. Right-Handers	179	45	9	0	4	17	9	49	.251	.369	.295
vs. Ground-Ballers	147	40	9	1	3	19	14	34	.272	.408	.337
vs. Fly-Ballers	202	53	13	0	8	25	11	65	.262	.446	.306
Home Games	189	56	15	0	6	26	9	60	.296	.471	.338
Road Games	160	37	7	1	5	18	16	39	.231	.381	.298
Grass Fields	80	20	5	0	0	3	6	22	.250	.313	.302
Artificial Turf	269	73	17	1	11	41	19	77	.271	.465	.324
April	72	18	4	0	1	7	0	26	.250	.347	.270
May	75	20	3	0	1	8	6	19	.267	.347	.317
June	64	18	5	0	4	11	6	23	.281	.547	.343
July	65	21	7	0	3	9	6	13	.323	.569	.380
August	42	9	1	0	1	3	2	8	.214	.310	.244
Sept./Oct.	31	7	2	1	1	6	5	10	.226	.452	.351
Leading Off Inn.	74	20	6	0	2	2	3	12	.270	.432	.308
Runners On	169	43	11	0	7	40	16	54	.254	.444	.323
Bases Empty	180	50	11	1	4	4	9	45	.278	.417	.316
Runners/Scor. Pos.	92	18	6	0	1	25	11	36	.196	.293	.290
Runners On/2 Out	70	14	2	0	3	13	6	26	.200	.357	.273
Scor. Pos./2 Out	44	7	2	0	1	9	5	18	.159	.273	.260
Late-Inning Pressure	57	13	5	0	1	5	6	19	.228	.368	.302
Leading Off	9	2	0	0	1	1	1	0	.222	.556	.300
Runners On	30	7	3	0	0	4	3	12	.233	.333	.303
Runners/Scor. Pos.	18	3	1	0	0	2	1	9	.167	.222	.211

RUNS BATTED IN	From 1B	From 2B	From 3B	Scoring Position
Totals	10/115	11/77	12/43	23/120
Percentage	8.7%	14.3%	27.9%	19.2%

Loves to face: Bud Black (.524, 11-for-21, 3 2B, 4 HR)
Dave Righetti (.400, 4-for-10, 2 2B, 2 HR)
Randy Tomlin (.667, 6-for-9, 3 2B)

Hates to face: Tom Candiotti (.143, 5-for-35)
Dan Plesac (.063, 1-for-16)
Greg Swindell (.061, 2-for-33, 3 BB, 16 SO)

Miscellaneous statistics: Ground outs-to-air outs ratio: 0.77 last season, 1.10 for career.... Grounded into 6 double plays in 78 opportunities (one per 13).... Drove in 8 of 20 runners from third base with less than two outs (40%), 5th-lowest rate in N.L.... Direction of balls hit to the outfield: 39% to left field, 36% to center, 26% to right.... Base running: Advanced from first base to third on 6 of 17 outfield singles (35%); scored from second on 5 of 8 (63%).... Made 2.58 putouts per nine innings in left field.

Comments: His home-run rate has decreased in every year since his debut in 1986: one every 18.0 at-bats as a rookie, followed by 18.9, 19.0, 21.6, 22.0, 30.6, and 31.7. Only five other players in major league history have seen their home-run rate fall in six consecutive years: Joe Gordon (1939–46, interrupted by military service), Gil Coan (1951–56), Wes Westrum (1952–57), and Amos Otis (1979–84). This year in Philadelphia, the Inkster goes for the record.... Batted .296 at the Astrodome last year, his highest batting average at home in any of his seven seasons in the majors. This year, he plays in his fourth different home stadium in as many years.... Hit six homers in the Astrodome last season, as many as he hit at Tiger Stadium while playing for Detroit in 1991; he also hit five on the road each year.... Owns .174 career average as a pinch hitter (8-for-46, 3 HR).... Rob Deer is the only other player in the majors to drive in fewer than 20 percent of teammates from scoring position in each of the last two seasons (minimum: 100 opportunities in both 1991 and 1992).... One of five players to appear in at least 100 games for both Texas and Houston. The others: Danny Darwin, Leon Roberts, Nolan Ryan, and Rusty Staub.... Remember 1986, when five A.L. rookies (Incaviglia, Jose Canseco, Wally Joyner, Cory Snyder, Danny Tartabull) hit 20 or more homers? Two other rookies from that class, each of whom hit only 16 homers that year, were the biggest bank breakers this past off-season: Barry Bonds and Ruben Sierra.

Darrin Jackson
Bats Right

San Diego Padres	AB	H	2B	3B	HR	RBI	BB	SO	BA	SA	OBA
Season	587	146	23	5	17	70	26	106	.249	.392	.283
vs. Left-Handers	188	38	6	4	7	19	9	33	.202	.388	.242
vs. Right-Handers	399	108	17	1	10	51	17	73	.271	.393	.302
vs. Ground-Ballers	254	67	9	2	9	34	13	41	.264	.421	.300
vs. Fly-Ballers	333	79	14	3	8	36	13	65	.237	.369	.270
Home Games	299	86	13	3	11	45	11	50	.288	.462	.313
Road Games	288	60	10	2	6	25	15	56	.208	.319	.252
Grass Fields	446	124	19	5	15	57	19	73	.278	.444	.309
Artificial Turf	141	22	4	0	2	13	7	33	.156	.227	.200
April	82	18	3	1	4	12	6	15	.220	.427	.278
May	100	27	4	0	3	13	2	18	.270	.400	.284
June	93	28	5	2	2	11	6	13	.301	.462	.347
July	99	26	3	2	3	11	3	18	.263	.424	.284
August	93	22	4	0	3	16	5	16	.237	.376	.280
Sept./Oct.	120	25	4	0	2	7	4	26	.208	.292	.236
Leading Off Inn.	144	41	6	2	5	5	4	28	.285	.458	.304
Runners On	236	60	9	2	7	60	14	36	.254	.398	.298
Bases Empty	351	86	14	3	10	10	12	70	.245	.387	.272
Runners/Scor. Pos.	136	41	8	2	6	57	12	22	.301	.522	.355
Runners On/2 Out	89	20	5	1	4	22	9	17	.225	.438	.303
Scor. Pos./2 Out	58	14	4	1	4	21	8	14	.241	.552	.343
Late-Inning Pressure	88	22	2	1	4	9	8	23	.250	.432	.316
Leading Off	26	8	0	1	3	3	2	9	.308	.731	.357
Runners On	30	8	1	0	1	6	5	7	.267	.400	.378
Runners/Scor. Pos.	21	6	1	0	1	6	5	5	.286	.476	.429

RUNS BATTED IN	From 1B	From 2B	From 3B	Scoring Position
Totals	7/184	23/113	23/55	46/168
Percentage	3.8%	20.4%	41.8%	27.4%

Loves to face: Bud Black (.545, 6-for-11, 1 HR)
Danny Jackson (.500, 9-for-18, 2 HR)
John Smoltz (.400, 8-for-20, 1 HR)
Hates to face: John Franco (0-for-10)
Ramon Martinez (.059, 1-for-17)
Terry Mulholland (.087, 2-for-23, 1 3B)

Miscellaneous statistics: Ground outs-to-air outs ratio: 0.84 last season, 0.89 for career.... Grounded into 21 double plays in 128 opportunities (one per 6.1).... Drove in 17 of 32 runners from third base with less than two outs (53%).... Direction of balls hit to the outfield: 44% to left field, 27% to center, 29% to right.... Base running: Advanced from first base to third on 8 of 23 outfield singles (35%); scored from second on 8 of 14 (57%).... Made 2.87 putouts per nine innings in center field.

Comments: Led major league outfielders with 18 assists, noteworthy for a center fielder. Of 812 outfield assists in the majors last year, 38 percent came from right field, 32 percent from left, only 30 percent from center.... Owns lowest career error rate (one every 104 chances) of any outfielder in Padres history (minimum: 250 games).... Grounded into 21 double plays to lead N.L. Gary Sheffield was runner-up with 19; Padres grounded into a league-high 126.... San Diego players had three of the five worst synthetic-turf averages in N.L. last year: Jackson (the lowest), Benito Santiago (3d lowest at .167), and Jerald Clark (5th lowest at .177). Santiago and Clark have split the California scene for expansion environs.... Batting average vs. lefties was 5th lowest in N.L. last season; his lefty/righty numbers showed a reversal of previous form and left his career average at .252 against both types.... Became Padres' 7th different opening-day center field starter in last seven years; Kevin McReynolds was last to start consecutive openers (1984–86). Starters since 1987: Marvell Wynne, Stan Jefferson, Tony Gwynn, Joe Carter, Shawn Abner, and Jackson.... Has .199 career batting average in Late-Inning Pressure Situations while driving in only 15 percent of LIPS runners from scoring position. Only two other active players have sub-.200 career LIPS averages and have driven in fewer than 20 percent of LIPS runners from scoring position (minimum: 50 chances): Junior Felix (.167, 14 percent) and Matt Williams (.191, 18 percent).

Chris James
Bats Right

San Francisco Giants	AB	H	2B	3B	HR	RBI	BB	SO	BA	SA	OBA
Season	248	60	10	4	5	32	14	45	.242	.375	.285
vs. Left-Handers	116	35	7	1	2	13	5	18	.302	.431	.333
vs. Right-Handers	132	25	3	3	3	19	9	27	.189	.326	.243
vs. Ground-Ballers	107	27	3	3	2	16	5	16	.252	.393	.287
vs. Fly-Ballers	141	33	7	1	3	16	9	29	.234	.362	.283
Home Games	127	27	5	3	3	19	5	26	.213	.370	.239
Road Games	121	33	5	1	2	13	9	19	.273	.380	.331
Grass Fields	186	43	6	4	4	28	10	31	.231	.371	.266
Artificial Turf	62	17	4	0	1	4	4	14	.274	.387	.338
April	25	4	2	0	0	3	3	7	.160	.240	.250
May	23	1	1	0	0	0	5	9	.043	.087	.241
June	30	8	1	0	2	5	2	6	.267	.500	.294
July	75	25	4	2	2	8	2	8	.333	.520	.351
August	34	8	1	0	0	3	1	9	.235	.265	.278
Sept./Oct.	61	14	1	2	1	13	1	6	.230	.361	.238
Leading Off Inn.	52	8	0	1	1	1	2	8	.154	.250	.185
Runners On	123	31	6	2	1	28	7	27	.252	.358	.291
Bases Empty	125	29	4	2	4	4	7	18	.232	.392	.278
Runners/Scor. Pos.	66	17	2	2	0	23	6	16	.258	.348	.316
Runners On/2 Out	66	14	2	1	1	11	2	17	.212	.318	.246
Scor. Pos./2 Out	34	8	1	1	0	8	1	12	.235	.324	.278
Late-Inning Pressure	39	9	2	0	2	3	4	11	.231	.436	.311
Leading Off	9	2	0	0	0	0	1	2	.222	.222	.300
Runners On	17	3	1	0	0	1	1	8	.176	.235	.211
Runners/Scor. Pos.	12	2	0	0	0	1	1	7	.167	.167	.214

RUNS BATTED IN	From 1B	From 2B	From 3B	Scoring Position
Totals	4/88	11/56	12/23	23/79
Percentage	4.5%	19.6%	52.2%	29.1%

Loves to face: Les Lancaster (.538, 7-for-13, 2 HR)
Zane Smith (.400, 6-for-15, 2 HR)
Mitch Williams (.667, 4-for-6)
Hates to face: Tom Browning (.192, 5-for-26)
Rob Dibble (0-for-8)
Danny Jackson (.125, 3-for-24, 1 HR)

Miscellaneous statistics: Ground outs-to-air outs ratio: 0.87 last season, 1.08 for career.... Grounded into 2 double plays in 40 opportunities (one per 20).... Drove in 9 of 11 runners from third base with less than two outs (82%).... Direction of balls hit to the outfield: 25% to left field, 39% to center, 37% to right.... Base running: Advanced from first base to third on 0 of 8 outfield singles (0%); scored from second on 8 of 11 (73%).... Made 2.22 putouts per nine innings in left field.

Comments: Signed with Houston in January; Astros would be his fifth major league team since June 1989.... Started only 57 games for Giants last season on a team whose outfielders combined for only 27 home runs and 169 RBIs. That was the 2d-lowest total of homers by any N.L. team's outfield (the Dodgers hit 26), and the RBI total matched the White Sox outfield for the lowest in the majors.... Acquired by the Padres from Philadelphia in June 1989 in exchange for both John Kruk and Randy Ready. That was a pretty hefty price to pay for a guy whose career with San Diego lasted just 87 games.... Batting average vs. left-handers was just a shade below his career high (.302 in 1990), while his average against right-handers was the lowest of his career.... Career average in day games (.274) is almost 20 points higher than at night (.255); last season's breakdown: .280 in day games, .216 in night games.... Had more pinch-hit appearances in 1992 (50) than he had over the previous six years of his career combined (41).... Percentage of runners driven in from scoring position was the 2d-highest of his career, but he drove in only one of 13 such runners in Late-Inning Pressure Situations. Over the last two seasons, he has driven in only two of 27 runners from scoring position in LIPS.... Grounded into 20 double plays in 1989, only one shy of the league lead, but only two last season.... Born October 4, 1962, the day Whitey Ford topped Billy O'Dell at Candlestick Park in the first World Series game in San Francisco.

Stan Javier — Bats Left and Right

Dodgers/Phillies	AB	H	2B	3B	HR	RBI	BB	SO	BA	SA	OBA
Season	334	83	17	1	1	29	37	54	.249	.314	.327
vs. Left-Handers	146	32	8	1	0	5	12	22	.219	.288	.283
vs. Right-Handers	188	51	9	0	1	24	25	32	.271	.335	.359
vs. Ground-Ballers	141	33	6	1	0	8	15	25	.234	.291	.314
vs. Fly-Ballers	193	50	11	0	1	21	22	29	.259	.332	.336
Home Games	150	41	11	0	1	16	14	22	.273	.367	.337
Road Games	184	42	6	1	0	13	23	32	.228	.272	.319
Grass Fields	123	26	3	0	1	9	14	16	.211	.260	.295
Artificial Turf	211	57	14	1	0	20	23	38	.270	.346	.346
April	21	4	0	0	0	2	1	2	.190	.190	.227
May	16	3	0	0	1	3	2	5	.188	.375	.316
June	20	3	3	0	0	0	3	4	.150	.300	.261
July	80	21	3	0	0	6	12	12	.262	.300	.372
August	92	26	6	0	0	9	8	14	.283	.348	.340
Sept./Oct.	105	26	5	1	0	9	11	17	.248	.314	.314
Leading Off Inn.	95	21	2	1	0	0	15	15	.221	.263	.327
Runners On	126	35	10	0	1	29	13	25	.278	.381	.340
Bases Empty	208	48	7	1	0	0	24	29	.231	.274	.319
Runners/Scor. Pos.	79	22	5	0	1	27	11	12	.278	.380	.359
Runners On/2 Out	55	12	5	0	1	13	7	12	.218	.364	.306
Scor. Pos./2 Out	38	8	3	0	1	11	6	8	.211	.368	.318
Late-Inning Pressure	64	12	2	0	0	4	6	14	.188	.219	.264
Leading Off	12	2	1	0	0	0	2	3	.167	.250	.286
Runners On	24	3	1	0	0	4	3	8	.125	.167	.214
Runners/Scor. Pos.	17	2	0	0	0	3	3	6	.118	.118	.238

RUNS BATTED IN	From 1B	From 2B	From 3B	Scoring Position
Totals	5/81	10/65	13/26	23/91
Percentage	6.2%	15.4%	50.0%	25.3%

Loves to face: Eric King (.500, 6-for-12)
Kirk McCaskill (.667, 4-for-6, 1 HR, 2 SO)
Dennis Rasmussen (.333, 3-for-9, 1 HR, 4 BB)

Hates to face: Mark Gubicza (0-for-11)
Dave Schmidt (0-for-9)
Frank Viola (.143, 3-for-21)

Miscellaneous statistics: Ground outs-to-air outs ratio: 1.42 last season, 1.63 for career.... Grounded into 4 double plays in 49 opportunities (one per 12).... Drove in 12 of 16 runners from third base with less than two outs (75%), 4th-highest rate in N.L.... Direction of balls hit to the outfield: 38% to left field, 38% to center, 23% to right batting left-handed; 24% to left field, 32% to center, 44% to right batting right-handed.... Base running: Advanced from first base to third on 8 of 22 outfield singles (36%); scored from second on 7 of 8 (88%).... Made 3.35 putouts per nine innings in center field.

Comments: Signed with Angels in off-season; they would be his fourth major league team in the nineties.... Has the lowest career pinch-hit batting average (.162) among active players with at least 100 pinch-hit at-bats, by .0001 over Dion James (Javier, .1618 on 22-for-136; James, .1619 on 17-for-105).... Has played over 100 games in each of the last five seasons, but has not had more than 35 RBIs in any of those years. Over the last 20 years, only one player has had a longer streak of consecutive seasons with at least 100 games but no more than 35 RBIs: Johnnie LeMaster (7 years, 1978–84).... His .944 stolen base percentage (17-for-18) with Phillies last year was the best in a single season in team history (minimum: 15 steals since 1950, when statistics for "caught stealing" became official in N.L.). Javier was one-for-three tries with Dodgers last season (April through July 1).... Career batting breakdown: .228 in day games, .257 at night; .229 on grass fields; .292 on artificial turf.... Made his major league debut for Yogi Berra's Yankees in 1984, and went on to play under Tony LaRussa, Tommy Lasorda, and Jim Fregosi. *That's* Italian.... Seven other players have been managed in the majors by both Lasorda and Berra: Al Downing, Jerry Grote, Jay Howell, Teddy Martinez, Willie Randolph, Mike Vail, and Hank Webb. You think they might have some stories to tell? Randolph, who was swapped for Javier in 1990, is the only one of them who has also played for LaRussa.

Howard Johnson — Bats Left and Right

New York Mets	AB	H	2B	3B	HR	RBI	BB	SO	BA	SA	OBA
Season	350	78	19	0	7	43	55	79	.223	.337	.329
vs. Left-Handers	132	30	8	0	4	21	23	30	.227	.379	.340
vs. Right-Handers	218	48	11	0	3	22	32	49	.220	.312	.323
vs. Ground-Ballers	172	39	10	0	3	25	28	34	.227	.337	.340
vs. Fly-Ballers	178	39	9	0	4	18	27	45	.219	.337	.319
Home Games	164	31	8	0	2	16	25	41	.189	.274	.293
Road Games	186	47	11	0	5	27	30	38	.253	.392	.361
Grass Fields	231	45	11	0	2	22	37	55	.195	.268	.304
Artificial Turf	119	33	8	0	5	21	18	24	.277	.471	.379
April	79	16	6	0	3	14	9	19	.203	.392	.297
May	85	17	4	0	1	11	21	21	.200	.282	.352
June	92	24	6	0	3	9	13	21	.261	.424	.352
July	86	20	2	0	0	9	12	15	.233	.256	.327
August	8	1	1	0	0	0	0	3	.125	.250	.125
Sept./Oct.	0	0	0	0	0	0	0	0	.000	.000	.000
Leading Off Inn.	75	20	3	0	1	1	7	25	.267	.347	.329
Runners On	164	37	12	0	2	38	30	33	.226	.335	.340
Bases Empty	186	41	7	0	5	5	25	46	.220	.339	.319
Runners/Scor. Pos.	95	23	8	0	1	35	23	20	.242	.358	.380
Runners On/2 Out	66	15	3	0	1	15	11	12	.227	.318	.338
Scor. Pos./2 Out	43	9	1	0	1	14	8	10	.209	.302	.333
Late-Inning Pressure	50	14	3	0	2	9	13	17	.280	.460	.422
Leading Off	9	3	1	0	0	0	2	6	.333	.444	.455
Runners On	24	7	1	0	1	8	7	7	.292	.458	.484
Runners/Scor. Pos.	12	3	1	0	1	8	5	4	.250	.583	.444

RUNS BATTED IN	From 1B	From 2B	From 3B	Scoring Position
Totals	5/126	14/69	17/48	31/117
Percentage	4.0%	20.3%	35.4%	26.5%

Loves to face: Mark Davis (.455, 5-for-11, 2 HR)
Kevin Gross (.359, 23-for-64, 5 HR)
Todd Worrell (.556, 5-for-9, 4 HR, 6 BB)

Hates to face: Jose DeJesus (0-for-16)
Ken Hill (.156, 5-for-32, 1 HR, 0 BB)
John Smiley (.103, 4-for-39)

Miscellaneous statistics: Ground outs-to-air outs ratio: 0.65 last season (5th lowest in N.L.), 0.57 for career.... Grounded into 7 double plays in 94 opportunities (one per 13).... Drove in 11 of 28 runners from third base with less than two outs (39%), 4th-lowest rate in N.L.... Direction of balls hit to the outfield: 23% to left field, 29% to center, 47% to right batting left-handed; 67% to left field, 16% to center, 18% to right batting right-handed.... Base running: Advanced from first base to third on 6 of 25 outfield singles (24%); scored from second on 4 of 5 (80%).... Made 2.28 putouts per nine innings in center field, 2d-lowest rate in N.L.

Comments: Home-run output dropped from 38 in 1991 to seven last season; that decrease of 31 homers was 2d-largest in major league history in consecutive seasons of at least 100 games.... Hack Wilson set N.L. record with 56 in 1930 and followed with only 13 in 1931.... Home-run rate (one every 50 at-bats) was the lowest of his career; his career-high rate (one every 14.8 at-bats) had come in 1991.... The last player with fewer than 50 RBIs in defense of N.L. RBI crown: Monte Irvin, who led N.L. in 1951 but fell to 21 the next year due to a broken ankle.... Became the 6th switch-hitter to hit 200 home runs, joining Mickey Mantle (536), Eddie Murray (414), Reggie Smith (314), Ted Simmons (248), and Ken Singleton (246); Chili Davis is next with 197.... Became 16th player with 200 home runs and 200 stolen bases; he had 157 homers and 160 steals from 1987 to 1991, joining Willie Mays and Bobby Bonds as only players to average 30/30 over a five-year span.... In 1992, six N.L. players hit 30 points below their career average coming into the year (minimums: 2000 at-bats coming in, 300 in 1992); three of them were the Mets' "power" switch-hitters: HoJo underperformed his previous career average by 33 points (.256 to .223), Bobby Bonilla by 34 points (.283 to .249), Eddie Murray by 31 points (.292 to .261). The others: Mike Scioscia (.262 to .221), Tim Wallach (.263 to .223), and Bill Doran (.269 to .235).

Ricky Jordan — Bats Right

Philadelphia Phillies	AB	H	2B	3B	HR	RBI	BB	SO	BA	SA	OBA
Season	276	84	19	0	4	34	5	44	.304	.417	.313
vs. Left-Handers	132	49	11	0	3	21	2	18	.371	.523	.372
vs. Right-Handers	144	35	8	0	1	13	3	26	.243	.319	.259
vs. Ground-Ballers	115	35	6	0	1	12	2	20	.304	.383	.314
vs. Fly-Ballers	161	49	13	0	3	22	3	24	.304	.441	.313
Home Games	116	37	7	0	2	20	3	15	.319	.431	.331
Road Games	160	47	12	0	2	14	2	29	.294	.406	.301
Grass Fields	79	24	6	0	1	5	0	16	.304	.418	.304
Artificial Turf	197	60	13	0	3	29	5	28	.305	.416	.317
April	0	0	0	0	0	0	0	0	—	—	—
May	47	10	3	0	1	8	1	6	.213	.340	.224
June	56	16	4	0	0	5	2	9	.286	.357	.305
July	41	9	0	0	1	5	1	15	.220	.293	.233
August	59	18	3	0	2	9	0	5	.305	.458	.305
Sept./Oct.	73	31	9	0	0	7	1	9	.425	.548	.432
Leading Off Inn.	65	22	4	0	2	2	1	8	.338	.492	.348
Runners On	134	37	9	0	2	32	3	17	.276	.388	.286
Bases Empty	142	47	10	0	2	2	2	27	.331	.444	.340
Runners/Scor. Pos.	79	21	2	0	1	27	2	9	.266	.329	.274
Runners On/2 Out	57	17	2	0	0	11	2	5	.298	.333	.322
Scor. Pos./2 Out	40	11	0	0	0	9	1	3	.275	.275	.293
Late-Inning Pressure	53	14	2	0	0	5	4	10	.264	.302	.316
Leading Off	13	4	1	0	0	0	1	3	.308	.385	.357
Runners On	24	8	0	0	0	5	2	3	.333	.333	.385
Runners/Scor. Pos.	13	6	0	0	0	5	1	1	.462	.462	.500

RUNS BATTED IN	From 1B	From 2B	From 3B	Scoring Position
Totals	6/99	12/63	12/34	24/97
Percentage	6.1%	19.0%	35.3%	24.7%

Loves to face: Tom Browning (.500, 9-for-18, 1 HR)
Tim Crews (.667, 4-for-6, 1 HR)
Ramon Martinez (.412, 7-for-17, 1 HR)
Hates to face: Rob Dibble (.083, 1-for-12, 1 2B)
Doug Drabek (.059, 1-for-17, 1 2B)
Greg Maddux (.182, 6-for-33)

Miscellaneous statistics: Ground outs-to-air outs ratio: 1.30 last season, 1.17 for career.... Grounded into 8 double plays in 61 opportunities (one per 7.6).... Drove in 11 of 20 runners from third base with less than two outs (55%).... Direction of balls hit to the outfield: 33% to left field, 36% to center, 31% to right.... Base running: Advanced from first base to third on 2 of 9 outfield singles (22%); scored from second on 6 of 8 (75%).... Made 0.55 assists per nine innings at first base.

Comments: Career rate of one walk every 28.9 trips to the plate is 2d lowest among active players (minimum: 1000 PA); only Ozzie Guillen (one every 33.0) has a lower rate. Last year, Jordan produced the lowest single-season rate by a Phillies player since 1925.... Owns a .305 career batting average from August 1 to the end of the season and a .318 career mark vs. left-handers.... His 1992 home-run rate (one every 69 at-bats) was the worst of his career, as was his strikeout rate (one every 6.5 plate appearances).... Increased his batting average 32 points from 1991 to 1992, but saw his slugging percentage drop 35 points in the process.... Finished season with 12-game hitting streak. Only Tony Fernandez (19 games) ended the season with a longer streak intact. To forestall the question of whether such streaks "carry over" to the next season, let's go through the drill. There are two different kinds of streak records, relating to hitting streaks or anything else: (1) those streaks that are contained within one season; (2) those that extend beyond one season. Examples: Tim Keefe and Rube Marquard share the all-time mark of 19 consecutive wins in one season; Carl Hubbell owns the record of 24 consecutive wins unrestricted by one season. Also, Pete Rose and Willie Keeler share the N.L. record of getting a hit in 44 games in a row in a season; but Keeler's unrestricted streak is 45 games (the last game of the 1896 season and the first 44 games in 1897). Jordan stands just 33 games shy of tying that record.

Felix Jose — Bats Left and Right

St. Louis Cardinals	AB	H	2B	3B	HR	RBI	BB	SO	BA	SA	OBA
Season	509	150	22	3	14	75	40	100	.295	.432	.347
vs. Left-Handers	182	68	11	2	6	31	15	33	.374	.555	.419
vs. Right-Handers	327	82	11	1	8	44	25	67	.251	.364	.306
vs. Ground-Ballers	213	57	7	1	4	28	18	43	.268	.366	.323
vs. Fly-Ballers	296	93	15	2	10	47	22	57	.314	.480	.364
Home Games	255	75	10	1	12	46	23	52	.294	.482	.354
Road Games	254	75	12	2	2	29	17	48	.295	.382	.339
Grass Fields	124	41	7	1	0	18	10	22	.331	.403	.381
Artificial Turf	385	109	15	2	14	57	30	78	.283	.442	.336
April	10	4	1	0	0	1	0	2	.400	.500	.400
May	104	36	4	2	4	25	13	20	.346	.538	.415
June	105	29	6	0	3	16	7	20	.276	.419	.321
July	78	20	2	0	1	3	7	19	.256	.321	.318
August	105	32	5	0	3	12	5	26	.305	.438	.342
Sept./Oct.	107	29	4	1	3	18	8	13	.271	.411	.322
Leading Off Inn.	128	49	10	0	3	3	8	19	.383	.531	.419
Runners On	224	62	9	2	4	65	21	48	.277	.388	.340
Bases Empty	285	88	13	1	10	10	19	52	.309	.467	.352
Runners/Scor. Pos.	153	40	6	1	1	56	18	36	.261	.333	.341
Runners On/2 Out	93	26	5	2	1	28	11	15	.280	.409	.356
Scor. Pos./2 Out	70	20	4	1	1	26	10	12	.286	.414	.375
Late-Inning Pressure	104	33	4	1	4	18	9	24	.317	.490	.372
Leading Off	23	9	1	0	0	1	0	5	.391	.435	.417
Runners On	44	16	3	0	2	16	6	9	.364	.568	.440
Runners/Scor. Pos.	29	8	1	0	1	11	5	8	.276	.310	.382

RUNS BATTED IN	From 1B	From 2B	From 3B	Scoring Position
Totals	10/137	26/117	25/66	51/183
Percentage	7.3%	22.2%	37.9%	27.9%

Loves to face: Tommy Greene (.571, 8-for-14, 4 2B, 1 3B)
John Smoltz (.435, 10-for-23)
Randy Tomlin (.440, 11-for-25, 1 HR, 0 BB)
Hates to face: Tom Glavine (0-for-9)
Mike Jackson (0-for-9)
Greg Maddux (0-for-16)

Miscellaneous statistics: Ground outs-to-air outs ratio: 1.56 last season, 1.49 for career.... Grounded into 9 double plays in 87 opportunities (one per 10).... Drove in 16 of 37 runners from third base with less than two outs (43%).... Direction of balls hit to the outfield: 41% to left field, 28% to center, 31% to right batting left-handed; 44% to left field, 33% to center, 23% to right batting right-handed.... Base running: Advanced from first base to third on 7 of 22 outfield singles (32%); scored from second on 11 of 17 (65%).... Made 2.20 putouts per nine innings in right field, 2d-highest rate in N.L.

Comments: Led N.L. in batting vs. left-handers last season; 123-point disparity between his marks vs. right- and left-handed pitchers was the largest among N.L. players who qualified for the batting title. Career marks: .323 vs. LHP, .266 vs. RHP; that career mark against left-handers is 4th-highest among players with at least 500 at-bats vs. southpaws since 1975. The top three: Kirby Puckett (.340), Edgar Martinez (.333), and Barry Larkin (.323).... His .331 average on grass fields was 3d highest in N.L.... On-base percentage leading off innings was 2d highest in N.L.... His .500 career average with the bases loaded (18-for-36) is highest in majors since 1975 among players with 15 bases-loaded hits; top five among active players: Jose, Pat Tabler (.489), Sandy Alomar (.476), Dave Magadan (.433), Frank Thomas (.429). Batted .467 with bags full last season (7-for-15), with four singles, a double, a triple, and a homer. The only other major leaguer to "hit for the cycle" with the bases loaded was Steve Sax.... Hit three homers in extra innings, tying Jeff Bagwell for most in majors.... With the Busch Stadium fences brought in last year, he became the first Cardinals player since the stadium opened in 1966 to hit at least 10 more homers at home than he did on the road.... Drove in 77 runs in 1991, followed by 75 last year. A rather modest achievement? We agree, but no St. Louis player has had three consecutive 75-RBI seasons since Ted Simmons did it for 10 years from 1971 to 1980.

David Justice — Bats Left

Atlanta Braves	AB	H	2B	3B	HR	RBI	BB	SO	BA	SA	OBA
Season	484	124	19	5	21	72	79	85	.256	.446	.359
vs. Left-Handers	159	45	9	1	5	17	16	28	.283	.447	.352
vs. Right-Handers	325	79	10	4	16	55	63	57	.243	.446	.362
vs. Ground-Ballers	203	60	11	2	8	33	37	32	.296	.488	.402
vs. Fly-Ballers	281	64	8	3	13	39	42	53	.228	.416	.326
Home Games	245	56	9	4	10	35	45	48	.229	.420	.346
Road Games	239	68	10	1	11	37	34	37	.285	.473	.373
Grass Fields	355	91	12	5	16	54	60	69	.256	.454	.363
Artificial Turf	129	33	7	0	5	18	19	16	.256	.426	.349
April	27	1	0	0	0	0	5	10	.037	.037	.188
May	99	23	3	0	4	11	17	18	.232	.384	.347
June	86	25	4	1	4	19	15	13	.291	.500	.388
July	90	25	5	1	1	7	12	11	.278	.389	.362
August	98	28	4	2	4	13	13	16	.286	.490	.369
Sept./Oct.	84	22	3	1	8	22	17	17	.262	.607	.382
Leading Off Inn.	119	22	4	2	3		15	26	.185	.328	.281
Runners On	230	67	9	3	13	64	53	32	.291	.526	.415
Bases Empty	254	57	10	2	8	8	26	53	.224	.374	.301
Runners/Scor. Pos.	127	29	6	2	7	50	41	22	.228	.402	.402
Runners On/2 Out	109	32	4	1	9	26	25	13	.294	.596	.425
Scor. Pos./2 Out	64	12	1	0	6	18	17	10	.188	.484	.358
Late-Inning Pressure	56	15	4	1	2	5	7	13	.268	.482	.344
Leading Off	11	5	1	1	1		2	1	.455	1.000	.538
Runners On	23	5	1	0	1	4	5	6	.217	.391	.345
Runners/Scor. Pos.	10	2	1	0	1	4	5	2	.200	.600	.438

RUNS BATTED IN	From 1B	From 2B	From 3B	Scoring Position
Totals	13/162	14/98	24/52	38/150
Percentage	8.0%	14.3%	46.2%	25.3%

Loves to face: Kevin Gross (.600, 6-for-10, 2 HR)
Danny Jackson (.333, 5-for-15, 2 HR)
Lee Smith (3-for-3, 1 2B, 1 3B)

Hates to face: Pete Harnisch (.091, 2-for-22, 1 2B, 1 HR, 3 BB)
Greg W. Harris (.091, 1-for-11)
Jose Rijo (.125, 3-for-24, 2 2B, 5 BB)

Miscellaneous statistics: Ground outs-to-air outs ratio: 0.76 last season, 0.71 for career.... Grounded into 1 double play in 105 opportunities, best rate in majors.... Drove in 17 of 22 runners from third base with less than two outs (77%), 2d-highest rate in N.L.... Direction of balls hit to the outfield: 20% to left field, 24% to center, 56% to right.... Base running: Advanced from first base to third on 8 of 28 outfield singles (29%); scored from second on 12 of 16 (75%).... Made 2.35 putouts per nine innings in right field, highest rate in majors.

Comments: Owns .316 career batting average with runners on base, .229 mark with bases empty. That 87-point difference is the largest of its kind among active players (minimum: 500 AB in each situation).... He's the left-handed hitter in the majors least put out by a change to a left-handed reliever; career figures: batting .254, slugging .479, one homer every 18.7 at-bats vs. right-handers; .301, .505, one every 20.7 vs. left-handers.... Career batting average with runners in scoring position: .365 with less than two outs, .211 with two outs.... Had uncommon success in the first inning of games last season: batted .404 with five homers, 20 RBIs in 52 at-bats. Among all major league players (minimum: 50 plate appearances), only Mike Felder (.434) had a higher first-inning batting average.... On-base percentage when leading off an inning was 2d-lowest in National League.... Made eight errors, most by an N.L. outfielder.... Had perhaps the least-important two-homer game in postseason history in Game 6 of the 1992 N.L. Championship Series. Bucs won that night, 13–4, but Justice joined Bob Elliott as the only Braves ever to hit two homers in a postseason game. A little difference in the pitchers they connected off: Justice hit his off 55-mph knuckleballer Tim Wakefield, while Elliott connected twice off Bob Feller in Game 5 of 1948 World Series.... World Series homer was the sixth of his postseason career, tying Hank Aaron for the most in Braves history.

Eric Karros — Bats Right

Los Angeles Dodgers	AB	H	2B	3B	HR	RBI	BB	SO	BA	SA	OBA
Season	545	140	30	1	20	88	37	103	.257	.426	.304
vs. Left-Handers	213	59	10	0	8	32	16	26	.277	.437	.325
vs. Right-Handers	332	81	20	1	12	56	21	77	.244	.419	.291
vs. Ground-Ballers	193	49	9	0	7	29	12	35	.254	.409	.300
vs. Fly-Ballers	352	91	21	1	13	59	25	68	.259	.435	.306
Home Games	251	65	14	1	6	35	23	45	.259	.394	.320
Road Games	294	75	16	0	14	53	14	58	.255	.452	.289
Grass Fields	388	102	23	1	13	62	30	72	.263	.428	.316
Artificial Turf	157	38	7	0	7	26	7	31	.242	.420	.273
April	35	10	2	0	2	6	2	5	.286	.514	.316
May	58	15	3	0	4	12	3	13	.259	.517	.290
June	106	29	5	0	3	9	6	20	.274	.406	.307
July	119	29	5	1	6	20	4	18	.244	.454	.280
August	106	24	3	0	3	21	11	22	.226	.387	.299
Sept./Oct.	121	33	7	0	2	20	11	25	.273	.380	.331
Leading Off Inn.	131	40	8	0	3	3	5	13	.305	.435	.331
Runners On	261	64	16	1	9	77	24	54	.245	.418	.306
Bases Empty	284	76	14	0	11	11	13	49	.268	.433	.302
Runners/Scor. Pos.	172	40	10	1	4	65	21	34	.233	.372	.312
Runners On/2 Out	129	22	4	0	2	23	13	30	.171	.248	.246
Scor. Pos./2 Out	86	15	3	0	0	18	11	17	.174	.209	.268
Late-Inning Pressure	91	19	4	0	4	12	8	24	.209	.385	.273
Leading Off	20	5	0	0	0		1	3	.250	.250	.286
Runners On	47	8	2	0	3	11	5	12	.170	.404	.250
Runners/Scor. Pos.	27	3	1	0	1	7		4	.111	.259	.226

RUNS BATTED IN	From 1B	From 2B	From 3B	Scoring Position
Totals	13/159	22/133	33/86	55/219
Percentage	8.2%	16.5%	38.4%	25.1%

Loves to face: Bruce Hurst (.600, 6-for-10)
Danny Jackson (.556, 5-for-9)
Jimmy Jones (.833, 5-for-6)

Hates to face: Rheal Cormier (0-for-11)
Butch Henry (.091, 1-for-11)
Greg Maddux (0-for-7)

Miscellaneous statistics: Ground outs-to-air outs ratio: 0.88 last season, 0.85 for career.... Grounded into 15 double plays in 95 opportunities (one per 6.3).... Drove in 24 of 49 runners from third base with less than two outs (49%).... Direction of balls hit to the outfield: 41% to left field, 30% to center, 28% to right.... Base running: Advanced from first base to third on 6 of 20 outfield singles (30%); scored from second on 8 of 16 (50%), 5th-lowest rate in N.L.... Made 0.94 assists per nine innings at first base, highest rate in N.L.

Comments: The only Dodgers player to reach double figures in home runs; the last time the Dodgers did not have at least two players reach double figures in home runs was in 1968, when Len Gabrielson led with 10 homers. Karros hit 20; Dave Hansen and Mitch Webster led his teammates with six. Last team with a 20-home run hitter but no one else with more than six: 1981 Mets (Dave Kingman 22, Lee Mazzilli 6 in the strike-interrupted season); last time it happened in a full season: Houston in 1968 (Jim Wynn, 26; Denis Menke, Norm Miller, Doug Rader, and Rusty Staub, 6 each).... Hit only six of his 20 home runs at Dodger Stadium, but that was still twice as many as any of his teammates. Darryl Strawberry came next in line with three.... Led N.L. with 55 RBIs after the All-Star break; was the only major leaguer to drive in at least 20 runs in each of the last three months of the season.... Led all major league rookies in home runs, RBIs, extra-base hits, and doubles.... Dodgers rookies combined for a total of 341 starts, tying Angels rookies for most in the majors.... Who was the last Dodgers rookie to play as many games at first base as Karros? Answer below.... Had only three hits in first 43 at-bats with runners in scoring position and two outs, but had 12 hits in last 43 at-bats in those situations.... Batted .625 (10-for-16) with the bases loaded, tying Eddie Murray for the most bases-loaded hits in N.L.... Played 143 games at first base, the most by a Dodgers rookie since Jackie Robinson broke in with 151 games at first base in 1947.

Jeff Kent
Bats Right

Blue Jays/Mets	AB	H	2B	3B	HR	RBI	BB	SO	BA	SA	OBA
Season	305	73	21	2	11	50	27	76	.239	.430	.312
vs. Left-Handers	92	20	5	0	3	14	10	20	.217	.370	.291
vs. Right-Handers	213	53	16	2	8	36	17	56	.249	.455	.321
vs. Ground-Ballers	146	35	10	1	7	27	14	33	.240	.466	.325
vs. Fly-Ballers	159	38	11	1	4	23	13	43	.239	.396	.299
Home Games	167	40	14	1	4	20	18	39	.240	.407	.317
Road Games	138	33	7	1	7	30	9	37	.239	.457	.305
Grass Fields	144	38	7	2	7	29	8	41	.264	.486	.318
Artificial Turf	161	35	14	0	4	21	19	35	.217	.379	.306
April	19	5	3	0	1	3	4	5	.263	.579	.400
May	10	3	2	0	0	1	2	2	.300	.500	.417
June	61	16	4	1	2	9	8	14	.262	.459	.366
July	65	12	3	0	2	14	5	16	.185	.323	.247
August	61	14	2	1	4	12	1	18	.230	.492	.262
Sept./Oct.	89	23	7	0	2	11	7	21	.258	.404	.320
Leading Off Inn.	67	22	7	0	2	2	5	17	.328	.522	.375
Runners On	150	35	11	2	6	45	8	37	.233	.453	.287
Bases Empty	155	38	10	0	5	5	19	39	.245	.406	.335
Runners/Scor. Pos.	90	23	7	2	5	42	7	21	.256	.544	.324
Runners On/2 Out	67	9	2	0	1	8	3	22	.134	.209	.171
Scor. Pos./2 Out	47	6	2	0	1	8	2	15	.128	.234	.163
Late-Inning Pressure	42	12	4	0	3	9	1	13	.286	.595	.318
Leading Off	7	3	2	0	0	0	0	2	.429	.714	.429
Runners On	20	6	2	0	2	8	0	6	.300	.700	.333
Runners/Scor. Pos.	16	5	2	0	2	8	0	5	.313	.813	.313

RUNS BATTED IN	From 1B	From 2B	From 3B	Scoring Position
Totals	8/98	13/73	18/39	31/112
Percentage	8.2%	17.8%	46.2%	27.7%

Loves to face: Doug Drabek (2-for-2, 1 2B)

Hates to face: Rob Dibble (0-for-4, 3 SO)
Chris Hammond (0-for-5)
Danny Jackson (0-for-5)

Miscellaneous statistics: Ground outs-to-air outs ratio: 0.79 last season, 0.79 for career.... Grounded into 5 double plays in 64 opportunities (one per 13).... Drove in 16 of 19 runners from third base with less than two outs (84%), 2nd-highest rate in majors.... Direction of balls hit to the outfield: 53% to left field, 28% to center, 19% to right.... Base running: Advanced from first base to third on 9 of 24 outfield singles (38%); scored from second on 5 of 8 (63%).... Made 1.90 assists per nine innings at third base.

Comments: Bud Harrelson, who scouted A.L. East for the Mets last season, must have submitted a glowing report on Kent based on his performance against that other New York club. He hit three homers in 33 at-bats against the Yankees, while averaging one every 34 at-bats against the rest of the majors.... Hit his first major league home run off Lee Guetterman last April and was his teammate on the Mets by the end of August.... Selected by the Blue Jays in 20th round of 1989 June draft. Joe Vitko is the only one of the Mets' choices in that draft to have already appeared in a major league game.... Compiled .257 average in three minor league seasons, but never played Triple-A ball. Made jump from Knoxville (Double-A) in 1991 to Toronto's 1992 opening-day roster on the strength of a strong spring training (.375, 15-for-40, 1 HR).... One of four rookies to play at least one game at all four infield positions last season. The others: Boston's Scott Cooper, Seattle's Rich Amaral, and Jeff McKnight of Mets.... Highest strikeout rates among major league rookies last season (minimum: 250 plate appearances): Eddie Taubensee (one SO every 4.2 PA); Reggie Sanders (4.5); Kent (4.5); Todd Hundley (5.1).... Mets' acquisitions over the past two years are heavy on guys who had played mostly or exclusively in the American League, including Eddie Murray, Bret Saberhagen, Bill Pecota, Dave Gallagher, Tony Fernandez, Joe Orsulak, Paul Gibson, Willie Randolph, Dick Schofield, Lee Guetterman, Frank Tanana, and Jeff Kent.

Jeff King
Bats Right

Pittsburgh Pirates	AB	H	2B	3B	HR	RBI	BB	SO	BA	SA	OBA
Season	480	111	21	2	14	65	27	56	.231	.371	.272
vs. Left-Handers	216	51	12	2	6	32	13	18	.236	.394	.277
vs. Right-Handers	264	60	9	0	8	33	14	38	.227	.352	.269
vs. Ground-Ballers	153	28	2	1	2	13	8	20	.183	.248	.227
vs. Fly-Ballers	327	83	19	1	12	52	19	36	.254	.428	.293
Home Games	247	59	12	0	6	37	14	26	.239	.360	.280
Road Games	233	52	9	2	8	28	13	30	.223	.382	.264
Grass Fields	135	34	8	1	4	19	7	18	.252	.415	.285
Artificial Turf	345	77	13	1	10	46	20	38	.223	.354	.268
April	50	9	0	2	0	2	5	4	.180	.260	.255
May	98	23	4	0	4	11	4	12	.235	.398	.262
June	65	8	1	0	2	7	2	9	.123	.231	.162
July	53	14	3	0	2	6	4	7	.264	.434	.310
August	97	28	8	0	3	17	4	11	.289	.464	.314
Sept./Oct.	117	29	5	0	3	22	8	13	.248	.368	.297
Leading Off Inn.	117	28	5	0	6	6	1	10	.239	.436	.246
Runners On	227	51	11	1	2	53	15	32	.225	.308	.273
Bases Empty	253	60	10	1	12	12	12	24	.237	.427	.272
Runners/Scor. Pos.	149	34	5	1	1	45	10	24	.228	.295	.277
Runners On/2 Out	96	20	3	0	0	15	12	15	.208	.240	.309
Scor. Pos./2 Out	67	14	1	0	0	13	8	13	.209	.224	.312
Late-Inning Pressure	79	18	3	0	3	12	5	13	.228	.380	.274
Leading Off	25	6	1	0	1	1	0	2	.240	.400	.240
Runners On	38	8	1	0	0	9	2	7	.211	.237	.250
Runners/Scor. Pos.	28	7	1	0	0	9	2	6	.250	.286	.300

RUNS BATTED IN	From 1B	From 2B	From 3B	Scoring Position
Totals	8/157	23/124	20/55	43/179
Percentage	5.1%	18.5%	36.4%	24.0%

Loves to face: Steve Avery (.455, 5-for-11, 3 2B, 1 HR)
Pete Schourek (.333, 6-for-18, 1 HR)
Steve Wilson (.333, 5-for-15, 2 HR)

Hates to face: Dennis Martinez (.133, 2-for-15)
Chris Nabholz (.133, 2-for-15)
Mel Rojas (0-for-8)

Miscellaneous statistics: Ground outs-to-air outs ratio: 0.74 last season, 0.80 for career.... Grounded into 8 double plays in 103 opportunities (one per 13).... Drove in 16 of 26 runners from third base with less than two outs (62%).... Direction of balls hit to the outfield: 42% to left field, 33% to center, 26% to right.... Base running: Advanced from first base to third on 14 of 28 outfield singles (50%); scored from second on 11 of 13 (85%).... Made 2.21 assists per nine innings at third base, 3d-highest rate in N.L.

Comments: Demoted to Buffalo on Independence Day with a .187 batting average; recalled after 10 days, he went 0-for-8 dropping his average to its nadir (.181) on the Sunday after the All-Star Game. After that, he batted .277; he collected 39 RBIs after August 1, just two fewer than that Bonds guy.... Batted .152 with runners in scoring position through July 21; .289 in those situations over the balance of the season.... Had three game-winning RBIs in extra innings, one behind major league leader Jeff Bagwell.... Made 64 starts at third base, 30 at first, 23 at second, and three at shortstop last season; Rene Gonzales and Jeff McKnight were the only other players to start at all four infield positions.... King was not only all over the infield, but all over the batting order as well; he started at least two games from every batting order position with the exception of the ninth spot last season; only one other N.L. player did that (Reggie Sanders).... Had the lowest on-base percentage among qualifiers for N.L. batting title.... His .227 batting average vs. right-handers was a career *high*.... Rate of walks last season (one every 19.3 plate appearances) was less than half of his 1991 rate (one every 8.9 PA).... Helped Mickey Morandini earn his 15 minutes of fame as King joined the exclusive "I Hit Into an Unassisted Triple Play Club." The other members: Amby McConnell, Frank Brower, Walter Holke, Jim Bottomley, Paul Waner, Homer Summa, and Jose Azcue. Hey, 25 percent of them made the Hall of Fame!

John Kruk

Bats Left

Philadelphia Phillies	AB	H	2B	3B	HR	RBI	BB	SO	BA	SA	OBA
Season	507	164	30	4	10	70	92	88	.323	.458	.423
vs. Left-Handers	210	66	9	1	1	18	37	42	.314	.381	.414
vs. Right-Handers	297	98	21	3	9	52	55	46	.330	.512	.430
vs. Ground-Ballers	224	76	15	2	6	37	38	38	.339	.504	.432
vs. Fly-Ballers	283	88	15	2	4	33	54	50	.311	.420	.416
Home Games	248	76	11	1	7	37	46	39	.306	.444	.409
Road Games	259	88	19	3	3	33	46	49	.340	.471	.437
Grass Fields	134	43	8	1	3	17	29	29	.321	.463	.442
Artificial Turf	373	121	22	3	7	53	63	59	.324	.456	.416
April	81	33	3	1	0	16	11	12	.407	.469	.468
May	87	31	4	0	4	14	19	16	.356	.540	.472
June	85	29	8	1	1	7	12	11	.341	.494	.418
July	90	23	5	0	3	14	27	25	.256	.411	.420
August	86	24	5	0	1	9	12	11	.279	.372	.366
Sept./Oct.	78	24	5	2	1	10	11	13	.308	.462	.393
Leading Off Inn.	118	41	9	1	2	2	13	21	.347	.492	.412
Runners On	242	80	13	1	4	64	54	42	.331	.442	.442
Bases Empty	265	84	17	3	6	6	38	46	.317	.472	.405
Runners/Scor. Pos.	135	41	4	0	4	60	43	23	.304	.422	.454
Runners On/2 Out	104	32	6	1	1	22	27	19	.308	.413	.450
Scor. Pos./2 Out	64	19	2	0	1	19	21	11	.297	.375	.471
Late-Inning Pressure	80	27	7	0	0	5	14	14	.338	.425	.432
Leading Off	23	10	3	0	0	0	3	3	.435	.565	.500
Runners On	36	10	1	0	0	5	7	8	.278	.306	.386
Runners/Scor. Pos.	18	3	0	0	0	5	4	5	.167	.167	.304

RUNS BATTED IN	From 1B	From 2B	From 3B	Scoring Position
Totals	8/181	20/98	32/61	52/159
Percentage	4.4%	20.4%	52.5%	32.7%

Loves to face: John Burkett (.429, 9-for-21, 2 HR)
Randy Myers (.438, 7-for-16)
Francisco Oliveras (.600, 3-for-5, 2 HR)

Hates to face: Frank DiPino (.111, 2-for-18, 9 SO)
Lee Smith (0-for-15)
Zane Smith (.194, 6-for-31)

Miscellaneous statistics: Ground outs-to-air outs ratio: 1.76 last season, 1.50 for career.... Grounded into 11 double plays in 129 opportunities (one per 12).... Drove in 24 of 34 runners from third base with less than two outs (71%).... Direction of balls hit to the outfield: 45% to left field, 31% to center, 25% to right.... Base running: Advanced from first base to third on 13 of 39 outfield singles (33%); scored from second on 7 of 17 (41%), 2d-lowest rate in N.L.... Made 0.54 assists per nine innings at first base, lowest rate in N.L.

Comments: What do George Bush, the Houston Oilers, and Kruk have in common? Besides a late-night craving for pork rinds?... Bush blew a 50-point lead, Houston blew a 32-point lead, and Kruk blew a 46-point lead. Kruk led N.L. in batting from April 22 to August 10 (except for July 28, when Andy Van Slyke was king for a day) in bid to become Phillies' first N.L. batting champion since Richie Ashburn in 1958; his widest lead was 46 points on May 12, and he still led by 36 points on June 29. Gary Sheffield overtook him in August, and except for two days in the last week of August, Kruk never had the lead again.... Consolation prize: He did lead N.L. in batting in road games (.340) and in day games (.350).... Career-high batting average may have cost him in the power department. Although his average jumped from .294 to .323, his slugging percentage dipped by nearly the same amount (from .483 to .458) and his home-run total fell from 21 to 10. In the process, he became first N.L. player since Tom Haller (1967–68) to increase his batting average and decrease his slugging percentage, each by at least 25 points, from one qualifying season (502 PA) to the next.... Career breakdown: .311 on artificial turf, .279 on grass fields.... Has lowest error rate (one error every 212 chances) of any first baseman in Phillies history (minimum: 200 games).... Listed at 5'10", he was the shortest player to appear in more than 25 games at first base last season. It's a good bet he wasn't the lightest.

Ray Lankford

Bats Left

St. Louis Cardinals	AB	H	2B	3B	HR	RBI	BB	SO	BA	SA	OBA
Season	598	175	40	6	20	86	72	147	.293	.480	.371
vs. Left-Handers	216	55	11	2	4	32	27	61	.255	.380	.345
vs. Right-Handers	382	120	29	4	16	54	45	86	.314	.537	.385
vs. Ground-Ballers	252	76	13	2	10	38	29	51	.302	.488	.381
vs. Fly-Ballers	346	99	27	4	10	48	43	96	.286	.474	.363
Home Games	314	97	18	3	13	54	35	70	.309	.510	.375
Road Games	284	78	22	3	7	32	37	77	.275	.447	.366
Grass Fields	151	44	13	2	3	17	20	39	.291	.464	.376
Artificial Turf	447	131	27	4	17	69	52	108	.293	.485	.369
April	89	24	2	1	2	4	14	20	.270	.382	.387
May	103	32	6	1	3	13	11	25	.311	.476	.377
June	103	28	7	2	3	13	12	24	.272	.466	.345
July	95	32	12	0	3	13	9	26	.337	.558	.394
August	103	30	7	0	3	20	8	28	.291	.447	.342
Sept./Oct.	105	29	6	2	6	23	18	24	.276	.543	.381
Leading Off Inn.	178	47	5	2	5	5	13	43	.264	.399	.314
Runners On	241	77	18	3	11	77	42	62	.320	.556	.419
Bases Empty	357	98	22	3	9	9	30	85	.275	.429	.334
Runners/Scor. Pos.	162	53	13	2	7	67	28	44	.327	.562	.421
Runners On/2 Out	89	29	7	2	3	31	21	24	.326	.551	.459
Scor. Pos./2 Out	69	24	6	2	2	29	18	18	.348	.580	.489
Late-Inning Pressure	116	34	5	0	5	16	19	34	.293	.466	.391
Leading Off	35	8	0	0	1	1	0	8	.229	.314	.229
Runners On	44	14	2	0	1	12	15	15	.318	.432	.484
Runners/Scor. Pos.	29	10	2	0	1	12	9	10	.345	.517	.488

RUNS BATTED IN	From 1B	From 2B	From 3B	Scoring Position
Totals	12/131	36/136	18/48	54/184
Percentage	9.2%	26.5%	37.5%	29.3%

Loves to face: Tommy Greene (.389, 7-for-18, 2 2B, 1 3B, 2 HR)
Kevin Gross (.462, 6-for-13, 3 2B, 1 HR)
Chris Nabholz (.500, 8-for-16)

Hates to face: Frank Castillo (.125, 2-for-16)
Dave Righetti (0-for-6)
Randy Tomlin (.125, 2-for-16)

Miscellaneous statistics: Ground outs-to-air outs ratio: 0.69 last season, 0.91 for career.... Grounded into 5 double plays in 106 opportunities (one per 21).... Drove in 13 of 30 runners from third base with less than two outs (43%).... Direction of balls hit to the outfield: 38% to left field, 30% to center, 33% to right.... Base running: Advanced from first base to third on 12 of 32 outfield singles (38%); scored from second on 15 of 19 (79%).... Made 2.88 putouts per nine innings in center field.

Comments: Had 43 RBIs from August 1 to the end of the season; Terry Pendleton (46) was the only N.L. player with more.... Has some fine clutch-hitting numbers. Let's start with his .332 career average with runners on base and two outs (63-for-190) and his three consecutive .300 seasons in that category.... Then there's his .304 career average with runners on base, compared to .253 with the bases empty.... Not to mention his .417 career batting average with two outs and runners in scoring position in Late-Inning Pressure Situations, the highest among active players.... Ranked second among N.L. center fielders with 66 extra-base hits, behind Andy Van Slyke (71); that total led all major league sophomores.... Became only the second Cardinals hitter ever to lead N.L. in strikeouts; big Steve Bilko led in 1953.... Caught stealing 24 times, most in the majors. His stolen base percentage (.636 with 42 steals) was the lowest by a 40-base stealer since 1923, when George Grantham of the Cubs (.606) and Eddie Collins of the White Sox (.618) had lower marks.... Friendlier Busch Stadium confines contributed to both Lankford and Felix Jose hitting more homers there than on the road last year. Only one St. Louis player over the previous five years had hit at least five more homers at Busch than on the road: Terry Pendleton, who hit all six of his homers at home in 1990. Last season, Busch had a negligible effect on home runs (see page 331), after suppressing them by 22.5 percent over the previous five years.

Barry Larkin — Bats Right

Cincinnati Reds	AB	H	2B	3B	HR	RBI	BB	SO	BA	SA	OBA
Season	533	162	32	6	12	78	63	58	.304	.454	.377
vs. Left-Handers	200	71	20	4	6	29	33	18	.355	.585	.443
vs. Right-Handers	333	91	12	2	6	49	30	40	.273	.375	.336
vs. Ground-Ballers	214	61	14	3	5	37	16	26	.285	.449	.329
vs. Fly-Ballers	319	101	18	3	7	41	47	32	.317	.458	.408
Home Games	254	78	14	2	8	53	34	29	.307	.472	.389
Road Games	279	84	18	4	4	25	29	29	.301	.437	.366
Grass Fields	154	38	8	2	2	12	13	17	.247	.364	.304
Artificial Turf	379	124	24	4	10	66	50	41	.327	.491	.405
April	39	7	0	1	1	5	6	6	.179	.308	.319
May	86	26	5	0	1	9	5	14	.302	.395	.341
June	103	25	6	0	2	16	10	13	.243	.359	.307
July	95	37	9	2	3	14	13	9	.389	.621	.464
August	109	37	8	1	3	16	21	7	.339	.514	.443
Sept./Oct.	101	30	4	2	2	18	8	9	.297	.436	.339
Leading Off Inn.	99	26	0	3	4	4	10	13	.263	.444	.336
Runners On	236	79	15	2	4	70	36	25	.335	.466	.414
Bases Empty	297	83	17	4	8	8	27	33	.279	.444	.346
Runners/Scor. Pos.	145	49	8	1	2	65	27	17	.338	.448	.428
Runners On/2 Out	66	21	4	0	0	17	16	7	.318	.379	.458
Scor. Pos./2 Out	44	15	3	0	0	17	13	6	.341	.409	.500
Late-Inning Pressure	66	17	3	1	0	9	11	8	.258	.333	.359
Leading Off	20	3	0	1	0	0	3	5	.150	.250	.261
Runners On	26	9	1	0	0	9	6	1	.346	.385	.455
Runners/Scor. Pos.	16	7	1	0	0	9	5	1	.438	.500	.545

RUNS BATTED IN	From 1B	From 2B	From 3B	Scoring Position
Totals	5/162	25/113	36/60	61/173
Percentage	3.1%	22.1%	60.0%	35.3%

Loves to face: Steve Avery (.425, 17-for-40, 1 HR, 0 SO)
Butch Henry (.714, 5-for-7, 1 HR)
Zane Smith (.447, 17-for-38, 3 HR)
Hates to face: Jeff Brantley (.083, 1-for-12)
Marvin Freeman (0-for-13)
Mark Portugal (.071, 1-for-14)

Miscellaneous statistics: Ground outs-to-air outs ratio: 1.23 last season, 1.17 for career.... Grounded into 13 double plays in 121 opportunities (one per 9.3).... Drove in 26 of 38 runners from third base with less than two outs (68%).... Direction of balls hit to the outfield: 30% to left field, 32% to center, 38% to right.... Base running: Advanced from first base to third on 14 of 31 outfield singles (45%); scored from second on 10 of 11 (91%), 3d-highest rate in N.L.... Made 3.04 assists per nine innings at shortstop.

Comments: Became the fifth Reds player since 1900 to hit .300 in each of four consecutive seasons of at least 300 at-bats. The others: Pete Rose (twice), Edd Roush (twice), Ernie Lombardi, and Ted Kluszewski.... Yearly batting averages since 1990: .301, .302, .304. Actually, his .301 was .3013 and his .304 was .3039, meaning that his last three season averages have been separated by only .0026.... Only two other players in this century have produced such tightly bunched batting averages in three successive seasons of .300 or better (minimum: 450 at-bats): Harvey Kuenn (.308, .306, .306, an actual separation of 1.4 points, 1953–55), and Keith Hernandez (.311, .309, .310, a separation of 2.3 points, 1984–86).... Has a perfect career stolen-base log against Houston: 24-for-24, the most steals without being caught by any active player against any opponent; next come Marquis Grissom vs. Atlanta and Eric Davis vs. Philadelphia, both 19-for-19.... Among players with at least 600 at-bats vs. left-handers since 1975, only Kirby Puckett (.340) has hit them better than Larkin (.323). Had 4th-highest average in N.L. vs left-handed pitchers last season.... Career batting breakdown: .296 at Riverfront, .296 on the road.... Has started at shortstop on opening day for the Reds six straight years, following right on the heels of Dave Concepcion's 13-year streak from 1974–86. So who was the last Reds shortstop other than Concepcion or Larkin to start a season opener? Darrell Chaney in 1973.

Mike LaValliere — Bats Left

Pittsburgh Pirates	AB	H	2B	3B	HR	RBI	BB	SO	BA	SA	OBA
Season	293	75	13	1	2	29	44	21	.256	.328	.350
vs. Left-Handers	31	5	0	1	0	5	5	5	.161	.226	.297
vs. Right-Handers	262	70	13	0	2	24	39	16	.267	.340	.356
vs. Ground-Ballers	118	28	6	0	0	6	23	7	.237	.288	.357
vs. Fly-Ballers	175	47	7	1	2	23	21	14	.269	.354	.345
Home Games	135	35	2	1	1	16	26	12	.259	.311	.373
Road Games	158	40	11	0	1	13	18	9	.253	.342	.328
Grass Fields	70	21	6	0	1	6	10	5	.300	.429	.387
Artificial Turf	223	54	7	1	1	23	34	16	.242	.296	.338
April	39	12	2	1	0	4	5	4	.308	.410	.378
May	41	9	1	0	0	1	11	2	.220	.244	.385
June	56	11	3	0	1	9	8	5	.196	.304	.284
July	56	16	2	0	0	1	5	4	.286	.321	.344
August	46	17	4	0	1	10	6	3	.370	.522	.434
Sept./Oct.	55	10	1	0	0	4	9	3	.182	.200	.308
Leading Off Inn.	57	17	2	0	0	0	8	4	.298	.333	.385
Runners On	124	32	4	1	2	29	24	13	.258	.355	.370
Bases Empty	169	43	9	0	0	0	20	8	.254	.308	.333
Runners/Scor. Pos.	71	18	4	1	0	25	21	7	.254	.338	.408
Runners On/2 Out	46	9	1	1	1	11	13	5	.196	.326	.383
Scor. Pos./2 Out	25	5	1	1	0	9	12	2	.200	.320	.474
Late-Inning Pressure	41	10	2	0	0	5	9	4	.244	.293	.380
Leading Off	8	2	1	0	0	0	4	0	.250	.375	.500
Runners On	10	3	1	0	0	5	4	2	.300	.400	.500
Runners/Scor. Pos.	9	3	1	0	0	5	4	2	.333	.444	.538

RUNS BATTED IN	From 1B	From 2B	From 3B	Scoring Position
Totals	4/95	9/54	14/35	23/89
Percentage	4.2%	16.7%	40.0%	25.8%

Loves to face: Frank Castillo (.500, 8-for-16)
Tommy Greene (.444, 8-for-18)
John Smoltz (.550, 11-for-20, 1 HR, 0 SO)
Hates to face: Frank DiPino (.111, 2-for-18)
Scott Terry (.100, 1-for-10)
Bob Tewksbury (.138, 4-for-29)

Miscellaneous statistics: Ground outs-to-air outs ratio: 1.04 last season, 1.04 for career.... Grounded into 8 double plays in 70 opportunities (one per 8.8).... Drove in 12 of 23 runners from third base with less than two outs (52%).... Direction of balls hit to the outfield: 40% to left field, 33% to center, 27% to right.... Base running: Advanced from first base to third on 0 of 17 outfield singles (0%), worst rate in majors; scored from second on 1 of 6 (17%).... Opposing base stealers: 71-for-115 (62%), 5th-lowest rate in N.L.

Comments: Has a chance to challenge Johnny Edwards's standing as the N.L. catcher with the lowest career error rate. Edwards made one error for every 118.4 chances; LaValliere has averaged one every 123.6 chances, but has played in only 709 games (1000 games are needed to qualify).... His last 117 starts (including all 87 in 1992) have come against right-handers; he hasn't been in the starting lineup against a lefty since August 8, 1991 vs. Frank Viola.... Pittsburgh has faced 13 left-handed starters in its 20 postseason games over the past three years; accordingly, Spanky has started only seven postseason games. Career breakdown: .277 vs. right-handers, .230 vs. left-handers.... Bucs pitchers had a 2.98 ERA in the 767 innings that he caught last season, 3.32 with Tom Prince (114 innings), 3.83 with Don Slaught (598⅔ innings).... Pirates catchers hit .285 last year, 2d highest in the majors to Twins' .298. Combined N.L. average by catchers was .245, the lowest of any position except for pitchers.... Owns .407 career batting average with the bases loaded (22-for-54), 4th highest among active players (minimum: 50 at-bats).... Had driven in at least 30 percent of runners from scoring position in each of last four years prior to 1992.... One of two players in the majors to hit at least one, but no more than three homers in each of the last seven years. The other: Dave Anderson. The longest such streak since the introduction of the lively ball (1920) is nine years by Don Blasingame (1958–66).

Mark Lemke — Bats Left and Right

Atlanta Braves	AB	H	2B	3B	HR	RBI	BB	SO	BA	SA	OBA
Season	427	97	7	4	6	26	50	39	.227	.304	.307
vs. Left-Handers	145	33	1	1	5	14	13	11	.228	.352	.289
vs. Right-Handers	282	64	6	3	1	12	37	28	.227	.280	.316
vs. Ground-Ballers	184	39	3	2	0	6	23	19	.212	.250	.300
vs. Fly-Ballers	243	58	4	2	6	20	27	20	.239	.346	.313
Home Games	222	50	5	0	4	13	25	20	.225	.302	.302
Road Games	205	47	2	4	2	13	25	19	.229	.307	.312
Grass Fields	321	75	5	2	4	17	40	31	.234	.299	.318
Artificial Turf	106	22	2	2	2	9	10	8	.208	.321	.274
April	45	10	1	0	0	2	3	4	.222	.244	.271
May	93	20	3	1	1	2	2	7	.215	.301	.232
June	76	19	0	1	1	3	10	7	.250	.316	.337
July	50	9	2	1	0	6	9	3	.180	.260	.300
August	87	27	1	0	3	7	11	6	.310	.425	.388
Sept./Oct.	76	12	0	1	1	6	15	12	.158	.224	.293
Leading Off Inn.	96	20	1	1	3	3	9	3	.208	.333	.276
Runners On	184	41	3	3	0	20	25	18	.223	.272	.313
Bases Empty	243	56	4	1	6	6	25	21	.230	.329	.302
Runners/Scor. Pos.	105	22	3	2	0	19	17	12	.210	.276	.315
Runners On/2 Out	79	15	1	2	0	9	14	9	.190	.253	.312
Scor. Pos./2 Out	58	9	1	1	0	8	11	6	.155	.207	.290
Late-Inning Pressure	58	13	2	1	0	5	13	6	.224	.293	.361
Leading Off	11	3	0	0	0	0	1	1	.273	.273	.333
Runners On	25	6	1	1	0	5	8	2	.240	.360	.412
Runners/Scor. Pos.	15	4	1	1	0	5	5	1	.267	.467	.429

RUNS BATTED IN	From 1B	From 2B	From 3B	Scoring Position
Totals	2/130	10/76	8/43	18/119
Percentage	1.5%	13.2%	18.6%	15.1%

Loves to face: Tom Browning (.267, 4-for-15, 1 HR)
Denny Neagle (.500, 2-for-4, 2 HR)
Wally Whitehurst (.625, 5-for-8, 2 3B)

Hates to face: John Burkett (.091, 1-for-11)
Danny Jackson (0-for-11)
Bob Tewksbury (.077, 1-for-13, 1 2B)

Miscellaneous statistics: Ground outs-to-air outs ratio: 1.07 last season, 1.12 for career.... Grounded into 9 double plays in 100 opportunities (one per 11).... Drove in 7 of 16 runners from third base with less than two outs (44%).... Direction of balls hit to the outfield: 34% to left field, 34% to center, 31% to right batting left-handed; 44% to left field, 33% to center, 23% to right batting right-handed.... Base running: Advanced from first base to third on 4 of 19 outfield singles (21%); scored from second on 6 of 13 (46%), 3d-lowest rate in N.L.... Made 2.75 assists per nine innings at second base.

Comments: Has the 2d-lowest career batting average (.2261) of any nonpitcher in Atlanta Braves history (minimum: 1000 at-bats); if he goes hitless in his first two at-bats of 1993, he'll pass Darrell Chaney (.2259) as low man on the totem pole.... Has played in more postseason games over the last two years than Willie Mays played in his entire career. Who said life is fair?...On the other hand, Lemke (.298 with nine RBIs in 26 games) has done more in his postseason opportunities than Willie (.247, 10 RBIs in 25 games) did with his (save for one catch of some renown). Lemke's totals include a 9-for-21 burst with runners in scoring position. Two players batted over .500 with runners in scoring position in postseason play (minimum: 15 at-bats): Marty Barrett (12-for-18) and Fred Lynn (9-for-15). Lemke is one of 12 players to hit .400 or better; the difference between him and the rest of those guys is that Lemmer's regular-season career average is .226; the lowest regular-season average by any of the others is .263 by Dave Lopes.... Batted .205 in night games last season, 3d lowest in N.L.; career figures: .271 in day games, .211 at night.... Collected five hits in 12 at-bats during extra innings last season.... Has never been hit by a pitch in 1189 career plate appearances. The top five players active in 1992, who've never been nailed: Herm Winningham, 2069 PA; Bob Melvin, 1870; Lemke, 1189; Nolan Ryan, 957; and Dave Clark, 848. If no one has nailed Nolan by now, he may be in the clear.

Darren Lewis — Bats Right

San Francisco Giants	AB	H	2B	3B	HR	RBI	BB	SO	BA	SA	OBA
Season	320	74	8	1	1	18	29	46	.231	.272	.295
vs. Left-Handers	125	27	3	0	1	5	12	16	.216	.264	.285
vs. Right-Handers	195	47	5	1	0	13	17	30	.241	.277	.302
vs. Ground-Ballers	159	36	6	1	0	9	14	18	.226	.277	.287
vs. Fly-Ballers	161	38	2	0	1	9	15	28	.236	.267	.303
Home Games	142	25	2	0	1	8	13	18	.176	.211	.248
Road Games	178	49	6	1	0	10	16	28	.275	.320	.333
Grass Fields	214	44	5	0	1	11	22	27	.206	.243	.282
Artificial Turf	106	30	3	1	0	7	7	19	.283	.330	.325
April	91	29	2	1	0	6	12	14	.319	.363	.398
May	87	15	0	0	0	4	6	14	.172	.172	.229
June	51	9	2	0	1	4	5	8	.176	.275	.250
July	11	1	0	0	0	0	1	1	.091	.091	.167
August	8	1	0	0	0	0	0	1	.125	.125	.125
Sept./Oct.	72	19	4	0	0	4	5	8	.264	.319	.312
Leading Off Inn.	129	29	1	1	1		15	18	.225	.271	.306
Runners On	83	21	2	0	0	17	6	9	.253	.277	.297
Bases Empty	237	53	6	1	1	1	23	37	.224	.270	.295
Runners/Scor. Pos.	59	16	1	0	0	17	3	9	.271	.288	.297
Runners On/2 Out	38	8	0	0	0	8	3	5	.211	.211	.268
Scor. Pos./2 Out	32	7	0	0	0	8	1	5	.219	.219	.242
Late-Inning Pressure	51	11	3	0	0	2	3	9	.216	.275	.259
Leading Off	14	3	1	0	0	0	0	4	.214	.286	.214
Runners On	19	2	0	0	0	2	1	1	.105	.105	.150
Runners/Scor. Pos.	13	1	0	0	0	2	1	1	.077	.077	.143

RUNS BATTED IN	From 1B	From 2B	From 3B	Scoring Position
Totals	0/42	7/49	10/22	17/71
Percentage	0.0%	14.3%	45.5%	23.9%

Loves to face: Brian Barnes (3-for-3, 2 2B)
Tom Browning (.462, 6-for-13)
Steve Wilson (3-for-3)

Hates to face: Kip Gross (.100, 1-for-10)
Orel Hershiser (0-for-9)
Lee Smith (0-for-5, 3 SO)

Miscellaneous statistics: Ground outs-to-air outs ratio: 1.56 last season, 1.60 for career.... Grounded into 3 double plays in 37 opportunities (one per 12).... Drove in 5 of 9 runners from third base with less than two outs (56%).... Direction of balls hit to the outfield: 18% to left field, 33% to center, 49% to right.... Base running: Advanced from first base to third on 6 of 17 outfield singles (35%); scored from second on 11 of 14 (79%).... Made 2.81 putouts per nine innings in center field.

Comments: Probably wished the Giants' proposed move to Florida had gone through; he batted .176 at Candlestick last year, the lowest mark in home games by any N.L. player. Career numbers: .202 at The Stick, .238 on other grass fields, .292 on artificial surfaces.... Led Giants with 77 starts in center field; only three other teams didn't have a center fielder who started a majority of its games: Red Sox, Cubs, and Reds.... Has played 185 major league games in the outfield and still has not made Error One. Doug Dascenzo went 242 games from the start of his career before making an error, a major league record; the record for consecutive errorless games by an outfielder (any time in his career) is 266 by Don Demeter (1962–65), who, like Lewis, crossed league lines.... Lewis was the only center fielder in the majors to play errorless ball last season (minimum: 81 games).... Batted .220 from the leadoff spot in the lineup, lowest in the majors (minimum: 250 leadoff at-bats).... Despite the fact that center fielders Lewis and Mike Felder usually batted in the leadoff spot, Giants' center fielders finished tied with San Diego for the fewest runs scored in the league last season (75).... Matched San Francisco record for fewest RBIs in a 300-at-bat season, shared by Matty Alou (1965) and Mike Felder (1991).... One of 16 players to have roamed the outfields on both sides of San Francisco Bay. Included among them are Giants manager Dusty Baker and all three Alou brothers.

Jose Lind
Bats Right

Pittsburgh Pirates	AB	H	2B	3B	HR	RBI	BB	SO	BA	SA	OBA
Season	468	110	14	1	0	39	26	29	.235	.269	.275
vs. Left-Handers	177	42	6	1	0	14	11	16	.237	.282	.277
vs. Right-Handers	291	68	8	0	0	25	15	13	.234	.261	.273
vs. Ground-Ballers	186	44	4	0	0	14	14	6	.237	.258	.294
vs. Fly-Ballers	282	66	10	1	0	25	12	23	.234	.277	.262
Home Games	229	58	7	1	0	24	16	14	.253	.293	.298
Road Games	239	52	7	0	0	15	10	15	.218	.247	.251
Grass Fields	114	24	2	0	0	6	5	8	.211	.228	.244
Artificial Turf	354	86	12	1	0	33	21	21	.243	.282	.284
April	56	9	0	1	0	4	2	0	.161	.196	.186
May	74	22	2	0	0	13	0	6	.297	.324	.289
June	93	25	5	0	0	7	9	8	.269	.323	.333
July	88	14	3	0	0	2	4	7	.159	.193	.196
August	94	24	3	0	0	7	7	5	.255	.287	.307
Sept./Oct.	63	16	1	0	0	6	4	3	.254	.270	.304
Leading Off Inn.	103	26	4	0	0	0	2	4	.252	.291	.267
Runners On	236	58	6	0	0	39	21	16	.246	.271	.305
Bases Empty	232	52	8	1	0	0	5	13	.224	.267	.241
Runners/Scor. Pos.	136	35	5	0	0	38	17	9	.257	.294	.331
Runners On/2 Out	104	24	3	0	0	20	16	6	.231	.260	.339
Scor. Pos./2 Out	65	16	3	0	0	20	14	4	.246	.292	.380
Late-Inning Pressure	71	14	2	0	0	3	4	4	.197	.225	.250
Leading Off	12	4	1	0	0	0	0	1	.333	.417	.333
Runners On	32	8	0	0	0	3	2	3	.250	.250	.314
Runners/Scor. Pos.	17	6	0	0	0	3	2	2	.353	.353	.421

RUNS BATTED IN	From 1B	From 2B	From 3B	Scoring Position
Totals	3/173	15/109	21/58	36/167
Percentage	1.7%	13.8%	36.2%	21.6%

Loves to face: Joe Boever (.444, 8-for-18)
Bob Ojeda (.348, 16-for-46)
Dennis Rasmussen (.412, 7-for-17, 2 2B)

Hates to face: Danny Darwin (0-for-6, 3 SO)
Derek Lilliquist (.091, 1-for-11)
Bill Sampen (.167, 2-for-12, 5 SO)

Miscellaneous statistics: Ground outs-to-air outs ratio: 1.41 last season, 1.41 for career.... Grounded into 14 double plays in 106 opportunities (one per 7.6).... Drove in 11 of 26 runners from third base with less than two outs (42%).... Direction of balls hit to the outfield: 24% to left field, 31% to center, 45% to right.... Base running: Advanced from first base to third on 3 of 12 outfield singles (25%); scored from second on 11 of 15 (73%).... Made 3.24 assists per nine innings at second base.

Comments: Committed only six errors last season and became the first Pittsburgh second baseman since Bill Mazeroski in 1966 to lead N.L. in fielding. But he'd surely like to have one October ground ball as a do-over.... Leaves Pirates as their all-time leader in fielding at second base (one error every 79 chances). Dave Cash ranks second (one every 65 chances), Mazeroski third (58).... Has hit .290 or higher in eight months in his major league career; four of the eight are Septembers. Career breakdown: .244 before September 1, .295 after.... One of four players who appeared in all 20 N.L. Championship Series games over the past three years; ranked by RBIs in those games: Lind, 10; Andy Van Slyke, 9; Jay Bell, 6; Barry Bonds, 3.... Drove in six runs in extra innings last season, one fewer than major league leader Jeff Bagwell.... Career breakdown: .255 vs. right-handers, .254 vs. lefties.... Toughest right-handed batter to strike out in N.L. last season, with career-best rate of one strikeout every 17.5 times up.... Batted .158 in day games, lowest in the majors.... Drove in 39 runs from the eighth spot in the lineup, the most in the league. This year, he'll get a shot at the nine hole.... Of 91 walks drawn over the past three years, 41 were intentional; the over/under in that category will drop considerably this year.... Joins Wally Joyner, Greg Gagne, and Gregg Jefferies as projected starters in the Royals' infield; all four have postseason experience with other clubs.

Dave Magadan
Bats Left

New York Mets	AB	H	2B	3B	HR	RBI	BB	SO	BA	SA	OBA
Season	321	91	9	1	3	28	56	44	.283	.346	.390
vs. Left-Handers	120	37	3	0	0	7	16	22	.308	.333	.390
vs. Right-Handers	201	54	6	1	3	21	40	22	.269	.353	.390
vs. Ground-Ballers	147	35	4	1	2	11	36	24	.238	.320	.388
vs. Fly-Ballers	174	56	5	0	1	17	20	20	.322	.368	.392
Home Games	153	48	5	1	2	13	30	16	.314	.399	.426
Road Games	168	43	4	0	1	15	26	28	.256	.298	.356
Grass Fields	222	67	5	1	2	17	38	28	.302	.360	.404
Artificial Turf	99	24	4	0	1	11	18	16	.242	.313	.359
April	63	20	4	0	0	5	5	13	.317	.381	.368
May	90	27	2	1	1	7	16	11	.300	.378	.406
June	59	14	1	0	0	6	17	7	.237	.254	.408
July	81	25	2	0	2	9	15	10	.309	.407	.417
August	28	5	0	0	0	1	3	3	.179	.179	.258
Sept./Oct.	0	0	0	0	0	0	0	0	.000	.000	.000
Leading Off Inn.	73	20	1	0	1	1	12	14	.274	.329	.376
Runners On	134	41	2	0	2	27	29	18	.306	.366	.429
Bases Empty	187	50	7	1	1	1	27	26	.267	.332	.360
Runners/Scor. Pos.	69	20	0	0	2	26	23	12	.290	.377	.467
Runners On/2 Out	64	19	1	0	2	16	12	8	.297	.406	.408
Scor. Pos./2 Out	35	11	0	0	2	16	9	7	.314	.486	.455
Late-Inning Pressure	43	14	0	0	2	6	15	8	.326	.465	.500
Leading Off	11	5	0	0	1	1	5	3	.455	.727	.625
Runners On	21	7	0	0	1	5	6	4	.333	.476	.481
Runners/Scor. Pos.	14	3	0	0	1	5	4	4	.214	.429	.389

RUNS BATTED IN	From 1B	From 2B	From 3B	Scoring Position
Totals	3/100	15/53	7/26	22/79
Percentage	3.0%	28.3%	26.9%	27.8%

Loves to face: Tim Belcher (.529, 9-for-17)
Bill Landrum (.714, 5-for-7)
Mike Morgan (.478, 11-for-23)

Hates to face: Andy Benes (.154, 2-for-13, 2 BB)
Bud Black (.077, 1-for-13)
Danny Jackson (0-for-7)

Miscellaneous statistics: Ground outs-to-air outs ratio: 1.59 last season, 1.22 for career.... Grounded into 6 double plays in 60 opportunities (one per 10).... Drove in 3 of 11 runners from third base with less than two outs (27%).... Direction of balls hit to the outfield: 36% to left field, 33% to center, 31% to right.... Base running: Advanced from first base to third on 7 of 25 outfield singles (28%); scored from second on 4 of 6 (67%).... Made 1.61 assists per nine innings at third base, lowest rate in N.L.

Comments: His .327 career average with runners on base is 6th best in majors since 1975, behind Rod Carew (.348), Wade Boggs (.345), Tony Gwynn (.344), Frank Thomas (.334), and Kirby Puckett (.330). Has driven in 32.8 percent of runners from scoring position in his career, 5th-highest rate among active N.L. players (minimum: 500 opportunities), behind Will Clark (33.4), Pedro Guerrero (33.3), Eddie Murray (33.0), and Mark Grace (32.8).... Averaged one error every 17 chances at third base last season, after a previous career rate of one error every 33 chances there.... Career breakdown: .299 vs. right-handers, .278 vs. left-handers.... Leaves Mets with .292 career batting average, 2d best in team history among players with 1000 at-bats. Keith Hernandez is the Mets' all-time leader at .2968, the 2d-lowest average to lead any of the 26 established franchises. The only other franchise without a career .300 hitter is Houston, where Bob Watson leads at .2965.... With Magadan, Mackey Sasser, and Kevin Elster gone, Howard Johnson is the only nonpitcher remaining from the Mets' 1988 postseason squad.... No player has ever hit .300 for a first-year expansion team that played its home games in a country whose President plays alto sax. Rusty Staub (.302 in 1969) and Bob Bailor (.310 in 1977) did it on the Expos and Blue Jays, respectively. For more expansion-team records, see the Florida essay on page 56.

Kirt Manwaring   Bats Right

San Francisco Giants	AB	H	2B	3B	HR	RBI	BB	SO	BA	SA	OBA
Season	349	85	10	5	4	26	29	42	.244	.335	.311
vs. Left-Handers	131	40	4	3	0	6	10	12	.305	.382	.355
vs. Right-Handers	218	45	6	2	4	20	19	30	.206	.307	.285
vs. Ground-Ballers	164	37	5	3	2	13	14	14	.226	.329	.294
vs. Fly-Ballers	185	48	5	2	2	13	15	28	.259	.341	.325
Home Games	168	39	8	3	1	15	10	16	.232	.333	.275
Road Games	181	46	2	2	3	11	19	26	.254	.337	.341
Grass Fields	258	65	8	3	3	21	16	30	.252	.341	.298
Artificial Turf	91	20	2	2	1	5	13	12	.220	.319	.343
April	53	14	0	0	0	5	3	5	.264	.264	.304
May	55	15	3	2	0	5	11	3	.273	.400	.412
June	74	20	1	2	1	6	6	11	.270	.378	.325
July	54	10	1	0	0	3	2	11	.185	.204	.214
August	64	14	3	1	2	5	5	7	.219	.391	.275
Sept./Oct.	49	12	2	0	1	2	2	5	.245	.347	.315
Leading Off Inn.	72	18	0	1	3	3	10	13	.250	.403	.357
Runners On	141	31	5	2	0	22	9	13	.220	.284	.276
Bases Empty	208	54	5	3	4	4	20	29	.260	.370	.333
Runners/Scor. Pos.	84	18	5	2	0	22	8	7	.214	.321	.283
Runners On/2 Out	64	12	2	1	0	8	5	5	.188	.250	.246
Scor. Pos./2 Out	42	7	2	1	0	8	4	4	.167	.262	.239
Late-Inning Pressure	68	13	2	1	1	5	8	11	.191	.294	.295
Leading Off	18	3	0	0	1	1	4	4	.167	.333	.348
Runners On	21	4	1	1	0	4	2	2	.190	.333	.292
Runners/Scor. Pos.	11	2	1	1	0	4	2	1	.182	.455	.308

RUNS BATTED IN	From 1B	From 2B	From 3B	Scoring Position
Totals	3/98	14/69	5/24	19/93
Percentage	3.1%	20.3%	20.8%	20.4%

Loves to face: Kyle Abbott (.556, 5-for-9)
Barry Jones (.600, 3-for-5, 1 2B, 1 3B)
Randy Tomlin (3-for-3, 1 2B, 1 3B)

Hates to face: Doug Drabek (0-for-11)
Mike Morgan (.050, 1-for-20)
Zane Smith (0-for-13)

Miscellaneous statistics: Ground outs-to-air outs ratio: 1.61 last season, 1.55 for career.... Grounded into 12 double plays in 65 opportunities (one per 5.4), 4th-worst rate in N.L.... Drove in 4 of 12 runners from third base with less than two outs (33%).... Direction of balls hit to the outfield: 28% to left field, 25% to center, 48% to right.... Base running: Advanced from first base to third on 2 of 17 outfield singles (12%); scored from second on 3 of 5 (60%).... Opposing base stealers: 46-for-93 (49%), lowest rate in N.L.

Comments: Although he held opposing base stealers to the lowest success rate of any N.L. catcher, the performance of both Mark Bailey and Steve Decker in backup roles suggests that the Giants' pitching staff and the frequent pitchouts called by manager Roger Craig deserve some credit. Opponents averaged one steal every 19 innings with Manwaring catching, considerably better than the league average (one every 11), but opponents stole one base every 59⅓ innings against Decker and had no steals in 52⅓ innings against Bailey.... Tied Tony Pena for most double plays in majors by a catcher (12).... Had 3d-lowest average in N.L. vs. right-handed pitchers. Career mark vs. lefties (.259) is 50 points higher than vs. righties (.209).... Caught 69 percent of the innings pitched by major league ERA leader Bill Swift, but Swift had a 1.42 ERA with other catchers compared to 2.37 with Manwaring.... Giants have used a different opening-day starting catcher in each of the last six years. Since 1987: Bob Brenly, Bob Melvin, Terry Kennedy, Gary Carter, Steve Decker, and Manwaring.... There are 35 players in major league history who have caught 1000 games for one team; the Giants are the only one of the eight "old" N.L. teams (in existence from 1900 to 1961) who have not had a 1000-game catcher; Wes Westrum holds the franchise record with 902 games. Even two of the N.L. teams born since 1962 have had 1000-game catchers: Gary Carter with the Expos and Jerry Grote with the Mets.

Dave Martinez   Bats Left

Cincinnati Reds	AB	H	2B	3B	HR	RBI	BB	SO	BA	SA	OBA
Season	393	100	20	5	3	31	42	54	.254	.354	.323
vs. Left-Handers	59	16	5	0	0	8	7	15	.271	.356	.348
vs. Right-Handers	334	84	15	5	3	23	35	39	.251	.353	.319
vs. Ground-Ballers	178	43	6	1	0	9	20	25	.242	.287	.313
vs. Fly-Ballers	215	57	14	4	3	22	22	29	.265	.409	.332
Home Games	196	57	11	3	3	20	21	20	.291	.423	.355
Road Games	197	43	9	2	0	11	21	34	.218	.284	.292
Grass Fields	114	29	6	1	0	5	15	23	.254	.325	.338
Artificial Turf	279	71	14	4	3	26	27	31	.254	.366	.317
April	51	14	3	0	0	4	7	6	.275	.333	.362
May	64	14	1	1	0	5	9	9	.219	.266	.315
June	67	19	4	2	0	7	3	12	.284	.403	.306
July	84	21	2	1	1	2	6	10	.250	.333	.300
August	50	11	2	0	0	4	9	7	.220	.260	.333
Sept./Oct.	77	21	8	1	2	9	8	10	.273	.481	.337
Leading Off Inn.	75	21	4	2	0	0	9	10	.280	.387	.357
Runners On	174	41	8	2	1	29	24	24	.236	.322	.322
Bases Empty	219	59	12	3	2	2	18	30	.269	.379	.325
Runners/Scor. Pos.	111	23	5	2	1	28	19	19	.207	.315	.313
Runners On/2 Out	67	15	5	2	0	12	15	8	.224	.358	.366
Scor. Pos./2 Out	48	10	3	2	0	11	13	5	.208	.354	.377
Late-Inning Pressure	46	3	2	0	0	2	7	13	.065	.109	.189
Leading Off	9	1	0	0	0	0	3	2	.111	.111	.333
Runners On	23	1	1	0	0	2	4	4	.043	.087	.185
Runners/Scor. Pos.	15	0	0	0	0	2	3	3	.000	.000	.167

RUNS BATTED IN	From 1B	From 2B	From 3B	Scoring Position
Totals	3/115	10/88	15/43	25/131
Percentage	2.6%	11.4%	34.9%	19.1%

Loves to face: Frank Castillo (.500, 4-for-8, 2 HR)
Jose DeJesus (.444, 8-for-18, 2 HR)
Bob Walk (.341, 15-for-44, 2 HR)

Hates to face: Paul Assenmacher (.067, 1-for-15)
Greg Maddux (.159, 7-for-44)
Alejandro Pena (.077, 1-for-13)

Miscellaneous statistics: Ground outs-to-air outs ratio: 1.06 last season, 0.99 for career.... Grounded into 6 double plays in 89 opportunities (one per 15).... Drove in 10 of 21 runners from third base with less than two outs (48%).... Direction of balls hit to the outfield: 32% to left field, 35% to center, 33% to right.... Base running: Advanced from first base to third on 12 of 25 outfield singles (48%); scored from second on 5 of 8 (63%).... Made 2.65 putouts per nine innings in center field.

Comments: Batting average in Late-Inning Pressure Situations was the lowest in the majors. His 15 hitless LIPS at-bats with runners in scoring position fell one shy of the single-season "record" (since 1975) for futility in those situations, shared by Bill Sudakis (1975), Rennie Stennett (1979), and Ron Kittle (1984).... Homerless in 369 career at-bats in LIPS, the most at-bats without a LIPS home run by any active player; that's unusual because he has some pop (39 home runs in seven seasons).... Started 95 of the 101 games in which Reds faced a right-handed starter, but only three of 61 against lefties. If you look at the breakdown above, you might wonder why he didn't start more against southpaws, but his reputation has preceded him everywhere he has played. Still, though he batted only .193 against southpaws over his first four years in the majors, he has hit .248 against them in three years since.... Drove in career-low 19.1 percent of runners from scoring position last season; that put him 177th among 190 major league players who had 100 scoring-position opportunities.... Has played in 836 regular-season games without either a postseason or an All-Star appearance.... Hitless in 12 at-bats as a pinch hitter last season, lowering his career average in those situations to .200 (15-for-75) with no home runs.... Mr. Consistency: batted .254 last season: .254 on grass fields, .254 on artificial turf; owns a .269 career average: .269 on grass fields, .269 on artificial turf.

Derrick May — Bats Left

Chicago Cubs	AB	H	2B	3B	HR	RBI	BB	SO	BA	SA	OBA
Season	351	96	11	0	8	45	14	40	.274	.373	.306
vs. Left-Handers	76	19	2	0	2	9	3	13	.250	.355	.287
vs. Right-Handers	275	77	9	0	6	36	11	27	.280	.378	.311
vs. Ground-Ballers	147	44	5	0	2	18	8	15	.299	.374	.340
vs. Fly-Ballers	204	52	6	0	6	27	6	25	.255	.373	.282
Home Games	202	59	8	0	3	28	10	19	.292	.376	.327
Road Games	149	37	3	0	5	17	4	21	.248	.369	.277
Grass Fields	260	76	10	0	4	34	14	26	.292	.377	.332
Artificial Turf	91	20	1	0	4	11	0	14	.220	.363	.228
April	11	1	0	0	0	1	2	1	.091	.091	.231
May	57	13	2	0	0	2	3	8	.228	.263	.267
June	70	22	2	0	3	14	2	7	.314	.471	.333
July	28	4	0	0	1	2	2	4	.143	.250	.194
August	80	25	4	0	1	10	4	10	.313	.400	.368
Sept./Oct.	105	31	3	0	3	16	1	10	.295	.410	.302
Leading Off Inn.	76	18	2	0	1	1	4	5	.237	.303	.275
Runners On	165	47	6	0	6	43	5	21	.285	.430	.312
Bases Empty	186	49	5	0	2	2	9	19	.263	.323	.301
Runners/Scor. Pos.	92	26	4	0	4	38	5	12	.283	.457	.330
Runners On/2 Out	67	20	3	0	1	15	1	9	.299	.388	.319
Scor. Pos./2 Out	40	11	3	0	1	15	1	6	.275	.425	.310
Late-Inning Pressure	63	16	1	0	3	9	2	10	.254	.413	.273
Leading Off	14	1	1	0	0	0	0	1	.071	.143	.071
Runners On	26	10	0	0	3	9	1	5	.385	.731	.393
Runners/Scor. Pos.	15	4	0	0	2	7	1	3	.267	.667	.294

RUNS BATTED IN	From 1B	From 2B	From 3B	Scoring Position
Totals	9/132	12/67	16/36	28/103
Percentage	6.8%	17.9%	44.4%	27.2%

Loves to face: Brad Brink (3-for-3, 2 HR)
Ken Hill (.357, 5-for-14, 3 2B)
Dennis Martinez (.500, 4-for-8, 1 HR)
Hates to face: Doug Drabek (.071, 1-for-14, 1 HR)
John Smoltz (.091, 1-for-11)
John Wetteland (0-for-5, 3 SO)

Miscellaneous statistics: Ground outs-to-air outs ratio: 1.21 last season, 1.10 for career.... Grounded into 10 double plays in 85 opportunities (one per 8.5).... Drove in 12 of 22 runners from third base with less than two outs (55%).... Direction of balls hit to the outfield: 28% to left field, 32% to center, 40% to right.... Base running: Advanced from first base to third on 12 of 28 outfield singles (43%); scored from second on 8 of 13 (62%).... Made 1.81 putouts per nine innings in left field, 2d-lowest rate in majors.

Comments: Rookies generally do not draw a lot of bases on balls, but May's walk rate (one every 26.5 plate appearances) was low even for a rookie; teammate Rey Sanchez (one walk every 27.5 PA) was the only N.L. rookie (minimum: 250 PA) with a lower walk rate last year.... Drove in 28 of 103 runners he found in scoring position—exactly the same totals produced last season by Tony Gwynn. Only one N.L. rookie had a higher rate than May's 27.2 percent: Moises Alou drove in 28 percent (minimum: 100 opportunities).... Cubs gave him some shots at left-handers, including 12 starts; his total of 76 at-bats vs. lefties was the highest by any N.L. rookie who bats left-handed.... Seven of his 10 career homers have been hit with runners on base.... Son of Dave May, Derrick was Cubs' first-round selection in 1986 June draft; also chosen in that draft: Lee May, Jr., Jaime Roseboro (son of John), Dru Kosco (son of Andy), Bill Robinson (son of Bill), and Moises Alou (son of Felipe).... May played parts of the 1990 and 1991 seasons with the Cubs, and has already played 156 games in the majors at the age of 24; at the same age, his dad had only 36 games under his belt, on his way to an 11-year career in which he played 1253 games.... When Derrick was six years old, his dad was traded by the Brewers to the Braves, along with a minor league pitcher to be named later, in exchange for baseball's all-time home run king, Hank Aaron. Talk about bragging rights; how great must that have been for a first grader!

Willie McGee — Bats Left and Right

San Francisco Giants	AB	H	2B	3B	HR	RBI	BB	SO	BA	SA	OBA
Season	474	141	20	2	1	36	29	88	.297	.354	.339
vs. Left-Handers	159	45	6	2	1	12	4	36	.283	.365	.305
vs. Right-Handers	315	96	14	0	0	24	25	52	.305	.349	.355
vs. Ground-Ballers	206	73	12	2	0	20	12	36	.354	.432	.391
vs. Fly-Ballers	268	68	8	0	1	16	17	52	.254	.295	.298
Home Games	224	71	13	1	0	14	16	30	.317	.384	.361
Road Games	250	70	7	1	1	22	13	58	.280	.328	.318
Grass Fields	328	99	17	1	0	26	23	52	.302	.360	.347
Artificial Turf	146	42	3	1	1	10	6	36	.288	.342	.320
April	76	21	3	0	0	5	9	12	.276	.316	.349
May	85	25	5	1	0	10	2	18	.294	.376	.310
June	88	30	1	0	0	2	4	16	.341	.352	.370
July	83	21	6	0	1	4	4	22	.253	.361	.295
August	90	29	4	0	0	11	4	13	.322	.367	.351
Sept./Oct.	52	15	1	1	0	4	6	7	.288	.346	.362
Leading Off Inn.	132	34	3	0	0	0	7	32	.258	.280	.300
Runners On	171	60	10	1	0	35	17	23	.351	.421	.407
Bases Empty	303	81	10	1	1	1	12	65	.267	.317	.297
Runners/Scor. Pos.	101	34	3	0	0	29	11	13	.337	.366	.398
Runners On/2 Out	77	29	3	1	0	18	4	6	.377	.442	.407
Scor. Pos./2 Out	49	20	1	0	0	15	3	1	.408	.429	.442
Late-Inning Pressure	93	28	5	0	0	10	3	17	.301	.355	.323
Leading Off	16	3	1	0	0	0	0	4	.188	.250	.188
Runners On	47	14	3	0	0	10	2	7	.298	.362	.327
Runners/Scor. Pos.	30	9	2	0	0	9	2	3	.300	.367	.344

RUNS BATTED IN	From 1B	From 2B	From 3B	Scoring Position
Totals	7/105	8/82	20/37	28/119
Percentage	6.7%	9.8%	54.1%	23.5%

Loves to face: Darryl Kile (.571, 8-for-14)
Mike Morgan (.414, 12-for-29)
Mark Portugal (.524, 11-for-21)
Hates to face: Tom Browning (.163, 7-for-43, 1 HR)
John Candelaria (.130, 3-for-23, 1 HR)
Tom Candiotti (0-for-8)

Miscellaneous statistics: Ground outs-to-air outs ratio: 2.79 last season (highest in majors), 2.37 for career.... Grounded into 7 double plays in 74 opportunities (one per 11).... Drove in 11 of 18 runners from third base with less than two outs (61%).... Direction of balls hit to the outfield: 54% to left field, 28% to center, 18% to right batting left-handed; 20% to left field, 33% to center, 47% to right batting right-handed.... Base running: Advanced from first base to third on 15 of 32 outfield singles (47%); scored from second on 10 of 11 (91%), 3d-highest rate in N.L.... Made 2.06 putouts per nine innings in right field.

Comments: Even with a .337 batting average with runners in scoring position, he drove in only 23.5 percent of runners he found in scoring position; infield hits and outfielders playing him shallow cut down the number of RBIs. There were 43 major league players last season who had 100 or more RBI opportunities from scoring position and who batted .300 or higher in those at-bats; the only one with a lower RBI percentage than McGee was Omar Vizquel, who drove in only 15.1 percent of such runners (tied for the major league low) despite batting .307 with runners on second and/or third.... Batting average with two outs and runners on base was 3d highest in league.... His .329 career batting average in day games is 2d highest among active players behind Wade Boggs (.330); has .283 career mark at night.... More career numbers: he has succeeded on 77.9 percent of stolen base attempts on artificial turf, 69.0 percent on grass fields.... Pinch-hit 23 times last year, more than he had in the previous six years combined. Batted .524 in that role (11-for-21) with four extra-base hits; in his non-pinch-hit at-bats, he averaged one extra-base hit every 24 at-bats.... Stole only 13 bases last season, the fewest in any 100-game season in his career; his strikeout rate (one every 5.8 plate appearances) was also the worst of his career.... Has batted over .300 from the left side of the plate in each of the last three seasons.... In two seasons with the Giants, he has hit .414 (29-for-70) vs. his old team, the Cardinals.

Fred McGriff
Bats Left

San Diego Padres	AB	H	2B	3B	HR	RBI	BB	SO	BA	SA	OBA
Season	531	152	30	4	35	104	96	108	.286	.556	.394
vs. Left-Handers	205	58	10	3	13	50	28	49	.283	.551	.369
vs. Right-Handers	326	94	20	1	22	54	68	59	.288	.558	.409
vs. Ground-Ballers	232	71	14	1	15	40	46	48	.306	.569	.418
vs. Fly-Ballers	299	81	16	3	20	64	50	60	.271	.545	.374
Home Games	273	83	17	2	21	56	47	51	.304	.612	.406
Road Games	258	69	13	2	14	48	49	57	.267	.496	.381
Grass Fields	385	109	24	2	26	74	70	72	.283	.558	.392
Artificial Turf	146	43	6	2	9	30	26	36	.295	.548	.399
April	85	23	3	1	6	21	15	17	.271	.541	.376
May	97	38	8	1	6	16	16	18	.392	.680	.478
June	58	16	5	0	2	11	16	12	.276	.466	.434
July	93	24	2	1	7	16	14	16	.258	.527	.352
August	89	20	2	0	10	21	14	20	.225	.584	.330
Sept./Oct.	109	31	10	1	4	19	21	25	.284	.505	.397
Leading Off Inn.	151	47	8	0	10	10	13	25	.311	.563	.366
Runners On	235	69	17	4	16	85	67	48	.294	.604	.444
Bases Empty	296	83	13	0	19	19	29	60	.280	.517	.347
Runners/Scor. Pos.	131	39	12	3	7	63	49	27	.298	.595	.478
Runners On/2 Out	99	24	6	2	6	25	45	22	.242	.525	.479
Scor. Pos./2 Out	48	11	3	1	2	14	32	10	.229	.458	.538
Late-Inning Pressure	76	22	7	0	2	10	11	17	.289	.461	.371
Leading Off	26	5	2	0	1	1	2	6	.192	.385	.250
Runners On	32	14	5	0	1	9	9	9	.438	.688	.535
Runners/Scor. Pos.	16	5	1	0	1	7	7	6	.313	.563	.480

RUNS BATTED IN	From 1B	From 2B	From 3B	Scoring Position
Totals	19/182	24/103	26/50	50/153
Percentage	10.4%	23.3%	52.0%	32.7%

Loves to face: Terry Mulholland (.500, 11-for-22, 3 HR)
Jeff M. Robinson (.467, 7-for-15, 3 HR, 3 BB)
Trevor Wilson (.700, 7-for-10, 2 HR)

Hates to face: John Candelaria (.125, 3-for-24, 1 HR, 4 BB)
Orel Hershiser (.158, 3-for-19)
Randy Tomlin (0-for-19)

Miscellaneous statistics: Ground outs-to-air outs ratio: 1.26 last season, 1.14 for career.... Grounded into 14 double plays in 120 opportunities (one per 8.6).... Drove in 22 of 35 runners from third base with less than two outs (63%).... Direction of balls hit to the outfield: 32% to left field, 28% to center, 40% to right.... Base running: Advanced from first base to third on 2 of 29 outfield singles (7%), 2d-lowest rate in N.L.; scored from second on 9 of 19 (47%), 4th-lowest rate in N.L.... Made 0.73 assists per nine innings at first base.

Comments: Led A.L. in homers in 1989, led N.L. last year. Became the first player to lead both the American League and the National League in home runs since the Roosevelt administration—that's the *Teddy* Roosevelt administration. Buck Freeman led the N.L. in 1899 and the A.L. in 1903; Sam Crawford led the N.L. in 1901 and the A.L. in 1908.... In 1987 and 1988, the Blue Jays posted a starting lineup with both McGriff and Cecil Fielder 30 times.... The only N.L. first baseman to hit over 20 home runs last year.... Led N.L. with 10 opposite-field homers; that in itself isn't surprising, but what makes it noteworthy was his margin of victory: no other N.L. player hit more than four dingers to the off-field.... Career slugging percentage (.570) and home-run rate (one every 13.8 at-bats) vs. right-handed pitchers are both the best by any player since 1975.... Meanwhile, vs. left-handed pitchers, he has improved both his batting average and his slugging percentage in each of his six years in the majors.... Has hit at least 30 homers in five consecutive seasons, something that has been done 20 other times by 18 players (Aaron and Ruth each did it twice); 14 of those 18 players are in the Hall of Fame (Mike Schmidt is not yet eligible; Rocky Colavito, Gil Hodges, and Hank Sauer didn't get the votes). However, of the 11 players who extended their 30-homer streaks to six years, all are enshrined in Cooperstown except for Schmidt, who is a first-ballot sure shot in 1995.

Orlando Merced
Bats Left and Right

Pittsburgh Pirates	AB	H	2B	3B	HR	RBI	BB	SO	BA	SA	OBA
Season	405	100	28	5	6	60	52	63	.247	.385	.332
vs. Left-Handers	84	16	3	0	0	7	14	11	.190	.226	.306
vs. Right-Handers	321	84	25	5	6	53	38	52	.262	.427	.339
vs. Ground-Ballers	167	45	11	3	3	25	25	34	.269	.425	.366
vs. Fly-Ballers	238	55	17	2	3	35	27	29	.231	.357	.307
Home Games	199	50	15	2	4	25	29	27	.251	.407	.345
Road Games	206	50	13	3	2	35	23	36	.243	.364	.319
Grass Fields	108	23	7	0	0	12	12	22	.213	.278	.293
Artificial Turf	297	77	21	5	6	48	40	41	.259	.424	.346
April	41	8	1	0	0	5	11	7	.195	.220	.370
May	72	19	9	1	0	7	10	12	.264	.417	.349
June	76	19	5	2	3	13	5	9	.250	.487	.296
July	72	16	4	0	2	10	4	10	.222	.361	.260
August	62	13	2	1	0	11	11	15	.210	.274	.320
Sept./Oct.	82	25	7	1	1	14	11	10	.305	.451	.394
Leading Off Inn.	94	24	7	3	1	1	8	20	.255	.426	.314
Runners On	179	49	11	2	4	58	30	18	.274	.425	.372
Bases Empty	226	51	17	3	2	2	22	45	.226	.354	.297
Runners/Scor. Pos.	121	35	8	2	2	53	22	11	.289	.438	.389
Runners On/2 Out	86	20	8	0	1	24	14	11	.233	.360	.347
Scor. Pos./2 Out	63	16	7	0	0	21	10	7	.254	.365	.365
Late-Inning Pressure	73	17	5	1	1	12	10	16	.233	.370	.325
Leading Off	20	5	1	1	0	0	1	7	.250	.400	.286
Runners On	35	11	4	0	1	12	8	4	.314	.514	.442
Runners/Scor. Pos.	25	7	3	0	0	10	6	2	.280	.400	.419

RUNS BATTED IN	From 1B	From 2B	From 3B	Scoring Position
Totals	10/123	23/103	21/43	44/146
Percentage	8.1%	22.3%	48.8%	30.1%

Loves to face: Shawn Boskie (.800, 4-for-5, 1 HR)
Mark Portugal (.600, 6-for-10, 1 HR)
Bob Tewksbury (.391, 9-for-23, 1 HR)

Hates to face: John Burkett (.056, 1-for-18)
Kevin Gross (.100, 1-for-10)
Les Lancaster (0-for-8)

Miscellaneous statistics: Ground outs-to-air outs ratio: 1.25 last season, 1.49 for career.... Grounded into 6 double plays in 72 opportunities (one per 12).... Drove in 16 of 23 runners from third base with less than two outs (70%).... Direction of balls hit to the outfield: 39% to left field, 33% to center, 29% to right batting left-handed; 32% to left field, 28% to center, 40% to right batting right-handed.... Base running: Advanced from first base to third on 9 of 15 outfield singles (60%), 2d-highest rate in N.L.; scored from second on 7 of 11 (64%).... Made 0.79 assists per nine innings at first base.

Comments: One of three players in the majors to start at least 10 games from both the leadoff (17) and the cleanup (14) spots last season; the others were a couple of Royals, Jim Eisenreich and Gregg Jefferies. But Merced batted fifth or sixth in the vast majority of his starts (67 of 98).... Pirates first basemen batted only .236 last season, lowest in N.L.; first basemen on 11 other teams batted a combined .275.... A switch-hitter in name only; he's a career .193 hitter from the right side with no home runs in 145 at-bats. Started only three games against left-handed starters last year after making only one such start the previous season.... Had 14 game-winning RBIs last season, one behind team leader Andy Van Slyke. Merced tied Jeff Bagwell for the most game-winners among second-year players.... In two full years with Pittsburgh, he has had 28 go-ahead RBIs, 24 of which stood up as game-winners.... Has batted .381 as a pinch hitter over the last two seasons (16-for-42). His career mark in that role is .318 (21-for-66), 4th highest in Pirates history among players with at least that many at-bats, behind Smoky Burgess (.358), Erv Brame (.357), and Mike Easler (.326).... Has a .300 career batting average against the Braves during the regular season, but has batted only .158 against them in postseason play.... Career breakdown: .297 in day games, .245 at night; we suppose he, like many of us, would like to have more postseason games played under the sun.

Mickey Morandini   Bats Left

Philadelphia Phillies	AB	H	2B	3B	HR	RBI	BB	SO	BA	SA	OBA
Season	422	112	8	8	3	30	25	64	.265	.344	.305
vs. Left-Handers	121	24	1	1	1	8	7	19	.198	.248	.240
vs. Right-Handers	301	88	7	7	2	22	18	45	.292	.382	.331
vs. Ground-Ballers	193	63	4	5	2	17	10	25	.326	.430	.358
vs. Fly-Ballers	229	49	4	3	1	13	15	39	.214	.271	.261
Home Games	202	55	5	4	2	16	12	36	.272	.366	.313
Road Games	220	57	3	4	1	14	13	28	.259	.323	.298
Grass Fields	118	38	2	2	1	12	7	17	.322	.398	.354
Artificial Turf	304	74	6	6	2	18	18	47	.243	.322	.286
April	66	24	1	2	1	5	4	11	.364	.485	.400
May	54	12	1	0	1	6	6	16	.222	.296	.300
June	58	8	3	2	0	2	7	7	.138	.259	.227
July	78	24	2	2	0	7	3	16	.308	.385	.333
August	46	10	1	1	0	2	2	5	.217	.283	.250
Sept./Oct.	120	34	0	1	1	8	3	9	.283	.325	.298
Leading Off Inn.	100	23	2	1	1	1	3	11	.230	.300	.252
Runners On	167	43	3	4	2	29	18	31	.257	.359	.326
Bases Empty	255	69	5	4	1	1	7	33	.271	.333	.290
Runners/Scor. Pos.	101	24	1	3	1	25	14	23	.238	.337	.325
Runners On/2 Out	83	21	1	1	1	13	8	13	.253	.325	.319
Scor. Pos./2 Out	60	13	1	1	0	11	6	12	.217	.267	.288
Late-Inning Pressure	75	23	1	0	0	5	5	11	.307	.320	.346
Leading Off	22	7	1	0	0	0	1	2	.318	.364	.348
Runners On	29	8	0	0	0	5	3	4	.276	.276	.333
Runners/Scor. Pos.	14	2	0	0	0	5	2	3	.143	.143	.235

RUNS BATTED IN	From 1B	From 2B	From 3B	Scoring Position
Totals	3/114	9/73	15/50	24/123
Percentage	2.6%	12.3%	30.0%	19.5%

Loves to face: Dwight Gooden (.375, 9-for-24)
Greg Maddux (.433, 13-for-30)
Bryn Smith (.333, 3-for-9, 2 2B)
Hates to face: Dennis Martinez (.056, 1-for-18)
Mike Morgan (.125, 3-for-24)
Omar Olivares (.077, 1-for-13)

Miscellaneous statistics: Ground outs-to-air outs ratio: 1.37 last season, 1.39 for career.... Grounded into 4 double plays in 73 opportunities (one per 18).... Drove in 9 of 19 runners from third base with less than two outs (47%).... Direction of balls hit to the outfield: 36% to left field, 30% to center, 34% to right.... Base running: Advanced from first base to third on 6 of 23 outfield singles (26%); scored from second on 8 of 10 (80%).... Made 3.17 assists per nine innings at second base.

Comments: Sorry, but we're about to have a cow.... Morandini's unassisted triple play last Sept. 20 was the first of the Video Era. You know, the era that began without warning when the relative importance of what happens in sports is defined by its number of showings on made-for-squirrels highlight shows and tapes. So, of course, Don Mattingly grabbing some popcorn from an eight-year-old fan is more important than his six .300 seasons. There's a vital distinction between an unusual play and a significant performance. To put an unassisted triple play "into perspective," how much more do you need to know than this: When Morandini executed one last year, it was only the eighth such play in the 117-year history of major league baseball. You don't need to compare it with the number of perfect games or four-home-run games, legitimate achievements that are debased by comparing them to an act of serendipity. Morandini's play will give him and everyone else at Three Rivers Stadium that day a fine memory. But it isn't even an "achievement" of baseball skill at all; rather, through an integration of circumstances, he happened to catch a line drive near second base with none out on a hit-and-run play. That's not at all like pitching a perfect game—even though there have been more perfect games than unassisted triple plays. Remember: Reaching base on catcher's interference is *not* more of an achievement than hitting a grand-slam home run, even if it happens less frequently.

Hal Morris   Bats Left

Cincinnati Reds	AB	H	2B	3B	HR	RBI	BB	SO	BA	SA	OBA
Season	395	107	21	3	6	53	45	53	.271	.385	.347
vs. Left-Handers	139	35	5	0	1	11	13	30	.252	.309	.325
vs. Right-Handers	256	72	16	3	5	42	32	23	.281	.426	.359
vs. Ground-Ballers	156	44	9	0	3	20	19	17	.282	.397	.358
vs. Fly-Ballers	239	63	12	3	3	33	26	36	.264	.377	.340
Home Games	198	54	12	1	3	29	16	27	.273	.389	.333
Road Games	197	53	9	2	3	24	29	26	.269	.381	.360
Grass Fields	96	20	4	1	1	9	13	14	.208	.302	.297
Artificial Turf	299	87	17	2	5	44	32	39	.291	.411	.363
April	34	9	1	1	0	2	3	5	.265	.353	.342
May	37	12	3	1	0	9	8	3	.324	.459	.435
June	87	30	5	1	2	20	11	10	.345	.494	.418
July	103	26	5	0	2	8	12	16	.252	.359	.328
August	56	14	4	0	2	8	4	9	.250	.429	.300
Sept./Oct.	78	16	3	0	0	6	7	10	.205	.244	.279
Leading Off Inn.	75	17	2	2	0	0	8	11	.227	.307	.301
Runners On	179	52	11	0	3	50	22	19	.291	.402	.368
Bases Empty	216	55	10	3	3	3	23	34	.255	.370	.329
Runners/Scor. Pos.	110	33	9	0	2	48	19	14	.300	.436	.397
Runners On/2 Out	75	20	4	0	1	21	12	11	.267	.360	.368
Scor. Pos./2 Out	56	17	4	0	1	21	10	9	.304	.429	.409
Late-Inning Pressure	47	17	5	3	1	2	5	8	.362	.660	.423
Leading Off	15	7	1	2	0	0	0	3	.467	.800	.467
Runners On	17	3	1	0	0	1	3	2	.176	.235	.300
Runners/Scor. Pos.	7	1	1	0	0	1	3	1	.143	.286	.400

RUNS BATTED IN	From 1B	From 2B	From 3B	Scoring Position
Totals	8/123	18/73	21/55	39/128
Percentage	6.5%	24.7%	38.2%	30.5%

Loves to face: John Burkett (.381, 8-for-21, 2 HR)
Jimmy Jones (.636, 7-for-11, 1 HR)
Greg Maddux (.529, 9-for-17)
Hates to face: Pete Harnisch (.136, 3-for-22, 1 HR, 3 BB)
Bruce Hurst (.133, 2-for-15)
Chuck McElroy (0-for-7, 5 SO)

Miscellaneous statistics: Ground outs-to-air outs ratio: 1.32 last season, 1.29 for career.... Grounded into 12 double plays in 85 opportunities (one per 7.1).... Drove in 12 of 26 runners from third base with less than two outs (46%).... Direction of balls hit to the outfield: 41% to left field, 27% to center, 32% to right.... Base running: Advanced from first base to third on 7 of 17 outfield singles (41%); scored from second on 2 of 11 (18%), lowest rate in majors.... Made 0.85 assists per nine innings at first base.

Comments: His .328 lifetime average vs. right-handed pitchers is 4th highest in majors since 1975 behind Wade Boggs (.354), Rod Carew (.341), and Tony Gwynn (.336). But his career mark vs. left-handers is only .239, leaving him open to manipulation in the late innings by opposing managers with a decent lefty in the bullpen. While his career batting average with runners in scoring position is .303, his career average with runners in scoring position in Late-Inning Pressure Situations is only .189, and he has driven in only 11.6 percent of runners from scoring position in LIPS.... Reds first basemen combined for only eight home runs last season, the fewest of any team in the majors at that position.... Has the lowest error rate, one every 205 chances, of any first baseman in Reds history (minimum: 200 games).... By the way, no Reds first baseman has started the All-Star Game since Ted Kluszewski in 1955.... Had two disabled-list stays last year: 31 days with a broken hand in May; 16 days with a hamstring injury in August.... Batting average on grass fields fell from .369 in 1991 to .208, 7th lowest in N.L., last year.... His .308 average in the '90s is N.L.'s 4th highest.... A good first-half hitter: .323 career mark from April to July, .279 from August 1 to season's end.... Batting average has fallen by at least 20 points in each of the last two years; that has happened to only five other players (minimum: 300 at-bats), but since Morris started at the .340 plateau, he's guilty with an explanation.

Eddie Murray

Bats Left and Right

New York Mets	AB	H	2B	3B	HR	RBI	BB	SO	BA	SA	OBA
Season	551	144	37	2	16	93	66	74	.261	.423	.336
vs. Left-Handers	202	48	16	1	3	35	16	16	.238	.371	.286
vs. Right-Handers	349	96	21	1	13	58	50	58	.275	.453	.364
vs. Ground-Ballers	267	68	16	0	6	42	26	30	.255	.382	.316
vs. Fly-Ballers	284	76	21	2	10	51	40	44	.268	.461	.354
Home Games	266	60	16	2	7	43	30	39	.226	.380	.303
Road Games	285	84	21	0	9	50	36	35	.295	.463	.366
Grass Fields	387	99	24	2	14	62	42	53	.256	.437	.326
Artificial Turf	164	45	13	0	2	31	24	21	.274	.390	.358
April	78	21	8	0	1	19	11	11	.269	.410	.360
May	91	24	3	0	4	12	13	16	.264	.429	.346
June	97	22	5	1	3	20	11	16	.227	.392	.295
July	91	24	9	0	1	12	4	9	.264	.396	.295
August	94	23	4	0	4	11	9	9	.245	.415	.311
Sept./Oct.	100	30	8	1	3	19	18	13	.300	.490	.403
Leading Off Inn.	151	39	8	1	5	5	8	18	.258	.424	.296
Runners On	250	72	25	1	8	85	42	36	.288	.492	.380
Bases Empty	301	72	12	1	8	8	24	38	.239	.365	.295
Runners/Scor. Pos.	141	38	18	0	4	76	33	24	.270	.482	.390
Runners On/2 Out	114	27	11	0	3	29	17	15	.237	.412	.336
Scor. Pos./2 Out	71	14	10	0	0	23	13	11	.197	.338	.321
Late-Inning Pressure	79	16	6	0	1	15	14	9	.203	.316	.316
Leading Off	25	0	0	0	0	0	1	3	.000	.000	.038
Runners On	34	9	6	0	0	14	10	5	.265	.441	.413
Runners/Scor. Pos.	20	7	5	0	0	14	8	1	.350	.600	.500

RUNS BATTED IN	From 1B	From 2B	From 3B	Scoring Position
Totals	15/182	26/108	36/74	62/182
Percentage	8.2%	24.1%	48.6%	34.1%

Loves to face: Shawn Boskie (.400, 6-for-15, 2 2B, 2 HR)
Pete Harnisch (.500, 7-for-14, 1 HR)
Darryl Kile (.500, 6-for-12, 1 HR)
Hates to face: Bruce Hurst (.150, 12-for-80, 4 HR)
Curt Schilling (0-for-11)
Bryn Smith (.115, 3-for-26)

Miscellaneous statistics: Ground outs-to-air outs ratio: 1.06 last season, 1.04 for career.... Grounded into 15 double plays in 115 opportunities (one per 7.7).... Drove in 27 of 42 runners from third base with less than two outs (64%).... Direction of balls hit to the outfield: 26% to left field, 31% to center, 43% to right batting left-handed; 44% to left field, 31% to center, 25% to right batting right-handed.... Base running: Advanced from first base to third on 7 of 26 outfield singles (27%); scored from second on 10 of 14 (71%).... Made 0.66 assists per nine innings at first base, 2d-lowest rate in N.L.

Comments: First player in major league history with at least 75 RBIs in each of his first 16 seasons; only Hank Aaron had a longer streak of 75-RBI seasons anytime in his career: 19 years, 1955–73. In the postwar era, only Aaron, Stan Musial, Willie Mays, Ernie Banks, Mike Schmidt, and Murray have driven in 1500 runs over a 16-season span.... Last season marked 10th straight in which Murray posted a higher batting average batting left-handed than right-handed.... Led Mets with .261 average, lowest to lead any club in the majors last season.... Power starting to wane: He has set career-low home-run rates in each of the last two years.... Has played 2214 games at first base, third on all-time list behind Jake Beckley (2377) and Mickey Vernon (2237). Even a 162-game season in 1993 would leave him one game shy of the top.... Passed Keith Hernandez to become all-time leader in assists at first base (1717).... Career mark of 38.3 percent of runners driven in from scoring position in LIPS is 3d best among active players behind Albert Belle (44.2%) and Don Mattingly (39.3%).... Batted .667 (10-for-15) with bases loaded last season, tying Eric Karros for most bases-loaded hits in N.L. That lifted his career mark to .424 in 191 bases-loaded at-bats; he's the only player since 1975 to bat .400 in at least 100 at-bats.... Became the 24th player to reach 400 career home runs; of the 20 who have come up for Hall of Fame consideration, only Dave Kingman has been rejected.

Otis Nixon

Bats Left and Right

Atlanta Braves	AB	H	2B	3B	HR	RBI	BB	SO	BA	SA	OBA
Season	456	134	14	2	2	22	39	54	.294	.346	.348
vs. Left-Handers	178	61	8	1	2	16	11	15	.343	.433	.379
vs. Right-Handers	278	73	6	1	0	6	28	39	.263	.291	.329
vs. Ground-Ballers	173	51	7	0	2	9	23	22	.295	.370	.374
vs. Fly-Ballers	283	83	7	2	0	13	16	32	.293	.332	.331
Home Games	221	66	5	0	1	11	24	27	.299	.335	.366
Road Games	235	68	9	2	1	11	15	27	.289	.357	.331
Grass Fields	328	95	11	0	2	19	32	40	.290	.341	.351
Artificial Turf	128	39	3	2	0	3	7	14	.305	.359	.341
April	16	6	1	0	0	1	2	2	.375	.438	.444
May	75	28	2	0	0	2	5	3	.373	.400	.412
June	61	18	1	0	2	8	6	7	.295	.410	.353
July	73	22	5	0	0	2	5	8	.301	.370	.346
August	112	33	5	2	0	7	11	13	.295	.375	.358
Sept./Oct.	119	27	0	0	0	2	10	21	.227	.227	.285
Leading Off Inn.	197	61	11	1	0	0	15	29	.310	.376	.358
Runners On	134	33	2	0	2	22	10	11	.246	.306	.295
Bases Empty	322	101	12	2	0	0	29	43	.314	.363	.370
Runners/Scor. Pos.	86	21	2	0	1	20	5	8	.244	.302	.280
Runners On/2 Out	67	12	1	0	1	8	4	6	.179	.239	.225
Scor. Pos./2 Out	49	9	1	0	1	8	3	4	.184	.265	.231
Late-Inning Pressure	60	19	2	0	0	8	10	6	.317	.350	.414
Leading Off	17	4	1	0	0	0	2	3	.235	.294	.316
Runners On	24	7	1	0	0	8	2	1	.292	.333	.346
Runners/Scor. Pos.	16	7	1	0	0	8	1	1	.438	.500	.471

RUNS BATTED IN	From 1B	From 2B	From 3B	Scoring Position
Totals	1/90	10/73	9/31	19/104
Percentage	1.1%	13.7%	29.0%	18.3%

Loves to face: Ken Hill (.600, 9-for-15)
Zane Smith (.500, 7-for-14)
Randy Tomlin (.625, 5-for-8)
Hates to face: Tom Browning (.067, 2-for-30, 3 BB)
Sid Fernandez (.077, 1-for-13, 3 BB, 10 SO)
Greg W. Harris (0-for-10)

Miscellaneous statistics: Ground outs-to-air outs ratio: 2.00 last season (4th highest in N.L.), 1.55 for career.... Grounded into 4 double plays in 58 opportunities (one per 15).... Drove in 7 of 13 runners from third base with less than two outs (54%).... Direction of balls hit to the outfield: 56% to left field, 36% to center, 8% to right batting left-handed; 28% to left field, 39% to center, 33% to right batting right-handed.... Base running: Advanced from first base to third on 9 of 29 outfield singles (31%); scored from second on 15 of 21 (71%).... Made 3.18 putouts per nine innings in center field, highest rate in N.L.

Comments: Atlanta's leadoff batters scored 116 runs last season, second straight year they led N.L. Braves were one of three teams with at least 200 hits from that spot (others: Reds and Expos), one of two teams with fewer than 50 walks from the top spot (other: Cubs).... Batting average from the right side was highest of his career.... Had .343 average in day games, the 4th highest in N.L. last season.... Another spray hitter who, despite a strong batting average (.300) with runners in scoring position, did not drive in a lot of runs; he knocked in only 18.1 percent of runners he found in scoring position, 3d lowest among N.L. players with at least 100 opportunities.... Hasn't had more than one extra-base hit in a game since July 3, 1988—a span of 345 starts that's the longest current streak in the majors.... Since majors discovered RBIs in 1920, no Braves player has ever had so few RBIs in a 450-at-bat season.... Hit both 1992 home runs off Trevor Wilson six days apart. Had hit only four homers previously: three in 1985, one in 1990.... Didn't have his first 400-at-bat season until 1991, when he was 32 years old. Only two other players over the past 40 years have had their first 400-at-bat season at age 32 or older, and then followed with another 400-at-bat season the next year: Tom Paciorek (1980–81) and Lee Lacy (1984–85).

Jose Offerman
Bats Left and Right

Los Angeles Dodgers

	AB	H	2B	3B	HR	RBI	BB	SO	BA	SA	OBA
Season	534	139	20	8	1	30	57	98	.260	.333	.331
vs. Left-Handers	201	54	8	1	1	7	20	27	.269	.333	.332
vs. Right-Handers	333	85	12	7	0	23	37	71	.255	.333	.330
vs. Ground-Ballers	181	57	11	1	1	15	20	29	.315	.403	.383
vs. Fly-Ballers	353	82	9	7	0	15	37	69	.232	.297	.304
Home Games	283	77	14	5	1	20	33	44	.272	.367	.348
Road Games	251	62	6	3	0	10	24	54	.247	.295	.310
Grass Fields	410	104	14	5	1	26	43	68	.254	.320	.323
Artificial Turf	124	35	6	3	0	4	14	30	.282	.379	.355
April	74	16	3	2	0	4	7	14	.216	.311	.284
May	64	18	1	1	0	4	9	12	.281	.328	.370
June	91	26	3	2	0	5	9	15	.286	.363	.350
July	115	28	5	1	0	3	11	27	.243	.304	.310
August	97	30	4	2	1	8	12	15	.309	.423	.385
Sept./Oct.	93	21	4	0	0	6	9	15	.226	.269	.288
Leading Off Inn.	179	47	5	3	0	0	19	28	.263	.324	.333
Runners On	194	50	9	3	0	29	24	35	.258	.335	.336
Bases Empty	340	89	11	5	1	1	33	63	.262	.332	.327
Runners/Scor. Pos.	98	27	3	2	0	26	18	18	.276	.347	.381
Runners On/2 Out	83	21	6	0	0	13	11	16	.253	.325	.340
Scor. Pos./2 Out	48	13	3	0	0	11	9	9	.271	.333	.386
Late-Inning Pressure	101	25	1	1	0	5	3	22	.248	.277	.269
Leading Off	31	8	0	0	0	0	1	5	.258	.258	.281
Runners On	34	9	1	1	0	5	2	5	.265	.353	.306
Runners/Scor. Pos.	16	5	0	1	0	4	1	2	.313	.438	.353

RUNS BATTED IN	From 1B	From 2B	From 3B	Scoring Position
Totals	4/145	11/82	14/37	25/119
Percentage	2.8%	13.4%	37.8%	21.0%

Loves to face: Chris Hammond (.500, 4-for-8)
Dennis Martinez (.455, 5-for-11, 1 HR)
Shane Reynolds (.667, 4-for-6)

Hates to face: Steve Avery (.100, 1-for-10)
Bud Black (.083, 1-for-12)
Pete Smith (0-for-7)

Miscellaneous statistics: Ground outs-to-air outs ratio: 1.41 last season, 1.52 for career.... Grounded into 5 double plays in 98 opportunities (one per 20).... Drove in 11 of 19 runners from third base with less than two outs (58%).... Direction of balls hit to the outfield: 48% to left field, 34% to center, 18% to right batting left-handed; 31% to left field, 31% to center, 38% to right batting right-handed.... Base running: Advanced from first base to third on 8 of 21 outfield singles (38%); scored from second on 8 of 14 (57%).... Made 2.78 assists per nine innings at shortstop, 2d-lowest rate in N.L.

Comments: His 42 errors were the most by any shortstop since Robin Yount made 44 in 1975; the last N.L. shortstop with more errors in a season was Alvin Dark (45 in 1951).... Something to shoot for: No shortstop has made 40 or more errors in each of two consecutive seasons since 1943–44, when Joe Hoover (Detroit) and John Sullivan (Washington) were allowed to masquerade as major league shortstops during the war.... Had highest error rate among major league shortstops both on grass fields (one error every 16.2 chances) and on artificial turf (one every 13.3 chances).... And here's a scary thought: While Offerman committed errors at an overall rate of one every 15.4 chances, the four other Dodgers players who saw duty at short last year were even worse, averaging an error every 8.6 chances.... Team total of 52 errors by shortstops was the highest by any major league team at any position since third basemen on 1972 Dodgers, led by Steve (Please Move Me to First Base) Garvey, made 53 errors. The 1961 Cardinals (Alex Grammas, Bob Lillis, and other guys who went on to become instructors) were the last team to make so many errors at shortstop.... As if defense wasn't enough of a problem, L.A. shortstops had only 35 RBIs, the fewest by any N.L. team's shortstops last season.... Offerman's longest errorless streak last year: 14 games, June 26–July 8. Dodgers have signed Kevin Elster to compete for the job; he holds N.L. shortstops' mark of 88 consecutive errorless games.

Joe Oliver
Bats Right

Cincinnati Reds

	AB	H	2B	3B	HR	RBI	BB	SO	BA	SA	OBA
Season	485	131	25	1	10	57	35	75	.270	.388	.316
vs. Left-Handers	176	54	11	0	4	24	16	22	.307	.438	.359
vs. Right-Handers	309	77	14	1	6	33	19	53	.249	.359	.291
vs. Ground-Ballers	200	56	8	1	5	27	8	25	.280	.405	.305
vs. Fly-Ballers	285	75	17	0	5	30	27	50	.263	.375	.324
Home Games	245	68	16	0	7	36	17	37	.278	.429	.320
Road Games	240	63	9	1	3	21	18	38	.262	.346	.313
Grass Fields	141	37	5	1	2	14	5	21	.262	.355	.286
Artificial Turf	344	94	20	0	8	43	30	54	.273	.401	.328
April	58	13	3	1	1	9	6	7	.224	.362	.297
May	70	14	3	0	1	4	10	17	.200	.286	.309
June	75	18	2	0	3	8	4	10	.240	.387	.275
July	85	28	7	0	1	9	7	8	.329	.447	.372
August	97	28	5	0	3	18	4	20	.289	.433	.314
Sept./Oct.	100	30	5	0	1	9	4	13	.300	.380	.318
Leading Off Inn.	110	35	11	0	2	2	3	16	.318	.473	.336
Runners On	220	52	8	0	6	53	28	36	.236	.355	.316
Bases Empty	265	79	17	1	4	4	7	39	.298	.415	.316
Runners/Scor. Pos.	122	21	2	0	4	45	25	25	.172	.287	.303
Runners On/2 Out	94	22	5	0	4	26	15	16	.234	.415	.339
Scor. Pos./2 Out	61	13	2	0	2	19	13	14	.213	.344	.351
Late-Inning Pressure	64	16	2	0	1	5	6	12	.250	.328	.306
Leading Off	16	3	0	0	0	0	0	6	.188	.188	.188
Runners On	28	6	2	0	0	4	5	5	.214	.286	.314
Runners/Scor. Pos.	14	0	0	0	0	3	4	4	.000	.000	.200

RUNS BATTED IN	From 1B	From 2B	From 3B	Scoring Position
Totals	10/159	12/95	25/61	37/156
Percentage	6.3%	12.6%	41.0%	23.7%

Loves to face: Bud Black (.357, 5-for-14, 2 HR)
Zane Smith (.367, 11-for-30, 3 HR, 0 BB)
Steve Wilson (.800, 4-for-5, 2 HR, 1 SO)

Hates to face: John Burkett (.083, 1-for-12)
Pete Harnisch (.077, 1-for-13)
Joe Magrane (.083, 1-for-12)

Miscellaneous statistics: Ground outs-to-air outs ratio: 0.94 last season, 0.90 for career.... Grounded into 12 double plays in 102 opportunities (one per 8.5).... Drove in 18 of 35 runners from third base with less than two outs (51%).... Direction of balls hit to the outfield: 39% to left field, 29% to center, 33% to right.... Base running: Advanced from first base to third on 2 of 19 outfield singles (11%); scored from second on 5 of 10 (50%), 5th-lowest rate in N.L.... Opposing base stealers: 87-for-134 (65%).

Comments: The only active player whose career batting average shows an improvement every month: .218 in April, .226 in May, .235 in June, .259 in July, .261 in August, .262 in September.... A nice cap would be a postseason average higher than his September mark, but it's .250.... The best monthly batting average of his career came in his first full month in the majors, August 1989, when he hit .339.... Had 5th-lowest average in N.L. with runners in scoring position; he had to overcome a 5-for-51 start in that category just to battle back to the .172 mark. His scoring-position batting average has declined each season with the Reds, from .300 in 1989 to .274 to .258 to .172.... Tied Darren Daulton for the major league lead among catchers in games (141) and starts (137). No Reds catcher has played in more games since Johnny Bench in 1969 (147).... Career breakdowns: .289 in 105 day games, .233 in 302 night games; .287 vs. left-handers, .216 vs. right-handers. Last season's mark vs. righties was by far the best of his career.... Batted .330 when hitting sixth or seventh in the lineup, but only .224 in his more accustomed eighth spot. Hit six home runs while batting eighth, the second straight year he has led N.L. in that category.... Walked only 35 times last season; 19 were intentional. Of those 19 IBBs, 13 came from the 8th spot in the lineup. Still, he can proudly proclaim that over the last 20 years, only one Reds player has been purposely passed more often in one season: Dave Parker, 24 in 1985.

Greg Olson
Bats Right

Atlanta Braves	AB	H	2B	3B	HR	RBI	BB	SO	BA	SA	OBA
Season	302	72	14	2	3	27	34	31	.238	.328	.316
vs. Left-Handers	117	30	5	2	1	10	6	7	.256	.359	.288
vs. Right-Handers	185	42	9	0	2	17	28	24	.227	.308	.332
vs. Ground-Ballers	103	25	4	0	2	13	12	13	.243	.340	.316
vs. Fly-Ballers	199	47	10	2	1	14	22	18	.236	.322	.315
Home Games	135	32	6	0	0	11	19	11	.237	.281	.327
Road Games	167	40	8	2	3	16	15	20	.240	.365	.306
Grass Fields	203	50	9	1	1	17	25	21	.246	.315	.326
Artificial Turf	99	22	5	1	2	10	9	10	.222	.354	.294
April	43	10	3	0	0	2	7	8	.233	.302	.340
May	53	14	2	0	1	7	4	5	.264	.358	.316
June	57	14	3	0	1	3	6	5	.246	.351	.317
July	45	10	2	2	1	4	8	5	.222	.422	.340
August	65	15	3	0	0	8	7	6	.231	.277	.307
Sept./Oct.	39	9	1	0	0	3	2	2	.231	.256	.268
Leading Off Inn.	71	17	4	0	0	0	6	5	.239	.296	.299
Runners On	125	30	7	0	0	24	20	13	.240	.296	.340
Bases Empty	177	42	7	2	3	3	14	18	.237	.350	.297
Runners/Scor. Pos.	80	15	2	0	0	20	14	11	.188	.213	.302
Runners On/2 Out	57	15	4	0	0	12	6	5	.263	.333	.333
Scor. Pos./2 Out	35	9	1	0	0	9	4	3	.257	.286	.333
Late-Inning Pressure	42	9	2	0	2	6	10	3	.214	.405	.358
Leading Off	11	3	1	0	0	0	1	0	.273	.364	.333
Runners On	13	2	1	0	0	4	8	0	.154	.231	.455
Runners/Scor. Pos.	11	1	1	0	0	4	5	0	.091	.182	.353

RUNS BATTED IN	From 1B	From 2B	From 3B	Scoring Position
Totals	4/84	8/64	12/32	20/96
Percentage	4.8%	12.5%	37.5%	20.8%

Loves to face: Jeff Brantley (.714, 5-for-7)
Donovan Osborne (.500, 4-for-8, 1 2B, 1 3B)
Zane Smith (.444, 4-for-9)

Hates to face: Andy Benes (.130, 3-for-23)
Mike Morgan (0-for-11)
Bob Tewksbury (0-for-8)

Miscellaneous statistics: Ground outs-to-air outs ratio: 1.10 last season, 1.26 for career.... Grounded into 8 double plays in 53 opportunities (one per 6.6).... Drove in 8 of 18 runners from third base with less than two outs (44%).... Direction of balls hit to the outfield: 24% to left field, 46% to center, 30% to right.... Base running: Advanced from first base to third on 3 of 14 outfield singles (21%); scored from second on 10 of 13 (77%).... Opposing base stealers: 70-for-115 (61%), 4th-lowest rate in N.L.

Comments: Career batting average with runners in scoring position: .289 with two outs, .189 with less than two outs. He's the only active player to hit 100 points better with two outs than with less than two outs in that category (minimum: 100 at-bats in each category); 19 players have hit at least 100 points better with less than two outs than with two outs.... Became the fifth different catcher in the last five years to start opening day for the Braves. Assuming his ankle has healed, he could be the first Atlanta catcher to start consecutive openers since Ozzie Virgil's three-year run, 1986–88.... Career breakdowns: .288 vs. left-handers, .223 vs. right-handers; .273 in Atlanta, .223 in road games; .316 in April, .183 in September, and .256 in between.... Most impressively, while he's a .227 career hitter with the bases empty, he has hit .275 with runners on base. Numbers are even more diverse in Late-Inning Pressure Situations: .161 average with bases empty, .304 with runners on base.... Turned in 2d-lowest error rate (one in 566 chances) among N.L. catchers; Tom Pagnozzi set single-season league record with one error in 742 chances. Olson would have led N.L. in any other year except 1950 (Wes Westrum) or 1991 (Mike LaValliere). His only error came when his throw sailed into center field on a steal by Mike Felder, June 30.... Batted only .207 in night games, 5th lowest in N.L., while teammate Damon Berryhill had the 5th-lowest N.L. average in day games. A possible Lon Chaney, Jr., platoon here?

Paul O'Neill
Bats Left

Cincinnati Reds	AB	H	2B	3B	HR	RBI	BB	SO	BA	SA	OBA
Season	496	122	19	1	14	66	77	85	.246	.373	.346
vs. Left-Handers	173	39	6	0	2	26	14	46	.225	.295	.279
vs. Right-Handers	323	83	13	1	12	40	63	39	.257	.415	.379
vs. Ground-Ballers	182	46	4	0	6	27	40	26	.253	.374	.388
vs. Fly-Ballers	314	76	15	1	8	39	37	59	.242	.373	.319
Home Games	245	58	10	1	6	33	43	39	.237	.359	.354
Road Games	251	64	9	0	8	33	34	46	.255	.386	.338
Grass Fields	146	41	5	0	5	20	17	27	.281	.418	.352
Artificial Turf	350	81	14	1	9	46	60	58	.231	.354	.344
April	74	25	5	0	3	16	13	13	.338	.527	.456
May	80	20	3	0	3	20	14	16	.250	.400	.368
June	73	14	2	1	3	11	9	14	.192	.370	.286
July	80	19	3	0	1	9	14	14	.237	.313	.344
August	81	20	4	0	1	11	16	14	.247	.333	.360
Sept./Oct.	108	24	2	0	3	9	8	14	.222	.324	.276
Leading Off Inn.	114	29	1	1	7	7	13	21	.254	.465	.336
Runners On	232	56	9	0	2	54	50	29	.241	.306	.368
Bases Empty	264	66	10	1	12	12	27	56	.250	.432	.324
Runners/Scor. Pos.	141	31	5	0	0	47	43	18	.220	.255	.389
Runners On/2 Out	97	22	3	0	2	22	23	8	.227	.320	.375
Scor. Pos./2 Out	62	14	1	0	0	16	20	6	.226	.242	.415
Late-Inning Pressure	69	14	3	0	2	11	11	15	.203	.333	.305
Leading Off	12	2	0	0	1	1	3	6	.167	.417	.333
Runners On	32	8	1	0	1	10	5	2	.250	.375	.333
Runners/Scor. Pos.	19	3	0	0	0	7	5	1	.158	.158	.308

RUNS BATTED IN	From 1B	From 2B	From 3B	Scoring Position
Totals	9/163	16/107	27/68	43/175
Percentage	5.5%	15.0%	39.7%	24.6%

Loves to face: Ron Darling (.381, 8-for-21, 2 HR, 4 BB)
Jay Howell (.727, 8-for-11, 2 2B, 1 3B, 2 HR)
Tim Leary (.333, 8-for-24, 3 2B, 2 HR)

Hates to face: Jeff Parrett (0-for-15)
Bob Patterson (0-for-11)
Nolan Ryan (0-for-10, 5 SO)

Miscellaneous statistics: Ground outs-to-air outs ratio: 1.26 last season, 0.98 for career.... Grounded into 10 double plays in 114 opportunities (one per 11).... Drove in 20 of 38 runners from third base with less than two outs (53%).... Direction of balls hit to the outfield: 34% to left field, 33% to center, 32% to right.... Base running: Advanced from first base to third on 14 of 32 outfield singles (44%); scored from second on 7 of 11 (64%).... Made 2.16 putouts per nine innings in right field.

Comments: Even distribution of balls hit to the outfield is interesting, considering the history of left-handed batters at Yankee Stadium.... O'Neill may miss Riverfront more than you might think: 63 of his 96 career home runs were hit there; the only active players with a greater difference between home and road homers are Ryne Sandberg (135 home, 96 road) and Don Mattingly (115 home, 77 road).... Led Reds with 14 home runs last year, the lowest figure by a Cincinnati team leader since Grady Hatton led with the same total in 1946.... His .215 career batting average vs. left-handers has been an albatross. That's the 2d-lowest average vs. southpaws by any left-handed batter active in 1992 (minimum: 500 at-bats vs. LHP); Mike Pagliarulo (.206) had the lowest. Mel Hall, the player effectively replaced by O'Neill in the Yankees lineup, had a .221 career mark vs. lefties.... Led all N.L. outfielders in fielding with only one error in 304 chances. His fielding average has improved in each of the last three seasons.... Batting average has decreased in each of the last three seasons, but even more disturbing is his 108-point drop in slugging percentage from 1991 to 1992. Only six other players in the majors had a 100-point drop in slugging last season; two of them are now his teammates: Wade Boggs and Danny Tartabull.... His first month in the Bronx will be Steinbrenner's first month back; best thing Paul could do would be to duplicate his .338 mark of last April, the best monthly average of his career.

Spike Owen
Bats Left and Right

Montreal Expos	AB	H	2B	3B	HR	RBI	BB	SO	BA	SA	OBA
Season	386	104	16	3	7	40	50	30	.269	.381	.348
vs. Left-Handers	161	46	10	2	4	23	16	11	.286	.447	.346
vs. Right-Handers	225	58	6	1	3	17	34	19	.258	.333	.350
vs. Ground-Ballers	150	38	5	1	1	17	22	15	.253	.320	.341
vs. Fly-Ballers	236	66	11	2	6	23	28	15	.280	.419	.353
Home Games	173	42	9	0	3	19	23	11	.243	.347	.323
Road Games	213	62	7	3	4	21	27	19	.291	.408	.369
Grass Fields	104	28	1	0	3	11	17	8	.269	.365	.369
Artificial Turf	282	76	15	3	4	29	33	22	.270	.387	.341
April	69	17	4	1	1	9	7	8	.246	.377	.308
May	67	16	2	0	4	8	7	5	.239	.448	.311
June	68	20	5	1	1	8	10	3	.294	.441	.380
July	44	10	0	0	0	1	7	5	.227	.227	.327
August	66	26	5	1	0	10	8	5	.394	.500	.453
Sept./Oct.	72	15	0	0	1	4	11	4	.208	.250	.310
Leading Off Inn.	83	17	3	0	2	2	13	3	.205	.313	.313
Runners On	157	48	7	2	1	34	20	15	.306	.395	.372
Bases Empty	229	56	9	1	6	6	30	15	.245	.371	.332
Runners/Scor. Pos.	91	29	4	0	0	28	16	6	.319	.363	.398
Runners On/2 Out	66	15	3	0	1	11	9	6	.227	.318	.320
Scor. Pos./2 Out	45	9	3	0	0	9	8	3	.200	.267	.321
Late-Inning Pressure	51	15	4	0	0	4	12	1	.294	.373	.422
Leading Off	14	3	0	0	0	0	5	0	.214	.214	.421
Runners On	18	5	3	0	0	4	5	1	.278	.444	.417
Runners/Scor. Pos.	12	2	1	0	0	3	5	1	.167	.250	.389

RUNS BATTED IN	From 1B	From 2B	From 3B	Scoring Position
Totals	6/117	7/67	20/45	27/112
Percentage	5.1%	10.4%	44.4%	24.1%

Loves to face: Juan Agosto (.500, 6-for-12, 4 XBH, 6 BB)
Danny Darwin (.417, 10-for-24)
Frank Viola (.387, 24-for-62, 1 HR)
Hates to face: Mike Bielecki (0-for-22)
Tim Leary (.059, 1-for-17)
Dennis Rasmussen (.100, 3-for-30, 3 BB)

Miscellaneous statistics: Ground outs-to-air outs ratio: 1.08 last season, 1.13 for career.... Grounded into 10 double plays in 83 opportunities (one per 8.3).... Drove in 16 of 23 runners from third base with less than two outs (70%).... Direction of balls hit to the outfield: 33% to left field, 41% to center, 26% to right batting left-handed; 53% to left field, 26% to center, 21% to right batting right-handed.... Base running: Advanced from first base to third on 9 of 20 outfield singles (45%); scored from second on 8 of 10 (80%).... Made 2.78 assists per nine innings at shortstop, 3d-lowest rate in N.L.

Comments: Averaged one error every 62.9 chances in four years in N.L.; he didn't stick around to meet the 1000-game qualifier for official recognition, but it's the lowest error rate in N.L. history for shortstops who played at least 500 games.... Unlike new teammates O'Neill and Wade Boggs, who posted career-low batting averages last season, Owen hit for a career high. He is one of six players to increase his batting average by at least 10 points in each of the last two seasons (minimum: 300 AB in each of last three years). It's the second time in his career he has done that (the other: 1984–85).... In each of the last seven seasons, he has batted .259 or better from the right side, .258 or worse from the left side. Career breakdown: .274 right-handed, .228 left-handed.... Clip and save for Yankees' next division title: Owen went 9-for-21 with Red Sox in 1986 Championship Series; O'Neill went 8-for-17 in 1990 Championship Series.... Strikeout rate (one every 14.9 PA) was the best of his career.... Born on April 19, 1961, one day before new teammate Don Mattingly and three days before new teammate Jimmy Key.... With Owen and Bernie Williams around, Yankees should extend their streak of having at least two switch-hitters on the team in every season since 1961.... His final hit with the Expos was the 1000th of his career; anyone out there want to sign Gene Alley or Tommie Agee, each of whom finished their career with 999? Hey, now that Fay's gone, can the next Minnie Minoso comeback be far off?

Tom Pagnozzi
Bats Right

St. Louis Cardinals	AB	H	2B	3B	HR	RBI	BB	SO	BA	SA	OBA
Season	485	121	26	3	7	44	28	64	.249	.359	.290
vs. Left-Handers	176	43	9	1	5	15	11	28	.244	.392	.287
vs. Right-Handers	309	78	17	2	2	29	17	36	.252	.340	.292
vs. Ground-Ballers	224	51	12	0	3	17	16	23	.228	.321	.282
vs. Fly-Ballers	261	70	14	3	4	27	12	41	.268	.391	.297
Home Games	223	55	9	2	3	18	13	32	.247	.345	.291
Road Games	262	66	17	1	4	26	15	32	.252	.370	.289
Grass Fields	128	40	13	1	1	13	7	12	.313	.453	.343
Artificial Turf	357	81	13	2	6	31	21	52	.227	.325	.271
April	73	22	5	1	0	8	2	9	.301	.397	.320
May	90	26	5	1	1	7	6	13	.289	.400	.333
June	75	22	5	0	2	10	8	7	.293	.440	.357
July	84	19	4	1	3	9	4	13	.226	.405	.261
August	86	15	5	0	0	5	5	13	.174	.233	.217
Sept./Oct.	77	17	2	0	1	5	3	9	.221	.286	.256
Leading Off Inn.	105	17	2	1	1	1	6	19	.162	.229	.207
Runners On	215	59	12	2	3	40	18	31	.274	.391	.329
Bases Empty	270	62	14	1	4	4	10	33	.230	.333	.257
Runners/Scor. Pos.	128	31	8	1	1	32	16	24	.242	.344	.324
Runners On/2 Out	87	25	6	1	1	16	11	13	.287	.414	.374
Scor. Pos./2 Out	55	13	5	0	0	13	11	9	.236	.327	.373
Late-Inning Pressure	98	20	3	0	2	7	4	16	.204	.296	.243
Leading Off	24	1	0	0	0	0	1	6	.042	.042	.080
Runners On	38	7	1	0	0	5	2	5	.184	.211	.244
Runners/Scor. Pos.	25	4	1	0	0	5	2	5	.160	.200	.250

RUNS BATTED IN	From 1B	From 2B	From 3B	Scoring Position
Totals	9/148	14/94	14/49	28/143
Percentage	6.1%	14.9%	28.6%	19.6%

Loves to face: Dwight Gooden (.565, 13-for-23)
Terry Mulholland (.478, 11-for-23, 1 HR)
John Smiley (.368, 7-for-19, 1 HR)
Hates to face: John Franco (0-for-12)
Bill Landrum (0-for-11)
Zane Smith (.087, 2-for-23, 2 BB)

Miscellaneous statistics: Ground outs-to-air outs ratio: 1.04 last season, 1.10 for career.... Grounded into 15 double plays in 95 opportunities (one per 6.3).... Drove in 8 of 23 runners from third base with less than two outs (35%), 2d-lowest rate in N.L.... Direction of balls hit to the outfield: 32% to left field, 32% to center, 36% to right.... Base running: Advanced from first base to third on 6 of 17 outfield singles (35%); scored from second on 9 of 11 (82%).... Opposing base stealers: 87-for-123 (71%).

Comments: Set N.L. record for lowest error rate in a season by a catcher: one error in 742 chances. But there's this asterisk: According to today's standards, adopted in 1957, a catcher must play in half of his team's scheduled games to qualify. That's not a problem for Pagnozzi (138 games last year), but in 1939, Spud Davis of the Phillies caught in 85 games and had no errors in 300 chances. However, according to the more stringent rules of the day, a catcher needed to play 90 (of his team's 154) games to qualify.... Pagnozzi's only error came on an attempted pickoff at third base; he committed seven errors in 1991.... He and Tony Pena are the only major leaguers to have caught 1000 innings in each of the last two seasons.... Cardinals were 70–62 with Pagnozzi as starting catcher, 13–18 when Rich Gedman started. He and Gedman were the only duo in the majors last season to catch every inning for their club; they accounted for 98 percent of the Cardinals' innings caught in 1991. Last year, only one other club had just two players combine for all of their innings at any position: Steve Sax and Joey Cora handled all the second base duties for the White Sox.... Not much of a difference between the staff ERAs with Gedman (3.46) and Pagnozzi (3.36), but opposing base stealers went 37-for-40 vs. Gedman.... Pags owns a slightly better career batting average vs. right-handed pitchers (.259) than vs. left-handers (.249), but he has hit 10 of his 13 home runs off southpaws.

Bill Pecota

Bats Right

New York Mets	AB	H	2B	3B	HR	RBI	BB	SO	BA	SA	OBA
Season	269	61	13	0	2	26	25	40	.227	.297	.293
vs. Left-Handers	107	25	6	0	2	13	9	12	.234	.346	.291
vs. Right-Handers	162	36	7	0	0	13	16	28	.222	.265	.294
vs. Ground-Ballers	124	24	4	0	0	11	9	20	.194	.226	.246
vs. Fly-Ballers	145	37	9	0	2	15	16	20	.255	.359	.331
Home Games	125	34	10	0	1	17	13	20	.272	.376	.336
Road Games	144	27	3	0	1	9	12	20	.188	.229	.255
Grass Fields	173	44	11	0	2	25	19	28	.254	.353	.325
Artificial Turf	96	17	2	0	0	1	6	12	.177	.198	.233
April	32	6	1	0	0	4	2	2	.188	.219	.235
May	34	6	2	0	0	5	3	6	.176	.235	.263
June	50	14	3	0	0	4	7	10	.280	.340	.368
July	63	15	3	0	0	3	6	12	.238	.286	.304
August	48	12	2	0	2	7	4	4	.250	.417	.302
Sept./Oct.	42	8	2	0	0	3	3	6	.190	.238	.239
Leading Off Inn.	70	12	2	0	0	0	1	7	.171	.200	.183
Runners On	99	23	6	0	1	25	16	15	.232	.323	.333
Bases Empty	170	38	7	0	1	1	9	25	.224	.282	.267
Runners/Scor. Pos.	54	10	3	0	0	21	13	6	.185	.241	.333
Runners On/2 Out	43	10	3	0	1	13	7	10	.233	.372	.340
Scor. Pos./2 Out	28	6	3	0	0	11	5	5	.214	.321	.333
Late-Inning Pressure	48	14	3	0	1	5	5	6	.292	.417	.364
Leading Off	16	2	0	0	0	0	0	3	.125	.125	.125
Runners On	14	5	1	0	0	4	3	0	.357	.429	.444
Runners/Scor. Pos.	9	3	1	0	0	4	2	0	.333	.444	.417

RUNS BATTED IN	From 1B	From 2B	From 3B	Scoring Position
Totals	4/68	7/44	13/26	20/70
Percentage	5.9%	15.9%	50.0%	28.6%

Loves to face: Denis Boucher (4-for-4, 1 2B)
Greg Swindell (.304, 7-for-23, 2 2B)
Frank Tanana (.556, 5-for-9, 1 2B)

Hates to face: Greg Cadaret (0-for-8)
Jose DeLeon (.091, 1-for-11, 1 2B)
Curt Schilling (.111, 1-for-9)

Miscellaneous statistics: Ground outs-to-air outs ratio: 1.49 last season, 1.27 for career.... Grounded into 7 double plays in 48 opportunities (one per 6.9).... Drove in 9 of 13 runners from third base with less than two outs (69%).... Direction of balls hit to the outfield: 43% to left field, 25% to center, 32% to right.... Base running: Advanced from first base to third on 4 of 11 outfield singles (36%); scored from second on 4 of 6 (67%).... Made 3.71 assists per nine innings at second base.

Comments: From the 1992 *Analyst*: "Mets manager Jeff Torborg talked of Pecota as a semi-regular starter. But our model projects him as only a .230 hitter in slightly less than 100 games." Okay, we missed; he batted .227 in 117 games. (If you want to bring us down to size quickly, though, remind us of our Ryne Sandberg projection for 1992. Ouch!)... Mets employed eight different players at second base last season, the most by any team in the majors; their total of eight third basemen matched Cleveland and Seattle for the most in the majors; and their total of seven shortstops tied the Cubs for the N.L. high. Pecota was among the players at each of those positions.... By the way, without any help from Pecota, the Mets also used the most players in the National League in center field (eight), and tied for the most in right field (10).... For six consecutive seasons, he has appeared at shortstop, third base, and second base. That's a pretty good definition of a utility man. Four more years of doing that and he'll tie the major league record streak of 10 seasons playing those three positions, a mark shared by Tom Brookens and Ed Romero.... Became the first nonpitcher in Mets history to take the mound when he mopped up in a game at Pittsburgh in September; previously, the Mets had been the only current major league team that had never used a position player on the hill. Andy Van Slyke greeted him with a home run, but Pecota came back to get the next three guys.

Terry Pendleton

Bats Left and Right

Atlanta Braves	AB	H	2B	3B	HR	RBI	BB	SO	BA	SA	OBA
Season	640	199	39	1	21	105	37	67	.311	.473	.345
vs. Left-Handers	207	74	11	0	8	41	13	13	.357	.527	.390
vs. Right-Handers	433	125	28	1	13	64	24	54	.289	.448	.323
vs. Ground-Ballers	273	98	17	1	9	44	19	26	.359	.527	.397
vs. Fly-Ballers	367	101	22	0	12	61	18	41	.275	.433	.306
Home Games	306	94	19	1	13	56	22	36	.307	.503	.353
Road Games	334	105	20	0	8	49	15	31	.314	.446	.338
Grass Fields	471	153	30	1	19	83	29	51	.325	.514	.361
Artificial Turf	169	46	9	0	2	22	8	16	.272	.361	.300
April	85	26	9	0	1	15	2	7	.306	.447	.315
May	118	37	5	0	8	21	8	17	.314	.559	.354
June	105	33	3	1	3	14	2	10	.314	.442	.321
July	103	26	3	0	2	9	3	14	.252	.340	.274
August	112	39	8	0	4	27	10	8	.348	.527	.398
Sept./Oct.	117	38	11	0	3	19	12	11	.325	.496	.385
Leading Off Inn.	111	39	6	0	2	2	3	6	.351	.459	.368
Runners On	278	93	18	1	10	94	23	35	.335	.514	.377
Bases Empty	362	106	21	0	11	11	14	32	.293	.442	.319
Runners/Scor. Pos.	163	63	10	1	8	86	20	22	.387	.607	.437
Runners On/2 Out	85	28	8	0	4	32	7	9	.329	.565	.380
Scor. Pos./2 Out	52	18	4	0	3	27	6	6	.346	.596	.414
Late-Inning Pressure	67	19	2	0	5	14	6	6	.284	.537	.333
Leading Off	20	6	0	0	1	1	1	2	.300	.450	.333
Runners On	26	9	2	0	3	12	5	1	.346	.769	.424
Runners/Scor. Pos.	20	8	1	0	3	12	5	0	.400	.900	.481

RUNS BATTED IN	From 1B	From 2B	From 3B	Scoring Position
Totals	13/193	36/121	35/65	71/186
Percentage	6.7%	29.8%	53.8%	38.2%

Loves to face: Shawn Boskie (.545, 6-for-11, 4 2B, 1 HR)
Roger McDowell (.375, 12-for-32, 4 HR)
Zane Smith (.491, 26-for-53, 2 HR)

Hates to face: Pat Combs (.091, 1-for-11)
Ken Hill (0-for-14)
Scott Ruskin (0-for-6)

Miscellaneous statistics: Ground outs-to-air outs ratio: 1.20 last season, 1.24 for career.... Grounded into 16 double plays in 148 opportunities (one per 9.3).... Drove in 28 of 48 runners from third base with less than two outs (58%).... Direction of balls hit to the outfield: 36% to left field, 27% to center, 36% to right batting left-handed; 32% to left field, 34% to center, 33% to right batting right-handed.... Base running: Advanced from first base to third on 7 of 27 outfield singles (26%); scored from second on 21 of 26 (81%).... Made 2.11 assists per nine innings at third base.

Comments: Tied Andy Van Slyke for the National League lead in hits (199), becoming the first Braves player ever to lead the league in consecutive seasons.... Led N.L. with 17 games of three or more hits; ranked 2d with 62 multiple-hit games, trailing only Van Slyke (16).... Batting average with runners in scoring position was a major league high, as was the percentage of runners he knocked in from scoring position.... Batting average vs. left-handers was 3d-best in the N.L.... Batted .221 in 145 at-bats during the first inning last season, .337 from the second inning on.... Led the N.L. with 35 go-ahead RBIs; 20 stood up as game-winners, tying Gary Sheffield and Larry Walker for major league lead in that category.... Has killed ground-ball pitchers in his two seasons with Atlanta, posting a .370 mark against them, compared to a .277 average against fly-ball pitchers.... Has hit 43 home runs in his two seasons with the Braves; hit 44 in seven seasons with the Cardinals.... Career batting average is .291 on grass fields, .263 on artificial turf.... But he sure doesn't prefer grass when he's wearing leather. Has posted a much higher fielding percentage on artificial turf than on grass in each of the last four seasons. Four-year error rates: one every 19 chances on grass, one every 33 chances on plastic.... Career total of 46 postseason games at third base is 2d most in major league history, behind Graig Nettles (52).

Willie Randolph
Bats Right

New York Mets	AB	H	2B	3B	HR	RBI	BB	SO	BA	SA	OBA
Season	286	72	11	1	2	15	40	34	.252	.318	.352
vs. Left-Handers	105	29	2	1	2	8	21	5	.276	.371	.397
vs. Right-Handers	181	43	9	0	0	7	19	29	.238	.287	.324
vs. Ground-Ballers	137	37	5	1	1	5	22	15	.270	.343	.375
vs. Fly-Ballers	149	35	6	0	1	10	18	19	.235	.295	.329
Home Games	153	39	8	1	2	6	20	24	.255	.359	.349
Road Games	133	33	3	0	0	9	20	10	.248	.271	.355
Grass Fields	217	57	10	1	2	10	26	27	.263	.346	.347
Artificial Turf	69	15	1	0	0	5	14	7	.217	.232	.365
April	68	18	4	0	1	5	14	10	.265	.368	.390
May	87	20	2	0	0	5	8	7	.230	.253	.295
June	74	18	4	1	1	3	7	11	.243	.365	.333
July	36	11	0	0	0	2	4	3	.306	.306	.375
August	18	5	1	0	0	0	6	2	.278	.333	.480
Sept./Oct.	3	0	0	0	0	0	1	1	.000	.000	.250
Leading Off Inn.	79	18	2	0	1	1	7	7	.228	.291	.291
Runners On	99	23	4	0	0	13	18	12	.232	.273	.372
Bases Empty	187	49	7	1	2	2	22	22	.262	.342	.340
Runners/Scor. Pos.	58	10	2	0	0	11	13	10	.172	.207	.351
Runners On/2 Out	50	7	2	0	0	6	4	6	.140	.180	.204
Scor. Pos./2 Out	33	5	1	0	0	5	4	5	.152	.182	.243
Late-Inning Pressure	46	13	2	0	0	1	8	9	.283	.326	.400
Leading Off	9	3	1	0	0	0	1	0	.333	.444	.400
Runners On	20	4	0	0	0	1	4	5	.200	.200	.360
Runners/Scor. Pos.	14	2	0	0	0	1	3	5	.143	.143	.294

RUNS BATTED IN	From 1B	From 2B	From 3B	Scoring Position
Totals	3/67	3/47	7/22	10/69
Percentage	4.5%	6.4%	31.8%	14.5%

Loves to face: Tom Browning (.533, 8-for-15, 1 HR)
             Greg A. Harris (.524, 11-for-21)
             Bruce Hurst (.366, 34-for-93, 1 HR)
Hates to face: Roger Clemens (.186, 8-for-43)
             Mike Moore (.120, 3-for-25)
             Nolan Ryan (.115, 3-for-26, 5 BB)

Miscellaneous statistics: Ground outs-to-air outs ratio: 1.82 last season, 1.47 for career.... Grounded into 6 double plays in 50 opportunities (one per 8.3).... Drove in 5 of 12 runners from third base with less than two outs (42%).... Direction of balls hit to the outfield: 32% to left field, 29% to center, 39% to right.... Base running: Advanced from first base to third on 9 of 21 outfield singles (43%); scored from second on 9 of 10 (90%).... Made 2.69 assists per nine innings at second base, 3d-lowest rate in N.L.

Comments: Five current major league managers were once teammates of Willie Randolph: Don Baylor, Butch Hobson, Johnny Oates, Lou Piniella, and Art Howe (who teamed briefly with Randolph on the 1975 Pirates).... Fifth on all-time list of games at second base (2152), 45 shy of Charlie Gehringer's 4th-place total. The only other active player with more than 2000 games there is Lou Whitaker (2052).... Third in major league history with 1547 double plays at second base, behind only Bill Mazeroski (1706) and Nellie Fox (1619).... The Mets had a winning record with Randolph as starting second baseman (38–36), but were 20 games below .500 with their seven other starters (34–54).... Walked more often than he struck out for the 18th time in 18 seasons in the majors, but by the smallest margin since his debut season (7 BB, 6 SO in 1975).... Percentage of runners driven in from scoring position was the lowest in the majors (minimum: 60 opportunities). He had driven in 36 percent in 1991.... Batting average dropped by 75 points from 1991 (.327), the largest decrease in consecutive seasons of at least 275 at-bats by any player since John Shelby's 80-point crash in 1989.... The top three hitters in the A.L. two years ago (Julio Franco, Wade Boggs, and Randolph) combined for a .334 average in 1991, and a .254 average last season.... Was on the losing end of four postseason-series sweeps (1975 Pirates, 1976 Yankees, 1980 Yankees, 1990 A's). No other player was on the postseason roster of more than three teams that were swept.

Bip Roberts
Bats Left and Right

Cincinnati Reds	AB	H	2B	3B	HR	RBI	BB	SO	BA	SA	OBA
Season	532	172	34	6	4	45	62	54	.323	.432	.393
vs. Left-Handers	185	54	7	0	3	15	17	20	.292	.378	.350
vs. Right-Handers	347	118	27	6	1	30	45	34	.340	.461	.416
vs. Ground-Ballers	213	71	17	3	0	16	23	16	.333	.441	.395
vs. Fly-Ballers	319	101	17	3	4	29	39	38	.317	.426	.392
Home Games	252	89	22	3	3	23	36	24	.353	.500	.432
Road Games	280	83	12	3	1	22	26	30	.296	.371	.357
Grass Fields	173	54	6	3	1	16	15	19	.312	.399	.367
Artificial Turf	359	118	28	3	3	29	47	35	.329	.448	.405
April	83	23	4	2	0	6	12	8	.277	.373	.371
May	95	29	5	0	0	7	13	10	.305	.358	.385
June	99	32	8	0	0	7	7	12	.323	.404	.364
July	75	20	4	0	1	8	13	11	.267	.360	.375
August	87	27	6	1	1	6	7	7	.310	.437	.358
Sept./Oct.	93	41	7	3	2	11	10	6	.441	.645	.500
Leading Off Inn.	252	86	13	3	2	2	23	30	.341	.440	.396
Runners On	157	54	17	3	2	43	18	14	.344	.529	.406
Bases Empty	375	118	17	3	2	2	44	40	.315	.392	.388
Runners/Scor. Pos.	98	33	10	3	1	40	15	9	.337	.531	.415
Runners On/2 Out	77	28	11	2	1	23	8	5	.364	.597	.424
Scor. Pos./2 Out	52	18	7	2	0	20	8	4	.346	.558	.433
Late-Inning Pressure	68	20	4	0	1	5	8	9	.294	.397	.368
Leading Off	23	6	1	0	0	0	5	4	.261	.304	.393
Runners On	25	9	2	0	1	5	2	3	.360	.560	.407
Runners/Scor. Pos.	14	5	1	0	0	3	2	2	.357	.429	.438

RUNS BATTED IN	From 1B	From 2B	From 3B	Scoring Position
Totals	4/106	18/75	19/44	37/119
Percentage	3.8%	24.0%	43.2%	31.1%

Loves to face: Greg Maddux (.476, 10-for-21)
             Dennis Martinez (.469, 15-for-32, 0 BB)
             John Smoltz (.320, 8-for-25, 9 BB)
Hates to face: Stan Belinda (0-for-4, 3 SO)
             Bob Tewksbury (.176, 3-for-17)
             Wally Whitehurst (0-for-8)

Miscellaneous statistics: Ground outs-to-air outs ratio: 1.50 last season, 1.59 for career.... Grounded into 7 double plays in 64 opportunities (one per 9.1).... Drove in 10 of 21 runners from third base with less than two outs (48%).... Direction of balls hit to the outfield: 34% to left field, 39% to center, 26% to right batting left-handed; 36% to left field, 24% to center, 40% to right batting right-handed.... Base running: Advanced from first base to third on 16 of 27 outfield singles (59%), 4th-highest rate in N.L.; scored from second on 13 of 19 (68%).... Made 2.08 putouts per nine innings in left field.

Comments: Reds dominate the list of highest N.L. batting averages since 1989 (minimum: 1000 AB): Tony Gwynn, .320; Barry Larkin, .309; Hal Morris, .308; Will Clark, .308; Willie McGee, .306; Bip Roberts, .305.... Has batted leadoff in 434 of 453 starts over the past four years and assumed the title of "Best Leadoff Hitter in N.L." from Brett Butler. His average of .325 from the leadoff slot was the highest in either league last season (minimum: 100 PA). Reds batters from that spot combined for the highest batting, slugging, and on-base averages of any N.L. club.... Over the past 40 years, the only player to post a higher batting average in his first season with the Reds was Morris (.340 in 1990).... Had the highest average in majors from September 1 until season's end.... Hit .344 in day games (3d-best in N.L.), .314 at night (8th).... Batting average of .353 at Riverfront Stadium was 2d best home-game mark in the National League, behind Gary Sheffield (.365).... Career batting average at Riverfront is .342.... Among active players, only Kirby Puckett (.335) and Tony Gwynn (.333) have higher batting averages on artificial turf than Roberts (.324) (minimum: 150 hits).... Career average with two outs and runners on base is .336, the highest in Player Analysis history.... Career stolen-base percentage is .636 on grass (82 SB, 47 CS), .802 on artificial turf (69 SB, 17 CS).... Career batting average of .299 is two hits shy of the .300 mark.

Chris Sabo   Bats Right

Cincinnati Reds	AB	H	2B	3B	HR	RBI	BB	SO	BA	SA	OBA
Season	344	84	19	3	12	43	30	54	.244	.422	.302
vs. Left-Handers	146	36	8	1	6	21	14	23	.247	.438	.311
vs. Right-Handers	198	48	11	2	6	22	16	31	.242	.409	.295
vs. Ground-Ballers	125	31	8	1	6	23	7	19	.248	.472	.281
vs. Fly-Ballers	219	53	11	2	6	20	23	35	.242	.393	.313
Home Games	148	35	11	0	8	22	11	27	.236	.473	.282
Road Games	196	49	8	3	4	21	19	27	.250	.383	.317
Grass Fields	114	24	5	1	1	8	10	16	.211	.298	.272
Artificial Turf	230	60	14	2	11	35	20	38	.261	.483	.316
April	26	4	0	0	0	0	3	2	.154	.154	.241
May	92	24	7	2	2	10	9	14	.261	.446	.324
June	87	24	5	1	5	16	6	15	.276	.529	.319
July	55	13	1	0	1	5	4	9	.236	.309	.279
August	55	13	6	0	3	7	4	7	.236	.509	.283
Sept./Oct.	29	6	0	0	1	5	4	7	.207	.310	.314
Leading Off Inn.	89	23	8	0	4	4	6	14	.258	.483	.313
Runners On	170	37	3	0	5	36	15	22	.218	.324	.272
Bases Empty	174	47	16	3	7	7	15	32	.270	.517	.332
Runners/Scor. Pos.	108	23	2	0	4	33	14	17	.213	.343	.289
Runners On/2 Out	79	10	1	0	3	13	9	11	.127	.253	.216
Scor. Pos./2 Out	53	7	0	0	3	12	8	9	.132	.302	.246
Late-Inning Pressure	36	8	0	0	0	4	4	6	.222	.222	.286
Leading Off	12	4	0	0	0	0	2	2	.333	.333	.429
Runners On	16	3	0	0	0	4	2	2	.188	.188	.250
Runners/Scor. Pos.	9	2	0	0	0	4	2	1	.222	.222	.308

RUNS BATTED IN	From 1B	From 2B	From 3B	Scoring Position
Totals	5/122	9/83	17/53	26/136
Percentage	4.1%	10.8%	32.1%	19.1%

Loves to face: Steve Avery (.414, 12-for-29, 1 HR)
John Burkett (.417, 10-for-24, 1 HR)
Chris Nabholz (.538, 7-for-13, 3 2B, 1 3B, 2 HR)

Hates to face: Sid Fernandez (.042, 1-for-24, 1 2B, 2 BB)
Greg Maddux (.167, 6-for-36, 0 BB)
John Wetteland (0-for-9)

Miscellaneous statistics: Ground outs-to-air outs ratio: 0.68 last season, 0.73 for career.... Grounded into 12 double plays in 77 opportunities (one per 6.4).... Drove in 14 of 28 runners from third base with less than two outs (50%).... Direction of balls hit to the outfield: 51% to left field, 30% to center, 19% to right.... Base running: Advanced from first base to third on 5 of 11 outfield singles (45%); scored from second on 3 of 6 (50%).... Made 1.81 assists per nine innings at third base.

Comments: Spent only 15 days on the D.L. (Apr. 8–22, for a sprained right ankle), but played hurt throughout the season.... Didn't miss more than four straight games at any time from May through August, but was limited to a total of 96 games.... Stole only four bases in nine attempts after averaging 26 steals per season during the previous four years.... His 57-point decline in batting average (from .301 in 1991) was the largest by a Reds player in consecutive seasons of at least 300 at-bats since Nick Esasky batted .193 in 1984 coming off a .265 mark in '83.... Strikeout rate of one every 7.1 plate appearances was the worst of his career.... Had a ground outs-to-air outs ratio of 1.04 against left-handers, 0.48 against right-handers. That led to a GIDP rate of one every 12 opportunities against right-handers, one every 3.9 opportunities against left-handers.... Had the lowest batting average in majors with runners on base and two outs.... Career batting average is .287 with one home run every 23 at-bats at Riverfront Stadium, compared to .259 with one homer every 39 at-bats on the road.... No Cincinnati player has homered in their last eight games at Wrigley Field; the last Reds homer at Wrigley was hit by Sabo on July 23, 1991.... Was Cincinnati's opening-day third baseman in each of the last five seasons. The last third baseman with a longer streak for the Reds was Grady Hatton (1946–51), known to a later generation as the manager of the Astros (1966–68), and more or less unknown to the generation after that.

Luis Salazar   Bats Right

Chicago Cubs	AB	H	2B	3B	HR	RBI	BB	SO	BA	SA	OBA
Season	255	53	7	2	5	25	11	34	.208	.310	.237
vs. Left-Handers	156	39	6	2	4	18	6	16	.250	.391	.273
vs. Right-Handers	99	14	1	0	1	7	5	18	.141	.182	.181
vs. Ground-Ballers	93	21	2	2	2	12	6	19	.226	.355	.265
vs. Fly-Ballers	162	32	5	0	3	13	5	15	.198	.284	.220
Home Games	119	28	4	2	3	16	7	15	.235	.378	.271
Road Games	136	25	3	0	2	9	4	19	.184	.250	.206
Grass Fields	182	37	6	2	4	20	9	23	.203	.324	.237
Artificial Turf	73	16	1	0	1	5	2	11	.219	.274	.237
April	28	7	2	0	0	2	3	3	.250	.321	.323
May	65	10	2	0	1	6	3	11	.154	.231	.188
June	49	13	1	0	1	6	3	10	.265	.347	.302
July	19	4	0	0	1	2	0	1	.211	.368	.200
August	35	6	1	0	0	2	0	3	.171	.200	.167
Sept./Oct.	59	13	1	2	2	7	2	6	.220	.407	.246
Leading Off Inn.	50	10	1	0	1	1	2	4	.200	.280	.231
Runners On	111	22	2	2	1	21	6	16	.198	.279	.231
Bases Empty	144	31	5	0	4	4	5	18	.215	.333	.242
Runners/Scor. Pos.	62	14	1	2	0	18	5	11	.226	.306	.268
Runners On/2 Out	47	6	2	0	0	5	4	10	.128	.170	.196
Scor. Pos./2 Out	26	4	1	0	0	4	3	6	.154	.192	.241
Late-Inning Pressure	39	6	1	0	0	4	3	6	.154	.179	.205
Leading Off	7	1	0	0	0	0	1	1	.143	.143	.250
Runners On	17	1	1	0	0	4	2	5	.059	.118	.143
Runners/Scor. Pos.	12	0	0	0	0	3	2	4	.000	.000	.125

RUNS BATTED IN	From 1B	From 2B	From 3B	Scoring Position
Totals	3/82	6/50	11/29	17/79
Percentage	3.7%	12.0%	37.9%	21.5%

Loves to face: Bud Black (.391, 9-for-23, 3 HR)
Zane Smith (.333, 5-for-15, 2 HR)
Greg Swindell (.438, 7-for-16)

Hates to face: Brian Barnes (.056, 1-for-18)
Jose DeLeon (.136, 3-for-22, 2 2B)
John Smoltz (0-for-10)

Miscellaneous statistics: Ground outs-to-air outs ratio: 0.89 last season, 1.06 for career.... Grounded into 10 double plays in 48 opportunities (one per 4.8), worst rate in N.L.... Drove in 10 of 21 runners from third base with less than two outs (48%).... Direction of balls hit to the outfield: 35% to left field, 30% to center, 35% to right.... Base running: Advanced from first base to third on 3 of 10 outfield singles (30%); scored from second on 5 of 7 (71%).... Made 2.35 assists per nine innings at third base.

Comments: Started 47 of 61 games in which the Cubs faced left-handed starters, only 20 of 101 vs. right-handers.... Has posted a higher batting average against left-handed pitchers than vs. right-handers in every season since 1982.... Became the sixth different Cubs player in the last six years to start the opener in left field; in order: Rafael Palmeiro, Mitch Webster, Lloyd McClendon, George Bell, and Salazar. Brian Dayett (1986–87) was the last Cubs left fielder to start consecutive openers.... Home-run rate dropped from one every 24 at-bats in 1991 to one every 51 at-bats last season, breaking a streak of five consecutive increases. Only three players in major league history have had streaks of more than five seasons: Hack Wilson, 1924–30 (seven years); Ron Cey, 1972–77; and Cy Williams, 1918–23.... Although 137 players have appeared for both the Cubs and the White Sox, Salazar is one of only four to hit at least 10 career homers for both clubs. The others: George Bell, Jay Johnstone, and Vance Law.... Played 647 games in the majors prior to injuring his left knee in 1985; has played 655 since then. Stolen-base totals tell the story: 103 before, 14 after.... Batted .337 as a Padres rookie in 1980, .303 as a sophomore, only .253 since then. Over the past 50 years, only two other players have posted marks of .300 or better in each of their first two seasons, but batted below .260 thereafter: John Wathan and Jack Daugherty.

Rey Sanchez — Bats Right

Chicago Cubs	AB	H	2B	3B	HR	RBI	BB	SO	BA	SA	OBA
Season	255	64	14	3	1	19	10	17	.251	.341	.285
vs. Left-Handers	106	30	8	2	0	8	7	4	.283	.396	.327
vs. Right-Handers	149	34	6	1	1	11	3	13	.228	.302	.255
vs. Ground-Ballers	118	24	7	2	0	9	6	11	.203	.297	.254
vs. Fly-Ballers	137	40	7	1	1	10	4	6	.292	.380	.313
Home Games	130	39	9	1	1	11	5	11	.300	.408	.328
Road Games	125	25	5	2	0	8	5	6	.200	.272	.241
Grass Fields	189	48	13	1	1	12	7	13	.254	.349	.283
Artificial Turf	66	16	1	2	0	7	3	4	.242	.318	.292
April	9	0	0	0	0	0	0	1	.000	.000	.000
May	7	1	0	1	0	1	0	1	.143	.429	.125
June	48	14	3	2	0	8	1	3	.292	.438	.306
July	88	20	4	0	0	4	5	5	.227	.273	.292
August	90	28	7	0	1	6	4	6	.311	.422	.337
Sept./Oct.	13	1	0	0	0	0	0	1	.077	.077	.077
Leading Off Inn.	81	22	4	0	1	1	2	4	.272	.358	.306
Runners On	98	22	5	2	0	18	5	7	.224	.316	.264
Bases Empty	157	42	9	1	1	1	5	10	.268	.357	.299
Runners/Scor. Pos.	48	12	3	1	0	16	3	3	.250	.354	.296
Runners On/2 Out	43	12	3	1	0	6	5	1	.279	.395	.354
Scor. Pos./2 Out	25	4	1	0	0	4	3	1	.160	.200	.250
Late-Inning Pressure	51	10	3	0	0	2	2	2	.196	.255	.250
Leading Off	13	5	1	0	0	0	0	1	.385	.462	.429
Runners On	16	1	0	0	0	2	1	0	.063	.063	.158
Runners/Scor. Pos.	7	1	0	0	0	2	0	0	.143	.143	.222

RUNS BATTED IN	From 1B	From 2B	From 3B	Scoring Position
Totals	4/76	2/38	12/24	14/62
Percentage	5.3%	5.3%	50.0%	22.6%

Loves to face: Brian Barnes (.571, 4-for-7)
Sid Fernandez (.500, 2-for-4, 2 2B)
Ken Hill (.600, 3-for-5)

Hates to face: Tom Candiotti (0-for-4, 3 SO)
Doug Drabek (.125, 1-for-8)
Dennis Martinez (0-for-9)

Miscellaneous statistics: Ground outs-to-air outs ratio: 1.65 last season, 1.56 for career. . . . Grounded into 7 double plays in 51 opportunities (one per 7.3). . . . Drove in 9 of 12 runners from third base with less than two outs (75%). . . . Direction of balls hit to the outfield: 38% to left field, 29% to center, 33% to right. . . . Base running: Advanced from first base to third on 1 of 7 outfield singles (14%); scored from second on 7 of 7 (100%). . . . Made 3.00 assists per nine innings at shortstop.

Comments: Average of one walk every 27.5 plate appearances was 2d lowest among major league rookies (minimum: 250 PA), ahead of only Gary DiSarcina (one every 27.7 PA). But his strikeout rate (one every 16.2 PA) was the best among that group. . . . Sanchez put the ball in play on 245 of 275 plate appearances (89%). No rookie since Ozzie Guillen (1985) has reached the 90 percent mark; Sanchez came closest. . . . Seven of his 19 RBIs proved to be game-winners. . . . Posted similar figures to those of another Windy City rookie shortstop of not too long ago, Scott Fletcher (.237, 62-for-262, 3 HR, 31 RBI in 1983). . . . Shortstops for both Chicago clubs must have been under an evil spell last season. Shawon Dunston was placed on the disabled list on May 5 and never returned. His replacement, Jose Vizcaino, was on the D.L. with a thumb injury in late April; he returned just in time to replace Dunston in the lineup. Sanchez went down for 15 days in May with the chicken pox, and Vizcaino spent another 21 days on the list in August and September. . . . Of course, things were even worse on the South Side. Guillen went down for the season even before Dunston did; his replacement, Craig Grebeck, also spent 57 days on the D.L. . . . That combined total of 428 D.L. days by Chicago shortstops makes you yearn for 1960, when Luis Aparicio played all but one game at shortstop for the Sox, and Ernie Banks played the full schedule for the Cubs. Did someone say, "Let's play two today?"

Ryne Sandberg — Bats Right

Chicago Cubs	AB	H	2B	3B	HR	RBI	BB	SO	BA	SA	OBA
Season	612	186	32	8	26	87	68	73	.304	.510	.371
vs. Left-Handers	206	70	13	4	4	24	23	19	.340	.500	.403
vs. Right-Handers	406	116	19	4	22	63	45	54	.286	.515	.355
vs. Ground-Ballers	269	77	12	5	7	28	29	30	.286	.446	.355
vs. Fly-Ballers	343	109	20	3	19	59	39	43	.318	.560	.383
Home Games	300	92	19	6	16	46	41	35	.307	.570	.386
Road Games	312	94	13	2	10	41	27	38	.301	.452	.357
Grass Fields	423	127	23	7	20	62	49	50	.300	.530	.370
Artificial Turf	189	59	9	1	6	25	19	23	.312	.466	.374
April	64	16	3	1	2	11	8	5	.250	.422	.333
May	109	31	5	0	5	15	13	17	.284	.468	.361
June	109	32	8	2	3	18	10	13	.294	.486	.344
July	95	30	4	2	3	9	13	10	.316	.495	.398
August	118	34	6	2	3	11	12	8	.288	.449	.351
Sept./Oct.	117	43	6	1	10	23	12	20	.368	.692	.426
Leading Off Inn.	119	37	8	1	4	4	14	15	.311	.496	.383
Runners On	262	77	17	4	14	75	26	35	.294	.550	.350
Bases Empty	350	109	15	4	12	12	42	38	.311	.480	.387
Runners/Scor. Pos.	125	37	5	2	7	54	19	17	.296	.536	.373
Runners On/2 Out	101	24	5	1	5	22	14	11	.238	.455	.330
Scor. Pos./2 Out	55	13	1	1	2	15	12	5	.236	.400	.373
Late-Inning Pressure	101	33	3	0	5	14	9	16	.327	.505	.378
Leading Off	28	11	3	0	1	1	3	3	.393	.607	.452
Runners On	44	12	0	0	3	12	3	8	.273	.477	.313
Runners/Scor. Pos.	24	6	0	0	2	10	3	3	.250	.500	.321

RUNS BATTED IN	From 1B	From 2B	From 3B	Scoring Position
Totals	17/188	25/100	19/50	44/150
Percentage	9.0%	25.0%	38.0%	29.3%

Loves to face: Bob Tewksbury (.406, 13-for-32, 3 2B, 4 HR)
Randy Tomlin (.560, 14-for-25, 1 HR, 0 SO)
Wally Whitehurst (.450, 9-for-20, 2 HR)

Hates to face: Larry Andersen (.081, 3-for-37, 0 BB)
Ramon Martinez (.125, 3-for-24, 1 HR)
Jeff Reardon (.111, 2-for-18)

Miscellaneous statistics: Ground outs-to-air outs ratio: 1.02 last season, 1.11 for career. . . . Grounded into 13 double plays in 125 opportunities (one per 10). . . . Drove in 16 of 31 runners from third base with less than two outs (52%). . . . Direction of balls hit to the outfield: 42% to left field, 28% to center, 30% to right. . . . Base running: Advanced from first base to third on 15 of 37 outfield singles (41%); scored from second on 16 of 21 (76%). . . . Made 3.52 assists per nine innings at second base, highest rate in majors.

Comments: Career total of 135 homers at Wrigley Field, 96 elsewhere; with Alvin Davis gone, Sandberg becomes the active player with the largest home-field home-run surplus. In 11 seasons with the Cubs, he has never hit more homers on the road than he has at home. . . . Needs 62 hits to become 7th player in Cubs history to reach 2000. . . . Most hits after leaving the Phillies: Nap Lajoie, 2523; Sandberg, 1938; Julio Franco, 1622; Cupid Childs, 1727; Dave Bancroft, 1370. . . . Most home runs by ex-Phillies: Sandberg, 213; Dick Allen, 147; Larry Hisle, 136; Don Money, 134; Keith Moreland, 111. . . . Has collected 15 or more homers and 15 or more steals in the same season eight times. Only four players have done it more often: Bobby Bonds (10), Willie Mays (10), Hank Aaron (9), and Andre Dawson (9). . . . Has been caught stealing more times (90) than any player in Cubs history. . . . All-time leader in fielding percentage among second basemen, averaging one error every 98.2 chances (minimum: 1000 games). . . . Strikeout rate of one every 9.4 plate appearances last season was the best of his career. . . . Career total of 25 at-bats in All-Star competition without an RBI; only Billy Herman (30 AB) and Luis Aparicio (28) had more unproductive All-Star ABs. . . . He and Aparicio are two of six players with a career average under .200 in at least 25 All-Star Game ABs: Orlando Cepeda (1-for-27, .037); Aparicio (2-for-28, .071); Eddie Mathews (2-for-25, .080); Sandberg (3-for-25, .120); Hank Aaron (13-for-67, .194); and Yogi Berra (8-for-41, .195).

Deion Sanders
Bats Left

Atlanta Braves	AB	H	2B	3B	HR	RBI	BB	SO	BA	SA	OBA
Season	303	92	6	14	8	28	18	52	.304	.495	.346
vs. Left-Handers	48	13	1	4	2	5	2	12	.271	.583	.300
vs. Right-Handers	255	79	5	10	6	23	16	40	.310	.478	.354
vs. Ground-Ballers	140	39	2	6	4	13	7	23	.279	.464	.315
vs. Fly-Ballers	163	53	4	8	4	15	11	29	.325	.521	.371
Home Games	138	36	2	4	5	14	13	27	.261	.442	.329
Road Games	165	56	4	10	3	14	5	25	.339	.539	.360
Grass Fields	213	60	3	9	7	19	17	38	.282	.479	.336
Artificial Turf	90	32	3	5	1	9	1	14	.356	.533	.370
April	82	27	4	6	2	4	7	12	.329	.598	.382
May	61	21	0	3	0	5	3	9	.344	.443	.375
June	48	17	0	2	4	7	5	10	.354	.688	.415
July	41	9	0	2	2	6	1	9	.220	.463	.250
August	61	16	2	1	0	6	1	10	.262	.328	.286
Sept./Oct.	10	2	0	0	0	0	1	2	.200	.200	.273
Leading Off Inn.	118	40	2	3	5	5	5	21	.339	.534	.366
Runners On	101	29	2	5	1	21	11	19	.287	.436	.360
Bases Empty	202	63	4	9	7	7	7	33	.312	.525	.338
Runners/Scor. Pos.	64	17	1	5	0	19	7	11	.266	.438	.333
Runners On/2 Out	35	7	1	1	0	6	5	8	.200	.286	.317
Scor. Pos./2 Out	26	5	1	1	0	6	3	6	.192	.308	.276
Late-Inning Pressure	37	12	3	3	2	7	4	7	.324	.730	.419
Leading Off	8	3	1	0	1	1	2	1	.375	.875	.500
Runners On	15	5	2	1	1	6	2	4	.333	.800	.444
Runners/Scor. Pos.	9	2	1	1	0	4	2	2	.222	.556	.364

RUNS BATTED IN	From 1B	From 2B	From 3B	Scoring Position
Totals	2/59	6/50	12/23	18/73
Percentage	3.4%	12.0%	52.2%	24.7%

Loves to face: Tim Belcher (.474, 9-for-19, 1 HR)
John Burkett (.556, 5-for-9, 2 3B)
Kevin Gross (.556, 5-for-9)

Hates to face: Tom Browning (0-for-3, 3 SO)
Dennis Martinez (.133, 2-for-15)
Steve Wilson (0-for-4, 3 SO)

Miscellaneous statistics: Ground outs-to-air outs ratio: 1.18 last season, 1.23 for career.... Grounded into 5 double plays in 49 opportunities (one per 10).... Drove in 8 of 12 runners from third base with less than two outs (67%).... Direction of balls hit to the outfield: 30% to left field, 33% to center, 37% to right.... Base running: Advanced from first base to third on 7 of 15 outfield singles (47%); scored from second on 5 of 8 (63%).... Made 2.58 putouts per nine innings in center field.

Comments: Third player in this century to bat .300 coming off consecutive sub.-200 seasons (minimum: 100 AB in each). The others: Joe Rudi in 1970 (.177, .189, .309) and Ray Fosse in 1976 (.196, .140, .301).... Batting average was pretty much a straight-line decline after a torrid April, with only a slight rally in the first half of June.... Was still batting .355 on June 20, but went 31-for-131 thereafter (.237).... Dipped below .300 only twice, for one at-bat each time (Aug. 23 and Aug. 29).... Despite having only 303 at-bats, he led the majors with 14 triples—the lowest at-bat total by a league leader in any extra-base hit category in this century (excluding seasons of fewer than 154 games).... Led majors with six triples during month of April. The Mets as a team did not hit their sixth triple until July 29th.... Led N.L. in extra-base hits (12) during April, but had only 16 over the rest of the season.... Became the first player since Hall of Famer Edd Roush in 1916 to have more than twice as many triples as doubles in a season of at least 300 at-bats.... Started 66 games of the 110 in which Atlanta faced right-handed starters (59%), but only 4 of 52 vs. left-handers.... Career batting average is .232 on grass fields, .275 on artificial turf.... Has scored eight return touchdowns (that is, on kickoffs, punts, interceptions, and so on) in 59 NFL games, the highest ratio in league history (minimum: 50 games). And that, of course, doesn't even include his TD reception last November.

Reggie Sanders
Bats Right

Cincinnati Reds	AB	H	2B	3B	HR	RBI	BB	SO	BA	SA	OBA
Season	385	104	26	6	12	36	48	98	.270	.462	.356
vs. Left-Handers	175	55	15	4	7	18	19	30	.314	.566	.391
vs. Right-Handers	210	49	11	2	5	18	29	68	.233	.376	.328
vs. Ground-Ballers	144	42	12	2	3	11	16	40	.292	.465	.360
vs. Fly-Ballers	241	62	14	4	9	25	32	58	.257	.461	.354
Home Games	205	50	14	3	6	22	32	51	.244	.429	.353
Road Games	180	54	12	3	6	14	16	47	.300	.500	.360
Grass Fields	118	32	6	2	3	7	8	24	.271	.432	.323
Artificial Turf	267	72	20	4	9	29	40	74	.270	.476	.370
April	73	23	4	2	2	6	6	16	.315	.507	.367
May	38	12	4	0	0	7	6	9	.316	.421	.413
June	81	19	5	1	2	8	6	21	.235	.395	.287
July	28	9	3	2	0	0	2	9	.321	.571	.367
August	91	23	5	1	6	8	16	23	.253	.527	.376
Sept./Oct.	74	18	5	0	2	7	12	20	.243	.392	.356
Leading Off Inn.	86	21	5	0	2	2	14	23	.244	.372	.350
Runners On	166	38	8	1	3	27	21	51	.229	.343	.325
Bases Empty	219	66	18	5	9	9	27	47	.301	.553	.381
Runners/Scor. Pos.	99	18	3	1	0	19	11	39	.182	.232	.274
Runners On/2 Out	64	12	4	0	0	6	3	19	.188	.250	.246
Scor. Pos./2 Out	45	7	2	0	0	5	1	14	.156	.200	.208
Late-Inning Pressure	54	17	4	0	1	6	7	20	.315	.444	.393
Leading Off	8	3	1	0	0	0	2	3	.375	.500	.500
Runners On	28	8	1	0	1	6	5	10	.286	.429	.394
Runners/Scor. Pos.	16	4	0	0	0	4	3	7	.250	.250	.368

RUNS BATTED IN	From 1B	From 2B	From 3B	Scoring Position
Totals	6/113	6/75	12/42	18/117
Percentage	5.3%	8.0%	28.6%	15.4%

Loves to face: Doug Drabek (.571, 4-for-7, 1 HR)
Bruce Hurst (.462, 6-for-13, 2 2B)
Terry Mulholland (.750, 3-for-4, 1 2B, 1 HR)

Hates to face: Steve Avery (.136, 3-for-22, 1 2B, 1 3B)
Kevin Gross (0-for-6)
Greg W. Harris (0-for-8)

Miscellaneous statistics: Ground outs-to-air outs ratio: 0.83 last season, 0.80 for career.... Grounded into 6 double plays in 88 opportunities (one per 15).... Drove in 11 of 25 runners from third base with less than two outs (44%).... Direction of balls hit to the outfield: 51% to left field, 26% to center, 23% to right.... Base running: Advanced from first base to third on 8 of 17 outfield singles (47%); scored from second on 12 of 13 (92%), 2d-highest rate in N.L.... Made 3.07 putouts per nine innings in center field, 2d-highest rate in N.L.

Comments: His 12 home runs were the most by a Reds rookie since 1983, when Gary Redus hit 17 and Nick Esasky hit 12.... Who was the only Reds rookie of the past 25 years to hit 20 home runs? Not Johnny Bench, not Lee May, not George Foster; see the answer below.... Led major league rookies in slugging percentage.... Tied Moises Alou for the lead among N.L. rookies with 16 stolen bases.... Also led N.L. rookies with 11 assists from the outfield.... Started 70 games in center field, 26 in left—24 with Dave Martinez in center. Martinez has gone to the Giants, but the Reds have acquired Roberto Kelly, who was outspoken about his desire to play *center* field for the Yankees, not left. Could be interesting.... Batting average with runners in scoring position was 6th lowest in the N.L.... His percentage of runners driven in from scoring position was 2d lowest in the league (minimum: 100 opportunities), ahead of only Mark Lemke (15.1%).... One of only two N.L. players to start at least two games in each of the first eight lineup slots; Pittsburgh's Jeff King was the other.... Barely avoided becoming the third player in Reds history to strike out 100 times in his rookie season. Those who did it: Gary Redus (111 in 1983) and Rolando Roomes (100 in 1989).... His strikeout rate was nearly twice as high against right-handed pitchers (one per 3.1 PA) as vs. southpaws (one per 5.8 PA).... The last Reds rookie to hit 20 home runs was Bernie Carbo (21 in 1970).

Benito Santiago — Bats Right

San Diego Padres	AB	H	2B	3B	HR	RBI	BB	SO	BA	SA	OBA
Season	386	97	21	0	10	42	21	52	.251	.383	.287
vs. Left-Handers	130	38	7	0	7	17	7	17	.292	.508	.326
vs. Right-Handers	256	59	14	0	3	25	14	35	.230	.320	.267
vs. Ground-Ballers	191	47	9	0	3	23	8	19	.246	.340	.275
vs. Fly-Ballers	195	50	12	0	7	19	13	33	.256	.426	.299
Home Games	195	60	10	0	8	30	7	28	.308	.482	.328
Road Games	191	37	11	0	2	12	14	24	.194	.283	.246
Grass Fields	272	78	13	0	9	37	16	37	.287	.434	.324
Artificial Turf	114	19	8	0	1	5	5	15	.167	.263	.198
April	88	21	3	0	1	8	3	9	.239	.307	.264
May	95	26	7	0	3	16	6	12	.274	.442	.311
June	0	0	0	0	0	0	0	0	—	—	—
July	57	17	3	0	0	7	5	5	.298	.351	.349
August	90	20	5	0	5	7	1	11	.222	.444	.231
Sept./Oct.	56	13	3	0	1	4	6	15	.232	.339	.302
Leading Off Inn.	88	21	8	0	3	3	5	16	.239	.432	.280
Runners On	168	37	4	0	3	35	8	24	.220	.298	.250
Bases Empty	218	60	17	0	7	7	13	28	.275	.450	.316
Runners/Scor. Pos.	103	27	2	0	1	30	5	14	.262	.311	.286
Runners On/2 Out	80	15	3	0	0	13	2	11	.188	.225	.207
Scor. Pos./2 Out	58	12	2	0	0	12	2	7	.207	.241	.233
Late-Inning Pressure	67	17	6	0	3	7	3	12	.254	.478	.282
Leading Off	19	9	4	0	1	1	0	2	.474	.842	.474
Runners On	29	3	0	0	1	5	1	6	.103	.207	.129
Runners/Scor. Pos.	17	2	0	0	0	3	1	3	.118	.118	.158

RUNS BATTED IN	From 1B	From 2B	From 3B	Scoring Position
Totals	4/124	13/88	15/42	28/130
Percentage	3.2%	14.8%	35.7%	21.5%

Loves to face: Dwayne Henry (.800, 4-for-5, 1 HR)
Paul Miller (3-for-3, 2 2B)
Zane Smith (.429, 12-for-28, 5 HR)

Hates to face: Doug Drabek (.045, 1-for-22, 1 3B)
Sid Fernandez (.121, 4-for-33, 1 HR, 0 BB)
Pete Harnisch (.067, 1-for-15, 1 2B)

Miscellaneous statistics: Ground outs-to-air outs ratio: 0.88 last season, 0.88 for career.... Grounded into 14 double plays in 69 opportunities (one per 4.9), 2d-worst rate in N.L.... Drove in 12 of 16 runners from third base with less than two outs (75%), 4th-highest rate in N.L.... Direction of balls hit to the outfield: 36% to left field, 35% to center, 29% to right.... Base running: Advanced from first base to third on 3 of 18 outfield singles (17%); scored from second on 3 of 5 (60%).... Opposing base stealers: 73-for-115 (63%).

Comments: Led all N.L. catchers in errors (with 12, five on stolen bases) for the fifth time in the last six seasons.... Played 103 games behind the plate without a passed ball; his previous career average was one every 11 games.... Hit only .194 on the road, the 4th-lowest mark in the N.L.... Career batting average is .297 in day games, .256 at night. That's an issue because the Marlins, like the Rangers, will play a disproportionate number of their home games at night because of the climate. (They have only 10 day games on their home schedule, none from June through August.)... Leaves San Diego with 85 home runs, third in Padres history, behind Nate Colbert (163) and Dave Winfield (154). Every other franchise has at least three players with at least 100 home runs.... Five years ago, with Santiago coming off his .300 rookie season and Sandy Alomar, Jr., on the horizon, it would have been hard to imagine anyone else as San Diego's opening-day catcher in 1993. (Santiago has started six straight openers for the Padres since ending Terry Kennedy's six-year streak in 1987.)... Who were the best pairs of catchers launched by one team within such a short period of time? How about these (debut seasons in parentheses): Mickey Owen (1937) and Walker Cooper (1940) by the Cardinals; Jim Hegan (1941) and Sherm Lollar (1946) by the Indians; Tom Haller (1961) and Randy Hundley (1964) by the Giants; Johnny Edwards (1961) and Johnny Bench (1967) by the Reds; Manny Sanguillen (1967) and Milt May (1970) by the Pirates.

Dick Schofield — Bats Right

Angels/Mets	AB	H	2B	3B	HR	RBI	BB	SO	BA	SA	OBA
Season	423	87	18	2	4	36	61	82	.206	.286	.311
vs. Left-Handers	145	29	6	2	2	17	23	28	.200	.310	.316
vs. Right-Handers	278	58	12	0	2	19	38	54	.209	.273	.308
vs. Ground-Ballers	207	47	8	1	1	15	24	38	.227	.290	.315
vs. Fly-Ballers	216	40	10	1	3	21	37	44	.185	.282	.307
Home Games	204	44	7	1	3	18	33	37	.216	.304	.326
Road Games	219	43	11	1	1	18	28	45	.196	.269	.296
Grass Fields	308	69	12	2	3	26	42	55	.224	.305	.322
Artificial Turf	115	18	6	0	1	10	19	27	.157	.235	.283
April	47	13	5	0	0	1	9	12	.277	.383	.414
May	94	19	2	0	2	9	14	14	.202	.287	.306
June	89	16	3	0	0	3	12	13	.180	.213	.277
July	57	11	3	0	1	8	6	14	.193	.298	.281
August	75	16	2	1	0	7	10	16	.213	.267	.314
Sept./Oct.	61	12	3	1	1	8	10	13	.197	.328	.306
Leading Off Inn.	92	21	4	0	1	1	12	20	.228	.304	.317
Runners On	178	42	9	2	1	33	40	28	.236	.326	.379
Bases Empty	245	45	9	0	3	3	21	54	.184	.257	.254
Runners/Scor. Pos.	100	21	4	1	1	29	26	19	.210	.300	.374
Runners On/2 Out	69	13	6	1	0	7	22	15	.188	.304	.391
Scor. Pos./2 Out	41	5	2	1	0	5	18	10	.122	.220	.400
Late-Inning Pressure	74	13	2	0	0	4	5	14	.176	.203	.235
Leading Off	22	5	0	0	0	0	0	4	.227	.227	.227
Runners On	26	6	1	0	0	4	4	3	.231	.269	.344
Runners/Scor. Pos.	16	4	0	0	0	3	2	2	.250	.250	.350

RUNS BATTED IN	From 1B	From 2B	From 3B	Scoring Position
Totals	5/130	9/81	18/43	27/124
Percentage	3.8%	11.1%	41.9%	21.8%

Loves to face: Charlie Leibrandt (.366, 15-for-41)
Dave Schmidt (.300, 6-for-20, 1 HR)
Matt Young (.357, 5-for-14, 1 HR)

Hates to face: Bert Blyleven (.105, 2-for-19)
Mark Gubicza (0-for-27)
Nolan Ryan (0-for-13, 9 SO)

Miscellaneous statistics: Ground outs-to-air outs ratio: 0.89 last season, 0.92 for career.... Grounded into 11 double plays in 105 opportunities (one per 10).... Drove in 17 of 24 runners from third base with less than two outs (71%).... Direction of balls hit to the outfield: 38% to left field, 29% to center, 33% to right.... Base running: Advanced from first base to third on 8 of 23 outfield singles (35%); scored from second on 5 of 8 (63%).... Made 3.06 assists per nine innings at shortstop, 3d-highest rate in N.L.

Comments: Return to A.L. signals resumption of his epic battle with Gubicza.... Became the first Mets shortstop ever to lead N.L. in fielding percentage (one error every 86 chances). He led A.L. shortstops three times (1984 and 1987–88). Other shortstops who have led both leagues: Tim Foli, Leo Cardenas, and George Davis.... His father, Ducky, led N.L. shortstops in fielding in 1965.... The last New York shortstop to lead the N.L. in fielding was Pee Wee Reese of the 1949 Brooklyn Dodgers.... Mets shortstops combined for a .203 batting average last season, the lowest of any position other than pitcher on any team in the majors.... Had the 2d-lowest night-game batting average in the N.L. (.201); only teammate Todd Hundley had a lower mark (.200).... His average on artificial turf was also the 2d worst in the N.L.... And it didn't matter which side they threw from—his batting average was 4th lowest in N.L. vs. both lefties and righties.... Hit a pair of home runs within four days in May, less than 25 games into his Mets career; he hadn't homered in his last 230 games with the Angels (729 ABs), dating back to June 9, 1990.... Has hit for a higher average against ground-ball pitchers than he has against fly-ballers in each of his 10 seasons in the majors. Career breakdown: .254 vs. ground-ballers; .211 vs. fly-ballers.... Moves to a carpeted home field for the first time. Over the past five seasons, his error rate is almost twice as high on artificial turf (one every 37 chances) as on grass (one every 55).

Mike Scioscia — Bats Left

Los Angeles Dodgers	AB	H	2B	3B	HR	RBI	BB	SO	BA	SA	OBA
Season	348	77	6	3	3	24	32	31	.221	.282	.286
vs. Left-Handers	81	19	1	2	1	10	8	6	.235	.333	.297
vs. Right-Handers	267	58	5	1	2	14	24	25	.217	.266	.283
vs. Ground-Ballers	137	34	2	1	0	5	9	9	.248	.277	.295
vs. Fly-Ballers	211	43	4	2	3	19	23	22	.204	.284	.282
Home Games	178	44	3	3	1	17	13	16	.247	.315	.297
Road Games	170	33	3	0	2	7	19	15	.194	.247	.275
Grass Fields	257	60	3	3	3	23	24	24	.233	.304	.298
Artificial Turf	91	17	3	0	0	1	8	7	.187	.220	.253
April	63	13	2	0	1	7	9	7	.206	.286	.297
May	56	8	0	0	1	3	3	3	.143	.196	.186
June	53	13	2	1	0	3	7	6	.245	.321	.333
July	66	18	1	1	0	4	5	6	.273	.318	.319
August	54	15	0	0	0	2	5	6	.278	.278	.339
Sept./Oct.	56	10	1	1	1	5	3	3	.179	.286	.233
Leading Off Inn.	84	17	1	1	0	0	6	7	.202	.238	.256
Runners On	135	31	2	1	2	23	18	12	.230	.304	.318
Bases Empty	213	46	4	2	1	1	14	19	.216	.268	.264
Runners/Scor. Pos.	76	15	0	1	0	19	12	7	.197	.224	.297
Runners On/2 Out	57	10	0	1	1	9	11	3	.175	.263	.309
Scor. Pos./2 Out	38	6	0	1	0	7	9	2	.158	.211	.319
Late-Inning Pressure	63	13	1	0	1	4	6	8	.206	.270	.275
Leading Off	16	3	0	0	0	0	1	0	.188	.188	.235
Runners On	27	7	0	0	1	4	4	5	.259	.370	.355
Runners/Scor. Pos.	13	3	0	0	0	2	2	2	.231	.231	.333

RUNS BATTED IN	From 1B	From 2B	From 3B	Scoring Position
Totals	3/102	3/51	15/41	18/92
Percentage	2.9%	5.9%	36.6%	19.6%

Loves to face: Paul Assenmacher (.467, 7-for-15, 3 BB)
Jim Corsi (3-for-3, 1 HR)
Lee Smith (.389, 7-for-18, 1 HR)

Hates to face: Larry Andersen (0-for-17)
Steve Avery (0-for-11)
John Franco (.071, 1-for-14)

Miscellaneous statistics: Ground outs-to-air outs ratio: 1.27 last season, 1.06 for career.... Grounded into 9 double plays in 74 opportunities (one per 8.2).... Drove in 10 of 21 runners from third base with less than two outs (48%).... Direction of balls hit to the outfield: 34% to left field, 33% to center, 33% to right.... Base running: Advanced from first base to third on 5 of 13 outfield singles (38%); scored from second on 3 of 7 (43%).... Opposing base stealers: 87-for-130 (67%).

Comments: What do Scioscia, Barry Bonds, and Will Clark have in common? They've all played their entire big-league careers for one manager (Tommy Lasorda, Jim Leyland, and Roger Craig, respectively). But Bonds has left Pittsburgh, Craig has left Frisco, and as of late January, Scioscia was a free agent in search of employment.... Lasorda and Scioscia go together like pasta and primavera; Mike has played 1441 major league games, all for Tommy. No other player in major league history played more games, all for the same manager.... Several players reached higher totals before splitting with their first skippers: Willie Davis for Walter Alston (1952 games), Donie Bush for Hughie Jennings (1768), Jimmy Dykes for Connie Mack (1702), Tommy Leach for Fred Clarke (1653), Frank Crosetti for Joe McCarthy (1635), Bob Johnson for Mack (1459), and Bobby Lowe for Frank Selee (whom he then replaced, 1565).... Should Scioscia sign with another team for 1993, leadership would revert to Gil McDougald, who played his entire 1336-game career for Casey Stengel. (The new runner-up, just in case McDougald is considering a comeback, would be Wes Parker—1288 games, all for Walter Alston.) ... Scioscia was the opening-day catcher in each of the last nine seasons, equaling the L.A. record set by John Roseboro (1959–67). Roy Campanella started 10 in a row for Brooklyn.... Has never struck out three times in a game, in a career spanning 1441 games. For more on this, see the Ozzie Smith comments.

Mike Sharperson — Bats Right

Los Angeles Dodgers	AB	H	2B	3B	HR	RBI	BB	SO	BA	SA	OBA
Season	317	95	21	0	3	36	47	33	.300	.394	.387
vs. Left-Handers	199	62	13	0	3	22	27	15	.312	.422	.390
vs. Right-Handers	118	33	8	0	0	14	20	18	.280	.347	.381
vs. Ground-Ballers	107	36	8	0	0	14	17	11	.336	.411	.424
vs. Fly-Ballers	210	59	13	0	3	22	30	22	.281	.386	.368
Home Games	159	50	11	0	2	19	18	18	.314	.421	.382
Road Games	158	45	10	0	1	17	29	15	.285	.367	.392
Grass Fields	250	76	19	0	2	32	35	29	.304	.404	.387
Artificial Turf	67	19	2	0	1	4	12	4	.284	.358	.387
April	40	13	1	0	0	3	8	5	.325	.350	.429
May	37	15	4	0	0	6	9	2	.405	.514	.522
June	80	25	8	0	1	12	12	5	.313	.450	.398
July	86	21	4	0	2	13	11	13	.244	.360	.327
August	26	8	2	0	0	0	5	4	.308	.385	.419
Sept./Oct.	48	13	2	0	0	2	2	4	.271	.313	.300
Leading Off Inn.	42	15	2	0	0	0	4	5	.357	.405	.413
Runners On	175	52	13	0	2	35	24	18	.297	.406	.376
Bases Empty	142	43	8	0	1	1	23	15	.303	.380	.400
Runners/Scor. Pos.	91	23	8	0	0	30	23	13	.253	.341	.393
Runners On/2 Out	55	15	6	0	1	17	13	7	.273	.436	.412
Scor. Pos./2 Out	40	12	6	0	0	15	13	4	.300	.450	.472
Late-Inning Pressure	72	22	8	0	1	9	11	12	.306	.458	.393
Leading Off	13	5	2	0	0	0	0	3	.385	.538	.385
Runners On	41	11	3	0	1	9	10	7	.268	.415	.404
Runners/Scor. Pos.	25	4	2	0	0	7	10	5	.160	.240	.389

RUNS BATTED IN	From 1B	From 2B	From 3B	Scoring Position
Totals	5/129	6/64	22/45	28/109
Percentage	3.9%	9.4%	48.9%	25.7%

Loves to face: Tom Glavine (.360, 9-for-25, 5 2B)
Danny Jackson (.464, 13-for-28, 0 SO)
Randy Myers (.375, 6-for-16, 2 2B, 2 3B, 5 BB)

Hates to face: Brian Barnes (0-for-7)
Greg Swindell (.100, 1-for-10)
Mitch Williams (0-for-6)

Miscellaneous statistics: Ground outs-to-air outs ratio: 1.00 last season, 1.20 for career.... Grounded into 9 double plays in 101 opportunities (one per 11).... Drove in 12 of 22 runners from third base with less than two outs (55%).... Direction of balls hit to the outfield: 33% to left field, 37% to center, 30% to right.... Base running: Advanced from first base to third on 7 of 20 outfield singles (35%); scored from second on 8 of 13 (62%).... Made 2.31 assists per nine innings at third base.

Comments: Started 54 of the 62 games in which the Dodgers faced left-handed starters, but only 18 of 100 against right-handers.... The only National League player to hit .300 or better vs. southpaws in each of the last three seasons (.322, .323, .312; minimum: 100 AB each). Four A.L. players did so: Ken Griffey, Edgar Martinez, Paul Molitor, and Ruben Sierra.... Career batting average is .309 vs. left-handers, .247 vs. right-handers.... Has increased his slugging percentage—sometimes ever so slightly—in each of five years since his debut in 1987: .287, .288, .357, .373, .375, .394. Only seven nonpitchers in major league history have had longer streaks, and they form an elite club of which Sharperson would clearly not be a member: Joe Morgan (1969–76), Ty Cobb (1906–11), Steve Garvey (1970–75), Hank Greenberg (1933–38), Chick Hafey (1925–30), Tim McCarver (1961–67), and Zack Wheat (1919–24).... Had the highest walk rate (one every 7.9 PA) and the lowest strikeout rate (one every 11.3 PA) of his career last season.... Played 63 games at second base and 60 games at third base last season. The only other player in Dodgers history to play as many as 50 games at both of those positions in the same season: Jim Gilliam (1961–63).... Has stolen only three bases in eight attempts since stealing 15 bases in 1990.... We know you all hate this subject, but Sharperson's average was actually below .300 (.2997). Believe us, someday someone will sit out the final weekend with a .3996 average, and you'll think Hillary pushed the red button— all hell will break loose.

Gary Sheffield

Bats Right

San Diego Padres

	AB	H	2B	3B	HR	RBI	BB	SO	BA	SA	OBA
Season	557	184	34	3	33	100	48	40	.330	.580	.385
vs. Left-Handers	189	69	9	2	13	38	18	13	.365	.640	.420
vs. Right-Handers	368	115	25	1	20	62	30	27	.313	.549	.367
vs. Ground-Ballers	258	82	16	1	15	48	22	17	.318	.562	.376
vs. Fly-Ballers	299	102	18	2	18	52	26	23	.341	.595	.393
Home Games	288	105	19	2	23	58	30	18	.365	.684	.426
Road Games	269	79	15	1	10	42	18	22	.294	.468	.340
Grass Fields	402	139	27	3	30	77	40	29	.346	.652	.408
Artificial Turf	155	45	7	0	3	23	8	11	.290	.394	.323
April	84	28	6	1	3	15	16	9	.333	.536	.431
May	105	34	3	0	7	23	6	7	.324	.552	.357
June	94	28	5	0	5	17	7	5	.298	.511	.359
July	91	32	10	1	4	11	5	2	.352	.615	.390
August	97	35	6	0	10	26	6	10	.361	.732	.390
Sept./Oct.	86	27	4	1	4	8	8	7	.314	.523	.385
Leading Off Inn.	94	33	8	1	6	6	4	6	.351	.649	.384
Runners On	255	86	10	1	17	84	29	16	.337	.584	.401
Bases Empty	302	98	24	2	16	16	19	24	.325	.576	.370
Runners/Scor. Pos.	127	43	4	1	11	71	18	10	.339	.646	.409
Runners On/2 Out	83	32	2	0	7	36	9	7	.386	.663	.452
Scor. Pos./2 Out	55	21	1	0	7	35	7	6	.382	.782	.452
Late-Inning Pressure	70	25	2	1	1	9	6	3	.357	.457	.418
Leading Off	15	4	0	0	0	0	2	0	.267	.267	.353
Runners On	31	12	1	0	0	8	4	1	.387	.419	.474
Runners/Scor. Pos.	17	7	1	0	0	8	2	1	.412	.471	.476

RUNS BATTED IN	From 1B	From 2B	From 3B	Scoring Position
Totals	16/195	24/107	27/50	51/157
Percentage	8.2%	22.4%	54.0%	32.5%

Loves to face: Chris Hammond (.750, 3-for-4, 1 2B, 1 HR, 3 BB)
Dave Righetti (.556, 5-for-9, 2 HR)
Brian Williams (.667, 4-for-6, 1 2B, 2 HR)

Hates to face: Jose Rijo (0-for-7, 3 SO)
Bill Swift (.067, 1-for-15)
Bob Tewksbury (0-for-12)

Miscellaneous statistics: Ground outs-to-air outs ratio: 0.73 last season, 0.74 for career.... Grounded into 19 double plays in 152 opportunities (one per 8).... Drove in 17 of 25 runners from third base with less than two outs (68%).... Direction of balls hit to the outfield: 49% to left field, 28% to center, 23% to right.... Base running: Advanced from first base to third on 10 of 22 outfield singles (45%); scored from second on 9 of 12 (75%).... Made 2.16 assists per nine innings at third base.

Comments: His 33 homers were the most by a league batting champion since Fred Lynn in 1979 (.333 BA, 39 HR), and the most by an N.L. batting leader since Billy Williams in 1972 (.333 BA, 37 HR).... No other active player ever hit as many as 33 home runs in a season of 40 or fewer strikeouts. The last to do so: Ted Kluszewski, who did it four years in a row (1953–56).... Had the most extreme breakthrough in more than 20 years, rated at odds of more than 12,000-to-1. The last player with such an extreme resurgence: Bob Bailey of the Expos in 1970 (who batted .287 with 28 HR in 352 AB after hitting a total of 21 HR over the three previous seasons, in which he batted .227, .227, and .265).... Batted .194 in 1991; only two other players in major league history increased their batting average by more than 135 points in consecutive seasons of at least 200 plate appearances: Elmer Valo (.214 in 1954, .364 in 1955) and Silver Flint (.162 in 1880, .310 in 1881).... Shared the major league lead in game-winning RBIs (20) with Terry Pendleton and Larry Walker.... Had the majors' highest batting average with two outs and runners in scoring position.... Hit seven home runs vs. the Giants, the most by an N.L. player vs. any opponent.... None of his 33 home runs was hit to the opposite field, and only one was hit to center.... Most comparable offensive profiles at the same age: Reggie Smith, Joe Torre, Del Ennis.... His continued success would guarantee that the name Ricky Bones would live in baseball history along with Milt Pappas, Ernie Broglio, and Jim Fregosi.

Don Slaught

Bats Right

Pittsburgh Pirates

	AB	H	2B	3B	HR	RBI	BB	SO	BA	SA	OBA
Season	255	88	17	3	4	37	17	23	.345	.482	.384
vs. Left-Handers	174	56	9	1	3	21	11	13	.322	.437	.362
vs. Right-Handers	81	32	8	2	1	16	6	10	.395	.580	.429
vs. Ground-Ballers	87	29	4	0	1	7	5	14	.333	.414	.376
vs. Fly-Ballers	168	59	13	3	3	30	12	9	.351	.518	.387
Home Games	131	44	11	3	2	21	11	14	.336	.511	.379
Road Games	124	44	6	0	2	16	6	9	.355	.452	.388
Grass Fields	71	32	6	0	1	11	3	6	.451	.577	.468
Artificial Turf	184	56	11	3	3	26	14	17	.304	.446	.351
April	8	4	0	0	0	0	0	0	.500	.500	.500
May	54	22	3	2	1	9	4	4	.407	.593	.441
June	47	19	4	0	0	2	2	6	.404	.489	.429
July	36	5	1	0	0	7	5	5	.139	.167	.227
August	58	20	6	0	1	10	2	5	.345	.500	.371
Sept./Oct.	52	18	3	1	2	9	4	3	.346	.558	.404
Leading Off Inn.	66	17	4	1	3	3	2	4	.258	.485	.290
Runners On	126	44	9	1	1	34	9	11	.349	.460	.383
Bases Empty	129	44	8	2	3	3	8	12	.341	.504	.384
Runners/Scor. Pos.	71	21	3	0	0	27	8	7	.296	.338	.353
Runners On/2 Out	54	16	2	0	0	10	5	3	.296	.333	.367
Scor. Pos./2 Out	31	9	1	0	0	9	5	1	.290	.323	.405
Late-Inning Pressure	51	17	1	2	0	9	3	6	.333	.431	.368
Leading Off	18	5	0	1	0	0	1	1	.278	.389	.350
Runners On	22	8	1	0	0	9	1	2	.364	.409	.360
Runners/Scor. Pos.	16	6	1	0	0	9	1	1	.375	.438	.368

RUNS BATTED IN	From 1B	From 2B	From 3B	Scoring Position
Totals	6/92	12/56	15/33	27/89
Percentage	6.5%	21.4%	45.5%	30.3%

Loves to face: Joe Magrane (.556, 5-for-9, 1 HR)
Dennis Martinez (.500, 8-for-16)
Ben Rivera (4-for-4)

Hates to face: Tom Glavine (.111, 2-for-18)
Charlie Hough (.130, 3-for-23)
Dave Righetti (0-for-15)

Miscellaneous statistics: Ground outs-to-air outs ratio: 0.96 last season, 0.96 for career.... Grounded into 6 double plays in 57 opportunities (one per 10).... Drove in 13 of 21 runners from third base with less than two outs (62%).... Direction of balls hit to the outfield: 43% to left field, 26% to center, 31% to right.... Base running: Advanced from first base to third on 1 of 11 outfield singles (9%), 4th-lowest rate in N.L.; scored from second on 5 of 6 (83%).... Opposing base stealers: 45-for-70 (64%).

Comments: Over the past two seasons, he has batted .389 from August 15 to the end of the season, .288 before that.... Has caught 226 games in three seasons with the Pirates, compiling a .315 batting average. *No other player in N.L. history who has caught as many as 200 games has a batting average as high as Slaught's..* ..Should we repeat that, or would you prefer simply to read it again? The next highest mark belongs to Bubbles Hargrave (.312).... Batting average was the highest by a catcher in a 250-at-bat season since Elston Howard hit .348 for the 1961 Yankees. The last N.L. catcher to hit for that high an average was Smoky Burgess (.368 for 1954 Phillies).... Started 58 of 66 games in which the Pirates faced left-handed pitchers, but only 7 of 97 vs. left-handers.... Maybe it's time to halt the platoon: Sluggo not only batted .395 in limited action vs. right-handers last season, but he hit a cool .340 in 94 at-bats vs. RHP in 1991. He has outhit his platoonmate, Mike LaValliere, *vs. right-handed pitchers* in each of his three seasons with Pittsburgh. Their three-year BAs vs. RHP aren't even close: Slaught, .336; LaV., .269.... He's been with four teams, and has played between 200 and 300 games with each: Kansas City, 250; Texas, 292; Yankees, 214; Pittsburgh, 248.... Career total of 18 games in the League Championship Series is 5th highest among players who have never appeared in a World Series, behind Bobby Grich (24), Jay Bell (20), Barry Bonds (20), and Jose Lind (20).

Ozzie Smith
Bats Left and Right

St. Louis Cardinals	AB	H	2B	3B	HR	RBI	BB	SO	BA	SA	OBA
Season	518	153	20	2	0	31	59	34	.295	.342	.367
vs. Left-Handers	202	55	10	1	0	13	21	14	.272	.332	.339
vs. Right-Handers	316	98	10	1	0	18	38	20	.310	.348	.384
vs. Ground-Ballers	213	69	5	1	0	11	17	11	.324	.357	.374
vs. Fly-Ballers	305	84	15	1	0	20	42	23	.275	.331	.362
Home Games	278	93	10	1	0	18	29	15	.335	.378	.396
Road Games	240	60	10	1	0	13	30	19	.250	.300	.333
Grass Fields	124	29	5	0	0	5	15	9	.234	.274	.317
Artificial Turf	394	124	15	2	0	26	44	25	.315	.363	.383
April	60	16	1	0	0	5	9	4	.267	.283	.362
May	104	31	5	1	0	8	12	4	.298	.365	.371
June	57	17	0	0	0	6	2	2	.298	.298	.322
July	92	30	3	0	0	2	14	11	.326	.359	.415
August	100	26	4	1	0	2	11	6	.260	.320	.333
Sept./Oct.	105	33	7	0	0	8	11	7	.314	.381	.376
Leading Off Inn.	85	31	8	1	0	0	10	5	.365	.482	.432
Runners On	196	52	4	1	0	31	31	11	.265	.296	.364
Bases Empty	322	101	16	1	0	0	28	23	.314	.370	.369
Runners/Scor. Pos.	110	27	2	0	0	29	24	9	.245	.264	.378
Runners On/2 Out	75	14	0	0	0	13	15	6	.187	.187	.322
Scor. Pos./2 Out	52	10	0	0	0	13	11	6	.192	.192	.333
Late-Inning Pressure	102	29	3	0	0	10	13	7	.284	.314	.362
Leading Off	24	7	1	0	0	0	4	1	.292	.333	.393
Runners On	40	11	1	0	0	10	8	3	.275	.300	.388
Runners/Scor. Pos.	26	8	1	0	0	10	7	2	.308	.346	.441

RUNS BATTED IN	From 1B	From 2B	From 3B	Scoring Position
Totals	2/130	17/93	12/36	29/129
Percentage	1.5%	18.3%	33.3%	22.5%

Loves to face: Larry Andersen (.467, 7-for-15, 8 BB)
Tim Belcher (.542, 13-for-24)
Frank Castillo (.700, 7-for-10)

Hates to face: Tom Browning (.143, 6-for-42)
Sid Fernandez (.140, 7-for-50)
Bruce Hurst (.171, 7-for-41)

Miscellaneous statistics: Ground outs-to-air outs ratio: 1.77 last season, 1.55 for career.... Grounded into 11 double plays in 92 opportunities (one per 8.4).... Drove in 6 of 13 runners from third base with less than two outs (46%).... Direction of balls hit to the outfield: 52% to left field, 28% to center, 20% to right batting left-handed; 32% to left field, 47% to center, 21% to right batting right-handed.... Base running: Advanced from first base to third on 13 of 29 outfield singles (45%); scored from second on 16 of 20 (80%).... Made 3.27 assists per nine innings at shortstop, 2d-highest rate in N.L.

Comments: Needs only 35 more games at shortstop to move into 2d place in major league history; currently ranks 4th with 2187, behind Luis Aparicio (2581), Larry Bowa (2222) and Luke Appling (2218).... Has surpassed Roy McMillan to become the all-time N.L. leader in double plays at shortstop (1361).... With 43 stolen bases at the age of 37, he became the 2d-oldest player ever to reach the 40 mark; he'll have to do it again in *1994* to top Davey Lopes, who stole 47 in 1985 at the age of 39. Others to steal 40 at a "younger" 37 than Ozzie: Lou Brock (1976), Eddie Collins (1924), and Nixey Callahan (1911).... Has stolen at least 25 bases but was caught fewer than 10 times in each of the last 11 seasons. Since "caught stealing" became an official category (1920 in the A.L., 1950 in the N.L.), no other player has had a streak even half that long.... Ozzie is more than six years older than Spike Owen, the 2d-oldest regular shortstop in the N.L. last season.... Stole 11 bases in May, and 13 in September/October. Both were N.L. highs.... Cardinals shortstops did not hit a home run last season. Other than pitchers, every other major league club had at least one homer from every position.... Hasn't struck out three times in any of his last 1816 starts, dating back to May 22, 1980 (vs. Bert Blyleven)—the longest current streak in the majors, followed by Mike Scioscia (1278 starts), Tony Gwynn (995), and Kent Hrbek (900).

San Francisco Giants	AB	H	2B	3B	HR	RBI	BB	SO	BA	SA	OBA
Season	390	105	22	2	14	57	23	96	.269	.444	.311
vs. Left-Handers	170	50	12	0	6	20	9	31	.294	.471	.331
vs. Right-Handers	220	55	10	2	8	37	14	65	.250	.423	.295
vs. Ground-Ballers	194	54	11	1	9	33	12	46	.278	.485	.321
vs. Fly-Ballers	196	51	11	1	5	24	11	50	.260	.403	.301
Home Games	184	55	14	0	8	34	12	40	.299	.505	.342
Road Games	206	50	8	2	6	23	11	56	.243	.388	.283
Grass Fields	291	81	15	1	11	43	19	70	.278	.450	.322
Artificial Turf	99	24	7	1	3	14	4	26	.242	.424	.279
April	25	5	1	0	0	2	1	8	.200	.240	.231
May	46	10	2	0	3	7	4	10	.217	.457	.280
June	94	35	9	1	5	24	2	24	.372	.649	.388
July	92	23	3	0	3	11	5	18	.250	.380	.289
August	72	16	3	1	1	5	7	21	.222	.333	.296
Sept./Oct.	61	16	4	0	2	8	4	15	.262	.426	.303
Leading Off Inn.	91	25	6	0	7	7	6	20	.275	.571	.320
Runners On	182	48	11	0	5	48	12	54	.264	.407	.312
Bases Empty	208	57	11	2	9	9	11	42	.274	.476	.311
Runners/Scor. Pos.	118	30	8	0	2	41	11	38	.254	.373	.316
Runners On/2 Out	74	24	6	0	4	27	7	17	.324	.568	.390
Scor. Pos./2 Out	54	16	5	0	2	22	6	13	.296	.500	.367
Late-Inning Pressure	71	15	4	2	0	8	6	22	.211	.324	.269
Leading Off	15	2	2	0	0	2	2	2	.133	.267	.235
Runners On	32	6	2	0	0	8	2	13	.188	.250	.229
Runners/Scor. Pos.	23	4	1	0	0	7	2	9	.174	.217	.231

RUNS BATTED IN	From 1B	From 2B	From 3B	Scoring Position
Totals	9/129	16/89	18/52	34/141
Percentage	7.0%	18.0%	34.6%	24.1%

Loves to face: Bruce Hurst (.333, 7-for-21, 3 2B, 2 HR)
Chris Nabholz (.625, 5-for-8, 1 HR)
Jose Rijo (.400, 6-for-15, 1 2B, 3 HR, 5 SO)

Hates to face: Tom Filer (0-for-8)
Mike Jackson (0-for-10, 5 SO)
Frank Tanana (.086, 3-for-35, 3 BB)

Miscellaneous statistics: Ground outs-to-air outs ratio: 0.92 last season, 0.85 for career.... Grounded into 10 double plays in 88 opportunities (one per 8.8).... Drove in 12 of 30 runners from third base with less than two outs (40%), 5th-lowest rate in N.L.... Direction of balls hit to the outfield: 33% to left field, 36% to center, 32% to right.... Base running: Advanced from first base to third on 6 of 21 outfield singles (29%); scored from second on 11 of 11 (100%), best rate in N.L.... Made 1.81 putouts per nine innings in right field.

Comments: Snapped a streak of five consecutive seasons in which his home-run rate declined. For a list of those with longer streaks, see the Pete Incaviglia comments.... Led all N.L. players in extra-base hits (15) and RBIs during month of June. His seven RBIs on June 6 was matched eight days later by Pete Incaviglia for the N.L. high last season.... Can still wing the ball. He threw out six runners in only 332⅓ innings in right field, the highest rate in the N.L. (minimum: 3 assists).... Became the first Giants player since Andy Reese in 1928 to play all three outfield positions and all four infield positions in the same season.... Not a bad job for someone just passing through the Bay Area. The best one-season Giants: East Coast branch—Rogers Hornsby (.361, 26 HR, 125 RBI in 1927); West Coast branch—Reggie Smith (.284, 18 HR, 56 RBI in 1982).... His 14 home runs were the most of any N.L. player who had no homers in Late-Inning Pressure Situations last season.... Drove in 31 percent of runners from scoring position as a rookie in 1986, but hasn't reached the 25 percent level in six years since. Three other nonpitchers have been below 25 percent in each of the last six seasons: Greg Gagne, Lance Parrish, and one who will try to replace Snyder in San Francisco this season—Mark Carreon.... After consecutive 2-for-15 seasons as a pinch hitter, his career pinch-BA stands at .140, with no home runs in 50 at-bats; owns a career average of one homer every 22 ABs at other times.

Sammy Sosa
Bats Right

Chicago Cubs	AB	H	2B	3B	HR	RBI	BB	SO	BA	SA	OBA
Season	262	68	7	2	8	25	19	63	.260	.393	.317
vs. Left-Handers	75	21	3	0	0	5	8	19	.280	.320	.353
vs. Right-Handers	187	47	4	2	8	20	11	44	.251	.422	.302
vs. Ground-Ballers	101	35	3	1	4	13	5	23	.347	.515	.394
vs. Fly-Ballers	161	33	4	1	4	12	14	40	.205	.317	.270
Home Games	116	31	6	1	4	10	12	28	.267	.440	.344
Road Games	146	37	1	1	4	15	7	35	.253	.356	.295
Grass Fields	177	45	6	1	4	14	15	45	.254	.367	.321
Artificial Turf	85	23	1	1	4	11	4	18	.271	.447	.308
April	80	17	3	0	0	1	7	21	.213	.250	.284
May	109	29	3	1	2	10	8	25	.266	.367	.322
June	34	7	0	1	3	5	2	6	.206	.529	.270
July	15	7	1	0	2	5	0	4	.467	.933	.467
August	24	8	0	0	1	4	2	7	.333	.458	.385
Sept./Oct.	0	0	0	0	0	0	0	0	.000	.000	.000
Leading Off Inn.	76	20	3	1	2	2	6	17	.263	.408	.325
Runners On	93	24	3	1	4	21	7	25	.258	.441	.324
Bases Empty	169	44	4	1	4	4	12	38	.260	.367	.313
Runners/Scor. Pos.	48	11	2	0	2	16	4	14	.229	.396	.291
Runners On/2 Out	39	11	1	0	1	7	3	9	.282	.385	.378
Scor. Pos./2 Out	24	5	1	0	0	5	2	8	.208	.250	.296
Late-Inning Pressure	41	9	1	0	1	3	5	9	.220	.317	.319
Leading Off	5	1	0	0	0	0	2	3	.200	.200	.429
Runners On	19	4	1	0	1	3	2	3	.211	.421	.318
Runners/Scor. Pos.	11	1	0	0	0	1	2	2	.091	.091	.231

RUNS BATTED IN	From 1B	From 2B	From 3B	Scoring Position
Totals	5/67	8/44	4/16	12/60
Percentage	7.5%	18.2%	25.0%	20.0%

Loves to face: Mark Clark (.667, 2-for-3, 2 HR)
Randy Tomlin (.667, 6-for-9)
David West (.545, 6-for-11, 2 2B, 1 3B, 1 HR)
Hates to face: Bud Black (.143, 3-for-21)
Dave Burba (0-for-10)
Frank Tanana (.176, 3-for-17)

Miscellaneous statistics: Ground outs-to-air outs ratio: 0.88 last season, 1.16 for career.... Grounded into 4 double plays in 49 opportunities (one per 12).... Drove in 2 of 6 runners from third base with less than two outs (33%).... Direction of balls hit to the outfield: 40% to left field, 34% to center, 26% to right.... Base running: Advanced from first base to third on 5 of 7 outfield singles (71%); scored from second on 7 of 8 (88%).... Made 2.28 putouts per nine innings in center field, lowest rate in N.L.

Comments: Some good signs in 1992: career-best marks in batting average, on-base percentage, walk rate (one per 15 plate appearances), and strikeout rate (one per 4.6 PA).... Scored more runs in 67 games for the Cubs last season (41) than he did in 116 games for the White Sox in 1991 (39).... Committed six errors in 67 games in center field, 2d most in the N.L. to Marquis Grissom (who made one more error than Sosa playing 90 more games).... Career error rate of one every 28.4 chances in the outfield is 4th worst among active players (minimum: 300 games), ahead of only Lonnie Smith (one every 27.4 chances), Pete Incaviglia (27.9), and George Bell (28.0).... A batting breakdown worth noting: seven homers and 22 RBIs in 33 Cubs victories; one HR, three RBIs in 34 losses.... Had two separate stints on the Cubs disabled list totaling 84 days, with fractures in his right hand (June) and left ankle (August). Was officially removed from the D.L. in September, but didn't return to action.... Hit 16 of his first 21 career home runs off left-handed pitchers; since then, he has hit 13 of 16 off right-handers.... Sox and George Bell won Round 1 in the biggest crosstown trade in Chicago history (not counting Ken Kravec for Dennis Lamp), but Sosa could dominate the later rounds. He's nine years younger than Bell. In fact, Sammy is younger than seven of the eight rookies to play for the Cubs last season; he didn't turn 24 until after the season ended.

Kurt Stillwell
Bats Left and Right

San Diego Padres	AB	H	2B	3B	HR	RBI	BB	SO	BA	SA	OBA
Season	379	86	15	3	2	24	26	58	.227	.298	.274
vs. Left-Handers	112	28	1	2	1	8	7	19	.250	.321	.289
vs. Right-Handers	267	58	14	1	1	16	19	39	.217	.288	.268
vs. Ground-Ballers	168	47	6	2	2	14	10	23	.280	.375	.322
vs. Fly-Ballers	211	39	9	1	0	10	16	35	.185	.237	.237
Home Games	191	42	6	1	1	14	16	32	.220	.277	.274
Road Games	188	44	9	2	1	10	10	26	.234	.319	.275
Grass Fields	277	60	10	1	1	19	22	42	.217	.271	.270
Artificial Turf	102	26	5	2	1	5	4	16	.255	.373	.287
April	57	17	4	1	0	3	1	12	.298	.404	.305
May	64	18	6	0	0	4	5	12	.281	.375	.324
June	78	13	0	0	0	5	8	15	.167	.167	.241
July	77	16	3	2	2	7	5	5	.208	.377	.256
August	49	12	1	0	0	3	2	6	.245	.265	.264
Sept./Oct.	54	10	1	0	0	2	5	8	.185	.204	.267
Leading Off Inn.	100	26	8	1	1	1	5	20	.260	.390	.302
Runners On	150	33	2	1	1	23	14	25	.220	.267	.276
Bases Empty	229	53	13	2	1	1	12	33	.231	.319	.273
Runners/Scor. Pos.	87	16	1	0	0	20	12	15	.184	.195	.267
Runners On/2 Out	66	13	1	1	0	6	9	13	.197	.242	.293
Scor. Pos./2 Out	40	6	1	0	0	5	8	8	.150	.175	.292
Late-Inning Pressure	62	13	2	1	0	3	5	9	.210	.274	.265
Leading Off	19	4	1	1	0	0	0	3	.211	.368	.211
Runners On	19	5	0	0	0	3	5	3	.263	.263	.400
Runners/Scor. Pos.	13	3	0	0	0	3	4	1	.231	.231	.389

RUNS BATTED IN	From 1B	From 2B	From 3B	Scoring Position
Totals	2/104	7/70	13/32	20/102
Percentage	1.9%	10.0%	40.6%	19.6%

Loves to face: Jose Guzman (.250, 3-for-12, 2 2B, 1 HR, 4 BB)
Orel Hershiser (.368, 7-for-19)
Barry Jones (.545, 6-for-11)
Hates to face: Bud Black (0-for-12)
Sid Fernandez (0-for-7, 3 SO, 1 HBP)
John Smoltz (0-for-9)

Miscellaneous statistics: Ground outs-to-air outs ratio: 1.26 last season, 0.97 for career.... Grounded into 6 double plays in 67 opportunities (one per 11).... Drove in 11 of 18 runners from third base with less than two outs (61%).... Direction of balls hit to the outfield: 49% to left field, 25% to center, 27% to right batting left-handed; 46% to left field, 26% to center, 28% to right batting right-handed.... Base running: Advanced from first base to third on 1 of 11 outfield singles (9%), 4th-lowest rate in N.L.; scored from second on 5 of 9 (56%).... Made 2.55 assists per nine innings at second base, lowest rate in majors.

Comments: Played only second base last season, after appearing exclusively at shortstop in each of the previous four seasons. Only three other players have had a 100-game season at second base immediately following at least four straight years playing 100 games at shortstop: Julio Franco (switched to 2B in 1987), Dick McAuliffe (1967), and Rabbit Maranville, who hopped back and forth. Maranville was primarily a shortstop for the first 20 years of his career (1912–31), with the exception of 1924, when he played second base exclusively. Then, in 1932, he moved back to second for the final four years of his career.... So we know that such a switch is possible; but the question remains, is it advisable? Stillwell led N.L. second basemen with 16 errors; then again, he also led A.L. shortstops in errors in 1990.... Fielding percentage (one error every 33 chances) was the lowest of any second baseman in the majors (minimum: 108 games).... The Padres infield of McGriff, Stillwell, Fernandez, and Sheffield started 83 games together, the most of any infield in the majors last season.... Batting average, walk rate, and home-run rate were all career lows.... Career home-run rates show that he's twice as likely to homer from the left side of the plate (one every 77 at-bats) as he is from the right (one every 155 ABs).... Career batting-average breakdowns: .236 on grass fields, .260 on artificial turf; .226 with the bases empty, .283 with runners on base.

Eddie Taubensee

Bats Left

Houston Astros	AB	H	2B	3B	HR	RBI	BB	SO	BA	SA	OBA
Season	297	66	15	0	5	28	31	78	.222	.323	.299
vs. Left-Handers	47	11	3	0	2	5	6	12	.234	.426	.333
vs. Right-Handers	250	55	12	0	3	23	25	66	.220	.304	.292
vs. Ground-Ballers	139	30	8	0	1	14	14	43	.216	.295	.286
vs. Fly-Ballers	158	36	7	0	4	14	17	35	.228	.348	.311
Home Games	157	38	10	0	2	12	18	39	.242	.344	.324
Road Games	140	28	5	0	3	16	13	39	.200	.300	.271
Grass Fields	89	17	2	0	2	10	8	27	.191	.281	.265
Artificial Turf	208	49	13	0	3	18	23	51	.236	.341	.313
April	47	10	2	0	0	2	6	17	.213	.255	.302
May	60	9	3	0	0	4	6	10	.150	.200	.224
June	23	2	1	0	0	4	3	9	.087	.130	.192
July	34	14	3	0	1	4	1	5	.412	.588	.429
August	73	15	4	0	4	10	5	22	.205	.425	.275
Sept./Oct.	60	16	2	0	0	4	10	15	.267	.300	.371
Leading Off Inn.	62	16	4	0	1	1	7	17	.258	.371	.333
Runners On	128	28	6	0	2	25	17	29	.219	.313	.318
Bases Empty	169	38	9	0	3	3	14	49	.225	.331	.284
Runners/Scor. Pos.	74	14	2	0	0	18	15	23	.189	.216	.330
Runners On/2 Out	58	11	4	0	1	8	10	15	.190	.310	.319
Scor. Pos./2 Out	35	4	1	0	0	4	10	12	.114	.143	.326
Late-Inning Pressure	47	7	0	0	1	5	4	14	.149	.213	.216
Leading Off	12	1	0	0	0	0	1	5	.083	.083	.154
Runners On	21	3	0	0	1	5	2	5	.143	.286	.217
Runners/Scor. Pos.	14	2	0	0	0	3	2	4	.143	.143	.250

RUNS BATTED IN	From 1B	From 2B	From 3B	Scoring Position
Totals	5/88	5/58	13/30	18/88
Percentage	5.7%	8.6%	43.3%	20.5%

Loves to face: Jose DeLeon (.500, 2-for-4)
Jose Rijo (.333, 3-for-9, 1 2B, 1 HR, 5 SO)
Jeff M. Robinson (2-for-2, 1 2B, 1 HR)

Hates to face: Mike Morgan (0-for-10, 4 SO)
Omar Olivares (0-for-6, 3 SO)
Bob Tewksbury (0-for-6)

Miscellaneous statistics: Ground outs-to-air outs ratio: 0.90 last season, 0.88 for career.... Grounded into 4 double plays in 53 opportunities (one per 13).... Drove in 10 of 15 runners from third base with less than two outs (67%).... Direction of balls hit to the outfield: 38% to left field, 35% to center, 27% to right.... Base running: Advanced from first base to third on 4 of 9 outfield singles (44%); scored from second on 4 of 6 (67%).... Opposing base stealers: 67-for-102 (66%).

Comments: Started 81 of 98 games in which the Astros faced right-handed starters, but only 7 of 64 vs. left-handers.... Still, his total of 47 at-bats vs. southpaws was the 2d highest among lefty-swinging N.L. rookies last season; Derrick May had 76. The only A.L. rookie with 100+ ABs vs. southpaws from the left side last season: Kenny Lofton, who was traded by Houston for Taubensee.... May and Taubensee each hit two homers off lefties. Jeff Grotewold of the Phillies was the only other left-handed-batting N.L. rookie to take a left-hander deep even once.... Had the 2d-lowest batting average on grass fields in the majors, ahead of only Tim Wallach (.185).... Batting average with two outs and runners in scoring position was 3d lowest in the league.... Strikeout rate of one every 4.2 plate appearances was the worst among major league rookies (minimum: 250 PA).... Smacked the only five homers hit by Houston backstops last season, the fewest of any N.L. club at that position. Other N.L. clubs averaged 11 homers from their catchers.... Astros pitchers posted a 3.99 ERA in 804⅓ innings with Taubensee catching, 3.38 in 524 innings caught by Scott Servais, and 3.57 in the 131 innings Scooter Tucker worked.... Posted similar batting statistics to those of Todd Hundley (.209, 17 2B, 0 3B, 7 HR, 32 RBI, 19 BB, 76 SO), the only other rookie to catch 100 games last season. The last time at least two N.L. rookies each caught 100 games was 1984: Mark Bailey (Astros), Mike Fitzgerald (Mets), and Brad Gulden (Reds).

Tim Teufel

Bats Right

San Diego Padres	AB	H	2B	3B	HR	RBI	BB	SO	BA	SA	OBA
Season	246	55	10	0	6	25	31	45	.224	.337	.312
vs. Left-Handers	92	22	6	0	4	14	12	13	.239	.435	.333
vs. Right-Handers	154	33	4	0	2	11	19	32	.214	.279	.299
vs. Ground-Ballers	108	22	2	0	0	3	17	19	.204	.222	.312
vs. Fly-Ballers	138	33	8	0	6	22	14	26	.239	.428	.312
Home Games	109	28	6	0	2	14	16	14	.257	.367	.357
Road Games	137	27	4	0	4	11	15	31	.197	.314	.275
Grass Fields	189	46	8	0	4	17	24	30	.243	.349	.332
Artificial Turf	57	9	2	0	2	8	7	15	.158	.298	.246
April	37	9	2	0	1	1	4	4	.243	.297	.333
May	39	11	1	0	1	4	5	10	.282	.385	.356
June	46	11	3	0	1	8	4	7	.239	.370	.300
July	33	7	2	0	2	6	6	4	.212	.455	.333
August	30	7	0	0	0	1	6	5	.233	.233	.361
Sept./Oct.	61	10	2	0	2	5	6	15	.164	.295	.239
Leading Off Inn.	64	17	1	0	2	2	6	7	.266	.375	.338
Runners On	104	24	6	0	2	21	11	18	.231	.346	.302
Bases Empty	142	31	4	0	4	4	20	27	.218	.331	.319
Runners/Scor. Pos.	59	14	4	0	1	17	9	9	.237	.356	.333
Runners On/2 Out	47	7	2	0	1	8	8	15	.149	.255	.273
Scor. Pos./2 Out	31	6	2	0	0	6	7	8	.194	.258	.342
Late-Inning Pressure	54	10	1	0	0	3	11	7	.185	.204	.323
Leading Off	13	3	1	0	0	0	1	1	.231	.308	.286
Runners On	27	4	0	0	0	3	4	4	.148	.148	.258
Runners/Scor. Pos.	20	3	0	0	0	3	4	1	.150	.150	.292

RUNS BATTED IN	From 1B	From 2B	From 3B	Scoring Position
Totals	3/69	8/49	8/22	16/71
Percentage	4.3%	16.3%	36.4%	22.5%

Loves to face: Kyle Abbott (.667, 2-for-3, 2 HR)
Tom Browning (.429, 18-for-42, 4 HR)
Randy Tomlin (.250, 4-for-16, 1 2B, 2 HR, 4 BB)

Hates to face: Bud Black (.063, 1-for-16, 2 BB)
Greg Mathews (.056, 1-for-18, 2 BB)
Zane Smith (.174, 8-for-46)

Miscellaneous statistics: Ground outs-to-air outs ratio: 1.03 last season, 1.05 for career.... Grounded into 7 double plays in 41 opportunities (one per 5.9).... Drove in 6 of 10 runners from third base with less than two outs (60%).... Direction of balls hit to the outfield: 44% to left field, 28% to center, 28% to right.... Base running: Advanced from first base to third on 2 of 11 outfield singles (18%); scored from second on 4 of 8 (50%).... Made 2.88 assists per nine innings at second base.

Comments: Has batted below .230 in consecutive seasons of 399 and 279 at-bats. Only two players as old as Teufel (34) have ever gotten a 250-AB season under those circumstances. One was Reggie Jackson; the other was Rabbit Warstler.... Had 568 at-bats in his rookie season (1984 with Minnesota) and 434 as a sophomore, but never had another 400-AB season after that. The only other players to have done that over the past 50 years: Bernie Allen, Coco Laboy, Rick Bosetti, and Ron Kittle.... San Diego second basemen combined for a .232 average, the lowest of any team in the majors last season. Teufel batted .247 in 52 games at second; Kurt Stillwell posted a .227 mark in 111 games there.... Batting average with two outs and runners on base was 4th lowest in the league.... Hit two homers in a game against the Phillies in July, the fourth two-HR game of his career, but his first since 1987.... No triples in 762 at-bats over the last three seasons.... Was a valuable pinch hitter during his five-year stint with the Mets, posting a .271 average in that role, with five homers and 23 RBIs in 96 at-bats. Since joining the Padres, however, he has only three hits and no RBIs in 24 pinch ABs (.125).... Career average of .244 on grass fields, .267 on artificial turf.... Needs two more games with San Diego to join Chris Cannizzaro and Kevin McReynolds as the only players to appear in at least 200 games for both the Padres and the Mets (induction ceremony to be held at Joe McIlvaine's home).

Robby Thompson
Bats Right

San Francisco Giants	AB	H	2B	3B	HR	RBI	BB	SO	BA	SA	OBA
Season	443	115	25	1	14	49	43	75	.260	.415	.333
vs. Left-Handers	164	46	14	1	1	11	20	22	.280	.396	.357
vs. Right-Handers	279	69	11	0	13	38	23	53	.247	.427	.319
vs. Ground-Ballers	207	53	8	1	7	22	15	33	.256	.406	.314
vs. Fly-Ballers	236	62	17	0	7	27	28	42	.263	.424	.349
Home Games	236	64	14	1	8	27	22	38	.271	.441	.342
Road Games	207	51	11	0	6	22	21	37	.246	.386	.323
Grass Fields	356	95	22	1	12	42	31	58	.267	.435	.332
Artificial Turf	87	20	3	0	2	7	12	17	.230	.333	.337
April	68	24	5	0	3	11	10	7	.353	.559	.432
May	22	7	1	0	0	0	1	4	.318	.364	.348
June	81	11	4	0	1	5	11	19	.136	.222	.271
July	96	24	4	0	4	12	9	13	.250	.417	.324
August	101	26	6	1	4	14	6	14	.257	.455	.303
Sept./Oct.	75	23	5	0	2	7	6	18	.307	.453	.358
Leading Off Inn.	98	27	8	1	5	5	6	17	.276	.531	.343
Runners On	186	44	9	0	6	41	19	27	.237	.382	.311
Bases Empty	257	71	16	1	8	8	24	48	.276	.440	.350
Runners/Scor. Pos.	89	18	3	0	4	35	14	14	.202	.371	.306
Runners On/2 Out	76	17	4	0	4	20	9	16	.224	.434	.330
Scor. Pos./2 Out	46	10	2	0	2	15	5	9	.217	.391	.308
Late-Inning Pressure	83	14	2	0	2	9	4	14	.169	.265	.242
Leading Off	26	8	1	0	0	0	1	6	.308	.346	.379
Runners On	38	3	1	0	1	8	2	6	.079	.184	.167
Runners/Scor. Pos.	22	2	0	0	1	7	1	2	.091	.227	.167

RUNS BATTED IN	From 1B	From 2B	From 3B	Scoring Position
Totals	7/136	10/65	18/44	28/109
Percentage	5.1%	15.4%	40.9%	25.7%

Loves to face: Tom Glavine (.441, 15-for-34, 1 HR)
Les Lancaster (.467, 7-for-15)
Mike Maddux (.467, 7-for-15, 2 HR)

Hates to face: Jay Howell (.125, 2-for-16, 9 SO)
Ramon Martinez (.135, 5-for-37, 0 BB)
Todd Worrell (.077, 1-for-13)

Miscellaneous statistics: Ground outs-to-air outs ratio: 1.08 last season, 1.01 for career.... Grounded into 8 double plays in 92 opportunities (one per 12).... Drove in 12 of 18 runners from third base with less than two outs (67%).... Direction of balls hit to the outfield: 42% to left field, 24% to center, 34% to right.... Base running: Advanced from first base to third on 19 of 34 outfield singles (56%); scored from second on 6 of 7 (86%).... Made 3.27 assists per nine innings at second base, 3d-highest rate in N.L.

Comments: Thompson and Will Clark have been the opening-day right side of the Giants infield each year since 1987. Only one other team in the majors has used the same first and second basemen for even the last four season openers: Mark Grace and Ryne Sandberg for the Cubs.... Only one other second baseman has played more games for the Giants than Thompson, who is 37 games shy of 1000 at that position: Larry Doyle (1593).... No Giants second baseman has ever started the All-Star Game.... Has played 983 games for the Giants by the bay. Since the Giants left Manhattan, only Jim Davenport (1501 games) and Will Clark (1028) have played 1000 games for the team and none for any other.... Thompson and Sandberg were the only N.L. second basemen to reach double figures in home runs last season.... Batting average in June was lowest in the majors.... Batting average in Late-Inning Pressure Situations was 2d lowest in the league.... Stole only five bases after posting between 10 and 20 in each of his six previous seasons.... Has led N.L. second basemen in double plays each of the last three seasons. The last N.L. second baseman with a streak that long: Dave Cash (1974–76).... Set a career high with 101 DPs last season, the most by a Giants second baseman since Tito Fuentes in 1973.... Career batting average of .294 vs. left-handers, .240 vs. right-handers.... Just one of those crazy things: Thompson has batted .300 or better during the month of May five times in his seven seasons. Career BAs: .300 during May, .250 otherwise.

Andy Van Slyke
Bats Left

Pittsburgh Pirates	AB	H	2B	3B	HR	RBI	BB	SO	BA	SA	OBA
Season	614	199	45	12	14	89	58	99	.324	.505	.381
vs. Left-Handers	269	80	22	4	4	41	18	46	.297	.454	.341
vs. Right-Handers	345	119	23	8	10	48	40	53	.345	.545	.411
vs. Ground-Ballers	219	65	17	3	3	32	28	39	.297	.443	.379
vs. Fly-Ballers	395	134	28	9	11	57	30	60	.339	.539	.382
Home Games	315	101	24	6	6	40	22	44	.321	.492	.360
Road Games	299	98	21	6	8	49	36	55	.328	.518	.402
Grass Fields	153	51	11	1	6	23	21	25	.333	.536	.416
Artificial Turf	461	148	34	11	8	66	37	74	.321	.495	.369
April	67	19	4	1	0	12	16	17	.284	.373	.422
May	94	39	11	2	1	17	12	13	.415	.606	.486
June	103	31	5	2	2	11	8	19	.301	.447	.345
July	102	34	7	3	4	17	11	11	.333	.578	.391
August	108	34	6	2	4	18	8	18	.315	.519	.367
Sept./Oct.	140	42	12	2	3	14	3	21	.300	.479	.310
Leading Off Inn.	119	42	14	0	3	3	7	27	.353	.546	.398
Runners On	260	86	21	9	5	80	26	37	.331	.538	.382
Bases Empty	354	113	24	3	9	9	32	62	.319	.480	.380
Runners/Scor. Pos.	146	49	12	4	3	64	17	22	.336	.534	.387
Runners On/2 Out	72	20	5	2	2	20	14	13	.278	.486	.402
Scor. Pos./2 Out	46	13	4	0	1	15	10	9	.283	.435	.421
Late-Inning Pressure	96	27	5	0	1	13	10	20	.281	.365	.336
Leading Off	32	9	3	0	0	0	1	10	.281	.375	.303
Runners On	39	10	2	0	1	13	4	8	.256	.385	.298
Runners/Scor. Pos.	24	8	1	0	1	13	3	5	.333	.500	.355

RUNS BATTED IN	From 1B	From 2B	From 3B	Scoring Position
Totals	15/181	31/113	29/60	60/173
Percentage	8.3%	27.4%	48.3%	34.7%

Loves to face: Frank Castillo (.526, 10-for-19, 2 HR)
Greg Maddux (.382, 21-for-55, 4 HR)
Ben Rivera (.700, 7-for-10, 1 HR)

Hates to face: Rob Dibble (0-for-8, 5 SO)
Jeff Reardon (.111, 2-for-18, 2 BB)
Lee Smith (.069, 2-for-29, 1 HR, 4 BB)

Miscellaneous statistics: Ground outs-to-air outs ratio: 0.88 last season, 0.89 for career.... Grounded into 9 double plays in 138 opportunities (one per 15).... Drove in 24 of 40 runners from third base with less than two outs (60%).... Direction of balls hit to the outfield: 31% to left field, 29% to center, 40% to right.... Base running: Advanced from first base to third on 5 of 27 outfield singles (19%); scored from second on 23 of 29 (79%).... Made 2.76 putouts per nine innings in center field.

Comments: Van Slyke and Barry Bonds had played 17 postseason games together before they *combined* for three hits in a game (Game 5 of 1992 N.L.C.S.).... Increase of 59 batting average points from 1991 to 1992 was the 2d largest of any player who qualified for the batting title in both seasons (behind Mark McGwire), and the largest by a Pirates player since a 66-point jump by Ralph Kiner in 1947.... Brought career batting averages of .290 vs. right-handers and .219 vs. left-handers into 1992. Last year's average vs. right-handers was the best in the majors.... His career average of .233 against left-handers is the lowest among active players (minimum: 1000 AB), but he has improved: .208 from 1983 through 1988, .255 since then (including a career-high mark in 1992).... Career BA is .296 vs. RHP. The difference of 63 points between his career averages is 2d largest among active players (1000 ABs vs. both). Mariano Duncan has an 82-point spread.... Also has trouble with lefties on the bases. Over the last four seasons, he's stolen only 14 bases in 24 attempts against left-handers (.636), compared to 38-for-44 vs. RHP (.864).... Has the highest fielding percentage (one error every 84 chances) of any outfielder in Pirates history (minimum: 250 games).... Walk rate was the worst of his career (one every 11.8 PA), aided by his late-season quest for 200 hits. He drew only two walks in 104 trips to the plate after September 10, but to no avail; he got hit number 199 in the season finale, but went hitless in his final two at-bats.

Jose Vizcaino

Bats Left and Right

Chicago Cubs	AB	H	2B	3B	HR	RBI	BB	SO	BA	SA	OBA
Season	285	64	10	4	1	17	14	35	.225	.298	.260
vs. Left-Handers	88	19	3	3	0	5	3	7	.216	.318	.242
vs. Right-Handers	197	45	7	1	1	12	11	28	.228	.289	.268
vs. Ground-Ballers	126	29	3	2	1	6	6	17	.230	.310	.265
vs. Fly-Ballers	159	35	7	2	0	11	8	18	.220	.289	.256
Home Games	126	29	4	1	0	3	7	18	.230	.278	.269
Road Games	159	35	6	3	1	14	7	17	.220	.314	.253
Grass Fields	220	52	6	3	1	12	12	26	.236	.305	.275
Artificial Turf	65	12	4	1	0	5	2	9	.185	.277	.209
April	22	2	0	0	0	1	0	2	.091	.091	.087
May	56	10	0	2	0	1	4	5	.179	.250	.233
June	113	28	7	0	0	6	5	15	.248	.310	.280
July	45	7	3	0	0	0	3	7	.156	.222	.208
August	49	17	0	2	1	9	2	6	.347	.490	.373
Sept./Oct.	0	0	0	0	0	0	0	0	.000	.000	.000
Leading Off Inn.	100	19	5	1	1	1	7	16	.190	.290	.243
Runners On	87	22	1	2	0	16	5	9	.253	.310	.290
Bases Empty	198	42	9	2	1	1	9	26	.212	.293	.246
Runners/Scor. Pos.	56	15	0	0	0	14	5	6	.268	.268	.323
Runners On/2 Out	52	10	0	0	0	7	5	5	.192	.192	.263
Scor. Pos./2 Out	34	7	0	0	0	7	5	4	.206	.206	.308
Late-Inning Pressure	45	11	3	0	0	4	3	5	.244	.311	.292
Leading Off	14	3	1	0	0	0	2	3	.214	.286	.313
Runners On	15	5	1	0	0	4	0	1	.333	.400	.333
Runners/Scor. Pos.	11	4	0	0	0	4	0	0	.364	.364	.364

RUNS BATTED IN	From 1B	From 2B	From 3B	Scoring Position
Totals	2/56	5/41	9/23	14/64
Percentage	3.6%	12.2%	39.1%	21.9%

Loves to face: Doug Drabek (.556, 5-for-9)
Mark Portugal (3-for-3, 2 2B)
Curt Schilling (.429, 3-for-7, 1 2B)
Hates to face: Tim Burke (0-for-5)
Mark Clark (0-for-8)
Bob Tewksbury (.100, 1-for-10)

Miscellaneous statistics: Ground outs-to-air outs ratio: 1.51 last season, 1.76 for career.... Grounded into 4 double plays in 31 opportunities (one per 7.8).... Drove in 6 of 10 runners from third base with less than two outs (60%).... Direction of balls hit to the outfield: 30% to left field, 42% to center, 28% to right batting left-handed; 34% to left field, 31% to center, 34% to right batting right-handed.... Base running: Advanced from first base to third on 6 of 10 outfield singles (60%), 2d-highest rate in N.L.; scored from second on 4 of 7 (57%).... Made 3.33 assists per nine innings at shortstop.

Comments: Started 38 games from the leadoff spot, and while he batted only .205 from the top spot, the Cubs posted a winning record in those games (20–18).... Cubs leadoff hitters combined for a .248 batting average and a .289 on-base percentage, both N.L. lows last season. The only other Cubs player to start as often in the leadoff slot as Vizcaino was Doug Dascenzo.... Spent a total of 37 days on the disabled list; see the Rey Sanchez comments for more on this.... Career batting-average breakdowns: .222 before the All-Star break, .272 after the break; .247 on grass fields, .214 on artificial turf; .223 with bases empty, .276 with runners on base.... Career batting averages rise steadily from a low of .133 in April to a peak of .276 in August, before slipping back to .243 for September/October.... Acquired from the Dodgers in 1991. Against all odds, the myth persists that the Dodgers never trade promising prospects. The following all debuted for Los Angeles, and all played fewer than 100 games for the Dodgers and at least 600 games for other teams: Sid Bream, Ivan DeJesus, Jim Gentile, Mickey Hatcher, Tom Hutton, Jeffrey Leonard, Jerry Royster, Charley Smith, and Bob Stinson. Not an All-Star squad, but all useful players—and the list doesn't even include the following L.A. debutante pitchers, who won fewer than 25 games for the Dodgers, but 100 or more for others: Doyle Alexander, Jack Billingham, Dave Stewart, Rick Sutcliffe, and Geoff Zahn.

Chico Walker

Bats Left and Right

Cubs/Mets	AB	H	2B	3B	HR	RBI	BB	SO	BA	SA	OBA
Season	253	73	12	1	4	38	27	50	.289	.391	.351
vs. Left-Handers	90	29	4	0	0	13	4	13	.322	.367	.340
vs. Right-Handers	163	44	8	1	4	25	23	37	.270	.405	.356
vs. Ground-Ballers	118	36	6	0	3	21	11	22	.305	.432	.353
vs. Fly-Ballers	135	37	6	1	1	17	16	28	.274	.356	.349
Home Games	104	33	5	0	0	18	14	26	.317	.365	.388
Road Games	149	40	7	1	4	20	13	24	.268	.409	.323
Grass Fields	172	53	5	1	1	26	18	35	.308	.366	.366
Artificial Turf	81	20	7	0	3	12	9	15	.247	.444	.319
April	23	2	0	0	0	1	2	4	.087	.087	.160
May	37	11	0	0	1	5	2	6	.297	.378	.317
June	29	7	2	0	1	8	3	5	.241	.414	.313
July	34	11	3	0	1	3	3	5	.324	.500	.378
August	58	21	1	1	0	8	8	10	.362	.414	.433
Sept./Oct.	72	21	6	0	1	13	9	20	.292	.417	.361
Leading Off Inn.	58	13	1	0	1	6	14	14	.224	.293	.297
Runners On	109	37	4	1	2	36	18	20	.339	.450	.417
Bases Empty	144	36	8	0	2	2	9	30	.250	.347	.294
Runners/Scor. Pos.	70	20	3	1	2	36	15	14	.286	.443	.389
Runners On/2 Out	46	14	1	1	1	14	7	9	.304	.435	.396
Scor. Pos./2 Out	34	9	1	1	1	14	6	7	.265	.441	.375
Late-Inning Pressure	70	16	3	0	0	8	8	12	.229	.271	.308
Leading Off	20	5	1	0	0	0	1	5	.250	.300	.286
Runners On	31	7	1	0	0	8	6	4	.226	.258	.351
Runners/Scor. Pos.	26	6	0	0	0	8	5	4	.231	.231	.355

RUNS BATTED IN	From 1B	From 2B	From 3B	Scoring Position
Totals	4/78	12/55	18/33	30/88
Percentage	5.1%	21.8%	54.5%	34.1%

Loves to face: Tim Burke (.714, 5-for-7)
Dennis Martinez (.381, 8-for-21, 1 HR)
Trevor Wilson (.400, 4-for-10)
Hates to face: Brian Barnes (.071, 1-for-14)
Andy Benes (0-for-12)
Bob Tewksbury (0-for-8)

Miscellaneous statistics: Ground outs-to-air outs ratio: 1.44 last season, 1.22 for career.... Grounded into 9 double plays in 57 opportunities (one per 6.3).... Drove in 15 of 23 runners from third base with less than two outs (65%).... Direction of balls hit to the outfield: 46% to left field, 19% to center, 36% to right batting left-handed; 44% to left field, 25% to center, 31% to right batting right-handed.... Base running: Advanced from first base to third on 4 of 12 outfield singles (33%); scored from second on 5 of 6 (83%).... Made 2.08 assists per nine innings at third base.

Comments: Appeared in 69 games as a pinch hitter, tying Philadelphia's Jeff Grotewold for major league lead. But after batting .406 (13-for-32) as a pinch hitter in 1991, he hit only .175 (10-for-57) as an emergency swinger last year. That fits the pattern often demonstrated by pinch hitters, who rarely put two outstanding years back-to-back. But since 1975, only two pinch hitters have suffered larger declines (minimum: 25 at-bats each year): Jerry Mumphrey (.343 to .100, 1987–88) and Gary Varsho (.393 to .139, 1988–89).... Career switch-hitting breakdown: .249 batting right-handed, .250 batting left-handed.... Made 49 starts last season after a career-high 80 starts in 1991.... Stole 15 bases in 16 attempts, 2d-highest percentage in majors behind Eric Davis (minimum: 15 attempts). Chico was caught stealing by his old teammate, Rick Wilkins.... Mets third basemen combined for only four home runs (Walker and Dave Magadan each hit two), fewest in N.L.; other N.L. clubs averaged more than 16 homers from their third basemen.... Selected by Red Sox in same 1976 draft in which they chose Wade Boggs.... Pro career began that year; he played first major league game in 1980, but he didn't spend a full season in the majors until 1991, and only became a "three-year" player (in terms of accumulated major league service) in 1992. He spent all of the 1982, 1989, and 1990 seasons in the minors.... The major leaguers closest in age to Walker are Lee Smith and Bob Ojeda.

Larry Walker — Bats Left

Montreal Expos	AB	H	2B	3B	HR	RBI	BB	SO	BA	SA	OBA
Season	528	159	31	4	23	93	41	97	.301	.506	.353
vs. Left-Handers	209	66	8	2	10	42	10	38	.316	.517	.354
vs. Right-Handers	319	93	23	2	13	51	31	59	.292	.498	.353
vs. Ground-Ballers	214	65	11	1	6	30	14	32	.304	.449	.350
vs. Fly-Ballers	314	94	20	3	17	63	27	65	.299	.545	.355
Home Games	257	73	12	3	13	43	23	47	.284	.506	.349
Road Games	271	86	19	1	10	50	18	50	.317	.506	.357
Grass Fields	163	52	11	1	8	30	9	34	.319	.546	.356
Artificial Turf	365	107	20	3	15	63	32	63	.293	.488	.352
April	89	23	5	0	5	15	7	19	.258	.483	.327
May	75	22	4	1	4	15	9	15	.293	.533	.365
June	60	18	2	0	5	14	5	11	.300	.583	.338
July	98	29	3	1	4	15	4	21	.296	.469	.320
August	96	32	7	1	2	14	7	14	.333	.490	.377
Sept./Oct.	110	35	10	1	3	20	9	17	.318	.509	.382
Leading Off Inn.	135	40	6	2	9	9	7	25	.296	.570	.340
Runners On	253	80	17	0	10	80	26	44	.316	.502	.376
Bases Empty	275	79	14	4	13	13	15	53	.287	.509	.331
Runners/Scor. Pos.	159	49	10	0	6	68	24	29	.308	.484	.385
Runners On/2 Out	122	29	10	0	1	24	14	26	.238	.344	.331
Scor. Pos./2 Out	73	16	5	0	0	18	14	19	.219	.288	.352
Late-Inning Pressure	80	18	1	0	4	13	11	21	.225	.387	.315
Leading Off	21	4	0	0	2	2	4	7	.190	.476	.320
Runners On	33	8	0	0	1	10	5	7	.242	.333	.333
Runners/Scor. Pos.	21	5	0	0	1	10	5	6	.238	.381	.370

RUNS BATTED IN	From 1B	From 2B	From 3B	Scoring Position
Totals	10/162	24/116	36/76	60/192
Percentage	6.2%	20.7%	47.4%	31.3%

Loves to face: John Burkett (.412, 7-for-17, 3 HR)
Greg W. Harris (.643, 9-for-14, 3 HR)
Anthony Young (.600, 6-for-10, 2 HR)

Hates to face: Mark Portugal (0-for-9)
Bryn Smith (.067, 1-for-15)
Wally Whitehurst (0-for-9, 5 SO)

Miscellaneous statistics: Ground outs-to-air outs ratio: 1.17 last season, 1.34 for career.... Grounded into 9 double plays in 91 opportunities (one per 10).... Drove in 26 of 44 runners from third base with less than two outs (59%).... Direction of balls hit to the outfield: 29% to left field, 30% to center, 41% to right.... Base running: Advanced from first base to third on 8 of 21 outfield singles (38%); scored from second on 15 of 19 (79%).... Made 1.99 putouts per nine innings in right field, 3d-lowest rate in N.L.

Comments: The only nonpitcher in the National League to increase his batting average by at least 10 points in each of the last three seasons.... One of three left-handed batters who hit .300 with double-figure home runs vs. left-handed pitchers last season; the others: Ken Griffey (.358, 12) and Barry Bonds (.311, 13). Over the previous 17 years, there were only 10 such seasons turned in by left-handed hitters: Dave Parker in 1978 and 1986, Reggie Jackson in 1979, Ben Oglivie in 1980, George Brett in 1985 and 1988, Don Mattingly and Larry Sheets in 1987, and David Justice and Bonds in 1990.... Walker's career batting average and career home-run rate are both higher vs. left-handed pitchers (.278, one homer every 24.5 at-bats) than vs. righties (.275, one homer every 26.1 at-bats).... Tied Terry Pendleton and Gary Sheffield for major league lead with 20 game-winning RBIs.... Had more hits from the cleanup spot than any N.L. player (156).... Expos outfielders combined for 265 RBIs, the most by any N.L. club last season, and third in the majors behind Minnesota (274) and Toronto (266).... Hit .405 (17-for-42) vs. Braves and .429 (15-for-35) vs. Reds last season, the top mark by any N.L. player against each of those clubs.... Led major league right fielders with 16 assists.... One of the few active players who has a substantially higher stolen base percentage on grass fields (.840, 21-for-25) than on artificial turf (.635, 33-for-52). His career batting average is also higher on grass (.298) than on rugs (.267).

Tim Wallach — Bats Right

Montreal Expos	AB	H	2B	3B	HR	RBI	BB	SO	BA	SA	OBA
Season	537	120	29	1	9	59	50	90	.223	.331	.296
vs. Left-Handers	198	52	11	1	7	29	17	25	.263	.434	.329
vs. Right-Handers	339	68	18	0	2	30	33	65	.201	.271	.276
vs. Ground-Ballers	232	49	9	0	3	26	25	44	.211	.289	.297
vs. Fly-Ballers	305	71	20	1	6	33	25	46	.233	.364	.295
Home Games	262	69	19	0	5	41	24	47	.263	.393	.333
Road Games	275	51	10	1	4	18	26	43	.185	.273	.259
Grass Fields	146	27	5	1	3	11	14	24	.185	.295	.265
Artificial Turf	391	93	24	0	6	48	36	66	.238	.345	.307
April	85	19	7	0	1	8	12	16	.224	.341	.327
May	74	16	6	0	2	7	5	10	.216	.378	.289
June	103	30	5	0	0	13	6	12	.291	.340	.336
July	100	18	4	0	1	8	12	15	.180	.250	.265
August	90	20	3	1	2	8	7	21	.222	.344	.283
Sept./Oct.	85	17	4	0	3	15	8	16	.200	.353	.271
Leading Off Inn.	140	32	12	0	0	0	12	18	.229	.314	.294
Runners On	220	54	12	1	4	54	24	43	.245	.364	.322
Bases Empty	317	66	17	0	5	5	26	47	.208	.309	.277
Runners/Scor. Pos.	132	30	6	1	2	45	17	27	.227	.333	.314
Runners On/2 Out	95	20	7	0	1	18	11	20	.211	.316	.299
Scor. Pos./2 Out	64	12	5	0	0	14	10	12	.188	.266	.307
Late-Inning Pressure	89	19	8	0	1	7	5	13	.213	.337	.263
Leading Off	31	5	3	0	0	0	3	6	.161	.258	.235
Runners On	31	8	4	0	0	6	2	5	.258	.387	.303
Runners/Scor. Pos.	16	3	1	0	0	4	2	3	.188	.250	.278

RUNS BATTED IN	From 1B	From 2B	From 3B	Scoring Position
Totals	9/148	16/92	25/65	41/157
Percentage	6.1%	17.4%	38.5%	26.1%

Loves to face: Tom Browning (.347, 17-for-49, 4 2B, 3 HR)
Tom Glavine (.386, 17-for-44, 5 HR)
Joe Magrane (.364, 16-for-44, 2 HR)

Hates to face: Doug Drabek (.155, 11-for-71, 1 HR)
Omar Olivares (.091, 2-for-22)
Wally Whitehurst (0-for-12)

Miscellaneous statistics: Ground outs-to-air outs ratio: 0.91 last season, 0.84 for career.... Grounded into 10 double plays in 95 opportunities (one per 10).... Drove in 19 of 35 runners from third base with less than two outs (54%).... Direction of balls hit to the outfield: 36% to left field, 33% to center, 32% to right.... Base running: Advanced from first base to third on 11 of 28 outfield singles (39%); scored from second on 6 of 12 (50%), 5th-lowest rate in N.L.... Made 2.36 assists per nine innings at third base, highest rate in N.L.; 0.91 assists per nine innings at first base, 2d-highest rate in N.L.

Comments: Only player in majors who has batted below .230 in 500-at-bat seasons in each of the past two years; over the past 70 years, only five other players had similar repeat seasons: Rabbit Warstler (1936–37), Ed Brinkman (1971–72), Aurelio Rodriguez (1973–74), Ozzie Smith (1979–80), and Dale Murphy (1988–89).... Road batting average was 3d lowest in N.L.; average vs. right-handers was 2d lowest in N.L.; average on grass fields was worst in the majors.... Hitless in 15 at-bats in extra innings last season, the largest such zero in majors.... Leaves Expos as all-time leader in games, at-bats, hits, doubles, extra-base hits, and RBIs. He's also third in homers with 204, behind Andre Dawson (225) and Gary Carter (220); then comes Bob Bailey with 118.... Expos third basemen combined for 30 errors, the most by any N.L. club last season; Wallach made nine of them, Bret Barberie 12, Archi Cianfrocco five, and Sean Berry four.... Meanwhile, the Expos started eight different players at first base, the most by any N.L. club last season; they combined for only 56 RBIs last season, the fewest of any club in the majors at that position.... The durable Wallach has played 1691 games over the past 11 years; only three players have been in more: Cal Ripken (1777), Eddie Murray (1707), and Ryne Sandberg (1692). Perhaps those games have taken a toll: He has hit no higher than .227 in July, August or September in either of the past two years.

Mitch Webster

Bats Left and Right

Los Angeles Dodgers	AB	H	2B	3B	HR	RBI	BB	SO	BA	SA	OBA
Season	262	70	12	5	6	35	27	49	.267	.420	.334
vs. Left-Handers	130	38	8	1	3	17	15	18	.292	.438	.361
vs. Right-Handers	132	32	4	4	3	18	12	31	.242	.402	.309
vs. Ground-Ballers	88	21	4	3	1	9	6	15	.239	.386	.292
vs. Fly-Ballers	174	49	8	2	5	26	21	34	.282	.437	.355
Home Games	125	27	5	1	1	13	16	16	.216	.296	.308
Road Games	137	43	7	4	5	22	11	33	.314	.533	.360
Grass Fields	188	46	6	3	3	26	20	32	.245	.356	.316
Artificial Turf	74	24	6	2	3	9	7	17	.324	.581	.383
April	9	3	0	0	0	4	2	3	.333	.333	.385
May	46	10	1	3	2	5	4	17	.217	.500	.275
June	46	12	1	0	1	8	9	6	.261	.348	.393
July	54	16	3	1	0	5	2	6	.296	.389	.321
August	57	14	4	0	1	5	5	9	.246	.368	.302
Sept./Oct.	50	15	3	1	2	8	5	8	.300	.520	.368
Leading Off Inn.	58	15	4	2	0	0	4	9	.259	.397	.317
Runners On	122	28	5	2	2	31	13	21	.230	.352	.298
Bases Empty	140	42	7	3	4	4	14	28	.300	.479	.368
Runners/Scor. Pos.	70	15	4	1	1	28	10	15	.214	.343	.302
Runners On/2 Out	55	13	2	1	1	14	4	11	.236	.364	.300
Scor. Pos./2 Out	40	9	2	1	0	12	4	7	.225	.325	.311
Late-Inning Pressure	67	21	1	2	2	10	12	14	.313	.478	.420
Leading Off	15	7	1	1	0	0	1	1	.467	.667	.529
Runners On	37	9	0	1	0	8	6	9	.243	.297	.341
Runners/Scor. Pos.	21	5	0	1	0	8	4	7	.238	.333	.346

RUNS BATTED IN	From 1B	From 2B	From 3B	Scoring Position
Totals	6/87	11/58	12/32	23/90
Percentage	6.9%	19.0%	37.5%	25.6%

Loves to face: Larry Andersen (.750, 6-for-8, 2 2B)
Paul Assenmacher (.571, 4-for-7, 1 3B, 1 HR)
Zane Smith (.462, 12-for-26)

Hates to face: Tim Belcher (.059, 1-for-17)
Tim Burke (0-for-10)
Tom Glavine (.125, 2-for-16)

Miscellaneous statistics: Ground outs-to-air outs ratio: 0.60 last season (3d lowest in N.L.), 0.73 for career.... Grounded into 1 double play in 65 opportunities (one per 65), 2d-best rate in majors.... Drove in 9 of 13 runners from third base with less than two outs (69%).... Direction of balls hit to the outfield: 25% to left field, 37% to center, 37% to right batting left-handed; 35% to left field, 33% to center, 32% to right batting right-handed.... Base running: Advanced from first base to third on 4 of 12 outfield singles (33%); scored from second on 4 of 7 (57%).... Made 1.98 putouts per nine innings in right field.

Comments: You might think that he's a good candidate to become the first player to play against each of the 28 current major league clubs, including expansionists Colorado and Florida, but he has never played a game against the Indians. Maybe he'll be the first to play *with* all 28.... Played with six teams over seven years from 1985 to 1991: Blue Jays, Expos, Cubs, Indians, Pirates, and Dodgers.... Has hit at least 50 points higher from the right side of plate than from the left in each of the last four years. Four-year averages: .283 right-handed, .224 left-handed.... Fashioned career-high mark in Late-Inning Pressure Situations last year.... Led majors with 17 pinch hits last year; not surprisingly, Tommy Lasorda used more pinch hitters (344) than any manager in majors. That's just 19 shy of the major league record set by 1965 Mets. Aided by Webster, Dodgers pinch hitters batted .266, 2d best in N.L. to Cubs' .271.... He's an early-in-the-inning specialist; career batting: .296 leading off innings, .270 with runners on base, .260 with runners in scoring position, .242 with runners in scoring position and two outs.... Sign of the times: His six home runs last year put him second on team (tied with Dave Hansen) behind Eric Karros.... Three steadiest jobs on earth: Queen of England, host of *American Bandstand,* and backup to Eric Davis.

Rick Wilkins

Bats Left

Chicago Cubs	AB	H	2B	3B	HR	RBI	BB	SO	BA	SA	OBA
Season	244	66	9	1	8	22	28	53	.270	.414	.344
vs. Left-Handers	50	14	3	0	0	1	5	10	.280	.340	.345
vs. Right-Handers	194	52	6	1	8	21	23	43	.268	.433	.344
vs. Ground-Ballers	110	35	5	0	6	13	10	20	.318	.527	.372
vs. Fly-Ballers	134	31	4	1	2	9	18	33	.231	.321	.322
Home Games	129	34	3	0	3	9	18	26	.264	.357	.354
Road Games	115	32	6	1	5	13	10	27	.278	.478	.333
Grass Fields	173	47	6	0	5	16	21	35	.272	.393	.349
Artificial Turf	71	19	3	1	3	6	7	18	.268	.465	.333
April	10	2	0	0	0	0	1	2	.200	.200	.273
May	0	0	0	0	0	0	0	0	.000	.000	.000
June	22	9	2	0	1	5	1	4	.409	.636	.417
July	59	17	1	0	3	5	3	12	.288	.458	.323
August	66	15	0	0	1	2	7	17	.227	.273	.301
Sept./Oct.	87	23	6	1	3	10	16	18	.264	.460	.379
Leading Off Inn.	52	15	3	0	0	0	2	14	.288	.346	.315
Runners On	109	23	2	1	2	16	17	25	.211	.303	.315
Bases Empty	135	43	7	0	6	6	11	28	.319	.504	.370
Runners/Scor. Pos.	53	13	1	1	2	16	15	9	.245	.415	.406
Runners On/2 Out	55	10	0	0	1	7	13	13	.182	.236	.338
Scor. Pos./2 Out	29	5	0	0	1	7	13	5	.172	.276	.429
Late-Inning Pressure	48	14	0	0	2	4	5	11	.292	.417	.358
Leading Off	13	4	0	0	0	0	0	3	.308	.308	.308
Runners On	17	4	0	0	0	2	2	4	.235	.235	.316
Runners/Scor. Pos.	8	2	0	0	0	2	2	2	.250	.250	.400

RUNS BATTED IN	From 1B	From 2B	From 3B	Scoring Position
Totals	1/89	8/44	5/19	13/63
Percentage	1.1%	18.2%	26.3%	20.6%

Loves to face: Kevin Gross (.667, 4-for-6, 1 HR)
John Smoltz (.400, 4-for-10, 1 HR)
Bob Walk (.700, 7-for-10, 2 HR)

Hates to face: Chris Nabholz (0-for-5)
Omar Olivares (0-for-6)
Bryn Smith (0-for-5)

Miscellaneous statistics: Ground outs-to-air outs ratio: 0.64 last season (4th lowest in N.L.), 0.87 for career.... Grounded into 6 double plays in 47 opportunities (one per 7.8).... Drove in 2 of 9 runners from third base with less than two outs (22%).... Direction of balls hit to the outfield: 35% to left field, 26% to center, 39% to right.... Base running: Advanced from first base to third on 3 of 14 outfield singles (21%); scored from second on 3 of 6 (50%).... Opposing base stealers: 49-for-78 (63%).

Comments: Started each of the last 15 games of last year for the Cubs, not as a statement of 1993 policy but as a replacement for the injured Joe Girardi.... Cubs were the only N.L. team whose catchers didn't steal a base last year. Cubs catchers also combined for fewest RBIs in N.L. (44).... No Cubs catcher made more than 70 starts in either 1991 or 1992. Cubs had only three positions at which one player started a majority of their games last year: first base, second base, right field; no other team in the majors had so few.... While we're at it, let's note that no Cubs catcher since Gabby Hartnett in 1937 has started the All-Star Game. Gabby hit .357 that year; he's also the last Cubs backstop to hit .300 in a 300-at-bat season.... Only four left-handed hitters have caught more games for the Cubs than Wilkins (155): Tim Donahue (454), Sammy Taylor (320), Ken O'Dea (253), and Rube Walker (180). Honorable mention to Joe Garagiola (123).... Wilkins and Jerald Clark each hit six homers from 7th lineup spot; not many, but enough to tie for N.L. lead.... Career breakdown: .215 in day games, .289 at night; .281 with the bases empty, .206 with runners on base.... Major leaguers born on the Fourth of July include Hall of Fame pitcher Mickey Welch (1859), former managers Chuck Tanner (1929) and Hal Lanier (1942), Bill Tuttle (1929), Ed Armbrister (1948), Jim Beattie (1954), and current players Jose Oquendo (1963), Vinny Castilla (1967), and Wilkins (1967). And, of course, George Steinbrenner (1930).

Matt Williams   Bats Right

San Francisco Giants	AB	H	2B	3B	HR	RBI	BB	SO	BA	SA	OBA
Season	529	120	13	5	20	66	39	109	.227	.384	.286
vs. Left-Handers	164	37	2	2	10	21	13	30	.226	.445	.279
vs. Right-Handers	365	83	11	3	10	45	26	79	.227	.356	.290
vs. Ground-Ballers	270	60	5	0	10	34	23	56	.222	.352	.287
vs. Fly-Ballers	259	60	8	5	10	32	16	53	.232	.417	.286
Home Games	269	62	5	5	9	29	17	51	.230	.387	.283
Road Games	260	58	8	0	11	37	22	58	.223	.381	.290
Grass Fields	390	82	8	5	12	40	25	83	.210	.349	.264
Artificial Turf	139	38	5	0	8	26	14	26	.273	.482	.346
April	81	14	2	1	5	16	3	16	.173	.407	.221
May	87	23	2	1	6	18	15	22	.264	.517	.369
June	88	17	1	1	0	2	1	19	.193	.227	.202
July	78	20	2	1	2	7	10	18	.256	.385	.352
August	97	18	1	1	3	9	3	19	.186	.309	.210
Sept./Oct.	98	28	5	0	4	14	7	15	.286	.459	.346
Leading Off Inn.	131	34	4	1	7	7	11	18	.260	.466	.322
Runners On	232	49	6	4	10	56	20	57	.211	.401	.283
Bases Empty	297	71	7	1	10	10	19	52	.239	.370	.289
Runners/Scor. Pos.	149	31	4	2	8	49	17	42	.208	.423	.298
Runners On/2 Out	111	23	4	3	3	22	9	30	.207	.378	.279
Scor. Pos./2 Out	90	15	3	1	3	20	9	27	.167	.322	.250
Late-Inning Pressure	94	16	1	0	2	7	10	23	.170	.245	.257
Leading Off	25	3	0	0	1	1	2	3	.120	.240	.185
Runners On	39	6	1	0	1	6	8	13	.154	.256	.313
Runners/Scor. Pos.	20	4	0	0	1	5	8	9	.200	.350	.429

RUNS BATTED IN	From 1B	From 2B	From 3B	Scoring Position
Totals	12/157	18/113	16/61	34/174
Percentage	7.6%	15.9%	26.2%	19.5%

Loves to face: Shawn Boskie (.375, 6-for-16, 2 2B, 2 HR)
John Smiley (.429, 9-for-21, 4 HR)
Bryn Smith (.316, 6-for-19, 2 HR)
Hates to face: Greg W. Harris (0-for-14)
Orel Hershiser (.121, 4-for-33, 1 HR, 15 SO)
Mark Portugal (.081, 3-for-37)

Miscellaneous statistics: Ground outs-to-air outs ratio: 0.96 last season, 0.94 for career.... Grounded into 15 double plays in 98 opportunities (one per 6.5).... Drove in 10 of 22 runners from third base with less than two outs (45%).... Direction of balls hit to the outfield: 38% to left field, 37% to center, 25% to right.... Base running: Advanced from first base to third on 10 of 21 outfield singles (48%); scored from second on 9 of 11 (82%).... Made 2.08 assists per nine innings at third base.

Comments: Yearly strikeout rates since his debut in 1987: one every 3.9 plate appearances, followed by one every 4.1, 4.3, 4.8, 5.0, and 5.3. He and Andy Van Slyke are the only players in the majors whose rate of strikeouts has decreased in each of the last five seasons. The all-time record: eight consecutive decreases, shared by Rod Carew, Lou Piniella, Hank Gowdy, and Frank Welch.... Williams has also improved his walk rate in each of the last three seasons; the only other players to improve both walk and strikeout rates in 1990, 1991, and 1992 are Steve Finley and Barry Bonds (minimum: 300 PA). The last player to do it in four consecutive years: George Brett (1974–77).... With all this "improving," however, Matt has fallen dramatically since 1990 in two more important categories: RBIs (122 to 98 to 66) and his percentage of runners driven in from scoring position (35.4 to 26.8 to 19.5).... Batting average with runners on base was 3d lowest in league.... Led N.L. third basemen with 23 errors, but started more double plays than any third baseman in majors (31).... Owns .191 career batting average in Late-Inning Pressure Situations, the lowest in the majors over the past 18 years among players with at least 350 LIPS at-bats. Only two other players posted career averages below .200: Greg Brock (.193) and Bruce Benedict (.199).... Career home-run rate by month: one every 24.8 at-bats in April, one every 24.4 in May, 19.9 in June, 17.8 in July, 17.1 in August, 19.6 in September.

Todd Zeile   Bats Right

St. Louis Cardinals	AB	H	2B	3B	HR	RBI	BB	SO	BA	SA	OBA
Season	439	113	18	4	7	48	68	70	.257	.364	.352
vs. Left-Handers	133	37	5	1	1	15	26	16	.278	.353	.394
vs. Right-Handers	306	76	13	3	6	33	42	54	.248	.369	.333
vs. Ground-Ballers	205	56	11	1	3	28	40	35	.273	.380	.387
vs. Fly-Ballers	234	57	7	3	4	20	28	35	.244	.350	.320
Home Games	226	52	7	2	4	27	38	34	.230	.332	.337
Road Games	213	61	11	2	3	21	30	36	.286	.399	.368
Grass Fields	124	37	6	2	3	12	17	19	.298	.452	.375
Artificial Turf	315	76	12	2	4	36	51	51	.241	.330	.343
April	74	19	3	1	3	11	13	11	.257	.446	.356
May	88	16	4	0	0	7	15	19	.182	.227	.295
June	86	25	5	2	1	8	10	9	.291	.430	.361
July	91	27	3	0	1	10	15	14	.297	.363	.396
August	15	2	0	0	0	0	0	4	.133	.133	.133
Sept./Oct.	85	24	3	1	2	12	15	13	.282	.412	.386
Leading Off Inn.	95	28	1	1	3	14	14	19	.295	.421	.385
Runners On	201	50	9	0	2	43	35	32	.249	.323	.350
Bases Empty	238	63	9	4	5	5	33	38	.265	.399	.354
Runners/Scor. Pos.	131	28	6	0	1	39	28	26	.214	.282	.337
Runners On/2 Out	88	18	4	0	1	18	15	17	.205	.284	.320
Scor. Pos./2 Out	72	13	4	0	0	16	13	17	.181	.236	.306
Late-Inning Pressure	89	20	1	2	0	4	13	17	.225	.281	.320
Leading Off	25	6	0	1	0	0	4	5	.240	.320	.345
Runners On	38	6	0	0	0	4	7	6	.158	.158	.283
Runners/Scor. Pos.	23	3	0	0	0	4	5	5	.130	.130	.276

RUNS BATTED IN	From 1B	From 2B	From 3B	Scoring Position
Totals	6/123	11/97	24/62	35/159
Percentage	4.9%	11.3%	38.7%	22.0%

Loves to face: Pete Harnisch (.429, 6-for-14, 1 HR)
Terry Mulholland (.458, 11-for-24)
Bob Scanlan (.667, 6-for-9)
Hates to face: Tom Browning (.063, 1-for-16)
Doug Drabek (.167, 6-for-36)
Zane Smith (.095, 2-for-21, 1 3B, 3 BB)

Miscellaneous statistics: Ground outs-to-air outs ratio: 0.93 last season, 1.07 for career.... Grounded into 11 double plays in 92 opportunities (one per 8.4).... Drove in 14 of 26 runners from third base with less than two outs (54%).... Direction of balls hit to the outfield: 35% to left field, 30% to center, 36% to right.... Base running: Advanced from first base to third on 10 of 32 outfield singles (31%); scored from second on 9 of 17 (53%).... Made 1.96 assists per nine innings at third base.

Comments: Only three other players in baseball history have had 100-game seasons at both catcher and third base: Duke Farrell, Johnny Bench, and Joe Torre. Among them, only Torre ever posted as high a fielding percentage at third base as Zeile did last season. He reduced his error rate from one error every 17.6 chances in 1991 to one every 25.2 chances last season.... Moving the fences in at Busch Stadium didn't help him very much: Despite hitting two home runs in his first three home games, he hit only two other Busch homers the rest of the season.... Despite a 23-point decrease in batting average, his on-base percentage dropped only one point due to the best walk rate of his career.... Has been called on to pinch-hit 17 times in the majors; he's 0-for-11 with six walks.... Cardinals have provided N.L.'s starting All-Star third baseman 14 times, the most of any team, including at least once in each decade from the 1930s through the 1980s. The roll call: Pepper Martin in 1933 and 1935; Whitey Kurowski in 1946; Andy Kazak in 1949; Ray Jablonski in 1954; Ken Boyer six times between 1956 and 1964; Torre in 1971–72; Ken Reitz in 1980.... Born September 9, 1965, in Van Nuys, California; that's not too far from Dodger Stadium, where Sandy Koufax pitched a perfect game against the Cubs that night. (Chicago pitcher Bob Hendley went all the way and allowed one hit in a 1–0 loss; that's still the only game of nine or more innings in major league history in which both teams combined for only one hit.)

PITCHER SECTION

The Pitcher Section is an alphabetical listing of every pitcher who either faced 500 batters, started 15 games, or finished 25 games in relief in the major leagues last season. Pitchers who pitched in both leagues are listed in the league where they finished the season.

Column Headings Information

Jim Abbott

California Angels	W-L	ERA	AB	H	HR	BB	SO	BA	SA	OBA

W-L	Won-Lost Record
ERA	Earned Run Average
AB	At-Bats
H	Hits
HR	Home Runs
BB	Bases on Balls
SO	Strikeouts
BA	Batting Average
SA	Slugging Average
OBA	On-Base Average

In addition to the traditional statistics used to evaluate pitchers—won-lost record, ERA, walks, and strikeouts—this section provides the batting performance of the league against each pitcher. This enables us to break down his performance into the same types of categories used to measure batters' performance. We can identify those pitchers with huge platoon differentials, or those who give up a lot of hits and home runs but can bear down with runners on base and avoid giving up the clutch run-scoring hit. (Bear in mind that overall batting average increases with runners on base, as a result of the altered defensive alignment and the effects of pitching out of the stretch position. This makes any pitcher who holds opponents to a lower average with runners on all the more impressive.)

Season Summary Information

Season	7-15	2.77	790	208	12	68	130	.263	.349	.323
vs. Left-Handers			128	35	0	13	17	.273	.359	.343
vs. Right-Handers			662	173	12	55	113	.261	.347	.320
vs. Ground-Ballers			388	96	2	25	55	.247	.296	.294
vs. Fly-Ballers			402	112	10	43	75	.279	.400	.350
Home Games	2-8	3.32	363	107	6	28	56	.295	.386	.344
Road Games	5-7	2.33	427	101	6	40	74	.237	.319	.306
Grass Fields	5-13	3.19	651	177	11	58	98	.272	.364	.332
Artificial Turf	2-2	0.92	139	31	1	10	32	.223	.281	.280
April	1-3	1.80	132	35	0	9	23	.265	.280	.312
May	1-4	3.57	149	34	3	19	24	.228	.322	.318
June	2-2	3.49	149	44	2	11	24	.295	.409	.342
July	0-2	2.70	73	20	1	3	17	.274	.356	.308
August	2-1	2.02	134	33	3	11	17	.246	.351	.313
Sept./Oct.	1-3	2.83	153	42	3	15	25	.275	.373	.337

Each pitcher's performance for the season is broken down into a variety of special categories. The first line given for each pitcher is his season total. This is followed by a breakdown of his performance against left- and right-handed hitters, against ground-ball and

fly-ball hitters (defined by whether their ground outs-to-air outs ratio is above or below the league average), in home and road games, on grass fields and artificial turf, and by month (regular-season October games are combined with September). For pitchers who pitched with more than one team, all totals are combined; the "home" totals for David Cone, for example, include all games pitched in New York while with the Mets, and in Toronto while with the Blue Jays.

Leading Off Inn.	204	61	3	13	29	.299	.392	.344
Bases Empty	452	119	5	41	75	.263	.336	.329
Runners On	338	89	7	27	55	.263	.367	.316
Runners/Scor. Pos.	169	43	4	21	34	.254	.385	.333
Runners On/2 Out	136	35	4	14	23	.257	.382	.331
Scor. Pos./2 Out	83	22	3	11	16	.265	.434	.358

Following these breakdowns, each pitcher's performance is divided into specific game situations. Totals are given for each pitcher against batters who lead off an inning (for relievers, this would not include the first batter faced if not leading off an inning), with bases empty and runners on base, with runners in scoring position (on second or third, or both), with runners on base and two out, and with runners in scoring position and two out.

Late-Inning Pressure	41	18	1	4	8	.439	.585	.489
Leading Off	11	6	0	1	2	.545	.636	.583
Runners On	22	7	1	2	6	.318	.500	.375
Runners/Scor. Pos.	9	4	0	2	3	.444	.556	.545

The next group shows the pitcher's performance in Late-Inning Pressure Situations (LIPS). These are the flip side of the batters' pressure situations: any at-bats in the seventh inning or later, with the score tied, or the pitcher's team leading by one, two, or three runs (or four if there are two or more runners on base).

The statistics for Late-Inning Pressure Situations are then broken down for each pitcher's performance when the hitter is leading off an inning, batting with runners on base, or with runners in scoring position.

First 9 Batters	234	51	3	21	39	.218	.274	.287
Second 9 Batters	231	54	0	21	45	.234	.268	.298
All Batters Thereafter	325	103	9	26	46	.317	.462	.368

The last set of breakdowns tracks a pitcher's performance through each appearance by listing the opponents' record in his first time through the batting order, his second time through, and all at-bats thereafter. This spotlights those pitchers who get stronger as the game progresses, as well as those who breeze through the first time around but falter on repeated viewing.

Following the statistics for each pitcher is a list of batters he "loves and hates to face." The stats listed for each match-up include all regular-season games since 1975 inclusive. Next are miscellaneous statistics given in text form; these include: the pitcher's ground outs-to-air outs ratio; the number of double-play grounders he induced and the number of opportunities he faced (runner on first, less than two out); the number of doubles and triples he allowed in his innings pitched; and the performance of opposing base stealers, along with his totals of pickoffs and balks. In addition, for starting pitchers there are his totals of first-inning runs allowed, and the batting support per start given him by his team. For relievers, the number of inherited runners he stranded and allowed to score are given.

As with batters, for purposes of comparison the league totals in all these categories are listed in the introduction to the Team Section (see page 2).

Jim Abbott

Throws Left

California Angels	W-L	ERA	AB	H	HR	BB	SO	BA	SA	OBA
Season	7-15	2.77	790	208	12	68	130	.263	.349	.323
vs. Left-Handers			128	35	0	13	17	.273	.359	.343
vs. Right-Handers			662	173	12	55	113	.261	.347	.320
vs. Ground-Ballers			388	96	2	25	55	.247	.296	.294
vs. Fly-Ballers			402	112	10	43	75	.279	.400	.350
Home Games	2-8	3.32	363	107	6	28	56	.295	.386	.344
Road Games	5-7	2.33	427	101	6	40	74	.237	.319	.306
Grass Fields	5-13	3.19	651	177	11	58	98	.272	.364	.332
Artificial Turf	2-2	0.92	139	31	1	10	32	.223	.281	.280
April	1-3	1.80	132	35	0	9	23	.265	.280	.312
May	1-4	3.57	149	34	3	19	24	.228	.322	.318
June	2-2	3.49	149	44	2	11	24	.295	.409	.342
July	0-2	2.70	73	20	1	3	17	.274	.356	.308
August	2-1	2.02	134	33	3	11	17	.246	.351	.313
Sept./Oct.	1-3	2.83	153	42	3	15	25	.275	.373	.337
Leading Off Inn.			204	61	3	13	29	.299	.392	.344
Bases Empty			452	119	5	41	75	.263	.336	.329
Runners On			338	89	7	27	55	.263	.367	.316
Runners/Scor. Pos.			169	43	4	21	34	.254	.385	.333
Runners On/2 Out			136	35	4	14	23	.257	.382	.331
Scor. Pos./2 Out			83	22	3	11	16	.265	.434	.358
Late-Inning Pressure			41	18	1	4	8	.439	.585	.489
Leading Off			11	6	0	1	2	.545	.636	.583
Runners On			22	7	1	2	6	.318	.500	.375
Runners/Scor. Pos.			9	4	0	2	3	.444	.556	.545
First 9 Batters			234	51	3	21	39	.218	.274	.287
Second 9 Batters			231	54	0	21	45	.234	.268	.298
All Batters Thereafter			325	103	9	26	46	.317	.462	.368

Loves to face: Scott Fletcher (.045, 1-for-22)
Gary Thurman (.100, 2-for-20, 2 BB)
Devon White (.143, 3-for-21)
Hates to face: George Brett (.545, 12-for-22, 3 HR)
Juan Gonzalez (.588, 10-for-17, 1 HR)
Dave Henderson (.529, 9-for-17, 1 2B, 5 HR)

Miscellaneous statistics: Ground outs-to-air outs ratio: 1.53 last season, 1.70 for career.... Opponents grounded into 22 double plays in 172 opportunities (one per 7.8).... Allowed 28 doubles, 2 triples in 211 innings.... Allowed 10 first-inning runs in 29 starts (2.48 ERA).... Batting support: 2.55 runs per start, lowest average in majors.... Opposing base stealers: 14-for-27 (52%); 10 pickoffs (2d most in A.L.), 0 balks.

Comments: That run-support figure was not only the lowest in the majors last year, it was the lowest in the A.L. in the DH era and the lowest in team history.... No starting pitcher since Harry Harper in 1920 had a season in which both his ERA and his winning percentage were as low as Abbott's last year (minimum: 150 IP).... Fell from seven games over .500 in 1991 to eight games under last season, but that's not without recent precedent; Allan Anderson and Jeff Ballard had similar drops from 1989 to 1990.... Among pitchers who have qualified for A.L. ERA title each year since 1990, only three have lowered their ERAs in each of the last two years: Abbott, Jack McDowell, and Charlie Hough.... His 2.45 ERA after the All-Star break was 2d lowest in the league, behind Cal Eldred (1.79).... Career breakdown: 19–27, 3.78 ERA at Anaheim; 28–25, 3.20 ERA elsewhere.... Bad news: Left-handed batters have a .304 career batting average against him, the highest against any active pitcher (minimum: 500 AB by LHB); good news: their average has decreased every year since he was a rookie: .325, .318, .303, .273.... Also, he has not allowed a home run to a left-handed batter in his last 30 games, since Rafael Palmeiro tagged him on Sept. 19, 1991.... Almost won A.L. fielding title for pitchers last season; he handled 46 chances without an error, second to Ben McDonald's 51 errorless chances.... He has a 2–10 career record in April; a start like that this year and the Principal Owner might throw him from the top of the World Trade Center.

Rick Aguilera

Throws Right

Minnesota Twins	W-L	ERA	AB	H	HR	BB	SO	BA	SA	OBA
Season	2-6	2.84	252	60	7	17	52	.238	.353	.287
vs. Left-Handers			129	32	3	11	29	.248	.326	.310
vs. Right-Handers			123	28	4	6	23	.228	.382	.262
vs. Ground-Ballers			123	28	3	9	23	.228	.325	.278
vs. Fly-Ballers			129	32	4	8	29	.248	.380	.295
Home Games	1-3	4.25	116	32	5	6	30	.276	.440	.315
Road Games	1-3	1.70	136	28	2	11	22	.206	.279	.264
Grass Fields	1-2	1.84	108	22	2	10	16	.204	.287	.271
Artificial Turf	1-4	3.62	144	38	5	7	36	.264	.403	.299
April	0-2	5.73	47	16	2	2	9	.340	.553	.360
May	0-2	2.63	53	13	0	3	9	.245	.283	.286
June	1-0	1.59	43	10	1	3	11	.233	.302	.277
July	0-1	2.79	35	6	1	4	8	.171	.257	.256
August	0-1	4.00	31	5	2	3	5	.161	.387	.257
Sept./Oct.	1-0	0.75	43	10	1	2	10	.233	.326	.267
Leading Off Inn.			51	13	0	4	11	.255	.294	.309
Bases Empty			119	29	2	8	23	.244	.336	.291
Runners On			133	31	5	9	29	.233	.368	.283
Runners/Scor. Pos.			85	18	5	8	17	.212	.400	.274
Runners On/2 Out			57	11	2	3	10	.193	.316	.233
Scor. Pos./2 Out			42	9	2	3	5	.214	.357	.267
Late-Inning Pressure			194	47	7	16	38	.242	.387	.299
Leading Off			39	11	0	4	9	.282	.333	.349
Runners On			109	24	5	8	21	.220	.376	.271
Runners/Scor. Pos.			74	15	5	7	15	.203	.419	.268
First 9 Batters			252	60	7	17	52	.238	.353	.287
Second 9 Batters			0	0	0	0	0	—	—	—
All Batters Thereafter			0	0	0	0	0	—	—	—

Loves to face: Dave Henderson (.071, 1-for-14, 8 SO)
Don Mattingly (.067, 1-for-15)
Tim Raines (.138, 4-for-29)
Hates to face: Mark McGwire (.500, 4-for-8, 1 2B, 2 HR)
Randy Milligan (.571, 4-for-7, 2 2B, 1 HR, 2 SO)
Paul Molitor (.556, 5-for-9, 1 HR)

Miscellaneous statistics: Ground outs-to-air outs ratio: 0.76 last season, 1.06 for career.... Opponents grounded into 7 double plays in 64 opportunities (one per 9.1).... Allowed 8 doubles, 0 triples in 66⅔ innings.... Saved 41 games in 48 opportunities (85%).... Stranded 33 inherited runners, allowed 7 to score (83%), 5th-highest rate in A.L.... Opposing base stealers: 5-for-5 (100%); 0 pickoffs, 0 balks.

Comments: Has earned a franchise career record 115 saves over the past three seasons; only four pitchers in history have had higher three-year totals: Dennis Eckersley, 142 (1990–92); Dan Quisenberry, 126 (1983–85); Bobby Thigpen, 125 (1988–90); and Lee Smith, 121 (1990–92).... Entered 19 games in eighth inning, 41 games in ninth inning, four games in extra innings last season. In 183 relief appearances since joining the Twins, he has never entered a game before the eighth inning; his last "early entry": July 30, 1989, his final game with Mets.... Career strikeout rate: 8.30 per nine innings as a reliever, 6.06 as a starter.... Strikeout rate has decreased in each of the last three seasons, from a career-high 8.50 per nine innings in 1989 to 7.02 last season.... Owns 17–7 record and 2.80 ERA from September 1 to the end of the season, his best record and ERA in any month.... Odd 1992 breakdown: 0.93 ERA in day games, 4.30 at night.... Has not allowed a run in 13⅔ career innings vs. Toronto during the regular season; added another 3⅓ scoreless innings vs. Jays in 1991 A.L. Championship Series. He owns the lowest career Championship Series ERA (0.59) among all relievers who have worked at least 15 innings in L.C.S. play.... Has not made an error in three and one-half years with Minnesota.... Has held opponents to .137 career batting average (7-for-51) with the bases loaded, 3d lowest among all pitchers since 1975 (minimum: 50 at-bats), behind Jeff Brantley (.088) and Bryan Harvey (.123).

Kevin Appier   Throws Right

Kansas City Royals	W-L	ERA	AB	H	HR	BB	SO	BA	SA	OBA
Season	15-8	2.46	771	167	10	68	150	.217	.319	.281
vs. Left-Handers			370	76	7	41	67	.205	.324	.283
vs. Right-Handers			401	91	3	27	83	.227	.314	.278
vs. Ground-Ballers			392	83	4	33	65	.212	.301	.272
vs. Fly-Ballers			379	84	6	35	85	.222	.338	.289
Home Games	8-5	2.60	387	83	4	31	82	.214	.302	.276
Road Games	7-3	2.33	384	84	6	37	68	.219	.336	.286
Grass Fields	5-2	2.14	301	62	4	33	57	.206	.322	.283
Artificial Turf	10-6	2.68	470	105	6	35	93	.223	.317	.280
April	0-2	1.27	121	18	1	12	23	.149	.264	.231
May	4-1	2.54	170	40	2	15	32	.235	.353	.296
June	4-0	3.24	128	32	2	7	22	.250	.367	.289
July	4-0	1.55	172	35	0	11	33	.203	.238	.254
August	3-3	3.57	151	34	5	18	36	.225	.377	.306
Sept./Oct.	0-2	3.86	29	8	0	5	4	.276	.310	.382
Leading Off Inn.			194	50	2	19	31	.258	.381	.324
Bases Empty			442	107	5	42	74	.242	.355	.309
Runners On			329	60	5	26	76	.182	.271	.242
Runners/Scor. Pos.			180	30	2	18	50	.167	.233	.243
Runners On/2 Out			139	23	3	15	33	.165	.273	.252
Scor. Pos./2 Out			89	12	0	12	26	.135	.157	.245
Late-Inning Pressure			76	10	2	9	8	.132	.224	.224
Leading Off			21	4	1	3	3	.190	.333	.292
Runners On			25	5	1	1	3	.200	.360	.231
Runners/Scor. Pos.			8	3	0	1	2	.375	.375	.444
First 9 Batters			242	49	1	22	47	.202	.289	.271
Second 9 Batters			244	65	2	16	49	.266	.365	.312
All Batters Thereafter			285	53	7	30	54	.186	.305	.263

Loves to face: Albert Belle (.118, 2-for-17, 10 SO)
Joe Carter (.150, 3-for-20)
Mike Devereaux (.053, 1-for-19)
Hates to face: Chili Davis (.364, 4-for-11, 3 HR)
Leo Gomez (.500, 7-for-14, 1 HR)
Ruben Sierra (.391, 9-for-23, 2 HR)

Miscellaneous statistics: Ground outs-to-air outs ratio: 0.89 last season, 1.01 for career. . . . Opponents grounded into 11 double plays in 156 opportunities (one per 14). . . . Allowed 37 doubles, 6 triples in 208⅓ innings. . . . Allowed 10 first-inning runs in 30 starts (2.70 ERA). . . . Batting support: 3.47 runs per start, 3d-lowest average in A.L. . . . Opposing base stealers: 18-for-27 (67%); 1 pickoff, 0 balks.

Comments: One of five pitchers with a record at least three games above .500 in each of the last three seasons. The others: Roger Clemens (seven years), Jack McDowell, Jose Rijo, and Kevin Tapani. . . . Had 2d-lowest ERA in A.L. behind Roger Clemens (2.46); also stands second to Clemens among A.L. starters over past three years (2.89 to 2.34). . . . Opponents' batting average with runners in scoring position was not only lowest in majors last season, it was the 2d-lowest such average against any A.L. 200-inning pitcher since we started keeping track of such things in 1975. Nolan Ryan held hitters to a .156 scoring-position average in 1990 with Texas. . . . Among A.L.'s bottom 20 pitchers in average batting support last season, only three had winning records: Appier (15–8), Scott Erickson and Frank Viola (each 13–12). . . . He became only the second pitcher in the last 20 years to finish at least seven games above the .500 mark in a season in which he was supported with an average of fewer than 3.5 runs per game; the other was Jim Palmer, 22–13 in 1976, when the Orioles averaged only 3.38 runs in his starts. . . . Has lowered his rate of home runs allowed in every season since his 1989 debut; career home-run rate: one home run allowed every 45 at-bats by left-handed batters, one every 89 at-bats by right-handed batters. He has allowed only 14 home runs in 290⅔ innings at Royals Stadium. . . . His nine-game winning streak (May 30 to July 29) was the longest by a Royals pitcher over the last 10 years.

Jack Armstrong   Throws Right

Cleveland Indians	W-L	ERA	AB	H	HR	BB	SO	BA	SA	OBA
Season	6-15	4.64	654	176	23	67	114	.269	.430	.337
vs. Left-Handers			277	76	10	39	39	.274	.433	.366
vs. Right-Handers			377	100	13	28	75	.265	.427	.315
vs. Ground-Ballers			318	83	10	37	51	.261	.406	.336
vs. Fly-Ballers			336	93	13	30	63	.277	.452	.339
Home Games	5-5	4.54	286	73	12	32	51	.255	.437	.330
Road Games	1-10	4.72	368	103	11	35	63	.280	.424	.343
Grass Fields	6-13	4.55	567	152	21	58	102	.268	.436	.337
Artificial Turf	0-2	5.24	87	24	2	9	12	.276	.391	.343
April	0-3	4.13	94	26	5	10	10	.277	.500	.349
May	1-3	5.34	132	39	3	15	19	.295	.447	.369
June	1-3	4.54	128	30	6	17	29	.234	.445	.324
July	1-4	6.75	121	40	3	8	12	.331	.446	.371
August	2-1	3.48	75	15	3	7	15	.200	.333	.268
Sept./Oct.	1-1	3.00	104	26	3	10	29	.250	.375	.313
Leading Off Inn.			159	43	8	14	29	.270	.465	.333
Bases Empty			380	90	13	42	66	.237	.400	.316
Runners On			274	86	10	25	48	.314	.471	.367
Runners/Scor. Pos.			156	47	5	19	26	.301	.449	.370
Runners On/2 Out			120	36	5	14	22	.300	.475	.373
Scor. Pos./2 Out			76	22	4	11	10	.289	.513	.379
Late-Inning Pressure			17	5	0	1	5	.294	.294	.333
Leading Off			6	4	0	0	0	.667	.667	.667
Runners On			7	0	0	3	0	.000	.000	.125
Runners/Scor. Pos.			3	0	0	0	1	.000	.000	.000
First 9 Batters			256	60	9	35	55	.234	.379	.324
Second 9 Batters			207	56	7	18	29	.271	.430	.333
All Batters Thereafter			191	60	7	14	30	.314	.497	.361

Loves to face: Eric Anthony (0-for-6, 5 SO)
Craig Biggio (.143, 3-for-21)
Lonnie Smith (.067, 1-for-15, 1 HR, 6 SO)
Hates to face: Jay Bell (.545, 6-for-11)
Gerald Perry (4-for-4, 1 2B, 1 BB)
Phil Plantier (3-for-3, 1 HR)

Miscellaneous statistics: Ground outs-to-air outs ratio: 0.99 last season, 0.86 for career. . . . Opponents grounded into 8 double plays in 123 opportunities (one per 15). . . . Allowed 28 doubles, 4 triples in 166⅔ innings. . . . Allowed 25 first-inning runs in 23 starts (8.22 ERA, 3d highest in A.L.) . . . Batting support: 3.83 runs per start. . . . Opposing base stealers: 15-for-24 (63%); 2 pickoffs, 3 balks (2d most in A.L.).

Comments: Career record of 0–28 in 33 starts in which his team scored fewer than three runs. Only two active pitchers have longer current losing streaks of that type: Mike Boddicker (39) and Bruce Ruffin (25). . . . His 5.02 ERA over the past two years is the highest by any of the 78 major leaguers who threw 300 innings over that span. . . . In the 1992 Analyst, we pointed out that he had never won a game west of Houston. Amazingly, he continued that streak in 1992, losing in Anaheim, Arlington, and Oakland to extend his record to 0–12 west of the Astrodome. . . . Relief win at Tiger Stadium in September snapped a streak of 13 consecutive road losses dating back to July 2, 1991, when he led Reds to victory at Atlanta. . . . Fewest career victories by pitchers who at any time in their career started an All-Star Game: Dave Stenhouse, 16; Mark Fidrych, 29; Armstrong, 31 (and counting); Jerry Walker, 37; Ken McBride, 40. . . . Averaged one walk for every 6.8 batters faced during the first inning of his starts, his worst rate in any inning last season; averaged one walk every 12.6 batters faced after the first inning. . . . Career ERA by month: April, 3.11; May, 3.66; June, 5.15; July, 5.69; August, 6.43; Sept./Oct., 4.03. . . . One of six pitchers whose strikeout rate has increased in each of the last three years (minimum: 100 IP in each season). The others: Tom Candiotti, Doug Drabek, Randy Johnson, Ben McDonald, and Dave Stewart. . . . Career breakdown: 3–0, 1.72 ERA in 19 relief appearances (no saves); 28–47, 4.88 ERA in 95 starts.

Bert Blyleven
Throws Right

California Angels	W-L	ERA	AB	H	HR	BB	SO	BA	SA	OBA
Season	8-12	4.74	526	150	17	29	70	.285	.439	.326
vs. Left-Handers			253	66	6	17	38	.261	.387	.305
vs. Right-Handers			273	84	11	12	32	.308	.487	.345
vs. Ground-Ballers			252	65	6	16	34	.258	.385	.306
vs. Fly-Ballers			274	85	11	13	36	.310	.489	.344
Home Games	4-6	4.31	250	67	5	17	36	.268	.360	.319
Road Games	4-6	5.14	276	83	12	12	34	.301	.511	.332
Grass Fields	7-9	4.07	435	122	12	22	57	.280	.402	.318
Artificial Turf	1-3	8.06	91	28	5	7	13	.308	.615	.360
April	0-0	—	0	0	0	0	0	—	—	—
May	1-0	1.93	53	12	2	4	9	.226	.377	.276
June	2-2	4.88	91	23	5	6	16	.253	.462	.299
July	1-3	8.10	100	35	3	8	16	.350	.530	.391
August	3-2	3.38	131	34	3	8	11	.260	.389	.305
Sept./Oct.	1-5	4.86	151	46	4	3	18	.305	.430	.333
Leading Off Inn.			137	39	7	5	17	.285	.496	.310
Bases Empty			318	81	12	16	47	.255	.425	.297
Runners On			208	69	5	13	23	.332	.462	.368
Runners/Scor. Pos.			131	45	3	9	16	.344	.496	.377
Runners On/2 Out			86	28	0	5	11	.326	.442	.363
Scor. Pos./2 Out			60	20	0	4	7	.333	.483	.375
Late-Inning Pressure			8	3	0	1	3	.375	.625	.444
Leading Off			4	1	0	0	1	.250	.500	.250
Runners On			1	1	0	0	0	1.000	1.000	1.000
Runners/Scor. Pos.			1	1	0	0	0	1.000	1.000	1.000
First 9 Batters			201	54	10	11	27	.269	.478	.310
Second 9 Batters			191	53	4	11	25	.277	.393	.317
All Batters Thereafter			134	43	3	7	18	.321	.448	.361

Loves to face: Dave Henderson (.080, 2-for-25)
Terry Steinbach (0-for-8, 4 SO)
Mickey Tettleton (.048, 1-for-21, 9 SO)

Hates to face: Jay Buhner (4-for-4, 1 HR)
Don Mattingly (.409, 18-for-44, 3 HR)
Randy Velarde (.600, 6-for-10)

Miscellaneous statistics: Ground outs-to-air outs ratio: 0.93 last season, 1.19 for career. . . . Opponents grounded into 11 double plays in 98 opportunities (one per 8.9). . . . Allowed 24 doubles, 3 triples in 133 innings. . . . Allowed 16 first-inning runs in 24 starts (6.17 ERA). . . . Batting support: 3.17 runs per start, 2d-lowest average in A.L. . . . Opposing base stealers: 10-for-14 (71%); 0 pickoffs, 1 balk.

Comments: The first pitcher in major league history to make a successful comeback after age 40 after missing an entire season due to injury. ("Successful" is defined here as either 10 starts, 10 wins, or 100 innings.) Of note: Red Ruffing spent more than two years in military service before his return in 1945 at the age of 41. He won his first three starts and compiled a record of 12–4 over two seasons for the Yankees before breaking his ankle. . . . Became only the 2d pitcher ever to win a game in both his teens and in his forties. Hall of Famer Herb Pennock won 162 games in 11 years with the Yankees (1923–33); he also won three games for the Athletics before turning 20 (1912–13), and two at age 40 for the Red Sox in 1934. Ty Cobb and Rusty Staub did that with home runs. . . . Needs 13 wins for 300; four pitchers in the postwar era have seen their career peter out in the 280s: Tommy John, 288; Robin Roberts, 286; Fergie Jenkins, 284; Jim Kaat, 283. John had the highest win total shy of 300 of any pitcher in history. . . . Bly was the only pitcher in the majors with an ERA above 6.00 in both the first (6.17) and second (6.26) innings last season (minimum: 15 starts). . . . What does Blyleven have in common with Fran Tarkenton? Each pitched his team to a victory at RFK Stadium in 1970. Blyleven did it in his major league debut at age 19; replacing the injured Luis Tiant on Minnesota's roster, he beat the Senators, 2–1, after allowing a home run to Lee Maye, the first batter he faced in the majors. (He is the last active pitcher to have beaten Nats II.)

Ricky Bones
Throws Right

Milwaukee Brewers	W-L	ERA	AB	H	HR	BB	SO	BA	SA	OBA
Season	9-10	4.57	641	169	27	48	65	.264	.448	.321
vs. Left-Handers			302	81	9	21	22	.268	.421	.321
vs. Right-Handers			339	88	18	27	43	.260	.472	.322
vs. Ground-Ballers			322	82	14	26	29	.255	.438	.313
vs. Fly-Ballers			319	87	13	22	36	.273	.458	.330
Home Games	6-4	3.25	374	84	10	26	41	.225	.366	.277
Road Games	3-6	6.64	267	85	17	22	24	.318	.562	.381
Grass Fields	7-8	4.19	523	134	17	41	59	.256	.402	.317
Artificial Turf	2-2	6.30	118	35	10	7	6	.297	.653	.341
April	1-0	2.38	85	17	3	4	11	.200	.341	.258
May	0-2	5.34	109	25	5	9	14	.229	.404	.300
June	3-2	5.83	115	32	8	12	7	.278	.557	.344
July	2-3	5.53	120	41	2	7	11	.342	.475	.380
August	1-2	3.56	115	29	6	8	13	.252	.470	.298
Sept./Oct.	2-1	4.38	97	25	3	8	9	.258	.402	.330
Leading Off Inn.			160	39	7	15	12	.244	.469	.324
Bases Empty			400	106	18	32	35	.265	.470	.329
Runners On			241	63	9	16	30	.261	.411	.309
Runners/Scor. Pos.			122	27	3	13	19	.221	.328	.296
Runners On/2 Out			96	17	3	6	15	.177	.281	.233
Scor. Pos./2 Out			51	6	1	5	10	.118	.176	.196
Late-Inning Pressure			39	8	2	2	4	.205	.410	.244
Leading Off			11	2	1	2	2	.182	.545	.308
Runners On			9	2	0	0	1	.222	.333	.222
Runners/Scor. Pos.			3	0	0	0	1	.000	.000	.000
First 9 Batters			251	58	11	18	29	.231	.398	.295
Second 9 Batters			220	67	11	21	20	.305	.545	.367
All Batters Thereafter			170	44	5	9	16	.259	.394	.301

Loves to face: Dean Palmer (0-for-5, 5 SO)
Andy Stankiewicz (0-for-6)
Danny Tartabull (0-for-7)

Hates to face: Kevin McReynolds (.500, 4-for-8, 2 HR)
Jeff Reboulet (2-for-2, 1 HR)
Paul Sorrento (.444, 4-for-9)

Miscellaneous statistics: Ground outs-to-air outs ratio: 1.00 last season, 1.08 for career. . . . Opponents grounded into 11 double plays in 114 opportunities (one per 10). . . . Allowed 27 doubles, 5 triples in 163⅓ innings. . . . Allowed 8 first-inning runs in 28 starts (2.25 ERA). . . . Batting support: 4.21 runs per start. . . . Opposing base stealers: 13-for-15 (87%); 1 pickoff, 2 balks.

Comments: Averaged 3.58 strikeouts per nine innings, 3d lowest among A.L. pitchers (minimum: 162 IP)—but don't tell that to Dean Palmer. Deano's five strikeouts in five plate appearances vs. Bones represents the 2d-worst all-whiff performance of any active batter against any active pitcher; Andres Galarraga has fanned in all eight trips to the plate against Rob Dibble. But at least Dibble is a strikeout pitcher!. . .Bones was knocked out of nine starts before pitching five innings, the most early kayos in the majors last season. . . . Has made 39 starts but has never thrown a complete game; that's the 5th-highest total of starts among active pitchers who have never gone the distance. He pitched 8⅔ innings against the Yankees in May, a game in which Don Mattingly spoiled his shutout bid with a game-tying homer leading off the ninth inning. . . . First-inning ERA was his lowest in any inning. . . . Allowed an average of one home run every 6.1 innings last season, the 3d-worst rate in Pilots/Brewers franchise history, ahead of only Marty Pattin (one HR every 5.5 innings in 1969 for the Pilots, who played their home games in the Sicks Stadium bandbox) and Bill Travers (one HR every 5.7 innings in 1979). . . . Born on April 7, 1969, which may someday be looked upon as the beginning of baseball's modern era. No, not because of Bones, but because that was the opening day of the 1969 season, the year of baseball's largest expansion to date, and the first year of divisional play.

Chris Bosio   Throws Right

Milwaukee Brewers	W-L	ERA	AB	H	HR	BB	SO	BA	SA	OBA
Season	16-6	3.62	878	223	21	44	120	.254	.376	.291
vs. Left-Handers			421	115	10	24	40	.273	.399	.310
vs. Right-Handers			457	108	11	20	80	.236	.354	.273
vs. Ground-Ballers			434	115	7	21	53	.265	.359	.299
vs. Fly-Ballers			444	108	14	23	67	.243	.392	.283
Home Games	9-3	3.03	476	116	10	22	63	.244	.351	.280
Road Games	7-3	4.34	402	107	11	22	57	.266	.405	.304
Grass Fields	14-5	3.58	764	194	16	43	104	.254	.365	.295
Artificial Turf	2-1	3.86	114	29	5	1	16	.254	.447	.261
April	2-1	4.60	112	32	3	7	16	.286	.446	.328
May	1-2	6.23	159	48	5	14	24	.302	.465	.364
June	3-1	2.36	128	25	2	7	14	.195	.281	.237
July	2-1	2.23	149	37	3	1	15	.248	.362	.257
August	4-0	3.77	161	40	3	10	27	.248	.360	.293
Sept./Oct.	4-1	2.78	169	41	5	5	24	.243	.343	.263
Leading Off Inn.			228	57	3	12	25	.250	.329	.287
Bases Empty			540	125	12	30	67	.231	.339	.273
Runners On			338	98	9	14	53	.290	.435	.319
Runners/Scor. Pos.			174	43	6	8	27	.247	.414	.280
Runners On/2 Out			128	34	3	4	17	.266	.430	.288
Scor. Pos./2 Out			78	16	2	2	11	.205	.359	.225
Late-Inning Pressure			71	23	1	1	11	.324	.465	.329
Leading Off			22	10	1	0	2	.455	.773	.455
Runners On			28	9	0	1	5	.321	.357	.333
Runners/Scor. Pos.			17	5	0	1	4	.294	.353	.316
First 9 Batters			277	63	7	18	36	.227	.343	.273
Second 9 Batters			275	77	4	14	37	.280	.382	.321
All Batters Thereafter			326	83	10	12	47	.255	.399	.282

Loves to face: Travis Fryman (.071, 1-for-14, 7 SO)
       Juan Gonzalez (.067, 1-for-15)
       Kevin Reimer (.087, 2-for-23)
Hates to face: George Bell (.433, 13-for-30, 1 HR)
       George Brett (.429, 15-for-35, 1 HR)
       Harold Reynolds (.524, 11-for-21)

Miscellaneous statistics: Ground outs-to-air outs ratio: 1.11 last season, 1.25 for career.... Opponents grounded into 24 double plays in 179 opportunities (one per 7.5).... Allowed 38 doubles, 3 triples in 231⅓ innings.... Allowed 11 first-inning runs in 33 starts (2.73 ERA).... Batting support: 5.12 runs per start, 6th-highest average in majors.... Opposing base stealers: 12-for-19 (63%); 0 pickoffs, 2 balks.

Comments: Bosio is the only pitcher to post a winning record in April in each of the last six seasons; he is also the only pitcher to post a losing record in May in each of the last six seasons. His career marks: 18–5 in April, 8–16 in May.... The only pitcher to defeat the Blue Jays three times last season.... One of eight major league pitchers to finish with at least 10 more wins than losses in 1992; of that group, only Bob Tewksbury (3.52) had a lower rate of strikeouts per nine innings than the Bos (4.67).... Averaged 1.71 walks per nine innings, lowest in A.L. last season, the best of his career, and the lowest by a Milwaukee starter since Moose Haas set the club record of 1.39 in 1985.... Walked only one batter over the course of eight starts (58⅔ innings) from late June to early August.... Has not lost consecutive starts since May 1991.... Did not allow a run during the first inning of his last 18 starts; allowed only one first-inning hit over his last seven starts.... Winning percentage has increased by more than 125 points in each of the last two seasons (from .308 to .583 to .727); he and Jack Morris are the only pitchers to accomplish that.... Had never won more than four straight games until he reeled off 10 in a row starting on July 25. The winning streak was snapped in his final game of the season, a game in which he allowed three homers at the Kingdome. But he liked the ballpark so much, he decided to make it his home.

Kevin Brown   Throws Right

Texas Rangers	W-L	ERA	AB	H	HR	BB	SO	BA	SA	OBA
Season	21-11	3.32	1007	262	11	76	173	.260	.335	.316
vs. Left-Handers			488	131	7	51	75	.268	.365	.339
vs. Right-Handers			519	131	4	25	98	.252	.306	.294
vs. Ground-Ballers			508	133	8	46	90	.262	.350	.327
vs. Fly-Ballers			499	129	3	30	83	.259	.319	.304
Home Games	11-4	2.71	464	118	4	27	89	.254	.328	.297
Road Games	10-7	3.85	543	144	7	49	84	.265	.341	.332
Grass Fields	15-10	3.19	768	199	9	57	138	.259	.340	.314
Artificial Turf	6-1	3.73	239	63	2	19	35	.264	.318	.323
April	4-1	3.08	135	32	0	11	25	.237	.281	.295
May	4-2	3.50	182	49	1	8	30	.269	.352	.302
June	4-1	3.20	166	37	1	18	32	.223	.265	.314
July	2-3	4.03	143	39	4	9	21	.273	.399	.312
August	3-1	2.83	182	52	1	17	28	.286	.341	.345
Sept./Oct.	4-3	3.38	199	53	4	13	37	.266	.362	.321
Leading Off Inn.			256	71	0	12	42	.277	.328	.315
Bases Empty			574	138	4	39	98	.240	.301	.294
Runners On			433	124	7	37	75	.286	.379	.344
Runners/Scor. Pos.			246	65	5	28	47	.264	.370	.335
Runners On/2 Out			172	48	2	15	29	.279	.355	.340
Scor. Pos./2 Out			110	29	2	11	20	.264	.345	.336
Late-Inning Pressure			132	41	0	8	22	.311	.348	.347
Leading Off			34	11	0	4	4	.324	.382	.324
Runners On			61	22	0	5	11	.361	.377	.391
Runners/Scor. Pos.			37	13	0	3	7	.351	.378	.372
First 9 Batters			287	73	3	25	43	.254	.328	.316
Second 9 Batters			284	67	3	22	57	.236	.313	.304
All Batters Thereafter			436	122	5	29	73	.280	.353	.324

Loves to face: Gary Gaetti (.130, 3-for-23)
       Ozzie Guillen (0-for-22)
       Terry Steinbach (.136, 3-for-22)
Hates to face: George Brett (.440, 11-for-25, 1 HR, 0 BB)
       John Olerud (.478, 11-for-23, 1 HR)
       Dave Winfield (.417, 10-for-24, 4 HR)

Miscellaneous statistics: Ground outs-to-air outs ratio: 2.22 last season (2d highest in A.L.), 2.42 for career.... Opponents grounded into 28 double plays in 220 opportunities (one per 7.9).... Allowed 40 doubles, 1 triple in 265⅔ innings.... Allowed 22 first-inning runs in 35 starts (5.66 ERA).... Batting support: 4.60 runs per start.... Opposing base stealers: 7-for-19 (37%), 2d-lowest rate in A.L.; 3 pickoffs, 2 balks.

Comments: Ozzie Guillen has faced Brown 22 times without ever reaching base, the highest total by any active batter against any active pitcher.... Yielded 11 home runs in 265⅔ innings (one every 24), 2d-lowest rate among A.L. starters; only Juan Guzman (one every 30) had a lower rate. Brown has not allowed a home run to the last 350 batters faced leading off an inning, the longest current streak of its type among active pitchers.... Allowed one stolen base for every 38 innings, best rate among A.L. starters last season.... His ground outs-to-air outs ratio (2.22) was 2d highest among A.L. pitchers who qualified for ERA title. He recorded more air outs than ground outs in only one of 35 starts last season.... Led major league pitchers in putouts (37) and led A.L. pitchers in fielding chances (81), but his eight errors ranked second among A.L. pitchers to Melido Perez, who made 10.... Opponents' batting average with runners on base in Late-Inning Pressure Situations was the highest in the majors last season.... Tied Jack Morris for major league high in wins; Fergie Jenkins (25 wins in 1974) is the only other pitcher in franchise history to top the majors in that category.... Also joined Charlie Hough (1987) as the only pitchers in franchise history to lead A.L. in innings.... Career breakdown: 7–11 with a 5.14 ERA in day games, 49–32 with a 3.30 ERA at night.... Allowed most hits of any pitcher in majors; that sometimes happens when you face the most batters of any pitcher in the majors (1108).

Roger Clemens

Throws Right

Boston Red Sox	W-L	ERA	AB	H	HR	BB	SO	BA	SA	OBA
Season	18-11	2.41	907	203	11	62	208	.224	.308	.279
vs. Left-Handers			447	101	6	30	98	.226	.304	.277
vs. Right-Handers			460	102	5	32	110	.222	.311	.280
vs. Ground-Ballers			507	107	2	28	101	.211	.264	.260
vs. Fly-Ballers			400	96	9	34	107	.240	.363	.302
Home Games	8-6	2.88	486	117	5	36	115	.241	.323	.299
Road Games	10-5	1.90	421	86	6	26	93	.204	.290	.254
Grass Fields	14-10	2.55	759	175	7	56	181	.231	.307	.289
Artificial Turf	4-1	1.70	148	28	4	6	27	.189	.311	.226
April	3-2	1.38	134	25	0	9	45	.187	.216	.241
May	5-1	1.76	175	33	2	8	35	.189	.263	.232
June	1-2	2.43	142	35	3	14	32	.246	.345	.314
July	2-2	4.00	134	31	2	12	26	.231	.328	.295
August	5-1	1.90	177	40	4	8	40	.226	.322	.266
Sept./Oct.	2-3	3.47	145	39	0	11	30	.269	.372	.331
Leading Off Inn.			238	56	3	11	50	.235	.307	.278
Bases Empty			553	124	8	25	133	.224	.304	.268
Runners On			354	79	3	37	75	.223	.314	.295
Runners/Scor. Pos.			209	42	0	26	49	.201	.258	.286
Runners On/2 Out			134	27	1	15	32	.201	.284	.287
Scor. Pos./2 Out			96	19	0	12	24	.198	.250	.294
Late-Inning Pressure			95	19	2	5	22	.200	.284	.248
Leading Off			26	4	0	2	6	.154	.154	.241
Runners On			30	9	0	2	5	.300	.333	.344
Runners/Scor. Pos.			14	4	0	2	3	.286	.286	.375
First 9 Batters			264	60	1	19	67	.227	.288	.283
Second 9 Batters			263	57	4	18	61	.217	.300	.272
All Batters Thereafter			380	86	6	25	80	.226	.326	.280

Loves to face: Cecil Fielder (.048, 1-for-21, 2 BB, 11 SO)
Mark McGwire (.036, 1-for-28, 1 2B, 3 BB)
Greg Vaughn (.056, 1-for-18, 10 SO)

Hates to face: Ken Griffey, Jr. (.407, 11-for-27, 1 HR)
Alan Trammell (.353, 18-for-51, 2 HR)
Lou Whitaker (.345, 20-for-58, 2 HR)

Miscellaneous statistics: Ground outs-to-air outs ratio: 1.67 last season, 1.10 for career.... Opponents grounded into 28 double plays in 188 opportunities (one per 6.7).... Allowed 39 doubles, 2 triples in 246⅔ innings.... Allowed 11 first-inning runs in 32 starts (3.09 ERA).... Batting support: 4.06 runs per start.... Opposing base stealers: 24-for-36 (67%); 2 pickoffs, 0 balks.

Comments: Second pitcher to lead the A.L. in ERA three years in a row; Lefty Grove had a four-year streak (1929–32).... Led A.L. pitchers in shutouts (with 5), the third straight year (and fifth in last six) that he's done that.... First pitcher since Juan Marichal, and first in A.L. since Whitey Ford, to start his career with nine straight winning seasons.... Career total of 272 starts is 2d highest in team history behind Cy Young (297); he trails Cy in Sox shutouts, 34 to 30.... Has started five straight season openers, matching Sox record shared by Cy (1904–08) and Eck (1979–83).... Turned 30 years of age last August with career totals of 146 wins and 1808 strikeouts; the only active pitcher who had totals that high in either category at age 30 is Bert Blyleven (156 wins, 2250 strikeouts). The highest such totals since 1900: Walter Johnson (253 wins, 2304 whiffs).... Hasn't allowed a home run in the first inning in his last 49 starts.... Career April marks in won-lost record (25–8), ERA (1.96), opponents' batting average (.190), and strikeouts per nine innings (9.34) are all his best in any month.... Among all pitchers who pitched at least 81 innings on the road in 1992, Clemens was only one with a road ERA under 2.00.... Owns an 80–16 career mark in starts in which he walked fewer than two batters, including 44–4 since June 1989.... Man vs. boys: Has held rookies to .168 batting average over past two years. The last rookie to homer off Clemens: Beau Allred in June 1990; they're homerless in 260 at-bats since then.

David Cone

Throws Right

Mets/Blue Jays	W-L	ERA	AB	H	HR	BB	SO	BA	SA	OBA
Season	17-10	2.81	916	201	15	111	261	.219	.321	.309
vs. Left-Handers			505	116	10	72	123	.230	.339	.331
vs. Right-Handers			411	85	5	39	138	.207	.299	.281
vs. Ground-Ballers			435	92	6	47	128	.211	.313	.293
vs. Fly-Ballers			481	109	9	64	133	.227	.328	.323
Home Games	8-6	3.38	453	103	9	57	137	.227	.344	.317
Road Games	9-4	2.26	463	98	6	54	124	.212	.298	.302
Grass Fields	11-6	2.71	560	119	8	66	169	.213	.302	.299
Artificial Turf	6-4	2.97	356	82	7	45	92	.230	.351	.324
April	2-1	2.23	139	26	0	16	41	.187	.245	.274
May	3-2	2.55	157	33	3	18	42	.210	.287	.299
June	2-1	2.83	132	33	3	9	43	.250	.386	.310
July	5-0	3.20	166	35	5	28	60	.211	.349	.325
August	1-4	4.65	158	42	1	18	33	.266	.373	.343
Sept./Oct.	4-2	1.55	164	32	3	22	42	.195	.287	.298
Leading Off Inn.			232	58	5	19	54	.250	.392	.312
Bases Empty			507	122	9	58	132	.241	.353	.326
Runners On			409	79	6	53	129	.193	.281	.290
Runners/Scor. Pos.			238	43	4	37	74	.181	.277	.292
Runners On/2 Out			174	30	3	22	51	.172	.253	.276
Scor. Pos./2 Out			114	20	2	16	36	.175	.272	.288
Late-Inning Pressure			63	13	2	10	15	.206	.365	.316
Leading Off			16	3	1	4	2	.188	.500	.350
Runners On			28	4	1	4	7	.143	.286	.257
Runners/Scor. Pos.			16	1	1	3	6	.063	.250	.227
First 9 Batters			281	54	4	25	92	.192	.270	.272
Second 9 Batters			261	57	2	35	84	.218	.299	.317
All Batters Thereafter			374	90	9	51	85	.241	.374	.331

Loves to face: Bill Doran (.156, 5-for-32)
Shane Mack (.111, 1-for-9, 5 SO)
Rafael Ramirez (.067, 1-for-15)

Hates to face: Chili Davis (.364, 4-for-11, 2 2B, 1 HR)
John Morris (.435, 10-for-23, 1 HR)
Franklin Stubbs (.375, 6-for-16, 3 2B, 1 HR)

Miscellaneous statistics: Ground outs-to-air outs ratio: 0.82 last season, 0.84 for career.... Opponents grounded into 9 double plays in 187 opportunities (one per 21), 4th-worst rate in majors.... Allowed 30 doubles, 9 triples (most in majors) in 249⅔ innings.... Allowed 9 first-inning runs in 34 starts (1.32 ERA).... Batting support: 4.12 runs per start (4.30 in N.L., 9th-highest average in league).... Opposing base stealers: 49-for-59 (83%), most steals in majors; 2 pickoffs, 1 balk.

Comments: First pitcher since Nolan Ryan (1972–74) to lead majors in strikeouts three years in a row. Cone has 45–34 (.570) record since 1990; Ryan had a nearly identical winning percentage (.564, 62–48) in his three years in a row atop the leader board. All-time record for consecutive years leading the majors in strikeouts: five by Rube Waddell, 1903–07.... Over last three years, Cone has fanned 370 left-handed batters, 365 right-handed batters.... Posted his lowest ERA since 1988, when he had a 2.22 ERA and a 20–3 record. But he averaged 4.00 walks per nine innings in 1992 after never before averaging more than 3.11 in any full season.... Had a 14–4 record with a 2.36 ERA in games in which he recorded more outs on balls hit in the air than on grounders. When ground outs outnumbered air outs, he had a 3–6 record with a 3.59 ERA.... His ERA from September 1 to the end of the season was 2d lowest in A.L. (Dennis Rasmussen, believe it or not, had a 1.43 ERA over that span.)... Traded after winning 13 games for Mets; only one pitcher in this century was traded in-season after winning more games: Rick Honeycutt (traded to L.A. in 1983 after winning 14 for Texas).... Hit 12 batters with pitches last season, more than he did over the previous three seasons combined.... Has 8–8 career record in April and a winning record in every other month.... His 84 career victories are the most ever by a pitcher after leaving the Royals. He surpassed Jim Rooker's total of 81 last September.

Dennis Cook — Throws Left

Cleveland Indians	W-L	ERA	AB	H	HR	BB	SO	BA	SA	OBA
Season	5-7	3.82	611	156	29	50	96	.255	.463	.312
vs. Left-Handers			98	23	4	3	10	.235	.408	.257
vs. Right-Handers			513	133	25	47	86	.259	.474	.322
vs. Ground-Ballers			315	76	12	17	45	.241	.422	.281
vs. Fly-Ballers			296	80	17	33	51	.270	.507	.344
Home Games	4-3	4.04	349	87	18	25	58	.249	.467	.298
Road Games	1-4	3.51	262	69	11	25	38	.263	.458	.331
Grass Fields	4-4	3.74	528	133	26	46	89	.252	.460	.310
Artificial Turf	1-3	4.29	83	23	3	4	7	.277	.482	.326
April	1-2	4.50	73	21	4	3	8	.288	.507	.321
May	0-2	7.31	70	24	5	5	7	.343	.643	.387
June	0-1	3.13	88	18	7	11	19	.205	.443	.293
July	2-0	2.48	132	32	1	7	26	.242	.356	.281
August	2-1	4.85	113	28	6	12	17	.248	.513	.323
Sept./Oct.	0-1	2.70	135	33	6	12	19	.244	.422	.304
Leading Off Inn.			154	36	8	13	21	.234	.474	.293
Bases Empty			395	94	18	30	62	.238	.435	.293
Runners On			216	62	11	20	34	.287	.514	.346
Runners/Scor. Pos.			129	33	5	13	17	.256	.419	.317
Runners On/2 Out			95	28	5	10	15	.295	.558	.362
Scor. Pos./2 Out			62	13	1	7	8	.210	.323	.290
Late-Inning Pressure			26	6	1	4	3	.231	.423	.333
Leading Off			11	3	1	1	2	.273	.545	.333
Runners On			2	1	0	2	0	.500	1.500	.750
Runners/Scor. Pos.			1	0	0	2	0	.000	.000	.667
First 9 Batters			249	64	17	20	48	.257	.518	.311
Second 9 Batters			213	52	9	15	26	.244	.441	.296
All Batters Thereafter			149	40	3	15	22	.268	.403	.337

Loves to face: Juan Gonzalez (0-for-6)
Kevin McReynolds (.071, 1-for-14, 2 BB)
Devon White (.111, 1-for-9, 1 HR)

Hates to face: Joe Carter (.364, 4-for-11, 1 HR, 4 BB)
Jack Clark (.571, 4-for-7, 1 2B, 2 HR, 2 SO)
Mike Fitzgerald (.727, 8-for-11, 2 HR)

Miscellaneous statistics: Ground outs-to-air outs ratio: 0.65 last season (4th lowest in A.L.), 0.71 for career. . . . Opponents grounded into 7 double plays in 93 opportunities (one per 13). . . . Allowed 34 doubles, 3 triples in 158 innings. . . . Allowed 19 first-inning runs in 25 starts (3.96 ERA). . . . Batting support: 4.52 runs per start. . . . Opposing base stealers: 8-for-18 (44%); 6 pickoffs, 5 balks (most in A.L.).

Comments: Averaged 5.52 innings per start, the fewest by any major league pitcher who started at least 25 games last season. . . . Led A.L. with 14 no-decision starts. No other pitcher started at least 20 games and failed to gain a decision in half of them. . . . Next, some long-ball numbers: Gave up 3d-highest total of home runs in majors (29), behind only Bill Gullickson (35) and Ben McDonald (32). Each of those fellows pitched more than 220 innings; Cook threw 158. . . . That's the most homers ever allowed in one season by a Cleveland left-hander. . . . Allowed eight first-inning homers last season, the most off any pitcher in the majors. . . . Has allowed 68 home runs in 474⅔ career innings, the highest ratio among active pitchers with at least 400 innings pitched. . . . Committed five balks; no other A.L. pitcher had more than three. . . . Has played for four teams whose franchise histories date back to 1901 and further (Indians, Dodgers, Phillies, and Giants). If you think that at least one other player in baseball history must have played for all four of those clubs, you're wrong. . . . Okay, we've established that he led the league in early knockouts, no-decision starts, and home-run rate. What can we say to his family? Well, of all the pitchers in the A.L. who faced at least 100 left-handed batters in 1992, your Dennis had the lowest rate of walks (three walks in 102 PAs by left-handers).

Ron Darling — Throws Right

Oakland A's	W-L	ERA	AB	H	HR	BB	SO	BA	SA	OBA
Season	15-10	3.66	783	198	15	72	99	.253	.379	.318
vs. Left-Handers			371	100	6	45	40	.270	.402	.348
vs. Right-Handers			412	98	9	27	59	.238	.359	.290
vs. Ground-Ballers			388	97	4	31	43	.250	.358	.308
vs. Fly-Ballers			395	101	11	41	56	.256	.400	.327
Home Games	8-6	3.57	384	85	7	36	49	.221	.333	.292
Road Games	7-4	3.77	399	113	8	36	50	.283	.424	.343
Grass Fields	14-10	3.66	693	175	14	61	91	.253	.378	.316
Artificial Turf	1-0	3.70	90	23	1	11	8	.256	.389	.333
April	1-1	4.80	119	33	3	12	17	.277	.429	.346
May	3-2	3.06	115	26	2	12	17	.226	.339	.297
June	3-2	5.74	106	29	1	8	10	.274	.396	.328
July	2-3	2.92	150	35	4	15	17	.233	.387	.307
August	3-0	3.53	144	46	3	11	13	.319	.458	.368
Sept./Oct.	3-2	2.81	149	29	2	14	25	.195	.275	.268
Leading Off Inn.			201	49	4	16	30	.244	.353	.303
Bases Empty			469	112	10	38	66	.239	.367	.301
Runners On			314	86	5	34	33	.274	.398	.342
Runners/Scor. Pos.			178	47	3	23	25	.264	.404	.343
Runners On/2 Out			143	47	2	20	18	.329	.448	.411
Scor. Pos./2 Out			96	29	2	15	12	.302	.427	.396
Late-Inning Pressure			36	4	0	3	8	.111	.111	.179
Leading Off			12	3	0	1	1	.250	.250	.308
Runners On			8	0	0	2	1	.000	.000	.200
Runners/Scor. Pos.			5	0	0	1	1	.000	.000	.167
First 9 Batters			264	63	6	30	38	.239	.364	.320
Second 9 Batters			269	71	3	17	30	.264	.375	.309
All Batters Thereafter			250	64	6	25	31	.256	.400	.325

Loves to face: Joe Carter (.105, 2-for-19)
Brian McRae (0-for-12)
John Morris (0-for-10)

Hates to face: Andre Dawson (.333, 19-for-57, 4 HR)
Carlos Martinez (3-for-3, 2 HR)
John Valentin (4-for-4)

Miscellaneous statistics: Ground outs-to-air outs ratio: 0.94 last season, 1.06 for career. . . . Opponents grounded into 15 double plays in 133 opportunities (one per 8.9). . . . Allowed 44 doubles, 5 triples in 206⅓ innings. . . . Allowed 22 first-inning runs in 33 starts (4.64 ERA). . . . Batting support: 4.24 runs per start. . . . Opposing base stealers: 10-for-23 (43%), 4th-lowest rate in A.L.; 3 pickoffs, 0 balks.

Comments: Took no-hitters into the fifth inning six times and into the seventh inning four times last season. . . . When does a team usually get its first hit? In 1992, it came in the first inning 58.6 percent of the time, 23.1 percent in the second inning, 9.4 percent in the third, 5.3 percent in the fourth, and 2.1 percent in the fifth; that leaves only 59 total times last season (1.4 percent) that a team had no hits entering the sixth inning. Of those 59 times, the potential no-hitter was broken in the sixth inning 31 times, in the seventh 17 times, in the eighth seven times, and in the ninth twice. In two games, a team finished with no hits: Matt Young's non-no-hitter and Kevin Gross's real one. . . . Darling was the first pitcher since Frank Tanana in 1987 to shut out Toronto twice in one season. Both of Ron's shutouts vs. Jays, and another vs. Bosox, were two-hitters; the last A.L. pitcher with three complete games allowing fewer than three hits was Dave Stieb in 1989. . . . Completed four of 33 starts last season after posting only one CG in 50 starts over the previous two years. . . . Allowed an average of one home run every 13.8 innings pitched, the lowest rate of his career. . . . Yearly rate of strikeouts per nine innings since 1990: 7.07, 5.97, 4.32. In recent years, Mike Scott, Dwight Gooden, and Fernando Valenzuela have all seen their rates drop by more than a strikeout every nine innings in two consecutive seasons; the last pitcher to do that three years in a row (minimum: 125 innings in each season): Johnny Vander Meer.

Danny Darwin — Throws Right

Boston Red Sox	W-L	ERA	AB	H	HR	BB	SO	BA	SA	OBA
Season	9-9	3.96	618	159	11	53	124	.257	.380	.319
vs. Left-Handers			274	77	1	28	47	.281	.387	.345
vs. Right-Handers			344	82	10	25	77	.238	.375	.297
vs. Ground-Ballers			328	83	0	30	71	.253	.338	.316
vs. Fly-Ballers			290	76	11	23	53	.262	.428	.322
Home Games	6-4	4.26	292	86	4	23	62	.295	.411	.352
Road Games	3-5	3.69	326	73	7	30	62	.224	.353	.289
Grass Fields	9-8	3.65	553	138	10	41	117	.250	.365	.306
Artificial Turf	0-1	6.89	65	21	1	12	7	.323	.508	.412
April	1-0	2.45	66	17	0	3	19	.258	.364	.296
May	1-1	9.31	40	13	1	7	6	.325	.425	.426
June	2-3	5.49	79	23	4	4	14	.291	.532	.333
July	1-1	4.24	86	19	0	10	15	.221	.302	.306
August	2-1	2.36	171	37	3	12	44	.216	.298	.276
Sept./Oct.	2-3	4.23	176	50	3	17	26	.284	.426	.342
Leading Off Inn.			149	40	4	9	28	.268	.403	.314
Bases Empty			338	83	6	27	73	.246	.358	.311
Runners On			280	76	5	26	51	.271	.407	.328
Runners/Scor. Pos.			174	41	3	19	31	.236	.356	.303
Runners On/2 Out			117	23	2	8	17	.197	.316	.248
Scor. Pos./2 Out			80	15	1	7	13	.188	.300	.253
Late-Inning Pressure			118	31	3	12	22	.263	.398	.336
Leading Off			29	7	1	2	4	.241	.379	.290
Runners On			50	15	1	8	8	.300	.420	.397
Runners/Scor. Pos.			29	7	0	8	5	.241	.276	.405
First 9 Batters			302	74	5	27	65	.245	.387	.312
Second 9 Batters			152	43	4	10	27	.283	.395	.327
All Batters Thereafter			164	42	2	16	32	.256	.354	.324

Loves to face: Kirby Puckett (.143, 4-for-28, 0 BB)
Harold Reynolds (.071, 1-for-14)
Curtis Wilkerson (0-for-10)

Hates to face: Rafael Palmeiro (.500, 8-for-16, 1 HR)
Terry Steinbach (.500, 5-for-10, 3 HR)
Dave Winfield (.366, 15-for-41, 4 HR)

Miscellaneous statistics: Ground outs-to-air outs ratio: 0.62 last season (3d lowest in A.L.), 0.79 for career. . . . Opponents grounded into 7 double plays in 135 opportunities (one per 19), 2d-worst rate in A.L. . . . Allowed 31 doubles, 6 triples in 161⅓ innings. . . . Allowed 9 first-inning runs in 15 starts (5.40 ERA). . . . Batting support: 3.67 runs per start. . . . Record of 4–5, 3.53 ERA as a starter; 5–4, 4.80 ERA in 36 relief appearances. . . . Stranded 23 inherited runners, allowed 12 to score (66%). . . . Opposing base stealers: 14-for-20 (70%); 0 pickoffs, 0 balks.

Comments: Career breakdown: 73–96, 3.74 ERA in 235 starts; 50–28, 2.82 ERA in 316 relief games. He's the only player in major league history who stands 20 games below .500 as a starter and 20 games above .500 as a reliever. Closest to him: John Klippstein went 42–78 as a starter, 59–40 in relief. . . . Danny's overall record: 123–124; among pitchers active in majors in 1992, only two have more wins but a losing record: Floyd Bannister (134–143) and Mike Moore (132–142). Two old-timers won more than 200 games and had a losing record: Jack Powell (246–255) and Bobo Newsom (211–222). . . . Made first 36 appearances last season in relief, last 15 appearances as a starter. . . . Allowed fewer home runs in 161⅓ innings last season (11) than he did in 68 innings in 1991 (15). . . . Has been used as both a starter and a reliever in all but three of his 15 seasons in the majors. Has appeared in at least 15 games as both a starter and a reliever four times in his career. The last pitcher to do it as often: Larry McWilliams, between 1978 and 1990. . . . His 18 decisions were the most by any A.L. pitcher who did not have either a winning streak or a losing streak of more than two games last season. . . . Allowed only one home run in 274 at-bats to left-handed batters (Mickey Tettleton), 3d-lowest rate in the majors (minimum: 200 at-bats by LHB). Had a similar breakdown in 1991: Allowed only three homers in 139 at-bats to left-handed batters, but 12 in 131 at-bats (yikes!) to right-handers.

John Dopson — Throws Right

Boston Red Sox	W-L	ERA	AB	H	HR	BB	SO	BA	SA	OBA
Season	7-11	4.08	554	159	17	38	55	.287	.437	.334
vs. Left-Handers			257	71	5	18	17	.276	.389	.324
vs. Right-Handers			297	88	12	20	38	.294	.478	.343
vs. Ground-Ballers			265	78	2	13	18	.294	.366	.329
vs. Fly-Ballers			289	81	15	25	37	.280	.502	.339
Home Games	5-5	2.69	327	91	6	16	31	.278	.398	.313
Road Games	2-6	6.09	227	68	11	22	24	.300	.493	.363
Grass Fields	7-10	3.89	517	147	16	35	52	.284	.435	.332
Artificial Turf	0-1	6.75	37	12	1	3	3	.324	.459	.366
April	0-0	—	0	0	0	0	0	—	—	—
May	1-2	4.05	74	19	1	3	7	.257	.365	.282
June	3-1	2.90	113	28	5	8	7	.248	.442	.295
July	2-1	3.28	151	47	3	7	14	.311	.437	.342
August	0-3	4.15	133	38	4	13	16	.286	.414	.354
Sept./Oct.	1-4	7.20	83	27	4	7	11	.325	.530	.385
Leading Off Inn.			137	37	2	15	14	.270	.401	.342
Bases Empty			326	95	10	26	34	.291	.445	.346
Runners On			228	64	7	12	21	.281	.425	.317
Runners/Scor. Pos.			132	36	2	8	13	.273	.379	.315
Runners On/2 Out			87	24	2	5	6	.276	.448	.315
Scor. Pos./2 Out			56	13	1	5	3	.232	.393	.295
Late-Inning Pressure			25	8	1	1	0	.320	.600	.346
Leading Off			8	3	0	0	0	.375	.875	.375
Runners On			8	1	0	0	0	.125	.125	.125
Runners/Scor. Pos.			5	1	0	0	0	.200	.200	.200
First 9 Batters			213	56	5	10	28	.263	.380	.299
Second 9 Batters			188	51	7	16	13	.271	.426	.327
All Batters Thereafter			153	52	5	12	14	.340	.529	.389

Loves to face: Brady Anderson (0-for-10)
Rafael Palmeiro (.067, 1-for-15, 1 2B)
Mickey Tettleton (0-for-10)

Hates to face: Paul Molitor (.385, 5-for-13, 2 2B)
Omar Vizquel (.556, 5-for-9)
Devon White (.500, 5-for-10, 1 HR)

Miscellaneous statistics: Ground outs-to-air outs ratio: 1.89 last season, 1.90 for career. . . . Opponents grounded into 17 double plays in 101 opportunities (one per 5.9), 4th-best rate in A.L. . . . Allowed 30 doubles, 1 triple in 141⅓ innings. . . . Allowed 10 first-inning runs in 25 starts (3.60 ERA). . . . Batting support: 3.72 runs per start, 9th-lowest average in A.L. . . . Opposing base stealers: 17-for-24 (71%); 0 pickoffs, 3 balks (2d most in A.L.).

Comments: One of four A.L. pitchers with at least 25 starts who didn't pitch past the eighth inning in any start last season. The others: Bobby Witt, Greg Hibbard, and Joe Hesketh. . . . His 1992 home/road ERA breakdown was the most extreme in the majors among pitchers who made 10 or more starts both at home and on the road. The top five: Dopson (2.69/6.09), Ricky Bones (3.25/6.64), Danny Jackson (2.85/6.00), Pete Harnisch (2.75/5.61), and Bud Black (2.91/5.76). Boston's three other regular starters—Clemens, Viola, and Hesketh—all had better ERAs on the road than at Fenway; but thanks chiefly to Dopson's numbers, the Sox staff finished the season with a lower ERA at Fenway (3.52) than on the road (3.65) for the third straight year. . . . Ground outs-to-air outs ratio was much higher during the first two innings of his starts (2.93) than in later innings (1.53). . . . Although he has almost identical career ERAs in both day and night games, he has a much better won-lost record in day games (10–6, 3.86 ERA) than at night (12–26, 3.83). . . . Averaged only 3.50 strikeouts per nine innings last season (6th lowest among A.L. pitchers with at least 100 innings), after averaging more than five strikeouts per nine innings in both 1988 and 1989 (his only other major league seasons of at least 100 innings). . . . The throwing elbow has placed him on the disabled list in each of the last five seasons; although he spent the first 41 days of last season on the DL, he did not miss a start after he was activated on May 17.

Kelly Downs   Throws Right

Giants/A's	W-L	ERA	AB	H	HR	BB	SO	BA	SA	OBA
Season	6-7	3.37	540	137	8	70	71	.254	.348	.343
vs. Left-Handers			262	71	1	36	25	.271	.344	.356
vs. Right-Handers			278	66	7	34	46	.237	.353	.331
vs. Ground-Ballers			270	71	2	23	33	.263	.352	.323
vs. Fly-Ballers			270	66	6	47	38	.244	.344	.362
Home Games	4-2	3.23	228	50	2	31	36	.219	.263	.312
Road Games	2-5	3.47	312	87	6	39	35	.279	.410	.367
Grass Fields	6-6	2.88	405	92	5	57	57	.227	.301	.323
Artificial Turf	0-1	5.12	135	45	3	13	14	.333	.489	.408
April	0-2	2.32	112	26	1	10	12	.232	.304	.304
May	1-0	6.43	59	21	3	9	8	.356	.576	.449
June	0-0	3.12	65	18	0	5	13	.277	.323	.324
July	2-2	4.03	90	26	1	9	14	.289	.400	.373
August	1-3	3.92	142	36	3	26	11	.254	.352	.366
Sept./Oct.	2-0	1.31	72	10	0	11	13	.139	.181	.250
Leading Off Inn.			139	34	1	13	11	.245	.302	.318
Bases Empty			300	82	4	35	37	.273	.367	.353
Runners On			240	55	4	35	34	.229	.325	.332
Runners/Scor. Pos.			136	24	2	27	22	.176	.243	.310
Runners On/2 Out			103	21	2	10	18	.204	.311	.293
Scor. Pos./2 Out			66	6	1	9	13	.091	.136	.221
Late-Inning Pressure			37	7	0	4	11	.189	.189	.268
Leading Off			12	1	0	1	5	.083	.083	.154
Runners On			11	3	0	1	0	.273	.273	.333
Runners/Scor. Pos.			4	1	0	1	0	.250	.250	.400
First 9 Batters			260	67	3	26	33	.258	.362	.329
Second 9 Batters			177	50	4	26	21	.282	.373	.379
All Batters Thereafter			103	20	1	18	17	.194	.272	.320

Loves to face: Joey Cora (0-for-11)
            Alfredo Griffin (.077, 2-for-26)
            Shane Mack (.125, 1-for-8)
Hates to face: Kevin McReynolds (.385, 5-for-13, 1 HR)
            Luis Quinones (.600, 3-for-5, 1 2B, 1 3B, 1 HR)
            Danny Tartabull (2-for-2, 1 2B, 1 HR)

Miscellaneous statistics: Ground outs-to-air outs ratio: 0.87 last season, 1.17 for career.... Opponents grounded into 9 double plays in 137 opportunities (one per 15).... Allowed 23 doubles, 2 triples in 144⅓ innings.... Allowed 10 first-inning runs in 20 starts (3.60 ERA).... Batting support: 3.85 runs per start.... Record of 4–7, 3.65 ERA as a starter; 2–0, 2.58 ERA in 17 relief appearances.... Stranded 4 inherited runners, allowed 5 to score (44%).... Opposing base stealers: 17-for-25 (68%); 0 pickoffs, 1 balk.

Comments: Opponents' batting average with runners in scoring position and two outs was the 2d-lowest single-season mark since 1975 (minimum: 75 BFP); Jack Morris held opponents to an .082 average in those situations in 1987. Opponents went 4-for-32 vs. Downs in N.L., 2-for-34 in A.L.; they finished the season hitless in their last 23 at-bats against him with runners in scoring position and two outs.... Released by the Giants on June 24 and signed by the A's on June 30 to become the first player ever to appear for both Bay Area teams in the same season.... Career won-lost breakdown: 29–16 in the Bay Area (26–14 at Candlestick), 23–27 elsewhere.... One of three pitchers whose rate of walks has increased in each of the last four seasons (minimum: 50 IP in each season); the others: Tom Candiotti and Tim Leary. Downs has produced career-high marks in that category in each of the last two seasons.... Averaged 5.30 innings in his 20 starts, 2d lowest among major league pitchers who started at least that many games.... His first 13 appearances for the A's were starts, but he moved to the bullpen in September after they traded for Bobby Witt.... Has a 9–0 record as a reliever over the last two regular seasons, compared to 7–11 in starting roles. His nine-game winning streak as a reliever is intact going into 1993, even though he was the losing pitcher in the pivotal Game 4 of last fall's A.L. Championship Series. He lost that one in relative anonymity, after the Eck shocked everyone by blowing a lead.

Dennis Eckersley   Throws Right

Oakland A's	W-L	ERA	AB	H	HR	BB	SO	BA	SA	OBA
Season	7-1	1.91	294	62	5	11	93	.211	.306	.242
vs. Left-Handers			149	39	3	8	33	.262	.369	.299
vs. Right-Handers			145	23	2	3	60	.159	.241	.181
vs. Ground-Ballers			132	33	1	9	42	.250	.341	.298
vs. Fly-Ballers			162	29	4	2	51	.179	.278	.194
Home Games	7-0	2.76	158	37	4	8	55	.234	.354	.271
Road Games	0-1	0.96	136	25	1	3	38	.184	.250	.207
Grass Fields	7-1	2.06	244	54	5	10	78	.221	.316	.255
Artificial Turf	0-0	1.26	50	8	0	1	15	.160	.260	.176
April	1-0	0.82	39	7	0	1	13	.179	.205	.200
May	0-0	0.79	42	8	1	0	17	.190	.262	.190
June	1-0	3.31	64	17	1	3	16	.266	.328	.299
July	1-0	0.87	37	6	1	1	11	.162	.297	.184
August	3-1	3.21	53	13	0	4	13	.245	.358	.298
Sept./Oct.	1-0	1.59	59	11	2	2	23	.186	.339	.226
Leading Off Inn.			64	14	1	1	19	.219	.313	.231
Bases Empty			162	38	4	4	52	.235	.358	.257
Runners On			132	24	1	7	41	.182	.242	.223
Runners/Scor. Pos.			76	12	1	7	28	.158	.237	.229
Runners On/2 Out			68	12	1	3	18	.176	.250	.211
Scor. Pos./2 Out			41	7	1	3	13	.171	.293	.227
Late-Inning Pressure			251	47	3	8	83	.187	.267	.215
Leading Off			55	11	1	1	19	.200	.291	.214
Runners On			105	16	0	6	32	.152	.190	.198
Runners/Scor. Pos.			62	9	0	6	22	.145	.194	.221
First 9 Batters			294	62	5	11	93	.211	.306	.242
Second 9 Batters			0	0	0	0	0	—	—	—
All Batters Thereafter			0	0	0	0	0	—	—	—

Loves to face: Gary Gaetti (.152, 5-for-33)
            Kirby Puckett (.063, 1-for-16)
            Mickey Tettleton (.077, 1-for-13)
Hates to face: Greg Briley (.667, 4-for-6, 1 HR)
            Kent Hrbek (.360, 9-for-25, 4 2B, 2 HR)
            Geno Petralli (.500, 4-for-8, 1 HR)

Miscellaneous statistics: Ground outs-to-air outs ratio: 0.67 last season, 0.71 for career.... Opponents grounded into 3 double plays in 48 opportunities (one per 16).... Allowed 11 doubles, 1 triple in 80 innings.... Saved 51 games in 54 opportunities (94%), highest rate in majors.... Stranded 29 inherited runners, allowed 2 to score (94%), highest rate in majors.... Opposing base stealers: 9-for-10 (90%); 0 pickoffs, 0 balks.

Comments: Although Eck holds neither the single-season nor the career record for saves, he has the most saves by anyone in major league history over a two-year span (94, 1991–92); over a three-year span (142, 1990–92); over a four-year span (175, 1989–92), over a five-year span (220, 1988–92), and over a six-year span (236, 1987–92).... To call him the Babe Ruth of Saves would be appropriate: While Ruth holds neither the single-season nor the career record for home runs, he does hold the marks for homers over two years (114, 1927–28), three years (161, 1926–28), four years (209, 1927–30), five years (256, 1926–30), and six years (302, 1926–31).... Left-handed batters hit .275 vs. Eck over his first 13 years in majors; he has held them to a .215 mark over the past five years.... Held right-handed batters to a .159 average last year, 2d lowest among major league pitchers (minimum: 100 at-bats by RHB), behind Yankees rookie Sam Militello (.132).... Among those who have pitched at least 300 innings in Athletics' 92-year franchise history, Eck has the lowest rate of walks (1.04) and hits (6.55) and the highest rate of strikeouts (9.30) per nine innings.... Has averaged fewer than two walks per nine innings in each of the last 11 seasons, 4th-longest streak in major league history, behind Cy Young (16 years), Babe Adams (15), and Robin Roberts (13).... In six years with Oakland, he has never walked the leadoff batter in an inning more than once in any season.

Mark Eichhorn — Throws Right

Angels/Blue Jays	W-L	ERA	AB	H	HR	BB	SO	BA	SA	OBA
Season	4-4	3.08	337	86	3	25	61	.255	.338	.306
vs. Left-Handers			129	44	2	14	25	.341	.450	.400
vs. Right-Handers			208	42	1	11	36	.202	.269	.246
vs. Ground-Ballers			163	43	0	9	24	.264	.344	.297
vs. Fly-Ballers			174	43	3	16	37	.247	.333	.314
Home Games	3-0	3.79	163	46	2	8	32	.282	.399	.312
Road Games	1-4	2.47	174	40	1	17	29	.230	.282	.301
Grass Fields	3-3	3.03	249	59	2	20	45	.237	.313	.296
Artificial Turf	1-1	3.22	88	27	1	5	16	.307	.409	.337
April	0-0	2.76	64	16	1	3	6	.250	.297	.275
May	1-3	2.00	66	14	1	6	14	.212	.303	.278
June	0-0	0.96	35	9	0	0	4	.257	.286	.257
July	1-1	3.46	49	12	0	9	18	.245	.388	.356
August	2-0	4.79	80	23	0	6	11	.287	.375	.344
Sept./Oct.	0-0	3.48	43	12	1	1	8	.279	.372	.295
Leading Off Inn.			77	18	1	3	14	.234	.338	.272
Bases Empty			182	43	2	7	28	.236	.313	.268
Runners On			155	43	1	18	33	.277	.368	.346
Runners/Scor. Pos.			106	27	1	18	24	.255	.340	.349
Runners On/2 Out			69	18	1	7	16	.261	.377	.329
Scor. Pos./2 Out			55	13	1	7	14	.236	.364	.323
Late-Inning Pressure			96	28	2	8	20	.292	.385	.346
Leading Off			25	5	1	0	8	.200	.400	.200
Runners On			37	12	0	6	8	.324	.351	.419
Runners/Scor. Pos.			25	8	0	6	7	.320	.360	.452
First 9 Batters			320	80	3	23	57	.250	.331	.300
Second 9 Batters			17	6	0	2	4	.353	.471	.421
All Batters Thereafter			0	0	0	0	0	—	—	—

Loves to face: Randy Bush (.050, 1-for-20, 1 2B)
Rob Deer (.118, 2-for-17, 10 SO)
Cecil Fielder (0-for-12)

Hates to face: Mark McGwire (.438, 7-for-16, 1 HR)
Mickey Tettleton (.364, 4-for-11, 4 HR, 5 SO)
Robin Yount (.440, 11-for-25, 0 BB, 0 SO)

Miscellaneous statistics: Ground outs-to-air outs ratio: 2.00 last season, 1.75 for career.... Opponents grounded into 6 double plays in 75 opportunities (one per 13).... Allowed 11 doubles, 4 triples in 87⅔ innings.... Stranded 23 inherited runners, allowed 19 to score (55%).... Opposing base stealers: 6-for-8 (75%); 0 pickoffs, 1 balk.

Comments: Batting average by opposing left-handed batters was 3d highest vs. any A.L. pitcher (minimum: 100 AB by LHB), ahead of only Les Lancaster (.358) and Shawn Hillegas (.358). Left-handed batters have been a problem for Eich throughout his eight years in the majors; they own a .283 career average against him, while right-handers have hit only .216. Take a good look at those numbers; since we started keeping track in 1975, that 67-point left/right disparity is the largest for any major league pitcher (minimum: 1000 at-bats by batters of each type). Eichhorn is followed on that list by Jose DeLeon (.255 by LHB, .190 by RHB), Terry Leach (.295 by LHB, .233 by RHB), John Smoltz (.259 by LHB, .197 by RHB), and Elias ("Sports Bureau") Sosa (.295 by LHB, .233 by RHB).... Became the fifth player in Blue Jays history to have a second tour of duty with team; the others: Jim Acker, Rico Carty, Alfredo Griffin, and Cliff Johnson.... Issued eight intentional passes in 42 games with the Angels last season, after issuing only one over the previous two seasons. That's one reason why his rate of walks allowed per nine innings increased from 1.43 in 1991 to 2.57 last year.... Posted records of 5–5 in 1989, 3–3 in 1991, and 4–4 last season. The "record" for most seasons with a .500 winning percentage is five, shared by Marty Pattin and Tippy Martinez. Two active pitchers have had four .500 seasons: Orel Hershiser and Larry Andersen.

Scott Erickson — Throws Right

Minnesota Twins	W-L	ERA	AB	H	HR	BB	SO	BA	SA	OBA
Season	13-12	3.40	781	197	18	83	101	.252	.371	.328
vs. Left-Handers			410	99	7	41	41	.241	.337	.311
vs. Right-Handers			371	98	11	42	60	.264	.410	.345
vs. Ground-Ballers			384	94	2	44	45	.245	.307	.328
vs. Fly-Ballers			397	103	16	39	56	.259	.433	.327
Home Games	8-6	3.43	464	123	7	36	57	.265	.369	.323
Road Games	5-6	3.35	317	74	11	47	44	.233	.375	.334
Grass Fields	5-5	2.81	275	64	7	43	37	.233	.349	.337
Artificial Turf	8-7	3.73	506	133	11	40	64	.263	.383	.322
April	0-3	5.10	109	27	2	13	9	.248	.358	.328
May	3-1	4.82	111	32	3	10	18	.288	.423	.363
June	3-1	3.52	113	33	4	14	12	.292	.434	.366
July	1-2	2.25	128	27	4	13	17	.211	.344	.289
August	2-3	2.76	150	33	3	20	21	.220	.313	.310
Sept./Oct.	4-2	2.80	170	45	2	13	24	.265	.376	.323
Leading Off Inn.			199	54	5	17	16	.271	.417	.338
Bases Empty			445	117	11	49	50	.263	.396	.345
Runners On			336	80	7	34	51	.238	.339	.304
Runners/Scor. Pos.			185	41	6	23	31	.222	.341	.298
Runners On/2 Out			139	33	4	18	20	.237	.353	.325
Scor. Pos./2 Out			86	20	3	12	11	.233	.360	.327
Late-Inning Pressure			78	27	4	8	10	.346	.590	.407
Leading Off			21	7	3	3	2	.333	.810	.417
Runners On			35	12	1	2	7	.343	.486	.378
Runners/Scor. Pos.			20	4	1	2	4	.200	.350	.273
First 9 Batters			260	61	7	23	31	.235	.358	.297
Second 9 Batters			249	61	3	27	27	.245	.321	.327
All Batters Thereafter			272	75	8	33	43	.276	.430	.356

Loves to face: Mike Greenwell (.063, 1-for-16)
Kevin Seitzer (0-for-12)
Joel Skinner (0-for-8, 7 SO)

Hates to face: Ken Griffey, Jr. (.526, 10-for-19)
Mark McGwire (.444, 8-for-18, 2 2B, 3 HR)
Dan Pasqua (.400, 6-for-15, 1 2B, 3 HR)

Miscellaneous statistics: Ground outs-to-air outs ratio: 2.36 last season (highest in A.L.), 2.15 for career.... Opponents grounded into 32 double plays in 156 opportunities (one per 4.9), 2d-best rate in A.L.... Allowed 29 doubles, 5 triples in 212 innings.... Allowed 14 first-inning runs in 32 starts (3.94 ERA).... Batting support: 3.91 runs per start.... Opposing base stealers: 23-for-30 (77%); 0 pickoffs, 1 balk.

Comments: Induced 32 double-play grounders, 2d-highest total in majors behind Charles Nagy (34).... Has made only eight career starts in which he has recorded fewer outs on grounders than he has on balls hit in the air, but in those eight starts he has a 7–1 record and 0.99 ERA.... At 24, he was the youngest opening-day starting pitcher in the A.L. last season.... Strikeout rate during the first inning of his starts (one every 13 batters faced) was his lowest in any inning.... Highest winning percentages in Washington/Minnesota franchise history (minimum: 50 decisions): Stan Coveleski (.679, 36–17); Erickson (.631, 41–24); Firpo Marberry (.617, 116–72); Kevin Tapani (.605, 46–30); Bill Campbell (.604, 32–21).... First Twins pitcher since Tom Hall (1968–70) to have a winning record in each of his first three seasons in the majors.... Career breakdown: 25–11 at the Metrodome, 16–13 on the road, despite an ERA that's 62 points higher at home (3.47) than elsewhere (2.85). No real mystery; there's been an even larger difference in his batting support: Twins have averaged 5.27 runs in his home starts, 4.08 runs in his road starts.... April record listed above represents his first five starts of the season. The last A.L. pitcher to start 0–3 coming off a 20-win season was Frank Viola, who went 0–5 in his first five decisions in 1989 after a 24–7 mark the previous year. In the N.L., Doug Drabek went 22–6 in 1990, then dropped his first three decisions in 1991; he fell to 1–6 before he got going.

Steve Farr   Throws Right

New York Yankees	W-L	ERA	AB	H	HR	BB	SO	BA	SA	OBA
Season	2-2	1.56	183	34	2	19	37	.186	.240	.267
vs. Left-Handers			83	18	1	15	14	.217	.253	.347
vs. Right-Handers			100	16	1	4	23	.160	.230	.190
vs. Ground-Ballers			91	15	1	8	19	.165	.209	.245
vs. Fly-Ballers			92	19	1	11	18	.207	.272	.288
Home Games	1-1	1.86	99	17	1	12	17	.172	.212	.265
Road Games	1-1	1.17	84	17	1	7	20	.202	.274	.269
Grass Fields	1-1	1.40	156	26	2	14	28	.167	.218	.243
Artificial Turf	1-1	2.57	27	8	0	5	9	.296	.370	.394
April	0-1	1.50	26	8	0	2	6	.308	.308	.357
May	0-0	1.08	28	4	0	4	4	.143	.179	.273
June	0-0	2.45	37	7	1	1	11	.189	.324	.205
July	1-0	0.00	13	3	0	4	2	.231	.308	.412
August	0-1	1.98	47	6	1	5	7	.128	.191	.212
Sept./Oct.	1-0	0.96	32	6	0	3	7	.188	.188	.270
Leading Off Inn.			47	9	1	2	6	.191	.277	.240
Bases Empty			114	24	1	8	24	.211	.263	.274
Runners On			69	10	1	11	13	.145	.203	.256
Runners/Scor. Pos.			35	7	1	8	3	.200	.314	.333
Runners On/2 Out			34	4	0	4	6	.118	.147	.211
Scor. Pos./2 Out			20	3	0	4	2	.150	.200	.292
Late-Inning Pressure			141	28	2	13	30	.199	.262	.268
Leading Off			35	7	1	2	5	.200	.314	.263
Runners On			55	9	1	7	11	.164	.236	.250
Runners/Scor. Pos.			31	6	1	5	3	.194	.323	.289
First 9 Batters			183	34	2	19	37	.186	.240	.267
Second 9 Batters			0	0	0	0	0	—	—	—
All Batters Thereafter			0	0	0	0	0	—	—	—

Loves to face: Kelly Gruber (.077, 1-for-13)
Mickey Tettleton (.071, 1-for-14, 2 BB, 9 SO)
Dave Winfield (.143, 3-for-21)

Hates to face: Harold Baines (.400, 6-for-15, 5 BB)
Harold Reynolds (.450, 9-for-20)
Ruben Sierra (.500, 9-for-18, 1 HR, 6 SO)

Miscellaneous statistics: Ground outs-to-air outs ratio: 0.74 last season, 1.08 for career.... Opponents grounded into 3 double plays in 38 opportunities (one per 13).... Allowed 4 doubles, 0 triples in 52 innings.... Saved 30 games in 36 opportunities (83%).... Stranded 10 inherited runners, allowed 8 to score (56%).... Opposing base stealers: 7-for-7 (100%); 0 pickoffs, 0 balks.

Comments: Had the 2d-lowest total of innings pitched (52) in a 30-save season in major league history; Tom Henke recorded 32 saves in only 50⅓ innings in 1991.... Pitched one inning or less in 28 of his 30 saves. In the majors last season, 65.3 percent of all saves went to closers pitching one inning or less; just two years ago, one-inning-or-less saves accounted for only 53.4 percent of the major league total. That percentage has risen since the early 1980s, with the biggest increases coming in the last two years: 37.0 in 1982, gradually up to 53.4 in 1990, then 60.3 in 1991 and 65.3 last year.... Entered four games with the bases loaded, and it was all or nothing: Twice he stranded all three runners, twice he let all three score.... Has walked only three of 111 batters faced leading off innings since joining Yankees in 1991.... Strikeout rate fell from 7.71 per nine innings in 1991 to 6.40 last season, but he established career bests in opponents' batting average, home-run rate, and ERA. In fact, his was the 2d-lowest one-season ERA in team history among pitchers who had thrown at least 50 innings; Steve Hamilton had a 1.40 ERA in 58 innings in 1965.... Breakdown of Yankees' 4.03 bullpen ERA last season: Farr, 1.56; Steve Howe, 2.45; everybody else, 4.50.... Yearly batting averages by opposing right-handers since 1989: .313, .215, .201, .160. Farr finished last season allowing right-handed batters only two hits in their last 36 at-bats, although one was a three-run homer by Carney Lansford on August 20.

Alex Fernandez   Throws Right

Chicago White Sox	W-L	ERA	AB	H	HR	BB	SO	BA	SA	OBA
Season	8-11	4.27	736	199	21	50	95	.270	.405	.322
vs. Left-Handers			351	88	9	19	45	.251	.385	.295
vs. Right-Handers			385	111	12	31	50	.288	.423	.346
vs. Ground-Ballers			375	105	10	29	44	.280	.408	.341
vs. Fly-Ballers			361	94	11	21	51	.260	.402	.302
Home Games	4-7	4.39	424	110	12	35	50	.259	.394	.320
Road Games	4-4	4.09	312	89	9	15	45	.285	.420	.325
Grass Fields	6-11	4.53	617	168	19	46	77	.272	.415	.328
Artificial Turf	2-0	2.93	119	31	2	4	18	.261	.353	.290
April	1-2	4.44	102	28	3	10	15	.275	.461	.336
May	1-3	3.19	136	31	2	12	20	.228	.346	.300
June	1-2	5.23	128	34	1	10	17	.266	.344	.329
July	1-0	3.86	79	21	3	5	12	.266	.418	.318
August	2-1	5.10	122	39	3	4	11	.320	.410	.351
Sept./Oct.	2-3	3.98	169	46	9	9	20	.272	.456	.307
Leading Off Inn.			184	42	4	11	21	.228	.342	.279
Bases Empty			439	113	16	23	59	.257	.412	.300
Runners On			297	86	5	27	36	.290	.394	.352
Runners/Scor. Pos.			177	47	3	19	25	.266	.350	.340
Runners On/2 Out			113	27	3	9	14	.239	.372	.301
Scor. Pos./2 Out			68	16	2	9	11	.235	.353	.333
Late-Inning Pressure			62	17	4	1	8	.274	.484	.286
Leading Off			19	4	1	0	2	.211	.368	.211
Runners On			14	2	0	1	2	.143	.143	.200
Runners/Scor. Pos.			9	1	0	1	1	.111	.111	.111
First 9 Batters			244	64	4	12	38	.262	.369	.305
Second 9 Batters			222	61	6	25	20	.275	.401	.353
All Batters Thereafter			270	74	11	13	37	.274	.441	.310

Loves to face: Jose Canseco (.071, 1-for-14, 2 BB, 9 SO)
Franklin Stubbs (0-for-11, 7 SO)
Dave Winfield (.158, 3-for-19)

Hates to face: Travis Fryman (.375, 6-for-16, 2 2B, 1 3B, 1 HR)
Rene Gonzales (.800, 4-for-5)
Kevin Seitzer (.750, 3-for-4, 2 HR)

Miscellaneous statistics: Ground outs-to-air outs ratio: 0.82 last season, 0.89 for career.... Opponents grounded into 15 double plays in 154 opportunities (one per 10).... Allowed 30 doubles, 3 triples in 187⅔ innings.... Allowed 18 first-inning runs in 29 starts (4.97 ERA).... Batting support: 4.79 runs per start.... Opposing base stealers: 15-for-19 (79%); 0 pickoffs, 0 balks.

Comments: Improved his rate of walks allowed per nine innings from 4.13 in 1991 to 2.40 in 1992, the top drop by any pitcher in the majors last year (minimum: 150 IP in consecutive years), and the largest by a White Sox pitcher since Billy Pierce, 1950–51. But his strikeout rate also took a fall, from 6.81 per nine innings in 1991 to 4.56 in 1992. That, too, was the largest drop by any pitcher last year, and the 2d largest in team history to Floyd Bannister's, 1985–86. Only one other pitcher in baseball history ever had as large a decrease in both rates in the same season (minimum: 150 IP in consecutive seasons): Jim Bibby, whose walk rate fell from 5.65 to 3.85 while his strikeout rate fell from 7.67 to 5.08 from 1973 to 1974.... Fernandez struck out 50 fewer batters in 1992 than in 1991, accounting for nearly half of the 113-strikeout drop experienced by the White Sox staff.... Strikeout rate during the first inning (one every 6.1 batters faced) was his highest in any inning last season, as it was the year before. Averaged one strikeout every 9.2 batters faced from the second inning on.... Career breakdown: 3–7, 5.40 ERA in 16 starts during the daytime; 19–22, 4.00 ERA at night.... His 6.29 career ERA in April is his worst in any month; 3.11 mark in September is his lowest in any month.... Allowed at least two home runs in four of his last five starts after doing that in only three of his previous 49 starts.... Allowed only one home run in 29 first innings pitched.

Chuck Finley

Throws Left

California Angels	W-L	ERA	AB	H	HR	BB	SO	BA	SA	OBA
Season	7-12	3.96	762	212	24	98	124	.278	.425	.359
vs. Left-Handers			87	35	1	6	9	.402	.517	.441
vs. Right-Handers			675	177	23	92	115	.262	.413	.349
vs. Ground-Ballers			349	96	8	42	49	.275	.393	.353
vs. Fly-Ballers			413	116	16	56	75	.281	.453	.363
Home Games	3-5	3.93	398	110	9	48	70	.276	.394	.355
Road Games	4-7	4.00	364	102	15	50	54	.280	.459	.363
Grass Fields	5-11	3.97	665	187	20	85	111	.281	.421	.360
Artificial Turf	2-1	3.90	97	25	4	13	13	.258	.454	.345
April	1-1	5.00	32	7	5	5	6	.219	.688	.324
May	0-3	6.12	129	45	8	17	21	.349	.581	.420
June	1-4	5.35	146	48	3	16	18	.329	.486	.390
July	1-1	3.67	127	33	3	18	18	.260	.354	.352
August	1-2	2.87	167	41	4	26	34	.246	.365	.342
Sept./Oct.	3-1	2.42	161	38	1	16	27	.236	.311	.309
Leading Off Inn.			183	58	6	27	33	.317	.497	.410
Bases Empty			415	126	14	63	69	.304	.472	.399
Runners On			347	86	10	35	55	.248	.369	.309
Runners/Scor. Pos.			196	44	5	24	38	.224	.332	.296
Runners On/2 Out			139	33	5	14	21	.237	.374	.307
Scor. Pos./2 Out			92	19	4	9	12	.207	.380	.277
Late-Inning Pressure			58	16	1	6	7	.276	.345	.344
Leading Off			16	3	0	2	3	.188	.188	.278
Runners On			23	6	1	3	4	.261	.435	.346
Runners/Scor. Pos.			9	1	1	1	1	.111	.444	.200
First 9 Batters			236	59	9	34	36	.250	.415	.341
Second 9 Batters			235	68	7	34	40	.289	.438	.379
All Batters Thereafter			291	85	8	30	48	.292	.423	.357

Loves to face: Jerry Browne (.050, 1-for-20, 1 2B)
Terry Shumpert (0-for-14)
Greg Vaughn (0-for-14)

Hates to face: Leo Gomez (.750, 6-for-8, 1 HR)
Shane Mack (.464, 13-for-28, 1 HR)
Mike Stanley (.455, 15-for-33, 1 HR)

Miscellaneous statistics: Ground outs-to-air outs ratio: 1.04 last season, 1.06 for career.... Opponents grounded into 28 double plays in 172 opportunities (one per 6.1), 5th-best rate in A.L.... Allowed 34 doubles, 3 triples in 204⅓ innings.... Allowed 15 first-inning runs in 31 starts (4.35 ERA).... Batting support: 4.06 runs per start.... Opposing base stealers: 21-for-39 (54%); 4 pick-offs, 0 balks.

Comments: Not many left-handed batters stayed in opponents' lineups to face him, but those that did tore him up. That .402 batting average was the highest allowed by any left-handed pitcher to lefty batters since 1979, when a southpaw named Gary Serum, pitching for Minnesota, also allowed 35 hits in 87 at-bats to his left-handed brethren (minimum: 50 at-bats by LHB).... Reminds us of that Come-to-the-Caymans commercial: "Just a few know of us, but those that know us love us."...Opponents' yearly batting averages since 1989: .233, .243, .244, .278. Ramon Martinez is the only other pitcher whose opponents' average has risen in each of the last three years (minimum: 150 innings each year).... Opponents' on-base percentage leading off innings was highest in majors last season.... Opposing base runners were caught stealing 18 times, tying Melido Perez for most in majors.... Among 39 pitchers who opened last season on the disabled list, Finley was the only one who went on to start 30 games or pitch 200 innings.... Owns a winning record on artificial turf in each of his five years as a regular starter. Career breakdown: 16–5, 3.11 ERA on artificial turf; 57–57, 3.79 ERA on grass fields.... Finally settled down toward the end of last season, fashioning sub-3.00 ERAs in consecutive months for only the second time in his career.... His 2.61 career ERA in April is his lowest in any month; his May ERA takes a big jump, pitch then it's a downward progession from May through September: 4.20, 3.79, 3.64, 3.23, 3.10.

Dave Fleming

Throws Left

Seattle Mariners	W-L	ERA	AB	H	HR	BB	SO	BA	SA	OBA
Season	17-10	3.39	877	225	13	60	112	.257	.371	.306
vs. Left-Handers			142	35	2	11	24	.246	.359	.305
vs. Right-Handers			735	190	11	49	88	.259	.373	.307
vs. Ground-Ballers			404	105	4	28	51	.260	.356	.311
vs. Fly-Ballers			473	120	9	32	61	.254	.383	.303
Home Games	7-5	3.53	425	108	9	29	56	.254	.384	.306
Road Games	10-5	3.26	452	117	4	31	56	.259	.358	.307
Grass Fields	8-3	3.49	337	89	4	22	42	.264	.377	.310
Artificial Turf	9-7	3.33	540	136	9	38	70	.252	.367	.304
April	2-1	6.53	85	25	2	9	15	.294	.447	.362
May	5-0	1.87	166	38	1	20	16	.229	.307	.312
June	3-2	3.23	152	40	1	10	20	.263	.342	.309
July	2-1	2.50	148	33	4	3	16	.223	.331	.238
August	3-2	3.00	175	41	5	8	27	.234	.400	.278
Sept./Oct.	2-4	5.02	151	48	0	10	18	.318	.430	.362
Leading Off Inn.			221	61	4	14	26	.276	.407	.322
Bases Empty			516	137	8	31	61	.266	.386	.310
Runners On			361	88	5	29	51	.244	.349	.302
Runners/Scor. Pos.			212	49	1	16	27	.231	.307	.289
Runners On/2 Out			148	34	2	15	21	.230	.338	.301
Scor. Pos./2 Out			94	20	1	9	13	.213	.298	.282
Late-Inning Pressure			81	22	3	7	8	.272	.457	.330
Leading Off			26	9	1	1	0	.346	.577	.370
Runners On			30	5	1	4	4	.167	.300	.265
Runners/Scor. Pos.			11	2	0	3	1	.182	.273	.357
First 9 Batters			274	73	2	18	41	.266	.372	.319
Second 9 Batters			260	60	4	23	32	.231	.335	.295
All Batters Thereafter			343	92	7	19	39	.268	.397	.306

Loves to face: Glenn Davis (.091, 1-for-11)
Leo Gomez (.100, 1-for-10, 1 2B)
Andy Stankiewicz (0-for-8)

Hates to face: Dean Palmer (.500, 7-for-14, 1 HR)
Terry Steinbach (.667, 4-for-6, 1 HR)
Robin Yount (3-for-3, 1 BB)

Miscellaneous statistics: Ground outs-to-air outs ratio: 1.03 last season, 1.09 for career.... Opponents grounded into 16 double plays in 161 opportunities (one per 10).... Allowed 53 doubles (most in majors), 4 triples in 228⅓ innings.... Allowed 15 first-inning runs in 33 starts (3.82 ERA).... Batting support: 4.27 runs per start.... Opposing base stealers: 18-for-32 (56%); 6 pickoffs, 1 balk.

Comments: Only the fifth pitcher in major league history to finish seven games above .500 for a team with a won-lost percentage as low as Seattle had last season (.395). The others, none of whom were rookies: Ray Scarborough, 1948 Senators; Ned Garver, 1951 Browns; Steve Carlton, 1972 Phillies; Mike Henneman, 1989 Tigers.... Over the last 40 years, only one other rookie has finished even *five* games above .500 for a team that finished at least 30 games below: That was Larry Hardy, a reliever for the 1974 Padres. The last rookie *starter* to win *four* more games than he lost while pitching for a club with a record as bad as the Mariners': Tom Seaver, 16–12 as a starter for the 1967 Mets.... Before the All-Star break, opposing right-handers had outhit left-handers, .263 to .143; but during the season's second half, it was opposing left-handers who gave Fleming more trouble, .329 to .253.... The last A.L. pitcher to hurl as many innings in a season at an age as young as Fleming's was Bret Saberhagen in 1985.... The only left-handed pitcher to shut out the Red Sox last year. Okay, so it wasn't at Fenway, but it was one of three shutouts he threw at the Kingdome.... Tied Pedro Astacio for most shutouts in majors by a rookie last season (four); Astacio, it should be noted, started only 11 games.... Career mark of 2–5 with a 5.98 ERA in day games, 16–5 with a 2.93 ERA at night.... Not to take anything away from Flem, but we'll take Cal Eldred's second half over Fleming's first half.

Mike Gardiner — Throws Right

Boston Red Sox	W-L	ERA	AB	H	HR	BB	SO	BA	SA	OBA
Season	4-10	4.75	498	126	12	58	79	.253	.380	.330
vs. Left-Handers			221	57	3	23	38	.258	.380	.327
vs. Right-Handers			277	69	9	35	41	.249	.379	.333
vs. Ground-Ballers			226	51	3	21	32	.226	.314	.292
vs. Fly-Ballers			272	75	9	37	47	.276	.434	.361
Home Games	2-1	4.41	195	50	2	25	26	.256	.338	.338
Road Games	2-9	4.97	303	76	10	33	53	.251	.406	.326
Grass Fields	4-6	4.27	423	103	10	49	67	.243	.362	.320
Artificial Turf	0-4	7.58	75	23	2	9	12	.307	.480	.388
April	2-0	1.62	59	9	0	4	19	.153	.271	.206
May	1-3	4.37	131	35	1	15	22	.267	.344	.342
June	0-5	6.15	132	37	5	17	16	.280	.439	.364
July	0-2	10.00	42	15	2	7	3	.357	.571	.449
August	0-0	4.26	24	6	1	1	1	.250	.375	.269
Sept./Oct.	1-0	3.90	110	24	3	14	18	.218	.336	.304
Leading Off Inn.			120	24	3	14	22	.200	.292	.284
Bases Empty			278	57	4	33	47	.205	.291	.289
Runners On			220	69	8	25	32	.314	.491	.381
Runners/Scor. Pos.			115	32	2	21	22	.278	.409	.380
Runners On/2 Out			98	32	4	15	14	.327	.541	.416
Scor. Pos./2 Out			65	21	2	12	10	.323	.538	.429
Late-Inning Pressure			36	10	0	5	10	.278	.306	.381
Leading Off			8	0	0	2	4	.000	.000	.200
Runners On			15	7	0	2	3	.467	.467	.556
Runners/Scor. Pos.			10	4	0	1	2	.400	.400	.455
First 9 Batters			210	50	9	29	36	.238	.414	.325
Second 9 Batters			173	46	0	14	25	.266	.306	.324
All Batters Thereafter			115	30	3	15	18	.261	.426	.348

Loves to face: Kevin Mitchell (0-for-6)

Hates to face: Mark Carreon (.667, 2-for-3, 1 HR)
Roberto Kelly (.429, 3-for-7, 1 2B)

Tom Gordon — Throws Right

Kansas City Royals	W-L	ERA	AB	H	HR	BB	SO	BA	SA	OBA
Season	6-10	4.59	449	116	9	55	98	.258	.379	.340
vs. Left-Handers			202	58	3	22	45	.287	.391	.352
vs. Right-Handers			247	58	6	33	53	.235	.368	.331
vs. Ground-Ballers			236	60	1	29	53	.254	.318	.336
vs. Fly-Ballers			213	56	8	26	45	.263	.446	.346
Home Games	5-4	3.36	224	54	2	28	44	.241	.339	.327
Road Games	1-6	5.83	225	62	7	27	54	.276	.418	.354
Grass Fields	1-4	6.28	167	48	7	17	40	.287	.461	.354
Artificial Turf	5-6	3.62	282	68	2	38	58	.241	.330	.332
April	0-3	4.25	122	34	3	8	19	.279	.410	.328
May	0-3	9.30	80	29	3	11	15	.363	.563	.417
June	1-1	4.35	40	11	1	6	6	.275	.375	.362
July	2-2	1.32	95	15	1	10	26	.158	.242	.252
August	2-0	3.21	51	12	0	9	15	.235	.275	.361
Sept./Oct.	1-1	6.19	61	15	1	11	17	.246	.377	.361
Leading Off Inn.			103	20	2	14	22	.194	.272	.297
Bases Empty			234	60	4	31	54	.256	.376	.348
Runners On			215	56	5	24	44	.260	.381	.332
Runners/Scor. Pos.			128	37	1	15	24	.289	.367	.353
Runners On/2 Out			91	21	3	11	21	.231	.385	.327
Scor. Pos./2 Out			60	15	1	8	12	.250	.350	.348
Late-Inning Pressure			34	14	1	5	8	.412	.676	.512
Leading Off			10	2	0	1	4	.200	.300	.273
Runners On			15	7	1	3	4	.467	.800	.579
Runners/Scor. Pos.			11	5	0	2	3	.455	.545	.538
First 9 Batters			287	69	6	39	70	.240	.369	.333
Second 9 Batters			115	35	1	9	22	.304	.374	.354
All Batters Thereafter			47	12	2	7	6	.255	.447	.352

Loves to face: Dave Henderson (0-for-12, 9 SO)
John Olerud (.056, 1-for-18, 1 HR)
Harold Reynolds (.080, 2-for-25, 5 BB)

Hates to face: Juan Gonzalez (.438, 7-for-16, 2 2B, 2 3B, 1 HR)
Ken Griffey, Jr. (.400, 8-for-20, 3 HR)
Alan Trammell (.455, 5-for-11, 2 HR)

Miscellaneous statistics: Ground outs-to-air outs ratio: 1.04 last season, 1.11 for career.... Opponents grounded into 12 double plays in 113 opportunities (one per 9.4).... Allowed 15 doubles, 6 triples in 130⅔ innings.... Allowed 6 first-inning runs in 18 starts (2.50 ERA).... Batting support: 3.28 runs per start.... Opposing base stealers: 3-for-5 (60%); 2 pickoffs, 0 balks.

Comments: One of a handful of ex-Mariners pitchers to come out of the gates flying last season. At the beginning of May, Gardiner, Bill Krueger, Jose Melendez, Mike Moore, and Bill Swift had a combined record of 17–0.... Stood second to Roger Clemens in strikeouts per nine innings as of late May—not just on the Red Sox staff, but in the American League as a whole. But his strikeout rate slipped away throughout the rest of the season: April, 10.26 per nine innings; May, 5.66; June, 4.28; July, 3.00; August, 1.42; September, 5.40.... Has held opponents to .238 career batting average with the bases empty, but they've hit .312 with runners on base, not a good sign over a career than has now encompassed more than 1000 opponents' at-bats.... At least he starts out strong: He allowed a .100 batting average (6-for-60) in the first inning of his starts, lowest such average allowed by anyone who made at least 15 starts last season.... Has made 43 starts in his career without completing any of them, 3d-highest total of starts among active pitchers who have never completed one.... Stranded 17 of 21 inherited runners, including each of his last nine.... His nine-game losing streak was longest in A.L. last season. He ended it with a win in relief, meaning that he'll carry a seven-game losing streak as a starter into 1993. But during those seven straight losses as a starter, his teammates gave him a total of only eight runs to work with, scoring no more than two in any of those games.

Miscellaneous statistics: Ground outs-to-air outs ratio: 1.32 last season, 1.17 for career.... Opponents grounded into 12 double plays in 101 opportunities (one per 8.4).... Allowed 23 doubles, 2 triples in 117⅔ innings.... Allowed 8 first-inning runs in 11 starts (6.75 ERA).... Batting support: 3.91 runs per start.... Record of 0–5, 6.08 ERA as a starter; 6–5, 3.48 ERA in 29 relief appearances.... Stranded 14 inherited runners, allowed 5 to score (74%).... Opposing base stealers: 5-for-12 (42%), 3d-lowest rate in A.L.; 1 pickoff, 2 balks.

Comments: Yearly won-lost records since 1989: 17–9, 12–11, 9–14, 6–10; he's the only pitcher in the majors whose winning percentage has dropped in each of the last three seasons (minimum: 15 decisions each year).... Still, he had the lowest ERA in the league in July.... Although he turned in the lowest strikeout rate of his career in 1992, his career average of 8.46 strikeouts per nine innings is still the highest in team history among pitchers with at least 300 innings, just ahead of Jeff Montgomery (8.13).... Had averaged 7.17 whiffs per nine at the time of his visit to the DL with tendinitis (August 12 to Sept. 1), but returned to average over a strikeout per inning in September.... Removed from Royals' rotation in late May after nine starts, with an 0–5 record and 5.64 ERA; his record as a starter since June 1991 is a sorry 1–11 over 19 starts.... Career breakdown: 24–32, 4.36 ERA in 75 starts; 20–14, 3.03 ERA, two saves in 96 relief appearances.... Pitched more than two innings in 17 relief appearances last season; Alan Mills (19) was the only pitcher in the majors with more "long" relief appearances.... Joins Greg Cadaret and Randy Johnson as the only pitchers in the majors to average more than four walks per nine innings in each of the last four seasons (minimum: 100 innings in each season). Inquiring minds may ask, "Why isn't Bobby Witt on that list?" Answer to inquiring minds: Because he pitched only 88⅔ innings in 1991; otherwise, he's there, baby.

Joe Grahe — Throws Right

California Angels	W-L	ERA	AB	H	HR	BB	SO	BA	SA	OBA
Season	5-6	3.52	346	85	5	39	39	.246	.324	.329
vs. Left-Handers			157	45	1	16	16	.287	.338	.365
vs. Right-Handers			189	40	4	23	23	.212	.312	.300
vs. Ground-Ballers			153	37	2	15	24	.242	.307	.326
vs. Fly-Ballers			193	48	3	24	15	.249	.337	.332
Home Games	2-4	3.94	163	40	4	22	17	.245	.350	.335
Road Games	3-2	3.12	183	45	1	17	22	.246	.301	.324
Grass Fields	4-6	3.49	318	77	5	38	38	.242	.324	.332
Artificial Turf	1-0	3.86	28	8	0	1	1	.286	.321	.300
April	2-2	7.14	113	34	2	15	12	.301	.398	.393
May	0-1	2.53	38	11	1	7	5	.289	.447	.400
June	0-0	0.68	45	7	0	1	12	.156	.156	.188
July	1-0	1.15	55	11	2	5	3	.200	.309	.267
August	1-1	0.75	38	5	0	8	4	.132	.132	.298
Sept./Oct.	1-2	4.50	57	17	0	3	3	.298	.368	.333
Leading Off Inn.			81	18	0	11	9	.222	.272	.323
Bases Empty			192	45	3	20	22	.234	.313	.310
Runners On			154	40	2	19	17	.260	.338	.352
Runners/Scor. Pos.			89	22	2	14	14	.247	.360	.355
Runners On/2 Out			61	11	1	7	7	.180	.262	.286
Scor. Pos./2 Out			43	8	1	3	5	.186	.302	.271
Late-Inning Pressure			157	31	2	20	16	.197	.255	.292
Leading Off			36	6	0	6	3	.167	.167	.286
Runners On			73	12	1	10	8	.164	.247	.274
Runners/Scor. Pos.			35	5	1	7	5	.143	.286	.302
First 9 Batters			238	57	3	27	25	.239	.315	.320
Second 9 Batters			62	18	1	5	8	.290	.355	.343
All Batters Thereafter			46	10	1	7	6	.217	.326	.357

Loves to face: Scott Livingstone (0-for-7)
Alan Trammell (0-for-7)
Greg Vaughn (.091, 1-for-11)
Hates to face: Lance Johnson (.467, 7-for-15)
Paul Molitor (.400, 4-for-10, 1 HR)
Lou Whitaker (.364, 4-for-11, 3 2B, 1 HR)

Miscellaneous statistics: Ground outs-to-air outs ratio: 1.92 last season, 1.77 for career.... Opponents grounded into 12 double plays in 86 opportunities (one per 7.2).... Allowed 12 doubles, 0 triples in 94⅔ innings.... Saved 21 games in 24 opportunities (88%), 5th-highest rate in majors.... Stranded 15 inherited runners, allowed 3 to score (83%).... Opposing base stealers: 7-for-12 (58%); 0 pickoffs, 0 balks.

Comments: Started seven games for the Angels in April and May before a brief demotion to Edmonton.... Was recalled in June and sent straight to the pen to replace closer Bryan Harvey, who was disabled with a bad elbow. Grahe had made 40 starts without a relief appearance over four minor league seasons; his bullpen experience had been limited to eight games of long mop-up relief for the Angels in 1991.... Faced 530 batters in 1990–91, only 32 in Late-Inning Pressure Situations.... Grahe led the Angels in saves (21), and his total of 17 after the All-Star break ranked 5th in the American League, behind the big boys: Dennis Eckersley (21), Tom Henke (19), Steve Farr and Jeff Montgomery (18 each).... Pitched at least two innings in nine of the games in which he recorded a save. Among major league pitchers, only Jeff Montgomery did that more often (11 times).... Career record of 7–14 with a 5.40 ERA in 25 starts; 4–3 (2.18 ERA) with 21 saves in 47 relief appearances.... Only four other pitchers recorded more than 20 saves in a season in which they walked at least as many batters as they struck out: Don Stanhouse (1978 and 1979), Ed Farmer (1980), Greg Minton (1981 and 1983), and Ted Power (1985).... Opposing left-handed batters have a career average of .310 against him, compared to a .237 mark by right-handers.... Pitched the most innings (94⅔) of any A.L. pitcher not charged with an unearned run last season.

Mark Gubicza — Throws Right

Kansas City Royals	W-L	ERA	AB	H	HR	BB	SO	BA	SA	OBA
Season	7-6	3.72	425	110	8	36	81	.259	.374	.316
vs. Left-Handers			215	49	5	18	39	.228	.363	.285
vs. Right-Handers			210	61	3	18	42	.290	.386	.348
vs. Ground-Ballers			199	52	2	8	35	.261	.347	.288
vs. Fly-Ballers			226	58	6	28	46	.257	.398	.339
Home Games	5-2	2.88	261	64	2	19	38	.245	.333	.297
Road Games	2-4	5.06	164	46	6	17	43	.280	.439	.346
Grass Fields	1-4	6.06	142	43	6	15	37	.303	.486	.367
Artificial Turf	6-2	2.62	283	67	2	21	44	.237	.318	.290
April	1-2	4.76	88	26	1	11	15	.295	.443	.374
May	4-1	2.61	152	33	1	11	30	.217	.276	.268
June	2-3	4.57	164	46	6	12	32	.280	.439	.330
July	0-0	1.50	21	5	0	2	4	.238	.286	.304
August	0-0	0.00	0	0	0	0	0	.000	.000	.000
Sept./Oct.	0-0	0.00	0	0	0	0	0	.000	.000	.000
Leading Off Inn.			109	24	4	5	24	.220	.385	.254
Bases Empty			253	60	6	20	54	.237	.360	.296
Runners On			172	50	2	16	27	.291	.395	.346
Runners/Scor. Pos.			95	29	2	14	17	.305	.463	.384
Runners On/2 Out			78	21	1	9	14	.269	.346	.345
Scor. Pos./2 Out			49	13	1	8	10	.265	.388	.368
Late-Inning Pressure			37	10	1	5	4	.270	.378	.349
Leading Off			10	3	0	0	1	.300	.300	.300
Runners On			18	3	1	2	3	.167	.333	.238
Runners/Scor. Pos.			7	1	1	2	1	.143	.571	.300
First 9 Batters			149	32	1	4	39	.215	.282	.240
Second 9 Batters			133	32	2	17	22	.241	.338	.322
All Batters Thereafter			143	46	5	15	20	.322	.503	.384

Loves to face: Geno Petralli (.053, 1-for-19, 2 BB)
Dick Schofield (0-for-27)
Joel Skinner (0-for-19)
Hates to face: Wade Boggs (.379, 22-for-58, 1 HR)
Ivan Calderon (.400, 6-for-15, 3 2B, 2 HR)
Don Mattingly (.418, 28-for-67, 4 HR)

Miscellaneous statistics: Ground outs-to-air outs ratio: 1.15 last season, 1.65 for career.... Opponents grounded into 10 double plays in 79 opportunities (one per 7.9).... Allowed 19 doubles, 3 triples in 111⅓ innings.... Allowed 2 first-inning runs in 18 starts (1.00 ERA, lowest in A.L.).... Batting support: 4.06 runs per start.... Opposing base stealers: 4-for-8 (50%); 1 pickoff, 1 balk.

Comments: Pitched more than 240 innings in three straight seasons from 1987 to 1989. Has spent at least a month on the disabled list in each of the three seasons since then (for a total of 215 days).... Didn't pitch after the All-Star break in either 1990 or 1992.... Pitched back-to-back complete games in May, his only CGs since undergoing rotator-cuff surgery in 1990.... Hasn't allowed a first-inning home run in his last 32 starts, dating back to July 17, 1991.... Control was at its best early in the game: one walk for every 43 batters faced over the first two innings, one every 10 batters thereafter.... Given his medical history and his early-game success, could he benefit from the "Joe Grahe treatment"? Gubicza's last relief appearance was July 29, 1986; he's made 179 consecutive starts since then.... Posted a 3.02 ERA in 53⅔ innings with Brent Mayne catching last season, compared to 4.37 in 57⅔ innings with Mike Macfarlane behind the plate.... Career record of 7–17 (.292) in April, 97–75 (.564) from May through October.... Career average of one home run allowed every 17.0 innings is the 7th best among active pitchers (minimum: 1000 IP). Of course, Royals Stadium provides him a tremendous advantage; his home-game average (one HR per 25.4 IP) is less than half his road-game figure (one per 12.1 IP).... Schofield's 27 hitless at-bats against him are the most of any active batter against any active pitcher.

Bill Gullickson   Throws Right

Detroit Tigers	W-L	ERA	AB	H	HR	BB	SO	BA	SA	OBA
Season	14-13	4.34	853	228	35	50	64	.267	.447	.305
vs. Left-Handers			414	116	18	28	21	.280	.473	.322
vs. Right-Handers			439	112	17	22	43	.255	.421	.288
vs. Ground-Ballers			409	107	15	25	23	.262	.435	.302
vs. Fly-Ballers			444	121	20	25	41	.273	.457	.307
Home Games	6-9	4.28	509	137	24	25	32	.269	.466	.302
Road Games	8-4	4.43	344	91	11	25	32	.265	.419	.309
Grass Fields	11-11	4.30	714	192	30	40	53	.269	.450	.305
Artificial Turf	3-2	4.58	139	36	5	10	11	.259	.432	.303
April	3-2	3.94	125	32	7	7	12	.256	.472	.295
May	3-1	2.09	161	37	2	5	13	.230	.304	.253
June	3-1	3.81	104	25	2	10	13	.240	.375	.299
July	2-3	4.89	159	40	7	9	7	.252	.453	.287
August	3-1	3.92	153	42	4	8	8	.275	.412	.307
Sept./Oct.	0-5	7.79	151	52	13	11	11	.344	.656	.387
Leading Off Inn.			220	66	8	15	19	.300	.495	.345
Bases Empty			540	151	19	30	41	.280	.448	.318
Runners On			313	77	16	20	23	.246	.444	.284
Runners/Scor. Pos.			163	43	6	17	10	.264	.429	.317
Runners On/2 Out			135	33	7	11	14	.244	.444	.301
Scor. Pos./2 Out			74	17	2	10	6	.230	.365	.321
Late-Inning Pressure			65	17	3	6	2	.262	.415	.319
Leading Off			22	6	0	2	1	.273	.318	.333
Runners On			19	7	1	0	1	.368	.526	.350
Runners/Scor. Pos.			6	4	0	0	0	.667	.667	.571
First 9 Batters			277	69	10	12	19	.249	.422	.277
Second 9 Batters			253	66	9	20	21	.261	.427	.310
All Batters Thereafter			323	93	16	18	24	.288	.483	.324

Loves to face: Jay Buhner (.063, 1-for-16, 2 BB)
    Manuel Lee (0-for-13)
    Jim Thome (0-for-9)
Hates to face: Wade Boggs (.750, 6-for-8)
    Rafael Palmeiro (.600, 6-for-10, 2 HR)
    Tim Raines (.394, 13-for-33, 3 HR, 0 SO)

Miscellaneous statistics: Ground outs-to-air outs ratio: 0.73 last season (5th lowest in A.L.), 0.90 for career.... Opponents grounded into 15 double plays in 125 opportunities (one per 8.3).... Allowed 38 doubles, 5 triples in 221⅓ innings.... Allowed 22 first-inning runs in 34 starts (5.73 ERA).... Batting support: 5.06 runs per start, 8th-highest average in majors.... Opposing base stealers: 20-for-28 (71%); 0 pickoffs, 0 balks.

Comments: Earned 33 victories in his first 50 decisions after joining Detroit. Only three Tigers pitchers won more games in their first 50 decisions with the team: Bobo Newsom, 36; Denny McLain, 34; and Earl Wilson, 34.... Led the majors in home runs allowed (35), joining Ferguson Jenkins as the only pitchers over the last 40 years to have led both the A.L. and N.L. in that category. (Gullickson led the N.L. in 1984.)... Total of 343 air outs was 2d highest in majors (two fewer than Rick Sutcliffe).... Allowed 78 extra-base hits, the 3d-highest total in majors.... Struck out 7.66 batters per nine innings as an Expos freshman in 1980 (and set a rookie record with 18 strikeouts in one game). His strikeout rate declined steadily after that; year by year from 1981 through 1985: 6.59, 5.89, 4.46, 3.97, 3.38.... His strikeout rate in three seasons with the Tigers has been 3.20 per nine innings, the lowest in the majors during that period (minimum: 300 innings). His mark of 2.60 last season was the major league low, a personal career low, and the lowest by a Detroit pitcher since Dave Rozema in 1978 (2.45).... No other active pitcher has had a season with a strikeout rate above 7.00 and another with a rate below 3.00.... Tigers pitchers struck out 693 batters last season, 100 fewer than any other team in the majors. (Of course, they don't get to face the Tigers.) Detroit has the two pitchers with the lowest individual rates in the A.L. (minimum: 100 IP): Gullickson and John Doherty (2.88).... Tied Bert Blyleven for the most losses in the league from Sept. 1 on.

Jose Guzman   Throws Right

Texas Rangers	W-L	ERA	AB	H	HR	BB	SO	BA	SA	OBA
Season	16-11	3.66	853	229	17	73	179	.268	.399	.327
vs. Left-Handers			399	111	6	29	65	.278	.409	.323
vs. Right-Handers			454	118	11	44	114	.260	.390	.330
vs. Ground-Ballers			431	115	4	32	76	.267	.360	.313
vs. Fly-Ballers			422	114	13	41	103	.270	.438	.340
Home Games	6-7	4.28	394	113	12	31	79	.287	.434	.341
Road Games	10-4	3.12	459	116	5	42	100	.253	.368	.314
Grass Fields	12-11	3.90	721	201	17	65	145	.279	.413	.339
Artificial Turf	4-0	2.34	132	28	0	8	34	.212	.318	.255
April	2-2	2.43	122	26	1	11	22	.213	.303	.276
May	2-1	3.89	163	45	1	12	32	.276	.380	.326
June	3-2	5.70	119	39	5	9	20	.328	.555	.379
July	1-3	4.65	124	37	2	14	27	.298	.403	.374
August	4-2	2.36	167	41	6	9	43	.246	.389	.279
Sept./Oct.	4-1	3.61	158	41	2	18	35	.259	.380	.337
Leading Off Inn.			215	57	6	18	35	.265	.456	.322
Bases Empty			493	139	15	47	107	.282	.448	.346
Runners On			360	90	2	26	72	.250	.331	.301
Runners/Scor. Pos.			208	51	1	18	41	.245	.332	.302
Runners On/2 Out			147	28	2	12	38	.190	.286	.256
Scor. Pos./2 Out			86	15	1	9	24	.174	.256	.260
Late-Inning Pressure			86	27	0	4	16	.314	.349	.344
Leading Off			24	8	0	0	5	.333	.417	.333
Runners On			39	9	0	3	6	.231	.231	.286
Runners/Scor. Pos.			23	5	0	3	3	.217	.217	.308
First 9 Batters			260	65	6	28	55	.250	.423	.324
Second 9 Batters			260	68	3	26	50	.262	.369	.328
All Batters Thereafter			333	96	8	19	74	.288	.402	.328

Loves to face: Alex Cole (0-for-8, 3 SO)
    Roberto Kelly (.167, 4-for-24, 1 HR)
    Kevin Mitchell (0-for-5)
Hates to face: Dante Bichette (.444, 4-for-9)
    Fred McGriff (.600, 3-for-5, 1 HR, 2 BB)
    Joe Orsulak (.357, 5-for-14, 1 HR)

Miscellaneous statistics: Ground outs-to-air outs ratio: 1.21 last season, 1.27 for career.... Opponents grounded into 20 double plays in 163 opportunities (one per 8.2).... Allowed 52 doubles (3d most in majors), 4 triples in 224 innings.... Allowed 12 first-inning runs in 33 starts (3.27 ERA).... Batting support: 4.52 runs per start.... Opposing base stealers: 16-for-31 (52%); 0 pickoffs, 0 balks.

Comments: Was 11–2 with a 2.63 ERA in 11 starts last season in which he recorded more outs in the air than on the ground, compared to 9–7 with a 4.22 ERA when he induced more ground outs than fly outs. That could change at Wrigley Field.... By the way, Wrigley doesn't necessarily inflate the ERAs of incoming pitchers. Among those who thrived in their first season pitching for the Cubs: Mike Morgan (14–10, 2.78 for Dodgers in 1991; 16–8, 2.55 for Cubs in '92); Rick Sutcliffe (4–5, 5.15 for Indians before his mid-1984 trade to the Cubs; 16–1, 2.69 thereafter); Larry Jackson (16–11, 3.75 for the Cardinals in 1963; 14–18, 2.55 for the Cubs in '64); Claude Passeau (16–11, 4.26 for the Phillies in 1939; 13–9, 3.05 for the Cubs in '40); and Larry French (12–18, 3.58 for the Pirates in 1935; 17–10, 2.96 for the Cubs in '36).... Last season's strikeout rate was the highest of his career (7.19 per nine innings), and coincided with the lowest walk rate of his career (2.93 per nine innings).... Has allowed an average of one home run every 14.6 innings over the last two seasons, compared to one every 8.2 innings prior to his two-year, injury-related hiatus.... Left- and right-handed batters both have career batting averages of .255 against him.... Was called for five balks in 1987 and 12 in 1988, but has balked only once in almost 400 innings since then (none in 224 innings last season). Balks are called more frequently in the National League: one every 136 innings last season, compared to one every 226 innings in the A.L.

Juan Guzman

Throws Right

Toronto Blue Jays	W-L	ERA	AB	H	HR	BB	SO	BA	SA	OBA
Season	16-5	2.64	652	135	6	72	165	.207	.275	.286
vs. Left-Handers			323	69	1	34	58	.214	.245	.288
vs. Right-Handers			329	66	5	38	107	.201	.304	.284
vs. Ground-Ballers			305	74	4	36	69	.243	.321	.323
vs. Fly-Ballers			347	61	2	36	96	.176	.233	.253
Home Games	7-2	2.89	306	67	2	30	75	.219	.284	.288
Road Games	9-3	2.42	346	68	4	42	90	.197	.266	.284
Grass Fields	7-2	2.11	271	52	3	35	69	.192	.258	.286
Artificial Turf	9-3	3.03	381	83	3	37	96	.218	.286	.286
April	3-0	1.82	124	23	1	17	39	.185	.258	.284
May	3-0	1.95	131	23	1	12	26	.176	.229	.245
June	4-1	2.65	123	24	1	10	31	.195	.260	.252
July	2-1	1.71	110	22	1	11	37	.200	.255	.279
August	0-1	6.48	34	8	1	5	7	.235	.412	.333
Sept./Oct.	4-2	4.11	130	35	1	17	25	.269	.331	.351
Leading Off Inn.			173	37	2	12	39	.214	.283	.265
Bases Empty			393	80	3	42	105	.204	.262	.282
Runners On			259	55	3	30	60	.212	.293	.291
Runners/Scor. Pos.			156	31	2	23	39	.199	.282	.297
Runners On/2 Out			104	15	1	11	27	.144	.212	.226
Scor. Pos./2 Out			73	11	1	9	19	.151	.219	.244
Late-Inning Pressure			66	7	0	11	14	.106	.121	.234
Leading Off			20	1	0	1	3	.050	.050	.095
Runners On			21	3	0	2	4	.143	.143	.217
Runners/Scor. Pos.			12	2	0	1	4	.167	.167	.231
First 9 Batters			218	41	1	30	66	.188	.239	.285
Second 9 Batters			225	50	4	19	48	.222	.311	.285
All Batters Thereafter			209	44	1	23	51	.211	.273	.288

Loves to face: Dan Gladden (.091, 1-for-11)
Matt Nokes (.083, 1-for-12)
Tony Phillips (0-for-12)

Hates to face: Bob Melvin (.571, 4-for-7, 1 HR)
Danny Tartabull (.250, 2-for-8, 1 HR, 7 BB)
Omar Vizquel (.556, 5-for-9)

Miscellaneous statistics: Ground outs-to-air outs ratio: 0.84 last season, 0.88 for career.... Opponents grounded into 7 double plays in 124 opportunities (one per 18), 3d-worst rate in A.L.... Allowed 24 doubles, 1 triple in 180⅔ innings.... Allowed 5 first-inning runs in 28 starts (1.61 ERA), 2d lowest in A.L.... Batting support: 4.46 runs per start.... Opposing base stealers: 27-for-35 (77%), 4th-most steals in A.L.; 2 pickoffs, 2 balks.

Comments: Posted a 10–3 record in 1991, followed by a 16–5 mark last season. The only other active pitchers who were at least seven games above the .500-mark in both their rookie and sophomore seasons are Mike Boddicker, Ted Higuera, and Dwight Gooden.... Only one other pitcher in this century posted a winning percentage of .750 or higher in both his rookie and sophomore seasons (minimum: 10 wins in each season): Howie Krist (1941–42).... Allowed six home runs in 180⅔ innings last season, the lowest rate among A.L. starting pitchers; in 1991, he yielded just six homers in 138⅔ innings.... Has never allowed more than one homer in any of his 51 regular-season and four postseason starts.... Hasn't allowed a first-inning home run in his last 33 starts, dating back to September 13, 1991.... Has allowed only two home runs in 561 at-bats to left-handed batters (Paul Sorrento in 1991, Eric Fox in 1992).... Average of 6.73 hits allowed per nine innings was 2d lowest in the A.L. last season, behind Randy Johnson (6.59).... Averaged 8.22 strikeouts per nine innings, 2d-best rate in the league.... Opponents' slugging percentage was the lowest against any pitcher in the majors who qualified for the ERA title.... Threw 14 wild pitches, 2d-highest total in the A.L., behind Mike Moore (22).... The only pitcher ever to defeat the Twins in a postseason game at the Metrodome (Game 2, 1991 A.L.C.S.); Minnesota has won 11 of its 12 postseason contests there.... Comparable statistical profiles at the same age: David Cone and John Montefusco.

Erik Hanson

Throws Right

Seattle Mariners	W-L	ERA	AB	H	HR	BB	SO	BA	SA	OBA
Season	8-17	4.82	728	209	14	57	112	.287	.402	.341
vs. Left-Handers			365	88	5	26	56	.241	.329	.291
vs. Right-Handers			363	121	9	31	56	.333	.477	.390
vs. Ground-Ballers			357	95	3	30	54	.266	.347	.326
vs. Fly-Ballers			371	114	11	27	58	.307	.456	.356
Home Games	6-6	4.78	357	104	8	28	56	.291	.412	.351
Road Games	2-11	4.86	371	105	6	29	56	.283	.394	.331
Grass Fields	2-9	4.55	313	86	5	25	50	.275	.387	.325
Artificial Turf	6-8	5.04	415	123	9	32	62	.296	.414	.353
April	1-3	5.04	122	33	4	9	17	.270	.410	.328
May	1-4	4.74	148	41	4	14	27	.277	.426	.343
June	3-3	2.80	169	45	3	13	25	.266	.343	.315
July	3-3	3.70	153	37	2	9	25	.242	.333	.285
August	0-2	15.92	65	28	1	5	4	.431	.646	.472
Sept./Oct.	0-2	4.26	71	25	0	7	14	.352	.408	.412
Leading Off Inn.			187	54	5	8	24	.289	.417	.321
Bases Empty			438	114	7	26	69	.260	.352	.305
Runners On			290	95	7	31	43	.328	.479	.391
Runners/Scor. Pos.			148	55	5	20	28	.372	.568	.436
Runners On/2 Out			122	44	4	15	21	.361	.525	.435
Scor. Pos./2 Out			75	28	3	13	14	.373	.560	.472
Late-Inning Pressure			33	13	1	3	6	.394	.576	.444
Leading Off			10	5	0	1	2	.500	.600	.545
Runners On			15	6	1	2	3	.400	.733	.471
Runners/Scor. Pos.			5	2	0	1	2	.400	.600	.500
First 9 Batters			254	69	3	16	39	.272	.366	.320
Second 9 Batters			222	67	3	22	37	.302	.401	.367
All Batters Thereafter			252	73	8	19	36	.290	.440	.338

Loves to face: Rob Deer (0-for-16, 9 SO)
Travis Fryman (.063, 1-for-16)
Sam Horn (0-for-21)

Hates to face: Ellis Burks (.545, 12-for-22, 2 HR)
Paul Molitor (.500, 16-for-32, 1 HR)
Frank Thomas (.533, 8-for-15, 1 HR)

Miscellaneous statistics: Ground outs-to-air outs ratio: 2.08 last season (3d highest in A.L.), 1.38 for career.... Opponents grounded into 25 double plays in 155 opportunities (one per 6.2).... Allowed 34 doubles, 4 triples in 186⅔ innings.... Allowed 14 first-inning runs in 30 starts (2.10 ERA).... Batting support: 3.63 runs per start, 6th-lowest average in A.L.... Opposing base stealers: 15-for-19 (79%); 1 pickoff, 0 balks.

Comments: Posted a 3.18 ERA as a rookie in 1989, but it has risen in every season since then: 3.24, 3.81, 4.82. The only other pitchers with an increase in each of the last three seasons (minimum: 100 IP in each): Tom Gordon and Bruce Hurst.... Became the third different Mariners pitcher in the last nine years to lead the majors in losses. Mike Moore led in 1987, Matt Young in 1985.... Career record still stands above the .500-mark (45–42); in fact, he has the 2d-highest winning percentage in Mariners history, behind Mark Langston (74–67, .525).... His 11 road defeats were most of any pitcher in majors.... Opponents' batting average with runners in scoring position was the highest in the majors last season.... Struck out almost two fewer batters per nine innings last year (5.40) than he did in 1991 (7.37).... Ratio of ground outs to air outs rose sharply last season from a previous career rate of 1.20. That produced a career-high 25 double-play grounders; he induced a total of 33 GIDPs over the two previous seasons.... Since 1975, only five pitchers have faced as many as 50 batters with the bases loaded without ever walking in a run: Steve Crawford (95 BFP), Paul Gibson (69), Tim Crews (63), Todd Worrell (56), and Hanson (52).... Posted a 1–5 record in six complete games last season. Did you know that a complete game is much more likely to result in victory for N.L. starters than for A.L. starters? Last season, N.L. pitchers won 89 percent of their CGs, compared to only 59 percent in the American League.

Tom Henke
Throws Right

Toronto Blue Jays	W-L	ERA	AB	H	HR	BB	SO	BA	SA	OBA
Season	3-2	2.26	203	40	5	22	46	.197	.315	.272
vs. Left-Handers			105	20	2	14	23	.190	.286	.279
vs. Right-Handers			98	20	3	8	23	.204	.347	.264
vs. Ground-Ballers			86	21	1	11	16	.244	.337	.327
vs. Fly-Ballers			117	19	4	11	30	.162	.299	.231
Home Games	2-0	2.48	100	18	4	10	20	.180	.310	.250
Road Games	1-2	2.03	103	22	1	12	26	.214	.320	.293
Grass Fields	1-2	2.84	76	19	1	11	18	.250	.382	.341
Artificial Turf	2-0	1.96	127	21	4	11	28	.165	.276	.229
April	1-1	2.57	28	6	1	4	6	.214	.393	.313
May	1-0	3.38	27	4	2	5	4	.148	.407	.273
June	0-0	0.00	26	4	0	2	9	.154	.192	.214
July	1-1	3.12	30	5	0	4	8	.167	.233	.257
August	0-0	2.45	40	7	1	3	7	.175	.250	.227
Sept./Oct.	0-0	2.08	52	14	1	4	12	.269	.385	.321
Leading Off Inn.			50	11	2	3	9	.220	.400	.264
Bases Empty			124	23	3	11	29	.185	.306	.252
Runners On			79	17	2	11	17	.215	.329	.301
Runners/Scor. Pos.			53	12	2	8	10	.226	.377	.313
Runners On/2 Out			33	5	1	4	5	.152	.242	.243
Scor. Pos./2 Out			22	4	1	3	2	.182	.318	.280
Late-Inning Pressure			148	30	4	11	37	.203	.331	.256
Leading Off			37	8	2	1	8	.216	.432	.237
Runners On			53	11	1	6	14	.208	.302	.283
Runners/Scor. Pos.			37	7	1	4	8	.189	.297	.262
First 9 Batters			203	40	5	22	46	.197	.315	.272
Second 9 Batters			0	0	0	0	0	—	—	—
All Batters Thereafter			0	0	0	0	0	—	—	—

Loves to face: Dave Bergman (0-for-17)
    Randy Bush (.130, 3-for-23, 3 BB, 12 SO)
    Lou Whitaker (.071, 2-for-28)
Hates to face: Wade Boggs (.417, 5-for-12, 6 BB)
    Don Mattingly (.368, 7-for-19, 2 HR)
    David Segui (.833, 5-for-6, 1 HR)

Miscellaneous statistics: Ground outs-to-air outs ratio: 0.68 last season, 0.73 for career.... Opponents grounded into 3 double plays in 37 opportunities (one per 12).... Allowed 9 doubles, 0 triples in 55⅔ innings.... Saved 34 games in 38 opportunities (89%), 3d-highest rate in majors.... Stranded 5 inherited runners, allowed 2 to score (71%).... Opposing base stealers: 2-for-3 (67%); 0 pick-offs, 0 balks.

Comments: Leaves the Blue Jays as their all-time leader in ERA (2.48) among pitchers with at least 300 innings.... Returns to the Rangers, for whom he made his major league debut on September 10, 1982, in relief of Frank Tanana. He last pitched for Texas (also in relief of Tanana) on September 29, 1984; his teammates at that time included Mickey Rivers and Jim Bibby.... Will become the 23d player to serve a second tour of duty with the Washington/Texas franchise. That group includes Buddy Bell, Ferguson Jenkins, Gaylord Perry, and Jim Sundberg.... Rate of walks increased from 1.97 per nine innings in 1991 to 3.56 last season, a career high.... His ratio of 46 strikeouts in 55⅔ innings sounds great, but it, too, represented a personal worst.... Has struck out a batter per inning in seven of his 11 seasons in the majors. Only Nolan Ryan (16) and Sandy Koufax (7) have done so as often.... Won-lost records for relievers are often misleading, but here's an interesting breakdown: Henke has a career record of 20–8 in home games (10–1 over the last four years), 12–22 on the road (1–8 over the last three years).... Enters 1993 with 487 career appearances, all in relief. Only seven pitchers have started their careers with at least 500 appearances out of the bullpen: Kent Tekulve, Sparky Lyle, Jeff Reardon, Dan Quisenberry, Bruce Sutter, Bob Locker, and John Franco. No pitcher who began his career with that many relief appearances went on to start even one game in the majors.

Mike Henneman
Throws Right

Detroit Tigers	W-L	ERA	AB	H	HR	BB	SO	BA	SA	OBA
Season	2-6	3.96	293	75	6	20	58	.256	.369	.299
vs. Left-Handers			144	40	2	9	22	.278	.389	.314
vs. Right-Handers			149	35	4	11	36	.235	.349	.284
vs. Ground-Ballers			142	30	1	12	24	.211	.282	.271
vs. Fly-Ballers			151	45	5	8	34	.298	.450	.325
Home Games	1-4	3.19	160	40	4	9	34	.250	.363	.288
Road Games	1-2	4.89	133	35	2	11	24	.263	.376	.311
Grass Fields	2-5	4.01	255	65	6	18	52	.255	.384	.300
Artificial Turf	0-1	3.60	38	10	0	2	6	.263	.263	.293
April	0-0	6.23	32	10	0	4	9	.313	.406	.368
May	0-2	3.55	50	14	1	4	11	.280	.360	.327
June	0-1	2.60	60	10	2	4	11	.167	.283	.219
July	0-2	7.36	45	15	1	3	6	.333	.489	.367
August	1-1	2.45	54	12	1	2	10	.222	.333	.246
Sept./Oct.	1-0	3.46	52	14	1	3	11	.269	.385	.309
Leading Off Inn.			70	16	0	3	14	.229	.257	.260
Bases Empty			168	43	4	7	32	.256	.369	.286
Runners On			125	32	2	13	26	.256	.368	.315
Runners/Scor. Pos.			65	19	2	11	18	.292	.415	.370
Runners On/2 Out			52	9	0	2	11	.173	.173	.204
Scor. Pos./2 Out			29	7	0	2	8	.241	.241	.290
Late-Inning Pressure			176	48	5	11	37	.273	.415	.311
Leading Off			44	9	0	2	10	.205	.250	.239
Runners On			70	20	2	6	13	.286	.429	.329
Runners/Scor. Pos.			35	12	2	6	8	.343	.571	.409
First 9 Batters			286	75	6	19	57	.262	.378	.303
Second 9 Batters			7	0	0	1	1	.000	.000	.125
All Batters Thereafter			0	0	0	0	0	—	—	—

Loves to face: Joe Carter (.118, 2-for-17)
    Bo Jackson (0-for-9, 3 SO)
    Danny Tartabull (.077, 1-for-13, 3 BB)
Hates to face: Paul Molitor (.385, 5-for-13, 2 2B, 2 HR)
    Kirby Puckett (.500, 5-for-10)
    Harold Reynolds (.615, 8-for-13, 1 HR)

Miscellaneous statistics: Ground outs-to-air outs ratio: 1.50 last season, 1.37 for career.... Opponents grounded into 7 double plays in 71 opportunities (one per 10).... Allowed 11 doubles, 2 triples in 77⅓ innings.... Saved 24 games in 26 opportunities (92%), 2d-highest rate in majors.... Stranded 9 inherited runners, allowed 4 to score (69%).... Opposing base stealers: 2-for-3 (67%); 0 pick-offs, 0 balks.

Comments: After five seasons in which he was at least three games above .500, his career winning percentage fell by 46 points to .654 (51–27). That still ranks 5th among relievers in A.L. history, and it's the highest by any relief pitcher since Doug Bird posted a .672 mark with a 43–21 record (minimum: 50 decisions).... Functioned much more as a 9th-inning closer last season than in the past. He entered 39 of 60 games in the 9th or later (65%), compared to 23 of 60 (38%) in 1991, 23 of 69 (33%) in 1990, and 14 of 60 (23%) in 1989.... Entered only five of 60 games with runners in scoring position, the lowest percentage in the American League (minimum: 40 relief games).... Still, he pitched at least two innings in seven of his 24 saves; only four pitchers in the majors had more saves in which they worked at least two innings.... Has appeared in *exactly* 60 games in three of the last four seasons, and never pitched in as many as 70 in one year. The two longest streaks of 60- to 69-game seasons belong to two of the most durable and successful relievers ever: Lee Smith (10 years, 1982–91) and Jeff Reardon (7, 1983–89).... Posted a career-low rate of 2.33 walks per nine innings last season; half of the walks he allowed were intentional.... Career breakdown: 35–10 (2.73 ERA) at Tiger Stadium, 16–17 (3.41 ERA) on the road.... Opponents have a career batting average of .201 with two outs and runners on base, and are homerless in 438 at-bats in those situations.

Doug Henry — Throws Right

Milwaukee Brewers	W-L	ERA	AB	H	HR	BB	SO	BA	SA	OBA
Season	1-4	4.02	250	64	6	24	52	.256	.400	.319
vs. Left-Handers			106	22	1	16	17	.208	.274	.306
vs. Right-Handers			144	42	5	8	35	.292	.493	.329
vs. Ground-Ballers			119	29	0	10	23	.244	.294	.300
vs. Fly-Ballers			131	35	6	14	29	.267	.496	.336
Home Games	0-1	2.72	136	30	3	10	28	.221	.375	.270
Road Games	1-3	5.65	114	34	3	14	24	.298	.430	.375
Grass Fields	1-4	2.89	208	48	4	18	46	.231	.365	.289
Artificial Turf	0-0	11.00	42	16	2	6	6	.381	.571	.458
April	0-0	5.63	34	14	0	3	4	.412	.441	.447
May	1-1	2.31	40	6	1	6	8	.150	.300	.261
June	0-0	0.66	46	6	0	4	13	.130	.174	.200
July	0-0	4.35	40	12	1	4	10	.300	.475	.364
August	0-1	10.22	56	18	4	5	9	.321	.679	.371
Sept./Oct.	0-2	1.00	34	8	0	2	8	.235	.235	.278
Leading Off Inn.			58	11	1	4	13	.190	.293	.242
Bases Empty			155	33	2	6	34	.213	.303	.242
Runners On			95	31	4	18	18	.326	.558	.426
Runners/Scor. Pos.			57	22	4	14	9	.386	.702	.493
Runners On/2 Out			46	14	1	12	9	.304	.500	.448
Scor. Pos./2 Out			31	12	1	11	6	.387	.613	.548
Late-Inning Pressure			149	38	1	14	33	.255	.349	.315
Leading Off			35	7	0	3	9	.200	.257	.263
Runners On			57	17	1	9	10	.298	.439	.382
Runners/Scor. Pos.			30	10	1	7	5	.333	.567	.436
First 9 Batters			243	63	6	23	50	.259	.403	.321
Second 9 Batters			7	1	0	1	2	.143	.286	.250
All Batters Thereafter			0	0	0	0	0	—	—	—

Loves to face: Jack Clark (0-for-5, 3 SO)
John Olerud (0-for-5, 3 SO)
Hates to face: Craig Grebeck (.400, 2-for-5, 1 2B, 1 HR)
Danny Tartabull (.750, 3-for-4, 3 2B)
Dave Winfield (4-for-4)

Miscellaneous statistics: Ground outs-to-air outs ratio: 0.85 last season, 0.75 for career. . . . Opponents grounded into 2 double plays in 43 opportunities (one per 22). . . . Allowed 14 doubles, 2 triples in 65 innings. . . . Saved 29 games in 33 opportunities (88%), 4th-highest rate in majors. . . . Stranded 16 inherited runners, allowed 9 to score (64%). . . . Opposing base stealers: 4-for-7 (57%); 0 pickoffs, 0 balks.

Comments: Brewers relievers posted the lowest ERA of any bullpen in the majors last season (2.78). Although Henry accounted for 29 of their 39 saves, give credit for the ERA title to James Austin (1.85), Mike Fetters (1.87), and Dan Plesac (2.17). . . . Reached the 100-inning mark for his career on September 27, the same game in which he recorded his 43d career save. No pitcher in major league history had ever picked up that many saves in his first 100 innings pitched; in fact, no one even came close. Mike Schooler was the only other pitcher to earn even 30 saves during his first 100 innings (36). . . . Has made 100 career appearances; entered only three of those games prior to the 8th inning, 75 in the 9th inning or later. . . . Saved 29 games in both 1991 and 1992. The difference: in 1991, 14 were at the Triple-A level. . . . Has a career ERA of 0.42 in 21⅔ innings pitched during September and October. . . . A late-blooming 8th-round selection from the 1985 June draft—the same year the Brewers drafted B.J. Surhoff in the first round. . . . "Clinton/Quayle Syndrome", Part I: As Henry's career takes off, it's worth noting that two other players born the same day (December 10, 1963), Gilberto Reyes and Rick Wrona, have probably completed their major league careers. . . . Career total of 101 innings is the highest of any active A.L. pitcher who has never hit a batter with a pitch. . . . Henke, Henneman, and Henry have a combined career total of 956 games, all in relief. That's still not as many as Kent Tekulve (1050).

Roberto Hernandez — Throws Right

Chicago White Sox	W-L	ERA	AB	H	HR	BB	SO	BA	SA	OBA
Season	7-3	1.65	250	45	4	20	68	.180	.272	.249
vs. Left-Handers			107	20	1	11	36	.187	.280	.264
vs. Right-Handers			143	25	3	9	32	.175	.266	.237
vs. Ground-Ballers			108	20	0	9	29	.185	.231	.256
vs. Fly-Ballers			142	25	4	11	39	.176	.303	.244
Home Games	5-1	0.44	138	23	0	7	42	.167	.196	.215
Road Games	2-2	3.26	112	22	4	13	26	.196	.366	.289
Grass Fields	7-2	1.55	223	39	3	20	63	.175	.256	.252
Artificial Turf	0-1	2.57	27	6	1	0	5	.222	.407	.222
April	0-0	5.40	11	1	0	6	2	.091	.091	.412
May	0-0	0.00	8	0	0	0	3	.000	.000	.000
June	2-0	2.00	33	4	0	3	10	.121	.182	.216
July	1-2	2.35	58	16	1	6	14	.276	.379	.354
August	2-0	0.51	58	7	1	2	20	.121	.207	.175
Sept./Oct.	2-1	1.59	82	17	2	3	19	.207	.329	.233
Leading Off Inn.			57	10	3	5	16	.175	.351	.242
Bases Empty			142	24	3	12	43	.169	.268	.234
Runners On			108	21	1	8	25	.194	.278	.268
Runners/Scor. Pos.			64	11	1	6	11	.172	.250	.263
Runners On/2 Out			52	14	0	5	9	.269	.346	.367
Scor. Pos./2 Out			33	7	0	4	6	.212	.273	.350
Late-Inning Pressure			173	38	3	14	43	.220	.335	.292
Leading Off			40	8	2	4	13	.200	.375	.273
Runners On			82	18	1	5	16	.220	.329	.293
Runners/Scor. Pos.			50	10	1	4	7	.200	.300	.293
First 9 Batters			230	41	4	19	62	.178	.278	.250
Second 9 Batters			20	4	0	1	6	.200	.200	.238
All Batters Thereafter			0	0	0	0	0	—	—	—

Loves to face: Luis Polonia (0-for-5)
Danny Tartabull (0-for-5)
Mickey Tettleton (0-for-4, 4 SO)
Hates to face: Juan Gonzalez (2-for-2, 1 HR)

Miscellaneous statistics: Ground outs-to-air outs ratio: 0.69 last season, 0.78 for career. . . . Opponents grounded into 2 double plays in 46 opportunities (one per 23). . . . Allowed 11 doubles, 0 triples in 71 innings. . . . Saved 12 games in 15 opportunities (80%). . . . Stranded 23 inherited runners, allowed 13 to score (64%). . . . Opposing base stealers: 4-for-8 (50%); 0 pickoffs, 0 balks.

Comments: ERA was the 2d lowest by a White Sox pitcher over the last 70 years (minimum: 50 IP), behind Hoyt Wilhelm's 1.31 mark in 1967. . . . His ERA in home games was the lowest over the last 10 years (minimum: 40 IP). Career breakdown: 0.91 at Comiskey Park, 5.20 on the road. . . . The last American League rookie with an ERA as low as Hernandez in as many innings as he pitched was Jerry Bell of the Brewers in 1972. (He posted the exact same figures as Hernandez.) . . . Led A.L. rookies with 12 saves; the only N.L. rookie with more: Anthony Young (15). . . . Batting average by opposing left-handed hitters was the 3d lowest in the league, behind those of a pair of southpaws: Mark Langston and Jimmy Key (minimum: 100 AB). . . . Posted a 3–0 record against the Angels. . . . Was one of California's five first-round selections in the June 1986 draft, but didn't make his major league debut until 1991. (For more on this subject, see the Lee Stevens comments.) Of the first 18 selections in that draft, only two have never played in the majors. . . . Has allowed five homers in his career, all to fly-ball hitters. . . . Opponents have a career batting average of .339 with two outs and runners on base (21-for-62), .168 at other times. . . . "Clinton/Quayle Syndrome", Part II: Born November 11, 1964, one day after Junior Noboa. Funny how two guys can be the same age, and while one is already over the hill the other is just taking off.

Joe Hesketh

Throws Left

Boston Red Sox	W-L	ERA	AB	H	HR	BB	SO	BA	SA	OBA
Season	8-9	4.36	588	162	15	58	104	.276	.425	.339
vs. Left-Handers			98	25	2	4	20	.255	.367	.288
vs. Right-Handers			490	137	13	54	84	.280	.437	.349
vs. Ground-Ballers			275	81	6	17	36	.295	.425	.333
vs. Fly-Ballers			313	81	9	41	68	.259	.425	.344
Home Games	4-4	4.50	269	81	5	31	43	.301	.431	.370
Road Games	4-5	4.25	319	81	10	27	61	.254	.420	.313
Grass Fields	7-7	4.37	463	128	9	50	82	.276	.408	.345
Artificial Turf	1-2	4.31	125	34	6	8	22	.272	.488	.319
April	0-0	3.86	63	18	0	7	9	.286	.365	.347
May	1-2	2.65	129	31	1	9	24	.240	.357	.288
June	2-3	4.54	131	32	5	12	29	.244	.427	.308
July	2-3	6.39	109	38	5	10	15	.349	.560	.405
August	1-1	6.86	88	32	3	10	16	.364	.523	.420
Sept./Oct.	2-0	2.29	68	11	1	10	11	.162	.265	.278
Leading Off Inn.			149	43	8	10	25	.289	.537	.333
Bases Empty			338	93	10	28	53	.275	.435	.334
Runners On			250	69	5	30	51	.276	.412	.346
Runners/Scor. Pos.			141	37	3	19	31	.262	.369	.337
Runners On/2 Out			97	21	2	16	22	.216	.340	.327
Scor. Pos./2 Out			56	9	1	10	16	.161	.214	.288
Late-Inning Pressure			16	5	0	3	2	.313	.500	.421
Leading Off			6	2	0	1	2	.333	.667	.429
Runners On			4	2	0	1	0	.500	.750	.600
Runners/Scor. Pos.			2	1	0	0	0	.500	1.000	.500
First 9 Batters			234	62	8	19	46	.265	.419	.322
Second 9 Batters			206	55	4	15	34	.267	.437	.313
All Batters Thereafter			148	45	3	24	24	.304	.419	.401

Loves to face: Henry Cotto (.077, 1-for-13, 1 2B)
Leo Gomez (0-for-6)
Don Mattingly (.071, 1-for-14)

Hates to face: Shane Mack (.571, 8-for-14, 2 HR)
Mickey Tettleton (.462, 6-for-13, 2 2B, 2 HR)
Frank Thomas (.833, 5-for-6, 2 2B, 2 HR, 1 SO)

Miscellaneous statistics: Ground outs-to-air outs ratio: 1.35 last season, 1.26 for career.... Opponents grounded into 10 double plays in 116 opportunities (one per 12).... Allowed 39 doubles, 2 triples in 148⅔ innings.... Allowed 11 first-inning runs in 25 starts (2.52 ERA).... Batting support: 4.25 runs per start.... Opposing base stealers: 17-for-21 (81%); 3 pickoffs, 0 balks.

Comments: Started 25 games last season, matching his career high, set in 1985 with the Expos.... Walked an average of one batter for every 15.1 he faced over the first four innings of his starts last season; that rate increased to one every 8.9 batters faced from the fifth inning on.... Of the six A.L. pitchers who had both a save and a complete game last season, three were Red Sox: Hesketh, Danny Darwin, and Greg A. Harris. The other three A.L. swing men: Russ Swan, Greg Cadaret, Tim Fortugno.... Career record of 35-26 with a 3.46 ERA in 89 starts, 14-12 with a 3.96 ERA and 20 saves in 197 relief appearances.... Threw two shutouts in his first 25 major league starts, but has not had one in 64 starts since. (Last season, he didn't even reach the 9th inning in any of 25 starts.)... Career ERA of 3.87 from April through August, 2.47 from September 1 on.... Allowed 36 home runs in 466⅔ innings in his National League career (one every 13 innings); has allowed the same number of homers in only 327⅔ innings with the Red Sox (one every 9.1 innings).... Posted only one other losing record in his nine seasons in the majors—a 1-6 mark in 1990, when he played for three clubs (Montreal, Atlanta, and Boston).... During the 52 years that the Red Sox and Braves cohabited Boston, only one player appeared for both teams in the same season (Gene Bailey in 1920). Since the Braves left Beantown, eight players have done so, including five in the past four seasons: Ed Romero (1989), Hesketh and Dan Petry (1991), and Steve Lyons and Jeff Reardon last season.

Greg Hibbard

Throws Left

Chicago White Sox	W-L	ERA	AB	H	HR	BB	SO	BA	SA	OBA
Season	10-7	4.40	675	187	17	57	69	.277	.404	.337
vs. Left-Handers			85	19	1	6	15	.224	.271	.302
vs. Right-Handers			590	168	16	51	54	.285	.424	.342
vs. Ground-Ballers			339	89	4	28	39	.263	.357	.319
vs. Fly-Ballers			336	98	13	29	30	.292	.452	.355
Home Games	7-3	3.44	361	89	11	29	39	.247	.374	.305
Road Games	3-4	5.56	314	98	6	28	30	.312	.439	.374
Grass Fields	9-5	4.35	584	158	16	49	63	.271	.401	.330
Artificial Turf	1-2	4.70	91	29	1	8	6	.319	.429	.380
April	4-0	2.83	102	23	2	9	7	.225	.314	.283
May	1-3	5.45	146	46	7	16	15	.315	.527	.392
June	1-1	4.42	146	40	4	6	12	.274	.411	.305
July	1-1	5.14	95	23	2	15	16	.242	.379	.351
August	2-1	3.21	108	26	1	8	11	.241	.296	.299
Sept./Oct.	1-1	5.40	78	29	1	3	8	.372	.462	.395
Leading Off Inn.			171	41	5	15	21	.240	.368	.305
Bases Empty			399	104	12	35	47	.261	.388	.325
Runners On			276	83	5	22	22	.301	.428	.354
Runners/Scor. Pos.			144	39	2	14	12	.271	.403	.339
Runners On/2 Out			119	33	2	6	14	.277	.412	.323
Scor. Pos./2 Out			66	18	1	4	9	.273	.409	.333
Late-Inning Pressure			62	20	2	7	7	.323	.452	.403
Leading Off			20	6	1	1	2	.300	.450	.364
Runners On			27	9	0	2	3	.333	.370	.367
Runners/Scor. Pos.			11	3	0	1	0	.273	.364	.308
First 9 Batters			238	61	4	24	32	.256	.340	.328
Second 9 Batters			230	62	6	14	21	.270	.400	.310
All Batters Thereafter			207	64	7	19	16	.309	.483	.375

Loves to face: Dante Bichette (.154, 4-for-26)
Pete Incaviglia (.125, 2-for-16)
Lee Stevens (0-for-11)

Hates to face: Jim Eisenreich (.400, 4-for-10)
Dave Gallagher (.667, 4-for-6, 2 2B, 3 BB)
Felix Jose (.500, 4-for-8)

Miscellaneous statistics: Ground outs-to-air outs ratio: 1.99 last season (4th highest in A.L.), 1.53 for career.... Opponents grounded into 19 double plays in 150 opportunities (one per 7.9).... Allowed 25 doubles, 5 triples in 176 innings.... Allowed 13 first-inning runs in 28 starts (3.54 ERA).... Batting support: 4.36 runs per start.... Opposing base stealers: 9-for-15 (60%); 1 pickoff, 1 balk.

Comments: One of three pitchers to win at least 10 starts with fewer than 100 strikeouts in each of the last three seasons. The others: Bill Gullickson and Bob Tewksbury.... Lowest career strikeout rates among active pitchers (minimum: 500 IP): Bob Tewksbury, 3.50 per nine innings; Bill Swift, 3.60; Hibbard, 3.60; Lee Guetterman, 3.87; Chuck Crim, 4.10.... The White Sox used only seven starting pitchers last season, the fewest of any team in the majors. All but 10 games were started by the core of McDowell (34), McCaskill (34), Fernandez (29), Hibbard (28), and Hough (27), marking the first time in franchise history that five pitchers have started more than 25 games each.... Moves to Waveland Avenue having pitched 119 games for the Sox. The only players to pitch 100 games for both teams: Dennis Lamp, Turk Lown, Mike Proly, and Steve Trout.... He and Bobby Witt were the only A.L. pitchers to start more than 25 games without ever making it past the eighth inning.... The *Elias Baseball Analyst* S.A.T. Preparation Exam: Opponents' batting averages year by year since 1990: .255, .266, .277. What comes next?. ..Has allowed 50 home runs to right-handed batters (one per 47 at-bats), only 6 to left-handed hitters (one per 61 AB).... In four seasons in the big leagues, he has never had a streak of more than two losses without a victory.... Like David Cone and Melido Perez, another pitcher who got away from Kansas City for very little. In fact, Hibbard and Perez were packaged together in the deal that brought Floyd Bannister from the Sox to the Royals.

Darren Holmes — Throws Right

Milwaukee Brewers	W-L	ERA	AB	H	HR	BB	SO	BA	SA	OBA
Season	4-4	2.55	156	35	1	11	31	.224	.308	.284
vs. Left-Handers			67	15	0	5	11	.224	.284	.278
vs. Right-Handers			89	20	1	6	20	.225	.326	.289
vs. Ground-Ballers			88	23	0	3	13	.261	.341	.286
vs. Fly-Ballers			68	12	1	8	18	.176	.265	.282
Home Games	3-2	3.26	71	17	0	3	13	.239	.282	.280
Road Games	1-2	1.96	85	18	1	8	18	.212	.329	.287
Grass Fields	4-4	2.88	129	30	1	10	24	.233	.318	.293
Artificial Turf	0-0	1.13	27	5	0	1	7	.185	.259	.241
April	0-0	—	0	0	0	0	0	—	—	—
May	2-1	1.93	18	4	0	3	6	.222	.389	.333
June	0-2	5.79	41	14	1	4	6	.341	.439	.413
July	1-1	3.86	36	8	0	0	8	.222	.306	.222
August	0-0	0.00	26	3	0	1	5	.115	.154	.179
Sept./Oct.	1-0	0.87	35	6	0	3	6	.171	.229	.237
Leading Off Inn.			32	10	1	2	4	.313	.531	.353
Bases Empty			73	21	1	2	13	.288	.411	.307
Runners On			83	14	0	9	18	.169	.217	.266
Runners/Scor. Pos.			50	7	0	7	11	.140	.160	.259
Runners On/2 Out			37	3	0	3	7	.081	.108	.150
Scor. Pos./2 Out			26	1	0	1	6	.038	.038	.074
Late-Inning Pressure			64	16	0	8	13	.250	.313	.333
Leading Off			12	3	0	2	3	.250	.417	.357
Runners On			37	8	0	6	7	.216	.270	.326
Runners/Scor. Pos.			24	3	0	4	6	.125	.125	.250
First 9 Batters			153	34	1	10	31	.222	.307	.279
Second 9 Batters			3	1	0	1	0	.333	.333	.500
All Batters Thereafter			0	0	0	0	0	—	—	—

Loves to face: Jim Eisenreich (0-for-3, 1 SO)
Chris James (0-for-3, 1 SO)

Hates to face: Roberto Kelly (.500, 2-for-4, 1 2B)
Joe Orsulak (.333, 3-for-9)
Jody Reed (.600, 3-for-5)

Miscellaneous statistics: Ground outs-to-air outs ratio: 1.55 last season, 1.17 for career.... Opponents grounded into 3 double plays in 45 opportunities (one per 15).... Allowed 6 doubles, 2 triples in 42⅓ innings.... Stranded 28 inherited runners, allowed 6 to score (82%).... Opposing base stealers: 4-for-5 (80%); 0 pickoffs, 0 balks.

Comments: Pitched in one more game for the Brewers last season than in 1991, but threw 34 fewer innings (76⅓–42⅓). He faced more than 10 batters in 15 of 40 appearances in 1991, but did so only once in 41 games last season.... The only home run he allowed last season was hit by Glenn Davis. He hasn't allowed a homer to any of the 126 left-handed batters he's faced since George Brett tagged him August 1, 1991. Let's see him extend that streak at Mile High.... Opposing ground-ball hitters have batted .315 over three seasons, 98 points higher than fly-ball hitters.... Career ERA is far lower on artificial turf (1.55) than on grass (4.79).... Was drafted by the Dodgers in 1984; he has never played a full season in the majors.... Stranded 67 of the 90 runners he inherited in his three-year career (74%), well above the major league average during that time (66%).... Appears that he and Bryan Harvey will be the respective (if not respected) closers for Colorado and Florida this season; if so, they'll be about as busy as the Maytag repairman. Saves leaders for expansion teams (including unofficial figures for the pre-1969 teams): Art Fowler, L.A. (11 in 1961); Dave Sisler, Wash. (11 in 1961); Don McMahon, Hou. (8 in 1962); Craig Anderson, N.Y. (4 in 1962); Moe Drabowsky, K.C. (11 in 1969); Diego Segui, Sea. (12 in 1969); Dan McGinn, Mon. (6 in 1969); Billy McCool, S.D. (7 in 1969); Pete Vuckovich, Tor. (8 in 1977); Enrique Romo, Sea. (16 in 1977).

Charlie Hough — Throws Right

Chicago White Sox	W-L	ERA	AB	H	HR	BB	SO	BA	SA	OBA
Season	7-12	3.93	670	160	19	66	76	.239	.373	.311
vs. Left-Handers			267	63	7	26	25	.236	.352	.304
vs. Right-Handers			403	97	12	40	51	.241	.387	.316
vs. Ground-Ballers			334	80	8	35	26	.240	.359	.312
vs. Fly-Ballers			336	80	11	31	50	.238	.387	.310
Home Games	6-4	3.49	380	91	8	30	40	.239	.334	.299
Road Games	1-8	4.52	290	69	11	36	36	.238	.424	.326
Grass Fields	7-8	3.94	541	132	15	47	60	.244	.366	.309
Artificial Turf	0-4	3.89	129	28	4	19	16	.217	.403	.318
April	0-1	6.43	61	20	2	3	4	.328	.459	.359
May	1-1	3.38	91	17	3	14	7	.187	.286	.306
June	3-2	2.31	141	24	3	17	17	.170	.284	.259
July	0-3	3.18	146	30	4	18	16	.205	.329	.297
August	2-4	6.23	149	46	5	9	20	.309	.497	.360
Sept./Oct.	1-1	3.63	82	23	2	5	12	.280	.415	.311
Leading Off Inn.			174	36	2	9	23	.207	.293	.250
Bases Empty			410	92	11	36	48	.224	.349	.295
Runners On			260	68	8	30	28	.262	.412	.336
Runners/Scor. Pos.			136	36	4	24	14	.265	.412	.361
Runners On/2 Out			123	36	6	19	15	.293	.496	.387
Scor. Pos./2 Out			74	22	4	15	8	.297	.514	.416
Late-Inning Pressure			57	14	4	6	6	.246	.526	.328
Leading Off			18	5	0	1	2	.278	.389	.316
Runners On			17	3	2	4	2	.176	.588	.364
Runners/Scor. Pos.			12	3	2	4	1	.250	.833	.438
First 9 Batters			206	41	1	29	27	.199	.248	.298
Second 9 Batters			210	56	9	18	19	.267	.443	.328
All Batters Thereafter			254	63	9	19	30	.248	.417	.309

Loves to face: Gary Sheffield (0-for-7)
Don Slaught (.130, 3-for-23)
Sammy Sosa (1-for-9)

Hates to face: Daryl Boston (.394, 13-for-33, 2 HR)
Steve Finley (.455, 5-for-11)
Jody Reed (.321, 9-for-28, 3 2B)

Miscellaneous statistics: Ground outs-to-air outs ratio: 0.94 last season, 1.03 for career.... Opponents grounded into 13 double plays in 115 opportunities (one per 8.8).... Allowed 25 doubles, 4 triples in 176⅓ innings.... Allowed 24 first-inning runs in 27 starts (6.75 ERA).... Batting support: 3.70 runs per start, 8th-lowest average in A.L.... Opposing base stealers: 17-for-20 (85%); 2 pickoffs, 1 balk.

Comments: Here's a 20/20 Club that really means something: Hough has pitched at least 20 games in 20 consecutive seasons. (That eliminates the Reuss-style hangers-on who extend their participation streaks with an otherwise meaningless single appearance in a given season or decade.) Other members: Nolan Ryan, 25 years; Phil Niekro, 23; Don Sutton, 22; Tommy John and Gaylord Perry, 21; Hough, Goose Gossage, Lindy McDaniel, Eppa Rixey, Tom Seaver, Warren Spahn, and Cy Young, 20.... Hough and Carlton Fisk were never paired as batterymates in two seasons together with the White Sox. Too bad—each was over 44 years of age, so they would have comprised the oldest battery in major league history. Only twice previously have pitchers and catchers even 41 or older worked together: Curt Davis (41) pitched to Clyde Sukeforth (43) on the 1945 Dodgers; Ellis Kinder (41) pitched to Walker Cooper (41) for the 1956 Cardinals.... One of five players to have lowered his ERA in each of the last three seasons (minimum: 100 innings in each). The others: Jack McDowell, Melido Perez, Bob Walk, and Duane Ward. Hough's ERA year by year since 1989: 4.35, 4.07, 3.95, 3.93. (Who knows how low it'll be by the time he turns 50!)...Had trouble finding the plate in the first inning, averaging one walk every 4.6 batters (the highest mark in the A.L.), compared to one every 12.9 thereafter. Posted an ERA of 6.75 in the first inning, 0.69 in the second inning.... We thought you were supposed to move to Florida *after* you retired.

Randy Johnson   Throws Left

Seattle Mariners	W-L	ERA	AB	H	HR	BB	SO	BA	SA	OBA
Season	12-14	3.77	749	154	13	144	241	.206	.307	.344
vs. Left-Handers			75	14	1	12	19	.187	.240	.303
vs. Right-Handers			674	140	12	132	222	.208	.315	.348
vs. Ground-Ballers			369	84	5	77	117	.228	.331	.372
vs. Fly-Ballers			380	70	8	67	124	.184	.284	.316
Home Games	8-6	2.76	403	72	4	68	146	.179	.253	.308
Road Games	4-8	5.03	346	82	9	76	95	.237	.370	.383
Grass Fields	3-7	5.49	288	70	8	68	79	.243	.375	.398
Artificial Turf	9-7	2.77	461	84	5	76	162	.182	.265	.307
April	3-0	1.53	107	21	3	10	30	.196	.336	.265
May	2-5	5.40	143	31	1	35	34	.217	.287	.385
June	0-2	5.73	37	7	2	13	11	.189	.405	.455
July	2-4	4.28	152	39	4	33	43	.257	.388	.398
August	4-1	3.27	150	28	1	26	56	.187	.240	.309
Sept./Oct.	1-2	3.33	160	28	2	27	67	.175	.269	.298
Leading Off Inn.			186	42	3	29	60	.226	.333	.339
Bases Empty			397	81	4	80	132	.204	.285	.351
Runners On			352	73	9	64	109	.207	.332	.336
Runners/Scor. Pos.			212	41	5	49	71	.193	.297	.351
Runners On/2 Out			152	32	4	23	49	.211	.349	.326
Scor. Pos./2 Out			106	21	2	19	36	.198	.283	.336
Late-Inning Pressure			80	14	2	20	32	.175	.300	.337
Leading Off			25	5	0	3	11	.200	.280	.286
Runners On			25	5	2	9	9	.200	.480	.395
Runners/Scor. Pos.			12	4	2	6	6	.333	.917	.476
First 9 Batters			222	40	2	47	77	.180	.266	.344
Second 9 Batters			229	47	4	39	71	.205	.301	.321
All Batters Thereafter			298	67	7	58	93	.225	.342	.360

Loves to face: Rob Deer (.105, 2-for-19, 10 SO)
               Rafael Palmeiro (.059, 1-for-17)
               Steve Sax (.038, 1-for-26, 1 2B, 2 BB)

Hates to face: Bob Melvin (.464, 13-for-28)
               Ruben Sierra (.441, 15-for-34, 2 HR)
               Frank Thomas (.400, 6-for-15, 1 HR, 8 BB, 5 SO)

Miscellaneous statistics: Ground outs-to-air outs ratio: 0.80 last season, 0.95 for career. . . . Opponents grounded into 14 double plays in 187 opportunities (one per 13). . . . Allowed 33 doubles, 2 triples in 210⅓ innings. . . . Allowed 19 first-inning runs in 31 starts (3.48 ERA). . . . Batting support: 3.97 runs per start. . . . Opposing base stealers: 42-for-58 (72%), most steals in A.L.; 9 pickoffs, 1 balk.

Comments: Averaged 10.3 strikeouts per nine innings, the highest rate in majors (minimum: 162 IP). . . . Became the fourth pitcher to strike out at least 10 batters per nine innings in two consecutive seasons. The others: Sandy Koufax, Sam McDowell, and Nolan Ryan. . . . Career strikeout rate is lowest in April (7.77 per nine innings), highest in September (9.96). . . . Led A.L. pitchers in both walks and strikeouts; the last pitcher to do so: Mark Langston (1984). . . . It was the third consecutive season in which he led the majors in walks, tying a record held by Nolan Ryan (1972–74 and 1976–78), Tommy Byrne (1949–51), and Togie Pittinger (1902–04). . . . Earned decisions in 22 consecutive starts (Apr. 11–Aug. 21), the longest streak in the majors since 1990 (Bob Welch, 27). . . . Has made 129 career starts, completing 16; but he has never pitched a complete game without allowing at least one walk. . . . Hit 18 batters with pitches, the highest total since 1987, when Charlie Hough plunked 19 batters. . . . Opponents' batting average was the lowest in league (minimum: 162 IP). . . . The battery of Johnson and Lance Parrish worked 42⅔ innings, the most of any battery that didn't allow a home run last season. . . . His eight-game losing streak (May 26–July 21) was the longest by any A.L. starter last season. (Mike Gardiner lost nine in a row, but two were in relief.) . . . Opposing left-handed batters have a .198 career batting average (one home run per 67 at-bats); right-handers have batted .257 (one HR per 43 AB).

Scott Kamieniecki   Throws Right

New York Yankees	W-L	ERA	AB	H	HR	BB	SO	BA	SA	OBA
Season	6-14	4.36	717	193	13	74	88	.269	.379	.340
vs. Left-Handers			337	94	5	35	43	.279	.380	.345
vs. Right-Handers			380	99	8	39	45	.261	.379	.335
vs. Ground-Ballers			362	91	5	30	39	.251	.340	.308
vs. Fly-Ballers			355	102	8	44	49	.287	.420	.370
Home Games	6-4	4.03	365	97	7	42	44	.266	.378	.342
Road Games	0-10	4.70	352	96	6	32	44	.273	.381	.337
Grass Fields	6-13	4.37	661	178	12	71	82	.269	.377	.342
Artificial Turf	0-1	4.20	56	15	1	3	6	.268	.411	.305
April	0-0	—	0	0	0	0	0	—	—	—
May	1-2	3.40	160	39	0	18	16	.244	.294	.324
June	0-3	6.21	115	36	3	14	16	.313	.478	.388
July	1-3	4.98	135	40	4	9	13	.296	.422	.345
August	2-3	3.95	151	36	4	16	18	.238	.364	.311
Sept./Oct.	2-3	3.92	156	42	2	17	25	.269	.372	.341
Leading Off Inn.			183	52	6	11	24	.284	.415	.332
Bases Empty			416	108	8	34	46	.260	.363	.320
Runners On			301	85	5	40	42	.282	.402	.365
Runners/Scor. Pos.			181	51	3	29	29	.282	.403	.372
Runners On/2 Out			114	30	2	16	17	.263	.368	.359
Scor. Pos./2 Out			74	25	1	12	11	.338	.432	.430
Late-Inning Pressure			40	15	0	4	4	.375	.475	.432
Leading Off			11	2	0	1	3	.182	.182	.250
Runners On			15	9	0	2	1	.600	.800	.647
Runners/Scor. Pos.			7	4	0	2	1	.571	.714	.667
First 9 Batters			220	58	5	30	27	.264	.386	.357
Second 9 Batters			228	57	2	19	30	.250	.325	.307
All Batters Thereafter			269	78	6	25	31	.290	.420	.352

Loves to face: Jack Clark (0-for-6, 4 SO)
               Rickey Henderson (0-for-9)
               Kevin Seitzer (.077, 1-for-13)

Hates to face: Randy Bush (.500, 4-for-8, 1 2B, 2 HR)
               Luis Polonia (.556, 5-for-9)
               Bill Spiers (3-for-3)

Miscellaneous statistics: Ground outs-to-air outs ratio: 1.12 last season, 1.14 for career. . . . Opponents grounded into 20 double plays in 143 opportunities (one per 7.2). . . . Allowed 38 doubles, 1 triple in 188 innings. . . . Allowed 18 first-inning runs in 28 starts (4.82 ERA). . . . Batting support: 4.46 runs per start. . . . Opposing base stealers: 29-for-35 (83%), 2d-most steals in A.L.; 1 pickoff, 1 balk.

Comments: His 10 road losses tied him with Melido Perez, Jack Armstrong, and Orel Hershiser for 2d highest total in majors. Erik Hanson was the losingest pitcher away from home (2–11). . . . The last pitcher to post a worse single-season record in road games was Terry Felton, who was 0–11 away from Minnesota in 1982. . . . Pitched four complete games last season, but has never pitched nine innings; all of his CGs were road losses. . . . Among pitchers who opened the season on the disabled list, only Chuck Finley started more games or threw more innings last season than Kamieniecki. . . . Career record of 6–7 with a 3.51 ERA in games in which he has recorded more outs on grounders than on fly balls. In other starts, he has a 4–11 record with a 4.99 ERA. . . . Won four of his first five decisions in the majors, but has a 6–17 record since then. . . . Only two pitchers in Yankees history posted lower winning percentages in a season of at least 20 decisions: Bill Hogg (4–16, .200) and Joe Lake (9–22, .290), both in 1908. . . . Was two months past his 27th birthday when he made his major league debut on June 18, 1991. Over the past quarter-century, only two pitchers 27 or older when they debuted eventually won as many as 100 games: Jim Bibby and Geoff Zahn. (Both had 111 career wins.) It's worth noting that two Yankees pitchers did so during a 10-year period: Spud Chandler, who debuted at age 29 in 1937 and won 109 games; and Vic Raschi, 27 for his debut in 1946, who won 132 games.

Jimmy Key
Throws Left

Toronto Blue Jays	W-L	ERA	AB	H	HR	BB	SO	BA	SA	OBA
Season	13-13	3.53	828	205	24	59	117	.248	.391	.298
vs. Left-Handers			131	23	2	6	19	.176	.252	.216
vs. Right-Handers			697	182	22	53	98	.261	.418	.314
vs. Ground-Ballers			399	95	8	28	55	.238	.358	.289
vs. Fly-Ballers			429	110	16	31	62	.256	.422	.307
Home Games	7-5	3.35	397	99	11	34	63	.249	.393	.310
Road Games	6-8	3.70	431	106	13	25	54	.246	.390	.288
Grass Fields	4-5	4.03	294	74	8	20	35	.252	.395	.300
Artificial Turf	9-8	3.26	534	131	16	39	82	.245	.390	.298
April	1-0	3.58	106	28	3	7	10	.264	.443	.316
May	2-3	2.88	151	36	6	10	14	.238	.424	.282
June	1-3	3.25	141	37	2	8	20	.262	.369	.302
July	3-2	3.75	139	37	6	9	17	.266	.453	.309
August	1-4	6.25	125	34	4	12	21	.272	.424	.338
Sept./Oct.	5-1	2.22	166	33	3	13	35	.199	.271	.260
Leading Off Inn.			217	44	5	7	26	.203	.313	.228
Bases Empty			528	119	15	34	70	.225	.366	.276
Runners On			300	86	9	25	47	.287	.437	.336
Runners/Scor. Pos.			155	41	6	22	27	.265	.445	.342
Runners On/2 Out			130	31	3	11	28	.238	.362	.303
Scor. Pos./2 Out			69	14	2	10	16	.203	.362	.304
Late-Inning Pressure			29	12	3	3	2	.414	.828	.469
Leading Off			11	5	2	0	1	.455	1.182	.455
Runners On			7	4	0	2	0	.571	.714	.667
Runners/Scor. Pos.			2	1	0	2	0	.500	.500	.750
First 9 Batters			274	71	4	19	42	.259	.354	.306
Second 9 Batters			260	64	8	18	43	.246	.408	.293
All Batters Thereafter			294	70	12	22	32	.238	.412	.296

Loves to face: Ellis Burks (.080, 2-for-25)
Darnell Coles (.077, 2-for-26, 2 BB)
Kent Hrbek (.143, 3-for-21)
Hates to face: Dave Henderson (.417, 20-for-48, 3 HR)
Rickey Henderson (.380, 27-for-71, 5 HR)
Tony Pena (.476, 10-for-21, 2 HR)

Miscellaneous statistics: Ground outs-to-air outs ratio: 0.96 last season, 1.16 for career. . . . Opponents grounded into 11 double plays in 138 opportunities (one per 13). . . . Allowed 45 doubles, 1 triple in 216⅔ innings. . . . Allowed 16 first-inning runs in 33 starts (4.09 ERA). . . . Batting support: 5.00 runs per start, 10th-highest average in majors. . . . Opposing base stealers: 14-for-23 (61%); 3 pickoffs, 0 balks.

Comments: Led the Jays with five wins during their 21–9 spurt from September 1 to the end of the season, but didn't start again until Game 4 of the World Series. . . . Became the 14th pitcher to win games as both a starter and a reliever in the same World Series. Only four others did it over the last 40 years: Bob Turley (1958), Harvey Haddix (1960), Dave McNally (1971), and Catfish Hunter (1972). . . . Career record is 79–47 in night games, but only 37–34 in day games. . . . Career rate of 2.14 walks per nine innings is 6th lowest among active pitchers (minimum: 1000 innings), behind Bret Saberhagen (1.83), Greg Swindell (1.91), Dennis Eckersley (2.06), Bill Wegman (2.07), and John Candelaria (2.09). . . . Rate of walks allowed per nine innings has risen in each of the last three seasons. Rates since 1989: 1.13, 1.28, 1.89, 2.45. . . . Limited left-handed batters to a .176 batting average, 2d lowest among left-handed pitchers last season (minimum: 100 AB). The leader? Look to the right. . . . Held leadoff hitters to a .228 on-base percentage, lowest among A.L. starters. . . . Someone in Ft. Lauderdale better introduce Key to his new batterymate, Matt Nokes. Although both have played in the same division in each of the last seven seasons, Nokes has never batted against Key during a regular-season game. . . . Most career innings among active pitchers who have never allowed a grand slam: Mike Boddicker (2069⅔), Roger Clemens (2031), Key (1695⅔), Greg Maddux (1442), Ted Higuera (1291⅓).

Mark Langston
Throws Left

California Angels	W-L	ERA	AB	H	HR	BB	SO	BA	SA	OBA
Season	13-14	3.66	852	206	14	74	174	.242	.343	.305
vs. Left-Handers			110	19	2	9	21	.173	.282	.252
vs. Right-Handers			742	187	12	65	153	.252	.352	.313
vs. Ground-Ballers			407	92	4	26	83	.226	.295	.273
vs. Fly-Ballers			445	114	10	48	91	.256	.387	.333
Home Games	9-7	3.61	492	122	9	31	97	.248	.346	.294
Road Games	4-7	3.71	360	84	5	43	77	.233	.339	.320
Grass Fields	12-12	3.69	741	177	13	64	150	.239	.341	.302
Artificial Turf	1-2	3.41	111	29	1	10	24	.261	.351	.328
April	1-1	10.29	67	25	2	3	11	.373	.582	.408
May	4-1	2.53	167	34	4	15	32	.204	.323	.272
June	3-3	2.47	170	40	4	15	33	.235	.329	.296
July	1-4	6.97	121	38	3	13	16	.314	.455	.375
August	3-2	2.90	144	30	1	16	31	.208	.292	.299
Sept./Oct.	1-3	2.52	183	39	0	12	51	.213	.251	.265
Leading Off Inn.			219	49	2	16	45	.224	.297	.286
Bases Empty			521	115	7	45	108	.221	.305	.288
Runners On			331	91	7	29	66	.275	.402	.332
Runners/Scor. Pos.			170	48	2	20	40	.282	.382	.355
Runners On/2 Out			132	30	3	15	32	.227	.326	.306
Scor. Pos./2 Out			78	15	1	10	22	.192	.244	.284
Late-Inning Pressure			103	21	1	9	22	.204	.282	.268
Leading Off			30	8	1	4	7	.267	.400	.353
Runners On			32	6	0	3	6	.188	.250	.257
Runners/Scor. Pos.			17	3	0	1	5	.176	.176	.222
First 9 Batters			260	65	3	23	51	.250	.319	.319
Second 9 Batters			260	61	4	20	53	.235	.342	.288
All Batters Thereafter			332	80	7	31	70	.241	.361	.308

Loves to face: Harold Baines (.139, 5-for-36, 1 HR, 0 BB)
Scott Leius (0-for-10)
Mickey Tettleton (.140, 6-for-43)
Hates to face: Dave Henderson (.421, 16-for-38, 3 HR)
Danny Tartabull (.360, 9-for-25, 2 HR, 8 BB)
Frank Thomas (.444, 8-for-18, 2 HR, 9 BB)

Miscellaneous statistics: Ground outs-to-air outs ratio: 1.31 last season, 1.03 for career. . . . Opponents grounded into 23 double plays in 161 opportunities (one per 7.0). . . . Allowed 38 doubles, 3 triples in 229 innings. . . . Allowed 19 first-inning runs in 32 starts (5.34 ERA). . . . Batting support: 3.53 runs per start, 5th-lowest average in A.L. . . . Opposing base stealers: 21-for-31 (68%); 11 pickoffs (most in A.L.), 0 balks.

Comments: Held left-handed batters to .173 batting average, lowest in the majors (minimum: 100 AB). Career average of .197 by opposing left-handed batters is the lowest in *Player Analysis* history (minimum: 750 AB). . . . Hasn't allowed more than two home runs to left-handers since 1986 and 1987, when he gave up his career high: four. Career totals: 183 HRs by right-handers (one per 35 at-bats); 20 by left-handers (one per 54 AB). . . . ERA was more than one run lower last season with John Orton catching (2.54 in 92 innings) than with Mike Fitzgerald (3.63 in 94⅓ innings). . . . Posted the major leagues' highest ERA during April; it was the 2d consecutive season in which he had a higher ERA in April than in any other month. . . . Allowed only one home run over his last 103 innings. . . . Averaged 2.91 walks per nine innings last season, more than a half-walk lower than his previous best mark (3.51 in 1991). That marks the 2d straight season in which he has improved by at least a half-walk per nine innings. . . . Has pitched no fewer than 223 innings in any of the last seven years. The only other pitchers to do that are Frank Viola and Roger Clemens. . . . Total of 13 wins matched Melido Perez for the lowest total to lead any A.L. club. . . . Was the Angels' only representative at last year's All-Star game. The last Angels player to start an All-Star game was Wally Joyner in 1986; every other club in the majors has had at least one starter since then.

Tim Leary
Throws Right

Yankees/Mariners	W-L	ERA	AB	H	HR	BB	SO	BA	SA	OBA
Season	8-10	5.36	511	131	12	87	46	.256	.386	.367
vs. Left-Handers			244	57	7	39	24	.234	.393	.336
vs. Right-Handers			267	74	5	48	22	.277	.378	.395
vs. Ground-Ballers			255	57	2	38	24	.224	.314	.323
vs. Fly-Ballers			256	74	10	49	22	.289	.457	.410
Home Games	3-5	5.37	206	52	3	44	19	.252	.359	.381
Road Games	5-5	5.36	305	79	9	43	27	.259	.403	.357
Grass Fields	3-7	5.16	291	73	8	51	26	.251	.378	.370
Artificial Turf	5-3	5.64	220	58	4	36	20	.264	.395	.363
April	2-1	3.14	97	23	1	8	6	.237	.309	.287
May	2-2	6.57	88	19	2	17	12	.216	.375	.336
June	1-2	3.57	116	24	4	20	15	.207	.336	.340
July	0-1	25.58	34	16	2	11	0	.471	.765	.600
August	1-0	4.09	39	10	0	11	5	.256	.282	.426
Sept./Oct.	2-4	4.89	137	39	3	20	8	.285	.423	.380
Leading Off Inn.			121	36	4	25	8	.298	.471	.426
Bases Empty			278	66	5	51	27	.237	.342	.361
Runners On			233	65	7	36	19	.279	.438	.374
Runners/Scor. Pos.			137	40	4	26	11	.292	.467	.386
Runners On/2 Out			87	27	3	19	4	.310	.494	.444
Scor. Pos./2 Out			61	17	2	14	3	.279	.459	.421
Late-Inning Pressure			17	5	0	5	2	.294	.353	.435
Leading Off			4	1	0	2	0	.250	.250	.500
Runners On			10	4	0	0	0	.400	.500	.364
Runners/Scor. Pos.			5	1	0	0	0	.200	.200	.167
First 9 Batters			180	54	6	34	19	.300	.439	.417
Second 9 Batters			177	36	5	25	11	.203	.362	.304
All Batters Thereafter			154	41	1	28	16	.266	.351	.378

Loves to face: Milt Cuyler (0-for-12)
              Gary Gaetti (.056, 1-for-18)
              Spike Owen (.059, 1-for-17)
Hates to face: Joe Carter (.611, 11-for-18, 4 HR)
              Andre Dawson (.360, 9-for-25, 3 HR, 0 BB)
              Luis Rivera (.700, 7-for-10, 1 HR)

Miscellaneous statistics: Ground outs-to-air outs ratio: 1.28 last season, 1.30 for career.... Opponents grounded into 18 double plays in 129 opportunities (one per 7.2).... Allowed 26 doubles, 2 triples in 141 innings.... Allowed 19 first-inning runs in 23 starts (7.04 ERA, 4th highest in A.L.).... Batting support: 4.35 runs per start.... Opposing base stealers: 27-for-32 (84%), 4th-most steals in A.L.; 0 pickoffs, 0 balks.

Comments: Averaged 6.19 strikeouts per nine innings in 1991, but only 2.94 last season, 2d lowest among pitchers with at least 120 innings. Only one other pitcher in major league history has had consecutive 120-inning seasons in which his average fell from above 6.00 to below 3.00: Charlie Sweeney (1885).... Walks per nine innings year by year since 1988: 2.20, 2.96, 3.38, 4.25, 5.55. He is the only pitcher in major league history whose average has risen by at least four-tenths of a walk in four straight seasons.... Walked 41 more batters than he struck out last season. Only three other pitchers have done that in the expansion era: Pete Broberg (1976), John D'Acquisto (1976), and Steve Blass (1973).... His ERA in road games was the highest in the majors.... Posted a 6.49 ERA in 1991, followed by a 5.36 mark last season. Since the end of World War II, only two other pitchers have had ERAs that high in consecutive seasons of at least 120 innings pitched: Al Nipper (1986–87) and Camilo Pascual (1955–56).... Compiled a record of 18–35 in three seasons with the Yankees; his .340 winning percentage was the lowest in franchise history (minimum: 50 decisions).... Ask yourself the following questions: *(1)* Am I good at my job? *(2)* How much did I earn last year? Then clear the room of any children and other breakable objects and consider this: Leary will make nearly six million dollars over the course of his current three-year contract. Ladies and gentlemen, we live in a strange society.

Craig Lefferts
Throws Left

Padres/Orioles	W-L	ERA	AB	H	HR	BB	SO	BA	SA	OBA
Season	14-12	3.76	759	214	19	41	104	.282	.411	.316
vs. Left-Handers			123	30	2	3	25	.244	.350	.258
vs. Right-Handers			636	184	17	38	79	.289	.424	.327
vs. Ground-Ballers			365	97	7	16	63	.266	.364	.295
vs. Fly-Ballers			394	117	12	25	41	.297	.454	.336
Home Games	7-6	3.67	365	103	9	20	48	.282	.405	.315
Road Games	7-6	3.84	394	111	10	21	56	.282	.416	.317
Grass Fields	10-9	3.80	555	156	13	31	77	.281	.398	.316
Artificial Turf	4-3	3.63	204	58	6	10	27	.284	.446	.318
April	2-2	5.09	73	23	3	5	10	.315	.548	.350
May	4-1	3.52	154	44	9	4	22	.286	.416	.325
June	3-2	2.62	126	32	2	5	18	.254	.341	.278
July	3-1	3.16	141	40	2	7	18	.284	.369	.318
August	1-3	4.75	138	41	5	9	13	.297	.478	.338
Sept./Oct.	1-3	4.09	127	34	3	6	23	.268	.370	.299
Leading Off Inn.			201	61	8	6	24	.303	.453	.324
Bases Empty			456	131	12	20	56	.287	.408	.317
Runners On			303	83	7	21	48	.274	.416	.315
Runners/Scor. Pos.			158	44	2	11	32	.278	.392	.314
Runners On/2 Out			130	41	4	11	21	.315	.477	.369
Scor. Pos./2 Out			85	26	1	7	15	.306	.424	.359
Late-Inning Pressure			48	17	1	0	2	.354	.438	.347
Leading Off			13	3	1	0	1	.231	.462	.231
Runners On			20	5	0	0	0	.250	.300	.238
Runners/Scor. Pos.			6	1	0	0	0	.167	.167	.143
First 9 Batters			264	66	7	14	47	.250	.386	.287
Second 9 Batters			259	77	5	13	35	.297	.405	.328
All Batters Thereafter			236	71	7	14	22	.301	.445	.336

Loves to face: Roberto Alomar (.091, 1-for-11)
              Keith Miller (0-for-6)
              Tony Pena (.174, 4-for-23)
Hates to face: Jack Clark (.455, 5-for-11, 1 2B, 4 HR)
              Glenn Davis (.318, 7-for-22, 4 2B, 3 HR)
              Tim Raines (.500, 11-for-22, 1 HR)

Miscellaneous statistics: Ground outs-to-air outs ratio: 1.02 last season, 0.87 for career.... Opponents grounded into 17 double plays in 145 opportunities (one per 8.5).... Allowed 33 doubles, 4 triples in 196⅓ innings.... Allowed 19 first-inning runs in 32 starts (4.60 ERA).... Batting support: 4.00 runs per start, (4.30 in N.L., 9th-highest average in league).... Opposing base stealers: 20-for-30 (67%); 6 pickoffs, 1 balk.

Comments: Pitched exclusively as a starter last season after making 542 consecutive relief appearances—the most *between starts* in major league history. He last started as a Cubs rookie in 1983. (Dave Righetti had a streak of 522 games between starts snapped last season, the 2d longest ever.)... Became the first pitcher in major league history to start 30 games in a season after having already accumulated at least 100 career saves.... Pitched the first and only complete game of his career on September 6, in his first start in the American League, having never pitched longer than five innings in relief in his nine-year career; he was three weeks shy of his 35th birthday. Only nine pitchers were older at the time of their first complete game; the most recent were Hoyt Wilhelm (1958 at 35), outfielder-turned-pitcher Johnny Lindell (1953 at 36), and the record holder: 42-year-old Satchel Paige (1948).... Pitched 609 games in the National League before making his A.L. debut. Nine other pitchers played at least 600 N.L. games before switching leagues, most recently Ron Reed and Phil Niekro in 1984. This April, Frank Tanana will become only the 2d pitcher to do so in the other direction; the other was Sparky Lyle.... Went 4–1 in May last season; had lost 16 of 17 decisions during May in his first nine seasons.... Has walked only three of the last 157 left-handed batters he has faced, dating back to July 26, 1991.

Kirk McCaskill — Throws Right

Chicago White Sox	W-L	ERA	AB	H	HR	BB	SO	BA	SA	OBA
Season	12-13	4.18	796	193	11	95	109	.242	.343	.325
vs. Left-Handers			379	106	6	47	43	.280	.391	.358
vs. Right-Handers			417	87	5	48	66	.209	.300	.295
vs. Ground-Ballers			421	99	3	50	57	.235	.297	.317
vs. Fly-Ballers			375	94	8	45	52	.251	.395	.334
Home Games	6-7	3.54	413	99	7	48	61	.240	.332	.321
Road Games	6-6	4.88	383	94	4	47	48	.245	.355	.330
Grass Fields	11-10	4.32	656	161	11	79	89	.245	.349	.328
Artificial Turf	1-3	3.50	140	32	0	16	20	.229	.314	.312
April	1-3	6.85	88	25	3	16	10	.284	.443	.390
May	2-1	2.30	159	33	1	12	23	.208	.258	.267
June	2-2	3.21	122	25	2	12	20	.205	.295	.287
July	1-2	7.63	118	36	3	20	10	.305	.441	.401
August	3-2	2.39	138	29	1	13	22	.210	.275	.282
Sept./Oct.	3-3	4.54	171	45	1	22	24	.263	.392	.347
Leading Off Inn.			194	39	0	23	25	.201	.247	.292
Bases Empty			445	95	4	55	61	.213	.281	.306
Runners On			351	98	7	40	48	.279	.422	.350
Runners/Scor. Pos.			171	51	3	26	27	.298	.468	.383
Runners On/2 Out			152	40	4	20	19	.263	.434	.349
Scor. Pos./2 Out			82	26	3	14	11	.317	.537	.417
Late-Inning Pressure			54	15	1	6	6	.278	.463	.365
Leading Off			17	4	0	2	3	.235	.353	.316
Runners On			16	5	0	2	0	.313	.500	.429
Runners/Scor. Pos.			7	3	0	1	0	.429	.857	.545
First 9 Batters			260	53	3	39	38	.204	.277	.307
Second 9 Batters			277	61	3	22	39	.220	.303	.281
All Batters Thereafter			259	79	5	34	32	.305	.452	.389

Loves to face: John Olerud (.056, 1-for-18)
Tony Pena (.053, 1-for-19)
Mike Stanley (0-for-11)

Hates to face: Greg Briley (.407, 11-for-27, 1 HR)
Jose Canseco (.325, 13-for-40, 4 HR)
Mike Devereaux (.409, 9-for-22, 2 HR)

Miscellaneous statistics: Ground outs-to-air outs ratio: 1.34 last season, 1.22 for career. . . . Opponents grounded into 12 double plays in 176 opportunities (one per 15). . . . Allowed 31 doubles, 8 triples (3d most in A.L.) in 209 innings. . . . Allowed 12 first-inning runs in 34 starts (2.91 ERA). . . . Batting support: 4.44 runs per start. . . . Opposing base stealers: 12-for-21 (57%); 4 pickoffs, 2 balks.

Comments: Opposing base stealers were 7-for-8 with Carlton Fisk behind the plate, but only 5-for-12 with Ron Karkovice catching. . . . For the fourth consecutive season, McCaskill's team scored fewer runs per game in his starts (4.44) than for other starters (4.59). . . . Ground outs-to-air outs ratio was 2.10 on his first pass through the batting order, 1.34 on his second pass, 0.82 thereafter. . . . Didn't throw a double-play grounder after the 6th inning. . . . Struck out at least a batter per inning in 28 starts over his first four seasons, but in only five starts in his four seasons since then. . . . Pitched 27 complete games in his first five seasons, but only three in 93 starts over the last three years. That includes 34 starts without a complete game last season, an American League record. . . . McCaskill and teammate Greg Hibbard (28 starts) became the first pitchers in White Sox history to start at least 25 games in a season without a complete game. The old Chisox "record" belonged to Cisco Carlos, who went 0-for-21 in 1968. . . . Has gone 69 starts since his last shutout, on August 28, 1990. . . . Allowed three homers to the Mariners in his second start of the 1992 season, but didn't allow more than one in any game for the rest of the season. . . . Career record is 11 games above .500 in day games (25–14), eight games below at night (65–73). . . . Career record is 10–2 vs. the Twins, 80–85 vs. the rest of the American League.

Ben McDonald — Throws Right

Baltimore Orioles	W-L	ERA	AB	H	HR	BB	SO	BA	SA	OBA
Season	13-13	4.24	863	213	32	74	158	.247	.421	.311
vs. Left-Handers			405	95	14	44	74	.235	.398	.311
vs. Right-Handers			458	118	18	30	84	.258	.441	.311
vs. Ground-Ballers			417	111	10	33	84	.266	.417	.322
vs. Fly-Ballers			446	102	22	41	74	.229	.424	.301
Home Games	5-8	4.90	453	113	21	39	73	.249	.455	.314
Road Games	8-5	3.54	410	100	11	35	85	.244	.383	.308
Grass Fields	12-11	4.02	786	186	27	72	141	.237	.399	.305
Artificial Turf	1-2	7.02	77	27	5	2	17	.351	.636	.370
April	2-0	3.47	86	18	3	12	19	.209	.349	.303
May	4-2	4.32	153	37	8	8	31	.242	.477	.279
June	1-3	6.08	147	38	8	9	26	.259	.524	.306
July	3-2	3.98	159	39	6	14	29	.245	.415	.318
August	2-3	4.58	155	45	5	13	21	.290	.465	.351
Sept./Oct.	1-3	3.02	163	36	2	18	32	.221	.276	.304
Leading Off Inn.			227	55	11	12	39	.242	.463	.289
Bases Empty			552	128	21	43	98	.232	.404	.296
Runners On			311	85	11	31	60	.273	.450	.337
Runners/Scor. Pos.			179	51	7	20	35	.285	.475	.350
Runners On/2 Out			130	31	6	18	33	.238	.408	.331
Scor. Pos./2 Out			83	21	4	11	20	.253	.434	.340
Late-Inning Pressure			33	7	2	4	6	.212	.424	.316
Leading Off			12	2	1	1	1	.167	.417	.231
Runners On			7	2	0	1	1	.286	.429	.444
Runners/Scor. Pos.			5	2	0	1	1	.400	.600	.500
First 9 Batters			283	55	8	27	50	.194	.311	.271
Second 9 Batters			280	73	11	21	62	.261	.464	.320
All Batters Thereafter			300	85	13	26	46	.283	.483	.340

Loves to face: Milt Cuyler (0-for-7, 4 SO)
Ron Karkovice (0-for-9)
Lou Whitaker (.063, 1-for-16)

Hates to face: Rickey Henderson (.500, 8-for-16, 2 HR)
Steve Sax (.545, 6-for-11, 1 HR)
Dave Winfield (.438, 7-for-16, 3 2B, 2 HR)

Miscellaneous statistics: Ground outs-to-air outs ratio: 1.01 last season, 0.97 for career. . . . Opponents grounded into 14 double plays in 131 opportunities (one per 9.4). . . . Allowed 44 doubles, 5 triples in 227 innings. . . . Allowed 8 first-inning runs in 35 starts (1.80 ERA, 4th lowest in A.L.) . . . Batting support: 5.06 runs per start, 9th-highest average in majors. . . . Opposing base stealers: 20-for-28 (71%); 1 pickoff, 2 balks.

Comments: Allowed 81 extra-base hits, the most in the majors. The last Orioles pitcher to allow that many XBHs: Scott McGregor (86 in 1983). . . . Total of 32 home runs was 2d highest in the majors; only Bill Gullickson allowed more (35). . . . Allowed 11 homers to batters leading off innings, the most in the majors. . . . His ERA was lower in the first inning than in any other last season. . . . One of eight pitchers with winning and losing streaks of at least five games last season. The others: Dave Fleming, Rheal Cormier, Bill Gullickson, Bill Krueger, Tom Gordon, Nolan Ryan, and Rick Sutcliffe. . . . Opposing base stealers were 13-for-16 with Chris Hoiles catching (81.3%), 6-for-10 with Jeff Tackett (60%). . . . ERA in home games was 2d highest in the majors, behind only Scott Sanderson (5.47). . . . Strikeout rate has risen every season since his debut in 1989; year by year: 3.68, 4.93, 6.06, 6.26. . . . Although he throws right-handed, opposing right-handed batters have hit for a higher average than left-handers in each of his four seasons in the majors. Career breakdown: .216 (one HR every 37 at-bats) by left-handed batters; .266 (one HR every 26 AB) by right-handers. . . . Career record of 22–26 since winning the first six decisions of his career (1989–90). . . . Most comparable statistical profile after each season suggests his disappointing career track to date: 1990—Juan Marichal; 1991—Carl Erskine; 1992—Reggie Cleveland.

Jack McDowell · Throws Right

Chicago White Sox	W-L	ERA	AB	H	HR	BB	SO	BA	SA	OBA
Season	20-10	3.18	983	247	21	75	178	.251	.379	.307
vs. Left-Handers			486	128	13	44	85	.263	.409	.328
vs. Right-Handers			497	119	8	31	93	.239	.350	.287
vs. Ground-Ballers			508	133	10	38	85	.262	.378	.317
vs. Fly-Ballers			475	114	11	37	93	.240	.381	.297
Home Games	9-5	2.77	439	103	9	35	83	.235	.346	.291
Road Games	11-5	3.53	544	144	12	40	95	.265	.406	.320
Grass Fields	18-9	3.30	806	199	20	63	148	.247	.378	.303
Artificial Turf	2-1	2.60	177	48	1	12	30	.271	.384	.328
April	5-0	3.00	140	31	6	4	24	.221	.393	.247
May	2-3	5.08	134	35	5	7	25	.261	.448	.308
June	4-0	3.14	167	44	4	16	26	.263	.407	.332
July	3-2	3.07	154	39	0	12	29	.253	.318	.308
August	4-2	2.25	178	44	5	18	33	.247	.371	.313
Sept./Oct.	2-3	3.05	210	54	1	18	41	.257	.357	.320
Leading Off Inn.			253	68	7	14	44	.269	.419	.307
Bases Empty			596	156	12	40	117	.262	.388	.313
Runners On			387	91	9	35	61	.235	.367	.299
Runners/Scor. Pos.			208	46	6	27	39	.221	.380	.311
Runners On/2 Out			161	31	3	19	32	.193	.292	.278
Scor. Pos./2 Out			96	16	2	15	21	.167	.260	.279
Late-Inning Pressure			103	23	1	8	23	.223	.282	.274
Leading Off			30	9	1	2	6	.300	.433	.344
Runners On			37	7	0	3	9	.189	.216	.238
Runners/Scor. Pos.			17	3	0	3	5	.176	.235	.273
First 9 Batters			286	78	8	16	48	.273	.441	.309
Second 9 Batters			274	64	9	25	56	.234	.394	.308
All Batters Thereafter			423	105	4	34	74	.248	.329	.305

Loves to face: Rafael Palmeiro (.107, 3-for-28)
Kevin Reimer (.053, 1-for-19, 1 3B)
Kevin Seitzer (.045, 1-for-22, 3 BB)

Hates to face: Roberto Alomar (.615, 8-for-13, 1 HR)
Rickey Henderson (.440, 11-for-25, 1 HR)
Don Mattingly (.435, 10-for-23, 1 HR)

Miscellaneous statistics: Ground outs-to-air outs ratio: 0.83 last season, 0.90 for career.... Opponents grounded into 12 double plays in 173 opportunities (one per 14).... Allowed 45 doubles, 9 triples (most in majors) in 260⅔ innings.... Allowed 18 first-inning runs in 34 starts (4.76 ERA).... Batting support: 4.85 runs per start.... Opposing base stealers: 29-for-45 (64%), 2d-most steals in A.L.; 8 pickoffs, 0 balks.

Comments: Became the White Sox's first 20-game-winner since 1983, when both LaMarr Hoyt (24) and Richard Dotson (22) reached that plateau. No White Sox pitcher has posted consecutive 20-win seasons since Jim Kaat (1974–75).... One of three pitchers to increase his total of wins in each of his last four seasons. The others: Mike Morgan and Bob Tewksbury. The last pitcher with a longer streak was Bob Walk (6 years, 1984–89).... His ERA has declined in each of those seasons as well; year by year since 1988: 3.97, 3.82, 3.41, 3.18.... One of three pitchers at least five games above the .500 mark in each of the last three seasons. The others: Jose Rijo and Roger Clemens (whose streak dates back to 1986).... He and Greg Maddux are the only pitchers to work 250-plus innings in each of the last two seasons.... Led majors in complete games for second consecutive season. The last White Sox pitcher to lead the majors in CGs in consecutive years was Red Faber (1921–22).... Completed four consecutive starts (Aug. 7–23); the only other pitcher with four in a row last season was Mark Langston. The last pitcher with a five-CG streak: Tom Browning (1989).... Was the only pitcher to throw two complete games against the Athletics last season.... His total of eight pickoffs ranked 2d among right-handed pitchers, behind Melido Perez (9).... Tied with Mike Mussina for A.L. lead in road wins.... Career total of 132 starts ranks third among active pitchers who have never appeared in relief, behind Tom Glavine (172) and John Smoltz (146).

Jose Mesa · Throws Right

Orioles/Indians	W-L	ERA	AB	H	HR	BB	SO	BA	SA	OBA
Season	7-12	4.59	619	169	14	70	62	.273	.397	.348
vs. Left-Handers			328	100	8	29	23	.305	.436	.363
vs. Right-Handers			291	69	6	41	39	.237	.354	.332
vs. Ground-Ballers			294	86	4	29	28	.293	.401	.361
vs. Fly-Ballers			325	83	10	41	34	.255	.394	.337
Home Games	2-5	4.40	297	84	6	32	26	.283	.391	.355
Road Games	5-7	4.77	322	85	8	38	36	.264	.404	.342
Grass Fields	4-9	4.98	471	130	11	60	44	.276	.399	.359
Artificial Turf	3-3	3.35	148	39	3	10	18	.264	.392	.311
April	1-2	3.26	81	23	3	3	9	.284	.469	.310
May	1-3	6.75	92	29	5	15	8	.315	.511	.414
June	1-3	5.32	88	23	1	5	5	.261	.386	.298
July	1-1	1.96	81	20	1	9	9	.247	.346	.319
August	1-1	4.38	138	36	2	20	15	.261	.355	.363
Sept./Oct.	2-2	5.35	139	38	2	18	16	.273	.360	.354
Leading Off Inn.			164	42	3	10	17	.256	.390	.303
Bases Empty			360	89	9	42	34	.247	.381	.328
Runners On			259	80	5	28	28	.309	.421	.376
Runners/Scor. Pos.			152	45	3	16	17	.296	.421	.356
Runners On/2 Out			108	34	3	14	12	.315	.472	.398
Scor. Pos./2 Out			71	21	2	9	7	.296	.479	.383
Late-Inning Pressure			31	9	0	2	4	.290	.355	.333
Leading Off			11	4	0	1	1	.364	.455	.417
Runners On			9	2	0	0	2	.222	.333	.222
Runners/Scor. Pos.			4	0	0	0	1	.000	.000	.000
First 9 Batters			222	57	6	25	27	.257	.378	.331
Second 9 Batters			212	55	4	28	18	.259	.382	.347
All Batters Thereafter			185	57	4	17	17	.308	.438	.371

Loves to face: Jeff Huson (0-for-9)
Edgar Martinez (0-for-10)
Matt Nokes (0-for-15)

Hates to face: Gregg Jefferies (.615, 8-for-13, 1 HR)
Kevin Maas (.615, 8-for-13, 1 HR)
Danny Tartabull (.833, 5-for-6, 3 2B)

Miscellaneous statistics: Ground outs-to-air outs ratio: 0.85 last season, 0.89 for career.... Opponents grounded into 15 double plays in 135 opportunities (one per 9.0).... Allowed 33 doubles, 1 triple in 160⅔ innings.... Allowed 12 first-inning runs in 27 starts (3.67 ERA).... Batting support: 4.44 runs per start.... Opposing base stealers: 14-for-22 (64%); 2 pickoffs, 0 balks.

Comments: Among active pitchers with at least 45 decisions, only Joe Boever (14–31, .311) and Matt Young (54–89, .378) have lower winning percentages than Mesa (17–28, .378).... Owns a 5.09 career ERA; only one other pitcher active in 1992 has a career ERA above 5.00 in 300 + innings: David West (5.45).... Among that same group, only three pitchers have walked more batters than they have struck out: Mesa (174 BB/167 SO), Pat Clements (160/158), and Mike Dunne (225/205).... No pitcher who has made his debut within the last 40 years and had a higher career total of walks than strikeouts won even 50 starts. The last to do so: Mickey McDermott, who pitched from 1948–61, with 840 walks and 757 strikeouts; 60 of his 69 career victories came as a starting pitcher. The last such pitchers to win 100 or more starts: Kirby Higbe (1937–50) and Mel Parnell (1947–56).... So for those with Jose Mesa rookie cards sheathed in two-ply plastic, this will come as good news: His walk rate has decreased in each of the last two seasons: 5.21 per nine innings in 1990, 4.51 in 1991, 3.92 last season.... Only A.L. pitcher with a record five games below .500 in each of the last two seasons.... Waived by the Orioles with a 3–8 record and a 5.19 ERA three days before the All-Star break, picked up by Cleveland, and started their first game after the break. That had to be a real confidence boost for the rest of the Indians staff.... Posted a 1–8 record with a 5.99 ERA in day games last season.

Bob Milacki   Throws Right

Baltimore Orioles	W-L	ERA	AB	H	HR	BB	SO	BA	SA	OBA
Season	6-8	5.84	472	140	16	44	51	.297	.481	.357
vs. Left-Handers			211	55	6	22	25	.261	.431	.329
vs. Right-Handers			261	85	10	22	26	.326	.521	.380
vs. Ground-Ballers			244	70	7	19	28	.287	.471	.336
vs. Fly-Ballers			228	70	9	25	23	.307	.491	.379
Home Games	4-4	6.00	254	76	10	17	33	.299	.492	.342
Road Games	2-4	5.66	218	64	6	27	18	.294	.468	.373
Grass Fields	6-8	5.77	451	133	15	41	51	.295	.477	.353
Artificial Turf	0-0	7.20	21	7	1	3	0	.333	.571	.440
April	1-2	5.33	107	28	5	12	14	.262	.467	.342
May	3-1	4.66	121	40	4	10	12	.331	.479	.382
June	1-2	6.90	127	39	5	11	15	.307	.535	.360
July	0-2	15.63	30	12	2	3	4	.400	.667	.441
August	0-0	0.00	0	0	0	0	0	.000	.000	.000
Sept./Oct.	1-1	3.86	87	21	0	8	6	.241	.356	.309
Leading Off Inn.			113	31	2	9	14	.274	.416	.328
Bases Empty			257	75	9	25	31	.292	.486	.357
Runners On			215	65	7	19	20	.302	.474	.357
Runners/Scor. Pos.			130	37	3	10	10	.285	.431	.333
Runners On/2 Out			82	23	6	8	5	.280	.549	.344
Scor. Pos./2 Out			53	15	2	5	3	.283	.434	.345
Late-Inning Pressure			24	7	3	1	3	.292	.708	.320
Leading Off			7	0	0	0	1	.000	.000	.000
Runners On			3	1	1	0	0	.333	1.333	.333
Runners/Scor. Pos.			0	0	0	0	0	—	—	—
First 9 Batters			185	63	5	14	26	.341	.508	.385
Second 9 Batters			156	47	6	16	11	.301	.519	.366
All Batters Thereafter			131	30	5	14	14	.229	.397	.308

Loves to face: Sandy Alomar, Jr. (0-for-13)
    Mike Gallego (.071, 1-for-14)
    Greg Vaughn (.105, 2-for-19, 1 HR)
Hates to face: Kent Hrbek (.375, 9-for-24, 3 2B, 3 HR)
    Carlos Martinez (.500, 9-for-18, 5 2B, 1 HR)
    Rafael Palmeiro (.571, 8-for-14, 1 HR)

Miscellaneous statistics: Ground outs-to-air outs ratio: 1.05 last season, 1.09 for career. . . . Opponents grounded into 13 double plays in 98 opportunities (one per 7.5). . . . Allowed 31 doubles, 4 triples in 115⅔ innings. . . . Allowed 21 first-inning runs in 20 starts (8.55 ERA, 2d highest in A.L.) . . . Batting support: 4.50 runs per start. . . . Opposing base stealers: 11-for-12 (92%); 0 pickoffs, 1 balk.

Comments: It may not have been *Five Guys Named Moe,* but the Orioles' rotation before the All-Star break included Rick Sutcliffe and four "Ms": Milacki, McDonald, Mesa, and Mussina. (Maniacs with masterful memories might mention the 1969 California Angels rotation: McGlothlin, Murphy, Messersmith, and May.) . . . ERA was the 3d highest in Orioles history (minimum: 100 innings), ahead of only Ken Dixon (6.43 in 1987) and Jose Mesa (5.97 in 1991). Remember, that's *Baltimore* history, not including the St. Louis Browns. . . . Failed to last five innings in seven of his 20 starts (35%), tying Kelly Downs for the highest such rate in the majors (minimum: 20 GS). . . . His average of 5.32 innings pitched per start was the 3d lowest among major league pitchers who started at least 20 games last season. . . . Orioles finally pulled the plug after he was bombed out in the 3d inning on July 12, the sixth consecutive start in which he failed to complete six innings. . . . Sent to Rochester at the All-Star break, posting a 7-1 record in nine starts there before his recall in September. . . . Allowed 16 home runs last season, all prior to his demotion. He pitched 22⅓ innings without a home run after his return. That's not too surprising, at least in this sense: His career record in September and October is seven games above .500 (11-4); for the rest of the calendar, it's seven below (26-33). . . . He even recorded the first and only save of his career in the Orioles' 1992 season finale.

Jeff Montgomery   Throws Right

Kansas City Royals	W-L	ERA	AB	H	HR	BB	SO	BA	SA	OBA
Season	1-6	2.18	297	61	5	27	69	.205	.279	.277
vs. Left-Handers			146	30	2	16	36	.205	.274	.293
vs. Right-Handers			151	31	3	11	33	.205	.285	.261
vs. Ground-Ballers			147	38	2	17	39	.259	.347	.333
vs. Fly-Ballers			150	23	3	10	30	.153	.213	.220
Home Games	1-4	1.85	187	44	4	8	44	.235	.337	.269
Road Games	0-2	2.65	110	17	1	19	25	.155	.182	.288
Grass Fields	0-2	3.08	86	15	1	16	20	.174	.209	.314
Artificial Turf	1-4	1.76	211	46	4	11	49	.218	.308	.259
April	0-2	2.45	41	10	0	3	8	.244	.293	.311
May	0-2	2.84	45	10	1	5	9	.222	.311	.294
June	0-0	0.00	50	7	0	1	11	.140	.180	.157
July	1-1	2.40	54	10	2	6	10	.185	.296	.279
August	0-1	3.55	43	7	2	8	12	.163	.302	.294
Sept./Oct.	0-0	2.12	64	17	0	4	19	.266	.297	.314
Leading Off Inn.			67	12	1	9	21	.179	.254	.276
Bases Empty			164	34	3	17	42	.207	.293	.286
Runners On			133	27	2	10	27	.203	.263	.265
Runners/Scor. Pos.			68	13	1	7	12	.191	.250	.260
Runners On/2 Out			59	11	1	6	8	.186	.271	.273
Scor. Pos./2 Out			34	5	0	5	5	.147	.176	.256
Late-Inning Pressure			229	52	4	23	55	.227	.301	.298
Leading Off			52	12	1	6	16	.231	.327	.310
Runners On			107	23	2	10	24	.215	.280	.283
Runners/Scor. Pos.			54	10	1	7	11	.185	.241	.270
First 9 Batters			292	61	5	26	69	.209	.284	.279
Second 9 Batters			5	0	0	1	0	.000	.000	.167
All Batters Thereafter			0	0	0	0	0	—	—	—

Loves to face: Chili Davis (0-for-12)
    Darryl Hamilton (0-for-11)
    Mike Stanley (0-for-9, 5 SO)
Hates to face: Jose Canseco (.444, 4-for-9, 1 HR)
    Greg Myers (3-for-3, 2 2B)
    Lou Whitaker (.625, 5-for-8, 1 HR)

Miscellaneous statistics: Ground outs-to-air outs ratio: 1.22 last season, 1.22 for career. . . . Opponents grounded into 7 double plays in 71 opportunities (one per 10). . . . Allowed 7 doubles, 0 triples in 82⅔ innings. . . . Saved 39 games in 46 opportunities (85%). . . . Stranded 13 inherited runners, allowed 7 to score (65%). . . . Opposing base stealers: 5-for-7 (71%); 0 pickoffs, 0 balks.

Comments: Recorded 11 saves in games in which he pitched at least two innings; no one else reached double figures in that category last season. . . . Total of saves has increased in every year since his debut for Pete Rose's Reds in 1987; year by year: 0, 1, 18, 24, 33, 39. Sammy Stewart is the only pitcher ever to post six consecutive increases in saves (1979-84). Others with five-year streaks are Tom Henke (1983-87) and Craig Lefferts (1986-90). . . . This goes with the territory: His winning percentage has decreased in each of the last four seasons; year-by-year records since 1988: 7-2 (.788), 7-3 (.700), 6-5 (.545), 4-4 (.500), 1-6 (.143). . . . Since saves became an official category in 1969, only two pitchers have increased both their saves total and their winning percentage in three consecutive seasons: Tippy Martinez (1981-83) and Greg A. Harris (1984-86). For more on this topic, see the Jeff Russell comments. . . . Strikeout rate has decreased in each of the last three seasons; from a career high of 9.20 per nine innings in 1989, it has dropped steadily: 8.97, 7.70, 7.51. . . . His 2.39 ERA with the Royals is the lowest in team history (minimum: 300 innings). . . . Career record is 19-11 with a 2.06 ERA at Royals Stadium, 8-11 with a 3.13 ERA elsewhere. . . . Royals relievers combined for 31 losses, tying the Mets for the most in the majors last season. Five different pitchers contributed at least four losses each: Montgomery (6), Tom Gordon (5), Mike Magnante, Rusty Meacham, and Steve Shifflett (4 each).

Mike Moore

Throws Right

Oakland A's	W-L	ERA	AB	H	HR	BB	SO	BA	SA	OBA
Season	17-12	4.12	852	229	20	103	117	.269	.399	.349
vs. Left-Handers			445	116	8	41	48	.261	.364	.326
vs. Right-Handers			407	113	12	62	69	.278	.437	.373
vs. Ground-Ballers			423	111	7	50	50	.262	.376	.342
vs. Fly-Ballers			429	118	13	53	67	.275	.422	.356
Home Games	7-4	3.55	400	112	12	42	48	.280	.412	.351
Road Games	10-8	4.61	452	117	8	61	69	.259	.387	.347
Grass Fields	13-11	4.28	715	199	17	88	99	.278	.408	.358
Artificial Turf	4-1	3.32	137	30	3	15	18	.219	.350	.301
April	4-0	1.51	132	31	0	13	19	.235	.303	.306
May	2-3	6.31	148	45	4	24	23	.304	.507	.408
June	1-4	6.75	124	39	6	22	15	.315	.532	.412
July	3-2	4.91	125	34	7	12	17	.272	.480	.343
August	3-1	2.79	157	38	1	15	23	.242	.293	.312
Sept./Oct.	4-2	3.22	166	42	2	17	20	.253	.319	.316
Leading Off Inn.			218	53	7	18	36	.243	.422	.307
Bases Empty			488	137	16	50	65	.281	.443	.355
Runners On			364	92	4	53	52	.253	.341	.342
Runners/Scor. Pos.			201	54	3	42	29	.269	.378	.383
Runners On/2 Out			155	36	1	28	24	.232	.310	.350
Scor. Pos./2 Out			97	26	1	23	13	.268	.381	.408
Late-Inning Pressure			63	9	1	5	7	.143	.206	.214
Leading Off			20	1	0	2	4	.050	.050	.174
Runners On			13	3	0	1	1	.231	.308	.267
Runners/Scor. Pos.			5	1	0	1	0	.200	.200	.286
First 9 Batters			286	78	5	30	47	.273	.385	.341
Second 9 Batters			265	70	5	41	35	.264	.385	.365
All Batters Thereafter			301	81	10	32	35	.269	.425	.342

Loves to face: Juan Gonzalez (.050, 1-for-20, 6 SO)
Gary Pettis (.152, 10-for-66)
Carlos Quintana (0-for-10)

Hates to face: Mike Greenwell (.517, 15-for-29)
Dan Pasqua (.415, 22-for-53, 2 HR)
Dave Winfield (.444, 16-for-36, 2 HR, 13 BB)

Miscellaneous statistics: Ground outs-to-air outs ratio: 1.38 last season, 1.28 for career.... Opponents grounded into 26 double plays in 178 opportunities (one per 6.8).... Allowed 43 doubles, 4 triples in 223 innings.... Allowed 18 first-inning runs in 36 starts (4.00 ERA).... Batting support: 4.94 runs per start.... Opposing base stealers: 19-for-32 (59%); 0 pickoffs, 0 balks.

Comments: The average time of his nine-inning starts was 3 hours, 7 minutes, the longest of any pitcher in the majors last season (minimum: 20 GS). Give Tony LaRussa a bit of the blame for that; under his strategic guidance, last season's A's became the first team in major league history to average more than three hours per nine-inning game.... Moore, David Cone, and Frank Tanana were the only starters to post winning records despite averages of more than four walks per nine innings (minimum: 15 decisions). Moore did so in 1991 as well; only two active pitchers have had more than two such seasons in their careers: Ron Darling (3) and, of course, Nolan Ryan (9).... Led the majors with 22 wild pitches, two shy of Jack Morris's A.L. record. Over the last four seasons, he has thrown 66 wild pitches; only one pitcher in major league history has had a higher four-year total: Tony Cloninger (73, 1963–66).... Started five double plays in the field, 2d most of any major league pitcher, behind Frank Viola (6).... Was 20 games above .500 during four seasons with the Athletics (66–46), but is still 10 games under the .500 mark for his career (132–142).... Has started at least 32 games (every fifth game over 162) in each of the last nine seasons. The only other active pitcher to have done that at any time during his career: Frank Viola, whose current 10-year streak is the longest since Gaylord Perry and Steve Carlton had their respective 15- and 11-year streaks snapped by Marvin Miller in 1981.

Jack Morris

Throws Right

Toronto Blue Jays	W-L	ERA	AB	H	HR	BB	SO	BA	SA	OBA
Season	21-6	4.04	902	222	18	80	132	.246	.358	.312
vs. Left-Handers			460	121	10	42	61	.263	.389	.322
vs. Right-Handers			442	101	8	38	71	.229	.326	.302
vs. Ground-Ballers			418	98	2	35	57	.234	.292	.301
vs. Fly-Ballers			484	124	16	45	75	.256	.415	.322
Home Games	11-2	3.09	464	98	7	43	63	.211	.310	.284
Road Games	10-4	5.11	438	124	11	37	69	.283	.409	.342
Grass Fields	8-4	5.27	334	93	8	30	51	.278	.398	.341
Artificial Turf	13-2	3.36	568	129	10	50	81	.227	.335	.295
April	3-1	3.69	142	31	6	13	24	.218	.401	.285
May	2-2	4.99	148	38	5	21	15	.257	.439	.353
June	4-0	4.11	131	35	3	14	15	.267	.344	.340
July	3-1	5.45	129	35	1	6	20	.271	.349	.319
August	5-1	3.07	153	38	1	15	28	.248	.327	.322
Sept./Oct.	4-1	3.40	199	45	2	11	30	.226	.307	.269
Leading Off Inn.			222	46	6	21	39	.207	.338	.279
Bases Empty			539	119	10	52	84	.221	.317	.294
Runners On			363	103	8	28	48	.284	.419	.339
Runners/Scor. Pos.			201	52	2	22	34	.259	.368	.330
Runners On/2 Out			141	27	3	17	19	.191	.312	.292
Scor. Pos./2 Out			83	14	0	13	15	.169	.229	.296
Late-Inning Pressure			103	23	3	6	12	.223	.369	.273
Leading Off			25	3	0	3	3	.120	.160	.241
Runners On			34	10	1	3	5	.294	.500	.351
Runners/Scor. Pos.			15	5	1	2	2	.333	.733	.412
First 9 Batters			274	71	5	26	37	.259	.365	.329
Second 9 Batters			266	69	6	32	39	.259	.368	.339
All Batters Thereafter			362	82	7	22	56	.227	.345	.279

Loves to face: Randy Milligan (.053, 1-for-19, 1 2B)
Steve Sax (.100, 2-for-20)
Paul Sorrento (0-for-15)

Hates to face: George Brett (.333, 27-for-81, 5 HR)
Cecil Fielder (.375, 6-for-16, 1 2B, 3 HR)
Wally Joyner (.432, 19-for-44, 1 HR)

Miscellaneous statistics: Ground outs-to-air outs ratio: 1.08 last season, 1.12 for career.... Opponents grounded into 15 double plays in 175 opportunities (one per 12).... Allowed 41 doubles, 3 triples in 240⅔ innings.... Allowed 26 first-inning runs in 34 starts (6.88 ERA, 5th highest in A.L.)... Batting support: 5.44 runs per start, 2d-highest average in majors.... Opposing base stealers: 22-for-38 (58%); 0 pickoffs, 2 balks.

Comments: Yearly won-lost records and winning percentages since 1989: 6–14 (.300); 15–18 (.455); 18–12 (.600); 21–6 (.778).... Became the 17th pitcher in major league history with three consecutive 15-win seasons at age 35 or older. Two pitchers had three-year streaks in their forties: Cy Young (1907–09) and Warren Spahn (1961–63).... Only four other starters have *increased* their victories in three consecutive seasons after the age of 35: Mordecai Brown (1913–15), Spahn (1956–58), Cal McLish (1961–63), and Tom Seaver (1983–85).... Became the first pitcher *of any age* to increase his winning percentage by at least 140 points in three consecutive seasons (minimum: 15 decisions each).... Second pitcher in this century to post three consecutive 15-win seasons for three different teams. Mike Torrez won 15 for Montreal in 1974, 20 for Balitmore in 1975, and 16 for Oakland in 1976. (Torrez then won 14 games for the Yankees in 1977, after arriving in late April.)... Shared the league lead in victories with Kevin Brown, becoming the 2d-oldest pitcher ever to lead the A.L. in wins. The oldest: Early Wynn, at 39 for the 1959 White Sox.... Was the only pitcher to defeat the Tigers four times last season (4–0). Lost his only decision against his longtime mates in 1991.... Went from 4–0 during the 1991 postseason to 0–3 in 1992; Tommy John remains the only pitcher in major league history to win a postseason game for three different clubs (Dodgers, Yankees, and Angels).

Mike Mussina — Throws Right

Baltimore Orioles	W-L	ERA	AB	H	HR	BB	SO	BA	SA	OBA
Season	18-5	2.54	888	212	16	48	130	.239	.348	.278
vs. Left-Handers			422	93	1	29	64	.220	.280	.269
vs. Right-Handers			466	119	15	19	66	.255	.410	.286
vs. Ground-Ballers			427	115	5	20	50	.269	.370	.299
vs. Fly-Ballers			461	97	11	28	80	.210	.328	.258
Home Games	7-3	2.65	419	100	9	19	66	.239	.356	.272
Road Games	11-2	2.44	469	112	7	29	64	.239	.341	.283
Grass Fields	15-4	2.25	708	161	10	38	116	.227	.323	.267
Artificial Turf	3-1	3.83	180	51	6	10	14	.283	.444	.319
April	3-0	2.37	112	27	2	8	10	.241	.357	.289
May	2-1	3.03	109	24	1	4	14	.220	.312	.246
June	3-2	2.01	157	33	3	8	24	.210	.306	.251
July	2-1	3.05	163	44	4	6	23	.270	.393	.294
August	3-1	3.56	165	44	5	11	27	.267	.424	.315
Sept./Oct.	5-0	1.56	182	40	1	11	32	.220	.291	.263
Leading Off Inn.			237	59	3	11	39	.249	.342	.282
Bases Empty			558	140	8	33	82	.251	.351	.294
Runners On			330	72	8	15	48	.218	.342	.250
Runners/Scor. Pos.			154	27	1	11	19	.175	.260	.227
Runners On/2 Out			140	24	2	7	22	.171	.264	.211
Scor. Pos./2 Out			77	11	0	5	9	.143	.182	.195
Late-Inning Pressure			90	18	1	4	12	.200	.267	.229
Leading Off			28	3	0	0	2	.107	.107	.107
Runners On			19	2	0	1	2	.105	.105	.136
Runners/Scor. Pos.			4	1	0	0	0	.250	.250	.167
First 9 Batters			269	67	3	16	50	.249	.331	.290
Second 9 Batters			262	62	9	16	36	.237	.397	.283
All Batters Thereafter			357	83	4	16	44	.232	.325	.264

Loves to face: Cecil Fielder (.063, 1-for-16)
Dan Pasqua (0-for-14)
Lou Whitaker (.056, 1-for-18, 1 2B)

Hates to face: Chuck Knoblauch (.545, 6-for-11, 1 HR)
Kirby Puckett (.400, 6-for-15, 1 HR)
Frank Thomas (.625, 10-for-16, 3 HR)

Miscellaneous statistics: Ground outs-to-air outs ratio: 0.75 last season, 0.76 for career.... Opponents grounded into 18 double plays in 161 opportunities (one per 8.9).... Allowed 39 doubles, 5 triples in 241 innings.... Allowed 6 first-inning runs in 32 starts (1.69 ERA), 3d lowest in A.L.... Batting support: 4.44 runs per start.... Opposing base stealers: 9-for-18 (50%); 1 pickoff, 0 balks.

Comments: The last American League sophomore pitcher to win as many as 18 games with an ERA as low as Mussina's was Ron Guidry (25–3, 1.74 in 1978). Three N.L. sophs did so in the interim: Orel Hershiser (19–3, 2.03 in 1985), Dwight Gooden (24–4, 1.53 in 1985), and David Cone (20–3, 2.22 in 1988).... His .783 winning percentage was the highest in the majors (minimum: 15 decisions).... Won 11 games on the road, tying Jack McDowell for most in the A.L.... Posted a 1.90 ERA in 123 innings with Chris Hoiles catching, compared to 3.26 in 116 innings with Jeff Tackett behind the plate.... Allowed an average of 9.78 base runners per nine innings, lowest rate of any A.L. pitcher who qualified for ERA title.... Averaged 1.79 walks per nine innings, 2d-lowest rate in A.L., behind Chris Bosio (1.71).... All-time Browns/Orioles franchise leaders, fewest walks per nine innings (minimum: 300 IP): Dick Hall, 1.47; Bill Reidy, 1.68; Red Donahue, 1.75; Robin Roberts, 1.81; Mussina, 1.89.... Scott Cooper hit the only home run against him in 422 at-bats by left-handed batters, the best rate by any pitcher in the majors last season.... Opponents' batting average with runners in scoring position was 2d lowest in majors, behind Kevin Appier (.167).... Career record is 7–1 with a 1.61 ERA in 12 starts on or after September 1.... Most comparable statistical profile, decade by decade: 1930s—Lon Warneke; 1940s—Don Newcombe; 1950s—Gene Conley; 1960s—Mel Stottlemyre; 1970s—Jon Matlack; 1980s—Jimmy Key; 1990s—Scott Erickson.

Charles Nagy — Throws Right

Cleveland Indians	W-L	ERA	AB	H	HR	BB	SO	BA	SA	OBA
Season	17-10	2.96	944	245	11	57	169	.260	.346	.300
vs. Left-Handers			424	106	5	27	68	.250	.330	.292
vs. Right-Handers			520	139	6	30	101	.267	.360	.308
vs. Ground-Ballers			521	144	3	29	83	.276	.345	.314
vs. Fly-Ballers			423	101	8	28	86	.239	.348	.284
Home Games	8-4	2.34	503	126	5	29	95	.250	.330	.291
Road Games	9-6	3.67	441	119	6	28	74	.270	.365	.312
Grass Fields	15-7	2.64	778	194	9	45	140	.249	.330	.289
Artificial Turf	2-3	4.53	166	51	2	12	29	.307	.422	.352
April	3-1	1.63	142	32	0	8	27	.225	.282	.270
May	3-2	3.38	173	51	2	11	27	.295	.376	.333
June	3-1	1.99	148	38	1	4	22	.257	.304	.273
July	2-2	2.95	136	39	1	11	22	.287	.382	.336
August	2-4	4.34	186	48	3	13	40	.258	.382	.307
Sept./Oct.	4-0	3.14	159	37	4	10	31	.233	.340	.278
Leading Off Inn.			248	64	3	13	49	.258	.359	.295
Bases Empty			567	152	8	31	106	.268	.376	.307
Runners On			377	93	3	26	63	.247	.302	.291
Runners/Scor. Pos.			208	56	2	16	46	.269	.337	.312
Runners On/2 Out			147	31	0	14	28	.211	.252	.284
Scor. Pos./2 Out			99	24	0	11	22	.242	.283	.324
Late-Inning Pressure			91	29	0	4	13	.319	.352	.351
Leading Off			29	10	0	3	.345	.379	.345	
Runners On			37	8	0	2	5	.216	.216	.268
Runners/Scor. Pos.			13	2	0	1	1	.154	.154	.250
First 9 Batters			274	61	2	22	69	.223	.318	.283
Second 9 Batters			273	72	3	17	41	.264	.341	.303
All Batters Thereafter			397	112	6	18	59	.282	.370	.311

Loves to face: Jose Canseco (0-for-12)
Matt Nokes (.067, 1-for-15, 1 2B)
David Segui (0-for-8)

Hates to face: Greg Gagne (.529, 9-for-17)
Luis Polonia (.556, 10-for-18)
Luis Sojo (.700, 7-for-10, 1 HR)

Miscellaneous statistics: Ground outs-to-air outs ratio: 1.95 last season (5th highest in A.L.), 1.65 for career.... Opponents grounded into 34 double plays in 185 opportunities (one per 5.4), 3d-best rate in A.L.... Allowed 41 doubles, 4 triples in 252 innings.... Allowed 7 first-inning runs in 33 starts (1.91 ERA).... Batting support: 4.09 runs per start.... Opposing base stealers: 12-for-27 (44%); 2 pickoffs, 0 balks.

Comments: The average time of his nine-inning starts was 2 hours, 38 minutes—15 minutes shorter than the major league average (2:53). The only A.L. pitcher with a lower average (minimum: 20 GS) was Bert Blyleven (2:34). Rounding out the fastest five: Dave Fleming (2:40), Scott Erickson (2:40), and Erik Hanson (2:41).... Nagy and Fleming went head to head on August 25 and produced one of only two A.L. games played in less than two hours last season (1:55). In 1984, there were 40 nine-inning games played in less than two hours, compared to only six last season.... Hasn't allowed a first-inning home run in his last 40 starts (since Sept. 12, 1991).... Allowed one home run every 22.9 innings, the 3d-lowest rate in the league. The two lower marks: Juan Guzman (one every 30.1 IP) and Kevin Brown (24.2).... ERA in home games was 3d lowest in league.... Has posted a lower ERA in home games than he has on the road in each of his three seasons in the majors. Career ERA at Cleveland Stadium (3.18) is more than a run lower than elsewhere (4.30).... Career record is 27–20 on grass fields, 2–9 on artificial turf. And that's more than a home-field advantage; even on foreign grass, he's 11–8.... A key to Nagy's success: He recorded more ground outs than fly outs in 30 of 33 starts last season, including each of his last 18. Career figures: 24–20 with a 2.84 ERA in 54 starts with more ground outs than fly outs; 5–9 with a 6.75 ERA in 20 other starts.... Most comparable statistical profile: Dennis Leonard (through 1976).

Jaime Navarro

Throws Right

Milwaukee Brewers	W-L	ERA	AB	H	HR	BB	SO	BA	SA	OBA
Season	17-11	3.33	912	224	14	64	100	.246	.351	.295
vs. Left-Handers			435	112	6	32	46	.257	.370	.304
vs. Right-Handers			477	112	8	32	54	.235	.333	.288
vs. Ground-Ballers			434	114	5	30	50	.263	.357	.309
vs. Fly-Ballers			478	110	9	34	50	.230	.345	.283
Home Games	9-4	3.29	411	104	6	26	49	.253	.341	.299
Road Games	8-7	3.36	501	120	8	38	51	.240	.359	.293
Grass Fields	14-7	3.18	722	180	8	55	82	.249	.339	.303
Artificial Turf	3-4	3.88	190	44	6	9	18	.232	.395	.266
April	1-2	4.50	107	29	0	9	6	.271	.299	.333
May	3-2	3.95	172	45	4	8	16	.262	.436	.293
June	4-2	3.77	159	41	6	14	16	.258	.415	.318
July	3-0	1.60	131	18	0	10	15	.137	.168	.196
August	3-3	2.35	164	39	3	7	22	.238	.341	.276
Sept./Oct.	3-2	4.09	179	52	1	16	25	.291	.385	.343
Leading Off Inn.			244	58	5	12	25	.238	.352	.276
Bases Empty			589	139	11	36	68	.236	.350	.282
Runners On			323	85	3	28	32	.263	.353	.318
Runners/Scor. Pos.			180	45	2	20	18	.250	.350	.312
Runners On/2 Out			142	34	2	13	17	.239	.366	.308
Scor. Pos./2 Out			90	23	2	11	10	.256	.400	.343
Late-Inning Pressure			92	20	1	6	13	.217	.326	.263
Leading Off			30	7	1	1	5	.233	.367	.258
Runners On			23	8	0	2	0	.348	.565	.385
Runners/Scor. Pos.			11	5	0	2	0	.455	.818	.500
First 9 Batters			271	58	3	28	34	.214	.284	.284
Second 9 Batters			277	71	3	16	27	.256	.339	.303
All Batters Thereafter			364	95	8	20	39	.261	.409	.298

Loves to face: Albert Belle (0-for-9, 5 SO)
Ron Karkovice (0-for-10)
Tim Raines (.067, 1-for-15)

Hates to face: Julio Franco (.563, 9-for-16)
Steve Sax (.464, 13-for-28, 0 SO)
Danny Tartabull (.643, 9-for-14, 3 HR, 3 SO)

Miscellaneous statistics: Ground outs-to-air outs ratio: 1.10 last season, 1.18 for career. . . . Opponents grounded into 23 double plays in 157 opportunities (one per 6.8). . . . Allowed 42 doubles, 6 triples in 246 innings. . . . Allowed 12 first-inning runs in 34 starts (3.18 ERA). . . . Batting support: 4.50 runs per start. . . . Opposing base stealers: 17-for-28 (61%); 0 pickoffs, 0 balks.

Comments: Every one of Milwaukee's top five starters averaged fewer than 2.7 walks per nine innings: Ricky Bones, 2.64; Chris Bosio, 1.71; Cal Eldred, 2.06; Jaime Navarro, 2.34; Bill Wegman, 1.89. The last teams to do that, both in 1977: Boston (Tiant, Jenkins, Cleveland, Wise, and Lee) and Los Angeles (Sutton, Rau, John, Hooton, and Rhoden). . . . Didn't walk any of the last 107 batters he faced leading off innings. . . . Made 10 consecutive starts without allowing a home run (June 28–Aug. 16), one short of the league high for last season, set by Eric King (May 31–Sept. 8). Two other pitchers had 10-game streaks: Cal Eldred (July 19–Sept. 13) and Mark Gubicza (July 23–Sept. 10). . . . Threw three shutouts, all during the second half of the season. His ERA of 2.64 after the All-Star break ranked 5th in the league. . . . Posted a 2.75 ERA in 163⅔ innings with B. J. Surhoff catching, compared to a 4.48 mark in 81⅓ innings with other catchers. . . . Strikeout rate has decreased in each season since his debut in 1989, from a high of 4.60 to last season's 3.66 mark. But who cares—his winning percentage has increased in each of those seasons. That's an unlikely parlay; no other active pitcher has ever raised his winning percentage for three straight seasons with a declining strikeout rate (minimum: 100 innings in each). The last pitcher to do so was Bob Forsch (1979–81); only one pitcher ever had a four-year streak: Rick Langford (1977–80). . . . Career record is 28–15 at County Stadium, 19–23 on the road.

Jeff Nelson

Throws Right

Seattle Mariners	W-L	ERA	AB	H	HR	BB	SO	BA	SA	OBA
Season	1-7	3.44	290	71	7	44	46	.245	.372	.353
vs. Left-Handers			108	31	2	25	18	.287	.398	.418
vs. Right-Handers			182	40	5	19	28	.220	.357	.311
vs. Ground-Ballers			148	37	2	23	24	.250	.345	.366
vs. Fly-Ballers			142	34	5	21	22	.239	.401	.339
Home Games	1-2	3.46	146	34	2	14	23	.233	.336	.309
Road Games	0-5	3.43	144	37	5	30	23	.257	.410	.393
Grass Fields	0-4	4.06	116	32	5	26	15	.276	.466	.418
Artificial Turf	1-3	3.06	174	39	2	18	31	.224	.310	.305
April	0-1	3.24	29	6	0	4	3	.207	.241	.361
May	0-1	4.91	42	12	1	3	6	.286	.429	.326
June	0-1	4.02	59	17	2	10	8	.288	.458	.400
July	0-1	3.86	52	15	2	6	8	.288	.462	.356
August	1-0	0.53	53	6	0	7	11	.113	.208	.230
Sept./Oct.	0-3	4.80	55	15	2	14	10	.273	.382	.423
Leading Off Inn.			60	18	0	5	9	.300	.417	.373
Bases Empty			136	35	5	13	23	.257	.426	.344
Runners On			154	36	2	31	23	.234	.325	.360
Runners/Scor. Pos.			103	22	1	26	16	.214	.282	.364
Runners On/2 Out			63	10	1	20	13	.159	.238	.369
Scor. Pos./2 Out			44	6	0	19	11	.136	.182	.397
Late-Inning Pressure			112	26	1	23	19	.232	.313	.374
Leading Off			23	6	0	3	4	.261	.261	.370
Runners On			60	16	0	18	8	.267	.367	.430
Runners/Scor. Pos.			39	9	0	15	5	.231	.308	.436
First 9 Batters			275	69	6	43	44	.251	.375	.355
Second 9 Batters			15	2	1	1	2	.133	.333	.316
All Batters Thereafter			0	0	0	0	0	—	—	—

Loves to face: Gary Gaetti (0-for-5)
Leo Gomez (0-for-4, 2 SO)

Hates to face: Harold Baines (1-for-1, 1 HR, 1 BB)
Robin Yount (.600, 3-for-5, 1 2B, 1 HR)

Miscellaneous statistics: Ground outs-to-air outs ratio: 1.27 last season, 1.27 for career. . . . Opponents grounded into 10 double plays in 75 opportunities (one per 7.5). . . . Allowed 10 doubles, 3 triples in 81 innings. . . . Stranded 45 inherited runners, allowed 18 to score (71%). . . . Opposing base stealers: 4-for-7 (57%); 0 pickoffs, 0 balks.

Comments: Led American League rookie pitchers with 66 appearances; the only N.L. rookie with a higher total: St. Louis's Mike Perez (77). . . . Total of six saves ranked second among A.L. rookies to Roberto Hernandez (12). . . . His ERA ranked fourth among A.L. rookies (minimum: 81 innings), behind Cal Eldred (1.79), Rusty Meacham (2.74), and Dave Fleming (3.39). . . . Fleming and Nelson combined for 17 of the 23 losses by Mariners rookies last season. (Of course, the difference in wins—Fleming had 17, Nelson 1—made it a little easier for Seattle to accept Fleming's 10 losses than Nelson's seven.) Only Phillies rookies posted a higher total of losses (35). . . . The last rookie with more losses in relief than Nelson was Mike Schooler, who dropped eight decisions for Seattle in 1988. The Mariners record for losses by a rookie reliever is nine, by Enrique Romo (1977). . . . Only four rookies ever lost 10 or more games in relief: Frank Funk (11–11 as a reliever in 1961), Ken Sanders (6–10 in 1966), Dan McGinn (7–10 in 1969), and Todd Worrell (9–10 in 1986). . . . Wasn't on the Mariners' opening-day roster, but joined the team on April 16. . . . Listed in the Mariners' media guide at six feet, eight inches tall. Only three players active in 1992 are taller: Terry Bross (6'9"), Eric Hillman (6'10"), and Randy Johnson (6'10", who probably calls his teammate Nelson "Shorty"). . . . Anyone remember the early Lite Beer ad with Wilt and Lurch?

Steve Olin
Throws Right

Cleveland Indians	W-L	ERA	AB	H	HR	BB	SO	BA	SA	OBA
Season	8-5	2.34	321	80	8	27	47	.249	.355	.314
vs. Left-Handers			145	47	1	13	19	.324	.400	.385
vs. Right-Handers			176	33	7	14	28	.188	.318	.254
vs. Ground-Ballers			141	35	0	13	20	.248	.277	.316
vs. Fly-Ballers			180	45	8	14	27	.250	.417	.311
Home Games	4-3	4.37	176	53	8	16	27	.301	.472	.361
Road Games	4-2	0.21	145	27	0	11	20	.186	.214	.256
Grass Fields	8-4	2.67	283	73	8	22	40	.258	.378	.318
Artificial Turf	0-1	0.00	38	7	0	5	7	.184	.184	.279
April	0-1	2.53	36	8	1	4	6	.222	.306	.317
May	0-2	3.86	44	12	1	5	6	.273	.364	.353
June	2-0	1.46	42	9	1	5	6	.214	.357	.306
July	3-0	1.42	74	19	1	2	9	.257	.338	.276
August	1-1	4.38	46	11	3	4	8	.239	.457	.300
Sept./Oct.	2-1	1.61	79	21	1	7	12	.266	.329	.333
Leading Off Inn.			65	15	0	3	11	.231	.277	.275
Bases Empty			167	44	3	11	27	.263	.359	.317
Runners On			154	36	5	16	20	.234	.351	.310
Runners/Scor. Pos.			87	16	1	10	15	.184	.230	.277
Runners On/2 Out			78	24	3	5	11	.308	.436	.357
Scor. Pos./2 Out			50	11	1	4	10	.220	.280	.291
Late-Inning Pressure			213	56	7	20	30	.263	.380	.335
Leading Off			43	12	0	2	6	.279	.326	.326
Runners On			107	23	4	15	15	.215	.346	.317
Runners/Scor. Pos.			61	11	1	9	11	.180	.246	.297
First 9 Batters			297	74	7	24	45	.249	.350	.310
Second 9 Batters			24	6	1	3	2	.250	.417	.357
All Batters Thereafter			0	0	0	0	0	—	—	—

Loves to face: Mike Devereaux (.100, 1-for-10)
Mike Macfarlane (0-for-7)
Terry Steinbach (.077, 1-for-13)
Hates to face: Harold Baines (6-for-6, 1 BB)
Wade Boggs (.364, 4-for-11, 2 HR)
Juan Gonzalez (.600, 6-for-10, 2 2B, 2 HR)

Miscellaneous statistics: Ground outs-to-air outs ratio: 1.81 last season, 2.45 for career. . . . Opponents grounded into 15 double plays in 76 opportunities (one per 5.1). . . . Allowed 8 doubles, 1 triple in 88⅓ innings. . . . Saved 29 games in 36 opportunities (81%). . . . Stranded 38 inherited runners, allowed 11 to score (78%). . . . Opposing base stealers: 2-for-6 (33%); 0 pickoffs, 1 balk.

Comments: Baines's perfect mark against him is the only performance of 6-for-6 or better (if that's the right word) of any active batter against any active pitcher. The only 5-for-5 among A.L. players is Ken Griffey vs. Carl Willis. . . . Maybe Baines will be able to help his new Baltimore teammates score a run against Olin, something the Orioles haven't managed in the 25⅔ innings Olin has worked against them. . . . Three of his eight victories followed blown save opportunities. The only other relievers to "vulture" three wins: Stan Belinda and Jeff Reardon. . . . Indians relievers won 32 games, a club record, and the most of any bullpen in the A.L. last season. The last time Cleveland's bullpen led the league in wins was 1961. . . . Has earned either a save or a victory in more than half of Cleveland's wins since the 1991 All-Star break (9 wins, 46 saves in 107 Indians victories). . . . Has earned more saves on the road than he has at home in each of his four seasons in the majors. . . . Opposing left-handed batters have hit .300 or better in each of his four seasons; right-handers have never batted above .251. Career breakdown: .319 by left-handers, .221 by right-handers. . . . Most appearances in a season by Cleveland pitchers: Sid Monge, 76 (1979); Olin, 72 (1992); Derek Lilliquist, 71 (1992); Don McMahon, 70 (1964). . . . Didn't walk any of the last 46 batters he faced leading off innings. . . . Faced just one batter in five of his saves. Jeff Reardon was the only pitcher in either league with more one-batter saves (6).

Gregg Olson
Throws Right

Baltimore Orioles	W-L	ERA	AB	H	HR	BB	SO	BA	SA	OBA
Season	1-5	2.05	218	46	3	24	58	.211	.280	.287
vs. Left-Handers			113	22	0	9	30	.195	.230	.252
vs. Right-Handers			105	24	3	15	28	.229	.333	.322
vs. Ground-Ballers			102	21	1	9	25	.206	.255	.270
vs. Fly-Ballers			116	25	2	15	33	.216	.302	.301
Home Games	1-1	1.38	111	20	2	12	28	.180	.261	.258
Road Games	0-4	2.83	107	26	1	12	30	.243	.299	.317
Grass Fields	1-2	1.33	184	32	2	21	51	.174	.228	.257
Artificial Turf	0-3	7.36	34	14	1	3	7	.412	.559	.447
April	0-1	2.35	27	8	1	4	9	.296	.444	.387
May	0-1	1.15	58	14	1	5	13	.241	.293	.302
June	1-0	1.86	30	3	1	4	11	.100	.267	.206
July	0-2	6.75	24	8	0	4	5	.333	.375	.429
August	0-1	2.19	46	10	0	2	9	.217	.261	.240
Sept./Oct.	0-0	0.84	33	3	0	5	11	.091	.091	.211
Leading Off Inn.			44	10	0	5	10	.227	.318	.306
Bases Empty			112	26	2	13	29	.232	.330	.312
Runners On			106	20	1	11	29	.189	.226	.261
Runners/Scor. Pos.			63	11	0	7	18	.175	.190	.250
Runners On/2 Out			47	8	0	5	13	.170	.170	.250
Scor. Pos./2 Out			29	5	0	5	7	.172	.172	.294
Late-Inning Pressure			173	36	3	17	46	.208	.295	.276
Leading Off			35	8	0	4	8	.229	.343	.308
Runners On			83	16	1	7	22	.193	.241	.250
Runners/Scor. Pos.			46	8	0	5	13	.174	.196	.245
First 9 Batters			218	46	3	24	58	.211	.280	.287
Second 9 Batters			0	0	0	0	0	—	—	—
All Batters Thereafter			0	0	0	0	0	—	—	—

Loves to face: Ellis Burks (0-for-10)
Pete O'Brien (.071, 1-for-14)
Ruben Sierra (0-for-10)
Hates to face: Brian Harper (.625, 5-for-8, 3 SO)
Mark McGwire (.444, 4-for-9, 1 HR, 3 SO)
Danny Tartabull (.417, 5-for-12, 4 SO)

Miscellaneous statistics: Ground outs-to-air outs ratio: 1.64 last season, 1.06 for career. . . . Opponents grounded into 8 double plays in 52 opportunities (one per 6.5). . . . Allowed 4 doubles, 1 triple in 61⅓ innings. . . . Saved 36 games in 45 opportunities (80%). . . . Stranded 25 inherited runners, allowed 5 to score (83%), 4th-highest rate in A.L. . . . Opposing base stealers: 10-for-10 (100%); 2 pickoffs, 0 balks.

Comments: Career rate of one home run every 33.9 innings pitched is the best among active players (minimum: 300 IP). The last pitcher with a better career rate was Doug Sisk (one HR every 34.9 IP). . . . Hasn't allowed a home run to a left-handed batter since Mel Hall took him deep on May 26, 1991, a span of 108 LH batters. . . . Selected in the June 1988 draft; was the only player chosen in that draft to appear in the majors that season. Played only 16 games in the minors before debuting with the Orioles. . . . Recorded the 100th save of his career on May 3 last season, at the age of 25—more than a year younger than anyone else in major league history at the time of his 100th save. . . . Four weeks later, he became the all-time franchise leader in saves (131), but he ranks only 16th in relief wins (17). The leader: Dick Hall (58). Olson ranks eighth with 19 relief losses; the leader: Tippy Martinez (40). . . . Career average of 8.93 strikeouts per nine innings is the best in franchise history, more than a strikeout better than the runner-up, junkballer Stu Miller (7.76). . . . Strikeout rate has decreased in each of the last three seasons; year by year since 1989: 9.53, 8.96, 8.80, 8.51. . . . Opposing left-handed batters have a career batting average of .187, 2d lowest in *Player Analysis* history (minimum: 500 AB), behind Bryan Harvey (.177). . . . Some career breakdowns: 14–10 with a 1.94 ERA on grass fields; 3–9, 4.23 ERA on artificial turf; 2–10, 3.98 ERA in day games; 15–9, 1.75 ERA at night.

Dave Otto

Throws Left

Cleveland Indians	W-L	ERA	AB	H	HR	BB	SO	BA	SA	OBA
Season	5-9	7.06	330	110	12	33	32	.333	.494	.395
vs. Left-Handers			54	19	1	5	3	.352	.481	.407
vs. Right-Handers			276	91	11	28	29	.330	.496	.392
vs. Ground-Ballers			147	55	4	16	12	.374	.510	.439
vs. Fly-Ballers			183	55	8	17	20	.301	.481	.358
Home Games	3-2	6.63	149	48	8	14	18	.322	.550	.380
Road Games	2-7	7.42	181	62	4	19	14	.343	.448	.406
Grass Fields	5-7	5.99	294	93	9	30	31	.316	.463	.382
Artificial Turf	0-2	18.90	36	17	3	3	1	.472	.750	.500
April	2-2	6.00	99	32	3	7	10	.323	.434	.374
May	1-1	8.40	60	21	3	7	9	.350	.567	.412
June	1-4	5.65	114	32	2	12	12	.281	.395	.349
July	0-0	0.00	0	0	0	0	0	.000	.000	.000
August	1-2	10.66	57	25	4	7	1	.439	.719	.500
Sept./Oct.	0-0	0.00	0	0	0	0	0	.000	.000	.000
Leading Off Inn.			84	27	2	5	9	.321	.452	.360
Bases Empty			186	57	3	16	19	.306	.409	.361
Runners On			144	53	9	17	13	.368	.604	.436
Runners/Scor. Pos.			89	33	6	9	6	.371	.640	.424
Runners On/2 Out			57	24	4	6	7	.421	.702	.484
Scor. Pos./2 Out			37	15	2	5	4	.405	.649	.476
Late-Inning Pressure			5	3	1	0	0	.600	1.200	.600
Leading Off			1	0	0	0	0	.000	.000	.000
Runners On			3	2	1	0	0	.667	1.667	.667
Runners/Scor. Pos.			1	1	1	0	0	1.000	4.000	1.000
First 9 Batters			133	40	5	19	14	.301	.436	.390
Second 9 Batters			118	42	1	9	11	.356	.458	.402
All Batters Thereafter			79	28	6	5	7	.354	.646	.393

Loves to face: Mike Devereaux (.100, 1-for-10)
Mark McGwire (0-for-8)
Kevin Seitzer (0-for-7)

Hates to face: Chris Hoiles (.714, 5-for-7, 2 HR)
Kirby Puckett (.571, 4-for-7, 2 HR)
Gary Thurman (.556, 5-for-9, 3 SO)

Miscellaneous statistics: Ground outs-to-air outs ratio: 1.60 last season, 1.70 for career.... Opponents grounded into 16 double plays in 74 opportunities (one per 4.6).... Allowed 17 doubles, 0 triples in 80⅓ innings.... Allowed 9 first-inning runs in 16 starts (5.06 ERA).... Batting support: 3.06 runs per start.... Opposing base stealers: 11-for-13 (85%); 1 pickoff, 0 balks.

Comments: Only two other pitchers in Indians history posted ERAs of 7.00 or higher in a season of 80-plus innings: Milt Shoffner (7.94) and Jake Miller (7.16), both in 1930.... Was 0-4 with a 9.59 ERA in seven appearances in day games last season (5 starts). Career day-game figures: 0-5, 5.91 ERA in 14 games (8 starts).... His 16 starts were the most of any A.L. pitcher who didn't last into the eighth inning even once last season.... Only two A.L. pitchers averaged fewer than five innings per start (minimum: 15 GS): Otto (4.92) and teammate Scott Scudder (4.91). Only five other teams in major league history had two 15-game starters who lasted less than five innings per start: 1935 Browns (Fay Thomas, 4.53, and Dick Coffman, 4.91); 1956 Senators (Bob Wiesler, 4.68, and Dean Stone, 4.70); 1976 Expos (Clay Kirby, 4.38, and Dan Warthen, 4.94); 1982 Red Sox (Bruce Hurst, 4.54, and Chuck Rainey, 4.99); 1985 Braves (Len Barker, 3.94, and Pascual Perez, 4.33).... Batting average by opposing ground-ball hitters was the highest against any A.L. pitcher in the 18-year history of *The Player Analysis*.... Made his major league debut on Sept. 8, 1987—two days after Tim Belcher, three days before Jay Buhner. Pitched for Oakland in every season from 1987 through 1990, but in a total of only nine games.... There have been seven players in major league history with palindromic surnames (don't worry—it's curable): Truck Hannah, Toby Harrah, Eddie Kazak, Dick Nen, Dave Otto, Johnny Reder, and Mark Salas.

Melido Perez

Throws Right

New York Yankees	W-L	ERA	AB	H	HR	BB	SO	BA	SA	OBA
Season	13-16	2.87	901	212	16	93	218	.235	.332	.308
vs. Left-Handers			430	106	8	50	99	.247	.344	.324
vs. Right-Handers			471	106	8	43	119	.225	.321	.293
vs. Ground-Ballers			494	122	4	44	102	.247	.312	.306
vs. Fly-Ballers			407	90	12	49	116	.221	.356	.310
Home Games	5-6	3.01	352	79	7	42	94	.224	.315	.310
Road Games	8-10	2.78	549	133	9	51	124	.242	.342	.307
Grass Fields	12-10	2.94	714	166	13	74	173	.232	.325	.306
Artificial Turf	1-6	2.61	187	46	3	19	45	.246	.358	.316
April	1-2	2.36	92	20	1	16	26	.217	.293	.336
May	3-2	2.82	166	40	3	19	36	.241	.319	.323
June	3-2	3.51	150	37	3	21	34	.247	.367	.341
July	2-3	3.29	139	34	3	16	36	.245	.353	.321
August	2-4	2.39	172	38	3	11	42	.221	.302	.269
Sept./Oct.	2-3	2.81	182	43	3	10	44	.236	.346	.275
Leading Off Inn.			225	60	4	24	50	.267	.373	.337
Bases Empty			542	132	10	48	136	.244	.347	.307
Runners On			359	80	6	45	82	.223	.309	.308
Runners/Scor. Pos.			199	42	3	30	54	.211	.271	.307
Runners On/2 Out			154	37	1	23	29	.240	.299	.343
Scor. Pos./2 Out			101	22	1	17	20	.218	.267	.331
Late-Inning Pressure			65	17	1	7	17	.262	.369	.333
Leading Off			16	4	1	1	2	.250	.500	.294
Runners On			28	8	0	3	9	.286	.321	.355
Runners/Scor. Pos.			18	4	0	2	6	.222	.278	.300
First 9 Batters			258	68	6	30	64	.264	.376	.340
Second 9 Batters			269	61	6	21	65	.227	.327	.289
All Batters Thereafter			374	83	4	42	89	.222	.305	.298

Loves to face: Felix Fermin (.077, 1-for-13)
Travis Fryman (0-for-16)
Carlos Quintana (0-for-11)

Hates to face: Ellis Burks (.333, 6-for-18, 2 HR)
Brian McRae (.600, 6-for-10)
Kirby Puckett (.488, 20-for-41, 2 HR)

Miscellaneous statistics: Ground outs-to-air outs ratio: 1.12 last season, 0.96 for career.... Opponents grounded into 19 double plays in 177 opportunities (one per 9.3).... Allowed 33 doubles, 3 triples in 247⅔ innings.... Allowed 17 first-inning runs in 33 starts (4.64 ERA).... Batting support: 3.85 runs per start.... Opposing base stealers: 18-for-36 (50%); 9 pickoffs, 0 balks.

Comments: Led the Yankees with 13 victories. Five former Yankees pitchers won more games than that for other clubs, and they all had winning records: Doug Drabek (15-11), Bill Gullickson (14-13), Mike Morgan (16-8), Jose Rijo (15-10), and Bob Tewksbury (16-5).... His 16 losses were 2d most in the majors, behind only Erik Hanson (17).... Nine complete-game losses were the most since Bert Blyleven lost nine CGs in 1985.... The Yankees scored fewer than three runs in 12 of his 16 losses. So what? Good pitchers win at least occasionally despite poor support. Rick Sutcliffe won five starts last season when the O's scored two runs or fewer; Steve Avery, Andy Benes, Doug Drabek, Charlie Leibrandt, and Dave Fleming all won four such starts, and nine other pitchers won three. Perez has lost 19 consecutive starts in which his team scored two runs or fewer.... Made 10 consecutive starts with Mike Stanley catching (Aug. 6–Sept. 25). For the season, he went 6-9 with a 2.63 ERA for Stanley; 6-4, 3.34 for the jilted Matt Nokes.... Has lowered his ERA by at least 20 points in each of the last three seasons. Only three pitchers since 1900 have continued such streaks for a fourth season (minimum: 125 IP each): Camilo Pascual (1956–59), Jerry Reuss (1972–75), and Mark Langston (1986–89).... Strikeout total was 2d highest ever by a Yankees right-hander, behind Jack Chesbro (239 in 1904).... Picked off nine base runners, to lead right-handed pitchers in both leagues; had only two pickoffs over the previous two years.

Hipolito Pichardo

Throws Right

Kansas City Royals	W-L	ERA	AB	H	HR	BB	SO	BA	SA	OBA
Season	9-6	3.95	554	148	9	49	59	.267	.379	.327
vs. Left-Handers			244	70	3	23	21	.287	.406	.346
vs. Right-Handers			310	78	6	26	38	.252	.358	.313
vs. Ground-Ballers			252	71	4	28	25	.282	.385	.347
vs. Fly-Ballers			302	77	5	21	34	.255	.374	.310
Home Games	5-2	3.94	294	75	4	16	30	.255	.357	.297
Road Games	4-4	3.95	260	73	5	33	29	.281	.404	.359
Grass Fields	3-4	4.15	217	61	5	28	24	.281	.419	.360
Artificial Turf	6-2	3.81	337	87	4	21	35	.258	.353	.305
April	0-0	7.36	14	4	0	1	2	.286	.286	.333
May	1-2	3.51	97	22	2	7	11	.227	.330	.279
June	2-1	2.79	112	29	0	11	13	.259	.321	.323
July	2-1	2.14	124	28	3	8	13	.226	.339	.271
August	3-1	5.90	116	35	3	10	10	.302	.466	.367
Sept./Oct.	1-1	5.56	91	30	1	12	10	.330	.462	.402
Leading Off Inn.			132	38	1	17	17	.288	.402	.377
Bases Empty			299	73	4	31	37	.244	.348	.321
Runners On			255	75	5	18	22	.294	.416	.335
Runners/Scor. Pos.			140	40	3	11	16	.286	.400	.327
Runners On/2 Out			100	25	2	9	9	.250	.360	.312
Scor. Pos./2 Out			61	10	1	7	9	.164	.246	.250
Late-Inning Pressure			9	3	0	1	0	.333	.333	.400
Leading Off			4	2	0	0	0	.500	.500	.500
Runners On			2	0	0	1	0	.000	.000	.333
Runners/Scor. Pos.			2	0	0	0	0	.000	.000	.000
First 9 Batters			235	58	0	26	30	.247	.298	.326
Second 9 Batters			191	50	5	12	16	.262	.377	.304
All Batters Thereafter			128	40	4	11	13	.313	.531	.364

Loves to face: Carlos Baerga (0-for-7)
Albert Belle (0-for-6, 3 SO)
Hubie Brooks (0-for-6)

Hates to face: Jack Clark (.600, 3-for-5, 1 HR)
Paul Sorrento (.500, 3-for-6, 1 2B, 1 HR)
Omar Vizquel (.571, 4-for-7)

Miscellaneous statistics: Ground outs-to-air outs ratio: 1.39 last season, 1.39 for career. . . . Opponents grounded into 15 double plays in 116 opportunities (one per 7.7). . . . Allowed 31 doubles, 2 triples in 143⅔ innings. . . . Allowed 10 first-inning runs in 24 starts (3.38 ERA). . . . Batting support: 5.21 runs per start, 5th-highest average in majors. . . . Opposing base stealers: 11-for-14 (79%); 0 pickoffs, 1 balk.

Comments: His first seven appearances last season were in relief, but he was used exclusively as a starter thereafter (starting May 20). . . . Hasn't allowed a home run during the first two innings of any of his 24 career starts. . . . Went 5–0 with a 2.34 ERA in eight starts in which he recorded more air outs than ground outs; was 4–4 with a 4.70 ERA in 13 starts in which the opposite was true. . . . Average of 5.43 innings pitched per start was 4th lowest in the majors (minimum: 20 GS). . . . Was the 3d-youngest pitcher to start at least 20 games last season, behind Steve Avery and Dave Fleming. . . . Ranked fifth among rookie pitchers in wins, starts (24), and innings (143⅔). Royals rookie pitchers combined for 20 wins, tying Seattle's rookies for most in the league. . . . Who posted a lower ERA last season, A.L. rookie pitchers or A.L. veterans? A no-brainer, right? Well, it was closer than you think. Rookies: 3.97; vets: 3.94. . . . In the 24-year history of the Royals franchise, only four other rookies had winning percentages of .600 or better (minimum: 15 decisions): Dennis Leonard in 1975 (.682, 15–7); Tom Gordon in 1989 (.654, 17–9); Rich Gale in 1978 (.636, 14–8); Kevin Appier in 1990 (.600, 12–8). . . . Owns a 6.31 ERA in nine appearances in day games, 3.17 in 22 games at night. . . . Posted a career record of 9–21 over five seasons in the minors, without ever reaching the Triple-A level.

Scott Radinsky

Throws Left

Chicago White Sox	W-L	ERA	AB	H	HR	BB	SO	BA	SA	OBA
Season	3-7	2.73	222	54	3	34	48	.243	.351	.347
vs. Left-Handers			66	12	2	8	24	.182	.318	.280
vs. Right-Handers			156	42	1	26	24	.269	.365	.375
vs. Ground-Ballers			101	27	2	18	21	.267	.396	.375
vs. Fly-Ballers			121	27	1	16	27	.223	.314	.324
Home Games	3-2	1.17	116	28	1	12	30	.241	.302	.313
Road Games	0-5	4.40	106	26	2	22	18	.245	.406	.382
Grass Fields	3-3	1.44	180	39	1	25	44	.217	.267	.312
Artificial Turf	0-4	9.64	42	15	2	9	4	.357	.714	.481
April	0-1	1.29	25	5	0	2	7	.200	.240	.259
May	2-0	1.35	47	8	0	10	15	.170	.234	.316
June	0-4	6.00	32	6	2	6	5	.188	.438	.350
July	0-1	3.48	40	10	1	7	13	.250	.350	.362
August	1-0	0.00	36	9	0	3	4	.250	.250	.308
Sept./Oct.	0-1	4.35	42	16	0	6	4	.381	.571	.449
Leading Off Inn.			41	7	0	6	15	.171	.195	.292
Bases Empty			89	19	1	16	23	.213	.270	.346
Runners On			133	35	2	18	25	.263	.406	.349
Runners/Scor. Pos.			77	18	1	12	19	.234	.390	.333
Runners On/2 Out			57	14	0	9	13	.246	.333	.348
Scor. Pos./2 Out			38	7	0	6	13	.184	.289	.295
Late-Inning Pressure			145	32	3	19	30	.221	.317	.313
Leading Off			29	4	0	4	11	.138	.138	.265
Runners On			83	20	2	8	13	.241	.373	.304
Runners/Scor. Pos.			45	8	1	4	11	.178	.289	.240
First 9 Batters			222	54	3	34	48	.243	.351	.347
Second 9 Batters			0	0	0	0	0	—	—	—
All Batters Thereafter			0	0	0	0	0	—	—	—

Loves to face: George Brett (0-for-10)
Ken Griffey, Jr. (0-for-9, 5 SO)
Lou Whitaker (0-for-8, 4 SO)

Hates to face: Kirby Puckett (3-for-3)
Jeff Reboulet (2-for-2, 1 BB)
Ruben Sierra (.429, 3-for-7, 3 BB)

Miscellaneous statistics: Ground outs-to-air outs ratio: 1.02 last season, 1.05 for career. . . . Opponents grounded into 4 double plays in 67 opportunities (one per 17). . . . Allowed 11 doubles, 2 triples in 59⅓ innings. . . . Saved 15 games in 37 opportunities (41%). . . . Stranded 32 inherited runners, allowed 22 to score (59%). . . . Opposing base stealers: 1-for-4 (25%); 0 pickoffs, 0 balks.

Comments: Made 32 appearances in which he pitched less than one inning, facing a single batter 11 times. Boston's Tony Fossas had the most one-batter appearances in the majors (32), pitching less than one inning in 48 of his 60 games. . . . Has faced more than nine batters in only three of his 197 career appearances (0-for-68 in 1992). . . . Entered 22 games with his team leading by one run, most by any A.L. reliever. . . . Walk rate per nine innings rose from 2.90 in 1991 to 5.16 last season. Of the 10 relievers in the majors who walked more than five per nine innings (minimum: 50 IP), three were with the White Sox: Radinsky, Bobby Thigpen (5.40), and Wilson Alvarez (6.27). . . . Has a career ERA of 2.20 in Chicago (1.37 at the "new" Comiskey Park), 4.04 on the road. . . . In 11 appearances on artificial turf last season, he was 0–4 with a 9.64 ERA. . . . Opponents have a career batting average of .190 with runners on base in Late-Inning Pressure Situations, 4th lowest among active pitchers (minimum: 150 AB), behind Mike Boddicker (.181), Bryan Harvey (.185), and John Wetteland (.189). . . . With runners in scoring position in LIPS, he's even tougher, holding opponents to a .155 mark, 2d lowest in *Player Analysis* history (minimum: 100 AB), behind Roger Clemens (.144). . . . Left-handers have a career batting average of .189 against him, but have averaged one home run every 41.2 at-bats. Opposing right-handed batters have a higher batting average (.246), but a much lower home-run rate (one per 156 AB).

Rick Reed
Throws Right

Kansas City Royals	W-L	ERA	AB	H	HR	BB	SO	BA	SA	OBA
Season	3-7	3.68	387	105	10	20	49	.271	.413	.312
vs. Left-Handers			169	34	5	9	27	.201	.367	.236
vs. Right-Handers			218	71	5	11	22	.326	.450	.370
vs. Ground-Ballers			202	50	4	9	26	.248	.371	.285
vs. Fly-Ballers			185	55	6	11	23	.297	.459	.340
Home Games	1-2	4.53	176	54	3	7	18	.307	.455	.333
Road Games	2-5	3.02	211	51	7	13	31	.242	.379	.294
Grass Fields	2-4	2.60	168	40	4	8	23	.238	.345	.283
Artificial Turf	1-3	4.55	219	65	6	12	26	.297	.466	.333
April	0-0	—	0	0	0	0	0	—	—	—
May	0-0	—	0	0	0	0	0	—	—	—
June	1-3	3.80	89	26	4	4	8	.292	.461	.326
July	1-1	5.01	88	22	1	6	9	.250	.386	.306
August	0-1	2.70	72	15	2	4	16	.208	.319	.256
Sept./Oct.	1-2	3.28	138	42	3	6	16	.304	.449	.336
Leading Off Inn.			103	30	3	2	8	.291	.437	.318
Bases Empty			234	62	9	12	31	.265	.427	.306
Runners On			153	43	1	8	18	.281	.392	.320
Runners/Scor. Pos.			84	20	0	7	13	.238	.286	.289
Runners On/2 Out			56	14	1	3	7	.250	.411	.300
Scor. Pos./2 Out			38	7	0	2	5	.184	.263	.225
Late-Inning Pressure			12	1	0	1	1	.083	.083	.154
Leading Off			4	0	0	0	0	.000	.000	.000
Runners On			0	0	0	1	0	—	—	1.000
Runners/Scor. Pos.			0	0	0	0	0	—	—	—
First 9 Batters			149	42	1	9	22	.282	.356	.325
Second 9 Batters			148	34	6	6	23	.230	.399	.266
All Batters Thereafter			90	29	3	5	4	.322	.533	.365

Loves to face: Alfredo Griffin (0-for-7)
Von Hayes (.059, 1-for-17)
Mickey Tettleton (0-for-5, 2 SO)
Hates to face: Keith Miller (3-for-3)
Pedro Munoz (.600, 3-for-5, 1 2B, 1 HR, 1 BB)
Cal Ripken (3-for-3, 1 2B, 1 HR)

Miscellaneous statistics: Ground outs-to-air outs ratio: 1.13 last season, 0.94 for career.... Opponents grounded into 11 double plays in 85 opportunities (one per 7.7).... Allowed 21 doubles, 2 triples in 100⅓ innings.... Allowed 8 first-inning runs in 18 starts (3.18 ERA).... Batting support: 3.61 runs per start.... Opposing base stealers: 6-for-9 (67%); 3 pickoffs, 0 balks.

Comments: One of baseball's least-known pinpoint-control pitchers. He has walked more than two batters only once in 36 career starts.... Ranks 5th among active pitchers with a rate of 1.84 walks per nine innings (minimum: 25 GS), trailing only Rheal Cormier (1.45), Bob Tewksbury (1.56), Kevin Tapani (1.75), and Bret Saberhagen (1.83).... Of the 46 walks that Reed has allowed in his career, 12 have been intentional.... Picked off three runners in only 100⅓ innings pitched. Melido Perez led right-handers with nine pickoffs, one every 28 innings; that's only slightly better than Reed's rate (one every 33 innings).... The only pitcher in the A.L. to pitch at least 100 innings last season without a wild pitch. His career total of 225 innings is the highest among active pitchers who've never "uncorked" one.... Hasn't allowed a first-inning home run in 22 starts since July 22, 1990.... Made 18 starts, the most of any A.L. pitcher who didn't win consecutive decisions at any time last season.... Average of 5.20 innings per start was 3d lowest in the A.L. (minimum: 15 GS).... The only complete games of his career have both been shutouts: against Philadelphia in 1990, and against California in his final appearance of 1992.... Has pitched in the majors in parts of the last five seasons, but has never been active on opening day. In fact, the earliest he has pitched in the majors in any season was June 7 (in both 1990 and 1992).

Arthur Rhodes
Throws Left

Baltimore Orioles	W-L	ERA	AB	H	HR	BB	SO	BA	SA	OBA
Season	7-5	3.63	348	87	6	38	77	.250	.382	.325
vs. Left-Handers			40	10	0	6	9	.250	.250	.348
vs. Right-Handers			308	77	6	32	68	.250	.399	.322
vs. Ground-Ballers			186	47	3	21	44	.253	.355	.332
vs. Fly-Ballers			162	40	3	17	33	.247	.414	.317
Home Games	4-4	4.81	216	59	4	26	47	.273	.421	.354
Road Games	3-1	1.73	132	28	2	12	30	.212	.318	.276
Grass Fields	6-4	3.84	294	76	5	36	66	.259	.388	.340
Artificial Turf	1-1	2.45	54	11	1	2	11	.204	.352	.232
April	0-0	—	0	0	0	0	0	—	—	—
May	0-0	—	0	0	0	0	0	—	—	—
June	0-0	—	0	0	0	0	0	—	—	—
July	3-0	1.76	104	19	1	11	24	.183	.260	.259
August	2-4	6.00	131	38	4	12	28	.290	.489	.354
Sept./Oct.	2-1	2.93	113	30	1	15	25	.265	.372	.352
Leading Off Inn.			93	24	2	9	22	.258	.398	.324
Bases Empty			208	53	5	20	42	.255	.409	.323
Runners On			140	34	1	18	35	.243	.343	.327
Runners/Scor. Pos.			83	18	1	11	22	.217	.301	.305
Runners On/2 Out			51	11	1	8	16	.216	.353	.322
Scor. Pos./2 Out			36	8	1	7	11	.222	.389	.349
Late-Inning Pressure			25	7	0	1	4	.280	.400	.308
Leading Off			9	3	0	0	1	.333	.333	.333
Runners On			7	3	0	0	0	.429	.857	.429
Runners/Scor. Pos.			4	1	0	0	0	.250	.250	.250
First 9 Batters			122	25	2	11	30	.205	.311	.271
Second 9 Batters			111	29	2	14	26	.261	.432	.349
All Batters Thereafter			115	33	2	13	21	.287	.409	.357

Loves to face: Juan Gonzalez (0-for-7)
Ken Griffey, Jr. (0-for-5)
Manuel Lee (0-for-5)
Hates to face: Albert Belle (.400, 4-for-10, 2 2B, 2 HR)
Mark Lewis (.667, 4-for-6, 2 2B, 1 HR)
Shane Mack (.833, 5-for-6, 1 SO)

Miscellaneous statistics: Ground outs-to-air outs ratio: 0.83 last season, 0.84 for career.... Opponents grounded into 10 double plays in 79 opportunities (one per 7.9).... Allowed 20 doubles, 4 triples in 94⅓ innings.... Allowed 4 first-inning runs in 15 starts (2.40 ERA).... Batting support: 4.53 runs per start.... Opposing base stealers: 4-for-8 (50%); 1 pickoff, 1 balk.

Comments: One of five major leaguers born within five weeks of Baltimore's loss to the Mets in the 1969 World Series. You could do a lot worse than to start a team with that group: Juan Gonzalez (Oct. 16), Rhodes (Oct. 24), Dave Fleming (Nov. 7), Damion Easley (Nov. 11), and Ken Griffey, Jr. (Nov. 21).... The September acquisition of Craig Lefferts gave the Orioles two left-handed starters in their rotation for the first time since the days of Mike Flanagan and Scott McGregor.... Became the first Orioles left-hander to throw a shutout or a complete game since Jeff Ballard in 1989.... Has never allowed an extra-base hit to a left-handed batter (53 career at-bats), but opposing right-handers have averaged one XBH every 10.3 ABs.... Only two left-handed batters have even driven in a run against him: Scott Livingstone (2 RBIs on a bases-loaded single in 1992) and Cleveland's Wayne Kirby (an RBI ground out in 1991). Opposing left-handers are 1-for-16 with runners in scoring position.... Strikeout rate was higher in the first inning last season (one every 3.1 batters faced) than in any other (one per 5.8 batters thereafter).... Career record of 5–4 in 11 starts in which he walked fewer than three batters, compared to 2–4 in 12 starts with three or more walks.... The left-hander with the most similar rookie season to Rhodes's at the same age was Sid Fernandez in 1984 (6–6, 3.50 ERA, 34 BB, 62 SO in 90 IP).

Kenny Rogers
Throws Left

Texas Rangers	W-L	ERA	AB	H	HR	BB	SO	BA	SA	OBA
Season	3-6	3.09	306	80	7	26	70	.261	.392	.318
vs. Left-Handers			92	24	1	3	21	.261	.348	.284
vs. Right-Handers			214	56	6	23	49	.262	.411	.332
vs. Ground-Ballers			156	42	3	11	35	.269	.397	.317
vs. Fly-Ballers			150	38	4	15	35	.253	.387	.319
Home Games	1-4	3.53	172	46	4	17	38	.267	.407	.333
Road Games	2-2	2.55	134	34	3	9	32	.254	.373	.299
Grass Fields	3-5	3.15	268	70	6	24	60	.261	.399	.321
Artificial Turf	0-1	2.70	38	10	1	2	10	.263	.342	.300
April	0-0	2.45	44	13	1	1	10	.295	.455	.311
May	0-2	4.00	68	18	3	8	18	.265	.471	.342
June	1-1	1.59	43	9	1	3	7	.209	.326	.261
July	0-1	4.91	48	16	2	4	6	.333	.563	.377
August	1-1	2.25	45	12	0	4	11	.267	.289	.327
Sept./Oct.	1-1	2.93	58	12	0	6	18	.207	.241	.281
Leading Off Inn.			63	18	0	3	13	.286	.349	.318
Bases Empty			146	35	2	9	34	.240	.342	.284
Runners On			160	45	5	17	36	.281	.438	.348
Runners/Scor. Pos.			94	29	5	15	18	.309	.543	.400
Runners On/2 Out			63	13	1	11	10	.206	.317	.324
Scor. Pos./2 Out			41	11	1	9	5	.268	.415	.400
Late-Inning Pressure			146	43	4	9	35	.295	.473	.335
Leading Off			32	9	0	2	8	.281	.375	.324
Runners On			75	26	4	6	17	.347	.600	.395
Runners/Scor. Pos.			47	17	4	6	10	.362	.723	.434
First 9 Batters			304	78	7	26	70	.257	.388	.314
Second 9 Batters			2	2	0	0	0	1.000	1.000	1.000
All Batters Thereafter			0	0	0	0	0	—	—	—

Loves to face: Mike Greenwell (.067, 1-for-15, 1 2B)
Ozzie Guillen (.071, 1-for-14)
Luis Polonia (0-for-14)

Hates to face: Roberto Alomar (.500, 3-for-6, 1 3B, 1 HR)
Craig Grebeck (.750, 3-for-4, 1 2B, 2 HR)
Luis Rivera (.500, 6-for-12, 3 2B, 1 3B)

Miscellaneous statistics: Ground outs-to-air outs ratio: 0.82 last season, 0.99 for career.... Opponents grounded into 3 double plays in 82 opportunities (one per 27).... Allowed 17 doubles, 1 triple in 78⅔ innings.... Stranded 31 inherited runners, allowed 29 to score (52%), 5th-lowest rate in A.L.... Opposing base stealers: 2-for-5 (40%); 3 pickoffs, 1 balk.

Comments: Led A.L. pitchers with 81 appearances, tying Joe Boever for the major league lead. His total of 286 appearances over the last four seasons ranks 2d in the majors, behind Duane Ward (299). The only pitcher ever to make more appearances in his *first* four seasons in the majors is Mitch Williams (308).... Rogers's total certainly could have been higher had he not started 12 games during the 1990 and 1991 seasons.... Career record is 21–20 with a 3.32 ERA and 28 saves in 274 relief appearances; 5–6, 6.17 ERA in 12 starts.... Rangers relievers posted the highest ERA of any bullpen in the majors last season (4.53).... He's a new man: Walk rate dropped from 5.01 per nine innings in 1991 to a career-low 2.97 last season; his strikeout rate rose from 5.99 to a career-high 8.01. Only two other pitchers in major league history increased their strikeout rate by at least two per nine innings and decreased their walk rate by that amount in the same season (minimum: 75 IP): Pete Falcone (1979) and Victor Cruz (1980).... Walked only three left-handed batters last season, all with two outs and first base open. ... Career batting average is .220 by opposing left-handed batters, .273 by right-handers. The only homer he allowed to a left-handed batter last season was a grand slam by Franklin Stubbs.... Career ERA is 4.71 before the All-Star break, 2.66 after.

Jeff Russell
Throws Right

Rangers/A's	W-L	ERA	AB	H	HR	BB	SO	BA	SA	OBA
Season	4-3	1.63	246	55	3	25	48	.224	.309	.298
vs. Left-Handers			110	27	1	14	17	.245	.355	.339
vs. Right-Handers			136	28	2	11	31	.206	.272	.264
vs. Ground-Ballers			121	26	0	8	16	.215	.289	.269
vs. Fly-Ballers			125	29	3	17	32	.232	.328	.324
Home Games	2-1	0.94	136	23	2	10	26	.169	.235	.230
Road Games	2-2	2.57	110	32	1	15	22	.291	.400	.378
Grass Fields	3-1	1.07	213	42	2	21	42	.197	.258	.274
Artificial Turf	1-2	6.14	33	13	1	4	6	.394	.636	.447
April	1-1	2.16	34	9	0	4	7	.265	.294	.333
May	1-1	2.12	65	17	1	6	9	.262	.354	.319
June	0-0	0.71	42	5	0	7	14	.119	.119	.260
July	0-1	2.31	46	13	0	4	8	.283	.413	.340
August	0-0	2.57	27	7	2	1	5	.259	.519	.310
Sept./Oct.	2-0	0.00	32	4	0	3	5	.125	.156	.200
Leading Off Inn.			45	10	1	4	6	.222	.333	.300
Bases Empty			109	27	2	12	20	.248	.349	.328
Runners On			137	28	1	13	28	.204	.277	.275
Runners/Scor. Pos.			77	15	1	10	15	.195	.286	.281
Runners On/2 Out			73	17	0	11	15	.233	.288	.341
Scor. Pos./2 Out			51	10	0	8	10	.196	.275	.305
Late-Inning Pressure			199	45	2	20	40	.226	.312	.297
Leading Off			36	9	0	2	6	.250	.306	.308
Runners On			115	23	1	12	24	.200	.287	.271
Runners/Scor. Pos.			65	12	1	10	13	.185	.292	.286
First 9 Batters			245	55	3	24	48	.224	.310	.297
Second 9 Batters			1	0	0	1	0	.000	.000	.500
All Batters Thereafter			0	0	0	0	0	—	—	—

Loves to face: Joe Carter (.067, 1-for-15)
Gary Gaetti (.053, 1-for-19)
Dan Gladden (.125, 4-for-32, 0 BB)

Hates to face: George Brett (.400, 6-for-15, 3 HR, 5 BB)
Mike Greenwell (.615, 8-for-13, 2 HR)
Dave Winfield (.538, 7-for-13, 4 SO)

Miscellaneous statistics: Ground outs-to-air outs ratio: 0.83 last season, 1.20 for career.... Opponents grounded into 4 double plays in 53 opportunities (one per 13).... Allowed 10 doubles, 1 triple in 66⅓ innings.... Saved 30 games in 39 opportunities (77%).... Stranded 31 inherited runners, allowed 12 to score (72%).... Opposing base stealers: 1-for-4 (25%); 0 pickoffs, 0 balks.

Comments: Among the 110 seasons of 30 saves since 1969 (when saves became an official statistic), there have been more pitchers with losing records (50) than winning records (46). That makes sense: Closers usually enter the game in a literal "can't-win" situation. That's what makes Russell so exceptional; last season was the third 30-save season of his career, and he's posted winning records in every one. The only pitchers with more 30-save/winning-record seasons are Dennis Eckersley (all 5 of his 30-save seasons) and Dan Quisenberry (4 of his 5). Lee Smith also had three, but with four other 30-save seasons in which his record was at .500 or below. Honorable mention: Kent Tekulve was 2-for-2.... One of four active pitchers with career totals of at least 75 starts and 75 saves. The others: Mark Davis, Dennis Eckersley, and Dave Righetti.... Left the Rangers as their all-time franchise leader in saves (111); he shares the franchise lead for relief wins with Steve Foucault and Ron Kline (26 each).... By the time the Athletics acquired Russell last August, Goose Goosage was already through for the season. But technically, they had three pitchers on their roster with 100 career saves each. That's happened just three other times, even including pre-1969 saves totals from the *Baseball Encyclopedia*: the 1968 Tigers (Roy Face, Don McMahon, and John Wyatt); 1973 Yankees (Lindy McDaniel, Wayne Granger, and Sparky Lyle); 1985 Braves (Terry Forster, Gene Garber, and Bruce Sutter).

Nolan Ryan — Throws Right

Texas Rangers	W-L	ERA	AB	H	HR	BB	SO	BA	SA	OBA
Season	5-9	3.72	580	138	9	69	157	.238	.341	.328
vs. Left-Handers			294	72	5	43	69	.245	.364	.339
vs. Right-Handers			286	66	4	26	88	.231	.318	.316
vs. Ground-Ballers			316	82	4	28	77	.259	.361	.326
vs. Fly-Ballers			264	56	5	41	80	.212	.318	.330
Home Games	3-6	3.40	336	73	5	39	99	.217	.333	.312
Road Games	2-3	4.18	244	65	4	30	58	.266	.352	.350
Grass Fields	5-9	3.96	519	124	8	64	141	.239	.343	.331
Artificial Turf	0-0	1.65	61	14	1	5	16	.230	.328	.300
April	0-1	10.80	28	10	0	6	7	.357	.464	.457
May	0-0	3.21	99	21	1	8	33	.212	.323	.273
June	1-2	3.46	101	26	1	15	26	.257	.317	.364
July	4-0	1.96	128	23	2	13	34	.180	.258	.262
August	0-5	7.16	126	36	5	22	37	.286	.452	.403
Sept./Oct.	0-1	0.99	98	22	0	5	20	.224	.316	.283
Leading Off Inn.			145	32	3	14	39	.221	.345	.307
Bases Empty			330	76	5	37	94	.230	.339	.319
Runners On			250	62	4	32	63	.248	.344	.339
Runners/Scor. Pos.			150	34	3	19	44	.227	.340	.324
Runners On/2 Out			102	22	1	14	27	.216	.294	.328
Scor. Pos./2 Out			68	14	1	9	20	.206	.294	.325
Late-Inning Pressure			30	8	0	2	5	.267	.400	.313
Leading Off			9	3	0	0	1	.333	.556	.333
Runners On			11	3	0	1	1	.273	.455	.333
Runners/Scor. Pos.			6	3	0	1	1	.500	.833	.571
First 9 Batters			203	44	5	25	62	.217	.350	.318
Second 9 Batters			200	49	3	20	55	.245	.335	.318
All Batters Thereafter			177	45	1	24	40	.254	.339	.349

Loves to face: Rob Deer (0-for-14, 10 SO)
              Edgar Martinez (.053, 1-for-19, 10 SO)
              Dan Pasqua (.120, 3-for-25, 0 BB, 12 SO)
Hates to face: Carlos Baerga (.750, 6-for-8, 1 HR)
              Harold Baines (.368, 7-for-19, 1 2B, 4 HR)
              Jack Clark (.250, 11-for-44, 4 2B, 1 3B, 4 HR)

Miscellaneous statistics: Ground outs-to-air outs ratio: 0.61 last season (2d lowest in A.L.), 1.00 for career. . . . Opponents grounded into 5 double plays in 118 opportunities (one per 24), worst rate in A.L. . . . Allowed 27 doubles, 3 triples in 157⅓ innings. . . . Allowed 14 first-inning runs in 27 starts (4.85 ERA). . . . Batting support: 3.81 runs per start, 10th-lowest average in A.L. . . . Opposing base stealers: 26-for-38 (68%); 2 pickoffs, 0 balks.

Comments: Only four pitchers in major league history are within one strikeout of Ryan's career average of 9.59 per nine innings (minimum: 1000 innings): Sandy Koufax (9.27), Sam McDowell (8.86), Lee Smith (8.85), and David Cone (8.72). . . . Struck out more batters before the age of 35 than anyone else, but by only a small margin (3249 to 2939 over runner-up Walter Johnson). It's what he's done since then that separates him from the pack: Only 21 pitchers struck out as many batters during their entire careers as Ryan has struck out since turning 35. Ryan's total of 2419 strikeouts since his 35th birthday is higher than the career totals of Koufax (2396), Juan Marichal (2303), Lefty Grove (2266), Jim Palmer (2212), and Grover Cleveland Alexander (2199). . . . Strikeout rate has been higher in his 40s than in his 20s or his 30s. As we pointed out in the 1987 *Analyst*, most great strikeout pitchers were nearly as strong in their late 30s as in their early 30s; only Ryan was dominant in his 40s. His strike-outs per nine innings by age: 20–24, 8.64; 25–29, 10.05; 30–34, 9.19; 35–39, 8.89; 40-up, 10.39. . . . Since Ryan turned 40 in 1987, only one pitcher has more strikeouts; the top three: Roger Clemens, 1435; Ryan, 1391; Mark Langston, 1284. . . . Has more SOs since turning 40 than the career total of Three Finger Brown (1375) or Bob Lemon (1277). . . . Has won 290 games since being traded (with Leroy Stanton and others) by the Mets to the Angels for Jim Fregosi in 1971. Only two other pitchers won even 100 games for other clubs after leaving the Mets: Tom Seaver (113) and Mike Scott (110).

Scott Sanderson — Throws Right

New York Yankees	W-L	ERA	AB	H	HR	BB	SO	BA	SA	OBA
Season	12-11	4.93	769	220	28	64	104	.286	.464	.340
vs. Left-Handers			367	110	13	38	40	.300	.466	.362
vs. Right-Handers			402	110	15	26	64	.274	.463	.319
vs. Ground-Ballers			405	115	9	35	43	.284	.420	.341
vs. Fly-Ballers			364	105	19	29	61	.288	.514	.338
Home Games	5-6	5.47	396	117	20	32	51	.295	.505	.346
Road Games	7-5	4.39	373	103	8	32	53	.276	.421	.333
Grass Fields	11-11	5.03	705	203	27	55	98	.288	.470	.339
Artificial Turf	1-0	4.00	64	17	1	9	6	.266	.406	.347
April	2-1	5.34	115	36	7	10	15	.313	.530	.365
May	2-1	4.66	150	45	7	12	23	.300	.527	.348
June	3-3	3.65	141	33	4	14	22	.234	.390	.308
July	1-3	6.99	120	42	3	8	13	.350	.525	.394
August	3-0	2.79	138	29	3	13	19	.210	.319	.279
Sept./Oct.	1-3	7.88	105	35	4	7	12	.333	.524	.362
Leading Off Inn.			189	62	7	13	23	.328	.545	.371
Bases Empty			431	132	16	29	55	.306	.497	.351
Runners On			338	88	12	35	49	.260	.423	.326
Runners/Scor. Pos.			162	50	5	22	24	.309	.475	.376
Runners On/2 Out			137	37	4	16	24	.270	.438	.355
Scor. Pos./2 Out			79	23	2	11	16	.291	.481	.385
Late-Inning Pressure			12	5	0	3	0	.417	.583	.563
Leading Off			4	2	0	0	0	.500	.750	.500
Runners On			4	1	0	3	0	.250	.250	.625
Runners/Scor. Pos.			3	1	0	3	0	.333	.333	.667
First 9 Batters			271	70	9	18	43	.258	.417	.301
Second 9 Batters			261	74	7	26	37	.284	.429	.351
All Batters Thereafter			237	76	12	20	24	.321	.557	.372

Loves to face: Greg Briley (0-for-20)
              John Olerud (.105, 2-for-19)
              Herm Winningham (0-for-11)
Hates to face: Scott Fletcher (.550, 11-for-20, 2 HR)
              Julio Franco (.500, 8-for-16, 2 HR)
              Shane Mack (.700, 7-for-10, 3 HR)

Miscellaneous statistics: Ground outs-to-air outs ratio: 0.83 last season, 0.80 for career. . . . Opponents grounded into 17 double plays in 169 opportunities (one per 10). . . . Allowed 35 doubles, 9 triples (most in majors) in 193⅓ innings. . . . Allowed 18 first-inning runs in 33 starts (4.64 ERA). . . . Batting support: 5.12 runs per start, 6th-highest average in majors. . . . Opposing base stealers: 18-for-26 (69%); 2 pickoffs, 1 balk.

Comments: One of nine pitchers with a winning record in each of the last four seasons. . . . Became the 10th pitcher in major league history to follow four consecutive losing seasons with four straight winners. The others: Tully Sparks, Cy Morgan, Bump Hadley, Alex Kellner, Sam Jones, Ralph Terry, Ron Kline (off 10 straight losing seasons), Joe Coleman, and Jim Rooker. . . . Still unsigned at this writing; we hope he lands with an established N.L. team, which would make him the favorite in the race to defeat all 28 major league teams. He has already beaten the first 26, which no active N.L. pitcher has done. Active A.L. pitchers to do so: Goose Gossage, Nolan Ryan, and Rick Sutcliffe. . . . In two seasons in New York, he posted a .571 winning percentage in 49 decisions; the Yankees played .434 ball in other games. . . . Only three other starters posted winning records for teams with losing marks in each of the last two seasons (minimum: 25 GS in each): John Burkett, Greg Maddux, and Terry Mulholland. The last pitchers with three-year streaks: Tom Candiotti and Greg Swindell (1988–90). . . . Walked as many batters in his first 13 starts last season as he did in all 34 starts in 1991 (29). . . . His ERA in home games was the highest in the majors; he was the only pitcher in either league with a home-game ERA above 5.00 (minimum: 81 innings). . . . A victory over Texas last July 5 was the 139th of his career, making him the Greatest Scott of 'em all. Career wins: Scott Sanderson, 143; Scott McGregor, 138; Mike Scott, 124.

Mike Schooler

Throws Right

Seattle Mariners	W-L	ERA	AB	H	HR	BB	SO	BA	SA	OBA
Season	2-7	4.70	200	55	7	24	33	.275	.420	.351
vs. Left-Handers			79	22	3	15	10	.278	.468	.394
vs. Right-Handers			121	33	4	9	23	.273	.388	.321
vs. Ground-Ballers			86	20	2	16	12	.233	.326	.350
vs. Fly-Ballers			114	35	5	8	21	.307	.491	.352
Home Games	1-4	4.55	104	27	3	9	17	.260	.385	.319
Road Games	1-3	4.88	96	28	4	15	16	.292	.458	.384
Grass Fields	1-2	4.43	80	23	4	12	15	.287	.475	.376
Artificial Turf	1-5	4.88	120	32	3	12	18	.267	.383	.333
April	0-1	4.15	30	7	1	6	6	.233	.367	.361
May	0-2	6.94	47	13	3	6	7	.277	.489	.370
June	0-2	3.75	48	13	0	2	4	.271	.292	.300
July	1-0	3.00	10	1	1	3	5	.100	.400	.308
August	0-1	5.63	33	13	1	1	6	.394	.576	.389
Sept./Oct.	1-1	3.24	32	8	1	6	5	.250	.406	.359
Leading Off Inn.			40	8	0	4	10	.200	.300	.273
Bases Empty			98	21	1	14	21	.214	.296	.319
Runners On			102	34	6	10	12	.333	.539	.383
Runners/Scor. Pos.			64	26	6	9	7	.406	.734	.461
Runners On/2 Out			47	13	4	6	3	.277	.553	.358
Scor. Pos./2 Out			29	10	4	6	1	.345	.793	.457
Late-Inning Pressure			99	29	6	16	17	.293	.515	.388
Leading Off			19	4	0	3	4	.211	.316	.318
Runners On			59	19	5	7	7	.322	.610	.388
Runners/Scor. Pos.			39	14	5	7	4	.359	.795	.447
First 9 Batters			199	55	7	24	33	.276	.422	.352
Second 9 Batters			1	0	0	0	0	.000	.000	.000
All Batters Thereafter			0	0	0	0	0	—	—	—

Loves to face: Wade Boggs (0-for-5)
Paul Molitor (0-for-8)
Dean Palmer (0-for-4, 4 SO)

Hates to face: Randy Bush (.385, 5-for-13, 2 HR)
Greg Gagne (3-for-3, 2 2B)
Terry Steinbach (.500, 6-for-12)

Miscellaneous statistics: Ground outs-to-air outs ratio: 0.79 last season, 1.01 for career.... Opponents grounded into 3 double plays in 50 opportunities (one per 17).... Allowed 6 doubles, 1 triple in 51⅔ innings.... Saved 13 games in 17 opportunities (76%).... Stranded 22 inherited runners, allowed 17 to score (56%).... Opposing base stealers: 8-for-9 (89%); 0 pickoffs, 0 balks.

Comments: Hasn't posted a winning record in any of his five major league seasons. Mike Flanagan has the longest current streak of consecutive nonwinning seasons (9); the all-time record is 13, by George Brunet (1956–69).... The longest career by a pitcher who never posted a winning record is 10 years, by Phil Ortega and Bobby Tiefenauer.... Career winning percentage of .293 (12–29) is the lowest in Mariners history (minimum: 40 decisions).... Needed a record 226 career appearances to reach the 250-inning mark (on July 4 vs. Detroit). Prior to Schooler, the most appearances needed to reach 250 innings was 223, by Juan Agosto.... He pitched less than one inning in 56 of his 243 appearances, more than two innings only eight times. Has made 90 appearances since the last time he pitched more than two innings (August 11, 1990).... Returned in August from a five-week stay on the D.L. (strained right bicep) and found his role had changed. Was called on in the 7th inning or earlier in 9 of 16 appearances after his return; was brought in that early only twice in his previous 166 games.... Struck out 54 batters in 48⅓ innings (10.06 per nine innings) as a rookie in 1988, but fanned only 33 batters in 51⅔ innings last season (5.75 per nine).... Seattle's bullpen was the wildest in the American League last season, averaging 4.62 walks per nine innings. Schooler's rate (4.18) was slightly below the team average, but was sharply higher than in any of the past three seasons (2.22 in 1989, 2.57 in 1990, 2.62 in 1991).

Scott Scudder

Throws Right

Cleveland Indians	W-L	ERA	AB	H	HR	BB	SO	BA	SA	OBA
Season	6-10	5.28	442	134	10	55	66	.303	.432	.380
vs. Left-Handers			251	75	5	31	30	.299	.410	.376
vs. Right-Handers			191	59	5	24	36	.309	.461	.384
vs. Ground-Ballers			226	65	1	26	33	.288	.350	.361
vs. Fly-Ballers			216	69	9	29	33	.319	.519	.399
Home Games	2-5	5.06	222	77	3	22	33	.347	.455	.404
Road Games	4-5	5.50	220	57	7	33	33	.259	.409	.356
Grass Fields	6-8	5.68	362	115	10	44	57	.318	.464	.391
Artificial Turf	0-2	3.54	80	19	0	11	9	.237	.287	.330
April	1-2	5.89	75	22	3	6	11	.293	.453	.341
May	2-3	2.72	140	33	2	18	20	.236	.321	.327
June	2-2	5.87	129	45	2	16	20	.349	.473	.415
July	1-2	5.79	91	29	3	12	14	.319	.495	.400
August	0-0	0.00	0	0	0	0	0	.000	.000	.000
Sept./Oct.	0-1	162.0	7	5	0	3	1	.714	.857	.800
Leading Off Inn.			111	28	1	9	18	.252	.324	.308
Bases Empty			235	71	4	26	39	.302	.426	.376
Runners On			207	63	6	29	27	.304	.440	.383
Runners/Scor. Pos.			120	35	3	18	17	.292	.408	.373
Runners On/2 Out			82	23	3	16	8	.280	.427	.398
Scor. Pos./2 Out			58	16	1	11	6	.276	.362	.391
Late-Inning Pressure			23	10	0	1	3	.435	.609	.458
Leading Off			9	3	0	0	2	.333	.333	.333
Runners On			7	4	0	1	1	.571	1.000	.625
Runners/Scor. Pos.			2	2	0	0	0	1.000	2.000	1.000
First 9 Batters			168	48	5	28	27	.286	.435	.388
Second 9 Batters			138	42	3	15	19	.304	.428	.377
All Batters Thereafter			136	44	2	12	20	.324	.434	.373

Loves to face: Carlton Fisk (0-for-6)
Mark McGwire (0-for-7)
B.J. Surhoff (0-for-5)

Hates to face: George Bell (.625, 5-for-8, 1 2B, 1 HR)
Andre Dawson (.750, 3-for-4, 1 2B, 2 HR, 4 BB)
Brian McRae (.556, 5-for-9)

Miscellaneous statistics: Ground outs-to-air outs ratio: 1.20 last season, 0.94 for career.... Opponents grounded into 14 double plays in 104 opportunities (one per 7.4).... Allowed 23 doubles, 2 triples in 109 innings.... Allowed 24 first-inning runs in 22 starts (10.07 ERA), highest in majors.... Batting support: 3.86 runs per start.... Opposing base stealers: 14-for-21 (67%); 0 pickoffs, 0 balks.

Comments: Career total of 63 starts is the most of any pitcher in major league history who never completed a game. (He's pitched into the ninth inning only twice.) Completing the top five: Chris Hammond (47 GS), Steve Bedrosian (46), Mike Gardiner (43), Eric Plunk (41).... Even among pitchers who eventually pitched a complete game, only one made as many as 50 starts before going all the way for the first time: Bobby Witt, who pitched his first CG in his 56th start.... Opponents batted .345 during the first inning last season, the highest average against any A.L. pitcher.... Didn't allow an earned run during the first inning of his first eight starts, but finished the season with the highest first-inning ERA in the majors. Over his last 12 starts, he allowed 22 runs in the first inning, all but one of which were earned (19.55 ERA).... Failed to complete the first inning in three of his 22 starts, including his only two appearances after returning from a 49-day visit to the disabled list. In his final start of the season, he faced three batters and walked them all.... Average of 4.91 innings pitched per start was the lowest in the majors (minimum: 20 GS). For more on this, see the Dave Otto comments.... Was charged with 16 unearned runs; only two pitchers were victimized by higher totals: Kevin Brown and Kirk McCaskill (19 each).... Has allowed more than one home run only once in his last 40 starts.

John Smiley
Throws Left

Minnesota Twins	W-L	ERA	AB	H	HR	BB	SO	BA	SA	OBA
Season	16-9	3.21	886	205	17	65	163	.231	.356	.286
vs. Left-Handers			139	36	1	12	16	.259	.367	.316
vs. Right-Handers			747	169	16	53	147	.226	.353	.280
vs. Ground-Ballers			396	95	4	28	66	.240	.328	.292
vs. Fly-Ballers			490	110	13	37	97	.224	.378	.280
Home Games	10-4	2.83	501	117	8	40	94	.234	.353	.294
Road Games	6-5	3.71	385	88	9	25	69	.229	.358	.275
Grass Fields	5-4	3.20	307	66	8	23	56	.215	.355	.271
Artificial Turf	11-5	3.22	579	139	9	42	107	.240	.356	.294
April	0-2	6.84	93	24	3	17	13	.258	.452	.368
May	4-1	3.79	137	36	4	11	24	.263	.438	.320
June	4-0	1.34	169	34	4	8	35	.201	.331	.242
July	2-2	3.25	127	26	3	11	28	.205	.339	.270
August	4-1	2.91	197	48	3	11	35	.244	.371	.287
Sept./Oct.	2-3	3.02	163	37	0	7	28	.227	.252	.259
Leading Off Inn.			236	61	5	12	37	.258	.419	.300
Bases Empty			552	130	11	38	105	.236	.373	.288
Runners On			334	75	6	27	58	.225	.326	.282
Runners/Scor. Pos.			193	52	3	14	29	.269	.383	.315
Runners On/2 Out			139	29	3	10	28	.209	.331	.272
Scor. Pos./2 Out			79	20	2	8	12	.253	.418	.337
Late-Inning Pressure			84	14	1	6	14	.167	.250	.222
Leading Off			24	3	0	1	5	.125	.167	.160
Runners On			25	2	0	2	3	.080	.080	.148
Runners/Scor. Pos.			13	2	0	0	1	.154	.154	.154
First 9 Batters			279	64	6	24	56	.229	.351	.293
Second 9 Batters			270	56	7	25	54	.207	.341	.278
All Batters Thereafter			337	85	4	16	53	.252	.371	.286

Loves to face: Howard Johnson (.103, 4-for-39)
Lloyd McClendon (.167, 3-for-18)
Gerald Young (.056, 1-for-18, 4 BB)
Hates to face: Felix Jose (.444, 8-for-18)
Tom Pagnozzi (.368, 7-for-19, 1 HR)
Matt Williams (.429, 9-for-21, 4 HR)

Miscellaneous statistics: Ground outs-to-air outs ratio: 0.91 last season, 0.91 for career.... Opponents grounded into 14 double plays in 147 opportunities (one per 11).... Allowed 51 doubles (4th most in majors), 4 triples in 241 innings.... Allowed 13 first-inning runs in 34 starts (3.18 ERA).... Batting support: 4.09 runs per start.... Opposing base stealers: 25-for-41 (61%); 10 pickoffs (2d most in A.L.), 0 balks.

Comments: Made 32 starts for the Pirates in 1991, 34 for the Twins last season. This season, pitching for the Reds, Smiley could become the second pitcher in this century to make 30-plus starts for three different teams in three consecutive years. The first: Mike Torrez (four teams in four years, 1974–77).... Joined the Twins coming off a 20-win season; over the last 75 years, the only pitcher younger than Smiley to be traded following a 20-win season was Steve Carlton, who went on to win another 252 games after being traded from St. Louis to Philadelphia in 1972.... Twins were the first defending World Series champions ever to add an incumbent 20-game winner to their staff in the off-season.... Winless in five consecutive starts after recording his 14th victory on August 26; no pitcher has won 20 games in consecutive seasons in the American and National Leagues since Jack Chesbro in 1902–03.... Had a 7–1 record with a 2.25 ERA in 11 starts in which he recorded more ground outs than air outs; he was 9–8 with a 3.55 ERA when the opposite was true.... Completed five of his last 15 starts after going the distance only once in his previous 49 starts. A big part of that story: holding opponents to .167 batting average in Late-Inning Pressure Situations, 4th lowest among major league starters (minimum: 50 LIPS ABs).... Could spearhead a Players Association demand for one-month mid-season sabbaticals: He owns a 9–14 career record during July, 67–37 in all other months combined.

Dave Stewart
Throws Right

Oakland A's	W-L	ERA	AB	H	HR	BB	SO	BA	SA	OBA
Season	12-10	3.66	737	175	25	79	130	.237	.393	.315
vs. Left-Handers			340	89	11	46	51	.262	.415	.349
vs. Right-Handers			397	86	14	33	79	.217	.375	.284
vs. Ground-Ballers			394	105	16	40	63	.266	.444	.333
vs. Fly-Ballers			343	70	9	39	67	.204	.335	.294
Home Games	4-5	3.73	363	82	14	38	76	.226	.383	.304
Road Games	8-5	3.58	374	93	11	41	54	.249	.404	.325
Grass Fields	10-8	3.87	579	130	21	69	112	.225	.382	.311
Artificial Turf	2-2	2.79	158	45	4	10	18	.285	.437	.331
April	1-2	3.86	137	32	4	15	17	.234	.394	.312
May	2-3	4.65	144	30	9	24	36	.208	.465	.326
June	4-0	3.24	126	32	5	11	20	.254	.421	.319
July	0-0	5.23	50	19	0	1	7	.380	.460	.404
August	3-3	3.18	140	29	3	16	20	.207	.300	.283
Sept./Oct.	2-2	2.84	140	33	4	12	30	.236	.364	.305
Leading Off Inn.			188	46	7	20	37	.245	.399	.324
Bases Empty			454	98	16	51	85	.216	.366	.303
Runners On			283	77	9	28	45	.272	.438	.333
Runners/Scor. Pos.			149	38	6	18	29	.255	.443	.328
Runners On/2 Out			121	31	6	12	20	.256	.471	.323
Scor. Pos./2 Out			72	18	5	9	13	.250	.542	.333
Late-Inning Pressure			49	13	3	9	9	.265	.469	.373
Leading Off			15	4	2	4	4	.267	.667	.353
Runners On			21	6	1	1	2	.286	.476	.304
Runners/Scor. Pos.			10	2	1	0	2	.200	.600	.182
First 9 Batters			245	52	8	24	53	.212	.359	.296
Second 9 Batters			238	57	6	29	40	.239	.378	.321
All Batters Thereafter			254	66	11	26	37	.260	.441	.327

Loves to face: Dean Palmer (0-for-12)
Harold Reynolds (.113, 7-for-62, 7 BB)
Gary DiSarcina (0-for-9)
Hates to face: Wade Boggs (.371, 23-for-62, 2 HR)
Danny Tartabull (.417, 15-for-36, 5 HR)
Greg Vaughn (.333, 8-for-24, 2 2B, 5 HR, 7 BB)

Miscellaneous statistics: Ground outs-to-air outs ratio: 0.60 last season (lowest in A.L.), 0.84 for career.... Opponents grounded into 14 double plays in 149 opportunities (one per 11).... Allowed 28 doubles, 6 triples in 199⅓ innings.... Allowed 17 first-inning runs in 31 starts (3.77 ERA).... Batting support: 4.61 runs per start.... Opposing base stealers: 15-for-25 (60%); 1 pickoff, 1 balk.

Comments: The 1992 Athletics were the first team since the 1984 Tigers not to use a left-handed starting pitcher. Even the bullpen was predominantly right-handed; the club's total of only 91⅔ innings pitched by lefties was the lowest by any team since the 1983 Blue Jays.... Starting assignment in the first game of the 1992 A.L.C.S. was his seventh in the opening game of a postseason series; only Whitey Ford (eight) and Don Gullett (seven) had as many. Stew is 3–1 with three no-decisions in those openers.... Holds the major league record for most L.C.S. wins (6) without any losses; only two other pitchers are even 4–0 in L.C.S. play (Bruce Kison and John Smoltz).... Has balked only once in 950 innings since setting major league record with 16 balks in 1987.... First Athletics pitcher with a winning percentage of at least .500 in seven consecutive seasons since Lefty Grove had an eight-year streak (1926–33).... Leaves Oakland with 116 wins in six-plus seasons, including 107 over the last six years; Roger Clemens (112) and Frank Viola (100) are the only other pitchers who have won 100 games since 1987.... If they can't beat you, join 'em? Stew is the 2d pitcher in as many years to join the Jays during the offseason after starting against them in the previous postseason; Jack Morris was the first. The only other pitchers to make a similar switch: Don Gullett (1976 Reds to '77 Yankees) and Tommy John (1978 Dodgers to '79 Yankees). Those four were a combined 5–0 in those postseason series.

Todd Stottlemyre — Throws Right

Toronto Blue Jays	W-L	ERA	AB	H	HR	BB	SO	BA	SA	OBA
Season	12-11	4.50	669	175	20	63	98	.262	.398	.329
vs. Left-Handers			284	80	6	32	21	.282	.394	.355
vs. Right-Handers			385	95	14	31	77	.247	.400	.310
vs. Ground-Ballers			365	106	7	36	42	.290	.400	.354
vs. Fly-Ballers			304	69	13	27	56	.227	.395	.300
Home Games	7-5	4.79	322	87	10	26	50	.270	.410	.331
Road Games	5-6	4.24	347	88	10	37	48	.254	.386	.328
Grass Fields	5-4	3.43	280	63	8	28	43	.225	.354	.301
Artificial Turf	7-7	5.33	389	112	12	35	55	.288	.429	.350
April	3-1	4.50	134	33	3	16	21	.246	.358	.322
May	1-3	5.28	123	31	5	14	17	.252	.415	.338
June	1-2	6.75	91	31	4	10	9	.341	.516	.404
July	1-1	3.00	64	17	0	9	10	.266	.344	.342
August	3-2	3.76	140	32	3	11	23	.229	.336	.296
Sept./Oct.	3-2	3.94	117	31	5	3	18	.265	.436	.301
Leading Off Inn.			166	44	4	14	13	.265	.373	.326
Bases Empty			394	94	10	29	52	.239	.363	.297
Runners On			275	81	10	34	46	.295	.447	.371
Runners/Scor. Pos.			151	47	6	21	29	.311	.477	.388
Runners On/2 Out			108	30	1	18	19	.278	.343	.391
Scor. Pos./2 Out			74	21	1	15	15	.284	.365	.411
Late-Inning Pressure			33	8	0	4	10	.242	.303	.324
Leading Off			10	3	0	2	1	.300	.400	.417
Runners On			11	3	0	1	4	.273	.364	.333
Runners/Scor. Pos.			5	1	0	1	3	.200	.200	.333
First 9 Batters			219	57	11	17	35	.260	.461	.318
Second 9 Batters			212	55	4	24	28	.259	.354	.333
All Batters Thereafter			238	63	5	22	35	.265	.378	.336

Loves to face: Scott Fletcher (.056, 1-for-18, 2 BB)
Lance Johnson (.130, 3-for-23, 0 SO)
Pete O'Brien (.105, 2-for-19, 2 2B)

Hates to face: George Brett (.571, 12-for-21)
Jose Canseco (.375, 9-for-24, 7 HR)
Rafael Palmeiro (.400, 8-for-20, 2 HR)

Miscellaneous statistics: Ground outs-to-air outs ratio: 0.93 last season, 0.94 for career.... Opponents grounded into 9 double plays in 157 opportunities (one per 17), 4th-worst rate in A.L.... Allowed 31 doubles, 0 triples in 174 innings.... Allowed 19 first-inning runs in 27 starts (5.33 ERA).... Batting support: 5.30 runs per start (4th-highest average in majors).... Opposing base stealers: 17-for-20 (85%); 0 pickoffs, 0 balks.

Comments: One of three major league pitchers to win at least 10 games and show a winning record despite a season ERA of 4.50 or higher; the others: Scott Sanderson (12–11, 4.93) and Bill Krueger (10–8, 4.53).... Jimmy Key won each of his last five regular-season decisions while Stot won five of seven down the stretch, but they started only one postseason game between them.... Opponents' batting average with runners in scoring position was 3d highest in A.L.; the bottom five: Erik Hanson (.372), Walt Terrell (.344), Stottlemyre (.344), Scott Sanderson (.309), Jack Armstrong (.301).... Left-handed batters are no longer the nightmare they were in his first three years in the majors, when they hit .300 or better each year; however, lefties' .292 career mark vs. Stot is 3d highest among pitchers active in 1992. Only Bill Swift (.303) and Dennis Lamp (.296) have allowed higher averages.... His 7–0 career record vs. Baltimore makes him the only active pitcher who is undefeated in at least four decisions against the Birds.... Stottlemyres became second father/son combination to pitch in World Series: Mel Sr. with 1964 Yankees, Todd with four scoreless relief stints last fall. The Jim Bagbys pitched in the 1920 and 1946 World Series with Indians and Red Sox, respectively.... Todd will turn 28 years of age on May 20. Dad: "Back in my day, by the time I turned 28, I had already had three 20-win seasons." Todd: "Yeah, but you had also had a 20-loss season and you never won a World Series. Besides, let's compare dollars."

Rick Sutcliffe — Throws Right

Baltimore Orioles	W-L	ERA	AB	H	HR	BB	SO	BA	SA	OBA
Season	16-15	4.47	920	251	20	74	109	.273	.393	.328
vs. Left-Handers			431	114	13	37	44	.265	.418	.320
vs. Right-Handers			489	137	7	37	65	.280	.372	.335
vs. Ground-Ballers			478	127	6	37	58	.266	.374	.318
vs. Fly-Ballers			442	124	14	37	51	.281	.414	.339
Home Games	9-8	4.17	497	117	12	45	63	.235	.346	.301
Road Games	7-7	4.85	423	134	8	29	46	.317	.449	.361
Grass Fields	12-12	4.69	723	188	19	61	85	.260	.385	.320
Artificial Turf	4-3	3.65	197	63	1	13	24	.320	.426	.360
April	3-2	2.65	140	34	0	7	21	.243	.293	.279
May	4-2	6.33	174	52	8	12	17	.299	.523	.344
June	3-2	3.21	159	43	1	12	15	.270	.327	.311
July	0-5	5.85	164	49	3	16	23	.299	.445	.363
August	4-0	1.60	163	39	1	17	19	.239	.288	.313
Sept./Oct.	2-4	8.31	120	34	7	10	14	.283	.483	.356
Leading Off Inn.			229	74	3	21	22	.323	.419	.387
Bases Empty			516	148	10	42	65	.287	.403	.346
Runners On			404	103	10	32	44	.255	.381	.305
Runners/Scor. Pos.			207	52	8	21	29	.251	.401	.311
Runners On/2 Out			154	33	2	13	17	.214	.318	.280
Scor. Pos./2 Out			100	18	2	9	12	.180	.270	.255
Late-Inning Pressure			92	25	1	6	15	.272	.337	.310
Leading Off			27	6	0	2	6	.222	.222	.276
Runners On			25	7	0	3	1	.280	.320	.333
Runners/Scor. Pos.			10	3	0	1	1	.300	.300	.308
First 9 Batters			291	67	3	25	47	.230	.313	.294
Second 9 Batters			288	90	6	26	28	.313	.441	.371
All Batters Thereafter			341	94	11	23	34	.276	.422	.321

Loves to face: George Brett (.048, 1-for-21, 3 BB)
Spike Owen (.100, 2-for-20, 2 BB)
Kirby Puckett (.071, 1-for-14)

Hates to face: Edgar Martinez (.538, 7-for-13)
Rafael Palmeiro (.625, 5-for-8, 2 2B, 2 HR)
Dave Winfield (.400, 14-for-35, 5 HR)

Miscellaneous statistics: Ground outs-to-air outs ratio: 0.73 last season, 0.96 for career.... Opponents grounded into 20 double plays in 217 opportunities (one per 11).... Allowed 37 doubles, 7 triples in 237⅓ innings.... Allowed 22 first-inning runs in 36 starts (5.25 ERA).... Batting support: 4.06 runs per start.... Opposing base stealers: 22-for-27 (81%); 3 pickoffs, 2 balks.

Comments: Became the 12th pitcher to win more than 15 games in a season for four different teams. Among the more familiar names on that list: Burleigh Grimes, Cy Young, and Mike Torrez (the only other pitcher in the postwar era to have done it).... His 1992 won-lost record: 0–10 in games in which he allowed a first-inning run, 16–5 in his other starts.... His 4.47 season ERA was the highest by any major league pitcher to win at least 16 games since Frank Viola had a 16–13 record and a 4.51 ERA in 1986.... Ground outs-to-air outs ratio (0.73) was 3d lowest among A.L. starters, behind fly-ballers Dave Stewart (0.60) and Bill Gullickson (0.73); ground outs-to-air outs ratio of Orioles starters (0.88) was the lowest by starters of any A.L. team.... Allowed the most runs (123) and the most earned runs (118) in the majors last season; it's the first time since the Browns moved to Baltimore in 1954 that an Orioles pitcher has led the A.L. in runs allowed.... Was the youngest pitcher in the majors at the time of his debut in 1976.... Since 1947, when Jackie Robinson won the first Rookie of the Year award, 23 major league pitchers have been honored as the top rookie in their league. Among them, Sutcliffe and Tom Seaver are the only ones to win 150 games. Most wins by past winners: Seaver, 311–205 (1967 N.L. Rookie of the Year); Sutcliffe, 155–125 (1979 N.L.); Don Newcombe, 149–90 (1949 N.L.); Stan Bahnsen, 146–149 (1968 A.L.); Dwight Gooden, 142–66 (1984 N.L.); Fernando Valenzuela, 141–118 (1981 N.L.)

Russ Swan   Throws Left

Seattle Mariners	W-L	ERA	AB	H	HR	BB	SO	BA	SA	OBA
Season	3-10	4.74	397	104	8	45	45	.262	.398	.338
vs. Left-Handers			81	16	0	8	15	.198	.222	.275
vs. Right-Handers			316	88	8	37	30	.278	.443	.354
vs. Ground-Ballers			187	57	2	27	19	.305	.417	.392
vs. Fly-Ballers			210	47	6	18	26	.224	.381	.288
Home Games	1-6	6.44	186	60	5	15	20	.323	.500	.376
Road Games	2-4	3.54	211	44	3	30	25	.209	.308	.306
Grass Fields	2-4	3.26	171	35	2	23	20	.205	.287	.296
Artificial Turf	1-6	6.09	226	69	6	22	25	.305	.482	.370
April	2-3	4.94	113	24	1	10	11	.212	.363	.286
May	0-2	7.40	101	31	3	14	12	.307	.505	.388
June	0-0	2.92	50	14	0	5	5	.280	.320	.345
July	1-2	2.41	66	14	2	5	9	.212	.303	.264
August	0-2	6.30	39	13	2	5	5	.333	.538	.409
Sept./Oct.	0-1	2.25	28	8	0	6	3	.286	.321	.405
Leading Off Inn.			92	23	2	8	6	.250	.348	.310
Bases Empty			211	51	3	23	23	.242	.336	.316
Runners On			186	53	5	22	22	.285	.468	.361
Runners/Scor. Pos.			115	30	2	15	16	.261	.417	.338
Runners On/2 Out			79	19	2	8	11	.241	.418	.310
Scor. Pos./2 Out			52	10	1	6	10	.192	.327	.276
Late-Inning Pressure			125	33	4	9	15	.264	.384	.311
Leading Off			31	6	0	1	1	.194	.194	.219
Runners On			57	15	3	6	10	.263	.456	.328
Runners/Scor. Pos.			29	5	1	4	6	.172	.310	.265
First 9 Batters			265	67	5	32	33	.253	.355	.330
Second 9 Batters			70	21	1	7	7	.300	.529	.380
All Batters Thereafter			62	16	2	6	5	.258	.435	.324

Loves to face: Mike Greenwell (.091, 1-for-11)
Lance Johnson (0-for-10)
Lou Whitaker (0-for-11)

Hates to face: Ellis Burks (.375, 3-for-8, 1 2B, 1 HR)
Carlton Fisk (.750, 3-for-4, 1 HR)
Shane Mack (.571, 4-for-7, 2 3B, 1 BB)

Miscellaneous statistics: Ground outs-to-air outs ratio: 2.13 last season, 2.28 for career. . . . Opponents grounded into 9 double plays in 94 opportunities (one per 10). . . . Allowed 22 doubles, 4 triples in 104⅓ innings. . . . Stranded 27 inherited runners, allowed 11 to score (71%). . . . Opposing base stealers: 5-for-7 (71%); 1 pickoff, 0 balks.

Comments: Quietly, he has become one of the most effective pitchers in baseball against left-handed batters. Over the past two seasons, only three A.L. pitchers have held lefties to a lower batting average (minimum: 200 at-bats by LHB): Bryan Harvey, .180; Tom Henke, .185; Duane Ward, .195; Swan .195 (39-for-200). No pitcher in either league has held left-handed batters to as low a slugging percentage: Swan, .225; Juan Guzman, .242; Gregg Olson, .250; Rob Dibble, .266; Tim Wakefield, .270 (same minimum as above). . . . Has held opposing left-handed batters to a sub-.200 batting average in each of the last two seasons; over his career, left-handed batters have reached him for only five extra-base hits in 240 at-bats; the only home run among those five was hit by John Olerud in July 1991. Right-handed batters have a .292 career average against him, with one extra-base hit every 9.2 at-bats. . . . Getting lefties out is a useful specialty in Seattle, considering that lefties raked the Mariners staff for a .274 average last season, 2d highest against any A.L. team. . . . Career breakdown: 4–11, 5.27 ERA in 20 starts; 7–7, 3.51 ERA in 113 games in relief. . . . Doesn't look like he's a big fan of either Candlestick or the Kingdome, the two major league stadiums he has called home; career ERA: 5.58 at home (3–9 record, including four straight losses), 3.28 on the road (8–9). . . . One of five pitchers active in 1992 with more career walks than strikeouts (minimum: 200 IP). The others: Mike Dunne, Jose DeJesus, Jose Mesa, and Pat Clements.

Frank Tanana   Throws Left

Detroit Tigers	W-L	ERA	AB	H	HR	BB	SO	BA	SA	OBA
Season	13-11	4.39	704	188	22	90	91	.267	.415	.351
vs. Left-Handers			102	23	2	8	15	.225	.333	.282
vs. Right-Handers			602	165	20	82	76	.274	.429	.362
vs. Ground-Ballers			350	90	8	38	40	.257	.386	.333
vs. Fly-Ballers			354	98	14	52	51	.277	.444	.369
Home Games	7-5	4.98	300	84	12	37	41	.280	.457	.360
Road Games	6-6	3.96	404	104	10	53	50	.257	.384	.345
Grass Fields	12-11	4.55	652	176	20	84	85	.270	.416	.354
Artificial Turf	1-0	2.45	52	12	2	6	6	.231	.404	.322
April	0-2	9.20	60	22	2	13	8	.367	.550	.473
May	3-2	4.18	121	32	4	17	15	.264	.438	.350
June	4-1	3.96	141	35	5	17	20	.248	.433	.331
July	2-1	2.65	118	26	3	17	14	.220	.331	.326
August	2-2	4.00	140	39	4	13	17	.279	.393	.344
Sept./Oct.	2-3	5.13	124	34	4	13	17	.274	.411	.345
Leading Off Inn.			176	42	8	20	17	.239	.420	.323
Bases Empty			401	108	15	51	43	.269	.429	.359
Runners On			303	80	7	39	48	.264	.396	.342
Runners/Scor. Pos.			157	35	3	27	30	.223	.312	.323
Runners On/2 Out			126	28	2	17	20	.222	.302	.315
Scor. Pos./2 Out			75	16	2	15	14	.213	.307	.344
Late-Inning Pressure			35	10	3	10	3	.286	.657	.444
Leading Off			11	3	2	2	0	.273	.909	.385
Runners On			14	3	0	6	3	.214	.214	.450
Runners/Scor. Pos.			11	2	0	4	2	.182	.182	.400
First 9 Batters			241	70	7	34	42	.290	.432	.379
Second 9 Batters			227	54	6	28	31	.238	.348	.326
All Batters Thereafter			236	64	9	28	18	.271	.462	.347

Loves to face: Alex Cole (0-for-6, 3 SO)
Phil Plantier (0-for-3, 3 SO)
Cory Snyder (.086, 3-for-35, 3 BB)

Hates to face: Cecil Espy (.556, 5-for-9)
Junior Felix (.400, 6-for-15, 3 2B, 1 HR)
Bill Pecota (.556, 5-for-9)

Miscellaneous statistics: Ground outs-to-air outs ratio: 0.88 last season, 0.98 for career. . . . Opponents grounded into 21 double plays in 164 opportunities (one per 7.8). . . . Allowed 34 doubles, 2 triples in 186⅔ innings. . . . Allowed 23 first-inning runs in 31 starts (5.52 ERA). . . . Batting support: 4.61 runs per start. . . . Opposing base stealers: 21-for-32 (66%); 10 pickoffs (2d most in A.L.), 1 balk.

Comments: Rickey Henderson's 11 career home runs against him are the most of any batter/pitcher combination active in the majors. . . . The nine-inning games he started last season lasted an average of 3:03, 4th highest in the majors among pitchers with at least 20 starts; only Mike Moore (3:07), Ben McDonald (3:05), and Nolan Ryan (3:04) had higher averages. Considering that Sid Fernandez had the highest average of any N.L. pitcher last season (3:00), and that the Mets played longer nine-inning games than any N.L. team last season (2:52), "Kiner's Korner" could become legitimate competition for Leno and Letterman. . . . Struck out 25 batters during the first innings of his 31 starts, an average of 7.26 per nine innings, almost twice his average from the second inning on (3.80 per nine innings). His strikeout rate has decreased in each of the last three seasons. . . . Much of his success, or lack of it, in recent years can be measured by the rate at which his opponents have grounded out. Over the last three seasons, he has a 14–6 record in games in which ground outs outnumbered air outs; in his other starts, he has a 20–25 mark. . . . Owned the 2d-highest ERA in the majors last April, while three other Detroit pitchers stood among the five worst. . . . Pitched 3984 innings in the American League, the highest total ever amassed by a pitcher exclusively in the A.L. before switching to the N.L.; six pitchers have started their careers with at least that many N.L. innings before switching to the A.L.: Cy Young, Burleigh Grimes, Tom Seaver, Don Sutton, Phil Niekro, and Steve Carlton.

Kevin Tapani — Throws Right

Minnesota Twins	W-L	ERA	AB	H	HR	BB	SO	BA	SA	OBA
Season	16-11	3.97	839	226	17	48	138	.269	.405	.309
vs. Left-Handers			434	121	12	24	78	.279	.452	.313
vs. Right-Handers			405	105	5	24	60	.259	.356	.304
vs. Ground-Ballers			434	113	6	26	59	.260	.380	.304
vs. Fly-Ballers			405	113	11	22	79	.279	.432	.314
Home Games	11-4	3.48	487	135	6	24	83	.277	.400	.312
Road Games	5-7	4.63	352	91	11	24	55	.259	.412	.305
Grass Fields	5-5	4.25	271	68	9	17	41	.251	.402	.295
Artificial Turf	11-6	3.83	568	158	8	31	97	.278	.407	.316
April	1-2	4.81	91	28	1	7	14	.308	.484	.353
May	4-2	5.35	146	43	6	7	28	.295	.486	.325
June	3-1	3.02	158	39	2	5	26	.247	.323	.270
July	4-1	2.95	149	37	3	9	21	.248	.369	.298
August	2-3	4.15	162	42	5	11	28	.259	.407	.299
Sept./Oct.	2-2	4.04	133	37	0	9	21	.278	.398	.329
Leading Off Inn.			216	53	6	11	31	.245	.394	.285
Bases Empty			514	136	13	32	89	.265	.407	.311
Runners On			325	90	4	16	49	.277	.403	.305
Runners/Scor. Pos.			191	54	2	12	34	.283	.408	.315
Runners On/2 Out			142	35	3	8	27	.246	.345	.287
Scor. Pos./2 Out			95	22	1	6	21	.232	.295	.277
Late-Inning Pressure			40	10	2	4	4	.250	.450	.318
Leading Off			12	3	2	2	1	.250	.750	.357
Runners On			11	4	0	0	0	.364	.545	.364
Runners/Scor. Pos.			3	1	0	0	0	.333	.333	.333
First 9 Batters			283	72	7	14	59	.254	.392	.290
Second 9 Batters			280	77	4	15	46	.275	.400	.312
All Batters Thereafter			276	77	6	19	33	.279	.424	.325

Loves to face: Jeff Huson (.056, 1-for-18, 1 2B)
Don Mattingly (.091, 2-for-22)
Luis Rivera (0-for-11)

Hates to face: Travis Fryman (.667, 6-for-9, 1 HR)
Paul Sorrento (.625, 5-for-8, 2 2B, 2 HR, 2 SO)
Robin Ventura (.421, 8-for-19, 2 HR)

Miscellaneous statistics: Ground outs-to-air outs ratio: 1.24 last season, 1.13 for career.... Opponents grounded into 17 double plays in 127 opportunities (one per 7.5).... Allowed 53 doubles (most in majors), 5 triples in 220 innings.... Allowed 12 first-inning runs in 34 starts (2.38 ERA).... Batting support: 5.35 runs per start, 3d-highest average in majors.... Opposing base stealers: 26-for-37 (70%); 0 pickoffs, 0 balks.

Comments: Has averaged fewer than two walks per nine innings in each of the last three seasons. Only four other pitchers in this century have done that in three straight seasons starting with their rookie year (minimum: 150 innings each season): Fred Glade (1904–06), Ray Kremer (1924–26), Bill Swift (the other one—four years, 1932–35), and Hank Wyse (1943–45).... Has walked more than two batters in only 15 of 101 career starts, and has walked more than three only twice.... Career walk rate is just about the same vs. left-handed batters (one every 21.2 plate appearances) as vs. right-handed batters (one every 20.9 PA).... Brian Harper caught all but seven of his 220 innings last season.... His 11 wins at the Metrodome tied Kevin Brown and Jack Morris for most home victories in A.L. Career breakdown: 30–13, 3.31 ERA at the Metrodome; 16–17, 3.97 ERA elsewhere. Among active starters, only Dwight Gooden (81–28) and Ted Higuera (54–22) have better records at their home parks (minimum: 15 home wins).... Owns 25–9 career record in June, July, and August; he's 21–21 in the other months.... Three of his four complete games last year came in consecutive starts; only nine other pitchers hurled three straight CGs last season.... Yearly won-lost records since 1990: 12–8, 16–9, 16–11. Only three other pitchers have compiled a "plus-four" record in each of the past three years: Roger Clemens, Jack McDowell, and Jose Rijo. Jim Kaat is the only other Twins starter with at least three straight plus-fours in a row since the team moved to the Midwest in 1961.

Walt Terrell — Throws Right

Detroit Tigers	W-L	ERA	AB	H	HR	BB	SO	BA	SA	OBA
Season	7-10	5.20	547	163	14	48	61	.298	.431	.354
vs. Left-Handers			235	67	3	20	20	.285	.387	.342
vs. Right-Handers			312	96	11	28	41	.308	.465	.362
vs. Ground-Ballers			272	81	4	23	25	.298	.390	.349
vs. Fly-Ballers			275	82	10	25	36	.298	.473	.358
Home Games	4-3	4.76	247	68	9	22	32	.275	.445	.331
Road Games	3-7	5.57	300	95	5	26	29	.317	.420	.372
Grass Fields	6-9	5.22	474	141	14	41	53	.297	.437	.352
Artificial Turf	1-1	5.09	73	22	0	7	8	.301	.397	.366
April	0-3	5.74	97	26	4	11	13	.268	.412	.339
May	0-3	8.44	65	25	0	12	5	.385	.477	.481
June	1-2	2.43	112	25	5	14	5	.223	.384	.263
July	3-1	7.02	78	27	0	7	5	.346	.474	.400
August	1-0	5.89	75	23	2	4	10	.307	.480	.338
Sept./Oct.	2-1	4.30	120	37	3	9	14	.308	.408	.351
Leading Off Inn.			127	28	2	12	15	.220	.331	.293
Bases Empty			306	75	7	21	34	.245	.366	.298
Runners On			241	88	7	27	27	.365	.515	.420
Runners/Scor. Pos.			131	45	2	24	16	.344	.435	.429
Runners On/2 Out			97	30	3	13	15	.309	.454	.396
Scor. Pos./2 Out			65	18	2	12	10	.277	.415	.397
Late-Inning Pressure			45	15	2	2	6	.333	.489	.375
Leading Off			13	5	1	1	0	.385	.615	.429
Runners On			16	6	0	1	4	.375	.438	.444
Runners/Scor. Pos.			8	3	0	1	1	.375	.375	.500
First 9 Batters			251	85	8	23	18	.339	.494	.392
Second 9 Batters			178	46	1	11	30	.258	.331	.301
All Batters Thereafter			118	32	5	14	13	.271	.449	.351

Loves to face: Kevin McReynolds (0-for-9)
Tony Pena (.097, 3-for-31)
Billy Ripken (0-for-19)

Hates to face: Carlos Baerga (.526, 10-for-19, 1 HR)
Wade Boggs (.433, 26-for-60, 2 HR)
Paul Molitor (.477, 21-for-44, 2 HR)

Miscellaneous statistics: Ground outs-to-air outs ratio: 1.17 last season, 1.37 for career.... Opponents grounded into 11 double plays in 131 opportunities (one per 12).... Allowed 27 doubles, 2 triples in 136⅔ innings.... Allowed 10 first-inning runs in 14 starts (6.92 ERA).... Batting support: 5.07 runs per start.... Record of 3–6, 6.63 ERA as a starter; 4–4, 3.34 ERA in 22 relief appearances.... Stranded 10 inherited runners, allowed 6 to score (63%).... Opposing base stealers: 7-for-10 (70%); 0 pickoffs, 0 balks.

Comments: Two reasons why Sparky's hair is whiter than ever: (1) Terrell's 6.92 ERA during the first inning last season; (2) his 10.38 ERA in the second inning.... Opponents' batting average with runners on base was the highest in the majors last season; average with runners in scoring position was 2d highest in the league.... Last year marked his fifth straight sub-.500 season, with at least 15 decisions in each of those years. Kevin Gross has done that in each of the last six years; no one else has had five straight since Eric Rasmussen (1976–80).... For the sixth time in his career, Terrell had a winning record at home and a losing record on the road; his road record has been below .500 eight years in a row. Career breakdown: 65–49 in home games, 46–75 on the road.... Don't you love when people talk about the value of "taking the ball" or "throwing innings" without any consideration of the *quality* of the innings that a guy throws? Is it valuable to have a guy throw 240 innings in which he gets creamed? Okay, Terrell takes the ball; he pitches innings. But he's the first pitcher in major league history who, starting with his rookie season, has pitched 10 consecutive seasons with at least 100 innings and an ERA above 3.50 every year. Only two other pitchers have done that anytime during their careers: Rube Walberg (11 years, 1927–37) and Milt Gaston (1925–34). Those guys, of course, pitched in an era in which ERAs were very high throughout baseball; even so, neither one answered the bell the next season.

Bobby Thigpen

Throws Right

Chicago White Sox	W-L	ERA	AB	H	HR	BB	SO	BA	SA	OBA
Season	1-3	4.75	211	58	4	33	45	.275	.374	.375
vs. Left-Handers			80	27	1	15	10	.338	.400	.429
vs. Right-Handers			131	31	3	18	35	.237	.359	.340
vs. Ground-Ballers			92	30	3	19	17	.326	.446	.447
vs. Fly-Ballers			119	28	1	14	28	.235	.319	.314
Home Games	1-2	3.77	116	33	1	12	28	.284	.336	.354
Road Games	0-1	5.81	95	25	3	21	17	.263	.421	.397
Grass Fields	1-2	4.10	199	52	3	29	43	.261	.337	.357
Artificial Turf	0-1	19.29	12	6	1	4	2	.500	1.000	.625
April	0-0	2.89	31	7	0	6	5	.226	.258	.342
May	0-2	6.17	44	13	1	5	14	.295	.432	.346
June	0-0	0.00	39	8	0	7	9	.205	.231	.326
July	1-0	8.71	42	13	2	6	9	.310	.524	.408
August	0-0	5.40	31	11	1	4	5	.355	.452	.459
Sept./Oct.	0-1	5.68	24	6	0	5	3	.250	.292	.379
Leading Off Inn.			37	8	1	9	10	.216	.297	.370
Bases Empty			98	24	2	11	24	.245	.337	.321
Runners On			113	34	2	22	21	.301	.407	.415
Runners/Scor. Pos.			72	19	1	13	12	.264	.375	.367
Runners On/2 Out			54	13	1	12	10	.241	.352	.379
Scor. Pos./2 Out			40	9	1	8	8	.225	.375	.354
Late-Inning Pressure			145	36	2	25	35	.248	.331	.358
Leading Off			24	4	0	8	8	.167	.167	.375
Runners On			78	23	1	15	14	.295	.385	.404
Runners/Scor. Pos.			52	13	1	9	10	.250	.365	.348
First 9 Batters			209	57	4	33	45	.273	.373	.373
Second 9 Batters			2	1	0	0	0	.500	.500	.500
All Batters Thereafter			0	0	0	0	0	—	—	—

Loves to face: George Brett (.067, 1-for-15, 2 BB)
Joe Carter (.077, 1-for-13, 1 2B)
Geno Petralli (.063, 1-for-16)

Hates to face: Julio Franco (.636, 7-for-11, 1 HR)
Mark McGwire (.385, 5-for-13, 2 HR)
Matt Nokes (.400, 6-for-15, 1 HR)

Miscellaneous statistics: Ground outs-to-air outs ratio: 0.83 last season, 0.91 for career.... Opponents grounded into 5 double plays in 65 opportunities (one per 13).... Allowed 9 doubles, 0 triples in 55 innings.... Saved 22 games in 32 opportunities (69%).... Stranded 26 inherited runners, allowed 12 to score (68%).... Opposing base stealers: 3-for-3 (100%); 0 pickoffs, 0 balks.

Comments: Became the first pitcher ever to reach the 200-save mark before his 30th birthday. The youngest pitcher to reach that plateau previously was Bruce Sutter in 1983 (30 years, 5 months); Thigpen did it at the age of 29 years, 2 months.... Recorded the 200th save of his career in his 397th relief appearance. Only two pitchers reached the 200 mark in fewer appearances; the five fastest: Dennis Eckersley, 324; Dan Quisenberry, 393; Thigpen, 397; Dave Righetti, 411; Bruce Sutter, 444.... Recorded only one save in seven opportunities from July 2 to September 14; August was his first saveless month since June 1987.... Saved 22 games despite an average of 5.40 walks per nine innings. Only four pitchers have saved as many games in a season with a walk rate as high: Mitch Williams (1989, 1991, 1992), Bryan Harvey (1989), Don Stanhouse (1978), and Ted Abernathy (1971).... Two other White Sox pitchers saved more than 10 games: Scott Radinsky (15) and Roberto Hernandez (12). Eight other teams had three pitchers in double figures, including the 1968 White Sox—if you accept pre-1969 save figures—with Wilbur Wood (16), Hoyt Wilhelm (12), and Bob Locker (10). But no previous team had three pitchers with as many as 12 each.... Career total of 28 relief wins is tied for 5th most in White Sox history, behind Wilhelm (41), Wood (32), Gerry Staley (31), and Clint Brown (29). Only Wood (35) suffered more losses in relief than Thigpen (33).

Julio Valera

Throws Right

California Angels	W-L	ERA	AB	H	HR	BB	SO	BA	SA	OBA
Season	8-11	3.73	718	188	15	64	113	.262	.386	.323
vs. Left-Handers			336	98	4	27	33	.292	.387	.343
vs. Right-Handers			382	90	11	37	80	.236	.385	.306
vs. Ground-Ballers			339	95	5	27	52	.280	.398	.333
vs. Fly-Ballers			379	93	10	37	61	.245	.375	.314
Home Games	6-3	2.34	354	84	4	21	53	.237	.333	.284
Road Games	2-8	5.18	364	104	11	43	60	.286	.437	.359
Grass Fields	8-7	2.99	624	156	9	50	100	.250	.354	.307
Artificial Turf	0-4	9.27	94	32	6	14	13	.340	.596	.422
April	1-1	3.46	46	10	1	3	11	.217	.348	.265
May	1-2	2.94	120	26	0	14	21	.217	.258	.296
June	2-4	4.08	150	37	3	12	21	.247	.420	.302
July	1-1	3.86	161	48	6	10	25	.298	.453	.337
August	1-1	4.50	118	32	3	15	14	.271	.407	.353
Sept./Oct.	2-2	3.38	123	35	2	10	21	.285	.374	.348
Leading Off Inn.			181	58	4	16	29	.320	.459	.379
Bases Empty			414	115	10	30	67	.278	.423	.330
Runners On			304	73	5	34	46	.240	.336	.315
Runners/Scor. Pos.			168	39	1	27	21	.232	.280	.335
Runners On/2 Out			115	27	1	16	17	.235	.322	.328
Scor. Pos./2 Out			76	18	0	14	10	.237	.250	.356
Late-Inning Pressure			43	7	0	1	9	.163	.209	.182
Leading Off			14	4	0	1	5	.286	.357	.333
Runners On			12	2	0	0	3	.167	.250	.167
Runners/Scor. Pos.			3	0	0	0	1	.000	.000	.000
First 9 Batters			248	66	5	20	40	.266	.379	.322
Second 9 Batters			230	51	4	17	38	.222	.330	.278
All Batters Thereafter			240	71	6	27	35	.296	.446	.366

Loves to face: Leo Gomez (0-for-7)
Rickey Henderson (.091, 1-for-11)
Pedro Munoz (0-for-7)

Hates to face: George Brett (.778, 7-for-9)
Wally Joyner (.444, 4-for-9, 1 HR)
Tony Phillips (.857, 6-for-7)

Miscellaneous statistics: Ground outs-to-air outs ratio: 0.97 last season, 0.97 for career.... Opponents grounded into 15 double plays in 150 opportunities (one per 10).... Allowed 38 doubles, 3 triples in 188 innings.... Allowed 10 first-inning runs in 28 starts (2.89 ERA).... Batting support: 3.68 runs per start, 7th-lowest average in A.L.... Opposing base stealers: 14-for-18 (78%); 1 pickoff, 0 balks.

Comments: The only pitcher to defeat the Athletics three times last season (3–0); he and Shawn Hillegas of the Yankees were the only pitchers to throw shutouts vs. Oakland.... One of only four rookies in the majors to qualify for the ERA title (translation: "to pitch 162 or more innings"); the others: Dave Fleming, Donovan Osborne, and Butch Henry. That doesn't seem like too many, but it was actually one more than the number of rookies who qualified in 1991; the last season with a substantially greater number of qualifying rookies was 1984, when 10 rookies qualified for the ERA title.... Valera led major league rookies with 113 strikeouts, one more than Fleming, and pitched 188 innings, the most by a California rookie since Kirk McCaskill in 1985 (189⅔); Angels' rookie record is 269 by Frank Tanana in 1974.... Opponents' on-base percentage leading off innings was the 3d highest in A.L. last season; Angels pitchers allowed the league's highest batting average to batters leading off an inning (.280).... His ERA in home games was 2d lowest in league, behind only Bill Wegman (2.26); but his ERA in road games was 2d worst in the league, ahead of only Tim Leary (5.36).... Career numbers in six games on artificial turf: 0–5 record, 9.99 ERA.... Has hit only two batters in over 200 innings pitched in the majors; they came in consecutive innings against Minnesota last September (Derek Parks and Shane Mack). Guess he liked it.

Frank Viola — Throws Left

Boston Red Sox	W-L	ERA	AB	H	HR	BB	SO	BA	SA	OBA
Season	13-12	3.44	886	214	13	89	121	.242	.331	.313
vs. Left-Handers			109	23	1	10	9	.211	.294	.281
vs. Right-Handers			777	191	12	79	112	.246	.336	.317
vs. Ground-Ballers			418	93	3	35	61	.222	.282	.285
vs. Fly-Ballers			468	121	10	54	60	.259	.374	.336
Home Games	8-7	4.08	454	121	7	44	65	.267	.355	.328
Road Games	5-5	2.83	432	93	6	45	56	.215	.306	.296
Grass Fields	10-10	3.36	748	183	11	73	104	.245	.334	.312
Artificial Turf	3-2	3.89	138	31	2	16	17	.225	.312	.316
April	2-2	3.06	121	27	1	11	19	.223	.298	.289
May	3-1	2.86	132	32	3	8	20	.242	.333	.286
June	2-2	4.28	150	38	4	14	21	.253	.400	.315
July	2-1	2.32	164	40	1	17	16	.244	.287	.321
August	2-5	4.25	177	44	3	20	24	.249	.373	.322
Sept./Oct.	2-1	3.63	142	33	1	19	21	.232	.282	.331
Leading Off Inn.			231	54	2	16	32	.234	.307	.283
Bases Empty			517	125	6	45	77	.242	.315	.307
Runners On			369	89	7	44	44	.241	.352	.319
Runners/Scor. Pos.			193	48	4	32	24	.249	.378	.346
Runners On/2 Out			155	39	5	18	22	.252	.419	.337
Scor. Pos./2 Out			96	24	3	14	13	.250	.427	.351
Late-Inning Pressure			87	16	1	9	10	.184	.241	.258
Leading Off			25	4	0	3	2	.160	.160	.250
Runners On			26	6	1	4	2	.231	.385	.323
Runners/Scor. Pos.			11	2	1	4	1	.182	.455	.375
First 9 Batters			279	57	4	28	48	.204	.283	.278
Second 9 Batters			272	82	4	27	35	.301	.419	.362
All Batters Thereafter			335	75	5	34	38	.224	.299	.301

Loves to face: Henry Cotto (.136, 3-for-22)
Chili Davis (.100, 2-for-20, 2 BB)
Mickey Tettleton (.059, 1-for-17, 3 BB)

Hates to face: Jose Canseco (.394, 13-for-33, 2 HR)
Chuck Knoblauch (.714, 5-for-7, 1 BB)
Danny Tartabull (.417, 10-for-24, 2 HR)

Miscellaneous statistics: Ground outs-to-air outs ratio: 1.44 last season, 0.95 for career. . . . Opponents grounded into 28 double plays in 192 opportunities (one per 6.9). . . . Allowed 40 doubles, 0 triples in 238 innings. . . . Allowed 14 first-inning runs in 35 starts (3.34 ERA). . . . Batting support: 3.49 runs per start, 4th-lowest average in A.L. . . . Opposing base stealers: 12-for-17 (71%); 2 pickoffs, 2 balks.

Comments: Has made 354 starts over the past 10 years, the most in the majors; Jack Morris stands second (339). Only eight other pitchers in major league history have made 34 or more starts for 10 straight seasons; Cy Young did it 14 years in a row, 1891–1904, and Pud Galvin 11 years, 1879–89; no pitcher in this century has a longer streak than Frankie Vee. . . . First pitcher with 200 innings pitched in 10 straight seasons since the 1981 strike season snapped streaks of at least 10 years by Gaylord Perry, Don Sutton, Phil Niekro, Steve Carlton, and Bert Blyleven. . . . Led A.L. pitchers with 47 assists last season; started six double plays, the most by any pitcher in the majors. . . . Strikeout rate has decreased in each of the last three seasons to a career-low 4.58 per nine innings last season. . . . Career numbers: 95–56, 3.39 ERA before the All-Star break, 68–81, 4.04 ERA after the hiatus. . . . Allowed one home run every 18.3 innings last season, the lowest rate of his career; that he did it in his first season in Boston shouldn't surprise our regular readers: Although Fenway Park increases run production, it does not increase home-run rate. . . . He's had a nice career for a guy who posted an ERA over 5.00 in each of his first two seasons. Six other pitchers have started their career with two such seasons (minimum: 100 innings pitched in each), and among them, only one went on to win more than 33 games in his career: Ed Brandt, who had a 121–146 record during 11 seasons in the majors (1928–38).

Duane Ward — Throws Right

Toronto Blue Jays	W-L	ERA	AB	H	HR	BB	SO	BA	SA	OBA
Season	7-4	1.95	367	76	5	39	103	.207	.286	.282
vs. Left-Handers			183	36	5	25	61	.197	.322	.289
vs. Right-Handers			184	40	0	14	42	.217	.250	.275
vs. Ground-Ballers			174	47	3	23	37	.270	.374	.352
vs. Fly-Ballers			193	29	2	16	66	.150	.207	.217
Home Games	6-1	1.57	187	37	3	21	56	.198	.273	.281
Road Games	1-3	2.36	180	39	2	18	47	.217	.300	.284
Grass Fields	0-3	2.88	150	35	2	16	36	.233	.333	.302
Artificial Turf	7-1	1.34	217	41	3	23	67	.189	.253	.269
April	1-1	4.22	42	10	1	6	10	.238	.310	.333
May	1-1	2.60	67	17	0	10	14	.254	.284	.359
June	1-2	2.12	59	9	1	6	11	.153	.220	.231
July	2-0	1.37	74	18	1	7	23	.243	.365	.305
August	1-0	1.72	53	13	1	2	16	.245	.358	.259
Sept./Oct.	1-0	0.86	72	9	1	8	23	.125	.194	.213
Leading Off Inn.			80	15	1	10	25	.188	.237	.278
Bases Empty			191	44	2	20	59	.230	.288	.303
Runners On			176	32	3	19	44	.182	.284	.260
Runners/Scor. Pos.			101	18	3	12	24	.178	.327	.263
Runners On/2 Out			87	17	2	11	20	.195	.287	.293
Scor. Pos./2 Out			58	10	2	8	13	.172	.293	.284
Late-Inning Pressure			228	45	2	19	60	.197	.254	.260
Leading Off			49	8	0	6	14	.163	.184	.255
Runners On			113	19	1	9	29	.168	.230	.232
Runners/Scor. Pos.			68	9	1	6	19	.132	.206	.208
First 9 Batters			359	74	5	38	100	.206	.287	.281
Second 9 Batters			8	2	0	1	3	.250	.250	.333
All Batters Thereafter			0	0	0	0	0	—	—	—

Loves to face: Jose Canseco (0-for-17, 10 SO)
Carlos Quintana (.091, 1-for-11, 8 SO)
Kevin Reimer (0-for-6, 5 SO)

Hates to face: Mike Greenwell (.500, 8-for-16)
Rickey Henderson (.478, 11-for-23)
Robin Yount (.409, 9-for-22)

Miscellaneous statistics: Ground outs-to-air outs ratio: 1.20 last season, 1.72 for career. . . . Opponents grounded into 5 double plays in 77 opportunities (one per 15), 5th-worst rate in A.L. . . . Allowed 10 doubles, 2 triples in 101⅓ innings. . . . Saved 12 games in 26 opportunities (46%). . . . Stranded 21 inherited runners, allowed 9 to score (70%). . . . Opposing base stealers: 14-for-18 (78%); 0 pickoffs, 0 balks.

Comments: The 10th pitcher in history, and the first since Rawly Eastwick in 1975, to earn victories in consecutive World Series games (Games 2 and 3 of the 1992 Series). . . . Both he and Tom Henke have at least 10 saves in each of the last five seasons. No other pair of teammates has ever had a streak of longer than three years. Gary Lavelle and Randy Moffitt both reached double figures three years in a row for the Giants (1976–78); Jesse Orosco and Roger McDowell had a three-year streak for Mets (1985–87). . . . He is the Blue Jays' all-time leader in relief wins (30) and relief losses (31), but he's far behind Henke in saves (217 to 76). No other pitcher has saved more than 31 games for the Jays. . . . Opponents' batting average has decreased in each of the last five seasons, equaling the longest streaks in major league history (minimum: 100 innings in each). Others with five-year streaks: Jim Bunning (1963–67), Joe Coleman (1968–72), and Art Ditmar (1955–59). . . . Hasn't allowed a home run to a right-handed batter in his last 161 appearances, since Tom Brunansky homered off him on Sept. 29, 1990. Opposing right-handed batters have a career average of one home run every 149 at-bats. . . . Batting average of opposing fly-ball hitters was the lowest in the majors last season. . . . The only pitcher to work at least 100 innings out of the bullpen in each of the last five seasons. Only two pitchers in major league history have had longer streaks: Rollie Fingers (7 years, 1972–78) and Pedro Borbon (6 years, 1972–77).

Bill Wegman — Throws Right

Milwaukee Brewers	W-L	ERA	AB	H	HR	BB	SO	BA	SA	OBA
Season	13-14	3.20	1004	251	28	55	127	.250	.387	.294
vs. Left-Handers			469	98	7	25	30	.209	.296	.247
vs. Right-Handers			535	153	21	30	97	.286	.467	.334
vs. Ground-Ballers			452	104	10	25	48	.230	.350	.274
vs. Fly-Ballers			552	147	18	30	79	.266	.418	.310
Home Games	9-5	2.26	547	127	14	33	59	.232	.346	.282
Road Games	4-9	4.35	457	124	14	22	68	.271	.438	.309
Grass Fields	12-12	2.93	894	220	25	48	110	.246	.381	.289
Artificial Turf	1-2	5.40	110	31	3	7	17	.282	.436	.331
April	2-1	2.38	149	34	1	13	14	.228	.302	.303
May	3-3	2.77	188	46	9	5	25	.245	.426	.270
June	2-1	4.50	125	31	5	11	19	.248	.408	.319
July	2-3	3.78	211	60	8	7	21	.284	.460	.306
August	2-4	3.24	162	43	3	8	25	.265	.370	.305
Sept./Oct.	2-2	2.78	169	37	2	11	23	.219	.331	.267
Leading Off Inn.			260	61	10	8	33	.235	.400	.263
Bases Empty			632	156	19	26	91	.247	.388	.281
Runners On			372	95	9	29	36	.255	.387	.315
Runners/Scor. Pos.			204	52	5	23	20	.255	.377	.333
Runners On/2 Out			158	32	4	17	16	.203	.323	.284
Scor. Pos./2 Out			98	19	3	15	10	.194	.327	.307
Late-Inning Pressure			114	31	3	6	14	.272	.439	.311
Leading Off			30	10	1	1	5	.333	.533	.375
Runners On			46	13	2	4	3	.283	.500	.333
Runners/Scor. Pos.			28	5	1	4	2	.179	.357	.273
First 9 Batters			293	73	9	18	35	.249	.386	.297
Second 9 Batters			294	72	8	16	45	.245	.371	.287
All Batters Thereafter			417	106	11	21	47	.254	.400	.297

Loves to face: Pat Kelly (.083, 1-for-12)
Lou Whitaker (.140, 8-for-57, 4 2B, 1 HR)
Mark Whiten (0-for-8)

Hates to face: Joe Carter (.415, 17-for-41, 4 2B, 2 3B, 5 HR)
Kent Hrbek (.400, 14-for-35, 4 HR)
Billy Ripken (.647, 11-for-17, 1 HR)

Miscellaneous statistics: Ground outs-to-air outs ratio: 1.43 last season, 1.02 for career.... Opponents grounded into 22 double plays in 177 opportunities (one per 8.0).... Allowed 50 doubles (5th most in majors), 2 triples in 261⅔ innings.... Allowed 13 first-inning runs in 35 starts (1.80 ERA, 4th lowest in A.L.)... Batting support: 4.29 runs per start.... Opposing base stealers: 18-for-24 (75%); 2 pickoffs, 2 balks.

Comments: Averaged 1.89 walks per nine innings, 3d-lowest rate among A.L. pitchers (minimum: 162 IP), behind teammate Chris Bosio (1.71 walks per nine) and Mike Mussina (1.79). Each of the Brewers' top five starters (Bosio, Wegman, Navarro, Bones, and Eldred) averaged fewer than 2.7 walks per nine innings; no team had done that since 1977, when it was done by both the Red Sox (Tiant, Jenkins, Cleveland, Wise, and Lee) and the Dodgers (Sutton, Rau, John, Hooton, and Rhoden).... Weggy walked only eight of 270 batters leading off innings, the lowest ratio by any A.L. pitcher last year.... Combined with B. J. Surhoff for 238 innings last season, the most by any battery in the majors. The next two: Roger Clemens and Tony Pena (230⅓); Jack Morris and Pat Borders (221⅓).... Allowed 80 extra-base hits, 2d most in majors; only Ben McDonald (81) surrendered more.... Allowed 21 homers to right-handed batters, the most by any right-handed pitcher last season.... ERA in home games was lowest in A.L. last season; career breakdown: 35–27, 3.62 ERA at County Stadium; 29–38, 4.53 ERA on the road, including 9–13, 5.17 ERA on artificial turf.... Batting average by opposing left-handers was the lowest of his career; right-handers have a career mark of .276 against him, compared to a .253 career mark by left-handers.... Has faced Wade Boggs and Don Mattingly 35 times each in his career, but has never struck out either of them.

Bob Welch — Throws Right

Oakland A's	W-L	ERA	AB	H	HR	BB	SO	BA	SA	OBA
Season	11-7	3.27	461	114	13	43	47	.247	.360	.312
vs. Left-Handers			241	64	6	22	20	.266	.373	.325
vs. Right-Handers			220	50	7	21	27	.227	.345	.299
vs. Ground-Ballers			239	55	5	20	29	.230	.322	.291
vs. Fly-Ballers			222	59	8	23	18	.266	.401	.335
Home Games	4-3	2.94	192	45	5	15	20	.234	.339	.292
Road Games	7-4	3.52	269	69	8	28	27	.257	.375	.327
Grass Fields	7-6	3.32	337	85	13	28	37	.252	.398	.309
Artificial Turf	4-1	3.15	124	29	0	15	10	.234	.258	.321
April	0-0	—	0	0	0	0	0	—	—	—
May	2-3	3.00	122	31	5	8	9	.254	.393	.301
June	3-1	2.70	97	20	3	12	13	.206	.320	.294
July	3-1	3.69	121	32	4	12	14	.264	.405	.328
August	2-0	2.08	51	16	0	2	5	.314	.373	.340
Sept./Oct.	1-2	4.66	70	15	1	9	6	.214	.271	.313
Leading Off Inn.			116	30	5	12	9	.259	.405	.333
Bases Empty			279	69	9	29	22	.247	.384	.323
Runners On			182	45	4	14	25	.247	.324	.296
Runners/Scor. Pos.			87	24	3	8	14	.276	.379	.327
Runners On/2 Out			77	18	2	7	9	.234	.312	.298
Scor. Pos./2 Out			45	8	2	5	7	.178	.311	.260
Late-Inning Pressure			19	1	0	1	0	.053	.053	.053
Leading Off			6	0	0	0	0	.000	.000	.000
Runners On			2	0	0	0	0	.000	.000	.000
Runners/Scor. Pos.			2	0	0	0	0	.000	.000	.000
First 9 Batters			166	42	5	12	22	.253	.386	.311
Second 9 Batters			160	36	3	12	12	.225	.294	.277
All Batters Thereafter			135	36	5	19	13	.267	.407	.353

Loves to face: Brady Anderson (.059, 1-for-17. 1 HR)
Wade Boggs (.037, 1-for-27, 1 2B, 3 BB)
Joey Cora (0-for-12)

Hates to face: Carlos Baerga (.474, 9-for-19, 1 HR)
Brian Harper (.414, 12-for-29, 2 HR)
Lou Whitaker (.308, 12-for-39, 5 2B, 4 HR)

Miscellaneous statistics: Ground outs-to-air outs ratio: 0.86 last season, 0.93 for career.... Opponents grounded into 14 double plays in 98 opportunities (one per 7.0).... Allowed 11 doubles, 1 triple in 123⅔ innings.... Allowed 7 first-inning runs in 20 starts (3.15 ERA).... Batting support: 4.50 runs per start.... Opposing base stealers: 8-for-13 (62%); 1 pickoff, 0 balks.

Comments: Among the 39 pitchers who started last season on the disabled list, Welch was the only one to win more than 10 games. Alert to rotisserie players: Those guys combined for a 89–120 record; Welch was the only A.L. pitcher to start the season on the D.L. and end it with a winning record.... Welch, with 199 career wins, started against Jack Morris (237 career wins) in Game 4 of the 1992 A.L.C.S., coming within an eyelash of making that only the fifth postseason game in baseball history in which 200-game winners started against each other. It happened in the 1913 World Series, when Christy Mathewson (with 337 wins) twice opposed Eddie Plank (270); and it happened in 1978, when Don Sutton (205) faced Steve Carlton (207) in the Championship Series and Catfish Hunter (222) in the World Series.... After we found that Dan Marino and Mark Clayton had combined for more TD passes than any other duo in NFL history, we got to thinking about baseball. We found that Welch and Dennis Eckersley are the most prolific win/save duo in major league history; no other pitcher has had as many of his victories saved by a single reliever. The top five win/save combinations: Welch and Eck, 49; Dave Stewart and Eck, 41; Jimmy Key and Tom Henke, 37; Mike Moore and Eck, 32; Ron Guidry and Goose Gossage, 31. Bet you'll see that one on a few full-screen graphics this year; let's see who attributes it properly.... Has posted a winning record in each of the last six Aprils. (He spent April 1992 on the disabled list.)

David Wells

Throws Left

Toronto Blue Jays	W-L	ERA	AB	H	HR	BB	SO	BA	SA	OBA
Season	7-9	5.40	478	138	16	36	62	.289	.471	.346
vs. Left-Handers			92	27	3	4	13	.293	.446	.363
vs. Right-Handers			386	111	13	32	49	.288	.477	.342
vs. Ground-Ballers			248	70	4	12	27	.282	.403	.321
vs. Fly-Ballers			230	68	12	24	35	.296	.543	.372
Home Games	4-3	3.60	231	61	8	12	30	.264	.437	.312
Road Games	3-6	7.20	247	77	8	24	32	.312	.502	.377
Grass Fields	2-5	8.18	198	67	7	22	23	.338	.540	.406
Artificial Turf	5-4	3.59	280	71	9	14	39	.254	.421	.301
April	1-1	4.15	66	14	2	5	8	.212	.379	.297
May	1-1	2.93	57	17	1	5	7	.298	.386	.344
June	1-1	1.99	90	26	0	7	11	.289	.367	.354
July	3-1	4.22	119	29	6	3	14	.244	.454	.264
August	1-4	13.14	117	45	6	15	9	.385	.667	.463
Sept./Oct.	0-1	2.45	29	7	1	1	7	.241	.448	.267
Leading Off Inn.			114	33	3	5	19	.289	.447	.325
Bases Empty			277	72	11	14	38	.260	.444	.305
Runners On			201	66	5	22	24	.328	.507	.398
Runners/Scor. Pos.			119	41	2	19	17	.345	.529	.438
Runners On/2 Out			87	30	3	11	11	.345	.540	.430
Scor. Pos./2 Out			54	21	1	11	8	.389	.593	.507
Late-Inning Pressure			66	19	1	4	11	.288	.364	.333
Leading Off			16	4	0	1	4	.250	.313	.294
Runners On			27	9	1	2	3	.333	.444	.367
Runners/Scor. Pos.			14	4	1	2	1	.286	.500	.353
First 9 Batters			258	72	6	16	41	.279	.426	.323
Second 9 Batters			142	39	5	13	15	.275	.465	.352
All Batters Thereafter			78	27	5	7	6	.346	.628	.409

Loves to face: Carlos Baerga (.067, 1-for-15, 1 2B)
Jay Buhner (0-for-11)
Omar Vizquel (0-for-9)

Hates to face: Chili Davis (.429, 12-for-28, 3 HR)
Ken Griffey, Jr. (.444, 8-for-18, 2 HR)
Cal Ripken (.421, 8-for-19, 2 2B, 3 HR)

Miscellaneous statistics: Ground outs-to-air outs ratio: 0.80 last season, 0.87 for career.... Opponents grounded into 8 double plays in 88 opportunities (one per 11).... Allowed 35 doubles, 2 triples in 120 innings.... Allowed 6 first-inning runs in 14 starts (3.86 ERA).... Batting support: 4.50 runs per start.... Record of 6–7, 6.39 ERA as a starter; 1–2, 3.68 ERA in 27 relief appearances.... Stranded 13 inherited runners, allowed 6 to score (68%).... Opposing base stealers: 14-for-20 (70%); 4 pick-offs, 1 balk.

Comments: What is 22.74? (a) The TV rating for the latest Amy Fisher/Joey Buttafuoco movie; (b) The combined passer rating for New England quarterbacks; (c) Wells's ERA against the Brewers last season. Answer: (c). It was the highest by any pitcher against any team last year (minimum: five innings).... The only pitcher in the majors who has at least 10 starts and at least 10 relief appearances in each of the past three years. Career breakdown: 30–24, 4.11 ERA in 69 starts; 13–13, 3.24 ERA in 168 relief appearances.... Did not last into the eighth inning in any of his 14 starts last season.... Rate of homers allowed has increased in each of the last three seasons, from one every 17.3 innings in 1989 to one every 13.5, 8.3, and 7.5 in the last three years.... Meanwhile, his strikeout rate has declined since 1989: 8.13 per nine innings, followed by 5.48, 4.81, and 4.65. And in each of those years, his opponents' batting average has risen: .207, .235, .252, .289.... Has faced 63 batters with the bases loaded in his career and has walked only one (Mickey Tettleton last June).... Okay, we'll give you another chance. What is 13.14? (a) The number after 11.12; (b) The over/under on how many weeks Buck Showalter lasts; (c) Wells's ERA in August last year. Answer: (c). Not only was it the highest in the majors that month, but it contributed to the Blue Jays' 5.93 team ERA that month, the highest team ERA by any team in any month in the past four years. And you wondered why they rented David Cone?

Bobby Witt

Throws Right

Rangers/A's	W-L	ERA	AB	H	HR	BB	SO	BA	SA	OBA
Season	10-14	4.29	715	183	16	114	125	.256	.371	.356
vs. Left-Handers			292	71	4	63	52	.243	.342	.373
vs. Right-Handers			423	112	12	51	73	.265	.390	.342
vs. Ground-Ballers			380	97	8	53	67	.255	.382	.346
vs. Fly-Ballers			335	86	8	61	58	.257	.358	.366
Home Games	7-8	3.76	455	113	8	67	82	.248	.341	.342
Road Games	3-6	5.24	260	70	8	47	43	.269	.423	.379
Grass Fields	10-11	4.02	648	162	14	100	112	.250	.360	.348
Artificial Turf	0-3	7.31	67	21	2	14	13	.313	.478	.427
April	2-2	3.12	103	27	3	11	20	.262	.408	.333
May	3-2	3.40	149	33	4	22	30	.221	.336	.320
June	3-3	3.92	143	30	2	26	21	.210	.315	.329
July	1-1	6.04	87	24	3	9	13	.276	.437	.351
August	0-5	6.75	116	38	2	27	16	.328	.440	.442
Sept./Oct.	1-1	3.41	117	31	2	19	25	.265	.333	.362
Leading Off Inn.			180	52	5	23	24	.289	.444	.369
Bases Empty			404	109	12	58	64	.270	.408	.361
Runners On			311	74	4	56	61	.238	.322	.348
Runners/Scor. Pos.			165	36	2	39	39	.218	.297	.353
Runners On/2 Out			135	31	2	21	32	.230	.319	.338
Scor. Pos./2 Out			79	16	1	18	23	.203	.291	.351
Late-Inning Pressure			48	10	2	9	8	.208	.354	.345
Leading Off			15	4	0	3	3	.267	.333	.389
Runners On			16	2	1	5	3	.125	.313	.364
Runners/Scor. Pos.			6	1	1	5	3	.167	.667	.583
First 9 Batters			229	57	5	45	43	.249	.371	.367
Second 9 Batters			225	59	4	33	39	.262	.364	.352
All Batters Thereafter			261	67	7	36	43	.257	.375	.348

Loves to face: Greg Gagne (.147, 5-for-34, 1 HR)
Dan Gladden (.147, 5-for-34)
Pedro Munoz (.083, 1-for-12, 7 SO)

Hates to face: Felix Fermin (.611, 11-for-18)
Leo Gomez (.667, 4-for-6, 1 HR)
Pete O'Brien (.474, 9-for-19, 1 HR, 3 BB, 0 SO)

Miscellaneous statistics: Ground outs-to-air outs ratio: 1.30 last season, 1.01 for career.... Opponents grounded into 22 double plays in 173 opportunities (one per 7.9).... Allowed 28 doubles, 3 triples in 193 innings.... Allowed 15 first-inning runs in 31 starts (3.77 ERA).... Batting support: 3.87 runs per start.... Opposing base stealers: 22-for-32 (69%); 0 pickoffs, 1 balk.

Comments: Career turned around after he was optioned to Oklahoma City in May 1988. Prior to that, he had averaged 8.49 walks per nine innings; since then, his rate is 5.15 per nine. He completed only two of 62 starts prior to his demotion, compared to 25 of his next 88 after his return. His won-lost record: 19–24 before, 50–49 after.... But he hasn't pitched a complete game in 38 starts since suffering a partial rotator cuff tear on May 26, 1991, and now his career again seems in doubt. His record since the injury: 10–18, with a 5.02 ERA.... Made 31 starts last season, the most of any pitcher who failed to reach the 9th inning. In fact, he saw the eighth inning only once—and that was as a reliever during garbage time in the A.L.C.S. finale at the Skydome, when Tony LaRussa cleared his bench and bullpen.... Career average of 6.11 walks per nine innings is 2d worst in major league history (minimum: 1000 innings), ahead of only Tommy Byrne (6.85).... Hasn't allowed more than two home runs in one game since May 14, 1986—a span of 181 consecutive starts, the 2d-longest current streak in the American League, behind Storm Davis (199, not including 10 more in the National League). Longer streaks that include N.L. games: Danny Jackson (231) and Greg Maddux (208).... Recorded the 1000th strikeout of his career last season, needing 1047⅓ innings to reach that milestone, one-third of an inning less than Roger Clemens needed. Three pitchers reached 1000 strikeouts in fewer than 1000 innings: Sam McDowell, Nolan Ryan, and Sandy Koufax.

Kyle Abbott

Throws Left

Philadelphia Phillies	W-L	ERA	AB	H	HR	BB	SO	BA	SA	OBA
Season	1-14	5.13	520	147	20	45	88	.283	.460	.338
vs. Left-Handers			129	42	3	8	28	.326	.426	.370
vs. Right-Handers			391	105	17	37	60	.269	.471	.328
vs. Ground-Ballers			224	63	5	18	50	.281	.406	.335
vs. Fly-Ballers			296	84	15	27	38	.284	.500	.340
Home Games	1-7	5.64	293	86	11	25	54	.294	.488	.347
Road Games	0-7	4.47	227	61	9	20	34	.269	.423	.327
Grass Fields	0-6	4.72	185	49	8	17	28	.265	.427	.325
Artificial Turf	1-8	5.36	335	98	12	28	60	.293	.478	.345
April	0-4	5.76	91	22	4	11	17	.242	.418	.320
May	0-3	5.11	97	26	4	10	21	.268	.464	.336
June	0-2	5.40	45	15	1	2	4	.333	.467	.354
July	1-2	3.58	146	39	4	12	22	.267	.404	.319
August	0-2	6.64	84	27	4	7	16	.321	.560	.376
Sept./Oct.	0-1	5.79	57	18	3	3	8	.316	.509	.350
Leading Off Inn.			126	34	4	8	23	.270	.437	.313
Bases Empty			298	78	10	30	49	.262	.413	.329
Runners On			222	69	10	15	39	.311	.523	.350
Runners/Scor. Pos.			119	30	4	10	20	.252	.420	.299
Runners On/2 Out			91	24	4	10	16	.264	.429	.337
Scor. Pos./2 Out			56	11	4	8	9	.196	.446	.297
Late-Inning Pressure			9	4	0	0	0	.444	.778	.444
Leading Off			2	1	0	0	0	.500	1.000	.500
Runners On			4	2	0	0	0	.500	.500	.500
Runners/Scor. Pos.			4	2	0	0	0	.500	.500	.500
First 9 Batters			219	61	10	18	47	.279	.489	.329
Second 9 Batters			156	43	4	15	26	.276	.397	.335
All Batters Thereafter			145	43	6	12	15	.297	.483	.354

Loves to face: Moises Alou (0-for-7)
Fred McGriff (0-for-7, 4 SO)
Ryne Sandberg (0-for-8)
Hates to face: Will Clark (.583, 7-for-12)
Dave Gallagher (.500, 3-for-6, 3 BB)
Tim Teufel (.667, 2-for-3, 2 HR)

Miscellaneous statistics: Ground outs-to-air outs ratio: 0.85 last season, 0.91 for career.... Opponents grounded into 11 double plays in 104 opportunities (one per 9.5).... Allowed 16 doubles, 8 triples (3d most in N.L.) in 133⅓ innings.... Allowed 14 first-inning runs in 19 starts (6.63 ERA, 5th highest in N.L.)... Batting support: 3.21 runs per start.... Opposing base stealers: 9-for-16 (56%); 2 pickoffs, 1 balk.

Comments: Tied Danny Jackson and Dennis Martinez for the most losses in April, and it didn't get much better. That was the beginning of an 11-game losing streak, the 2d longest in the majors last season (to Anthony Young's 14-game streak), and the longest to start a season since Terry Felton went 0-13 in 1982.... Only five pitchers in major league history have posted lower single-season winning percentages than Abbott's (minimum: 15 decisions): Art Hagan, 1883 (1-16); Frank Bates, 1899 (1-18); Jack Nabors, 1916 (1-20); Tom Sheehan, 1916 (1-16); and Mike Parrott, 1980 (1-16).... Abbott tied Young for the major league high in losses by a rookie.... His nine wild pitches tied Roger Pavlik for the most among the same group.... Allowed the most home runs of any rookie pitcher; his total of 17 to right-handed batters was the 2d most in the N.L. (Bud Black allowed 19).... Phillies rookie pitchers started 63 games, the highest total by any team since the 1990 Phillies, whose rookies (Pat Combs, Jose DeJesus, Jason Grimsley, and Tommy Greene) combined for 71 starts. Other rookie starters for the Phillies last season were Ben Rivera (14), Cliff Brantley (9), Andy Ashby (8), Brad Brink (7), Mike Williams (5), and Mickey Weston (1).... Batting average by opposing left-handed batters was the highest vs. any left-handed pitcher in majors (minimum: 100 BFP).... Opponents' batting average in the first inning (.342) was 3d highest in the league.... Von Hayes for Abbott and Ruben Amaro, Jr.? Is that one of those deals that hurt both clubs?

Steve Avery

Throws Left

Atlanta Braves	W-L	ERA	AB	H	HR	BB	SO	BA	SA	OBA
Season	11-11	3.20	878	216	14	71	129	.246	.343	.300
vs. Left-Handers			155	40	3	20	38	.258	.348	.341
vs. Right-Handers			723	176	11	51	91	.243	.342	.291
vs. Ground-Ballers			380	89	5	31	61	.234	.308	.291
vs. Fly-Ballers			498	127	9	40	68	.255	.369	.307
Home Games	6-4	2.51	408	107	5	29	61	.262	.343	.307
Road Games	5-7	3.79	470	109	9	42	68	.232	.343	.294
Grass Fields	9-7	2.58	635	150	8	53	89	.236	.313	.292
Artificial Turf	2-4	4.88	243	66	6	18	40	.272	.420	.321
April	1-2	3.08	97	22	1	9	13	.227	.340	.287
May	2-3	3.22	171	43	3	22	29	.251	.345	.337
June	3-1	2.04	130	32	2	8	17	.246	.308	.288
July	2-1	2.79	175	36	2	15	25	.206	.297	.267
August	2-2	4.72	160	51	1	11	19	.319	.400	.358
Sept./Oct.	1-2	3.23	145	32	5	6	26	.221	.366	.248
Leading Off Inn.			228	63	6	17	30	.276	.395	.327
Bases Empty			540	128	9	41	75	.237	.333	.291
Runners On			338	88	5	30	54	.260	.358	.314
Runners/Scor. Pos.			199	46	2	24	36	.231	.307	.303
Runners On/2 Out			144	31	3	13	21	.215	.333	.280
Scor. Pos./2 Out			93	16	1	12	16	.172	.247	.267
Late-Inning Pressure			81	22	0	10	6	.272	.321	.348
Leading Off			25	9	0	2	1	.360	.440	.407
Runners On			28	8	0	5	4	.286	.357	.382
Runners/Scor. Pos.			15	3	0	4	3	.200	.267	.350
First 9 Batters			287	59	6	24	52	.206	.303	.265
Second 9 Batters			284	75	5	21	49	.264	.384	.312
All Batters Thereafter			307	82	3	26	28	.267	.342	.321

Loves to face: Moises Alou (0-for-9)
Juan Samuel (.120, 3-for-25, 0 BB)
Darryl Strawberry (.118, 2-for-17)
Hates to face: Barry Larkin (.425, 17-for-40, 1 HR, 0 SO)
Kevin Mitchell (4-for-4, 1 HR)
Chris Sabo (.414, 12-for-29, 1 HR)

Miscellaneous statistics: Ground outs-to-air outs ratio: 1.08 last season, 1.19 for career.... Opponents grounded into 16 double plays in 151 opportunities (one per 9.4).... Allowed 31 doubles, 6 triples in 233⅔ innings.... Allowed 16 first-inning runs in 35 starts (3.86 ERA).... Batting support: 3.97 runs per start.... Opposing base stealers: 42-for-56 (75%), most steals in N.L.; 7 pickoffs, 3 balks.

Comments: The youngest pitcher to take a regular turn in a starting rotation throughout last season. (He was 22 years, 5 months when the 1992 season ended.)... One of three pitchers to share the league lead with 35 starts. Two were Braves, Avery and John Smoltz; the other is the newest member of the Atlanta starting rotation: Greg Maddux.... Was the first pitcher since Dwight Gooden to accumulate two 200-inning seasons at such a young age. The only other active pitchers to have done that are now two of the oldest players in the majors: Bert Blyleven and Frank Tanana.... Has made eight postseason starts before his 23d birthday, the most by any pitcher in major league history.... Had a 3.51 ERA in 133⅓ innings with Greg Olson catching, 2.77 in 94⅓ innings with Damon Berryhill behind the plate.... Braves left-handers combined for 99 starts and 801⅔ innings last season, both major league highs, but both lower than the figures their southpaws posted in 1991 (109 starts, 846⅔ innings).... Opponents batted .234 through the first six innings of his starts, .311 from the seventh inning on.... Career statistics (32-30, 3.71 ERA) are deceiving due to a dreadful start at age 20. He was 9-15 with a 5.03 ERA through mid-June 1991; he is 23-15 with a 3.18 ERA since then.... Southpaws with the most comparable statistical profiles at the same age as Avery: Dave McNally (through 1965), Tommy John (1966), and Ken Holtzman (1968).

Brian Barnes — Throws Left

Montreal Expos	W-L	ERA	AB	H	HR	BB	SO	BA	SA	OBA
Season	6-6	2.97	362	77	9	46	65	.213	.329	.306
vs. Left-Handers			62	14	2	9	14	.226	.371	.338
vs. Right-Handers			300	63	7	37	51	.210	.320	.299
vs. Ground-Ballers			167	35	3	20	30	.210	.299	.296
vs. Fly-Ballers			195	42	6	26	35	.215	.354	.314
Home Games	4-3	2.47	207	41	4	25	42	.198	.300	.289
Road Games	2-3	3.67	155	36	5	21	23	.232	.368	.328
Grass Fields	2-1	2.35	114	27	3	12	18	.237	.360	.315
Artificial Turf	4-5	3.25	248	50	6	34	47	.202	.315	.302
April	0-0	—	0	0	0	0	0	—	—	—
May	0-0	—	0	0	0	0	0	—	—	—
June	1-1	2.77	49	11	0	6	6	.224	.286	.321
July	1-2	1.91	117	26	4	13	25	.222	.376	.305
August	2-2	4.21	96	22	3	13	16	.229	.354	.324
Sept./Oct.	2-1	3.18	100	18	2	14	18	.180	.270	.281
Leading Off Inn.			96	20	2	10	16	.208	.313	.290
Bases Empty			230	46	3	24	40	.200	.278	.281
Runners On			132	31	6	22	25	.235	.417	.346
Runners/Scor. Pos.			78	15	3	14	21	.192	.346	.319
Runners On/2 Out			52	9	0	9	10	.173	.231	.295
Scor. Pos./2 Out			34	6	0	6	9	.176	.235	.300
Late-Inning Pressure			10	1	0	1	3	.100	.100	.182
Leading Off			4	1	0	1	2	.250	.250	.400
Runners On			0	0	0	0	0	—	—	—
Runners/Scor. Pos.			0	0	0	0	0	—	—	—
First 9 Batters			154	31	3	19	37	.201	.292	.287
Second 9 Batters			128	31	6	15	17	.242	.445	.326
All Batters Thereafter			80	15	0	12	11	.188	.213	.309

Loves to face: Wes Chamberlain (.056, 1-for-18, 3 BB)
Luis Salazar (.056, 1-for-18)
Chico Walker (.071, 1-for-14)

Hates to face: Barry Bonds (.667, 4-for-6, 2 2B, 2 HR)
Charlie Hayes (.400, 6-for-15, 1 HR)
John Kruk (.400, 6-for-15, 1 HR)

Miscellaneous statistics: Ground outs-to-air outs ratio: 0.91 last season, 1.05 for career.... Opponents grounded into 7 double plays in 71 opportunities (one per 10).... Allowed 15 doubles, 0 triples in 100 innings.... Allowed 2 first-inning runs in 17 starts (0.53 ERA, 2d lowest in majors).... Batting support: 4.12 runs per start.... Opposing base stealers: 14-for-21 (67%); 4 pickoffs, 2 balks.

Comments: Had a 4.53 ERA in 49⅔ innings with Gary Carter catching, 1.43 in 50⅓ innings with other catchers.... Failed to complete six innings in each of his last eight starts, the 2d-longest streak in the N.L. last season. The only pitcher with a longer streak: Ryan Bowen (9).... Averaged 5.53 innings pitched per start last season, 4th lowest in the N.L. (minimum: 15 GS).... Made several impressive relief appearances late last season, striking out nine batters with only one walk and three hits in a total of six scoreless innings.... Opponents' batting average in the first inning (.138) was 2d lowest in the league.... Batting average by opposing right-handed batters was the lowest vs. any left-handed pitcher in the N.L. (minimum: 200 BFP).... One of 13 active southpaws who held right-handers to a lower batting average than left-handers in each of his first three seasons in the majors. Career marks: RHB, .224; LHB, .235.... Struck out 23 batters in 28 innings in his debut season, but his rate has dropped since then; year by year: 7.39 per nine innings in 1990, 6.58 in 1991, 5.85 in 1992.... Allowed two home runs at Olympic Stadium in his major league debut (Sept. 14, 1990, both to Barry Bonds), but has allowed more than one homer in only one of 24 home games since then.... Has a career record of 5–1 in games on grass fields.... Ended the season with a four-game hitting streak, 3d longest of any pitcher last season, behind Don Robinson (6) and Doug Drabek (5).

Rod Beck — Throws Right

San Francisco Giants	W-L	ERA	AB	H	HR	BB	SO	BA	SA	OBA
Season	3-3	1.76	327	62	4	15	87	.190	.257	.228
vs. Left-Handers			180	32	2	6	47	.178	.256	.212
vs. Right-Handers			147	30	2	9	40	.204	.259	.248
vs. Ground-Ballers			145	29	1	3	44	.200	.269	.216
vs. Fly-Ballers			182	33	3	12	43	.181	.247	.237
Home Games	2-3	2.06	158	35	1	4	43	.222	.291	.248
Road Games	1-0	1.49	169	27	3	11	44	.160	.225	.210
Grass Fields	2-3	1.66	234	50	2	7	62	.214	.278	.241
Artificial Turf	1-0	2.00	93	12	2	8	25	.129	.204	.198
April	0-0	0.00	56	8	0	3	16	.143	.143	.186
May	0-0	4.76	66	16	1	1	21	.242	.333	.271
June	0-2	2.19	44	11	1	3	9	.250	.409	.298
July	1-1	2.35	55	13	1	2	22	.236	.327	.263
August	0-0	0.77	41	7	0	2	7	.171	.171	.205
Sept./Oct.	2-0	0.48	65	7	1	4	12	.108	.169	.159
Leading Off Inn.			76	15	2	3	17	.197	.289	.237
Bases Empty			190	37	4	9	50	.195	.284	.235
Runners On			137	25	0	6	37	.182	.219	.219
Runners/Scor. Pos.			82	16	0	4	24	.195	.232	.236
Runners On/2 Out			70	10	0	4	24	.143	.157	.189
Scor. Pos./2 Out			43	6	0	3	17	.140	.163	.196
Late-Inning Pressure			178	35	2	10	50	.197	.270	.238
Leading Off			43	8	0	2	11	.186	.209	.222
Runners On			73	13	0	4	22	.178	.205	.218
Runners/Scor. Pos.			53	9	0	2	18	.170	.189	.196
First 9 Batters			314	58	4	13	85	.185	.255	.221
Second 9 Batters			13	4	0	2	2	.308	.308	.375
All Batters Thereafter			0	0	0	0	0	—	—	—

Loves to face: Darren Daulton (0-for-4, 3 SO, 1 HBP)
Marquis Grissom (.111, 1-for-9, 3 SO)
Dave Hansen (0-for-5)

Hates to face: Steve Finley (.500, 4-for-8, 2 2B, 1 HR)
John Kruk (.500, 3-for-6, 1 2B, 1 HR)
Gary Sheffield (2-for-2, 1 HR)

Miscellaneous statistics: Ground outs-to-air outs ratio: 1.00 last season, 0.93 for career.... Opponents grounded into 2 double plays in 54 opportunities (one per 27).... Allowed 8 doubles, 1 triple in 92 innings.... Saved 17 games in 25 opportunities (68%).... Stranded 32 inherited runners, allowed 9 to score (78%).... Opposing base stealers: 2-for-6 (33%); 0 pickoffs, 2 balks.

Comments: In seven full seasons as manager of the Giants, Roger Craig used seven different pitchers as many as 65 times in a season, none of them more than once: Mark Davis (1986), Scott Garrelts (1988), Craig Lefferts (1989), Steve Bedrosian (1990), Jeff Brantley (1991), Mike Jackson and Beck (1992).... For a franchise with a record book dominated by names like Mathewson and Hubbell, Beck's 1.76 ERA is a footnote. But since the move to the coast, only three Giants have posted lower marks (minimum: 75 innings): Frank Linzy (1.43 in 1965, 1.50 in 1967), Jeff Brantley (1.56 in 1990), and Al Holland (1.76 in 1980).... Opponents' batting average during his first pass through the order was the lowest in the majors (minimum: 200 AB). He faced at least 10 batters five times in his first 10 appearances, but only once in his next 53 games.... Saved only one game each in April and May, but became the closer of choice in June and earned 15 of San Francisco's last 17 saves thereafter.... Pitched almost exclusively as a starter in the minors from 1988 through 1990 (76 starts, seven games in relief); was moved to the bullpen in '91.... Batting average by opposing left-handed batters was the lowest in the N.L. last season, and the 3d lowest by an N.L. right-hander over the last 10 years (minimum: 175 BFP). The lower marks belong to Lance McCullers (.153 in 1988) and Bill Landrum (.176 in 1989).... Has allowed only two home runs in 69⅓ innings pitched at Candlestick Park.

Tim Belcher — Throws Right

Cincinnati Reds	W-L	ERA	AB	H	HR	BB	SO	BA	SA	OBA
Season	15-14	3.91	843	201	17	80	149	.238	.368	.303
vs. Left-Handers			508	141	9	59	78	.278	.411	.351
vs. Right-Handers			335	60	8	21	71	.179	.301	.228
vs. Ground-Ballers			410	106	6	38	75	.259	.368	.322
vs. Fly-Ballers			433	95	11	42	74	.219	.367	.286
Home Games	11-7	3.43	461	104	10	47	88	.226	.369	.297
Road Games	4-7	4.51	382	97	7	33	61	.254	.366	.310
Grass Fields	3-4	3.84	263	58	4	21	43	.221	.319	.278
Artificial Turf	12-10	3.95	580	143	13	59	106	.247	.390	.314
April	1-3	4.98	130	32	1	8	30	.246	.400	.291
May	3-2	2.55	124	23	2	16	28	.185	.266	.277
June	3-1	3.02	146	34	4	17	20	.233	.377	.313
July	2-3	3.92	159	44	4	18	19	.277	.428	.346
August	2-3	5.20	142	38	2	13	21	.268	.380	.327
Sept./Oct.	4-2	3.96	142	30	4	8	31	.211	.338	.252
Leading Off Inn.			217	46	7	19	34	.212	.387	.275
Bases Empty			523	107	11	46	94	.205	.325	.269
Runners On			320	94	6	34	55	.294	.438	.356
Runners/Scor. Pos.			184	50	5	20	33	.272	.457	.329
Runners On/2 Out			133	26	1	13	25	.195	.271	.277
Scor. Pos./2 Out			85	13	1	7	18	.153	.247	.226
Late-Inning Pressure			71	22	1	8	9	.310	.423	.383
Leading Off			20	5	0	2	3	.250	.300	.318
Runners On			31	12	1	3	1	.387	.581	.444
Runners/Scor. Pos.			19	4	1	1	1	.211	.421	.273
First 9 Batters			274	56	4	34	58	.204	.303	.289
Second 9 Batters			272	72	7	15	51	.265	.404	.307
All Batters Thereafter			297	73	6	31	40	.246	.394	.313

Loves to face: Steve Decker (0-for-9)
Jose Uribe (.095, 2-for-21)
Mitch Webster (.059, 1-for-17)

Hates to face: Vince Coleman (.500, 11-for-22)
Deion Sanders (.474, 9-for-19, 1 HR)
Ozzie Smith (.542, 13-for-24)

Miscellaneous statistics: Ground outs-to-air outs ratio: 0.85 last season, 0.84 for career. . . . Opponents grounded into 9 double plays in 165 opportunities (one per 18). . . . Allowed 42 doubles (4th most in N.L.), 8 triples (3d most in N.L.) in 227⅔ innings. . . . Allowed 23 first-inning runs in 34 starts (6.15 ERA). . . . Batting support: 4.32 runs per start, 8th-highest average in N.L. . . . Opposing base stealers: 6-for-17 (35%), 3d-lowest rate in N.L.; 1 pickoff, 1 balk.

Comments: One of only four active pitchers with at least six years in the majors who has never posted a losing record. The others: Roger Clemens (9 years), Randy St. Claire (8), and Ted Higuera (7). . . . Has thrown at least one shutout in each of the last five seasons; only Greg Maddux and Doug Drabek have longer N.L. streaks (6 years each). . . . Has had a winning record in home games and a losing record on the road in each of the past four seasons. Career breakdown: 44–22 at home, 21–30 on the road. Posted a 3.43 ERA at Riverfront Stadium last season, after five straight years with an ERA below 3.00 at Dodger Stadium, his old address. . . . Allowed the most runs (104), earned runs (99), and extra-base hits (67) in the N.L. last season; his teammate Tom Browning hit the same trifecta in 1991. That's the price of being a workhorse for a team that plays in a hitters' ballpark. . . . Held right-handed batters to the 2d-lowest average in the majors (minimum: 200 BFPs). Only Greg Maddux (.176) compiled a lower mark. . . . Opposing left-handers batted .222 over his first four seasons, .276 over the last two. . . . Career record of 16–7 with a 2.31 ERA after August 31. . . . Has faced 67 batters with the bases loaded, walked in only one run. . . . One of six active pitchers who has a career winning percentage of 1.000 in both the World Series (1–0) and the League Championship Series (2–0). The others: John Smoltz, Orel Hershiser, Rick Honeycutt, Bob Ojeda, and Jose Rijo.

Stan Belinda — Throws Right

Pittsburgh Pirates	W-L	ERA	AB	H	HR	BB	SO	BA	SA	OBA
Season	6-4	3.15	260	58	8	29	57	.223	.381	.295
vs. Left-Handers			135	26	4	17	21	.193	.326	.277
vs. Right-Handers			125	32	4	12	36	.256	.440	.314
vs. Ground-Ballers			103	26	3	12	19	.252	.398	.322
vs. Fly-Ballers			157	32	5	17	38	.204	.369	.277
Home Games	2-1	1.89	126	27	2	11	27	.214	.325	.277
Road Games	4-3	4.26	134	31	6	18	30	.231	.433	.310
Grass Fields	2-3	6.63	75	21	5	9	13	.280	.560	.353
Artificial Turf	4-1	1.89	185	37	3	20	44	.200	.308	.271
April	0-0	0.00	23	1	0	2	8	.043	.043	.120
May	2-2	7.50	51	17	4	5	9	.333	.686	.379
June	1-0	0.00	42	6	0	3	11	.143	.190	.200
July	2-1	3.60	47	11	3	8	11	.234	.468	.322
August	0-0	1.93	36	8	0	8	10	.222	.306	.364
Sept./Oct.	1-1	4.20	61	15	1	3	8	.246	.361	.281
Leading Off Inn.			61	11	1	4	18	.180	.311	.231
Bases Empty			148	30	1	15	38	.203	.284	.276
Runners On			112	28	7	14	19	.250	.509	.318
Runners/Scor. Pos.			79	19	6	11	14	.241	.544	.313
Runners On/2 Out			55	11	3	4	13	.200	.418	.254
Scor. Pos./2 Out			38	7	3	4	9	.184	.474	.262
Late-Inning Pressure			189	41	6	23	36	.217	.349	.296
Leading Off			46	7	0	2	13	.152	.174	.188
Runners On			77	18	6	11	12	.234	.506	.315
Runners/Scor. Pos.			50	10	5	8	8	.200	.540	.290
First 9 Batters			251	52	7	27	57	.207	.351	.278
Second 9 Batters			9	6	1	2	0	.667	1.222	.727
All Batters Thereafter			0	0	0	0	0	—	—	—

Loves to face: Andres Galarraga (.176, 3-for-17)
Mickey Morandini (0-for-7)
Robby Thompson (0-for-6)

Hates to face: Mark Grace (.333, 3-for-9, 5 BB)
Fred McGriff (2-for-2, 1 HR, 1 BB)
Ryne Sandberg (.417, 5-for-12, 1 HR)

Miscellaneous statistics: Ground outs-to-air outs ratio: 0.58 last season, 0.68 for career. . . . Opponents grounded into 1 double play in 46 opportunities (one per 46). . . . Allowed 13 doubles, 2 triples in 71⅓ innings. . . . Saved 18 games in 25 opportunities (72%). . . . Stranded 10 inherited runners, allowed 18 to score (36%), lowest rate in majors. . . . Opposing base stealers: 12-for-14 (86%); 0 pickoffs, 0 balks.

Comments: That stranded-runners rate of 36 percent was the worst in the majors, and it cost the Bucs in the ninth inning of Game 7 of the N.L.C.S. See the Braves essay for more on this. . . . Belinda is in the netherland between setup man and closer, having saved between 15 and 20 games in each of the last two seasons. . . . Has held opponents to a .203 batting average in Late-Inning Pressure Situations, 4th lowest among active pitchers (minimum: 400 BFP). The top five: Bryan Harvey (.196), Roger Clemens (.198), Nolan Ryan (.199), Belinda (.203), and Mitch Williams (.205). . . . Opposing batters have a career on-base percentage of .180 leading off innings in LIPS—the lowest by far in *Player Analysis* history. The next-lowest belongs to Craig Swan (.225), followed by Woodie Fryman (.234), Greg W. Harris (.239), and Ross Grimsley (.245). . . . His strikeout rate has decreased in each of last three seasons: 8.71 per nine innings in 1989, followed by 8.49, 8.16, and 7.19. . . . Opponents have a career batting average of .258 in day games, but night-game average of .198 is 3d lowest in *Player Analysis* history (minimum: 500 BFP). Only Bryan Harvey (.192) and Rob Dibble (.196) have held batters to a lower average at night. Belinda has a career ERA of 5.03 in day games, 2.94 at night. . . . His ERA has been below 2.00 at home and above 4.00 on the road in each of the past two seasons. Career figures: home, 3.10; road, 3.89.

Andy Benes
Throws Right

San Diego Padres	W-L	ERA	AB	H	HR	BB	SO	BA	SA	OBA
Season	13-14	3.35	870	230	14	61	169	.264	.371	.314
vs. Left-Handers			533	147	10	45	94	.276	.394	.333
vs. Right-Handers			337	83	4	16	75	.246	.335	.283
vs. Ground-Ballers			414	116	3	27	71	.280	.360	.327
vs. Fly-Ballers			456	114	11	34	98	.250	.382	.303
Home Games	7-6	3.55	445	126	8	25	84	.283	.391	.322
Road Games	6-8	3.14	425	104	6	36	85	.245	.351	.306
Grass Fields	10-9	3.64	637	176	11	43	121	.276	.375	.323
Artificial Turf	3-5	2.60	233	54	3	18	48	.232	.361	.291
April	2-2	3.97	126	35	2	6	29	.278	.413	.313
May	3-1	3.31	134	34	2	6	28	.254	.351	.289
June	1-2	3.40	165	49	2	12	25	.297	.388	.348
July	2-4	3.48	155	42	2	13	30	.271	.374	.331
August	2-2	4.45	118	31	2	11	15	.263	.347	.321
Sept./Oct.	3-3	2.06	172	39	4	13	42	.227	.355	.281
Leading Off Inn.			226	67	5	12	39	.296	.416	.338
Bases Empty			514	132	8	34	97	.257	.358	.305
Runners On			356	98	6	27	72	.275	.390	.327
Runners/Scor. Pos.			206	55	2	20	46	.267	.369	.329
Runners On/2 Out			138	30	1	17	28	.217	.290	.308
Scor. Pos./2 Out			94	17	0	13	21	.181	.234	.280
Late-Inning Pressure			71	21	1	7	13	.296	.437	.359
Leading Off			23	8	0	0	7	.348	.478	.348
Runners On			23	7	0	5	2	.304	.348	.429
Runners/Scor. Pos.			15	5	0	5	1	.333	.400	.500
First 9 Batters			284	64	4	16	67	.225	.310	.269
Second 9 Batters			276	64	4	18	57	.232	.326	.284
All Batters Thereafter			310	102	6	27	45	.329	.468	.380

Loves to face: Steve Finley (.125, 3-for-24)
                  Greg Olson (.130, 3-for-23)
                  Chico Walker (0-for-12)
Hates to face: Jeff Bagwell (.471, 8-for-17, 1 HR)
                  Barry Bonds (.385, 5-for-13, 3 HR)
                  Kevin Mitchell (.350, 7-for-20, 2 2B, 4 HR)

Miscellaneous statistics: Ground outs-to-air outs ratio: 0.78 last season, 0.76 for career. . . . Opponents grounded into 12 double plays in 179 opportunities (one per 15). . . . Allowed 39 doubles, 6 triples in 231⅓ innings. . . . Allowed 10 first-inning runs in 34 starts (2.38 ERA). . . . Batting support: 2.82 runs per start, lowest average in N.L. . . . Opposing base stealers: 20-for-31 (65%); 2 pickoffs, 1 balk.

Comments: Only Sid Fernandez among N.L. pitchers recorded more fly outs (309) than Benes (286) last season. . . . Allowed more hits than any N.L. pitcher, including a league-high total of singles (171). . . . Has lost six straight decisions to the Expos; he went 0–4 against them last season. . . . Career record is 15–6 with a 2.59 ERA in day games, 29–33 and a 3.63 ERA at night. . . . Career ERA is nearly one run higher in home games (3.79) than on the road (2.87). . . . Hasn't allowed more than two home runs in his last 66 starts, dating back to April 11, 1991. . . . Don't overlook the breakdown listed at the bottom of his statistics grid; late-game problems have become part of a career-long pattern. Career opponents' batting averages: .205 on the first pass, .218 on the second, .307 after that. . . . Broke a streak of 54 consecutive hitless at-bats at the plate with a double against Butch Henry on April 19 that started a streak of four hits in four ABs. No other pitcher had a 4-for-4 streak last season; Steve Avery and Trevor Wilson did so in 1991. . . . Update on the first-round selections from the June 1988 draft. Most career wins: Jim Abbott (47–52), Andy Benes (44–39), Steve Avery (32–30), Charles Nagy (29–29), Alex Fernandez (22–29). Last season was the first in which Abbott did not lead the group in wins. Benes is the only member to win at least 10 games in each of the last three seasons.

Bud Black
Throws Left

San Francisco Giants	W-L	ERA	AB	H	HR	BB	SO	BA	SA	OBA
Season	10-12	3.97	677	178	23	59	82	.263	.422	.321
vs. Left-Handers			140	32	4	10	20	.229	.364	.281
vs. Right-Handers			537	146	19	49	62	.272	.438	.332
vs. Ground-Ballers			287	58	4	17	35	.202	.282	.247
vs. Fly-Ballers			390	120	19	42	47	.308	.526	.374
Home Games	8-5	2.91	422	104	13	32	58	.246	.382	.300
Road Games	2-7	5.76	255	74	10	27	24	.290	.490	.356
Grass Fields	9-8	3.36	538	135	14	45	68	.251	.379	.309
Artificial Turf	1-4	6.43	139	43	9	14	14	.309	.590	.368
April	0-0	—	0	0	0	0	0	—	—	—
May	2-1	4.26	115	27	6	10	11	.235	.452	.294
June	2-1	3.48	122	34	0	12	16	.279	.344	.343
July	5-1	1.59	166	34	3	10	20	.205	.307	.249
August	1-3	3.72	150	43	6	12	20	.287	.453	.341
Sept./Oct.	0-6	8.01	124	40	8	15	15	.323	.589	.393
Leading Off Inn.			179	47	4	11	17	.263	.363	.305
Bases Empty			430	118	15	29	49	.274	.440	.320
Runners On			247	60	8	30	33	.243	.393	.323
Runners/Scor. Pos.			137	34	3	20	21	.248	.380	.340
Runners On/2 Out			96	14	1	13	12	.146	.250	.248
Scor. Pos./2 Out			60	11	1	10	10	.183	.333	.300
Late-Inning Pressure			51	12	3	5	4	.235	.451	.304
Leading Off			17	3	0	1	2	.176	.176	.222
Runners On			9	2	1	3	2	.222	.556	.417
Runners/Scor. Pos.			4	0	0	2	2	.000	.000	.333
First 9 Batters			238	60	7	10	30	.252	.399	.282
Second 9 Batters			219	63	9	23	32	.288	.493	.352
All Batters Thereafter			220	55	7	26	20	.250	.377	.329

Loves to face: Mariano Duncan (0-for-9)
                  Tony Fernandez (.197, 13-for-66)
                  Kurt Stillwell (0-for-12, 5 SO)
Hates to face: Pete Incaviglia (.524, 11-for-21, 3 2B, 4 HR)
                  Darrin Jackson (.545, 6-for-11, 2 2B, 1 HR)
                  Juan Samuel (.500, 8-for-16, 2 HR)

Miscellaneous statistics: Ground outs-to-air outs ratio: 1.01 last season, 1.08 for career. . . . Opponents grounded into 17 double plays in 138 opportunities (one per 8.1). . . . Allowed 27 doubles, 6 triples in 177 innings. . . . Allowed 3 first-inning runs in 28 starts (0.64 ERA, 4th lowest in majors). . . . Batting support: 3.11 runs per start, 4th-lowest average in N.L. . . . Opposing base stealers: 7-for-21 (33%), 2d-lowest rate in N.L.; 9 pickoffs (3d most in N.L.), 7 balks (most in majors).

Comments: Allowed 23 home runs to lead the National League. The last Giants pitcher to lead the league was Mike McCormick in 1961. . . . His 10 wins ranked 2d in the majors among pitchers who started the season on the disabled list; Bob Welch led with 11. Among those pitchers, only Chuck Finley and Scott Kamieniecki pitched more innings than Black. . . . Shared the major league lead with five wins in July, but led both leagues in losses after August 31. His ERA over that period was a National League high. . . . Posted a record of 7–3 with a 2.88 ERA in 12 starts in which he recorded more ground outs than fly outs, compared to 3–9 with a 4.82 ERA when the opposite was true. . . . Over the last two seasons, he has a 12–3 record in day games, 10–25 at night. . . . Committed seven balks, tying teammate Trevor Wilson for the most in the majors. Last season was the fifth in which he balked at least five times; only Steve Carlton has had more such seasons (9). . . . Hasn't made an error in 94 chances since joining the Giants; in franchise history, only two pitchers have handled more chances without an error: Slim Sallee (133) and Andy Hansen (122). . . . Held opponents to the lowest first-inning batting average in the league (.109), but didn't overpower anyone; he had the league's lowest first-inning strikeout rate (one every 12.1 batters). . . . Had three hits in 54 at-bats for the 3d-lowest batting average by an N.L. pitcher last year (.056). Giants pitchers combined for an .086 mark, the lowest in the league.

Joe Boever
Throws Right

Houston Astros	W-L	ERA	AB	H	HR	BB	SO	BA	SA	OBA
Season	3-6	2.51	416	103	3	45	67	.248	.310	.324
vs. Left-Handers			185	45	1	28	30	.243	.319	.347
vs. Right-Handers			231	58	2	17	37	.251	.303	.304
vs. Ground-Ballers			189	56	0	21	30	.296	.339	.367
vs. Fly-Ballers			227	47	3	24	37	.207	.286	.290
Home Games	1-2	1.32	226	55	2	19	37	.243	.288	.308
Road Games	2-4	3.96	190	48	1	26	30	.253	.337	.342
Grass Fields	0-3	5.46	109	32	1	17	16	.294	.422	.391
Artificial Turf	3-3	1.51	307	71	2	28	51	.231	.270	.299
April	0-0	0.00	43	6	0	6	10	.140	.140	.245
May	1-1	3.09	89	22	0	10	11	.247	.303	.320
June	1-2	4.43	80	23	0	8	8	.287	.375	.363
July	0-1	2.20	65	21	1	7	11	.323	.400	.397
August	1-2	2.87	56	11	1	6	11	.196	.250	.274
Sept./Oct.	0-0	1.64	83	20	1	8	16	.241	.313	.309
Leading Off Inn.			92	27	1	6	11	.293	.370	.343
Bases Empty			191	55	3	19	27	.288	.382	.355
Runners On			225	48	0	26	40	.213	.249	.298
Runners/Scor. Pos.			135	30	0	21	27	.222	.274	.327
Runners On/2 Out			99	23	0	12	20	.232	.273	.327
Scor. Pos./2 Out			67	16	0	11	16	.239	.299	.363
Late-Inning Pressure			102	31	1	15	9	.304	.392	.392
Leading Off			27	10	0	3	5	.370	.481	.433
Runners On			51	13	0	8	3	.255	.294	.355
Runners/Scor. Pos.			25	8	0	7	2	.320	.360	.441
First 9 Batters			388	95	3	44	62	.245	.307	.325
Second 9 Batters			28	8	0	1	5	.286	.357	.310
All Batters Thereafter			0	0	0	0	0	—	—	—

Loves to face: Mike Felder (.111, 1-for-9)
Gregg Jefferies (0-for-10)
Spike Owen (0-for-9)

Hates to face: Andre Dawson (.350, 7-for-20, 3 2B, 2 HR)
Billy Hatcher (.438, 7-for-16, 1 HR)
Jose Lind (.444, 8-for-18)

Miscellaneous statistics: Ground outs-to-air outs ratio: 0.85 last season, 0.82 for career.... Opponents grounded into 7 double plays in 111 opportunities (one per 16).... Allowed 13 doubles, 2 triples in 111⅓ innings.... Stranded 49 inherited runners, allowed 10 to score (83%), 3d-highest rate in N.L.... Opposing base stealers: 7-for-12 (58%); 0 pickoffs, 0 balks.

Comments: Led N.L. pitchers with 81 games pitched. Houston pitchers finished one-two-three in the N.L. in appearances in 1992, the fifth time in league history that one team took the top three spots. The last to do so: the 1979 Pirates (Kent Tekulve, Enrique Romo, and Grant Jackson); others were the 1977 Padres, 1937 Phillies, and 1921 Braves.... He and Duane Ward are the only pitchers to make more than 65 appearances in each of the last four seasons.... Pitched in 11 games for the Cardinals in 1986, and has increased that total in every season since: 14, 16, 66, 67, 68, 81. The only pitcher in major league history with a seven-year streak is Nolan Ryan (1968–74).... Made 29 saves in his last 100 appearances for the Braves (1989–90), but only eight more in 183 games since then.... After making 68 relief appearances without a save in 1991 (which at the time was one game shy of the record), he earned only two saves last season. The only other pitcher ever to make more than 80 appearances and save fewer than three: Frank Williams, who was 2-for-85 as John Franco's setup man in 1987.... Total of 189 at-bats by opposing ground-ball hitters was the most against any pitcher who didn't allow a home run to them last season.... Allowed the lowest home-run rate of his career: one every 37 innings; his previous career rate was one every 11 innings. The Astrodome can do that for you, and he should find Oakland Coliseum just as spacious.

Shawn Boskie
Throws Right

Chicago Cubs	W-L	ERA	AB	H	HR	BB	SO	BA	SA	OBA
Season	5-11	5.01	338	96	14	36	39	.284	.482	.354
vs. Left-Handers			195	59	10	31	27	.303	.538	.392
vs. Right-Handers			143	37	4	5	12	.259	.406	.296
vs. Ground-Ballers			157	47	4	15	21	.299	.478	.362
vs. Fly-Ballers			181	49	10	21	18	.271	.486	.348
Home Games	3-3	5.40	147	42	8	16	15	.286	.503	.358
Road Games	2-8	4.70	191	54	6	20	24	.283	.466	.352
Grass Fields	3-7	5.28	217	64	9	25	24	.295	.507	.367
Artificial Turf	2-4	4.50	121	32	5	11	15	.264	.438	.331
April	3-1	4.82	67	15	4	7	14	.224	.493	.297
May	1-2	4.88	105	31	3	8	9	.295	.467	.345
June	1-1	2.79	30	6	0	4	4	.200	.300	.324
July	0-2	2.08	60	15	1	8	7	.250	.333	.329
August	0-0	0.00	0	0	0	0	0	.000	.000	.000
Sept./Oct.	0-5	9.33	76	29	6	9	5	.382	.684	.448
Leading Off Inn.			89	26	5	7	10	.292	.528	.351
Bases Empty			212	57	9	20	26	.269	.462	.338
Runners On			126	39	5	16	13	.310	.516	.380
Runners/Scor. Pos.			66	20	2	12	8	.303	.455	.388
Runners On/2 Out			54	19	5	8	7	.352	.704	.435
Scor. Pos./2 Out			35	11	2	6	5	.314	.543	.415
Late-Inning Pressure			16	3	1	5	1	.188	.438	.409
Leading Off			5	2	1	2	0	.400	1.000	.571
Runners On			6	0	0	2	1	.000	.000	.333
Runners/Scor. Pos.			3	0	0	1	1	.000	.000	.400
First 9 Batters			153	41	8	22	22	.268	.490	.369
Second 9 Batters			118	35	4	9	14	.297	.483	.341
All Batters Thereafter			67	20	2	5	3	.299	.463	.342

Loves to face: Pedro Guerrero (0-for-10)
Dave Martinez (.087, 2-for-23, 3 BB)
Jose Uribe (0-for-10)

Hates to face: Orlando Merced (.800, 4-for-5, 1 HR)
Terry Pendleton (.545, 6-for-11, 4 2B, 1 HR)
Andy Van Slyke (.462, 6-for-13, 2 HR)

Miscellaneous statistics: Ground outs-to-air outs ratio: 0.90 last season, 1.00 for career.... Opponents grounded into 12 double plays in 74 opportunities (one per 6.2).... Allowed 25 doubles, 0 triples in 91⅔ innings.... Allowed 18 first-inning runs in 18 starts (9.72 ERA, highest in N.L.)... Batting support: 3.06 runs per start.... Opposing base stealers: 2-for-3 (67%); 2 pickoffs, 1 balk.

Comments: Won his first two starts of the 1992 season (the only time he's won consecutive starts), then went downhill.... Was one of two Cubs pitchers to go 0–5 after August 31. The other: Jim Bullinger.... Was 0–6 with an 8.10 ERA after the All-Star break; ended the season with an eight-game losing streak that straddled a 46-day visit to the disabled list (July 17–Sept. 1).... Allowed six runs without retiring a batter against the Cardinals on September 20, the 2d-highest such total in the N.L. last season. (He faced seven batters, allowing six hits and a walk.)... Average of 4.70 innings per start was the lowest in the majors last season (minimum: 15 GS).... Started 18 games, 2d most of any pitcher who didn't reach the eighth inning last season; Kyle Abbott went 0-for-19.... Allowed five first-inning home runs; only one N.L. pitcher allowed more: Doug Drabek (6).... Last May he snapped a streak of 11 consecutive starts in which he allowed a home run.... Career record is 0–6 vs. Pittsburgh; he's also winless against Atlanta and Los Angeles (0–4 vs. each).... Career record is 8–13 at Wrigley Field, 1–7 on other grass fields, 5–6 on artificial turf.... Career batting average of .301 by opposing left-handed hitters is the 3d highest among active pitchers (minimum: 500 AB), ahead of only southpaw Jim Abbott (.304) and right-hander Bill Swift (.303).

Jeff Brantley

Throws Right

San Francisco Giants	W-L	ERA	AB	H	HR	BB	SO	BA	SA	OBA
Season	7-7	2.95	323	67	8	45	86	.207	.319	.307
vs. Left-Handers			193	35	4	32	58	.181	.280	.300
vs. Right-Handers			130	32	4	13	28	.246	.377	.320
vs. Ground-Ballers			138	28	1	23	34	.203	.275	.321
vs. Fly-Ballers			185	39	7	22	52	.211	.351	.297
Home Games	4-3	2.30	165	31	3	21	42	.188	.291	.280
Road Games	3-4	3.63	158	36	5	24	44	.228	.348	.335
Grass Fields	6-4	2.50	256	54	7	32	64	.211	.332	.304
Artificial Turf	1-3	4.58	67	13	1	13	22	.194	.269	.321
April	1-0	2.00	30	4	2	6	7	.133	.333	.270
May	1-2	2.63	43	8	0	5	9	.186	.186	.265
June	1-2	3.86	38	7	3	9	9	.184	.421	.347
July	0-0	5.40	49	14	1	4	17	.286	.408	.340
August	0-2	4.26	71	19	2	12	11	.268	.408	.388
Sept./Oct.	4-1	1.01	92	15	0	9	33	.163	.217	.238
Leading Off Inn.			76	12	0	7	18	.158	.184	.229
Bases Empty			180	34	4	24	53	.189	.289	.291
Runners On			143	33	4	21	33	.231	.357	.327
Runners/Scor. Pos.			92	20	3	16	24	.217	.370	.324
Runners On/2 Out			64	11	2	11	17	.172	.313	.303
Scor. Pos./2 Out			44	8	2	9	13	.182	.364	.321
Late-Inning Pressure			91	26	2	17	17	.286	.385	.396
Leading Off			22	6	0	3	5	.273	.318	.360
Runners On			48	14	2	8	10	.292	.438	.390
Runners/Scor. Pos.			33	10	2	7	6	.303	.515	.405
First 9 Batters			272	61	7	42	72	.224	.338	.329
Second 9 Batters			43	3	1	2	11	.070	.186	.130
All Batters Thereafter			8	3	0	1	3	.375	.375	.444

Loves to face: Casey Candaele (0-for-8)
Darren Daulton (.100, 1-for-10)
Barry Larkin (.083, 1-for-12)

Hates to face: Brett Butler (.417, 5-for-12)
Ron Gant (.313, 5-for-16, 1 2B, 3 HR)
Tony Gwynn (.647, 11-for-17)

Miscellaneous statistics: Ground outs-to-air outs ratio: 0.72 last season, 0.99 for career. . . . Opponents grounded into 6 double plays in 76 opportunities (one per 13). . . . Allowed 12 doubles, 0 triples in 91⅔ innings. . . . Stranded 21 inherited runners, allowed 11 to score (66%). . . . Opposing base stealers: 4-for-5 (80%); 0 pickoffs, 1 balk.

Comments: All seven of his saves came before the All-Star break, six by the end of May. . . . Lost seven games in relief last season, compared to only five losses in 188 relief appearances over his four previous seasons. . . . Left the bullpen in September for the first time since 1989 and was a smash, going 3–0 and allowing only one earned run in 20⅔ innings, with 27 strikeouts and 11 hits. Granted, it was only four starts, but only one pitcher *ever* compiled an ERA that low (0.44) in a season of four or more starts: Buck O'Brien, with the 1911 Red Sox. (O'Brien, incidentally, was a 20-game winner in 1912.) . . . Brantley was a starting pitcher throughout his minor league career. . . . Ended the season with a scoreless streak of 19⅔ innings. . . . Averaged a career-high rate of 8.44 strikeouts per nine innings last season, up from 6.33 in 1990 and 7.65 in '91. . . . Career rate of 7.08 strikeouts per nine innings is 3d highest in Giants history (minimum: 300 IP), behind Mark Davis (7.77) and "Toothpick" Sam Jones (7.17). . . . Batting average by opposing left-handed batters, year by year since 1989: .302, .274, .205, .181. Last season's mark was the lowest in the majors (minimum: 200 BFP). He and bullpen mate Rod Beck, a pair of right-handers, held opposing lefties to a .180 average in 373 at-bats. . . . Opponents own a career batting average of .088 with the bases loaded (5-for-57, 1 HR), the lowest vs. any pitcher over the last 18 years (minimum: 50 BFP).

Tom Browning

Throws Left

Cincinnati Reds	W-L	ERA	AB	H	HR	BB	SO	BA	SA	OBA
Season	6-5	5.07	347	108	6	28	33	.311	.484	.362
vs. Left-Handers			83	27	1	8	8	.325	.470	.385
vs. Right-Handers			264	81	5	20	25	.307	.489	.355
vs. Ground-Ballers			137	40	1	4	15	.292	.409	.308
vs. Fly-Ballers			210	68	5	24	18	.324	.533	.395
Home Games	5-1	5.03	129	34	6	8	20	.264	.512	.302
Road Games	1-4	5.09	218	74	0	20	13	.339	.468	.397
Grass Fields	0-4	5.52	133	49	0	11	9	.368	.519	.418
Artificial Turf	6-1	4.82	214	59	6	17	24	.276	.463	.328
April	3-1	5.33	103	32	2	10	16	.311	.466	.368
May	1-2	6.23	108	34	3	7	11	.315	.519	.359
June	2-2	4.11	120	36	1	8	5	.300	.467	.346
July	0-0	3.60	16	6	0	3	1	.375	.500	.450
August	0-0	0.00	0	0	0	0	0	.000	.000	.000
Sept./Oct.	0-0	0.00	0	0	0	0	0	.000	.000	.000
Leading Off Inn.			87	27	2	5	11	.310	.494	.348
Bases Empty			201	60	3	10	24	.299	.468	.335
Runners On			146	48	3	18	9	.329	.507	.396
Runners/Scor. Pos.			97	29	1	14	7	.299	.433	.379
Runners On/2 Out			55	12	1	9	3	.218	.364	.338
Scor. Pos./2 Out			41	9	1	6	2	.220	.415	.333
Late-Inning Pressure			9	2	0	0	1	.222	.222	.222
Leading Off			3	1	0	0	0	.333	.333	.333
Runners On			2	1	0	0	0	.500	.500	.500
Runners/Scor. Pos.			1	0	0	0	0	.000	.000	.000
First 9 Batters			130	42	1	8	11	.323	.438	.362
Second 9 Batters			119	36	3	12	18	.303	.521	.364
All Batters Thereafter			98	30	2	8	4	.306	.500	.361

Loves to face: Steve Lake (.095, 2-for-21)
Otis Nixon (.067, 2-for-30, 3 BB)
Todd Zeile (.063, 1-for-16)

Hates to face: Barry Bonds (.325, 13-for-40, 3 2B, 5 HR, 11 BB)
Bobby Bonilla (.390, 16-for-41, 4 2B, 1 3B, 8 HR)
Tim Teufel (.429, 18-for-42, 4 HR)

Miscellaneous statistics: Ground outs-to-air outs ratio: 0.80 last season, 0.66 for career. . . . Opponents grounded into 10 double plays in 61 opportunities (one per 6.1). . . . Allowed 28 doubles, 7 triples in 87 innings. . . . Allowed 16 first-inning runs in 16 starts (9.19 ERA, 2d highest in N.L.) . . . Batting support: 3.94 runs per start. . . . Opposing base stealers: 11-for-12 (92%); 2 pickoffs, 1 balk.

Comments: His 271 career starts is the 7th-highest total in Reds history; he needs only eight more to move past Johnny Vander Meer into fifth place. The top five: Eppa Rixey, 356; Paul Derringer, 322; Dolf Luque, 319; Bucky Walters, 296; Vander Meer, 278. . . . Batting average by opposing right-handed batters was the highest vs. any N.L. pitcher (minimum: 200 BFP). . . . Opponents' batting average during the first inning (.419) was the highest in majors. . . . Averaged 3.41 strikeouts per nine innings, the lowest rate of his career. . . . His rate of one double-play grounder every 6.1 chances was the best last season among fly-ball starters (pitchers with more fly outs than ground outs and a minimum of 10 starts). . . . Average of one home run allowed every 14.5 innings was the best rate of his career (with the exception of his debut in 1984, when he allowed no homers in 23⅓ innings). Notice that he didn't allow any homers in 53 innings away from Riverfront Stadium last season; that's the sixth consecutive season in which he's allowed more homers at home than on the road. . . . Career record is 36–34 in day games, 77–46 at night. . . . Average of innings per start has decreased in every year since 1988: 6.96, 6.74, 6.50, 6.40, 5.44 in 1992 (3d lowest in the league among pitchers with at least 15 starts last season). . . . Bobby Bonilla's eight career homers against him are 2d most of any active batter against any active pitcher. (Rickey Henderson has hit 11 against Frank Tanana, now pitching for the Mets.)

John Burkett — Throws Right

San Francisco Giants	W-L	ERA	AB	H	HR	BB	SO	BA	SA	OBA
Season	13-9	3.84	735	194	13	45	107	.264	.382	.308
vs. Left-Handers			466	138	11	27	56	.296	.448	.334
vs. Right-Handers			269	56	2	18	51	.208	.268	.265
vs. Ground-Ballers			334	85	6	15	51	.254	.374	.290
vs. Fly-Ballers			401	109	7	30	56	.272	.389	.323
Home Games	10-2	3.09	382	89	5	17	56	.233	.317	.267
Road Games	3-7	4.72	353	105	8	28	51	.297	.453	.351
Grass Fields	13-6	3.65	560	143	7	32	82	.255	.354	.297
Artificial Turf	0-3	4.50	175	51	6	13	25	.291	.474	.344
April	2-1	4.97	111	27	2	11	19	.243	.387	.311
May	3-0	2.43	123	28	3	4	21	.228	.333	.252
June	0-4	6.56	104	35	3	9	12	.337	.529	.400
July	2-1	2.83	127	29	2	10	18	.228	.331	.288
August	4-1	2.75	133	33	1	4	13	.248	.308	.271
Sept./Oct.	2-2	4.64	137	42	2	7	24	.307	.431	.338
Leading Off Inn.			187	47	3	9	23	.251	.337	.289
Bases Empty			442	112	8	17	64	.253	.342	.284
Runners On			293	82	5	28	43	.280	.444	.343
Runners/Scor. Pos.			169	51	3	20	31	.302	.485	.374
Runners On/2 Out			123	33	2	13	19	.268	.415	.343
Scor. Pos./2 Out			80	22	1	8	15	.275	.425	.348
Late-Inning Pressure			46	12	2	3	8	.261	.478	.294
Leading Off			14	4	1	1	2	.286	.643	.333
Runners On			15	5	1	0	3	.333	.667	.294
Runners/Scor. Pos.			8	4	0	0	2	.500	.750	.400
First 9 Batters			263	58	5	15	59	.221	.323	.271
Second 9 Batters			256	73	5	15	31	.285	.430	.325
All Batters Thereafter			216	63	3	15	17	.292	.398	.335

Loves to face: Andujar Cedeno (0-for-8, 4 SO)
Mariano Duncan (.100, 2-for-20)
Orlando Merced (.056, 1-for-18)

Hates to face: Darren Daulton (.571, 8-for-14)
Ryne Sandberg (.583, 7-for-12, 1 HR)
Larry Walker (.412, 7-for-17, 3 HR)

Miscellaneous statistics: Ground outs-to-air outs ratio: 1.14 last season, 1.22 for career.... Opponents grounded into 13 double plays in 137 opportunities (one per 11).... Allowed 34 doubles, 7 triples in 189⅔ innings... Allowed 14 first-inning runs in 32 starts (3.94 ERA).... Batting support: 4.69 runs per start, highest average in N.L.... Opposing base stealers: 17-for-24 (71%); 1 pickoff, 0 balks.

Comments: Had the lowest batting average (.018, 1-for-55) of any N.L. pitcher last season; in fact, it was the 4th-lowest single-season batting average in N.L. history (minimum: 50 AB). The bottom five: Bob Buhl, 1962 (0-for-70); Roger Craig, 1956 (.016, 1-for-61); Bill Hands, 1972 (.018, 1-for-57); Burkett, 1992; and Carl Willey, 1961 (.019, 1-for-54).... Allowed 11 homers to left-handed batters, 2d most in the N.L. The top five: Omar Olivares (13); Burkett, Doug Drabek, Greg W. Harris, and Orel Hershiser (11 each).... Allowed eight home runs and had a 4.41 ERA in 69⅓ innings with Kirt Manwaring catching; gave up only five homers and had a 3.05 ERA in 112 innings caught by Craig Colbert or Jim McNamara.... Started eight games in which he failed to pitch at least five innings, tied for the most in the N.L.... His ERA in road games was 4th highest in the league.... Opponents' batting average with runners in scoring position was 2d highest in the league.... Career record is 16–5 in starts in which he recorded more fly outs than ground outs, but he has only a .500 record (19–19) in starts in which the opposite is true.... He was unique in Roger Craig's stable—a pitcher healthy enough to make at least 30 starts in three consecutive seasons. During Craig's seven-year tenure in San Francisco, only one other pitcher started at least 30 games in even *two* straight seasons: Rick Reuschel.

Tom Candiotti — Throws Right

Los Angeles Dodgers	W-L	ERA	AB	H	HR	BB	SO	BA	SA	OBA
Season	11-15	3.00	746	177	13	63	152	.237	.347	.297
vs. Left-Handers			408	100	6	47	75	.245	.343	.321
vs. Right-Handers			338	77	7	16	77	.228	.352	.267
vs. Ground-Ballers			318	71	4	28	68	.223	.305	.290
vs. Fly-Ballers			428	106	9	35	84	.248	.379	.303
Home Games	6-6	2.33	327	80	3	17	65	.245	.324	.283
Road Games	5-9	3.53	419	97	10	46	87	.232	.365	.307
Grass Fields	7-12	3.11	531	125	12	37	107	.235	.358	.286
Artificial Turf	4-3	2.75	215	52	1	26	45	.242	.321	.322
April	3-0	3.62	121	28	4	8	31	.231	.421	.279
May	2-3	3.60	110	27	0	10	17	.245	.291	.306
June	1-3	2.11	156	36	3	12	28	.231	.365	.287
July	2-3	2.92	132	27	5	13	35	.205	.348	.279
August	1-3	2.75	74	18	0	5	15	.243	.284	.291
Sept./Oct.	2-3	3.21	153	41	1	15	26	.268	.340	.333
Leading Off Inn.			198	60	4	9	43	.303	.470	.333
Bases Empty			457	119	7	29	90	.260	.381	.306
Runners On			289	58	6	34	62	.201	.294	.284
Runners/Scor. Pos.			189	40	6	28	38	.212	.339	.311
Runners On/2 Out			128	23	2	19	26	.180	.266	.291
Scor. Pos./2 Out			93	17	2	16	17	.183	.280	.309
Late-Inning Pressure			102	27	4	9	18	.265	.431	.321
Leading Off			29	10	1	0	7	.345	.552	.345
Runners On			37	7	1	6	6	.189	.270	.295
Runners/Scor. Pos.			29	5	1	5	5	.172	.276	.286
First 9 Batters			242	60	3	21	44	.248	.335	.311
Second 9 Batters			233	55	4	17	49	.236	.352	.286
All Batters Thereafter			271	62	6	25	59	.229	.354	.294

Loves to face: Tony Gwynn (.091, 1-for-11)
Pete Incaviglia (.143, 5-for-35)
Felix Jose (0-for-9)

Hates to face: Jay Bell (.400, 4-for-10, 2 2B)
Barry Bonds (.500, 5-for-10, 3 BB)
Scott Servais (.500, 4-for-8)

Miscellaneous statistics: Ground outs-to-air outs ratio: 1.31 last season, 1.24 for career.... Opponents grounded into 17 double plays in 123 opportunities (one per 7.2).... Allowed 35 doubles, 4 triples in 203⅔ innings.... Allowed 23 first-inning runs in 30 starts (5.76 ERA).... Batting support: 3.13 runs per start, 6th-lowest average in N.L.... Opposing base stealers: 30-for-35 (86%), 3d-most steals in N.L.; 1 pickoff, 2 balks.

Comments: Candiotti and teammate Orel Hershiser shared the N.L. lead in losses. You don't have to look back too far to find the last N.L. team with the league's top two losers: the 1990 Cardinals (Jose DeLeon, 19; and Joe Magrane, 17). The last time teammates *tied* for the N.L. lead was 1951, when Ken Raffensberger and Willie Ramsdell each lost 17 games for the Cincinnati Reds.... Led the Dodgers with 11 wins, the lowest total to lead the club since 1944 when Curt Davis led the wartime Bums with 10 wins. Even in the strike-shortened season of 1981, the Dodgers had a 13-game winner named Fernando.... Won each of his first three starts for the Dodgers, but didn't have a two-game winning streak for the rest of the season.... Over the last five seasons, he has a record of 14–2 during April, but a losing mark thereafter (52–55).... Has a career record of 56–42 in home games (wherever they may be), and 39–51 on the road.... Has pitched for last-place clubs in Milwaukee (1984), Cleveland (1987), and Los Angeles (1992). The only active players to have finished last more often than Candiotti: Mark Grant, Greg A. Harris, and Dave Schmidt (4 times each).... A previously unknown fact: Six players in major league history have finished nine or more seasons with last-place teams; the leader: Nate Colbert (10). Those with nine include current Blue Jays manager Cito Gaston, Hall of Famer Chuck Klein, Dale Murphy, Frank Thomas the Elder, and Elmer Valo.

Frank Castillo
Throws Right

Chicago Cubs	W-L	ERA	AB	H	HR	BB	SO	BA	SA	OBA
Season	10-11	3.46	770	179	19	63	135	.232	.371	.294
vs. Left-Handers			448	102	10	49	73	.228	.346	.303
vs. Right-Handers			322	77	9	14	62	.239	.407	.281
vs. Ground-Ballers			362	65	5	29	69	.180	.260	.242
vs. Fly-Ballers			408	114	14	34	66	.279	.471	.339
Home Games	6-7	3.63	457	106	12	37	82	.232	.372	.294
Road Games	4-4	3.21	313	73	7	26	53	.233	.371	.294
Grass Fields	9-10	3.50	596	136	15	51	106	.228	.362	.293
Artificial Turf	1-1	3.33	174	43	4	12	29	.247	.402	.296
April	0-2	3.65	88	16	2	6	19	.182	.352	.250
May	3-2	2.01	117	26	2	9	24	.222	.299	.276
June	3-2	3.96	145	37	4	14	22	.255	.421	.319
July	0-1	2.83	110	27	3	11	18	.245	.409	.309
August	2-3	4.35	142	31	5	12	18	.218	.366	.291
Sept./Oct.	2-1	3.59	168	42	3	11	34	.250	.369	.300
Leading Off Inn.			202	49	7	14	30	.243	.411	.298
Bases Empty			504	116	12	28	89	.230	.363	.276
Runners On			266	63	7	35	46	.237	.387	.325
Runners/Scor. Pos.			144	33	3	32	23	.229	.361	.363
Runners On/2 Out			108	19	2	23	19	.176	.278	.321
Scor. Pos./2 Out			69	11	0	21	12	.159	.217	.356
Late-Inning Pressure			63	17	2	9	9	.270	.381	.365
Leading Off			18	3	1	3	2	.167	.333	.318
Runners On			16	6	0	4	3	.375	.438	.476
Runners/Scor. Pos.			5	1	0	4	1	.200	.200	.500
First 9 Batters			272	57	2	19	55	.210	.279	.266
Second 9 Batters			263	64	11	22	45	.243	.441	.304
All Batters Thereafter			235	58	6	22	35	.247	.400	.313

Loves to face: Jeff Bagwell (0-for-13)
Mariano Duncan (.091, 1-for-11, 1 2B)
Felix Jose (0-for-9)

Hates to face: Mike LaValliere (.500, 8-for-16)
Ozzie Smith (.700, 7-for-10)
Andy Van Slyke (.526, 10-for-19, 2 HR)

Miscellaneous statistics: Ground outs-to-air outs ratio: 0.95 last season, 1.03 for career.... Opponents grounded into 6 double plays in 122 opportunities (one per 20), 4th-worst rate in N.L.... Allowed 42 doubles (4th most in N.L.), 4 triples in 205⅓ innings.... Allowed 8 first-inning runs in 33 starts (1.36 ERA).... Batting support: 3.45 runs per start.... Opposing base stealers: 18-for-27 (67%); 0 pickoffs, 0 balks.

Comments: Allowed 65 extra-base hits, 2d-highest total in the N.L.... His ERA was lower in the first inning than in any other. He hasn't allowed a first-inning home run in his last 35 starts, dating back to Sept. 22, 1991.... Threw 11 wild pitches, tied for 3d most in the league.... Batting average of opposing ground-ball hitters was 2d lowest in the majors (minimum: 150 BFP). Career average of ground-ball hitters (.197) is the lowest against any pitcher over the last 18 years (minimum: 500 AB). Fly-ball hitters have batted .272 against him.... Completed four of his first 11 starts in the majors (1991), but has gone 0-for-40 since then.... Has a career record of 14–9 in games in which he has walked fewer than three batters, compared to a 2–9 record when he walked three or more.... Has allowed more than one home run four times in 27 starts at Wrigley Field, but only once in 24 starts on the road. His career rate is one home run every 11 innings at home, one every 18 innings on the road.... As a borderline fly-ball pitcher, he may find it difficult to win at Wrigley Field. No Cubs pitcher has recorded more fly outs than ground outs and won as many as 12 games since Lynn McGlothen in 1980; since then, there have been 18 seasons of 12-plus wins by ground-ball pitchers for the Cubs.... Most comparable two-year statistical profile belongs to a Cubs pitcher of 30 years earlier; anyone remember Bob Hendley?

Norm Charlton
Throws Left

Cincinnati Reds	W-L	ERA	AB	H	HR	BB	SO	BA	SA	OBA
Season	4-2	2.99	302	79	7	26	90	.262	.397	.323
vs. Left-Handers			71	21	2	6	11	.296	.465	.359
vs. Right-Handers			231	58	5	20	79	.251	.377	.313
vs. Ground-Ballers			135	34	3	10	35	.252	.378	.301
vs. Fly-Ballers			167	45	4	16	55	.269	.413	.340
Home Games	2-1	2.27	148	37	3	10	40	.250	.372	.300
Road Games	2-1	3.67	154	42	4	16	50	.273	.422	.345
Grass Fields	2-1	2.45	94	24	1	9	24	.255	.330	.327
Artificial Turf	2-1	3.23	208	55	6	17	66	.264	.428	.322
April	0-0	2.70	45	9	2	6	13	.200	.378	.308
May	1-0	2.30	62	18	2	3	21	.290	.435	.328
June	2-0	1.84	54	12	2	5	17	.222	.389	.300
July	0-0	2.40	52	11	0	2	14	.212	.288	.241
August	0-1	5.87	61	20	1	7	18	.328	.492	.386
Sept./Oct.	1-1	2.45	28	9	0	3	7	.321	.357	.387
Leading Off Inn.			65	21	2	8	14	.323	.508	.397
Bases Empty			161	39	4	11	47	.242	.373	.299
Runners On			141	40	3	15	43	.284	.426	.350
Runners/Scor. Pos.			95	26	3	13	34	.274	.453	.351
Runners On/2 Out			55	11	2	5	16	.200	.364	.279
Scor. Pos./2 Out			41	7	2	5	13	.171	.366	.261
Late-Inning Pressure			202	50	5	22	58	.248	.376	.326
Leading Off			46	12	1	5	13	.261	.391	.333
Runners On			84	25	2	14	22	.298	.452	.394
Runners/Scor. Pos.			57	15	2	13	19	.263	.456	.394
First 9 Batters			295	77	6	24	89	.261	.390	.320
Second 9 Batters			7	2	1	2	1	.286	.714	.444
All Batters Thereafter			0	0	0	0	0	—	—	—

Loves to face: Andre Dawson (.188, 3-for-16)
Bill Doran (.100, 1-for-10)

Hates to face: Roberto Alomar (.333, 5-for-15, 5 BB)
Rafael Ramirez (.381, 8-for-21)

Miscellaneous statistics: Ground outs-to-air outs ratio: 1.34 last season, 1.32 for career.... Opponents grounded into 7 double plays in 70 opportunities (one per 10).... Allowed 18 doubles, 1 triple in 81⅓ innings.... Saved 26 games in 34 opportunities (76%).... Stranded 17 inherited runners, allowed 10 to score (63%).... Opposing base stealers: 15-for-19 (79%); 3 pickoffs, 0 balks.

Comments: Raised his strikeout rate from 6.40 per nine innings in 1991 to 9.96 last season, the largest increase since 1987, when Scott Garrelts's rate rose from 6.48 to 10.75 when he moved to the bullpen (minimum: 75 innings each season).... Saved 26 games last season, compared to a total of three saves in 137 relief appearances over the three previous years.... He and Rob Dibble became the first teammates in major league history to save at least 25 games each in the same season. Only four other pairs reached the 20 mark together: Tom Henke and Duane Ward (1991 Blue Jays), Roger McDowell and Jesse Orosco (1986 Mets), Greg Minton and Gary Lavelle (1983 Giants), and Eddie Fisher and Hoyt Wilhelm (1965 White Sox, when saves were unofficial).... Made 69 appearances without a save in 1989, a record at the time for most relief appearances in a season without a save. Jeff Innis matched that total in 1991, and two pitchers broke it in 1992: Mike Perez (77 games) and Bob McClure (71 games); Jeff Parrett also set an A.L. record last season (66 games).... Only two pitchers have made 30 starts or won 10 starts coming off 20-save seasons: Wilbur Wood (21 saves in 1970, 22 wins in 42 starts in 1971) and Craig Lefferts (23 saves in 1991, 14 wins in 32 starts in 1992). Goose Gossage was a near miss on both counts (26 saves in 1975, 9 wins in 29 starts in 1976).... Career breakdown: 13–15 with a 3.43 ERA in 37 starts (5.31 strikeouts per nine innings); 18–9, 2.63 ERA in 201 relief appearances (9.50 SO per 9 IP).... Career record is 7–0 during the month of June.

Mark Clark

Throws Right

St. Louis Cardinals	W-L	ERA	AB	H	HR	BB	SO	BA	SA	OBA
Season	3-10	4.45	441	117	12	36	44	.265	.406	.318
vs. Left-Handers			263	70	6	25	25	.266	.395	.326
vs. Right-Handers			178	47	6	11	19	.264	.421	.305
vs. Ground-Ballers			232	55	2	12	21	.237	.310	.272
vs. Fly-Ballers			209	62	10	24	23	.297	.512	.366
Home Games	1-6	5.25	185	45	9	15	16	.243	.427	.297
Road Games	2-4	3.86	256	72	3	21	28	.281	.391	.333
Grass Fields	2-2	2.41	138	34	2	11	13	.246	.333	.300
Artificial Turf	1-8	5.45	303	83	10	25	31	.274	.439	.326
April	0-0	—	0	0	0	0	0	—	—	—
May	0-0	—	0	0	0	0	0	—	—	—
June	0-2	4.71	109	28	5	9	9	.257	.459	.311
July	2-3	2.25	150	32	1	11	15	.213	.280	.267
August	1-2	5.16	81	17	2	8	9	.210	.321	.275
Sept./Oct.	0-3	7.36	101	40	4	8	11	.396	.604	.436
Leading Off Inn.			111	30	3	7	11	.270	.414	.314
Bases Empty			262	72	8	20	22	.275	.416	.326
Runners On			179	45	4	16	22	.251	.391	.307
Runners/Scor. Pos.			103	22	2	10	16	.214	.359	.274
Runners On/2 Out			72	15	2	12	12	.208	.375	.321
Scor. Pos./2 Out			48	7	1	6	10	.146	.271	.241
Late-Inning Pressure			13	8	0	0	0	.615	.923	.615
Leading Off			4	2	0	0	0	.500	.750	.500
Runners On			6	5	0	0	0	.833	1.333	.833
Runners/Scor. Pos.			4	3	0	0	0	.750	1.500	.750
First 9 Batters			161	34	6	14	20	.211	.373	.273
Second 9 Batters			154	44	0	17	15	.286	.331	.353
All Batters Thereafter			126	39	6	5	9	.310	.540	.333

Loves to face: Jose Offerman (0-for-6)
  Gary Sheffield (0-for-6)
  Jose Vizcaino (0-for-8)
Hates to face: Ruben Amaro (.750, 3-for-4, 1 HR, 1 SO)
  Ryne Sandberg (.500, 3-for-6, 1 3B, 1 HR, 3 BB)
  Sammy Sosa (.667, 2-for-3, 2 HR)

Miscellaneous statistics: Ground outs-to-air outs ratio: 0.95 last season, 0.89 for career.... Opponents grounded into 8 double plays in 79 opportunities (one per 10).... Allowed 18 doubles, 4 triples in 113⅓ innings.... Allowed 7 first-inning runs in 20 starts (3.15 ERA).... Batting support: 3.60 runs per start.... Opposing base stealers: 17-for-19 (89%); 2 pickoffs, 0 balks.

Comments: St. Louis was the only team in the majors to have two rookie pitchers who each started at least 20 games; the other was Donovan Osborne, who led all N.L. rookies with 29 starts. In the last 50 years, only two other pairs of Cardinals rookies started at least 20 games in the same season: Larry Jackson and Luis Arroyo in 1955; Dave LaPoint and John Stuper in 1982. (Rheal Cormier, who started 30 games for St. Louis last season, lost his rookie status with 67⅔ innings in 1991, 17⅔ over the limit.)... Clark, Osborne, Cormier, and Omar Olivares all started at least 20 games for St. Louis last season; all were 25 or younger at the end of the season. The last three teams with four 20-start pitchers under the age of 26 have all been perennial contenders ever since: the 1987 Pirates (Doug Drabek, Brian Fisher, Mike Dunne, and Bob Kipper), the 1989 Braves (Derek Lilliquist, Tom Glavine, John Smoltz, and Pete Smith), and the 1989 White Sox (Melido Perez, Eric King, Greg Hibbard, and Steve Rosenberg).... Clark was one of three N.L. rookies to lose at least 10 games last season. If you don't know the others, check the first and last pitchers in this section.... His ERA after August 31 was the 2d highest in the National League, and his opponents' batting average in September was the highest in the majors.... Allowed nine home runs in 48 innings at Busch Stadium. The last Cardinals pitcher to yield homers at a higher rate there: Buddy Schultz in 1979 (5 HR in 16 innings).

Rheal Cormier

Throws Left

St. Louis Cardinals	W-L	ERA	AB	H	HR	BB	SO	BA	SA	OBA
Season	10-10	3.68	720	194	15	33	117	.269	.387	.305
vs. Left-Handers			132	38	1	5	25	.288	.402	.324
vs. Right-Handers			588	156	14	28	92	.265	.384	.301
vs. Ground-Ballers			325	90	4	13	45	.277	.369	.307
vs. Fly-Ballers			395	104	11	20	72	.263	.403	.303
Home Games	7-4	3.98	360	108	6	19	46	.300	.411	.337
Road Games	3-6	3.38	360	86	9	14	71	.239	.364	.272
Grass Fields	1-3	3.30	170	43	5	7	31	.253	.382	.289
Artificial Turf	9-7	3.79	550	151	10	26	86	.275	.389	.310
April	0-3	4.50	73	21	1	10	15	.288	.370	.373
May	0-2	7.80	127	38	4	6	16	.299	.472	.336
June	1-1	2.63	90	26	3	3	11	.289	.422	.312
July	2-2	4.18	117	38	4	2	19	.325	.470	.339
August	2-2	1.91	145	30	1	8	22	.207	.283	.258
Sept./Oct.	5-0	2.47	168	41	2	4	34	.244	.345	.262
Leading Off Inn.			186	49	3	6	31	.263	.376	.290
Bases Empty			444	113	6	15	78	.255	.342	.284
Runners On			276	81	9	18	39	.293	.460	.338
Runners/Scor. Pos.			159	40	5	14	28	.252	.409	.315
Runners On/2 Out			117	33	4	9	18	.282	.436	.333
Scor. Pos./2 Out			74	22	3	9	13	.297	.459	.373
Late-Inning Pressure			50	17	1	3	5	.340	.440	.377
Leading Off			15	5	0	0	1	.333	.333	.333
Runners On			18	6	1	2	3	.333	.556	.400
Runners/Scor. Pos.			6	1	1	2	1	.167	.667	.375
First 9 Batters			259	64	3	10	48	.247	.340	.277
Second 9 Batters			241	71	9	12	38	.295	.469	.333
All Batters Thereafter			220	59	3	11	31	.268	.355	.306

Loves to face: Archi Cianfrocco (.100, 1-for-10)
  Eric Karros (0-for-11)
  John Kruk (0-for-6)
Hates to face: Delino DeShields (.500, 5-for-10, 1 HR, 3 SO)
  Tony Gwynn (.667, 4-for-6)
  Barry Larkin (.800, 4-for-5)

Miscellaneous statistics: Ground outs-to-air outs ratio: 1.55 last season, 1.35 for career.... Opponents grounded into 19 double plays in 124 opportunities (one per 6.5).... Allowed 34 doubles, 3 triples in 186 innings.... Allowed 12 first-inning runs in 30 starts (3.30 ERA).... Batting support: 3.97 runs per start.... Opposing base stealers: 11-for-15 (73%); 1 pickoff, 2 balks.

Comments: Averaged 1.95 walks per nine innings in his minor league career, then 1.60 last season, 2d-lowest rate in majors behind teammate Bob Tewksbury (0.77). That's not as rare as you might think; it's the fifth time in the past 30 years that the one-two pitchers in this category have come from the same team, most recently the 1986 Cubs with Dennis Eckersley and Scott Sanderson.... His career rate of 1.45 walks per nine innings is the lowest among all active pitchers with a minimum of 250 innings pitched. He reached the 250-IP mark in his final start, having walked only 41 batters; the last major league pitcher to reach 250 innings with as few walks was Dave Rozema in 1978, with the same total.... As a whole, the Cardinals' staff walk rate (2.43 per nine innings) was the lowest in the majors last season, and the lowest by any N.L. staff since 1968.... Finished with a flourish: Cormier's season-ending seven-game winning streak tied for 3d longest in the N.L. last season; Mel Rojas of Montreal and Pete Smith of Atlanta also won each of their last seven decisions; in Smith's case, they were his only decisions of the season.... Five of his wins came from September 1 on; Doug Drabek (5–1) and Jose Rijo (5–1) were the only other N.L. pitchers to win five games in that period.... Born April 23, 1967; the Cardinals were beaten that day by the Dodgers' Claude Osteen, the same type of smallish, good-control left-hander that Cormier may turn out to be.

Jose DeLeon   Throws Right

Cardinals/Phillies	W-L	ERA	AB	H	HR	BB	SO	BA	SA	OBA
Season	2-8	4.37	444	111	7	48	79	.250	.374	.322
vs. Left-Handers			245	69	5	26	38	.282	.424	.351
vs. Right-Handers			199	42	2	22	41	.211	.312	.286
vs. Ground-Ballers			218	55	1	21	35	.252	.330	.313
vs. Fly-Ballers			226	56	6	27	44	.248	.416	.331
Home Games	2-3	3.33	252	57	3	24	47	.226	.317	.296
Road Games	0-5	5.80	192	54	4	24	32	.281	.448	.355
Grass Fields	0-3	5.70	86	21	1	14	9	.244	.349	.340
Artificial Turf	2-5	4.04	358	90	6	34	70	.251	.380	.317
April	1-2	3.64	108	22	2	15	18	.204	.343	.304
May	1-2	5.53	114	32	1	8	21	.281	.386	.331
June	0-2	3.78	61	18	1	3	14	.295	.475	.313
July	0-1	4.00	67	15	2	9	12	.224	.358	.312
August	0-0	6.97	37	8	1	8	7	.216	.405	.356
Sept./Oct.	0-1	3.00	57	16	0	5	7	.281	.298	.339
Leading Off Inn.			106	28	1	13	20	.264	.387	.345
Bases Empty			232	59	3	29	42	.254	.384	.342
Runners On			212	52	4	19	37	.245	.363	.300
Runners/Scor. Pos.			135	30	3	12	24	.222	.348	.275
Runners On/2 Out			89	23	3	9	14	.258	.438	.327
Scor. Pos./2 Out			65	15	2	8	10	.231	.385	.315
Late-Inning Pressure			4	1	0	0	0	.250	.250	.400
Leading Off			1	0	0	0	0	.000	.000	.000
Runners On			2	1	0	0	0	.500	.500	.500
Runners/Scor. Pos.			1	1	0	0	0	1.000	1.000	1.000
First 9 Batters			212	45	3	26	43	.212	.325	.295
Second 9 Batters			146	37	4	12	31	.253	.418	.313
All Batters Thereafter			86	29	0	10	5	.337	.419	.404

Loves to face: Mark Bailey (0-for-9)
Shawon Dunston (.180, 9-for-50, 0 BB)
Andres Galarraga (.061, 2-for-33, 1 HR, 3 BB)

Hates to face: Barry Bonds (.400, 12-for-30, 4 HR)
Eddie Murray (.364, 12-for-33, 4 HR)
Terry Pendleton (.542, 13-for-24)

Miscellaneous statistics: Ground outs-to-air outs ratio: 0.65 last season (3d lowest in N.L.), 0.77 for career.... Opponents grounded into 5 double plays in 103 opportunities (one per 21), 3d-worst rate in N.L.... Allowed 26 doubles, 4 triples in 117⅓ innings.... Allowed 8 first-inning runs in 18 starts (4.00 ERA).... Batting support: 3.67 runs per start.... Opposing base stealers: 12-for-17 (71%); 0 pickoffs, 0 balks.

Comments: Right-handed batters have a career average of .1904 against him, 2d lowest against any pitcher since 1975, behind J. R. Richard (.1901). If right-handers go hitless in their next four at-bats against DeLeon, he will move past J.R.... Made 18 starts last season, 2d most among major league pitchers who did not last into the eighth inning in any of them. Averaged 5.33 innings per start, 2d lowest among N.L. pitchers with at least 15 starts last season.... Strikeout rate fell to a career-low 6.06 per nine innings last year. DeLeon debuted for the 1983 Pirates averaging 9.83 strikeouts per nine innings. At the time, only two starting pitchers in the N.L.'s 108-year history had posted a rate as high (minimum: 100 innings): Sandy Koufax (four times), and J. R. Richard (1978). In nine years since, another four N.L. starters have done it: Dwight Gooden (1984), Mike Scott (1986), Nolan Ryan (1987), and David Cone (1990).... Career record (75–113) gives him the 2d-lowest winning percentage (.399) among pitchers with at least 150 decisions during the expansion era; Skip Lockwood had the lowest (57–97, .370). Last year marked his sixth season with a winning percentage below .400 in a season of at least 10 decisions; Curt Simmons, who retired in the late 1960s, was the last pitcher to do that. DeLeon needs only one more season like that to tie the all-time mark of seven, shared by baseball luminaries Milt Gaston, Long Tom Hughes, Si Johnson, and Jack Russell.

Jim Deshaies   Throws Left

San Diego Padres	W-L	ERA	AB	H	HR	BB	SO	BA	SA	OBA
Season	4-7	3.28	356	92	6	33	46	.258	.360	.321
vs. Left-Handers			59	21	1	11	10	.356	.458	.451
vs. Right-Handers			297	71	5	22	36	.239	.340	.293
vs. Ground-Ballers			146	30	1	12	28	.205	.253	.266
vs. Fly-Ballers			210	62	5	21	18	.295	.433	.359
Home Games	2-4	4.11	189	49	5	24	27	.259	.360	.341
Road Games	2-3	2.36	167	43	1	9	19	.257	.359	.298
Grass Fields	3-6	3.62	282	74	6	27	40	.262	.369	.325
Artificial Turf	1-1	2.11	74	18	0	6	6	.243	.324	.309
April	0-0	—	0	0	0	0	0	—	—	—
May	0-0	—	0	0	0	0	0	—	—	—
June	0-0	—	0	0	0	0	0	—	—	—
July	1-1	1.83	67	12	2	9	14	.179	.299	.276
August	2-3	3.92	148	39	1	20	20	.264	.351	.353
Sept./Oct.	1-3	3.34	141	41	3	4	12	.291	.397	.308
Leading Off Inn.			89	25	2	12	14	.281	.404	.366
Bases Empty			208	52	3	21	27	.250	.351	.322
Runners On			148	40	3	12	19	.270	.372	.321
Runners/Scor. Pos.			70	21	1	10	8	.300	.357	.378
Runners On/2 Out			60	16	2	5	9	.267	.400	.323
Scor. Pos./2 Out			32	7	0	4	6	.219	.250	.306
Late-Inning Pressure			17	8	3	0	0	.471	.588	.550
Leading Off			3	1	0	2	0	.333	.667	.600
Runners On			10	5	0	1	0	.500	.500	.545
Runners/Scor. Pos.			7	3	0	1	0	.429	.429	.500
First 9 Batters			122	23	2	12	19	.189	.262	.267
Second 9 Batters			122	32	0	10	19	.262	.336	.313
All Batters Thereafter			112	37	4	11	8	.330	.491	.390

Loves to face: Doug Dascenzo (.100, 2-for-20)
Tim Raines (.111, 2-for-18)
Luis Rivera (0-for-9)

Hates to face: Andre Dawson (.400, 8-for-20, 3 2B, 2 HR)
Von Hayes (.533, 8-for-15, 6 BB)
Keith Miller (.667, 4-for-6, 1 HR)

Miscellaneous statistics: Ground outs-to-air outs ratio: 0.58 last season, 0.62 for career.... Opponents grounded into 7 double plays in 72 opportunities (one per 10).... Allowed 16 doubles, 1 triple in 96 innings.... Allowed 0 first-inning runs in 15 starts (0.00 ERA, lowest in majors).... Batting support: 2.87 runs per start.... Opposing base stealers: 6-for-16 (38%), 4th-lowest rate in N.L.; 8 pickoffs, 2 balks.

Comments: Pitched two games in both 1984 and 1985, and has made at least 15 starts each of the past seven years. Opposing left-handed batters had a higher batting average than right-handers in every year that he's been in the majors. A streak of that length would be rare for a right-handed pitcher; it's incredible for a lefty. Over the last 18 years, only one other lefty has had a streak of at least seven such seasons: that old screwball himself, Fernando Valenzuela.... Career numbers: Lefties have hit .276 vs. Deshaies, righties .232. Managers should do some reverse platooning against him and against Jim Abbott and Brian Barnes, lefties who have similar tendencies.... After calling the Astrodome home from 1985 to 1991, he set a career best by allowing one home run every 16.0 innings last season with San Diego. But the difference wasn't what he did in his home park; he gave up 15 homers in road games in 1991, only one last year.... Our annual checkup on his hitting: His career batting average (.090, 33-for-367) is the lowest among active players and the 10th-lowest all-time among players with 350 at-bats; Dean Chance (.066) is at the bottom of that list. Right below Deshaies is Bob Buhl at .089; but averages drop slowly when you're so low. Deshaies will need to go 0-for-6 just to drop that one point. But he may not get another six at-bats; he has sought refuge with the Twins, in the DH League, a Chapter 11 for poor-hitting pitchers.

Rob Dibble

Throws Right

Cincinnati Reds	W-L	ERA	AB	H	HR	BB	SO	BA	SA	OBA
Season	3-5	3.07	249	48	3	31	110	.193	.265	.285
vs. Left-Handers			128	23	2	22	64	.180	.258	.298
vs. Right-Handers			121	25	1	9	46	.207	.273	.271
vs. Ground-Ballers			100	20	1	16	49	.200	.230	.319
vs. Fly-Ballers			149	28	2	15	61	.188	.289	.261
Home Games	2-1	1.47	125	19	0	11	67	.152	.176	.221
Road Games	1-4	4.81	124	29	3	20	43	.234	.355	.345
Grass Fields	0-2	4.64	79	19	2	13	22	.241	.367	.358
Artificial Turf	3-3	2.39	170	29	1	18	88	.171	.218	.249
April	0-0	0.00	15	1	0	4	3	.067	.133	.263
May	0-2	5.54	50	13	0	7	20	.260	.280	.356
June	0-1	4.91	56	12	0	8	22	.214	.304	.313
July	1-1	1.46	43	9	1	4	19	.209	.279	.292
August	1-1	3.38	41	4	2	5	22	.098	.293	.191
Sept./Oct.	1-0	0.75	44	9	0	3	24	.205	.205	.255
Leading Off Inn.			51	6	1	7	25	.118	.176	.224
Bases Empty			126	19	1	17	61	.151	.206	.252
Runners On			123	29	2	14	49	.236	.325	.319
Runners/Scor. Pos.			90	19	2	11	37	.211	.311	.298
Runners On/2 Out			55	12	1	6	24	.218	.345	.306
Scor. Pos./2 Out			45	11	1	4	18	.244	.378	.306
Late-Inning Pressure			164	26	3	18	82	.159	.238	.249
Leading Off			34	5	1	4	20	.147	.235	.237
Runners On			75	14	2	10	32	.187	.293	.295
Runners/Scor. Pos.			61	12	2	8	25	.197	.328	.296
First 9 Batters			247	48	3	31	110	.194	.267	.287
Second 9 Batters			2	0	0	0	0	.000	.000	.000
All Batters Thereafter			0	0	0	0	0	—	—	—

Loves to face: Andres Galarraga (0-for-8, 8 SO)
Dale Murphy (.150, 3-for-20, 11 SO)
Matt Williams (.071, 1-for-14, 9 SO)
Hates to face: Tony Gwynn (.333, 5-for-15)
Willie McGee (.455, 5-for-11)
Ozzie Smith (.455, 5-for-11)

Miscellaneous statistics: Ground outs-to-air outs ratio: 0.81 last season, 0.95 for career.... Opponents grounded into 3 double plays in 62 opportunities (one per 21).... Allowed 5 doubles, 2 triples in 70⅓ innings.... Saved 25 games in 32 opportunities (78%).... Stranded 31 inherited runners, allowed 10 to score (76%).... Opposing base stealers: 8-for-10 (80%); 1 pickoff, 0 balks.

Comments: Among all pitchers in major league history who have pitched at least 400 innings, Dibble owns the lowest career rate of hits allowed (6.21 per nine innings) and the highest career rate of strikeouts (12.54 per nine innings).... His strikeout rate in 1992 (14.08 per nine) was also a major league single-season record for relievers, breaking his own mark of 13.55 set the previous year.... His 2.35 career ERA is the lowest among active pitchers (same 400-IP minimum).... Opponents' batting average in Late-Inning Pressure Situations was the lowest in the majors last year (minimum: 150 BFP in LIPS).... Opponents' career averages in many categories rank at or near the top of our lists: .148 with runners on base and two outs is the lowest, as is opponents' average on artificial turf (.188); .185 with runners in scoring postion is 2d best to Bryan Harvey (.156); .191 by left-handed batters ranks third.... Right-handed batters have hit 10 of the 17 home runs Dibble has allowed in the majors.... He has fanned Andres Galarraga in each of their eight career meetings, the highest all-K total for any matchup of an active batter and an active pitcher.... Has at least 100 strikeouts in each of the past four seasons, as does Toronto's Duane Ward; prior to 1992, Dick Radatz (1962–65) was the only reliever ever to have four successive seasons of 100 strikeouts. Rollie Fingers and Goose Gossage each had five 100-strikeout seasons, although not consecutive; Dibble and Ward can shoot for that mark in '93.

Doug Drabek

Throws Right

Pittsburgh Pirates	W-L	ERA	AB	H	HR	BB	SO	BA	SA	OBA
Season	15-11	2.77	945	218	17	54	177	.231	.330	.274
vs. Left-Handers			544	141	11	42	90	.259	.369	.313
vs. Right-Handers			401	77	6	12	87	.192	.277	.220
vs. Ground-Ballers			444	97	5	24	87	.218	.304	.259
vs. Fly-Ballers			501	121	12	30	90	.242	.353	.288
Home Games	8-3	2.44	403	92	3	27	87	.228	.303	.279
Road Games	7-8	3.02	542	126	14	27	90	.232	.351	.271
Grass Fields	1-6	4.35	226	58	11	16	34	.257	.434	.303
Artificial Turf	14-5	2.29	719	160	6	38	143	.223	.298	.265
April	3-2	2.75	131	29	2	9	21	.221	.328	.273
May	0-2	3.19	157	36	6	5	35	.229	.382	.256
June	3-2	3.02	168	37	2	10	38	.220	.286	.268
July	2-2	1.76	148	35	2	8	21	.236	.324	.270
August	2-2	2.98	167	42	5	13	31	.251	.377	.306
Sept./Oct.	5-1	2.85	174	39	0	9	31	.224	.287	.271
Leading Off Inn.			252	58	2	9	53	.230	.298	.257
Bases Empty			605	145	11	26	113	.240	.340	.271
Runners On			340	73	6	28	64	.215	.312	.280
Runners/Scor. Pos.			192	34	4	24	40	.177	.260	.269
Runners On/2 Out			143	25	2	7	33	.175	.280	.229
Scor. Pos./2 Out			92	13	1	6	21	.141	.207	.210
Late-Inning Pressure			130	28	0	11	21	.215	.269	.274
Leading Off			39	7	0	1	10	.179	.205	.200
Runners On			41	8	0	7	3	.195	.293	.302
Runners/Scor. Pos.			20	1	0	6	3	.050	.100	.258
First 9 Batters			290	67	7	9	60	.231	.359	.262
Second 9 Batters			283	68	5	17	53	.240	.329	.281
All Batters Thereafter			372	83	5	28	64	.223	.309	.279

Loves to face: Lenny Harris (.048, 1-for-21)
Ricky Jordan (.059, 1-for-17, 1 2B)
Benito Santiago (.045, 1-for-22, 1 3B)
Hates to face: Brett Butler (.410, 16-for-39, 1 HR)
Kevin Elster (.370, 10-for-27, 2 HR)
Tony Gwynn (.429, 15-for-35)

Miscellaneous statistics: Ground outs-to-air outs ratio: 1.63 last season, 1.17 for career.... Opponents grounded into 20 double plays in 167 opportunities (one per 8.4).... Allowed 35 doubles, 4 triples in 256⅔ innings.... Allowed 19 first-inning runs in 34 starts (5.03 ERA).... Batting support: 3.94 runs per start.... Opposing base stealers: 18-for-32 (56%); 3 pickoffs, 1 balk.

Comments: Has a winning record in each of the past five seasons; five others have that distinction: Roger Clemens, Dennis Eckersley, Bruce Hurst, Jose Rijo, and Bob Walk. Related note: Drabek is 81–50 over the past five years; only six others stand "plus-30" over that span: Clemens (92–50), Bob Welch (84–43), David Cone (79–45), Dave Stewart (87–53), Hurst (73–43), and Greg Maddux (87–57).... Career won-lost record: 31–36 in April, May, and June; 68–34 from July 1 to the end of the season.... Allowed six first-inning home runs last season, most in N.L.... Allowed only three first-inning walks in 34 starts, 2d-best rate among N.L. pitchers, behind Zane Smith (one in 22 starts).... Averaged 1.89 walks per nine innings last year, a career-low rate. Meanwhile, his rate of strikeouts per nine innings has increased in every year since 1989 to a career high in 1992: 4.53, 5.10, 5.45, 6.21.... Opponents' batting average with runners in scoring position was 2d lowest in the league, behind Curt Schilling (.176).... Opponents had 10 steals in 14 attempts with Don Slaught catching, but only eight in 18 tries with Mike LaValliere.... Has lost eight of his last nine regular-season decisions on grass fields; also lost two games in Atlanta in the 1992 Championship Series.... Lasted just 4⅔ and 4⅓ innings in first two starts of the 1992 N.L.C.S.; before that, he had made 217 regular-season and four postseason starts and had never lasted fewer than five innings in any two consecutive starts.

Sid Fernandez
Throws Left

New York Mets	W-L	ERA	AB	H	HR	BB	SO	BA	SA	OBA
Season	14-11	2.73	771	162	12	67	193	.210	.328	.273
vs. Left-Handers			152	28	0	16	48	.184	.289	.267
vs. Right-Handers			619	134	12	51	145	.216	.338	.275
vs. Ground-Ballers			326	69	1	26	98	.212	.288	.272
vs. Fly-Ballers			445	93	11	41	95	.209	.357	.274
Home Games	7-4	2.17	360	68	5	26	101	.189	.286	.248
Road Games	7-7	3.20	411	94	7	41	92	.229	.365	.294
Grass Fields	11-6	2.60	505	105	8	38	127	.208	.327	.265
Artificial Turf	3-5	2.95	266	57	4	29	66	.214	.331	.287
April	1-2	5.54	92	20	3	13	39	.217	.370	.309
May	2-3	1.89	119	22	4	6	31	.185	.311	.224
June	3-2	2.38	157	34	4	10	37	.217	.363	.263
July	3-1	2.08	112	19	0	11	31	.170	.268	.236
August	2-1	3.63	151	39	0	15	24	.258	.371	.327
Sept./Oct.	3-2	1.60	140	28	1	12	31	.200	.279	.269
Leading Off Inn.			211	45	5	12	49	.213	.351	.256
Bases Empty			514	107	9	31	131	.208	.331	.257
Runners On			257	55	3	36	62	.214	.323	.302
Runners/Scor. Pos.			146	28	1	22	40	.192	.267	.279
Runners On/2 Out			117	24	2	22	29	.205	.291	.336
Scor. Pos./2 Out			77	13	0	13	22	.169	.208	.289
Late-Inning Pressure			60	17	1	5	8	.283	.417	.348
Leading Off			19	4	0	0	3	.211	.316	.211
Runners On			18	4	1	5	1	.222	.389	.391
Runners/Scor. Pos.			11	2	0	2	0	.182	.182	.308
First 9 Batters			254	52	4	24	86	.205	.327	.270
Second 9 Batters			244	47	2	27	64	.193	.291	.276
All Batters Thereafter			273	63	6	16	43	.231	.363	.274

Loves to face: Chris Sabo (.042, 1-for-24, 1 2B, 2 BB)
Benito Santiago (.121, 4-for-33, 1 HR, 0 BB)
Matt Williams (.091, 2-for-22)

Hates to face: Will Clark (.357, 10-for-28, 2 2B, 2 HR)
Mariano Duncan (.405, 17-for-42)
Dale Murphy (.289, 11-for-38, 4 HR)

Miscellaneous statistics: Ground outs-to-air outs ratio: 0.44 last season (lowest in majors), 0.46 for career.... Opponents grounded into 5 double plays in 112 opportunities (one per 22), 2d-worst rate in N.L.... Allowed 37 doubles, 9 triples (most in majors) in 214⅔ innings.... Allowed 16 first-inning runs in 32 starts (4.22 ERA).... Batting support: 4.34 runs per start, 6th-highest average in N.L.... Opposing base stealers: 17-for-26 (65%); 3 pickoffs, 0 balks.

Comments: Nine-inning games he started last season averaged three hours, longest in N.L. (minimum: 10 starts); no fewer than 19 A.L. starters averaged more than three hours for nine-inning games.... Career record: 56–29 at Shea, 37–44 elsewhere. Opponents' .183 career batting average in his home games (including six innings at Dodger Stadium in 1983) is the lowest since 1975.... Has allowed 6.68 hits per nine innings, lowest career rate in N.L. history (minimum: 1000 innings), and 2d-lowest rate in major league history behind Nolan Ryan (6.54).... Struck out 36 batters in the first inning of his 32 starts, best rate in N.L.... Struck out more right-handed batters than any N.L. pitcher last season.... Averaged 8.09 strikeouts per nine innings, 2d-highest rate in N.L. behind David Cone (9.79).... Threw the most innings among major league pitchers who didn't throw a wild pitch last season; has thrown only two wild pitches in 657⅓ innings over the past four years.... Opponents' on-base percentage leading off innings was 3d lowest in the league.... Has not allowed a home run to a left-handed batter in 40 games since Darryl Strawberry hit one in July 1991.... Recorded more outs on balls hit in the air than he did on grounders in all but one of 32 starts last year. His 0.46 career ground outs-to-air outs ratio is the lowest by any pitcher in the majors since 1975.... Has come to bat 205 times since he last drew a walk, in July 1989. How long ago was that? The guy who walked him was Kent Tekulve.

John Franco
Throws Left

New York Mets	W-L	ERA	AB	H	HR	BB	SO	BA	SA	OBA
Season	6-2	1.64	115	24	1	11	20	.209	.304	.273
vs. Left-Handers			28	7	0	7	6	.250	.286	.389
vs. Right-Handers			87	17	1	4	14	.195	.310	.228
vs. Ground-Ballers			50	10	1	6	9	.200	.280	.286
vs. Fly-Ballers			65	14	0	5	11	.215	.323	.264
Home Games	4-1	0.92	66	13	0	3	8	.197	.258	.229
Road Games	2-1	2.70	49	11	1	8	12	.224	.367	.328
Grass Fields	4-1	1.01	89	15	1	5	14	.169	.258	.211
Artificial Turf	2-1	4.26	26	9	0	6	6	.346	.462	.455
April	2-0	0.00	26	1	0	1	6	.038	.038	.074
May	1-0	0.00	15	1	0	0	4	.067	.133	.067
June	3-1	3.18	44	15	0	6	4	.341	.432	.404
July	0-0	0.00	0	0	0	0	0	.000	.000	.000
August	0-1	2.25	30	7	1	4	4	.233	.433	.324
Sept./Oct.	0-0	0.00	0	0	0	0	0	.000	.000	.000
Leading Off Inn.			29	6	0	0	3	.207	.276	.207
Bases Empty			69	13	1	4	15	.188	.290	.233
Runners On			46	11	0	7	5	.239	.326	.327
Runners/Scor. Pos.			26	5	0	7	4	.192	.192	.343
Runners On/2 Out			21	7	0	5	3	.333	.524	.462
Scor. Pos./2 Out			12	3	0	5	2	.250	.250	.471
Late-Inning Pressure			101	21	0	9	16	.208	.287	.268
Leading Off			25	5	0	0	2	.200	.200	.200
Runners On			42	10	0	6	5	.238	.333	.320
Runners/Scor. Pos.			24	5	0	6	4	.208	.208	.344
First 9 Batters			114	23	1	10	20	.202	.298	.262
Second 9 Batters			1	1	0	1	0	1.000	1.000	1.000
All Batters Thereafter			0	0	0	0	0	—	—	—

Loves to face: Delino DeShields (0-for-8, 5 SO)
Darrin Jackson (0-for-10)
Tom Pagnozzi (0-for-12)

Hates to face: Mariano Duncan (.500, 8-for-16)
Kevin Mitchell (.333, 4-for-12, 1 HR, 5 BB)
Ryne Sandberg (.333, 6-for-18, 6 BB)

Miscellaneous statistics: Ground outs-to-air outs ratio: 2.16 last season, 1.91 for career.... Opponents grounded into 6 double plays in 20 opportunities (one per 3.3).... Allowed 6 doubles, 1 triple in 33 innings.... Saved 15 games in 18 opportunities (83%), 3d-highest rate in N.L.... Stranded 7 inherited runners, allowed 5 to score (58%).... Opposing base stealers: 2-for-5 (40%); 2 pickoffs, 0 balks.

Comments: Limited to 31 games and 33 innings last season by a combination of injury, lack of Mets leads, and perhaps his own choosiness about which games someone of his stature should enter.... Prior to 1992, he had tied a major league record with five consecutive 30-save seasons.... In 1990, he pitched one inning or less in only 16 of 33 saves; but in 1991, one-inning saves accounted for 27 of 30, and in 1992, for 14 of 15.... Has walked only one of the last 83 batters he has faced leading off innings.... Allowed one home run in 33 innings last season, the lowest rate of his career.... In three years with the Mets, he has allowed only one home run in 313 opponents' at-bats with runners on base (a two-run shot by Bobby Bonilla in 1991).... Opposing left-handers have hit for a higher batting average than right-handers in each of the last two years.... Finished 30 of 31 games in which he appeared last year; he hasn't been removed from the mound during an inning since June 1991.... For someone used to finishing, he doesn't finish his seasons very well: His ERA from September 1 to the end of the season had been above 5.00 in five of his eight seasons; then last year, he didn't even make it to September, making his last appearance on August 25.... Last year, he was quoted to the effect that if it was not a save situation, he'd rather not pitch. Maybe that has something to do with his total of games and innings decreasing in each of the last four seasons.

Mark Gardner — Throws Right

Montreal Expos	W-L	ERA	AB	H	HR	BB	SO	BA	SA	OBA
Season	12-10	4.36	690	179	15	60	132	.259	.386	.324
vs. Left-Handers			396	108	7	31	62	.273	.399	.330
vs. Right-Handers			294	71	8	29	70	.241	.367	.315
vs. Ground-Ballers			345	90	6	27	62	.261	.386	.318
vs. Fly-Ballers			345	89	9	33	70	.258	.386	.329
Home Games	6-5	4.80	406	104	8	32	89	.256	.392	.319
Road Games	6-5	3.74	284	75	7	28	43	.264	.377	.330
Grass Fields	4-2	2.45	147	34	4	15	22	.231	.354	.299
Artificial Turf	8-8	4.91	543	145	11	45	110	.267	.394	.331
April	2-1	3.48	112	27	2	14	25	.241	.357	.323
May	1-3	3.64	112	29	2	12	28	.259	.366	.341
June	3-2	4.34	113	29	3	10	18	.257	.398	.320
July	4-2	3.12	155	39	5	8	28	.252	.413	.288
August	1-1	5.93	108	25	2	10	18	.231	.333	.317
Sept./Oct.	1-1	6.85	90	30	1	6	15	.333	.444	.374
Leading Off Inn.			171	44	7	16	27	.257	.444	.332
Bases Empty			408	102	11	29	71	.250	.390	.306
Runners On			282	77	4	31	61	.273	.379	.348
Runners/Scor. Pos.			178	47	3	26	43	.264	.371	.361
Runners On/2 Out			115	24	2	15	23	.209	.287	.311
Scor. Pos./2 Out			83	18	1	13	19	.217	.277	.337
Late-Inning Pressure			47	15	3	7	10	.319	.553	.407
Leading Off			13	4	2	4	3	.308	.923	.471
Runners On			8	3	0	2	2	.375	.375	.500
Runners/Scor. Pos.			3	2	0	2	1	.667	.667	.800
First 9 Batters			247	66	4	27	53	.267	.381	.358
Second 9 Batters			239	59	6	16	51	.247	.368	.291
All Batters Thereafter			204	54	5	17	28	.265	.412	.318

Loves to face: Alfredo Griffin (.182, 2-for-11)

Hates to face: George Bell (.400, 4-for-10)
Andre Dawson (.348, 8-for-23, 4 2B, 3 HR)
Von Hayes (.400, 4-for-10, 1 HR)

Miscellaneous statistics: Ground outs-to-air outs ratio: 0.75 last season (4th lowest in N.L.), 0.81 for career.... Opponents grounded into 2 double plays in 131 opportunities (one per 66), worst rate in majors.... Allowed 36 doubles, 3 triples in 179⅔ innings.... Allowed 21 first-inning runs in 30 starts (6.00 ERA).... Batting support: 4.13 runs per start.... Opposing base stealers: 29-for-40 (73%), 5th-most steals in N.L.; 0 pickoffs, 0 balks.

Comments: In what category does Mark Gardner rank among the top five active pitchers? Keep reading.... Career hitting by opponents: left-handed batters have batted .242 and slugged .365; right-handed batters .241 and .368. No other active N.L. pitcher shows differences of fewer than three points in each category (minimum: 2000 batters faced).... Career record is 21–21 with a 3.04 ERA from April through July, compared to 7–21 with a 5.93 ERA from August through October. His 7.26 ERA for September and October is the worst by any pitcher over the last 10 years (minimum: 50 IP).... Pitched a shutout on July 12, 1990, and has made 67 starts since then without even a complete game. The only pitcher with a longer current streak of incomplete starts: Danny Jackson (70 starts since July 18, 1989). Other streaks longer than 50 starts: Scott Scudder (63 career GS without a CG), Kelly Downs (58, since Aug. 9, 1988), Shawn Boskie (52, since May 20, 1990), and Kirk McCaskill (51, since June 16, 1991).... 1992 ERA by battery mate (2.88 in 84⅓ innings with Gary Carter, 5.66 in 95⅓ with other catchers) doesn't bode well for 1993; Carter's now an announcer.... Answer to top-five tease question: He has the 5th-highest hit-batter frequency among active pitchers (minimum: 1000 batters faced). The top five: Mitch Williams (one HBP every 55.9 batters); Donn Pall (83.0), Juan Agosto (89.6), Todd Stottlemyre (90.5), and Gardner (92.9).

Tom Glavine — Throws Left

Atlanta Braves	W-L	ERA	AB	H	HR	BB	SO	BA	SA	OBA
Season	20-8	2.76	839	197	6	70	129	.235	.310	.293
vs. Left-Handers			176	48	1	23	32	.273	.341	.353
vs. Right-Handers			663	149	5	47	97	.225	.302	.277
vs. Ground-Ballers			357	73	1	27	62	.204	.241	.259
vs. Fly-Ballers			482	124	5	43	67	.257	.361	.318
Home Games	13-4	2.31	524	124	2	37	72	.237	.303	.285
Road Games	7-4	3.49	315	73	4	33	57	.232	.321	.307
Grass Fields	14-6	2.69	621	151	5	45	90	.243	.329	.293
Artificial Turf	6-2	2.95	218	46	1	25	39	.211	.257	.295
April	3-1	2.48	141	31	2	5	30	.220	.319	.247
May	4-2	3.51	154	40	0	13	18	.260	.299	.314
June	4-0	2.49	161	31	1	17	23	.193	.273	.268
July	5-0	1.42	145	33	1	12	21	.228	.297	.291
August	3-2	4.01	131	37	1	12	22	.282	.382	.338
Sept./Oct.	1-3	2.79	107	25	1	11	15	.234	.299	.308
Leading Off Inn.			208	47	1	20	39	.226	.293	.297
Bases Empty			496	113	4	40	81	.228	.302	.287
Runners On			343	84	2	30	48	.245	.321	.303
Runners/Scor. Pos.			172	44	2	24	27	.256	.355	.340
Runners On/2 Out			143	33	1	20	17	.231	.336	.329
Scor. Pos./2 Out			80	21	1	17	8	.262	.387	.398
Late-Inning Pressure			105	23	0	7	17	.219	.276	.274
Leading Off			25	9	0	3	3	.360	.480	.448
Runners On			50	13	0	2	9	.260	.320	.288
Runners/Scor. Pos.			27	6	0	1	5	.222	.259	.250
First 9 Batters			267	69	1	25	47	.258	.341	.319
Second 9 Batters			266	60	2	24	34	.226	.297	.288
All Batters Thereafter			306	68	3	21	48	.222	.294	.276

Loves to face: Mark Carreon (.083, 1-for-12)
Shawon Dunston (.150, 3-for-20)
Don Slaught (.111, 2-for-18)

Hates to face: Lloyd McClendon (.407, 11-for-27, 2 HR)
Robby Thompson (.441, 15-for-34, 1 HR)
Tim Wallach (.386, 17-for-44, 5 HR)

Miscellaneous statistics: Ground outs-to-air outs ratio: 1.13 last season, 1.28 for career.... Opponents grounded into 18 double plays in 162 opportunities (one per 9.0).... Allowed 37 doubles, 4 triples in 225 innings.... Allowed 21 first-inning runs in 33 starts (5.45 ERA).... Batting support: 4.61 runs per start, 3d-highest average in N.L.... Opposing base stealers: 13-for-23 (57%); 4 pickoffs, 0 balks.

Comments: This season, he can become the first N.L. pitcher since Fergie Jenkins to win at least 20 games in three straight years; Jenkins did it six years in a row, 1967–72.... Winning streak of 13 games was longest in the majors last season; no other N.L. pitcher had a streak longer than eight games.... Tied for major league lead with five shutouts; he's the first Braves pitcher to lead the majors since Lew Burdette in 1956.... Over the past two years, he is 30–8 (.789) from April to July, 10–11 (.476) from August 1 to the end of the season, and 2–6 in postseason. Became first pitcher in major league history to lose six postseason games over a two-year span.... After allowing six home runs in 225 innings last season, he allowed five in 24⅓ postseason innings.... Batted .247 (19-for-77) last season, second to Dwight Gooden among N.L. pitchers. More impressively, Glavine had the lowest strikeout rate among pitchers (minimum: 40 plate appearances): he fanned only 10 times in 90 trips to the plate.... No pitcher since 1900 has started his career with as many games started (172) without a relief appearance. Back in horse 'n' buggy days, a guy named Terry Larkin made 176 starts in a row, 1876–80.... With Steve Bedrosian and Mark Davis joining Glavine and Greg Maddux in training camp, the 1993 Braves could be the first team ever with four past Cy Young Award winners on its roster. Only two teams have had even three: the 1980 Rangers (Ferguson Jenkins, Sparky Lyle, and Gaylord Perry) and the 1981 Orioles (Mike Flanagan, Steve Stone, and Jim Palmer).

Dwight Gooden   Throws Right

New York Mets	W-L	ERA	AB	H	HR	BB	SO	BA	SA	OBA
Season	10-13	3.67	773	197	11	70	145	.255	.371	.317
vs. Left-Handers			445	120	9	47	62	.270	.384	.339
vs. Right-Handers			328	77	2	23	83	.235	.354	.286
vs. Ground-Ballers			381	92	2	32	65	.241	.336	.300
vs. Fly-Ballers			392	105	9	38	80	.268	.406	.333
Home Games	7-5	4.25	364	95	6	34	63	.261	.398	.325
Road Games	3-8	3.15	409	102	5	36	82	.249	.347	.309
Grass Fields	9-9	3.88	546	143	8	49	92	.262	.379	.323
Artificial Turf	1-4	3.19	227	54	3	21	53	.238	.352	.302
April	2-1	3.16	91	20	0	12	17	.220	.319	.317
May	2-4	4.10	148	40	3	15	30	.270	.399	.335
June	1-2	3.95	150	36	1	16	28	.240	.313	.310
July	1-2	4.08	67	17	1	6	13	.254	.418	.320
August	2-2	4.60	118	35	3	11	22	.297	.458	.357
Sept./Oct.	2-2	2.78	199	49	3	10	35	.246	.352	.281
Leading Off Inn.			198	60	3	12	40	.303	.424	.346
Bases Empty			439	109	6	41	89	.248	.364	.315
Runners On			334	88	5	29	56	.263	.380	.318
Runners/Scor. Pos.			207	49	2	22	40	.237	.309	.304
Runners On/2 Out			123	29	1	18	22	.236	.325	.333
Scor. Pos./2 Out			84	21	1	14	15	.250	.321	.357
Late-Inning Pressure			64	14	3	4	8	.219	.406	.261
Leading Off			17	3	1	1	3	.176	.412	.222
Runners On			20	5	1	1	1	.250	.400	.273
Runners/Scor. Pos.			12	3	1	1	1	.250	.500	.286
First 9 Batters			243	54	1	27	58	.222	.300	.298
Second 9 Batters			249	67	3	23	47	.269	.394	.331
All Batters Thereafter			281	76	7	20	40	.270	.413	.320

Loves to face: Casey Candaele (.148, 4-for-27)
               Jose Oquendo (.077, 2-for-26)
               Tracy Woodson (0-for-8, 3 SO)

Hates to face: Barry Bonds (.357, 20-for-56, 3 HR)
               Ray Lankford (.421, 8-for-19, 1 HR)
               Tom Pagnozzi (.565, 13-for-23)

Miscellaneous statistics: Ground outs-to-air outs ratio: 1.45 last season, 1.32 for career. . . . Opponents grounded into 20 double plays in 152 opportunities (one per 7.6). . . . Allowed 43 doubles (2d most in N.L.), 7 triples in 206 innings. . . . Allowed 15 first-inning runs in 31 starts (3.77 ERA). . . . Batting support: 3.26 runs per start, 8th-lowest average in N.L. . . . Opposing base stealers: 22-for-33 (67%); 3 pickoffs, 1 balk.

Comments: Made 31 starts following off-season surgery; his strikeout rate was a career-low 6.33 per nine innings, and his 10–13 record broke a major league record-tying streak of eight consecutive years with a winning percentage of at least .650; he shares that mark with Vic Raschi (1946–53). . . . Career winning percentage (.683) is highest among active pitchers (minimum: 100 decisions) and 6th highest all-time. . . . Never had a losing record in consecutive months before last season. . . . Has pitched only one shutout in his last 77 starts (dating back to June 28, 1990), with a 3.61 ERA during that period. He threw 13 shutouts with a 2.00 ERA in the first 77 starts of his career. . . . One very big difference between Old Doc and New Doc: In 1984 and 1985, batters leading off an inning hit .178 and .196 against him; in 1991 and 1992, they hit .301 and .303. He's the only pitcher in the majors who has let batters leading off an inning hit better than .300 against him in each of the last two years. . . . Has had a better record in road games than he has at home only once in nine years in majors. Last year, he went 7–5 at home and 3–8 on the road despite being one of two N.L. pitchers with a road ERA a full run *lower* than his home ERA. His teammates averaged 3.93 runs in his Shea starts, 2.63 on the road. . . . Career breakdown: 43–29, 3.70 ERA in day games; 99–37, 2.65 at night. . . . Followed .238 batting average in 1991 with .264 (19-for-72) in 1992, best among N.L. pitchers (minimum: 40 PA); also led in hits, RBIs (nine), and extra-base hits (five).

Jim Gott   Throws Right

Los Angeles Dodgers	W-L	ERA	AB	H	HR	BB	SO	BA	SA	OBA
Season	3-3	2.45	320	72	4	41	75	.225	.287	.314
vs. Left-Handers			148	39	3	28	39	.264	.365	.382
vs. Right-Handers			172	33	1	13	36	.192	.221	.249
vs. Ground-Ballers			126	29	1	18	25	.230	.294	.331
vs. Fly-Ballers			194	43	3	23	50	.222	.284	.303
Home Games	1-1	1.79	148	33	1	15	39	.223	.277	.293
Road Games	2-2	3.02	172	39	3	26	36	.227	.297	.332
Grass Fields	2-1	2.22	246	53	3	31	58	.215	.276	.305
Artificial Turf	1-2	3.32	74	19	1	10	17	.257	.324	.345
April	0-1	1.32	52	13	0	4	12	.250	.269	.304
May	0-0	2.70	36	6	0	4	12	.167	.167	.250
June	1-1	1.80	70	15	1	10	16	.214	.271	.313
July	0-0	2.12	61	14	1	7	14	.230	.311	.309
August	1-0	0.90	68	10	1	10	14	.147	.206	.266
Sept./Oct.	1-1	11.05	33	14	1	6	7	.424	.606	.500
Leading Off Inn.			73	25	3	10	14	.342	.521	.422
Bases Empty			160	40	3	18	39	.250	.331	.326
Runners On			160	32	1	23	36	.200	.244	.303
Runners/Scor. Pos.			92	17	0	20	21	.185	.217	.327
Runners On/2 Out			60	10	0	15	6	.167	.167	.342
Scor. Pos./2 Out			37	7	0	15	3	.189	.189	.423
Late-Inning Pressure			112	24	2	18	27	.214	.286	.328
Leading Off			25	10	2	6	3	.400	.720	.516
Runners On			58	10	0	10	18	.172	.172	.304
Runners/Scor. Pos.			36	6	0	8	9	.167	.167	.318
First 9 Batters			311	71	4	40	75	.228	.293	.317
Second 9 Batters			9	1	0	1	0	.111	.111	.200
All Batters Thereafter			0	0	0	0	0	—	—	—

Loves to face: Mariano Duncan (.077, 1-for-13)
               Marquis Grissom (0-for-7)
               Kevin Mitchell (0-for-10)

Hates to face: Vince Coleman (.455, 5-for-11)
               Mark Grace (.500, 5-for-10)
               Tony Gwynn (.450, 9-for-20)

Miscellaneous statistics: Ground outs-to-air outs ratio: 1.91 last season, 1.37 for career. . . . Opponents grounded into 6 double plays in 84 opportunities (one per 14). . . . Allowed 6 doubles, 1 triple in 88 innings. . . . Stranded 22 inherited runners, allowed 12 to score (65%). . . . Opposing base stealers: 6-for-11 (55%); 0 pickoffs, 3 balks.

Comments: ERA doesn't mean as much for relief pitchers as for starters; nevertheless, Gott's has been below 3.00 in each of the past three years. Only 12 pitchers in the majors have that distinction (minimum: 50 innings each year). . . . Held opposing right-handed batters to a career-low batting average last season. . . . Has not allowed more than one home run in any of his last 236 appearances, dating back to April 17, 1988. . . . Opponents batted only .214 in Late-Inning Pressure Situations; it breaks down this way: .400 to lead off an inning, .172 with runners on base. It certainly wasn't Gott's fault, but the Dodgers allowed the highest LIPS batting average (.282) by any team in the majors last year. . . . Allowed only one hit in nine at-bats with the bases loaded; the Dodgers held opponents to a .191 batting average with the bags full last season, the lowest such average against any major league team. . . . Tied with Orel Hershiser and Roger McDowell for the major league lead in intentional walks (13), the first time that three teammates have finished tied for the lead in that category. (That's since 1955, a year remembered for the opening of Disneyland, the establishment of the Warsaw Pact, and baseball's decision to start keeping track of intentional walks.) Tom Lasorda had his pitchers issue 95 free passes, the most in the majors last season, and the most by the Dodgers since 1967. . . . Has hit four home runs in 71 career at-bats; his rate of one every 17.8 at-bats is better than Kevin Mitchell's (one HR every 18.2 AB).

Kevin Gross — Throws Right

Los Angeles Dodgers	W-L	ERA	AB	H	HR	BB	SO	BA	SA	OBA
Season	8-13	3.17	756	182	11	77	158	.241	.337	.311
vs. Left-Handers			409	113	5	52	75	.276	.389	.356
vs. Right-Handers			347	69	6	25	83	.199	.277	.255
vs. Ground-Ballers			327	83	2	39	75	.254	.324	.332
vs. Fly-Ballers			429	99	9	38	83	.231	.347	.295
Home Games	5-9	3.35	412	95	4	35	91	.231	.320	.291
Road Games	3-4	2.95	344	87	7	42	67	.253	.358	.334
Grass Fields	6-10	3.41	574	143	7	61	122	.249	.341	.320
Artificial Turf	2-3	2.39	182	39	4	16	36	.214	.324	.281
April	0-3	4.01	99	33	0	4	17	.333	.404	.356
May	3-1	1.65	113	19	1	10	42	.168	.230	.242
June	0-4	5.76	111	30	5	11	21	.270	.468	.328
July	2-2	2.79	147	38	1	22	24	.259	.333	.353
August	1-3	3.21	122	23	2	15	24	.189	.262	.288
Sept./Oct.	2-0	2.38	164	39	2	15	30	.238	.341	.300
Leading Off Inn.			190	50	2	23	42	.263	.347	.346
Bases Empty			437	105	6	44	101	.240	.327	.313
Runners On			319	77	5	33	57	.241	.351	.309
Runners/Scor. Pos.			182	41	3	23	39	.225	.335	.303
Runners On/2 Out			134	31	4	19	27	.231	.396	.327
Scor. Pos./2 Out			89	20	2	16	19	.225	.371	.343
Late-Inning Pressure			86	24	1	6	16	.279	.349	.333
Leading Off			25	11	0	2	4	.440	.560	.500
Runners On			37	9	1	3	6	.243	.324	.300
Runners/Scor. Pos.			21	5	1	3	4	.238	.381	.333
First 9 Batters			251	57	2	33	51	.227	.307	.316
Second 9 Batters			244	56	4	18	57	.230	.324	.285
All Batters Thereafter			261	69	5	26	50	.264	.379	.330

Loves to face: Mark Bailey (.077, 1-for-13, 6 SO)
Rafael Belliard (.111, 2-for-18, 2 BB)
Craig Biggio (.074, 2-for-27, 2 BB)

Hates to face: Sid Bream (.353, 18-for-51, 4 HR)
Howard Johnson (.359, 23-for-64, 5 HR)
David Justice (.600, 6-for-10, 2 HR)

Miscellaneous statistics: Ground outs-to-air outs ratio: 1.49 last season, 1.04 for career.... Opponents grounded into 12 double plays in 156 opportunities (one per 13).... Allowed 30 doubles, 5 triples in 204⅔ innings.... Allowed 17 first-inning runs in 30 starts (4.80 ERA).... Batting support: 3.40 runs per start, 10th-lowest average in N.L.... Opposing base stealers: 18-for-27 (67%); 1 pickoff, 2 balks.

Comments: Pitched the only no-hitter in the majors last season, but finished 8–13. No big deal there; in 1952, Virgil Trucks of the Tigers pitched two no-hitters and finished 5–19.... Joins Bruce Ruffin as the only pitchers with a losing record in each of the last six seasons. No pitcher has done that in seven straight seasons since Ernie Camacho (1981–88; he wasn't in the majors in 1982); the all-time record of 10 straight losing seasons belongs to Bill Bailey (1908–22) and Ron Kline (1952–63).... Despite those poor records, he has had a winning record in May in each of the last seven seasons; career breakdown: 23–13 in May, 75–101 in less lusty months.... Streak of eight straight years with at least 11 losses is the longest by anyone since Nolan Ryan's 10-year streak, 1970–79.... Gross went 8–13 last season despite a career-low ERA.... Opponents' batting average in April was tied with Danny Jackson for highest in N.L., but Gross turned things around quickly: His ERA and opponents' average in May were both best in the majors.... Tied Bill Gullickson and Trevor Wilson for major league lead in losses at home.... Walked one of every 9.3 batters he faced leading off innings, 2d-highest rate among N.L. starters, ahead of only Danny Jackson (one every 9.26 BFP).... Held opposing right-handed batters to a career-low batting average last season.... In the nineties, he's 14–12 in starts in which he has recorded more ground outs than air outs; in other games during that time, he has a 6–18 mark.

Chris Hammond — Throws Left

Cincinnati Reds	W-L	ERA	AB	H	HR	BB	SO	BA	SA	OBA
Season	7-10	4.21	561	149	13	55	79	.266	.399	.333
vs. Left-Handers			117	34	5	12	20	.291	.504	.356
vs. Right-Handers			444	115	8	43	59	.259	.372	.327
vs. Ground-Ballers			225	60	3	18	35	.267	.400	.318
vs. Fly-Ballers			336	89	10	37	44	.265	.399	.342
Home Games	5-4	3.92	312	79	7	31	42	.253	.388	.322
Road Games	2-6	4.59	249	70	6	24	37	.281	.414	.347
Grass Fields	1-2	4.25	114	31	1	13	17	.272	.360	.349
Artificial Turf	6-8	4.21	447	118	12	42	62	.264	.409	.329
April	2-1	3.20	93	20	2	8	20	.215	.355	.277
May	2-1	2.59	86	18	1	13	7	.209	.279	.320
June	1-2	5.08	110	31	2	13	13	.282	.391	.355
July	0-2	6.33	90	32	3	10	12	.356	.567	.420
August	2-3	4.70	120	34	4	7	17	.283	.433	.328
Sept./Oct.	0-1	3.12	62	14	1	4	10	.226	.339	.273
Leading Off Inn.			147	33	2	8	15	.224	.327	.269
Bases Empty			354	83	3	29	54	.234	.322	.296
Runners On			207	66	10	26	25	.319	.531	.392
Runners/Scor. Pos.			106	31	4	22	19	.292	.472	.409
Runners On/2 Out			86	26	4	10	11	.302	.477	.375
Scor. Pos./2 Out			47	13	1	9	11	.277	.383	.393
Late-Inning Pressure			21	9	0	5	0	.429	.619	.538
Leading Off			8	3	0	0	0	.375	.500	.375
Runners On			8	4	0	3	0	.500	.625	.636
Runners/Scor. Pos.			2	1	0	3	0	.500	1.000	.800
First 9 Batters			226	64	5	17	38	.283	.420	.332
Second 9 Batters			205	47	6	17	32	.229	.351	.296
All Batters Thereafter			130	38	2	21	9	.292	.438	.388

Loves to face: Craig Biggio (.167, 3-for-18)
Ken Caminiti (.083, 2-for-24)
Kirt Manwaring (0-for-7)

Hates to face: Barry Bonds (.353, 6-for-17, 1 HR)
Bernard Gilkey (.778, 7-for-9)
Todd Zeile (.455, 5-for-11)

Miscellaneous statistics: Ground outs-to-air outs ratio: 1.44 last season, 1.53 for career.... Opponents grounded into 11 double plays in 104 opportunities (one per 9.5).... Allowed 20 doubles, 8 triples (3d most in N.L.) in 147⅓ innings.... Allowed 17 first-inning runs in 26 starts (5.19 ERA).... Batting support: 3.58 runs per start.... Opposing base stealers: 7-for-11 (64%); 5 pickoffs, 0 balks.

Comments: Had the most starts (26) of any N.L. pitcher who did not pitch into ninth inning in any game last season; Jimmy Jones was the only other N.L. pitcher who started 20 games without going beyond the eighth inning.... Averaged 5.55 innings pitched per start, the lowest average by any N.L. pitcher with at least 20 starts.... Has made 47 career starts, 2d most among active pitchers who have never pitched a complete game; only ex-teammate Scott Scudder (63) has more.... Allowed five home runs in 117 at-bats to left-handed batters last season; only Bruce Hurst (eight in 157 at-bats) had a higher lefty-to-lefty home run rate in N.L. last season (minimum: five home runs allowed to LHB). Hammond ranked first (.504) and Hurst second (.478) in majors in lefty-vs.-lefty slugging percentage (minimum: 100 at-bats by LHB).... In 13 starts in which he registered more ground outs than air outs, he had a 5–3 record and 3.38 ERA; in his 13 other starts, he went 2–7 with 5.24 ERA.... Opponents batted .319 with runners on base last season, the highest average allowed by any N.L. starter (minimum: 200 opponents' at-bats with runners on base). Reds' staff allowed .262 average with runners aboard; Padres (.270) were only N.L. team that allowed a higher average.... Career record: 14–19, with five wins vs. Houston and five losses vs. Pittsburgh. He's 5–1 in April, 9–18 thereafter.... He was called for three balks in his first seven innings in the majors (1990) but has not balked in 251⅓ innings since then.

Pete Harnisch

Throws Right

Houston Astros	W-L	ERA	AB	H	HR	BB	SO	BA	SA	OBA
Season	9-10	3.70	779	182	18	64	164	.234	.371	.294
vs. Left-Handers			461	106	10	41	77	.230	.356	.297
vs. Right-Handers			318	76	8	23	87	.239	.393	.290
vs. Ground-Ballers			370	86	6	30	79	.232	.338	.295
vs. Fly-Ballers			409	96	12	34	85	.235	.401	.294
Home Games	7-4	2.75	505	106	7	38	107	.210	.319	.270
Road Games	2-6	5.61	274	76	11	26	57	.277	.467	.338
Grass Fields	2-4	4.35	191	51	8	20	38	.267	.440	.333
Artificial Turf	7-6	3.50	588	131	10	44	126	.223	.349	.281
April	1-3	2.41	124	28	2	8	23	.226	.331	.269
May	1-2	5.50	137	32	5	11	30	.234	.380	.296
June	1-2	4.04	136	32	6	16	24	.235	.456	.316
July	1-1	3.00	113	25	1	11	22	.221	.336	.290
August	1-1	4.26	101	27	2	6	27	.267	.416	.308
Sept./Oct.	4-1	3.13	168	38	2	12	38	.226	.321	.288
Leading Off Inn.			206	49	3	9	45	.238	.320	.270
Bases Empty			484	105	10	36	107	.217	.341	.277
Runners On			295	77	8	28	57	.261	.420	.322
Runners/Scor. Pos.			172	46	4	22	37	.267	.430	.342
Runners On/2 Out			121	25	1	18	32	.207	.298	.314
Scor. Pos./2 Out			78	20	1	13	21	.256	.385	.363
Late-Inning Pressure			52	11	1	3	13	.212	.346	.250
Leading Off			16	4	0	0	3	.250	.313	.250
Runners On			15	2	0	3	5	.133	.200	.263
Runners/Scor. Pos.			8	0	0	1	5	.000	.000	.100
First 9 Batters			272	56	6	23	62	.206	.327	.269
Second 9 Batters			270	62	5	17	61	.230	.359	.282
All Batters Thereafter			237	64	7	24	41	.270	.435	.336

Loves to face: Darren Daulton (.077, 1-for-13)
Tommy Gregg (0-for-8)
Benito Santiago (.067, 1-for-15, 1 2B)

Hates to face: Tony Fernandez (.417, 15-for-36)
Eddie Murray (.500, 7-for-14, 1 HR)
Todd Zeile (.429, 6-for-14, 1 HR)

Miscellaneous statistics: Ground outs-to-air outs ratio: 0.65 last season (2d lowest in N.L.), 0.72 for career.... Opponents grounded into 8 double plays in 125 opportunities (one per 16).... Allowed 37 doubles, 8 triples (3d most in N.L.) in 206⅔ innings.... Allowed 17 first-inning runs in 34 starts (3.74 ERA).... Batting support: 4.50 runs per start, 4th-highest average in N.L.... Opposing base stealers: 27-for-33 (82%); 0 pickoffs, 1 balk.

Comments: The only pitcher in the majors to lower his rate of walks in each of the last four years (minimum: 100 IP in each season). We're not talking about a slight improvement, but rather, to use the vogue phrase, "a sea change." Annual walks per nine innings since he broke into the majors in 1988: 6.23, 5.57, 4.10, 3.45, 2.79.... The last pitcher with a longer streak of improvement: Dennis Leonard (five years, 1975–79).... Has allowed 7.46 hits per nine innings in two years with Houston, 4th-lowest average in team history (minimum: 300 IP), behind J. R. Richard (6.88), Nolan Ryan (6.99), and Joe Sambito (7.41).... Allowed 63 extra-base hits, 3d-highest total in league; on the other hand, his total of five extra-base hits as a batter tied for the lead among N.L. pitchers. He had eight RBIs, one fewer than N.L. leader Dwight Gooden.... Had 4.11 ERA in 114 innings caught by Scott Servais, 3.20 in 92⅔ innings with either Eddie Taubensee or Scooter Tucker catching.... His 3.70 ERA led the Astros, but that was the highest ERA to lead any N.L. club last season.... Led majors with 15 no-decision starts.... The average length of the nine-inning games he started last season was 2 hours, 59 minutes, 2d longest among N.L. pitchers (minimum 10 starts); that'll come as a surprise to anyone who saw him duel Pedro Astacio in the season finale, the shortest nine-inning game in the majors last season (1:44). Those bags were packed and ready to go!

Greg W. Harris

Throws Right

San Diego Padres	W-L	ERA	AB	H	HR	BB	SO	BA	SA	OBA
Season	4-8	4.12	448	113	13	35	66	.252	.384	.307
vs. Left-Handers			287	80	11	23	34	.279	.436	.330
vs. Right-Handers			161	33	2	12	32	.205	.292	.267
vs. Ground-Ballers			216	58	6	10	28	.269	.398	.304
vs. Fly-Ballers			232	55	7	25	38	.237	.371	.310
Home Games	2-3	3.36	232	54	6	15	37	.233	.345	.278
Road Games	2-5	4.95	216	59	7	20	29	.273	.426	.338
Grass Fields	2-4	3.52	284	66	6	21	44	.232	.338	.284
Artificial Turf	2-4	5.23	164	47	7	14	22	.287	.463	.346
April	1-1	2.06	127	29	3	7	19	.228	.323	.272
May	1-3	6.67	121	36	7	15	20	.298	.521	.372
June	0-0	0.00	5	0	0	1	1	.000	.000	.167
July	0-0	0.00	0	0	0	0	0	.000	.000	.000
August	0-2	5.84	51	14	1	2	5	.275	.373	.296
Sept./Oct.	2-2	3.69	144	34	2	10	21	.236	.340	.290
Leading Off Inn.			116	34	3	5	21	.293	.431	.322
Bases Empty			282	74	6	15	47	.262	.387	.300
Runners On			166	39	7	20	19	.235	.380	.319
Runners/Scor. Pos.			100	27	5	16	12	.270	.430	.372
Runners On/2 Out			68	13	2	12	11	.191	.294	.329
Scor. Pos./2 Out			44	12	2	10	6	.273	.432	.429
Late-Inning Pressure			24	5	1	2	2	.208	.333	.269
Leading Off			8	0	0	0	2	.000	.000	.000
Runners On			3	1	1	1	0	.333	1.333	.500
Runners/Scor. Pos.			0	0	0	0	0	—	—	—
First 9 Batters			155	40	1	13	28	.258	.329	.316
Second 9 Batters			157	41	6	12	22	.261	.420	.312
All Batters Thereafter			136	32	6	10	16	.235	.404	.293

Loves to face: Len Dykstra (.118, 2-for-17)
Otis Nixon (0-for-10)
Matt Williams (0-for-14)

Hates to face: John Kruk (.429, 6-for-14, 1 HR)
Darryl Strawberry (.360, 9-for-25, 3 HR)
Larry Walker (.643, 9-for-14, 3 HR)

Miscellaneous statistics: Ground outs-to-air outs ratio: 1.01 last season, 1.13 for career.... Opponents grounded into 4 double plays in 75 opportunities (one per 19).... Allowed 18 doubles, 1 triple in 118 innings.... Allowed 8 first-inning runs in 20 starts (3.60 ERA).... Batting support: 3.90 runs per start.... Opposing base stealers: 18-for-23 (78%); 2 pickoffs, 1 balk.

Comments: After being used exclusively in relief in 73 games in 1990, he has pitched only as a starter the last two seasons (20 starts each year).... His 2.72 career ERA is lowest in Padres history (minimum: 300 IP); his career rate of hits allowed (7.60 per nine innings) is 2d lowest, behind Lance McCullers (7.14).... Career breakdown of those rates: as a reliever, 2.19 ERA and 6.86 hits allowed per nine innings; as a starter, 3.12 ERA and 8.09 hits per nine.... As is true for most pitchers who have had considerable experience as both a starter and a reliever, his career strikeout rate in starts (6.21 per nine innings) is lower than his rate out of the pen (7.03).... One of six active pitchers who has held right-handed batters to a career batting average below .200; the six: Jose DeLeon (.190), Mike Jackson (.196), Tommy Greene (.196), John Smoltz (.197), Harris (.198), and Rob Dibble (.199).... Allowed 11 home runs to left-handed batters, second in N.L. to Omar Olivares (13).... Speaking of lefties and righties, study these numbers and see if you can properly match these 1992 overall major league batting averages— .266, .260, .255, .244—with the proper combination of lefty pitcher/righty batter; lefty pitcher/lefty batter; righty pitcher/righty batter; righty pitcher/lefty batter. (Insert "Jeopardy!" music here.) Time's up; the answers: in the majors in 1992, right-handed batters hit .266 vs. lefties and .244 vs. righties; left-handed batters hit .260 vs. righties and .255 vs. lefties.

Butch Henry

Throws Left

Houston Astros	W-L	ERA	AB	H	HR	BB	SO	BA	SA	OBA
Season	6-9	4.02	649	185	16	41	96	.285	.433	.325
vs. Left-Handers			141	42	2	12	14	.298	.411	.351
vs. Right-Handers			508	143	14	29	82	.281	.439	.318
vs. Ground-Ballers			306	85	4	21	42	.278	.386	.322
vs. Fly-Ballers			343	100	12	20	54	.292	.475	.328
Home Games	3-3	3.27	338	91	7	19	51	.269	.382	.307
Road Games	3-6	4.87	311	94	9	22	45	.302	.489	.344
Grass Fields	1-3	4.50	154	45	3	14	23	.292	.442	.345
Artificial Turf	5-6	3.88	495	140	13	27	73	.283	.430	.319
April	0-2	4.37	93	28	2	9	14	.301	.441	.363
May	1-2	5.24	134	40	3	6	16	.299	.463	.326
June	1-2	5.32	94	26	1	12	14	.277	.404	.352
July	1-1	3.03	149	42	3	8	25	.282	.403	.316
August	2-2	3.29	160	46	6	6	25	.287	.456	.311
Sept./Oct.	1-0	1.69	19	3	1	0	2	.158	.368	.158
Leading Off Inn.			166	44	3	10	25	.265	.410	.307
Bases Empty			393	119	9	20	61	.303	.453	.338
Runners On			256	66	7	21	35	.258	.402	.306
Runners/Scor. Pos.			129	32	4	18	16	.248	.372	.325
Runners On/2 Out			103	18	2	10	15	.175	.272	.248
Scor. Pos./2 Out			57	10	1	9	7	.175	.263	.288
Late-Inning Pressure			32	8	0	1	5	.250	.313	.265
Leading Off			10	3	0	0	1	.300	.500	.300
Runners On			10	2	0	0	1	.200	.200	.182
Runners/Scor. Pos.			3	0	0	0	0	.000	.000	.000
First 9 Batters			230	57	3	14	41	.248	.343	.289
Second 9 Batters			213	58	9	13	29	.272	.469	.310
All Batters Thereafter			206	70	4	14	26	.340	.495	.381

Loves to face: Mark Grace (.100, 1-for-10)
Eric Karros (.091, 1-for-11)
Mitch Webster (0-for-6)
Hates to face: David Hollins (.875, 7-for-8, 1 2B, 4 HR, 1 SO)
Barry Larkin (.714, 5-for-7, 1 HR)
Mike Sharperson (.667, 6-for-9)

Miscellaneous statistics: Ground outs-to-air outs ratio: 1.13 last season, 1.13 for career.... Opponents grounded into 10 double plays in 131 opportunities (one per 13).... Allowed 38 doubles, 5 triples in 165⅔ innings.... Allowed 10 first-inning runs in 28 starts (3.29 ERA).... Batting support: 3.32 runs per start, 9th-lowest average in N.L.... Opposing base stealers: 10-for-17 (59%); 4 pickoffs, 2 balks.

Comments: Second among N.L. rookies in innings, starts, and strikeouts; Donovan Osborne led N.L. rooks in each of those categories.... His innings total is 7th highest in team history by a rookie, and the most since Mark Lemongello set the team rookie mark with 215 in 1977. Other Astros rookies to pitch more innings than Henry: Don Wilson (184 in 1967), Tom Griffin (188 in 1969), Ken Forsch (188 in 1971), Doug Konieczny (171 in 1975), and Joaquin Andujar (172 in 1976).... Held opponents to a .175 mark with runners on base and two outs. Astros led the N.L. in that category, holding hitters to a .201 mark in those situations.... Despite playing his home games in one of the toughest home run parks in the majors, he allowed more homers than any rookie except Kyle Abbott.... Faced 114 batters in first innings, the most by any rookie pitcher who did not surrender a first-inning home run last season.... Had a 5–1 record, 2.45 ERA in day games; 1–8, 5.16 at night. Some might pooh-pooh day/night figures for players whose home games are played in domes, where artificial lights are used day or night. But there's more to day/night figures than the difference between sunshine or artificial light; as Max McGee can tell you, there's a certain matter of the "body clock" that must also be considered.... Born October 7, 1968, the day that Lou Brock's failure to slide on a play at home plate became the turning point of the World Series against the Tigers.

Xavier Hernandez

Throws Right

Houston Astros	W-L	ERA	AB	H	HR	BB	SO	BA	SA	OBA
Season	9-1	2.11	404	81	5	42	96	.200	.275	.279
vs. Left-Handers			209	44	2	29	51	.211	.292	.310
vs. Right-Handers			195	37	3	13	45	.190	.256	.245
vs. Ground-Ballers			174	32	1	17	45	.184	.236	.259
vs. Fly-Ballers			230	49	4	25	51	.213	.304	.295
Home Games	6-1	1.83	214	44	2	14	50	.206	.266	.255
Road Games	3-0	2.42	190	37	3	28	46	.195	.284	.305
Grass Fields	3-0	2.64	110	22	2	16	30	.200	.309	.307
Artificial Turf	6-1	1.90	294	59	3	26	66	.201	.262	.269
April	2-0	0.00	44	7	0	7	13	.159	.182	.275
May	1-0	4.08	69	14	2	5	10	.203	.290	.267
June	2-0	2.25	92	21	1	8	23	.228	.315	.290
July	1-1	1.23	54	11	0	4	7	.204	.241	.267
August	2-0	2.33	67	12	1	12	26	.179	.284	.300
Sept./Oct.	1-0	2.05	78	16	1	6	17	.205	.282	.271
Leading Off Inn.			88	17	0	8	16	.193	.227	.260
Bases Empty			224	44	0	20	46	.196	.232	.265
Runners On			180	37	5	22	50	.206	.328	.296
Runners/Scor. Pos.			107	17	2	19	32	.159	.234	.281
Runners On/2 Out			92	18	3	15	23	.196	.315	.308
Scor. Pos./2 Out			59	9	2	13	15	.153	.254	.306
Late-Inning Pressure			132	29	1	16	27	.220	.303	.311
Leading Off			29	9	0	5	5	.310	.379	.412
Runners On			66	11	1	7	14	.167	.258	.263
Runners/Scor. Pos.			41	4	0	7	10	.098	.146	.224
First 9 Batters			386	78	5	42	92	.202	.277	.284
Second 9 Batters			18	3	0	0	4	.167	.222	.167
All Batters Thereafter			0	0	0	0	0	—	—	—

Loves to face: Jerald Clark (0-for-8)
Tim Wallach (0-for-6)
Jerome Walton (0-for-8)
Hates to face: Barry Bonds (2-for-2, 1 HR, 2 BB)
Daryl Boston (.500, 3-for-6, 1 2B, 2 HR)
Darryl Strawberry (.444, 4-for-9, 2 HR)

Miscellaneous statistics: Ground outs-to-air outs ratio: 1.14 last season, 1.27 for career.... Opponents grounded into 5 double plays in 72 opportunities (one per 14).... Allowed 11 doubles, 2 triples in 111 innings.... Stranded 34 inherited runners, allowed 12 to score (74%).... Opposing base stealers: 10-for-14 (71%); 0 pickoffs, 0 balks.

Comments: Roughly once each season, some pitcher wins as many as four games against one opponent all in relief; it's happened 23 times in the last 23 years. Last season, the reliever was Hernandez, and his victim was the Giants. But it's rare for a reliever to defeat one opponent *five* times in one year; the last occurrence: the unlikely combo of Wilbur Wood beating the Seattle Pilots five times in 1969.... Winning percentage of .900 was the highest ever by an Astros reliever (minimum: five wins). The previous best: .846, by Charlie Kerfeld (11–2 in 1986).... Hernandez and Doug Jones became the first pair of N.L. teammates to win at least nine games each from the bullpen since Craig Lefferts and Lance McCullers of the Padres in 1986.... Compiled a 2.84 ERA in 57 innings with Eddie Taubensee catching, compared to a 1.33 mark in 54 innings with either Scott Servais or Scooter Tucker catching.... Batting average of .190 by opposing right-handed batters was 5th lowest in the majors last season (minimum: 200 BFP), behind Greg Maddux (.176), Tim Belcher (.178), Kent Mercker (.185), and Doug Drabek (.189).... Opponents' batting average with runners in scoring position was 2d lowest in majors (minimum: 125 BFP).... Has allowed only four home runs at the Astrodome in three seasons with Houston, compared to 15 on the road.... Has faced 34 batters with the bases loaded in his career without issuing a walk.

Orel Hershiser   Throws Right

Los Angeles Dodgers	W-L	ERA	AB	H	HR	BB	SO	BA	SA	OBA
Season	10-15	3.67	812	209	15	69	130	.257	.372	.320
vs. Left-Handers			455	130	11	56	60	.286	.418	.366
vs. Right-Handers			357	79	4	13	70	.221	.314	.257
vs. Ground-Ballers			354	96	6	33	62	.271	.370	.332
vs. Fly-Ballers			458	113	9	36	68	.247	.373	.310
Home Games	7-5	2.75	452	111	7	31	70	.246	.345	.295
Road Games	3-10	4.86	360	98	8	38	60	.272	.406	.349
Grass Fields	10-8	3.30	632	157	11	50	98	.248	.358	.307
Artificial Turf	0-7	4.98	180	52	4	19	32	.289	.422	.361
April	2-2	4.13	121	26	2	11	22	.215	.322	.296
May	2-1	2.89	109	26	2	12	18	.239	.349	.314
June	2-2	2.78	128	26	2	12	19	.203	.289	.275
July	1-4	5.19	153	54	3	9	19	.353	.484	.388
August	2-2	3.67	158	39	2	15	22	.247	.354	.316
Sept./Oct.	1-4	3.32	143	38	4	10	30	.266	.406	.316
Leading Off Inn.			207	59	6	13	36	.285	.449	.327
Bases Empty			469	120	12	32	78	.256	.399	.310
Runners On			343	89	3	37	52	.259	.335	.332
Runners/Scor. Pos.			205	48	1	29	41	.234	.293	.329
Runners On/2 Out			140	33	0	17	34	.236	.264	.323
Scor. Pos./2 Out			90	18	0	14	26	.200	.222	.314
Late-Inning Pressure			55	14	1	6	7	.255	.345	.328
Leading Off			20	6	1	1	3	.300	.500	.333
Runners On			13	4	0	3	2	.308	.308	.438
Runners/Scor. Pos.			11	3	0	1	2	.273	.273	.333
First 9 Batters			269	73	5	17	45	.271	.387	.320
Second 9 Batters			262	65	5	22	49	.248	.374	.313
All Batters Thereafter			281	71	5	30	36	.253	.356	.326

Loves to face: Damon Berryhill (.095, 2-for-21)
Benito Santiago (.167, 7-for-42, 0 BB)
Matt Williams (.121, 4-for-33, 1 HR, 15 SO)

Hates to face: Craig Biggio (.465, 20-for-43)
Bobby Bonilla (.306, 11-for-36, 3 2B, 4 HR)
Steve Finley (.450, 9-for-20, 1 HR)

Miscellaneous statistics: Ground outs-to-air outs ratio: 1.72 last season (5th highest in N.L.), 2.03 for career.... Opponents grounded into 19 double plays in 161 opportunities (one per 8.5).... Allowed 42 doubles (4th most in N.L.), 3 triples in 210⅔ innings.... Allowed 19 first-inning runs in 33 starts (4.36 ERA).... Batting support: 3.12 runs per start, 5th-lowest average in N.L.... Opposing base stealers: 13-for-20 (65%); 1 pickoff, 0 balks.

Comments: Has completed only one of his last 66 starts.... Pitched an average of 6.38 innings per start last season, his first full season back from arm surgery. From 1984–89, before the injury, he averaged 7.28 innings.... Posted a losing record for the first time in 10 major league seasons. Over the last 50 years, only seven other pitchers started their careers with streaks of at least nine nonlosing seasons: Carl Erskine, Whitey Ford, Milt Pappas, Juan Marichal, Tom Seaver, Doug Bird, and Roger Clemens.... *Doug Bird?*... Allowed 15 unearned runs, a total exceeded by only one N.L. pitcher (Donovan Osborne, 16). Over the past 10 years, six different Dodgers pitchers have been victimized a total of 11 times (a major league high) by seasons of 15 or more unearned runs. Hershiser went the entire 1991 season (112 innings) without allowing an unearned run; this was the third time he allowed 15 or more.... Didn't allow a stolen base in 51⅔ innings with Carlos Hernandez catching, the most innings of any N.L. battery that didn't allow a steal. In fact, no player even attempted to steal a base against them.... His ERA in road games was 2d highest in the league, ahead of only Danny Jackson (5.21).... He and Jim Bullinger were the only N.L. pitchers to steal a base last season.... His .221 batting average (15-for-68) was 4th highest among N.L. pitchers; he tied Pete Harnisch for most doubles (5).... Has made 77 starts since he last allowed more than one home run (June 19, 1989), the longest streak in the majors.

Ken Hill   Throws Right

Montreal Expos	W-L	ERA	AB	H	HR	BB	SO	BA	SA	OBA
Season	16-9	2.68	812	187	13	75	150	.230	.335	.297
vs. Left-Handers			465	104	6	49	80	.224	.320	.299
vs. Right-Handers			347	83	7	26	70	.239	.354	.294
vs. Ground-Ballers			365	83	3	24	59	.227	.301	.278
vs. Fly-Ballers			447	104	10	51	91	.233	.362	.311
Home Games	6-6	3.15	358	91	4	39	62	.254	.360	.330
Road Games	10-3	2.33	454	96	9	36	88	.211	.315	.270
Grass Fields	4-2	2.14	200	38	3	16	42	.190	.280	.250
Artificial Turf	12-7	2.87	612	149	10	59	108	.243	.353	.312
April	2-2	1.42	141	30	1	8	20	.213	.277	.253
May	2-0	3.81	107	26	2	15	17	.243	.374	.347
June	4-2	2.92	138	31	2	13	22	.225	.348	.292
July	4-0	3.41	119	25	5	14	30	.210	.403	.293
August	2-3	2.28	161	40	1	12	30	.248	.323	.301
Sept./Oct.	2-2	2.72	146	35	2	13	31	.240	.308	.302
Leading Off Inn.			210	48	2	13	41	.229	.319	.277
Bases Empty			463	113	8	43	88	.244	.367	.312
Runners On			349	74	5	32	62	.212	.292	.276
Runners/Scor. Pos.			226	45	3	28	40	.199	.270	.284
Runners On/2 Out			152	33	2	16	25	.217	.309	.292
Scor. Pos./2 Out			104	22	2	14	16	.212	.317	.305
Late-Inning Pressure			62	16	4	5	10	.258	.468	.309
Leading Off			19	3	0	1	6	.158	.158	.200
Runners On			18	4	2	1	2	.222	.556	.250
Runners/Scor. Pos.			7	1	1	0	2	.143	.571	.125
First 9 Batters			262	56	3	30	65	.214	.309	.294
Second 9 Batters			270	66	2	18	48	.244	.326	.294
All Batters Thereafter			280	65	8	27	37	.232	.368	.302

Loves to face: Shawon Dunston (.125, 2-for-16)
Dale Murphy (0-for-12)
Terry Pendleton (0-for-14)

Hates to face: Len Dykstra (.600, 12-for-20, 1 HR)
Fred McGriff (.333, 5-for-15, 3 HR, 5 BB)
Otis Nixon (.600, 9-for-15)

Miscellaneous statistics: Ground outs-to-air outs ratio: 1.43 last season, 1.31 for career.... Opponents grounded into 12 double plays in 134 opportunities (one per 11).... Allowed 36 doubles, 5 triples in 218 innings.... Allowed 21 first-inning runs in 33 starts (5.45 ERA).... Batting support: 3.85 runs per start.... Opposing base stealers: 30-for-38 (79%), 3d-most steals in N.L.; 3 pickoffs, 4 balks (3d most in N.L.).

Comments: Acquired from the Cardinals prior to the 1992 season for Andres Galarraga and immediately made the Expos look good: He compiled the N.L.'s best ERA during the month of April, while Galarraga was sidelined April 8–May 21 with a fractured wrist.... At the All-Star break, Hill was batting .324, 138 points higher than Galarraga (.186). Although Hill went 0-for-28 after the break, Le Gros Chat didn't pass him until August 11.... Scored 10 runs last season, the 2d-highest total among pitchers, behind Tom Glavine (11).... Had a 2.12 ERA with Darrin Fletcher catching (106 innings), compared to 3.21 in 112 innings with either Gary Carter, Rick Cerone, or Tim Laker behind the plate.... His ERA in road games was the lowest in the league; he tied John Smoltz for most road wins.... Average of one home run allowed every 16.8 innings was better than the rate he posted in either of the previous two seasons, while pitching his home games at Busch Stadium.... Average of 3.10 walks allowed per nine innings was the best rate of his career.... Has completed only six of 111 career starts, including four shutouts (three last season).... Career ERA is 2.77 in day games (15–13 record), 4.08 at night (24–28).... Career record is 22–13 with a 3.22 ERA before the All-Star break, 17–28 with a 3.96 ERA after.... Winning percentage has increased in each of four seasons since he made his debut in 1988. The only other pitchers with current four-year streaks are Mike Morgan and Steve Howe.

Jay Howell
Throws Right

Los Angeles Dodgers	W-L	ERA	AB	H	HR	BB	SO	BA	SA	OBA
Season	1-3	1.54	178	41	2	18	36	.230	.281	.303
vs. Left-Handers			91	22	2	8	19	.242	.330	.310
vs. Right-Handers			87	19	0	10	17	.218	.230	.296
vs. Ground-Ballers			69	15	0	10	21	.217	.232	.316
vs. Fly-Ballers			109	26	2	8	15	.239	.312	.294
Home Games	1-2	1.57	83	19	0	8	19	.229	.241	.293
Road Games	0-1	1.52	95	22	2	10	17	.232	.316	.311
Grass Fields	1-2	1.52	110	26	0	12	23	.236	.264	.309
Artificial Turf	0-1	1.59	68	15	2	6	13	.221	.309	.293
April	0-0	—	0	0	0	0	0	—	—	—
May	0-0	0.00	7	1	0	4	2	.143	.143	.455
June	0-0	0.69	47	7	0	7	10	.149	.191	.259
July	1-1	2.25	62	16	1	4	11	.258	.306	.313
August	0-2	1.17	29	7	0	2	5	.241	.241	.290
Sept./Oct.	0-0	2.25	33	10	1	1	8	.303	.424	.314
Leading Off Inn.			43	10	1	2	9	.233	.326	.267
Bases Empty			99	21	2	8	21	.212	.293	.278
Runners On			79	20	0	10	15	.253	.266	.333
Runners/Scor. Pos.			43	10	0	8	9	.233	.233	.346
Runners On/2 Out			34	9	0	7	7	.265	.294	.390
Scor. Pos./2 Out			20	5	0	6	4	.250	.250	.423
Late-Inning Pressure			67	25	1	7	15	.373	.448	.432
Leading Off			16	5	0	0	4	.313	.313	.313
Runners On			32	15	0	4	5	.469	.500	.528
Runners/Scor. Pos.			18	9	0	4	3	.500	.500	.591
First 9 Batters			172	39	2	18	35	.227	.279	.298
Second 9 Batters			6	2	0	0	1	.333	.333	.429
All Batters Thereafter			0	0	0	0	0	—	—	—

Loves to face: Howard Johnson (0-for-10)
Robby Thompson (.125, 2-for-16, 9 SO)
Larry Walker (0-for-7)

Hates to face: Eric Davis (.400, 4-for-10, 3 BB)
Luis Salazar (.571, 4-for-7, 1 HR)
Andy Van Slyke (.444, 4-for-9)

Miscellaneous statistics: Ground outs-to-air outs ratio: 0.96 last season, 1.00 for career. . . . Opponents grounded into 1 double play in 42 opportunities (one per 42). . . . Allowed 3 doubles, 0 triples in 46⅔ innings. . . . Stranded 10 inherited runners, allowed 7 to score (59%). . . . Opposing base stealers: 7-for-8 (88%); 0 pickoffs, 1 balk.

Comments: Has the 4th-lowest average of hits allowed per nine innings in team history (minimum: 300 innings); the top five: Sandy Koufax, 6.79; Jim Brewer, 6.91; Andy Messersmith, 7.02; Howell, 7.09; Rex Barney, 7.12. . . . His 2.07 ERA is the lowest in franchise history. (Last season's ERA was the lowest of his career.) . . . Total of 85 saves with Los Angeles is 3d most in Dodgers history behind Jim Brewer (125) and Ron Perranoski (101). . . . Pitched an average of only 1.14 innings per game last season, his lowest rate since he debuted in the majors with three innings in five appearances for John McNamara's Reds in 1980. . . . Only 37 percent of the batters he faced last season came in Late-Inning Pressure Situations; his rates for the previous seven seasons ranged from 75 to 85 percent. . . . Only three N.L. pitchers had more at-bats by opposing right-handed batters without allowing a home run, and two of them were teammates: Jeff Fassero, 232 AB vs. RHB; Roger McDowell, 183; and Pedro Astacio, 134. . . . The last right-hander to homer off Howell was Dale Murphy on May 11, 1991. . . . Has spent at least three weeks on the disabled list in each of the past three seasons, for a total of 99 days. . . . Has pitched 415 games since his last start, June 16, 1984, when he defeated the Baltimore Orioles at Yankee Stadium. The managers were Yogi Berra and Joe Altobelli, and the game was Lou Piniella's last.

Bruce Hurst
Throws Left

San Diego Padres	W-L	ERA	AB	H	HR	BB	SO	BA	SA	OBA
Season	14-9	3.85	835	223	22	51	131	.267	.390	.308
vs. Left-Handers			157	46	8	10	28	.293	.478	.335
vs. Right-Handers			678	177	14	41	103	.261	.370	.302
vs. Ground-Ballers			397	113	7	22	53	.285	.378	.322
vs. Fly-Ballers			438	110	15	29	78	.251	.402	.295
Home Games	5-4	4.38	386	99	15	26	65	.256	.409	.302
Road Games	9-5	3.39	449	124	7	25	66	.276	.374	.313
Grass Fields	11-5	3.48	610	154	17	37	99	.252	.369	.294
Artificial Turf	3-4	4.89	225	69	5	14	32	.307	.449	.346
April	1-2	4.83	122	34	4	10	24	.279	.434	.333
May	3-2	2.84	166	40	4	13	27	.241	.337	.294
June	4-1	1.93	175	39	3	7	35	.223	.320	.251
July	3-1	4.32	162	48	5	12	24	.296	.407	.345
August	2-1	4.91	110	30	3	6	10	.273	.409	.308
Sept./Oct.	1-2	6.08	100	32	3	3	11	.320	.500	.337
Leading Off Inn.			211	51	8	13	35	.242	.379	.286
Bases Empty			510	132	13	39	82	.259	.363	.311
Runners On			325	91	9	12	49	.280	.434	.302
Runners/Scor. Pos.			174	47	1	7	26	.270	.345	.292
Runners On/2 Out			145	34	3	5	27	.234	.331	.260
Scor. Pos./2 Out			81	19	0	4	13	.235	.284	.271
Late-Inning Pressure			83	21	2	2	6	.253	.361	.271
Leading Off			23	4	0	1	4	.174	.174	.208
Runners On			26	8	1	0	0	.308	.500	.308
Runners/Scor. Pos.			13	4	0	0	0	.308	.308	.308
First 9 Batters			266	73	4	16	47	.274	.368	.314
Second 9 Batters			264	69	9	19	41	.261	.413	.309
All Batters Thereafter			305	81	9	16	43	.266	.390	.301

Loves to face: Steve Lake (0-for-8)
Ozzie Smith (.171, 7-for-41)
Darryl Strawberry (.125, 3-for-24)

Hates to face: Barry Bonds (.462, 12-for-26, 3 HR)
Eric Karros (.600, 6-for-10)
Kevin Mitchell (.333, 7-for-21, 1 2B, 5 HR)

Miscellaneous statistics: Ground outs-to-air outs ratio: 1.07 last season, 1.16 for career. . . . Opponents grounded into 8 double plays in 139 opportunities (one per 17). . . . Allowed 31 doubles, 3 triples in 217⅓ innings. . . . Allowed 15 first-inning runs in 32 starts (4.22 ERA). . . . Batting support: 4.34 runs per start, 6th-highest average in N.L. . . . Opposing base stealers: 18-for-28 (64%); 4 pickoffs, 3 balks.

Comments: Ranks 2d in Padres history among pitchers with 40+ decisions with a .598 winning percentage (55–37), behind Gaylord Perry (.660, 33–17). . . . Has posted winning records in each of his four seasons with San Diego (15–11, 11–9, 15–8, 14–9). In fact, he and Roger Clemens are the only pitchers to post winning records in every season since 1986. (Clemens has done it in every year since 1984.) . . . Only two other pitchers in Padres history reached double figures in wins in four consecutive seasons: Eric Show (1982–85) and Ed Whitson (1987–90), neither of whom got a fifth. . . . Average of one home run allowed every 9.9 innings was the worst in his four seasons with San Diego. He allowed 22 home runs, 2d most in the league, ahead of only Bud Black (23). . . . Had the 2d-highest ERA in home games in the National League. . . . Has won his last nine decisions against the Mets; last season he was 4–0 against them, including three shutouts and a scoreless string of 33 consecutive innings. . . . Has set a career-best mark in walks allowed per nine innings in each of the last two seasons (2.40 in 1991, 2.11 last season). . . . His strikeout rate has declined in every season since 1986, one year short of the longest such streak in major league history (minimum: 100 IP each season), shared by Bob Feller (1947–53) and Bill Doak (1914–20). The last pitcher with a streak as long as Hurst's: Doc Medich (1974–79). . . . Career record is 126–83 on grass fields (.603), 17–27 on artificial turf (.386).

Jeff Innis
Throws Right

New York Mets	W-L	ERA	AB	H	HR	BB	SO	BA	SA	OBA
Season	6-9	2.86	319	85	4	36	39	.266	.357	.348
vs. Left-Handers			159	46	2	28	16	.289	.390	.399
vs. Right-Handers			160	39	2	8	23	.244	.325	.291
vs. Ground-Ballers			148	42	1	9	17	.284	.345	.325
vs. Fly-Ballers			171	43	3	27	22	.251	.368	.366
Home Games	3-5	2.81	176	46	2	19	24	.261	.347	.342
Road Games	3-4	2.92	143	39	2	17	15	.273	.371	.356
Grass Fields	4-5	2.80	223	60	3	24	28	.269	.363	.345
Artificial Turf	2-4	3.00	96	25	1	12	11	.260	.344	.355
April	3-1	2.61	38	11	1	3	10	.289	.395	.386
May	1-0	3.21	50	14	1	8	3	.280	.380	.373
June	0-3	3.32	75	22	0	6	11	.293	.373	.341
July	1-3	3.06	61	15	1	6	6	.246	.344	.313
August	0-1	0.73	41	5	0	2	4	.122	.122	.182
Sept./Oct.	1-1	3.68	54	18	1	11	5	.333	.481	.449
Leading Off Inn.			73	22	2	6	8	.301	.425	.354
Bases Empty			174	46	2	14	22	.264	.351	.323
Runners On			145	39	2	22	17	.269	.366	.375
Runners/Scor. Pos.			96	23	1	18	13	.240	.323	.364
Runners On/2 Out			67	14	1	12	6	.209	.328	.338
Scor. Pos./2 Out			53	9	1	9	5	.170	.302	.290
Late-Inning Pressure			165	49	2	20	20	.297	.418	.389
Leading Off			44	14	0	2	4	.318	.364	.348
Runners On			67	20	2	15	7	.299	.507	.449
Runners/Scor. Pos.			46	11	1	12	6	.239	.413	.413
First 9 Batters			310	83	4	35	38	.268	.361	.350
Second 9 Batters			9	2	0	1	1	.222	.222	.273
All Batters Thereafter			0	0	0	0	0	—	—	—

Loves to face: Otis Nixon (0-for-8)
　　　　　　　　Benito Santiago (0-for-9)
　　　　　　　　Matt Williams (.100, 1-for-10)
Hates to face: Marquis Grissom (.556, 5-for-9, 1 HR)
　　　　　　　　David Justice (.500, 3-for-6, 2 HR)
　　　　　　　　Orlando Merced (.667, 4-for-6, 2 2B)

Miscellaneous statistics: Ground outs-to-air outs ratio: 2.67 last season, 2.52 for career.... Opponents grounded into 14 double plays in 81 opportunities (one per 5.8).... Allowed 11 doubles, 3 triples in 88 innings.... Stranded 34 inherited runners, allowed 15 to score (69%).... Opposing base stealers: 8-for-13 (62%); 1 pickoff, 0 balks.

Comments: Among the 383 pitchers in major league history with at least 200 games out of the bullpen, Innis's two saves in 220 appearances represents the the lowest rate. The 2d-worst average: Charlie Williams, 4-for-235 (one per 59).... Became the first pitcher in major league history to earn fewer than three saves in his first 200 relief appearances. Two pitchers had three saves after 200 games: Tony Fossas and Steve Ridzik.... Innis's nine relief losses last season contributed to a total of 31 by Mets relievers, tying the Royals for highest in the majors. That conjured memories of the Mets bullpens that lost 33, 34, and 34 from 1978 to 1980—the only time in major league history that a team's relievers lost 30-plus games in three straight seasons.... The only Mets pitchers ever to lose more games in relief in one season: Skip Lockwood (7–13 in 1978) and Neil Allen (7–10 in 1980). Lockwood had 15 saves, Allen had 22.... Only one other reliever in major league history lost as many as nine games in a season in which he saved fewer than two: Bill Fleming (6–10, one save for the 1944 Cubs).... Batting average by opposing right-handers was a career high, following a pair of sub-.200 seasons.... Opponents have a career batting average of .298 in Late-Inning Pressure Situations, compared to a .229 average in other at-bats. The difference of 69 points is 3d largest among active pitchers (minimum: 250 LIPS AB), beating only Chuck McElroy (75 points, .289/.214) and Mike Jeffcoat (69 points, .351/.282).

Danny Jackson
Throws Left

Cubs/Pirates	W-L	ERA	AB	H	HR	BB	SO	BA	SA	OBA
Season	8-13	3.84	775	211	6	77	97	.272	.361	.337
vs. Left-Handers			119	29	2	16	21	.244	.311	.331
vs. Right-Handers			656	182	4	61	76	.277	.370	.338
vs. Ground-Ballers			333	89	1	30	49	.267	.342	.327
vs. Fly-Ballers			442	122	5	47	48	.276	.376	.345
Home Games	6-4	2.85	440	116	1	44	54	.264	.334	.330
Road Games	2-9	5.21	335	95	5	33	43	.284	.397	.347
Grass Fields	2-8	3.28	354	86	5	39	41	.243	.350	.316
Artificial Turf	6-5	4.36	421	125	1	38	56	.297	.371	.355
April	0-4	6.39	108	36	0	10	12	.333	.435	.397
May	0-3	3.86	133	35	2	16	18	.263	.368	.338
June	4-1	3.54	152	36	1	17	19	.237	.316	.312
July	1-2	1.91	111	25	3	12	12	.225	.324	.302
August	1-1	4.85	102	28	0	10	18	.275	.353	.336
Sept./Oct.	2-2	3.48	169	51	0	12	18	.302	.379	.346
Leading Off Inn.			187	56	3	23	22	.299	.439	.385
Bases Empty			405	110	4	42	48	.272	.380	.346
Runners On			370	101	2	35	49	.273	.341	.328
Runners/Scor. Pos.			216	60	0	22	31	.278	.343	.331
Runners On/2 Out			141	31	0	11	18	.220	.284	.276
Scor. Pos./2 Out			91	19	0	9	13	.209	.275	.280
Late-Inning Pressure			42	17	1	3	5	.405	.500	.444
Leading Off			12	7	1	3	0	.583	.917	.667
Runners On			18	7	0	0	3	.389	.389	.389
Runners/Scor. Pos.			9	3	0	0	2	.333	.333	.333
First 9 Batters			255	60	3	38	38	.235	.310	.333
Second 9 Batters			270	70	2	24	31	.259	.352	.319
All Batters Thereafter			250	81	1	15	28	.324	.424	.362

Loves to face: Jerald Clark (0-for-13)
　　　　　　　　Todd Hundley (0-for-8)
　　　　　　　　Mark Lemke (0-for-11)
Hates to face: Craig Biggio (.667, 6-for-9)
　　　　　　　　Darrin Jackson (.500, 9-for-18, 2 HR)
　　　　　　　　Jose Uribe (.462, 12-for-26)

Miscellaneous statistics: Ground outs-to-air outs ratio: 1.49 last season, 1.66 for career.... Opponents grounded into 17 double plays in 203 opportunities (one per 12).... Allowed 39 doubles, 6 triples in 201⅓ innings.... Allowed 21 first-inning runs in 34 starts (5.03 ERA).... Batting support: 3.79 runs per start.... Opposing base stealers: 21-for-34 (62%); 6 pickoffs, 2 balks.

Comments: His victory over the Expos on June 5 broke a streak of 20 consecutive starts without a win, the longest in the majors in roughly 10 years since Ross Baumgarten had a 20-start winless streak that ended his career (June 2, 1981–Aug. 23, 1982). The last longer streak: Matt Keough, 0-for-28 (Sept. 6, 1978–Aug. 8, 1979).... Jackson was 0–10 with a 6.05 ERA over those 20 starts, but went 8–6 with a 3.38 ERA thereafter.... His road-game ERA was highest in the National League.... Opponents' on-base percentage leading off innings was the highest in the N.L., as was his walk rate to leadoff batters.... Has made 70 regular-season starts since his last complete game (July 18, 1989), the longest current streak.... Career record is 19–34 in day games, 62–58 at night.... Has a record of 0–10 in his last 15 starts during April; his last win in that month was April 3, 1989.... Allowed only six home runs in 201⅓ innings (one per 33.6 innings) last season, the 3d-lowest rate in the majors, and the best of his career. With the Cubs in 1991, he had the worst rate of his career: one every 8.8 innings (one every 5.0 innings at Wrigley Field).... Has made 231 career starts, the most among active pitchers who've never allowed more than two home runs in a game. Others with 100-plus starts, none with three HRs: Greg Maddux (208 GS), Kevin Brown (127), Terry Mulholland (126), Kelly Downs (123), Joe Magrane (119), Bob Tewksbury (116), Erik Hanson (113), Jimmy Jones (112), Ken Hill (111), Bill Swift (108).

Doug Jones

Houston Astros — Throws Right

	W-L	ERA	AB	H	HR	BB	SO	BA	SA	OBA
Season	11-8	1.85	409	96	5	17	93	.235	.320	.274
vs. Left-Handers			215	55	3	12	41	.256	.358	.298
vs. Right-Handers			194	41	2	5	52	.211	.278	.246
vs. Ground-Ballers			173	40	1	9	41	.231	.277	.273
vs. Fly-Ballers			236	56	4	8	52	.237	.352	.274
Home Games	6-5	2.42	230	54	3	13	59	.235	.326	.282
Road Games	5-3	1.12	179	42	2	4	34	.235	.313	.263
Grass Fields	3-3	0.89	113	28	1	3	23	.248	.319	.280
Artificial Turf	8-5	2.21	296	68	4	14	70	.230	.321	.272
April	1-1	1.62	63	17	1	2	21	.270	.349	.303
May	2-2	3.38	66	17	1	3	14	.258	.409	.290
June	1-2	1.10	60	15	0	4	13	.250	.267	.308
July	4-2	2.21	72	14	1	4	14	.194	.292	.237
August	0-1	2.00	68	15	2	1	14	.221	.309	.254
Sept./Oct.	3-0	0.83	80	18	0	3	17	.225	.300	.262
Leading Off Inn.			91	22	0	3	17	.242	.275	.281
Bases Empty			215	62	2	6	44	.288	.372	.317
Runners On			194	34	3	11	49	.175	.263	.227
Runners/Scor. Pos.			109	22	0	8	26	.202	.275	.263
Runners On/2 Out			90	12	1	9	21	.133	.200	.228
Scor. Pos./2 Out			58	9	0	7	13	.155	.207	.258
Late-Inning Pressure			316	74	5	14	78	.234	.329	.275
Leading Off			72	19	0	2	14	.264	.292	.303
Runners On			149	24	3	9	39	.161	.255	.219
Runners/Scor. Pos.			79	15	0	7	18	.190	.253	.264
First 9 Batters			391	93	5	16	89	.238	.327	.277
Second 9 Batters			18	3	0	1	4	.167	.167	.211
All Batters Thereafter			0	0	0	0	0	—	—	—

Loves to face: Jay Bell (0-for-8)
Pete Incaviglia (.158, 3-for-19)
Fred McGriff (0-for-11)

Hates to face: Sid Bream (.500, 3-for-6, 2 2B)
Willie McGee (.571, 4-for-7)
Eddie Murray (.385, 5-for-13, 3 2B)

Miscellaneous statistics: Ground outs-to-air outs ratio: 1.54 last season, 1.38 for career.... Opponents grounded into 7 double plays in 86 opportunities (one per 12).... Allowed 14 doubles, 3 triples in 111⅔ innings.... Saved 36 games in 42 opportunities (86%), highest rate in N.L.... Stranded 26 inherited runners, allowed 11 to score (70%).... Opposing base stealers: 5-for-9 (56%); 0 pickoffs, 1 balk.

Comments: His ERA dropped from 5.54 in 1991 to 1.85 last season, the largest decrease in consecutive seasons of 60-plus innings since 1986, when Jeff Russell got his career in gear by slicing his ERA from 7.55 in 1985 to 3.40.... Led the majors with 11 relief wins, a total made all the more impressive by his 36 saves. No other pitcher in major league history posted totals as high as Jones in both categories.... Led the Astros in both wins and saves. The last pitcher to lead his team in both: Lee Smith in 1986 (nine wins, 31 saves for the Cubs).... Tied Houston's club record for relief wins in a season; the coholders: Hal Woodeshick (1963), Bill Dawley (1984), Charlie Kerfeld (1986), and Danny Darwin (1989).... None of his victories resulted from blown save opportunities.... Entered 23 games with the score tied, the most of any relief pitcher in the majors last season.... Led N.L. pitchers in games finished with 70, the highest total by an N.L. pitcher since Mike Marshall set the league record in 1974 (83).... Average of 1.37 walks per nine innings was the best of his career, and the 2d-lowest single-season rate in franchise history (minimum: 100 IP), behind Hal Brown, who walked only eight batters in 141 innings in 1963 (0.51 per 9 IP).... Opponents' batting average with runners on base was 2d lowest in majors, behind Mel Rojas (.143).... Houston's bullpen worked 535 innings last season (2d most in the league; one fewer than San Francisco). Astros relievers led the N.L. in wins (39) and ERA (2.89).

Jimmy Jones

Houston Astros — Throws Right

	W-L	ERA	AB	H	HR	BB	SO	BA	SA	OBA
Season	10-6	4.07	524	135	13	39	69	.258	.403	.313
vs. Left-Handers			297	85	9	27	33	.286	.458	.347
vs. Right-Handers			227	50	4	12	36	.220	.330	.268
vs. Ground-Ballers			270	71	6	15	38	.263	.404	.310
vs. Fly-Ballers			254	64	7	24	31	.252	.402	.316
Home Games	5-2	3.33	193	45	1	21	29	.233	.301	.318
Road Games	5-4	4.54	331	90	12	18	40	.272	.462	.310
Grass Fields	2-1	5.62	167	49	6	9	18	.293	.497	.333
Artificial Turf	8-5	3.41	357	86	7	30	51	.241	.359	.304
April	0-0		0	0	0	0	0	—	—	—
May	2-0	3.55	91	19	1	8	15	.209	.275	.273
June	2-1	4.72	131	39	3	6	18	.298	.466	.336
July	0-3	3.72	111	29	2	12	12	.261	.378	.349
August	4-1	3.57	136	33	7	10	17	.243	.441	.293
Sept./Oct.	2-1	5.28	55	15	0	3	7	.273	.418	.300
Leading Off Inn.			136	42	4	8	15	.309	.478	.356
Bases Empty			323	87	9	19	41	.269	.418	.316
Runners On			201	48	4	20	28	.239	.378	.308
Runners/Scor. Pos.			112	26	2	17	15	.232	.366	.333
Runners On/2 Out			82	16	2	6	14	.195	.317	.258
Scor. Pos./2 Out			50	9	2	5	9	.180	.360	.268
Late-Inning Pressure			38	11	1	0	7	.289	.447	.325
Leading Off			10	2	0	0	1	.200	.300	.273
Runners On			12	3	0	0	3	.250	.417	.250
Runners/Scor. Pos.			2	0	0	0	1	.000	.000	.000
First 9 Batters			187	54	2	20	28	.289	.385	.360
Second 9 Batters			187	36	5	14	24	.193	.326	.248
All Batters Thereafter			150	45	6	5	17	.300	.520	.333

Loves to face: Rafael Belliard (.143, 2-for-14)
Mark Grace (.083, 1-for-12)
Robby Thompson (.056, 1-for-18, 3 BB)

Hates to face: Fred McGriff (.389, 7-for-18, 4 HR)
Orlando Merced (.462, 6-for-13, 1 HR)
Andy Van Slyke (.429, 12-for-28, 3 HR)

Miscellaneous statistics: Ground outs-to-air outs ratio: 1.41 last season, 1.59 for career.... Opponents grounded into 11 double plays in 93 opportunities (one per 8.5).... Allowed 27 doubles, 5 triples in 139⅓ innings.... Allowed 21 first-inning runs in 23 starts (7.83 ERA, 3d highest in N.L.).... Batting support: 4.17 runs per start.... Opposing base stealers: 20-for-25 (80%); 0 pickoffs, 1 balk.

Comments: He and Chris Hammond were the only N.L. pitchers to start at least 20 games last season without reaching the 9th inning.... Has had career-long late-game problems: Opponents have batted .257 on his first two passes through the order (one HR per 47 at-bats), compared to .320 thereafter (one HR per 33 AB).... Has completed only one of his last 65 starts, a span dating back to August 1988.... Opponents' batting average in the first inning (.348) was 2d highest in majors.... Posted the lowest ERA of his career (with the exception of his 2.50 in three starts in 1986). Also established career bests in wins and hits per nine innings (8.72).... Don't underestimate the role that his home field played in those superlatives: During two seasons with Houston, his ERA was 3.17 at the Astrodome (5 HR in 150⅓ innings), 5.50 elsewhere (17 HR in 124⅓ innings).... Over the last two seasons, he's allowed a batting average of .293 to left-handers, .212 to right-handers.... Made only two relief appearances last season, and was the winning pitcher in both; his career record as a reliever is 5–1.... The most relief appearances in a season by a pitcher who won them all is seven, by none other than Cy Young in 1895. How 'bout in this century, you ask? It's Young again, with five in 1905. Eight different pitchers won all three relief appearances in a season; the most recent of them is Max Lanier, who did it in 1944.

Darryl Kile

Throws Right

Houston Astros	W-L	ERA	AB	H	HR	BB	SO	BA	SA	OBA
Season	5-10	3.95	476	124	8	63	90	.261	.391	.348
vs. Left-Handers			271	69	5	46	45	.255	.391	.361
vs. Right-Handers			205	55	3	17	45	.268	.390	.329
vs. Ground-Ballers			226	59	3	27	45	.261	.367	.344
vs. Fly-Ballers			250	65	5	36	45	.260	.412	.352
Home Games	3-5	3.53	241	61	1	36	51	.253	.336	.350
Road Games	2-5	4.38	235	63	7	27	39	.268	.447	.346
Grass Fields	1-2	3.35	139	30	3	15	29	.216	.345	.297
Artificial Turf	4-8	4.21	337	94	5	48	61	.279	.409	.368
April	2-2	1.89	120	24	1	13	29	.200	.292	.278
May	0-3	6.08	95	33	3	18	12	.347	.547	.440
June	0-1	7.56	30	7	1	10	5	.233	.400	.429
July	0-0	0.00	0	0	0	0	0	.000	.000	.000
August	0-3	5.47	100	31	2	8	16	.310	.490	.366
Sept./Oct.	3-1	2.55	131	29	1	14	28	.221	.290	.301
Leading Off Inn.			115	35	3	16	29	.304	.530	.394
Bases Empty			250	65	5	35	54	.260	.404	.353
Runners On			226	59	3	28	36	.261	.376	.342
Runners/Scor. Pos.			138	28	2	23	28	.203	.297	.314
Runners On/2 Out			79	10	2	13	16	.127	.215	.266
Scor. Pos./2 Out			55	6	1	13	13	.109	.182	.290
Late-Inning Pressure			18	4	1	1	3	.222	.444	.300
Leading Off			5	2	1	0	2	.400	1.200	.500
Runners On			6	2	0	0	0	.333	.333	.333
Runners/Scor. Pos.			4	2	0	0	0	.500	.500	.500
First 9 Batters			168	46	1	24	35	.274	.381	.369
Second 9 Batters			164	41	6	21	28	.250	.396	.335
All Batters Thereafter			144	37	1	18	27	.257	.396	.337

Loves to face: Dave Hansen (.091, 1-for-11, 1 2B)
Howard Johnson (.100, 1-for-10, 1 2B)
Fred McGriff (0-for-10)

Hates to face: Ray Lankford (.455, 5-for-11, 1 HR)
Willie McGee (.571, 8-for-14)
Eddie Murray (.500, 6-for-12, 1 HR)

Miscellaneous statistics: Ground outs-to-air outs ratio: 0.86 last season, 0.98 for career.... Opponents grounded into 8 double plays in 114 opportunities (one per 14).... Allowed 26 doubles, 6 triples in 125⅓ innings.... Allowed 7 first-inning runs in 22 starts (2.86 ERA).... Batting support: 3.09 runs per start, 3d-lowest average in N.L.... Opposing base stealers: 6-for-9 (67%); 1 pickoff, 4 balks (3d most in N.L.).

Comments: Allowed one homer in 63⅔ innings at home—an unusually low rate even for the Astrodome. Only two Houston pitchers in the last 10 years had lower home-run rates there (minimum: 50 IP): Mike LaCoss in 1984 (no HR in 70⅓ IP) and Danny Darwin in 1989 (one HR in 72⅔ IP).... Walked 15 batters in the first inning of his 22 starts; teammate Brian Williams was the only N.L. pitcher with a worse rate (13 first-inning walks in 16 starts).... Pitched an average of 5.70 innings per start, 3d lowest in the N.L. (minimum: 20 GS).... The Astros scored more than one run per game more for Jimmy Jones than for Kile, who finished five games below the .500-mark despite posting a 3.95 ERA in 22 starts. Jones had a record of 8–6 in his 23 starts, despite a 4.15 ERA.... Career record is 12–19 with a 3.50 ERA in 44 career starts. His winning percentage (.387) is the lowest of any active pitcher with an ERA below 4.00 (minimum: 40 GS). Only two other active starting pitchers with ERAs lower than Kile's have losing records: Jim Abbott (47–52, 3.49 ERA) and Joe Magrane (43–44, 3.06 ERA).... He's the only N.L. pitcher to average more than 4.50 walks per nine innings in each of the last two seasons (minimum: 100 IP in each). The last N.L. pitcher with rates that high in each of his first two seasons in the majors: Dick Ruthven (1973–74).

Bill Krueger

Throws Left

Twins/Expos	W-L	ERA	AB	H	HR	BB	SO	BA	SA	OBA
Season	10-8	4.53	703	189	18	53	99	.269	.404	.323
vs. Left-Handers			104	32	1	4	13	.308	.442	.345
vs. Right-Handers			599	157	17	49	86	.262	.397	.320
vs. Ground-Ballers			313	89	7	27	42	.284	.419	.343
vs. Fly-Ballers			390	100	11	26	57	.256	.392	.307
Home Games	2-4	4.80	260	69	9	25	42	.265	.427	.334
Road Games	8-4	4.38	443	120	9	28	57	.271	.391	.316
Grass Fields	6-3	4.45	338	88	8	20	47	.260	.393	.301
Artificial Turf	4-5	4.61	365	101	10	33	52	.277	.414	.343
April	4-0	0.84	109	18	1	4	16	.165	.220	.195
May	1-0	3.15	159	41	6	8	25	.258	.409	.298
June	3-2	3.49	146	39	4	11	19	.267	.397	.323
July	1-0	6.20	101	28	2	12	12	.277	.416	.354
August	1-4	9.69	115	40	5	11	14	.348	.574	.406
Sept./Oct.	0-2	6.75	73	23	0	7	13	.315	.397	.383
Leading Off Inn.			181	45	6	7	27	.249	.376	.280
Bases Empty			434	109	10	20	61	.251	.373	.287
Runners On			269	80	8	33	38	.297	.454	.377
Runners/Scor. Pos.			160	45	7	23	27	.281	.469	.373
Runners On/2 Out			115	31	4	20	19	.270	.443	.378
Scor. Pos./2 Out			78	20	3	16	16	.256	.436	.383
Late-Inning Pressure			50	12	1	6	9	.240	.340	.321
Leading Off			15	2	1	2	2	.133	.333	.235
Runners On			10	4	0	2	0	.400	.400	.500
Runners/Scor. Pos.			4	2	0	2	0	.500	.500	.667
First 9 Batters			279	81	9	11	44	.290	.455	.325
Second 9 Batters			221	56	4	22	26	.253	.362	.321
All Batters Thereafter			203	52	5	20	29	.256	.379	.323

Loves to face: Ellis Burks (0-for-14)
Ozzie Guillen (.158, 3-for-19)
Harold Reynolds (.118, 2-for-17, 3 BB)

Hates to face: Mike Devereaux (.476, 10-for-21, 2 HR)
Mike Greenwell (.625, 10-for-16)
Danny Tartabull (.455, 5-for-11, 3 HR)

Miscellaneous statistics: Ground outs-to-air outs ratio: 0.85 last season, 1.05 for career.... Opponents grounded into 13 double plays in 122 opportunities (one per 9.4).... Allowed 37 doubles, 2 triples in 178⅔ innings.... Allowed 17 first-inning runs in 29 starts (4.34 ERA).... Batting support: 5.69 runs per start, highest average in majors.... Opposing base stealers: 22-for-26 (85%); 4 pickoffs, 0 balks.

Comments: Won four times as many games last April as he had in the previous six Aprils *combined*.... Won his first four starts for Minnesota; the last pitcher to start his Twins career with a longer streak was Jerry Koosman (five wins in five starts in 1979).... Threw the first shutout of his career in his second start of the season. He had come within 13 starts of Roy Mahaffey's mark of 128 career starts without a shutout. Only one other pitcher began the 1992 season with at least 100 career starts and no shutouts: Todd Stottlemyre, who recorded his first shutout 12 days after Krueger's. The new leader: Greg A. Harris (98 career starts without a shutout); the runner-up: John Dopson (86).... The longest current streak of starts since a pitcher's last SHO: Danny Cox, 107 (since Aug. 26, 1985); Curt Young, 106 (Oct. 5, 1986); Harris (see previous note); and Danny Jackson, 94 (Sept. 4, 1988).... Started eight games in which he failed to pitch at least five innings last season; only Ricky Bones suffered more early knockouts (9).... Has set career-best marks in walks allowed per nine innings in each of the last two seasons (3.09 in 1991, 2.67 last year).... Last year was the second in which he pitched in both the American and National Leagues in the same season. Sal Maglie did it in four straight seasons (1955–58). Five pitchers did it three times: George Brunet, John Candelaria, Dave LaPoint, Dave Stewart, and Tom Sturdivant.

Charlie Leibrandt — Throws Left

Atlanta Braves	W-L	ERA	AB	H	HR	BB	SO	BA	SA	OBA
Season	15-7	3.36	741	191	9	42	104	.258	.351	.301
vs. Left-Handers			173	39	1	9	25	.225	.266	.273
vs. Right-Handers			568	152	8	33	79	.268	.377	.309
vs. Ground-Ballers			327	84	3	18	41	.257	.355	.297
vs. Fly-Ballers			414	107	6	24	63	.258	.348	.303
Home Games	9-4	3.76	429	114	5	21	55	.266	.347	.304
Road Games	6-3	2.82	312	77	4	21	49	.247	.356	.296
Grass Fields	11-5	3.32	550	144	5	29	69	.262	.340	.301
Artificial Turf	4-2	3.46	191	47	4	13	35	.246	.382	.298
April	2-1	3.05	77	21	0	8	14	.273	.286	.341
May	2-1	5.70	117	36	1	5	12	.308	.436	.339
June	2-1	3.14	115	31	3	8	11	.270	.383	.317
July	2-1	1.67	134	26	1	9	18	.194	.284	.250
August	3-1	2.92	137	29	4	3	23	.212	.350	.232
Sept./Oct.	4-2	3.92	161	48	0	9	26	.298	.354	.339
Leading Off Inn.			195	51	2	5	19	.262	.359	.284
Bases Empty			458	122	4	14	56	.266	.341	.293
Runners On			283	69	5	28	48	.244	.367	.312
Runners/Scor. Pos.			154	37	1	22	30	.240	.318	.328
Runners On/2 Out			129	27	3	17	23	.209	.341	.301
Scor. Pos./2 Out			80	18	1	15	14	.225	.300	.347
Late-Inning Pressure			51	12	0	4	4	.235	.294	.291
Leading Off			14	3	0	0	0	.214	.357	.214
Runners On			16	3	0	4	2	.188	.188	.350
Runners/Scor. Pos.			9	2	0	3	0	.222	.222	.417
First 9 Batters			268	73	2	11	44	.272	.340	.305
Second 9 Batters			245	62	3	17	40	.253	.363	.299
All Batters Thereafter			228	56	4	14	20	.246	.351	.297

Loves to face: Gary Gaetti (.103, 4-for-39, 1 HR, 0 BB)
Alfredo Griffin (.167, 8-for-48)
Mike Pagliarulo (.118, 2-for-17)
Hates to face: Wade Boggs (.388, 19-for-49, 3 HR)
Greg Litton (.545, 6-for-11)
Alan Trammell (.394, 13-for-33, 3 HR)

Miscellaneous statistics: Ground outs-to-air outs ratio: 0.98 last season, 1.15 for career.... Grounded into 6 double plays in 121 opportunities (one per 20, 5th-worst rate in N.L.) ... Allowed 34 doubles, 4 triples in 193 innings.... Allowed 15 first-inning runs in 31 starts (3.48 ERA).... Batting support: 4.16 runs per start.... Opposing base stealers: 28-for-44 (64%); 16 pickoffs (most in majors), 2 balks.

Comments: His loss in the final game of the World Series dropped his career postseason record to 1–7; that .125 winning percentage is the lowest in postseason history among pitchers with more than five decisions.... Ended the 1992 regular season with a scoreless streak of 23 consecutive innings; he can continue that streak in 1993 (regardless of his postseason performance).... One of two pitchers to have thrown at least one shutout in each of the last eight seasons; Roger Clemens has a nine-year streak.... Allowed nine home runs in 193 innings pitched (one per 21.4 innings), the 5th-lowest rate in the National League. The only left-handed batter to homer against him was Fred McGriff.... Walked only five of 201 batters leading off an inning (one every 40.2 BFP), lowest rate in majors.... Had a 3.55 ERA with nine home runs allowed in 157⅓ innings with Greg Olson catching, compared to a 2.52 ERA with no homers in 35⅔ innings caught by Damon Berryhill.... Opposing base runners were caught stealing 16 times with Leibrandt pitching, 2d-highest total in the N.L., behind Dennis Martinez (17).... How often does a pitcher get his team's first hit? Last season, that happened only 29 times in 972 N.L. games—an average of once every 34 games. None occurred in the 7th inning or later; three came in the 6th inning: Leibrandt (vs. Frank Castillo, Apr. 28), Jimmy Jones (vs. Mike Morgan, May 12), and Jose Rijo (vs. Curt Schilling, Aug. 18).

Greg Maddux — Throws Right

Chicago Cubs	W-L	ERA	AB	H	HR	BB	SO	BA	SA	OBA
Season	20-11	2.18	959	201	7	70	199	.210	.279	.272
vs. Left-Handers			563	131	6	51	117	.233	.320	.303
vs. Right-Handers			396	70	1	19	82	.177	.222	.227
vs. Ground-Ballers			424	96	1	26	91	.226	.276	.281
vs. Fly-Ballers			535	105	6	44	108	.196	.282	.266
Home Games	12-4	1.91	485	92	4	36	110	.190	.252	.256
Road Games	8-7	2.47	474	109	3	34	89	.230	.308	.290
Grass Fields	15-8	1.95	695	140	5	49	157	.201	.265	.261
Artificial Turf	5-3	2.74	264	61	2	21	42	.231	.318	.302
April	3-1	2.79	103	23	0	7	18	.223	.252	.283
May	1-4	2.49	155	31	1	14	36	.200	.271	.279
June	5-2	2.45	193	33	1	16	40	.171	.233	.241
July	4-1	1.13	136	29	1	11	26	.213	.279	.270
August	3-2	1.91	198	41	2	13	37	.207	.278	.259
Sept./Oct.	4-1	2.45	174	44	2	9	42	.253	.356	.312
Leading Off Inn.			250	50	2	18	51	.200	.252	.265
Bases Empty			609	120	5	31	126	.197	.253	.243
Runners On			350	81	2	39	73	.231	.326	.320
Runners/Scor. Pos.			211	43	0	30	43	.204	.275	.316
Runners On/2 Out			153	33	1	24	36	.216	.307	.333
Scor. Pos./2 Out			105	21	0	18	23	.200	.257	.333
Late-Inning Pressure			109	26	0	15	20	.239	.275	.333
Leading Off			30	6	0	4	8	.200	.200	.294
Runners On			38	9	0	10	7	.237	.316	.388
Runners/Scor. Pos.			20	5	0	7	5	.250	.300	.429
First 9 Batters			282	49	1	19	58	.174	.213	.238
Second 9 Batters			290	72	3	20	58	.248	.352	.304
All Batters Thereafter			387	80	3	31	83	.207	.274	.275

Loves to face: Charlie Hayes (.087, 2-for-23)
Felix Jose (0-for-16)
Dale Murphy (.059, 2-for-34)
Hates to face: Luis Gonzalez (.409, 9-for-22, 3 HR)
Tony Gwynn (.500, 22-for-44, 0 SO)
Andy Van Slyke (.382, 21-for-55, 4 HR)

Miscellaneous statistics: Ground outs-to-air outs ratio: 2.41 last season (2d highest in majors), 2.00 for career.... Opponents grounded into 19 double plays in 162 opportunities (one per 8.5).... Allowed 36 doubles, 5 triples in 268 innings.... Allowed 9 first-inning runs in 35 starts (2.06 ERA).... Batting support: 3.77 runs per start.... Opposing base stealers: 26-for-39 (67%); 1 pickoff, 0 balks.

Comments: Has won 20 consecutive starts in which his team scored more than three runs, the longest streak of its type since Denny McLain won 24 in a row (1968–69), fueling the majors' last 30-win season.... Allowed one home run per 38.3 innings, the best rate in the National League last season, and the lowest by a Cubs pitcher since 1949, when Dutch Leonard allowed only four home runs in 180 innings (one per 45).... A surprise: It was the 7th time in the last 50 years that a Cubs pitcher led the N.L. in home-run rate. The others: Claude Passeau (1945), Leonard (1949), Bob Rush (1950 and 1954), Rick Reuschel (1977), and Steve Trout (1986).... Has made 208 career starts, the 2d most among active pitchers who've never allowed more than two home runs in a game, behind Danny Jackson (231).... Has led N.L. pitchers in putouts each of the last four seasons, tying the league record held by Grover Cleveland Alexander (1914–17).... Led all major league pitchers with 64 assists, 12 more than runner-up Randy Tomlin.... Becomes the third incumbent 20-game winner to join a defending league champion during the offseason. The others: Sad Sam Jones (23–16 for the Red Sox in 1921, joined the Yankees) and John Smiley (20–8 for the Pirates in 1991, joined the Twins). Some other big winners to go that route: Burleigh Grimes (19–8 for the Giants in 1927, joined the Pirates); Tommy John (17–10 for the Dodgers in 1978; joined the Yankees); Ferguson Jenkins (17–18 for the Rangers in 1975; joined the Red Sox); Eddie Lopat (16–13 for the White Sox in 1947; joined the Yankees).

Dennis Martinez — Montreal Expos   Throws Right

Montreal Expos	W-L	ERA	AB	H	HR	BB	SO	BA	SA	OBA
Season	16-11	2.47	814	172	12	60	147	.211	.287	.271
vs. Left-Handers			503	106	8	34	94	.211	.288	.261
vs. Right-Handers			311	66	4	26	53	.212	.286	.288
vs. Ground-Ballers			370	81	6	25	74	.219	.289	.274
vs. Fly-Ballers			444	91	6	35	73	.205	.286	.269
Home Games	8-4	2.09	408	73	5	28	74	.179	.243	.236
Road Games	8-7	2.85	406	99	7	32	73	.244	.333	.306
Grass Fields	4-4	3.29	194	55	3	17	33	.284	.366	.355
Artificial Turf	12-7	2.22	620	117	9	43	114	.189	.263	.244
April	1-4	2.65	116	20	1	12	20	.172	.233	.258
May	4-0	1.83	124	25	1	8	19	.202	.266	.261
June	3-2	3.51	147	34	3	16	29	.231	.320	.315
July	2-4	3.76	150	41	5	11	27	.273	.413	.329
August	4-0	1.42	134	24	1	7	25	.179	.224	.220
Sept./Oct.	2-1	1.55	143	28	1	6	27	.196	.245	.230
Leading Off Inn.			219	48	4	15	35	.219	.311	.275
Bases Empty			530	109	8	34	92	.206	.285	.259
Runners On			284	63	4	26	55	.222	.292	.294
Runners/Scor. Pos.			165	37	2	15	34	.224	.279	.289
Runners On/2 Out			127	29	2	10	25	.228	.299	.295
Scor. Pos./2 Out			81	17	1	7	17	.210	.272	.281
Late-Inning Pressure			82	16	3	5	13	.195	.317	.275
Leading Off			26	8	1	1	2	.308	.462	.333
Runners On			23	3	2	1	5	.130	.391	.259
Runners/Scor. Pos.			12	2	2	1	2	.167	.667	.231
First 9 Batters			254	50	3	24	57	.197	.256	.269
Second 9 Batters			263	55	2	19	59	.209	.278	.265
All Batters Thereafter			297	67	7	17	31	.226	.323	.280

Loves to face: Jay Bell (.150, 9-for-60)
     Mickey Morandini (.056, 1-for-18)
     Matt Williams (.120, 3-for-25)
Hates to face: Kevin Mitchell (.320, 8-for-25, 5 HR)
     Ryne Sandberg (.355, 22-for-62, 4 HR)
     Don Slaught (.500, 8-for-16)

Miscellaneous statistics: Ground outs-to-air outs ratio: 1.54 last season, 1.23 for career.... Opponents grounded into 9 double plays in 129 opportunities (one per 14).... Allowed 26 doubles, 0 triples in 226⅓ innings.... Allowed 6 first-inning runs in 32 starts (1.13 ERA, 5th lowest in N.L.).... Batting support: 3.88 runs per start.... Opposing base stealers: 22-for-39 (56%); 3 pickoffs, 0 balks.

Comments: Appeared to be through after 1985, the last of three consecutive seasons in which he posted ERAs over 5.00 in at least 100 innings each. *No other pitcher in the last 50 years has had three such seasons consecutively; of the 11 who did it from 1876 to 1941, only one went on to record even 40 more career victories....* Posted a career-low ERA in 1991 and the 2d lowest of his career last season, his 17th in the majors. Only one other pitcher in major league history had his two lowest single-season ERAs (minimum: 20 GS) after having already pitched 15 seasons: Ted Lyons, who compiled a career-low ERA of 2.10 in 1942 at age 41. Others who had their two lowest ERAs at least 12 years into their careers: Tommy Bridges, Jim Bunning, Don Cardwell, Charlie Hough, Dutch Leonard, Joe Niekro, Claude Osteen, Jerry Reuss, Red Ruffing, Ed Whitson, Whitlow Wyatt, Early Wynn, and Cy Young.... Allowed 6.84 hits per nine innings last season, the 4th-lowest rate in the National League.... Opposing base runners were caught stealing 17 times with Martinez on the mound, most of any N.L. pitcher.... He needs 15 more wins in the National League to join Jim Bunning, Fergie Jenkins, Gaylord Perry, Nolan Ryan, and Cy Young as the only pitchers to win at least 100 games in both the National and American Leagues.... The only pitcher in major league history to work at least three innings in both All-Star and postseason play and compiled ERAs above 6.00 in each (6.75 and 6.10, respectively).

Ramon Martinez — Los Angeles Dodgers   Throws Right

Los Angeles Dodgers	W-L	ERA	AB	H	HR	BB	SO	BA	SA	OBA
Season	8-11	4.00	575	141	11	69	101	.245	.362	.331
vs. Left-Handers			316	81	9	54	47	.256	.415	.367
vs. Right-Handers			259	60	2	15	54	.232	.297	.282
vs. Ground-Ballers			252	59	2	33	46	.234	.310	.328
vs. Fly-Ballers			323	82	9	36	55	.254	.402	.333
Home Games	4-7	4.29	354	90	10	42	61	.254	.390	.338
Road Games	4-4	3.55	221	51	1	27	40	.231	.317	.319
Grass Fields	7-7	3.57	453	104	10	52	74	.230	.344	.314
Artificial Turf	1-4	5.76	122	37	1	17	27	.303	.426	.390
April	0-1	3.64	111	27	1	15	13	.243	.315	.339
May	3-0	3.06	135	34	2	18	31	.252	.385	.340
June	1-4	4.33	108	31	2	13	14	.287	.407	.366
July	2-3	4.30	111	26	2	13	23	.234	.342	.315
August	2-3	4.91	110	23	4	10	20	.209	.355	.293
Sept./Oct.	0-0	0.00	0	0	0	0	0	.000	.000	.000
Leading Off Inn.			140	35	4	17	24	.250	.379	.331
Bases Empty			321	76	6	35	54	.237	.358	.316
Runners On			254	65	5	34	47	.256	.366	.349
Runners/Scor. Pos.			155	42	4	21	30	.271	.400	.363
Runners On/2 Out			111	27	3	17	21	.243	.387	.349
Scor. Pos./2 Out			75	22	2	12	12	.293	.440	.398
Late-Inning Pressure			43	11	0	5	6	.256	.349	.333
Leading Off			11	2	0	0	1	.182	.273	.182
Runners On			21	7	0	2	2	.333	.476	.391
Runners/Scor. Pos.			13	3	0	2	1	.231	.308	.333
First 9 Batters			198	43	2	19	32	.217	.298	.292
Second 9 Batters			187	55	6	22	32	.294	.460	.373
All Batters Thereafter			190	43	3	28	37	.226	.332	.329

Loves to face: Craig Biggio (.087, 2-for-23, 1 HR)
     Darrin Jackson (.059, 1-for-17)
     Lonnie Smith (0-for-12)
Hates to face: Will Clark (.368, 14-for-38, 3 HR)
     Delino DeShields (.429, 9-for-21, 1 HR)
     Chris Sabo (.333, 7-for-21, 2 2B, 3 HR)

Miscellaneous statistics: Ground outs-to-air outs ratio: 1.04 last season, 0.84 for career.... Opponents grounded into 7 double plays in 125 opportunities (one per 18).... Allowed 30 doubles, 2 triples in 150⅔ innings.... Allowed 12 first-inning runs in 25 starts (3.60 ERA).... Batting support: 3.60 runs per start.... Opposing base stealers: 19-for-26 (73%); 0 pickoffs, 0 balks.

Comments: Career average of 7.13 strikeouts per nine innings is 3d highest in Dodgers history (minimum: 500 innings), behind Sandy Koufax (9.27) and Jim Brewer (7.37).... Averaged 5.33 strikeouts per nine innings on his first pass through the order last season, 6.26 on his second pass, and 6.57 after that. Only two other N.L. pitchers increased their strikeout rate with each pass last season (minimum: 100 IP): Jose Rijo and Tom Candiotti.... The average time of his nine-inning starts was 2 hours, 55 minutes, 5th longest in the N.L. last season (minimum: 10 GS).... Had a 3.32 ERA in 78⅔ innings with Mike Scioscia catching, compared to 4.75 in 72 innings with Carlos Hernandez behind the plate.... His home-game ERA was 4th highest in the N.L.; he had posted ERAs below 3.00 at Dodger Stadium in each of the previous three seasons.... Started 15 games at Dodger Stadium, allowing an average of one home run every 9.2 innings; allowed only one home run all season in 10 starts on the road (58⅓ IP).... Career record is 28–19 at home, 13–8 on other grass fields, 11–10 on artificial turf.... Over the last three seasons, he's posted a record of 33–15 with a 2.82 ERA in starts in which he recorded more fly outs than ground outs; in starts in which the opposite was true, he was 8–12 record with a 4.39 ERA.... Opponents' batting average has increased every year since his debut in 1988: .216, .219, .221, .229, .245.... Was the youngest opening-day starting pitcher in the majors last season.

Roger Mason
Throws Right

Pittsburgh Pirates	W-L	ERA	AB	H	HR	BB	SO	BA	SA	OBA
Season	5-7	4.09	325	80	11	33	56	.246	.409	.320
vs. Left-Handers			162	35	2	22	26	.216	.333	.306
vs. Right-Handers			163	45	9	11	30	.276	.485	.333
vs. Ground-Ballers			129	33	2	17	15	.256	.380	.347
vs. Fly-Ballers			196	47	9	16	41	.240	.429	.301
Home Games	2-1	3.60	163	39	4	12	26	.239	.368	.292
Road Games	3-6	4.60	162	41	7	21	30	.253	.451	.346
Grass Fields	1-1	3.42	86	20	1	11	11	.233	.326	.330
Artificial Turf	4-6	4.34	239	60	10	22	45	.251	.439	.316
April	1-1	2.45	41	10	1	9	5	.244	.366	.392
May	0-2	3.68	78	17	2	7	11	.218	.346	.287
June	1-0	3.68	57	18	1	3	11	.316	.491	.339
July	0-3	5.23	38	8	3	6	5	.211	.500	.311
August	2-0	5.28	58	15	3	2	9	.259	.414	.306
Sept./Oct.	1-1	4.30	53	12	1	6	15	.226	.377	.305
Leading Off Inn.			76	19	2	5	10	.250	.395	.296
Bases Empty			180	49	5	15	27	.272	.439	.342
Runners On			145	31	6	18	29	.214	.372	.293
Runners/Scor. Pos.			83	19	4	16	18	.229	.422	.340
Runners On/2 Out			66	8	0	7	15	.121	.136	.205
Scor. Pos./2 Out			39	5	0	7	8	.128	.154	.261
Late-Inning Pressure			153	42	7	19	30	.275	.484	.352
Leading Off			39	10	0	4	5	.256	.359	.326
Runners On			70	15	4	11	16	.214	.414	.310
Runners/Scor. Pos.			43	9	3	9	10	.209	.442	.327
First 9 Batters			295	69	10	32	51	.234	.400	.312
Second 9 Batters			19	8	0	1	5	.421	.474	.429
All Batters Thereafter			11	3	1	0	0	.273	.545	.333

Loves to face: Jerald Clark (0-for-5)
Ron Gant (.125, 1-for-8)
Dave Hollins (0-for-6, 4 SO)

Hates to face: John Kruk (.500, 4-for-8, 1 HR)
Ray Lankford (.600, 3-for-5, 2 2B, 1 HR)
Milt Thompson (.462, 6-for-13)

Miscellaneous statistics: Ground outs-to-air outs ratio: 0.88 last season, 0.97 for career.... Opponents grounded into 4 double plays in 71 opportunities (one per 18).... Allowed 14 doubles, 3 triples in 88 innings.... Stranded 33 inherited runners, allowed 9 to score (79%).... Opposing base stealers: 4-for-9 (44%); 1 pickoff, 0 balks.

Comments: We told you in the Xavier Hernandez comments that roughly once each season, a pitcher wins as many as four games against one opponent, all in relief; the same is true for relief losses. It's happened 10 times in the last 15 years; last season, the reliever was Mason and his conqueror was Houston. But it's rare for a reliever to lose to one opponent five times in one year; the last occurrence: Larry Sherry lost five games in relief to the Cardinals in 1960.... Allowed seven home runs in Late-Inning Pressure Situations last season, the most in the National League. Two A.L. pitchers allowed seven: Rick Aguilera and Steve Olin.... Three of those LIPS homers were hit in overtime; no other pitcher allowed as many as three extra-inning homers.... Career ERA is 2.93 in home games, 5.38 on the road. Only two active pitchers have gaps that wide between their home and road marks (minimum: 300 IP): David West (6.93 at home, 4.26 on the road) and Pat Clements (2.60 at home, 5.25 on the road). The funny thing is, all three have moved around quite a bit. Mason has pitched for the Tigers, Giants, Astros, and Pirates, and spent a few days during the offseason on the Mets roster before being moved along to San Diego. Clements has played for the Angels, Pirates, Yankees, Padres, and Orioles in an eight-year career. West pitched for the Mets and Twins, and joined the Phillies last winter. So why do we mention this random spread in their home and road ERAs? A simple reminder that some statistics don't really mean anything; they just are.

Roger McDowell
Throws Right

Los Angeles Dodgers	W-L	ERA	AB	H	HR	BB	SO	BA	SA	OBA
Season	6-10	4.09	337	103	3	42	50	.306	.374	.381
vs. Left-Handers			154	49	3	30	20	.318	.422	.428
vs. Right-Handers			183	54	0	12	30	.295	.333	.337
vs. Ground-Ballers			129	40	2	22	18	.310	.395	.412
vs. Fly-Ballers			208	63	1	20	32	.303	.361	.361
Home Games	2-2	2.92	146	41	0	12	27	.281	.322	.333
Road Games	4-8	5.01	191	62	3	30	23	.325	.414	.415
Grass Fields	5-8	4.01	271	83	3	30	38	.306	.380	.375
Artificial Turf	1-2	4.41	66	20	0	12	12	.303	.348	.405
April	3-2	1.59	36	7	0	6	9	.194	.194	.302
May	0-3	3.52	57	18	1	5	11	.316	.386	.371
June	1-1	3.86	37	10	0	7	4	.270	.297	.378
July	0-1	4.26	52	15	1	4	14	.288	.404	.333
August	1-1	6.89	75	28	1	7	5	.373	.440	.427
Sept./Oct.	1-2	3.72	80	25	0	13	7	.313	.400	.415
Leading Off Inn.			75	25	0	5	12	.333	.387	.375
Bases Empty			154	48	0	12	22	.312	.351	.365
Runners On			183	55	3	30	28	.301	.393	.394
Runners/Scor. Pos.			128	34	2	29	21	.266	.359	.394
Runners On/2 Out			77	21	2	16	14	.273	.390	.398
Scor. Pos./2 Out			60	17	1	16	10	.283	.383	.434
Late-Inning Pressure			193	52	2	23	30	.269	.337	.345
Leading Off			43	14	0	4	8	.326	.349	.383
Runners On			104	28	2	15	18	.269	.375	.352
Runners/Scor. Pos.			78	22	1	15	12	.282	.372	.385
First 9 Batters			311	93	3	38	47	.299	.373	.374
Second 9 Batters			24	9	0	3	3	.375	.375	.444
All Batters Thereafter			2	1	0	1	0	.500	.500	.667

Loves to face: Steve Buechele (0-for-6)
Andres Galarraga (.150, 3-for-20)
Gerald Young (0-for-12)

Hates to face: Bobby Bonilla (.462, 6-for-13, 6 BB)
Terry Pendleton (.375, 12-for-32, 4 HR)
Andy Van Slyke (.478, 11-for-23, 2 HR)

Miscellaneous statistics: Ground outs-to-air outs ratio: 2.96 last season, 2.95 for career.... Opponents grounded into 9 double plays in 98 opportunities (one per 11).... Allowed 10 doubles, 2 triples in 83⅔ innings.... Saved 14 games in 25 opportunities (56%).... Stranded 26 inherited runners, allowed 10 to score (72%).... Opposing base stealers: 3-for-5 (60%); 0 pickoffs, 1 balk.

Comments: Career ground outs-to-air outs ratio (2.95) is the highest among active pitchers (minimum: 1000 BFP). Strange, then, that his average of one double-play grounder for every 11 opportunities was below the league average.... Batting average by opposing right-handers was 2d highest in N.L. (minimum: 200 BFPs vs. RH batters); Tom Browning (.307) led.... Opponents' batting average and slugging average, as well as rate of walks allowed (4.52 per nine innings), were all the highest of his career.... Led team with six relief wins. The L.A. bullpen won only 15 games last year, 2d fewest in the majors; Seattle (14) brought up the rear.... His career home-run rate—one allowed every 24.13 innings—stands 2d lowest among active pitchers (minimum: 500 IP), behind Joe Magrane (one every 25.16). If we drop the minimum to 300 innings, then Gregg Olson (one every 33.93 innings), Steve Howe (one every 29.98), and Juan Guzman (one every 26.61) rank one-two-three.... Did not allow a home run in 39⅓ innings with Mike Scioscia catching, the most innings any N.L. battery worked together without allowing a homer last year.... Has allowed only two homers to right-handed batters since 1988 (his last full year in New York). Both were hit in 1991, by renowned sluggers Rick Cerone and Javier Ortiz.... Dodgers allowed the fewest home runs in N.L. for the second straight year, the first time they have led two years in a row since 1910–11 in Brooklyn. See, Tommy, if we looked long enough, we knew we'd find a silver lining.

Chuck McElroy — Throws Left

Chicago Cubs	W-L	ERA	AB	H	HR	BB	SO	BA	SA	OBA
Season	4-7	3.55	308	73	5	51	83	.237	.367	.341
vs. Left-Handers			102	28	2	12	30	.275	.422	.345
vs. Right-Handers			206	45	3	39	53	.218	.340	.339
vs. Ground-Ballers			138	39	1	18	36	.283	.428	.358
vs. Fly-Ballers			170	34	4	33	47	.200	.318	.327
Home Games	3-4	3.64	154	36	3	20	43	.234	.357	.313
Road Games	1-3	3.46	154	37	2	31	40	.240	.377	.368
Grass Fields	3-4	3.36	217	49	4	29	56	.226	.350	.311
Artificial Turf	1-3	4.01	91	24	1	22	27	.264	.407	.407
April	1-0	0.82	36	4	0	8	12	.111	.111	.267
May	1-3	4.60	61	16	0	9	17	.262	.361	.357
June	1-1	0.96	33	7	1	5	9	.212	.424	.316
July	0-2	3.50	63	14	1	9	14	.222	.365	.311
August	1-0	3.95	54	15	2	6	10	.278	.444	.350
Sept./Oct.	0-1	5.63	61	17	1	14	21	.279	.426	.403
Leading Off Inn.			70	17	0	6	22	.243	.343	.303
Bases Empty			159	39	4	16	44	.245	.415	.314
Runners On			149	34	1	35	39	.228	.315	.365
Runners/Scor. Pos.			96	24	1	27	27	.250	.375	.398
Runners On/2 Out			72	16	1	15	18	.222	.347	.356
Scor. Pos./2 Out			51	12	1	12	13	.235	.412	.381
Late-Inning Pressure			126	37	1	26	39	.294	.437	.409
Leading Off			32	10	0	3	11	.313	.469	.371
Runners On			61	18	0	18	19	.295	.393	.444
Runners/Scor. Pos.			40	11	0	15	14	.275	.400	.456
First 9 Batters			305	71	4	50	83	.233	.351	.336
Second 9 Batters			3	2	1	1	0	.667	2.000	.750
All Batters Thereafter			0	0	0	0	0	—	—	—

Loves to face: Andres Galarraga (0-for-6, 4 SO)
Hal Morris (0-for-7, 5 SO)
Ozzie Smith (0-for-9)

Hates to face: Jay Bell (.625, 5-for-8, 1 HR)
Brett Butler (.500, 3-for-6, 6 BB, 2 SO)
Ken Caminiti (.750, 6-for-8, 1 HR)

Miscellaneous statistics: Ground outs-to-air outs ratio: 0.78 last season, 0.96 for career. . . . Opponents grounded into 2 double plays in 73 opportunities (one per 37). . . . Allowed 19 doubles, 3 triples in 83⅔ innings. . . . Stranded 32 inherited runners, allowed 15 to score (68%). . . . Opposing base stealers: 4-for-7 (57%); 0 pickoffs, 0 balks.

Comments: He did something unusual on April 11: Entering the game in relief, he not only had two at-bats, but picked up two hits. That was the only case last season in which a reliever had two hits in game. Relievers get so few at-bats that very few have been able to produce any memorable moments as hitters. Terry Forster was an exception; with the White Sox in 1972, he pitched in 62 games in relief and batted .526 (10-for-19). Three relief pitchers went McElroy one better and hit two home runs in a game: Detroit's Jess Doyle in 1925 and Babe Birrer in 1955, and Dixie Howell of the White Sox in 1957. And can late-night cable addicts ever forget Atlanta reliever Rick Camp homering in the 18th inning to extend what would be the latest-finishing game in major league history, the Mets-Braves game of July 4–5, 1985?. . .Has pitched 209⅓ innings in the majors and has never hit a batter, nor has he balked. He's the only active pitcher with that many innings who hasn't nailed anyone; Mark Guthrie (375 innings) is the only other active left-hander with as many innings who has never balked. . . . Has averaged 5.25 walks per nine innings; he's one of seven active pitchers with a career rate of more than five walks per nine innings (minimum: 200 innings). . . . His 1.53 ERA at Wrigley Field in 1991 was then the lowest single-season ERA by any pitcher there in 10 years (minimum: 50 innings). But Mike Morgan topped it last season, when he led the N.L. with a 1.38 ERA in home games. And now, for more on Morgan. . . .

Mike Morgan — Throws Right

Chicago Cubs	W-L	ERA	AB	H	HR	BB	SO	BA	SA	OBA
Season	16-8	2.55	868	203	14	79	123	.234	.334	.298
vs. Left-Handers			489	122	8	57	56	.249	.356	.330
vs. Right-Handers			379	81	6	22	67	.214	.306	.256
vs. Ground-Ballers			410	87	3	33	53	.212	.268	.274
vs. Fly-Ballers			458	116	11	46	70	.253	.393	.320
Home Games	9-2	1.38	459	100	3	40	62	.218	.288	.279
Road Games	7-6	3.94	409	103	11	39	61	.252	.386	.319
Grass Fields	13-3	1.85	613	141	9	50	81	.230	.325	.288
Artificial Turf	3-5	4.26	255	62	5	29	42	.243	.357	.323
April	0-2	5.63	88	23	1	14	16	.261	.352	.369
May	5-0	2.32	159	34	2	15	25	.214	.302	.282
June	2-0	1.93	131	31	2	12	17	.237	.351	.297
July	2-2	1.18	139	31	1	11	25	.223	.302	.285
August	4-2	2.11	174	51	3	15	22	.293	.391	.349
Sept./Oct.	3-2	3.18	177	33	5	12	18	.186	.311	.237
Leading Off Inn.			222	47	0	21	27	.212	.261	.283
Bases Empty			532	123	4	41	72	.231	.310	.289
Runners On			336	80	10	38	51	.238	.372	.313
Runners/Scor. Pos.			174	39	3	32	39	.224	.310	.340
Runners On/2 Out			130	26	5	21	16	.200	.354	.311
Scor. Pos./2 Out			79	15	2	18	12	.190	.304	.340
Late-Inning Pressure			61	12	0	3	8	.197	.262	.234
Leading Off			16	1	0	1	0	.063	.063	.118
Runners On			18	1	0	1	4	.056	.111	.105
Runners/Scor. Pos.			9	0	0	0	3	.000	.000	.000
First 9 Batters			279	54	1	21	50	.194	.240	.252
Second 9 Batters			271	69	7	31	36	.255	.391	.333
All Batters Thereafter			318	80	6	27	37	.252	.368	.308

Loves to face: Vince Coleman (.105, 2-for-19)
Kirt Manwaring (.050, 1-for-20)
Greg Olson (0-for-11)

Hates to face: Brett Butler (.429, 18-for-42, 0 SO)
Will Clark (.400, 10-for-25, 4 2B, 1 3B, 7 BB)
David Hollins (.400, 8-for-20, 3 2B, 2 HR)

Miscellaneous statistics: Ground outs-to-air outs ratio: 1.76 last season (4th highest in N.L.), 1.82 for career. . . . Opponents grounded into 29 double plays in 178 opportunities (one per 6.1), 5th-best rate in N.L. . . . Allowed 39 doubles, 3 triples in 240 innings. . . . Allowed 8 first-inning runs in 34 starts (0.53 ERA, 2d lowest in majors). . . . Batting support: 4.06 runs per start. . . . Opposing base stealers: 6-for-15 (40%), 5th-lowest rate in N.L.; 1 pickoff, 0 balks.

Comments: What are the chances that a pitcher with a career 53–94 won-lost record—that's 41 games below .500—and a 4.37 ERA would turn around to produce consecutive winning seasons with ERAs below 3.00 each year? No starting pitcher had done that since the leagues began to keep track of ERAs in the second decade of this century. And Morgan didn't just meet those specs by the skin of his teeth; he went 14–10 and 16–8 with 2.78 and 2.55 ERAs. . . . Remember, this is the chap who never had a winning season over his first 10 years in the majors; even after the last two years, he still stands 29 games in the red. . . . He has added at least two wins to his season totals in each of the last four years. Only two pitchers in major league history have done that for five straight years: Phil Niekro (1965–69) and Mario Soto (1979–83). Jack McDowell also enters 1993 with a four-year streak. Morgan's winning percentage has also increased in each of the last four years. No pitcher has had a longer streak in seasons of at least 15 decisions since Bobo Newsom, 1936–40. . . . Induced 29 double-play grounders to lead N.L. . . . Morgan and Greg Maddux went 36–19 in 69 starts; their rotation mates went 23–37 in 93 starts and the relief pitchers went 19–28. . . . Has balked only twice in 1625⅓ career innings pitched, the lowest rate among active pitchers (minimum: 500 innings). . . . Has struck out only 4.34 batters per nine innings in his career, 4th-lowest rate among active pitchers with 1500 innings.

Terry Mulholland — Throws Left

Philadelphia Phillies	W-L	ERA	AB	H	HR	BB	SO	BA	SA	OBA
Season	13-11	3.81	871	227	14	46	125	.261	.365	.298
vs. Left-Handers			161	34	4	11	25	.211	.342	.263
vs. Right-Handers			710	193	10	35	100	.272	.370	.306
vs. Ground-Ballers			315	69	3	16	51	.219	.286	.258
vs. Fly-Ballers			556	158	11	30	74	.284	.410	.320
Home Games	9-6	3.63	557	145	9	31	78	.260	.368	.297
Road Games	4-5	4.14	314	82	5	15	47	.261	.360	.298
Grass Fields	1-2	5.93	105	30	4	6	22	.286	.438	.324
Artificial Turf	12-9	3.53	766	197	10	40	103	.257	.355	.294
April	0-3	7.28	120	34	3	13	24	.283	.408	.351
May	5-1	2.16	191	49	2	9	23	.257	.325	.297
June	3-0	2.79	137	28	2	7	19	.204	.299	.241
July	3-3	2.47	186	44	5	2	28	.237	.366	.243
August	1-1	5.76	122	40	1	8	11	.328	.426	.361
Sept./Oct.	1-3	4.80	115	32	1	7	20	.278	.400	.323
Leading Off Inn.			224	60	4	9	29	.268	.366	.299
Bases Empty			535	138	8	18	70	.258	.355	.283
Runners On			336	89	6	28	55	.265	.381	.319
Runners/Scor. Pos.			171	59	3	15	28	.345	.480	.387
Runners On/2 Out			134	30	1	8	20	.224	.291	.273
Scor. Pos./2 Out			72	22	0	7	11	.306	.333	.375
Late-Inning Pressure			95	27	1	2	9	.284	.411	.299
Leading Off			26	6	0	0	2	.231	.269	.231
Runners On			33	12	1	1	7	.364	.545	.382
Runners/Scor. Pos.			15	8	0	1	3	.533	.733	.563
First 9 Batters			268	66	7	15	42	.246	.377	.283
Second 9 Batters			262	72	2	15	43	.275	.340	.317
All Batters Thereafter			341	89	5	16	40	.261	.375	.294

Loves to face: Darrin Jackson (.087, 2-for-23, 1 3B)
Geronimo Pena (0-for-9)
Craig Wilson (0-for-9)

Hates to face: Barry Bonds (.321, 9-for-28, 2 2B, 5 HR)
Fred McGriff (.500, 11-for-22, 3 HR)
Ryne Sandberg (.333, 15-for-45, 6 HR)

Miscellaneous statistics: Ground outs-to-air outs ratio: 1.09 last season, 1.18 for career.... Opponents grounded into 14 double plays in 184 opportunities (one per 13).... Allowed 43 doubles (2d most in N.L.), 3 triples in 229 innings.... Allowed 16 first-inning runs in 32 starts (3.94 ERA).... Batting support: 4.63 runs per start, 2d-highest average in N.L.... Opposing base stealers: 2-for-7 (29%); 16 pickoffs (most in majors), 0 balks.

Comments: Became only the fourth Phillies pitcher to lead N.L. in complete games (12); none of the others was a one-termer: Grover Alexander and Robin Roberts did it five times and Steve Carlton three times.... Mulholland won nine of those 12 CGs; the overall won-lost record for major league pitchers throwing complete games last season was 300–119 (.716).... Had worst ERA among N.L. pitchers in April, but tied for major league high in wins in May.... Averaged 1.81 walks per nine innings, 4th-best rate in N.L. Walked only two of 99 batters faced in Late-Inning Pressure Situations, compared to one every 19 batters at other times.... Since joining the Phillies, he owns a 25–15 record at the Vet, 17–26 on the road; career numbers: 11–21 in day games, 34–28 at night.... Has made 126 career starts and has never allowed more than two home runs in any of them; the only active pitchers with more starts without a three-gong job: Danny Jackson (231), Greg Maddux (208), and Kevin Brown (127).... His Achilles' heel: pitching with runners in scoring position. He allowed the highest opponents' batting average in N.L. in those situations in 1992; he and Walt Terrell are the only major league pitchers against whom opponents have hit .300 or better at those times in three of the past four years (minimum: 100 at-bats each year with RISP). Mulholland has allowed a .290 career average with runners in scoring position; the only active pitchers who have allowed higher averages (minimum: 100 starts) are Jimmy Jones (.308) and Bruce Ruffin (.301).

Randy Myers — Throws Left

San Diego Padres	W-L	ERA	AB	H	HR	BB	SO	BA	SA	OBA
Season	3-6	4.29	301	84	7	34	66	.279	.402	.349
vs. Left-Handers			63	17	0	13	20	.270	.365	.390
vs. Right-Handers			238	67	7	21	46	.282	.412	.337
vs. Ground-Ballers			127	32	2	10	26	.252	.315	.304
vs. Fly-Ballers			174	52	5	24	40	.299	.466	.379
Home Games	2-3	4.58	158	46	4	14	31	.291	.411	.347
Road Games	1-3	4.02	143	38	3	20	35	.266	.392	.351
Grass Fields	3-3	3.49	219	56	5	21	45	.256	.361	.318
Artificial Turf	0-3	6.64	82	28	2	13	21	.341	.512	.424
April	1-1	5.02	57	18	1	5	14	.316	.404	.371
May	1-0	6.17	45	13	0	6	11	.289	.400	.365
June	0-1	7.20	41	14	3	5	8	.341	.610	.417
July	0-1	1.50	43	9	1	9	8	.209	.326	.346
August	0-1	2.31	42	9	1	2	11	.214	.310	.239
Sept./Oct.	1-2	4.05	73	21	1	7	14	.288	.384	.346
Leading Off Inn.			57	19	2	5	14	.333	.491	.387
Bases Empty			136	40	4	12	28	.294	.426	.351
Runners On			165	44	3	22	38	.267	.382	.347
Runners/Scor. Pos.			101	26	0	15	19	.257	.307	.344
Runners On/2 Out			71	16	0	15	13	.225	.282	.360
Scor. Pos./2 Out			51	11	0	9	8	.216	.255	.333
Late-Inning Pressure			243	68	6	28	55	.280	.403	.348
Leading Off			45	17	2	5	10	.378	.578	.440
Runners On			134	36	3	19	34	.269	.381	.348
Runners/Scor. Pos.			86	23	0	14	17	.267	.302	.352
First 9 Batters			292	81	6	33	63	.277	.394	.347
Second 9 Batters			9	3	1	1	3	.333	.667	.400
All Batters Thereafter			0	0	0	0	0			

Loves to face: Craig Biggio (.071, 1-for-14)
Eddie Murray (.118, 2-for-17, 2 BB)
Andy Van Slyke (.161, 5-for-31)

Hates to face: Jeff Bagwell (.455, 5-for-11, 3 2B, 2 HR)
Kevin Bass (.385, 5-for-13, 2 HR)
Bobby Bonilla (.429, 9-for-21, 1 HR)

Miscellaneous statistics: Ground outs-to-air outs ratio: 0.82 last season, 0.76 for career.... Opponents grounded into 6 double plays in 85 opportunities (one per 14).... Allowed 16 doubles, 0 triples in 79⅔ innings.... Saved 38 games in 46 opportunities (83%), 4th-highest rate in N.L.... Stranded 24 inherited runners, allowed 16 to score (60%).... Opposing base stealers: 2-for-5 (40%); 1 pickoff, 0 balks.

Comments: Low ERAs for relief pitchers can be misleading; a high ERA is not. That's why it's odd to see a career high for Myers in both ERA and saves (38).... That's the most saves ever accumulated by a pitcher with an ERA above 4.00; only one other pitcher had even 30 saves in a season with an ERA that high: Jeff Reardon (31 saves, 4.48 ERA in 1987; 31 saves, 4.07 ERA in 1989).... He was charged with at least one run in nine of the games he saved, the most such saves since Dan Quisenberry had 10 in 1984.... Led majors with 23 saves after the All-Star break. He had saves in 10 straight appearances starting on July 20, the longest streak of his career.... His most enjoyable saves may have been his five vs. Cincinnati, his old team; no other pitcher had more than three against the Reds.... Increase from six saves (in 1991) to 38 was the 4th-largest one-season increase in history; Jeff Russell (0 to 38, 1988–89), John Wetteland (0 to 37, 1991–92), and John Hiller (3 to 38, 1972–73) had larger increases.... Opponents' on-base percentage leading off innings in Late-Inning Pressure Situations (.440) was the 2d highest over the past 18 years (minimum: 50 batters faced); Duane Ward had the highest (.441) in 1989.... Opponents' batting average has risen by more than 35 points in each of last two seasons (from .193 to .242 to .279); that hasn't happened to any N.L. pitcher since Jeff D. Robinson in 1988–89.... Annual batting average by opposing left-handed batters since 1987: .175, .180, .164, .181, then .287 and .270 the last two years.

Chris Nabholz — Throws Left

Montreal Expos

	W-L	ERA	AB	H	HR	BB	SO	BA	SA	OBA
Season	11-12	3.32	722	176	11	74	130	.244	.349	.317
vs. Left-Handers			134	35	3	12	35	.261	.358	.329
vs. Right-Handers			588	141	8	62	95	.240	.347	.314
vs. Ground-Ballers			285	62	2	23	57	.218	.305	.278
vs. Fly-Ballers			437	114	9	51	73	.261	.378	.341
Home Games	5-7	3.09	355	79	5	31	59	.223	.332	.291
Road Games	6-5	3.56	367	97	6	43	71	.264	.365	.341
Grass Fields	2-4	4.22	187	51	2	16	32	.273	.374	.327
Artificial Turf	9-8	3.02	535	125	9	58	98	.234	.340	.313
April	1-2	3.62	105	26	1	14	20	.248	.333	.347
May	2-2	4.65	112	24	2	13	21	.214	.339	.299
June	2-2	3.26	115	27	0	15	31	.235	.330	.328
July	1-1	3.58	118	33	3	11	17	.280	.390	.346
August	3-2	2.18	147	33	4	13	20	.224	.333	.287
Sept./Oct.	2-3	3.06	125	33	1	8	21	.264	.368	.301
Leading Off Inn.			187	48	4	20	36	.257	.374	.332
Bases Empty			417	101	6	43	69	.242	.353	.320
Runners On			305	75	5	31	61	.246	.344	.312
Runners/Scor. Pos.			158	41	1	21	37	.259	.348	.339
Runners On/2 Out			124	34	2	14	28	.274	.363	.348
Scor. Pos./2 Out			83	21	1	11	21	.253	.313	.340
Late-Inning Pressure			43	14	1	3	4	.326	.442	.370
Leading Off			15	6	0	1	0	.400	.467	.438
Runners On			15	2	0	2	1	.133	.133	.235
Runners/Scor. Pos.			5	1	0	1	2	.200	.200	.333
First 9 Batters			254	55	4	24	60	.217	.319	.289
Second 9 Batters			261	64	5	20	44	.245	.349	.300
All Batters Thereafter			207	57	2	30	26	.275	.386	.370

Loves to face: Ken Caminiti (0-for-13)
Will Clark (0-for-12)
Tony Fernandez (0-for-12)
Hates to face: Ray Lankford (.500, 8-for-16)
Fred McGriff (.625, 5-for-8, 2 HR)
Chris Sabo (.538, 7-for-13, 3 2B, 1 3B, 2 HR)

Miscellaneous statistics: Ground outs-to-air outs ratio: 1.51 last season, 1.17 for career.... Opponents grounded into 21 double plays in 154 opportunities (one per 7.3).... Allowed 29 doubles, 7 triples in 195 innings.... Allowed 11 first-inning runs in 32 starts (2.81 ERA).... Batting support: 4.13 runs per start.... Opposing base stealers: 23-for-29 (79%); 6 pickoffs, 1 balk.

Comments: His 23 decisions were the most among major league pitchers who did not have either a winning streak or a losing streak of more than two games last season. In fact, his last 16 decisions of the season followed a win-loss-win-loss pattern exclusively. We checked back to 1958 and did not find another win-loss-win-loss pattern that extended for 16 decisions in a single season; overlapping two seasons, we found only one: Chuck Finley went win-loss-win-loss for 16 straight decisions in 1991–92. For those of you looking for Nabholz to continue his pattern into 1993, he's due to win his next decision.... But prior to last year, Nabholz was Mr. Streak himself, with 21 of his 23 major league decisions connected to either a winning streak or a losing streak of at least four games in length.... He's the only active pitcher whose career ERA, broken down by months, gets lower with each passing month: April, 4.08; May, 4.07; June, 3.81; July, 3.58; August, 3.10; September, 2.65.... Has pitched 418⅔ innings in majors across three seasons, all with Montreal; it's an indication of the Expos' recent catching woes that he has not yet pitched 100 innings to any one catcher. He threw 89 innings to Darrin Fletcher last year, and Fletcher immediately moved to the top of the list; Nabholz has also thrown 80⅔ innings to Gary Carter, 76⅔ to Mike Fitzgerald, 62⅔ to Gilberto Reyes, 58⅔ to Nelson Santovenia, 17⅔ to Jerry Goff, 14⅓ to Rick Cerone, 11 to Tim Laker, and eight to Orlando Mercado.

Bob Ojeda — Throws Left

Los Angeles Dodgers

	W-L	ERA	AB	H	HR	BB	SO	BA	SA	OBA
Season	6-9	3.63	631	169	8	81	94	.268	.371	.349
vs. Left-Handers			116	25	1	13	27	.216	.276	.290
vs. Right-Handers			515	144	7	68	67	.280	.392	.362
vs. Ground-Ballers			271	68	2	29	46	.251	.321	.321
vs. Fly-Ballers			360	101	6	52	48	.281	.408	.368
Home Games	4-2	2.40	307	81	2	36	44	.264	.340	.340
Road Games	2-7	4.84	324	88	6	45	50	.272	.414	.357
Grass Fields	4-6	3.22	463	124	6	59	66	.268	.356	.349
Artificial Turf	2-3	4.78	168	45	2	22	28	.268	.411	.347
April	1-2	4.01	95	29	3	15	15	.305	.495	.400
May	2-1	2.60	95	19	0	18	12	.200	.263	.330
June	1-1	4.23	108	29	3	15	22	.269	.426	.355
July	1-1	2.48	129	34	1	10	15	.264	.333	.314
August	1-1	3.41	105	26	0	13	19	.248	.295	.325
Sept./Oct.	0-3	5.47	99	32	1	10	11	.323	.424	.378
Leading Off Inn.			157	29	5	15	25	.185	.331	.256
Bases Empty			362	93	7	35	54	.257	.370	.324
Runners On			269	76	1	46	40	.283	.372	.379
Runners/Scor. Pos.			167	45	1	38	30	.269	.383	.392
Runners On/2 Out			117	30	1	23	18	.256	.333	.379
Scor. Pos./2 Out			84	21	1	17	15	.250	.357	.376
Late-Inning Pressure			15	5	0	4	4	.333	.333	.474
Leading Off			4	0	0	0	1	.000	.000	.000
Runners On			6	2	0	3	1	.333	.333	.556
Runners/Scor. Pos.			5	1	0	2	1	.200	.200	.429
First 9 Batters			234	53	4	20	40	.226	.329	.285
Second 9 Batters			215	53	3	28	28	.247	.358	.331
All Batters Thereafter			182	63	1	33	26	.346	.440	.444

Loves to face: Roberto Alomar (.176, 3-for-17)
Bill Doran (.111, 2-for-18)
Kent Hrbek (.167, 3-for-18)
Hates to face: Carlton Fisk (.391, 9-for-23, 3 HR)
Lou Whitaker (.440, 11-for-25, 5 2B, 1 3B)
Dave Winfield (.450, 9-for-20, 3 2B, 1 3B)

Miscellaneous statistics: Ground outs-to-air outs ratio: 1.24 last season, 1.13 for career.... Opponents grounded into 15 double plays in 134 opportunities (one per 8.9).... Allowed 29 doubles, 6 triples in 166⅓ innings.... Allowed 16 first-inning runs in 29 starts (3.72 ERA).... Batting support: 3.72 runs per start.... Opposing base stealers: 20-for-35 (57%); 9 pickoffs (3d most in N.L.), 0 balks.

Comments: Received no decision in 14 of his 29 starts, the highest rate of no-decision starts for any N.L. pitcher with at least 20 starts last season.... Pitched almost 75 percent of the 258⅓ innings thrown by Dodgers left-handers last season, the fewest innings by lefties on any N.L. team.... Issued 81 walks, second most in N.L.; David Cone walked 82 before heading north.... Opponents' on-base percentage leading off innings was 4th lowest among N.L. pitchers, behind Bob Tewksbury (.225), Curt Schilling (.237), and Sid Fernandez (.256).... Has 13–17 career record in April, his only sub-.500 month; his best work has come in September (26–16), despite 0–3 mark last year.... ERA was 2.92 in 49⅓ innings with Carlos Hernandez catching, 3.92 in 177 innings with either Mike Scioscia or Mike Piazza. However, the Ojeda-Scioscia battery allowed only 10 steals in 22 attempts; with other catchers, Ojeda allowed 10 in 13 tries.... In all, opposing base runners were caught stealing 15 times with Ojeda on the mound, a total exceeded by only two N.L. pitchers, Dennis Martinez (17) and Charlie Leibrandt (16). Eight runners were caught stealing on pickoffs, a scoring rule that is often misunderstood. If a runner is picked off and retired without attempting to advance from his original base, he is not caught stealing; but if he is put out after a pickoff, either trying to advance a base or in a rundown trying to return to his original base, he is caught stealing. Either way, the pitcher is credited with a pickoff.

Omar Olivares

St. Louis Cardinals   Throws Right

St. Louis Cardinals	W-L	ERA	AB	H	HR	BB	SO	BA	SA	OBA
Season	9-9	3.84	736	189	20	63	124	.257	.394	.316
vs. Left-Handers			425	122	13	40	64	.287	.454	.347
vs. Right-Handers			311	67	7	23	60	.215	.312	.272
vs. Ground-Ballers			368	91	10	23	74	.247	.383	.295
vs. Fly-Ballers			368	98	10	40	50	.266	.405	.336
Home Games	5-6	3.96	450	113	12	36	77	.251	.391	.310
Road Games	4-3	3.64	286	76	8	27	47	.266	.399	.326
Grass Fields	3-2	3.92	164	42	4	19	29	.256	.384	.332
Artificial Turf	6-7	3.82	572	147	16	44	95	.257	.397	.312
April	2-2	3.65	136	33	2	9	20	.243	.338	.295
May	0-1	7.20	80	23	6	7	12	.287	.575	.352
June	2-0	1.95	94	17	2	13	14	.181	.319	.275
July	2-3	3.41	128	34	5	8	17	.266	.461	.312
August	2-2	3.43	149	41	2	16	27	.275	.349	.341
Sept./Oct.	1-1	4.42	149	41	3	10	34	.275	.383	.321
Leading Off Inn.			195	59	5	9	20	.303	.441	.337
Bases Empty			450	119	10	36	72	.264	.382	.323
Runners On			286	70	10	27	52	.245	.413	.305
Runners/Scor. Pos.			152	30	5	17	26	.197	.336	.271
Runners On/2 Out			115	24	2	12	17	.209	.339	.289
Scor. Pos./2 Out			67	7	0	7	9	.104	.149	.200
Late-Inning Pressure			64	19	2	8	13	.297	.469	.375
Leading Off			16	6	0	3	2	.375	.438	.474
Runners On			32	9	2	2	7	.281	.531	.324
Runners/Scor. Pos.			15	3	1	2	4	.200	.400	.294
First 9 Batters			249	61	10	23	44	.245	.410	.314
Second 9 Batters			242	60	6	15	48	.248	.355	.290
All Batters Thereafter			245	68	4	25	32	.278	.416	.343

Loves to face: Wes Chamberlain (0-for-9)
Tony Gwynn (0-for-10)
Tim Wallach (.091, 2-for-22)
Hates to face: Ron Gant (.600, 6-for-10, 2 2B, 2 HR)
Terry Pendleton (.538, 7-for-13, 1 HR)
Dwight Smith (.500, 7-for-14, 3 2B, 1 3B, 1 HR)

Miscellaneous statistics: Ground outs-to-air outs ratio: 1.49 last season, 1.39 for career.... Opponents grounded into 16 double plays in 144 opportunities (one per 9.0).... Allowed 35 doubles, 3 triples in 197 innings.... Allowed 15 first-inning runs in 30 starts (4.50 ERA).... Batting support: 3.83 runs per start.... Opposing base stealers: 11-for-24 (46%); 3 pickoffs, 0 balks.

Comments: A triple threat who can pitch, hit, and field.... Had the 3d-highest batting average (.231, 15-for-65) by any N.L. pitcher last season (minimum: 40 plate appearances), behind Dwight Gooden (.264) and Tom Glavine (.247).... Led all major league pitchers in fielding, handling 55 chances without an error last season.... His good glovework must be contagious: His teammates made only five errors in the 197 innings he pitched last season; he did not allow an unearned run all season.... In 18 starts last year in which he recorded more ground outs than air outs, he had a 7–2 record and 2.69 ERA; in 11 starts in which the opposite was true, he went 2–6 with a 6.35 ERA.... Allowed 20 home runs, tying Kyle Abbott for 3d most in league.... Allowed more home runs to left-handed batters than any N.L. pitcher.... In each of previous two years, opposing right-handed batters had hit for a higher average than left-handed batters; career breakdown: .256 by lefty batters, .244 by righties; .228 by ground-ball hitters, .270 by fly-ball hitters.... Career numbers: 2–5, 4.96 ERA in day games, 19–12, 3.28 ERA at night.... Has completed only one of 60 career starts.... Omar's father, Ed, had 35 at-bats with the Cardinals in 1960–61. He had led the Carolina League with 35 home runs and 125 RBIs for Winston-Salem in 1960, but he drove in only one run in his brief major league career. (At least it was off a Hall of Famer, Warren Spahn, and it drove in a future National League president, Bill White!)

Donovan Osborne

St. Louis Cardinals   Throws Left

St. Louis Cardinals	W-L	ERA	AB	H	HR	BB	SO	BA	SA	OBA
Season	11-9	3.77	703	193	14	38	104	.275	.404	.312
vs. Left-Handers			151	48	3	8	23	.318	.464	.348
vs. Right-Handers			552	145	11	30	81	.263	.388	.302
vs. Ground-Ballers			323	85	5	17	52	.263	.372	.301
vs. Fly-Ballers			380	108	9	21	52	.284	.432	.321
Home Games	5-3	3.42	311	84	4	17	49	.270	.389	.306
Road Games	6-6	4.05	392	109	10	21	55	.278	.416	.317
Grass Fields	4-3	3.91	207	57	5	9	27	.275	.386	.304
Artificial Turf	7-6	3.71	496	136	9	29	77	.274	.411	.315
April	2-0	1.71	74	17	1	5	9	.230	.311	.278
May	3-2	2.84	167	39	4	6	26	.234	.353	.260
June	0-2	3.86	120	32	4	8	16	.267	.400	.318
July	2-2	7.20	107	37	3	7	19	.346	.551	.383
August	2-1	3.47	89	22	2	3	20	.247	.404	.272
Sept./Oct.	2-2	3.86	146	46	0	9	14	.315	.404	.353
Leading Off Inn.			177	46	4	11	22	.260	.401	.307
Bases Empty			422	105	10	16	68	.249	.382	.278
Runners On			281	88	4	22	36	.313	.438	.360
Runners/Scor. Pos.			172	51	2	13	28	.297	.401	.339
Runners On/2 Out			111	33	2	7	17	.297	.432	.345
Scor. Pos./2 Out			80	24	2	4	13	.300	.463	.333
Late-Inning Pressure			65	16	1	9	9	.246	.369	.258
Leading Off			21	7	0	0	2	.333	.524	.333
Runners On			20	4	0	4	0	.200	.200	.200
Runners/Scor. Pos.			12	3	0	0	2	.250	.250	.250
First 9 Batters			272	62	4	15	52	.228	.331	.272
Second 9 Batters			234	79	5	12	28	.338	.491	.365
All Batters Thereafter			197	52	5	11	24	.264	.401	.303

Loves to face: Jerald Clark (0-for-10)
Fred McGriff (.167, 2-for-12)
Benito Santiago (0-for-9)
Hates to face: Darren Daulton (.571, 4-for-7, 1 HR, 2 SO)
Brian Hunter (.625, 5-for-8, 2 HR)
Barry Larkin (.375, 3-for-8, 2 HR)

Miscellaneous statistics: Ground outs-to-air outs ratio: 1.05 last season, 1.05 for career.... Opponents grounded into 19 double plays in 137 opportunities (one per 7.2).... Allowed 39 doubles, 5 triples in 179 innings.... Allowed 21 first-inning runs in 29 starts (5.90 ERA).... Batting support: 3.52 runs per start.... Opposing base stealers: 15-for-18 (83%); 0 pickoffs, 0 balks.

Comments: Led N.L. rookies in wins; he and teammate Mike Perez (nine) were the only N.L. rookies to win more than eight games. Not bad for two guys listed in the nonroster section of the team media guide last season. The Cardinals had 23 wins by rookies last season, the most by any team in the majors. Osborne also led all N.L. rookies in innings, starts, strikeouts, and lowest walk rate (1.91 per nine innings).... Became only the seventh rookie since 1969 to average fewer than two walks per nine innings while pitching at least 162 innings; the three N.L. pitchers who did it were left-handers (Atlee Hammaker, Derek Lilliquist, and Osborne); the four A.L. pitchers who did it were right-handers (Mark Fidrych, Dave Rozema, Bill Wegman, and Bill Long).... One of three left-handers in the majors against whom left-handed batters batted .300 last season (minimum: 100 AB by LHB). The others: Kyle Abbott (.326) and Bill Krueger (.308).... Opponents' batting average with runners in scoring position was 3d highest in league, behind Terry Mulholland (.345) and John Burkett (.302).... Osborne might have a hard time believing that the Cardinals made the fewest errors in the league last season; he was charged with 16 unearned runs, the most among N.L. pitchers, and one-third of the total against the entire St. Louis staff.... Turned 23 years of age last June; only one younger pitcher made at least 15 starts in the National League last year: Steve Avery, in his third season in 1992, is about 10 months younger than Osborne.

Bob Patterson   Throws Left

Pittsburgh Pirates	W-L	ERA	AB	H	HR	BB	SO	BA	SA	OBA
Season	6-3	2.92	240	59	7	23	43	.246	.400	.309
vs. Left-Handers			78	20	1	9	15	.256	.359	.330
vs. Right-Handers			162	39	6	14	28	.241	.420	.299
vs. Ground-Ballers			98	24	3	13	22	.245	.378	.330
vs. Fly-Ballers			142	35	4	10	21	.246	.415	.294
Home Games	4-2	3.47	133	30	5	14	25	.226	.398	.297
Road Games	2-1	2.22	107	29	2	9	18	.271	.402	.325
Grass Fields	0-0	0.87	42	13	0	5	9	.310	.405	.383
Artificial Turf	6-3	3.31	198	46	7	18	34	.232	.399	.294
April	1-0	0.00	23	3	0	0	3	.130	.217	.130
May	1-0	4.38	51	17	2	4	7	.333	.569	.382
June	2-0	1.54	40	8	0	5	6	.200	.225	.277
July	1-1	3.14	52	11	2	3	13	.212	.346	.255
August	0-1	0.75	42	11	0	6	7	.262	.333	.354
Sept./Oct.	1-1	7.56	32	9	3	5	7	.281	.656	.378
Leading Off Inn.			54	17	2	4	10	.315	.500	.362
Bases Empty			136	34	2	9	22	.250	.375	.297
Runners On			104	25	5	14	21	.240	.433	.325
Runners/Scor. Pos.			55	14	5	10	11	.255	.600	.358
Runners On/2 Out			47	13	1	10	4	.277	.362	.404
Scor. Pos./2 Out			29	7	1	7	4	.241	.379	.389
Late-Inning Pressure			117	32	5	13	17	.274	.479	.344
Leading Off			28	11	2	2	4	.393	.679	.433
Runners On			54	13	3	9	9	.241	.481	.344
Runners/Scor. Pos.			32	9	3	6	5	.281	.688	.385
First 9 Batters			226	56	7	23	40	.248	.403	.315
Second 9 Batters			14	3	0	0	3	.214	.357	.214
All Batters Thereafter			0	0	0	0	0	—	—	—

Loves to face: Roberto Alomar (0-for-6)
              Von Hayes (.190, 4-for-21, 1 HR)
              Paul O'Neill (0-for-11)
Hates to face: Gregg Jefferies (.500, 5-for-10, 1 2B)
              Kevin McReynolds (.389, 7-for-18, 1 2B, 2 HR)

Miscellaneous statistics: Ground outs-to-air outs ratio: 0.68 last season, 0.83 for career. . . . Opponents grounded into 5 double plays in 47 opportunities (one per 9.4). . . . Allowed 12 doubles, 2 triples in 64⅔ innings. . . . Stranded 17 inherited runners, allowed 13 to score (57%). . . . Opposing base stealers: 1-for-4 (25%); 1 pickoff, 0 balks.

Comments: A good example of why all baseball-loving parents should encourage their two-year olds to pick up spoons, toys, and balls—yes, especially balls—with their left hands: Patterson is still in the majors because he has held left-handed batters to a .221 career average; right-handed hitters have a .290 career mark against him. . . . Averaged 6.44 strikeouts per nine innings in his career with the Pirates, a rate exceeded by only five pitchers in team history (minimum: 300 IP): Rod Scurry (8.22), Jose DeLeon (8.09), Bob Veale (7.96), Cecilio Guante (7.41), and Bert Blyleven (6.73). In his career, Patterson has fanned 22.4 of every 100 left-handed batters he has faced; he has fanned 14.6 of every 100 right-handed batters he has faced. . . . Allowed homers to both Ray Knight and Keith Hernandez in his first major league game in 1985, but has not allowed more than one in any of 209 appearances since then. . . . Patterson and Dennis Eckersley are the only relievers who have had a winning record in each of the past four years. Two other Pirates pitchers also had winning records in each of the past four years: starters Doug Drabek and Bob Walk. That marked the first time that the same three teammates each had a winning record in four straight seasons since four Tigers pitchers—Jack Morris, Dan Petry, Milt Wilcox, and Aurelio Lopez—had a six-year streak from 1979 to 1984. The Pirates' last such streak was from 1973 to 1976, with Dave Giusti, Bruce Kison, and Jim Rooker.

Alejandro Pena   Throws Right

Atlanta Braves	W-L	ERA	AB	H	HR	BB	SO	BA	SA	OBA
Season	1-6	4.07	157	40	7	13	34	.255	.420	.310
vs. Left-Handers			78	16	5	6	19	.205	.436	.262
vs. Right-Handers			79	24	2	7	15	.304	.405	.356
vs. Ground-Ballers			60	14	1	2	13	.233	.300	.254
vs. Fly-Ballers			97	26	6	11	21	.268	.495	.343
Home Games	0-2	4.42	67	17	4	4	13	.254	.463	.296
Road Games	1-4	3.80	90	23	3	9	21	.256	.389	.320
Grass Fields	0-4	4.39	101	28	6	7	18	.277	.475	.321
Artificial Turf	1-2	3.52	56	12	1	6	16	.214	.321	.290
April	0-1	4.26	23	6	2	1	8	.261	.565	.292
May	0-3	9.72	40	17	4	5	4	.425	.750	.478
June	0-0	2.25	14	2	0	0	4	.143	.214	.143
July	1-1	2.35	52	9	1	5	10	.173	.250	.246
August	0-1	1.59	20	4	0	2	6	.200	.250	.273
Sept./Oct.	0-0	3.86	8	2	0	0	2	.250	.250	.250
Leading Off Inn.			36	5	3	2	8	.139	.389	.184
Bases Empty			99	22	4	4	23	.222	.374	.252
Runners On			58	18	3	9	11	.310	.500	.397
Runners/Scor. Pos.			35	10	1	9	7	.286	.400	.422
Runners On/2 Out			23	9	2	5	3	.391	.652	.500
Scor. Pos./2 Out			16	6	1	5	2	.375	.563	.524
Late-Inning Pressure			100	27	4	12	24	.270	.420	.345
Leading Off			22	3	1	2	6	.136	.273	.208
Runners On			46	14	2	8	11	.304	.457	.400
Runners/Scor. Pos.			30	9	1	8	7	.300	.433	.436
First 9 Batters			156	39	7	12	34	.250	.417	.304
Second 9 Batters			1	1	0	1	0	1.000	1.000	.667
All Batters Thereafter			0	0	0	0	0	—	—	—

Loves to face: Delino DeShields (0-for-8, 5 SO)
              Ron Gant (0-for-11)
              Joe Girardi (0-for-8)
Hates to face: Ken Caminiti (.429, 6-for-14, 1 HR)
              Will Clark (.333, 5-for-15, 2 HR, 7 SO)
              Ryne Sandberg (.341, 15-for-44, 3 HR)

Miscellaneous statistics: Ground outs-to-air outs ratio: 0.75 last season, 0.98 for career. . . . Opponents grounded into 5 double plays in 33 opportunities (one per 6.6). . . . Allowed 5 doubles, 0 triples in 42 innings. . . . Saved 15 games in 21 opportunities (71%). . . . Stranded 10 inherited runners, allowed 3 to score (77%). . . . Opposing base stealers: 5-for-6 (83%); 0 pickoffs, 0 balks.

Comments: For the second straight year, right-handed hitters batted much better against him than left-handed hitters; in 1991, righties out-hit lefties, .296 to .193. . . . Last year's 99-point difference was the 2d highest among N.L. pitchers (minimum: 75 AB by both LHB and RHB); only Bob McClure, a left-hander against whom right-handed batters hit .315 and lefties .198, had a wider disparity. The nearest N.L. right-hander to Pena in terms of a disparity running counter to the conventional lefty/righty rules is Jeff Brantley, with a 65-point difference (.246 by right-handed batters, .181 by lefties). . . . Had nine of his 15 saves in July, one shy of the team record for one month set by Rick Camp in September 1980. Only two N.L. pitchers had more saves in a month last year (Lee Smith, 12 in August; John Wetteland, 10 in July). . . . Among active pitchers with at least 900 N.L. innings, only Orel Hershiser (2.87), Dennis Martinez (2.93), Pena (2.95), and Dwight Gooden (2.99) have career N.L. ERAs under 3.00. . . . Has started 56 innings in Late-Inning Pressure Situations over the past two years; only 10 of those 56 leadoff batters have reached base, a .179 on-base percentage. Over the last two seasons, among pitchers who faced at least 50 leadoff batters in LIPS, only Stan Belinda (.157) and Jeff Reardon (.165) allowed a lower LIPS on-base percentage to batters leading off an inning. Ironically, those were the two relievers who came up short in the 1992 postseason; Pena will join Belinda in the Bucs pen in 1993.

Mark Portugal
Throws Right

Houston Astros	W-L	ERA	AB	H	HR	BB	SO	BA	SA	OBA
Season	6-3	2.66	357	76	7	41	62	.213	.331	.295
vs. Left-Handers			205	50	5	26	40	.244	.395	.328
vs. Right-Handers			152	26	2	15	22	.171	.243	.250
vs. Ground-Ballers			182	41	3	16	34	.225	.335	.291
vs. Fly-Ballers			175	35	4	25	28	.200	.326	.299
Home Games	4-0	1.86	202	41	3	23	37	.203	.287	.283
Road Games	2-3	3.74	155	35	4	18	25	.226	.387	.310
Grass Fields	1-2	3.24	88	20	2	12	19	.227	.375	.320
Artificial Turf	5-1	2.48	269	56	5	29	43	.208	.316	.287
April	2-1	3.19	108	25	0	16	21	.231	.324	.331
May	2-1	3.06	114	23	4	14	20	.202	.377	.295
June	1-1	1.71	75	17	1	5	10	.227	.280	.272
July	0-0	1.00	31	6	1	4	5	.194	.355	.286
August	0-0	0.00	0	0	0	0	0	.000	.000	.000
Sept./Oct.	1-0	3.38	29	5	1	2	6	.172	.276	.226
Leading Off Inn.			96	24	5	10	15	.250	.479	.321
Bases Empty			224	48	6	27	42	.214	.371	.299
Runners On			133	28	1	14	20	.211	.263	.289
Runners/Scor. Pos.			78	21	1	8	12	.269	.346	.341
Runners On/2 Out			53	6	0	5	9	.113	.113	.190
Scor. Pos./2 Out			33	5	0	3	5	.152	.152	.222
Late-Inning Pressure			25	6	2	4	4	.240	.520	.345
Leading Off			8	1	1	1	2	.125	.500	.222
Runners On			7	1	0	1	0	.143	.143	.250
Runners/Scor. Pos.			3	1	0	0	0	.333	.333	.333
First 9 Batters			128	30	2	17	23	.234	.344	.322
Second 9 Batters			121	24	2	16	24	.198	.314	.297
All Batters Thereafter			108	22	3	8	15	.204	.333	.259

Loves to face: Barry Larkin (.071, 1-for-14)
Larry Walker (0-for-9)
Matt Williams (.081, 3-for-37)

Hates to face: Jeff Blauser (.462, 6-for-13, 3 HR)
Ron Gant (.474, 9-for-19, 1 HR)
Darryl Strawberry (.421, 8-for-19, 3 HR, 7 SO)

Miscellaneous statistics: Ground outs-to-air outs ratio: 1.37 last season, 1.28 for career.... Opponents grounded into 10 double plays in 63 opportunities (one per 6.3).... Allowed 13 doubles, 4 triples in 101⅓ innings.... Allowed 11 first-inning runs in 16 starts (5.63 ERA).... Batting support: 3.31 runs per start.... Opposing base stealers: 7-for-13 (54%); 0 pickoffs, 1 balk.

Comments: Batting average by opposing right-handed batters was lowest in the league (minimum: 150 BFP).... Last season's breakdown of opposing left- and right-handed batters seems normal for a right-handed pitcher, but it's actually a dramatic departure from his previous career performance. Right-handed batters had hit for a higher average than left-handed batters in each of the previous three seasons, and own a career average (.271) that is 31 points higher than left-handed batters' (.240). He and Erik Hanson are the only active right-handed pitchers against whom right-handed batters have a career average at least 30 points higher than their lefty counterparts (minimum: 1000 AB by both RHB and LHB). Over the last 18 years, only three other right-handed pitchers preferred left-handed batters to such a degree: Mike Norris, Bobby Castillo, and Donnie Moore.... Set career bests in ERA and opponents' batting average.... Opponents batted .113 with runners on base and two outs; Cal Eldred (.105, 6-for-57) was the only major league pitcher who held batters to a lower average in such situations (minimum: 50 at-bats).... In four seasons with Houston, he has allowed 16 homers at the Astrodome, 38 homers on the road, while posting a 20–8 record in home games, 14–18 on the road.... Owns a 33–24 record in 90 starts for a Houston team that has a composite .474 won-lost percentage over those years.

Jeff Reardon
Throws Right

Red Sox/Braves	W-L	ERA	AB	H	HR	BB	SO	BA	SA	OBA
Season	5-2	3.41	230	67	6	9	39	.291	.426	.321
vs. Left-Handers			108	33	5	5	12	.306	.509	.342
vs. Right-Handers			122	34	1	4	27	.279	.352	.302
vs. Ground-Ballers			101	35	3	4	16	.347	.515	.364
vs. Fly-Ballers			129	32	3	5	23	.248	.357	.287
Home Games	3-1	3.60	140	41	4	3	22	.293	.450	.306
Road Games	2-1	3.13	90	26	2	6	17	.289	.389	.343
Grass Fields	5-2	3.35	211	60	6	8	37	.284	.427	.315
Artificial Turf	0-0	4.15	19	7	0	1	2	.368	.421	.381
April	0-0	1.13	28	7	1	1	4	.250	.393	.300
May	1-0	3.00	35	8	1	1	7	.229	.343	.250
June	0-0	7.50	29	12	0	1	6	.414	.517	.433
July	1-0	2.25	46	12	2	2	7	.261	.457	.280
August	0-2	6.97	44	15	2	3	9	.341	.591	.396
Sept./Oct.	3-0	1.42	48	13	0	1	6	.271	.271	.286
Leading Off Inn.			48	11	1	2	7	.229	.313	.275
Bases Empty			123	33	4	3	18	.268	.423	.297
Runners On			107	34	2	6	21	.318	.430	.348
Runners/Scor. Pos.			61	21	2	5	13	.344	.492	.382
Runners On/2 Out			58	19	1	6	13	.328	.483	.391
Scor. Pos./2 Out			36	12	1	5	7	.333	.500	.415
Late-Inning Pressure			172	51	5	5	31	.297	.436	.322
Leading Off			36	7	1	1	7	.194	.306	.237
Runners On			76	27	2	4	14	.355	.500	.383
Runners/Scor. Pos.			42	17	2	3	8	.405	.595	.435
First 9 Batters			230	67	6	9	39	.291	.426	.321
Second 9 Batters			0	0	0	0	0	—	—	—
All Batters Thereafter			0	0	0	0	0	—	—	—

Loves to face: Dave Gallagher (0-for-8)
Willie McGee (.143, 3-for-21)
Ryne Sandberg (.111, 2-for-18)

Hates to face: Tony Fernandez (.364, 4-for-11, 1 HR)
Dale Murphy (.400, 6-for-15)
Darryl Strawberry (.400, 4-for-10, 1 3B, 1 HR)

Miscellaneous statistics: Ground outs-to-air outs ratio: 0.47 last season, 0.54 for career.... Opponents grounded into 6 double plays in 40 opportunities (one per 6.7).... Allowed 11 doubles, 1 triple in 58 innings.... Saved 30 games in 40 opportunities (75%).... Stranded 15 inherited runners, allowed 15 to score (50%); stranded 14 of 28 in A.L., 2d-lowest rate in league.... Opposing base stealers: 4-for-4 (100%); 0 pickoffs, 0 balks.

Comments: Became the all-time major league leader in saves last June, but may have trouble staying ahead of Lee Smith, who trails him by only two, 357 to 355, heading into 1993.... All 30 of his saves last season were of the one-inning-max variety; 208 of his 357 career saves fall into that category. By the way, in only 140 of his 341 saves did Rollie Fingers pitch one inning or less.... Reardon has saved games for 70 different winning pitchers in his five-team career. And the fellow for whom he has saved more games than any other is Joe Hesketh: The (ex-)Beard has saved 25 of Joe's 49 career wins. Runners-up: Frank Viola, 22; Bill Gullickson, 20; Bryn Smith, 19; Roger Clemens, 17.... Opponents' batting average with runners on base in Late-Inning Pressure Situations was 2d highest in majors (minimum: 60 batters faced).... He and Jeff Russell were both traded in late August after having saved more than 25 games for their old teams, something never before done in major league history. Reardon had 27 saves for Boston, then added three for Atlanta; Russell had 28 for Texas, then got two for Oakland. The only other pitcher ever to switch teams after already having even 20 saves that season: Mudcat Grant in 1970 (24 for Oakland, none for Pittsburgh).... Has not started a game since tossing a one-hitter in his only start for Tidewater in 1979.... Has pitched in postseason play for four different teams (Expos, Twins, Red Sox, and Braves), tying Doyle Alexander's major league record. For nonpitchers, the record is five by Don Baylor.

Jose Rijo
Throws Right

Cincinnati Reds	W-L	ERA	AB	H	HR	BB	SO	BA	SA	OBA
Season	15-10	2.56	776	185	15	44	171	.238	.340	.281
vs. Left-Handers			426	114	6	32	87	.268	.371	.319
vs. Right-Handers			350	71	9	12	84	.203	.303	.232
vs. Ground-Ballers			351	87	4	21	85	.248	.319	.289
vs. Fly-Ballers			425	98	11	23	86	.231	.358	.274
Home Games	6-4	2.74	331	79	9	17	77	.239	.363	.277
Road Games	9-6	2.43	445	106	6	27	94	.238	.324	.283
Grass Fields	5-3	2.53	236	58	5	11	44	.246	.360	.282
Artificial Turf	10-7	2.57	540	127	10	33	127	.235	.331	.280
April	0-3	4.30	88	26	2	4	20	.295	.409	.323
May	1-1	3.10	112	28	2	7	24	.250	.339	.294
June	3-2	3.19	124	33	4	3	41	.266	.403	.289
July	4-1	2.37	136	34	3	13	25	.250	.390	.313
August	2-2	2.41	145	30	4	4	34	.207	.317	.237
Sept./Oct.	5-1	1.29	171	34	0	13	27	.199	.240	.254
Leading Off Inn.			200	54	9	11	35	.270	.445	.311
Bases Empty			473	121	12	24	93	.256	.368	.293
Runners On			303	64	3	20	78	.211	.297	.261
Runners/Scor. Pos.			160	32	0	16	49	.200	.244	.275
Runners On/2 Out			121	18	2	12	41	.149	.256	.226
Scor. Pos./2 Out			75	13	0	10	29	.173	.240	.271
Late-Inning Pressure			50	14	5	1	13	.280	.600	.288
Leading Off			15	7	3	0	2	.467	1.133	.467
Runners On			14	3	1	1	5	.214	.429	.250
Runners/Scor. Pos.			8	2	0	1	3	.250	.250	.300
First 9 Batters			271	67	5	18	56	.247	.351	.301
Second 9 Batters			283	72	3	11	61	.254	.329	.282
All Batters Thereafter			222	46	7	15	54	.207	.342	.253

Loves to face: Andujar Cedeno (0-for-14)
                 Jerald Clark (.053, 1-for-19)
                 Todd Zeile (0-for-11)
Hates to face: Bobby Bonilla (.348, 8-for-23, 3 HR)
                 Mark Grace (.455, 15-for-33, 1 HR)
                 Cory Snyder (.400, 6-for-15, 1 2B, 3 HR, 5 SO)

Miscellaneous statistics: Ground outs-to-air outs ratio: 1.64 last season, 1.21 for career.... Opponents grounded into 16 double plays in 150 opportunities (one per 9.4).... Allowed 26 doubles, 4 triples in 211 innings.... Allowed 6 first-inning runs in 33 starts (1.64 ERA).... Batting support: 4.00 runs per start.... Opposing base stealers: 17-for-29 (59%); 2 pickoffs, 1 balk.

Comments: He and Jack McDowell have each finished at least five games above .500 in each of the last three seasons; the only other pitcher to do that, Roger Clemens, has done it in each of the last seven years.... Has a winning record in each of his five seasons with Reds; only three pitchers have had a winning mark in each of their first six years with the Rhinelanders: Eppa Rixey (eight years, 1921–28), Pete Donohue (1921–26), and Fred Norman (1973–78).... Has a winning record in only two of his eight major league Aprils (3–1 in 1988, 1–0 in 1989), but has had a winning record in each of six Septembers in which he has a decision. Career records: 7–12 in April, 22–9 in September.... ERA after August 31 was lowest in the majors last season.... Has set a career best for walks allowed per nine innings in each of the last two years. Annual rates since 1989: 3.89, 3.56, 2.42, 1.88. Pretty impressive for a guy who averaged more than five walks per nine innings in his first full season in the majors (1986 with Oakland).... Averaged 7.29 strikeouts per nine innings, 4th-best rate in N.L.... Road-game ERA was 2d lowest in league, behind only Ken Hill (2.33).... Allowed nine home runs to batters leading off innings, the most by any N.L. pitcher.... Allowed five homers in 50 at-bats in Late-Inning Pressure Situations, after previously yielding three in 326 LIPS at-bats.... Owns 2.58 ERA in five seasons in National League, lowest by any pitcher over the last 50 years (minimum: 850 N.L. innings).

Mel Rojas
Throws Right

Montreal Expos	W-L	ERA	AB	H	HR	BB	SO	BA	SA	OBA
Season	7-1	1.43	357	71	2	34	70	.199	.269	.271
vs. Left-Handers			199	39	1	20	40	.196	.246	.268
vs. Right-Handers			158	32	1	14	30	.203	.297	.274
vs. Ground-Ballers			159	27	0	13	31	.170	.214	.233
vs. Fly-Ballers			198	44	2	21	39	.222	.313	.300
Home Games	5-0	1.72	187	39	1	14	39	.209	.289	.265
Road Games	2-1	1.12	170	32	1	20	31	.188	.247	.277
Grass Fields	1-0	1.80	69	14	0	9	12	.203	.217	.295
Artificial Turf	6-1	1.34	288	57	2	25	58	.198	.281	.265
April	0-1	2.25	30	9	0	6	4	.300	.333	.417
May	1-0	0.51	61	10	0	7	14	.164	.197	.261
June	0-0	1.59	61	13	1	4	10	.213	.361	.262
July	2-0	0.90	70	15	0	3	13	.214	.271	.240
August	2-0	1.31	70	12	1	3	13	.171	.271	.205
Sept./Oct.	2-0	2.60	65	12	0	11	16	.185	.215	.312
Leading Off Inn.			81	22	0	5	18	.272	.370	.314
Bases Empty			182	46	2	14	38	.253	.374	.306
Runners On			175	25	0	20	32	.143	.160	.236
Runners/Scor. Pos.			115	14	0	20	23	.122	.130	.254
Runners On/2 Out			81	11	0	14	15	.136	.160	.278
Scor. Pos./2 Out			58	8	0	14	11	.138	.155	.315
Late-Inning Pressure			149	33	0	17	31	.221	.255	.301
Leading Off			35	13	0	3	8	.371	.457	.421
Runners On			78	11	0	10	13	.141	.141	.239
Runners/Scor. Pos.			45	6	0	10	8	.133	.133	.291
First 9 Batters			332	63	0	32	68	.190	.238	.264
Second 9 Batters			25	8	2	2	2	.320	.680	.370
All Batters Thereafter			0	0	0	0	0	—	—	—

Loves to face: Wes Chamberlain (0-for-8)
                 David Hollins (0-for-7)
                 Jeff King (0-for-8)
Hates to face: Barry Bonds (.500, 5-for-10, 1 HR)
                 Bobby Bonilla (.400, 4-for-10, 1 HR)
                 Mike Sharperson (.667, 2-for-3, 1 2B, 1 HR)

Miscellaneous statistics: Ground outs-to-air outs ratio: 1.08 last season, 0.96 for career.... Opponents grounded into 7 double plays in 70 opportunities (one per 10).... Allowed 15 doubles, 2 triples in 100⅔ innings.... Saved 10 games in 14 opportunities (71%).... Stranded 47 inherited runners, allowed 10 to score (82%), 4th-highest rate in N.L.... Opposing base stealers: 12-for-15 (80%); 0 pickoffs, 0 balks.

Comments: His ERA was the lowest by any major leaguer in a season of at least 100 innings pitched since Bruce Sutter's 1.35 in 1977.... Held opponents to the lowest batting average with runners on base over the past 18 years (minimum: 125 batters faced). Opponents' average with runners in scoring position was 2d lowest (same minimum) in any season during that time; Mitch Williams held hitters to a .108 scoring-position average in 1991.... Opponents' career average: .271 with the bases empty, .157 with runners on base, .156 with runners in scoring position.... Opponents' batting average with runners on base in Late-Inning Pressure Situations was lowest in majors last season (minimum: 60 batters faced).... Batting average by left-handed hitters was 2d lowest in N.L. (minimum: 200 batters faced), behind Jeff Brantley (.181); Montreal pitchers led N.L., holding left-handed batters to .242 average, nine points lower than 2d-place Pittsburgh.... Held ground-ball hitters to .170 average, lowest in majors (minimum: 150 batters faced).... Seven-game winning streak was longest by an N.L. relief pitcher last season; Jeff Parrett had a seven-game relief-win streak in A.L.... Pitched more than two innings in 12 of his relief appearances, the most by any N.L. reliever last season. There were 14 A.L. pitchers who had at least that many "long" relief appearances.... Signed by one uncle, Jesus Alou, in 1985, and spent last year making the bullpen moves of another uncle, Felipe Alou, look good.

Bret Saberhagen — Throws Right

New York Mets	W-L	ERA	AB	H	HR	BB	SO	BA	SA	OBA
Season	3-5	3.50	360	84	6	27	81	.233	.344	.292
vs. Left-Handers			210	48	3	19	48	.229	.348	.292
vs. Right-Handers			150	36	3	8	33	.240	.340	.292
vs. Ground-Ballers			184	48	2	13	44	.261	.364	.310
vs. Fly-Ballers			176	36	4	14	37	.205	.324	.273
Home Games	1-2	2.41	209	42	3	15	49	.201	.287	.264
Road Games	2-3	5.21	151	42	3	12	32	.278	.424	.331
Grass Fields	2-2	2.53	240	50	5	18	57	.208	.317	.272
Artificial Turf	1-3	5.70	120	34	1	9	24	.283	.400	.333
April	1-2	5.52	120	30	2	9	31	.250	.367	.308
May	2-0	1.29	74	14	1	4	23	.189	.311	.228
June	0-0	—	0	0	0	0	0	—	—	—
July	0-1	5.00	32	9	0	6	7	.281	.375	.410
August	0-0	0.00	11	3	0	1	3	.273	.364	.333
Sept./Oct.	0-2	2.94	123	28	3	7	17	.228	.333	.276
Leading Off Inn.			93	18	1	7	23	.194	.226	.250
Bases Empty			225	51	4	10	48	.227	.316	.272
Runners On			135	33	2	17	33	.244	.393	.323
Runners/Scor. Pos.			65	13	1	12	14	.200	.369	.313
Runners On/2 Out			65	21	1	8	18	.323	.508	.397
Scor. Pos./2 Out			41	10	1	7	11	.244	.415	.354
Late-Inning Pressure			52	12	1	2	8	.231	.327	.259
Leading Off			14	2	0	0	1	.143	.143	.143
Runners On			14	4	0	2	2	.286	.286	.375
Runners/Scor. Pos.			7	1	0	2	2	.143	.143	.333
First 9 Batters			136	32	3	11	36	.235	.360	.305
Second 9 Batters			122	30	1	11	32	.246	.328	.313
All Batters Thereafter			102	22	2	5	13	.216	.343	.248

Loves to face: Todd Benzinger (0-for-9, 5 SO)
Steve Finley (.091, 1-for-11, 1 2B)
Luis Gonzalez (0-for-7, 3 SO)
Hates to face: Steve Buechele (.462, 12-for-26, 2 2B, 1 HR)
Ray Lankford (.556, 5-for-9)
Fred McGriff (.414, 12-for-29, 2 2B, 1 3B, 2 HR)

Miscellaneous statistics: Ground outs-to-air outs ratio: 1.09 last season, 1.10 for career.... Opponents grounded into 4 double plays in 66 opportunities (one per 17).... Allowed 14 doubles, 4 triples in 97⅔ innings.... Allowed 9 first-inning runs in 15 starts (5.40 ERA).... Batting support: 3.13 runs per start.... Opposing base stealers: 6-for-11 (55%); 3 pickoffs, 2 balks.

Comments: For the few who are unaware, he has a winning record in each of four odd-numbered years in the majors, and a losing record in each of five even-numbered years. Composite records: 74–30 in odds, 39–53 in evens.... Mets fans: If you're putting your eggs in that basket, you'll love the fact that he has won the Cy Young Award in the season following each of the last two presidential inaugurations.... Owns 21–22 record over three years since 23-win season earned him the A.L. Cy Young Award in 1989. He's the first Cy Young winner since Pete Vuckovich in 1982 to amass more wins in his Cy Young season than in the next three years combined.... Got off on the wrong foot last season, allowing seven runs in each of his first two starts; he had done that only twice in 96 starts with Kansas City. By allowing "only" five runs in his third start, he lowered his ERA to a snappy 13.15. In all, he allowed 19 earned runs over his first 10 innings; he then allowed 19 earned runs in his next 87⅔ innings. That stretch included a 26-inning scoreless streak, the 3d longest in the league last season.... His rates of walks per nine innings (2.49) and strikeouts per nine innings (7.46) last season were the highest of his career.... Career numbers: 21–26 in day games, 92–57 at night.... Has won his last 10 decisions during May, dating back to 1990.... Although he spent 99 days on the disabled list, he finished the season with reason for optimism, pitching eight full innings in each of his last three starts.

Bob Scanlan — Throws Right

Chicago Cubs	W-L	ERA	AB	H	HR	BB	SO	BA	SA	OBA
Season	3-6	2.89	323	76	4	30	42	.235	.319	.301
vs. Left-Handers			157	35	3	20	20	.223	.338	.313
vs. Right-Handers			166	41	1	10	22	.247	.301	.288
vs. Ground-Ballers			137	31	1	17	17	.226	.314	.312
vs. Fly-Ballers			186	45	3	13	25	.242	.323	.292
Home Games	1-2	2.66	153	37	3	10	20	.242	.366	.287
Road Games	2-4	3.09	170	39	1	20	22	.229	.276	.313
Grass Fields	2-2	2.16	213	48	3	17	28	.225	.319	.281
Artificial Turf	1-4	4.34	110	28	1	13	14	.255	.318	.336
April	0-1	1.74	34	7	1	2	4	.206	.324	.243
May	1-0	1.80	51	10	0	9	12	.196	.275	.311
June	1-3	3.60	58	15	0	6	4	.259	.293	.328
July	1-1	1.10	56	6	1	2	10	.107	.161	.138
August	0-0	0.66	44	8	0	5	5	.182	.205	.265
Sept./Oct.	0-1	7.41	80	30	2	6	7	.375	.538	.425
Leading Off Inn.			75	19	0	3	10	.253	.320	.282
Bases Empty			168	42	2	16	23	.250	.345	.315
Runners On			155	34	2	14	19	.219	.290	.285
Runners/Scor. Pos.			101	21	0	13	15	.208	.248	.293
Runners On/2 Out			72	17	1	8	11	.236	.319	.321
Scor. Pos./2 Out			49	11	0	7	9	.224	.286	.321
Late-Inning Pressure			174	48	2	16	18	.276	.356	.339
Leading Off			42	13	0	2	3	.310	.381	.341
Runners On			88	23	1	9	9	.261	.341	.333
Runners/Scor. Pos.			56	14	0	9	7	.250	.304	.348
First 9 Batters			311	73	4	29	39	.235	.322	.300
Second 9 Batters			12	3	0.	1	3	.250	.250	.308
All Batters Thereafter			0	0	0	0	0	—	—	—

Loves to face: Bret Barberie (.111, 1-for-9)
Sid Bream (0-for-5)
Royce Clayton (0-for-5)
Hates to face: Andres Galarraga (.455, 5-for-11)
Darrin Jackson (.600, 3-for-5, 1 HR)
Todd Zeile (.667, 6-for-9)

Miscellaneous statistics: Ground outs-to-air outs ratio: 1.61 last season, 1.74 for career.... Opponents grounded into 8 double plays in 64 opportunities (one per 8.0).... Allowed 13 doubles, 1 triple in 87⅓ innings.... Saved 14 games in 19 opportunities (74%).... Stranded 27 inherited runners, allowed 12 to score (69%).... Opposing base stealers: 6-for-9 (67%); 0 pickoffs, 4 balks (3d most in N.L.).

Comments: He was the Cubs' closer after the All-Star break, and led the team with 14 saves.... Had 3d-highest ground outs-to-air outs ratio among N.L. pitchers with at least 10 saves; only Roger McDowell (2.96) and John Franco (2.16) were more groundball-oriented. The 15 N.L. pitchers with 10 or more saves last season had a combined 1.12 ground outs-to-air outs ratio, slightly higher than their A.L. counterparts (1.03).... Cubs staff finished with 1.38 ground outs-to-air outs ratio last season, 2d highest in the N.L. to the Dodgers (1.40).... Fourteen players in the majors last season were listed at 6'7" or taller; of those 14, all but one were pitchers (6'7" Billy Ashley, an outfielder for the Dodgers). An additional 16 players were listed at 6'6", and all but two of them were pitchers (Dave Winfield and Darryl Strawberry). That means 27 of the 30 tallest players in the majors last season were pitchers.... According to the Cubs' public relations department, he grew an inch sometime during 1991, and at six feet, eight inches, is now the tallest man ever to play for the Cubs. He still needs to grow a couple of inches to catch Eric Hillman and Randy Johnson, allegedly the tallest players of all time. We should say "allegedly" to the entire topic of player heights and weights; it's hard to believe some of the numbers listed on the team rosters. Perhaps we'll have all players stop by the Elias Sports Bureau offices when they play in New York and we'll do the measurements ourselves.

Curt Schilling
Throws Right

Philadelphia Phillies	W-L	ERA	AB	H	HR	BB	SO	BA	SA	OBA
Season	14-11	2.35	819	165	11	59	147	.201	.288	.254
vs. Left-Handers			456	90	7	39	77	.197	.289	.259
vs. Right-Handers			363	75	4	20	70	.207	.287	.247
vs. Ground-Ballers			356	76	5	24	66	.213	.309	.260
vs. Fly-Ballers			463	89	6	35	81	.192	.272	.249
Home Games	8-6	2.21	465	87	8	33	84	.187	.271	.240
Road Games	6-5	2.53	354	78	3	26	63	.220	.311	.271
Grass Fields	4-3	3.00	180	41	2	17	37	.228	.322	.294
Artificial Turf	10-8	2.17	639	124	9	42	110	.194	.279	.242
April	2-1	2.76	56	10	1	8	17	.179	.250	.279
May	1-2	2.78	118	23	2	10	26	.195	.314	.258
June	3-2	2.30	159	33	1	11	28	.208	.308	.259
July	3-1	2.03	147	31	1	5	26	.211	.252	.235
August	2-3	3.02	168	38	5	14	25	.226	.333	.284
Sept./Oct.	3-2	1.62	171	30	1	11	25	.175	.251	.222
Leading Off Inn.			216	42	5	12	35	.194	.296	.237
Bases Empty			521	107	6	34	92	.205	.286	.254
Runners On			298	58	5	25	55	.195	.292	.253
Runners/Scor. Pos.			148	26	1	20	34	.176	.223	.266
Runners On/2 Out			140	24	3	12	28	.171	.293	.237
Scor. Pos./2 Out			79	14	1	10	18	.177	.241	.270
Late-Inning Pressure			69	19	2	6	12	.275	.478	.329
Leading Off			21	7	1	0	1	.333	.667	.333
Runners On			28	7	1	3	6	.250	.464	.313
Runners/Scor. Pos.			15	2	0	3	5	.133	.200	.263
First 9 Batters			298	58	4	31	69	.195	.258	.269
Second 9 Batters			229	46	4	9	37	.201	.297	.228
All Batters Thereafter			292	61	3	19	41	.209	.312	.256

Loves to face: Craig Biggio (0-for-10)
       Darrin Fletcher (0-for-14)
       Andres Galarraga (0-for-10)
Hates to face: Delino DeShields (.400, 6-for-15, 2 HR)
       Tony Fernandez (.500, 5-for-10, 3 SO)
       Marquis Grissom (.688, 11-for-16, 1 HR)

Miscellaneous statistics: Ground outs-to-air outs ratio: 0.89 last season, 0.90 for career.... Opponents grounded into 11 double plays in 141 opportunities (one per 13).... Allowed 30 doubles, 4 triples in 226⅓ innings.... Allowed 10 first-inning runs in 26 starts (3.12 ERA).... Batting support: 3.46 runs per start.... Record of 12–9, 2.27 ERA as a starter; 2–2, 2.86 ERA in 16 relief appearances.... Stranded 2 inherited runners, allowed 2 to score (50%).... Opposing base stealers: 7-for-14 (50%); 0 pickoffs, 0 balks.

Comments: Pitched exclusively as a reliever through May 13 (as he had in the two previous seasons), exclusively as a starter after that.... Made his first start on May 19; from that point on, he led the National League in complete games (with 10, one more than Greg Maddux, Doug Drabek, and Terry Mulholland) and shared the league lead in shutouts (with four, tying Maddux and Pedro Astacio).... Became the first pitcher in 18 years to finish at least 10 games as both a starter and a reliever; the last to do that was Reggie Cleveland in 1974.... Opponents' batting average and on-base percentage were the lowest in the majors (minimum: 162 IP); opponents' average with runners in scoring position was lowest in the National League.... Compiled a 29-inning scoreless streak (July 17–Aug. 1), 2d longest in the majors last season to John Smoltz (29⅓).... Darren Daulton caught 217⅓ of the 226⅓ innings that Schilling worked; Todd Pratt caught the leftovers. Only two other N.L. batteries combined for 200+ innings, both for the Reds: Tim Belcher/Joe Oliver (206⅔) and Greg Swindell/Oliver (201⅓).... Marquis Grissom's .688 batting average vs. Schilling is the 5th highest of any active batter vs. any active pitcher (minimum: 10 AB). The top four: Felix Fermin vs. Mark Guthrie (.909, 10-for-11); Gary Gaetti vs. Greg Cadaret (.733, 11-for-15); Pedro Guerrero vs. Dennis Rasmussen (.733, 11-for-15); Tim Raines vs. Ken Hill (.714, 10-for-14).

Pete Schourek
Throws Left

New York Mets	W-L	ERA	AB	H	HR	BB	SO	BA	SA	OBA
Season	6-8	3.64	524	137	9	44	60	.261	.385	.319
vs. Left-Handers			120	31	2	16	14	.258	.358	.341
vs. Right-Handers			404	106	7	28	46	.262	.394	.312
vs. Ground-Ballers			192	43	1	14	23	.224	.286	.280
vs. Fly-Ballers			332	94	8	30	37	.283	.443	.341
Home Games	5-3	2.89	342	83	6	29	36	.243	.357	.301
Road Games	1-5	5.12	182	54	3	15	24	.297	.440	.351
Grass Fields	5-4	2.99	366	89	8	29	42	.243	.369	.298
Artificial Turf	1-4	5.22	158	48	1	15	18	.304	.424	.365
April	0-0	—	0	0	0	0	0	—	—	—
May	0-1	1.50	20	5	0	3	3	.250	.350	.348
June	1-2	2.83	113	31	0	11	16	.274	.336	.344
July	1-1	3.08	98	22	1	5	6	.224	.337	.260
August	1-2	4.08	112	30	3	9	16	.268	.411	.323
Sept./Oct.	3-2	4.47	181	49	5	16	19	.271	.431	.328
Leading Off Inn.			132	30	5	6	20	.227	.386	.271
Bases Empty			307	78	8	18	30	.254	.414	.300
Runners On			217	59	1	26	30	.272	.346	.344
Runners/Scor. Pos.			127	36	1	20	18	.283	.362	.371
Runners On/2 Out			94	24	0	12	11	.255	.330	.340
Scor. Pos./2 Out			61	17	0	9	8	.279	.377	.371
Late-Inning Pressure			39	9	2	5	4	.231	.462	.311
Leading Off			12	2	1	1	2	.167	.417	.231
Runners On			9	2	0	3	1	.222	.444	.385
Runners/Scor. Pos.			4	1	0	2	0	.250	.500	.429
First 9 Batters			182	47	2	12	27	.258	.346	.299
Second 9 Batters			179	49	2	15	20	.274	.397	.337
All Batters Thereafter			163	41	5	17	13	.252	.417	.320

Loves to face: Marquis Grissom (0-for-9)
       Tony Gwynn (0-for-10)
       Fred McGriff (.100, 1-for-10)
Hates to face: Jay Bell (.368, 7-for-19)
       John Kruk (.455, 5-for-11)
       Todd Zeile (.438, 7-for-16)

Miscellaneous statistics: Ground outs-to-air outs ratio: 0.87 last season, 0.73 for career.... Opponents grounded into 12 double plays in 105 opportunities (one per 8.8).... Allowed 28 doubles, 5 triples in 136 innings.... Allowed 8 first-inning runs in 21 starts (3.00 ERA).... Batting support: 3.19 runs per start, 7th-lowest average in N.L.... Opposing base stealers: 15-for-20 (75%); 2 pickoffs, 2 balks.

Comments: Quiz for Mets fans: What follow are two sets of career statistics. One is Schourek's; the other belongs to another active pitcher, also 24 years old. Your job: Guess which is which. Player One: 11–12 record, 3.89 ERA, 3.52 walks and 5.14 strikeouts per nine innings. Player Two: 9–12 record, 3.90 ERA, 3.33 walks and 5.32 strikeouts per nine innings.... We'll give you some thinking time.... Schourek is one of three left-handed pitchers in the majors who walked more lefty batters than he struck out last year (minimum: 100 lefties faced); the others: Lee Guetterman and Frank Viola.... Averaged 6.98 strikeouts per nine innings in 1991, 3.97 in 1992; among pitchers with at least 75 innings each year, only Tim Leary had a larger drop (6.19 to 2.94). Schourek became the first Mets pitcher since Ed Lynch in 1985 with fewer than four strikeouts per nine innings in a season of at least 100 innings.... Time's up. Answer: Player One is Schourek; Player Two is former teammate Julio Valera. Quite similar numbers, huh? ... Career record: 9–4, 3.04 ERA at Shea Stadium; 2–8, 5.31 ERA on the road. Difference of 2.27 between them is 5th largest among active pitchers with at least 200 innings pitched, and it's the largest for any pitcher who has spent his entire career in the same home park.... Allowed only one home run in 217 opponents' at-bats with runners on base last season; Schourek's rate was the best by a Mets pitcher since Doug Sisk held opponents homerless in 205 at-bats with runners on base in 1983.

Frank Seminara
Throws Right

San Diego Padres	W-L	ERA	AB	H	HR	BB	SO	BA	SA	OBA
Season	9-4	3.68	380	98	5	46	61	.258	.345	.341
vs. Left-Handers			204	60	4	32	24	.294	.407	.390
vs. Right-Handers			176	38	1	14	37	.216	.273	.282
vs. Ground-Ballers			180	40	1	19	29	.222	.272	.295
vs. Fly-Ballers			200	58	4	27	32	.290	.410	.381
Home Games	6-1	3.04	207	53	1	33	37	.256	.319	.360
Road Games	3-3	4.50	173	45	4	13	24	.260	.376	.317
Grass Fields	8-3	3.46	313	80	3	41	53	.256	.329	.345
Artificial Turf	1-1	4.76	67	18	2	5	8	.269	.418	.324
April	0-0	—	0	0	0	0	0	—	—	—
May	0-0	—	0	0	0	0	0	—	—	—
June	3-2	5.46	118	31	2	17	17	.263	.373	.358
July	3-1	1.64	124	30	0	12	17	.242	.266	.309
August	0-0	8.22	36	16	0	7	5	.444	.500	.535
Sept./Oct.	3-1	2.86	102	21	3	10	22	.206	.353	.287
Leading Off Inn.			94	23	1	11	11	.245	.330	.336
Bases Empty			223	53	2	25	35	.238	.300	.320
Runners On			157	45	3	21	26	.287	.408	.370
Runners/Scor. Pos.			86	22	1	16	16	.256	.360	.365
Runners On/2 Out			66	16	1	10	8	.242	.364	.351
Scor. Pos./2 Out			45	11	1	7	6	.244	.356	.346
Late-Inning Pressure			10	3	0	2	1	.300	.300	.417
Leading Off			4	1	0	0	0	.250	.250	.250
Runners On			2	0	0	0	0	.000	.000	.000
Runners/Scor. Pos.			0	0	0	0	0	—	—	—
First 9 Batters			149	30	1	12	30	.201	.242	.268
Second 9 Batters			133	42	3	22	20	.316	.429	.410
All Batters Thereafter			98	26	1	12	11	.265	.388	.351

Loves to face: Craig Biggio (0-for-8)
Marquis Grissom (0-for-6)
Tim Wallach (0-for-6)

Hates to face: Will Clark (.444, 4-for-9, 1 2B, 2 HR)
David Justice (.750, 3-for-4, 1 2B, 1 3B, 1 HR)
Larry Walker (.667, 4-for-6)

Miscellaneous statistics: Ground outs-to-air outs ratio: 1.37 last season, 1.37 for career.... Opponents grounded into 11 double plays in 88 opportunities (one per 8.0).... Allowed 12 doubles, 3 triples in 100⅓ innings.... Allowed 5 first-inning runs in 18 starts (2.50 ERA).... Batting support: 5.06 runs per start.... Opposing base stealers: 10-for-16 (63%); 2 pickoffs, 1 balk.

Comments: He and St. Louis rookie Mike Perez each went 3–0 vs. San Francisco last season. The Giants had the worst record in the majors against rookie pitchers: They were 3–0 against Kyle Abbott and 3–19 against other N.L. rookies.... The Astros had the best record in the majors against rookie pitchers last year (14–4), but Seminara was one of the guys who beat Houston, too.... Allowed one home run in 176 at-bats by right-handed batters (Barry Larkin hit it), 5th-lowest rate in N.L. (minimum: 150 at-bats by RHB). The top four: left-hander Jeff Fassero (no home runs allowed in 232 at-bats by right-handers), Roger McDowell (none in 183), Greg Maddux (one in 393), and Bill Swift (one in 218).... Didn't get his first win until June 18; from then on, he led Padres (and also N.L. rookies) in wins, and matched Roger Clemens.... His .692 winning percentage tied him with Larry Hardy (9–4 in 1974) for the 3d highest by a Padres rookie (minimum: 10 decisions). The top two: Butch Metzger, .733 (11–4 in 1976, the year he shared N.L. Rookie of the Year Award with Pat Zachry); and Mark Thurmond, .700 (7–3 in 1983).... Received the most robust batting support among all major league pitchers with at least 15 starts last season, and matched the all-time team record. The Padres scored 91 runs in 18 starts for Seminara, as they did for Mike Corkins in 1970. The difference: Corkins, despite that support, went 5–6.

Lee Smith
Throws Right

St. Louis Cardinals	W-L	ERA	AB	H	HR	BB	SO	BA	SA	OBA
Season	4-9	3.12	281	62	4	26	60	.221	.320	.286
vs. Left-Handers			163	36	2	19	38	.221	.337	.301
vs. Right-Handers			118	26	2	7	22	.220	.297	.264
vs. Ground-Ballers			122	27	0	13	22	.221	.279	.296
vs. Fly-Ballers			159	35	4	13	38	.220	.352	.277
Home Games	3-8	3.25	170	40	1	17	44	.235	.312	.305
Road Games	1-1	2.93	111	22	3	9	16	.198	.333	.256
Grass Fields	1-0	2.70	58	10	2	4	5	.172	.328	.222
Artificial Turf	3-9	3.24	223	52	2	22	55	.233	.318	.302
April	0-1	2.38	40	7	1	1	7	.175	.275	.195
May	1-1	3.72	38	9	1	4	13	.237	.421	.310
June	1-1	4.50	49	14	1	6	11	.286	.490	.364
July	1-0	0.82	38	6	0	2	6	.158	.158	.200
August	0-2	2.87	56	12	0	5	14	.214	.250	.274
Sept./Oct.	1-4	4.11	60	14	1	8	9	.233	.317	.324
Leading Off Inn.			73	17	1	0	11	.233	.342	.233
Bases Empty			165	32	2	11	31	.194	.279	.244
Runners On			116	30	2	15	29	.259	.379	.341
Runners/Scor. Pos.			74	19	1	12	22	.257	.365	.356
Runners On/2 Out			52	15	0	5	13	.288	.365	.351
Scor. Pos./2 Out			41	11	0	5	12	.268	.317	.348
Late-Inning Pressure			254	51	3	20	54	.201	.276	.259
Leading Off			69	14	0	0	11	.203	.246	.203
Runners On			96	23	2	10	23	.240	.365	.311
Runners/Scor. Pos.			56	13	1	8	16	.232	.339	.328
First 9 Batters			279	62	4	26	59	.222	.323	.288
Second 9 Batters			2	0	0	0	1	.000	.000	.000
All Batters Thereafter			0	0	0	0	0	—	—	—

Loves to face: John Kruk (0-for-15, 6 SO)
John Vanderwal (0-for-4, 4 SO)
Andy Van Slyke (.069, 2-for-29, 1 HR, 4 BB)

Hates to face: Mariano Duncan (.500, 7-for-14)
Willie McGee (.333, 8-for-24)
Tim Wallach (.259, 7-for-27, 2 HR)

Miscellaneous statistics: Ground outs-to-air outs ratio: 0.61 last season, 1.01 for career.... Opponents grounded into 4 double plays in 59 opportunities (one per 15).... Allowed 8 doubles, 4 triples in 75 innings.... Saved 43 games in 51 opportunities (84%), 2d-highest rate in N.L.... Stranded 9 inherited runners, allowed 4 to score (69%).... Opposing base stealers: 12-for-13 (92%); 0 pickoffs, 0 balks.

Comments: Became the first pitcher to lead the National League in saves in consecutive seasons since Bruce Sutter's four-year reign as N.L. saves champ ended in 1982.... Should break Sutter's N.L. record of 300 career saves in April. Of Smith's 355 career saves, 297 have come in the N.L.... Needs only 13 more saves to pass Todd Worrell as the Cardinals' all-time leader. The top three: Worrell (129), Sutter (127), Smith (117).... Has saved games for 69 different winning pitchers; the greatest benefactor has been Rick Sutcliffe (18), followed by Steve Trout and Bob Tewksbury (16 each), Omar Olivares (14), and Scott Sanderson (12). And here's a cute kicker: Smith saved 11 Cubs wins for Dennis Eckersley.... Has made at least 60 appearances in each of the past 11 seasons, but hasn't pitched more than 100 innings since 1984.... Hasn't entered a game in which the Cardinals were trailing since July 14, 1990.... Entered 64 of 70 games in the ninth inning or later, the highest percentage in the majors (91%); hasn't been called prior to the eighth inning since June 6, 1990.... Faced 89 percent of his opposing batters in Late-Inning Pressure Situations, the highest rate by an N.L. pitcher in *Player Analysis* history (minimum: 50 BFP), and probably the highest in league history.... Career total of 787 games is 4th highest among pitchers who've never appeared in a World Series, behind Lindy McDaniel (987 games), Gene Garber (931), and Phil Niekro (864). The next-most among active pitchers: Dave Smith (609) and Frank Tanana (606).

Zane Smith
Throws Left

Pittsburgh Pirates	W-L	ERA	AB	H	HR	BB	SO	BA	SA	OBA
Season	8-8	3.06	529	138	8	19	56	.261	.365	.287
vs. Left-Handers			93	20	2	2	17	.215	.312	.232
vs. Right-Handers			436	118	6	17	39	.271	.376	.298
vs. Ground-Ballers			244	63	4	9	30	.258	.352	.286
vs. Fly-Ballers			285	75	4	10	26	.263	.375	.288
Home Games	4-4	3.25	249	69	3	10	32	.277	.394	.303
Road Games	4-4	2.91	280	69	5	9	24	.246	.339	.273
Grass Fields	0-2	5.09	87	25	4	5	6	.287	.460	.323
Artificial Turf	8-6	2.67	442	113	4	14	50	.256	.346	.280
April	4-1	2.02	132	30	2	2	16	.227	.311	.243
May	1-3	4.66	154	48	5	7	13	.312	.461	.337
June	0-3	3.82	124	33	1	7	18	.266	.371	.303
July	3-0	0.39	80	14	0	2	5	.175	.225	.205
August	0-1	8.44	25	12	0	0	4	.480	.640	.480
Sept./Oct.	0-0	0.00	14	1	0	1	0	.071	.071	.133
Leading Off Inn.			139	38	1	6	19	.273	.367	.303
Bases Empty			340	80	4	11	38	.235	.324	.261
Runners On			189	58	4	8	18	.307	.439	.332
Runners/Scor. Pos.			105	35	4	6	11	.333	.562	.362
Runners On/2 Out			82	28	1	2	8	.341	.463	.357
Scor. Pos./2 Out			47	15	1	2	6	.319	.511	.347
Late-Inning Pressure			63	15	0	3	4	.238	.270	.273
Leading Off			15	4	0	3	1	.267	.333	.389
Runners On			28	7	0	0	3	.250	.286	.250
Runners/Scor. Pos.			13	3	0	0	2	.231	.308	.231
First 9 Batters			188	46	0	4	20	.245	.314	.267
Second 9 Batters			162	42	3	5	17	.259	.370	.280
All Batters Thereafter			179	50	5	10	19	.279	.413	.314

Loves to face: Shawon Dunston (.147, 5-for-34)
Kirt Manwaring (0-for-13)
Tom Pagnozzi (.087, 2-for-23, 2 BB)

Hates to face: Barry Larkin (.447, 17-for-38, 3 HR)
Terry Pendleton (.491, 26-for-53, 2 HR)
Benito Santiago (.429, 12-for-28, 3 2B, 5 HR)

Miscellaneous statistics: Ground outs-to-air outs ratio: 2.08 last season (3d highest in N.L.), 2.08 for career.... Opponents grounded into 19 double plays in 90 opportunities (one per 4.7), best rate in N.L.... Allowed 23 doubles, 4 triples in 141 innings.... Allowed 11 first-inning runs in 22 starts (3.80 ERA).... Batting support: 3.82 runs per start.... Opposing base stealers: 9-for-13 (69%); 2 pickoffs, 0 balks.

Comments: Average time of his nine-inning starts was 2 hours, 28 minutes, the fastest in the majors (minimum: 10 GS). Only two other pitchers in either league averaged less than two and one-half hours: Greg Maddux (2:29) and Mike Morgan (2:29).... His average of 1.15 walks per nine innings since joining the Pirates is the lowest in franchise history (minimum: 300 innings).... Had a 5.58 ERA with Don Slaught catching (40⅓ innings), 2.06 in 100⅔ innings with Mike LaValliere or Tom Prince behind the plate. That's a reversal; in two previous seasons, Smith had been more effective for Sluggo (1.82) than for Spanky (3.35).... Didn't walk more than two batters in any of his 22 starts last season. Every other pitcher who started at least 15 games last season walked three batters at least once.... Walked only one batter in the first inning of his 22 starts, lowest rate in the majors.... Walks allowed per nine innings in three-year periods: 1984–86, 4.79; 1987–89, 3.18; 1990–92, 1.51.... Unless his control is sharp, Smith is a losing proposition; career records as a starting pitcher: 19–6 when he walks no one, 22–21 with one walk, 30–54 with two or more.... Has recorded more outs on the ground than in the air in 58 of his last 63 starts, dating back to September 1990.... Career record is 33–52 with a 3.95 ERA on grass fields, 43–34 with a 3.10 ERA on artificial turf; record is even more lopsided over the last four seasons: 3–18 on grass, 34–22 on artificial turf.

John Smoltz
Throws Right

Atlanta Braves	W-L	ERA	AB	H	HR	BB	SO	BA	SA	OBA
Season	15-12	2.85	921	206	17	80	215	.224	.332	.287
vs. Left-Handers			541	133	9	49	103	.246	.338	.309
vs. Right-Handers			380	73	8	31	112	.192	.324	.255
vs. Ground-Ballers			434	89	5	34	90	.205	.281	.261
vs. Fly-Ballers			487	117	12	46	122	.240	.378	.310
Home Games	5-6	2.87	380	81	12	33	87	.213	.355	.279
Road Games	10-6	2.83	541	125	5	47	128	.231	.316	.293
Grass Fields	11-8	2.65	659	140	15	60	144	.212	.331	.279
Artificial Turf	4-4	3.36	262	66	2	20	71	.252	.336	.306
April	2-2	3.24	123	29	1	14	33	.236	.358	.312
May	3-2	3.33	170	39	1	20	44	.229	.324	.313
June	4-1	2.96	168	34	3	11	34	.202	.298	.257
July	3-1	0.94	141	30	3	9	32	.213	.291	.263
August	2-3	3.43	160	35	6	12	33	.219	.394	.276
Sept./Oct.	1-3	3.05	159	39	3	14	39	.245	.333	.303
Leading Off Inn.			231	48	2	20	52	.208	.294	.274
Bases Empty			552	125	10	41	123	.226	.348	.284
Runners On			369	81	7	39	92	.220	.309	.292
Runners/Scor. Pos.			199	38	5	26	58	.191	.291	.281
Runners On/2 Out			163	37	6	17	33	.227	.387	.308
Scor. Pos./2 Out			103	22	4	12	23	.214	.379	.308
Late-Inning Pressure			105	19	4	5	21	.181	.343	.218
Leading Off			27	6	1	2	3	.222	.370	.276
Runners On			35	5	1	2	11	.143	.286	.189
Runners/Scor. Pos.			16	0	0	1	8	.000	.000	.059
First 9 Batters			286	59	5	25	85	.206	.301	.269
Second 9 Batters			271	67	5	26	55	.247	.365	.313
All Batters Thereafter			364	80	7	29	75	.220	.332	.281

Loves to face: Jay Bell (.077, 2-for-26)
Jerald Clark (0-for-11)
Dwight Smith (0-for-15)

Hates to face: Brett Butler (.400, 16-for-40, 13 BB)
Eric Davis (.556, 10-for-18, 4 HR)
Mike LaValliere (.550, 11-for-20, 1 HR, 0 SO)

Miscellaneous statistics: Ground outs-to-air outs ratio: 0.94 last season, 0.87 for career.... Opponents grounded into 10 double plays in 182 opportunities (one per 18).... Allowed 39 doubles, 5 triples in 246⅔ innings.... Allowed 17 first-inning runs in 35 starts (3.86 ERA).... Batting support: 4.00 runs per start.... Opposing base stealers: 11-for-18 (61%); 2 pickoffs, 1 balk.

Comments: One of four pitchers in major league history to win as many as five postseason games without a loss. The others all pitched before World War II: Lefty Gomez 6–0; Jack Coombs, Herb Pennock, and Smoltz, each 5–0.... Has started Game 7 of three postseason series (two in 1991, one in 1992); the only other pitcher in postseason history to have started three rubber games: Bob Gibson.... Trailed David Cone by 44 strikeouts when Cone was traded to Toronto on August 26, and needed every one of his eight remaining starts to win the title. Passed Cone by striking out Andy Benes in the third inning of his final start; he left the game after the fourth.... Became only the second Braves pitcher in the last 40 years to lead the N.L. in strikeouts. Phil Niekro led the league in 1977.... Had the longest scoreless streak in the majors last season (29⅓ innings).... His 10 road wins tied him with Ken Hill for most in league.... Threw 17 wild pitches, to lead the N.L. for a third consecutive season. Only two other pitchers have led their league for three years running: Larry Cheney (1912–14 and 1916–18) and Jack Morris (1983–85).... Fourth pitcher in *Player Analysis* history to hold opposing right-handed hitters to under a .200 batting average in three consecutive seasons (minimum: 300 AB in each season). The others: Tom Seaver (1975–77), J. R. Richard (1977–79), and Sid Fernandez (1988–90).... Career record is 16–9 with a 2.76 ERA in day games, 41–45 with a 3.71 ERA at night.

Bill Swift
Throws Right

San Francisco Giants	W-L	ERA	AB	H	HR	BB	SO	BA	SA	OBA
Season	10-4	2.08	602	144	6	43	77	.239	.314	.292
vs. Left-Handers			384	101	5	38	36	.263	.359	.331
vs. Right-Handers			218	43	1	5	41	.197	.234	.219
vs. Ground-Ballers			289	69	2	25	36	.239	.298	.301
vs. Fly-Ballers			313	75	4	18	41	.240	.329	.284
Home Games	4-3	2.55	306	75	5	25	38	.245	.324	.307
Road Games	6-1	1.58	296	69	1	18	39	.233	.304	.276
Grass Fields	7-4	2.21	460	112	5	37	62	.243	.320	.303
Artificial Turf	3-0	1.63	142	32	1	6	15	.225	.296	.255
April	4-0	1.55	153	34	1	9	17	.222	.275	.265
May	2-0	3.60	89	22	1	9	12	.247	.337	.316
June	0-0	2.45	42	10	0	2	3	.238	.310	.273
July	2-2	2.25	131	34	3	11	12	.260	.382	.326
August	1-1	1.69	115	28	1	9	18	.243	.304	.294
Sept./Oct.	1-1	1.35	72	16	0	3	15	.222	.264	.263
Leading Off Inn.			154	38	2	10	15	.247	.305	.297
Bases Empty			361	90	2	27	47	.249	.305	.307
Runners On			241	54	4	16	30	.224	.328	.270
Runners/Scor. Pos.			114	19	2	12	16	.167	.298	.242
Runners On/2 Out			101	18	0	8	13	.178	.257	.239
Scor. Pos./2 Out			58	9	0	6	8	.155	.259	.234
Late-Inning Pressure			74	19	2	1	10	.257	.378	.276
Leading Off			20	6	0	1	1	.300	.300	.333
Runners On			25	6	2	0	6	.240	.520	.240
Runners/Scor. Pos.			6	1	1	0	1	.167	.667	.167
First 9 Batters			240	61	3	15	38	.254	.338	.302
Second 9 Batters			181	40	1	21	16	.221	.298	.304
All Batters Thereafter			181	43	2	7	23	.238	.298	.266

Loves to face: Steve Buechele (.063, 1-for-16)
Gary Sheffield (.067, 1-for-15)
Willie Wilson (.129, 4-for-31, 4 BB)

Hates to face: Ruben Amaro (2-for-2, 1 3B, 1 HR)
Darren Daulton (.667, 4-for-6, 2 2B, 1 HR)
Tony Fernandez (.421, 8-for-19, 2 2B, 4 BB)

Miscellaneous statistics: Ground outs-to-air outs ratio: 2.45 last season (highest in majors), 2.80 for career.... Opponents grounded into 26 double plays in 129 opportunities (one per 5.0), 2d-best rate in N.L.... Allowed 19 doubles, 4 triples in 164⅔ innings.... Allowed 14 first-inning runs in 22 starts (5.32 ERA).... Batting support: 4.05 runs per start.... Opposing base stealers: 5-for-9 (56%); 0 pickoffs, 1 balk.

Comments: Became the first pitcher to lead the N.L. in ERA in his first season in the league since rookie Hoyt Wilhelm did it in 1952. The last A.L. refugee to lead in his first N.L. season: Hank Borowy, who started 1945 with the Yankees, but ended it as the N.L. ERA leader with the Cubs.... Swift's 2.08 mark was lower than those of any of San Francisco's six previous ERA leaders: Stu Miller (2.47 in 1958), Sam Jones (2.82 in 1959), Mike McCormick (2.70 in 1960), Juan Marichal (2.10 in 1969), Atlee Hammaker (2.25 in 1983), and Scott Garrelts (2.28 in 1989). But the lowest ERA in San Francisco history belongs to Bobby Bolin, whose 1.98 mark in 1968 ranked a distant 2d in the N.L. to Bob Gibson's 1.12.... Became the third pitcher to win each of his first six decisions for the Giants since they moved to San Francisco. The others: Billy Pierce (won his first eight, 1962) and John Cumberland (won his first seven, 1970-71).... Allowed six home runs in 164⅔ innings, for the 4th-lowest rate in league.... Career ratio of 2.80 ground outs per fly out is 2d highest among active pitchers (minimum: 1000 BFP), behind only Roger McDowell (2.96).... Has recorded more ground outs than air outs in 29 of 30 starts over the last three seasons, including all 22 starts he made in 1992.... Career record is 29-38 with a 4.34 ERA in 108 starts, 11-6 with a 2.35 ERA in 175 relief appearances.... Over the last three seasons, he's 11-2 with a 1.67 ERA in day games, 6-8 with a 2.43 ERA at night.

Greg Swindell
Throws Left

Cincinnati Reds	W-L	ERA	AB	H	HR	BB	SO	BA	SA	OBA
Season	12-8	2.70	808	210	14	41	138	.260	.365	.295
vs. Left-Handers			168	41	2	9	30	.244	.345	.285
vs. Right-Handers			640	169	12	32	108	.264	.370	.297
vs. Ground-Ballers			336	77	5	13	67	.229	.313	.259
vs. Fly-Ballers			472	133	9	28	71	.282	.403	.320
Home Games	7-2	2.31	408	107	6	23	68	.262	.348	.300
Road Games	5-6	3.10	400	103	8	18	70	.257	.382	.289
Grass Fields	2-4	4.38	198	60	6	12	32	.303	.465	.341
Artificial Turf	10-4	2.19	610	150	8	29	106	.246	.333	.280
April	1-1	4.78	102	29	3	6	18	.284	.441	.318
May	3-1	1.77	170	41	3	8	31	.241	.318	.272
June	3-0	3.32	157	46	5	9	26	.293	.439	.331
July	2-2	2.13	142	36	0	8	18	.254	.317	.288
August	3-2	1.66	142	35	2	5	26	.246	.352	.277
Sept./Oct.	0-2	3.60	95	23	1	5	19	.242	.337	.287
Leading Off Inn.			211	54	6	9	40	.256	.417	.293
Bases Empty			506	141	10	24	87	.279	.403	.314
Runners On			302	69	4	17	51	.228	.301	.264
Runners/Scor. Pos.			154	41	2	12	27	.266	.338	.306
Runners On/2 Out			137	30	1	11	24	.219	.285	.277
Scor. Pos./2 Out			77	18	1	9	14	.234	.312	.314
Late-Inning Pressure			76	26	3	4	14	.342	.526	.370
Leading Off			23	10	2	0	4	.435	.870	.435
Runners On			31	8	0	1	6	.258	.258	.273
Runners/Scor. Pos.			17	6	0	1	3	.353	.353	.368
First 9 Batters			254	52	3	14	47	.205	.283	.251
Second 9 Batters			249	64	3	14	47	.257	.349	.294
All Batters Thereafter			305	94	8	13	44	.308	.446	.332

Loves to face: Pete Incaviglia (.061, 2-for-33, 3 BB, 16 SO)
Lonnie Smith (0-for-9)
Ozzie Smith (0-for-7)

Hates to face: Jeff Blauser (.417, 5-for-12, 3 BB)
Bernard Gilkey (.714, 5-for-7, 1 BB)
Fred McGriff (.368, 7-for-19, 2 HR, 7 BB)

Miscellaneous statistics: Ground outs-to-air outs ratio: 0.76 last season (5th lowest in N.L.), 0.76 for career.... Opponents grounded into 16 double plays in 126 opportunities (one per 7.9).... Allowed 37 doubles, 3 triples in 213⅔ innings.... Allowed 9 first-inning runs in 30 starts (2.70 ERA).... Batting support: 4.40 runs per start, 5th-highest average in N.L.... Opposing base stealers: 17-for-26 (65%); 9 pickoffs (3d most in N.L.), 2 balks.

Comments: Last season marked only the second time since the opening of Riverfront Stadium that two Reds pitchers compiled ERAs below 3.00: Swindell and Jose Rijo, who posted a 2.56 mark. The other time was in 1988: Rijo (2.39) and Danny Jackson (2.73).... Was hardly intimidated by Riverfront, posting the 2d-lowest ERA there over the past 10 years, behind Rijo's 2.24 mark in 1990.... Will take career records of 41-28 in home games and 31-35 on the road to the Astrodome, his third different home in as many years.... Houston's 1993 rotation will apparently include at least three pitchers who made their major league debuts in the American League: Swindell, Pete Harnisch, and Doug Drabek. Among the 14 pitchers who've won at least 45 games for Houston, only one made his debut in the A.L.: Jim Deshaies.... Could have been 17-7 last season, as he failed to win five games in which he handed a lead to the bullpen.... Averaged 1.73 walks per nine innings last season, the 3d-lowest rate in the N.L. His career rate of 1.91 per nine innings is 2d lowest among active pitchers (minimum: 1000 innings), behind only Bret Saberhagen (1.83).... Has walked fewer than two batters per nine innings in three consecutive seasons of at least 200 innings pitched. The last pitcher with a longer streak was LaMarr Hoyt (4 years, 1982-85).... Opponents' career batting averages increase markedly with each pass through the order: .232 on his first pass, .261 on his second pass, .291 thereafter.

Bob Tewksbury — Throws Right

St. Louis Cardinals	W-L	ERA	AB	H	HR	BB	SO	BA	SA	OBA
Season	16-5	2.16	876	217	15	20	91	.248	.353	.265
vs. Left-Handers			517	125	10	7	57	.242	.344	.250
vs. Right-Handers			359	92	5	13	34	.256	.365	.286
vs. Ground-Ballers			411	96	4	8	39	.234	.299	.250
vs. Fly-Ballers			465	121	11	12	52	.260	.400	.278
Home Games	10-2	1.52	451	99	8	8	49	.220	.322	.236
Road Games	6-3	2.90	425	118	7	12	42	.278	.386	.295
Grass Fields	3-2	2.52	276	72	6	6	30	.261	.384	.276
Artificial Turf	13-3	2.00	600	145	9	14	61	.242	.338	.260
April	2-0	1.61	101	26	1	1	11	.257	.356	.260
May	4-1	1.88	176	39	4	5	18	.222	.352	.240
June	3-1	2.23	175	47	3	3	15	.269	.366	.283
July	1-2	2.04	135	36	2	5	17	.267	.341	.293
August	4-1	2.18	165	38	1	2	17	.230	.315	.237
Sept./Oct.	2-0	3.09	124	31	4	4	13	.250	.395	.285
Leading Off Inn.			229	46	2	6	22	.201	.288	.225
Bases Empty			567	148	11	14	60	.261	.383	.281
Runners On			309	69	4	6	31	.223	.298	.235
Runners/Scor. Pos.			162	32	3	5	13	.198	.278	.213
Runners On/2 Out			141	25	1	3	13	.177	.234	.194
Scor. Pos./2 Out			75	13	0	3	6	.173	.187	.205
Late-Inning Pressure			90	17	2	1	10	.189	.311	.198
Leading Off			26	5	1	0	2	.192	.462	.192
Runners On			20	3	0	0	4	.150	.150	.150
Runners/Scor. Pos.			10	1	0	0	2	.100	.100	.100
First 9 Batters			279	78	4	7	34	.280	.380	.298
Second 9 Batters			276	63	6	4	25	.228	.348	.240
All Batters Thereafter			321	76	5	9	32	.237	.333	.257

Loves to face: Andres Galarraga (0-for-13)
Joe Girardi (.063, 1-for-16)
Gary Sheffield (0-for-12)

Hates to face: Orlando Merced (.391, 9-for-23, 1 HR)
Ryne Sandberg (.406, 13-for-32, 3 2B, 4 HR)
Andy Van Slyke (.406, 13-for-32)

Miscellaneous statistics: Ground outs-to-air outs ratio: 1.49 last season, 1.43 for career.... Opponents grounded into 25 double plays in 130 opportunities (one per 5.2), 3d-best rate in N.L.... Allowed 39 doubles, 4 triples in 233 innings.... Allowed 18 first-inning runs in 32 starts (4.50 ERA).... Batting support: 4.06 runs per start.... Opposing base stealers: 7-for-11 (64%); 0 pickoffs, 0 balks.

Comments: His average of 0.77 walks per nine innings was the lowest in the majors since Cincinnati's Red Lucas walked just 18 batters in 220 innings in 1933 (0.74 per nine innings). *Only three other pitchers in this century posted rates that low:* Babe Adams (0.62 in 1920), Christy Mathewson (0.62 in 1913 and 0.66 in 1914), and Cy Young (0.69 in 1904).... Also had the lowest strikeout rate in the N.L. last season (3.52 per nine innings). The last pitchers to own their league's lowest rates in both walks and strikeouts were Dick Donovan with the Indians in 1962 and Lew Burdette with the Braves in 1960.... Of 915 opposing batters, 801 put the ball into play (87.5%), a career high for Tewksbury, but not the highest rate in the majors last season. That distinction belonged to Bill Gullickson (805 of 919, 87.6%).... Tewksbury's career rate of 1.56 walks per nine innings is the lowest among active pitchers. He is the only active pitcher in the all-time top 50 (minimum: 750 IP); in fact, only four other pitchers on that list of 50 debuted within the last 40 years: Dick Hall (1.69, 1955–71), Juan Marichal (1.82, 1960–75), Fritz Peterson (1.73, 1966–76), and Dan Quisenberry (1.40, 1979–90).... Was the first Cardinals pitcher to lead the N.L. in winning percentage since Al Hrabosky in 1975 (minimum: 15 decisions). The last Cardinals starter to lead the league was Nelson Briles in 1967.... Opponents grounded into 27 double plays, 2d-highest total of any N.L. pitcher.... ERA in home games was 2d lowest in the majors, behind Mike Morgan (1.38).

Randy Tomlin — Throws Left

Pittsburgh Pirates	W-L	ERA	AB	H	HR	BB	SO	BA	SA	OBA
Season	14-9	3.41	801	226	11	42	90	.282	.397	.320
vs. Left-Handers			150	38	2	11	26	.253	.327	.307
vs. Right-Handers			651	188	9	31	64	.289	.413	.323
vs. Ground-Ballers			368	104	5	18	44	.283	.378	.318
vs. Fly-Ballers			433	122	6	24	46	.282	.413	.322
Home Games	7-3	2.37	418	111	4	13	56	.266	.364	.288
Road Games	7-6	4.56	383	115	7	29	34	.300	.433	.353
Grass Fields	4-4	4.50	223	67	3	17	16	.300	.439	.350
Artificial Turf	10-5	2.99	578	159	8	25	74	.275	.381	.308
April	4-0	1.67	91	19	1	10	10	.209	.264	.305
May	1-3	7.33	107	42	2	10	8	.393	.561	.444
June	5-1	2.22	161	42	4	5	22	.261	.379	.283
July	0-3	5.45	135	45	1	6	11	.333	.496	.361
August	3-1	2.68	163	40	2	6	19	.245	.319	.271
Sept./Oct.	1-1	2.68	144	38	1	5	20	.264	.375	.291
Leading Off Inn.			206	69	4	8	17	.335	.461	.369
Bases Empty			471	134	6	22	55	.285	.393	.321
Runners On			330	92	5	20	35	.279	.403	.319
Runners/Scor. Pos.			194	52	3	17	21	.268	.392	.323
Runners On/2 Out			135	35	0	13	16	.259	.341	.329
Scor. Pos./2 Out			98	22	0	12	12	.224	.316	.309
Late-Inning Pressure			72	20	2	4	14	.278	.403	.316
Leading Off			20	5	0	1	4	.250	.250	.286
Runners On			21	8	1	2	3	.381	.619	.435
Runners/Scor. Pos.			7	3	1	1	0	.429	.857	.500
First 9 Batters			282	77	4	15	34	.273	.397	.311
Second 9 Batters			273	76	1	13	24	.278	.355	.311
All Batters Thereafter			246	73	6	14	32	.297	.443	.340

Loves to face: Vince Coleman (.050, 1-for-20)
Darrin Jackson (0-for-11)
Fred McGriff (0-for-19)

Hates to face: Tony Gwynn (.450, 9-for-20, 1 HR)
Charlie Hayes (.600, 6-for-10)
Ryne Sandberg (.560, 14-for-25, 1 HR, 0 SO)

Miscellaneous statistics: Ground outs-to-air outs ratio: 1.65 last season, 1.52 for career.... Opponents grounded into 27 double plays in 154 opportunities (one per 5.7), 4th-best rate in N.L.... Allowed 45 doubles (most in N.L.), 7 triples in 208⅔ innings.... Allowed 12 first-inning runs in 33 starts (3.00 ERA).... Batting support: 4.24 runs per start.... Opposing base stealers: 21-for-29 (72%); 7 pickoffs, 2 balks.

Comments: He owns Fred McGriff and Darrin Jackson, but no other active player is hitless in more than eight at-bats against Tomlin.... Career record is 6–0 in April (all in the last two seasons); no other active pitcher has more than five April wins without at least one loss. Over the last two years, two other pitchers have April records as good as Tomlin's: Mike Moore (7–0) and Greg Hibbard (6–0).... Averaged 1.81 walks per nine innings, the 5th-lowest rate in the N.L.... Only two N.L. pitchers who qualified for the ERA title averaged fewer than four strikeouts per nine innings: Bob Tewksbury (3.52 SO per nine) and Tomlin (3.88).... No Pirates pitcher had rates as low as Tomlin's in both strikeouts and walks since Vern Law in 1959.... Gave up 63 extra-base hits, 3d-highest total among N.L. pitchers.... Started eight games in which he failed to pitch at least five innings, tied for the most in the N.L.... ERA in road games was 5th highest in the league.... Allowed 17 stolen bases in 21 attempts with Mike LaValliere catching (81%), but only four in eight attempts with Don Slaught behind the plate.... Started 10 games in which he did not walk a batter last season; only four pitchers had more starts without a walk: Bob Tewksbury (19), Chris Bosio (12), and Rheal Cormier (11).... Career record is 4–10 with a 3.71 ERA in day games, 22–10 with a 2.82 ERA at night.... Tough on lefties, who own a .222 career batting average against him, compared to a .271 mark by opposing right-handed batters.

Bob Walk — Throws Right

Pittsburgh Pirates	W-L	ERA	AB	H	HR	BB	SO	BA	SA	OBA
Season	10-6	3.20	512	132	10	43	60	.258	.379	.322
vs. Left-Handers			286	82	6	28	21	.287	.423	.353
vs. Right-Handers			226	50	4	15	39	.221	.323	.282
vs. Ground-Ballers			242	60	2	16	27	.248	.347	.304
vs. Fly-Ballers			270	72	8	27	33	.267	.407	.338
Home Games	8-3	2.82	288	71	5	24	40	.247	.358	.304
Road Games	2-3	3.70	224	61	5	19	20	.272	.406	.332
Grass Fields	1-2	3.32	163	44	3	15	16	.270	.399	.335
Artificial Turf	9-4	3.14	349	88	7	28	44	.252	.370	.316
April	1-1	2.76	58	12	0	8	11	.207	.259	.324
May	0-2	5.66	84	22	2	9	14	.262	.429	.333
June	0-0	0.00	29	8	0	2	4	.276	.310	.323
July	2-1	4.21	103	31	1	5	10	.301	.369	.333
August	5-0	1.65	116	26	3	7	9	.224	.353	.286
Sept./Oct.	2-2	3.34	122	33	4	12	12	.270	.451	.338
Leading Off Inn.			132	38	4	5	11	.288	.424	.314
Bases Empty			305	79	7	16	27	.259	.393	.305
Runners On			207	53	3	27	33	.256	.357	.346
Runners/Scor. Pos.			128	37	2	20	21	.289	.422	.387
Runners On/2 Out			91	26	0	15	15	.286	.363	.393
Scor. Pos./2 Out			64	21	0	11	10	.328	.438	.434
Late-Inning Pressure			69	26	1	4	5	.377	.493	.427
Leading Off			16	10	0	1	1	.625	.813	.647
Runners On			41	13	1	2	2	.317	.439	.364
Runners/Scor. Pos.			26	7	1	1	2	.269	.462	.296
First 9 Batters			240	69	5	17	30	.287	.387	.344
Second 9 Batters			152	28	3	14	21	.184	.289	.253
All Batters Thereafter			120	35	2	12	9	.292	.475	.366

Loves to face: Jose Uribe (.120, 3-for-25)
Tim Wallach (.161, 10-for-62, 1 HR)
Matt Williams (0-for-12)

Hates to face: Daryl Boston (.545, 6-for-11, 1 2B, 2 HR, 3 BB)
Darryl Strawberry (.400, 8-for-20, 1 2B, 4 HR)
Rick Wilkins (.700, 7-for-10, 2 HR)

Miscellaneous statistics: Ground outs-to-air outs ratio: 1.61 last season, 1.28 for career.... Opponents grounded into 13 double plays in 92 opportunities (one per 7.1).... Allowed 26 doubles, 3 triples in 135 innings.... Allowed 8 first-inning runs in 19 starts (3.79 ERA).... Batting support: 5.05 runs per start.... Record of 6–6, 3.38 ERA as a starter; 4–0, 2.45 ERA in 17 relief appearances.... Stranded 2 inherited runners, allowed 4 to score (33%).... Opposing base stealers: 19-for-24 (79%); 2 pickoffs, 2 balks.

Comments: The only National League pitcher to finish each of the last six seasons at least two games above the .500 level. The last Pirates pitcher with a longer streak was Ray Kremer, who did it in his first seven seasons in the majors (1924–30).... His career-average support of 4.70 runs per start is the highest in the National League among all active pitchers (minimum: 50 GS). In fact, only three N.L. pitchers have received greater support during the expansion era (minimum: 200 GS): Tony Cloninger (4.97), Jack Billingham (4.78), and Steve Blass (4.75).... Has a career record of 2–24 in 51 starts in which his team scored fewer than three runs. Pittsburgh has scored at least three runs in 52 of his last 61 starts (85%); the league average during that time: 66 percent.... Had a 2.43 ERA in 55⅔ innings with Don Slaught catching last season, compared to 3.74 in 79⅓ innings with Mike LaValliere or Tom Prince behind the plate.... Career total of 46 RBIs is 4th highest among active pitchers, behind Dwight Gooden (54), Rick Sutcliffe (54), and John Candelaria (48).... Pitched a three-hit complete-game victory in Game 5 of the 1992 N.L.C.S., to keep the series alive and headed back to Atlanta. He had pitched only one complete game of less than four hits in his career—way back on July 16, 1980.... Has spent time on the disabled list in each of the last four seasons.... He is the only N.L. pitcher to make at least 25 appearances for the same club in each of the last seven seasons.

John Wetteland — Throws Right

Montreal Expos	W-L	ERA	AB	H	HR	BB	SO	BA	SA	OBA
Season	4-4	2.92	301	64	6	36	99	.213	.306	.304
vs. Left-Handers			174	35	3	21	66	.201	.293	.289
vs. Right-Handers			127	29	3	15	33	.228	.323	.324
vs. Ground-Ballers			135	27	1	14	43	.200	.252	.280
vs. Fly-Ballers			166	37	5	22	56	.223	.349	.323
Home Games	2-3	3.83	164	35	4	15	50	.213	.305	.291
Road Games	2-1	1.86	137	29	2	21	49	.212	.307	.319
Grass Fields	2-0	1.37	66	14	2	8	21	.212	.318	.303
Artificial Turf	2-4	3.39	235	50	4	28	78	.213	.302	.305
April	0-1	4.50	33	9	0	4	10	.273	.333	.368
May	0-1	5.93	53	13	3	5	19	.245	.472	.328
June	0-0	4.50	35	7	0	2	9	.200	.229	.243
July	2-0	0.57	52	10	0	4	15	.192	.192	.263
August	1-1	2.93	55	12	2	12	19	.218	.345	.358
Sept./Oct.	1-1	1.31	73	13	1	9	27	.178	.260	.268
Leading Off Inn.			65	17	2	3	19	.262	.415	.294
Bases Empty			143	31	3	17	45	.217	.315	.300
Runners On			158	33	3	19	54	.209	.297	.308
Runners/Scor. Pos.			101	24	3	15	30	.238	.356	.339
Runners On/2 Out			73	14	2	8	23	.192	.315	.280
Scor. Pos./2 Out			55	11	2	5	16	.200	.345	.267
Late-Inning Pressure			227	50	6	29	80	.220	.330	.313
Leading Off			46	14	2	3	14	.304	.500	.347
Runners On			132	25	3	16	49	.189	.280	.285
Runners/Scor. Pos.			85	20	3	13	27	.235	.365	.340
First 9 Batters			295	63	6	34	97	.214	.308	.302
Second 9 Batters			6	1	0	2	2	.167	.167	.375
All Batters Thereafter			0	0	0	0	0			

Loves to face: Todd Benzinger (0-for-5, 5 SO, 1 HBP)
Chris Sabo (0-for-9)
Dwight Smith (0-for-6)

Hates to face: Craig Biggio (.556, 5-for-9, 2 HR, 3 SO)
Ken Caminiti (.500, 4-for-8, 1 2B, 1 HR)
Ozzie Smith (.667, 4-for-6, 1 BB)

Miscellaneous statistics: Ground outs-to-air outs ratio: 0.76 last season, 0.76 for career.... Opponents grounded into 4 double plays in 75 opportunities (one per 19).... Allowed 8 doubles, 1 triple in 83⅓ innings.... Saved 37 games in 46 opportunities (80%).... Stranded 29 inherited runners, allowed 8 to score (78%).... Opposing base stealers: 14-for-17 (82%); 0 pickoffs, 0 balks.

Comments: Saved 37 games last season after earning no saves in six appearances for the Dodgers in 1991 (although he did save 20 games for Albuquerque). Other 30-save seasons by pitchers who had zero the previous season: Dave Righetti (30 in 1984) and Jeff Russell (38 in 1989); both had spent the previous season as starters.... Only two other pitchers saved more than 25 games without at least 10 appearances in the majors the year before: Fred Gladding (1969) and Bill Landrum (1988).... After one season with Montreal, his saves total ranks fifth in Expos franchise history. Next on his hit list: Woodie Fryman (52).... Career record is 2–9 with a 5.49 ERA in 17 starts; 10–7, 2.48 ERA in 109 relief appearances.... Difference between the career batting averages of opposing ground-ball and fly-ball hitters (.202 and .241, respectively) is far greater than that between left- and right-handed batters (.222 and .225, respectively).... Opponents' career batting average of .189 with runners on base in Late-Inning Pressure Situations is 3d lowest among active pitchers (minimum: 150 BFP), behind Mike Boddicker (.181) and Bryan Harvey (.185).... Career ERA is 5.11 in day games (79⅓ innings), 2.72 in 158⅔ innings at night.... Career ERA is 6.80 over the first two months of the season, 2.78 from June through October.... Although he never played in the Tigers or Reds system, he had brief stays in both organizations. He was selected by the Tigers from Los Angeles in the Rule-5 draft in December 1987, but was returned to the Dodgers the next spring. In November 1991, he was sent to Cincinnati with Tim Belcher in the deal that brought Eric Davis to L.A., but was dealt to the Expos two weeks later.

Brian Williams   Throws Right

Houston Astros	W-L	ERA	AB	H	HR	BB	SO	BA	SA	OBA
Season	7-6	3.92	361	92	10	42	54	.255	.393	.330
vs. Left-Handers			218	57	5	27	28	.261	.385	.340
vs. Right-Handers			143	35	5	15	26	.245	.406	.314
vs. Ground-Ballers			187	51	2	17	23	.273	.369	.332
vs. Fly-Ballers			174	41	8	25	31	.236	.420	.328
Home Games	3-3	4.10	160	43	3	23	24	.269	.381	.359
Road Games	4-3	3.79	201	49	7	19	30	.244	.403	.306
Grass Fields	2-2	3.77	118	29	6	9	17	.246	.449	.299
Artificial Turf	5-4	3.99	243	63	4	33	37	.259	.366	.344
April	0-0	—	0	0	0	0	0	—	—	—
May	0-0	—	0	0	0	0	0	—	—	—
June	3-0	1.29	71	13	1	8	8	.183	.296	.266
July	0-1	3.04	98	24	1	6	14	.245	.337	.286
August	3-3	4.64	130	36	6	17	25	.277	.462	.356
Sept./Oct.	1-2	7.47	62	19	2	11	7	.306	.452	.411
Leading Off Inn.			93	26	1	7	15	.280	.355	.330
Bases Empty			200	54	5	24	30	.270	.425	.348
Runners On			161	38	5	18	24	.236	.354	.308
Runners/Scor. Pos.			101	20	2	11	17	.198	.287	.270
Runners On/2 Out			63	13	4	6	10	.206	.429	.275
Scor. Pos./2 Out			48	10	2	3	7	.208	.354	.255
Late-Inning Pressure			28	7	0	2	1	.250	.286	.300
Leading Off			8	3	0	1	0	.375	.375	.444
Runners On			12	2	0	0	1	.167	.167	.167
Runners/Scor. Pos.			4	1	0	0	0	.250	.250	.250
First 9 Batters			123	31	4	18	20	.252	.431	.345
Second 9 Batters			124	29	2	14	24	.234	.306	.309
All Batters Thereafter			114	32	4	10	10	.281	.447	.336

Loves to face: Sid Bream (0-for-7)
               Jerald Clark (0-for-5)
               John Kruk (0-for-5)
Hates to face: Will Clark (.667, 4-for-6, 1 HR)
               Terry Pendleton (.667, 6-for-9)
               Gary Sheffield (.667, 4-for-6, 1 2B, 2 HR)

Miscellaneous statistics: Ground outs-to-air outs ratio: 1.06 last season, 1.15 for career.... Opponents grounded into 10 double plays in 88 opportunities (one per 8.8).... Allowed 16 doubles, 2 triples in 96⅓ innings.... Allowed 13 first-inning runs in 16 starts (6.75 ERA, 4th highest in N.L.).... Batting support: 4.06 runs per start.... Opposing base stealers: 7-for-10 (70%); 0 pickoffs, 1 balk.

Comments: Was 4–0 with a 1.81 ERA in six starts in which he recorded more ground outs than fly outs, compared to 3–6 with a 5.75 ERA when the opposite was true.... Walked an average of one of every 5.8 batters he faced during the first inning of his 16 starts, the highest rate in the National League.... Failed to induce a double-play grounder in 16 first-inning opportunities; his rate was one every 7.2 opportunities thereafter.... Ground outs-to-air outs ratio was lower in the first inning than in any other.... Thanks in part to last summer's Republican convention, Williams had a streak of 10 starts from June 27 to August 21 in which he pitched in nine different ballparks, missing only Shea Stadium, Olympic Stadium, and Busch Stadium.... Allowed seven homers in 25 innings in California ballparks, including back-to-back homers twice in the same game, to the same two batters: Gary Sheffield and Fred McGriff, on August 6 at Jack Murphy Stadium. That was the only National League game last season in which one pitcher allowed four home runs.... Rookie-season statistical profile is similar to that of Baltimore pitcher Arthur Rhodes (7–5 with a 3.63 ERA in 15 starts; 87 hits, 38 BB, 77 SO in 94⅓ innings). Other similar recent rookies: Kevin Ritz in 1989, Shawn Boskie in 1990, Chris Haney and Kevin Morton in 1991; none won more than four games as a sophomore.

Mitch Williams   Throws Left

Philadelphia Phillies	W-L	ERA	AB	H	HR	BB	SO	BA	SA	OBA
Season	5-8	3.78	287	69	4	64	74	.240	.359	.386
vs. Left-Handers			49	13	0	8	9	.265	.286	.379
vs. Right-Handers			238	56	4	56	65	.235	.374	.387
vs. Ground-Ballers			102	25	1	22	27	.245	.314	.378
vs. Fly-Ballers			185	44	3	42	47	.238	.384	.391
Home Games	3-5	4.29	149	37	1	35	43	.248	.356	.399
Road Games	2-3	3.23	138	32	3	29	31	.232	.362	.372
Grass Fields	2-2	3.72	70	19	3	16	14	.271	.471	.398
Artificial Turf	3-6	3.79	217	50	1	48	60	.230	.323	.382
April	2-0	4.91	41	12	0	7	5	.293	.439	.400
May	0-1	1.20	48	7	0	15	15	.146	.208	.349
June	0-1	1.98	44	8	1	13	13	.182	.273	.383
July	1-1	8.18	46	15	2	9	13	.326	.565	.436
August	0-3	5.14	53	15	0	5	14	.283	.340	.367
Sept./Oct.	2-2	2.76	55	12	1	15	14	.218	.345	.389
Leading Off Inn.			61	15	1	15	18	.246	.328	.403
Bases Empty			129	33	2	33	33	.256	.357	.422
Runners On			158	36	2	31	41	.228	.361	.356
Runners/Scor. Pos.			107	26	2	20	25	.243	.402	.364
Runners On/2 Out			71	14	0	11	19	.197	.268	.313
Scor. Pos./2 Out			49	11	0	8	12	.224	.306	.345
Late-Inning Pressure			205	45	2	47	49	.220	.317	.370
Leading Off			44	11	0	11	12	.250	.295	.400
Runners On			114	21	2	22	28	.184	.316	.317
Runners/Scor. Pos.			75	16	2	12	15	.213	.387	.322
First 9 Batters			280	64	4	64	73	.229	.343	.380
Second 9 Batters			7	5	0	0	1	.714	1.000	.714
All Batters Thereafter			0	0	0	0	0	—	—	—

Loves to face: Mark Grace (.083, 1-for-12)
               Marquis Grissom (0-for-11)
               Darryl Strawberry (0-for-12, 7 SO)
Hates to face: Kevin Bass (.455, 5-for-11, 2 2B, 2 HR)
               Ken Caminiti (.500, 5-for-10, 1 HR, 3 BB)
               Lonnie Smith (.500, 2-for-4, 1 2B, 1 3B, 7 BB)

Miscellaneous statistics: Ground outs-to-air outs ratio: 0.60 last season, 0.66 for career.... Opponents grounded into 3 double plays in 77 opportunities (one per 26).... Allowed 16 doubles, 3 triples in 81 innings.... Saved 29 games in 36 opportunities (81%), 5th-highest rate in N.L.... Stranded 8 inherited runners, allowed 4 to score (67%).... Opposing base stealers: 9-for-15 (60%); 6 pickoffs, 3 balks.

Comments: Has allowed 436 hits and walked 448 batters in his seven-year major league career. He's one of only three pitchers in major league history who had allowed fewer than 400 hits at the time of their 400th walk; Tommy Byrne and Bob Turley were the others. Here's something to shoot for: No pitcher in major league history has finished a career of more than 250 innings with a higher total of walks than hits allowed. The longest career among pitchers who did so: Dick Weik (213 innings, 237 walks, 203 hits); Tommy Lasorda is among the guys who did that in a shorter career.... Averaged 7.11 walks per nine innings last year, the highest rate in history for a 20-game saver. Old record: 6.71 by Bryan Harvey in 1989; Williams (1991–92) and Don ("Full Pack") Stanhouse (1978–79) are the only pitchers who twice averaged six walks per game in 20-save seasons.... Had highest rate of hit batters (one every 61.3 batters faced) among N.L. pitchers in 1992 (minimum: 50 innings); his career rate of one every 55.9 batters is highest among active pitchers (minimum: 200 innings).... Phillies bullpen had 4.20 ERA last year, worst in N.L.; besides Williams, their other lefty relievers combined for 5.05 ERA.... Entered only five of 66 games with runners in scoring position; among relievers in at least 40 games, only Todd Worrell, who entered only four of his 67 games with RISP, had a lower rate.... Has allowed only two home runs to left-handed batters in the past five years: Paul O'Neill and Andy Van Slyke hit them in 1990.

Trevor Wilson — Throws Left

San Francisco Giants	W-L	ERA	AB	H	HR	BB	SO	BA	SA	OBA
Season	8-14	4.21	574	152	18	64	88	.265	.416	.342
vs. Left-Handers			135	35	3	15	30	.259	.356	.348
vs. Right-Handers			439	117	15	49	58	.267	.435	.339
vs. Ground-Ballers			254	77	10	23	41	.303	.484	.365
vs. Fly-Ballers			320	75	8	41	47	.234	.363	.323
Home Games	4-9	4.17	322	87	11	30	45	.270	.435	.338
Road Games	4-5	4.26	252	65	7	34	43	.258	.393	.346
Grass Fields	5-13	4.40	454	125	15	41	63	.275	.436	.337
Artificial Turf	3-1	3.51	120	27	3	23	25	.225	.342	.356
April	1-1	3.38	72	21	3	5	10	.292	.472	.342
May	3-3	4.91	118	29	3	20	21	.246	.364	.353
June	1-4	4.63	130	33	6	17	19	.254	.438	.349
July	1-3	3.41	119	31	3	11	24	.261	.403	.333
August	2-3	4.29	135	38	3	11	14	.281	.422	.331
Sept./Oct.	0-0	0.00	0	0	0	0	0	.000	.000	.000
Leading Off Inn.			144	38	2	16	27	.264	.375	.342
Bases Empty			313	83	7	42	53	.265	.393	.356
Runners On			261	69	11	22	35	.264	.444	.324
Runners/Scor. Pos.			131	34	6	17	19	.260	.435	.344
Runners On/2 Out			94	22	4	14	11	.234	.436	.351
Scor. Pos./2 Out			59	13	3	12	6	.220	.441	.378
Late-Inning Pressure			24	4	0	1	9	.167	.250	.231
Leading Off			8	1	0	0	3	.125	.250	.125
Runners On			6	0	0	0	3	.000	.000	.143
Runners/Scor. Pos.			5	0	0	0	3	.000	.000	.167
First 9 Batters			207	54	5	20	36	.261	.391	.325
Second 9 Batters			202	56	6	24	25	.277	.431	.357
All Batters Thereafter			165	42	7	20	27	.255	.430	.344

Loves to face: Eric Anthony (.091, 1-for-11)
Darryl Strawberry (0-for-16)
Milt Thompson (0-for-8)

Hates to face: Ken Caminiti (.333, 8-for-24, 2 2B, 3 HR, 0 SO)
Mariano Duncan (.435, 10-for-23, 1 HR)
Fred McGriff (.700, 7-for-10, 2 HR)

Miscellaneous statistics: Ground outs-to-air outs ratio: 1.25 last season, 1.51 for career.... Opponents grounded into 20 double plays in 147 opportunities (one per 7.4).... Allowed 25 doubles, 4 triples in 154 innings.... Allowed 12 first-inning runs in 26 starts (3.81 ERA).... Batting support: 3.08 runs per start, 2d-lowest average in N.L.... Opposing base stealers: 6-for-13 (46%); 2 pickoffs, 7 balks (most in majors).

Comments: From 1991 to 1992, his rate of strikeouts decreased while his rates of walks, hits, and home runs allowed increased (minimum: 20 starts each year). That was the 3d straight year that a Giants pitcher had undergone such a breakdown: It happened to Scott Garrelts in 1990 and to Bud Black in 1991.... Wilson and Black both opened the season on the disabled list, but went on to start 26 and 28 games, respectively. Only one other N.L. pitcher who started the season on the DL went on to start more than 10 games (Jimmy Jones, 23).... Wilson and Black not only returned, but they went on to finish tied with each other for the major league lead in balks (seven).... Allowed two home runs to Otis Nixon, the only two homers hit by Nixon all season. Also gave up a pair of homers to three more likely players: Gary Sheffield, Eric Karros, and Fred McGriff. McGriff's homers are noteworthy because before last season, Wilson had allowed only two home runs in 261 at-bats by left-handed batters.... Although his overall career rate of walks per nine innings is 3.79—a little high, to be sure, but nothing to be ashamed of—he has been a veritable wild man when facing the first guy up in an inning. Over the past four years, he has walked 65 of 524 leadoff batters, or one every 8.06, the highest rate among N.L. pitchers (minimum: 500 batters faced). To provide added perspective, consider that renowned walkmeister Bobby Witt has an almost identical rate over that span (8.03).

Anthony Young — Throws Right

New York Mets	W-L	ERA	AB	H	HR	BB	SO	BA	SA	OBA
Season	2-14	4.17	470	134	8	31	64	.285	.423	.328
vs. Left-Handers			257	83	3	18	31	.323	.463	.365
vs. Right-Handers			213	51	5	13	33	.239	.376	.284
vs. Ground-Ballers			224	63	2	17	30	.281	.411	.332
vs. Fly-Ballers			246	71	6	14	34	.289	.435	.325
Home Games	0-7	3.96	210	66	3	17	28	.314	.467	.364
Road Games	2-7	4.33	260	68	5	14	36	.262	.388	.298
Grass Fields	0-9	3.98	318	95	5	25	46	.299	.443	.349
Artificial Turf	2-5	4.54	152	39	3	6	18	.257	.382	.283
April	2-0	2.96	91	25	0	4	12	.275	.374	.299
May	0-3	5.91	127	39	4	9	24	.307	.496	.350
June	0-5	4.68	109	36	1	7	11	.330	.495	.368
July	0-1	1.80	36	8	0	2	6	.222	.278	.282
August	0-0	0.44	67	10	0	5	8	.149	.164	.208
Sept./Oct.	0-5	11.00	40	16	3	4	3	.400	.675	.455
Leading Off Inn.			118	31	1	7	18	.263	.373	.304
Bases Empty			270	72	2	19	44	.267	.381	.317
Runners On			200	62	6	12	20	.310	.480	.343
Runners/Scor. Pos.			109	36	5	9	12	.330	.541	.369
Runners On/2 Out			97	31	2	8	11	.320	.443	.371
Scor. Pos./2 Out			60	20	2	5	8	.333	.533	.385
Late-Inning Pressure			119	27	3	12	14	.227	.319	.298
Leading Off			29	5	0	4	3	.172	.207	.273
Runners On			51	14	3	2	4	.275	.471	.302
Runners/Scor. Pos.			21	7	2	1	1	.333	.619	.364
First 9 Batters			274	68	5	20	38	.248	.361	.301
Second 9 Batters			114	36	0	8	20	.316	.412	.358
All Batters Thereafter			82	30	3	3	6	.366	.646	.379

Loves to face: Wes Chamberlain (.100, 1-for-10)
Cory Snyder (0-for-5)
Tim Wallach (0-for-7)

Hates to face: Bret Barberie (4-for-4, 2 BB)
Delino DeShields (.417, 5-for-12, 2 3B)
Larry Walker (.600, 6-for-10, 2 HR)

Miscellaneous statistics: Ground outs-to-air outs ratio: 1.52 last season, 1.67 for career.... Opponents grounded into 10 double plays in 87 opportunities (one per 8.7).... Allowed 23 doubles, 9 triples (most in majors) in 121 innings.... Allowed 10 first-inning runs in 13 starts (2.77 ERA).... Batting support: 3.69 runs per start.... Record of 1–7, 4.81 ERA as a starter; 1–7, 3.19 ERA in 39 relief appearances.... Saved 15 games in 21 opportunities (71%).... Stranded 13 inherited runners, allowed 4 to score (76%).... Opposing base stealers: 10-for-16 (63%); 1 pickoff, 1 balk.

Comments: His first major league victory came in a night game at Shea Stadium in 1991; since then he has lost 10 straight at Shea and 13 straight at night.... Tied Kyle Abbott for the most losses by a major league rookie last season, but led rookies with 15 saves. If 15 saves and 14 losses seems an odd pairing, it is; only three other pitchers have lost 14 and saved 15 in a season: Darold Knowles in 1970 (2–14, 27 saves), Gene Garber in 1979 (6–16, 25 saves), and Mike Marshall in 1979 (10–15, 32 saves).... Became only the second pitcher in the last 50 years to lose at least seven games as both a starter and a reliever in the same season. Tom Gordon did it in 1991.... Finished season with 14 straight losses, the longest single-season losing streak in the majors since Mike Parrott's 16-game streak for Seattle in 1980. Since 1911, only three N.L. pitchers have lost 14 in a row in one season; all three pitched for the Mets: Craig Anderson (16 in 1962), Roger Craig (18 in 1963), and Young. Anderson went on to lose three more games in 1963–64 (a streak that's *still* alive) to post a 19-game losing streak that no one has equaled since.... Only two N.L. pitchers allowed a higher batting average with runners in scoring position: Terry Mulholland (.345) and Zane Smith (.333).... Batting average by opposing left-handed batters was highest in majors among pitchers who faced at least 200 lefties. Meanwhile, right-handers went 1-for-36 during a scoreless streak of 23⅔ innings in July and August.

ROOKIES AND PROSPECTS SECTION

Is it possible to predict how a player will do in an upcoming season based on his past performance? The concept may seem foreign to baseball fans, but that's exactly how the country's horseplayers make their living—or try to. At least one baseball publication prints projected batting statistics for the upcoming season for every player in the majors—an inane endeavor that melts the peaks and valleys off each player's range of possibilities until three-quarters of them look like clones of Ken Caminiti. No one we know takes those predictions seriously, and for good reason—they simply have no reason to trust them. The better question is, can such a system be done well?

We once observed that baseball predictions provide cheap thrills, and that unlike stock market recommendations and weather forecasts, at least no one loses money or gets wet when they're wrong. But the proliferation of fantasy leagues has changed that. Our readers now want and deserve something better—a system that acknowledges the wide range of career paths that a player might subsequently take, but one that nevertheless identifies the most likely middle road. Toward that end, we field-tested a series of forecasting routines against more than 100 years of baseball history. By matching the projections for hundreds of rookies from the past against their subsequent performances, we were able to fine-tune the process. The model that resulted proved surprisingly accurate—so accurate, in fact, that we felt these projections deserved a section of their own. From our own experience, we guarantee that those who don't play in fantasy leagues will find this information as fascinating as those who do will find it useful.

The Rookies and Prospects Section's *raison d'etre* is not fact but fantasy. On the other hand, the forecasts are based on an analysis of past players so comprehensive and fact-based that it would have been inconceivable even two or three years ago—as unlikely as, say, a Japanese League refugee tearing up the American League, or nearly 20 no-hitters over a two-year period.

Our forecasts here are limited to rookies—the players about whom we have the most to learn. (We could try to project Cecil Fielder's 1993 season, but would it really tell you anything you don't already know?) By modifying various characteristics of the forecasting model, we were able to make accurate projections not only for rookies who played throughout the season, but also for late-season arrivals—prospects recalled in September who played regularly during the final month. Specifically, this section will include rookies with at least 100 plate appearances for the season, and others who batted at least 50 times from September 1 on.

For each player, basic batting totals and a few pertinent breakdowns are shown. (For rookies with at least 250 plate appearances, this will duplicate a few lines also found in the Batters Section.) That information is followed by a listing of the five rookies since 1960 with the most comparable batting statistics. (When fewer than five *recent* comparable rookies were found, players were listed without regard to when they played.) The projections follow, based on an analysis of the careers of not only the five statistical clones shown above them, but also those of dozens or perhaps hundreds more, regardless of when they played.

Projections are made for the upcoming season and for the players' career totals on both a best-guess and a best-case basis. The latter is a purposely optimistic forecast representing a statistical appraisal of the upper limits that the player might reasonably attain—not an absolute limit, but one that he stands roughly one chance in five of achieving. Beyond that, who knows?

A final issue: When should the optimistic forecast be given greater consideration? The best-case projections are especially pertinent for rookies who won starting jobs after the All-Star break. That was the case with Hal Morris, who spent most of the first half of 1990 in the minors but started regularly for Cincinnati for the last three months of the season. Remember that the projections are based on an analysis of players with similar batting statistics in their own rookie seasons. Morris's forecast was therefore based on rookies who, among their other characteristics, had roughly 300 at-bats. Some, like Morris himself, might have played regularly for a half-season. But others (and most likely the majority of the group) were part-timers who pulled several hundred at-bats together over the course of six months. The prognosis for the former group is obviously much better, but the best-guess forecast is based primarily on the latter group. Compare the estimates below for Morris's 1991 season to his actual performance:

	AB	H	2B	3B	HR	RBI	BB	SO	BA	SA	OBA
Best Guess	458	126	23	7	9	59	33	53	.275	.420	.324
Optimistic	537	168	32	14	16	94	58	28	.313	.516	.382
1991 Actual	505	164	42	2	14	68	44	61	.324	.495	.375

Morris's actual performance ultimately approximated the optimistic estimate. So, for best results, give more weight to the optimistic scenario for players who are significantly more productive after the All-Star break than before it. That would include the prospects who batted at least 50 times in September and October, but less than 100 times for the season.

Did someone mention pitchers? They are included in this section as well, although without projections. (Believe us—if we develop a forecasting model as accurate for pitchers as the one for batters, you'll read about it here first.) Each season, there are a dozen or so pitchers who take regular turns in the rotation over the final month of the season but fail to pitch enough over the entire season to be included in our Pitcher Section. Often they become regular starters a year later; such was the case with Mike Mussina and Rheal Cormier last season. They will appear in the Rookies and Prospects Section on a basis similar to those found in the Pitcher Section—basic statistics, significant breakdowns, and miscellaneous statistics.

Have fun!

Moises Alou
Bats Right

Born Jul. 3, 1966

Montreal Expos	AB	H	2B	3B	HR	RBI	BB	SO	BA	SA	OBA
Season	341	96	28	2	9	56	25	46	.282	.455	.328
vs. Left-Handers	136	40	11	0	2	14	7	13	.294	.419	.329
vs. Right-Handers	205	56	17	2	7	42	18	33	.273	.478	.327
vs. Ground-Ballers	139	42	12	1	3	27	15	15	.302	.468	.367
vs. Fly-Ballers	202	54	16	1	6	29	10	31	.267	.446	.299

Most Comparable Rookie Seasons:

	AB	H	2B	3B	HR	RBI	BB	SO	BA	SA	OBA
Mickey Brantley	351	106	23	2	14	54	24	44	.302	.499	.348
Tracy Jones	359	104	17	3	10	44	23	40	.290	.437	.334
Carlos Lopez	297	84	18	1	8	34	14	61	.283	.431	.316
Pat Putnam	426	118	19	2	18	64	23	50	.277	.458	.315
Terry Steinbach	391	111	16	3	16	56	32	66	.284	.463	.339

Projections for 1993:

	AB	H	2B	3B	HR	RBI	BB	SO	BA	SA	OBA
Best Guess	351	92	15	2	8	39	25	44	.263	.388	.314
Optimistic	502	146	27	5	17	76	45	44	.291	.470	.351

Projections for career:

	AB	H	2B	3B	HR	RBI	BB	SO	BA	SA	OBA
Best Guess	1234	321	64	8	27	158	85	170	.260	.391	.309
Optimistic	2115	569	113	20	69	317	193	230	.269	.439	.331

Rich Amaral
Bats Right

Born Apr. 1, 1962

Seattle Mariners	AB	H	2B	3B	HR	RBI	BB	SO	BA	SA	OBA
Season	100	24	3	0	1	7	5	16	.240	.300	.276
vs. Left-Handers	37	8	1	0	1	4	2	3	.216	.324	.256
vs. Right-Handers	63	16	2	0	0	3	3	13	.254	.286	.288
vs. Ground-Ballers	45	17	2	0	1	7	1	5	.378	.489	.391
vs. Fly-Ballers	55	7	1	0	0	0	4	11	.127	.145	.186

Most Comparable Rookie Seasons:

	AB	H	2B	3B	HR	RBI	BB	SO	BA	SA	OBA
Larry Cox	93	23	6	0	2	6	10	12	.247	.376	.322
Don LeJohn	78	20	2	0	0	7	5	13	.256	.282	.302
Mike Sadek	106	25	5	2	0	9	14	14	.236	.321	.326
Ron Washington	84	19	3	1	0	5	4	14	.226	.286	.263
Matt Winters	107	25	6	0	2	9	14	23	.234	.346	.323

Projections for 1993:

	AB	H	2B	3B	HR	RBI	BB	SO	BA	SA	OBA
Best Guess	28	5	1	0	0	2	1	5	.179	.200	.204
Optimistic	164	46	8	2	5	24	8	24	.278	.444	.314

Projections for career:

	AB	H	2B	3B	HR	RBI	BB	SO	BA	SA	OBA
Best Guess	372	84	13	2	5	35	14	63	.226	.309	.256
Optimistic	2539	739	109	38	60	372	115	326	.291	.434	.323

Ruben Amaro Jr.
Bats Left and Right

Born Feb. 12, 1965

Philadelphia Phillies	AB	H	2B	3B	HR	RBI	BB	SO	BA	SA	OBA
Season	374	82	15	6	7	34	37	54	.219	.348	.303
vs. Left-Handers	154	39	8	3	2	17	18	14	.253	.383	.343
vs. Right-Handers	220	43	7	3	5	17	19	40	.195	.323	.275
vs. Ground-Ballers	187	41	11	3	5	17	16	30	.219	.390	.301
vs. Fly-Ballers	187	41	4	3	2	17	21	24	.219	.305	.305

Most Comparable Rookie Seasons:

	AB	H	2B	3B	HR	RBI	BB	SO	BA	SA	OBA
Bobby Cox	437	100	15	1	7	41	41	85	.229	.316	.296
Brad Gulden	292	66	8	2	4	33	33	35	.226	.308	.306
Bobby Klaus	302	68	13	4	4	17	29	43	.225	.334	.294
Steve Lombardozzi	453	103	20	5	8	33	52	76	.227	.347	.308
Ernie Whitt	295	70	12	2	6	34	22	30	.237	.353	.291

Projections for 1993:

	AB	H	2B	3B	HR	RBI	BB	SO	BA	SA	OBA
Best Guess	200	48	8	1	2	18	19	26	.238	.321	.305
Optimistic	432	115	19	6	9	47	75	50	.266	.398	.377

Projections for career:

	AB	H	2B	3B	HR	RBI	BB	SO	BA	SA	OBA
Best Guess	768	172	30	9	11	69	84	114	.225	.331	.302
Optimistic	1580	399	68	21	33	167	233	195	.252	.384	.350

Alex Arias
Bats Right

Born Nov. 20, 1967

Chicago Cubs	AB	H	2B	3B	HR	RBI	BB	SO	BA	SA	OBA
Season	99	29	6	0	0	7	11	13	.293	.354	.375
vs. Left-Handers	41	13	4	0	0	2	4	3	.317	.415	.378
vs. Right-Handers	58	16	2	0	0	5	7	10	.276	.310	.373
vs. Ground-Ballers	38	10	2	0	0	4	8	8	.263	.316	.417
vs. Fly-Ballers	61	19	4	0	0	3	3	5	.311	.377	.344

Most Comparable Rookie Seasons:

	AB	H	2B	3B	HR	RBI	BB	SO	BA	SA	OBA
Jim Barbieri	82	23	5	0	0	3	9	7	.280	.341	.353
Jeff Branson	115	34	7	1	0	15	5	16	.296	.374	.326
Jim Dwyer	86	24	1	0	2	11	11	16	.279	.360	.362
Gary Holman	85	25	5	1	0	7	13	15	.294	.376	.389
David Hulse	92	28	4	0	0	2	3	18	.304	.348	.327

Projections for 1993:

	AB	H	2B	3B	HR	RBI	BB	SO	BA	SA	OBA
Best Guess	136	30	4	0	1	9	14	21	.224	.277	.299
Optimistic	369	100	17	5	6	40	62	29	.272	.390	.378

Projections for career:

	AB	H	2B	3B	HR	RBI	BB	SO	BA	SA	OBA
Best Guess	1046	265	42	5	9	103	139	109	.253	.329	.342
Optimistic	3192	870	148	33	54	376	519	212	.273	.390	.375

Billy Ashley
Bats Right

Born Jul. 11, 1970

Los Angeles Dodgers	AB	H	2B	3B	HR	RBI	BB	SO	BA	SA	OBA
Season	95	21	5	0	2	6	5	34	.221	.337	.260
vs. Left-Handers	30	10	2	0	2	4	1	6	.333	.600	.355
vs. Right-Handers	65	11	3	0	0	2	4	28	.169	.215	.217
vs. Ground-Ballers	31	3	2	0	0	0	1	8	.097	.161	.125
vs. Fly-Ballers	64	18	3	0	2	6	4	26	.281	.422	.324

Most Comparable Rookie Seasons:

	AB	H	2B	3B	HR	RBI	BB	SO	BA	SA	OBA
Jesse Barfield	95	22	3	2	2	9	4	19	.232	.368	.264
Steve Brye	107	24	1	0	3	11	7	15	.224	.318	.273
Jose Gonzalez	93	20	5	1	2	6	7	29	.215	.355	.271
Joe Keough	98	21	2	1	2	18	6	11	.214	.316	.275
Gary Roenicke	90	20	3	1	2	4	5	18	.222	.344	.256

Projections for 1993:

	AB	H	2B	3B	HR	RBI	BB	SO	BA	SA	OBA
Best Guess	121	26	4	1	1	11	6	46	.214	.284	.250
Optimistic	333	86	17	4	11	46	27	76	.257	.433	.313

Projections for career:

	AB	H	2B	3B	HR	RBI	BB	SO	BA	SA	OBA
Best Guess	1974	484	79	11	36	209	119	597	.245	.350	.289
Optimistic	4120	1072	193	35	147	576	362	849	.260	.431	.321

Kim Batiste
Bats Right

Born Mar. 15, 1968

Philadelphia Phillies	AB	H	2B	3B	HR	RBI	BB	SO	BA	SA	OBA
Season	136	28	4	0	1	10	4	18	.206	.257	.224
vs. Left-Handers	73	15	2	0	0	4	2	10	.205	.233	.224
vs. Right-Handers	63	13	2	0	1	6	2	8	.206	.286	.224
vs. Ground-Ballers	59	11	3	0	0	2	1	5	.186	.237	.200
vs. Fly-Ballers	77	17	1	0	1	8	3	13	.221	.273	.241

Most Comparable Rookie Seasons:

	AB	H	2B	3B	HR	RBI	BB	SO	BA	SA	OBA
Carmen Castillo	120	25	4	0	2	11	6	17	.208	.292	.247
Fernando Gonzalez	142	29	6	1	1	9	7	11	.204	.282	.243
Bob W. Johnson	146	30	4	0	1	9	19	23	.205	.253	.298
Dave Rosello	148	30	7	0	0	10	28	28	.203	.250	.254
Rob Sperring	107	22	3	0	1	5	9	28	.206	.262	.268

Projections for 1993:

	AB	H	2B	3B	HR	RBI	BB	SO	BA	SA	OBA
Best Guess	58	13	1	0	0	4	1	12	.219	.244	.236
Optimistic	180	48	8	2	4	22	7	23	.267	.393	.296

Projections for career:

	AB	H	2B	3B	HR	RBI	BB	SO	BA	SA	OBA
Best Guess	974	229	35	4	11	87	30	142	.235	.313	.259
Optimistic	2906	759	125	26	64	362	135	312	.261	.387	.295

Derek Bell
Bats Right

Born Dec. 11, 1968

Toronto Blue Jays	AB	H	2B	3B	HR	RBI	BB	SO	BA	SA	OBA
Season	161	39	6	3	2	15	15	34	.242	.354	.324
vs. Left-Handers	47	12	3	1	2	6	3	9	.255	.489	.333
vs. Right-Handers	114	27	3	2	0	9	12	25	.237	.298	.320
vs. Ground-Ballers	80	16	3	0	2	6	5	16	.200	.313	.256
vs. Fly-Ballers	81	23	3	3	0	9	10	18	.284	.395	.385

Most Comparable Rookie Seasons:

	AB	H	2B	3B	HR	RBI	BB	SO	BA	SA	OBA
Mike Felder	155	37	2	4	1	13	13	16	.239	.323	.299
Nelson Liriano	158	38	6	2	2	10	16	22	.241	.342	.312
Jeff Reed	165	39	6	1	2	9	16	19	.236	.321	.305
David Segui	123	30	7	0	2	15	11	15	.244	.350	.307
Jeff Torborg	150	36	5	1	3	13	10	26	.240	.347	.289

Projections for 1993:

	AB	H	2B	3B	HR	RBI	BB	SO	BA	SA	OBA
Best Guess	173	40	6	0	1	15	16	36	.231	.285	.298
Optimistic	348	94	18	4	8	44	52	43	.270	.413	.365

Projections for career:

	AB	H	2B	3B	HR	RBI	BB	SO	BA	SA	OBA
Best Guess	1387	336	51	10	17	136	149	266	.242	.331	.317
Optimistic	3370	928	161	33	89	410	526	430	.275	.422	.374

Esteban Beltre
Bats Right

Born Dec. 26, 1967

Chicago White Sox	AB	H	2B	3B	HR	RBI	BB	SO	BA	SA	OBA
Season	110	21	2	0	1	10	3	18	.191	.236	.211
vs. Left-Handers	51	12	1	0	1	5	1	7	.235	.314	.245
vs. Right-Handers	59	9	1	0	0	5	2	11	.153	.169	.180
vs. Ground-Ballers	47	7	0	0	0	6	1	5	.149	.149	.167
vs. Fly-Ballers	63	14	2	0	1	4	2	13	.222	.302	.242

Most Comparable Rookie Seasons:

	AB	H	2B	3B	HR	RBI	BB	SO	BA	SA	OBA
Lance Johnson	124	23	4	1	0	6	6	11	.185	.234	.224
Tom Kelly	127	23	5	0	1	11	15	22	.181	.244	.269
Terry McGriff	96	19	3	0	1	4	12	31	.198	.260	.288
Andy Mota	90	17	2	0	1	6	1	17	.189	.244	.199
John Wehner	123	22	6	0	0	4	12	22	.179	.228	.253

Projections for 1993:

	AB	H	2B	3B	HR	RBI	BB	SO	BA	SA	OBA
Best Guess	36	7	1	0	0	1	1	8	.203	.218	.222
Optimistic	180	49	9	2	2	18	8	21	.272	.369	.304

Projections for career:

	AB	H	2B	3B	HR	RBI	BB	SO	BA	SA	OBA
Best Guess	647	146	21	3	5	57	26	90	.226	.289	.257
Optimistic	2096	542	95	20	41	272	127	193	.259	.381	.302

Freddie Benavides
Bats Right

Born Apr. 7, 1966

Cincinnati Reds	AB	H	2B	3B	HR	RBI	BB	SO	BA	SA	OBA
Season	173	40	10	1	1	17	10	34	.231	.318	.277
vs. Left-Handers	90	23	7	0	1	15	8	15	.256	.367	.323
vs. Right-Handers	83	17	3	1	0	2	2	19	.205	.265	.224
vs. Ground-Ballers	65	14	3	0	0	3	3	13	.215	.262	.261
vs. Fly-Ballers	108	26	7	1	1	14	7	21	.241	.352	.287

Most Comparable Rookie Seasons:

	AB	H	2B	3B	HR	RBI	BB	SO	BA	SA	OBA
Oscar Brown	164	37	5	1	3	16	4	29	.226	.323	.245
John Jaha	133	30	3	1	2	10	12	30	.226	.308	.291
Ron Lolich	140	32	7	0	2	15	7	27	.229	.321	.266
Edgar Martinez	171	41	5	0	2	20	17	26	.240	.304	.310
Keith A. Miller	143	33	7	0	1	7	5	27	.231	.301	.258

Projections for 1993:

	AB	H	2B	3B	HR	RBI	BB	SO	BA	SA	OBA
Best Guess	80	19	3	0	0	6	3	18	.233	.267	.261
Optimistic	266	72	14	3	5	31	19	40	.270	.394	.319

Projections for career:

	AB	H	2B	3B	HR	RBI	BB	SO	BA	SA	OBA
Best Guess	752	183	32	3	7	72	36	158	.243	.320	.279
Optimistic	1868	497	90	18	38	222	122	256	.266	.396	.313

Sean Berry
Bats Right

Born Mar. 22, 1966

Montreal Expos	AB	H	2B	3B	HR	RBI	BB	SO	BA	SA	OBA
Season	57	19	1	0	1	4	1	11	.333	.404	.345
vs. Left-Handers	3	2	0	0	0	0	0	0	.667	.667	.667
vs. Right-Handers	54	17	1	0	1	4	1	11	.315	.389	.327
vs. Ground-Ballers	28	10	1	0	1	3	0	4	.357	.500	.357
vs. Fly-Ballers	29	9	0	0	0	1	1	7	.310	.310	.333

Most Comparable Rookie Seasons:

	AB	H	2B	3B	HR	RBI	BB	SO	BA	SA	OBA
Chris Arnold	54	16	2	0	1	13	8	11	.296	.389	.388
Jerry Davis	68	17	3	1	0	2	5	7	.293	.379	.350
Bobby Floyd	45	14	4	0	0	9	4	11	.311	.400	.369
Terry Jorgensen	58	18	1	0	0	5	3	11	.310	.328	.345
Chris Smith	67	22	6	1	1	11	7	12	.328	.493	.393

Projections for 1993:

	AB	H	2B	3B	HR	RBI	BB	SO	BA	SA	OBA
Best Guess	24	4	0	0	0	1	1	9	.152	.152	.184
Optimistic	195	49	9	2	2	21	12	50	.250	.347	.294

Projections for career:

	AB	H	2B	3B	HR	RBI	BB	SO	BA	SA	OBA
Best Guess	427	98	14	3	4	40	25	117	.229	.306	.272
Optimistic	2105	549	98	26	41	272	149	345	.261	.390	.311

Bret Boone
Bats Right

Born Apr. 6, 1969

Seattle Mariners	AB	H	2B	3B	HR	RBI	BB	SO	BA	SA	OBA
Season	129	25	4	0	4	15	4	34	.194	.318	.224
vs. Left-Handers	40	6	1	0	0	1	2	12	.150	.175	.190
vs. Right-Handers	89	19	3	0	4	14	2	22	.213	.382	.239
vs. Ground-Ballers	69	11	3	0	2	5	2	15	.159	.290	.194
vs. Fly-Ballers	60	14	1	0	2	10	2	19	.233	.350	.258

Most Comparable Rookie Seasons:

	AB	H	2B	3B	HR	RBI	BB	SO	BA	SA	OBA
Todd Cruz	118	24	7	0	2	15	3	19	.203	.314	.224
Jack Howell	137	27	4	0	5	18	16	33	.197	.336	.282
Reggie Jefferson	108	21	3	0	3	13	4	24	.194	.306	.224
Tino Martinez	112	23	2	0	4	9	11	24	.205	.330	.278
Dave Schneck	123	23	3	2	3	10	10	26	.187	.317	.249

Projections for 1993:

	AB	H	2B	3B	HR	RBI	BB	SO	BA	SA	OBA
Best Guess	138	33	4	0	1	12	4	34	.237	.304	.259
Optimistic	333	89	16	4	12	46	15	59	.267	.453	.299

Projections for career:

	AB	H	2B	3B	HR	RBI	BB	SO	BA	SA	OBA
Best Guess	1436	343	55	7	29	146	45	309	.239	.346	.263
Optimistic	3463	914	155	31	114	465	165	602	.264	.426	.299

Jeff Branson
Bats Left

Born Jan. 26, 1967

Cincinnati Reds	AB	H	2B	3B	HR	RBI	BB	SO	BA	SA	OBA
Season	115	34	7	1	0	15	5	16	.296	.374	.322
vs. Left-Handers	8	1	0	0	0	0	0	3	.125	.125	.125
vs. Right-Handers	107	33	7	1	0	15	5	13	.308	.393	.336
vs. Ground-Ballers	61	19	3	1	0	7	4	7	.311	.393	.354
vs. Fly-Ballers	54	15	4	0	0	8	1	9	.278	.352	.286

Most Comparable Rookie Seasons:

	AB	H	2B	3B	HR	RBI	BB	SO	BA	SA	OBA
Alex Arias	99	29	6	0	0	7	11	13	.293	.354	.365
Scott Livingstone	127	37	5	0	2	11	10	25	.291	.378	.344
Domingo Ramos	127	36	4	0	2	10	7	12	.283	.362	.322
Milt Thompson	99	30	1	0	2	4	11	11	.303	.374	.374
Rick Wrona	92	26	2	1	2	14	2	21	.283	.391	.299

Projections for 1993:

	AB	H	2B	3B	HR	RBI	BB	SO	BA	SA	OBA
Best Guess	99	21	3	0	0	6	4	15	.212	.248	.241
Optimistic	271	73	12	3	5	33	20	26	.270	.390	.321

Projections for career:

	AB	H	2B	3B	HR	RBI	BB	SO	BA	SA	OBA
Best Guess	878	216	34	4	7	95	48	118	.246	.320	.287
Optimistic	2955	794	137	24	76	352	202	247	.269	.408	.317

Rod Brewer
Bats Left

Born Feb. 24, 1966

St. Louis Cardinals	AB	H	2B	3B	HR	RBI	BB	SO	BA	SA	OBA
Season	103	31	6	0	0	10	8	12	.301	.359	.354
vs. Left-Handers	24	7	2	0	0	2	0	3	.292	.375	.292
vs. Right-Handers	79	24	4	0	0	8	8	9	.304	.354	.371
vs. Ground-Ballers	45	12	2	0	0	5	4	9	.267	.311	.340
vs. Fly-Ballers	58	19	4	0	0	5	4	3	.328	.397	.365

Most Comparable Rookie Seasons:

Jeff Branson	115	34	7	1	0	15	5	16	.296	.374	.326
Keith Drumright	86	25	1	1	0	11	4	4	.291	.326	.323
Bill Heath	123	37	6	0	0	8	9	11	.301	.350	.350
John Knox	88	27	1	1	0	6	6	13	.307	.341	.352
Scott Livingstone	127	37	5	0	2	11	10	25	.291	.378	.344

Projections for 1993:

Best Guess	65	14	1	0	0	4	3	13	.212	.232	.248
Optimistic	213	54	9	2	4	27	19	24	.255	.376	.318

Projections for career:

Best Guess	590	144	21	2	5	54	40	95	.244	.313	.294
Optimistic	1499	395	66	15	31	191	132	167	.264	.389	.324

Chuck Carr
Bats Left and Right

Born Aug. 10, 1968

St. Louis Cardinals	AB	H	2B	3B	HR	RBI	BB	SO	BA	SA	OBA
Season	64	14	3	0	0	3	9	6	.219	.266	.315
vs. Left-Handers	24	6	1	0	0	0	1	3	.250	.292	.280
vs. Right-Handers	40	8	2	0	0	3	8	3	.200	.250	.333
vs. Ground-Ballers	27	9	2	0	0	2	3	3	.333	.407	.400
vs. Fly-Ballers	37	5	1	0	0	1	6	3	.135	.162	.256

Most Comparable Rookie Seasons:

Doug Dascenzo	75	16	3	0	0	4	9	4	.213	.253	.299
Mike Devereaux	54	12	3	0	0	4	3	10	.222	.278	.264
Rob Ducey	76	16	4	0	0	7	9	25	.211	.263	.295
Lance Johnson	59	13	2	1	0	7	4	6	.220	.288	.271
Carlos Quintana	77	16	5	0	0	6	7	12	.208	.273	.275

Projections for 1993:

Best Guess	87	20	2	0	0	7	8	13	.225	.268	.295
Optimistic	322	88	16	3	8	42	50	30	.275	.423	.374

Projections for career:

Best Guess	1277	312	50	7	15	129	158	159	.244	.331	.328
Optimistic	2918	762	142	24	77	400	489	230	.261	.405	.368

Braulio Castillo
Bats Right

Born May 13, 1968

Philadelphia Phillies	AB	H	2B	3B	HR	RBI	BB	SO	BA	SA	OBA
Season	76	15	3	1	2	7	4	15	.197	.342	.237
vs. Left-Handers	33	6	0	1	1	4	0	5	.182	.333	.182
vs. Right-Handers	43	9	3	0	1	3	4	10	.209	.349	.277
vs. Ground-Ballers	40	8	2	1	1	3	3	8	.200	.375	.256
vs. Fly-Ballers	36	7	1	0	1	4	1	7	.194	.306	.216

Most Comparable Rookie Seasons:

Mike Gallego	77	16	5	1	1	9	12	14	.208	.338	.316
Danny Goodwin	91	19	6	1	1	8	5	19	.209	.330	.251
Bo Jackson	82	17	2	1	2	9	7	34	.207	.329	.271
Johnny Rabb	82	16	1	0	3	9	10	33	.195	.317	.284
Otto Velez	67	14	1	1	2	10	15	24	.209	.343	.355

Projections for 1993:

Best Guess	83	19	3	0	1	8	3	20	.235	.288	.260
Optimistic	312	85	17	2	10	42	18	49	.271	.435	.312

Projections for career:

Best Guess	663	152	27	4	10	69	25	142	.229	.327	.258
Optimistic	2500	643	123	27	99	356	130	381	.257	.446	.295

Archi Cianfrocco
Bats Right

Born Oct. 6, 1966

Montreal Expos	AB	H	2B	3B	HR	RBI	BB	SO	BA	SA	OBA
Season	232	56	5	2	6	30	11	66	.241	.358	.276
vs. Left-Handers	97	24	2	2	4	17	6	25	.247	.433	.286
vs. Right-Handers	135	32	3	0	2	13	5	41	.237	.304	.270
vs. Ground-Ballers	101	17	0	0	0	7	4	28	.168	.168	.206
vs. Fly-Ballers	131	39	5	2	6	23	7	38	.298	.504	.331

Most Comparable Rookie Seasons:

Oscar Azocar	214	53	8	0	5	19	2	15	.248	.355	.256
Curt Ford	214	53	15	2	2	29	23	29	.248	.364	.322
Tommy Gregg	276	67	8	0	6	23	18	45	.243	.337	.290
Garth Iorg	222	55	10	1	2	14	12	39	.248	.329	.287
John Vanderwal	213	51	8	2	4	20	24	36	.239	.352	.318

Projections for 1993:

Best Guess	207	50	7	1	3	24	8	61	.244	.324	.275
Optimistic	338	95	17	5	10	48	22	67	.280	.457	.325

Projections for career:

Best Guess	1107	273	41	8	21	127	54	322	.247	.355	.283
Optimistic	2533	680	120	26	76	332	161	487	.268	.427	.313

Royce Clayton
Bats Right

Born Jan. 2, 1970

San Francisco Giants	AB	H	2B	3B	HR	RBI	BB	SO	BA	SA	OBA
Season	321	72	7	4	4	24	26	63	.224	.308	.281
vs. Left-Handers	96	24	4	2	0	4	11	21	.250	.333	.327
vs. Right-Handers	225	48	3	2	4	20	15	42	.213	.298	.260
vs. Ground-Ballers	182	34	4	2	2	14	11	34	.187	.264	.232
vs. Fly-Ballers	139	38	3	2	2	10	15	29	.273	.367	.342

Most Comparable Rookie Seasons:

Ollie Brown	348	81	7	1	7	33	33	66	.233	.319	.300
Rudi Meoli	305	68	12	1	2	23	31	38	.223	.289	.296
Rey Quinones	312	68	16	1	2	22	24	57	.218	.295	.275
Lee Richard	260	60	7	3	2	17	20	46	.231	.304	.287
Roy Smalley Jr.	250	57	8	0	3	33	30	42	.228	.296	.312

Projections for 1993:

Best Guess	254	62	9	1	1	21	18	54	.245	.308	.296
Optimistic	469	129	22	6	10	57	47	68	.275	.412	.343

Projections for career:

Best Guess	2152	526	81	15	25	214	172	402	.244	.331	.302
Optimistic	5612	1487	255	64	132	670	637	765	.265	.404	.341

Craig Colbert
Bats Right

Born Feb. 13, 1965

San Francisco Giants	AB	H	2B	3B	HR	RBI	BB	SO	BA	SA	OBA
Season	126	29	5	2	1	16	9	22	.230	.325	.277
vs. Left-Handers	56	13	2	1	1	10	3	3	.232	.357	.267
vs. Right-Handers	70	16	3	1	0	6	6	19	.229	.300	.286
vs. Ground-Ballers	46	10	2	0	0	6	2	10	.217	.261	.245
vs. Fly-Ballers	80	19	3	2	1	10	7	12	.237	.363	.295

Most Comparable Rookie Seasons:

Fritz Connally	112	26	4	0	3	15	19	21	.232	.348	.345
Ross Jones	114	29	4	2	0	10	5	15	.254	.325	.287
Charlie O'Brien	118	26	6	0	2	9	5	16	.220	.322	.253
Jim Paciorek	101	23	5	0	2	10	12	20	.228	.337	.311
Mike Ja. Ramsey	125	29	4	2	0	12	10	32	.232	.296	.290

Projections for 1993:

Best Guess	14	2	0	0	0	1	0	5	.125	.125	.148
Optimistic	126	31	6	0	2	15	10	17	.243	.345	.301

Projections for career:

Best Guess	344	81	13	2	4	37	24	64	.236	.318	.286
Optimistic	1158	303	54	10	26	157	109	141	.261	.393	.326

Greg Colbrunn — Bats Right
Born Jul. 26, 1969

Montreal Expos	AB	H	2B	3B	HR	RBI	BB	SO	BA	SA	OBA
Season	168	45	8	0	2	18	6	34	.268	.351	.294
vs. Left-Handers	72	16	2	0	1	9	2	14	.222	.292	.237
vs. Right-Handers	96	29	6	0	1	9	4	20	.302	.396	.337
vs. Ground-Ballers	66	16	2	0	1	6	2	15	.242	.318	.261
vs. Fly-Ballers	102	29	6	0	1	12	4	19	.284	.373	.315

Most Comparable Rookie Seasons:

	AB	H	2B	3B	HR	RBI	BB	SO	BA	SA	OBA
Bruce Bochy	154	41	8	0	3	15	11	35	.266	.377	.316
Mike Colbern	141	38	5	1	2	20	1	36	.270	.362	.276
Damion Easley	151	39	5	0	1	12	8	26	.258	.311	.297
Donnie Hill	158	42	7	0	2	15	4	21	.266	.348	.285
Max Venable	138	37	5	0	0	10	15	22	.268	.304	.341

Projections for 1993:

	AB	H	2B	3B	HR	RBI	BB	SO	BA	SA	OBA
Best Guess	186	44	6	0	1	17	6	42	.236	.291	.260
Optimistic	375	102	18	5	7	47	19	48	.271	.396	.307

Projections for career:

	AB	H	2B	3B	HR	RBI	BB	SO	BA	SA	OBA
Best Guess	1582	394	68	8	18	169	56	299	.249	.335	.276
Optimistic	4255	1186	215	41	101	574	221	507	.279	.420	.316

Scott Cooper — Bats Left
Born Oct. 13, 1967

Boston Red Sox	AB	H	2B	3B	HR	RBI	BB	SO	BA	SA	OBA
Season	337	93	21	0	5	33	37	33	.276	.383	.346
vs. Left-Handers	41	11	3	0	1	5	7	6	.268	.415	.375
vs. Right-Handers	296	82	18	0	4	28	30	27	.277	.378	.341
vs. Ground-Ballers	160	45	15	0	0	15	18	18	.281	.375	.352
vs. Fly-Ballers	177	48	6	0	5	18	19	15	.271	.390	.340

Most Comparable Rookie Seasons:

	AB	H	2B	3B	HR	RBI	BB	SO	BA	SA	OBA
Damon Berryhill	309	80	19	1	7	38	17	56	.259	.395	.299
Gil Flores	342	95	19	4	1	26	23	39	.278	.365	.324
Al Gallagher	282	75	15	2	4	28	30	37	.266	.376	.338
Derrick May	351	96	11	0	8	45	14	40	.274	.373	.303
Rich McKinney	369	100	11	2	8	46	35	37	.271	.377	.335

Projections for 1993:

	AB	H	2B	3B	HR	RBI	BB	SO	BA	SA	OBA
Best Guess	312	77	11	2	5	31	28	31	.246	.336	.310
Optimistic	473	135	24	6	12	63	58	31	.284	.434	.364

Projections for career:

	AB	H	2B	3B	HR	RBI	BB	SO	BA	SA	OBA
Best Guess	1355	358	63	9	19	140	139	135	.264	.366	.334
Optimistic	3384	914	168	33	76	409	434	248	.270	.407	.354

Wil Cordero — Bats Right
Born Oct. 3, 1971

Montreal Expos	AB	H	2B	3B	HR	RBI	BB	SO	BA	SA	OBA
Season	126	38	4	1	2	8	9	31	.302	.397	.353
vs. Left-Handers	34	16	1	0	0	2	3	4	.471	.500	.514
vs. Right-Handers	92	22	3	1	2	6	6	27	.239	.359	.293
vs. Ground-Ballers	60	18	3	0	1	3	5	15	.300	.400	.354
vs. Fly-Ballers	66	20	1	1	1	5	4	16	.303	.394	.352

Most Comparable Rookie Seasons:

	AB	H	2B	3B	HR	RBI	BB	SO	BA	SA	OBA
Jose Canseco	96	29	3	0	5	13	4	31	.302	.490	.331
Howard Johnson	155	49	5	0	4	14	16	30	.316	.426	.381
Greg Luzinski	100	30	8	0	3	15	12	32	.300	.470	.376
Milt May	126	35	1	0	6	25	9	16	.278	.429	.327
Dave Winfield	141	39	4	1	3	12	12	19	.277	.383	.335

Projections for 1993:

	AB	H	2B	3B	HR	RBI	BB	SO	BA	SA	OBA
Best Guess	279	74	11	2	3	30	19	73	.267	.354	.315
Optimistic	548	161	31	7	18	72	57	84	.294	.474	.361

Projections for career:

	AB	H	2B	3B	HR	RBI	BB	SO	BA	SA	OBA
Best Guess	3659	990	148	31	43	405	290	745	.271	.363	.325
Optimistic	6263	1793	300	83	129	794	755	1008	.286	.423	.364

Chad Curtis — Bats Right
Born Nov. 6, 1968

California Angels	AB	H	2B	3B	HR	RBI	BB	SO	BA	SA	OBA
Season	441	114	16	2	10	46	51	71	.259	.372	.341
vs. Left-Handers	122	33	6	1	6	22	26	18	.270	.484	.393
vs. Right-Handers	319	81	10	1	4	24	25	53	.254	.329	.318
vs. Ground-Ballers	204	47	6	0	1	11	19	33	.230	.275	.306
vs. Fly-Ballers	237	67	10	2	9	35	32	38	.283	.456	.370

Most Comparable Rookie Seasons:

	AB	H	2B	3B	HR	RBI	BB	SO	BA	SA	OBA
Craig Biggio	443	114	21	2	13	60	49	64	.257	.402	.332
Von Hayes	527	132	25	3	14	82	42	63	.250	.389	.307
Gerald Perry	347	92	12	2	7	47	61	38	.265	.372	.376
Rick Schu	416	105	21	4	7	24	38	78	.252	.373	.316
Rick Sofield	417	103	18	4	9	49	24	92	.247	.374	.289

Projections for 1993:

	AB	H	2B	3B	HR	RBI	BB	SO	BA	SA	OBA
Best Guess	411	104	16	3	7	40	48	66	.254	.355	.332
Optimistic	534	147	27	6	13	71	82	65	.276	.425	.374

Projections for career:

	AB	H	2B	3B	HR	RBI	BB	SO	BA	SA	OBA
Best Guess	3045	783	125	19	56	322	383	473	.257	.365	.341
Optimistic	4813	1311	220	43	143	607	749	607	.272	.426	.372

Gary DiSarcina — Bats Right
Born Nov. 19, 1967

California Angels	AB	H	2B	3B	HR	RBI	BB	SO	BA	SA	OBA
Season	518	128	19	0	3	42	20	50	.247	.301	.283
vs. Left-Handers	114	26	4	0	0	4	5	12	.228	.263	.264
vs. Right-Handers	404	102	15	0	3	38	15	38	.252	.312	.288
vs. Ground-Ballers	248	63	9	0	0	16	10	22	.254	.290	.289
vs. Fly-Ballers	270	65	10	0	3	26	10	28	.241	.311	.277

Most Comparable Rookie Seasons:

	AB	H	2B	3B	HR	RBI	BB	SO	BA	SA	OBA
Glenn Beckert	614	147	21	3	3	30	28	52	.239	.298	.274
Larry Bowa	547	137	17	6	0	34	21	48	.250	.303	.279
Craig Reynolds	420	104	12	3	4	28	15	23	.248	.319	.275
Manny Trillo	545	135	12	2	7	70	45	78	.248	.316	.306
Walter Weiss	452	113	17	3	3	39	35	56	.250	.321	.305

Projections for 1993:

	AB	H	2B	3B	HR	RBI	BB	SO	BA	SA	OBA
Best Guess	445	106	15	3	3	38	21	45	.239	.305	.274
Optimistic	559	153	26	7	7	61	34	43	.274	.383	.317

Projections for career:

	AB	H	2B	3B	HR	RBI	BB	SO	BA	SA	OBA
Best Guess	2346	576	80	16	12	189	104	247	.246	.308	.279
Optimistic	4598	1183	188	53	47	427	262	369	.257	.352	.298

Chris Donnels — Bats Left
Born Apr. 21, 1966

New York Mets	AB	H	2B	3B	HR	RBI	BB	SO	BA	SA	OBA
Season	121	21	4	0	0	6	17	25	.174	.207	.275
vs. Left-Handers	24	4	1	0	0	1	2	8	.167	.208	.231
vs. Right-Handers	97	17	3	0	0	5	15	17	.175	.206	.286
vs. Ground-Ballers	57	9	2	0	0	3	5	11	.158	.193	.226
vs. Fly-Ballers	64	12	2	0	0	3	12	14	.188	.219	.316

Most Comparable Rookie Seasons:

	AB	H	2B	3B	HR	RBI	BB	SO	BA	SA	OBA
Mike Compton	110	18	0	1	1	7	9	22	.164	.209	.228
Paul Faries	130	23	3	1	0	7	14	21	.177	.215	.258
Craig Grebeck	119	20	3	1	1	9	8	24	.168	.235	.222
John Patterson	103	19	1	1	0	4	5	24	.184	.214	.223
David Rohde	98	18	4	0	0	5	9	20	.184	.224	.254

Projections for 1993:

	AB	H	2B	3B	HR	RBI	BB	SO	BA	SA	OBA
Best Guess	41	8	0	0	0	1	4	12	.197	.197	.274
Optimistic	192	49	8	2	4	23	35	35	.253	.368	.369

Projections for career:

	AB	H	2B	3B	HR	RBI	BB	SO	BA	SA	OBA
Best Guess	489	103	16	1	3	38	76	105	.210	.264	.317
Optimistic	1875	465	80	14	41	228	355	271	.248	.371	.369

Damion Easley — Bats Right
Born Nov. 11, 1969

California Angels	AB	H	2B	3B	HR	RBI	BB	SO	BA	SA	OBA
Season	151	39	5	0	1	12	8	26	.258	.311	.307
vs. Left-Handers	36	10	1	0	0	3	2	6	.278	.306	.316
vs. Right-Handers	115	29	4	0	1	9	6	20	.252	.313	.304
vs. Ground-Ballers	56	13	1	0	0	2	5	10	.232	.250	.317
vs. Fly-Ballers	95	26	4	0	1	10	3	16	.274	.347	.300

Most Comparable Rookie Seasons:

	AB	H	2B	3B	HR	RBI	BB	SO	BA	SA	OBA
Shooty Babitt	156	40	1	3	0	14	13	13	.256	.301	.315
Boots Day	116	31	4	0	0	5	6	21	.267	.302	.304
Kirt Manwaring	116	29	7	0	1	15	2	21	.250	.336	.264
Max Venable	138	37	5	0	0	10	15	22	.268	.304	.341
Mark Wagner	115	30	2	3	0	12	6	18	.261	.330	.299

Projections for 1993:

	AB	H	2B	3B	HR	RBI	BB	SO	BA	SA	OBA
Best Guess	138	32	4	0	0	12	7	25	.230	.270	.266
Optimistic	294	79	13	4	4	32	23	31	.268	.382	.322

Projections for career:

	AB	H	2B	3B	HR	RBI	BB	SO	BA	SA	OBA
Best Guess	1073	261	39	5	9	101	57	186	.243	.313	.282
Optimistic	3505	916	161	33	70	408	273	378	.261	.386	.316

Monty Fariss — Bats Right
Born Oct. 13, 1967

Texas Rangers	AB	H	2B	3B	HR	RBI	BB	SO	BA	SA	OBA
Season	166	36	7	1	3	21	17	51	.217	.325	.297
vs. Left-Handers	75	14	1	0	2	11	8	30	.187	.280	.274
vs. Right-Handers	91	22	6	1	1	10	9	21	.242	.363	.317
vs. Ground-Ballers	67	17	3	1	1	8	9	18	.254	.373	.351
vs. Fly-Ballers	99	19	4	0	2	13	8	33	.192	.293	.259

Most Comparable Rookie Seasons:

	AB	H	2B	3B	HR	RBI	BB	SO	BA	SA	OBA
Billy Beane	183	39	6	0	3	15	11	54	.213	.295	.259
Pat Corrales	174	39	8	1	2	15	25	42	.224	.316	.323
Ron Hodges	136	30	4	0	4	14	19	11	.221	.338	.317
Henry Rodriguez	146	32	7	0	3	14	8	30	.219	.329	.261
Tracy Woodson	136	31	8	1	1	11	9	21	.228	.324	.277

Projections for 1993:

	AB	H	2B	3B	HR	RBI	BB	SO	BA	SA	OBA
Best Guess	91	20	3	0	0	8	8	32	.217	.255	.280
Optimistic	316	84	16	3	8	39	59	73	.264	.413	.381

Projections for career:

	AB	H	2B	3B	HR	RBI	BB	SO	BA	SA	OBA
Best Guess	872	204	33	4	11	92	106	265	.234	.319	.318
Optimistic	2177	564	94	20	51	269	395	497	.259	.390	.374

Eric Fox — Bats Left and Right
Born Aug. 15, 1963

Oakland A's	AB	H	2B	3B	HR	RBI	BB	SO	BA	SA	OBA
Season	143	34	5	2	3	13	13	29	.238	.364	.299
vs. Left-Handers	22	5	1	0	0	1	2	6	.227	.273	.292
vs. Right-Handers	121	29	4	2	3	12	11	23	.240	.380	.301
vs. Ground-Ballers	68	19	3	1	1	4	4	10	.279	.397	.319
vs. Fly-Ballers	75	15	2	1	2	9	9	19	.200	.333	.282

Most Comparable Rookie Seasons:

	AB	H	2B	3B	HR	RBI	BB	SO	BA	SA	OBA
Terry Bulling	154	38	3	0	2	15	21	20	.247	.305	.338
Joe Hicks	174	39	4	2	6	14	15	34	.224	.374	.287
Jeff Newman	162	36	9	0	4	15	4	24	.222	.352	.242
Bob Perry	166	42	9	0	3	14	9	31	.253	.361	.293
Eddie Sadowski	164	38	13	0	4	12	11	33	.232	.384	.281

Projections for 1993:

	AB	H	2B	3B	HR	RBI	BB	SO	BA	SA	OBA
Best Guess	56	12	1	0	1	4	3	18	.209	.264	.256
Optimistic	220	57	10	1	6	30	25	39	.260	.394	.335

Projections for career:

	AB	H	2B	3B	HR	RBI	BB	SO	BA	SA	OBA
Best Guess	364	86	13	3	6	34	33	82	.236	.341	.301
Optimistic	545	138	23	5	16	69	77	88	.253	.397	.347

Jeff Frye — Bats Right
Born Aug. 31, 1966

Texas Rangers	AB	H	2B	3B	HR	RBI	BB	SO	BA	SA	OBA
Season	199	51	9	1	1	12	16	27	.256	.327	.320
vs. Left-Handers	68	21	5	0	1	6	5	10	.309	.426	.356
vs. Right-Handers	131	30	4	1	0	6	11	17	.229	.275	.301
vs. Ground-Ballers	64	21	1	1	0	3	8	4	.328	.375	.411
vs. Fly-Ballers	135	30	8	0	1	9	8	23	.222	.304	.274

Most Comparable Rookie Seasons:

	AB	H	2B	3B	HR	RBI	BB	SO	BA	SA	OBA
Carlos Hernandez	173	45	4	0	3	17	11	21	.260	.335	.306
Garth Iorg	222	55	10	1	2	14	12	39	.248	.329	.287
Jim Lentine	171	43	8	1	1	18	28	32	.251	.327	.358
Dave Marshall	174	46	5	1	1	16	20	37	.264	.322	.341
Rich Severson	240	60	11	1	1	22	16	33	.250	.317	.298

Projections for 1993:

	AB	H	2B	3B	HR	RBI	BB	SO	BA	SA	OBA
Best Guess	129	31	5	1	1	12	9	19	.242	.302	.292
Optimistic	337	94	17	5	7	43	41	30	.278	.418	.356

Projections for career:

	AB	H	2B	3B	HR	RBI	BB	SO	BA	SA	OBA
Best Guess	1077	276	45	7	11	100	93	143	.256	.341	.316
Optimistic	2378	649	118	25	52	285	271	222	.273	.408	.348

Willie Greene — Bats Left
Born Sep. 23, 1971

Cincinnati Reds	AB	H	2B	3B	HR	RBI	BB	SO	BA	SA	OBA
Season	93	25	5	2	2	13	10	23	.269	.430	.337
vs. Left-Handers	28	7	0	1	0	4	2	7	.250	.321	.290
vs. Right-Handers	65	18	5	1	2	9	8	16	.277	.477	.356
vs. Ground-Ballers	38	11	2	1	1	5	5	10	.289	.474	.364
vs. Fly-Ballers	55	14	3	1	1	8	5	13	.255	.400	.317

Most Comparable Rookie Seasons:

	AB	H	2B	3B	HR	RBI	BB	SO	BA	SA	OBA
Mike Anderson	89	22	5	1	2	5	13	28	.247	.393	.344
Darnell Coles	92	26	7	0	1	6	7	12	.283	.391	.335
Steve Garvey	93	25	5	0	1	6	6	17	.269	.355	.314
Rafael Palmeiro	73	18	4	0	3	12	4	6	.247	.425	.287
Jim Thome	98	25	4	2	1	9	5	16	.255	.367	.292

Projections for 1993:

	AB	H	2B	3B	HR	RBI	BB	SO	BA	SA	OBA
Best Guess	221	56	11	2	4	25	31	59	.252	.373	.344
Optimistic	545	154	34	6	23	74	99	87	.283	.491	.395

Projections for career:

	AB	H	2B	3B	HR	RBI	BB	SO	BA	SA	OBA
Best Guess	1494	372	67	12	39	167	174	305	.249	.389	.328
Optimistic	6486	1876	325	70	230	965	931	909	.289	.467	.380

Juan Guerrero — Bats Right
Born Feb. 1, 1967

Houston Astros	AB	H	2B	3B	HR	RBI	BB	SO	BA	SA	OBA
Season	125	25	4	2	1	14	10	32	.200	.288	.261
vs. Left-Handers	61	12	3	0	0	8	8	14	.197	.246	.286
vs. Right-Handers	64	13	1	2	1	6	2	18	.203	.328	.235
vs. Ground-Ballers	45	8	1	1	0	3	4	13	.178	.244	.245
vs. Fly-Ballers	80	17	3	1	1	11	6	19	.213	.313	.270

Most Comparable Rookie Seasons:

	AB	H	2B	3B	HR	RBI	BB	SO	BA	SA	OBA
Steve Balboni	107	20	2	1	2	4	6	34	.187	.280	.231
Tommy Dunbar	104	21	4	0	1	5	12	9	.202	.269	.286
Mario Ramirez	107	21	6	3	0	12	20	23	.196	.308	.324
Rob Sperring	144	30	4	1	1	9	16	31	.208	.271	.289
Chris Ward	137	28	4	0	1	15	18	13	.204	.255	.298

Projections for 1993:

	AB	H	2B	3B	HR	RBI	BB	SO	BA	SA	OBA
Best Guess	50	10	1	0	0	3	3	16	.200	.217	.247
Optimistic	173	47	8	1	5	23	18	37	.271	.412	.339

Projections for career:

	AB	H	2B	3B	HR	RBI	BB	SO	BA	SA	OBA
Best Guess	682	153	24	4	7	67	57	173	.225	.303	.286
Optimistic	1915	484	84	18	51	251	208	339	.253	.395	.327

Carlos Hernandez — Bats Right
Born May 24, 1967

Los Angeles Dodgers	AB	H	2B	3B	HR	RBI	BB	SO	BA	SA	OBA
Season	173	45	4	0	3	17	11	21	.260	.335	.316
vs. Left-Handers	108	31	3	0	3	9	7	9	.287	.398	.336
vs. Right-Handers	65	14	1	0	0	8	4	12	.215	.231	.284
vs. Ground-Ballers	56	15	1	0	0	3	2	6	.268	.286	.328
vs. Fly-Ballers	117	30	3	0	3	14	9	15	.256	.359	.310

Most Comparable Rookie Seasons:

	AB	H	2B	3B	HR	RBI	BB	SO	BA	SA	OBA
Geronimo Berroa	136	36	4	0	2	9	7	32	.265	.338	.302
Bob Gallagher	148	39	3	1	2	10	3	27	.264	.338	.279
Joe Girardi	157	39	10	0	1	14	11	26	.248	.331	.299
Bruce Kimm	152	40	8	0	1	6	15	20	.263	.336	.331
Gus Polidor	137	36	3	0	2	15	2	15	.263	.328	.275

Projections for 1993:

	AB	H	2B	3B	HR	RBI	BB	SO	BA	SA	OBA
Best Guess	173	41	7	0	1	16	9	25	.239	.299	.277
Optimistic	354	94	18	4	7	46	33	37	.266	.398	.329

Projections for career:

	AB	H	2B	3B	HR	RBI	BB	SO	BA	SA	OBA
Best Guess	970	237	36	3	10	94	58	136	.244	.321	.288
Optimistic	2158	575	99	18	41	250	175	212	.267	.386	.323

Steve Hosey — Bats Right
Born Apr. 2, 1969

San Francisco Giants	AB	H	2B	3B	HR	RBI	BB	SO	BA	SA	OBA
Season	56	14	1	0	1	6	0	15	.250	.321	.241
vs. Left-Handers	29	8	0	0	1	3	0	8	.276	.379	.267
vs. Right-Handers	27	6	1	0	0	3	0	7	.222	.259	.214
vs. Ground-Ballers	28	9	1	0	0	3	0	8	.321	.357	.310
vs. Fly-Ballers	28	5	0	0	1	3	0	7	.179	.286	.172

Most Comparable Rookie Seasons:

	AB	H	2B	3B	HR	RBI	BB	SO	BA	SA	OBA
Billy Bean	66	17	2	0	0	4	5	11	.258	.288	.311
Geronimo Pena	45	11	2	0	0	2	4	14	.244	.289	.307
Mike Piazza	69	16	3	0	1	7	4	12	.232	.319	.275
Chris Pittaro	62	15	3	1	0	7	5	13	.242	.323	.300
Eddie Taubensee	66	16	2	1	0	8	5	16	.242	.303	.297

Projections for 1993:

	AB	H	2B	3B	HR	RBI	BB	SO	BA	SA	OBA
Best Guess	103	23	4	0	0	7	0	32	.227	.267	.228
Optimistic	297	80	15	4	6	32	0	54	.271	.415	.272

Projections for career:

	AB	H	2B	3B	HR	RBI	BB	SO	BA	SA	OBA
Best Guess	1337	324	53	8	15	132	0	335	.242	.327	.243
Optimistic	2977	796	151	28	69	360	0	481	.267	.406	.268

David Hulse — Bats Left
Born Feb. 25, 1968

Texas Rangers	AB	H	2B	3B	HR	RBI	BB	SO	BA	SA	OBA
Season	92	28	4	0	0	2	3	18	.304	.348	.326
vs. Left-Handers	21	6	1	0	0	1	1	5	.286	.333	.318
vs. Right-Handers	71	22	3	0	0	1	2	13	.310	.352	.329
vs. Ground-Ballers	33	10	2	0	0	0	1	10	.303	.364	.324
vs. Fly-Ballers	59	18	2	0	0	2	2	8	.305	.339	.328

Most Comparable Rookie Seasons:

	AB	H	2B	3B	HR	RBI	BB	SO	BA	SA	OBA
Alex Arias	99	29	6	0	0	7	11	13	.293	.354	.365
Jim Barbieri	82	23	5	0	0	3	9	7	.280	.341	.353
Hubie Brooks	81	25	2	1	1	10	5	9	.309	.395	.350
Gary Holman	85	25	5	1	0	7	13	15	.294	.376	.389
Terry Shumpert	91	25	6	1	0	8	2	17	.275	.363	.291

Projections for 1993:

	AB	H	2B	3B	HR	RBI	BB	SO	BA	SA	OBA
Best Guess	151	34	5	0	0	11	5	31	.226	.275	.252
Optimistic	369	100	17	5	6	41	19	43	.272	.392	.309

Projections for career:

	AB	H	2B	3B	HR	RBI	BB	SO	BA	SA	OBA
Best Guess	769	196	30	4	6	72	29	123	.255	.331	.283
Optimistic	2637	722	121	29	44	321	129	269	.274	.392	.309

Todd Hundley — Bats Left and Right
Born May 27, 1969

New York Mets	AB	H	2B	3B	HR	RBI	BB	SO	BA	SA	OBA
Season	358	75	17	0	7	32	19	76	.209	.316	.256
vs. Left-Handers	113	20	3	0	4	10	4	32	.177	.310	.217
vs. Right-Handers	245	55	14	0	3	22	15	44	.224	.318	.274
vs. Ground-Ballers	170	38	9	0	1	10	10	40	.224	.294	.272
vs. Fly-Ballers	188	37	8	0	6	22	9	36	.197	.335	.241

Most Comparable Rookie Seasons:

	AB	H	2B	3B	HR	RBI	BB	SO	BA	SA	OBA
Mark Bailey	344	73	16	1	9	34	53	71	.212	.343	.319
Kevin Elster	406	87	11	1	9	37	35	47	.214	.313	.278
Brad Komminsk	301	61	10	0	8	36	29	77	.203	.316	.274
Rey Quinones	312	68	16	1	2	22	24	57	.218	.295	.275
Eddie Taubensee	297	66	15	0	5	28	31	78	.222	.323	.297

Projections for 1993:

	AB	H	2B	3B	HR	RBI	BB	SO	BA	SA	OBA
Best Guess	300	72	12	2	4	29	17	65	.240	.331	.283
Optimistic	458	121	24	6	12	55	40	76	.265	.418	.326

Projections for career:

	AB	H	2B	3B	HR	RBI	BB	SO	BA	SA	OBA
Best Guess	2679	639	111	15	53	288	179	563	.239	.350	.287
Optimistic	4499	1160	217	43	127	553	388	752	.258	.410	.318

John Jaha — Bats Right
Born Mar. 12, 1966

Milwaukee Brewers	AB	H	2B	3B	HR	RBI	BB	SO	BA	SA	OBA
Season	133	30	3	1	2	10	12	30	.226	.308	.291
vs. Left-Handers	46	8	1	0	1	5	6	10	.174	.261	.268
vs. Right-Handers	87	22	2	1	1	5	6	20	.253	.333	.305
vs. Ground-Ballers	54	14	1	1	0	3	8	11	.259	.315	.354
vs. Fly-Ballers	79	16	2	0	2	7	4	19	.203	.304	.244

Most Comparable Rookie Seasons:

	AB	H	2B	3B	HR	RBI	BB	SO	BA	SA	OBA
Beau Allred	125	29	3	0	3	12	25	35	.232	.328	.361
Jerry Goff	119	27	1	0	3	7	21	36	.227	.311	.344
Keith A. Miller	143	33	7	0	1	7	5	27	.231	.301	.258
Mike Ja. Ramsey	125	29	4	2	0	12	10	32	.232	.296	.290
John Stefero	120	28	2	0	2	13	16	25	.233	.300	.325

Projections for 1993:

	AB	H	2B	3B	HR	RBI	BB	SO	BA	SA	OBA
Best Guess	50	10	1	0	0	3	3	14	.191	.202	.237
Optimistic	157	41	8	0	2	16	20	25	.258	.353	.344

Projections for career:

	AB	H	2B	3B	HR	RBI	BB	SO	BA	SA	OBA
Best Guess	404	94	13	2	4	33	36	94	.232	.304	.296
Optimistic	1540	400	69	14	38	177	203	238	.260	.396	.347

Reggie Jefferson — Bats Left and Right
Born Sep. 25, 1968

Cleveland Indians	AB	H	2B	3B	HR	RBI	BB	SO	BA	SA	OBA
Season	89	30	6	2	1	6	1	17	.337	.483	.352
vs. Left-Handers	19	5	1	1	1	3	1	7	.263	.579	.300
vs. Right-Handers	70	25	5	1	0	3	0	10	.357	.457	.366
vs. Ground-Ballers	31	9	0	0	0	1	0	5	.290	.290	.313
vs. Fly-Ballers	58	21	6	2	1	5	1	12	.362	.586	.373

Most Comparable Rookie Seasons:

	AB	H	2B	3B	HR	RBI	BB	SO	BA	SA	OBA
Vic Mata	70	23	5	0	1	6	0	12	.329	.443	.330
Lee May	75	25	5	1	2	10	0	14	.333	.507	.335
Kevin Seitzer	96	31	4	1	2	11	19	14	.323	.448	.436
Jeff Treadway	84	28	4	0	2	4	2	6	.333	.452	.350
John Wehner	106	36	7	0	0	7	7	17	.340	.406	.382

Projections for 1993:

	AB	H	2B	3B	HR	RBI	BB	SO	BA	SA	OBA
Best Guess	253	66	12	2	4	33	8	58	.262	.370	.285
Optimistic	447	129	30	6	14	63	19	63	.290	.473	.319

Projections for career:

	AB	H	2B	3B	HR	RBI	BB	SO	BA	SA	OBA
Best Guess	2201	570	99	13	27	258	66	365	.259	.352	.282
Optimistic	4944	1398	273	52	159	797	180	575	.283	.455	.309

Brian Jordan — Bats Right
Born Mar. 29, 1967

St. Louis Cardinals	AB	H	2B	3B	HR	RBI	BB	SO	BA	SA	OBA
Season	193	40	9	4	5	22	10	48	.207	.373	.250
vs. Left-Handers	64	14	2	0	4	10	6	14	.219	.438	.286
vs. Right-Handers	129	26	7	4	1	12	4	34	.202	.341	.231
vs. Ground-Ballers	98	18	5	2	1	6	1	27	.184	.306	.200
vs. Fly-Ballers	95	22	4	2	4	16	9	21	.232	.442	.298

Most Comparable Rookie Seasons:

Steve Decker	233	48	7	1	5	24	16	44	.206	.309	.258
Jeff King	215	42	13	3	5	19	20	34	.195	.353	.265
Gene Leek	199	45	9	1	5	20	7	54	.226	.357	.254
Jim Lindeman	207	43	13	0	8	28	11	56	.208	.386	.249
Don Pavletich	183	38	11	0	5	18	17	12	.208	.350	276

Projections for 1993:

Best Guess	156	37	6	0	2	19	6	38	.236	.314	.265
Optimistic	419	111	22	4	16	66	29	75	.265	.456	.314

Projections for career:

Best Guess	967	224	41	9	19	111	53	244	.232	.352	.273
Optimistic	2372	626	123	25	82	336	163	445	.264	.441	.313

Terry Jorgensen — Bats Right
Born Sep. 2, 1966

Minnesota Twins	AB	H	2B	3B	HR	RBI	BB	SO	BA	SA	OBA
Season	58	18	1	0	0	5	3	11	.310	.328	.349
vs. Left-Handers	27	8	1	0	0	2	1	4	.296	.333	.333
vs. Right-Handers	31	10	0	0	0	3	2	7	.323	.323	.364
vs. Ground-Ballers	24	8	0	0	0	3	1	6	.333	.333	.360
vs. Fly-Ballers	34	10	1	0	0	2	2	5	.294	.324	.342

Most Comparable Rookie Seasons:

Chris Arnold	54	16	2	0	1	13	8	11	.296	.389	.388
Freddie Benavides	63	18	1	0	0	3	1	15	.286	.302	.298
Mario Diaz	72	22	5	0	0	9	3	5	.306	.375	.335
Cesar Hernandez	51	14	4	0	0	4	0	10	.275	.353	.276
Thomas Howard	44	12	2	0	0	0	0	11	.273	.318	.274

Projections for 1993:

Best Guess	26	5	0	0	0	1	1	8	.178	.178	.224
Optimistic	201	51	9	2	3	24	23	31	.253	.356	.330

Projections for career:

Best Guess	519	127	17	3	2	52	47	97	.246	.304	.310
Optimistic	1701	460	76	23	27	216	190	197	.271	.390	.345

Eric Karros — Bats Right
Born Nov. 4, 1967

Los Angeles Dodgers	AB	H	2B	3B	HR	RBI	BB	SO	BA	SA	OBA
Season	545	140	30	1	20	88	37	103	.257	.426	.304
vs. Left-Handers	213	59	10	0	8	32	16	26	.277	.437	.325
vs. Right-Handers	332	81	20	1	12	56	21	77	.244	.419	.291
vs. Ground-Ballers	193	49	9	0	7	29	12	35	.254	.409	.300
vs. Fly-Ballers	352	91	21	1	13	59	25	68	.259	.435	.306

Most Comparable Rookie Seasons:

Sam Bowens	501	132	25	2	22	71	42	99	.263	.453	.322
Lee May	438	116	29	2	12	57	19	80	.265	.422	.297
Bill Melton	556	142	26	2	23	87	56	106	.255	.433	.325
Craig Worthington	497	123	23	0	15	70	61	114	.247	.384	.331
Todd Zeile	495	121	25	3	15	57	67	77	.244	.398	.336

Projections for 1993:

Best Guess	472	124	22	3	12	60	31	87	.263	.399	.309
Optimistic	568	164	31	6	24	88	55	77	.289	.493	.353

Projections for career:

Best Guess	3094	782	136	17	96	405	216	588	.253	.401	.303
Optimistic	4998	1327	241	44	195	748	483	783	.265	.448	.331

Jeff Kent — Bats Right
Born Mar. 7, 1968

Blue Jays/Mets	AB	H	2B	3B	HR	RBI	BB	SO	BA	SA	OBA
Season	305	73	21	2	11	50	27	76	.239	.430	.312
vs. Left-Handers	92	20	5	0	3	14	10	20	.217	.370	.291
vs. Right-Handers	213	53	16	2	8	36	17	56	.249	.455	.321
vs. Ground-Ballers	146	35	10	1	7	27	14	33	.240	.466	.325
vs. Fly-Ballers	159	38	11	1	4	23	13	43	.239	.396	.299

Most Comparable Rookie Seasons:

Dann Bilardello	298	71	18	0	9	38	15	49	.238	.389	.276
Randy Bush	373	93	24	3	11	56	34	51	.249	.418	.313
Darrell Evans	260	63	11	1	12	38	39	54	.242	.431	.342
Dave Henderson	324	82	17	1	14	48	36	67	.253	.441	.329
Syd O'Brien	263	64	10	5	9	29	15	37	.243	.422	.285

Projections for 1993:

Best Guess	250	62	10	1	6	28	21	61	.247	.365	.306
Optimistic	442	121	24	5	20	68	47	78	.274	.482	.345

Projections for career:

Best Guess	2431	604	108	13	84	333	213	584	.248	.407	.310
Optimistic	3791	978	185	32	173	603	443	704	.258	.461	.337

Kevin Koslofski — Bats Left
Born Sep. 24, 1966

Kansas City Royals	AB	H	2B	3B	HR	RBI	BB	SO	BA	SA	OBA
Season	133	33	0	2	3	13	12	23	.248	.346	.313
vs. Left-Handers	14	6	0	0	0	1	4	3	.429	.429	.556
vs. Right-Handers	119	27	0	2	3	12	8	20	.227	.336	.279
vs. Ground-Ballers	46	7	0	1	1	3	6	8	.152	.261	.259
vs. Fly-Ballers	87	26	0	1	2	10	6	15	.299	.391	.344

Most Comparable Rookie Seasons:

Beau Allred	125	29	3	0	3	12	25	35	.232	.328	.361
Mike Gallego	124	31	6	0	2	14	12	21	.250	.347	.317
Clarence Jones	135	34	7	0	2	16	14	33	.252	.348	.323
Donell Nixon	132	33	4	0	3	12	13	28	.250	.348	.318
Gus Polidor	137	36	3	0	2	15	2	15	.263	.328	.275

Projections for 1993:

Best Guess	81	17	2	0	0	6	5	15	.209	.239	.259
Optimistic	271	71	14	2	5	32	35	33	.263	.380	.349

Projections for career:

Best Guess	782	190	24	5	8	74	74	136	.243	.318	.310
Optimistic	2279	603	103	23	61	286	311	260	.264	.410	.354

Pat Listach — Bats Left and Right
Born Sep. 12, 1967

Milwaukee Brewers	AB	H	2B	3B	HR	RBI	BB	SO	BA	SA	OBA
Season	579	168	19	6	1	47	55	124	.290	.349	.352
vs. Left-Handers	148	51	7	3	1	18	8	25	.345	.453	.382
vs. Right-Handers	431	117	12	3	0	29	47	99	.271	.313	.342
vs. Ground-Ballers	266	68	6	1	0	21	22	65	.256	.286	.311
vs. Fly-Ballers	313	100	13	5	1	26	33	59	.319	.403	.385

Most Comparable Rookie Seasons:

Bill Almon	613	160	18	11	2	43	37	114	.261	.336	.304
Dick Howser	611	171	29	6	3	45	92	38	.280	.362	.375
Kenny Lofton	576	164	15	8	5	42	68	54	.285	.365	.361
Ricky Peters	477	139	19	7	2	42	54	48	.291	.373	.365
Gene Richards	525	152	16	11	5	32	60	80	.290	.390	.364

Projections for 1993:

Best Guess	515	135	21	5	4	46	53	106	.263	.347	.333
Optimistic	555	167	28	9	9	59	69	59	.300	.433	.379

Projections for career:

Best Guess	3068	820	117	24	21	278	292	670	.267	.341	.332
Optimistic	4699	1341	208	70	53	478	529	733	.285	.393	.359

Scott Livingstone   Bats Left
Born Jul. 15, 1965

Detroit Tigers	AB	H	2B	3B	HR	RBI	BB	SO	BA	SA	OBA
Season	354	100	21	0	4	46	21	36	.282	.376	.319
vs. Left-Handers	45	13	2	0	1	7	4	8	.289	.400	.340
vs. Right-Handers	309	87	19	0	3	39	17	28	.282	.372	.316
vs. Ground-Ballers	164	48	9	0	1	22	5	18	.293	.366	.310
vs. Fly-Ballers	190	52	12	0	3	24	16	18	.274	.384	.327

Most Comparable Rookie Seasons:

	AB	H	2B	3B	HR	RBI	BB	SO	BA	SA	OBA
Barbaro Garbey	327	94	17	1	5	52	17	35	.287	.391	.324
Eddie Milner	407	109	23	5	4	31	41	40	.268	.378	.336
Jody Reed	338	99	23	1	1	28	45	21	.293	.376	.377
George Vukovich	335	91	18	2	6	42	32	47	.272	.391	.336
Bob Zupcic	392	108	19	1	3	43	25	60	.276	.352	.320

Projections for 1993:

	AB	H	2B	3B	HR	RBI	BB	SO	BA	SA	OBA
Best Guess	312	80	12	2	3	32	18	42	.257	.338	.299
Optimistic	481	137	27	6	11	59	50	43	.286	.436	.354

Projections for career:

	AB	H	2B	3B	HR	RBI	BB	SO	BA	SA	OBA
Best Guess	1330	349	60	6	17	140	79	171	.262	.353	.305
Optimistic	2442	656	120	23	45	292	215	220	.269	.392	.329

Kenny Lofton   Bats Left
Born May 31, 1967

Cleveland Indians	AB	H	2B	3B	HR	RBI	BB	SO	BA	SA	OBA
Season	576	164	15	8	5	42	68	54	.285	.365	.362
vs. Left-Handers	122	45	6	1	0	12	21	15	.369	.434	.466
vs. Right-Handers	454	119	9	7	5	30	47	39	.262	.346	.331
vs. Ground-Ballers	261	68	6	1	2	17	30	15	.261	.314	.339
vs. Fly-Ballers	315	96	9	7	3	25	38	39	.305	.406	.380

Most Comparable Rookie Seasons:

	AB	H	2B	3B	HR	RBI	BB	SO	BA	SA	OBA
Bill D. Doran	535	145	12	7	8	39	86	67	.271	.364	.373
Pat Listach	579	168	19	6	1	47	55	124	.290	.349	.353
Ricky Peters	477	139	19	7	2	42	54	48	.291	.373	.365
Johnny Ray	647	182	30	7	7	63	36	34	.281	.382	.320
Bump Wills	541	155	28	6	9	62	65	96	.287	.410	.364

Projections for 1993:

	AB	H	2B	3B	HR	RBI	BB	SO	BA	SA	OBA
Best Guess	531	140	22	6	5	49	63	61	.263	.351	.342
Optimistic	555	167	30	11	9	60	78	28	.300	.446	.388

Projections for career:

	AB	H	2B	3B	HR	RBI	BB	SO	BA	SA	OBA
Best Guess	3262	864	121	27	32	294	364	387	.265	.348	.340
Optimistic	5022	1445	240	76	64	548	657	398	.288	.404	.371

Tom Marsh   Bats Right
Born Dec. 27, 1965

Philadelphia Phillies	AB	H	2B	3B	HR	RBI	BB	SO	BA	SA	OBA
Season	125	25	3	2	2	16	2	23	.200	.304	.215
vs. Left-Handers	66	12	1	1	1	6	1	14	.182	.273	.203
vs. Right-Handers	59	13	2	1	1	10	1	9	.220	.339	.230
vs. Ground-Ballers	46	9	2	0	1	3	2	8	.196	.304	.229
vs. Fly-Ballers	79	16	1	2	1	13	0	15	.203	.304	.207

Most Comparable Rookie Seasons:

	AB	H	2B	3B	HR	RBI	BB	SO	BA	SA	OBA
Adams	121	23	3	1	2	10	5	23	.190	.281	.223
Mark Bradley	104	21	4	0	3	5	11	35	.202	.327	.279
Marty Castillo	119	23	4	0	2	10	7	22	.193	.277	.239
Jeff Manto	128	27	7	0	2	13	14	22	.211	.313	.290
Mario Ramirez	107	21	6	3	0	12	20	23	.196	.308	.324

Projections for 1993:

	AB	H	2B	3B	HR	RBI	BB	SO	BA	SA	OBA
Best Guess	43	8	0	0	0	2	0	12	.176	.176	.186
Optimistic	172	43	8	0	4	21	4	23	.248	.354	.265

Projections for career:

	AB	H	2B	3B	HR	RBI	BB	SO	BA	SA	OBA
Best Guess	347	75	11	2	5	35	6	69	.217	.302	.231
Optimistic	1461	371	66	13	38	192	32	186	.254	.395	.271

Derrick May   Bats Left
Born Jul. 14, 1968

Chicago Cubs	AB	H	2B	3B	HR	RBI	BB	SO	BA	SA	OBA
Season	351	96	11	0	8	45	14	40	.274	.373	.306
vs. Left-Handers	76	19	2	0	2	9	3	13	.250	.355	.287
vs. Right-Handers	275	77	9	0	6	36	11	27	.280	.378	.311
vs. Ground-Ballers	147	44	5	0	2	18	8	15	.299	.374	.340
vs. Fly-Ballers	204	52	6	0	6	27	6	25	.255	.373	.282

Most Comparable Rookie Seasons:

	AB	H	2B	3B	HR	RBI	BB	SO	BA	SA	OBA
Scott Cooper	337	93	21	0	5	33	37	33	.276	.383	.349
Rich McKinney	369	100	11	2	8	46	35	37	.271	.377	.335
Ron Oester	303	84	16	2	2	20	26	44	.277	.363	.336
Gerald Perry	347	92	12	2	7	47	61	38	.265	.372	.376
Scot Thompson	346	100	13	5	2	29	17	37	.289	.373	.323

Projections for 1993:

	AB	H	2B	3B	HR	RBI	BB	SO	BA	SA	OBA
Best Guess	307	77	12	1	4	30	12	33	.250	.338	.279
Optimistic	474	135	25	6	12	63	25	36	.284	.435	.321

Projections for career:

	AB	H	2B	3B	HR	RBI	BB	SO	BA	SA	OBA
Best Guess	1833	470	71	9	33	201	77	207	.256	.358	.287
Optimistic	3741	1015	173	34	97	477	202	313	.271	.413	.310

Dave Nilsson   Bats Left
Born Dec. 14, 1969

Milwaukee Brewers	AB	H	2B	3B	HR	RBI	BB	SO	BA	SA	OBA
Season	164	38	8	0	4	25	17	18	.232	.354	.304
vs. Left-Handers	27	6	2	0	0	7	2	3	.222	.296	.276
vs. Right-Handers	137	32	6	0	4	18	15	15	.234	.365	.309
vs. Ground-Ballers	66	19	4	0	3	13	3	7	.288	.485	.319
vs. Fly-Ballers	98	19	4	0	1	12	14	11	.194	.265	.295

Most Comparable Rookie Seasons:

	AB	H	2B	3B	HR	RBI	BB	SO	BA	SA	OBA
George A. Bell	163	38	2	1	5	12	5	27	.233	.350	.257
Craig Biggio	123	26	6	1	3	5	7	29	.211	.350	.255
Denny Gonzalez	124	28	4	0	4	12	13	27	.226	.355	.300
Jeff Hamilton	147	33	5	0	5	19	2	43	.224	.361	.236
Rich Murray	194	42	8	2	4	24	11	48	.216	.340	.260

Projections for 1993:

	AB	H	2B	3B	HR	RBI	BB	SO	BA	SA	OBA
Best Guess	120	27	4	0	1	10	12	13	.225	.270	.296
Optimistic	284	75	13	4	8	34	40	17	.265	.426	.357

Projections for career:

	AB	H	2B	3B	HR	RBI	BB	SO	BA	SA	OBA
Best Guess	1362	329	55	6	26	154	139	133	.242	.347	.313
Optimistic	5589	1508	261	49	179	712	857	422	.270	.430	.368

John Patterson   Bats Left and Right
Born Feb. 11, 1967

San Francisco Giants	AB	H	2B	3B	HR	RBI	BB	SO	BA	SA	OBA
Season	103	19	1	1	0	4	5	24	.184	.214	.229
vs. Left-Handers	25	6	1	0	0	1	1	6	.240	.280	.269
vs. Right-Handers	78	13	0	1	0	3	4	18	.167	.192	.217
vs. Ground-Ballers	54	12	1	1	0	2	2	10	.222	.278	.250
vs. Fly-Ballers	49	7	0	0	0	2	3	14	.143	.143	.208

Most Comparable Rookie Seasons:

	AB	H	2B	3B	HR	RBI	BB	SO	BA	SA	OBA
Lance Johnson	124	23	4	1	0	6	6	11	.185	.234	.224
Andy Mota	90	17	2	0	1	6	1	17	.189	.244	.199
Johnny Paredes	91	17	2	0	1	10	9	17	.187	.242	.261
David Rohde	98	18	4	0	0	5	9	20	.184	.224	.254
John Wehner	123	22	6	0	0	4	12	22	.179	.228	.253

Projections for 1993:

	AB	H	2B	3B	HR	RBI	BB	SO	BA	SA	OBA
Best Guess	54	11	1	0	0	3	2	15	.197	.211	.226
Optimistic	200	54	10	2	3	23	12	34	.272	.382	.315

Projections for career:

	AB	H	2B	3B	HR	RBI	BB	SO	BA	SA	OBA
Best Guess	428	92	12	2	3	33	21	97	.216	.275	.253
Optimistic	1227	313	53	11	24	127	78	180	.255	.377	.301

Mike Piazza
Bats Right

Born Sep. 4, 1968

Los Angeles Dodgers	AB	H	2B	3B	HR	RBI	BB	SO	BA	SA	OBA
Season	69	16	3	0	1	7	4	12	.232	.319	.284
vs. Left-Handers	30	8	2	0	0	4	2	5	.267	.333	.313
vs. Right-Handers	39	8	1	0	1	3	2	7	.205	.308	.262
vs. Ground-Ballers	25	4	0	0	1	3	0	5	.160	.280	.192
vs. Fly-Ballers	44	12	3	0	0	4	4	7	.273	.341	.333

Most Comparable Rookie Seasons:

Steve Hosey	56	14	1	0	1	6	0	15	.250	.321	.251
Vance Law	74	17	2	2	0	3	3	7	.230	.311	.261
Mickey Morandini	79	19	4	0	1	3	6	19	.241	.329	.295
Don Pavletich	63	14	3	0	1	7	8	18	.222	.317	.311
Chris Pittaro	62	15	3	1	0	7	5	13	.242	.323	.300

Projections for 1993:

Best Guess	87	19	3	0	0	7	4	16	.222	.254	.259
Optimistic	322	87	16	4	6	42	27	38	.271	.402	.328

Projections for career:

Best Guess	1378	343	56	8	17	145	86	232	.249	.338	.294
Optimistic	2990	797	158	31	80	387	238	336	.266	.421	.322

Jeff Reboulet
Bats Right

Born Apr. 30, 1964

Minnesota Twins	AB	H	2B	3B	HR	RBI	BB	SO	BA	SA	OBA
Season	137	26	7	1	1	16	23	26	.190	.277	.311
vs. Left-Handers	27	6	1	0	0	2	5	6	.222	.259	.364
vs. Right-Handers	110	20	6	1	1	14	18	20	.182	.282	.297
vs. Ground-Ballers	54	9	2	0	0	3	8	11	.167	.204	.274
vs. Fly-Ballers	83	17	5	1	1	13	15	15	.205	.325	.333

Most Comparable Rookie Seasons:

Chuck Brinkman	139	26	6	0	1	10	11	37	.187	.252	.248
Russ Gibson	138	28	7	0	1	15	12	31	.203	.275	.268
Glenn Gulliver	145	29	7	0	1	5	37	18	.200	.269	.364
Marc Sullivan	119	23	4	0	1	14	7	32	.193	.252	.239
Bill Voss	148	29	8	1	1	9	16	22	.196	.284	.276

Projections for 1993:

Best Guess	0	0	0	0	0	0	0	0	—	—	—
Optimistic	102	22	4	0	1	8	18	17	.213	.288	.331

Projections for career:

Best Guess	362	75	15	2	3	36	48	64	.208	.283	.303
Optimistic	1267	306	62	9	24	160	278	182	.241	.360	.379

Darren Reed
Bats Right

Born Oct. 16, 1965

Expos/Twins	AB	H	2B	3B	HR	RBI	BB	SO	BA	SA	OBA
Season	114	20	4	0	5	14	8	34	.175	.342	.232
vs. Left-Handers	66	11	3	0	3	6	4	21	.167	.348	.208
vs. Right-Handers	48	9	1	0	2	8	4	13	.188	.333	.264
vs. Ground-Ballers	51	11	1	0	3	9	5	12	.216	.412	.293
vs. Fly-Ballers	63	9	3	0	2	5	3	22	.143	.286	.179

Most Comparable Rookie Seasons:

Bill Bathe	103	19	3	0	5	11	2	20	.184	.359	.201
Mark Bradley	104	21	4	0	3	5	11	35	.202	.327	.279
Mark Parent	118	23	3	0	6	15	6	23	.195	.373	.235
Jim Price	132	23	4	0	3	13	13	14	.174	.273	.249
Randy Velarde	115	20	6	0	5	12	8	24	.174	.357	.229

Projections for 1993:

Best Guess	38	7	1	0	0	2	2	16	.188	.204	.224
Optimistic	187	48	10	0	5	27	16	49	.255	.391	.314

Projections for career:

Best Guess	371	76	17	1	11	41	25	120	.206	.345	.257
Optimistic	1409	358	73	7	52	186	133	355	.254	.427	.319

Henry Rodriguez
Bats Left

Born Nov. 8, 1967

Los Angeles Dodgers	AB	H	2B	3B	HR	RBI	BB	SO	BA	SA	OBA
Season	146	32	7	0	3	14	8	30	.219	.329	.258
vs. Left-Handers	15	6	0	0	0	1	1	5	.400	.400	.438
vs. Right-Handers	131	26	7	0	3	13	7	25	.198	.321	.237
vs. Ground-Ballers	65	16	5	0	3	8	2	11	.246	.462	.269
vs. Fly-Ballers	81	16	2	0	0	6	6	19	.198	.222	.250

Most Comparable Rookie Seasons:

Monty Fariss	166	36	7	1	3	21	17	51	.217	.325	.291
Darrin Fletcher	136	31	8	0	1	12	5	15	.228	.309	.256
Ron Hodges	136	30	4	0	4	14	19	11	.221	.338	.317
Andre Robertson	118	26	5	0	2	9	8	19	.220	.314	.271
Tracy Woodson	136	31	8	1	1	11	9	21	.228	.324	.277

Projections for 1993:

Best Guess	92	20	3	0	0	7	4	21	.217	.255	.248
Optimistic	322	86	16	3	9	40	26	48	.267	.417	.323

Projections for career:

Best Guess	957	227	38	4	11	93	52	185	.237	.319	.278
Optimistic	2284	594	101	21	56	277	190	331	.260	.397	.318

Rico Rossy
Bats Right

Born Feb. 16, 1964

Kansas City Royals	AB	H	2B	3B	HR	RBI	BB	SO	BA	SA	OBA
Season	149	32	8	1	1	12	20	20	.215	.302	.310
vs. Left-Handers	50	10	5	0	0	6	9	5	.200	.300	.317
vs. Right-Handers	99	22	3	1	1	6	11	15	.222	.303	.306
vs. Ground-Ballers	70	11	1	0	0	4	10	7	.157	.171	.268
vs. Fly-Ballers	79	21	7	1	1	8	10	13	.266	.418	.348

Most Comparable Rookie Seasons:

Rick Bladt	117	26	3	1	1	11	11	8	.222	.291	.290
Rick Joseph	155	34	5	0	3	12	16	35	.219	.310	.294
Steve Lubratich	156	34	9	0	0	7	4	17	.218	.276	.239
Roberto Pena	170	37	5	1	2	12	16	19	.218	.294	.286
Ronn Reynolds	126	27	4	0	3	10	5	30	.214	.317	.245

Projections for 1993:

Best Guess	0	0	0	0	0	0	0	0	—	—	—
Optimistic	147	33	7	0	2	13	18	20	.223	.301	.307

Projections for career:

Best Guess	474	106	20	2	4	42	48	70	.223	.297	.295
Optimistic	1375	347	62	9	27	168	219	154	.252	.371	.356

Tim Salmon
Bats Right

Born Aug. 24, 1968

California Angels	AB	H	2B	3B	HR	RBI	BB	SO	BA	SA	OBA
Season	79	14	1	0	2	6	11	23	.177	.266	.283
vs. Left-Handers	13	3	0	0	1	2	3	4	.231	.462	.375
vs. Right-Handers	66	11	1	0	1	4	8	19	.167	.227	.263
vs. Ground-Ballers	32	4	0	0	0	0	5	14	.125	.125	.243
vs. Fly-Ballers	47	10	1	0	2	6	6	9	.213	.362	.309

Most Comparable Rookie Seasons:

Gary Alexander	73	13	1	1	2	7	10	16	.178	.301	.278
Dave Cochrane	62	12	2	0	1	2	5	22	.194	.274	.255
Andres Galarraga	75	14	1	0	2	4	3	18	.187	.280	.219
Gary Scott	96	15	2	0	2	11	5	14	.156	.240	.199
Craig Worthington	81	15	2	0	2	4	9	24	.185	.284	.268

Projections for 1993:

Best Guess	77	17	2	0	2	7	9	24	.225	.270	.308
Optimistic	272	74	14	3	8	38	51	50	.271	.437	.387

Projections for career:

Best Guess	614	143	22	4	9	65	83	156	.233	.323	.325
Optimistic	2909	768	142	27	110	415	537	491	.264	.445	.380

Rey Sanchez — Bats Right
Born Oct. 5, 1967

Chicago Cubs	AB	H	2B	3B	HR	RBI	BB	SO	BA	SA	OBA
Season	255	64	14	3	1	19	10	17	.251	.341	.285
vs. Left-Handers	106	30	8	2	0	8	7	4	.283	.396	.327
vs. Right-Handers	149	34	6	1	1	11	3	13	.228	.302	.255
vs. Ground-Ballers	118	24	7	2	0	9	6	11	.203	.297	.254
vs. Fly-Ballers	137	40	7	1	1	10	4	6	.292	.380	.313

Most Comparable Rookie Seasons:

Ron E. Davis	194	48	10	1	2	19	13	26	.247	.340	.296
Tom Foley	277	70	8	3	5	27	24	36	.253	.357	.313
Tommy Herr	222	55	12	5	0	15	16	21	.248	.347	.299
R.J. Reynolds	240	62	12	2	2	24	14	38	.258	.350	.300
Mickey Tettleton	211	53	12	0	3	15	28	59	.251	.351	.340

Projections for 1993:

Best Guess	228	56	9	1	3	23	10	18	.247	.328	.281
Optimistic	353	98	18	6	8	47	26	16	.276	.430	.327

Projections for career:

Best Guess	1226	303	52	10	11	115	72	95	.247	.334	.290
Optimistic	2561	684	134	27	51	294	192	132	.267	.400	.319

Reggie Sanders — Bats Right
Born Dec. 1, 1967

Cincinnati Reds	AB	H	2B	3B	HR	RBI	BB	SO	BA	SA	OBA
Season	385	104	26	6	12	36	48	98	.270	.462	.356
vs. Left-Handers	175	55	15	4	7	18	19	30	.314	.566	.391
vs. Right-Handers	210	49	11	2	5	18	29	68	.233	.376	.328
vs. Ground-Ballers	144	42	12	2	3	11	16	40	.292	.465	.360
vs. Fly-Ballers	241	62	14	4	9	25	32	58	.257	.461	.354

Most Comparable Rookie Seasons:

Greg Briley	394	105	22	4	13	52	39	82	.266	.442	.334
Gates Brown	426	116	22	6	15	54	31	53	.272	.458	.323
Steve Henderson	350	104	16	6	12	65	43	79	.297	.480	.375
Kevin Mitchell	328	91	22	2	12	43	33	61	.277	.466	.345
Adolfo Phillips	419	109	29	1	16	36	43	135	.260	.449	.330

Projections for 1993:

Best Guess	444	118	21	3	11	59	48	98	.266	.402	.339
Optimistic	552	160	31	7	25	89	76	96	.289	.506	.377

Projections for career:

Best Guess	2965	768	136	21	82	343	352	676	.259	.402	.339
Optimistic	4819	1318	235	52	204	700	688	879	.273	.471	.365

Gary Scott — Bats Right
Born Aug. 22, 1968

Chicago Cubs	AB	H	2B	3B	HR	RBI	BB	SO	BA	SA	OBA
Season	96	15	2	0	1	11	5	14	.156	.240	.198
vs. Left-Handers	30	5	2	0	1	6	1	4	.167	.333	.194
vs. Right-Handers	66	10	0	0	1	5	4	10	.152	.197	.200
vs. Ground-Ballers	50	10	2	0	1	6	0	2	.200	.300	.200
vs. Fly-Ballers	46	5	0	0	1	5	5	12	.109	.174	.196

Most Comparable Rookie Seasons:

Kelvin Chapman	80	12	1	2	0	4	5	15	.150	.213	.201
Tom Prince	74	13	2	0	0	6	4	15	.176	.203	.219
Mike Ryan	107	17	0	1	3	9	5	19	.159	.262	.198
Tim Salmon	79	14	1	0	2	6	11	23	.177	.266	.279
Gary Scott	79	13	3	0	1	5	13	14	.165	.241	.284

Projections for 1993:

Best Guess	54	11	2	0	0	4	4	11	.212	.242	.271
Optimistic	293	79	15	3	7	37	37	32	.269	.407	.351

Projections for career:

Best Guess	768	163	27	4	10	75	78	103	.213	.296	.286
Optimistic	2028	497	99	17	42	246	277	183	.245	.372	.337

Scott Servais — Bats Right
Born Jun. 4, 1967

Houston Astros	AB	H	2B	3B	HR	RBI	BB	SO	BA	SA	OBA
Season	205	49	9	0	0	15	11	25	.239	.283	.294
vs. Left-Handers	145	36	8	0	0	15	8	14	.248	.303	.297
vs. Right-Handers	60	13	1	0	0	0	3	11	.217	.233	.288
vs. Ground-Ballers	80	25	4	0	0	5	3	9	.313	.363	.353
vs. Fly-Ballers	125	24	5	0	0	10	8	16	.192	.232	.257

Most Comparable Rookie Seasons:

Onix Concepcion	205	48	9	1	0	15	5	18	.234	.288	.254
Jim Essian	199	49	7	0	0	21	23	28	.246	.281	.325
Pepe Frias	225	52	10	1	0	22	10	24	.231	.284	.265
Terry Harmon	201	48	8	1	0	16	22	31	.239	.289	.315
Duane Josephson	189	45	5	1	1	9	6	24	.238	.291	.263

Projections for 1993:

Best Guess	127	31	5	0	0	12	6	19	.242	.293	.278
Optimistic	298	80	15	4	5	37	24	27	.270	.394	.326

Projections for career:

Best Guess	1016	243	42	5	7	95	66	134	.239	.309	.286
Optimistic	2193	577	105	21	38	255	191	208	.263	.381	.323

Andy Stankiewicz — Bats Right
Born Aug. 10, 1964

New York Yankees	AB	H	2B	3B	HR	RBI	BB	SO	BA	SA	OBA
Season	400	107	22	2	2	25	38	42	.268	.348	.338
vs. Left-Handers	136	37	5	1	0	10	10	11	.272	.324	.336
vs. Right-Handers	264	70	17	1	2	15	28	31	.265	.360	.339
vs. Ground-Ballers	179	50	11	1	1	11	15	24	.279	.369	.338
vs. Fly-Ballers	221	57	11	1	1	14	23	18	.258	.330	.337

Most Comparable Rookie Seasons:

Don Buford	442	116	14	6	4	30	46	62	.262	.348	.333
Mike Ferraro	381	97	18	1	2	29	17	41	.255	.323	.288
Eddie Milner	407	109	23	5	4	31	41	40	.268	.378	.336
Jim Norris	440	119	23	6	2	37	64	57	.270	.364	.364
Bob Randall	475	127	18	4	1	34	28	38	.267	.328	.309

Projections for 1993:

Best Guess	263	67	10	2	2	22	23	31	.254	.322	.315
Optimistic	501	140	26	7	11	59	75	40	.279	.424	.373

Projections for career:

Best Guess	1188	304	51	8	8	99	116	121	.256	.332	.323
Optimistic	2072	555	97	24	36	210	278	172	.268	.391	.356

Jeff Tackett — Bats Right
Born Dec. 1, 1965

Baltimore Orioles	AB	H	2B	3B	HR	RBI	BB	SO	BA	SA	OBA
Season	179	43	8	1	5	24	17	28	.240	.380	.307
vs. Left-Handers	52	15	1	0	4	7	6	5	.288	.538	.373
vs. Right-Handers	127	28	7	1	1	17	11	23	.220	.315	.280
vs. Ground-Ballers	88	21	4	0	3	12	8	15	.239	.386	.303
vs. Fly-Ballers	91	22	4	1	2	12	9	13	.242	.374	.311

Most Comparable Rookie Seasons:

Randy Elliott	167	40	5	1	7	26	8	24	.240	.407	.275
Randy Kutcher	186	44	9	1	7	16	11	41	.237	.409	.280
John Vanderwal	213	51	8	2	4	20	24	36	.239	.352	.318
Dan Walters	179	45	11	1	4	22	10	28	.251	.391	.292
Larry Whisenton	143	34	7	2	4	17	23	33	.238	.399	.345

Projections for 1993:

Best Guess	95	23	4	0	1	9	9	17	.240	.305	.304
Optimistic	338	97	17	4	9	50	50	39	.287	.444	.380

Projections for career:

Best Guess	840	201	35	4	17	97	85	137	.240	.351	.310
Optimistic	2193	585	111	22	70	300	317	261	.267	.433	.361

Eddie Taubensee — Bats Left
Born Oct. 31, 1968

Houston Astros	AB	H	2B	3B	HR	RBI	BB	SO	BA	SA	OBA
Season	297	66	15	0	5	28	31	78	.222	.323	.299
vs. Left-Handers	47	11	3	0	2	5	6	12	.234	.426	.333
vs. Right-Handers	250	55	12	0	3	23	25	66	.220	.304	.292
vs. Ground-Ballers	139	30	8	0	1	14	14	43	.216	.295	.286
vs. Fly-Ballers	158	36	7	0	4	14	17	35	.228	.348	.311

Most Comparable Rookie Seasons:

Alan Ashby	254	57	10	1	5	32	30	42	.224	.331	.308
Buddy Bradford	281	61	11	0	5	24	23	67	.217	.310	.277
Greg Gagne	293	66	15	3	2	23	20	57	.225	.317	.276
Todd Hundley	358	75	17	0	7	32	19	76	.209	.316	.251
Hensley Meulens	288	64	8	1	6	29	18	97	.222	.319	.269

Projections for 1993:

Best Guess	231	55	8	1	3	23	24	65	.240	.326	.313
Optimistic	385	103	20	4	10	50	54	76	.266	.415	.359

Projections for career:

Best Guess	1694	406	69	9	27	174	173	437	.239	.338	.311
Optimistic	3647	936	164	35	102	446	508	755	.257	.405	.349

Jim Thome — Bats Left
Born Aug. 27, 1970

Cleveland Indians	AB	H	2B	3B	HR	RBI	BB	SO	BA	SA	OBA
Season	117	24	3	1	2	12	10	34	.205	.299	.275
vs. Left-Handers	14	3	0	0	0	0	0	8	.214	.214	.214
vs. Right-Handers	103	21	3	1	2	12	10	26	.204	.311	.282
vs. Ground-Ballers	63	9	2	1	1	8	4	21	.143	.254	.188
vs. Fly-Ballers	54	15	1	0	1	4	6	13	.278	.352	.371

Most Comparable Rookie Seasons:

Brian Giles	138	29	5	0	3	10	12	29	.210	.312	.275
Jeff Kunkel	142	29	2	3	3	7	2	35	.204	.324	.216
Johnnie LeMaster	100	21	3	2	0	9	2	21	.210	.280	.227
Jorge Orta	124	25	3	1	3	11	6	37	.202	.315	.240
Mel D. Queen	95	19	2	0	2	12	4	19	.200	.284	.233

Projections for 1993:

Best Guess	134	30	3	0	0	10	9	31	.226	.265	.277
Optimistic	339	90	16	4	10	43	36	49	.266	.423	.338

Projections for career:

Best Guess	1812	431	70	12	27	181	153	356	.238	.334	.298
Optimistic	5140	1335	239	48	151	655	608	728	.260	.413	.339

Ryan Thompson — Bats Right
Born Nov. 4, 1967

New York Mets	AB	H	2B	3B	HR	RBI	BB	SO	BA	SA	OBA
Season	108	24	7	1	3	10	8	24	.222	.389	.274
vs. Left-Handers	37	8	4	0	0	0	6	4	.216	.324	.326
vs. Right-Handers	71	16	3	1	3	10	2	20	.225	.423	.243
vs. Ground-Ballers	55	16	4	0	2	6	4	10	.291	.473	.339
vs. Fly-Ballers	53	8	3	1	1	4	4	14	.151	.302	.207

Most Comparable Rookie Seasons:

Bobby Baldwin	95	21	3	0	4	8	5	14	.221	.379	.261
Jim R. Campbell	86	19	4	0	3	6	6	23	.221	.372	.273
Dave Clark	87	18	5	0	3	12	2	24	.207	.368	.226
Rick Renick	97	21	5	2	3	13	9	42	.216	.402	.284
Paul Sorrento	121	25	4	1	5	13	12	31	.207	.380	.279

Projections for 1993:

Best Guess	104	25	3	0	1	10	6	25	.236	.304	.279
Optimistic	322	88	16	3	12	49	33	44	.273	.457	.342

Projections for career:

Best Guess	695	165	28	4	13	76	50	137	.238	.349	.290
Optimistic	2254	600	106	25	74	311	220	292	.266	.434	.332

John Valentin — Bats Right
Born Feb. 18, 1967

Boston Red Sox	AB	H	2B	3B	HR	RBI	BB	SO	BA	SA	OBA
Season	185	51	13	0	5	25	20	17	.276	.427	.351
vs. Left-Handers	33	7	3	0	1	3	8	2	.212	.394	.381
vs. Right-Handers	152	44	10	0	4	22	12	15	.289	.434	.343
vs. Ground-Ballers	82	18	3	0	0	5	9	14	.220	.256	.304
vs. Fly-Ballers	103	33	10	0	5	20	11	3	.320	.563	.388

Most Comparable Rookie Seasons:

Pat Borders	154	42	6	3	5	21	3	24	.273	.448	.288
Jack Hiatt	153	42	6	0	6	26	27	37	.275	.431	.385
Darrin Jackson	188	50	11	3	6	20	5	28	.266	.452	.286
Mickey Klutts	197	53	14	0	4	21	13	41	.269	.401	.315
Scott Leius	199	57	7	2	5	20	30	35	.286	.417	.381

Projections for 1993:

Best Guess	224	54	10	1	4	26	21	22	.242	.342	.308
Optimistic	355	101	19	4	11	54	54	23	.285	.452	.380

Projections for career:

Best Guess	1026	254	47	4	19	119	109	94	.247	.358	.321
Optimistic	2171	585	109	18	70	294	322	135	.270	.433	.365

John Vanderwal — Bats Left
Born Apr. 29, 1966

Montreal Expos	AB	H	2B	3B	HR	RBI	BB	SO	BA	SA	OBA
Season	213	51	8	2	4	20	24	36	.239	.352	.316
vs. Left-Handers	29	7	0	0	0	1	2	6	.241	.241	.290
vs. Right-Handers	184	44	8	2	4	19	22	30	.239	.370	.320
vs. Ground-Ballers	94	20	3	2	1	7	8	13	.213	.319	.275
vs. Fly-Ballers	119	31	5	0	3	13	16	23	.261	.378	.348

Most Comparable Rookie Seasons:

Duke Carmel	193	45	6	3	4	20	25	48	.233	.358	.322
Ossie Chavarria	191	46	10	0	2	10	18	43	.241	.325	.307
Archi Cianfrocco	232	56	5	2	6	30	11	66	.241	.358	.277
Curt Ford	214	53	15	2	2	29	23	29	.248	.364	.322
Jeff Tackett	179	43	8	1	5	24	17	28	.240	.380	.307

Projections for 1993:

Best Guess	106	26	4	0	1	11	9	23	.244	.306	.297
Optimistic	330	94	17	5	8	45	42	43	.285	.443	.367

Projections for career:

Best Guess	1048	257	44	8	18	114	95	209	.245	.353	.309
Optimistic	2575	691	127	28	67	327	306	355	.268	.418	.347

Dan Walters — Bats Right
Born Aug. 15, 1966

San Diego Padres	AB	H	2B	3B	HR	RBI	BB	SO	BA	SA	OBA
Season	179	45	11	1	4	22	10	28	.251	.391	.295
vs. Left-Handers	61	16	4	0	1	8	1	9	.262	.377	.270
vs. Right-Handers	118	29	7	1	3	14	9	19	.246	.398	.308
vs. Ground-Ballers	66	20	3	1	2	9	4	6	.303	.470	.356
vs. Fly-Ballers	113	25	8	0	2	13	6	22	.221	.345	.258

Most Comparable Rookie Seasons:

Mike Aldrete	216	54	18	3	2	25	33	34	.250	.389	.351
Ed J. Hearn	136	36	5	0	4	10	12	19	.265	.390	.325
Merv Rettenmund	190	47	10	3	4	25	28	28	.247	.395	.345
Jeff Tackett	179	43	8	1	5	24	17	28	.240	.380	.307
Larry Whisenton	143	34	7	2	4	17	23	33	.238	.399	.345

Projections for 1993:

Best Guess	179	43	7	1	1	19	8	28	.242	.314	.275
Optimistic	357	100	19	5	9	52	31	43	.280	.441	.338

Projections for career:

Best Guess	878	214	40	4	14	99	53	139	.243	.345	.288
Optimistic	2358	629	124	24	62	301	196	282	.267	.419	.324

Lenny Webster
Born Feb. 10, 1965   Bats Right

Minnesota Twins	AB	H	2B	3B	HR	RBI	BB	SO	BA	SA	OBA
Season	118	33	10	1	1	13	9	11	.280	.407	.331
vs. Left-Handers	28	9	4	0	1	7	4	4	.321	.571	.406
vs. Right-Handers	90	24	6	1	0	6	5	7	.267	.356	.305
vs. Ground-Ballers	58	16	6	0	0	7	4	5	.276	.379	.323
vs. Fly-Ballers	60	17	4	1	1	6	5	6	.283	.433	.338

Most Comparable Rookie Seasons:

	AB	H	2B	3B	HR	RBI	BB	SO	BA	SA	OBA
Ramon Aviles	101	28	6	0	2	9	10	9	.277	.396	.344
Angel Bravo	90	26	4	2	1	3	3	5	.289	.411	.313
Jose Herrera	126	36	5	0	2	12	3	14	.286	.373	.303
Bob Stinson	111	29	6	1	3	12	17	15	.261	.414	.361
Ned Yost	98	27	6	3	1	8	7	20	.276	.429	.325

Projections for 1993:

	AB	H	2B	3B	HR	RBI	BB	SO	BA	SA	OBA
Best Guess	65	15	2	0	0	6	5	12	.229	.254	.280
Optimistic	208	57	10	2	6	31	32	23	.276	.425	.374

Projections for career:

	AB	H	2B	3B	HR	RBI	BB	SO	BA	SA	OBA
Best Guess	448	117	23	2	7	52	53	70	.262	.367	.341
Optimistic	1124	302	58	11	29	152	171	112	.269	.418	.366

Eric Wedge
Born Jan. 27, 1968   Bats Right

Boston Red Sox	AB	H	2B	3B	HR	RBI	BB	SO	BA	SA	OBA
Season	68	17	2	0	5	11	13	18	.250	.500	.370
vs. Left-Handers	36	11	1	0	4	8	5	8	.306	.667	.390
vs. Right-Handers	32	6	1	0	1	3	8	10	.188	.313	.350
vs. Ground-Ballers	23	6	0	0	2	5	4	7	.261	.522	.370
vs. Fly-Ballers	45	11	2	0	3	6	9	11	.244	.489	.370

Most Comparable Rookie Seasons:

	AB	H	2B	3B	HR	RBI	BB	SO	BA	SA	OBA
Steve Decker	54	16	2	0	3	8	1	10	.296	.500	.310
Duffy Dyer	74	19	3	1	3	12	4	22	.257	.446	.296
Pete M. O'Brien	67	16	4	1	4	13	6	8	.239	.507	.303
Gary Roenicke	58	15	3	0	3	15	8	3	.259	.466	.350
Ty Waller	71	19	2	1	3	13	4	18	.268	.451	.308

Projections for 1993:

	AB	H	2B	3B	HR	RBI	BB	SO	BA	SA	OBA
Best Guess	159	35	6	1	4	16	31	45	.222	.337	.350
Optimistic	376	98	19	4	13	52	104	71	.261	.436	.422

Projections for career:

	AB	H	2B	3B	HR	RBI	BB	SO	BA	SA	OBA
Best Guess	546	131	20	2	17	70	111	134	.239	.380	.369
Optimistic	2560	635	122	19	101	376	630	438	.248	.429	.398

John Wehner
Born Jun. 29, 1967   Bats Right

Pittsburgh Pirates	AB	H	2B	3B	HR	RBI	BB	SO	BA	SA	OBA
Season	123	22	6	0	0	4	12	22	.179	.228	.252
vs. Left-Handers	56	10	3	0	0	3	5	9	.179	.232	.246
vs. Right-Handers	67	12	3	0	0	1	7	13	.179	.224	.257
vs. Ground-Ballers	58	10	4	0	0	2	4	6	.172	.241	.226
vs. Fly-Ballers	65	12	2	0	0	2	8	16	.185	.215	.274

Most Comparable Rookie Seasons:

	AB	H	2B	3B	HR	RBI	BB	SO	BA	SA	OBA
Craig Grebeck	119	20	3	1	1	9	8	24	.168	.235	.222
Lance Johnson	124	23	4	1	0	6	6	11	.185	.234	.224
Tom Kelly	127	23	5	0	1	11	15	22	.181	.244	.269
John Patterson	103	19	1	1	0	4	5	24	.184	.214	.223
Dave Van Gorder	137	25	3	1	0	7	14	19	.182	.219	.259

Projections for 1993:

	AB	H	2B	3B	HR	RBI	BB	SO	BA	SA	OBA
Best Guess	59	12	1	0	0	3	3	13	.201	.218	.246
Optimistic	180	49	9	2	3	21	18	22	.273	.393	.339

Projections for career:

	AB	H	2B	3B	HR	RBI	BB	SO	BA	SA	OBA
Best Guess	628	150	27	2	4	46	53	97	.238	.305	.299
Optimistic	2390	612	115	21	46	268	279	241	.256	.380	.335

Eric Young
Born Nov. 26, 1966   Bats Right

Los Angeles Dodgers	AB	H	2B	3B	HR	RBI	BB	SO	BA	SA	OBA
Season	132	34	1	0	1	11	8	9	.258	.288	.300
vs. Left-Handers	66	18	0	0	1	6	3	4	.273	.318	.304
vs. Right-Handers	66	16	1	0	0	5	5	5	.242	.258	.296
vs. Ground-Ballers	53	15	0	0	0	5	2	1	.283	.283	.309
vs. Fly-Ballers	79	19	1	0	1	6	6	8	.241	.291	.294

Most Comparable Rookie Seasons:

	AB	H	2B	3B	HR	RBI	BB	SO	BA	SA	OBA
Horace Clarke	108	28	1	0	1	9	6	6	.259	.296	.299
John D. Morris	100	24	0	1	1	14	7	15	.240	.290	.291
Kelly Paris	120	30	6	0	0	7	15	22	.250	.300	.335
Geno Petralli	100	27	2	0	0	11	8	12	.270	.290	.325
Craig Wilson	121	30	2	0	0	7	8	14	.248	.264	.296

Projections for 1993:

	AB	H	2B	3B	HR	RBI	BB	SO	BA	SA	OBA
Best Guess	87	18	2	0	0	6	5	6	.212	.240	.254
Optimistic	261	69	12	3	4	29	24	12	.266	.382	.329

Projections for career:

	AB	H	2B	3B	HR	RBI	BB	SO	BA	SA	OBA
Best Guess	689	166	21	2	5	57	47	45	.242	.300	.291
Optimistic	2083	559	89	21	36	233	197	94	.268	.383	.333

Bob Zupcic
Born Aug. 18, 1966   Bats Right

Boston Red Sox	AB	H	2B	3B	HR	RBI	BB	SO	BA	SA	OBA
Season	392	108	19	1	3	43	25	60	.276	.352	.322
vs. Left-Handers	133	39	8	1	0	15	13	14	.293	.368	.356
vs. Right-Handers	259	69	11	0	3	28	12	46	.266	.344	.304
vs. Ground-Ballers	197	60	10	1	1	21	11	27	.305	.381	.352
vs. Fly-Ballers	195	48	9	0	2	22	14	33	.246	.323	.292

Most Comparable Rookie Seasons:

	AB	H	2B	3B	HR	RBI	BB	SO	BA	SA	OBA
Joey Amalfitano	328	91	15	3	1	27	26	31	.277	.351	.332
Casey Candaele	449	122	23	4	1	23	38	28	.272	.347	.330
Tim Hulett	395	106	19	4	5	37	30	81	.268	.375	.321
George Vukovich	335	91	18	2	6	42	32	47	.272	.391	.336
Reggie Williams	303	84	14	2	4	32	23	57	.277	.376	.329

Projections for 1993:

	AB	H	2B	3B	HR	RBI	BB	SO	BA	SA	OBA
Best Guess	356	89	14	2	3	32	21	58	.250	.330	.293
Optimistic	506	140	25	6	11	65	46	58	.277	.411	.339

Projections for career:

	AB	H	2B	3B	HR	RBI	BB	SO	BA	SA	OBA
Best Guess	1470	375	59	7	17	154	91	233	.255	.341	.300
Optimistic	2595	696	120	22	44	307	214	319	.268	.382	.325

Pedro Astacio — Throws Right

Born Nov. 28, 1969

Los Angeles Dodgers	W-L	ERA	AB	H	HR	BB	SO	BA	SA	OBA
Season	5-5	1.98	314	80	1	20	43	.255	.303	.302
vs. Left-Handers			180	44	1	18	17	.244	.300	.315
vs. Right-Handers			134	36	0	2	26	.269	.306	.283
vs. Ground-Ballers			150	38	1	13	21	.253	.320	.315
vs. Fly-Ballers			164	42	0	7	22	.256	.287	.289
Home Games	3-3	1.68	184	47	1	10	22	.255	.304	.298
Road Games	2-2	2.41	130	33	0	10	21	.254	.300	.307
Grass Fields	4-4	2.25	233	62	1	15	28	.266	.309	.313
Artificial Turf	1-1	1.23	81	18	0	5	15	.222	.284	.267
First 9 Batters			95	21	0	4	15	.221	.242	.253
Second 9 Batters			90	19	0	7	17	.211	.256	.276
All Batters Thereafter			129	40	1	9	11	.310	.380	.355

Miscellaneous statistics: Ground outs-to-air outs ratio: 1.45 last season, 1.45 for career.... Grounded into 12 double plays in 71 opportunities (one per 5.9).... Allowed 8 doubles, 2 triples in 82 innings.... Allowed 5 first-inning runs in 11 starts (3.27 ERA).... Batting support: 3.36 runs per start.... Opposing base stealers: 5-for-8 (63%); 0 pickoffs, 0 balks.

Cliff Brantley — Throws Right

Born Apr. 12, 1968

Philadelphia Phillies	W-L	ERA	AB	H	HR	BB	SO	BA	SA	OBA
Season	2-6	4.60	283	71	6	58	32	.251	.353	.382
vs. Left-Handers			153	46	3	32	13	.301	.405	.420
vs. Right-Handers			130	25	3	26	19	.192	.292	.338
vs. Ground-Ballers			127	28	1	25	14	.220	.276	.357
vs. Fly-Ballers			156	43	5	33	18	.276	.417	.402
Home Games	1-2	3.66	122	30	0	21	18	.246	.270	.359
Road Games	1-4	5.28	161	41	6	37	14	.255	.416	.399
Grass Fields	1-2	7.40	73	19	3	16	8	.260	.452	.398
Artificial Turf	1-4	3.56	210	52	3	42	24	.248	.319	.376
First 9 Batters			157	32	1	37	21	.204	.242	.359
Second 9 Batters			78	25	3	13	5	.321	.513	.419
All Batters Thereafter			48	14	2	8	6	.292	.458	.404

Miscellaneous statistics: Ground outs-to-air outs ratio: 1.56 last season, 1.56 for career.... Grounded into 9 double plays in 76 opportunities (one per 8.4).... Allowed 9 doubles, 1 triple in 76⅓ innings.... Stranded 8 inherited runners, allowed 2 to score (80%).... Opposing base stealers: 10-for-15 (67%); 0 pickoffs, 1 balk.

Bobby Ayala — Throws Right

Born Jul. 8, 1969

Cincinnati Reds	W-L	ERA	AB	H	HR	BB	SO	BA	SA	OBA
Season	2-1	4.34	111	33	1	13	23	.297	.414	.376
vs. Left-Handers			63	18	0	8	14	.286	.381	.366
vs. Right-Handers			48	15	1	5	9	.313	.458	.389
vs. Ground-Ballers			56	16	0	7	12	.286	.375	.365
vs. Fly-Ballers			55	17	1	6	11	.309	.455	.387
Home Games	2-0	3.86	70	20	0	6	17	.286	.386	.351
Road Games	0-1	5.23	41	13	1	7	6	.317	.463	.417
Grass Fields	0-1	5.23	41	13	1	7	6	.317	.463	.417
Artificial Turf	2-0	3.86	70	20	0	6	17	.286	.386	.351
First 9 Batters			40	12	0	5	10	.300	.350	.378
Second 9 Batters			40	13	1	3	7	.325	.475	.386
All Batters Thereafter			31	8	0	5	6	.258	.419	.361

Miscellaneous statistics: Ground outs-to-air outs ratio: 2.59 last season, 2.59 for career.... Grounded into 4 double plays in 20 opportunities (one per 5.0).... Allowed 10 doubles, 0 triples in 29 innings.... Opposing base stealers: 2-for-5 (40%); 1 pickoff, 0 balks.

Jim Bullinger — Throws Right

Born Aug. 21, 1965

Chicago Cubs	W-L	ERA	AB	H	HR	BB	SO	BA	SA	OBA
Season	2-8	4.66	309	72	9	54	36	.233	.382	.350
vs. Left-Handers			168	36	6	33	16	.214	.405	.346
vs. Right-Handers			141	36	3	21	20	.255	.355	.355
vs. Ground-Ballers			129	25	4	18	15	.194	.326	.295
vs. Fly-Ballers			180	47	5	36	21	.261	.422	.387
Home Games	2-6	3.48	192	43	4	31	23	.224	.365	.330
Road Games	0-2	6.75	117	29	5	23	13	.248	.410	.382
Grass Fields	2-6	3.84	226	51	6	33	26	.226	.376	.323
Artificial Turf	0-2	7.06	83	21	3	21	10	.253	.398	.417
First 9 Batters			185	45	4	29	22	.243	.378	.347
Second 9 Batters			79	13	1	12	11	.165	.241	.287
All Batters Thereafter			45	14	4	13	3	.311	.644	.459

Miscellaneous statistics: Ground outs-to-air outs ratio: 1.32 last season, 1.32 for career.... Grounded into 6 double plays in 79 opportunities (one per 13).... Allowed 9 doubles, 5 triples in 85 innings.... Stranded 12 inherited runners, allowed 5 to score (71%).... Opposing base stealers: 8-for-10 (80%); 0 pickoffs, 0 balks.

Willie Banks — Throws Right

Born Feb. 27, 1969

Minnesota Twins	W-L	ERA	AB	H	HR	BB	SO	BA	SA	OBA
Season	4-4	5.70	278	80	6	37	37	.288	.428	.370
vs. Left-Handers			140	41	3	16	22	.293	.421	.363
vs. Right-Handers			138	39	3	21	15	.283	.435	.377
vs. Ground-Ballers			135	43	1	20	17	.319	.437	.408
vs. Fly-Ballers			143	37	5	17	20	.259	.420	.333
Home Games	1-2	3.48	118	29	0	13	22	.246	.314	.321
Road Games	3-2	7.43	160	51	6	24	15	.319	.512	.403
Grass Fields	3-2	6.87	146	44	6	22	15	.301	.493	.391
Artificial Turf	1-2	4.46	132	36	0	15	22	.273	.356	.345
First 9 Batters			118	32	1	15	19	.271	.373	.350
Second 9 Batters			94	28	3	15	10	.298	.457	.393
All Batters Thereafter			66	20	2	7	8	.303	.485	.370

Miscellaneous statistics: Ground outs-to-air outs ratio: 1.00 last season, 1.00 for career.... Grounded into 2 double plays in 57 opportunities (one per 29).... Allowed 15 doubles, 3 triples in 71 innings.... Allowed 6 first-inning runs in 12 starts (4.50 ERA).... Batting support: 3.83 runs per start.... Opposing base stealers: 8-for-12 (67%); 0 pickoffs, 1 balk.

Kevin Campbell — Throws Right

Born Dec. 6, 1964

Oakland A's	W-L	ERA	AB	H	HR	BB	SO	BA	SA	OBA
Season	2-3	5.12	247	66	4	45	38	.267	.372	.378
vs. Left-Handers			108	28	2	25	20	.259	.361	.396
vs. Right-Handers			139	38	2	20	18	.273	.381	.363
vs. Ground-Ballers			116	32	1	18	18	.276	.371	.370
vs. Fly-Ballers			131	34	3	27	20	.260	.374	.384
Home Games	1-1	3.11	139	31	2	20	24	.223	.309	.319
Road Games	1-2	7.90	108	35	2	25	14	.324	.454	.448
Grass Fields	2-3	4.87	245	65	4	44	38	.265	.371	.375
Artificial Turf	0-0	54.00	2	1	0	1	0	.500	.500	.667
First 9 Batters			179	49	4	28	30	.274	.413	.368
Second 9 Batters			54	15	0	13	5	.278	.296	.418
All Batters Thereafter			14	2	0	4	3	.143	.143	.333

Miscellaneous statistics: Ground outs-to-air outs ratio: 0.66 last season, 0.66 for career.... Grounded into 5 double plays in 76 opportunities (one per 15).... Allowed 12 doubles, 1 triple in 65 innings.... Stranded 18 inherited runners, allowed 3 to score (86%).... Opposing base stealers: 2-for-7 (29%); 1 pickoff, 0 balks.

Larry Carter
Throws Right
Born May 22, 1965

San Francisco Giants	W-L	ERA	AB	H	HR	BB	SO	BA	SA	OBA
Season	1-5	4.64	126	34	6	18	21	.270	.532	.359
vs. Left-Handers			79	21	5	8	11	.266	.582	.330
vs. Right-Handers			47	13	1	10	10	.277	.447	.404
vs. Ground-Ballers			57	11	2	8	9	.193	.368	.288
vs. Fly-Ballers			69	23	4	10	12	.333	.667	.418
Home Games	0-1	5.06	23	7	1	2	2	.304	.565	.360
Road Games	1-4	4.55	103	27	5	16	19	.262	.524	.358
Grass Fields	1-2	2.45	69	16	1	8	6	.232	.362	.308
Artificial Turf	0-3	7.36	57	18	5	10	15	.316	.737	.418
First 9 Batters			48	10	0	6	10	.208	.354	.296
Second 9 Batters			45	15	3	7	4	.333	.600	.423
All Batters Thereafter			33	9	3	5	7	.273	.697	.359

Miscellaneous statistics: Ground outs-to-air outs ratio: 0.57 last season, 0.57 for career.... Grounded into 3 double plays in 24 opportunities (one per 8.0).... Allowed 9 doubles, 3 triples in 33 innings.... Opposing base stealers: 1-for-2 (50%); 0 pickoffs, 0 balks.

David Haas
Throws Right
Born Oct. 19, 1965

Detroit Tigers	W-L	ERA	AB	H	HR	BB	SO	BA	SA	OBA
Season	5-3	3.94	246	68	8	16	29	.276	.419	.323
vs. Left-Handers			116	33	3	9	12	.284	.397	.336
vs. Right-Handers			130	35	5	7	17	.269	.438	.312
vs. Ground-Ballers			116	28	3	9	15	.241	.362	.296
vs. Fly-Ballers			130	40	5	7	14	.308	.469	.348
Home Games	2-1	4.65	126	35	4	10	13	.278	.413	.336
Road Games	3-2	3.23	120	33	4	6	16	.275	.425	.310
Grass Fields	4-1	3.21	189	48	5	11	20	.254	.376	.299
Artificial Turf	1-2	6.43	57	20	3	5	9	.351	.561	.403
First 9 Batters			96	23	4	5	10	.240	.406	.284
Second 9 Batters			87	26	2	4	11	.299	.402	.330
All Batters Thereafter			63	19	2	7	8	.302	.460	.371

Miscellaneous statistics: Ground outs-to-air outs ratio: 0.88 last season, 0.88 for career.... Grounded into 4 double plays in 51 opportunities (one per 13).... Allowed 9 doubles, 1 triple in 61⅓ innings.... Allowed 7 first-inning runs in 11 starts (5.73 ERA).... Batting support: 4.82 runs per start.... Opposing base stealers: 1-for-2 (50%); 0 pickoffs, 0 balks.

John Doherty
Throws Right
Born Jun. 11, 1967

Detroit Tigers	W-L	ERA	AB	H	HR	BB	SO	BA	SA	OBA
Season	7-4	3.88	457	131	4	25	37	.287	.346	.328
vs. Left-Handers			200	48	1	8	17	.240	.285	.267
vs. Right-Handers			257	83	3	17	20	.323	.393	.374
vs. Ground-Ballers			226	56	1	12	22	.248	.292	.287
vs. Fly-Ballers			231	75	3	13	15	.325	.398	.367
Home Games	5-1	3.83	223	65	4	15	21	.291	.368	.342
Road Games	2-3	3.92	234	66	0	10	16	.282	.325	.315
Grass Fields	6-4	3.98	387	113	4	21	32	.292	.349	.332
Artificial Turf	1-0	3.38	70	18	0	4	5	.257	.329	.307
First 9 Batters			272	76	2	19	22	.279	.342	.333
Second 9 Batters			112	30	0	6	10	.268	.304	.306
All Batters Thereafter			73	25	2	0	5	.342	.425	.342

Miscellaneous statistics: Ground outs-to-air outs ratio: 2.70 last season, 2.70 for career.... Grounded into 24 double plays in 97 opportunities (one per 4.0).... Allowed 13 doubles, 1 triple in 116 innings.... Allowed 6 first-inning runs in 11 starts (4.35 ERA).... Batting support: 5.64 runs per start.... Record of 5-2, 3.67 ERA as a starter; 2-2, 4.12 ERA in 36 relief appearances.... Stranded 22 inherited runners, allowed 11 to score (67%).... Opposing base stealers: 4-for-8 (50%); 0 pickoffs, 0 balks.

Eric Hillman
Throws Left
Born Apr. 27, 1966

New York Mets	W-L	ERA	AB	H	HR	BB	SO	BA	SA	OBA
Season	2-2	5.33	211	67	9	10	16	.318	.502	.353
vs. Left-Handers			37	11	0	2	6	.297	.351	.350
vs. Right-Handers			174	56	9	8	10	.322	.534	.353
vs. Ground-Ballers			101	32	0	1	9	.317	.386	.330
vs. Fly-Ballers			110	35	9	9	7	.318	.609	.372
Home Games	1-1	3.99	120	36	6	1	11	.300	.492	.311
Road Games	1-1	7.04	91	31	3	9	5	.341	.516	.402
Grass Fields	2-1	4.20	161	48	7	4	14	.298	.478	.323
Artificial Turf	0-1	9.26	50	19	2	6	2	.380	.580	.439
First 9 Batters			86	30	4	7	6	.349	.547	.394
Second 9 Batters			65	19	3	2	5	.292	.462	.324
All Batters Thereafter			60	18	2	1	5	.300	.483	.323

Miscellaneous statistics: Ground outs-to-air outs ratio: 2.07 last season, 2.07 for career.... Grounded into 6 double plays in 38 opportunities (one per 6.3).... Allowed 10 doubles, 1 triple in 52⅓ innings.... Opposing base stealers: 4-for-9 (44%); 2 pickoffs, 0 balks.

Cal Eldred
Throws Right
Born Nov. 24, 1967

Milwaukee Brewers	W-L	ERA	AB	H	HR	BB	SO	BA	SA	OBA
Season	11-2	1.79	367	76	4	23	62	.207	.283	.258
vs. Left-Handers			154	29	2	11	21	.188	.240	.251
vs. Right-Handers			213	47	2	12	41	.221	.315	.262
vs. Ground-Ballers			169	33	2	14	28	.195	.278	.261
vs. Fly-Ballers			198	43	2	9	34	.217	.288	.255
Home Games	7-0	0.76	212	40	2	16	30	.189	.241	.246
Road Games	4-2	3.27	155	36	2	7	32	.232	.342	.274
Grass Fields	9-2	1.67	314	63	2	22	52	.201	.264	.257
Artificial Turf	2-0	2.57	53	13	2	1	10	.245	.396	.259
First 9 Batters			120	21	1	4	23	.175	.250	.208
Second 9 Batters			116	19	2	10	14	.164	.241	.230
All Batters Thereafter			131	36	1	9	25	.275	.351	.326

Miscellaneous statistics: Ground outs-to-air outs ratio: 0.67 last season, 0.67 for career.... Grounded into 5 double plays in 71 opportunities (one per 14).... Allowed 10 doubles, 3 triples in 100⅓ innings.... Allowed 2 first-inning runs in 14 starts (1.29 ERA).... Batting support: 5.64 runs per start.... Opposing base stealers: 8-for-12 (67%); 1 pickoff, 0 balks.

Kurt Knudsen
Throws Right
Born Feb. 20, 1967

Detroit Tigers	W-L	ERA	AB	H	HR	BB	SO	BA	SA	OBA
Season	2-3	4.58	265	70	9	41	51	.264	.423	.362
vs. Left-Handers			109	29	4	16	7	.266	.422	.357
vs. Right-Handers			156	41	5	25	44	.263	.423	.366
vs. Ground-Ballers			135	41	5	20	21	.304	.474	.397
vs. Fly-Ballers			130	29	4	21	30	.223	.369	.327
Home Games	2-1	3.93	136	36	4	17	29	.265	.404	.351
Road Games	0-2	5.29	129	34	5	24	22	.264	.442	.374
Grass Fields	2-2	5.17	200	51	7	33	43	.255	.420	.360
Artificial Turf	0-1	2.70	65	19	2	8	8	.292	.431	.370
First 9 Batters			227	58	7	36	50	.256	.410	.357
Second 9 Batters			38	12	2	5	1	.316	.500	.395
All Batters Thereafter			0	0	0	0	0	—	—	—

Miscellaneous statistics: Ground outs-to-air outs ratio: 0.39 last season, 0.39 for career.... Grounded into 4 double plays in 71 opportunities (one per 18).... Allowed 13 doubles, 1 triple in 70⅔ innings.... Stranded 26 inherited runners, allowed 13 to score (67%).... Opposing base stealers: 6-for-11 (55%); 1 pickoff, 0 balks.

Pat Mahomes   Throws Right
Born Aug. 9, 1970

Minnesota Twins	W-L	ERA	AB	H	HR	BB	SO	BA	SA	OBA
Season	3-4	5.04	262	73	5	37	44	.279	.439	.364
vs. Left-Handers			135	38	3	17	17	.281	.437	.355
vs. Right-Handers			127	35	2	20	27	.276	.441	.374
vs. Ground-Ballers			137	35	1	20	20	.255	.328	.346
vs. Fly-Ballers			125	38	4	17	24	.304	.560	.385
Home Games	1-2	7.02	135	41	3	18	26	.304	.504	.381
Road Games	2-2	3.22	127	32	2	19	18	.252	.370	.347
Grass Fields	0-2	4.00	64	18	1	11	8	.281	.422	.387
Artificial Turf	3-2	5.40	198	55	4	26	36	.278	.444	.357
First 9 Batters			106	25	1	15	23	.236	.340	.331
Second 9 Batters			103	29	1	10	18	.282	.417	.336
All Batters Thereafter			53	19	3	12	3	.358	.679	.477

Miscellaneous statistics: Ground outs-to-air outs ratio: 0.66 last season, 0.66 for career.... Grounded into 6 double plays in 62 opportunities (one per 10).... Allowed 19 doubles, 4 triples in 69⅔ innings.... Allowed 9 first-inning runs in 13 starts (6.23 ERA).... Batting support: 5.31 runs per start.... Opposing base stealers: 9-for-17 (53%); 2 pickoffs, 1 balk.

Roger Pavlik   Throws Right
Born Oct. 4, 1967

Texas Rangers	W-L	ERA	AB	H	HR	BB	SO	BA	SA	OBA
Season	4-4	4.21	236	66	3	34	45	.280	.381	.375
vs. Left-Handers			133	36	1	18	26	.271	.353	.353
vs. Right-Handers			103	30	2	16	19	.291	.417	.402
vs. Ground-Ballers			96	30	1	14	16	.313	.427	.393
vs. Fly-Ballers			140	36	2	20	29	.257	.350	.362
Home Games	2-2	6.95	94	31	2	13	18	.330	.468	.413
Road Games	2-2	2.70	142	35	1	21	27	.246	.324	.349
Grass Fields	4-3	3.81	213	56	3	31	40	.263	.366	.359
Artificial Turf	0-1	8.44	23	10	0	3	5	.435	.522	.519
First 9 Batters			87	22	1	15	18	.253	.310	.375
Second 9 Batters			77	21	1	11	18	.273	.442	.367
All Batters Thereafter			72	23	1	8	9	.319	.403	.383

Miscellaneous statistics: Ground outs-to-air outs ratio: 0.78 last season, 0.78 for career.... Grounded into 5 double plays in 63 opportunities (one per 13).... Allowed 7 doubles, 4 triples in 62 innings.... Allowed 8 first-inning runs in 12 starts (6.97 ERA).... Batting support: 4.67 runs per start.... Opposing base stealers: 3-for-11 (27%); 2 pickoffs, 0 balks.

Sam Militello   Throws Right
Born Nov. 26, 1969

New York Yankees	W-L	ERA	AB	H	HR	BB	SO	BA	SA	OBA
Season	3-3	3.45	221	43	6	32	42	.195	.335	.302
vs. Left-Handers			107	28	5	15	12	.262	.467	.352
vs. Right-Handers			114	15	1	17	30	.132	.211	.256
vs. Ground-Ballers			100	22	1	12	16	.220	.330	.316
vs. Fly-Ballers			121	21	5	20	26	.174	.339	.291
Home Games	2-1	2.50	139	21	3	22	31	.151	.273	.272
Road Games	1-2	5.31	82	22	3	10	11	.268	.439	.355
Grass Fields	3-2	3.09	201	36	6	26	38	.179	.318	.276
Artificial Turf	0-1	7.71	20	7	0	6	4	.350	.500	.519
First 9 Batters			70	17	2	11	14	.243	.443	.346
Second 9 Batters			71	9	0	10	16	.127	.155	.235
All Batters Thereafter			80	17	4	11	12	.213	.400	.323

Miscellaneous statistics: Ground outs-to-air outs ratio: 0.52 last season, 0.52 for career.... Grounded into 4 double plays in 43 opportunities (one per 11).... Allowed 13 doubles, 0 triples in 60 innings.... Opposing base stealers: 7-for-7 (100%); 1 pickoff, 0 balks.

Tim Pugh   Throws Right
Born Jan. 26, 1967

Cincinnati Reds	W-L	ERA	AB	H	HR	BB	SO	BA	SA	OBA
Season	4-2	2.58	170	47	2	13	18	.276	.400	.330
vs. Left-Handers			86	24	0	12	8	.279	.384	.367
vs. Right-Handers			84	23	2	1	10	.274	.417	.287
vs. Ground-Ballers			76	27	2	6	6	.355	.539	.402
vs. Fly-Ballers			94	20	0	7	12	.213	.287	.272
Home Games	2-2	3.68	116	38	2	10	11	.328	.483	.383
Road Games	2-0	0.56	54	9	0	3	7	.167	.222	.211
Grass Fields	2-0	0.56	54	9	0	3	7	.167	.222	.211
Artificial Turf	2-2	3.68	116	38	2	10	11	.328	.483	.383
First 9 Batters			55	17	1	5	5	.309	.436	.371
Second 9 Batters			58	15	0	4	6	.259	.345	.306
All Batters Thereafter			57	15	1	4	7	.263	.421	.311

Miscellaneous statistics: Ground outs-to-air outs ratio: 1.04 last season, 1.04 for career.... Grounded into 6 double plays in 41 opportunities (one per 6.8).... Allowed 11 doubles, 2 triples in 45⅓ innings.... Opposing base stealers: 1-for-2 (50%); 1 pickoff, 0 balks.

Denny Neagle   Throws Left
Born Sep. 13, 1968

Pittsburgh Pirates	W-L	ERA	AB	H	HR	BB	SO	BA	SA	OBA
Season	4-6	4.48	328	81	9	43	77	.247	.387	.335
vs. Left-Handers			92	21	2	16	27	.228	.348	.349
vs. Right-Handers			236	60	7	27	50	.254	.403	.330
vs. Ground-Ballers			150	35	2	25	40	.233	.327	.350
vs. Fly-Ballers			178	46	7	18	37	.258	.438	.322
Home Games	1-5	6.05	157	47	6	21	39	.299	.478	.381
Road Games	3-1	3.21	171	34	3	22	38	.199	.304	.292
Grass Fields	2-1	2.29	70	14	1	11	16	.200	.300	.309
Artificial Turf	2-5	5.13	258	67	8	32	61	.260	.411	.342
First 9 Batters			248	59	6	39	60	.238	.379	.341
Second 9 Batters			60	15	1	3	15	.250	.317	.281
All Batters Thereafter			20	7	2	1	2	.350	.700	.409

Miscellaneous statistics: Ground outs-to-air outs ratio: 0.81 last season, 0.81 for career.... Grounded into 2 double plays in 66 opportunities (one per 33).... Allowed 17 doubles, 1 triple in 86⅓ innings.... Stranded 21 inherited runners, allowed 4 to score (84%).... Opposing base stealers: 14-for-17 (82%); 2 pickoffs, 2 balks.

Ben Rivera   Throws Right
Born Jan. 11, 1969

Braves/Phillies	W-L	ERA	AB	H	HR	BB	SO	BA	SA	OBA
Season	7-4	3.07	431	99	9	45	77	.230	.357	.307
vs. Left-Handers			250	59	4	27	32	.236	.356	.317
vs. Right-Handers			181	40	5	18	45	.221	.359	.294
vs. Ground-Ballers			189	47	1	19	34	.249	.349	.325
vs. Fly-Ballers			242	52	8	26	43	.215	.364	.293
Home Games	5-0	2.01	193	39	1	23	35	.202	.275	.289
Road Games	2-4	3.96	238	60	8	22	42	.252	.424	.322
Grass Fields	1-1	4.28	134	37	5	7	24	.276	.440	.315
Artificial Turf	6-3	2.58	297	62	4	38	53	.209	.320	.304
First 9 Batters			200	51	4	23	39	.255	.370	.338
Second 9 Batters			115	29	3	12	17	.252	.383	.326
All Batters Thereafter			116	19	2	10	21	.164	.310	.234

Miscellaneous statistics: Ground outs-to-air outs ratio: 1.15 last season, 1.15 for career.... Grounded into 9 double plays in 81 opportunities (one per 9.0).... Allowed 18 doubles, 5 triples in 117⅓ innings.... Allowed 4 first-inning runs in 14 starts (2.57 ERA).... Batting support: 5.86 runs per start.... Opposing base stealers: 15-for-19 (79%); 2 pickoffs, 0 balks.

Kevin Rogers
Throws Left

Born Aug. 20, 1968

San Francisco Giants	W-L	ERA	AB	H	HR	BB	SO	BA	SA	OBA
Season	0-2	4.24	132	37	4	13	26	.280	.386	.349
vs. Left-Handers			25	7	0	0	4	.280	.280	.280
vs. Right-Handers			107	30	4	13	22	.280	.411	.364
vs. Ground-Ballers			59	16	1	6	13	.271	.356	.348
vs. Fly-Ballers			73	21	3	7	13	.288	.411	.350
Home Games	0-1	4.76	67	21	2	7	14	.313	.433	.378
Road Games	0-1	3.71	65	16	2	6	12	.246	.338	.319
Grass Fields	0-1	4.76	67	21	2	7	14	.313	.433	.378
Artificial Turf	0-1	3.71	65	16	2	6	12	.246	.338	.319
First 9 Batters			48	9	2	4	12	.188	.333	.264
Second 9 Batters			49	15	2	4	10	.306	.429	.358
All Batters Thereafter			35	13	0	5	4	.371	.400	.450

Miscellaneous statistics: Ground outs-to-air outs ratio: 0.68 last season, 0.68 for career.... Grounded into 3 double plays in 28 opportunities (one per 9.3).... Allowed 2 doubles, 0 triples in 34 innings.... Opposing base stealers: 1-for-3 (33%); 2 pickoffs, 0 balks.

Matt Whiteside
Throws Right

Born Aug. 8, 1967

Texas Rangers	W-L	ERA	AB	H	HR	BB	SO	BA	SA	OBA
Season	1-1	1.93	106	26	1	11	13	.245	.330	.314
vs. Left-Handers			51	15	1	5	2	.294	.412	.357
vs. Right-Handers			55	11	0	6	11	.200	.255	.274
vs. Ground-Ballers			48	14	0	2	4	.292	.333	.320
vs. Fly-Ballers			58	12	1	9	9	.207	.328	.309
Home Games	1-0	1.10	61	14	0	5	9	.230	.295	.284
Road Games	0-1	3.09	45	12	1	6	4	.267	.378	.353
Grass Fields	1-0	1.48	90	22	0	8	12	.244	.311	.303
Artificial Turf	0-1	4.91	16	4	1	3	1	.250	.438	.368
First 9 Batters			103	26	1	11	12	.252	.340	.322
Second 9 Batters			3	0	0	0	1	.000	.000	.000
All Batters Thereafter			0	0	0	0	0	—	—	—

Miscellaneous statistics: Ground outs-to-air outs ratio: 1.03 last season, 1.03 for career.... Grounded into 3 double plays in 18 opportunities (one per 6.0).... Allowed 6 doubles, 0 triples in 28 innings.... Stranded 15 inherited runners, allowed 2 to score (88%).... Opposing base stealers: 1-for-1 (100%); 0 pickoffs, 0 balks.

Mike Trombley
Throws Right

Born Apr. 14, 1967

Minnesota Twins	W-L	ERA	AB	H	HR	BB	SO	BA	SA	OBA
Season	3-2	3.30	174	43	5	17	38	.247	.402	.318
vs. Left-Handers			79	22	2	10	17	.278	.443	.360
vs. Right-Handers			95	21	3	7	21	.221	.368	.282
vs. Ground-Ballers			86	18	1	7	13	.209	.302	.269
vs. Fly-Ballers			88	25	4	10	25	.284	.500	.364
Home Games	1-0	3.50	66	15	3	5	17	.227	.394	.282
Road Games	2-2	3.18	108	28	2	12	21	.259	.407	.339
Grass Fields	1-1	3.18	66	18	1	7	15	.273	.394	.351
Artificial Turf	2-1	3.38	108	25	4	10	23	.231	.407	.297
First 9 Batters			79	9	1	6	26	.114	.165	.176
Second 9 Batters			59	19	0	6	7	.322	.424	.385
All Batters Thereafter			36	15	4	5	5	.417	.889	.500

Miscellaneous statistics: Ground outs-to-air outs ratio: 1.02 last season, 1.02 for career.... Grounded into 2 double plays in 29 opportunities (one per 15).... Allowed 12 doubles, 0 triples in 46⅓ innings.... Opposing base stealers: 2-for-5 (40%); 1 pickoff, 0 balks.

Bob Wickman
Throws Right

Born Feb. 6, 1969

New York Yankees	W-L	ERA	AB	H	HR	BB	SO	BA	SA	OBA
Season	6-1	4.11	187	51	2	20	21	.273	.385	.344
vs. Left-Handers			89	25	1	10	8	.281	.427	.347
vs. Right-Handers			98	26	1	10	13	.265	.347	.342
vs. Ground-Ballers			83	23	0	10	8	.277	.373	.351
vs. Fly-Ballers			104	28	2	10	13	.269	.394	.339
Home Games	2-1	5.09	87	25	1	6	8	.287	.425	.337
Road Games	4-0	3.29	100	26	1	14	13	.260	.350	.351
Grass Fields	4-1	4.00	134	38	2	13	15	.284	.418	.349
Artificial Turf	2-0	4.40	53	13	0	7	6	.245	.302	.333
First 9 Batters			64	22	0	5	7	.344	.453	.389
Second 9 Batters			61	12	1	8	8	.197	.279	.296
All Batters Thereafter			62	17	1	7	6	.274	.419	.348

Miscellaneous statistics: Ground outs-to-air outs ratio: 2.46 last season, 2.46 for career.... Grounded into 9 double plays in 47 opportunities (one per 5.2).... Allowed 9 doubles, 3 triples in 50⅓ innings.... Opposing base stealers: 8-for-9 (89%); 1 pickoff, 0 balks.

Tim Wakefield
Throws Right

Born Aug. 2, 1966

Pittsburgh Pirates	W-L	ERA	AB	H	HR	BB	SO	BA	SA	OBA
Season	8-1	2.15	327	76	3	35	51	.232	.309	.305
vs. Left-Handers			198	42	1	22	35	.212	.268	.290
vs. Right-Handers			129	34	2	13	16	.264	.372	.329
vs. Ground-Ballers			171	44	0	15	30	.257	.287	.317
vs. Fly-Ballers			156	32	3	20	21	.205	.333	.293
Home Games	5-0	2.09	165	42	1	19	26	.255	.333	.332
Road Games	3-1	2.20	162	34	2	16	25	.210	.284	.278
Grass Fields	3-1	2.31	114	22	2	13	17	.193	.263	.273
Artificial Turf	5-0	2.05	213	54	1	22	34	.254	.333	.322
First 9 Batters			106	23	1	7	18	.217	.321	.270
Second 9 Batters			90	21	0	16	15	.233	.267	.346
All Batters Thereafter			131	32	2	12	18	.244	.328	.303

Miscellaneous statistics: Ground outs-to-air outs ratio: 0.89 last season, 0.89 for career.... Grounded into 4 double plays in 68 opportunities (one per 17).... Allowed 12 doubles, 2 triples in 92 innings.... Allowed 2 first-inning runs in 13 starts (1.38 ERA).... Batting support: 4.08 runs per start.... Opposing base stealers: 4-for-13 (31%); 4 pickoffs, 1 balk.

BALLPARKS

The Ballparks Section lists, for all 26 parks in use last season, a variety of statistics about the games played there over the past several years.

The effect of each ballpark on performance has become an almost obsessively discussed topic in the last decade. Even the simplest conversation about an off-season trade these days is likely to touch on such factors as the relative dimensions of the two parks involved, whether they have natural or artificial turf, the size of their foul territory, and how far they are above sea level. Without going into the sometimes sticky question of the reasons for such differences, we present here the facts of those differences, park by park.

For each stadium, a box contains the basic statistics for the games played there, as contrasted with that home team's games played on the road. The totals listed are the complete statistics *for both teams* in those games. Totals and percentage differences are listed for the 1992 season, and for the five-year period from 1988 through 1992. (The differences, in many cases, don't reflect the change between the actual raw totals printed, but rather between related per-game averages. For instance, we print the number of runs scored in home and road games, but compute the difference between the average number of runs *per game*.) Since the statistics represent performances by roughly the same set of players, the differences can be attributed to the peculiarities of the park. (The one case where this assumption does not hold is Toronto's Skydome, which opened during the 1989 season. Excluded from the home totals for 1989 are the following games that were played at Exhibition Stadium: three each against Kansas City, New York, Texas, Seattle, California, Minnesota, Cleveland, and Chicago; and two against Oakland. This may create a skew in the statistics; we are confident that this is not a major problem, and it will shrink in significance as the years progress.)

Following the pages of ballpark data are tables that rank the stadiums according to their effects on various elements of play. To illustrate, let's say that you find that the Oakland Coliseum reduced scoring by 11.3 percent over the past five seasons. You won't have to look through twenty-five other boxes to see where this ranks; the table marked "Ranked by Effect on Runs" will show that it stands dead last, with a negative percentage more than twice that of the next-lowest American League park.

In addition to scoring, we've ranked the parks in seven other categories. The fields with artificial playing surfaces are marked with an asterisk, giving you a quick read on what kind of impact they have had on the category in question. While the effect on batting average is open to question, the effects on such categories as extra-base hit percentage, stolen base percentage, and errors are unmistakable.

BALTIMORE ORIOLES · ORIOLE PARK AT CAMDEN YARDS

	1992 SEASON				1992 SEASON		
	Home Games	Road Games	Pct. Diff.		Home Games	Road Games	Pct. Diff.
G	81	81	0.0		81	81	0.0
AB	5508	5508	0.0		5508	5508	0.0
1B	978	1032	-5.2		978	1032	-5.2
2B	227	266	-14.7		227	266	-14.7
3B	34	33	3.0		34	33	3.0
HR	144	128	12.5		144	128	12.5
R	672	689	-2.5		672	689	-2.5
BA	.251	.265	-5.2		.251	.265	-5.2
SLG	.383	.395	-3.0		.383	.395	-3.0
XB%	.211	.225	-6.2		.211	.225	-6.2
E	80	104	-23.1		80	104	-23.1
SHO	11	11	0.0		11	11	0.0

CHICAGO WHITE SOX · COMISKEY PARK

	1992 SEASON			1991–1992		
	Home Games	Road Games	Pct. Diff.	Home Games	Road Games	Pct. Diff.
G	82	80	2.5	163	161	1.2
AB	5542	5507	0.6	11022	11069	-0.4
1B	1023	1015	0.2	2018	1983	2.2
2B	216	277	-22.5	437	497	-11.7
3B	31	39	-21.0	65	74	-11.8
HR	116	117	-1.5	269	257	5.1
R	682	746	-10.8	1397	1470	-6.1
BA	.250	.263	-4.9	.253	.254	-0.4
SLG	.363	.391	-7.2	.378	.382	-1.1
XB%	.194	.237	-18.1	.199	.224	-10.9
E	116	128	-11.6	230	253	-10.2
SHO	10	6	62.6	20	16	23.5

BOSTON RED SOX · FENWAY PARK

	1992 SEASON			1988–1992		
	Home Games	Road Games	Pct. Diff.	Home Games	Road Games	Pct. Diff.
G	81	81	0.0	405	405	0.0
AB	5544	5413	2.4	27897	27339	2.0
1B	1050	937	9.4	5323	4996	4.4
2B	292	227	25.6	1595	1214	28.8
3B	24	25	-6.3	136	149	-10.6
HR	91	100	-11.2	604	564	5.0
R	669	599	11.7	3742	3343	11.9
BA	.263	.238	10.4	.275	.253	8.4
SLG	.373	.345	8.3	.406	.370	9.7
XB%	.231	.212	9.1	.245	.214	14.5
E	132	117	12.8	659	571	15.4
SHO	11	13	-15.4	59	64	-7.8

CLEVELAND INDIANS · CLEVELAND STADIUM

	1992 SEASON			1988–1992		
	Home Games	Road Games	Pct. Diff.	Home Games	Road Games	Pct. Diff.
G	81	81	0.0	406	404	0.5
AB	5701	5534	3.0	27874	27533	1.2
1B	1147	1046	6.4	5489	5098	6.4
2B	252	220	11.2	1214	1240	-3.3
3B	25	26	-6.7	151	170	-12.3
HR	156	130	16.5	578	658	-13.2
R	763	657	16.1	3510	3369	3.7
BA	.277	.257	7.9	.267	.260	2.4
SLG	.412	.377	9.5	.383	.389	-1.6
XB%	.195	.190	2.2	.199	.217	-8.1
E	143	103	38.8	621	586	5.5
SHO	8	10	-20.0	56	52	7.2

CALIFORNIA ANGELS · ANAHEIM STADIUM

	1992 SEASON			1988–1992		
	Home Games	Road Games	Pct. Diff.	Home Games	Road Games	Pct. Diff.
G	81	81	0.0	405	405	0.0
AB	5467	5381	1.6	27514	27486	0.1
1B	1086	991	7.9	5173	5197	-0.6
2B	204	219	-8.3	1072	1238	-13.5
3B	17	20	-16.3	115	160	-28.2
HR	104	114	-10.2	658	586	12.2
R	651	599	8.7	3262	3418	-4.6
BA	.258	.250	3.3	.255	.261	-2.4
SLG	.359	.361	-0.8	.374	.382	-2.0
XB%	.169	.194	-13.0	.187	.212	-12.0
E	153	124	23.4	617	623	-1.0
SHO	12	16	-25.0	67	53	26.4

DETROIT TIGERS · TIGER STADIUM

	1992 SEASON			1988–1992		
	Home Games	Road Games	Pct. Diff.	Home Games	Road Games	Pct. Diff.
G	80	82	-2.4	404	406	-0.5
AB	5490	5571	-1.5	27228	27740	-1.8
1B	1007	1049	-2.6	4794	5149	-5.1
2B	256	254	2.3	1150	1298	-9.7
3B	19	23	-16.2	134	150	-9.0
HR	181	156	17.7	856	723	20.6
R	788	797	1.3	3739	3755	0.1
BA	.266	.266	0.2	.255	.264	-3.5
SLG	.419	.404	3.7	.401	.400	0.3
XB%	.215	.209	2.7	.211	.219	-3.8
E	106	136	-20.1	612	610	0.8
SHO	5	8	-35.9	37	47	-20.9

KANSAS CITY ROYALS · ROYALS STADIUM

	1992 SEASON			1988–1992		
	Home Games	Road Games	Pct. Diff.	Home Games	Road Games	Pct. Diff.
G	81	81	0.0	404	404	0.0
AB	5501	5502	0.0	27651	27482	0.6
1B	1033	1004	2.9	5194	5079	1.6
2B	282	267	5.6	1424	1261	12.2
3B	42	28	50.0	244	145	67.2
HR	65	116	−44.0	396	633	−37.8
R	650	627	3.7	3396	3423	−0.8
BA	.258	.257	0.5	.262	.259	1.3
SLG	.360	.379	−4.9	.375	.385	−2.6
XB%	.239	.227	5.1	.243	.217	12.1
E	130	103	26.2	616	573	7.5
SHO	12	13	−7.7	56	62	−9.7

NEW YORK YANKEES · YANKEE STADIUM

	1992 SEASON			1988–1992		
	Home Games	Road Games	Pct. Diff.	Home Games	Road Games	Pct. Diff.
G	81	81	0.0	404	404	0.0
AB	5598	5512	1.6	27762	27644	0.4
1B	1022	999	0.7	5127	5064	0.8
2B	272	279	−4.0	1310	1355	−3.7
3B	23	28	−19.1	107	166	−35.8
HR	158	134	16.1	770	697	10.0
R	772	707	9.2	3680	3612	1.9
BA	.263	.261	0.9	.263	.263	0.0
SLG	.405	.395	2.5	.402	.400	0.4
XB%	.224	.235	−4.7	.217	.231	−6.3
E	108	121	−10.7	596	594	0.3
SHO	9	8	12.5	44	45	−2.2

MILWAUKEE BREWERS · COUNTY STADIUM

	1992 SEASON			1988–1992		
	Home Games	Road Games	Pct. Diff.	Home Games	Road Games	Pct. Diff.
G	81	81	0.0	404	406	−0.5
AB	5327	5645	−5.6	27467	27863	−1.4
1B	981	1048	−0.8	5138	5336	−2.3
2B	223	299	−21.0	1178	1266	−5.6
3B	25	36	−26.4	142	176	−18.2
HR	86	123	−25.9	588	626	−4.7
R	593	751	−21.0	3448	3615	−4.1
BA	.247	.267	−7.5	.257	.266	−3.5
SLG	.347	.398	−12.9	.374	.391	−4.4
XB%	.202	.242	−16.7	.204	.213	−3.9
E	124	111	11.7	656	604	9.1
SHO	10	9	11.1	50	50	0.5

OAKLAND A'S · OAKLAND–ALAMEDA COUNTY COLISEUM

	1992 SEASON			1988–1992		
	Home Games	Road Games	Pct. Diff.	Home Games	Road Games	Pct. Diff.
G	81	81	0.0	405	405	0.0
AB	5338	5495	−2.9	26917	27630	−2.6
1B	955	1050	−6.4	4811	5000	−1.2
2B	198	256	−20.4	1031	1281	−17.4
3B	25	30	−14.2	116	156	−23.7
HR	149	122	25.7	643	731	−9.7
R	691	726	−4.8	3274	3690	−11.3
BA	.249	.265	−6.3	.245	.259	−5.5
SLG	.379	.389	−2.7	.364	.396	−8.2
XB%	.189	.214	−11.6	.193	.223	−13.8
E	127	121	5.0	606	597	1.5
SHO	7	8	−12.5	64	48	33.3

MINNESOTA TWINS · METRODOME

	1992 SEASON			1988–1992		
	Home Games	Road Games	Pct. Diff.	Home Games	Road Games	Pct. Diff.
G	81	81	0.0	405	405	0.0
AB	5549	5505	0.8	27820	27427	1.4
1B	1053	1050	−0.5	5333	5140	2.3
2B	289	258	11.1	1499	1273	16.1
3B	39	21	84.2	196	131	47.5
HR	112	113	−1.7	647	644	−1.0
R	701	699	0.3	3747	3385	10.7
BA	.269	.262	2.7	.276	.262	5.3
SLG	.396	.378	4.7	.414	.388	6.5
XB%	.238	.210	13.1	.241	.215	12.4
E	90	127	−29.1	518	586	−11.6
SHO	12	9	33.3	43	58	−25.9

SEATTLE MARINERS · KINGDOME

	1992 SEASON			1988–1992		
	Home Games	Road Games	Pct. Diff.	Home Games	Road Games	Pct. Diff.
G	81	81	0.0	405	404	0.2
AB	5605	5478	2.3	27641	27152	1.8
1B	1008	1017	−3.1	4887	4975	−3.5
2B	338	243	35.9	1422	1208	15.6
3B	24	25	−6.2	147	133	8.6
HR	141	137	0.6	701	606	13.6
R	753	725	3.9	3603	3401	5.7
BA	.270	.260	3.9	.259	.255	1.6
SLG	.414	.388	6.7	.397	.376	5.6
XB%	.264	.209	26.7	.243	.212	14.5
E	115	105	9.5	565	577	−2.3
SHO	11	12	−8.3	53	59	−10.4

TEXAS RANGERS · ARLINGTON STADIUM

| | 1992 SEASON | | | 1988–1992 | | |
	Home Games	Road Games	Pct. Diff.	Home Games	Road Games	Pct. Diff.
G	81	81	0.0	406	403	0.7
AB	5571	5534	0.7	27517	27521	0.0
1B	985	996	−1.8	4979	4902	1.6
2B	274	279	−2.4	1239	1310	−5.4
3B	25	27	−8.0	164	143	14.7
HR	134	138	−3.5	676	629	7.5
R	693	742	−6.6	3626	3605	−0.2
BA	.255	.260	−2.2	.256	.254	1.1
SLG	.385	.395	−2.6	.387	.380	1.8
XB%	.233	.235	−0.9	.220	.229	−3.8
E	126	136	−7.4	625	624	−0.6
SHO	8	9	−11.1	46	45	1.5

TORONTO BLUE JAYS · SKYDOME

| | 1992 SEASON | | | 1989–1992 | | |
	Home Games	Road Games	Pct. Diff.	Home Games	Road Games	Pct. Diff.
G	81	81	0.0	298	324	−8.0
AB	5406	5562	−2.8	20255	22143	−8.5
1B	920	1014	−6.7	3517	3978	−3.3
2B	273	252	11.5	986	1024	5.3
3B	33	25	35.8	146	133	20.0
HR	139	148	−3.4	545	517	15.2
R	724	738	−1.9	2564	2787	0.0
BA	.252	.259	−2.4	.256	.255	0.5
SLG	.392	.393	−0.1	.400	.384	4.4
XB%	.250	.215	16.3	.243	.225	8.1
E	106	120	−11.7	386	490	−14.4
SHO	15	9	66.7	43	41	14.0

ATLANTA BRAVES · ATLANTA–FULTON COUNTY STADIUM

	1992 SEASON			1988–1992		
	Home Games	Road Games	Pct. Diff.	Home Games	Road Games	Pct. Diff.
G	81	81	0.0	401	406	-1.2
AB	5416	5531	-2.1	27593	27194	1.5
1B	996	952	6.8	5118	4734	6.5
2B	224	235	-2.7	1221	1171	2.8
3B	28	50	-42.8	134	177	-25.4
HR	117	110	8.6	656	566	14.2
R	633	618	2.4	3527	3180	12.3
BA	.252	.244	3.5	.258	.244	5.7
SLG	.369	.364	1.3	.384	.363	5.7
XB%	.202	.230	-12.4	.209	.222	-5.6
E	130	116	12.1	736	625	19.2
SHO	18	14	28.6	55	58	-4.0

HOUSTON ASTROS · ASTRODOME

	1992 SEASON			1988–1992		
	Home Games	Road Games	Pct. Diff.	Home Games	Road Games	Pct. Diff.
G	81	81	0.0	406	404	0.5
AB	5576	5406	3.1	27561	27349	0.8
1B	975	954	-0.9	4845	4828	-0.4
2B	251	259	-6.0	1224	1164	4.3
3B	42	45	-9.5	205	168	21.1
HR	90	120	-27.3	418	645	-35.7
R	595	681	-12.6	3055	3336	-8.9
BA	.244	.255	-4.5	.243	.249	-2.4
SLG	.352	.386	-8.8	.348	.374	-7.2
XB%	.231	.242	-4.4	.228	.216	5.3
E	97	116	-16.4	595	663	-10.7
SHO	19	11	72.7	74	58	27.0

CHICAGO CUBS · WRIGLEY FIELD

	1992 SEASON			1988–1992		
	Home Games	Road Games	Pct. Diff.	Home Games	Road Games	Pct. Diff.
G	81	81	0.0	408	401	1.7
AB	5585	5445	2.6	28300	27230	3.9
1B	983	1005	-4.6	5402	4873	6.7
2B	242	240	-1.7	1218	1243	-5.7
3B	47	29	58.0	209	186	8.1
HR	108	103	2.2	678	524	24.5
R	612	605	1.2	3637	3152	13.4
BA	.247	.253	-2.3	.265	.251	5.8
SLG	.365	.364	0.2	.395	.368	7.4
XB%	.227	.211	7.6	.209	.227	-7.8
E	124	122	1.6	745	585	25.2
SHO	14	17	-17.6	46	54	-16.3

LOS ANGELES DODGERS · DODGER STADIUM

	1992 SEASON			1988–1992		
	Home Games	Road Games	Pct. Diff.	Home Games	Road Games	Pct. Diff.
G	81	81	0.0	405	403	0.5
AB	5404	5421	-0.3	27133	27242	-0.4
1B	1072	1014	6.1	5185	4860	7.1
2B	201	226	-10.8	951	1181	-19.2
3B	34	33	3.4	122	150	-18.3
HR	59	95	-37.7	459	532	-13.4
R	558	626	-10.9	2964	3125	-5.6
BA	.253	.252	0.2	.248	.247	0.3
SLG	.335	.359	-6.5	.342	.360	-4.8
XB%	.180	.203	-11.6	.171	.215	-20.2
E	169	144	17.4	722	635	13.1
SHO	15	13	15.4	70	70	-0.5

CINCINNATI REDS · RIVERFRONT STADIUM

	1992 SEASON			1988–1992		
	Home Games	Road Games	Pct. Diff.	Home Games	Road Games	Pct. Diff.
G	81	81	0.0	404	405	-0.2
AB	5378	5501	-2.2	27216	27409	-0.7
1B	926	1024	-7.5	4749	4912	-2.6
2B	266	264	3.1	1299	1207	8.4
3B	41	51	-17.8	154	181	-14.3
HR	120	88	39.5	720	524	38.4
R	644	625	3.0	3373	3126	8.2
BA	.252	.259	-3.0	.254	.249	2.2
SLG	.383	.374	2.5	.393	.364	8.0
XB%	.249	.235	5.8	.234	.220	6.3
E	103	119	-13.4	541	640	-15.3
SHO	9	12	-25.0	46	66	-30.1

MONTREAL EXPOS · OLYMPIC STADIUM

	1992 SEASON			1988–1992		
	Home Games	Road Games	Pct. Diff.	Home Games	Road Games	Pct. Diff.
G	81	81	0.0	392	418	-6.2
AB	5382	5547	-3.0	26436	28251	-6.4
1B	929	989	-3.2	4551	4994	-2.6
2B	272	222	26.3	1239	1162	13.9
3B	39	32	25.6	195	198	5.2
HR	98	96	5.2	500	590	-9.4
R	665	564	17.9	2992	3213	-0.7
BA	.249	.241	3.0	.245	.246	-0.2
SLG	.368	.345	6.8	.364	.364	0.0
XB%	.251	.204	22.7	.240	.214	11.9
E	121	118	2.5	635	664	2.0
SHO	11	14	-21.4	51	68	-20.0

NEW YORK METS · SHEA STADIUM

	1992 SEASON			1988–1992		
	Home Games	Road Games	Pct. Diff.	Home Games	Road Games	Pct. Diff.
G	81	81	0.0	405	402	0.7
AB	5405	5409	−0.1	27084	27179	−0.3
1B	919	949	−3.1	4642	4760	−2.1
2B	260	266	−2.2	1155	1296	−10.6
3B	36	37	−2.6	154	160	−3.4
HR	91	100	−8.9	576	623	−7.2
R	593	659	−10.0	3089	3350	−8.5
BA	.242	.250	−3.3	.241	.252	−4.2
SLG	.354	.368	−4.0	.359	.380	−5.5
XB%	.244	.242	0.7	.220	.234	−6.1
E	110	112	−1.8	643	627	1.8
SHO	18	11	63.6	72	48	48.9

ST. LOUIS CARDINALS · BUSCH STADIUM

	1992 SEASON			1988–1992		
	Home Games	Road Games	Pct. Diff.	Home Games	Road Games	Pct. Diff.
G	81	81	0.0	410	402	2.0
AB	5663	5516	2.7	27846	27004	3.1
1B	1044	1021	−0.4	5048	5005	−2.2
2B	253	261	−5.6	1330	1242	3.8
3B	40	38	2.5	262	169	50.3
HR	107	105	−0.7	401	483	−19.5
R	625	610	2.5	3207	3075	2.3
BA	.255	.258	−1.3	.253	.255	−1.0
SLG	.370	.377	−1.6	.363	.368	−1.4
XB%	.219	.227	−3.3	.240	.220	9.0
E	98	93	5.4	560	595	−7.7
SHO	10	10	0.0	55	69	−21.8

PHILADELPHIA PHILLIES · VETERANS STADIUM

	1992 SEASON			1988–1992		
	Home Games	Road Games	Pct. Diff.	Home Games	Road Games	Pct. Diff.
G	81	81	0.0	407	404	0.7
AB	5437	5464	−0.5	27478	27175	1.1
1B	959	993	−2.9	4758	4918	−4.3
2B	253	265	−4.1	1342	1213	9.4
3B	45	33	37.0	178	158	11.4
HR	116	115	1.4	598	556	6.4
R	700	703	−0.4	3438	3344	2.1
BA	.253	.257	−1.9	.250	.252	−0.7
SLG	.380	.381	−0.4	.377	.370	2.1
XB%	.237	.231	2.7	.242	.218	11.1
E	122	130	−6.2	556	684	−19.3
SHO	7	9	−22.2	60	45	32.4

SAN DIEGO PADRES · SAN DIEGO/JACK MURPHY STADIUM

	1992 SEASON			1988–1992		
	Home Games	Road Games	Pct. Diff.	Home Games	Road Games	Pct. Diff.
G	81	81	0.0	405	404	0.2
AB	5522	5489	0.6	27220	27466	−0.9
1B	1073	989	7.8	4960	5033	−0.6
2B	228	247	−8.2	1050	1195	−11.3
3B	25	32	−22.3	146	169	−12.8
HR	151	95	58.0	689	546	27.3
R	673	580	16.0	3204	3122	2.4
BA	.267	.248	7.7	.251	.253	−0.5
SLG	.400	.357	12.0	.377	.368	2.3
XB%	.191	.220	−13.3	.194	.213	−8.9
E	108	110	−1.8	648	659	−1.9
SHO	9	14	−35.7	56	49	14.0

PITTSBURGH PIRATES · THREE RIVERS STADIUM

	1992 SEASON			1988–1992		
	Home Games	Road Games	Pct. Diff.	Home Games	Road Games	Pct. Diff.
G	81	81	0.0	408	402	1.5
AB	5510	5566	−1.0	27353	27465	−0.4
1B	1015	973	5.4	4754	4956	−3.7
2B	284	252	13.8	1316	1234	7.1
3B	46	42	10.6	204	208	−1.5
HR	88	119	−25.3	539	618	−12.4
R	640	648	−1.2	3219	3405	−6.9
BA	.260	.249	4.4	.249	.255	−2.5
SLG	.376	.374	0.7	.371	.383	−3.1
XB%	.245	.232	5.7	.242	.225	7.5
E	110	99	11.1	597	624	−5.7
SHO	12	17	−29.4	48	54	−12.4

SAN FRANCISCO GIANTS · CANDLESTICK PARK

	1992 SEASON			1988–1992		
	Home Games	Road Games	Pct. Diff.	Home Games	Road Games	Pct. Diff.
G	81	81	0.0	405	405	0.0
AB	5470	5453	0.3	27241	27497	−0.9
1B	959	987	−3.1	4826	4965	−1.9
2B	233	230	1.0	1139	1176	−2.2
3B	36	37	−3.0	168	207	−18.1
HR	117	116	0.5	623	650	−3.3
R	601	620	−3.1	3157	3434	−8.1
BA	.246	.251	−2.1	.248	.255	−2.6
SLG	.366	.371	−1.3	.371	.383	−3.3
XB%	.219	.213	2.9	.213	.218	−2.2
E	109	122	−10.7	631	608	3.8
SHO	15	15	0.0	60	54	11.1

RANKED BY EFFECT ON RUNS

	1992 SEASON			1988–1992		
	Home Games	Road Games	Pct. Diff.	Home Games	Road Games	Pct. Diff.
Wrigley Field	612	605	1.2	3637	3152	13.4
Atlanta Stadium	633	618	2.4	3527	3180	12.3
Fenway Park	669	599	11.7	3742	3343	11.9
*Metrodome	701	699	0.3	3747	3385	10.7
*Riverfront Stadium	644	625	3.0	3373	3126	8.2
*Kingdome	753	725	3.9	3603	3401	5.7
Cleveland Stadium	763	657	16.1	3510	3369	3.7
San Diego Stadium	673	580	16.0	3204	3122	2.4
*Busch Stadium	625	610	2.5	3207	3075	2.3
*Veterans Stadium	700	703	−0.4	3438	3344	2.1
Yankee Stadium	772	707	9.2	3680	3612	1.9
Tiger Stadium	788	797	1.3	3739	3755	0.1
*Skydome	724	738	−1.9	2564	2787	0.0
Arlington Stadium	693	742	−6.6	3626	3605	−0.2
*Olympic Stadium	665	564	17.9	2992	3213	−0.7
*Royals Stadium	650	627	3.7	3396	3423	−0.8
Oriole Park	672	689	−2.5	672	689	−2.5
County Stadium	593	751	−21.0	3448	3615	−4.1
Anaheim Stadium	651	599	8.7	3262	3418	−4.6
Dodger Stadium	558	626	−10.9	2964	3125	−5.6
Comiskey Park	682	746	−10.8	1397	1470	−6.1
*Three Rivers Stadium	640	648	−1.2	3219	3405	−6.9
Candlestick Park	601	620	−3.1	3157	3434	−8.1
Shea Stadium	593	659	−10.0	3089	3350	−8.5
*Astrodome	595	681	−12.6	3055	3336	−8.9
Oakland Coliseum	691	726	−4.8	3274	3690	−11.3

RANKED BY EFFECT ON HOME RUNS

	1992 SEASON			1988–1992		
	Home Games	Road Games	Pct. Diff.	Home Games	Road Games	Pct. Diff.
*Riverfront Stadium	120	88	39.5	720	524	38.4
San Diego Stadium	151	95	58.0	689	546	27.3
Wrigley Field	108	103	2.2	678	524	24.5
Tiger Stadium	181	156	17.7	856	723	20.6
*Skydome	139	148	−3.4	545	517	15.2
Atlanta Stadium	117	110	8.6	656	566	14.2
*Kingdome	141	137	0.6	701	606	13.6
Oriole Park	144	128	12.5	144	128	12.5
Anaheim Stadium	104	114	−10.2	658	586	12.2
Yankee Stadium	158	134	16.1	770	697	10.0
Arlington Stadium	134	138	−3.5	676	629	7.5
*Veterans Stadium	116	115	1.4	598	556	6.4
Comiskey Park	116	117	−1.5	269	257	5.1
Fenway Park	91	100	−11.2	604	564	5.0
*Metrodome	112	113	−1.7	647	644	−1.0
Candlestick Park	117	116	0.5	623	650	−3.3
County Stadium	86	123	−25.9	588	626	−4.7
Shea Stadium	91	100	−8.9	576	623	−7.2
*Olympic Stadium	98	96	5.2	500	590	−9.4
Oakland Coliseum	149	122	25.7	643	731	−9.7
*Three Rivers Stadium	88	119	−25.3	539	618	−12.4
Cleveland Stadium	156	130	16.5	578	658	−13.2
Dodger Stadium	59	95	−37.7	459	532	−13.4
*Busch Stadium	107	105	−0.7	401	483	−19.5
*Astrodome	90	120	−27.3	418	645	−35.7
*Royals Stadium	65	116	−44.0	396	633	−37.8

RANKED BY EFFECT ON BATTING AVERAGE

	1992 SEASON			1988–1992		
	Home Games	Road Games	Pct. Diff.	Home Games	Road Games	Pct. Diff.
Fenway Park	.263	.238	10.4	.275	.253	8.4
Wrigley Field	.247	.253	−2.3	.265	.251	5.8
Atlanta Stadium	.252	.244	3.5	.258	.244	5.7
*Metrodome	.269	.262	2.7	.276	.262	5.3
Cleveland Stadium	.277	.257	7.9	.267	.260	2.4
*Riverfront Stadium	.252	.259	−3.0	.254	.249	2.2
*Kingdome	.270	.260	3.9	.259	.255	1.6
*Royals Stadium	.258	.257	0.5	.262	.259	1.3
Arlington Stadium	.255	.260	−2.2	.256	.254	1.1
*Skydome	.252	.259	−2.4	.256	.255	0.5
Dodger Stadium	.253	.252	0.2	.248	.247	0.3
Yankee Stadium	.263	.261	0.9	.263	.263	0.0
*Olympic Stadium	.249	.241	3.0	.245	.246	−0.2
Comiskey Park	.250	.263	−4.9	.253	.254	−0.4
San Diego Stadium	.267	.248	7.7	.251	.253	−0.5
*Veterans Stadium	.253	.257	−1.9	.250	.252	−0.7
*Busch Stadium	.255	.258	−1.3	.253	.255	−1.0
Anaheim Stadium	.258	.250	3.3	.255	.261	−2.4
*Astrodome	.244	.255	−4.5	.243	.249	−2.4
*Three Rivers Stadium	.260	.249	4.4	.249	.255	−2.5
Candlestick Park	.246	.251	−2.1	.248	.255	−2.6
County Stadium	.247	.267	−7.5	.257	.266	−3.5
Tiger Stadium	.266	.266	0.2	.255	.264	−3.5
Shea Stadium	.242	.250	−3.3	.241	.252	−4.2
Oriole Park	.251	.265	−5.2	.251	.265	−5.2
Oakland Coliseum	.249	.265	−6.3	.245	.259	−5.5

RANKED BY EFFECT ON SLUGGING PERCENTAGE

	1992 SEASON			1988–1992		
	Home Games	Road Games	Pct. Diff.	Home Games	Road Games	Pct. Diff.
Fenway Park	.373	.345	8.3	.406	.370	9.7
*Riverfront Stadium	.383	.374	2.5	.393	.364	8.0
Wrigley Field	.365	.364	0.2	.395	.368	7.4
*Metrodome	.396	.378	4.7	.414	.388	6.5
Atlanta Stadium	.369	.364	1.3	.384	.363	5.7
*Kingdome	.414	.388	6.7	.397	.376	5.6
*Skydome	.392	.393	−0.1	.400	.384	4.4
San Diego Stadium	.400	.357	12.0	.377	.368	2.3
*Veterans Stadium	.380	.381	−0.4	.377	.370	2.1
Arlington Stadium	.385	.395	−2.6	.387	.380	1.8
Yankee Stadium	.405	.395	2.5	.402	.400	0.4
Tiger Stadium	.419	.404	3.7	.401	.400	0.3
*Olympic Stadium	.368	.345	6.8	.364	.364	0.0
Comiskey Park	.363	.391	−7.2	.378	.382	−1.1
*Busch Stadium	.370	.377	−1.6	.363	.368	−1.4
Cleveland Stadium	.412	.377	9.5	.383	.389	−1.6
Anaheim Stadium	.359	.361	−0.8	.374	.382	−2.0
*Royals Stadium	.360	.379	−4.9	.375	.385	−2.6
Oriole Park	.383	.395	−3.0	.383	.395	−3.0
*Three Rivers Stadium	.376	.374	0.7	.371	.383	−3.1
Candlestick Park	.366	.371	−1.3	.371	.383	−3.3
County Stadium	.347	.398	−12.9	.374	.391	−4.4
Dodger Stadium	.335	.359	−6.5	.342	.360	−4.8
Shea Stadium	.354	.368	−4.0	.359	.380	−5.5
*Astrodome	.352	.386	−8.8	.348	.374	−7.2
Oakland Coliseum	.379	.389	−2.7	.364	.396	−8.2

RANKED BY EFFECT ON EXTRA-BASE HIT PERCENTAGE

	1992 SEASON			1988–1992		
	Home Games	Road Games	Pct. Diff.	Home Games	Road Games	Pct. Diff.
Fenway Park	.231	.212	9.1	.245	.214	14.5
*Kingdome	.264	.209	26.7	.243	.212	14.5
*Metrodome	.238	.210	13.1	.241	.215	12.4
*Royals Stadium	.239	.227	5.1	.243	.217	12.1
*Olympic Stadium	.251	.204	22.7	.240	.214	11.9
*Veterans Stadium	.237	.231	2.7	.242	.218	11.1
*Busch Stadium	.219	.227	−3.3	.240	.220	9.0
*Skydome	.250	.215	16.3	.243	.225	8.1
*Three Rivers Stadium	.245	.232	5.7	.242	.225	7.5
*Riverfront Stadium	.249	.235	5.8	.234	.220	6.3
*Astrodome	.231	.242	−4.4	.228	.216	5.3
Candlestick Park	.219	.213	2.9	.213	.218	−2.2
Tiger Stadium	.215	.209	2.7	.211	.219	−3.8
Arlington Stadium	.233	.235	−0.9	.220	.229	−3.8
County Stadium	.202	.242	−16.7	.204	.213	−3.9
Atlanta Stadium	.202	.230	−12.4	.209	.222	−5.6
Shea Stadium	.244	.242	0.7	.220	.234	−6.1
Oriole Park	.211	.225	−6.2	.211	.225	−6.2
Yankee Stadium	.224	.235	−4.7	.217	.231	−6.3
Wrigley Field	.227	.211	7.6	.209	.227	−7.8
Cleveland Stadium	.195	.190	2.2	.199	.217	−8.1
San Diego Stadium	.191	.220	−13.3	.194	.213	−8.9
Comiskey Park	.194	.237	−18.1	.199	.224	−10.9
Anaheim Stadium	.169	.194	−13.0	.187	.212	−12.0
Oakland Coliseum	.189	.214	−11.6	.193	.223	−13.8
Dodger Stadium	.180	.203	−11.6	.171	.215	−20.2

RANKED BY EFFECT ON STRIKEOUT PERCENTAGE

	1992 SEASON			1988–1992		
	Home Games	Road Games	Pct. Diff.	Home Games	Road Games	Pct. Diff.
*Astrodome	.171	.152	12.7	.161	.150	7.4
Oakland Coliseum	.139	.129	7.5	.150	.142	5.8
Arlington Stadium	.176	.154	14.5	.168	.159	5.4
Tiger Stadium	.141	.137	3.2	.147	.140	5.0
Shea Stadium	.164	.162	1.3	.166	.159	4.2
San Diego Stadium	.145	.156	−6.9	.156	.151	3.4
*Metrodome	.149	.136	9.5	.137	.133	3.2
County Stadium	.125	.132	−5.3	.135	.131	2.9
*Veterans Stadium	.163	.148	10.2	.152	.150	1.9
*Olympic Stadium	.159	.166	−4.2	.164	.161	1.9
*Three Rivers Stadium	.140	.136	3.5	.143	.142	1.3
Anaheim Stadium	.142	.151	−5.7	.150	.149	0.2
Wrigley Field	.142	.136	4.6	.144	.144	−0.1
Candlestick Park	.154	.173	−10.9	.153	.154	−0.1
*Kingdome	.143	.134	6.8	.143	.144	−0.2
Dodger Stadium	.150	.157	−4.2	.160	.160	−0.3
Fenway Park	.142	.150	−5.2	.144	.146	−1.8
*Skydome	.152	.154	−1.7	.151	.155	−2.5
Yankee Stadium	.136	.145	−6.6	.141	.146	−3.0
*Riverfront Stadium	.163	.156	4.5	.157	.162	−3.4
Cleveland Stadium	.142	.141	0.6	.138	.144	−4.0
Oriole Park	.131	.137	−4.7	.131	.137	−4.7
Comiskey Park	.124	.131	−4.7	.133	.140	−4.9
*Busch Stadium	.147	.150	−1.9	.135	.146	−7.4
Atlanta Stadium	.149	.157	−5.2	.146	.158	−7.6
*Royals Stadium	.122	.135	−9.5	.140	.157	−10.6

RANKED BY EFFECT ON STOLEN BASE PERCENTAGE

	1992 SEASON			1988–1992		
	Home Games	Road Games	Pct. Diff.	Home Games	Road Games	Pct. Diff.
*Astrodome	.733	.688	6.5	.759	.697	9.0
*Busch Stadium	.725	.628	15.5	.721	.664	8.6
*Metrodome	.703	.634	11.0	.692	.644	7.5
*Olympic Stadium	.772	.732	5.5	.735	.705	4.2
Oakland Coliseum	.695	.613	13.4	.690	.668	3.3
*Skydome	.760	.702	8.3	.706	.684	3.2
*Riverfront Stadium	.675	.640	5.3	.701	.681	2.9
*Veterans Stadium	.762	.719	5.9	.724	.705	2.7
*Kingdome	.640	.703	−9.0	.670	.660	1.4
County Stadium	.679	.674	0.7	.698	.690	1.1
Tiger Stadium	.614	.612	0.3	.654	.647	1.1
San Diego Stadium	.618	.652	−5.1	.648	.654	−0.9
Cleveland Stadium	.631	.685	−7.9	.653	.659	−1.0
*Royals Stadium	.657	.661	−0.6	.676	.687	−1.5
Yankee Stadium	.684	.738	−7.3	.695	.710	−2.2
Fenway Park	.644	.587	9.6	.640	.657	−2.5
Atlanta Stadium	.679	.692	−2.0	.656	.679	−3.4
Arlington Stadium	.596	.544	9.5	.663	.691	−4.0
Dodger Stadium	.681	.655	4.1	.652	.680	−4.1
*Three Rivers Stadium	.649	.651	−0.3	.678	.711	−4.7
Comiskey Park	.688	.732	−6.0	.650	.684	−5.1
Candlestick Park	.558	.629	−11.3	.622	.661	−5.9
Shea Stadium	.624	.758	−17.6	.703	.747	−5.9
Oriole Park	.682	.728	−6.3	.682	.728	−6.3
Wrigley Field	.574	.646	−11.1	.639	.693	−7.9
Anaheim Stadium	.601	.645	−6.9	.595	.651	−8.6

RANKED BY EFFECT ON ERRORS

	1992 SEASON			1988–1992		
	Home Games	Road Games	Pct. Diff.	Home Games	Road Games	Pct. Diff.
Wrigley Field	124	122	1.6	745	585	25.2
Atlanta Stadium	130	116	12.1	736	625	19.2
Fenway Park	132	117	12.8	659	571	15.4
Dodger Stadium	169	144	17.4	722	635	13.1
County Stadium	124	111	11.7	656	604	9.1
*Royals Stadium	130	103	26.2	616	573	7.5
Cleveland Stadium	143	103	38.8	621	586	5.5
Candlestick Park	109	122	−10.7	631	608	3.8
*Olympic Stadium	121	118	2.5	635	664	2.0
Shea Stadium	110	112	−1.8	643	627	1.8
Oakland Coliseum	127	121	5.0	606	597	1.5
Tiger Stadium	106	136	−20.1	612	610	0.8
Yankee Stadium	108	121	−10.7	596	594	0.3
Arlington Stadium	126	136	−7.4	625	624	−0.6
Anaheim Stadium	153	124	23.4	617	623	−1.0
San Diego Stadium	108	110	−1.8	648	659	−1.9
*Kingdome	115	105	9.5	565	577	−2.3
*Three Rivers Stadium	110	99	11.1	597	624	−5.7
*Busch Stadium	98	93	5.4	560	595	−7.7
Comiskey Park	116	128	−11.6	230	253	−10.2
*Astrodome	97	116	−16.4	595	663	−10.7
*Metrodome	90	127	−29.1	518	586	−11.6
*Skydome	106	120	−11.7	386	490	−14.4
*Riverfront Stadium	103	119	−13.4	541	640	−15.3
*Veterans Stadium	122	130	−6.2	556	684	−19.3
Oriole Park	80	104	−23.1	80	104	−23.1